LIFE & HEALTH INSURANCE

Thirteenth
Edition

LIFE & HEALTH INSURANCE

Kenneth Black, Jr.
Georgia State University

Harold D. Skipper, Jr.
Georgia State University

PRENTICE HALL, UPPER SADDLE RIVER, NEW JERSEY 07458

VP/Editorial Director: Jim Boyd
Editor-in-Chief: P. J. Boardman
Senior Editor: Paul Donnelly
Editorial Assistant: Cheryl Clayton
Assistant Editor: Gladys Soto
Marketing Manager: Lori Braumberger
Director of Production: Michael Weinstein
Production Manager: Gail Steier de Acevedo
Production Coordinator: Kelly Warsak
Permissions Coordinator: Monica Stipanov
Manufacturing Buyer: Natacha St. Hill Moore
Senior Manufacturing Manager: Vincent Scelta
Cover Design: Bruce Kenselaar
Cover Art: Corbis Corporation Media
Full Service Composition: Omegatype Typography, Inc.

Library of Congress Cataloging-in-Publication Data
Black, Kenneth.
    Life and health insurance / Kenneth Black, Jr., Harold D.
Skipper, Jr. — 13th ed.
        p.   cm. — (The Prentice Hall series in security and
    insurance)
        Rev. ed. of: Life insurance. 12th ed. c1994.
        Includes bibliographical references and index.
        ISBN 0-13-891250-5
        1. Insurance, Life.   2. Insurance, Life—United States.
    3. Insurance, Health.   4. Insurance, Health—United States.
    I. Skipper, Harold D.   II. Black, Kenneth. Life
    insurance.   III. Title.   IV. Series.
    HG8771.B55   2000
    368.3'00973—dc21   99-22004
                                                         CIP

Prentice-Hall International (UK) Limited, London
Prentice-Hall of Australia Pty. Limited, Sydney
Prentice-Hall Canada, Inc., Toronto
Prentice-Hall Hispanoamericana, S.A., Mexico
Prentice-Hall of India Private Limited, New Delhi
Prentice-Hall of Japan, Inc., Tokyo
Prentice-Hall (Singapore) Pte. Ltd.
Editora Prentice-Hall do Brasil, Ltda., Rio de Janeiro

Printed in the United States of America

To
the memory of Kenneth Black, Sr.,
and Margaret Virginia Black
and
the memory of George W. Skipper, Jr.,
and Harold D. Skipper, Sr.

Solomon Stephen Huebner

Dr. Solomon Stephen Huebner was a distinguished professor of insurance at the Wharton School, University of Pennsylvania, and chairman of the Department of Insurance at that institution. He not only introduced the first university-level insurance courses in the United States but also wrote the first university-level insurance textbooks. Dr. Huebner wrote the first edition of this text, published in 1915, and since that time, succeeding editions have been in continuous use both at the university level and in professional designation programs. Through his strong leadership, he came to be known as the father of insurance education in the United States.

The authors are pleased to have been able to perpetuate this great educator's text. He built bridges of knowledge and understanding. The authors had the opportunity to cross one of his many bridges, moving from student to teacher, through the S. S. Huebner Foundation for Insurance Education at the University of Pennsylvania. We are grateful for the privilege that has been afforded us and hope that throughout this volume we have maintained the high standards of excellence and professionalism to which Dr. Huebner's entire career was committed.

Brief Contents

x

Contents

xi

Preface

This thirteenth edition is a major revision of its predecessors, the first of which was published by Solomon S. Huebner in 1915. The authors continue their emphasis on combining current information about the life and health insurance industry's products and their uses with careful consideration of the environment. We also continue to approach our presentation of life and health insurance simultaneously from the viewpoints of the buyer, the advisor, and the insurer.

The financial services industry continues to undergo unprecedented change. To permit a deeper understanding of the industry and the effects of these changes on life and health insurance, we have strengthened our treatment of fundamentals by building more economic and financial theory into this edition. Although the basis of this edition remains U.S. practice, comparisons with international practices are presented throughout the volume. Because of the growing importance of health care financing, we have expanded our treatment of health insurance and changed this edition's title to reflect this fact.

A financial management perspective has been adopted to explain how life and health insurance products fit into a broad framework of financial planning. In this context, these products have both unique advantages and some disadvantages. We have endeavored to present a forthright appraisal of them and to suggest how they may be evaluated from contractual, cost, and performance viewpoints.

This edition devotes entire chapters to the tax treatment of life and health insurance, to estate planning, to retirement planning, and to the business uses of life and health insurance. We recognize that these areas change continuously, but exposure to the topics is important to students and practitioners.

The chapters on health care have been significantly revised to reflect the growth of managed care and its impact on traditional health care programs. The rapidly aging U.S. population has moved insurer emphasis from protection to retirement products and focused the national debate over the future of Social Security and Medicare. All of these trends are reflected in this edition.

Life insurer management and the environment within which it operates are dealt with in the later chapters of the book. The entry of banks into the life and health insurance field has opened a new major distribution system. These and other developments reflect the strong movement toward eliminating the traditional barriers among commercial banks, investment banks, and insurers. The chapter on marketing life and health insurance reflects both the search for and the experiment with new distribution systems, including the growing impact of the Internet.

This edition provides a major effort to employ finance theory and concepts in understanding the management of risk by life and health insurers. In addition, the discussion of organization reflects the movement toward demutualizations and mutual holding companies as the need for capital has increased. The volume concludes with chapters on financial reporting and regulation and regulatory responses to the volatile financial environment.

In sum, we have attempted to provide a comprehensive, unbiased treatise on individual and group life, health, and retirement products, their appropriate uses and taxation, how to evaluate these products and their supplier insurers, along with a thorough examination of life insurance company operations and regulation.

ACKNOWLEDGMENTS

The authors benefited greatly from the constructive advice and criticism of many professionals including the following: Nathaniel B. Cabanilla, American Council of Life Insurance; William J. Danish and David Maslen, Aon Consulting Group, Inc.; Paul E. Barnhart; Dwight Bartlett, Bartlett Consulting Services; Joseph F. Quinn, Boston College; John M. Bragg, John M. Bragg and Associates; Andrea T. Sellers, Buck Consultants; Rajiv Basu and Albert Reznicek, Deloitte & Touche LLP; Julie F. Curry, Lori R. Noll, and Robert W. Stein, Ernst & Young LLP; William S. Custer and Martin F. Grace, Georgia State University; Peter L. Hutchings, Guardian Life Insurance Company; Loretta Jacobs, John Hancock Mutual Life Insurance; Richard Bush and Joseph Jordan, KPMG Peat Marwick; James C. Brooks, Jr., Harold Cohen, and W. Thomas Loftis, Life Insurance Company of Georgia; James O. Mitchell, LIMRA; Stephen W. Forbes, LOMA; Richard A. Hemming, Lord, Bissell & Brook; Peter Berry and Jerry E. Lusk, Milliman & Robertson, Inc.; Kevin M. Gallagher and Steven K. Thompson, Munich American Reassurance Company; Gerald Mischke, Mutual of Omaha Insurance Company; Robert J. Myers; Marina Boma, Martin Claire, Jane Hannick, Brian Lo, Elizabeth Lowell, Bruce Schobel, Mark Seliber, Joel Steinberg, and Steve Steinig, New York Life Insurance Company; Walter Zultowski, Phoenix Home Life; Thomas J. Graf, Principal Financial Group; Martin Brophy, The Prudential; Eli N. Donkar, Social Security Administration; Linden N. Cole and Robert Conover, Society of Actuaries; David Wittemore, Tillinghast/Towers Perrin; Elizabeth Borkhuis and James Durfee, Towers Perrin; Lisa Gardner, Bradley University; Randy Dumm, University of Georgia; Robert Hershbarger, Ferris State University; and Douglas Heeter, Mississippi State University.

Special acknowledgment is continued to Kenneth Black III for his efforts in preparing the initial draft of chapters 31, 32, and 33 in the twelfth edition and his review of the same chapters in this edition.

We are also indebted to several other Georgia State University colleagues, including Robert W. Batten, Joan T. A. Gabel, Bruce A. Palmer, Richard D. Phillips, and Fred A. Tillman. Each of these persons read individual chapters and shared his or her criticism and judgment.

Finally, the authors would like to record their appreciation of Anne Chamberlain Shaw, Janis Robson Wilcox, and Susan Holliman Fuller for their efforts and personal interests in helping with the many administrative duties associated with producing the manuscript. Special credit is due to Anne Chamberlain Shaw and Ian Webb for their major roles in developing the objectives, study questions, and glossary for this edition.

Naturally, none of those who reviewed the manuscript bears any responsibility for the deficiencies that may remain in the completed work.

Kenneth Black, Jr.
Harold D. Skipper, Jr.

CHAPTER

1

ECONOMIC SECURITY AND THE ECONOMICS OF LIFE AND HEALTH INSURANCE

Objectives

- Draw distinctions between social and private insurance, as well as between life and health insurance products.

- Describe the conditions required for competitive insurance markets.

- Describe market imperfections, giving examples of each within life and health insurance markets.

- Understand how economic theories of consumption may help explain the demand for life and health insurance.

- Describe the role of capital, financial management, and distribution systems in the production of life and health insurance.

ECONOMIC SECURITY AND THE NATURE OF LIFE AND HEALTH INSURANCE

Humans have always sought security. This quest for security was an important motivating force in the earliest formations of families, clans, tribes, and other groups. Indeed, groups have been the primary source of both emotional and physical security since the beginning of humankind. They ensured a less volatile source of life's necessities than that which isolated humans and families could provide and helped their less fortunate members in times of crises.

Humans today continue their quest to achieve security and reduce uncertainty. We still rely on groups for financial stability. The group may be our employer, the government, or an insurance company, but the concept is the same. In some ways, however, we today are more vulnerable than our ancestors. The physical and economic security formerly provided by the tribe or extended family diminished with industrialization. Our income-dependent, wealth-acquiring lifestyle renders us and our families more vulnerable to environmental and societal changes over which we have no control. More formalized means are required for mitigating the adverse consequences of unemployment,

1

loss of health, death, old age, lawsuits, and destruction of our property. As extensions of human activity, businesses are similarly vulnerable.

Humans are exposed to many serious perils, such as property losses from fire or windstorm, and personal losses from incapacity and death. Although individuals cannot predict or completely prevent such occurrences, they can provide for their financial effects. The function of insurance is to safeguard against such misfortunes by having contributions of the many pay for the losses of the unfortunate few. This is the essence of insurance—the sharing of losses and, in the process, the substitution of a certain, small "loss" called the premium for an uncertain, large loss.

Insurance Defined

Mastery of the subject of life and health insurance requires mastery of terminology and concepts. We begin our examination by noting that we can define private insurance from two perspectives—one economic and one legal. From an *economic* perspective, **insurance** is a financial intermediation function by which individuals exposed to a specified contingency each contribute to a pool from which covered events suffered by participating individuals are paid. Under this view, individuals purchase the right to collect from the pool if the insured contingency occurs. Insurance then is a contingent claim contract on the pool's assets.

From a *legal* perspective, **insurance** is an agreement, the **insurance policy** or **insurance contract,** by which one party, the **policyowner,** pays a stipulated consideration called the **premium** to the other party called the **insurer,** in return for which the insurer agrees to pay a defined amount of money or provide a defined service if a covered event occurs during the policy term. The person whose life, health, or property is the object of the insurance policy is referred to as the **insured.** In most instances, the insured is also the **policyowner**—the person who exercises contractual rights under the policy—but not invariably so, as discussed in chapter 9. Under life insurance policies, the person to whom the payment is made on the insured's death is the **beneficiary.**

Social versus Private Insurance

Governments provide some types of insurance. Thus, most countries have extensive government-administered social security schemes that provide survivor, retirement, disability, and unemployment benefits. Health insurance and benefits for job-related accidents and illnesses are typically provided by either government or the private sector, or some combination of the two.

Social insurance is distinguished from private insurance through its emphasis on social equity through income redistribution. Private insurance focuses on individual equity—each insured's premiums reflect the expected value of his or her losses. Also, participation in social insurance schemes is compulsory, and financing relies on government-mandated premiums. This book covers both social and private insurance, although it emphasizes private insurance.

Life versus Non-Life Insurance

The private insurance sector has historically divided itself between companies that sell insurance on the person, known as **life insurance,** and those that sell insurance to protect property, referred to variously as **non-life insurance, property/casualty insurance,** and **general insurance,** depending on the country. The non-life branch includes insurance to cover:

- property losses—damage to or destruction of homes, automobiles, businesses, aircraft

- liability losses—payments due to professional negligence, product defects, negligent automobile operation, or harm to others or their property
- workers' compensation and health insurance payments in some countries

This book, however, is concerned with the life branch of the private insurance business. The life branch includes insurance that pays benefits on a person's:

- death—usually called life insurance or life assurance
- living a certain length of time—called endowments, annuities, and pensions
- incapacity—called disability and long-term care insurance
- injury or incurring a disease—called health insurance, accident insurance, and medical expense insurance

The life and non-life branches of insurance perceive themselves differently, and with some justification. Many countries prohibit a single corporation from selling both types, although joint production via holding companies and affiliates usually is permitted.

Life and Health Insurance Defined

Definitions within the life branch can be inconsistent between countries and even within a single market. Thus, when referring to *life insurance* as a branch of private insurance, it is often understood to include all four classes of insurance coverages listed previously. Similarly, *life insurance companies* are insurers that may write any or all of the four classes of listed coverages. In many countries, the almost self-defining term **personal insurance** means life, accident, and other insurance covering a *person,* in contrast to insurance covering property, liability, and so forth.

When referring to the insurance policies, however, the term *life insurance* usually means the first category of coverages—policies that pay benefits on death—and, sometimes, also to the second category of coverages—policies that pay benefits on survival to a certain age or for a set number of years. Even here, we encounter some inconsistencies. In some markets, annuities and pension-related coverages often are classified separately from life insurance policies.

The term *health insurance* usually falls into the fourth category—policies covering the costs of injuries or sickness—and, sometimes, also for the third category of coverages—policies that pay benefits because of physical or mental incapacity. Many markets, most notably in Europe, classify health insurance as non-life insurance. In the United States, health insurance commonly falls within the life branch.

Types of Life and Health Insurance Policies

A life insurance policy that provides coverage for the whole of the insured's life is called **whole life insurance.** A policy that covers a set time period, such as five or ten years, is called term life insurance or endowment insurance. Endowments differ from **term insurance** in that term policies promise to pay benefits only if the insured dies during the policy term. Nothing is paid if the insured survives the term. In contrast, **endowment insurance** pays benefits if the insured dies during the policy term and also pays benefits if the insured survives the policy term.

An **annuity** is a contract that promises to pay the insured, or **annuitant,** a periodic (usually monthly) payment starting at a specified age, such as age 65. If payments cease on the annuitant's death, we call the contract a **life annuity.**

We will use the term *health insurance* to mean any form of insurance whose payment is contingent on the insured incurring additional expenses or losing income because of incapacity or loss of good health. Payment provoked because physical or mental incapacity prevents the insured from being able to work is called **disability income insurance.** If the incapacity prohibits the insured's activities of daily living, it is called **long-term care**

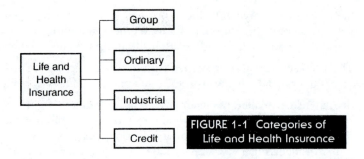

FIGURE 1-1 Categories of Life and Health Insurance

insurance. If the insured incurs hospital, physician, or other health care expenses, it is called **medical expense insurance.**

Life and Health Insurance Classifications

Much life and health insurance is purchased as **group insurance,** typically by employers for the benefit of their employees. Individually issued life or health insurance policies are classified as being either ordinary insurance or industrial insurance. **Industrial insurance** includes life and health insurance policies issued to individuals in small amounts, usually less than $2,000, with premiums payable on a weekly or monthly basis.

Ordinary insurance includes individual life and health insurance policies whose benefit amounts are larger than industrial insurance. Premiums are payable monthly or less frequently. The great majority of individually issued life and health insurance falls within the ordinary category. Finally, some life and health insurance—referred to as **credit insurance**—is issued through lending institutions to cover debtors' obligations if they die or become disabled. Figure 1-1 illustrates this classification scheme, which is used in the United States but not all countries.

Irrespective of classification of insurance or terminology, virtually all private life and health insurance in every market must be issued by an insurance organization, and every insurance organization is a mechanism for pooling losses. This is true whether a group of persons mutually insures each other—a mutual life insurer—or an independent contractor—a stock life insurer—assumes the risk and pays resulting losses.

AN ECONOMIC OVERVIEW OF LIFE AND HEALTH INSURANCE MARKETS

Economics underpins all business activity, with insurance being no exception. Almost all important insurance operations, practices, and regulation relate to economics. If we can gain an understanding of the economic principles that underpin insurance, we gain a logical structure for our examination of this vast subject.

Conditions for Competitive Insurance Markets

We begin with an examination of the conditions under which markets operate at optimum efficiency. The objective that a market-oriented economy would have for its insurance industry would be the same as that which it has for other industries—an efficient allocation of society's resources while maximizing consumer choice and value. At the same time, society desires an economic system that leads to continuous innovation and improvement. This objective is most likely to be achieved through reliance on competitive markets. As used here, a *market* exists whenever goods or services are bought and sold.

Competition not only leads to economic efficiency, it provides an automatic mechanism for fulfilling consumer needs and wants and for creating a great variety of choices. Additionally, in an effort always to secure an advantage over rivals in the market, suppliers engage in efforts to improve their products and services, thus further benefitting consumers. In the absence of severe imperfections, a competitive market requires no government direction or oversight to accomplish these desirable social goals. As we will see later, however, insurance markets have their share of imperfections.

For a *perfectly* competitive insurance—or any other—market to exist, certain conditions must be met. These conditions are shown in Box 1-1.

Neither insurance nor any other market fully meets these conditions. Fortunately, a market can meet them partially and still realize substantial competitive benefits. The more removed actual market functioning is from these ideal conditions, the more imperfect the resulting competition and the poorer the industry performance and attendant consumer value and choice. Variations of actual market performance and structure from the ideal are referred to as **market imperfections** or **market failures.**

Imperfections in Insurance Markets

If imperfections did not exist, insurers—if they existed at all—would be mere pass-through mechanisms akin to mutual funds, and no regulation would be necessary because all customers would have complete information. The existence of imperfections in insurance markets explains and justifies innumerable insurer practices and operations as well as most insurance regulation. An understanding of these imperfections, therefore, is essential to a sound conceptual foundation.[1]

No completely acceptable classification of market imperfections exists. Nonetheless, the four broad categories shown in Figure 1-2 provide a useful way of thinking about them. Each of the categories is explored next.

---

[1]This section draws from Harold D. Skipper, Jr., "Rationales for Government Intervention into Insurance Markets," in Harold D. Skipper, Jr., ed., *International Risk and Insurance: An Environmental-Managerial Approach* (Boston: Irwin McGraw-Hill, 1998), pp. 243–254. Hereafter, this book is cited as *International Risk and Insurance.*

BOX 1-1

CONDITIONS FOR A PERFECTLY COMPETITIVE INSURANCE MARKET

The following conditions are necessary for a perfectly competitive insurance market:

- *A sufficiently large number of buyers and sellers such that no one buyer or seller nor any group of them can influence the market.* This condition means that all buyers and sellers are price takers—none can influence the price of the product as determined by its supply and demand. Underlying this assumption is that neither sellers nor buyers engage in collusive behavior.

- *Sellers have freedom of entry into and exit from the market.* This condition means that new competitors can enter the market if they see that existing firms are making *excess* profits. Firms must not only respond to rivals after they enter the business, but they also must anticipate new competitors. Thus, if competitors know that entry barriers are low, they will tend automatically to hold the line on price increases even if no new competitors enter the market. The mere threat of new entry can be sufficient to ensure that firms will make only *normal* profits. Conversely, competitors will exit a market if they cannot make normal profits or if they can make greater profits elsewhere.

- *Sellers produce identical products.* This condition means that no seller can differentiate its products from those of its rivals. Hence, buyers have no incentive to pay more than the market price for any firm's products.

- *Buyers and sellers are well informed about the products.* This condition means that all firms and consumers possess full knowledge about the product or service under consideration and that none has knowledge unknown to others.

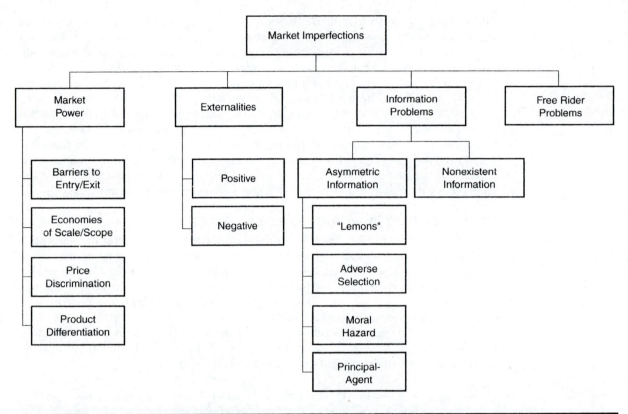

Market Power

The first assumption within the purely competitive model means that a sufficiently large number of buyers and sellers compete such that none is large enough to influence price. In fact, most sellers and some buyers can influence price, at least to some limited degree. The ability of one or a few sellers or buyers to influence the price of a product or service is called **market power.** If some players in a market can exercise market power, resource allocation will be suboptimal. Market power in insurance markets relates almost exclusively to sellers and can arise in at least four ways:

- barriers to entry or exit
- economies of scale or scope
- price discrimination
- product differentiation

Barriers to Entry or Exit　If a market has barriers to entry or to exit, suppliers have market power. Of course, governments often create such barriers for various reasons—some noble and some less so. For example, requirements that insurers secure a license to sell insurance within a jurisdiction and have a certain minimum financial capital base are barriers to entry, but they are justified on consumer protection grounds. When governments flatly prohibit the entry of new insurers, as is the situation in some developing countries, they create the opportunity for existing insurers to enjoy substantial market power (and higher prices and excess profits) but at almost certainly no benefit to society as a whole.

All firms want to create barriers to entry in their markets. Indeed, society benefits from firms attempting to create *legitimate* barriers. In this way, products and services undergo continuous improvement, and firms become more attuned to that which satisfies customers. Thus, if an insurer devotes great human, technical, and financial resources to developing highly skilled risk selection expertise, it may have created a barrier to entry for competitors because, to compete in their sophisticated lines of business, competitors must try to acquire this expertise—a difficult and expensive process. Similarly, any investment, marketing, product development, or other operation that requires substantial "learning by doing" can create barriers to competitor entry, giving the firm a (likely temporary) competitive edge, but also providing greater consumer choice or value—or both—in the process.

Not all market-created entry barriers are justified, however. For example, we would not condone a group of health insurance companies that agreed to set prices or apportion a geographic area among themselves. Nor would we condone a firm making misleading statements about itself or its products to gain market share. In general, market power that arises from concerted action of market suppliers will be suspect, whereas market power that arises from individual firm action will not be suspect provided its effects are not to mislead or harm customers. Indeed, society benefits when businesses use their skill, foresight, and acumen to gain market power in this way.

Neither entry nor exit barriers appear to be great in the insurance markets of the United States, Canada, the United Kingdom, and several other countries. Entry barriers exist in all countries in the form of licensing requirements and minimum capital requirements, but they usually are not onerous. Barriers to exit are comparatively rare worldwide, although some U.S. jurisdictions are known to exert pressure to discourage domestic insurers from attempting to redomesticate to other states.

Reasonable freedom of entry does not exist in many of the world's life and health insurance markets. Several countries prohibit or severely limit the creation of new domestic insurers, and many erect substantial entry barriers to foreign insurers, although the trend is toward more liberal markets.

Economies of Scale or Scope   Market power can emanate from a firm enjoying economies of scale or scope. **Economies of scale** exist when a firm's average cost of production falls with increasing production. With economies of scale, the larger the firm the more efficiently it can operate, thus putting new entrants at an immediate competitive disadvantage. Economies of scale become another type of entry barrier.

At a certain firm size—called the **minimum efficient scale** (MES)—further growth yields no additional efficiencies; that is, long-run average costs are at a minimum. If further growth neither adds to nor detracts from efficiency, the firm is operating at **constant returns to scale.** If further growth diminishes efficiency, the firm is operating at **decreasing returns to scale.** If, however, efficiency increases over an industry's entire relevant output range and if sunk costs are high (i.e., if fixed costs are high and cannot be recouped on exit), then conditions exist for a **natural monopoly.** The MES is so large relative to market size that only one firm can operate efficiently.

Studies on insurance scale economies generally find increasing returns to scale for small to moderate size firms and either constant, modestly increasing, or decreasing returns for larger firms.[2] Thus, market power because of scale economies might be minimal in insurance, with no compelling evidence of a natural monopoly. Even small insurers compete successfully with larger firms, usually as careful niche players. With market widening and deepening, there should be even less concern about market imperfections

---

[2]See ibid. for citations to studies on economies of scale and scope.

because of scale economies. An exception to this observation may exist in health insurance and in the provision of social insurance services.

Economies of scope exist when a single firm can produce multiple products or services at lower costs than can multiple firms. This too can also give rise to market power. Research suggests that scope economies exist for the joint production of some insurance lines. Little is known about the economies of joint marketing or production of insurance and banking services, although such economies are asserted to exist.

Whether an insurer possesses market power from scale or scope economies depends, of course, on its size relative to its market rather than its absolute size. A small firm in a tiny market may wield market power. A giant insurer in an international market may have little such power. Also, even a monopolist or oligopolist may be unable to exercise monopoly power if the market is *contestable,* meaning that entry barriers are low and exit is easy. In such instances, the mere threat of competition from possible new entrants may be sufficient to cause existing firms to behave as if the market were competitive.

Price Discrimination   The competitive model assumes that all firms charge the same price. **Price discrimination** occurs when a firm offers effectively identical products at different prices to different groups of customers. In this way, the firm can gain market power, which means higher profits.

Insurers often attempt price discrimination, although regulatory requirements may thwart this strategy. For example, an insurer may offer an identical long-term care insurance policy through its agents, through brokers, and through the Internet, with each carrying a different price. With increasing competition, insurers seek ways to segment their target markets to charge different prices in each. Insurance regulators become concerned about price discrimination when the insurer's underlying loss experience or expenses do not justify price differences on otherwise identical policies.

Product Differentiation   If an insurer can differentiate its products from those of its competitors in the minds of its customers, it gains market power and can secure higher profits. **Product differentiation** exists when buyers prefer one firm's products over those of its rivals. This preference may stem from perceived differences in product quality, service, reputation, convenience, or other attributes.

Like other firms, insurers routinely try to differentiate their products from those of their competitors. This is one of the reasons that insurers seek to establish and maintain good reputations. Some products—such as annuities or term life insurance—are more difficult to differentiate than others, such as whole life insurance and individual disability income insurance. In general, the more complex the product or, at least, the more complex the product is perceived to be in the minds of customers, the greater the likelihood of a successful product differentiation strategy. Regulators are concerned about product differentiation only if the effect is to mislead purchasers. Otherwise, product differentiation can lead to enhanced consumer choice and value and to continuous product improvement.

Externalities

Nature of Externalities   The conditions described earlier for a perfectly competitive market presume that all costs of production are fully included in each firm's costs. This is not always true. Producers can impose positive and negative spillover effects on others. The manufacturing facility that pollutes the surrounding air, water, or land imposes costs on the neighboring population in terms of a less pleasant environment, poorer health, and lower property values. Conversely, if a new business opens in an economically depressed area, its providing additional jobs may decrease the incentive for some people to resort to criminal activities, thereby providing a beneficial spillover effect to the local community.

The foregoing are examples of **externalities,** which can occur when a firm's production or an individual's consumption has direct and uncompensated effects on others. If others benefit, we have a **positive externality.** If costs are imposed on others, we have a **negative externality.**

The purely competitive economic model does not accommodate externalities easily because the price of goods and services that carry externalities fails to reflect the true benefits and costs of such goods and services. With the polluting manufacturing facility, its direct costs of production as measured by its expenses for labor, machinery, transportation, and so on, fail to capture the firm's true economic costs of production because the business imposes uncompensated costs on the surrounding community. This means that its production costs are understated, that the firm's prices are lower than they should be, and, therefore, that more of the firm's products will be manufactured than is socially desirable—further contributing to pollution. If the facility were forced to compensate the community for its lessened enjoyment, poorer health, and lower property values, its direct costs of production would align more closely to its true economic costs.

Herein lies the problem with allowing competitive markets to deal freely with goods and services that carry externalities. With negative externalities, too much of the good or service will be produced or consumed, the price will be too low, and too little effort and resources will be devoted to correcting or reducing the externality. Conversely, with positive externalities, too little of the good or service will be produced, its price will be too high, and too little effort will be devoted to enhancing the externality.

Externalities and Insurance   Both negative and positive externalities exist in life and health insurance. Perhaps the most significant insurance-related negative externality is the fraud associated with health insurance. From 5 to 15 percent of all health insurance claims in some markets (e.g., in Europe and North America) are believed to involve fraud. Fraudulent claims impose higher premiums for everyone.

An extreme example of a negative externality sometimes associated with life insurance is when murder is committed in an effort to collect death proceeds. In such instances, the lure of insurance money gave rise to a death and to great personal and possibly financial suffering on the part of those who cared about the murder victim.

Another example of a negative externality flows from the important role played by financial intermediaries, such as banks, securities firms, and insurers. **Systemic risks** exist if the difficulties of financial institutions cause disruptions elsewhere within an economy. Box 1-2 discusses systemic risks in insurance.

Positive externalities also exist in insurance. For example, insurers have only rarely sought protection under intellectual property law for their product, processing, and service innovations. Consequently, a tendency may exist for firms to engage in less such development than they would otherwise.

Finally, a society may determine that its interests are served best by ensuring that unemployed, sick, injured, or retired persons are provided with at least some base level of insurance coverage. In providing this insurance, government reduces the likelihood that relatives may have to relinquish their jobs to provide care and that such individuals would impose other costs on society, such as resorting to criminal activities.

Free Rider Problems

Some collectively consumed goods and services that are desired by the public—called **public goods**—carry extensive positive externalities. Examples include public education, lighthouses, police and fire protection services, basic research and development, and national defense. When such goods and services are available to others at low or zero cost, they can cause a **free rider problem.** Thus, the shipowner who operates a lighthouse cannot exclude other ships from using it.

BOX 1-2

SYSTEMIC RISKS IN INSURANCE MARKETS

We can identify two types of systemic risks. The first—*cascading failures*—exists when the failure of one financial institution is the cause of the failure of others. The potential for cascading failures exists in insurance, at least in theory, through risk pooling and reinsurance. Some reinsurer failures have led to direct-insurer failures. To date, these instances have been rare and their economic effects limited. They have been within the non-life branch only. The prevention of these types of cascading failures is within management control through careful selection of reinsurers.

The second type of systemic risk is a *run* in which many policyowners or other creditors de-mand their money at once. A loss of confidence stemming from the real or imagined fear of insol-vency usually causes runs. Runs have occurred in insurance. For example, policyowners of the two largest U.S. life insurer failures—Executive Life and Mutual Benefit Life—initiated runs, as have policyowners of smaller failed insurers. To date, runs on life insurers have been limited to insurers already in financial difficulty. They have not caused the failure of sound insurers. The possibil-ity of such contagion effects exists, however, and, with the continued move by life insurers to offer bank-life products and vice versa, we should not ignore the risk.

The problem with public goods is that left to itself, a competitive market is unlikely to provide as much of such goods and services as society really wants. Each shipowner has an incentive to encourage other shipowners to build the lighthouse, but each might wait for the others to do so, anticipating a "free ride." Consequently, governments gen-erally provide public goods, and they are appropriately financed by societal revenues—that is, taxes. Indeed, the existence of public goods is one of the primary justifications for having a tax system.

Free rider problems exist in insurance. For example, when an insurance trade asso-ciation lobbies for favorable legislation, all insurers—members and nonmembers alike—may benefit from its activities. Insurance-related free rider problems also can occur when individuals know or believe that others will make good any losses that they suffer. Thus, if individuals know that they will receive free emergency medical care, they have less in-centive to purchase private health insurance.

Insurance regulation itself may have characteristics of a public good. Persons and firms benefit from regulation, even if they pay little or nothing for it. The private market seems unlikely to provide the level of regulation that most countries' citizens seem to want.

Information Problems

A critically important assumption of the perfectly competitive model is that both buyers and sellers are well informed. As a practical matter, we know otherwise about in-surance buyers and sellers. Information problems abound in insurance and arguably are the industry's most important market imperfections.

Insurance is a complex business, with neither buyers nor sellers appearing to have as much information as they need. Two information problems are (1) asymmetric infor-mation and (2) nonexistent information problems, as shown in Figure 1-2.

Asymmetric Information Problems **Asymmetric information problems** arise when one party to a transaction has relevant information that the other does not have. Asym-metric information problems drive most insurer operations and also are the bane of most life and health insurance customers, driving much of the regulation in insurance. Four classes of such problems exist:

- "lemons" problems
- adverse selection problems
- moral hazard problems
- principal–agent problems

"Lemons" problems. In the first category of information problems, we have what economists refer to as a **"lemons" problem,** in which the insurance customer knows less than the seller about the seller and its products. The nature of the insurance transaction involves a contract that makes a present promise of future performance upon the occurrence of stipulated events. Although much has been done to simplify insurance contracts and to enhance their readability, life and health insurance contracts remain technical, complex documents.

Individuals purchase policies in good faith, relying on the integrity of the insurance company and its representatives. Even assuming that policyowners could be induced to take an interest in the financial condition of their insurers, few are sufficiently knowledgeable to do so. Life and health insurance is necessarily a technical, complicated subject, and the true financial condition of an insurance company can be determined only by expert examination.

The lemons problem for insurance customers provides the rationale for the great majority of insurance regulation. Insurers and their representatives have little incentive to disclose adverse information to potential customers. Doing so will hurt sales. Governments seek to rectify the unequal positions between insurance buyer and seller by mandating certain disclosures for insurers, by monitoring insurer financial condition, by regulating insurer marketing practices, and through other means.

Adverse selection problems. The second type of asymmetric information problem is the **adverse selection problem** in which the customer knows more than the seller about the customer's situation. It plagues insurers worldwide and is the principal reason that insurers seek such extensive information about proposed insureds. They want to know as much as practical about the loss potential of those to whom they issue insurance. In this way, they can charge equitable prices that reflect the expected value of the proposed insureds' losses.

The price charged will be fair to the proposed insured and to others in the insurance pool, each of whom is expected to pay premiums that reflect their loss potentials. If some insureds are able to secure a price that is lower than the expected value of their losses, they impose costs on other insureds and cause a distortion of pricing. In the extreme, adverse selection can cause the insurance mechanism to break down altogether.

Of course, the insurance company cannot be certain that the buyer is disclosing all relevant information. Proposed insureds have incentives to secure the most favorable possible terms, conditions, and prices. To do so, they may not disclose all that they know about their insurability, especially if the insurer does not ask. The challenge for insurers is to obtain sufficient information to assess insurability properly but to do so without incurring unwarranted expense.

The adverse selection problem can be so potentially severe that private insurers may refuse to offer certain insurance. For example, only highly limited private-sector coverage can be secured against the financial consequences of unemployment. Persons who are most likely to need unemployment insurance would tend to purchase it, thereby selecting against the insurer.

Moral hazard problems. Another critical information problem for insurers, the **moral hazard problem,** is the tendency of individuals to alter their behavior *because* of insurance. Moral hazard problems are of concern in both life and health insurance, but the nature of the problems differs somewhat. Insurers are not overly concerned that insureds for life insurance will engage in behavior that could take or shorten their lives just because they are insured. Also, they are not particularly concerned that those who purchase life annuities will engage in behavior to lengthen their lives just because they own annuities. For most of us, the desire to continue living is not influenced by whether we are insured!

On the other hand, insurers are greatly concerned about the possibility that the beneficiary under a life insurance policy might try to shorten the insured's life. They also are greatly concerned about selling a disability income policy whose benefit payment would provide more than the insured could earn from employment. Doing so would mean that the insurance itself provided an incentive for the insured to try to collect the benefits. It would create a moral hazard.

Insurers try to minimize this information asymmetry problem in several ways. For life insurance policies, they try to ensure that the beneficiary has a greater interest in the insured's living than in his or her dying. Also, the wording of insurance contracts is an important means of minimizing moral hazard. For example, to collect disability income benefits, the contract may require the insured to demonstrate the extent of the disability. One of the main rationales for insurer claims settlement departments is to discourage and identify incidents of moral hazard.

Principal–agent problems. A final asymmetric information problem in insurance can arise when one person represents another. The person who represents another is the **agent.** As used here, the term *agent* refers to anyone acting for another, not just to insurance agents representing insurance companies. The person whom the agent represents is the **principal.**

The **principal–agent problem** is when the agent knows more about his or her own actions than does the principal. Because of this information asymmetry, the agent can take advantage of the principal.[3] The agent's incentive is to maximize his or her personal gain, which is not always compatible with simultaneously maximizing the principal's gain.

Principal–agent problems lurk behind innumerable insurance relationships, operations, and practices. The issue of how to ensure that agents do not misrepresent or withhold required information about the company or its products from customers and, conversely, misrepresent or withhold key information about the customer from the company, are principal–agent problems. The typical insurance company (principal) cannot always depend on its agents being completely forthcoming to underwriters about applicants' insurability. After all, salespeople are interested in making the sale to secure a commission. Their personal interests may not align completely with the interests of the insurer (their principal).

At the public policy level, the issue of how to ensure that the insurance regulator (the public's agent) adequately protects the public (the principal) is a principal–agent problem. In these and a host of other situations, inefficiencies can arise when the interests of the agent and the interests of the principal diverge.

The key to minimizing the problem lies in arranging incentives (and disincentives) such that the interests of the agent align with those of the principal. This can be done, for example, by tying compensation as closely as possible to the principal's desired outcome or by requiring disclosure by the agent of potential conflicts between the agent's and principal's interests.

Asymmetric information problems, trade-offs, and solutions. By definition, solutions to information asymmetry problems rest in securing additional information. In each of

---

[3]Note that the other asymmetric information problems can be considered more generalized forms of the principal–agent problem.

the foregoing instances, the affected party could obtain more information to reduce the information asymmetry. An ill-informed buyer can engage in deeper research about his or her insurance needs and the quality and prices of insurance policies. The insurer considering the issuance of a policy can secure additional information about the proposed insured. An insurer's board of directors can establish a stricter system of monitoring managers, and managers can tighten supervision of salespeople. Insurers also can undertake deeper claims investigations to root out fraudulent or exaggerated claims.

Why don't the parties, therefore, simply obtain more information—indeed, simply secure as much information as they believe they need to make well-informed decisions? Contrary to the costless information assumption of the competitive model, securing more thorough information raises costs—either to the consumer in increased search costs or to the insurer in securing information from other sources. Trade-offs are inevitable between (1) the additional expenses incurred to become better informed and (2) the additional claim payments or other costs inherent in making decisions with less information.

The lemons problem is perhaps the most critical market failure in insurance. Individuals and small businesses are not well equipped to evaluate and monitor the financial condition of insurance enterprises. If an insurer is incurring financial difficulties, the principal–agent problem of managers withholding the bad news from its salespeople and shareholders exacerbates the consumer's asymmetric information problem. These problems are less prominent for sophisticated insurance purchasers, such as large businesses, which are better able to make their independent assessments.

Because insurance is a financial future-delivery product tied closely to the public interest, governments judge this information imbalance to warrant substantial oversight of the financial condition of insurers. The widely accepted view is that the public, especially poorly informed consumers, must be protected from the unscrupulous.

The market has some solutions to these problems. Rating agencies monitor insurers' financial condition, rendering opinions as to their solidity. Their services are widely used in Canada, the United Kingdom, and United States but less so in other countries. Also, insurance intermediaries, especially independent agents and brokers, often provide evaluations of insurers.

Even so, government often must provide information for the public good. Also, significant economies of scale and scope exist with respect to the consumption and production of regulatory services, further supporting a governmental role.[4]

Of course, the insurance buyer is often better informed than the seller with respect to other issues. Adverse selection and moral hazard problems exist for insurers. A central purpose of insurance companies' underwriting and claims settling processes is to minimize instances of adverse selection and moral hazard. Additionally, the extreme versions of these problems are addressed through laws that limit recovery under policies obtained through misrepresentation or in which the insured purposefully causes the loss.

Nonexistent Information In many aspects of insurance processes, neither the buyer nor the seller has complete information because the desired information simply does not exist. Insurance contracts promise future delivery and rely on pricing inversion; that is, the price is set before the costs of production (claims and expenses) are completely known. Insurers cannot know the future. Similarly, individuals cannot have complete knowledge about the consequences of their present and future choices. Both face uncertainty.

---

[4]Robert W. Klein, "Issues in Insurance Regulation and NAIC Services," unpublished paper, National Association of Insurance Commissioners, 1995. See also Martin F. Grace and Richard D. Phillips, "The Allocation of Government Regulatory Supervision within a Federal System of Government: Fiscal Federalism and the Case of Insurance Regulatory Oversight," Working Paper 96-2, Center for Risk Management and Insurance Research, Georgia State University (1997).

Environmental factors, such as the economy, inflation, new laws and regulations, and changing consumer attitudes and preferences, present great uncertainty to both buyers and sellers, thus rendering markets suboptimal. This uncertainty leads both buyers and sellers to support ameliorating actions intended to reduce their risk exposure, such as diversification and creation of funds to indemnify insureds of failed insurers.

Because of market failures, private insurers will not supply every type of insurance that consumers demand. Market failures occur when insurers perceive excessive adverse selection or moral hazard problems or when they cannot adequately diversify their loss exposures. Thus, the private insurance mechanism generally offers little unemployment insurance and little insurance for persons with extreme health problems. In each instance, insurers perceive too much uncertainty occasioned by a change in the state of nature or state of the world, coupled with prospects for severe adverse selection. If such exposures are to be insured, government itself or some government-subsidized private arrangement provides the insurance.

Nonexistent and asymmetric information problems also are responsible for individuals who are so completely ill-informed that they are unable to know their own best interests. One of the premises for social insurance programs is that individuals will not or cannot fully arrange for their own financial security, so government must do it for them.

THE ECONOMIC BASIS FOR LIFE AND HEALTH INSURANCE

As with all other products and services that are bought, sold, or traded, life and health insurance is subject to the laws of supply and demand. As with most other products and services, it is reasonable to assume that the higher the price, the less will be demanded and the more will be supplied, and vice versa.[5]

Figure 1-3 illustrates this simple but fundamental economic principle. The demand curve for this insurance policy shows that at a price of P^* and quantity Q^*, the market is in equilibrium—the quantity of insurance supplied equals the quantity demanded. At prices higher than P^*, say P^{**}, insurers would offer more insurance, Q^{**}. At that higher price, however, customers would reduce their insurance purchases to Q^{***}, creating pressure to drive prices back down toward P^*.

This section examines the demand and supply of life and health insurance. We begin with discussions of the conceptual nature of demand and supply and then discuss some of the environmental influences affecting supply and demand. We omit here any explicit discussion of the economics associated with group and social insurance.

The Demand for Life and Health Insurance

The Concept of Human Capital

Economists since Adam Smith have recognized that people are important elements of nations' wealth. The essence of human capital is that investments are made in oneself with an expectation of future benefits. Economic research related to investment in human capital has recently gained substantial recognition. Indeed, the 1991 Nobel Memorial Prize for economics was awarded to Gary S. Becker for his pioneering research on human capital.[6] Investment in human capital—education, for example—has become one of the most cogent explanations for the differences in

---

[5]Worth noting is that research on this issue for individually purchased life and health insurance is sparse. See David F. Babbel, "The Price Elasticity of Demand for Whole Life Insurance," *The Journal of Finance* (March 1985), pp. 225–239.

[6]See Gary S. Becker, "Investment in Human Capital: A Theoretical Analysis," *The Journal of Political Economy,* Vol. 70 (October 1962), pp. 9–49; and Gary S. Becker, *Human Capital,* 2nd ed. (New York: National Bureau of Economic Research, 1975).

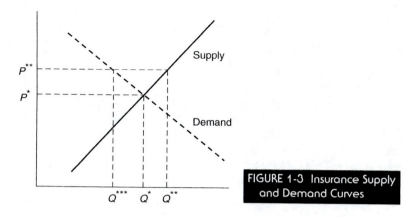

FIGURE 1-3 Insurance Supply and Demand Curves

countries' rates of economic growth as well as differences in wage rates between and within countries.

Estimating the value of human capital is complicated by the necessity to distinguish between expenditures for consumption and investment. Much of what is called consumption constitutes investment in human capital. Thus, expenditures on education, health, and migration to take advantage of better job opportunities are examples, as are workers acquiring on-the-job training. In these and other ways, the quality of human effort is greatly improved and productivity is enhanced.

One method for estimating human capital relies on its yield rather than its cost. The marketplace tends to reflect investment in personal development through wages and salaries. The resulting increase in earnings is viewed as the yield on the investment. Thus, those with university degrees typically earn more than those without them. This earnings differential can be thought of as the return on an investment in education.

The Human Life Value Concept

The human life value (HLV) concept is a part of the general theory of human capital. Although this has been an area of inquiry for more than four centuries, only recently has the interrelationship between human capital and life insurance been acknowledged.[7] Some semblance of the idea is expressed in the Code of Hammurabi, the Bible, the Koran, and early Anglo-Saxon law, in which it was used to determine the compensation allowed to the relatives of an individual killed by a third party. In recent years, the valuation of a human life in connection with legal actions seeking recovery for wrongful death has gained prominence. A considerable body of literature has developed in this area, contributing to a more scientific approach to the calculation of damages in wrongful-death cases.[8] Whatever philosophy is adopted, we must take care to avoid confusing human life valuation with ethical concepts of worth. See Box 1-3.

---

[7]William Petty (1623–1687) was the first economist credited with using the concept of the economic value of a man. Fifty years passed before another economist, Richard Cantillon (1680–1734), made a contribution to the concept of human capital. Then followed Adam Smith (1732–1790), Johann H. von Thunen (1783–1850), John Stuart Mill (1806–1873), and others. In 1853, William Farr, an economist and statistician, derived the first set of equations used to describe the human life value. In so doing, he laid the foundation of the theory as we know it today. See Alfred E. Hofflander, "The Human Life Value: An Historical Perspective," *The Journal of Risk and Insurance,* Vol. 33 (September 1966), pp. 381–391.

[8]On the other hand, welfare economists argue that the human capital approach is flawed. They assert that the appropriate HLV measure is an individual's willingness to pay to *avoid* death, incapacity, or ill health.

BOX 1-3

HUMAN LIFE VALUATION AND ETHICS

The market for property is well developed, and it is relatively easy to determine the price of goods and commodities, especially if they are homogeneous. Each human life, however, is unique. Some persons and cultures seem uneasy about human life valuation. They might contend that it is unethical to try to ascribe an economic value to a human life. Placing a value on human life is difficult because society does not condone the sale of persons. Society does, however, permit sale of a person's services. It is the value of a person's services that the human life value concept measures. Placing an economic value on a person's life (services) is not immoral; it is the concept of ownership of another person that society finds immoral.

Apparently, the HLV concept was first applied to life insurance in the 1880s through the efforts of Jacob L. Green, then president of the Connecticut Mutual Life Insurance Company. It was not, however, until the 1920s that the concept became established as an economic basis for life and health insurance.

In contrast to human capital, which is the production potential of an individual, **human life value** is a measure of the actual future earnings or values of services of an individual—that is, the capitalized value of an individual's future net earnings after subtracting self-maintenance costs such as food, clothing, and shelter.[9] From the standpoint of one's dependents, an individual's human life value is the measure of the value of benefits that the dependents can expect from their breadwinner or supporter. Similarly, from the viewpoint of an organization, the human life value of an employee is the value of his or her services to the firm. Thus, under this approach, there is not necessarily one single human life value. A given human life value is a function of its purpose and value to others.

In 1942, S. S. Huebner proposed the human life value concept as a philosophical framework for the analysis of basic economic risks individuals face. He argued that the human life value has qualitative aspects that give rise to its economic value. See Box 1-4. In Huebner's view, the concept meant more than just a statement that a human life has an economic value. Rather, it involved the five important concepts as shown in Box 1-5.

The human life value is subject to loss through (1) premature death, (2) incapacity, (3) retirement, and (4) unemployment. Any event affecting an individual's earning capacity has a corresponding impact on his or her human life value.

The probability of loss from death and incapacity is significantly greater than from the other commonly insured perils. Less than one building in every 100 ever experiences a significant fire or other loss throughout its entire history, whereas one of every six workers dies before age 65. Moreover, the average property loss in well-protected cities does not exceed 10 to 15 percent of the property value involved; that is, it is a partial loss. Perhaps only one of every 30 fires results in a total loss. The death peril, on the contrary, always results in a total loss to the potential estate. The same is true of some health events. Reasoning from this standpoint, it seems that the death peril is much more serious than fire or other perils. The same can be said for incapacity. Yet people routinely

---

[9]The human life can be viewed as having two components: economic and hedonic. The HLV approach focuses on the economic component. The hedonic approach places value on the enjoyment one derives from living.

BOX 1-4

HUEBNER'S QUALITATIVE AND QUANTITATIVE DIMENSIONS OF THE HUMAN LIFE VALUE

A person can be considered as possessing two estates—an acquired estate and a potential estate. The former refers to what one has acquired in property and financial assets. The latter refers to one's monetary worth as an economic force, that is, one's capability of earning for others beyond the limits of one's self-maintenance, and, if given time, the ability to accumulate surplus earnings into an acquired estate. The insurable value of an individual's economic possibilities is the monetary worth of the following qualitative forces incorporated within one's being: (1) ethical behavior;

(2) good health; (3) willingness to work; (4) willingness to make an investment in the mind; and (5) creative ability and judgment.

The human life value may be defined, quantitatively, as the present value of the expected net earnings of an individual. The same economic principles are applicable whether one is concerned with the appraisal of the value of property or the earning capacity of human beings. The appraisal of an individual's potential earnings involves taking the present value of future projected earnings.

purchase property insurance whereas they often avoid or purchase insufficient amounts of death, disability, and long-term care protection.[10]

Life insurance and health insurance make possible the preservation of an individual's human capital in the face of an uncertain lifetime. The human life value concept provides the philosophical basis for systematizing the insurance purchase decision.

Economic Theories of Consumption and Insurance

Individuals occupy their time either in activities that produce income (or its equivalent) or in those that do not. For the sake of simplicity, economists label these two states of nature as work and leisure. One's investment in self—in human capital—plus one's preferences, time, wealth, income, and a host of other factors influence how a given individual will divide his or her work and leisure time. As Figure 1-4 illustrates, work gives rise to income, which in turn is spent on consumption or is saved. Economic theories of consumption seek to explain consumer consumption and saving behavior over one's lifetime.

Economics is concerned with both positive and normative issues. *Positive issues* involve explanations of observed economic behavior—the "what is" questions. In contrast, *normative issues* are involved in questions relating to "what ought to be."

The human life value concept, therefore, provides a *normative* economic approach to life and health insurance planning. It suggests how one ought to behave. Stated differently, it provides an economic rationale for life and health insurance purchase from a replacement cost perspective. By this, we mean that individuals interested in complete *replacement* of themselves as wage earners would be drawn to its logic and simplicity.

As a *normative* economic concept, however, it can lead to results that are inconsistent with actual consumer behavior. The HLV concept provides an economic *rationale* for the purchase of life insurance, but not an economic *explanation* for its purchase.

---

[10]The economist would immediately want to know why this postulate may be true. Are individuals making provision for these loss potentials using informal mechanisms? Do they underestimate the likelihood of their own death or loss of health or perhaps their own economic value? Are their incomes too low? Are life insurance and disability insurance perceived as offering poor value? Although the following sections explore some of these issues, the fact remains that our knowledge is sketchy.

BOX 1-5

HUEBNER'S FIVE HUMAN LIFE VALUE ADMONITIONS

1. *The human life value should be carefully appraised and capitalized.* The human life value is based on the fact that persons who earn more than is necessary for their self-maintenance have a monetary value to those who are dependent upon them. Thus, it is the present value of that part of the earnings of individuals devoted to family dependents and others who benefit from these individuals' economic earning capacity. Whenever continuance of a life is financially valuable to others, an economic basis for life and health insurance exists.

2. *The human life value should be recognized as the creator of property values.* The human life value is key to turning property into a productive force. In other words, the human life value is the cause and property values are the effect.

3. *The family is an economic unit organized around the human life values of its members.* The family needs to be organized and managed, and its economic values finally liquidated, in the same manner that other enterprises are organized, operated, and liquidated.

4. *The human life value and its protection should be regarded as constituting the principal economic link between the present and succeeding generations.* The realization of the potential net earnings of the breadwinner constitutes the economic foundation for the proper education and development of the children in the event of the breadwinner's premature death or incapacity, and the protection of children against the burden of parent financial support.

5. *In view of the significance of human life values relative to property values, the scientific principles of business management utilized in connection with property values should be applied to life values.* Principles such as appraisal, conservation, indemnity, and depreciation should be applied to the organization, management, and liquidation of human life values. These principles have been applied to property values for decades.

With this in mind, it will prove insightful to examine briefly economic theories of consumption that explain the purchase of life and health insurance—that is, to focus on the positive economics of life insurance. Insurance purchases reduce current consumption (by virtue of the premium payment) to protect the later consumption ability of individuals or their dependents.

Economic Theories of Consumption Each consumption theory begins with the assumption that rational consumers seek to maximize their lifetime utility. **Utility** is a measure of consumer satisfaction derived from economic goods. Individuals seek to maximize their utility and minimize their disutility over their lifetimes—that is, to arrange their affairs to derive maximum enjoyment (and minimum discomfort) throughout their lives.

The maximization of lifetime utility, therefore, involves attempts by consumers to allocate their lifetime incomes in such a way as to achieve an optimum lifetime pattern of consumption. This means planning for the future and not living only for today. This

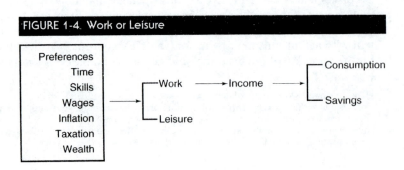

FIGURE 1-4. Work or Leisure

concept is rational, but on what basis would we expect individuals to make allocations between now and the future or, stated differently, between consumption now and consumption (saving) for the future? The economic literature has four hypotheses:

- the absolute income hypothesis
- the relative income hypothesis
- the life cycle hypothesis
- the permanent income hypothesis

Theories of consumption date from the era of the noted economist John Maynard Keynes. In 1935, he espoused what is referred to as the **absolute income hypothesis** when he observed that, on average, the larger a person's income, the smaller the proportion devoted to consumption (and the larger the proportion devoted to saving).[11] His theory suggests, in effect, that as average household income increases, the proportion consumed should decrease to that observed for other households within the new, higher-income bracket. The theory has strong intuitive appeal and formerly enjoyed wide acceptance among economists. With the passage of time, other theories have come to enjoy broader support.

A variation of the Keynesian view by Duesenberry, referred to as the **relative income hypothesis,** argues that consumption depends on the household's income *relative* to the income of households with which it identifies, rather than the *absolute* level of income.[12] Thus, if a household's income were to rise but its relative income position remained unchanged, its division between consumption and saving would remain unchanged. Similarly, if a household's income were to remain unchanged but the income of others with whom it identified rose, the greater would be current consumption in an effort to "keep up with the Joneses." An interesting recent extension of Duesenberry's work argues that certain consumption items typically cannot be readily observed by others (e.g., the amount spent on insurance) and that consumption expenditures thereby vary, depending on the observability of goods and services.[13]

Both the absolute and relative income hypotheses suggest that current consumption is some function of a household's current level of income. Consumption theories posed by Ando and Modigliani[14] and by Friedman[15] take a different view of income. According to the Ando-Modigliani **life cycle hypothesis** of consumption, an individual's income will be low in the beginning and end stages of life and high during the middle of life.

In spite of these life cycle changes in income, however, the individual can be expected to maintain a constant or modestly increasing level of consumption. Figure 1-5 is a presentation of a life cycle of income and consumption. The shaded areas in early and later life represent periods when consumption exceeds income—that is, periods of dissaving.

In early life, the family typically makes good the deficit. In later life, personal savings diminish. The area above the expenditure line and enclosed by the income curve represents periods of savings during which any earlier debts are repaid and amounts accumulated for retirement.

---

[11]In economic terms, the smaller the marginal propensity of a person to consume, the larger is his or her marginal propensity to save. See John Maynard Keynes, *The General Theory of Employment, Interest, and Money* (New York: Harcourt, Brace, and World, Inc., 1935), Chap. 8.

[12]James S. Duesenberry, *Income, Savings, and the Theory of Consumer Behavior* (Cambridge, MA: Harvard University Press, 1949).

[13]Robert H. Frank, "The Demand for Unobservable and Other Nonpositional Goods," *American Economic Review* (March 1985), pp. 101–115.

[14]Albert Ando and Franco Modigliani, "The 'Life Cycle' Hypothesis of Savings: Aggregate Implications and Tests," *American Economic Review* (March 1963).

[15]Milton Friedman, *A Theory of the Consumption Function* (Princeton, NJ: Princeton University Press, 1975).

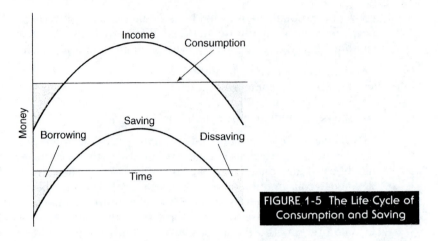

FIGURE 1-5 The Life-Cycle of Consumption and Saving

Friedman's **permanent income hypothesis** for consumption, like the life cycle hypothesis, assumes that individuals wish to smooth their level of lifetime consumption but do so through an assessment of their *permanent* level of income. Permanent income is stable, reflecting some type of weighted (for the time value of money) average of individuals' expected future income. It is an annualized measure of the consumer's expected future income or, stated differently, of the individual's human capital (as with the HLV concept, but with no diminution for self-maintenance expenses). Variations of actual from permanent income (so-called transitory income) are due to chance or accident and do not affect consumption—at least not unless they cease to be chance fluctuations.

Consumption also has its permanent and transitory components. The yearly difference between total income and total consumption is saving, which can fluctuate greatly from year to year under this hypothesis, because the transitory income and consumption components fluctuate independently of each other.

The life cycle and permanent income models are closely related. Households with large, positive transitory incomes in Friedman's model could be in the middle years of the Ando-Modigliani life cycle, and households with large, negative transitory incomes could be in the early or later life cycle states. As a result, the hypotheses often are viewed together or as different conceptualizations of the same issue. In any event, today they are widely accepted explanations of the consumer problem of dividing consumption (and, therefore, saving) between the present and the future.

Consumption Theories and Insurance   In their earliest forms, none of the consumption theories appropriately allowed for the possibility of bequests to heirs or for an uncertain time of death. Obviously, these two extensions make the theories more relevant.

In his seminal paper, Yaari examined the role of insurance within the context of the life cycle model by including the risk of dying. He showed *conceptually* that an individual increases expected lifetime utility by purchasing fair life insurance and fair annuities.[16] "Fair" means paying a premium equal to the expected value of payments to or on behalf of the individual, without charges for expenses or profits.

Pissarides extended Yaari's work by examining the joint motivation of saving for retirement and for bequests via life insurance.[17] He proved that life insurance was

---

[16]Menahem Yaari, "Uncertain Lifetime, Life Insurance, and the Theory of the Consumer," *Review of Economic Studies* (April 1965), pp. 137–150. This finding was confirmed by Stanley Fischer, "A Life Cycle Model of Life Insurance Purchases," *International Economic Review* (February 1973), pp. 132–152.

[17]C. A. Pissarides, "The Wealth-Age Relation with Life Insurance," *Economica* (November 1980), pp. 451–457.

theoretically capable of absorbing all fluctuations in lifetime income and, thereby, could enable consumption and bequests to be independent of the timing of income. As a result, the same effective consumption pattern could be achieved through the appropriate use of life insurance as could be achieved if the time of death were known with certainty.[18] Without life insurance, the lifetime consumption pattern would be different and involve less enjoyment (utility).

Lewis included the preferences of those dependent on the breadwinner's income.[19] His empirical estimates based on U.S. households were encouraging. He found that life insurance ownership was positively related to household income and to the number of dependent children. An important conclusion of his research was that social security substituted for privately purchased life insurance.

Research has established that highly risk-averse individuals will guard against a failure to have sufficient income later in life, so they will save more than individuals who are less risk-averse, and they would be expected to purchase more insurance. The degree of individual risk aversion, therefore, is an important determinant of individual consumption (and saving) patterns, as well as of aggregate national savings and insurance consumption.

Interest in mortality risk aversion has increased because some empirical research suggests that the elderly do not seem to dissave as the life cycle hypothesis would predict.[20] Such findings have led to further interest in the nature of bequests. This issue is of importance to our understanding of life insurance purchases because the demand for life insurance is positively related to motives for bequests.

Of course, bequests are consistent with the life cycle hypothesis because, with uncertainty about the date of death, individuals could die without having exhausted their assets, thus providing their heirs with what are termed *accidental bequests.* Some researchers have suggested that the magnitude of inherited wealth, however, is too large to be explained solely by accidental bequests.[21] At least a portion of bequests must, therefore, be intended—a thesis consistent with altruistic motivations or the desire to help dependents have more wealth so that they would be able to enjoy more leisure time throughout life.

However, other research, based on extensive survey data on retirees, suggests that (1) mortality risk aversion is not as large as previous researchers had assumed and, therefore, (2) most bequests are accidental.[22] The finding that average wealth of the elderly declines with age is further consistent with the life cycle hypothesis.

Another dimension of the life cycle hypothesis as discussed in the literature relates to the use of life annuities. Of course, life annuities offer insurance against the risk of outliving one's resources. Researchers have established that the purchase of actuarially fair annuities is welfare enhancing for risk-averse individuals. For individuals with high-mortality risk aversion, even high-priced annuities may be attractive.

As a practical matter, however, the market for individually purchased life annuities seems thin.[23] One of the hypotheses for this result is the presence of substantial adverse

[18]Ibid., p. 455. Pissarides introduces the concept of perfect life insurance, by which he means that the insurance is actuarially fair and is instantaneously adjustable to meet changing consumer desires and the transferability of budget constraints. In a more practical world, consumption would be affected.

[19]F. D. Lewis, "Dependents and the Demand for Life Insurance," *The American Economic Review* (June 1989), pp. 452–467.

[20]See, for example, S. Danziger, J. Van Der Gaag, E. Smolensky, and M. Taussig, "The Life-Cycle Hypothesis and the Consumption Behavior of the Elderly," *Journal of Post Keynesian Economics,* 5 (1982), pp. 208–227.

[21]L. Kotlikoff and L. Summers, "The Role of Intergenerational Transfers in Aggregate Capital Accumulation," *Journal of Political Economy,* 89 (1981), pp. 706–732.

[22]Michael D. Hurd, "Mortality Risk and Bequests," *Econometrica* (July 1989), pp. 779–813.

[23]Richard Disney, "Pensions as Insurance," *The Geneva Papers on Risk and Insurance* (April 1996), pp. 258–270.

selection. Individuals whose life expectancies are quite high would seek annuities, using their superior knowledge about their expected longevity to secure good deals for themselves. As insurers' annuity pricing schemes are not as refined as their life insurance pricing, adverse selection problems would be more prominent with annuities than with life insurance. Markets for annuities, therefore, would be even more imperfect.

The insurance market generally does not offer lower-priced annuities to individuals with lower survival probabilities. Such persons, therefore, would be expected to shun annuities in favor of holding greater proportions of their wealth in other assets—contrary to the expected utility-optimizing behavior implicit in the life cycle model. Therefore, the individual is not able to maximize lifetime utility because fairly priced annuities were unavailable to him or her. Because of this failure, some have suggested that government-mandated life annuities, such as through social insurance, are justified.[24]

The preceding economic findings probably come as no particular surprise to thoughtful students of insurance. This observation, however, in no way diminishes the importance of the research. Practical, real-world problems and consumer decision making can appear bewildering and confusing in the absence of a systematic theory. Theories lead to models, which lead to tests that confirm, refute, or cause modification of the models or theories. In so doing, we learn more about consumer preferences and choice.[25] Better-suited products and services offering good value often result.

The Production of Life and Health Insurance

Our intent here is to provide an overview of how the insurance supply evolves.[26] Insurance supply is a function of price, as Figure 1-3 suggests. The higher the unit price, the greater will be the quantity supplied. However, the supply of insurance is not subject to direct assessment because insurance output is not subject to precise definition or measurement. Even so, we know that insurance supply—however defined—is positively related to insurer risk-bearing capacity. Risk-bearing capacity, in turn, depends on insurer capital, that is the difference between assets and liabilities. Of course, insurer technical expertise and management capabilities also are important factors in determining insurance supply.

The production of insurance services—as with other financial services—relies on financial and human capital. Financial capital underpins all operations. The most important operations in the production process include insurance pricing, underwriting, and claims handling; investment management; and distribution, each of which is summarized next. Figure 1-6 illustrates important relationships in this process.

The Role of Capital

Financial capital provides a cushion against the possibility that actual expenses, claims, and investment results may deviate negatively from assumptions implicit in the insurer's pricing. Insurance policies are contingent claim contracts that rely on pricing inversion, which means the product is priced before actual production costs are known. Insurers, therefore, must provide a margin for unfavorable pricing deviations if the market is to perceive that the insurer can meet its obligations. Insurers, in effect, can borrow additional capital through the purchase of **reinsurance,** which is the purchase of insurance by the in-

---

[24]See ibid.

[25]See, for example, John J. Burnett and Bruce A. Palmer, "Examining Life Insurance Ownership Through Demographic and Psychographic Characteristics," *The Journal of Risk and Insurance,* Vol. 52 (September 1985), pp. 453–467 and Robert Ferber and Lucy Chao Lee, "Acquisition and Accumulation of Life Insurance in Early Married Life," *The Journal of Risk and Insurance,* Vol. 47 (December 1980), pp. 713–734.

[26]This section draws from Harold D. Skipper, Jr., "The Structure of Insurance Markets Worldwide," in *International Risk and Insurance,* pp. 81–87.

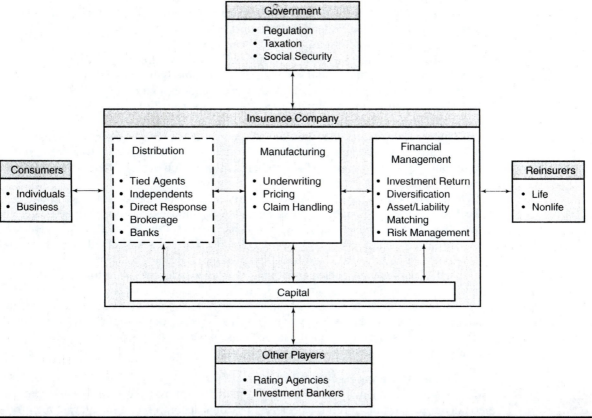

FIGURE 1-6 Insurer Operations and Relationships

surance company. Overall, the greater an insurer's capital, compared with its premium writings and liabilities, the greater the perceived security and the more favorable its reception among informed buyers, their representatives, and the public rating services.

Here lies the lemons problem, the most significant consumer problem in insurance. Consumers pay now for the promise of future payment under contractually defined conditions. Yet what assurance does the buyer have that the insurer will be able to pay? A strong capital position is desirable, but how does the consumer know what is "strong"?

A firm's capital (net worth) is the simple difference between its assets and liabilities. Even if the consumer determines what a strong capital position is, can the consumer be assured that the firm's apparent capital position is not inflated through asset overvaluation or liability undervaluation?

Insurance Production Process

The principal technical elements of the insurance production process (manufacturing) relate to pricing, underwriting, and claims handling. **Actuaries** determine insurance premiums and necessary reserves using their best estimates of future losses and expenses, with an eye toward competitiveness.

Because of time lags between the receipt of premiums and loss payments, the competitive premium will be the present value of expected losses, expenses, and profits. The greater the average period between premium payment and loss payout, the greater the influence of investment returns in setting rates. Thus, investment results can be exceedingly important in annuities, long-term care insurance, and some forms of disability income insurance. They are relatively less important in group life and health insurance, in term life insurance, and in some forms of health insurance.

Unlike the situation in non-life insurance, the premiums for most individually issued life insurance policies and some disability income policies are guaranteed at policy issuance. Thus, to the extent that the insurer includes a guaranteed, liberal discount factor—a high investment return—in its rates, its exposure to pricing errors and possible insolvency is heightened.

Underwriters determine whether and on what terms to issue a requested insurance policy. The underwriter must assemble information about the person to assess the loss potential—to rectify the insurer's asymmetric information problem. For high-value policies, the underwriting process can be quite complex.

The expertise required of **claims personnel**—those who negotiate and settle claims—varies directly with the nature of insurance. Claims under life insurance policies are settled when the beneficiary sends a claim form and a copy of the insured's death certificate to the insurer. Health insurance claims can be much more complex, with claims personnel being particularly attuned to possibilities of moral hazard, including fraud.

Claims personnel, sometimes with the assistance of an actuary, estimate amounts to be established as balance sheet liabilities for unpaid claims. This matter is more important for health than for life claims. In life insurance, the actuarial department establishes liabilities for future claims, known as **policy reserves,** or **mathematical reserves.** These reserves are based on mathematical formulas, mortality tables, and assumptions as to future investment earnings.

Financial Management

Life insurers manage significant investment portfolios. They have strong incentives to maximize investment returns because this can be a major factor in determining product competitiveness and profitability. A poorly diversified or low-quality portfolio can lead to financial difficulties and even failure, as several North American insurer failures demonstrate.

Financial management requires decisions on investment quality and quantity, including asset/liability matching and diversification. National insurance regulation places severe limits on insurer investments.

Distribution

Insurers sell insurance in one or a combination of three ways: (1) through direct response, (2) through agents, or (3) through banks. An insurer's success ties directly to the success of its distribution system. Some insurers sell directly to customers—**direct response**—without the use of intermediaries, via the Internet, mail, telephone solicitation, newspaper advertisements, or other direct means. Although relatively little insurance is sold worldwide through such direct solicitation, the proportion is growing in some markets, particularly in the United Kingdom, and is expected to continue.

The great majority of life insurance worldwide is sold through agents—called *intermediaries* in many markets. An **insurance agent** is a legal representative of the insurer. Two broad types of insurance agents are found internationally. Some agents—called variously **captive, exclusive,** or **tied agents**—sell exclusively for one company. **Independent agents** represent several insurers.

A **broker** is ordinarily thought of as the legal representative of the insurance purchaser. Brokers are expected to be knowledgeable about the overall insurance market and tend to work with larger or more complex cases. Insurance brokers, and also independent agents, reinforce product and price competition by rectifying, to some extent, the information asymmetry between buyers and sellers. In the United States, brokers who sell to individuals are considered legally as agents, and, therefore, they represent the insurer.

Banks are important insurance sellers in many markets. They sell approximately 25 percent of individual annuities in the United States and control more than 50 percent of the total life insurance market in France. In the majority of instances, the bank serves as an agent for either an affiliated insurer or an insurer with whom the bank has a special arrangement. In no major country are banks broadly permitted to underwrite insurance, although most countries allow them to do so through holding company arrangements. Restrictions in Japan and the United States limit banks' ability to sell insurance, much to the chagrin of national bankers. Banks have been most successful in selling simple, commodity-type life insurance products.

CONCLUSION

The life insurance business will continue to evolve. Indeed, change in insurance is occurring at an unprecedented pace. Many of yesterday's insurance practices differ from those of today, and many of tomorrow's practices will differ significantly from those of today. The fundamentals of risk and insurance, however, do not change, although our understanding of them deepens with time.

We should not study insurance as if we were examining sets of facts, figures, and operational details independent of their larger context. The fundamentals of risk and insurance provide this larger context as well as the foundation on which we construct our house of knowledge. The stronger that foundation, the more lasting will be our knowledge and the more easily we can add to it.

Questions

1. Insurance markets are imperfect and are often characterized by information problems that pose substantial challenges to life and health insurance providers. Explain how adverse selection and moral hazard complicate the supply of life and health insurance.
2. Give examples of how life and health insurers manage information problems that confront them in insurance markets. (There are many ways that life and health insurers manage information problems within marketing strategies, policy wording, claim settlement practices, and other aspects of their operations.)
3. How does the concept of human capital help explain the demand for life and health insurance?
4. The economic theories of consumption presented in this chapter purport to explain some of the variation in rates of consumption and savings over individual's lives. What do you believe each of the following theories predicts about an individual's demand for life insurance?
   a. absolute income hypothesis
   b. relative income hypothesis
   c. life cycle/permanent income hypothesis

CHAPTER

2

LIFE AND HEALTH INSURANCE PRICING FUNDAMENTALS

Objectives

- Understand the law of large numbers as it relates to insurance.

- Describe insurers' pricing objectives and explain why they are of relevance to the life insurer and consumer.

- Outline elements of life insurance rate making including the assumptions made in the absence of perfect information.

- Draw distinctions between participating and guaranteed cost, nonparticipating life insurance.

- Explain how asset share analysis is used to test the adequacy of life insurance rates.

PRINCIPLES OF INSURANCE

As noted in chapter 1, humans are exposed to many serious perils, such as property losses from fire and windstorm, and personal losses from disability and death. Although individuals cannot predict or completely prevent the occurrence of these perils, they can provide against their financial effects. Of course, the function of insurance is to safeguard against such misfortunes by having the losses of the unfortunate few paid by the contributions of the many who are exposed to the same peril. This is the essence of insurance—the sharing of losses.

Law of Large Numbers

Insurance relies on the law of large numbers to minimize the speculative element and reduce volatile fluctuations in year-to-year losses. The **law of large numbers,** applied to insurance, holds that the greater the number of similar exposures (e.g., lives insured) to a peril (e.g., death), the less observed loss experience will deviate from expected loss experience. Risk and uncertainty diminish as the number of exposure units increases.

The law of large numbers does not suggest that losses to particular individuals will become more predictable. Rather it states that the larger the group insured, the more predictable will be the loss experience for the group as a whole, other things being the same. (The fact that insurers issue policies of varying face amounts suggests that other things often are not the same.)

To insure a single life against death for $1,000 is clearly a gamble. If the number of persons insured is increased to 100, a large element of uncertainty is still present. If 500,000 similar persons are insured, however, observed death rates probably will vary from expected rates by less than 1 percent. Thus, the insurer should be able to determine its anticipated death claims with a manageable degree of accuracy. In theory, if the number of lives insured was so large as to make the application of the law of large numbers virtually perfect, and if no possibility of a catastrophe existed (e.g., war or epidemic), practically all uncertainty as to the accuracy of the estimated losses during a given period would be removed.

Nature of Perils Insured

Although all forms of insurance are alike in that they require a combination of many risks into a group, they differ with regard to the perils covered. A **peril** is a cause of loss, such as fire or windstorm, with respect to property, or an accident with respect to health. In the nonlife forms of insurance, perils may or may not happen. In life insurance, the event against which protection is granted—death—is uncertain for one year, but the probability of death generally increases with age until it becomes a virtual certainty. If a life insurance policy is to protect an insured during the whole of his or her life, an adequate fund must be accumulated to meet a claim that is certain to occur.

In the case of health insurance, not everyone becomes ill or suffers injury, and the risk does not follow as consistent a pattern as does the risk of dying. Under long-term health insurance contracts, however, the risk insured against increases over time, so it is necessary to charge steadily higher premiums or to accumulate an adequate fund to meet the relatively higher rates of claims that will develop as insureds grow older.

Gambling and Insurance

Some persons allege that insurance is a gamble. One hears such remarks as, "The insurance company is betting you won't have a loss, and you're betting that you will." From the insured's point of view, insurance is the antithesis of gambling. Gambling creates a risk where none existed. Insurance transfers an already existing exposure and, through the pooling of similar loss exposures, actually reduces risk. Insurance companies, of course, prefer that insureds not have losses. However, losses are inevitable and are planned for in insurers' rate structures.

PRICING INDIVIDUAL LIFE AND HEALTH INSURANCE

The preceding insurance concepts and principles are fundamental to understanding how insurance functions. This section provides an overview of how life insurance and health insurance are priced.

Life and Health Insurance Pricing Objectives

The three life and health insurance pricing objectives are: (1) Premium rates should be adequate, (2) they should be equitable, and (3) they should not be excessive. Each is discussed next.

Rate Adequacy

Insurance company rates must be adequate in light of the benefits promised under the company's insurance products. Rate inadequacy can lead to severe financial problems, if not insolvency.

Rate adequacy means that, for a given block of policies, total payments collected now and in the future by the insurer plus the investment earnings attributable to any net retained funds should be sufficient to fund the current and future benefits promised plus cover related expenses. A **block of policies** ordinarily constitutes all policies issued by the insurer under the same schedules of rates and values and on the same policy form.

An insurer cannot know with certainty the degree of rate adequacy until the final policy in the block has terminated. Because individually issued life insurance and health insurance may be issued at rates and on terms and conditions that may be guaranteed for many years, the issue of rate adequacy is especially important in establishing initial premium levels. In fact, as shown later, life insurance companies conduct tests to ensure that rates charged are adequate (as well as equitable and not excessive).

Life and health insurance rates are regulated to ensure adequacy in some countries, although the trend worldwide is toward deregulation of rates. Generally, life insurance rates are not regulated in the United States, but health insurance rates often are subject to regulation. A form of indirect regulation of both life and health insurance rates exists in the United States and most other countries in the form of requirements to establish minimum policy liabilities on insurer financial statements.

Rate Equity

Rates charged for life and health insurance should be equitable to policyowners. Equity means charging premiums commensurate with the expected losses and other costs that insureds bring to the insurance pool. Stated differently, no unfair subsidization should exist of any class of insureds by any other class of insureds.

The achievement of equity is a goal to be sought. In an imperfect world, it cannot be attained absolutely. Concepts of equity must give way to practical realities. These realities include the fact that the larger the number of separate classifications of insureds, the greater the expense in administering the plan. Also, a large enough group is necessary to permit reasonable prediction of losses within each classification. The assessment of the precise extra cost that each insured brings to the pool is simply impossible.

As discussed later, the pursuit of equity is one of the goals of underwriting. **Underwriting** is the process by which insurers decide whether to issue insurance to a person and the terms and prices. Life insurers strive toward equitable treatment of insureds by varying life and health insurance rates by factors such as age, sex, plan, health, and benefits provided. Generally, a greater degree of refinement in rate classes—and, therefore, more actuarial equity—exists for life insurance than for health insurance. Actuarial equity is sometimes in conflict with concepts of social equity. For example, some persons believe it to be socially unacceptable to charge different life and health insurance rates to otherwise identically situated men and women.

Rates Not Excessive

Life and health insurance rates should not be excessive in relation to the benefits provided. If the rate adequacy criterion can be considered as establishing conceptually a floor for rates, the "rates not excessive" criterion can be considered as establishing a ceiling.

Many countries and U.S. states define excessiveness with respect to some health insurance policies. These jurisdictions often provide that the insurer must reasonably expect to pay or actually pay in claims at least a certain minimum percentage (e.g., 50 percent) of the premiums collected.

Prices charged for life and health insurance in the United States and many other countries vary from company to company and, with some companies, prices are high. Even so, competition within insurance markets worldwide is keener than in times past, thus discouraging excessive prices. Simply put, in competitive markets life insurance companies are not likely to sell much insurance if the rates they charge or the interest rates they credit to policy cash values are not competitive.

Life and Health Insurance Pricing Elements

A sound understanding of life and health insurance requires a sound understanding of the elements used in their pricing. The calculation of life and health insurance rates and values requires information and assumptions regarding four elements:

1. the probability of the insured event occurring
2. the time value of money
3. the benefits promised
4. loadings to cover expenses, taxes, profits, and contingencies

Insurance pricing is based on the concept of pooling or loss sharing. Loss sharing in turn involves the accumulation of a fund from amounts paid by insureds to provide benefits to the unfortunate few who suffer loss. To establish the amount to be charged, the insurer must start with some idea as to the likelihood of losses for the group.

The likelihood of losses in life and health insurance is shown by specially constructed tables. **Mortality tables** show yearly probabilities of death. **Morbidity tables** show yearly probabilities or other information on loss of health. These tables show incidences of death and loss of health for a given group of insureds over time—often from birth to the death of the final persons in the group. These tables constitute the foundations of life and health insurance pricing.

Persons purchasing life insurance are not the same age. Generally, younger persons are less likely to die or suffer a morbidity condition within the next year than older persons. Equity, therefore, requires that premium rates charged be graded upward as the age at which the policy is issued increases.

Life and health insurance companies collect premiums in advance of providing insurance coverage. In longer-term coverages, that portion not needed immediately to cover losses and loadings is invested and produces earnings that are used to supplement premium income to fund future expected benefits and ongoing expenses. In such cases, insurers discount (lower) premiums in advance in recognition of the fact that they will earn interest on the accumulated funds.

Premium computation must take account of the coverage period, the level of coverage, as well as all other factors related to the benefits promised under the contract. Included here is the likelihood of policyowners voluntarily terminating their policies. With life insurance, the amount of benefit payout is typically fixed and known in advance. With health insurance contracts, the total benefit payout usually is not known in advance. This fact complicates health insurance pricing.

Many types of insurance policies are sold. Some insure against death, disability, or incapacity for a limited number of years only, whereas others cover the whole of life; some call for the payment of premiums for a stated number of years only, others for the entire duration of the contract; for some, premiums are fixed, whereas with others the policyowner determines the level of premiums to be paid, within certain guidelines. Some promise the payment of policy benefits in a single sum, whereas others provide for payment in a fixed number of installments, and so on. The rates for each coverage configuration are determined, not only with reference to estimated probabilities of death, illness, or injury, but also according to the nature of the benefits promised and the expected premium payment pattern.

These complex conditions cannot be gauged appropriately by companies unless they follow sound rate computation principles. Life insurance typically provides a definite benefit amount in the event of death or survival. Disability insurance typically promises a definite benefit. Other forms of health insurance provide benefits intended to finance long-term care or medical expenses because of a particular illness, injury, or incapacity. It is essential, therefore, that an accurate determination of the expected benefit cost be made and that an adequate amount be charged—an amount that is equitable as to claim likelihood, types of coverage, and other relevant factors. This is especially important because, unlike most other types of insurance, some life and health insurance contracts extend for long periods or even throughout life, and cannot be canceled by the company.

Net rates are insurance rates calculated to recognize (1) the probability of the insured event, (2) the time value of money, and (3) the benefits promised. They make no allowance for the expenses the insurer incurs in selling, issuing, and maintaining the policy, nor do they make provision for taxes, profits, or unforeseen contingencies. When **loadings**—amounts to cover expenses, taxes, contingencies, and profits—are added to the net rate, we obtain the **gross rate**—the amount charged policyowners.

The foregoing procedure for deriving gross premium rates, followed in principle by many insurers, is used here to illustrate insurance pricing concepts. However, a common method of deriving gross premium rate structures is for the insurer to select gross rates (based on market and competitive considerations), and then to test these rates against its objectives and expectations as to realistic future experience. If the test rate does not produce the profit and other desired results, the rate (or other policy elements) will be changed and the test repeated. With this procedure, the insurer does not calculate a net rate, then add amounts to cover loadings. Rather, the insurer simply selects a target gross rate to be tested. This amount, for example, may be the rate currently being charged by the company, or it may be a rate charged by competitors for similar coverage. (See chapter 30.)

Still another approach to establishing a gross premium rate structure is to calculate gross premium rates directly through the use of realistic interest, mortality, expense, taxes, and lapse assumptions, and a specific provision for contingencies and profit (or contribution to surplus). With cash values and a dividend scale assumed, the gross premium rate structure is determined by solving a mathematical equation.

No matter how the tentative gross rate is derived, it is tested against the company's anticipated future operating experience. The following discussion and examples focus on life insurance. The same principles and approaches, however, apply to health insurance pricing.

Life Insurance Rate Computation

The simplest form of life insurance protection is yearly renewable term (YRT) insurance. To illustrate the preceding principles, a brief explanation follows of the YRT plan, as well as of single-premium and flexible-premium plans.

Yearly Renewable Term Life Insurance

Yearly renewable term life insurance provides coverage for a period of one year only, but guarantees the policyowner the right to renew (i.e., continue) the policy even if the insured suffers poor health or otherwise becomes uninsurable. Each year's premium pays the policy's share of mortality costs for that year only. The renewal premium rate increases each year to reflect the annual rise in death rates as age advances.

The increasing probability of death may be seen in Table 2-1, which shows the annual male and female rates of mortality per 1,000 lives at various ages according to the *1980 Commissioners Standard Ordinary (CSO) Mortality Table,* the standard currently required by U.S. insurance regulatory authorities for the valuation (measurement) of certain policy liabilities. To derive life insurance premiums, insurers often use mortality rates that they judge to represent realistic expectations of future mortality experience for insured lives.

Table 2-1 shows that the rate of dying generally increases with age and at an increasing rate, rising ultimately to a certainty. Also, observe that female mortality experience is more favorable than that of males at every age. This relationship generally holds

TABLE 2-1	Rates of Mortality per 1,000 Lives	
	Rate of Mortality	
Age	*Male*	*Female*
10	0.73	0.68
20	1.90	1.05
30	1.73	1.38
40	3.02	2.42
50	6.71	4.96
60	16.08	9.47
70	36.51	22.11
80	98.84	65.99
90	221.77	190.75
99	1,000.00	1,000.00

for other U.S. mortality tables as well as for mortality tables used in other countries. As a result of these mortality differences, life insurers vary their premium charges by age, and the majority also vary them by the insured's sex, with females being charged lower rates for life insurance and higher rates for life annuities.

An example will illustrate YRT rate derivation. The mortality rate for males, age 30, according to the *1980 CSO Mortality Table,* is 1.73 per 1,000. If 100,000 males age 30 are insured for $1,000 each, an insurer would expect to pay 173 death claims for a total payment of $173,000. As 100,000 persons would be insured, the company would have to collect $1.73 from each insured individual to accumulate a fund sufficient to meet the expected 173 death claims. This rate is the same as the death rate.

This illustration includes only the mortality charge, as investment income as well as loadings are ignored. To derive a net rate, it is necessary to consider investment earnings.

Assume that the insurer credits a 5 percent annual return on all policyowner-related funds. To simplify the analysis, assume also that policyowner payments to the insurer are made at the beginning of the policy year (a realistic assumption) and that death claims are paid only at year end (an unrealistic assumption) and that, therefore, the insurer has use of the funds for a full year.

Ignoring other pricing components for now, the insurer need not now collect the full $173,000. In fact, the insurer need collect only $164,762. This amount, accumulated at 5 percent interest, will equal the $173,000 needed at the end of the year to honor all death claims ($164,762 × 1.05 = $173,000). Thus, the insurer need not charge each insured the full $1.73 per $1,000 of insurance. It can charge $1.65 per $1,000, relying on its investment income to contribute the additional $0.08 per $1,000.

To this net rate, we must add amounts necessary to provide reasonable allowances for expenses, taxes, contingencies, and profit. To keep the analysis simple, however, we will continue to ignore these elements.

As death rates increase with age, the premium rate that policyowners must pay each year increases proportionately. As surviving members of an insured group renew their insurance year after year, the increasing premium rate causes some to question the advisability of continuing the insurance. As the increases become more burdensome, those in good health tend to discontinue their coverage, whereas those in poor health have strong incentives to renew their policies even at the higher rates necessitated by advancing age. In other words, adverse selection sets in.

If insurers did not anticipate this phenomenon, it would eventually result in a continuing group of insureds whose mortality experience would exceed that implicit within the rate schedule. The combination of increasing mortality rates, caused by advancing age, plus adverse selection produces abnormally high mortality rates; consequently, insurance companies commonly place a limit on the period during which yearly renewable term insurance can be renewed, or, alternatively, they provide premium levels for later years that are high enough to cover the anticipated adverse selection.

The Single-Premium Plan

Another method of purchasing insurance is to pay for the policy with a single premium. In contrast to the yearly renewable term net rate of $1.65 for a male aged 30 (followed by rates each of which increases annually), the net premium for a single-premium whole life policy for a male aged 30, under the same mortality and interest assumptions as previously, is $150.45 for each $1,000 of coverage. This amount, when increased for expenses, taxes, profits, and contingencies, pays for the contract in full.

The single-premium whole life plan involves the payment of the policy's entire future mortality charges in a single sum. As the insurer will on average have use of these funds over an extended period of time, investment earnings constitute a major component from which benefits will be paid.

A highly simplified and admittedly unrealistic example will demonstrate the points made earlier. Assume that 100,000 males, all aged 95, purchase single-premium whole life policies whose face amounts are all $1,000. Assume further that the life insurer calculates its net rates based on the *1980 CSO Mortality Table*, with interest at 5 percent per year. A modified version of the *1980 CSO Mortality Table* is shown in Table 2-2.

Of the 100,000 males living at age 95, 33,000 are expected to die during the next year. These figures are based on a probability of death of 0.330 (i.e., 100,000 × 0.330 = 33,000), which is taken from the *1980 CSO Mortality Table*. This means that 67,000 males are expected to have survived to the age of 96.

Of the expected 67,000 survivors, an estimated 25,795 will die during the next year, based on the *1980 CSO Mortality Table* death probability of 0.385 (i.e., 67,000 × 0.385 = 25,795). Thus, 41,205 of the original group of 100,000 are estimated to survive to age 97, of which an estimated 19,778 are expected to die during the next year, and so on. Note that during age 99 all 7,328 of the survivors will be considered to have died.

From these data one can calculate the total amount that the insurer must collect today to be able to honor all future death claims in this group. Table 2-3 illustrates the calculation. Column 4 gives present value factors that convert a given amount to be paid in the future to its present-day equivalent, assuming a time value of money of 5 percent. For example, $1,000 to be paid in five years is equivalent to $783.50 today ($1,000 × 0.7835). Stated differently, $783.50 today will accumulate to $1,000 in five years if invested to earn 5 percent per year.

TABLE 2-2 Modified Version of *1980 CSO Mortality Table*

(1)	(2)	(3)	(4)
Age	*Number Living (Beginning of Year)*	*Probability of Death (During the Year)*	*Number Dying (During the Year)*
95	100,000	0.330	33,000
96	67,000	0.385	25,795
97	41,205	0.480	19,778
98	21,427	0.658	14,099
99	7,328	1.000	7,328
100	0		

TABLE 2-3 Present Value of Claims for 95-Year-Old Males

(1)	*(2)*	*(3)*	*(4)*	*(5)*
Policy Year	*Number Dying During the Year*	*Total Death Claims ($1,000 × Number Dying) For the Year*	*Present Value Factor at 5%*	*Present Value Total Death Claims*
1	33,000	$33,000,000	0.9525	$31,429,200
2	25,795	25,795,000	0.9070	23,396,065
3	19,778	19,778,000	0.8639	17,084,236
4	14,099	14,099,000	0.8227	11,599,247
5	7,328	7,328,000	0.7835	5,741,488
			Total Present Value	**$89,250,236**

During the first policy year (i.e., during age 95), 33,000 insureds of the original group of 100,000 are estimated to die, so the insurer will pay out a total of $33,000,000 in death claims ($1,000 × 33,000 deaths) at the end of the first year. However, the insurer needs only $31,429,200, as this amount accumulated at 5 percent interest equals $33,000,000 at the end of one year. Remember that premiums are assumed to be paid in advance and death claims are assumed to be paid at the end of the year of death.

During the second policy year, an estimated $25,795,000 is needed to honor the claims falling due during that year. However, those claims will not be paid for two years from the time of the issuance of the single-premium policy. Thus, the insurer needs to collect only $23,396,065 in advance ($25,795,000 × 0.9070) to have available $25,795,000 in two years.

The process is continued for the other three policy years, with the present value factor becoming smaller (i.e., the discount being larger) the greater the time period involved. The result of this process is that the insurer must collect $89,250,236 to be able to honor the $100,000,000 in claims as they occur; that is, the insurer needs to collect only $0.89 in premiums for each dollar of benefits to be paid out. The additional $0.11 is derived from investment income.

As we assumed an initial 100,000 insureds, the insurer would charge each insured a net single premium of $892.50 ($89,250,236 divided by 100,000) for each $1,000 of whole life insurance protection. To this net premium would be added amounts to cover loadings, the result of which may yield a gross premium in excess of $1,000! No one would logically purchase insurance at such advanced ages because it is not economically feasible. As in the case of other insured exposures, the loadings added to the value of the pure loss costs make insurance practicable only when the probability of loss is relatively low. Good risk management suggests avoiding merely exchanging funds with an insurance company.

This calculation also demonstrates clearly that a life insurance policy for the whole of life can be viewed as a series of yearly renewable term insurances continuing to the end of the mortality table. Note that the column 3 figures shown in Table 2-2, if multiplied by the policy face amounts of $1,000, give the year-by-year mortality charges, thus giving the yearly renewable term costs without the interest factor.

As all mortality charges with single-premium life insurance are prepaid, the life insurance company cannot consider the full premium earned when paid. As is clear from Table 2-3, the initial premium plus interest earned thereon will be utilized over the policy period to meet claims. The insurer must show a liability on its balance sheet equal to the then value of the unused fund. This value represents prefunded mortality charges and is the policy reserve referred to earlier.

Table 2-4 illustrates how these policy reserves evolve for this block of policies. The initial fund of $89,250,236 is developed from each of the 100,000 insureds, each age 95,

TABLE 2-4   Policy Reserves for Net Single-Premium Whole Life Insurance

(1)	(2)	(3)	(4)	(5)	(6)	(7)
Policy Year	Number Living at Beginning of Year	Fund Balance at Beginning of Policy Year	Interest Earned on Fund (at 5%) During Policy Year [(3) × 5%]	Death Claims Paid at End of Policy Year (See Table 2-3, Column 3)	Fund Balance at End of Policy Year [(3) + (4) − (5)]	Fund Balance per Policy [(6) ÷ (2) Next]
1	100,000	$89,250,236	$4,462,512	$33,000,000	$60,712,748	$906
2	67,000	60,712,747	3,035,637	25,795,000	37,953,384	921
3	41,205	37,953,384	1,897,669	19,778,000	20,073,053	937
4	21,427	20,073,053	1,003,653	14,099,000	6,977,706	952
5	7,328	6,977,705	348,885	7,328,000	0[a]	–

[a] Actually equals –$1,410 instead of $0. The cumulative effect of rounding causes this slight relative difference.

paying a net single premium of $892.50 for $1,000 of insurance coverage. (We ignore the $236 excess.) This fund earns interest (at 5 percent) of $4,462,512 during the first policy year. Death claims of $33,000,000 are paid at the end of the first year, resulting in a fund balance or aggregate policy reserve of $60,712,747 at the end of the first policy year.

Although policy reserves for a block of policies are an aggregate concept, the portion applicable to each policy can be calculated. This portion is found by dividing the aggregate reserve by the number of insureds surviving the first policy year (67,000) to yield a reserve per policy of $906.

At the beginning of the second year, the aggregate reserve liability is the same as the previous year's ending balance ($60,712,747). (This assumes that all surviving insureds continue their policies.) This fund is credited with $3,035,637 in interest, and $25,795,000 is paid out in death claims at year end. The aggregate reserve falls to $37,953,384, which represents the present value of the future benefits promised under the remaining policies. Note that the reserve per policy has increased to $921, even though the aggregate reserve has declined.

The foregoing process is continued through the third, fourth, and fifth policy years. Note that the aggregate policy reserve (column 6) continues to decline, but that the per-policy reserve must continue to grow. The per-policy reserve must equal the policy face amount the instant before the final policies mature as death claims at the end of age 99.

The last policy year deserves comment. The number of insureds living at the beginning of the year is 7,328. Based on the mortality table used here, it is assumed that all remaining insureds die during this year and that the full $1,000 face amount per policy is paid to the beneficiaries at year end.

The beginning reserve is $6,977,705. Interest of $348,885 is credited to the reserve. The $7,328,000 in death claims is paid even if, in reality, some insureds survive the period. The assumption within the premium computation is that all insureds died, so the insurer would pay the face amount on all policies, even if all insureds did not die.

The aggregate reserve at the end of the fifth policy year (i.e., at age 100) would be exactly zero were all rounding errors eliminated. In theory, the aggregate policy reserve balance the instant before the 7,328 claims were paid would, of course, exactly equal the death claims and the per-policy reserve would be $1,000 per policy.[1]

---

[1]The reader is cautioned that the preceding examples as well as others in this chapter have been simplified to illustrate the concepts involved and do not necessarily represent actual insurance company practice. For example, minimum policy reserve standards are established by law in many countries and may have little or no relationship to actual insurer results. Mortality and interest assumptions mandated by regulatory authorities coincide only rarely with those implicit within an insurer's gross premium rate structure.

In the preceding example, it was assumed that all 100,000 insureds paid their net single premiums for their $1,000 of insurance coverage, and none terminated their policies prior to death. In fact, policyowners regularly decide for various reasons to voluntarily terminate (other than by dying!) their insurance policies. In these situations, the question arises as to what, if anything, the terminating policyowner should be entitled, in terms of a refund of all or a portion of the prepayments made toward future mortality charges. Should the policyowner be considered as having forfeited these prepayments or should the insurer be required to provide some "nonforfeiture" benefit?

This important question has been settled by law in some countries and by industry practice in others. For example, U.S. law requires that all life insurance policies that involve *significant* prepayments of future mortality charges must provide for a type of partial refund of these prepayments to terminating policyowners. What is "significant" is defined by law, as discussed in chapter 29. Other countries' laws, such as those of Canada and the United Kingdom, do not mandate minimum amounts, but companies typically provide such nonforfeiture benefits as a matter of practice.

The amount of these prefunded mortality charges that is available to a terminating policyowner is referred to as a life insurance policy's **cash surrender value.** This value is the savings element in every cash-value insurance policy, and it is different from the policy reserve. The policy reserve is a pro rata share of the balance sheet representation of the company's future obligations to policyowners as a group. Cash surrender values are those amounts that are available to the policyowner upon voluntary policy termination (surrender). Thus, the policy reserve in year 3 for the policy in Table 2-4 was $937. The cash surrender value would be somewhere between zero and $937, depending on applicable law and company practice. More will be said on this point later in this chapter and in chapter 9.

The Level-Premium Plan

Few persons purchase their life insurance with a single-premium payment because of the relatively large initial outlay required. The practical difficulties arising from the single-premium plan and the fact that mortality rates increase with age have been solved through the use of the level-premium plan. The fundamental idea of the level-premium plan is that the company can accept the same premium each year (a level premium), provided that the level premiums collected are the mathematical equivalent of the corresponding single premium. As a result, the level premiums paid in the early years of the contract will be more than sufficient to pay current death claims but will be less than adequate to meet death claims that occur in later years. Life insurance was, thus, one of the first products marketed on the installment plan.

This leveling results in the creation of a fund from premiums paid in the early policy years, when mortality rates are low, just as a fund is created with single-premium policies. Naturally, the fund is smaller under level-premium plans than under single-premium plans, as the former involves less prefunding of future mortality charges. At any point in time, the fund, future interest, and future premiums together should be sufficient to enable the insurer to pay all death claims as they occur during the remaining coverage period provided by the class of policies.

The level-premium principle may be applied to life and health policies of any duration, from short-duration term policies to whole life policies. The level annual premium may amortize the single-premium cost of the insurance over the entire policy coverage period or over any shorter period. For example, a whole life policy can have premiums paid over the entire policy duration—that is, the whole of life. This is an **ordinary life policy.** Whole life policies can have level premiums paid over any shorter period, such as 10, 15, or 20 years or to a specified age—for example, to age 65. These policies are referred to as **10-, 15-,** and **20-payment whole life policies** and **life paid up at age 65 whole life policies,** respectively.

Net Level Premium Calculation   A brief, if (again) unrealistic, example will illustrate how level premiums are calculated. Recall that the life insurer would charge each of our 100,000 males at 95 years of age a net single premium of $892.50 per $1,000 of insurance for whole life coverage. In total, the insurer needed to collect $89,250,236 at date of issue.

The relevant question here is: If some of the 100,000 insureds preferred to pay premiums on an annual basis, how much must the insurer charge each insured to be indifferent as to whether an insured paid for the coverage with a single premium or level premiums (i.e., so that the two systems of payment were actuarially equivalent)? This is the fundamental question for beginning the analysis. Again, for simplicity, the illustration will ignore all loadings as well as competitive aspects.

The problem can be solved using simple algebra. We know that the present value of death claims equals $89,250,236. The insurer must collect this amount, in total, as net single premiums. The insurer must, therefore, collect the mathematical equivalent in net level premiums if it is to be indifferent as to method of premium payment. In other words, the present value of the net level premiums must equal the sum of the net single premiums, both of which, in turn, must equal the value of future death claims.

Table 2-5 illustrates the necessary calculation. The net level annual premium being sought is an unknown quantity, labeled P in column 2. It will be collected from each survivor each year. A total of 236,960 of these net level premiums (or 236,960P) is to be collected (the sum of column 3). However, the value today of these premiums is 225,722P.

Note that the present value factors for column 4 of this table differ from those shown in column 4 of Table 2-3. This is because premiums (unlike claims) are assumed to be paid at the beginning of each year. Thus, the present value of each dollar in premiums to be collected the first policy year is a dollar.

It was mentioned previously that the insurer must collect in net level premiums an amount equal, in present value terms, to the amount it expects to pay out in death claims. Thus, the present value of net level premiums (225,722P) must equal the present value of future claims ($89,250,236). This is shown in Table 2-5. Dividing both sides of the equation by 225,722 yields the net level premium of $395.40. This is the annualized equivalent of the single premium.[2]

The net level premium is considerably higher than one-fifth of the net single premium. This result should not be surprising because prior to the payment of the series of death claims, the insurer has use of far less money under the level-premium plan than under the single-premium plan and, therefore, interest income is not as large a factor in causing the premium to be lower. Also, note that the insurer collects premiums only from those who survive. This odd-seeming statement is highly important in explaining the level-premium concept. Under the level-premium plan, the insurer does not collect a full annual premium from 100,000 persons each year. It collects only from those who survive, thus necessitating a higher premium than would be the case otherwise. In other words, the level-premium plan discounts for both interest and mortality. It can be demonstrated that the net level premium of $395.40 is exactly sufficient, when combined with interest, to pay all death claims and to end the last policy year with a balance of zero, as was illustrated in Table 2-4 with the net single premium.

Net Amount at Risk   Policy reserves stated on a per-policy basis can be considered as "vanishing" or ending with the insured's death. As a result, the insurer can be considered to have less than the policy's face amount at risk. Under this view of the reserve, the actual

---

[2]An alternative but mathematically identical procedure to derive net level premiums is followed in chapter 28.

TABLE 2-5 Illustrative Net Level Premium Calculation

(1) *Policy Year*	*(2)* *Net Level Premium to Be Paid Annually by Each Survivor*	*(3)* *Number Living at the Beginning of Each Year*	*(4)* *Present Value Factor at 5%*	*(5)* *Present Value of Total Net Level Premiums [(2) × (3) × (4)]*
1	P	100,000	1.0000	100,000P
2	P	67,000	0.9524	63,811P
3	P	41,205	0.9070	37,373P
4	P	21,427	0.8638	18,509P
5	P	7,328	0.8227	6,029P
			Total Present Value	225,722P

Since   Present value of net level premiums $(PVP) = 225{,}722P$
Present value of claims (see Table 2-3) $(PVC) = \$89{,}250{,}236$
And $PVP = PVC$
Then $225{,}722P = \$89{,}250{,}236$
So $P = \$395.40$

amount of pure life insurance protection at any point is the difference between the policy reserve at that point and the face amount; this difference is called the **net amount at risk.**

Figure 2-1 shows a stylized whole life insurance policy of $1,000, which is payable on the death of the 30-year-old male insured. The net level premium of $8.43 is payable annually until death. The increasing reserve and the declining net amount at risk reflected in this view of the life insurance contract are apparent.

For example, at age 65, the reserve is $460 and the net amount at risk is $540. Remember that the sum of the net amount at risk and the reserve equals the face amount of the policy ($1,000 in the example). For all whole life policies, the net amount at risk declines as the reserve increases.

The foregoing analysis can be interpreted as dividing a life insurance policy into two parts: a decreasing amount of term insurance and an increasing savings element, which, when combined, always just equal the policy face amount. This can be a helpful way of viewing traditional cash-value insurance policies and is, in fact, an accurate way of viewing universal life policies, as discussed later.

The Flexible-Premium Plan

Many insurers sell policies that permit the policyowner the flexibility of deciding the amount of the premium he or she would like to pay. Universal life (UL) policies are examples of such flexible plans.

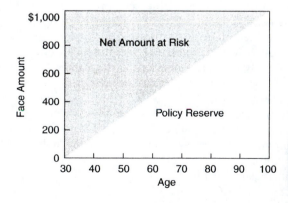

FIGURE 2-1 Relationship between Net Amount at Risk and Reserve

UL policy cash values are a function of past and present premium payments (and past and present expense and mortality charges as well as interest credits). Unlike traditional forms of cash-value insurance, the cash values of UL policies are not by-products of the leveling of premiums. Rather, they flow directly from the structure of the policy.

Subject to company rules regarding minimums and maximums, the policyowner may pay whatever premium that he or she wishes. An amount to cover the insurer's loadings and mortality charges is subtracted from the cash value. The balance remaining, plus any premium payments and the previous period's fund balance, then forms the next period's cash value. A penalty for early policy termination—a **surrender charge**—may be assessed on the policy's cash value. Mortality charges are based on the policy's net amount at risk calculated using the cash value instead of the reserve. Interest at the company's current rate is credited to the cash value. This process typically is repeated monthly.

No illustration is given here to demonstrate UL premium development, as the policyowner "develops" his or her own premium payment schedule. Of course, if the premium paid plus the current cash value are insufficient to cover fully all current mortality and loading charges, the UL policy will terminate.

THE SAVINGS ASPECT OF LIFE INSURANCE

Many life insurance policies have cash values. Conceptually, all life insurance policy cash values can be derived in the same way and all evolve for the same basic reason—prefunding of future mortality charges. As a practical matter, however, policies are usually viewed in different ways. Thus, with traditional forms of life insurance, the savings element is considered a by-product of the level-premium method of payment. With universal life and some other newer policy forms, the savings element is often considered as a more independent part of the policy, specifically designed to build a savings fund from which mortality and loading charges are withdrawn.

Traditional Cash-Value Insurance

Life insurance premiums traditionally have been computed by making assumptions regarding all elements impinging on the policy and deriving an indivisible premium to be charged for the policy. Much misunderstanding about traditional forms of cash-value life insurance flows from ascribing to individual policies concepts that apply to insurance companies' financial operations. The per-policy reserve referred to earlier is a prime example. If the policy reserve (a liability) is considered as a fund held on behalf of an individual policyowner, it is possible to consider the death benefit as a combination of that fund plus term insurance. This model, unless used carefully, can lead to false conclusions and to a general misunderstanding of the underlying realities of life insurance.

Economists and marketing personnel tend to view a level-premium whole life contract as a divisible contract providing financial protection to the policyowner's beneficiaries, with other contract benefits available, including cash surrender and loan values. A policyowner may discontinue the insurance and surrender the policy for its cash value. Alternatively, a policyowner may borrow from the insurer an amount up to the cash value, at a contractually stated rate of interest, using the cash value as collateral. Despite these and other living benefits, the whole life policy is an indivisible contract. It is not partly "protection" and partly "savings," with the premiums divisible between these components, as evidenced by the fact that the policyowner cannot withdraw the cash value without giving up the insurance protection. Even though the idea that the whole life contract is an indivisible entity is legally and actuarially correct, some companies and individuals continue to explain it as a combination of decreasing term insurance protection and increasing savings.

Universal Life Insurance

The distinguishing features of universal life policies are their (1) flexibility and (2) transparency. UL policies are flexible in that they permit policyowners, within limits, to increase or decrease (even to zero) premium payments as they wish, and also, subject to certain constraints, to increase or decrease the policy face amount.

UL policies are transparent in the sense that the three key elements of life insurance product pricing—mortality, interest, and loadings—are identified and disclosed to the consumer. The savings component of UL policies is a direct function of the premium payments made by the policyowner. Other things being equal, the higher the premium payments, the higher will be the cash value. With UL policies, the protection and savings components really are divisible and the methods used to derive them are apparent.

The fact that one policy is technically indivisible and another is divisible does not change the fundamental nature of the policies. They simply constitute different ways of viewing the same thing.

EXPERIENCE PARTICIPATION IN INSURANCE

Life and health insurance policies may be broadly classified based on whether policy values are (1) set at policy inception with no allowance for future deviations or (2) permit some variation from those illustrated at inception.

Guaranteed-Cost, Nonparticipating Insurance

Some life and health insurance policies—so-called **guaranteed-cost, nonparticipating insurance policies** (called **without profits policies** in many markets)—provide that all policy elements (i.e., the premium, the benefits, and the cash values, if any) are fixed at policy inception, guaranteed, and make no allowance for future values to differ from those set at inception. Such policies can offer advantages and disadvantages to policyowners, as discussed more fully later. The chief drawback of such cash-value policies is that, in periods of increasing investment return, they offer no means of passing excess returns to policyowners, with the result that they become viewed as expensive policies and may even be replaced.

A great proportion of insurance policies sold today provides that the policyowner will benefit (or suffer) from the favorable (or unfavorable) operating experience of the life insurance company. This experience is often based on the key elements of life insurance pricing—that is, mortality, interest, and loadings. Thus, a life insurance company may experience or expect to experience (1) lower mortality (morbidity), (2) greater investment earnings, or (3) lower expenses and taxes than the assumptions upon which its premiums are based. In this situation, it may share these favorable deviations with the policyowners producing or expected to produce them. In other words, policyowners can benefit from such favorable experience. Of course, the opposite can and does occur.

Participating Insurance

Participating insurance policies (called **with profits policies** in many markets) give their owners the right to share in surplus funds accumulated by the insurer because of deviations of actual from assumed experience. The distributable surplus is paid to policyowners as **dividends** (called **bonuses** in many markets). Dividends are paid on policies that base experience participation on deviations of actual from assumed operating experience relative to the mortality, interest, and loading assumptions built into the premium. Thus, if an insurer had calculated its premiums and reserves using an assumed interest rate of 3 percent and it actually earned 7 percent on its investments backing policy reserves, the insurer could pay some or all of the 4 percent additional investment return to policy-owners through dividends. It might credit, for example, 3½ percent, retaining the other 50 basis points for contingencies or profit. Similarly, if actual expenses incurred were less than those assumed in the premium loadings, the insurer could include such expense savings in that year's dividend payments. Also, any savings arising from paying fewer death claims than had been assumed could be passed to policyowners through dividends.

Note that participating life and health insurance policies adjust policy values—through the payment of dividends—only after the insurer's actual experience has materialized. It is in this sense that dividend payments represent each policy's share of accumulated surplus.

Premiums for participating policies are usually—but not always—based on fairly conservative mortality, interest, and loading assumptions, and they include a specific allowance for some level of dividend payments, with the result that the payment of some dividends over a policy's life may be reasonably assured. The actual amounts to be paid are not known and are never guaranteed. If future results follow exactly the assumptions on which premiums were derived, the dividends illustrated to be paid when the policy was issued should be paid. If future results are more favorable, dividends actually paid should be higher than were originally illustrated and vice versa. The term *dividend* as used in insurance should not be confused with the same term used to refer to earnings on shares of stock.

Current Assumption Insurance

Current assumption policies, like participating policies, allow policy values to deviate from those illustrated at policy inception—both favorably and unfavorably—but, unlike participating insurance in which adjustments are based on the insurer's past experience, current assumption policy adjustments are based on the insurer's anticipated future experience. Participating policies make adjustments, through the payment of dividends, only after the actual results have materialized. Current assumption policies make adjustments *in anticipation* of actual results being better than those assumed in policy pricing. Because the underlying guaranteed pricing assumptions usually are conservative, some favorable adjustments are almost certain with most current assumption policies, just as with participating policies.

Thus, a current assumption policy may guarantee to credit an interest rate of not less than 3 percent on policy cash values. If the insurer expects during the next year to earn 7 percent on its investments backing the policy's reserves, it could advise policyowners that it will credit their cash values with an interest rate of, say, 6½ percent during the next policy year. (The insurer ordinarily would maintain a margin between the policy crediting rate and its investment return to cover contingencies or profit—just as the insurer under the participating policy.) Adjustments might also be made in the policy loadings and in mortality charges for the coming year, in anticipation of actual experience being superior to that assumed in the premium.

It can be seen that participating policies allow for adjustments in policy elements based on the insurer's *actual* operating experience. These policies take a retrospective approach to experience participation. In contrast, current assumption policies allow adjustments to policy elements based on the insurer's *anticipated* operating experience. They take a prospective approach to experience participation—they, in effect, discount in advance for expected favorable results. These concepts are illustrated in the following diagram.

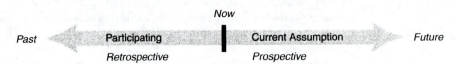

INTERACTION AMONG INSURANCE PRICING ELEMENTS

Earlier illustrations suggest that a life insurance company need only review its own experience carefully, calculate a net premium, and add allowances for expenses, taxes, profit, and contingencies. Although this can be a first step, many other facets enter into pricing in life and health insurance. For example, will the gross premium so developed be competitive? What proportion of the policyowners is expected voluntarily to terminate their policies, and when? What levels of cash value should be included (subject, of course, to any legally imposed minimums)? What level of dividends should be included, if any? How might inflation alter expected results, especially with health insurance claims? Are agent commissions sufficiently high to induce agents to sell the policy? What level of customer service is to be provided? The list of questions goes on and on, and the answers to them may suggest the need for further thought and change.

A life insurance company's raw materials—its operating experience in terms of mortality, morbidity, interest, expenses, and taxes and its philosophy regarding profits and contingencies—can be changed only so much. However, the elements derived from these raw materials can be altered and rearranged. For example, a company offering a participating policy could have a lower gross premium if it anticipated lower dividends.

The point is that an interaction exists among the various life and health insurance policy pricing elements. This section briefly explores this interaction to help the reader to understand better how a life insurance company functions from the standpoint of income and disbursements.

The following discussion can be considered as a microcosm of a life insurance company. It focuses on a simulated test of a block of policies, even though a typical life insurance company may have many policy blocks. The reader is invited to notice, in particular, the sources of the company's income for this block of policies (i.e., premiums and investment income) and how they interact with the disbursements. The reader also should recognize that the same type of analysis can be and is conducted for all forms of life and health insurance.

The Asset-Share Calculation

The testing of a tentative gross premium rate schedule and other policy elements is performed through an **asset-share calculation,** which is a simulation of the anticipated operating experience for a block of policies, using the best estimates of what the individual factors will be for each future policy year. The purpose of this calculation is to determine, for a block of policies, whether the insurer's profit, reserving, and other objectives can be met based on the anticipated operating experience. The calculation derives an expected fund (per $1,000 of insurance) held by the company at the end of each policy year after payment of death claims, expenses, dividends, or other nonguaranteed benefits or credits, cash surrender values, and allowance for actual interest earnings. The accumulated fund at the end of each policy year is divided by the number of surviving and persisting policyowners (lives exposed) to produce each policy's "share of assets" or asset share. Usually the test is for a maximum of 20 or 30 years.

Figure 2-2 shows, in simplified fashion, the mechanics of an asset-share calculation. Disbursements each year are netted against that year's income. The balance represents the net addition annually to the insurer's assets. Of course, most of the accumulated assets will be required to fund future death claims, expenses, and so on. In other words, they are required to back policy reserves, and, to the extent the accumulated assets are insufficient to do so, the insurer must, in essence, "loan" surplus to make good the deficit.

Asset-share calculations are made before the fact. As future experience is not known, estimates must be made that are thought to be reasonable representations of

Income ◄——— Premiums + Investment Earnings

Less: Disbursements ◄——— Expenses + Claims + Dividends + Surrender Payments

Equals: Net Assets

Time Period	Funds Flow
1	$\text{Income}_1 + \text{Disbursements}_1 = \text{Net Assets}_1$
2	$\text{Net Assets}_1 + \text{Income}_2 - \text{Disbursements}_2 = \text{Net Assets}_2$
3	$\text{Net Assets}_2 + \text{Income}_3 - \text{Disbursements}_3 = \text{Net Assets}_3$
n	$\text{Net Assets}_{n-1} + \text{Income}_n - \text{Disbursements}_n = \text{Net Assets}_n$

FIGURE 2-2 Insurance Company Funds Flow

future experience. Asset-share calculations seek to determine whether the individual elements of a policy result in a competitive product that is well balanced and produces acceptable results for both the insurance company and policyowners.

If the asset shares produced by the tentative gross premiums are deficient in light of company objectives, the premiums may be increased or some specific policy benefit (i.e., death benefit, dividends, or cash values) decreased. Alternatively, the insurer could decide to forgo changes in the policy itself, instead focusing on operational economies to reduce expenses, a change in its investment philosophy to allow riskier and thus higher-yielding assets, or other operational changes. If the fund accumulation appears excessive, especially in light of competitive considerations, the premium rate could be reduced or benefits increased. Naturally, for participating and current assumption policies, the available asset share may also be adjusted by modifying the tentative dividend scale or other nonguaranteed policy elements.

Illustrative Asset-Share Calculation

The process by which a gross premium rate structure is tested can be explained most effectively by means of an illustrative asset-share calculation. Table 2-6 shows the results of such an asset-share calculation. For purposes of this illustration, all assumptions have been simplified.

The tentative gross premium rate being tested is $15.00 per $1,000 for a participating ordinary life policy issued to males aged 35. Column 3 shows the expected number of deaths each year, based on 100,000 initial insureds and on what the insurer believes to be the most reasonable expected future mortality experience. Column 4 provides the insurer's best estimate as to the number of insureds who will lapse (voluntarily terminate) their insurance policies each year.

The insurer's expected expenses over each of the next 20 years are listed in column 6, and columns 7 and 8 show cash surrender values and illustrated dividends that the insurer is also testing. The dividend scale shown in column 8 can be changed as the insurer judges appropriate, depending on test results. The dividend scale ultimately decided upon would be the one illustrated in all sales materials and advertisements.

Column 9 shows the total asset fund value carried over from the previous year. In the first year, of course, it equals zero. Yearly premium income figures are shown in column 10; total yearly expense disbursements in column 11; total yearly death claim payments in column 12; total yearly cash surrender value payments in column 13; and total yearly

TABLE 2-6 Illustrative Asset-Share Calculation for $1,000 Ordinary Life Insurance Policies (35-Year-Old Males, Tentative Premium Rate of $15.00)

(1) Policy Year	(2) Number Paying Premiums at Beginning of Year	(3) Number Dying [a]	(4) Number Withdrawing [b]	(5) Number Alive at End of Year after Withdrawals [(2) − (3) − (4)]	(6) Expense Rate per $1,000	(7) Cash Value per $1,000 on Withdrawal [c]	(8) Dividend per $1,000	(9) Fund at Beginning of Year [(16) Prior Year]	(10) Premium Income [($15) × (2)]
1	100,000	88	10,000	89,912	$22.00	$ 0.00	$ 0.00	$ 0	$1,500,000
2	89,912	92	5,394	84,426	2.25	0.00	0.50	−847,520	1,348,680
3	84,426	101	4,221	80,104	2.25	4.31	1.00	184,874	1,266,390
4	80,104	111	3,524	76,469	2.25	13.91	1.50	1,158,880	1,201,560
5	76,469	118	3,058	73,293	2.25	22.86	2.00	2,075,460	1,147,035
6	73,293	132	2,638	70,523	2.25	34.16	2.50	2,952,205	1,099,395
7	70,523	142	2,256	68,125	2.25	44.81	3.10	3,793,912	1,057,845
8	68,125	152	1,975	65,998	2.25	55.82	3.70	4,608,568	1,021,875
9	65,998	164	1,781	64,053	2.25	67.19	4.30	5,402,814	989,970
10	64,053	175	1,601	62,277	2.25	78.94	5.90	6,178,176	960,795
11	62,277	198	1,494	60,585	2.25	91.05	6.60	6,878,629	934,155
12	60,585	212	1,393	58,980	2.25	103.56	7.30	7,544,662	908,775
13	58,980	226	1,297	57,457	2.25	116.46	7.90	8,187,202	884,700
14	57,457	240	1,206	56,011	2.25	129.78	8.50	8,814,332	861,855
15	56,011	256	1,120	54,635	2.25	143.51	9.20	9,428,453	840,165
16	54,635	273	1,092	53,270	2.25	157.66	9.90	10,024,390	819,525
17	53,270	293	1,065	51,912	2.25	172.19	10.60	10,595,210	799,050
18	51,912	315	1,038	50,559	2.25	187.10	11.40	11,137,980	778,680
19	50,559	340	1,011	49,208	2.25	202.35	12.20	11,645,660	758,385
20	49,208	368	984	47,856	2.25	217.92	13.00	12,114,990	738,120

[a] Deaths based on select and ultimate experience mortality table. Deaths assumed to occur in middle of policy year on the average.
[b] Withdrawals based on Linton A lapse rates. Assumed to occur on anniversary at end of policy year.
[c] Cash values: *1980 CSO Mortality Table*, 5½ percent.

(continued)

43

TABLE 2-6 *(cont.)*

(11) Expense Disbursements [(2) × (6)]	(12) Death Claims Paid [$1,000 × (3)]	(13) Amounts Paid on Surrender [(4) × (7)]	(14) Total Dividend Paid [(5) × (8)]	(15) Interest Earned During Year {0.08[(9) + (10) − (11) − (12) − (13) − (14) + (15)]}	(16) Fund at End of Year [(9) + (10) − (11) − (12) − (13) − (14) + (15)]	(17) Asset Share at End of Year [(16) ÷ (5)]	(18) Reserve^d at End of Year	(19) Surplus per $1,000 at End of Year [(17) − (18)]
$2,200,000	$ 88,000	$ 0	$ 0	$ −59,520	$ −847,520	$ −9.43	$ 9.15	−18.58
202,302	92,000	0	42,213	20,229	184,874	2.19	18.65	−16.46
189,959	101,000	18,185	80,104	96,864	1,158,880	14.47	28.49	−14.02
180,234	111,000	49,019	114,704	169,976	2,075,460	27.14	38.68	−11.54
172,055	118,000	72,965	146,586	239,315	2,952,205	40.28	49.20	−8.92
164,909	132,000	90,126	176,308	305,655	3,793,912	53.80	60.07	−6.27
158,677	142,000	101,091	211,188	369,766	4,608,568	67.65	71.25	−3.6
153,281	152,000	110,248	244,193	432,093	5,402,814	81.86	82.79	−0.93
148,496	164,000	119,667	275,428	492,983	6,178,176	96.45	94.67	1.78
144,119	175,000	126,377	367,434	552,588	6,878,629	110.45	106.90	3.55
140,123	198,000	136,030	399,861	605,893	7,544,662	124.53	119.48	5.05
136,316	212,000	144,255	430,554	656,890	8,187,202	138.81	132.43	6.38
132,705	226,000	151,050	453,910	706,096	8,814,332	153.41	145.75	7.66
129,278	240,000	156,514	476,094	754,153	9,428,453	168.33	159.45	8.88
126,025	256,000	160,729	502,642	801,167	10,024,390	183.48	173.54	9.94
122,929	273,000	172,162	527,373	846,759	10,595,210	198.90	188.01	10.89
119,858	293,000	183,387	550,267	890,232	11,137,980	214.56	202.83	11.73
116,802	315,000	194,213	576,273	931,389	11,645,660	230.34	217.99	12.35
113,758	340,000	204,581	600,338	969,623	12,114,990	246.20	233.45	12.75
110,718	368,000	214,430	622,128	1,004,672	12,542,510	262.09	249.19	12.90

^{d} Net level premium reserves, *1980 CSO Mortality Table,* 5 percent.

dividend payments in column 14. Note that, based on the cash-value schedule (shown in column 7) being tested, nothing would be paid to terminating policyowners until year 3.

Interest earned on net accumulated assets is shown in column 15, and the year-end fund balance is shown in column 16. Interest is earned (column 15) on the fund carried over from the previous year (column 9) plus premiums collected at the beginning of the year (column 10). However, from these two amounts one must subtract the expense disbursements (column 11)—assumed to be made at the beginning of each year—and one-half of the year's death claim payments. Why one-half? Recall that the focus here is interest earned (or forgone) during the year on the funds on hand for the year. Death claims are assumed to be paid uniformly throughout the year. Therefore, the company, on average, has use of only one-half of the funds throughout the year; hence, the one-half factor applied to the column 12 figures.

The first year's negative figures in both columns 15 and 16 indicate that the insurer's disbursements are greater than the income that it has received from premiums and interest earnings from this block of policies. Finally, the entire process translates into assets accumulated on a per $1,000 basis, as shown in column 17.

The asset-share fund for this block of policies is analogous to an income-outgo account. Each year, premiums and interest earnings are credited to the account as income, and death claims, surrender and dividend payments, and expense disbursements are charged against the account. The account balance at the end of each year (column 16) is divided by the number of surviving (i.e., those who did not die) and persisting (i.e., those who did not terminate) policyowners (column 5) to obtain the pro rata share of the account for each surviving and persisting policyowner—the asset share (column 17). For example, at the end of the tenth year, $110.45 in assets is expected to have been accumulated for each of the 62,277 surviving and persisting policyowners.

Several significant facts are shown by the asset-share study. First, the asset share is negative at the end of the first policy year. This outcome reflects the high first-year expenses involved in selling, underwriting, and issuing new business and the use of a level premium.

A comparison of columns 7 and 17 for the first policy year shows that, although terminating policyowners receive no cash value, the company nonetheless suffers an operating loss on each terminating policy. From the second year on, the company would experience a net gain on policies that are surrendered each year. Of course, future profits expected on such policies would be lost.

Column 18 shows the per-policy reserve established for this block of policies. Column 19 shows the year-by-year net cumulative effect on the company's surplus. Although policy reserves are not segregated on a company's balance sheet on a per-policy basis, they are shown on a per-policy basis here to illustrate better the concepts involved. Thus, during the first policy year, a reserve of $9.15 per policy is established. This amount is obviously greater than the increase (actually a net decrease) in assets (–$9.43) that results from the first year's operations. As a result, company surplus is lowered to the extent of the difference (a total of –$18.58).

Figure 2-3a shows the expected effect per policy on the company's balance sheet at the end of the first policy year, ignoring all other effects. Note the reduction in surplus by $18.58.

This "surplus strain" continues through the eighth policy year. From the ninth policy year onward, this block of policies, under the anticipated operating conditions, is expected to contribute positively to surplus, having "repaid" fully the amounts "borrowed" from surplus in the early policy years. After the eighth policy year, the increase in the asset side of the balance sheet more than offsets the increase in the reserve liability and does so increasingly as the years pass. Figure 2-3b shows the anticipated effect on a per-policy basis at the end of the second policy year, Figure 2-3c shows the effect at the end of the seventh year, and Figure 2-3d shows the effect at the end of the twentieth policy year.

Panel (a)
Balance Sheet at End of Year 1

Assets	Liabilities
−$9.43	$9.15
	Surplus −$18.68

Panel (c)
Balance Sheet at End of Year 7

Assets	Liabilities
$67.65	$71.25
	Surplus −$3.61

Panel (b)
Balance Sheet at End of Year 2

Assets	Liabilities
$2.19	$18.65
	Surplus −$16.46

Panel (d)
Balance Sheet at End of Year 20

Assets	Liabilities
$262.09	$249.19
	Surplus $12.90

FIGURE 2-3 Expected Effect on Insurer's Balance Sheet of New Policy at the End of Years 1, 2, 7, and 20 (from Table 2-6)

This example shows results for a single issue age. Blocks for other issue ages would also not show positive figures for several years under the assumptions used here.

As pointed out earlier, if the findings of the asset-share study do not develop satisfactory results for the company in terms of its objectives and the competitive environment, elements of the policy could be changed or the insurer could embark on a program to alter its expected mortality, lapse, or expense experience or to increase investment yields to achieve results judged acceptable. Asset shares are used to test premiums under various scenarios, including disaster conditions (i.e., extremely unfavorable investment earnings, mortality, or lapse experience, or expense inflation).[3] Computers have facilitated asset-share research, permitting prompt and economical analysis of the impact of possible changes in any factor affecting the financial experience of a block of life (or health) insurance policies.

Relation of Cash Surrender Values, Reserves, and Asset Shares

Previous discussions have attempted to make clear the differences among cash surrender values, reserves, and asset shares. To summarize: The *cash surrender value* represents the amount made available, contractually, to a withdrawing policyowner who is terminating his or her protection. This value is intended to represent an equitable distribution of the pro rata share of the amount accumulated on behalf of the particular block of policies from which the policyowner is withdrawing.

---

[3]The example here relies on accounting principles mandated by regulators. Insurers would make further analysis based on other accounting and cash flow analysis.

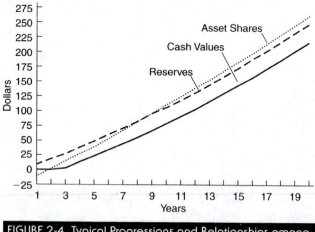

FIGURE 2-4 Typical Progressions and Relationships among Cash Values, Reserves, and Asset Shares

The *policy reserve,* generally a higher value, measures the company's liability for a given block of policies for financial statement purposes. Minimum liability values often are mandated by regulation in the interest of solvency, as discussed in chapter 29.

The *asset share* is the pro rata share of the assets accumulated on the basis of the company's anticipated operating experience, on behalf of the block of policies to which the particular policy belongs.

Figure 2-4 shows typical progressions for and relationships among cash values, reserves, and asset shares for a typical ordinary life policy. As shown, the asset share is typically less than the reserve in the early years because of the uneven incidence of expense outlay as compared with the expense provision in premiums. The length of time it takes the asset share to exceed the reserve is a management decision that reflects how soon the company wishes to recover its excess first-year expenses. After the asset share equals the reserve, under most cash-value policies both continue to increase, but with the asset share normally growing at a slightly faster rate.

In the United States and several other countries, the cash surrender value must not be less than legally prescribed minimums and cannot be negative. In the early years, it usually lies somewhere between the asset share and the policy reserve.

Questions

1. Why would a life insurer be interested in pricing its products so that the rates were fair, adequate, and not excessive? What competing concerns might lessen an insurer's compliance with these objectives? What difficulties might prevent an insurer from successfully achieving these objectives?
2. Effective pricing of life insurance products requires a considerable combination of information and assumptions on operational issues. Explain how and to what degree each of the following are important to the life insurer in pricing a product: (a) expected mortality, (b) administrative expenses, (c) lapse rates, (d) inflation rates, and (e) investment returns.
3. Explain why there are various premium payment plans in the market for life insurance policies.
4. What risks and returns are generally associated with guaranteed-cost versus participating life insurance?
5. Asset-share calculations provide a perspective on the relationship among the cash surrender value, policy reserve, and asset share of a life insurance policy. Describe this relationship over the life of a policy.

CHAPTER

3

THE HISTORY AND IMPORTANCE OF LIFE AND HEALTH INSURANCE

Objectives

- Depict several organizational practices in the near and distant past that could be considered historical origins of life insurance.

- Describe how an individual can benefit from a life insurance policy.

- Discuss ways that the economy as a whole may benefit from life insurance.

- Explain what is to be gained from an international perspective when trying to understand life and health insurance markets.

- Illustrate how economic, demographic, social, and political changes can affect the supply and demand of life insurance.

Life and health insurance is of great importance throughout the world. In general, the more economically developed a country, the greater the role of insurance as an economic security device. Indeed, a United Nations' committee has formally recognized that life insurance "can play an important role in providing individual economic security and in national development efforts, including the mobilization of personal savings."[1]

This chapter presents a brief history of life insurance and the potential benefits of life and health insurance to individuals and to society as a whole. It also provides an international overview of life and health insurance.

A BRIEF HISTORY OF LIFE INSURANCE

As Humbert O. Nelli wrote in his evaluation of the history of personal insurance, "History should explain the present and be a guide for the future."[2] As such, an understanding of the history of life insurance should be required of all serious students of insurance.

---

[1] *Resolution 21 (X), Life Insurance in Developing Countries,* adopted at the tenth session of the Committee on Invisibles and Financing Related to Trade, United Nations Conference on Trade and Development, December 1982.

[2] Humbert O. Nelli, "A New Look at the History of Personal Insurance," *Journal of the American Society of Chartered Life Underwriters,* Vol. XXIII (July 1969), p. 7. This historical overview is based on Nelli's work.

Introduction

A study of human history reveals a universal desire for security. The quest for security has been one of the most potent and motivating forces in material and cultural evolution. Early societies relied on family and tribe cohesiveness for their security. With economic progress, however, this security source weakens. Insurance, in some form, has been a universal response to societies' quests for security.

Insurance, as known today, did not exist in ancient or medieval times, although practices having important elements of insurance existed. From the standpoint of the individual, the most important insurance element is relief from the potential burden of financial loss, commonly known as a *transfer of risk.* Risk transfer is present to varying degrees in all instances presented in this section.

Greek Societies and Roman Collegia

The beginnings of personal insurance are generally attributed to the Greeks (although the Code of Hammurabi, c. 1750 B.C., provided for indemnity by the state for murder of a householder by a robber). The Greek societies—religious groups devoted to the observance and performance of prescribed feasts and sacrifices to their patron gods—practiced elementary insurance. Those societies gained their greatest popularity during the Greek classical period, from about 500 to 200 B.C.

An elaborate funeral ceremony was an important social and religious ritual of ancient times. (This view persists today to varying degrees in many cultures.) The belief was that the soul of the departed could gain entrance into the special paradise of his or her faith only if the funeral was conducted with all required rituals, sacrifices, and feasts. The Greek societies assumed this risk for its members by assuring them of a proper burial.

The Roman collegia, patterned after the Greek societies, were numerous during the period of the Roman Republic. These collegia evolved into mutual benefit associations with stated benefits and regular membership contributions. The dissolution of the Roman Empire brought an end to these societies, although similar organizations continued to exist in the Byzantine Empire.

The Guilds of the Middle Ages

The need for mutual protection and security not only continued but increased after Rome fell. The guilds evolved to meet this need. The guilds, particularly in England, provided mutual assistance to their members, as witnessed by the mentioning in most guild statutes of a host of perils for which members might qualify for relief (e.g., death, illness, capture by pirates, shipwreck, the burning of one's home, and the loss of one's tools of trade). Craftsmen's guilds evolved in Japan during the period from 1699 to 1868.

Guilds, however, were not organized primarily for benevolent or relief purposes. Their primary purposes were religious, social, and economic. Member benefits were neither a guarantee of aid nor an indemnity for accidental losses, but rather a system of organized charity. Even so, the risk transfer element was present.

The English Friendly Societies

Unlike the guilds, English Friendly Societies were true mutual benefit groups. Not concerned with trade, craft, or religion, they were operated by officers and a committee elected by the members and governed by a set of rules adopted and amended by the membership. Hardly a hamlet in England did not have at least one Friendly Society. All societies had some form of death or burial fund benefit. Many societies provided benefits for a variety of other perils. Unlike the guilds, however, benefit payments did not depend on the member's need, although they were often restricted by the funds available.

The beginnings of Friendly Societies predate, by some time, the first mortality tables, the laws of probability, and the mathematics of insurance. The societies operated on an **assessment basis** wherein the members were assessed as needed to provide the promised benefit payments. Contributions were not scaled according to the age or insurability of members, so a large share of the burden was placed on young, healthy members. As a result, many discontinued their memberships. Average mortality rates increased as the average age of the members increased, placing a still heavier burden upon those of advancing years—the ones least able to afford it. High failure rates were inevitable.

The Friendly Societies pioneered the formation of private life insurance in England. They provided insurance protection in limited amounts to persons of meager or limited means in return for periodic (often weekly) contributions. They were the proving ground for various forms of insuring organizations and insurance services. Freedom from political control allowed them to improvise, try, fail, and try again.

Early European Life Insurers

The earliest insurers were individual underwriters who either alone or in concert with others assumed various life insurance risks. Contracts were of short duration; they were seldom as long as a year. Obviously, long-term life insurance contracts could not be satisfactorily underwritten by individuals, for the insured could outlive the insurer!

During this early time, the practice of individuals writing their names under the amount of risk that they were willing to bear arose. This practice gave rise to the term **underwriting,** with the person making the contract being known as an **underwriter.**

Some early underwriters apparently were not always eager to meet their obligations. A 1584 dispute, the earliest on record, illustrates how the meaning of words can be critically important. A life insurance contract was issued on June 15, 1583, by the office of insurance within the Royal Exchange, for £383 6s 9d on the life of William Gybbons, for a term of 12 months. Thirteen individuals underwrote the contract. The premium was £75. The insured died shortly before the expiration of one year. The insurers refused to pay on the grounds that *their* intended 12 months were the shorter *lunar* months, not the more common *calendar* months. On this basis, the policy had expired. Mr. Gybbons' heirs brought suit against the underwriters. Not surprisingly, the heirs prevailed.

Individual underwriting gave way over time to corporate underwriting. The first true mutual insurance company was The Life Assurance and Annuity Association established by the Mystery of the Mercers of London on October 4, 1699. It failed 46 years later. Seven years later, The Amicable Society for a Perpetual Assurance Office was formed. It limited membership to 2,000, and it operated under a unique benefit system. The death benefit was not stated but depended upon the number dying each year.

By 1720, two English insurers, The Royal Exchange and The London (both major stock companies), had managed to receive a monopoly on British insurance. Thus, when the Equitable applied for a corporate charter to form a stock insurer in 1761, it was refused. Its founders, therefore, decided to form a mutual company that did not require a charter. Thus, in 1765, The Society for Equitable Assurances on Lives and Survivorships was born. The Equitable is said to be the first life insurer to operate on modern insurance principles.

Life insurance in the modern sense did not thrive until the corporate stock form gained acceptance and mathematicians developed the theory of probability and actuarial science. In 1803, The Globe was organized as a stock company. The first life insurance company in France was founded in 1787, but it failed in 1792. The Compagnie d'Assurance Générales sur la Vie was founded on December 29, 1819; it was followed by others, all of them stock companies and all successful. The first stock life insurer in Germany appears to have been the Deutsche Lebenversicherungs Gesellschaft, founded in 1828. It seems to have issued participating insurance. The Prudential (United Kingdom), formed in 1848, was the pioneer of industrial insurance, which it began to market about 1853.

The history of life insurance in Europe is intertwined with government in numerous ways. One of the most interesting was the effort to raise funds to support government expenditures through the use of a type of life annuity. Box 3-1 highlights the best known of these schemes.

Early Life Insurers in the United States

The growth of insurance in the American colonies was hampered by the monopoly on corporate insurers granted by the English Crown in 1720. The formation of new corporate insurers was prohibited and few, if any, individuals in the colonies were knowledgeable or rich enough then to compete as individual underwriters with the London insurers.

The English orders, such as the Odd Fellow and Foresters, had been introduced into the United States by English settlers before the Civil War, and they exerted a strong influence on the fraternal movement in the United States. Prior to that time, American associations were generally limited to political, literary, and commercial clubs. Some authorities credit the predominantly middle-class outlook of America for the absence of true Friendly Societies. The sparse population and wide expanse of territory in the eighteenth century may also have been a factor.

The first mutual life insurance corporation established in the United States was the Corporation for the Relief of the Poor and Distressed Presbyterian Ministers and for the Poor and Distressed Widows and Children of Presbyterian Ministers, organized in 1759 in Philadelphia. The insurer just recently merged into the Provident Mutual Life Insurance Company. The Mutual Life Insurance Company of New York was founded in 1842, followed by the Mutual Benefit Life Insurance Company of New Jersey in 1845. Mutual companies were popular during this period, until the New York legislature, at the prompting of the established mutuals in 1849, required all insurers to place a $100,000 security deposit with the state. Such a sum at that time acted as an effective barrier to entry, precluding the creation of further mutual insurers.

BOX 3-1

FRANCE AND TONTINES

The right to receive rent from land and to transfer this right to others was well established before Roman times. A landowner, for a consideration, could transfer the rent or income from a designated farm or landholding to a beneficiary, who might receive this rent in money or in kind for life or for a specified time. It was but a short step from life rents based upon land to annuities based upon the grantor's solvency. Governments, as well as monasteries and other religious organizations, used the sale of annuities as fund-raising devices. The religious prohibition against usury made the annuity a favored device for borrowing large sums.

In fact, in 1689, Louis XIV of France used an annuity scheme devised by Lorenzo Tonti—hence, the term *tontine*—to raise needed funds for the state. From the amounts contributed by the participants, a sum was set aside yearly to grant an annuity for life to the participants. As participants died and their attendant annuity obligations ceased, ever larger annuity amounts from the yearly sum became available to the survivors. The longer one lived, the larger grew the annuity payout. Other governments and private promoters continued this scheme almost into the twentieth century, when it was outlawed.

The first stock insurer in the United States, the Insurance Company of North America, was chartered in Pennsylvania on April 14, 1794. Originally organized to sell annuities, its plans changed. In five years, it issued only six life policies, so the company discontinued its life insurance business in 1804.

The Pennsylvania Company for the Insurance on Lives and Granting Annuities, chartered in 1812, was the first North American insurer organized for the sole purpose of selling life insurance and annuities to the general public and the first that sold an appreciable volume of insurance. It discontinued its insurance business in 1872. The Massachusetts Hospital Life Insurance Company was founded in 1818, and the New York Life and Trust Company in 1830. The latter company is notable as the first insurer to employ agents. All three companies were stock companies that later discontinued their insurance business and continued as banks or trust companies.

The Girard Life Insurance, Annuity and Trust Company of Philadelphia, established in 1836, used a new principle of granting policyowners participation in its profits, although it was a stock company. The first policy dividends were allotted in 1844 as insurance additions to policies in force three or more years.

An early market catalyst dates from 1875 when the Prudential Insurance Company of America introduced industrial life insurance in the United States. By 1879, the John Hancock Mutual Life Insurance Company and the Metropolitan Life Insurance Company were also selling industrial life insurance. Although of less economic importance today, industrial life insurance and its debit marketing system greatly enhanced public awareness of life insurance.

Early Asian Life Insurers

The first life insurance company to open for business in Japan was the Meiji Life Assurance Company, a stock corporation.[3] After seven years of monopoly by Meiji Life Assurance, two other modern life insurance companies were established. Teikoku Life Assurance Company was established in 1888, and Nippon Life Assurance Company Limited began in Osaka in July 1889. Many other stock companies followed, and life insurance spread throughout Japan as a result of the impact of World War II and the postwar occupation policies of the Allied forces ordering the dissolution of the *zaibatsu* (large conglomerates). Most major life insurers converted to mutuals.

Japanese and British insurers played a significant role in the development of life insurance in other Asian countries. In Korea, for example, British companies were most active in the insurance business until Japan gained control of Korea in 1905. The Cho-Sun Life Insurance Company, established in 1921, was the only company capitalized and owned by Koreans. The modern Korean life insurance industry really began in the 1960s.

British and other foreign companies played a major role in the development of the life insurance business in Singapore. The domestic Singapore life insurance industry was born in 1908 with the establishment of the Great Eastern Life Assurance Company Limited to compete with the overseas companies.[4] The industry's major development has occurred since 1965.

THE IMPORTANCE OF LIFE AND HEALTH INSURANCE

The preceding section has highlighted the evolution of life insurance. We now examine how life and health insurance can be important for individuals and for societies.

---

[3] *The 100-Year History of Nippon Life* (Tokyo: The Nippon Life Insurance Company, 1991), p. 5.

[4] Allen J. Pathmarajah, "Growth and Development of the Singapore Life Insurance Market and Its Future Outlook," *The Singapore Insurance Industry—Historical Perspective, Growth and Future Outlook* (Singapore: Singapore Insurance Training Centre, 1985), p. 195.

Life and Health Insurance and the Individual

Aside from the advantage of providing financial protection for individuals, families, and businesses, life and health insurance benefits policyowners in other important ways. Indeed, the policyowner can be considered as a "beneficiary" under his or her own life and health insurance. A number of potential advantages deserve mention in this respect.

Assists in Making Savings Possible

One occasionally hears those who argue that they prefer to save rather than purchase life insurance. Certainly, good savings habits should be encouraged, but saving involves time, resources, and discipline. A savings program can yield only a small amount at the start, whereas an insurance policy guarantees the full face value or other benefit from its beginning, and, thus, it can hedge the policyowner against failure through early death or incapacity to have sufficient working time to save adequately through other means. Thus, if one is able to save $1,000 annually, it would take nearly 16 years to accumulate a fund of $25,000, assuming that the accumulations are safely invested annually at 6.0 percent compound interest. Even at that, an individual's ability to accumulate such a savings fund is contingent upon his or her survival for the full period and may be defeated by death or disability before the savings have reached any appreciable sum.

To depend entirely on saving as a means of providing for the future could prove disastrous financially. It is generally accepted that the first requisite in providing for the future support of dependents is reasonable certainty. Life and health insurance (or a rich and sharing relative!) serves as a hedge against the possible failure to continue the annual accumulations of the savings fund because of early death or disability. Through life and health insurance, a fund of $25,000 can be assured in any case.

Furnishes a Safe and Profitable Investment

Life insurance policies and annuities are admirably adapted as accumulation devices and, with careful selection, can be reasonable, long-term savings instruments. The fact that interest credited to qualified policy cash values is typically tax deferred enhances the attractiveness of the contract as a savings vehicle.

Life insurance and annuities can furnish a profitable and safe investment service, but life insurance policies also make it possible for the policyowner to arrange for the safeguarding of the policy death proceeds and values. Many jurisdictions accord life insurance values special protection against the claims of the creditors of policyowners and beneficiaries.

Also, funds provided to heirs through life insurance death proceeds are lost by the beneficiary through speculation, unwise investments, or excessive, unnecessary expenditures. Sound financial planning suggests that such a contingency should be contemplated by the individual and can be discouraged or even prevented through judicious use of life insurance settlement options and trusts and in various other ways.

Encourages Thrift

Life insurance can constitute an excellent means of encouraging thrift for many persons. Many individuals who might not otherwise save regularly will nevertheless regularly pay premiums on a life insurance policy. If the policy is of the type that has a cash value, this can constitute a type of semicompulsory savings plan.

Minimizes Worry and Increases Initiative

Writers have frequently asserted that life and health insurance can be regarded not so much as producers of wealth but as mechanisms for distributing funds from the fortunate to the unfortunate. In reality, life and health insurance can be important forces in the production of wealth, in that they can relieve the policyowner of worry and increase his or her efficiency. Constant worry can inhibit productivity. To the extent that concern about the financial consequences of loss of life or health causes an individual uncertainty and worry, life and health insurance could help reduce this concern.

Furnishes an Assured Income in the Form of Annuities

Annuities can prove valuable to those older persons who have succeeded in saving only a limited amount of capital, and who have no one to whom they particularly care to transfer this sum on death. Assume that a person aged 65 has accumulated $100,000 and that this represents the entire funds available to the individual in his or her retirement years. Because of the limited size of the fund, the owner will be obliged to invest it in a most careful manner. Rates of return for such investments probably would not exceed 5 to 9 percent. Consequently, this individual would be limited to between $5,000 and $9,000 per year from the investment. Nor can he or she afford to take a portion of the principal for living expenses because this would reduce the available annual income in the future. The danger confronting this individual is just the opposite of that facing the person who wants insurance against premature death. The latter wants insurance because it is not known how long he or she will live; the former is confronted with the danger of living too long—that is, of outliving available income.

Just as the man or woman who felt that death or disability might intervene too soon could hedge against that risk, so the owner of the $100,000 fund who feels that the income is too limited or that he or she might outlive this income, can hedge against those risks by buying an annuity. A life annuity is a contract under which an insurance company promises to pay the owner a certain guaranteed minimum income every year for as long as the individual lives, with payment ceasing on death (unless a refund feature had been selected). The life insurance company is able to liquidate both the capital sum and the interest thereon in making these payments. Applying the law of large numbers to the probabilities of survival—instead of probabilities of death as in the case of life insurance—the insurer can further discount the cost of providing an annuity (i.e., guarantee a larger income payment) and, at the same time, guarantee that the annuitant will not outlive the payments.

Helps Preserve an Estate

Many persons will leave substantial estates on their deaths. In such instances, death taxes can be correspondingly substantial with, for example, large estates being subject to as much as a 55 percent marginal tax rate in the United States. As explained in chapter 13, the government expects taxes due to be paid in cash and within a reasonable time period. This payment often requires selling estate assets. Yet the heirs may prefer to retain these assets, either because of a depressed price occasioned by a down market or because of a desire to avoid loss of ownership.

Life insurance can be a natural means of providing funds to pay estate taxes. The heirs can be assured of having sufficient cash from the death proceeds to meet any tax obligations and thereby retain full ownership of estate assets. Chapter 16 outlines arrangements whereby the death proceeds themselves avoid taxation.

Life and Health Insurance and Society

Besides the benefits realized by individuals, life insurance and health insurance benefit society as a whole. Our focus here is on their role in assisting economic development, a topic of great interest worldwide. Later in this volume we discuss some of the other benefits to society that flow from health insurance programs and social insurance.

The Role of Insurance in Economies

Life insurance and health insurance provide at least three categories of services important to economies. We discuss each next.[5] Additionally, Box 3-2 highlights six benefits that a United Nations' agency asserted as flowing from a strong and efficient life insurance industry, some of which overlap with those discussed here.

Substitutes for Government Security Programs Life and health insurance can serve as a substitute for government security programs. A study by the Organization for Economic Cooperation and Development (OECD) highlighted this important point:

> The fact that so many life insurance policies are purchased undoubtedly relieves pressure on the social welfare systems in many states. To that extent, life insurance is an advantage in the context of public finance, and, as a result, is generally viewed with favor by governments. A number of governments acknowledge this in tangible form by granting tax relief to policyholders. At this point, tax incentives for life insurance contributions are widespread among OECD member countries.[6]

---

[5]This section draws from R. Levine, "Foreign Banks, Financial Development, and Economic Growth," in *International Financial Markets,* Claude E. Barfield, ed. (Washington, DC: The AEI Press, 1996) and Harold D. Skipper, Jr., "Risk Management and Insurance in Economic Development," in *International Risk and Insurance.*

[6]Organization for Economic Cooperation and Development, *Consumers and Life Insurance* (Paris: OECD, 1987).

BOX 3-2

SIX BENEFITS OF A STRONG LIFE INSURANCE MARKET TO ECONOMIC DEVELOPMENT

A study by the United Nations Conference on Trade and Development (UNCTAD) noted that a strong and efficient life insurance market can aid in overall economic development in the following ways:

- Life insurance can contribute to social stability by permitting individuals to minimize financial stress and worry.

- Life insurance can reduce the financial burden on the State of caring for the aged and for those made financially destitute because of the death of a family breadwinner.

- Through the accumulation from thousands of policyholders of small amounts of private savings, life insurers can accumulate sums to be invested in the public and private sectors. This can benefit an economy by creating a source of financing for new businesses, for new homeowners, and for farmers and their equipment.

- The life insurance business generates employment.

- Life insurance can permit more favorable credit terms to borrowers—both individuals and businesses—and can decrease the risk of default. Life insurance can also minimize the financial disruption to business caused by the death of key employees and owners.

- By making available a variety of employee benefit plans . . . life insurance companies can promote better employee/employer relations and can provide low-cost benefits to a broad spectrum of persons who may otherwise have been unable to obtain such protection.

The UNCTAD study introduction then notes: "Because of the foregoing reasons, the expansion and development of life insurance has been actively encouraged in many countries."

Source: UNCTAD, "The Promotion of Life Insurance in Developing Countries," pp. iii, 1–2.

A study by the Swiss Reinsurance Company reinforces the view that privately purchased life insurance can substitute for government-provided benefits and vice versa. For a group of 10 OECD countries, the study found a significant negative relationship between social expenditures and life insurance premiums. The study attributes the recent high growth in life insurance premiums, in part, ". . . to the growing financial difficulties of the social old-age pension systems. . . . Life insurers thus take an increasingly important role in relieving the burden of social pension schemes."[7]

Mobilizes Savings   The general financial services literature emphasizes the important role of savings in economic development. Countries that save more tend to grow faster. Savings can be either financial or nonfinancial. Nonfinancial savings take the form of real assets such as land, jewelry, buildings, and so on. Financial savings are held in financial assets such as savings accounts, bonds, shares, and life insurance policies. Generally, the more economically developed a country, the greater the proportion of its total wealth in financial savings. This result is not unexpected and is consistent with the view that financial development and overall economic development move in tandem.

Insurers, especially life insurers, offer the same advantages as other financial intermediaries in channeling savings into domestic investment. A **financial intermediary** is a firm (or other entity) that brings together providers and users of funds, such as commercial and investment banks and insurers. Financial intermediation of all types decouples the savings and investment functions. By doing so, investment is no longer confined to the sector in which the saving takes place. Funds can flow to the most productive sectors in an economy, which, in turn, implies the possibility of larger productivity gains.

Insurers enhance financial system efficiency in three ways.

1. As financial intermediaries, insurers reduce transaction costs associated with bringing together savers and borrowers. Thus, thousands of individuals each pay relatively small life insurance premiums, part of which typically represents savings. The insurers then invest these amassed funds as loans to businesses and other ventures. In performing this intermediation function, direct lending and investing by individual policyowners which would be exceptionally time consuming and costly, is avoided.

2. Insurers create liquidity. They "borrow" short term and lend long term. "Borrowing" for insurers means that they use funds entrusted to them by their policyholders to make long-term loans and other investments. Life and health insurers stand ready to provide policyowners (or third-party beneficiaries) with instant liquidity if a covered loss occurs. Additionally, they stand ready to provide policyowners with some or all of the savings accumulated within their policies. The creation of liquidity allows policyowners to have immediate access to loss payments and savings whereas borrowers need not repay their loans immediately. If all individuals instead undertook direct lending, they likely would find unacceptable the proportion of their personal wealth held in long-term, illiquid assets. Insurers and other financial intermediaries thereby reduce the illiquidity inherent in direct lending.

3. Insurers facilitate economies of scale in investment. Some investment projects are quite large, especially in relation to available financial capital in many emerging markets. They require correspondingly large amounts of financing. Such large projects often enjoy economies of scale, promote specialization, and stimulate technological innovations and, therefore, can be particularly important to economic development. By amassing large sums from thousands of smaller

---

[7]Swiss Reinsurance Company, "A Comparison of Social and Private Insurance, 1970–1985, in Ten Countries," *Sigma,* Zurich (1987).

premium payers, insurers can often meet the financing needs of such large projects, thereby helping the national economy by enlarging the set of feasible investment projects and encouraging economic efficiency.

The more developed (complete) a country's financial system, the greater the reliance on markets and the less the reliance on intermediaries. Financial markets are more developed in developed market-economy countries and, therefore, are of greater importance in such countries than in emerging countries. Even so, financial intermediaries, in all countries, are far more likely to be providers of investment funds than are financial markets. Only firms of a certain minimum size can easily tap into securities markets. Because of this fact and because financial markets are more complete in developed countries, one would expect financial intermediaries, such as insurers, to play a relatively greater role in investment finance in emerging markets than in developed market-economy countries.

A well-developed financial system will have a myriad of financial institutions and instruments. The greater the variety, other things being equal, the more efficient the system and the greater its contribution to economic development. Contractual savings institutions, such as life insurers and private pension funds, can be especially important financial intermediaries. In contrast with commercial banks, which often specialize in collecting short-term deposits and extending short-term credit, contractual saving institutions usually take a longer-term view. Their longer-term liabilities and stable cash flows are ideal sources of long-term finance for government and business.

Fosters a More Efficient Capital Allocation   Insurers gather substantial information to conduct their evaluations of firms, projects, and managers in their roles as lenders and investors. Although individual savers and investors may not have the time, resources, or ability to undertake this information gathering and processing, insurers have an advantage in this regard and are better at allocating financial capital. Insurers will choose to insure and to provide funds to the most attractive firms, projects, and managers.

Because insurers have a continuing interest in the firms, projects, and managers to whom they provide financial capital, they monitor managers and entrepreneurs to reduce the chances that they engage in unacceptable risk-increasing behavior. Insurers, thus, encourage managers and entrepreneurs to act in the best interests of their various stakeholders (customers, stockholders, creditors, etc.). In other words, insurers and other financial intermediaries help resolve the *principal–agent problem*—situations in which one party (the agent) does not always act in the best interests of its principal. By doing so, insurers tangibly signal the market's approval of promising, well-managed firms and foster a more efficient allocation of a country's scarce financial capital.

The Costs of Insurance

Although insurance offers societies great social and economic benefits, it also carries certain costs. First, insurers incur sales, servicing, administration, and investment management expenses. These expenses are an indispensable part of doing business but increase the cost of insurance. Such expenses may account for 10 to 40 percent or more of a policy's premium, with the loss payment portion accounting for the balance.

Second, the existence of insurance encourages *moral hazard,* as discussed in chapter 1. Some insureds inflate otherwise legitimate health claim payment requests. Moral hazard causes claim costs to be higher than they would be otherwise. For example, from 5 to 15 percent of health claims are believed to be fraudulent in many markets including the United States.

Each year, some insureds are murdered for life insurance proceeds. All such behavior causes premiums to be higher than they would be otherwise, represents a deadweight loss to society, can lead to disruptions in otherwise well-functioning markets, and truly is a "cost" of insurance.

LIFE INSURANCE INTERNATIONALLY

Life and health insurance is of great importance worldwide, with the earlier section on life insurance history setting its evolution in an international context. Although this text's material is oriented toward United States life insurance, all of the principles and the great majority of the practices outlined herein are of universal application. Only details vary from culture to culture. As a consequence, U.S. readers are cautioned to avoid ascribing a "Made in the USA" label to this text's material. This section examines some global dimensions of life and health insurance.

The Advantages of an International Perspective

The term *international insurance* traditionally is considered to encompass cross-border insurance transactions as well as foreign ownership of local insurers and reinsurers.[8] Insurers, agents, and policyowners not involved in international insurance (and the vast majority are *not* so involved) sometimes believe that understanding insurance practices and issues of other cultures is of little or no relevance to them. This view is myopic.

Life insurance products and the way they are sold naturally differ to suit each country's cultural, regulatory, tax, and economic environment. Yet term life insurance is still fundamentally limited-duration protection whether it is sold in Canada or Finland, and endowments are still high-value maturity instruments whether they are sold in Japan or Spain.

The operations of insurers around the world have numerous features in common. Although business environments vary dramatically, insurers in diverse markets often find themselves facing similar challenges. By exchanging ideas on how to meet these challenges, insurers can benefit themselves and their markets.

Insurance remains largely a local business, with nonlocal ownerships becoming increasingly common. Domestic companies and domestic subsidiaries of foreign insurers and reinsurers dominate many national insurance markets. Within any country market, products tend to be similar and distribution channels typically include some combination of exclusive agents, independent agents, direct response, and banks or securities firms. Insurers invest most of their funds domestically, yet lay off excess risk to reinsurers, many of whom are international. Governments set tax policy, approve policy forms (and, in some cases, rates), define the limits of the insurance activities of other financial institutions, and exercise surveillance over the financial condition and market conduct of insurers.

Notwithstanding these common features, each insurance market has evolved in its unique way. Many factors have shaped this evolution. For example:

- Variations in the importance of the concept of insurance in particular markets and the size of national economies have dictated how quickly local markets have grown and matured.
- Governments shape aspects of the industry through regulation, tax policies, financial requirements, social policies, and restrictions on other financial institutions.
- In some markets, cartels determine the rates (although their influence is steadily waning); in other markets, rate-making organizations prevail.
- The natural and social exposures within country markets—health care quality, lifestyle, litigation climate, quality of law enforcement—all shape a culture's security perceptions.

---

[8]This section draws in part from *International Insurance Society Value Statement.*

Any insurer concerned about trends in distribution channels, the potential role of banks and insurance companies, the erosion of cartels, or the impact of new products can invariably find country markets in which the change has already occurred and empirical evidence on the approaches that successful companies have used. Thus, idea transfer across country markets represents a major opportunity for insurance companies interested in improving performance within their own markets.

Insurers around the world confront many of the same competitive threats. For example, insurers concerned with changes in tax laws affecting their products can look to the United States, where sales of single-premium life declined after some tax benefits ended, but where sales of retirement annuities consequently grew. In one European country, many expect the removal of tax benefits for single-premium products to boost sales of group and pension products.

Insurance companies can also learn from their international counterparts about strategies for lowering costs and improving productivity. One European company added a direct-market channel to its branch office operations to spur new business development. A Japanese company creatively used technology to make its large sales force more productive. A United States company transformed its career agents into successful sellers of annuities.

Intergovernmental Trading Arrangements

So important is insurance that several important intergovernmental organizations have permanent insurance-related mandates. Thus, the *European Union* (EU) continues to adopt insurance directives, the intent of which is to harmonize insurance regulation and to eliminate regulatory inefficiencies that hinder competition among EU member countries. Table 3-1 lists the 15 EU member countries as of 1999.

Certain aspects of the codes of the *Organization for Economic Cooperation and Development* (OECD) set out obligations of member countries to liberalize their insurance markets progressively and to avoid discrimination against foreign insurers doing business within their markets. Table 3-2 lists the OECD member countries. The OECD's Insurance Committee conducts studies on and debates various regulatory issues of importance to life insurance.

The *General Agreement on Trade in Services* (GATS) is an international agreement that covers financial services, including insurance. The agreement binds signatory governments to have nondiscriminatory, clear, and publicly available regulatory rules and procedures. In excess of 100 countries participate in the GATS.

With the growing internationalization of markets generally and financial services markets in particular, one can expect the role of intergovernmental organizations to grow. Other important intergovernmental organizations whose work touches meaningfully on insurance include the *North American Free Trade Agreement* (NAFTA), composed of Canada, the United States, and Mexico; the *Association of Southeast Asian Nations* (ASEAN), composed of nine southeast Asian states; and the *Southern Cone Common Market* (MERCOSUR), composed of Argentina, Brazil, Paraguay, and Uruguay.

TABLE 3-1 Member Countries of the European Union		
Austria	Germany	The Netherlands
Belgium	Greece	Portugal
Denmark	Ireland	Spain
Finland	Italy	Sweden
France	Luxembourg	United Kingdom

TABLE 3-2 Member Countries of the Organization for Economic Cooperation and Development

European Union Countries:	European Free Trade Countries:
Austria	Iceland
Belgium	Norway
Denmark	Switzerland
Finland	**North American Free Trade Countries:**
France	Canada
Germany	Mexico
Greece	United States
Ireland	**Other Countries:**
Italy	Australia
Luxembourg	Czech Republic
The Netherlands	Hungary
Portugal	Japan
Spain	New Zealand
Sweden	Poland
United Kingdom	South Korea
	Turkey

The Importance of Life Insurance Worldwide

Figure 3-1 offers a breakdown of worldwide life premium income. Worth noting is that the source defines health insurance as property/casualty insurance, so these figures omit health premiums, an important segment in a few markets, especially in the United States. Thus, the Americas (both North America and Latin America) accounted for about 26 percent of the total world life premium volume in 1996. The European share stood at 30 percent and the Asian share at 41 percent. The shares accounted for by non-Japanese Asia, Latin America, Africa, and Europe are expected to grow in the future.

Life insurance is relatively more important in terms of premium income than is property/casualty insurance worldwide. Figure 3-2 shows the breakdown between life and nonlife premiums on both a worldwide and regional basis. Note, in particular, the large proportion of life insurance in Asia.

Two measures are used traditionally to show the relative importance of insurance within national economies. **Insurance density** indicates the average annual per capita premium within a country. Values are usually converted from national currency to U.S. dollars. As such, currency fluctuations affect comparisons, and this fact can lead to distortions, especially over time. Even so, this measure is a useful indicator of the importance of insurance purchases within national economies.

The other measure, **insurance penetration,** is the ratio of yearly direct premiums written to gross domestic product (GDP). It shows roughly the relative importance of insurance within national economies and is unaffected by currency fluctuations. Even so, it does not give a complete picture because it ignores differences in insurance price levels, national product mixes, and other market variations.

Figure 3-3 shows the insurance density for selected countries for 1996. As can be seen, the Japanese per capita expenditure of $3,236 is the world's highest, with Switzerland ($3,106), France ($1,559), the United States ($1,079), and most other OECD countries following. The OECD average is $1,037. The EU average is $881. Developing countries' figures fall uniformly at the end of the list.

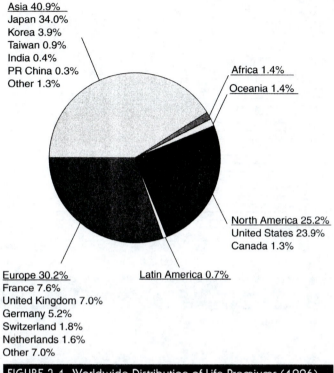

Asia 40.9%
Japan 34.0%
Korea 3.9%
Taiwan 0.9%
India 0.4%
PR China 0.3%
Other 1.3%

Africa 1.4%
Oceania 1.4%

North America 25.2%
United States 23.9%
Canada 1.3%

Europe 30.2%
France 7.6%
United Kingdom 7.0%
Germany 5.2%
Switzerland 1.8%
Netherlands 1.6%
Other 7.0%

Latin America 0.7%

FIGURE 3-1 Worldwide Distribution of Life Premiums (1996)

Source: Swiss Reinsurance Company, *Sigma* (1998).

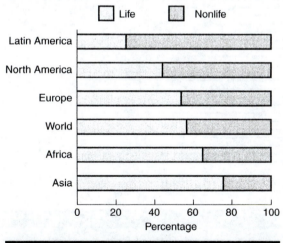

**FIGURE 3-2 Life and Nonlife Premium Proportions
Worldwide (1996)**

Source: Swiss Reinsurance Company, *Sigma* (1998).

Figure 3-4 shows insurance penetration figures for the same countries. Penetration is highest in South Africa (12.2 percent), followed by South Korea (10.0 percent) and Japan (9.2 percent). Ratios greater than 5 percent were recorded in several European

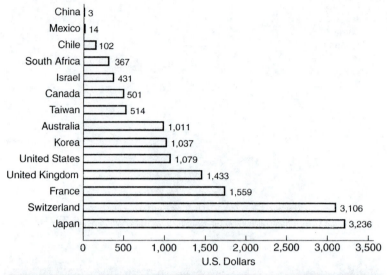

Source: Swiss Reinsurance Company, *Sigma* (1998).

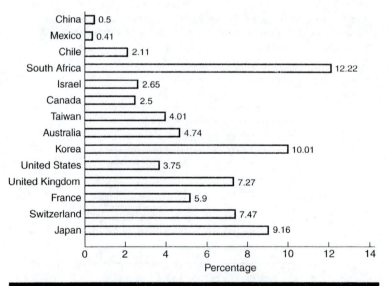

Source: Swiss Reinsurance Company, *Sigma* (1998).

countries, with the U.S. ratio at 3.8 and Canada at 2.5. The OECD average penetration is 4.8 percent, whereas the EU average is 3.8 percent. With important exceptions, developing countries' ratios are lower.

The differences in the relative importance of life insurance internationally are attributable to many factors such as taxation, religion, economic development, and culture. The role of the government as a source of personal economic security also greatly influences the role of the private sector. We discuss the factors shaping life insurance demand and supply in the following section.

Factors Affecting Life and Health Insurance Consumption

This section examines our understanding of the factors that affect life and health insurance consumption (and, therefore, production) worldwide.[9] As we explore these factors, we should recognize that national insurance markets will naturally differ, for each has evolved to suit its particular environment. Price and innumerable economic, demographic, sociocultural, political, and other factors determine each economy's consumption of life and health insurance.

Price

Of course, price is a critically important determinant of insurance demand and supply. The prices that insurers charge are influenced by their cost structures, by the competitiveness of the particular line of insurance, and by government tax and other policy. Unfortunately, no completely satisfactory national measures of price exist. Proxies are used, but the fact remains that the price elasticities of life and health insurance are not well understood.

Babbel examined the price elasticity of whole life insurance policies issued in the United States, using various price measures.[10] Under his methodology, he found prices to be negatively related to new sales, with elasticities ranging from –0.32 to –0.92, depending on policy type and the price index used. Another study found a negative relationship for term life insurance and an insignificant relationship for whole life insurance.[11]

A study that examined the price elasticity of group life insurance demand in the United States found it to be –0.7; meaning that a 10 percent increase (decrease) in price could be expected to cause a 7 percent decrease (increase) in quantity ($1,000 face amount units) demanded.[12]

The Economic Environment

Many economic factors influence life and health insurance consumption. Among those found to be the most consistently important is the level of a country's economic development.

Income   The level of a country's income has been found to be the most important factor in explaining the level of national life and health insurance consumption. The higher a country's income, other things being equal, the more its spends on all types of insurance. Also, at the microeconomic level, the higher a household's income, the greater the life insurance consumption.[13]

If we assume that countries follow an essentially common development path, a reasonable conclusion from the studies is that the income elasticity of insurance premiums

[9]This section draws from Skipper, "The Structure of Insurance Markets Worldwide," in *International Risk and Insurance;* and Harold D. Skipper, Jr. and Tara Skipper, "The Sociocultural Environment for Risk and Insurance," in *International Risk and Insurance.*

[10]D. F. Babbel, "The Price Elasticity of Demand for Whole Life Insurance," *Journal of Finance* 4, Issue 1 (1985), pp. 225–239.

[11]M. A. Boose and Gokhan R. Karahan, "An Empirical Estimation of the Market Demand for and Supply of Life Insurance," presented at the annual meeting of The American Risk and Insurance Association (1995).

[12]Swiss Reinsurance Company, "The Effects of Price Adjustment on Insurance Demand," *Sigma,* Zurich (1993).

[13]Frank D. Lewis, "Dependents and the Demand for Life Insurance," *American Economic Review* 79, Issue 3 (1989), pp. 452–466; D. B. Truett and Lila J. Truett, "The Demand for Life Insurance in Mexico and the United States: A Comparative Study," *The Journal of Risk and Insurance,* 57 (1990), pp. 321–328; and A. S. Gandolfi and L. Miners, "Gender-Based Differences in Life Insurance Ownership," *The Journal of Risk and Insurance,* 63 (1996), pp. 683–693.

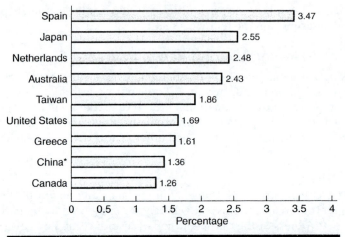

FIGURE 3-5 Income Elasticities of Life Insurance for Selected Countries (1984–1996)

*1987–1996
Source: Calculated by GSURMI Research Center from *Sigma* and IMF data.

is greater than 1.0. The **income elasticity of insurance premiums** tells us the relative change in insurance premiums written for a given change in national income.

Figure 3-5 gives income elasticities for life insurance for several countries over an 12-year period. Note that the income elasticity is greater than 1.0 for most of these countries, with some being substantially greater. This result is not unusual internationally or for the United States historically and, when coupled with strong economic growth for a country, might suggest great opportunities for insurers in such markets.

Inflation and interest rates   Inflation rates would be expected to have an influence on life and health insurance consumption. Of course, it is impossible to discuss inflation without also discussing interest rates, for inflation expectations drive interest rates.

Inflation has long been considered detrimental to life and health insurance supply and demand. It has been found to be negatively associated with life insurance consumption.[14] During the high inflation era in the United States in the late 1970s and 1980s, life insurers witnessed a diversion of premium dollars as consumers perceived better financial opportunities through other savings media. Cash flow problems were created for many insurers as dissatisfied policyowners either surrendered their policies or exercised their rights to obtain policy loans at below-market rates. High inflation rates and resulting high and volatile interest rates caused many existing and prospective policyowners to question whether their older insurance policies offered sufficient value and flexibility.

In times of high inflation and significant economic volatility, consumers seek shorter-term, more liquid investments and avoid longer-term, fixed commitments. Traditional cash-value insurance products have been perceived as long-term, fixed commitments and, therefore, demand for them often shrinks during inflationary or volatile times. Additionally, consumers perceive that inflation erodes life insurance values.

[14]D. F. Babbel, "Inflation, Indexation and Life Insurance Sales in Brazil," *The Journal of Risk and Insurance,* 48 (1981), pp. 115–135; and J. F. Outreville, "Life Insurance Markets in Developing Countries," *The Journal of Risk and Insurance,* 63 (1996), pp. 263–278.

BOX 3-3

POPULATION AGING IN THE UNITED STATES AND INSURANCE DEMAND

The U.S. population is aging. Persons in the 50-to-65 age category now represent 14 percent of the U.S. population, and this percentage will increase. More important, they already control one-third of U.S. disposable income. This group's greatest financial need is for products to provide for old age, and they have the money to spend for these products. Much of the future success of the U.S. life insurance business will hinge on its response to this and to the over-65 age groups' demand.

Roughly one in eight persons in the United States is now 65 or older. By the year 2030, approximately one in five persons will be 65 or older—the same ratio prevailing today in the state of Florida. This aging trend, coupled with medical advances, will mean that the demand for nursing homes and other types of extended care will grow enormously, for approximately two out of five persons aged 65 and over will need nursing home care during their lifetimes. The U.S. life insurance industry's response to this need for long-term care and its financing will continue to influence insurance product design and pricing.

The Demographic Environment

Changes in demographics affect insurance consumption. For example, the age of first marriage, for both men and women, is increasing in the United States and in many other countries, while the years of higher education lengthen. Married couples who have children—and many choose not to do so—are having fewer of them. Dual-income families are more common, as are single-parent families. The fitness trend results in healthier insureds, but also sometimes in a perception of less need for life and health insurance. These and other demographic trends alter insurance demand.

Aging Populations   The fact that much of the world's population, including that of the United States, is aging is well recognized. (See Box 3-3 dealing with the United States.) This aging results from a combination of decreasing fertility and decreasing mortality rates. Many countries, especially the United States, experienced atypically high birthrates following World War II, followed by a gradual but substantial decline in these rates. Figure 3-6 illustrates this phenomenon for the United States. Other developed

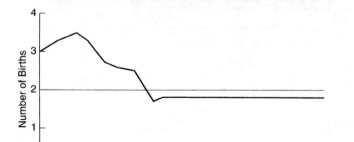

FIGURE 3-6 Fertility Rates in the United States: 1950 to 2010

*Projected fertility rates.
Source: U.S. Bureau of the Census.

countries—especially in Europe and Japan—have witnessed even lower fertility rates, to a point below that of the replacement rate.

As a consequence of the high post–World War II birthrate, many countries have a so-called "baby boom" generation, which, for the United States, is defined as the cohort of persons born between 1946 and 1964. "Baby boomers" represent a substantial bulge in the United States population, as illustrated in Figure 3-7.

A companion phenomenon of the past few decades has been an increase in life expectancy. Figure 3-8 shows how U.S. life expectancy has increased during the twentieth

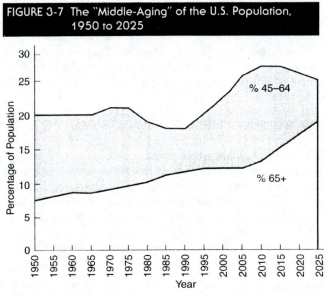

FIGURE 3-7 The "Middle-Aging" of the U.S. Population, 1950 to 2025

Source: United Nations (1989).

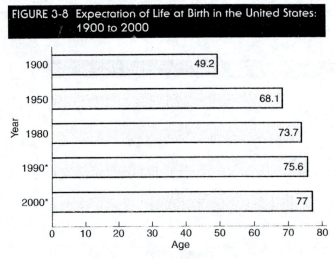

FIGURE 3-8 Expectation of Life at Birth in the United States: 1900 to 2000

*Projection using middle morality assumption.
Source: Metropolitan Life Statistical Bulletin, July–September 1985, and U.S. Bureau of the Census.

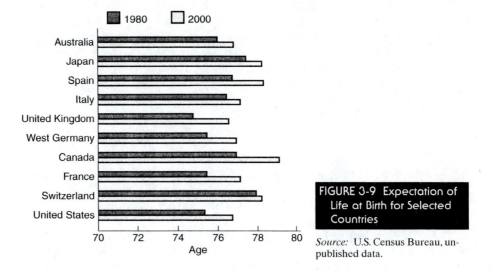

FIGURE 3-9 Expectation of Life at Birth for Selected Countries

Source: U.S. Census Bureau, unpublished data.

century. Figure 3-9 shows life expectancy for selected countries for 1980 and 2000. An increasing live expectancy has resulted in an increasing proportion of older persons in many societies. As discussed more fully in chapters 16 and 21, this growth will put new burdens on retirement systems worldwide.

Increasing life expectancy translates into a greater demand for savings-based life insurance products as well as for long-term care insurance.[15] Moreover, longer life should translate into lower-priced death-based life insurance, which should stimulate sales to the segment of populations needing such coverage.

Education   The educational level of a population or of a household affects insurance consumption. The expectation is that the more educated or literate a population or household the greater the likelihood of understanding the need for insurance. This seems to be true, even after allowing for the higher incomes associated with higher education.[16]

Household Structure   The structure of households continues to evolve. Families form the core of most households worldwide. The **nuclear family,** consisting of husband, wife, and dependent children, is perhaps the most familiar in Western societies. In an earlier, more agrarian era in Western societies and perhaps in most societies still in Asia and Africa, the **extended family**—consisting of one or more nuclear families plus grandparents and possibly aunts, uncles, and some cousins—lived and worked together. The extended family is a logical means of providing for the essentials of life and for taking care of the elderly and infirmed. Having many children could guarantee comfort in one's old age. Whether nuclear or extended, families remain perhaps the most fundamental source of physical and economic security in societies worldwide.

The nuclear family accounts for a declining majority of households in most developed market-economy countries. Within the United States, roughly one-half of nuclear families have no children under the age of 18 in the home. Research findings suggest,

---

[15]Ibid.

[16]John J. Burnett and Bruce A. Palmer, "Examining Life Insurance Ownership through Demographic and Psychographic Characteristics," *Journal of Risk and Insurance,* 51 (1984), pp. 453–467; and Truett and Truett, "The Demand for Life Insurance in Mexico and the United States."

unsurprisingly, that life insurance demand is related to the number of young children in the household.[17]

Double-income families are the rule rather than the exception in the United States and in many other (especially European) countries. In such situations, the death or incapacity of either spouse can disrupt the family's standard of living, although less so than in households with a single breadwinner. Research has shown that full-time labor force participation by the wife is associated with a reduction in life insurance owned by the husband.[18]

Single-parent householders are becoming more common because of divorce and, to a lesser extent, because of the spouse's death. Dependent children in such situations often give rise to substantial life and health insurance demand.

Because of lower mortality rates, there are fewer orphans today than in past times, more children who have living grandparents, and more adult children with elderly living parents. Thus, the likelihood of a 50-year-old U.S. citizen having at least one parent alive will have risen from 52 percent in 1940 to almost 80 percent by 2000. Because these parents are themselves older today than was the case several decades ago, the nature of any care-giving responsibility is likely to be greater, more complex, and more expensive.

Usually, the responsibility for care of elder parents falls on their children and more particularly on the daughter (or daughter-in-law). As one commentator observed:

> More and more women are on the Daughter Track, working, raising kids and helping aging parents. . . . Most [elderly U.S. citizens] are cared for by family members, at home, for free—and most families wouldn't have it any other way. . . . The average American woman will spend 17 years raising children and 18 years helping aged parents.[19]

Gerontologists refer to the phenomenon of middle-aged daughters caring for both teenage children and elderly parents as a "generation in the middle" or "the sandwich generation." Were the caregiver to die, the likelihood increases substantially that the elder parent(s) would then need more intensive (and expensive) professional care and possibly institutionalization. In the absence of substantial personal resources, life insurance coverage on the caregiver's life or long-term care insurance on the parents' lives often is a logical financial decision. The effects on insurance consumption of these demographic changes are not yet fully understood.

Industrialization and Urbanization   By revolutionizing agricultural production, the plow altered societies worldwide. It allowed economies of scale in food production, resulting in greater surpluses for exchange and accumulation and ushered in greater demand for material goods and services. The production of goods and services, thus, grew in importance and with it arose ever larger mining, manufacturing, and commercial enterprises. Business and employment specialization became even more important, thus rendering individuals more reliant on trade to obtain that which they and their families no longer produced themselves. Specialization implies vulnerability.

Industrialization brought urbanization. Villages became towns, which became cities. Urbanization brought about a new social order in which the predominant economic and

---

[17]Burnett and Palmer, "Examining Life Insurance Ownership through Demographic and Pyschographic Characteristics"; Lewis, "Dependents and the Demand for Life Insurance"; and Mark J. Browne and Kihong Kim, "An International Analysis of Life Insurance Demand," *The Journal of Risk and Insurance*, 60 (1993), pp. 616–634.

[18]Gandolfi and Miners, "Gender-Based Differences in Life Insurance Ownership."

[19]M. Beck, "Trading Places," *Newsweek*, July 16, 1990, pp. 48–54.

social security formerly provided by family, friends, and acquaintances was supplanted to varying degrees by formal public and private arrangements and a necessity for greater financial self-reliance. Research has documented the positive relationship between industrialization and urbanization, and insurance consumption.[20]

Greater formality, clear and enforceable rules, and bureaucracy accompanied industrialization and urbanization. Simultaneously, the adverse consequences of the damage to or the destruction of property or the loss of one's health, job, or life were magnified. With industrialization family units become smaller.

The Social Environment

Consumers today are better educated and more demanding. We know that higher educational levels are associated with increased insurance consumption, as indicated earlier. Education is but one dimension of the social environment that influences insurance consumption. Culture is another.

In some cultures and with certain relationships (as between close friends, for example), it might be socially unacceptable to refuse the offer to purchase insurance because saying no is considered impolite. Too often, in such circumstances, the policy is purchased, but it lapses shortly thereafter. This has been a particularly difficult issue in Korea, for example.

Cultural perceptions of the role of life and health products can vary substantially. In many countries, especially in Asia, life products are sought primarily as savings instruments, and this is consistent with a high cultural propensity to save. In other countries, especially those that are predominantly Muslim, life insurance is sometimes viewed as inappropriate because of religious beliefs (although life products and insurer operations can be made to comport fully with these beliefs). See Box 3-4. Within the United States, consumers by substantial margins view life insurance first and foremost as protection against premature death.

The Political Environment

Country political and economic stability influences insurance demand.[21] An unstable political environment depresses insurance demand because citizens cannot fully rely on insurers meeting their promises, as laws may be unenforceable. Citizens in unstable environments often avoid local insurance purchases but purchase insurance, especially life insurance policies denominated in strong currencies, from foreign companies that offer greater financial strength. They often make such purchases in spite of domestic prohibitions.

Therefore, the decisions made by public policymakers—insurance regulators, the courts, legislatures, and others—can have a profound impact on insurance consumption. Their decisions determine what life, health, and retirement products can be sold, who can sell them, and how they can be sold. Government policy also determines how attractive such products are from a tax standpoint and the extent to which government itself will supply life, health, and retirement benefits.

Thus, insurance regulators worldwide typically determine whether a given insurance product can be legally sold within their jurisdiction, through a policy review and approval process. Similarly, tax and other laws greatly influence product design and value. For

---

[20]Doocheol Kim, *The Determinants of Life Insurance Growth in Developing Countries, with Particular Reference to the Republic of Korea,* unpublished Ph.D. dissertation, Georgia State University (1988).

[21]Michael Beenstock, Gerry Dickinson, and Sajay Khajuria, "The Determination of Life Insurance Premiums: An International Cross-Section Analysis," *Insurance: Mathematics and Economics,* 5 (1986), pp. 261–270.

BOX 3-4

ISLAM AND INSURANCE

For devout Muslims, the Koran is the source and guide for all social and economic decisions and institutions. The Koran was God's final revelation of His law to humankind. After the Prophet Mohammed's death, Islamic scholars built a body of law—the Shari'a—around the Koran. Among other things, the Shari'a sets out rules for the allocation of resources, property rights, production and consumption, the working of markets, and the distribution of income and wealth. The Shari'a is central to Islamic economic theory and lies at the base of all Islamic financial and commercial activity. For example, an ethic in Islam is that wealthy Muslims contribute (*zabat*) to the less fortunate.

The Koran proscribes the payment of interest (*riba*) and gambling. Like Western banking, Western-style insurance may be dismissed by devout Muslims as a form of usury or gambling. Additionally, some Islamic scholars have argued that insurance is an attempt to defy fate as predetermined by God. Other Islamic scholars respond that, even if life's harmful events are a certainty, preparing for the inevitable is no defiance, especially for one's dependents. Indeed, this is both ethical and economically sound.

To be compatible with Islamic principles, Islamic insurance must incorporate *Mudarabad* and *Takaful*. **Mudarabad** is a form of partnership in which one party provides the funds while another provides the expertise and management.

The parties share any profits on a prearranged basis. Islamic insurers invest funds according to the Shari'a (no fixed-income securities; no investment in certain companies such as distilleries). By building a profit-sharing (rather than interest-paying) pooling arrangement, they fully respect the *riba* prohibition.

Islamic insurers establish a **Takaful**—a type of solidarity or mutual fund separate from the management operation, which relies on a pact among participants to guarantee each other. In this way, they respect the prohibition on gambling. The fund, as a collective rather than a one-on-one insuring arrangement, simply protects the investors and their heirs against events that would alter their economic status. The pooling arrangement is consistent with the *zabat* principle of helping those in need.

In a *Mudarabad* insurance contract, participants invest a fixed sum for a fixed term to be distributed between an investment fund and the *Takaful*. The insurer makes a clear distinction between shareholders and policyowners. They invest shareholder capital separately from policyowner funds. Underwriting is permitted to ensure fairness among participants, not to discriminate against or reject anyone. It would be unethical for *Mudarabad* participants to bear the risks of another without a contribution (*tabarru*) that reflects equitably those risks.

Source: Skipper and Skipper, "The Sociocultural Environment for Risk and Insurance," in *International Risk and Insurance.*

example, most countries law's permit a tax-deferred accumulation of interest on life product cash values. Repeal of this benefit would undoubtedly decrease the attractiveness of cash-value policies.

Governments also determine who can supply insurance products. Minimum capital or solvency margin standards plus other requirements for insurer licensing serve as marketplace gatekeepers (see chapter 35). Too lax a standard can result in financially unsound insurers operating within a market, thereby undermining consumer confidence in the industry. Too strict a standard can result in less consumer choice and value. A balance is needed.

Governments determine whether and under what circumstances foreign insurers and foreign-owned domestic insurers can enter and compete within their markets. The various U.S. state markets generally make few, if any, fundamental distinctions between

U.S. and non-U.S. firms or ownership, but many countries impose various barriers to foreign firms or ownership.

Besides determining which among several possible private insurers can operate within a market, policymakers also decide the appropriate role of the government itself within the economic security market, as alluded to earlier. Extensive government-provided security schemes depress the demand for private insurance.[22] Fortunately for private insurers, the trend worldwide is for governments to diminish their role as purveyors of individual financial security. Such actions increase the demand for private insurance.

Internationalization

The continuing internationalization of financial services adds a new dimension to insurance consumption, especially for markets that have been relatively closed in the past to new entrants. Countries can no longer view themselves as isolated economic islands. Important economic events in Asia and Europe cause economic fluctuations in the Americas, and vice versa. To appreciate this fact, one has but to witness the impact on the U.S. stock and bond markets of swings in interest rates and stock market values in Japan or the European Union.

With increasing internationalization can come increased capital from abroad, product and marketing innovations, and a different way of managing companies. Increased capital strengthens the financial capacity of insurers and can result in more competition and, therefore, consumption. Product and marketing innovations and different management styles can lead to greater consumer choice and value. The trend toward greater market internationalization almost certainly affects insurance consumption, although to date research on this issue is sparse.

Questions

1. The roots of modern life and health insurance are arguably found in Greek societies, Roman collegia, and the guilds of the Middle Ages. Compare and contrast the needs served by these organizations and those served by modern life insurers.
2. One life insurance policy can provide a number of benefits to a variety of people. Explain how a number of individuals may benefit from a policy on one individual's life.
3. How might one assess the impact of the life insurance industry on the general economy?
4. Choose two cities in the world and speculate as to how the economic, demographic, social, and political environments are affecting the life insurance markets in those cities.

---

[22]See ibid., and Lewis, "Dependents and the Demand for Life Insurance." Browne and Kim, "An International Analysis of Life Insurance Demand," found the relationship to be positive, although the authors suggested that data problems could have caused the surprising result.

CHAPTER

4

INTRODUCTION TO LIFE AND HEALTH INSURANCE PRODUCTS

Objectives

- Describe competitive pressures facing life insurers in the financial services marketplace.

- Give examples of how life insurers are responding to these competitive pressures through the design and marketing of their products.

- Identify distinguishing characteristics of term and endowment life insurance and give examples of appropriate uses for each.

- Describe the features of the term life insurance policy.

- Explain the mathematical and economic concepts behind endowment insurance.

This and the four following chapters present the principal types of individual life and health insurance and annuities. This chapter begins with an examination of recent life insurance product innovations. After a brief overview of the types of individual life insurance policies, a review of the nature and types of term life and endowment policies follows. Chapter 5 covers the nature and types of fixed-premium whole life policies, including variable life and current assumption whole life. Flexible-premium life insurance policies are presented in chapter 6. Chapter 7 examines individually issued health insurance policies. Annuities and optional benefits are reviewed in chapter 8.

RECENT LIFE INSURANCE PRODUCT INNOVATIONS

The discussion in the preceding chapter on life insurance consumption worldwide highlighted the many environmental factors affecting life and health insurance supply and demand. The confluence of various economic, sociocultural, demographic, technological, and other factors over the past two decades has created unprecedented pressure on life insurers in many markets to undertake various product innovations in an effort to gain market power and thereby to protect or enhance profitability.

It has been only within the past decade or two that life and health insurance product development has approached being an integrated, market-driven process in most

OECD countries, including Canada and the United States. As discussed in chapter 24, enlightened insurers today realize that the best means of developing competitive, innovative products is to develop a sound, clearly articulated strategy grounded in the needs of the market and that builds on the insurer's strengths.

The issue of product development and innovation, including pricing and marketing innovation, is all the more important with the continued convergence among financial service competitors. Important segments of the consumer market no longer consider life insurers as competing only with other life insurers. They ask about rates of return and about expenses inherent in products. Many consider carefully whether it is better to accumulate savings via their life insurance or through other media; in other words, they perceive many noninsurance savings media as substitutes for savings via insurance. This, in turn, means that the expense, tax, and profitability profiles of life insurers cannot differ negatively from such profiles of other financial intermediaries if life insurers are to compete effectively. As a result of these environmental pressures, life insurers have reacted in several important ways, as discussed next.

Insurance Company Reactions

The net effect of the preceding environmental influences is that competition among financial service retailers is increasing, particularly in the middle- and upper-income markets. This increased competition emanates from consumers, as discussed previously, and from agents and other advisors demanding lower-cost, higher-quality products and services for their customers.

Many consumers have demanded life insurance whose yields are competitive with returns on other investments. Some have stated a preference for flexible premium-payment schedules and the ability to alter other policy elements easily. Some have wanted transparent life insurance policies to show more clearly the various pricing components. Some have demanded greater disclosure and more up-to-date policy information. These are just a few of the types of "requests" that today's marketplace has made of insurers.

Potentially Lower-Cost Coverage

Life insurance today is potentially lower in cost than that offered in years past. Competition among life insurers (and agents), as well as between life insurers and other financial institutions, has put pressure on actuaries and insurer management to design and offer ever lower-cost policies. This pressure, in turn, has forced insurers to place great emphasis on expense control and improved productivity. Many insurers, in an effort to gain a competitive advantage, have sought riskier investments for their portfolios with the expectation that they would generate higher yields. This shift may be a sound strategy if appropriate proportions of assets are invested in this way, but some insurers have found that their aggressiveness has backfired because of excessive investment defaults and consumer concern about their financial solidity. Indeed, we have many recent examples of life insurer insolvencies in Canada, the United States, the United Kingdom and other markets because of poor investment results.

Besides internal expense control and other efforts, insurers have adopted several innovative product design approaches in order to be able to offer potentially lower-cost insurance. Three of these approaches are covered here: (1) indeterminate-premium plans, (2) more refined classification systems, and (3) provisions to encourage persistency.

Indeterminate-Premium Plans   Indeterminate-premium policies are usually nonparticipating but with nonguaranteed current premiums. A dual-premium structure is utilized whereby a scale of guaranteed maximum premiums is contained in the contract, but the insurance company reserves the right to and typically does charge lower premiums.

Some participating term policies sold in the United States carry indeterminate premiums. Such policies usually contemplate no dividend payments.

The lower current premium actually charged is subject to periodic change, but only on a classwide basis. Changes may be made if anticipated future interest, mortality, or expense experience differs from that implicit in the current premium charged. Premiums can be raised or lowered by the company but can never exceed the guaranteed maximum. The indeterminate-premium approach was first used with fixed-premium, cash-value life policies but has since found a larger usage with term and universal life policies, at least in the United States.

More Refined Classification Systems   In an effort to offer lower-priced insurance, insurers have adopted more refined risk-classification systems. Thus, whereas in the past otherwise similarly situated smokers and nonsmokers were charged the same premium, today most insurers in North America charge smokers more than nonsmokers in recognition of their higher average mortality.

Insurers have also provided lower rates for persons assessed to be preferred risks. Preferred risks may be defined as nonsmokers whose health, lifestyle, family history, and other characteristics are such as to suggest that they will exhibit mortality experience that is significantly better than average. Indeed, some insurers now have as many as six or more possible sets of rates for standard risks, ranging from a "superstandard," nonsmoker classification to a standard, smoker classification. Additionally, many insurers offer products that permit insureds to pay lower premiums than otherwise if they demonstrate periodically that they are still insurable. These reentry products are discussed later in this chapter.

Provisions to Encourage Persistency   The discussion on asset shares in chapter 2 made it clear that lapse rates have important implications for insurer product pricing. Other things being the same, the higher are early lapse rates, the greater are insurer losses, and, therefore, the more the insurer must charge for the policy. To discourage early lapses and thereby to be able to offer lower-cost policies, insurers are designing products with high charges for early surrender and with prescribed bonuses for policies that remain in force for a certain minimum number of years.

Increased Flexibility

Life insurance products offered today permit policyowners unprecedented flexibility. Many policies provide that the face amount may be decreased or increased (usually subject to insurability requirements) at any time. Increased flexibility in premium payment is permitted, with some policies allowing the owner to pay premiums as desired, subject to tax and procedural limitations. With the increasing use of accelerated death benefit provisions, life insurance policies assume even greater importance.

Life insurance policy provisions have always permitted policyowners certain flexibility. Insurers often allowed even greater flexibility on an extracontractual basis. Even so, product flexibility today is far superior to that which existed in the past. As stated earlier, pressure for this enhanced flexibility has come from several sources, but it has become feasible only because the needed technology support was developed.

Greater Disclosure

Only in the 1980s did insurers begin to incorporate disclosure as a key element of policy design and operation. This increased disclosure has had two dimensions. First, some new products (e.g., universal life and current assumption whole life) involve disclosure to potential purchasers of the product's various pricing elements. This transparency permits prospects to see clearly the portion of each premium payment applied toward mortality and loading charges and toward cash-value buildup. The interest credited to cash-value accumulations is also disclosed clearly in such products. Moreover, governments in some markets mandate that certain pricing information be given to prospective purchasers, sometimes including agent commissions, as discussed in chapter 11.

In addition to disclosure of the pricing and benefit elements at the time of purchase, policyowners often receive annual policy transaction summaries. They are thus able to monitor actual policy financial results and to compare these results against those that were illustrated at the time of policy purchase and against prevailing investment returns and other financial factors within the economy.

Increased Risk to Consumers

The purchaser of a life insurance policy today stands to benefit in some or all of the preceding ways. The benefits, however, are not without their price. For one thing, enhanced flexibility within a contract is more costly, even in the face of significant technological advances and lower unit costs of production.

Another highly important aspect of this "price" is that insurers cannot offer both lower-cost, interest-sensitive policies on the one hand and liberal, long-term guarantees on the other hand. Many life insurance products offer less liberal, traditional, insurance-type guarantees. Therefore, much of the investment, expense, and some of the mortality risk that traditionally have been borne almost exclusively by life insurers are shared increasingly by policyowners under these new products. This trend is even more evident as we witness a shift to variable (unit-linked) life insurance and annuity products in which potentially all of the investment risk is transferred to the policyowner.

In fact, many individuals who purchased life insurance during the high interest rate environment in the United States in the late 1970s and 1980s discovered the risks inherent in some of the newer, more interest-sensitive products. Policy values were projected at that time using double-digit interest rates. Many purchasers apparently were led to believe that future cash-value accumulations would be substantial enough such that no further premiums would be required after a few years. Actual policy interest rates fell short of those illustrated, as prevailing market rates declined and insurers could not sustain the high investment returns necessary to support high interest rates.

Many policyowners apparently were not fully aware of the interest rate risks that they were assuming and became disillusioned with their policies. In fact, U.S. and Canadian life insurers have found themselves facing severe fines and lawsuits as a result of the combination of (1) greater interest rate risk being borne by policyowners and (2) inadequate disclosure of these risks.

Some Japanese insurers encountered similar difficulties in connection with the sale of variable life insurance, which was financed through bank loans. Many policyowners complained that they did not fully understand the risks inherent in the purchase.

OVERVIEW OF TYPES OF LIFE INSURANCE POLICIES

As suggested in chapter 2, life insurance policies can be constructed and priced to fit a myriad of benefit and premium-payment patterns. Historically, however, life insurance benefit patterns have fit into one or a combination of three classes:

- term life insurance
- endowment insurance
- whole life insurance

Each of these was defined briefly in chapter 1. This life insurance classification scheme remains valid today, although it is not always possible to determine at policy issuance the exact class into which some types of policies fall. As discussed in chapter 6, some policies permit the policyowner flexibility effectively to alter the type of insurance during the policy term, thus allowing the policy to be classified as to form only at a particular point. For presentation purposes, these flexible forms of life insurance are discussed as if they were an additional classification, even though all can properly be placed (at a given point in time) into one or a combination of the three traditional classes.

The relative importance of each of these three types of life insurance varies from market to market and over time within a single market. For example, term life insurance is quite popular in the United States, accounting for about one-half of all individual life insurance sold based on face amount, yet little term is sold in most other markets worldwide. In contrast, endowment policies—which effectively are no longer sold in the United States—are quite popular in most Asian and many African, European, and Latin American countries.

TERM LIFE INSURANCE

Although its popularity varies substantially from market to market, some form of term life insurance is sold in the vast majority of markets worldwide. Here we explore the nature, common types, and uses of term life insurance policies.

Nature of Term Life Insurance

Term life insurance furnishes protection for a limited number of years at the end of which the policy **expires,** meaning that it terminates with no maturity value. The face amount of the policy is payable only if the insured's death occurs during the stipulated term, and nothing is paid in case of survival. Term policies may be issued for as short a period as one year but customarily provide protection for at least a set number of years, such as 10 or 20, or to a stipulated age, such as 65 or 70.

Term insurance is more comparable to property and liability insurance contracts than is any other life insurance contract. If a building valued at $100,000 is insured for that amount under a five-year term property policy, the insurer will pay this amount only if total destruction occurs during the term. Similarly, if a person insures his or her life for $100,000 under a five-year term life policy, the insurer will pay $100,000 only if the insured's death occurs before the expiration of the five years; nothing is paid if death does not occur during the policy term.

Initial premium rates per $1,000 of coverage are lower for term life insurance than for other life products issued on the same basis, as the period of protection is limited. Premiums for term coverage, however, can escalate rapidly as the duration of the policy lengthens.

Term product prices are more easily compared than are prices of other life products, as term policies are usually structurally simpler than other policies. As a consequence, buyers suffer fewer information problems with term insurance, thus rendering the term market more price competitive than the market for cash-value policies. Term products usually have no cash values and often no dividends, thus permitting policy comparisons on the basis of premiums.

Some insurers and an increasing number of buyers, in fact, treat term life insurance more as a commodity—an item that is essentially the same irrespective of the supplier and that, therefore, is sought at the lowest price. As commodity profit levels ordinarily are low, many insurers attempt product differentiation strategies. Even so, term insurance buyers as a group are price sensitive and consider term policies to be easily replaceable, as few penalties usually attach to early termination. Consequently, term lapse rates usually are higher than arc lapse rates for other policies.

High early lapse rates produce two types of losses for insurers. First, they may be unable to recoup fully underwriting and first-year commission expenses. Second, policyowners who replace their term policies tend to be those in good health; those who may no longer be insurable are more likely to retain their policies. This adverse selection problem results in poorer mortality among persisting insureds. For these reasons, insurers seek ways—via discounts for multiyear premium payments, more stringent underwriting for expected persistency, and other means—to minimize term lapse rates.

Three features applicable to many term life policies deserve special attention before discussing specific term products. These are the renewability, convertibility, and reentry features.

Renewability

Most one-year and five-year term policies and many 10-year and other duration policies contain an option—a *call* as understood in finance—that permits the policyowner to continue the policy for a limited number of additional periods of protection. This renewal option allows the policyowner, at the expiration of each term period, to continue the policy without reference to the insured's insurability status at renewal time. Usually, however, companies limit the age (generally to age 65 or 70) to which such term policies may be renewed.

The premium, although level for a given period, increases with each renewal and is based on the insured's attained age at renewal time. A scale of guaranteed future premium rates is contained in the contract, although the company charges a rate lower than that stated in the policy for some term policies.

As the premium rate increases with each renewal, mortality experience increasingly reflects adverse selection. Resistance to the higher premiums and lower-cost product opportunities cause many insureds in good health to fail to renew, whereas the majority of those in poor health will renew even in the face of higher premiums. Insurers try to accommodate this problem in their pricing structure or through other means, such as through altering dividends, by limiting renewability to stipulated maximum ages, or by product designs that encourage (or require) conversion.

From the policyowner's perspective, the term *renewability* means simply that the policy can be continued to the stipulated termination age. Renewal rates are fixed by contract and renewal is effected merely by the policyowner paying the billed premium. Therefore, renewable term policies can be viewed as increasing-premium, level-benefit term life insurance.

Convertibility

Most term insurance policies include a convertible feature. This feature is a call option that permits the policyowner to exchange the term policy for a cash-value insurance contract, without evidence of insurability. Often the period during which conversion is allowed is shorter than the maximum duration of the policy.

The conversion privilege increases the flexibility of term life insurance. For example, at the time a term policy was purchased, a policyowner may not have selected the type of policy best adapted to his or her needs. He or she may have preferred another type but, because of budget considerations, decided on low-premium term coverage. Following the issuance of the term policy, circumstances may have changed so as to enable the policyowner to purchase an adequate amount of other insurance. Alternatively, he or she may desire to utilize insurance to accumulate funds rather than entirely for the purpose of protection against death. If, therefore, an individual concludes that term insurance does not meet present and future needs, this conclusion could be implemented by exchanging the term contract for a type of insurance that conforms better to his or her needs.

A significant percentage of insureds become uninsurable or insurable only at higher than standard rates. Under such circumstances, a term policy that cannot be renewed beyond a certain point may fail to protect the insured in the desired manner. If, however, the policy contains a conversion privilege, and if the time limit for making an exchange of the policy has not yet expired, the exercise of this privilege can be to the insured's advantage and, thus, protect against the possibility that insurance may expire before death occurs. As with any call option, its value stems from the holder's (policyowner's) ability to exercise the option on conditions most favorable to him or her. Insurers can be expected to price the option accordingly.

If the insured is insurable at standard rates, there may be little or no financial advantage to exercising the conversion privilege compared to reentering the marketplace and shopping carefully. In effect, the value of the option is zero because the option exercise price is no lower than the market (spot) price. An exception to this statement can exist if the insurer provides a *conversion credit* against the new policy's premiums, such as $2 per $1,000 of insurance, as an amount equal to the previous year's term premium paid, or as a fixed percentage of the new policy's premium. The credit may apply only if the conversion takes place within a specified period (e.g., two years) from issue.

Conversion may be permitted on an attained age or original age basis. Box 4-1 discusses these bases.

Reentry

Many insurers include a **reentry** feature in their term policies, which allows the possibility of paying a lower premium than otherwise if insureds can demonstrate that they meet certain continuing insurability criteria. To understand the mechanics of reentry

---

BOX 4-1

ATTAINED-AGE VERSUS ORIGINAL-AGE CONVERSION

The **attained-age method** of conversion involves the issuance of a whole life or other cash-value policy of a form currently being issued by the insurer at the date of conversion. The premium rate for the new policy is that required at the insured's attained age and would be the same as that offered by the company to new insureds who could qualify for standard rates.

The **original-age method,** usually unavailable with universal life policies, involves a retroactive conversion, with the whole life or other cash-value policy bearing the date and premium rate that would have been paid had the cash-value policy been taken out originally instead of the term policy. Most companies offering this option require that retroactive conversion take place within five or so years of the issue date of the term contract. The policyowner is required to pay the difference between (1) the premiums (net of dividends or other credits) that would have been paid on the new policy had it been issued at the same time as the original policy and (2) the premiums actually paid for the term policy, with interest on the difference at a stipulated annual rate (e.g., 6 or 8 percent).

It was said that the policyowner, in making a choice between the two bases of conversion, might prefer an original-age conversion because he or she could obtain a lower premium rate and possibly more liberal contract provisions. However, with the trend toward lower premiums and better-valued products, it is far from clear whether either potential benefit would necessarily materialize. Even if the premium rate for the original-age conversion were less than the rate for current issues, the wisdom of making an original-age conversion may be doubtful because of having to pay the back premiums plus interest.

term, we must first understand the three types of mortality tables used by insurers. They are as follows:

- A **select mortality table** reflects the mortality experience of newly insured lives only. These persons exhibit superior (i.e., low) mortality relative to others of the same age and sex because to qualify for life insurance in the first place they must have been in good health and otherwise insurable. This select period or benefit of selection usually lasts from 5 to 15 years.
- An **ultimate mortality table** reflects the mortality experience beyond the select years (i.e., of those who already have been insured for several years). The benefit of selection has faded from the mortality experience of the ultimate group. Thus, a select table represents very favorable initial experience, whereas an ultimate table excludes this experience and, therefore, exhibits higher mortality.
- An **aggregate mortality table** includes data from both select and ultimate experience. Mortality experience under this table falls between that of the select and ultimate tables.

Traditional term premiums often are based on *aggregate* mortality experience. Reentry term premiums are based on a *select/ultimate* mortality split. This results in a scale of premium rates that varies not only by age but also by the duration since the insured last demonstrated insurability.

Figure 4-1 illustrates how an insurer might price a term policy with a reentry feature. The insurer uses a five-year select period. The insurer's expected ultimate mortality experience for ages 30 to 40 is shown graphically in panel a. It shows the expected mortality rate to be 1.35 per 1,000 lives insured for insureds now age 30 and who have been insured for more than five years. The mortality rate for insureds now age 35 and who have been insured for more than five years is expected to be 1.65; and the age 40 expected mortality rate is 2.42.

Panel b of Figure 4-1 superimposes the expected select mortality rates for new insureds now age 30. Their expected first-year (i.e., age 30) mortality rate is 0.6 per 1,000 insured lives. This rate is considerably lower than the rate that the insurer expects from those insureds who have been insured for more than five years but who are also now age 30.

The second-year select mortality rate is 0.75 (versus the ultimate rate of 1.4), the third-year select mortality rate is 0.9 (versus 1.45), the fourth-year rate is 1.1, and the fifth-year rate is 1.35 (versus an ultimate rate of 1.58). As from the end of the fifth policy year, the mortality rates for the two groups of insureds are expected to be identical.

Panel c superimposes on panel b the expected select mortality rates for new insureds now age 31. Their expected first-year (i.e., age 31) mortality rate is shown as 0.65 per 1,000 insured lives. Note that this rate is somewhat lower than the expected rate for those insured a year earlier and who are now 31 (i.e., who are exhibiting second-year select mortality). The same relative relationship holds throughout the five-year select period of this group of insureds, with their mortality rates grading into the ultimate curve at the end of their five-year select period.

Finally, panel d superimposes on panel c the expected select mortality rates for new insureds at ages 32, 33, and 34, illustrating the expected mortality progression for each of these insured cohorts relative to the earlier groups. It can be seen that, at any given age, the insurer expects insured cohorts to exhibit as many different sets of mortality as there are years in the select period, plus one for the ultimate mortality. At age 34, for example, the insurer expects six different sets of mortality experience. We anticipate those newly insured at age 34 to exhibit the lowest mortality. Those who are now age 34 but were insured a year earlier are expected to exhibit the next most favorable mortality, and so on, as shown on the vertical line at age 34.

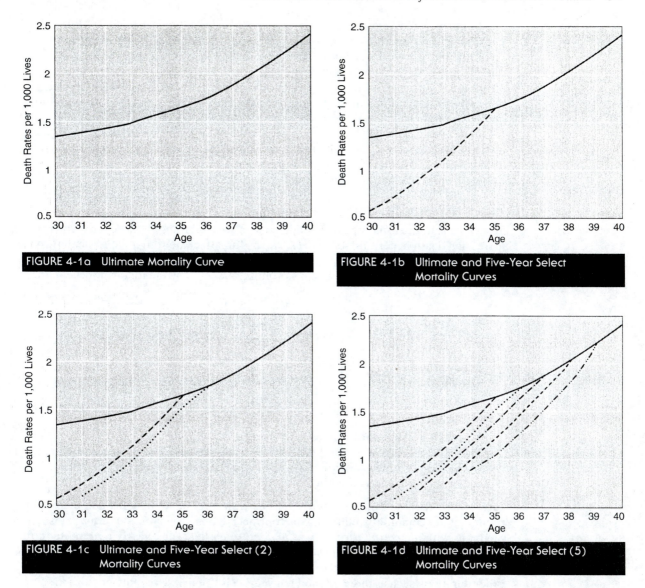

FIGURE 4-1a   Ultimate Mortality Curve

FIGURE 4-1b   Ultimate and Five-Year Select Mortality Curves

FIGURE 4-1c   Ultimate and Five-Year Select (2) Mortality Curves

FIGURE 4-1d   Ultimate and Five-Year Select (5) Mortality Curves

Knowing this result, the insurer can charge each group premiums that track its expected mortality rates. Thus, in the Figure 4-1 illustration, the insurer could be charging six otherwise identically situated insureds a different premium for the same coverage under the same policy form. The 34-year-old woman who just purchased a term policy using reentry pricing would pay the lowest rate; another woman, now age 34, who purchased the same policy type the year before (at age 33 and now age 34) would pay a somewhat higher rate; a third woman, who purchased her policy two years ago (at age 32 and who is now 34), would be paying a still higher rate; and so on, depending on the select mortality table used as the basis for the rates. Even though each insured would now be aged 34, the select/ultimate dichotomy leads to a premium schedule that permits the person most recently insured to pay the lowest rate.

Such policies are referred to as reentry term because the insured may be able to reenter the select group periodically—in our example, once every five years—if the insured resubmits to the insurer evidence of satisfactory insurability at that time. Thus, at the end of five years, insureds who can demonstrate continued insurability would be able to enjoy the much lower premium rates based on first-year select mortality for their attained age. For those insureds who fail to take advantage of the reentry provision or who fail to qualify for reentry because of insurability problems, ultimate rates are charged thereafter. These ultimate premiums are considerably higher than the select premiums, and higher than traditional aggregate term rates as well. A person who cannot qualify for select rates usually will be unable to qualify for a new policy based on aggregate rates and, therefore, must pay the higher ultimate rates if he or she wishes to continue insurance coverage. The reentry feature, in effect, encourages insureds to self-declare their expected mortality status, thus making for more refined risk classification.

Types of Term Life Insurance Policies

Term life insurance usually provides either a level or decreasing death benefit, with some increasing death benefit riders sold. (A **rider** is an attachment to a life or heath insurance policy that either adds benefits or excludes certain losses.) We center our discussion on the nature of the death benefit promise, as shown by the following schematic.

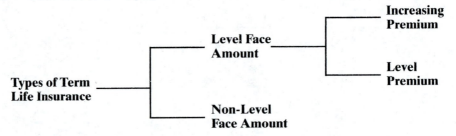

Level Face Amount Policies

Probably the vast majority of term life insurance sold worldwide, and certainly within the United States, provides for a level death benefit over the policy period. Premiums for such contracts either increase with age or remain level.

Increasing-Premium Policies Term policies with level death benefits and increasing premiums are commonly referred to as contracts that are *renewable*, a term that is synonymous with *increasing premium*, as alluded to earlier. Thus, **yearly renewable term** (YRT)—also called **annual renewable term** (ART)—and **five-year renewable term** policies are increasing-premium contracts. Some insurers offer renewable term policies of other durations, such as three, six, and ten years. YRT policies are quite popular in some markets, such as in the United States, but less so in most others. Many insurers have sought ways of minimizing the commodity aspects of term, with its high lapse rates and low profitability, and have moved away from YRT policies.

YRT product design has been of considerable interest, as particularly intense price competition has centered around these products. The trend in YRT design has been toward (1) lower premiums, (2) a greater number of rate bands (e.g., different rates at $100,000, $250,000, $500,000, and $1 million amount bands), and (3) differentiated pricing categories.

Differential pricing can be accomplished in several ways. One common method is through the use of separate smoker/nonsmoker rates. Most major North American writers of YRT offer either nonsmoker rates or a preferred risk category, although this is less common internationally.

YRT premium differences between smokers and nonsmokers can be substantial. Table 4-1 lists first-year YRT smoker and nonsmoker premiums for several companies.

TABLE 4-1	Selected Smoker and Nonsmoker YRT Premium Rates	
	Premium Amounts	
	Smoker	**Nonsmoker**
Company A	$204	$192
Company B	207	137
Company C	225	194
Company D	236	177
Company E	241	150
Company F	282	185
Company G	319	192

Source: Best's Flitcraft Compend.

As mentioned earlier, companies increasingly utilize a reentry feature to differentiate pricing. Table 4-2 illustrates two companies' YRT products. Policy A is a traditional aggregate-based product, and Policy B is a reentry product with a five-year reentry feature and with indeterminate premiums.

The Policy B reentry premiums are indeed low. The second column under Policy B shows the premiums that the insurer anticipates charging if the insured does not qualify for the lower reentry premiums. The third column shows the maximum premiums that the insurer could charge if it chose to do so and if the insured did not qualify for reentry. Note that the first five years of premiums are the same for each of the three premium sets.

TABLE 4-2		Reentry versus Aggregate-Based YRT Premiums				
			Policy A		**Policy B**	
Policy Year	**Age**	**Face Amount**	**Aggregate Premium**	**Current Reentry**	**Current Non-reentry**	**Failure to Reenter**
1	35	$100,000	$145	$111	$ 111	$ 111
2	36	100,000	148	132	132	132
3	37	100,000	154	147	147	147
4	38	100,000	162	165	165	165
5	39	100,000	172	185	185	185
6	40	100,000	185	138	210	228
7	41	100,000	200	176	256	291
8	42	100,000	219	204	312	372
9	43	100,000	242	236	400	470
10	44	100,000	268	272	499	597
11	45	100,000	288	181	616	770
12	46	100,000	333	241	777	972
13	47	100,000	373	287	945	1,182
14	48	100,000	417	337	1,121	1,401
15	49	100,000	466	393	1,305	1,631
16	50	100,000	521	238	1,495	1,869
17	51	100,000	581	327	1,699	2,124
18	52	100,000	646	395	1,911	2,389
19	53	100,000	716	466	2,133	2,667
20	54	100,000	791	544	2,362	2,953

Common minimum issue ages for YRT policies range from 15 to 20 years old, with common maximum issue ages of from 60 to 70. Some YRT contracts are now renewable to age 95 or 100 and convertible to age 65 or 70.

Level-Premium Policies   Term life insurance policies may have premium payment patterns that do not fit into the increasing-premium category discussed previously, although the face amount may remain level. Level-premium term contracts may be written for a set number of years or to cover the typical working lifetime. Contracts of the first type include *10-year* and *20-year* (level-premium, nonrenewable) *term* policies. Such policies have become more popular in the United States within the past few years. Contracts of the second type, providing essentially the same protection, are (1) life-expectancy term and (2) term-to-age 65.

Life-expectancy term provides protection for a number of years equal to the life expectancy for a person of the proposed insured's age and sex, based on some specific mortality table. The leveling of the premium over many years produces a cash value, which increases to a point and then declines to zero by policy expiration.

Term-to-age-65 (or **70**) policies provide protection for a somewhat shorter period than do life-expectancy policies and, consequently, have slightly lower premiums. The rationale for this policy is that it provides protection during the typical individual's most productive years, as 65 is often retirement age. As with the life-expectancy contract, a cash value often develops during the policy term, increasing for some years then decreasing to zero by policy expiry. Neither of these contracts is widely sold in most markets.

Non-Level Face Amount Policies

A significant amount of term life insurance sold in the United States and elsewhere involves policies (or riders) whose face amounts decrease or increase with time. Decreasing term policies are commonly used to pay off a loan balance on the death of the debtor/insured, be it in connection with a mortgage loan or a business or personal loan. Thus, **mortgage protection term** policies provide for face amount decreases that match the projected decreases in the principal amount owed under a mortgage loan. As the larger proportion of each early mortgage loan payment is applied to pay interest, the initial decrease in a mortgage loan's outstanding balance is slight, with later declines being substantial, as Figure 4-2 illustrates for a 30-year mortgage protection policy. Such policies' death benefits track this pattern and are available to cover a variety of mortgage loan durations (e.g, 10, 15, 20, 25, or 30 years) and amortization schedules. They usually provide for a conversion right. Level premiums are sometimes payable for a somewhat shorter period than the policy duration.

Term insurance that decreases by the same fixed amount each year is also available. Such policies are sold for durations of from 10 to 30 years but are not renewable.

A type of decreasing term, called **payor benefit** and available as a rider to a policy insuring the life of a juvenile, provides a death (and typically a waiver of premium) benefit on the life of the premium payor (usually a parent). The decreasing death benefit on the payor's life is exactly sufficient to pay all premiums that would be due from the payor's death until the insured's age 21. The benefit is designed to ensure that premiums due on the juvenile's life insurance policy will be paid even if the premium payor dies (or becomes disabled).

Another type of decreasing term life insurance, called a **family income policy,** is designed to appeal to young men and women whose family responsibilities call for a monthly income to be paid to the surviving spouse (typically) until a certain age or for a set period of usually 10, 15, or 20 years from the date of policy issuance. This policy, also

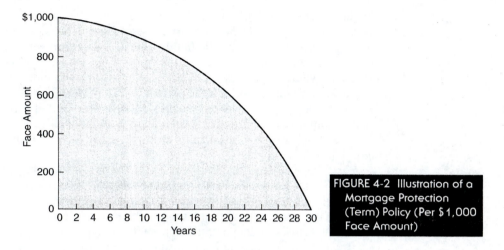

FIGURE 4-2 Illustration of a Mortgage Protection (Term) Policy (Per $1,000 Face Amount)

available as a rider to other forms of insurance, is often sold to protect the family during the child-rearing years. Of course, if the insured lives beyond the specified age or beyond the set number of years from issue, no further coverage is provided by this benefit.

Increasing term insurance is also sold but virtually never as a separate policy. Insurers offer increasing term coverage as a **cost-of-living-adjustment** (COLA) rider to many policies. COLA riders provide for automatic increases in the policy death benefit in accordance with increases in inflation, as measured by a national cost-of-living index, such as the consumer price index (CPI) in the United States. The policyowner is billed with the regular premium notice for the additional coverage. No evidence of insurability is required for these annual increases as long as the rider remains in force and is exercised fully each year. This requirement minimizes the possibility of adverse selection. Declines in the price index ordinarily do not result in declines in amounts purchased. Rather, the amount purchased in the previous year is carried forward to the current year.

Another type of increasing term insurance is provided by a so-called **return-of-premium feature** (or rider). This feature provides that, if the insured dies within a set number of years (e.g., 20 years) from the policy issue date, the death benefit will be augmented by an amount equal to the sum of all premiums paid to that point. Of course, the insurance company does not actually return the premiums paid and, in this sense, the feature's title might cause misunderstanding. Rather, the benefit is increasing term insurance whose annual death benefit is set to equal exactly the sum of the premiums paid to that year. The feature can be useful in certain business situations (see chapter 17), but it is also sometimes included to gain market power by differentiating the underlying policy from other similar contracts (thus making comparisons difficult) and to make the proposed policy seem more attractive to a prospect.

Increasing term insurance is also sometimes purchased through the use of policy dividends. This can be a valuable source of additional needed coverage and can render certain business arrangements more flexible, as discussed in chapter 17.

Uses and Limitations of Term Insurance

Term life insurance has long been the subject of debate. Some advocate the use of term insurance to the virtual exclusion of cash-value insurance, with others advocating the opposite viewpoint. Neither extreme position seems tenable. Term life insurance's uses and limitations should be understood.

Term insurance can be useful for persons with low incomes and high insurance needs (a situation that occurs often because of family obligations). Good risk management principles suggest that the family unit should be protected against catastrophic losses. If current family income does not permit the option of purchasing whole life or other cash-value life insurance in adequate amounts, the individual arguably has no choice but to purchase term, if adequate financial protection is to be provided.

Those who have a career to establish and have a temporarily limited income arguably should use their resources primarily to establish their careers. Investment in oneself for self-improvement, especially during the early career development years, clearly should have high priority.

Term life insurance can also prove useful for persons who have placed substantially all of their resources in a new business that is still in its formative stages. In such instances, death could result in loss of the invested capital. New enterprises are particularly speculative and become stable only with time. Term insurance can serve as a hedge, especially because of its low premium requirement in the initial stages of these undertakings.

Related to the preceding circumstances are situations in which life insurance is needed to indemnify the business for the death of one or more employees whose contributions to the firm are critical to its success. Also, owners of closely held businesses may wish to establish predeath arrangements to ensure that their business interests will be sold at a fair price at their death so as to provide family liquidity. Although cash-value policies are usually sold in each of the above preceding situations, term life insurance can also meet the need, especially if funds with which to pay premiums are not abundant.

Many persons use term insurance as a supplement to an existing life insurance program during the child-rearing period. Term insurance can also be appropriate to use as a hedge against a financial loss already sustained, when some time is required to recoup the loss.

Term life insurance is naturally suited for ensuring that mortgage and other loans are paid on the debtor/insured's death and as a vehicle for ensuring that education or other needs are available if death were to cut short the period needed for the provider/insured to earn the needed funds. Term insurance is also a natural for all situations that call for temporary income protection needs.

Term insurance can be the basis for one's permanent insurance program through a so-called **buy-term-and-invest-the-difference** (BTID) arrangement. With a BTID plan, the individual who has sufficient funds to purchase cash-value life insurance if he or she wished instead purchases a term policy, which will carry a lower premium initially than an equivalent amount of cash-value insurance. The difference between the higher-premium cash-value policy and the lower-premium term policy is to be invested separately, such as in a mutual fund, savings account, an annuity, or other investment media. The hope is that the term plus the separate investment will outperform the cash-value life insurance policy.

Such a program can be successful if it is well conceived and well executed. A well-conceived program is one that recognizes the increasing-premium nature of most term policies and devises a plan either to accommodate these increasing premiums or to minimize their impact (e.g., by having a program for reducing insurance needs over time). A well-conceived program realistically assesses the policyowner's willingness, ability, and commitment to follow through with the plan. A well-executed program is one that includes high-quality, reasonably priced coverage that provides the capability to adapt to changing circumstances. Similar care is needed with respect to the outside investment media.

Success requires the faithful execution—usually on an annual basis—of the devised BTID program. Thus, for example, if the decision is made to save through media other than life insurance, but the individual fails to set aside the planned amounts regularly, the program could be judged to have failed in its mission.

ENDOWMENT INSURANCE

Endowment insurance is widely sold in numerous markets (e.g., Germany, Japan, Korea, Taiwan, and Thailand), although not in the United States. Even in the United States, some endowment insurance is still found in tax-qualified retirement plans and many older endowment policies remain in force. More importantly, from the reader's perspective, an understanding of the concepts that underlie endowments is essential irrespective of the product's popularity in a given market.

Nature of Endowment Insurance

Term policies provide for the payment of the full policy amount only if the insured dies during the policy term. Endowment policies, in contrast, promise not only to pay the policy face amount on the death of the insured during a fixed term of years, but also to pay the full face amount at the end of the term if the insured survives the term. Whereas policies payable only in the event of death are purchased chiefly for the benefit of others, endowment policies, although affording protection to others against the death of the insured during the fixed term, usually pay to the insured if he or she survives the endowment period.

There are two equally valid ways of viewing endowment insurance: (1) the mathematical concept and (2) the economic concept. We cover each next.

Mathematical Concept

The insurer makes two mutually exclusive promises under endowment insurance: (1) to pay the face amount if the insured dies during the endowment period or (2) to pay the face (or some other) amount if the insured survives to the end of the endowment period. The first promise is identical to that made under a term policy for an equivalent face amount and period. The second promise introduces a new concept, the pure endowment. A **pure endowment** promises to pay the maturity amount only if the insured is living at the end of a specified period, with nothing paid in case of prior death. Pure endowment insurance is not often sold as a separate contract but rather often is embedded within policies that provide other benefits. In fact, most U.S. states prohibit the sale of a separate pure endowment insurance policy. It is said that few people are willing to risk the *apparent* loss of all premiums paid in the event of death before the end of the endowment period.

Thus, to provide a death benefit during the endowment period, only term insurance for the same period need be added to the pure endowment. It can be seen that these two elements—(1) level term insurance and (2) a pure endowment—together meet the two promises made under endowment insurance.

Endowment Insurance = Term Life Insurance + Pure Endowment

Economic Concept

Another analysis of endowment insurance, the economic concept, divides endowment insurance into two parts: decreasing term insurance and increasing savings. The savings part of the contract is available to the policyowner through surrender of the policy. This increasing savings feature is supplemented by decreasing term insurance, which, when added to the savings accumulation, equals the policy's face amount. This is the same analogy discussed in chapter 2 with respect to whole life insurance policies.

Insurance contracts have not always fit the increasing savings, decreasing term insurance model. In earlier times in the United States and in some other countries today, no nonforfeiture values existed for life insurance contracts. If an individual ceased premium payments, no return of any sort was available as a matter of contract. The contract promised to pay in the event of death or survival to a certain age, but if the contract was discontinued prior to the occurrence of these contingencies, all premiums were considered fully earned and any mortality prefunding was forfeited.

Types of Endowment Policies

Variations of endowment insurance are enormous worldwide. Many policies are for set durations of from 5 to 30 or more years, and others are arranged to mature at certain ages, such as at ages 60, 65, or 70. Endowment policies of from three to ten years' duration are common in many Asian countries. Premiums often are due throughout the term, although limited-payment plans, such as an endowment at age 65 paid up in 20 years, have been available. In several European countries, **single-premium endowment policies** are popular. In the United Kingdom, long-term endowment policies are commonly purchased as a mortgage loan companion, the idea being that the endowment maturity value will pay off the outstanding loan balance at a preset time.

Besides the standard contracts, other applications of the endowment principle are sometimes made. With a **retirement income policy,** the amount payable at death is the face amount or cash value, whichever is greater. The contract is used in insured pension plans utilizing individual contracts. A **semi-endowment policy** pays upon survival one-half the sum payable on death during the endowment period. **Modified endowment policies,** popular in some markets such as Thailand, provide for the payment periodically of a set percentage of the insured amount over the policy term, as well as a maturity amount.

Term life insurance riders are added to endowment policies in some markets, such as in Japan. Within the United States in the 1970s, a popular form of term insurance, known by the misleading name of **deposit term,** provided for payment of a modest endowment whose amount was set equal to a multiple of the difference between the first-year and renewal premiums. (First-year premiums on the policy were set to be higher than renewal premiums.) The marketing material suggested that this maturity amount was due to this premium differential, which was not correct.

Various kinds of **juvenile endowment policies** are sold in many markets, although they are not popular in the United States. These include policies maturing at specified ages and are designed to cover expenses associated with a child's education, marriage, or independence. Educational endowment policies are particularly popular in Korea, Japan, and certain other countries.

Because the company's liability under an endowment policy involves not only payment of the face amount upon death but also payment upon survival of the term, it follows that the annual premium on these policies must be higher than that for whole life or term policies, except for the very long endowment periods, in which the rate is only slightly higher than that charged on an ordinary life policy.

Uses and Limitations of Endowment Insurance

At one time in the United States, endowment insurance was considered an effective vehicle for accumulating savings. However, even before 1984 tax law changes effectively limited the endowment insurance market to qualified retirement plans, endowment insurance was having great difficulty competing against whole life and term insurance. The high first-year expenses associated with policies sold at that time rendered many of them less than stellar savings vehicles.

Endowments remain popular savings instruments in numerous other markets, although sales have declined in favor of whole life and term life sales in most markets. Even so, favorable tax treatment coupled with a strong savings impetus has resulted in a continuing strong demand for endowments in many markets. Endowments can be effective savings instruments provided loadings are competitive with those of other savings media.

Questions

1. Life insurers have actively responded to competitive pressures in the financial services marketplace with new premium plans, improved risk classification, and greater flexibility and disclosure in their products. How do some of these changes affect the attractiveness of life insurance from the savings and risk-pooling perspectives?
2. Reentry provisions in term insurance products allow life insurers to address adverse selection problems. Explain how these provisions can make term insurance products more attractive to consumers.
3. Explain the renewability and convertibility features of the term insurance policy.
4. Term and endowment are two forms of life insurance. Compare and contrast the product characteristics and objectives of these two coverages.

CHAPTER

5

WHOLE LIFE INSURANCE POLICIES

Objectives

- Understand mortality prefunding, participation in the experience of a life insurer, policy loans, and cash values as they apply to whole life policies.

- Understand how and for what uses ordinary and variable life insurance policies were designed.

- Describe the risks assumed by companies and individuals under ordinary and variable life policies.

- Understand the implications that policy loan provisions have for insureds and insurers.

- Recognize distinguishing features of modified, enhanced ordinary, graded premium, single-premium, indexed, and special-purpose whole life insurance policies.

In contrast with term, whole life insurance is intended to provide insurance protection over one's entire lifetime. Whole life insurance has been the mainstay of the North American life insurance business for more than a century and continues to be significant in these as well as other markets worldwide.

THE NATURE OF WHOLE LIFE INSURANCE

As discussed in chapters 1 and 2, the essence of *whole life insurance* is that it provides for the payment of the face amount upon the insured's death regardless of when death occurs. Its name describes its nature. It is insurance for the whole of life. As used in this text, the name refers not to any specific type of whole life policy—of which there are many—but rather is generic and describes any type of life insurance that can be maintained in effect indefinitely. By this definition, universal life policies can function as whole life insurance if they have sufficient cash value.

The face amounts payable under whole life policies typically remain at the same level throughout the policy duration, although dividends are often used to increase the total amount paid on death, especially in Europe. In most whole life insurance policies, the gross premium also remains at the same level throughout the premium payment period. Exceptions exist (e.g., graded premium whole life) wherein future premium changes are stipulated in the contract or by the insurer. With the indeterminate-premium approach, many whole life policies' future premium levels are unknown except that the maximum possible premium level is set by contract and near-term premiums may be guaranteed.

Whole Life as Endowment or Term Insurance

Much whole life insurance is priced on mortality tables that assume that all insureds die by a certain age. Age 100 is common, for example, in North America, as illustrated in chapter 2, and will be assumed hereafter to be the terminal age. Of course, all insureds do not, in fact, die by age 100 or whatever terminal age is used, but insurance companies price the insurance as if they do. It is only fair, therefore, that the company pay the policy face amount to those few persons who live to the terminal age—as if they had died. This fact is the reason that whole life policies are sometimes referred to, in the United States, as endowment-at-age-100 policies. The age-100 "endowment" really is not an endowment in the usual sense, but rather it is paid by the insurer in recognition that the underlying reserve and cash value of the policy equal the policy face amount at age 100 and, therefore, no pure insurance protection exists beyond that point. Thus, the insurer should terminate the policy. Even if the company did not do so, the policyowner could surrender the policy for its cash value—which equals the face amount.

Another equally valid viewpoint is that whole life policies are also term-to-age-100 policies. This view is justified by noting that the actuarial technique used for pricing whole life is the same, in concept, as that used to price any term policy. The age-100 payment, under this view, can be considered as a death benefit payment because the underlying mortality table assumes that all individuals surviving to age 99 die during this year.

Whole Life Cash Values

All whole life policies involve some prefunding of future mortality costs. The degree of prefunding is a function of the premium payment pattern and period. Because of this prefunding, all whole life policies sold in the United States and some other markets are required to have cash values and, as mentioned earlier, the cash value must build to the policy face amount, usually by age 100. Many countries' laws, such as Canada and the United Kingdom, do not require cash values, but insurers usually provide them by practice.

Whole life cash values are available to the policyowner at any time by the policyowner's surrendering (canceling) the policy. Alternatively, cash values can be used in other ways, providing flexibility to the policyowner, as discussed in chapter 9. Whole life policies usually contain cash-value schedules that show for selected time periods the guaranteed minimum amounts that the policyowner could receive from the company on surrender of the policy.

Owners of whole life insurance policies do not have to surrender their policies to have access to funds. Under participating whole life policies in which dividends have purchased paid-up additional insurance, such additions may be surrendered for their then value with no impact on the policy proper. Also, policyowners normally can obtain a loan from the insurer for amounts up to that of the policy's cash value. Of course, interest is charged for this loan, and the loan is deducted from the gross cash value if the policy is surrendered or from the face amount if the insured dies and a death claim is payable. Policy loans may, but need not, be repaid at any time and are a source of policy flexibility.

Par and Nonpar Whole Life

Most whole life insurance sold worldwide is participating. A significant proportion is nonparticipating but with some nonguaranteed element. The amount of guaranteed-cost, nonpar whole life sold in most OECD countries, including Canada, the United States,

France, Germany, Japan, and Korea, is small, although it remains popular in many developing countries. This small share is not surprising because companies are understandably unwilling to offer liberal pricing guaranteed for decades into the future. Conservatively priced products providing long-term guarantees do not compete well against those wherein the insurer does not guarantee every policy element.

Insurance companies usually provide a **dividend illustration** to prospective purchasers of participating policies, which shows the insurer dividends that would be paid under the policy if the mortality, expense, and interest experience implicit in the current scale of illustrated dividends were to be the actual basis for all future dividends. The dividend illustration is usually based on the recent past mortality, expense, and interest experience of the company. Important differences exist in the way insurers allocate amounts to be paid as dividends, and these differences can have a major impact on the dividend levels illustrated as well as on the dividends that are actually paid, as discussed later in this volume.

As mentioned in chapter 2, dividends are not guaranteed. **Dividends actually paid,** the schedule of which is a **dividend history,** are as its name implies amounts actually paid as dividends. Dividends actually paid equal those illustrated only if their experience basis is the same as that implicit in the illustration. Future experience rarely tracks past experience exactly and never over an extended period. On the other hand, some insurers have "frozen" their dividend scales (i.e., they have paid dividends almost exactly as illustrated regardless of the developing experience). This practice treats dividends more as a series of nonguaranteed pure endowments and is not in keeping with principles of equity underpinning participating life insurance. A widely accepted equitable concept is known as the **contribution principle,** which holds that insurers selling participating policies should distribute surplus accumulated on behalf of a block of policies in the same proportions as the policies are considered to have contributed to the surplus.

Dividends actually paid usually will exceed illustrated dividends in periods when investment returns are generally higher during the period after policy issuance than they were during the period prior thereto. Of course, the opposite also applies. Dividends illustrated during the high-yielding 1980s in the United States were quite high by historical standards. In fact, dividends actually paid were less than illustrated, giving rise to disappointment and even lawsuits, as alluded to earlier.

Some years ago, there were basically only two types of whole life insurance. One provided for level-premium payments to be made for the whole of life (ordinary life), and the other provided for premium payments to be made for a limited period of time only (limited-payment whole life). Today, however, whole life policies come with a great variety of premium payment patterns and options and benefits. The most common types are presented next.

TYPES OF WHOLE LIFE INSURANCE POLICIES

As a result of the pressures discussed earlier, many innovations have evolved in whole life insurance pricing and policy provisions. Because of the vast array of new whole life products and the even greater number of internal policy variations, the following discussion can highlight only some of the more important policies.

Ordinary Life Insurance

Ordinary life insurance provides whole life insurance with premiums that are payable for the whole of life. This oldest form of whole life may be referred to by several other names, including **straight life** and **continuous-premium whole life,** and often the term *whole life* itself is used to denote ordinary life insurance.

Product Design

Ordinary life policies are intended to afford permanent protection at a relatively modest annual outlay because the mortality costs are spread over the entire policy period. Table 5-1 lists gross premiums charged for several otherwise similar participating and guaranteed-cost, nonparticipating ordinary life insurance policies. Premium levels vary significantly. The premium paid for any cash-value policy, including whole life, is not a measure of the policy's cost. A policy can have a relatively high premium yet be low in cost by having large dividends, cash values, or excess interest credits, as discussed in chapter 12.

Ordinary life policy cash values normally increase at a fairly constant rate, reaching the policy face amount at age 100. As discussed more fully in chapter 9, cash values can be a source of policy flexibility. Early years' cash values are typically low, because the high costs associated with policy sale and issuance are charged off during the first years. These high costs result from the commission paid to the salesperson, which often is 40 to 80 percent or more of the first-year premium, as well as from underwriting and other administrative expenses.

Traditional whole life policies have lost market share in some countries to newer cash-value products including universal life (UL). Most UL and many of the newer variations of whole life use a new-money, interest rate crediting mechanism. These products were introduced at a time when interest rates were comparatively high, which meant that projections of potential future policy values were particularly attractive to prospective buyers. Many purchasers were not well enough informed about the risks inherent in policy illustrations or they chose to believe that high rates would prevail. As interest rates fell, many discovered that new-money rates could fall as fast as they rose. As discussed earlier, actual results did not meet expected results, with undesirable consequences for all concerned (except attorneys!).

At the same time, insurers issuing traditional participating whole life policies, whose excess interest credits are realized through dividends, discovered that they could credit steadily higher rates of interest. Their interest rate crediting mechanism—the portfolio average method (or variations thereon)—was predicated on their overall investment portfolio's return.

Although new-money rates move quickly, portfolio rates change slowly. Traditional par products produce more attractive returns in a falling interest rate environment for

TABLE 5-1	Gross Premiums Charged by Selected Par and Nonpar Policies	
Type of Policy	*Company*	*Gross Premium per $1,000*
Participating	A	$11.83
	B	13.95
	C	14.20
	D	15.66
	E	16.01
	F	21.68
Nonparticipating	G	10.70
	H	11.37
	I	12.22
	J	14.04
	K	17.00
	L	18.60

Source: A.M. Best Co.

the same reason that they produce less favorable returns—compared to new-money products—in a rising market. Thus, the advantage enjoyed by UL and other new-money-based products in a rising interest rate environment results in a disadvantage for them when interest rates fall—the very situation that prevailed during the late 1980s and the 1990s in several markets including Japan, Korea, and the United States. As interest rates stabilize, new money and portfolio yields converge.

To address those competitive dimensions, sellers of traditional whole life began creatively to introduce greater flexibility into their products. Many now offer prospective buyers the option of establishing their own level of future premium payments, subject to company-required minimum and tax-mandated maximum payments. This result is accomplished through several mechanisms. To enable the insured to pay a lower than usual premium, low-load term riders with face amounts of up to 10 times the base contract amount were introduced. For example, a 35-year-old male buying $100,000 of ordinary life insurance might pay a $1,400 premium. A combination ordinary life/term rider can reduce the annual outlay to $400. By blending the whole life and term elements, any premium between $400 and $1,400 can be derived. Alternatively, combinations of a decreasing term rider and paid-up additions from dividends can produce a level death benefit, but with a lower than usual premium outlay, similar to that used with enhanced ordinary life policies (see later in this chapter).

Greater than usual premium payments—either periodic or single—can be accommodated through a policy rider that permits such payments to be used to purchase paid-up additions analogous to those purchased with dividends. When the cash value of the paid-up additions (both those purchased through dividends and by additional premium payments) is of sufficient size, an organized program of surrendering pieces of these additions, coupled with further policy dividends, can be used to pay the policy's premiums. This method of arranging to meet future premium payments with the possibility of no further payments by the policyowner was referred to in the United States by the potentially misleading term, **vanish pay,** and sometimes by the erroneous name of *vanish premium*. If future dividends and surrenders of paid-up additions are sufficient, the policy would be self-sustaining with no further outlays required of the policyowner. If such dividends and surrenders prove insufficient to meet further premium payments—for example, if dividends prove to be lower than initially anticipated, the policyowner will be required to resume payments to maintain the policy in force. This same approach applies to nonparticipating policies containing nonguaranteed elements.

Finally, some insurers permit use of a **premium deposit rider** under which the policyowner deposits amounts to pay future premiums. Under this rider, funds are transferred automatically to cover each future premium payment, thus potentially relieving the policyowner of further policy payments at some point. Variations on each of the foregoing mechanisms exist. For example, some companies use immediate annuities as a premium repository to minimize taxation, but in all cases the purpose is to provide the policyowner with greater flexibility.

Policy Illustration

Table 5-2 shows a U.S. illustration for a traditional participating $100,000 ordinary life policy issued to a 35-year-old male nonsmoker. Dividends are shown both as being netted against the premium payment and as purchasing paid-up additional insurance. Of course, only one option would be selected. The negative impact on early cash values of the high front-end load is clear. The table shows that the guaranteed cash value at age 45 is $11,411, and at age 55 it will be $29,486.

TABLE 5-2	Illustration of Traditional Participating Ordinary Life Policy						
(1)	*(2)*	*(3)*	*(4)*	*(5)*	*(6)*	*(7)*	*(8)*
					If Dividends Used to Purchase Paid-Up Additions		
END OF YEAR	GROSS PREMIUM	ILLUSTRATED DIVIDENDS (YEAR END)[a]	PREMIUM LESS DIVIDEND (2–3 PREVIOUS YEARS)	GUARANTEED CASH SURRENDER VALUE	PAID-UP ADDITIONAL INSURANCE PURCHASED	TOTAL CASH VALUE[b]	TOTAL DEATH BENEFIT (YEAR END)[c]
1	$1,533	$ 16	$1,533	$ 0	$ 78	$ 15	$100,078
2	1,533	100	1,517	1,078	550	1,195	100,550
3	1,533	187	1,433	2,201	1,410	2,515	101,410
4	1,533	277	1,346	3,371	2,655	3,991	102,655
5	1,533	371	1,256	4,588	4,285	5,634	104,285
6	1,533	465	1,162	5,852	6,286	7,456	106,286
7	1,533	563	1,068	7,165	8,661	9,476	108,661
8	1,533	660	970	8,528	11,393	11,704	111,393
9	1,533	762	873	9,942	14,491	14,163	114,491
10	1,533	862	771	11,411	17,938	16,870	117,938
11	1,533	967	671	12,933	21,743	19,843	121,743
12	1,533	1,063	566	14,515	25,869	23,100	125,869
13	1,533	1,163	470	16,156	30,325	26,664	130,325
14	1,533	1,237	370	17,860	35,033	30,534	135,033
15	1,533	1,313	296	19,629	39,997	34,733	139,997
16	1,533	1,389	220	21,466	45,215	39,287	145,215
17	1,533	1,470	144	23,370	50,700	44,224	150,700
18	1,533	1,552	63	25,341	56,454	49,571	156,454
19	1,533	1,637	–19	27,380	62,486	55,359	162,486
20	1,533	1,726	–104	29,486	68,807	61,621	168,807

[a]Dividends assume no policy loans. Loans will reduce dividends. Based on current dividend scale but not an estimate or guarantee of future results. Loan provision is at 8 percent.
[b]Guaranteed cash surrender value (column 5) plus cash value of paid-up additional insurance.
[c]$100,000 plus column 6.

Uses of Ordinary Life

Contemporary ordinary life insurance policies offer greater flexibility and value than did most earlier versions. For persons whose life insurance need is expected to extend over 10 to 15 or more years and who are interested in accumulating savings via life insurance, ordinary life may prove to be the insurance of choice. By leveling premium payments over the entire policy duration, outlays can be relatively modest. Interest credited on cash values enjoys favorable income tax treatment in most countries, including the United States, thus rendering the policy a potentially attractive means of accumulating savings.

Most ordinary life policies prove costly for those whose life insurance need is less than 15 or so years, because the typically heavy front-end expenses penalize short- and medium-term values. Depending on the buyer's discipline and the availability of other means of accumulating funds, a buy-term-and-invest-the-difference program usually is superior for medium-term and shorter duration needs and also can prove an effective alternative for providing longer-term economic security, as discussed in chapter

4. For some persons, ordinary life and other whole life policies can serve as a quasi-forced savings plan.

For many persons whose careers are just beginning, the premium payment required for an adequate amount of ordinary life insurance may be too great, given other priorities. Rather than reduce the insurance amount to that with an affordable premium level, good risk management principles argue for placing primary emphasis on the insurance needed to cover the potential loss, with secondary emphasis on product type. The only effective choice, therefore, may be to purchase term insurance.

Limited-Payment Whole Life Insurance

With **limited-payment whole life insurance,** the policy remains in full force for the whole of life, but premiums are payable for a limited number of years only, after which the policy becomes paid up for its full face amount. The premium-paying period may be expressed as a set number of years or to a specified age. A paid-up policy should not be confused with a matured or an expired policy, both of which suggest that the policy is no longer in effect. A policy *matures* when the face amount becomes payable either as a death claim or because the policy cash value equals the face amount, as in an endowment policy. A policy *expires* when the policy term ends and the policy makes no benefit payment, as in a term policy. A **paid-up policy** is one for which no further premium payments are due contractually but the policy remains in effect.

Although potentially identical in practical effect, a paid-up policy differs in important ways from a so-called vanish pay policy. A paid-up policy is contractually guaranteed never to require premium payments beyond the stated premium payment period. No such guarantee exists with policies whose values *might* be such as to make them self-sustaining.

Premium payments may be fixed at almost any number of years—from 1 to 30, or even more. If premiums are limited to 20 years, for example, the policy is known as a **20-payment whole life** policy. The greater the number of premium payments, the more closely the contract resembles the ordinary life form.

Companies also make available contracts that limit premium payments to a certain age, such as to age 65, 70, or even higher. The objective typically would be to permit the owner to pay up the policy during his or her working lifetime. Thus, a policy that requires premiums to age 65 would be known as a **life-paid-up-at-age-65 whole life** policy (often abbreviated LP65). A 30-payment life and a LP65 policy both issued at age 35 (and based on the same pricing assumptions) would carry the same premium, because actually they would be the same policy.

As limited-payment policies require the payment of premiums for a period less than the contract term, it follows that the annual level premium under these plans must be larger than that necessary when premium payments continue throughout the life of the policy. Theoretically, the premiums payable under a limited-payment policy are the actuarial equivalent of the premiums payable for the insured's entire lifetime under an ordinary life plan.

Because of the higher premiums, limited-payment plans are not well adapted to those whose income is small and whose need for insurance protection is great. Furthermore, many persons who may be able to pay premiums may choose an ordinary life policy, as it may afford greater flexibility via riders permitting additional premium payments, or they may be able to invest the difference in the premiums more profitably. Limited-payment policies fit many business insurance situations in which it is desirable to ensure that the policy is fully paid for within a certain time period and are popular in many countries, although less so in the United States.

Of course, the disadvantage of higher premiums is offset to some degree by the availability of larger policy values. Other things being the same, the higher the premium for a policy, the greater the cash values (due to the greater prefunding of future mortality charges). All limited-payment policies contain the same nonforfeiture, dividend, and settlement options as well as other standard features of ordinary life policies that provide policyowner flexibility.

The extreme in limited-payment life insurance is the **single-premium whole life** policy wherein the policy is fully paid up from inception with but a single payment. Such a policy has immediate, substantial cash value. Consequently, such a contract requires a substantial outlay. The other extreme of whole life is represented by the ordinary life insurance policy, for which the premiums are payable until the maturity of the contract. Limited-payment contracts vary between these extremes. Thus, five- and 10-pay life policies are close to single-premium policies, whereas a policy paid up at age 85 or beyond is, for all practical purposes, an ordinary life policy. Other things being the same, as the number of premium payments increases, the annual premium and, consequently, the rate of growth of policy values become correspondingly smaller.

Figure 5-1 shows illustrative cash surrender values for various whole life insurance policies for a male aged 40. As is clear, the size of the cash value varies inversely with the length of the premium-paying period. Thus, the ordinary life plan with payments for life has the lowest cash values, and the single-premium plan, which involves only one premium payment, has the highest. Note that after premium payments cease under the 10-payment and 20-payment whole life plans, the cash values in each instance equal those under the single-premium plan. For policies using the same underlying pricing assumptions, this must be the case, because after any limited-payment period expires, the value to the company of future premiums is zero and all future mortality costs must be covered from existing funds and interest earnings thereon.

Current Assumption Whole Life Insurance

Current assumption whole life (CAWL) insurance policies provide (usually) nonpar whole life insurance under a nontraditional, transparent format that relies on an indeterminate-premium structure. The policy typically uses new-money interest rates and current mortality charges in cash-value determination. This fact has led to the product also being referred to as **interest-sensitive whole life** and as **fixed-premium universal life.**

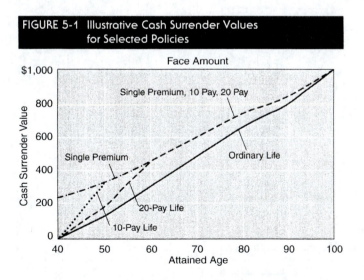

FIGURE 5-1 Illustrative Cash Surrender Values for Selected Policies

Traditional whole life relies on dividends as the mechanism for passing through deviations of actual operational experience from that implicit in the original policy pricing. CAWL, in contrast, relies on changes in the cash values and premiums to accommodate deviations in operational experience from that guaranteed in the contract.

CAWL policies are unbundled, meaning that an explicit allocation is made of premium payments and interest earnings to policy expenses, mortality charges, and cash values. Although this allocation may not accurately reflect the company's actual internal pricing components, the owner, nonetheless, can visualize the internal functioning of the policy in terms of how the premium payments and interest credits are allocated. In contrast, with so-called unbundled policies, such as traditional whole life, no visible allocation is made.

Figure 5-2 illustrates the funds flow of a CAWL policy. The premium is paid to the insurer. Expense charges (if any) are then deducted. The contract states the maximum expense charge that can be levied, but companies may charge less. Many CAWL policies have no explicitly identified expense charges; the charges are met through higher than needed mortality charges and through a margin in interest earnings.

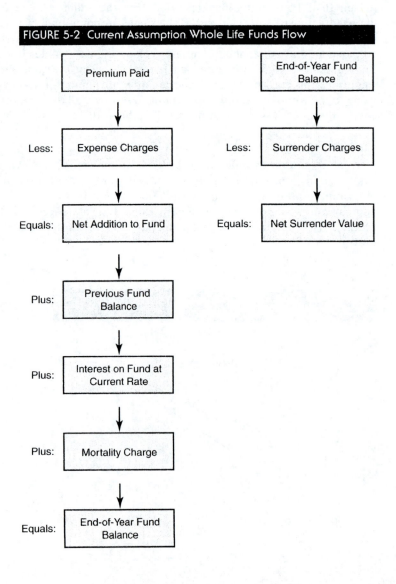

FIGURE 5-2 Current Assumption Whole Life Funds Flow

The amount remaining is added to the previous year's accumulated fund balance (if any) to constitute a beginning-year balance. To this balance is added interest based on the insurer's current crediting rate. Guaranteed minimum rates in the United States have ranged from 3.5 to 5.0 percent recently.

Next, mortality charges are assessed. These charges are based either on the maximum permissible rates as set forth in the contract or, more often, on lower current rates. The rate is applied to the policy's net amount at risk (face amount less cash value).

The remaining fund balance is the policy's gross cash value. Most contracts stipulate that surrender charges will be levied against this cash value (fund balance) to derive the cash *surrender* value. From the buyer's perspective, the lower the surrender charge the better the value, all else being equal. From the insurer's and persisting policyowners' perspectives, however, the higher the surrender charges the better. For the insurer, such charges permit a recoupment of some or all of the high first-year expenses, thus minimizing the strain on surplus. Stated in terms of the discussion on assets shares in chapter 2, surrender charges can permit a more equitable allocation of expenses between persisting and lapsing policyowners. In the absence of these charges and with other things being the same, terminating policyowners would depart with cash surrender values that, in all likelihood, greatly exceeded the corresponding asset share. The effect would be to require continuing policyowners to make good the deficit, thus reducing the long-term value of their policies.

Product Design

CAWL products can be classified as falling into either a low-premium or high-premium category. The low-premium version has several unique features. The initial, indeterminate premium is low by traditional ordinary life insurance standards. The policy's **redetermination provision** generally states that, after the initial guarantee period, the company can redetermine the premium using the same or new assumptions as to future interest and mortality. The policy contains specific quantitative guarantees as to the minimum interest rate to be credited and the maximum mortality charges to be levied. The premium is then redetermined, such that, together with the existing accumulation account value, it will be able to maintain a level death benefit to the end of life, if the new assumptions hold true. This will be recognized as a type of indeterminate-premium structure.

If the new assumptions are the same as those used at the time of issue or previous redetermination, the premiums and death benefits are guaranteed for another period of years. If the assumptions have changed since the last redetermination, the new redetermined premium will be higher or lower than previously.

If the new premium is lower than the previous premium, the policyowner often may elect one of these three options, one of which (usually option 2) is automatic but subject to policyowner change:

1. Pay the new, lower premium and maintain the previous death benefit.
2. Continue to pay the previous premium, maintain the previous death benefit, and have the difference in the two premiums added to the accumulation fund.
3. Continue to pay the previous premium and use the difference to pay for an increased death benefit, subject to evidence of insurability.

If the new premium is higher than the previous premium, the policyowner may elect one of three options, one of which (usually option 1) is automatic but subject to policyowner change:

1. Pay the new, higher premium and maintain the previous death benefit.
2. Continue to pay the previous premium but lower the policy death benefit to that which the new premium will sustain.

3. Continue to pay the previous premium and maintain the previous death benefit while using up some of the available cash value. (This option is not always available and, when available, requires the accumulation fund to be at or above a certain level for at least the next five policy years.)

The high-premium version also has several unique aspects. The premium is relatively high but typically guaranteed never to increase. An optional vanish pay provision is usually contained in the contract. This provision states that the policyowner may elect to cease paying premiums at some point in time and have the policy become self-sustaining. The point in time is determined by comparing the accumulation account to a net single premium needed to pay up the contract, but with the net single premium based on current interest and mortality rates. Once the accumulation account exceeds this net single premium, no further premium payments need be made but only if the current or more favorable interest and mortality levels are maintained until maturity of the contract. This provision is not mandatory and the vanish pay period is not guaranteed. The policy remains self-sustaining only so long as the accumulation account exceeds the minimum required cash value. Once it falls below this level, premium payments are required. As might be suspected, policyowners can easily confuse this vanish pay option, under which the policy *may* be self-sustaining, with a paid-up policy under which the policy is *guaranteed* to be self-sustaining.

The low-premium and high-premium versions are simply two different approaches applied to the same basic product. With the low-premium version, current assumptions as to interest, mortality, and expenses are used to lower the current premium charged. With the high-premium version, these favorable anticipated deviations result in a far more rapid increase in cash values, with the result that the policy can become self-sustaining quickly.

Numerous variations in CAWL product design are found. For example, some insurers offer a death benefit equal to a level, stated amount plus an additional amount equal to the accumulation fund balance. Some insurers make premium redeterminations every year or every three years instead of every five years, and some versions contain even longer guarantee periods. Some CAWL policies make adjustments based on interest alone and some index the policy's current interest rate to interest rates on money instruments, such as government securities or bond indexes.

Policy Illustration

Table 5-3 shows illustrated premiums and policy values based on one company's low-premium and high-premium CAWL policies. Note that the difference between the two premium levels is significant ($6.18 versus $13.00 per $1,000) and that the charge for the low-premium version is considerably less than the premiums illustrated in Table 5-1 for ordinary life policies. Premiums are subject to a five-year redetermination period.

At current rates and assumptions, the high-premium policy could be tentatively self-sustaining at the end of seven policy years. If premiums were stopped at that point, later-duration surrender values would be less than those shown in Table 5-3.

Uses of CAWL

Compared with universal life policies, which permit policyowners to pay whatever premium they wish, CAWL's premium allows for easier company and policyowner administration. The level premium also gives the company greater control over the cash-value buildup. It is a blend of new and old.

Unlike the universal life policy, the CAWL policy will lapse if a required premium is not paid. This fact may provide some incentive for policyowners to pay renewal premiums regularly and, therefore, could assist individuals who perceive themselves as not having the discipline to pay flexible premiums.

TABLE 5-3		Illustrative Premiums and Cash Values for CAWL Policy					

		Low-Premium Version (per $1,000)			High-Premium Version (per $1,000)		
Policy Year	Death Benefit	Current Premium	Guaranteed Surrender Value	Projected Surrender Value	Current Premium	Guaranteed Surrender Value	Projected Surrender Value[b]
1	$100,000	$6.18	$ 0	$ 0	$13.00	$ 0	$ 0
2	100,000	6.18	1	1	13.00	0	6
3	100,000	6.18	6	6	13.00	4	21
4	100,000	6.18	12	12	13.00	16	36
5[a]	100,000	6.18	17	17	13.00	28	54
10[a]	100,000	6.18	46	49	13.00	97	175
15[a]	100,000	6.18	78	93	13.00	176	373
20[a]	100,000	6.18	112	144	13.00	261	678

[a]Premium to be paid for next five years is redetermined by company.
[b]Assumes premiums continue to be paid each year and death benefit is kept at initial amount.

Variable Life Insurance

Variable life insurance (VLI), also called **unit-linked life insurance** in many markets, is a type of whole life insurance whose values may vary directly with the performance of a set of earmarked investments.[1] It was first offered in the United States in 1976, after being developed and sold successfully in The Netherlands, England, and Canada.[2] Its initial success in the United States was limited, with only the Equitable Life Assurance Society involved in pioneering marketing efforts. Since that time, many insurers, including some in Japan, have begun offering some version of it.

VLI was introduced as a product that could help offset the adverse effects of inflation on life insurance policy values. It was believed that, over the long term, the investment experience of common stocks supporting the policies would increase at a rate faster than the inflation rate, thus providing a hedge against inflation. Although true historically over periods of many years, short-term variations are inevitable, with inflation heading in one direction and investment performance in the other.

Product Design

A variable life policy provides whole life insurance under which the death benefits and cash values vary to reflect the experience of a distinct pool of investments—held in a so-called **separate account**—separate from those in the insurer's general account, which back reserves on all nonvariable contracts sold by the insurer. This separate account acts as a mutual fund (also called a unit trust in many markets). Traditional VLI policies carry fixed premiums—referred to as scheduled premium policies in many U.S. jurisdictions—similar to traditional whole life insurance. The focus of this discussion is on these traditional VLI policies. Flexible-premium VLI is discussed in chapter 6.

With VLI policies, premiums less expense loads and mortality charges are paid into the separate investment account. The policyowner may specify, within limits, where the assets backing the cash value are to be invested. Several options are generally available,

---

[1]Although discussed here exclusively as whole life insurance, variable life policies can and do exist as endowments in some markets, although not in the United States.

[2]This section draws from Gregory D. Jacobs, "Pricing Non-traditional Individual Life Products," *SOA Part 10 Study Note* (Schaumburg, IL: Society of Actuaries, 1984); Mary Jo Napoli, "Variable Annuities," *SOA Part 10 Study Note* (Schaumburg, IL: Society of Actuaries, 1985); and Frank L. Rainaldi, "Variable Life—An Investment Oriented Life Insurance Product with a Non-Investment Alternative," *Journal of the American Society of CLU*, Vol. XXXVIII (January 1985).

as with a mutual fund. Most companies offer money market funds, common stock funds, bond funds, as well as other fund types. The policy cash values and death benefits ordinarily are directly related to the investment performance. However, within the United States and Japan, regardless of the investment performance, the death benefit is guaranteed never to fall below a specified minimum. Cash values traditionally have not been guaranteed, although some newer VLI designs provide a guaranteed minimum return. The cash value at any point in time is based on the market value of the policy's share of the separate account's funds. Traditional VLI contracts pass all investment risk to the policyowner.

The death benefit is composed of two parts. The first is a guaranteed minimum death benefit that corresponds to the basic plan of insurance underlying the VLI contract. The second part of the death benefit is variable. Any positive excess interest credits (i.e., the excess of the return on the underlying funds over an assumed investment return) is used to buy additional units of VLI insurance. These additional units are generally purchased at net premium rates on a daily, monthly, or annual basis. If the excess interest credits are negative, previously purchased units are surrendered and the total death benefit lowered. Regulation in the United States provides that the total policy death benefit may not fall below the minimum guaranteed.

Variable life policies may be participating or nonparticipating. With participating VLI, the dividend is a function only of mortality and expense savings and includes no element of excess investment earnings. Excess investment earnings, less an asset management charge, are credited directly to policy cash values.

Regulatory Developments

VLI product design is influenced by regulation on more fronts than most insurance products. Issuers of VLI must, as with all insurance products, comply with insurance laws and regulations. In the United States, variable contracts and their issuers are also subject to federal securities laws and are regulated by the Securities and Exchange Commission (SEC).

U.S. Securities Regulation   Federal securities regulation of VLI has its basis principally in three laws and related regulations. The SEC administers these laws. The three laws are the Investment Company Act of 1940, the Securities Act of 1933, and the Securities Exchange Act of 1934.

Entities that invest VLI policyowner assets in securities are investment companies (mutual funds) as defined in the **Investment Company Act of 1940.** This act is the focal point of securities regulation of VLI. The act regulates investment company management and operation. It sets rules concerning security owners, maximum sales charges, investment management of contributions, and distribution of periodic financial reports.

The SEC provides limited exemptions from the sections of the 1940 act that require management accountability to contractholders, that impose limitations on sales loads, and that require issuers to offer refunds under certain circumstances. A 1996 law removed the provisions on the 1940 act, which strictly regulated VLI expense charges, and substituted a reasonableness requirement applicable to fees and charges in the aggregate. This change is expected to lead to more creative VLI design. A VLI policy must be funded by a life insurance company separate account and must provide cash values that vary to reflect the account's investment experience. The policy must also provide a minimum death benefit guarantee and have the mortality and expense risk borne by the insurer.

The **Securities Act of 1933** sets registration, financial, and disclosure standards for securities. A VLI policy is a security. This act's main impact on VLI (and variable annuities, see chapter 8) is the requirement that the potential purchaser be provided with a prospectus. This booklet includes the identity and nature of the insurer's business, the use to which the insurer will put the premiums, financial information on the insurer, the fees and expenses to be charged, and policyowner rights.

Whereas the 1933 act deals principally with new securities issues, the **Securities Exchange Act of 1934** regulates the secondary securities market (i.e., the exchange of securities). Under the 1934 act, the entity that distributes VLI—the insurance company or a sales company—usually must register as a broker-dealer. The act requires that associated persons pass an examination on the securities business. Associated persons include agents and many home office and agency employees. The 1934 act regulates advertising, annual reports to shareholders, shareholder proxies, and financial reporting requirements.

The Maloney Act, an amendment to the Securities Exchange Act of 1934, made provision for the securities industry to form one or more bodies to regulate itself in accordance with the act's standards. The National Association of Securities Dealers (NASD) was established for this purpose in 1939. All broker-dealers, including agents who sell VLI, must register with the NASD and pass an examination to be able to sell and offer advice about variable products.

U.S. State Regulation   VLI may be issued in all U.S. states, and all states make provision for separate accounts. The basis for VLI regulation is the **Variable Life Insurance Model Regulation** adopted by the National Association of Insurance Commissioners. The regulation establishes certain mandatory policy design characteristics and policy provisions. The regulation also covers the qualifications of a company to conduct a VLI business, operations of VLI separate accounts, reserve requirements, and necessary information to be furnished to applicants and policyowners.

Policy Provisions

In most aspects, the VLI policy operates in the same manner as a traditional whole life policy, including requirements that the policy contain the normal life insurance provisions discussed in chapters 8 and 9. With the traditional form, fixed premiums are payable on regular due dates, and, if they are not paid, the policy lapses and goes under an option on lapse. The policy may be reinstated subject to usual rules, except that the past-due premiums collected must not be less than 110 percent of the increase in cash value immediately available upon reinstatement. This condition is necessary because the reinstated policy reflects values associated with a policy that had never lapsed and, thus, would reflect any favorable investment experience during the period of lapse.

Policy loans are to be made available in an amount equal to at least 75 percent of the cash value at a fixed (often 8 percent) or a variable interest rate. Loans against policy cash values have the effect of creating an additional investment fund. Under this approach, variable benefits are affected, because the return reflected in benefits is a blend of the separate account investment return and the net return earned on any policy loan. An interesting characteristic of this provision is that it presents an opportunity for a policyowner to influence the policy's variable benefits. In making a loan, the policyowner withdraws funds from the separate account and may make the policy less variable (upward or downward) while the policy loan is outstanding.

Illustrations of Death Benefits and Cash Values

Although it is relatively easy to describe how variable life insurance policy benefits vary to reflect the investment experience of the underlying separate account, to describe the specific method of determining benefit variation is a challenge. To supplement the narrative descriptions in the policy and prospectus, illustrations of policy benefits (assuming hypothetical rates of return in the separate account) are developed. Currently, applicable U.S. regulations permit illustrations based on (1) annual gross rates of return (after any tax charges and before other deductions) of 0, 4, 6, 8, 10, and 12 percent and

(2) the Standard and Poor's 500 Stock Price Index with dividends reinvested. Table 5-4 summarizes an illustration for a $100,000 level face amount policy issued to a male non-smoker aged 35.

The Appropriateness of VLI

Traditional variable life insurance should be appealing to those who desire whole life insurance at a fixed, level premium and also the potential for important equity-type gains (and losses). Obviously, VLI is riskier than the more traditional forms of life insurance. As a result, regulations require greater disclosure than that required for other life policies, as discussed in chapter 10. Most sound financial plans have as one of their elements a savings program that is both highly liquid and relatively riskless. A VLI policy, at any point in time, may not meet this objective. Its cash value might be more appropriately considered as an element in one's long-term investment program.

Other Forms of Whole Life Insurance

Several other forms of whole life insurance policies are covered here. Although the market share of each of these policies is not great in most markets today, some of them were at one time quite important in some of the OECD country markets and remain important in selected other markets. Irrespective of their relative importance to a given market, they illustrate some important concepts.

Modified Life Insurance

A modified life policy provides whole life insurance under which premiums are redistributed so that they are lower than an otherwise identical ordinary life policy during the first three to five years, and higher thereafter. Thus, one company's "modified 5" policy carries a premium during the first five years that is one-half of the premiums thereafter. During the preliminary period, the premium is more than the equivalent level-term premium for such a period but less than the ordinary life premium at date of issue. Logically, after the preliminary period, the premium is somewhat larger than the ordinary life premium at the issue date but less than the ordinary life premium at the insured's attained age at the end of the preliminary period. Regardless of the redistribution arrangement utilized, the company expects to receive the actuarial equivalent of the regular ordinary life premiums, assuming that all underlying assumptions were equivalent.

TABLE 5-4   Illustration for $100,000 Variable Life Policy

Annual Premium: $1,570

	Death Benefit Assuming Hypothetical Gross Annual Investment Return of:					Cash Surrender Value Assuming Hypothetical Gross Annual Investment Return of:			
YEAR	0%	4%	8%	12%	YEAR	0%	4%	8%	12%
1	$100,000	$100,000	$100,064	$100,135	1	$ 379	$ 379	$ 418	$ 438
2	100,000	100,000	100,278	100,591	2	1,506	1,590	1,680	1,771
3	100,000	100,000	100,642	101,380	3	2,680	2,879	3,092	3,312
4	100,000	100,000	101,153	102,508	4	3,703	4,064	4,455	4,874
5	100,000	100,000	101,814	104,000	5	4,870	5,444	6,077	6,773
10	100,000	100,000	107,519	117,746	10	10,322	12,755	15,799	19,605
15	100,000	100,000	117,238	144,059	15	15,081	20,693	28,743	40,323
20	100,000	100,000	131,170	187,013	20	18,877	28,931	45,550	73,231
30	100,000	100,000	173,150	349,955	30	23,683	45,744	94,741	206,022

Enhanced Ordinary Life Insurance

Several mutual companies offer a participating whole life policy that uses dividends to provide some form of level coverage at a lower than usual premium. The details, including the name given the plan, vary from company to company, but the purpose is basically the same: to provide a whole life participating policy with a low premium. Under these policies, dividends are earmarked. Under one approach, the face amount of a special ordinary life policy is reduced after a few years. However, dividends are used to purchase deferred paid-up whole life additions, such that at the time the policy face amount is to be reduced, the paid-up additions fill the gap, with the result that the total death benefit is (intended to be) at least equal to the original face amount (based on illustrated dividends).

Under another approach, the actual policy face amount may be 60 to 80 percent of the initial death benefit, with the difference made up by the purchase of paid-up additions and term insurance in such proportions that the total death benefit is intended to remain equivalent to or greater than the initial death benefit. It is hoped that paid-up additions eventually are sufficient to require no further purchase of term insurance.

A guarantee period is used to ensure that the total death benefit during the early policy years does not fall below the original level, even if dividends prove insufficient to meet the desired targets. With most companies, if dividends actually paid exceed those needed to purchase the requisite amount of additional coverage, the excess purchases paid-up additions. If dividends paid are lower than illustrated, the majority of plans require the purchase of one-year term.

Graded Premium Whole Life Insurance

The traditional forms of **graded premium whole life (GPWL) insurance** provide that premiums begin at a level that is 50 percent or less than those for a comparable ordinary life policy. Premiums increase annually for a period of from 5 to 20 years and remain level thereafter. Cash values evolve much more slowly than with ordinary life, often not appearing for five or more years. Policies may be participating or nonparticipating and may have indeterminate premiums.

Many newer forms of GPWL are more akin to YRT policies than whole life insurance. These types of GPWL begin with premiums that are comparable to those charged for YRT, and they have YRT-type increases for periods ranging from 15 to 40 years. The premium levels off thereafter. Typically, no cash values evolve until well after the tenth policy year. For some policies, there are no cash values at policy year 20, or even by age 70 for a few. Such products resemble and compete with YRT policies that automatically convert to ordinary life at later ages. Premiums are often indeterminate and smoker/nonsmoker rates are typically used. A few companies also have reentry provisions.

Single-Premium Whole Life Insurance

Single-premium whole life (SPWL) insurance often uses the current assumption approach discussed earlier with respect to level premiums (see Figure 5-1). The purchaser pays a relatively large single premium to the insurer that credits current rates of interest to the fund value. Mortality and expense charges may be deducted annually from the cash value, or they may be netted against the interest credited to the fund. Thus, there may appear to be no specific deduction for these charges in the fund accumulation. Additional first-year policy expense charges might be levied against the premium.

Surrender charges are typically used. Some insurers include **bailout provisions** that provide that if the credited interest rate falls below a certain level, the policyowner may surrender and incur no surrender charge. The usual range of policy options is available, including policy loans. Insurers usually impose high (e.g., $10,000) minimum premiums.

SPWL insurance can be useful for individuals who have the funds to purchase such coverage, although its appropriate usage is limited. Wealthy, older persons often purchase it.

Indexed Whole Life Insurance

Several companies offer a whole life policy whose face amount increases with increases in the inflation as measured by some national price index, such as the CPI in the United States. These policies can be classified as to whether the policyowner or the company assumes the inflation risk. Under the approach in which the policyowner assumes the risk, the death benefit increases each year in accordance with the price index and the insurance company bills the policyowner each year for the new, higher amount of insurance. The company agrees, by contract, not to require evidence of insurability for these increases, provided each year's increase is exercised. If the policyowner declines in any year to purchase the increase, no further automatic increases are permitted.

The approach under which the insurer assumes the inflation risk is similar in effect to the preceding approach, except that the premium charged initially by the insurer anticipates future face amount increases. Thus, increases in face amount do not alter the premium level paid. Such policies often have a cap as to the maximum total increase permitted.

Special-Purpose Life Insurance

Insurers issue a wide variety of special policies and policy combinations. These special forms are based on the same principles that underpin all life insurance and typically rely on some type of whole life as the core insurance. They differ only in that they are typically oriented toward a particular market. The contracts typically were developed for specialized purposes and may not offer the same flexibility as do the more common forms of contracts.

Debit Insurance   Dating from the 1800s in the United States and with roots in seventeenth-century England, the debit insurance business was the backbone of the U.S. life insurance industry until early in the twentieth century. Originally, **debit insurance** was synonymous with **industrial insurance**—policies issued for small amounts, usually less than $2,000, with premiums payable weekly or monthly to an agent who called at the policyowner's home or place of employment. It was originally designed for low-income families who could not afford the amounts of protection and premium payments associated with ordinary life and individual health insurance. The agent's assigned territory was referred to as the *debit* (derived from the agent's "debiting" the client's records for each premium payment) and gave the name to both a class of insurance and a means of marketing. Today, the term *debit insurance* encompasses any type of insurance sold through the debit (home collection of premium) system of marketing.

Industrial insurance today represents a tiny share of most OECD country markets, with the U.S. share being 0.1 percent of all life insurance in force, compared with 14.1 percent in 1950. The decline in industrial insurance was due to its being narrowly defined legislatively and to the fact that life insurance amounts of less than $2,000 provide little economic security while being quite costly per unit of coverage. Other important factors have been the rapid expansion of group insurance, the significant growth in the government-provided survivorship benefits, and the adverse publicity given industrial insurance.

Debit life insurance today in the United States encompasses **monthly debit ordinary** (MDO) insurance—ordinary policies typically written in the $5,000 to $25,000 range with premiums collected monthly at the policyowner's home. MDO contracts are based on ordinary (as opposed to the more conservative industrial) mortality tables and offer more flexibility. Because MDO is sold in larger face amounts, more underwriting is involved than with industrial insurance. In recent years, industrial life insurance and MDO have come to be known as **home service life insurance.**

Whether a low-income person should purchase a debit life insurance policy is becoming a moot point as sales continue to stagnate and insurers emphasize premium-notice ordinary products. The continuing decline of industrial life insurance, in particular, seems assured in view of inflation, the legislative definition of industrial life insurance, and numerous other factors.

Debit life insurance was the focus of much public concern and debate in the late 1970s. Problems alleged to exist with this type of insurance in general and industrial insurance in particular have included the high cost of benefits compared to other forms of insurance, high lapse rates, unfair contract provisions, overloading (the practice of selling a person more policies than he or she can afford), churning of policies (the practice of repeatedly selling a person new policies to replace old policies), misleading and high-pressure sales tactics, and exorbitant profits. While acknowledging that some problems exist, particularly with the industrial product, industry spokespersons nonetheless have forcefully defended the home service system of marketing.

Family Policy/Rider   Many companies issue a policy or, more commonly, a rider that insures all or selected members of the family in one contract, commonly called a **family policy** or **family rider.** When issued as a policy, it provides whole life insurance on the father or the mother, designated as the principal insured, with a premium based on his or her age. Term insurance is generally provided on the spouse and children. When coverage is issued as a rider, no underlying insurance is provided through the rider on the principal insured's life. The policy to which the rider is attached provides the basic coverage, and the net result is possibly the same as with the family policy.

Coverage on the spouse may be a stated amount or may vary in amount with age. Insurance on the children is term for a fixed amount. All children living with the family are covered, even if they were adopted or born after the policy is issued. Coverage is afforded to children over a few days old (e.g., 15 days) and under a stated age, such as 18, 21, or 25, and it is usually convertible to any whole life plan of insurance, without evidence of insurability (and often for up to five times the amount of expiring term insurance). If the principal insured dies, the insurance on the spouse and children usually becomes paid up.

A unit of coverage under the policy typically consists of $5,000 whole life on the principal insured, $1,000 or $1,500 whole life or term on the spouse, and $1,000 term on each child. When the insurance is issued as a rider, a certain number of units of coverage on the spouse's life is purchased whereby a unit might provide $5,000 term-to-age-65 coverage on the spouse and $1,000 of term insurance on each child.

The premium does not change on the inclusion of additional children (i.e., via birth or adoption). The premium for the children's coverage is based on an average number of children. In the event of the spouse's death prior to the insured's death, the insurance is paid to his or her named beneficiary.

An optional benefit closely related to the family rider provides life insurance coverage on additional insureds. This *other insureds* rider is most frequently used to insure other family members, usually the spouse or children. If the rider insures only the children, it is often referred to as a *children's rider;* otherwise it is the same as the family rider.

Juvenile Insurance   Juvenile insurance typically is some form of whole life insurance (or endowment insurance in many Asian markets) written on the lives of children and issued on the application of a parent or other person responsible for the support of the child. In the past, most companies and some U.S. jurisdictions limited the amount of insurance that could be written on the lives of young children. This limitation is less common today.

Most companies permit the purchase of any reasonable amount of life insurance on a child's life, subject to underwriting requirements as to perceived need and adequacy of coverage on parents' and children's lives. Some companies will insure a child from the age of one day, but many require that the child be at least one month old. Because the insured under a juvenile policy is a minor, control of the policy typically vests in the applicant (usually a parent) until the child attains age 18 or until the prior death of the applicant. Many companies will issue regular policies to minors on their own application, provided they are above the juvenile age limit set by the particular state involved.

Juvenile insurance is sold to provide funds (1) for last-illness and funeral expenses, (2) for college education, (3) to start an insurance program for a child at a low premium rate, and (4) to assure that a child will have some life insurance even if he or she later becomes uninsurable. Whether any of these reasons is convincing to a parent or grandparent is a matter of judgment. Often, however, there is inadequate insurance coverage on the parents' lives, and the primary objective should be to insure fully against loss of income brought about by the death of the breadwinners. The death of a child, as sad as it is, rarely causes major financial loss to the family and, therefore, life insurance on a child's life is of questionable need.

Preneed Funeral Insurance   Life insurance benefits earmarked to prefund future funeral expenses are said to have first appeared in the United States in 1930. From a business that once evoked concerns about fairness and cost, it has evolved to what today is referred to as **preneed funeral insurance**—life insurance intended to fund a prearranged funeral. With this type of insurance, a funeral provider and a (typically older) person enter into an agreement whereby the details of the goods and services to be delivered by the funeral provider are set out. The funeral provider agrees to provide the service whenever death occurs, the services being paid by the insurance policy proceeds. The typical buyer is 65 to 70 years old and purchases a $2,500 to $5,000 single-premium whole life policy. Higher-issue age limits, lenient underwriting (and accompanying higher mortality), and a small policy size produce premium levels that reflect the realities of pricing. The market for these products is small but expanding.

Concern was expressed in the United States that consumers (1) did not understand that life insurance was being used to fund the funeral, (2) were unaware of certain restrictions on delivery of the goods and services, and (3) were unaware that they were dealing with a life insurance agent. As a result, the NAIC amended its life insurance advertising and disclosure model regulations to encompass funeral insurance and to require that these and certain other factors be made clear to purchasers.

Insurance Covering Multiple Lives

Life insurance most commonly insures the life of one person. It is theoretically possible to write a life insurance policy on any number of lives and to construct it to pay on the death of the first, second, third, and so on, or last of the group to die. In practice, two important plans have evolved: (1) the second-to-die policy and (2) the first-to-die life policy. We cover each briefly.

Survivorship Life Insurance

Survivorship life insurance—also referred to as **second-to-die life insurance**—insures two (or more) lives and pays the death proceeds only on the death of the second (or last) insured to die. Most survivorship life policies are whole life, but term and universal life survivorship policies exist. Blends of whole life and term are increasingly found as are variable second-to-die policies.

Because the policy promises to pay only on the death of the second of two insureds, the policy's premiums are quite low relative to those that would be charged for a separate policy on each insured. If this year's probability of death is, say, 0.001 for one insured and 0.002 for the other insured, the probability of both insureds dying and, therefore, the policy face amount having to be paid is only 0.00002 (i.e., 0.001 times 0.002). Premiums are based on such joint probabilities under survivorship policies and are correspondingly low.

Policies are priced in at least three ways. First, perhaps most policies charge the same level premium prior to and after the first death. Second, some policies provide that premiums increase after the first death. Finally, other policies provide that premiums cease at the first death.

When payment of the face amount is contingent upon two deaths rather than one, required reserves are quite low. However, after the first insured dies, the probability of the insurer paying the death benefit no longer rests on the low joint-death probability but is the single-life death probability. This fact necessitates that reserves increase substantially after the first death. With some insurers, cash values also increase.

A so-called split option is available in some policies. The **split option** allows the survivorship policy to be split into two individual policies, one on each insured. Some insurers levy a separate charge for this option. In an effort to minimize adverse selection, the option can be elected only under certain conditions whose occurrence would be expected to be unrelated to the policy. Thus, the option could typically be elected on divorce. Also, some policies provide that a dramatic change in estate tax laws can trigger the option, as the usual reason for having purchased the policy may have disappeared (discussed later).

Under U.S. estate tax law, assets bequeathed (in a qualifying manner) to a surviving spouse escape all federal estate taxation on the death of the first spouse. At the death of the surviving spouse (and assuming no remarriage), any remaining assets are subject to estate taxation at rates of up to 55 percent.

The second-to-die policy is particularly well situated to meet the need for cash to cover estate taxes and related expenses on the second death. These policies are also commonly used to provide financial security for a disabled child or dependent relative in situations in which one death would not necessarily result in financial disaster for survivors, but the deaths of both husband and wife (or other breadwinners) would. It is worth noting that some companies tend to offer more flexible underwriting with survivorship life in instances in which one of the proposed insureds has a health problem.

The face amount of the typical second-to-die policy issued in the United States is high, usually exceeding $1 million with premiums being comparatively low—perhaps $20,000 per year. The market for such high-value policies is competitive. As a result, prospective purchasers can find good value because many insurers offer special-policy benefits in an effort to differentiate their policies from those of their competitors.

First-to-Die Insurance

In contrast to the survivorship life insurance, **first-to-die insurance** (also called **joint life insurance**) promises to pay the face amount of the policy on the first death of one of two (or more) insureds covered by the contract. The policy is often used to insure both the husband and wife, with each being the beneficiary for the other, and in business buy-out situations involving multiple partners or major stockholders. The policy pays only on the death of the first to die and is terminated at that time.

The survivor(s) is (are) without life insurance coverage under this policy. Contracts usually provide, however, that the survivor has the right to purchase a whole life policy on his or her life without providing evidence of insurability. Some contracts continue insurance temporarily, and most provide that if both insureds die in a common disaster, the insurer will pay the face amount on each death. The importance of having a contingent beneficiary is clear.

The premium for a given face amount would be smaller than the total premiums that would be paid for two individual ordinary life policies covering each individual. Joint life coverage is also available under term and universal life plans.

EFFORTS TO ENHANCE VALUE WITHIN EXISTING POLICIES

As noted in this and the preceding chapters, life insurers in North America and elsewhere have begun to face unprecedented competitive pressure, and many product innovations have resulted. A further complexity faced by life insurers is how effectively to deal with policyowners who purchased older policies that may not offer as much value or flexibility as the insurers' contemporary products. We cover some approaches to this issue here.

Guaranteed-cost, nonparticipating, cash-value products have had great difficulty competing with the new generation of products. These products, which are necessarily priced on conservative assumptions, do not make provision for the pass-through to policyowners of a share in favorable experience. These products were and remain susceptible to replacement.

In theory, older participating policies should offer sound value even in inflationary times and, therefore, should be more resistive to replacement if the insurer's experience is at least average, and if the insurer distributes accumulated surplus in a reasonable and equitable manner. Not all insurers have met these two tests.

Many U.S. life insurers experienced massive cash flow and other financial difficulties during the 1980s and early 1990s. Some of these problems stemmed from product design difficulties and others grew out of a changed competitive environment. Box 5-1 highlights some of the key aspects of this period on the theory that history offers many lessons for contemporary management.

Unilateral Enhancements

Several insurance companies have made unilateral changes in certain classes of older policies, the intended effects of which are to enhance the policies' value. Enhancements have been made with both participating and nonparticipating policies, although the exact extent of this activity is not known.

Some companies have unilaterally increased policy death benefits either on a permanent basis or on a year-to-year basis. One company, for example, provides an increase in the death benefit of pre-1974 issues of whole life policies equal to one-half of 1 percent of the policy face amount for each year the policy has been in force. This additional insurance is provided by one-year term additions at no additional charge to policyowners.

Other companies have effected a permanent increase in policy face amount by changing the reserve (and usually cash value) interest assumptions underpinning the policies. Insurers gained some tax advantage from following this approach, which they used to partially offset the cost of the enhancement. If the reserve/cash-value bases are changed, cash values per $1,000 face amount can be less, but the total policy cash value is usually greater after the change.

Bilateral Enhancements

Several insurers have embarked on bilateral update programs. These programs have involved the insurer offering to change—usually improve—some benefit in the policy, in return for the policyowner's agreement to change some aspect of the life insurance contract itself.

Many U.S. bilateral update programs have revolved around the policy loan clause. The first types were simply requests by some insurers to increase the guaranteed policy loan interest rate on certain older policies, in return for which the insurer would place

BOX 5-1

LESSONS FROM U.S. EXPERIENCE

A problem with many older whole life policies in the United States is that they often, by contract, permit policy loans at interest rates below prevailing market rates. The right to a policy loan is a call option and, as with any call option, has value when the exercise price (the loan interest rate) is less than the spot price (the market interest rate). Naturally, when a person can borrow at below-market rates and invest the proceeds at market rates, he or she is wise to do so, other things being the same. This process called **disintermediation** is exactly what happened to life insurers in the United States during the late 1970s and 1980s and, when combined with record numbers of policy surrenders, it led to massive reductions in insurer cash inflows. In fact, many life insurers actually experienced negative cash flows for the first time since the 1930s' depression.

This fact meant that insurers had to liquidate bonds and other securities, usually at significant discounts from par. This action aggravated the problem. An additional important effect was that many insurers were forced to forgo investing in contemporary, high-yielding assets, because they needed the cash flow to fund not only the normal cash outflows, such as dividend payments, death claim payments, and expenses, but also to fund the greatly increased surrender and policy loan outflows. When an insurer makes a policy loan at 5, 6, or 8 percent, it is "investing" its assets in that loan at that rate, just as if it had made a commercial mortgage loan. The critical difference, of course, is

that the commercial loan would have earned a market rate of interest.

As a result of these lost investment opportunities and the increased level of investments in policy loans (reaching 25 percent and higher of assets with some insurers), many U.S. companies' overall portfolio earnings rates did not grow as fast as they otherwise would have. Because of this, dividends paid at that time on many participating policies were not competitive with excess interest and other credits on current assumption policies. Companies were keenly aware of these problems and many undertook efforts to enhance the value of their existing older policies to render them less prone to surrender and replacement or to retain the policyowner as a client.

During this period of high investment returns, companies began illustrating correspondingly high dividends or cash-value interest credits. When investment returns fell during the late 1980s, insurers realized that they would have to reduce dividends and interest credits below those which were illustrated. For the preceding decades, insurers had generally paid more not less than illustrated, so this action to pay less was resisted by insurers and agents alike. Many insurers actually maintained higher interest rate credits than were justified. Many also began to take on riskier investments in an effort to stem the decline in investment returns. By the early 1990s, however, neither strategy was working, with several large and dozens of smaller life insurers becoming insolvent.

the policy in a higher dividend classification. The amendment option typically was offered to those who owned policies that contained 5 and 6 percent loan clauses. The new loan rate was usually raised to 8 percent, although some companies opted to introduce a variable loan rate clause.

Another type of bilateral update program involved the direct recognition of policy loan activity within the policy's dividend formula. Under this approach, policyowners who borrowed heavily at low interest rates receive lower dividends than those who did not borrow as heavily. Most companies perceived the change to be of such significance as to warrant formal policyowner agreement.

Bilateral enhancements usually involve no change in premium or guaranteed cash values. The insurance coverage usually is unaffected. Dividends are usually the only item changed, besides the policy loan rate.

Policy Exchanges

Perhaps most life insurance companies have addressed the problems of enhancement of older policies through exchanging old policies for new ones. This process may involve a formalized company procedure for a systematic internal replacement program; it may involve revised procedures to accommodate internal replacements that agents initiate but with no company sponsorship; or it may involve the insurer being uninformed while agents effect internal replacements of their clients' policies. From the policyowner's viewpoint, the net result can be the same.

Companies that have formalized exchange programs usually offer existing policyowners the opportunity to replace their older policies with newer versions under favorable terms or conditions. For example, many insurers will forgo or streamline evidence of insurability requirements. Reduced loadings may be offered on the new policy or increased policy face amounts may be offered.

Insurers' older policies are a major source of profits. As the asset-share calculation in chapter 2 illustrated, policies' contributions to surplus (profit) typically increase over time. Thus, companies that undertake any meaningful enhancement programs usually forgo some current profit in hopes of future profit. This future profit is expected to be realized through existing improved policies because of higher earnings from higher loan interest rates. Increased profits may be expected to arise from increased business that flows from an improved company image among agents and the consumer. Tax savings might also partially offset current lost profits.

Questions

1. A young woman comes to your life agency and says she wants to buy a life policy. What questions would you ask her to try to help her decide whether a term, whole life, universal life, variable life, or endowment policy is best for her and her family?
2. Compare and contrast the risks assumed by companies and individuals under ordinary and variable life policies.
3. Explain why life insurance policy loans are offered, as well as why interest rate and maximum loan amount provisions are usually imposed upon them.
4. Both current assumption whole life (CAWL) and variable life policies are characterized by the use of new-money returns. How do they differ with respect to flexibility of premiums and cash values?

CHAPTER

6

UNIVERSAL LIFE
INSURANCE POLICIES

Objectives

- Describe the transparency and flexibility afforded by universal and variable life policies.

- Explain how differences in the design of universal and variable life policies meet different consumer needs.

- Understand the risks and returns associated with universal and variable life products.

- Discuss how the concept of net amount at risk applies to universal life policies and how it affects federal tax treatment of these policies.

- Describe the distinguishing characteristics of flexible enhanced ordinary life policies that permit the combination of whole life, term, and paid-up additions.

INTRODUCTION

Traditional life insurance policies have features that improve their ability to adapt to changing circumstances. The nonforfeiture and policy loan provisions, the dividend options of participating policies, and the renewable and convertible features of term insurance are all examples. Yet considerable rigidity exists in traditional life insurance products. It is usually not convenient to change either the face amount or the premium, except by lapsing or surrendering the old coverage and starting afresh.

Indeed, probably all life insurance policies sold in the United States and elsewhere before the 1970s were fixed-premium contracts issued on either a participating or guaranteed-cost, nonparticipating basis. With enhanced computer technology, more flexible policies became feasible.

The first major U.S. life insurance industry change in policy flexibility occurred during this period when the adjustable life (AL) policy was introduced in 1971. The policy permitted the policyowner to select, within limits, whatever premium he or she wished, and later to adjust, within limits, the premium and policy face amount.

The introduction of universal life (UL) in 1979 built on the strengths of adjustable life but provided greater premium payment flexibility, an adjustable face amount, contemporary interest rates, and an unbundling of the savings and protection elements and associated pricing. Increased disclosure to prospective purchasers and to existing policyowners accompanied the introduction of UL.

Some insurers, unsure whether UL policies were in their and their customers' best interests, sought a means of providing much of the UL flexibility but within a traditional, fixed-premium context. Thus, flexible enhanced ordinary life (FEOL) products, introduced as direct UL competitors in 1985, were born.

UL, AL, and FEOL are fixed-value contracts in the sense that they contain traditional insurance-type guarantees as to minimum cash values and death benefits. The marriage of flexibility and transparency with the equity-based potential of variable life insurance was expected. With the introduction of variable universal life in early 1985, this was reality.

These four types of life insurance policies are distinguishable from the fixed-premium contracts discussed in chapters 4 and 5. These policies permit the policyowner—not the insurer—to decide, with some restrictions, the premium level to be paid and the policy death benefit.

UNIVERSAL LIFE INSURANCE

Universal life insurance policies are flexible-premium, adjustable death benefit, unbundled life contracts. Their introduction in the late 1970s and early 1980s in North America caused great debates and perhaps as much media attention as any other contemporary life insurance product.

The Origins and Growth of Universal Life Insurance

The concepts upon which UL is based are as old as the concepts underlying level-premium payments and reserves. They are well over 100 years old. A key element—the use of the retrospective approach to cash value (and reserve) development—is analyzed and discussed, for example, in Spurgeon's 1922 authoritative book, *Life Contingencies,* long the standard for the study of this subject by North American actuarial students. Jordan's 1952 and 1957 editions of *Life Contingencies* continued the analysis.

It is said that the idea of universal life as a product was mentioned by H. L. Riedner in 1946 and by Alfred N. Guertin in 1964.[1] Ken E. Polk's 1974 article in the *Transactions of the Society of Actuaries,* along with the accompanying discussion papers, provided virtually all of the formulas needed for developing a workable UL policy. Polk referred to his hypothetical policy as variable premium life insurance.[2]

It seems, however, that principal credit for conceiving of UL as a product goes to George R. Dinney of the Great-West Life, a Canadian insurer.[3] He appears to have conceived of the idea as early as 1962, although a written description of the product, which he dubbed universal life plan, apparently was made public only in 1971.[4]

James C. H. Anderson, then president of the actuarial consulting firm of Tillinghast, Nelson and Warren, Inc., probably did more than anyone to publicize UL as a viable product and to stimulate serious thinking about the possible need and wisdom for developing such a product. His paper, entitled "The Universal Life Insurance Policy" and presented at the Seventh Pacific Insurance Conference in 1975, is considered by many to be the most

---

[1]Stuart J. Kingston, "On Universal Life," *The National Underwriter,* Life/Health ed., January 2, 1982, p. 25.

[2]Ken E. Polk, "Variable Premium Life Insurance," *Transactions of the Society of Actuaries,* Vol. XXVI (1974), pp. 449–465; and discussion, pp. 467–478.

[3]George R. Dinney, "Universal Life," *The Actuary,* Vol. XV, supplement (September 1981), p. 1; and J. Timothy Lynch, "Universal Life Insurance: A Primer," *The Journal of the American Society of Chartered Life Underwriters,* Vol. XXXVI (July 1982).

[4]Paper entitled, "A Descent into the Maelstrom of the Insurance Future," presented in 1971 at the Canadian Institute of Actuaries.

important step along the road to UL.[5] Embedded in the UL concept as articulated by Anderson and others was much lower agents' commissions than those found with traditional life products, thus rendering the policy more cost-effective and easier to sell.

In 1976 one insurer, American Agency Life, in fact developed and sold a UL policy of the type described in Anderson's paper. Because of adverse tax problems, the company soon discontinued sales. UL in its current form was not introduced and sold widely until its introduction by E.F. Hutton Life (then Life of California) in 1979.

The UL concept was at first not welcomed by most persons in the North American life insurance business. It was perceived as a threat to the orderly development of the industry, and as not being in consumers' or agents' best interests. Today few persons oppose UL. Most now see it simply as another, albeit important, life product that is available for consumers.

Universal life policy sales in the United States had a meteoric rise from an effective zero market share of new sales in 1979 to over 38 percent in 1985, its peak year. Since then, its share has declined to around a quarter of new individual life premiums—still a major proportion.

The initial high growth rate of UL was influenced by the high interest rate environment prevailing in the United States during the early to mid-1980s. During this time, interest rates on newly invested funds—those that backed UL products—were higher than those earned on established investment portfolios. In other words, new-money rates substantially exceeded portfolio rates.

Thus, life products such as UL that relied on new-money returns had a competitive advantage over portfolio-based, cash-value products—such as traditional participating whole life—because of the capability of showing higher future values in their sales illustrations. When interest rates peaked and then declined, new-money-based products no longer enjoyed this competitive advantage. This fact partially explains the relative decline in UL sales. Of course, over the longer term, otherwise similar new-money and portfolio products should perform similarly.

The Nature of Universal Life Insurance

UL policies offer flexibility in premium payments and adjustability of death benefits. After making an initial minimum premium payment, policyowners may thereafter pay whatever amounts and at whatever times they wish, or even skip premium payments, provided the cash value will cover policy charges. Also, policyowners may raise (usually subject to evidence of insurability) or lower their policies' death benefits as they deem appropriate, with minimum difficulty.

When UL policies were first conceived and designed, the hope was that they would offer not only greater flexibility but also superior value. Superior value was to be realized through reduced distribution costs. Because of the products' flexibility and superior value, agents were expected to increase substantially their sales rates from the industry average of about one policy per week. If agents sold more policies, their commission rates could be lower, thus resulting in better policy value to the buyer and ultimately higher total agent commissions.

Although many products did provide lower commissions than those applicable to more traditional whole life policies, in reality distribution costs did not remain low for most insurers, as agents resisted the lower commission structures. Many companies that entered the UL field failed to secure adequate margins because of lower than expected sales. The administrative costs associated with UL flexibility are high by traditional

---

[5]The paper was published in *Emphasis* (November 1975).

standards, and the uncertainty associated with UL cash flows has proven a challenge for many insurers.

UL policies are transparent in their operation, as noted in chapter 2. The policyowner is able to see how funds are allocated to the various policy elements. An illustration is provided to prospective purchasers describing how these elements—premiums, death benefits, interest credits, mortality charges, expenses, cash values—interact. Each year the policyowner receives similar information in an annual report. Transparency does not mean that the policyowner can necessarily evaluate the adequacy of projected values; it means only that the policyowner will be able to see, after the fact, the disposition made of policy funds.

Figure 6-1 illustrates the operation of a typical UL policy. Although similar in operation to current assumption whole life (CAWL) policies, UL policies differ from them in that neither the premium level nor the death benefit is fixed. Otherwise, the products are the same in concept. In fact, CAWL policies are sometimes referred to as fixed-premium UL policies.

Referring to Figure 6-1, the mechanics of a UL policy would be as follows: The policyowner pays a first premium of at least a certain required minimum amount. From this

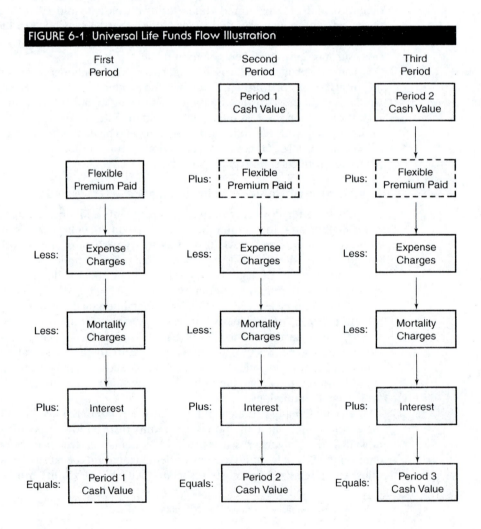

FIGURE 6-1 Universal Life Funds Flow Illustration

initial premium is subtracted first-period expense charges, although many UL policies have no identifiable front-end loadings.

Next, mortality charges based on the insured's attained age and the policy's net amount at risk and charges for any supplemental benefits (e.g., waiver of premium) would be subtracted. The mortality charges are usually indeterminate, the actual charge usually being less than the maximum rate shown in the policy.

After subtracting expense and mortality charges, the resulting fund is the initial policy cash value (not shown). This initial cash value is then credited with interest, usually at new-money rates, to arrive at the end-of-period cash value. Many UL policies levy high first-year surrender charges against any terminating policy. The cash value less surrender charges yields the policy's cash *surrender* value.

The second policy period (often a month) begins with the previous period's ending cash-value balance. To this amount the policyowner may add a further premium in an amount of his or her choosing. However, if the previous period's cash value is sufficient to cover the current expense and mortality charges, no premium need be paid. If the previous period's cash value is not sufficient, the policy will lapse in the absence of a further premium payment.

Expense and mortality charges are subtracted from the sum of the previous period's ending cash-value balance and any premium payment to arrive at the second-period initial cash value (not shown). Interest at the current rate would then be credited to this initial cash value to arrive at the end-of-period cash value for the second period.

The entire process is repeated in the third, fourth, and later periods. If the cash value at any time were insufficient to sustain the policy, it would lapse without further premium payments. No further premium need be paid, however, if the cash value is sufficient.

Universal Life Product Design

Numerous UL product design variations exist. For example, first-to-die and second-to-die UL policies exist. This section does not attempt to address all variations. Rather, an effort is made to describe the common product designs.

Death Benefit Patterns

Universal life policies typically offer two death benefit patterns from which the purchaser selects one. Of course, the pattern may be changed at any time, but, in the absence of a change request, the selected pattern will be followed during the policy term.

The two patterns are usually labeled options A and B. *Option A* provides a level death benefit pattern, and *option B* provides a level net amount at risk (NAR). Under option A, the NAR is adjusted each policy period (often monthly) so that the cash value and the NAR together always provide a level death benefit. Thus, if the cash value increases over time, the NAR decreases by the exact amount and vice versa. This option can result in the same policy benefit pattern as that provided by traditional cash-value policies.

Option B stipulates that the policy death benefit at any time will equal the sum of a stated, level NAR and the cash value at the time. Thus, if the cash value increases over time, the total policy death benefit increases exactly with the cash-value increase.

Figure 6-2 illustrates these two death benefit patterns, both of which assume that the cash value increases over time. It can be seen that with option A, the NAR decreases; whereas, with option B, it remains at a constant level.

The death benefit patterns provide for a *corridor* of NAR if the cash value becomes too large (as defined by tax law) relative to the NAR. This is illustrated in Figure 6-2 with option A. Without the corridor, a policy could effectively become an endowment and might not qualify for favorable tax treatment. In the United States, for example, if

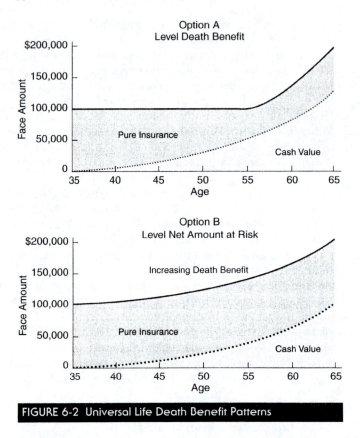

FIGURE 6-2 Universal Life Death Benefit Patterns

a policy's cash value builds more rapidly than would be necessary to cover future mortality charges, it could lose favorable tax treatment, as discussed in chapter 13.

Naturally, the greater the NAR, the higher will be the monthly mortality charges. Therefore, all else being equal, the option B pattern will result in higher mortality charges.

Decreases in the policy death benefit can be made by policyowner request at any time. As the insurer's NAR is lowered, no evidence of insurability is required for decreases. A lowering of the death benefit naturally also lowers the mortality charges, assuming no cash-value withdrawal.

Increases in UL policy death benefits, other than those provided for automatically under option B or any cost-of-living rider, typically require evidence of insurability. Otherwise, adverse selection could be a problem; that is, insureds in poor health would have an incentive to increase their policy's death benefits. Insurers often permit small increases without evidence, but this is usually done extracontractually. Increases in policy death benefits result in higher monthly mortality charges because the NAR increases.

Many companies permit policyowners to attach cost-of-living-adjustment (COLA) riders and future purchase options to their UL policies. Chapters 4 and 8, respectively, discuss the operation of these riders.

Premium Payments

UL policyowners pay premiums of whatever amount and whenever they desire, subject to company rules regarding minimums and maximums. Most companies require only that the first premium be sufficient to cover the first month's expense and mortality charges, although most purchasers pay an amount well in excess of this minimum.

One of the potential disadvantages of UL is that policyowners might too easily allow their policies to lapse because there are no required premiums, as is the situation with the products discussed in chapters 4 and 5. To overcome this concern, at least partially, companies bill for a **planned** or **target premium** in accordance with the policyowner's stated preference.

Thus, the buyer might agree to a monthly preauthorized draft of his or her bank account. Alternatively, the insurer might send a bill to the policyowner for the planned premium. The amount of the automatic bank draft or bill is set by the policyowner, usually at the agent's suggestion.

Because of policyowners' concerns about being ill-informed about their UL policies and especially about the uncertainty of future performance, many companies have introduced the concept of a *no-lapse guarantee,* which guarantees that the policy will not lapse if at least a stipulated minimum premium is paid. If this *minimum continuation premium* is paid, the contract will remain in force even with no (or even with negative) cash value. For example, a policy with a 10-year minimum continuation premium would guarantee that payment of this minimum premium would continue the policy in effect for up to 10 years, even if the insurer lowered interest credits or increased charges such that the policy would otherwise terminate at that premium level.

Figure 6-3 illustrates the flexible-premium feature of UL policies. In this illustration, Diane, a 35-year-old female policyowner, decides to pay $1,000 per year into her UL policy. She does this for five years, at which time she needs a lower outlay because she is sending her son to college. Diane, therefore, pays nothing for the next five policy years, with the cash value continuing to build based on the current interest rate, net of mortality and expense charges.

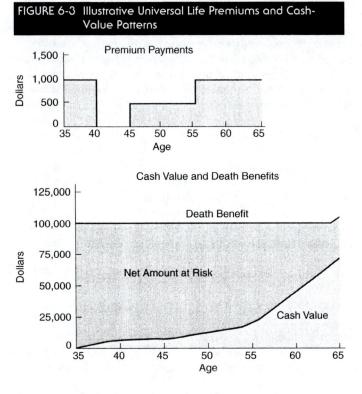

FIGURE 6-3 Illustrative Universal Life Premiums and Cash-Value Patterns

At the end of the five-year period, she resumes premium payments but at a lower level ($500), as she is undertaking an important, costly expansion of her business. At age 55, she decides to increase payments to $1,500 per year.

The option A death benefit pattern is assumed, and the interest rate and expense and mortality scales are assumed to remain on their current bases (an admittedly unrealistic assumption). The initial $1,000 premium payments cause a constant rise in cash value, to almost $5,000 by age 40. The cash value continues to build even with no premium payment to age 45—although the rate of growth is far lower—at which time the cash value is less than $6,000. The $500 per year payment, combined with current interest credits, is more than enough to cover mortality and expense charges for the next 10 years, so the age 55 cash value is about $20,000. The higher $1,500 premium payment causes a rapid buildup in cash value, so that by age 65 it stands at about $75,000.

Naturally, any premium payment pattern could be assumed, subject only to company rules and the need to have a sufficient cash value to maintain the policy in force. If insufficient cash value exists to continue the policy, the policyowner is provided a 30- or 60-day grace period in which to make a premium payment. Failure to do so results in the termination of coverage.

Policy Loadings

Figure 6-1 illustrated the nature of UL policy expense and other loading elements. *Identifiable* loadings are imposed on UL policies in one or both of two ways: (1) front-end loads and (2) back-end loads. The front-end load approach was more prevalent with earlier UL policies. Newer UL products rely more heavily or totally on back-end loadings (i.e., surrender charges). Some UL contracts are both back- and front-loaded, and a few have neither type of load.

The loading charges of a UL policy rarely match a company's actual expense pattern. Usually, the amount charged is insufficient to cover initial expenses, especially on policies with low or no front-end loadings. Excess first-year expenses, it is hoped, will be recouped through renewal expense charges, through surrender charges, through interest margins, through mortality margins, or through a combination of these. Indeed, for policies with little or no identifiable front-end load, it is incorrect to contend that the policy has no loading. A loading must somehow always be charged against the policy.

The margin between the actual investment earnings of the company and the rate it credits to UL policies is usually an important source of income for covering excess expenses and for profits. Regrettably for insurers, however, consumers have grown to expect high interest rate credits on their cash values, so these margins have been less than many insurers expected, because they have strived to meet policyowner expectations. Mortality margins also can be important, and because policyowners are not as sensitive to the level of mortality charges as they are to the level of interest rates credited to their cash values, insurers increasingly have relied on mortality margins to cover incurred expenses.

Most UL policies with identifiable expense charges have higher first-year than renewal expense charges. Both initial and renewal expense charges can be stated as a fixed amount per policy, as an amount for each $1,000 of face amount, or as a percentage of the premium. Some insurers use all three bases whereas others use two, one, or none.

For example, one company's expense loading for the first policy year is composed of a flat $96 policy assessment plus a charge of $0.15 per $1,000 of face amount per month (i.e., $1.80 per $1,000 per year), plus a further charge of 10 percent of the premiums paid. Renewal expense charges are based solely on the 10 percent premium charge. This front-loaded policy has very low surrender charges.

Most North American companies assess a percentage premium charge, with the majority having the same first-year and renewal percentage. Charges typically fall within the 2½ to 20 percent range, with most falling closer to the low end of the scale. Some insurers still assess a high first-year policy fee, with little or no fee thereafter, although the trend is to have the same policy fee for all years. Typical "high" first-year fees fall within the $200 to $400 range, with the newer levels falling in the $25 to $50 per-year range.

There appears to be a trend toward North American companies discontinuing the use of fees based on each $1,000 face amount; the trend is especially pronounced for renewal years. Many insurers now assess only a percentage of premium load.

For companies with low or no identifiable front-end loads, back-end loads tend to be high, although they cannot exceed those permitted by law. Surrender charges may be expressed as a percentage of the first-year premium (most common for policies with no front loads), as a loss of excess interest for one year, as a fixed assessment per unit of face amount (e.g., $10 per $1,000), as a flat assessment (e.g., $25), or as an amount equal to unpaid first-year expense charges. Policies that emphasize front loads usually have low or no back-end loads. The trend in North America is toward very low front-end loads and high back-end loads. Surrender charges are highest during the first policy years and grade downward with duration, often decreasing yearly after the first five policy years or sooner and typically reaching zero in 5 to 12 years. High back-end loads can create a tontine (see chapter 3) effect, as discussed in Box 6-1.

Mortality and Other Benefit Charges

Mortality charges are deducted each month from UL cash values. The total monthly mortality charge is derived by multiplying the applicable rate by the policy's NAR. The maximum rates per $1,000 are stated in the contract for all ages, and actual rates charged are guaranteed never to exceed these maximums. Most UL mortality charges are indeterminate, as mentioned previously, as well as differentiated according to cigarette smokers and nonsmokers and, in most jurisdictions, according to gender.

North American insurers typically base their maximum mortality charges on the *1980 CSO Mortality Table,* which is a conservative valuation table. The current and anticipated actual mortality charges are of greater importance than the level of the guaranteed rates because those are the fees actually charged.

BOX 6-1

LAPSE-SUPPORTED POLICIES

A tontine effect results whenever nonguaranteed death-related benefits (e.g., terminal dividends) or lapse-related benefits (e.g., cash surrender values) are low currently so as to afford higher values later. Thus, if a policy's cash surrender value in the early policy years is less than the assets accumulated by the insurer on behalf of that policy (i.e., the policy's asset share), the surrender or lapse of the policy will result in an increase in insurer surplus, as illustrated in chapter 2. This surplus can be accumulated and used to enhance later cash values of persisting policies.

Policies (UL or otherwise) so constructed that their future values are in part dependent on the assumption of incurring gains from such high early lapses and surrenders are said to be **lapse-supported policies.** The danger of this practice is that the expected rate of lapse may fail to materialize, thus resulting in less early surplus from which to enhance future values. Additionally, questions of the equitable treatment of terminating versus persisting policyowners arise.

The extent to which insurers market lapse-supported policies is unknown. This issue relates principally to nonguaranteed policy elements and applies equally to all types of life insurance policies, not just to UL, although much concern is focused on UL.

Mortality rates actually charged by issuers of UL vary considerably. Table 6-1 lists mortality charges levied by six companies for three different ages. These are monthly charges and, therefore, a difference of only a few dollars can mean a large amount over time. One could not conclude from these figures alone which of the various companies' policies might be a good buy. Interest credits and loadings also must be factored into the analysis. For example, Company F, with the highest mortality charges, has relatively low front-end loads and no surrender charges. Obviously, its mortality charges include provision for expense recovery.

Charges will be assessed for optional policy benefits. The COLA rider and the future purchase option rider were mentioned earlier. In addition, riders can be included that provide insurance on family members, provide waiver-of-premium (or waiver-of-mortality-charge) protection, offer accelerated death benefits, and afford additional insurance. None of these is unique to UL, and each is discussed in chapter 8.

Worth noting is the trend toward using the additional (term) insurance rider to lower overall mortality charges. Typically, these riders carry lower mortality charges than those of the UL policy itself and also lower commissions. By changing the mix of UL and such term insurance, policy cost and commissions can be made to vary.

Cash Values

Figure 6-1 shows that the cash value is simply the residual of each period's funds flow. It results from taking the previous period's ending cash-value balance (if any), adding to it any premium paid, subtracting expense and mortality charges, then adding current interest credits to the resulting fund balance. The result is the end-of-period cash value. All items except the current interest credit have been discussed previously.

UL policies sold in the United States guarantee the crediting of a minimum, contractually stated rate of interest to policy cash values. Guaranteed rates of 4 to 5 percent are commonly found. During a high interest rate environment, these rates may seem low, but they are reasonable, long-term guarantees and potentially of great value to the policyowner.

Some companies provide for a rolling interest rate guarantee. Under this approach, the insurer will guarantee to credit an interest rate not less than a moving average rate (less some basis points) of an external index, such as five-year Treasury bills.

Companies typically credit interest rates greater than the guaranteed rates. The first UL policies utilized a two-tiered interest approach wherein only the guaranteed rate was credited on the first $1,000 or so of cash values, with amounts in excess of $1,000 receiving the current rate. Most UL policies today do not make this distinction; they credit the entire cash value with the current rate.

Most UL policies provide that the current interest rate will be determined by the company. Others are indexed; these provide that the current interest rate will be set at

TABLE 6-1 Selected Companies' Current Mortality Charges			
	Age 25	*Age 40*	*Age 55*
Company A	$ 6.67	$14.43	$35.33
Company B	9.17	12.08	25.83
Company C	10.00	16.00	37.00
Company D	14.00	21.00	46.00
Company E	15.00	21.00	51.00
Company F	16.00	31.00	73.00

a level slightly below that being credited on some external, well-recognized money instrument such as three-month or one-year Treasury bills. A few insurers are using major stock market indices as the basis for determining the current crediting rate. This concept developed in connection with annuities and is discussed in chapter 8.

Most nonindexed UL policies receive interest credits that are based on the companies' new-money rates of return. As discussed in chapter 2, this rate represents what the company earns on its new investments. Many insurers, in contrast, use a portfolio rate of return, based on the earnings of the company's entire asset portfolio or the assets backing a given block of policies.

New-money rates are more responsive to changing market interest rates, and this can work for or against the policyowner. If market rates are generally rising, cash values credited with interest on this basis should be higher than those credited with portfolio rates during the period. On the other hand, when market rates fall, portfolio rates could be, and at some point will be, higher than new-money rates. In such circumstances, the portfolio-based policy should outperform its new-money brother, other things being the same.

Like most cash-value policies, UL policies permit policyowners to obtain policy loans on the security of the policy's cash value. The direct recognition provision in UL policies is important in this regard. In most policies, it provides that interest at the current rates will be credited only to the portion of the cash value that is not used to secure a policy loan. The portion backing any policy loan may be credited only with the contractually guaranteed interest rate or with a rate that is one or two percentage points below the policy loan interest rate, thus producing a guaranteed spread for the insurer.

Not all UL issuers use a direct recognition provision. A few credit the current interest rate on the entire cash value, irrespective of policy loan activity. If the UL policy contains a variable loan rate, little need exists for a direct recognition provision. Some UL policies also include a persistency bonus to reward customer loyalty. See Box 6-2.

Most UL policies permit partial surrenders. Usually, these surrenders must be for at least a minimum amount (e.g., $500) and may carry a processing charge (e.g., $25). The policy death benefit is reduced by the exact amount of any partial surrender. If it were not, the company would be inviting adverse selection. Total policy surrender, as discussed previously, often involves a surrender charge.

Uses and Limitations of Universal Life Insurance

Universal life offers the possibility of being the only life insurance policy a person ever needs. Its flexibility in premium payments and death benefits renders it well suited as an individual's "life cycle" policy.

Simplified Life Cycle Illustration

Figure 6-4 provides a simplified view of how this life cycle approach could work. This illustration ignores inflation and takes a simplistic view of insurance planning. In it, Larry Townsend, aged 25, purchases a $50,000 UL policy using option A (level death benefit) and pays a premium of $500. The purpose of this policy is to pay off education debts incurred while he was obtaining a law degree. This starting situation is depicted at point A.

At point B, Larry marries his longtime sweetheart, Barbara, and, because of additional obligations, believes the coverage amount under his UL policy should be increased to $75,000. At the same time, he increases the premium payment to $1,000. Cash values build slowly, as shown.

When Larry is 30, Barbara has a child, Emily (point C). Because this life event has major implications for Larry and Barbara, they increase coverage to $200,000, but with no increase in premium. Larry again meets the insurability requirements.

BOX 6-2

PERSISTENCY BONUSES: A REWARD FOR CUSTOMER LOYALTY?

With an increasing emphasis in sales presentation on later years' cash values, insurers have begun designing policies with *persistency bonuses,* the intent of which is to encourage policyowners to continue their policies. Two broad types of persistency bonuses, also called *enhancements,* are prevalent: an interest rate bonus and a mortality charge refund. The enhancement is credited to the policy's cash value after a minimum policy duration, after a minimum cash value has been attained, or after a minimum number of premiums has been paid. The interest rate bonus, stated as an additional interest rate, may be applied to the then accumulated cash value or it may be applied retroactively on a compounding basis.

The mortality charge bonus may involve a total or partial credit to the cash value of previously assessed mortality charges. Both the mortality charge refund and the interest rate bonus enhancements may be applied more than once (e.g., once every five years).

Other types of persistency bonuses exist. For example, some companies will increase the death benefit, pay special dividends, or provide COLA increases. Terminal dividends, in use for decades, are also enhancements. Terminal dividends are paid by some insurers on policy termination as either a surrender or a death claim, after a participating policy has been in force for a minimum number of years.

Persistency bonuses can serve a legitimate purpose; they can encourage and reward policy persistency. On the other hand, they also lend themselves to misuse. What assurance does the policyowner have that the insurer actually will credit a bonus? If a bonus is credited, is the amount solely at the discretion of the insurer, and, if so, what assurances does the policyowner have that the insurer will credit an appropriate amount?

Prospective policyowners can be misled by the use of bonuses if they are credited in such a way as to lead customers to believe a policy offers better value than it truly does. This can occur, for example, if the enhancement is credited at durations typically used by consumers and agents for product evaluation (e.g., at policy year 20) and if that year's value is not representative of surrounding years' values.

Two years later, at point D, Larry and Barbara withdraw $3,000 from the policy to help make a down payment on a new home. Such a cash withdrawal would normally reduce their death benefit by an equivalent amount, but they increase the coverage to maintain the previous amount. At this point, they also cease making premium payments to devote needed funds to the mortgage payment.

Two years later, they are able to resume $500 premium payments. Two years after that (point E), they are able to increase the payment to $1,000. Life continues merrily for the happy family, and when Larry is 48, Emily enters college (point F). They withdraw $2,500 per year for each of the next four years to help defray Emily's educational expenses, and they cease premium payments as well. They conclude that with the responsibilities of rearing Emily being essentially over, they can, simultaneously, decrease their total insurance amount to $100,000, although this amount will decrease each year by the amount of the $2,500 withdrawals.

Four years later, Emily is graduated from college and goes into the world to make her mark, independent of Larry and Barbara. The happy couple is now able to resume premium payments, and, with an eye toward accumulating a retirement fund, they make premium payments of $1,500 per year until Larry is 65, at which time (point H), they

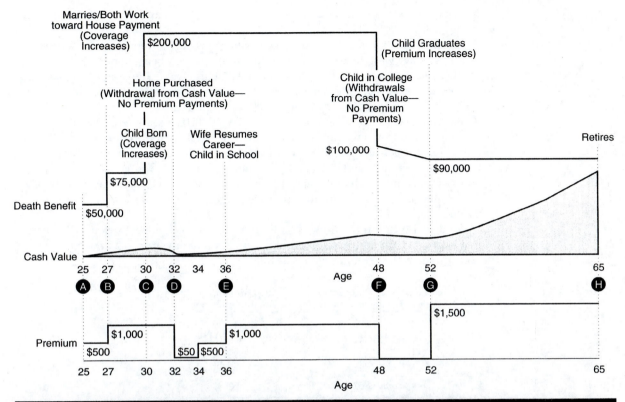

FIGURE 6-4 Hypothetical Life Cycle Using Universal Life Insurance Policy

Source: Modified from Universal Life Basics (Indianapolis, IN: Pictorial Publishers, 1983), pp. 6–70. Used with permission.

cease making premium payments and begin a systematic withdrawal program under their UL policy (and, of course, live happily ever after).

Notice that the single UL policy has served the needs of our hypothetical family well throughout their life cycle. The death benefit was altered as needed to suit their circumstances. Premium payments were similarly increased or decreased as financial circumstances dictated, and the cash value was a source of flexibility throughout life.

Although only one insured is shown in this figure, on close analysis (see chapter 14), significant amounts of insurance may be needed on Barbara's life also. A UL policy on her life, a joint life UL policy, or a spouse rider could have been illustrated, but, for simplicity, only one insured is considered here.

UL can be used in countless other ways as well, as can most other cash-value policies. A UL policy can be used in virtually every circumstance in which a whole life policy could be used.

Limitations on Illustrated Values

UL is undoubtedly flexible, and its operations are more transparent than most life products. As with other life policies that contain nonguaranteed elements, UL can be low in cost. However, whether it actually will be low cost can be determined only over time. An examination of how insurers have treated their past UL policyowners in terms of actual excess interest credits and actual mortality and expense charges can prove insightful.

Some argue that UL flexibility, especially with respect to premium payments, can lead to poor persistency, with the result that consumers lose money because of early UL policy terminations in the same way that they would with early whole life policy terminations. Results to date in North America suggest that early UL policy persistency is roughly equivalent to that for whole life policies, but later persistency lags.

Concern exists that UL (and CAWL) policy advertisements and sales aids place undue emphasis on the current interest rate, to the exclusion of other potentially important elements such as expense loadings, mortality charges, and surrender charges. For example, a $100,000 option B universal life policy that credits 9.0 percent has a projected 20-year cash surrender value of $46,191, based on a 45-year-old male nonsmoker, paying $1,500 per year, whereas another that credits 8.25 percent has a 20-year projected cash value of $56,617.

Consider also that the following policies, each of which advertises an 8.5 percent current interest credit and is based on similar policy and buyer profiles, have projected 10- and 20-year cash surrender values as follows:

UL Policy	10-Year Projected Cash Surrender Value	20-Year Projected Cash Surrender Value
A	$14,488	$41,379
B	15,541	46,916
C	16,826	52,054
D	18,742	68,134
E	19,862	56,131

Of course, these differences are all explainable to anyone who examines each element of these UL policies. To the great credit of UL policies, their operational transparency permits this examination; such an examination is not always easy with other cash-value products.

The concern does not rest with any deficiency related to transparency. Rather it rests with marketing approaches that place unwarranted emphasis on current interest rate credits, to the point that the average purchaser of the UL policy may be misled as to the product's future value.

Another concern results from the practice of projecting high interest rates for years and even decades into the future. These projections, unless carefully explained, can easily mislead customers into believing that actual future values will track projected values. Although no one can know such actual future interest rates, we know that it will almost certainly differ from the current rate.

The keys to avoiding misunderstanding (intended or otherwise) are carefully prepared illustrations and advertisements with appropriately worded caveats, illustrations that show policy value results using varying rates of interest, and, most important, well-informed agents and other financial advisors who carefully guide the client through a potentially misleading morass. Of course, these concerns apply to other products, including participating whole life policies. As noted in chapter 1, information asymmetries abound for life insurance consumers.

Policy illustrations remain widely used as a basis for comparing prospective policy performance. Because of the highly speculative nature of long-term illustrations, many now argue against such comparisons. Instead, it is argued, the focus of comparison shopping should shift more to the performance characteristics of the insurers themselves and to an examination of actual historical policy values.

Another concern with all interest-sensitive products, including traditional participating whole life policies, is that in competition today one finds that the prospective purchaser is often shown noncomparable comparisons of two or more policies' future values. We take up this and related topics in chapter 11.

VARIABLE UNIVERSAL LIFE INSURANCE

The next logical step in life insurance product evolution was to combine the flexible characteristics of universal life with the investment flexibility of variable life. The result was **variable universal life** (VUL)—also called **flexible-premium variable life**—first offered in 1985 in the United States by Pruco Life, a subsidiary of Prudential Life Insurance Company of America. With the strong North American stock market performance in the 1990s, VUL market share rose to about 20 percent—significantly higher than traditional variable life insurance (VLI) policies.

Nature of Variable Universal Life Insurance

VUL is subject to the same regulations as VLI, which were discussed in chapter 5. VUL tracks the UL model in that the policyowner decides, within limits, the premium to be paid each period, if any. The policyowner also has the option of increasing or decreasing the policy death benefit at will, subject to policy minimums and, with respect to death benefit increases, evidence of insurability requirements.

Cash Values

Unlike the situation with UL, the assets backing the VUL policy are maintained in one or more separate accounts. In this respect, VUL is identical to VLI. The cash values of VUL reflect exactly the policyowner's pro rata share of assets held in the separate account and are subject to fluctuation just like VLI cash values. Like cash values of VLI, there is no guarantee with respect to either a minimum rate of return or principal.

The cash value of the VUL operates as an account-balancing mechanism just as the cash value does with UL. Thus, it is the residual value in the policy after deduction of the costs of insurance and all selling, administrative, investment management, and other expenses. Investment income credited to the account ordinarily is tax deferred and possibly tax free (see chapter 13). In this respect, VUL (as well as all other cash-value policies) can be thought of as incorporating a savings accounts, the tax-deferred interest on which is used to purchase life insurance and cover policy expenses.

As the separate account is, in effect, a mutual fund (unit trust), the policy can be thought of as operating as if tax-free (or deferred) income is credited to the account. From this income is deducted policy expenses and costs of insurance. In other words, the expenses and mortality charges for the policy are paid with before-tax income. Of course, this result is opposite that for many buy-term-invest-the-difference situations. If the "difference" is invested in a typical mutual fund, the investment income would be fully taxable and the premiums for the term insurance would be paid with after-tax income.

The policyowner typically is offered a smorgasbord of funds into which he or she directs residual funds to be invested. These funds have different investment characteristics, just as with a family of mutual funds. Thus, one insurer offers the 14 investment options shown in Table 6-2 for its VUL policyowners. The first investment option allows policyowners to allocate some or all assets to the insurer's general fund, meaning that

TABLE 6-2 Typical Separate Account Investment Options	
General Account	Aggressive Stock
Common Stock	Global Securities
Equity Index	International Stock
Growth Asset	Growth and Income
Balanced	Conservative Allocation
High-Yield Bond	Quality Bond
Intermediate Government	Money Market

the policy's investment return would more or less mimic that of the insurer's traditional policies. The other options are self-explanatory. These 14 investment options are representative of those offered by competitor insurers, with some insurers offering many more options and others offering fewer. The typical VUL policyowner may hold investments in numerous accounts simultaneously in an effort to diversify his or her exposure. Increasingly, insurers are allowing policyowners to direct investment into funds not controlled by the insurer, such as those controlled by the large mutual fund companies.

The policyowner has the right of periodically transferring funds from one account to another. Most North American insurers will allow up to four transfers per year at no charge. Additional transfers often incur a $25 charge. Many insurers allow policyowners to establish automatic monthly transfers at no fee, usually from the money market account to one or several of the equity accounts. As all transfers are within a life insurance policy, no taxable gain (or loss) is realizable because of the transaction—a distinct advantage over taxable mutual fund transfers.

Death Benefits

The treatment of death benefits under most VUL policy designs differs from that under traditional VLI; instead, it follows the UL approach. VUL death benefits fluctuate with changes in the values of the underlying assets only under option B. With the option A death benefit pattern, the face amount remains constant unless it is changed by the policyowner. As a result, all variations in investment returns are reflected solely in the policy's cash values, with no part used to fund changes in the policy's net amount at risk.

Unlike VLI, VUL policies typically contain no minimum death benefit guarantee, as such would be inconsistent with the basic design of universal life. Additionally, VUL policies issued in the United States are required to offer a minimum grace period for the payment of premiums of 61 days rather than the more common 31 days for most other policies.

As with UL policies, mortality charges are assessed monthly against the fund account. These mortality charges are calculated by multiplying the relevant cost of insurance per unit of insurance (e.g., $1,000) by the policy's net amount at risk. The policy contains a schedule of maximum costs of insurance rates and the insurer reserves the right (and typically does) assess mortality charges at lower than guaranteed rates. A few insurers base mortality charges on select and ultimate mortality tables (see chapter 4).

Loadings and Expenses

VUL policies sold in North America typically carry both front-end and back-end loads. Typical front-end loads are in the range of 2 to 10 percent of premiums paid. In addition, a first-year administrative charge of perhaps $500 is assessed, with monthly administrative charges thereafter in the $4 to $15 range.

Back-end loads (surrender charges) on VUL policies serve the same function as they do with UL and other cash-value policies; they are intended to reimburse the insurer for unrecouped sales charges. Such loads typically are stated as a percentage of a target premium and grade to zero after a few years.

Besides the loadings assessed directly against the VUL policies, additional charges are levied to cover expenses associated with the operation and investment management of the separate account. These charges are netted against the account investment income, thus resulting in a net investment return. Of course, over the long run, high charges will significantly penalize investment yield. Such fees may reduce investment return by ½ to 1 percent. These (and other) charges are required to be disclosed to policyowners through the policy prospectus.

Finally, the separate account also is debited to compensate the insurer for certain guarantees provided within the VUL policy. These include (1) a guarantee of lifetime service, (2) maximum administration charge guarantee, (3) guarantee of maximum cost of insurance charges, and (4) guaranteed annuity rates. These charges are referred to collectively as mortality and expense (M&E) charges. Note that M&E charges are *not* designed to cover actual mortality charges and policy expenses, but rather to compensate the insurer for guaranteeing the various components of the policy. M&E charges are said to average between 1 and 1½ percent of account value.

Uses and Limitations of Variable Universal Life

VUL policies require the same type of discipline as does UL. The prospective purchaser should commit to ensuring that the policy always has sufficient funds to be self-sustaining, ideally with investment income sufficient to cover all policy charges with some residual to ensure cash-value growth. If this type of commitment is not likely, the individual probably would be in a superior financial position by purchasing term.

VUL policies are potentially useful for those persons who desire to treat their life insurance policy cash values more as an investment than a savings account. The owner assumes the investment risk. The danger is that, if separate account investment results are not favorable, the policy's cash value could be reduced substantially and the policy could require substantial additional premium payments. This risk should be considered most carefully. One of the strengths of the life insurance industry historically has been its investment guarantees. With all variable products, consumers are forgoing these guarantees. In a rising market, as has been the situation within North America in the decade of the 1990s, few would have reason to complain. However, with falling markets, consumers might take a different position, as many Japanese customers did in the early 1990s when the Japanese market tumbled.

On the other hand, funds held in insurer separate accounts are earmarked to back the policies to which the funds apply and are separate from the insurer's general-account assets. In the event that the insurer experiences financial difficulty, this separation could afford an additional margin of safety for the VUL policyowner.

OTHER FLEXIBLE PREMIUM POLICIES

Adjustable Life Insurance

Adjustable life insurance is a level-premium, level-death benefit life insurance policy that can assume the form of any traditional term or whole life policy (within certain guidelines) and that offers the policyowner the ability, within limits, to change the policy plan, premium payment, and face amount. In effect, its form ranges over a continuum of traditional level-premium life insurance, ranging from low-premium term through ordinary life to high-premium, limited-payment whole life.

The **adjustment provision** that distinguishes AL from more traditional life insurance contracts permits the policyowner to change the plan by requesting the insurer to change the policy configuration. Adjustments are made prospectively only. Premiums can be increased or decreased. The face amount can be increased (subject to evidence of insurability) or decreased. Some policies make allowance for unscheduled or extra premium payments. Whenever any of these adjustments occur, the plan of insurance will usually also change.

An increase in premium increases future cash values and, hence, (1) lengthens the period of coverage if the policy is in the term portion of the adjustable life range or (2) shortens the premium payment period if the policy is in the whole life range. A decrease in premium has the opposite effect.

The AL policy introduced a new concept to the life insurance business. The traditional approach to life insurance programming entailed first determining the face amount and plan of insurance; then, by entering a rate book at the insured's age, the premium was calculated. If the resulting premium was not consistent with premium-paying ability, adjustment to the face amount or a change to another insurance plan was considered. Under AL, the applicant selects the amount of insurance that then dictates the plan of insurance.

Although AL introduced some important new concepts, it retained many aspects of traditional products. The AL policyowner may alter the level of premiums paid, but premiums generally cannot be taken to zero without policy lapse. AL policies require certain minimum annual premium payments, usually equivalent to that for a five-year term policy. This is not the case with UL policies. Also, any change in the level of premium payments ordinarily requires formal notification of the company and a redefining of the resultant plan.

Once a particular premium payment level is decided upon, that premium is due at future due dates, unless the policyowner specifically requests a change. In this respect, AL is similar to fixed-premium policies. By contrast, UL policies require no implicit assumption regarding the level of future premium payments.

Flexible Enhanced Ordinary Life

The enhanced ordinary life (EOL) policy, presented in chapter 5, is a fixed-premium whole life policy that combines portions of ordinary life, term life, and paid-up additions. The mixture of whole life, term, and paid-up additions is fixed for the applicant of a given age and gender, as is the premium. As a response to the premium flexibility and death adjustability of universal life, some insurers have introduced an EOL-type policy with certain features of both UL and traditional products.

Concerns about Universal Life

Many companies perceived a need to offer products to compete with UL, but they did not believe that offering UL was the solution. They expressed concerns about the potential lack of premium commitment by the policyowner. In times of financial stringency, the policyowner might too easily cease paying the premium, thus endangering the life insurance program.

Additionally, because of a less certain premium stream and the ease of cash-value withdrawals from UL policies, insurers were compelled to adopt shorter-term investment strategies for the assets backing their UL policies. Shorter-duration investments should produce lower returns over the long term. This perceived problem could be expected to result in less stable and lower policyowner returns, in returns being subsidized by profits from other products or from insurer surplus, or in taking greater than normal investment risk (e.g., through junk bonds or risky mortgages) to enhance investment returns. The emphasis in UL marketing on its credited interest rate and on identifiable expense charges would only exacerbate the problem. To a degree, these companies' concerns proved to be valid.

Nature of Flexible Enhanced Ordinary Life

Some companies thus decided to offer a product built on the traditional participating model, but with added flexibility. **Flexible enhanced ordinary life** permits the combination of whole life, term, and paid-up additions in such proportions as to allow the policyowner to establish a comfortable premium level, within limits, and to adjust the policy face amount, also within limits.

The product requires a certain minimum amount of whole life insurance, then permits the addition of whatever amount of term insurance is desired. By varying the mixture, the effective premium rate per $1,000 is varied, subject to a minimum required fixed premium.

Policy dividends, regular additional premiums, and special additional premium payments (so-called dump-ins) all purchase single-premium (paid-up) insurance. The term insurance can be reduced on a one-for-one basis as the pieces of paid-up insurance grow. This effectively lowers internal (but not identified) mortality charges, thus rendering the policy death benefit more sustainable. Thus, a degree of flexibility in cash-value accumulation, mix of coverage, and premium is provided. Further flexibility is provided by allowing the policyowner to increase or decrease the amount of term insurance after issue and by allowing additional premium payments.

LIFE INSURANCE POLICY COMPARISON CHART

The great variety of life insurance products available today can seem bewildering. However, the vast majority of individual life insurance sold today is of one or more of six product types. These six types are listed in Table 6-3 in the order in which they were presented in this book. Beside each type is a summary of its basic features and a listing of its advantages and disadvantages, both to the buyer and to the seller. The table is intended to highlight key points only. As with all such shorthand charts, exceptions to the general statements exist.

Questions

1. Interest rate fluctuations in the late 1970s and 1980s heightened consumers' sensitivity to rates of return on savings and investments. Explain how UL and VL policies both give consumers greater disclosure and flexibility with regard to the investment aspect of life products and require consumers to assume greater risks.
2. In the United States the size of a policy's cash value in relation to its net amount at risk (NAR) can affect its tax treatment. Using the concept of NAR, explain how universal life and variable life policies may lose their favorable tax treatment. Are UL and VL policies more susceptible to losing favorable tax treatment than ordinary life policies?
3. How do flexible enhanced ordinary life policies combine aspects of whole life and term policies and the option for paid-up additions?
4. Discuss the advantages and disadvantages of purchasing a variable life policy versus buying term and investing the difference (BTID).

TABLE 6-3 Life Insurance Policy Comparison Chart

Product	Death Benefit	Premium	Cash Value	Cash Value or Dividends Use Current Interest?	Partial Surrenders Permitted?	Policy Elements Unbundled?	Direct Borrowing Recognition?	
Annual Renewable Term	Fixed, level	Fixed, increasing	No cash value	N.A.	N.A.	No	N.A.	
Par Ordinary Life	Fixed, level	Fixed, level	Fixed with minimum interest rate guaranteed. Excess through dividends.	Yes	Yes, but through paid-up additions only	No	Yes, with many policies	
Current Assumption Whole Life	Fixed, level	May change based on insurer's experience, cash value has guaranteed minimum percentage Maximum guaranteed, but insurer may charge less	Minimum guaranteed. Excess interest lowers premium or increases cash value.	Yes	Yes	Yes	Yes	
Variable Life	Guaranteed minimum can increase based on investment performance	Fixed, level	Based on investment performance. Not guaranteed.	Yes	No	No, but to some degree shown in prospectus	Yes	
Universal Life	Adjustable	Flexible	Varies depending on face amount and premium. Minimum guaranteed interest. Excess increases cash value.	Yes	Yes	Yes	Yes	
Variable Universal Life	Adjustable	Flexible	Based on investment performance. Not guaranteed.	Yes	Yes	Yes	Yes	

Advantages		Disadvantages		
To Buyer	To Seller	To Buyer	To Seller	Risks to Buyer
Low outlay. Can purchase large amounts. Buyer can develop outside investment program.	May be easier to sell.	Increasing outlay. Buyer may not invest difference or may realize lower return.	Low commission. Little profit. High lapse rates.	• Increasing premium. • Can buyer earn more on investments than insurer?
Familiar product. Predictable. Helps buyer discipline. Interest, mortality, and expense experience can be recognized.	Same as buyer. Traditional commissions. Greater margins.	Costly if lapsed early. Lack of flexibility. Can be more costly.	Can be less attractive to buyer.	• Failure to meet premium commitment.
Takes advantage of high current interest rates and improved mortality.	Same as buyer. Traditional whole life commissions. Responds to "buy term invest difference."	Premiums can increase or cash value be lower than projected. Buyer takes risk on high-premium version.	If projections are not met, can be negative client reaction.	If assumptions change adversely, • Premiums can be higher than with traditional products. • Cash value can be lower than with traditional products.
Takes advantage of growth in economy. More in control of growth.	Responds to inflation objections. Traditional whole life commissions. Shifts investment risk to buyer.	Buyer must decide on underlying investments and monitor them for change. Few guarantees.	Needs securities license.	• Investment risk is great. • Can be higher in cost than traditional products.
Greater transparency and more flexibility.	Consumer accepted. Widely publicized. May be easier to sell.	Flexibility places greater responsibility on buyer. Buyer assumes greater investment and mortality risks.	Generally, lower commissions. Renewals uncertain. Computer backup essential. Readily lapsable.	If assumptions change adversely, • Investment performance can affect satisfaction of long-term goal. • Cash value can be lower than with traditional products.
Takes advantage of growth of economy. More control of growth. Flexibility.	Shifts investment risk to buyer.	Fewer guarantees.	Same as variable life insurance, but more costly to administer.	• Will need to pay more if investment experiences are negative.

CHAPTER

7

HEALTH INSURANCE POLICIES

Objectives

- Highlight the differences between individual and group health insurance coverages.

- Describe the important features of comprehensive medical and special individual insurance coverages.

- Explain the need for long-term care and the extent to which it is met by the long-term care insurance market.

- Describe the market for disability income insurance.

- Outline the principal benefits included in disability insurance coverage.

INTRODUCTION TO HEALTH INSURANCE

Recall from the chapter 1 overview that we use the term *health insurance* to mean any form of insurance whose payment is contingent on the insured incurring additional expenses or losing income because of incapacity or loss of good health. Health insurance is sometimes called **accident and health insurance, accident and sickness insurance,** or **disability insurance** depending on the jurisdiction and customary practice. Whatever the term used, it often subsumes numerous distinctive plans of coverage to protect the insured against specific financial losses from injury, illness, or incapacity.

Health Insurance Coverages

As noted in chapter 1, we classify health insurance into three categories. First, *medical expense insurance*—often itself called simply *health insurance*—encompasses a broad range of benefit arrangements that can cover virtually any expenses connected with hospital and medical care and related services for the insured and covered family members. Plans may be limited to basic benefits for specific kinds of medical services or may provide comprehensive benefits for all major medical expenses associated with severe injury or long-term illness. Benefits may be paid directly to the health care provider or institution or as reimbursement of actual expenses incurred. Some benefits are paid as fixed amounts without regard to the actual costs of care.

Second, an increasingly popular coverage—*long-term care insurance*—provides financial protection against insureds incurring exceptional expenses because of their need for assistance in connection with the essential activities of daily living. Coverage is triggered by an insured's inability to perform such activities and usually is paid as fixed amounts.

Finally, *disability income insurance,* sometimes called **loss of time** or **loss of income insurance,** provides periodic payments when an insured loses income because of injury or sickness. Coverage customarily is directly related, at least in part, to the insured's occupational duties and earnings. Benefits are usually paid monthly as fixed amounts while the insured is disabled, although certain business insurance plans may provide reimbursement-type coverage, as discussed in chapter 17.

Health and life insurance policies share the common elements of general contract law and resemble each other in overall structure. However, individual health insurance contracts are more complex than life insurance contracts. More than one loss may occur while the policy is in force, a more varied spectrum of losses is present, and the cause of loss is more often subjective with health insurance. As a result, health insurance contracts require a much larger number of technical definitions and provide a greater range of optional coverages.

In addition, health insurance policies contain numerous provisions designed to remove any uncertainty as to how benefit entitlement is established and maintained. Thus, health contracts require that the insurer be provided with written notice of any claim within a certain time period, such as 20 days. The insurer is required to provide forms needed to file a proof of loss within 15 or so days, otherwise the claimant may simply provide his or her own statement of the loss. Proof of loss is to be provided typically within 90 days of the loss or, if the loss is continuing, every 90 days. The insurer may be required to pay the loss within a certain time period but also is usually given the right to have the claimant examined (or an autopsy performed) at the insurer's expense. These and several other provisions (see chapter 9) are common to all health insurance policies. Other provisions are specific to particular coverages, as discussed herein.

We cover each of these three types of health insurance in this chapter. We emphasize long-term care and disability income coverages because of their importance in the individual policy market.

Individual versus Group Coverages

Medical expense, long-term care insurance, and disability income insurance are available on either a group or individual basis in most OECD countries, including the United States. The distinctions between group and individual insurance arise primarily in the ways in which they are marketed and the manner in which coverage is finally issued and administered.

Distinctions between Individual and Group Coverages

Individual health insurance is an arrangement in which coverage is provided to a specific individual under a policy issued to the individual (and sometimes covering multiple family members). Except in mass-marketing approaches and in certain state-sponsored or mandated plans, insureds typically must furnish evidence of insurability for a policy to be issued. Companies maintain separate records for each policy and conduct all transactions, including premium collection, on a direct basis with each insured. With individual health insurance contracts, the ownership of the contract is vested in the insured.

Group health insurance refers to arrangements in which coverage is provided for groups of individuals under a single master contract issued to a group policyowner. The policyowner may be an employer, an association, a labor union, a trust, or any other legitimate entity not organized solely for the purpose of obtaining insurance. Members of larger groups generally obtain coverage without having to furnish evidence of insurability. Because of reduced marketing and administrative costs, group health insurance generally costs less than individual plans with comparable coverages. This chapter covers individually issued health insurance policies. Group insurance is covered in chapters 18 through 22.

The Individual Health Insurance Market

Fundamental differences exist between (1) the individual health insurance market and (2) the employer-sponsored group insurance market or government-provided coverages.[1] These differences make the individual health insurance market quite complex in comparison to group or government-sponsored health insurance, which makes information problems even worse for purchasers of individual health policies than those typically found for the purchasers of individual life policies. Individuals without government or employer-sponsored coverage usually access the individual health insurance market on their own and face a variety of ways of doing so. Individuals must choose from among a multitude of complex products that are often difficult to compare. Once a product is chosen, individuals must select from a wide range of cost-sharing arrangements and pay the full price of coverage with no assistance from government or an employer.

In contrast, employees eligible for group or governmental coverage do not face the task of accessing the insurance market. This is done for them with group insurance or is irrelevant with governmental insurance. Because employers typically offer only one or a few health plans, the task of identifying and comparing products is greatly simplified or eliminated. Finally, the burden of selecting cost-sharing options and paying for the products is significantly eased by employer contributions and payroll deduction.

Perhaps most consumers purchase individual health insurance through agents. Some health insurance is sold directly to consumers by insurers, especially when insurers have high name recognition. For example, several U.S. Blue Cross/Blue Shield plans (see chapter 20) and health maintenance organizations target individuals in their advertisements.

Another important access route is through business or social organizations, such as chambers of commerce, trade associations, unions, alumni associations, and religious organizations. Through pooled purchasing power, associations often can negotiate competitively priced products for their members.

INDIVIDUAL MEDICAL EXPENSE INSURANCE

Need for Individual Medical Expense Insurance

Individuals not covered by group or government health plans need protection through individual policies. Typical of this group are the following:

- self-employed persons
- students no longer covered by their parents' insurance
- persons under retirement age and not in the work force, such as early retirees and persons between jobs
- those whose employers do not choose to offer medical expense coverage
- part-time, temporary, or contract workers not eligible for coverage through their employers
- unemployed persons not eligible for government-sponsored health programs for the poor, such as Medicaid in the United States
- children, spouses, and other dependents ineligible for coverage or too costly to cover under an employer-sponsored plan

---

[1]This and the following sections draw from *Private Health Insurance* (Washington, DC: U.S. General Accounting Office, 1996), Chap. 3.

Some individuals falling into these categories rely on spouses or other family members to include them under the family coverage options of their employer-sponsored plan. Others do not have this alternative. For some the need for individual coverage is permanent; for others, it is temporary. It is estimated that almost 5 percent of the U.S. nonelderly population relies on private individual medical expense insurance as their only source of such insurance.[2] In spite of this, large proportions of the U.S. population and many other countries' populations have no medical expense insurance coverage. Some U.S. states have undertaken initiatives to increase access to such coverages, as Box 7-1 highlights.

Individuals whose basic need for health insurance is met through group or government plans may still find that individual policies are useful because they supplement their other coverages. Governmental health insurance schemes commonly do not cover all medical care expenses and insureds often incur delays in receiving government-provided care. In such instances, private supplemental health care policies are commonly purchased, as is the situation in the United Kingdom, France, Canada, the United States (with respect to Medicare), and several other countries.

Similarly, many individuals, even though they are covered by a medical expense insurance plan—whether it be group or individual insurance—find that their existing insurance is inadequate. The plan may pay less than current hospital charges for daily room and board. In addition, existing insurance may pay only limited amounts for various surgical procedures. Because of limitations in their existing medical expense insurance coverage, many persons need some kind of supplemental individual policy. They may merely need a hospital indemnity policy that will pay an additional fixed amount for each day of hospital confinement, or they may want a policy to cover truly catastrophic expenses, with a deductible of several thousand dollars.

Comprehensive Medical Insurance Coverage

Comprehensive medical insurance plans provide broad coverage and significant protection from large, unpredictable medical care expenses. From the beginning, most such plans covered a wide range of medical care charges with few internal limits and a high overall maximum benefit.

---

[2]Ibid., p. 25.

BOX 7-1

HIGH-RISK POOLS IN THE UNITED STATES

More than one-half of the states in the United States have created programs that allow so-called high-risk individuals to obtain needed medical expense insurance. To qualify for the pool, applicants generally must demonstrate that they have been rejected by at least one insurer for health reasons or have one of a number of specified health conditions. Premiums generally are 50 percent higher than that charged for standard, comparable coverage in the private market.

Most pools enroll only a limited number of individuals, usually less than 5 percent of those under age 65 with individual insurance. This low enrollment may be due to limited funding, lack of public awareness, and high premiums.

Source: Private Health Insurance, p. 59.

Insuring Arrangements

Comprehensive medical insurance plans are offered by a range of different insuring arrangements. The three most common are (1) traditional life insurers, (2) Blue Cross/Blue Shield insurers, and (3) health maintenance organizations (HMOs). Traditional life insurers have offered major medical expense insurance coverage for decades. We briefly cover these plans next.

Blue Cross/Blue Shield insurers are important sources of individual medical expense insurance in many states in the United States. These insurers offer relatively comprehensive individual coverage. A key distinction between the "Blues" and traditional life insurers is that life insurers rely largely on indemnity-type reimbursement plans whereas the Blues negotiate and pay hospital and health care provider fees directly, sometimes at a lower rate than that applicable to reimbursement plans. The chapter 20 discussion on Blue Cross/Blue Shield group plans is generally applicable to the individual market, except for obvious differences in administration and pricing as well as some other differences noted later.

Finally, HMOs continue to grow in importance as sources of comprehensive medical insurance coverage, especially in the United States. As discussed at length in chapter 20, HMOs combine the provision of health care and its financing into a single organization. Their individual coverage offerings are quite similar to their group offerings except for obvious differences in administration and pricing as well as some differences noted later.

Benefit Arrangements

Comprehensive medical insurance covers a wide range of health care benefits including inpatient and outpatient hospital services, physician and diagnostic services, specialty services such as physical therapy and radiology, and prescription drugs. Individuals choose from multiple cost-sharing arrangements. In the individual market, deductibles of between $250 and $2,500 are common, whereas limits on total out-of-pocket expenses typically begin at $1,200 and may exceed $6,000 annually.

Major Medical Expense Insurance Both life insurers and the Blues offer major medical expense insurance. Under such traditional expense plans, the reimbursement formula applies to the total covered expenses subject to a deductible and coinsurance. Thus, a plan could provide for the reimbursement of 80 percent of all combined covered expenses in a calendar year after a deductible of $500, up to a lifetime maximum of $1 million.

A variety of modified comprehensive designs was developed that provides some first-dollar coverage. In some plans, certain types of expenses, such as hospital expenses, are not subject to a deductible, and no coinsurance is applied on the initial hospital expenses, such as the first $2,000 or $5,000. Surgeons' fees may be treated similarly, subject to a usual and customary fee limitation. It is possible to waive or modify the deductible and coinsurance features for other services such as physicians' hospital visits and diagnostic tests. Most plans today provide a maximum annual **out-of-pocket cap** on expenses paid by the insured individual (a stop-loss provision). Diagrams of a comprehensive plan both with and without first-dollar coverage are presented in chapter 20 in Figure 20-2.

In 1996, a law was enacted in the United States permitting individuals (as well as small employers) to fund medical expenses in a new way. The law authorized the creation of up to 750,000 **medical savings accounts** (MSAs), which are savings accounts whose funds are limited to covering an individual's or family's medical expenses. Tax-deductible contributions may be made to the account, the interest on which is tax deferred. Withdrawals to cover medical expenses are not taxable income. Box 7-2 highlights other key aspects and some of the issues associated with MSAs.

BOX 7-2

MEDICAL SAVINGS ACCOUNTS IN THE UNITED STATES

High-deductible medical expense insurance is to be purchased along with the medical savings account. Deductibles range from $1,500 to $2,250 for single individuals and from $3,000 to $4,500 for families. The major medical expense insurance must have an out-of-pocket cap of $3,000 for individuals and $5,500 for families. No minimum lifetime benefit is required under the law. The idea is that relatively small medical expenses will be covered by the MSA with large expenses covered by the insurance. Yearly contributions to the MSA are limited to an amount equal to 65 percent of the deductible for individuals and 75 percent for families. No minimum is established.

Proponents of the MSA approach to funding individual and small group health care contend that it can lead to greater individual accountability because individuals will take greater care in deciding how to spend monies from the MSA. When medical expenses are paid by third parties such as insurers, individuals have little incentives to control expenditures. Proponents also contend that MSAs will permit individuals who previously had no health insurance coverage to secure it on favorable terms and will allow greater freedom of choice in health care service providers and in health care financing.

Opponents express concern that MSAs may actually discourage individuals from seeking needed medical care because they will be reluctant to spend their own money, instead wanting to save more. This concern applies particularly to preventive care. Opponents also argue that MSAs invite adverse selection in that mainly the wealthy and healthy will avail themselves of the option. Other insuring arrangements, therefore, will have less healthy groups, meaning higher costs for the least wealthy.

Health Maintenance Organizations   HMOs offer individual policies that provide coverage at least equal to that under major medical expense plans, and often their coverage is more comprehensive. HMOs are more likely to offer a broad range of preventive care services, such as periodic examinations, immunizations, and health education. Moreover, these benefits are generally more comparable with benefits covered under employer-sponsored group plans.

HMO copayment requirements typically are stated as a set amount per physician office visit (e.g., $10 or $15) and hospital admission (e.g., $100 to $500). Out-of-pocket caps similar to those under major medical expense plans are common with HMO coverage.

Special Individual Insurance Coverages

In addition to hospital-surgical and major medical insurance policies, insurers offer a number of special individual policies. These include (1) hospital confinement indemnity, (2) government supplemental insurance, and (3) specified disease policies.

Hospital Confinement Indemnity Policies

In contrast with basic hospital expense insurance that is provided on a reimbursement basis, **hospital confinement indemnity** coverage pays a fixed sum for each day of hospital confinement. The benefit is most commonly sold as monthly amounts between $1,000 and $6,000 for continuous confinement of up to one year or more. The monthly amount shown in this way actually is an aggregate of potential daily payments in any 30-day period of hospitalization. Thus, a policy that provides a $1,500 monthly payment would pay $50 for each day that the insured was hospitalized.

Government Supplemental Policies

As the name indicates, these health insurance products provide coverage that supplements the benefits provided by governmental medical insurance plans. Consider, for example, the U.S. Medicare system of insurance for the elderly. (The system is discussed in chapter 22.) In all states, the term **Medicare supplement** can apply only to a policy that meets specific minimum standards set out in insurance law or regulation. Health insurers generally offer two basic types of policies: (1) the Medicare Wraparound policy and (2) the Comprehensive Medicare Supplement policy.

The **Medicare Wraparound** policy provides benefits that cover the deductibles and coinsurance amounts that individuals must pay personally under Medicare. Such policies may continue to pay benefits for hospital and nursing home confinement after Medicare benefits are exhausted. They may also pay more than the Medicare Part B copayment of 20 percent of "reasonable charges." Coverage, however, is limited through the application of maximum benefit limits.

The Comprehensive Medicare Supplement policy is similar to a Medicare Wraparound policy except that it generally has significantly higher maximum benefit limits or is unlimited with respect to the duration of confinement in a hospital or skilled nursing facility. Some comprehensive policies pay benefits toward Medicare Part B expenses that exceed the amount deemed reasonable by Medicare (when the insurer's claim payment exceeds the Medicare payment). They also may provide benefits for a variety of health care expenses that the Medicare program does not cover.

U.S. law requires nationwide standardization of Medicare supplemental policies. The NAIC implemented the law in 1991 by designing 10 standard Medicare supplemental plans to replace the thousands then on the market. States are required to adopt the standards, and any company selling unapproved so-called medigap policies is subject to a fine.

Specified Disease Policies

So-called **dread disease** coverage refers to individual insurance that pays a variety of benefits up to substantial maximums solely for the treatment of a disease named in the policy, most typically cancer or heart disease. Benefits usually are paid as scheduled amounts of indemnity for designated events, such as hospital confinement, or for specific medical procedures, such as chemotherapy. Because insurance is limited to medical expenses associated with a single devastating disease, this coverage should be used only to supplement other health insurance.

Contract Provisions

The provisions common to all health insurance policies are discussed in chapters 9 and 10. The benefit and cost-sharing provisions applicable to medical expense insurance were discussed earlier. Of particular relevance to insureds and insurers is the contract provision regarding future premium levels and renewability.

Most individual medical expense policies provide that the insured has the contractual right to continue the policy by the timely payment of premiums to a specified age, such as 65. Future premiums are not guaranteed but are subject to change from year to year by the insurer. The insurer typically must secure regulatory approval for such changes. Importantly, premiums cannot be revised nor the policy nonrenewed based on any particular individual's claims experience. Rather premium revision is to be on a class basis.

Even with the guaranteed right to continue a policy and with insurers being unable to revise rates except on a class basis, concern has been expressed about certain insurer practices in this regard. Box 7-3 highlights one such practice.

BOX 7-3

CLOSED BLOCK DURATIONAL RATING

With *closed block durational rating,* an insurer can offer guaranteed renewable policies at artificially low rates to attract large numbers of new insureds and thereby increase market share. At some future time, the insurer closes the block of business by no longer accepting new applicants and then increases rates on that block. At about the same time, it begins selling a new policy (block) at low rates.

Without new, healthy insureds, rates for the closed block rise even faster. Healthy insureds lapse their policies and purchase new ones, often from the same insurer; that is, the block incurs adverse selection. The less healthy insureds must ei-

ther remain in the closed block with its spiral of poorer risks and increasing rates or lapse their policies and face the uncertain prospect of obtaining coverage on the open market.

Although legal in most jurisdictions, some insurance regulators have expressed concern about this practice. They observe that the effect is to transform a block of guaranteed renewable policies into policies whose premiums escalate with advancing age. Other jurisdictions have prohibited the practice through guaranteed-issue requirements and premium rate restrictions.

***

Source: Private Health Insurance, p. 50.

LONG-TERM CARE INSURANCE

The Need for Long-Term Care

As noted in chapter 3, many societies are experiencing rapid individual and population aging. With age comes a lessened ability to fully take care of oneself. Most elderly persons require no assistance with their activities of daily living, whereas many nonelderly require assistance. Even so, we know that a substantial proportion of elderly persons will require care at some point. Estimates for the United States, for example, suggest that some 40 percent of elderly will require nursing home care at some point in their lives. By age 75, the odds of requiring some long-term care increases to 60 percent. Because of these facts, our focus will be on the elderly, but note should be taken of the fact that middle-age and younger persons incur similar exposures through accidents or medical conditions. The long-term care need is not confined to the elderly.

Historically, any needed care was provided by family members through extended family living arrangements. Even today, families remain the primary source of care for the infirm, with the responsibility typically falling on females. However, numerous factors have converged both to decrease the ability of families to provide care and to increase the demand for such care, including the following:

- the continuing demise worldwide of the extended family
- the rise in single-parent households
- a growing proportion of adult women, who historically have been the primary family caregivers, working outside the home, making them less available to render care
- nuclear families' increasing reliance on the incomes of both spouses, making neither spouse available to assist elderly parents
- unprecedented numbers of individuals living into old age
- increasing life expectancy
- a more mobile society, meaning that children are less likely to live near elderly parents

- reduced fertility rates, which means fewer children to provide care
- modern medicine's ability to prolong life, which does not always translate into physical independence
- growing networks of desirable services available to those in need of long-term care

For these and other reasons, we have witnessed and will continue to witness a rapid growth in the demand for long-term care (LTC) services. The demand for long-term care insurance can be expected similarly to grow as more and more persons become aware of the extraordinary costs of long-term care. The average cost of a year's stay in a nursing home in the United States, for example, is about $30,000, with some easily costing twice that amount. Typical home care costs fall in the $10,000 to $15,000 range. The average confinement is between one and two years, with about one-fourth lasting more than three years. About 10 percent last more than five years. Of course, individual costs can be much higher than the averages suggest, meaning an even more rapid dissipation of personal assets and possibly even impoverishment. Of even greater importance to many persons is the concern about possible loss of dignity and a loss of control that accompany old-age wealth depletion.

Defining Long-Term Care

In the past, long-term care was synonymous with nursing home care and, for many people, this carried a somewhat negative connotation. Few elderly (or others) relish the idea of having to spend their last days in a nursing home. Today, however, long-term care has taken on a broad meaning and may even carry a positive connotation. Thus, for example, the New York State Insurance Department offers this comprehensive definition:

> Long-term care (LTC) refers to a broad range of supportive medical, personal, and social services needed by people who are unable to meet their basic living needs for an extended period of time because of accident, illness, or frailty. LTC involves receiving the assistance of another person(s) to perform the essential activities of daily living (ADLs) when these tasks can no longer be performed independently. . . . ADL assistance may be provided at home by formal (paid) caregivers, such as home health aids, by informal (unpaid) caregivers, such as family members or friends, or in a nursing home.[3]

This definition makes clear that LTC is more than nursing home care. It includes home care and community care. Thus, the essential elements of LTC include:

- the need for medical, personal, or social services
- the need results from an accident, illness, or frailty
- services are provided by other persons, either paid or unpaid, at home or in a nursing home
- services are to assist the individual in performing the essential ADLs

As might be expected, the intensity of needed care typically increases with time. By nature, it is stressful and demanding. As such, caregiving can have a significant impact on employees who are responsible for elderly parents. Employee productivity is adversely affected, and employee stress increases. In chapter 1 economic terms, LTC may carry a negative externality—that is, it imposes costs on others (in this instance, employers). As such, employers are increasingly investigating means of helping employees cope with the responsibilities of caregiving.

---

[3]*Affordable Financing for Long-Term Care* 2 (New York State, 1994).

Overview of Long-Term Care Insurance

Long-term care (LTC) insurance promises to pay expenses incurred if the insured is unable to engage safely in selected activities of daily living. The individual's inability to engage in these essential activities requires that someone provide the care, either in the home or in an institution such a nursing home. Such care is financed in a few countries by the government but, in the majority of countries worldwide, LTC expenses are met from individual or family resources and, increasingly, through long-term care insurance.

In the United States, Medicare pays for about 2 percent of long-term care costs. This low proportion is because this program is not designed to cover LTC expenses; instead it is designed to cover medical expenses of the aged (see chapter 22). LTC benefits are paid under Medicare only for medically necessary care in a skilled nursing facility and only when the facility-based care follows a period of hospitalization for the same condition. Additionally, even this coverage is limited to 100 days, of which only 20 are covered in full.

Another potential source of LTC funding in the United States is the state-based Medicaid program. Medicaid, an important part of the U.S. welfare program, provides certain payments or benefits to those in poverty. If one is impoverished and requires LTC, Medicaid often will meet the costs. It, however, is far from an acceptable alternative for most persons, as Box 7-4 makes clear.

Long-term care insurance was first introduced in the 1970s. At that time, it was designed and marketed as nursing home insurance without providing coverage for alternative care such as home health care. Because it was new, insurers knew neither how to define eligibility nor how to price it. With increasing experience, however, the market is beginning to stabilize, although products are still evolving to meet consumer needs.

LTC benefits are offered on both an individual and group basis. The LTC market developed initially through the individual product route, but group long-term care insurance is playing an increasingly important, yet still minority, role.

BOX 7-4

IS MEDICAID THE ANSWER TO LONG-TERM CARE EXPENSES IN THE U.S.?

Within the United States, Medicaid is the "provider of last resort" for the poor. In some states, it covers substantial proportions of LTC expenses. Medicaid recipients are those with desperately few assets.

Until recently in the United States, many financially well-off families facing the need to provide long-term care for an aged parent would arrange for the transfer of the parent's assets either to children or to a trust in order to voluntarily "impoverish" the parent who would then be eligible for Medicaid. The following provisions applicable to all potential Medicaid recipients are intended to minimize this type of financial manipulation:

- Property transferred within 60 months of application for Medicaid is considered to be owned by the applicant.
- State Medicaid programs are required to attempt to recover any Medicaid payments from the estates of recipients.
- Criminal sanctions apply to attempts to transfer property solely for purposes of qualifying for Medicaid.

Thus, although Medicaid continues to provide some financial security to the truly needy, it will no longer be subject to the same types of manipulation as formerly. The message is clear: If there is any way for the individual to cover his or her own LTC expenses, he or she must do so.

Source: Jacquelyn S. Coy and Paul J. Winn, "Long-Term Care—A Vital Product in an Evolving Environment," *Journal of the American Society of CLU & ChFC* (September 1967), pp. 72–73.

Coverage

Most individual LTC policies are underwritten on the basis of the application and the attending physician's statements.[4] Some insurers also interview the proposed insured by telephone, and some require a paramedical examination. Many companies that offer LTC policies utilize a single classification for all acceptable applicants. Some insurers have preferred, standard, and rated classifications.

Nursing Home Care

Policies often provide for three levels of nursing home care: (1) skilled nursing care, (2) intermediate nursing care, and (3) custodial care. Each of these is defined in Box 7-5. Formerly, most LTC policies required a hospital stay before admission to a nursing home. Also the stay must have been "medically necessary."

Policies issued today agree to pay benefits if the insured cannot perform basic living activities without assistance. The typical policy requires that the insured be unable to perform two of five or six ADLs, depending on the policy. LTC policies contain a list of **activities of daily living** (ADL), which typically includes five or six of the following:

- eating
- bathing
- dressing
- toileting
- continence
- transferring
- taking medicine

Of course, some individuals can physically perform all ADLs yet cannot be left alone safely. Thus, LTC policies also include a **cognitive impairment** clause, which permits benefit payments with respect to those who cannot safely perform essential ADLs.

---

[4]This discussion draws in part from Jacquelyn S. Coy and Paul J. Winn, "Long-Term Care—A Vital Product in an Evolving Environment," *Journal of the American Society of CLU & ChFC* (September 1997), pp. 68–75; *Disability Income Course* (Bethesda, MD: The Life Underwriter Training Council, 1996); and *Long-Term Care,* 3rd ed. (Indianapolis, IN: Pictorial, Inc., 1992).

BOX 7-5

LEVELS OF NURSING CARE

SKILLED NURSING CARE

Skilled nursing care is the highest level of nursing care and demands the greatest expertise. It is 24-hour care ordered by a physician and provided by a registered nurse, licensed practical nurse, or licensed therapist.

INTERMEDIATE NURSING CARE

Intermediate nursing care is similar to skilled nursing care except that the patient neither receives nor needs 24-hour attention. Thus, it is effectively noncontinuous skilled nursing care.

CUSTODIAL CARE

Custodial care, the most basic level of nursing care, typically takes the form of assistance with the activities of daily living. Individuals providing such nonmedical care usually are not medical personnel, although the care must have been ordered by a physician and supervised by a nurse.

Community Care

Most elderly are happier and healthier when they can maintain as much control over their own affairs and as much independence as possible. LTC policies usually provide benefit payments for insureds who require assistance but who are able to remain in their homes or communities. The benefits, usually stated as a percentage (e.g., 50 percent) of the full nursing home benefit, are available for a variety of programs and services, as described next.

- **Home health care** includes skilled nursing care, physical therapy, and related professional services as well as personal services such as assistance with ADLs. Care typically is on a part-time basis and may include payments to family members.
- **Adult day care** might be available in a long-term care facility or a community program. Individuals can receive assistance with ADLs and also benefit from socialization.
- **Respite care** provides temporary relief for family members providing care in the individual's home. The relief may involve placing the individual in a long-term care facility temporarily, such as a weekend, or having someone stay with the individual in his or her home temporarily.
- **Hospice care** involves special care and emotional support for persons diagnosed with terminal illnesses. The care may be provided in a facility or in the person's home.
- **Therapeutic devices,** such as equipment to help a person remain in the community, are paid for under some policies.

Two other evolving forms of community care that may be covered under the LTC policy deserve mention. **Assisted living facilities** (ALFs), which have been popular in the Scandinavian countries for years, provide supervision, assistance, and limited health services to relatively healthy senior citizens. ALFs provide less medical care than nursing homes but more care than through common living arrangements. They complement, not substitute for, nursing care.

Finally, **continuing care centers** (CCCs), also called **life care centers,** provide a range of sensitive living arrangements and services that reflect each person's level of needed care and assistance. In many instances, this type of living arrangement is not covered by the LTC policy; rather, individuals purchase the right to live and receive support in the center. The payments typically take the form of an initial, large, single amount plus monthly payments reflecting the level of care needed. An advantage of CCCs is that individuals can receive escalating levels of care while not having to move from the community.

Benefits

The benefit provisions in LTC policies set forth what will be payable by the insurer if an insured event occurs. These provisions relate to the types and levels of care for which benefits will be provided, any prerequisites for benefit eligibility, and the actual level of benefits payable. No policy covers all LTC expenses.

The policies offered by many companies provide a choice of **elimination (waiting) periods** before benefits become payable. Available elimination periods range from 0 to 365 days. Naturally, the longer the waiting period, the lower the premium, other things being the same.

The buyer is usually offered a choice from a schedule of maximum daily benefits and length of benefit periods. A typical LTC policy might offer the buyer a **daily benefit** schedule of $40 per day, increasing in $10 increments to a maximum of $250 per day. The schedule of the **benefit periods** offered might range from two to five years. Some insurers offer a lifetime benefit period, a not inexpensive option.

In the past, policies paid the daily benefit for a period of time up to the benefit period chosen at policy issuance. Today, a maximum lifetime approach to defining benefit payments is common. Thus, if the benefit amount is $100 per day and the benefit period is four years, the maximum lifetime payout would be $100 times 365 days times 4 years, for a total of $146,000. This $146,000 pool of money can be used for covered services in whatever way desired, subject to the daily maximum. In this way, the benefit period can extend beyond four years by using services costing less than $100 per day.

Some companies pay a set amount monthly, as with disability income insurance (see later in this chapter). Thus, the policy may agree to pay $5,000 per month regardless of actual charges.

Community-based care is less expensive than nursing home care, and it is typically preferred by the elderly themselves. The maximum daily benefit is often 50 percent of the maximum daily benefit for nursing home care. The length of the benefit period is often the same for both coverages, but some policies require a different waiting period.

The majority of LTC policies offer some kind of **inflation protection** for an additional premium, which is designed to ensure that the benefit amount more or less increases with the cost of living. Many companies offer four options: (1) purchase no inflation protection, with the benefit amount remaining at its original level; (2) increase the benefit amount by 5 percent of the original amount per year; (3) increase the benefit amount by 5 percent compounded annually; or (4) adjust the benefit amount annually according to increases in a price index, such as the consumer price index in the United States. The differences in premiums among these options can be substantial, with, for example, the third option requiring a premium of about twice that of a policy with no inflation protection, for persons in their forties and early fifties.

Contract Provisions

In addition to the basic benefit provisions discussed previously, LTC policies contain several other provisions that collectively define the quality of the policy. We cover some of the more important next.

Premiums

LTC premiums are determined by the applicant's age, sex, medical condition and history, and, of course, the benefits provided. Issue ages vary widely by company, such as 50–84, 55–79, 40–79, and 20–74. Some companies restrict LTC policies to the above-age-40 market, primarily because of concern over AIDS.

Actuaries remain uncertain about many aspects of LTC insurance pricing because they do not yet have a substantial body of experience on which to rely. The issue is further complicated because many LTC policies rely on lapse-supported pricing; that is, those who lapse early subsidize persisting policyholders. Higher persistency endangers profitability.

Many commentators believe that LTC premiums are too high, even in the face of evidence of their having declined in recent years. Typical first-year agent commissions in the 50 to 80 percent range are important factors in LTC insurance pricing. Of course, group commission rates are lower. With increasing awareness and innovative ways of marketing, such as worksite marketing, prices may decline further. However, the LTC policy is exceptionally complex for both insurer and customer. As such, care must be taken in pricing and in purchase.

Premiums usually are level, although a few companies utilize increasing premiums based on attained age, either annually or at periodic intervals. As would be expected, the annual premium differs greatly from one LTC policy to another, depending upon age at issue, waiting period, benefits, and other policy features. Box 7-6 summarizes the annual premium schedule of four LTC policies at various ages.

Nearly all LTC policies provide for a **waiver of premium,** usually after 60, 90, or 180 days of confinement or days of benefits paid. Some companies provide a discount if both spouses purchase a contract.

Renewability

Virtually all individually issued LTC policies are **guaranteed renewable,** meaning that the insured has a contractual right to renew the policy to some specified age, such as 79, but that the company retains the right to revise rates on a class basis. In other words, the insurer reserves the right to change the premium charged but can do so only for all insureds of the same class of policies. The insurer can neither cancel nor nonrenew the policy prior to the policy expiration unless the insured fails to pay a premium.

Some policies are guaranteed renewable for life. Very few are issued on a **noncancelable** basis, meaning the policy can neither be canceled nor the premium changed. Of course, group LTC policies are subject to nonrenewal and premiums for the group are subject to revision annually.

Nonforfeiture Options

Insurers in some United States states are required to offer individual LTC policies that contain nonforfeiture benefits. Such policies carry higher premiums than otherwise similar policies. Typical options include the right to cease premium payments and take a reduced paid-up policy that provides benefits for a shorter period or receive a partial refund of premiums.

Coverage Limitations

All LTC policies contain some exclusions and limitations of coverage. Common exclusions include war, self-inflicted injuries, and chemical or alcohol dependency. Policies also exclude coverage for mental illness that is not organically based. In the past, policies did not cover senile dementia, Alzheimer's disease, or Parkinson's disease. Virtually all LTC policies now cover these conditions and all other mental illnesses that can be demonstrated to be organically based.

Most LTC policies restrict coverage of **preexisting conditions**—sicknesses that started or injuries that occurred prior to the issuance of the policy. The most common preexisting condition restriction is for six months (some policies use 12 or 24 months), although a few policies have no preexisting condition exclusions.

BOX 7-6

ILLUSTRATIVE ANNUAL PREMIUMS FOR LONG-TERM CARE POLICIES WITH $100 DAILY BENEFIT

Insurer	*Benefit Period (Years)*	*Waiting Period (Days)*	*Annual Premiums by Age of Issue*		
			At Age 60	*At Age 65*	*At Age 70*
A	3	100	$ 910	$1,530	$2,120
B	3	90	1,080	1,500	2,160
C	3	90	856	1,168	1,696
D	3	100	1,090	1,480	2,210
E	4	100	1,320	1,740	2,590
F	3	90	1,875	2,495	3,207

Regulation

As the long-term care market developed, the NAIC wrote model legislation that has been adopted in many states. The **Long-Term-Care Insurance Model Act** specifies minimum standards that products must meet to be considered long-term care insurance. The model includes the following major provisions:

- Insurers must provide an outline of coverage and summarize the features of the policy.
- The individual policyowner must have a "free-look" period during which the policy can be canceled and the premiums returned for any reason.
- Waivers denying coverage for specific health conditions are prohibited.
- Insurers may not offer substantially greater benefits for skilled nursing care than for intermediate or custodial care.
- Policies must be guaranteed renewable, although state insurance commissioners may allow cancellation under limited circumstances.

The Long-Term Care Market

The long-term care insurance market is growing steadily. New products are being developed in an effort to meet the needs of the elderly. Of course, the need is not restricted to the United States. The projected age 65 and above population among member countries of the OECD shows a 91 percent increase between the years 1980 and 2050 and an increase in excess of 200 percent in the number of persons aged 80 and above during the same time period.

The number of insurers worldwide that provide any type of long-term care insurance continues to grow rapidly, and, given the demand for health care of the elderly, many more are likely to enter this market in the future. Reinsurance facilities have evolved to provide support programs and guidelines that will make it possible for more small insurers to enter this market. Product development has been evolving quite rapidly. Continued interest on the part of government regulators and consumer advocate groups ensure that this high level of activity will continue. As additional data are generated regarding claims experience and individual policy provisions, the life insurance industry will be able to continue to refine its underwriting and classification structure.

DISABILITY INCOME INSURANCE

Most individuals seem quite concerned about the possibility of incurring high medical bills and, therefore, diligently seek and maintain medical expense insurance coverage, whether group or individual. Observation would suggest that we might be only somewhat less concerned about the possibility of our deaths causing financial hardship for those dependent on us. Large proportions of the wage-earning population purchase group and individual life insurance.

Much smaller proportions of the wage-earning population, however, have either group or individual disability income coverage. Indeed, for the United States, only about one in four workers has private disability income coverage of any type. It is as if the possibility of losing one's income because of disability is not great or, if disabled, recovery will be swift and complete.

It is true that the majority of disabilities are short term, lasting less than one month. On the other hand, the probability of a disability lasting three months or longer is quite high for individuals in their typical wage-earning years. Figure 7-1 shows such probabilities for selected ages based on insured lives. We also show, for comparison, the probabilities of death prior to age 65 based on the *1980 CSO Mortality Table*.

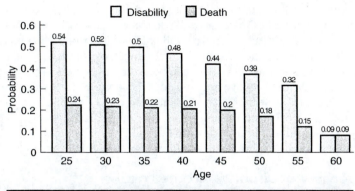

FIGURE 7-1 Probabilities of Disability for 90 Days or Longer
and Probabilities of Death: Prior to Age 65

Sources: 1980 CSO Mortality Table and *1985 Commissioners Disability Table.*

Note that the probabilities of a long-term disability, defined as having a duration of at least three months, is substantially greater than the likelihood of death until age 60, at which point the two events are equally likely (9 percent) before age 65. Additionally, if one is disabled for at least three months, the average duration of disability is in the five- to seven-year range, as illustrated in Figure 7-2.

Moreover, the need for disability income coverage has increased in most countries for the same reasons that the need for LTC coverage has increased. Informal support formerly provided by the family declines with economic development. Also, with unsupportably high government social insurance expenditures in many countries, we are witnessing a shift of responsibility for disability income (and other coverages) from government to the individual. In some markets, such as the United States, we observe similar trends in some areas of employer-sponsored benefit plans, including disability income

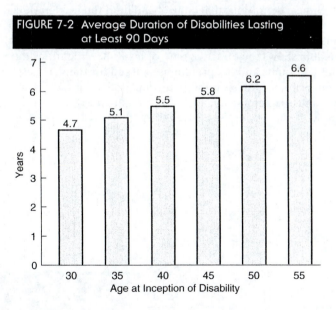

Source: 1985 Commissioners Disability Table.

insurance. At the same time, advances in medical care and technology have turned many of the greatest "killer" diseases into "disabler" diseases. In effect, in many instances, medical advances have substituted disability for what formerly would have been death.

It can be seen, therefore, that the financial consequences of a disability can be substantial. In some ways, disability can be even more financially debilitating on the family than death. With disability, not only does the income of the wage earner typically cease—as with death—but he or she continues to incur expenses—unlike the situation with death. Figure 7-3 illustrates this important financial planning concept. Adequate medical expense insurance should truncate the rise in expenses and adequate disability income (and perhaps LTC) insurance would do the same for the income stream.

Overview of Disability Income Policies

Disability income policies are designed to provide monthly benefits to replace lost income when the insured is disabled as the result of sickness or injury. Most disability income insurance is issued on a group basis, with a substantial portion issued to individuals.

Policies sold to individuals typically are issued on a guaranteed renewable or noncancelable basis. The definition of *guaranteed renewable* mentioned earlier in connection with LTC policies applies equally to disability income policies. A *noncancelable* policy is one in which the insurer cannot (1) cancel the policy, (2) refuse to renew it, or (3) unilaterally change the premium charged during the term of the policy.

The primary individual policy benefits usually are clustered together in the contract under a prominent heading, and any supplemental or optional benefits appear in rider forms attached to the policy. Many companies' systems integrate basic and optional coverages within a computer-printed policy that eliminates the need for riders.

The basic benefit arrangement in the policies of the major insurers consists of a monthly benefit for total disability and a waiver of premium benefit. Supplemental coverages may include a monthly benefit for residual or partial disability; a monthly benefit paid when certain social insurance programs fail to provide benefits; a cost of living benefit; and a guarantee for purchase of additional insurance at a later date. These provisions are augmented by a policy schedule that summarizes the available benefits and by a series of technical definitions that control and limit the way in which benefits are paid.

The policy schedule shows a summary of the principal policy benefits, including any supplemental coverages, and it usually appears immediately after the policy cover page. The schedule shows the effective date of insurance, identifies the insured, and displays the benefit amounts and the premiums charged for them.

Of all insurance lines, disability income policies are the least amenable to generalized analysis and comparison. Such contracts are designed to permit flexible adaptation to the individual needs of the insured through a broad range of interrelated benefit pat-

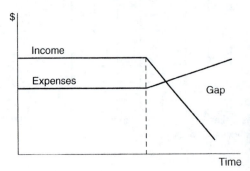

FIGURE 7-3 Effect of Total Disability on Income and Expenses.

terns and optional coverages. Probably no other type of insurance relies as heavily on subtle distinctions in benefits and the language used to describe them.

Contract design and language differ from insurer to insurer and, often, from policy to policy within the same company. Intense competitive pressures force insurers to find that unique provision or that more precise definition that will distinguish their policies in the marketplace. Companies constantly change contracts as they restate old concepts in new ways and introduce innovative coverages for the disability risk. Nonetheless, there are basic criteria to be used for thoughtful analysis and evaluation of all individual health insurance contracts.

Important Definitions

The technical definitions may be included in the benefit provisions, but more typically they form a separate part of the policy intended to define terms that are used to evaluate the claim and control payment of benefits. Among the most important of these are the definitions of injury, sickness, preexisting conditions, and disability.

The major North American insurance companies uniformly define injury to mean **accidental bodily injury** that occurs while the policy is in force. This definition employs "results" language and has replaced an older provision that was known as an "accidental means" clause. The distinction between the two definitions is important, as not all accidental bodily injuries result from accidental means.

Under the **accidental means** clause, a bodily injury must meet two tests to be a covered loss: Both the cause of the injury and the result (the injury itself) must be unforeseen or unexpected. For example, a person who deliberately jumps from a wall and breaks his or her leg would not have a covered loss under the accidental means clause. Although the result—a broken leg—was unexpected, the cause—a voluntary leap—was not. On the other hand, loss would be covered under the accidental bodily injury definition, as the broken leg was an unexpected result even though the precipitating act was intentional. Most U.S. jurisdictions now prohibit use of the accidental means clause in health insurance contracts.

Most insurers define **sickness** to mean sickness or disease that first manifests itself while the policy is in force. Some insurers use a modification of the "first manifest language" so that sickness means a sickness or disease that is first diagnosed and treated while the policy is in force. In either case, the intention is to cover only sickness that is first contracted after the policy takes effect.

Use of the preexisting condition limitation is customary in policies that contain a first-manifest or first-diagnosed definition of sickness. The *preexisting condition* limitation applies in the first two policy years to exclude benefits for any loss that results from a medical condition that the insured misrepresented or failed to disclose in the insurance application. The limitation varies from jurisdiction to jurisdiction, but the following is typical for the North American markets:

> Preexisting condition means a medical condition which exists on the Effective Date and during the past five years either:
> 1. caused you to receive medical advice or treatment; or
> 2. caused symptoms for which an ordinarily prudent person would seek medical advice or treatment.

Defining Disability

Traditionally, individual disability income policies have been called loss-of-time insurance because of the occupational definitions used to qualify the insured as disabled. A disabled person under these types of policies is presumed to have suffered a loss of income because he or she cannot work. The definitions of total disability and partial disability are premised on the inability of the insured to perform certain occupational tasks. In recent years, the concept of residual disability has largely replaced the partial disability provision as a means of paying proportionate benefits to an insured who works at reduced earnings as a result of sickness or injury. The residual concept differs from conventional indemnity plans, because it emphasizes protection of income rather than protection of occupational performance.

Essentially, insurance companies define **total disability** in two different ways. One is an any gainful occupation definition, which is popularly, if somewhat inaccurately, called "any occ." The other is an own occupation definition, which is usually referred to as "own occ."

An **own occupation** clause deems insureds to be totally disabled when they cannot perform the major duties of their regular occupations. A regular occupation is the one in which the insured was engaged at the time disability began. Under this definition, insureds can be at work in some other capacity and still be entitled to policy benefits if they cannot perform the important tasks of their own occupations in the usual way.

Under an **any gainful occupation** clause, insureds are considered totally disabled when they cannot perform the major duties of any gainful occupation for which they are reasonably suited because of education, training, or experience. Because the insured may be able to work at any of several suitable occupations, even though he or she is incapable of working at his or her regular job, this clause is a more restrictive definition of disability than the own occupation definition. It can limit recovery of benefits under the policy.

Many insurers in the past further defined regular occupation as the recognized specialty (or recognized subspecialty) in which a medical, dental, legal, or accounting professional was engaged at the time disability began—for example, an orthopedic surgeon will be totally disabled, even while at work in a general medical practice, as long as he or she cannot perform the customary duties associated with orthopedic surgery. This practice has diminished as insurers experienced severe moral hazard problems with this generous benefit provision.

The most common variation of the own occupation definition is the one that deems insureds to be totally disabled as long as they (1) cannot perform the major duties of their regular occupation and (2) are not at work in any other occupation. If insureds are disabled for their regular job, the insurance company can terminate disability benefits only if they voluntarily have chosen to work at some other job. If this provision is used, the company cannot insist that insureds resume work in some other suitable occupation.

Many disability insurers combine both occupation clauses in the same policy form, to provide an own occupation definition for a specified period of time and an any occupation definition thereafter. The specified period will vary between two and ten years in the policies of the major insurers. Many insurers allow own occupation coverage to age 65 for their most favorable classes of insureds, although recent trends are quite restrictive in the use of this liberal definition.

The following example is taken from a leading insurer's loss of time policy, which is available to its next-to-most-favorable rating class:

Total Disability, before age 55 or before benefits have been paid for five years for a period of disability, whichever is later, means that due to Injuries or Sickness:
  1. you are unable to perform the duties of your occupation; and
  2. you are under the care and attendance of a physician.

After you attain age 55 or after benefits have been paid for five years for a period of disability, whichever is later, Total Disability means that due to Injuries or Sickness:

1. you are unable to engage in any gainful occupation in which you might reasonably be expected to engage because of education, training, or experience, with due regard to your vocation and earnings at the start of disability; and
2. you are under the care and attendance of a physician.

Almost all insurers specify in the definition of disability or in a separate policy provision that an insured must be under the care and attendance of a physician to qualify for disability benefits. Most insurers do not interpret the medical care requirement literally, because common sense and various court decisions dictate that an insurer cannot deny benefits under this provision if medical care is not essential to the disabled insured's well-being or recovery. The insurer cannot insist that an insured maintain a physician-patient relationship for the sole purpose of certifying a disability.

It is common to include a definition of presumptive disability in policies that provide benefits for total disability. Under the **presumptive disability** clause, an insured is always considered totally disabled, even if he or she is at work, if sickness or injury results in the loss of the sight of both eyes, the hearing of both ears, the power of speech, or the use of any two limbs. Usually, the insurer begins benefits immediately upon the date of loss and waives the medical care requirement. The insured can work in any occupation and full benefits will be paid to the end of the policy's benefit period, while the loss continues.

Basic Components of the Benefit Provision

Three basic components establish the premium and define the payment of benefits under disability income policies: (1) the elimination period, (2) the benefit period, and (3) the amount of monthly indemnity. All other parts of the policy relate to these common elements and are used to limit or expand their value in meeting the specific needs of insureds at the time of loss. The strength of a particular disability income plan lies in how liberally the insurance company permits these elements to operate within the policy provisions and through its own administrative practices.

The Elimination Period

The *elimination period,* sometimes called the *waiting period,* refers to the number of days at the start of disability during which no benefits are paid. It is a limitation on benefits that is somewhat like a deductible in medical expense and property insurance policies. It is meant to exclude the inconsequential illness or injury that disables the insured for only a few days and that is more economically met from personal funds.

In general, insurers make available elimination periods of from 30 days to one year, with three months being common. Because indemnities of the policy are paid at the end of each month of continuing disability, a three-month elimination period usually means that a disabled insured will not receive benefits for at least 120 days from the time sickness began or injury occurred. Premiums are lower for policies with longer elimination periods. Most insurers require that the elimination period be the same for sickness and injury. Figure 7-4 shows how one insurer's premiums vary with different elimination periods.

The major insurers allow for a temporary break in the elimination period so that the insured will not be penalized for any brief attempt to return to work before the elimination period has expired at the start of disability. The brief recovery generally is limited to six months or, if less, to the length of the elimination period. If the insured is then again disabled because of the same or a different cause after the interruption, the insurer combines the two periods of disability to satisfy the elimination period.

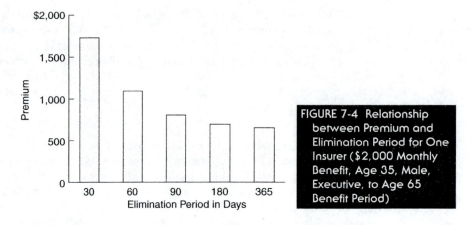

FIGURE 7-4 Relationship between Premium and Elimination Period for One Insurer ($2,000 Monthly Benefit, Age 35, Male, Executive, to Age 65 Benefit Period)

The Benefit Period

The *benefit period* is the longest period of time for which benefits will be paid under the disability policy. Usually, the benefit period is the same for sickness and injury and is available for durations of two or five years, to age 65, and for life provided continuous, total disability begins before age 55, age 60, or (less commonly) age 65.

Most disabilities are of short duration. Roughly 98 percent of all disabled persons recover before one year has elapsed, and most disabled individuals recover within six months of the time disability began. On the other hand, if disability lasts beyond 12 months, chances of a return to productive work diminish markedly, particularly at older ages. The effect of extended disability can be financially devastating. Long benefit periods are more consistent with sound personal risk management principles. Of course, the longer the benefit period, the higher the premium, other things being equal. Figure 7-5 shows how one insurer's premiums vary with the length of the benefit period chosen.

All insurers include a provision that is related to the benefit period and that deals with consecutive or recurrent episodes of disability and identifies whether the company is dealing with a new or continuing claim. The typical provision states that the company will consider **recurrent periods of disability** from the same cause to be one continuous period of disability, unless each period is separated by a recovery of six months or more.

Among the major insurers, use of a 12-month recurrent provision is common in policies with benefit periods to age 65 or longer. The provision is to an insured's advantage

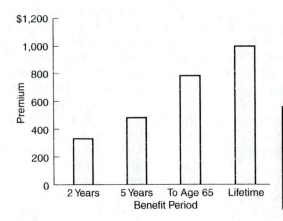

FIGURE 7-5 Relationship between Premium and Benefit Period for One Insurer ($2,000 Monthly Benefit, Age 35, Male, Executive, 90-Day Elimination Period)

because a new elimination period will not be required for disability that recurs more than six months, but less than a year, after a brief recovery in a long-term claim.

This recurrence language protects the insured from multiple elimination periods, so that benefits for recurring loss due to the same cause become payable immediately for the unused portion of the original benefit period. Conversely, the provision allows for a new benefit period, and a new elimination period, if loss results from a different cause at any time after an earlier disability, or if loss recurs due to the same cause more than six months after recovery.

The Benefit Amount

The benefit of the personal disability income policy is almost always payable as a fixed amount of **monthly indemnity.** The indemnity for total disability generally is written on a *valued basis,* which means that the stated policy benefit is presumed to equal the actual monetary loss sustained by the disabled insured. This amount is not adjusted to the insured's earnings or other insurance payments at the time of claim for total or partial disability. During a period of residual disability, however, indemnity may be reduced in proportion to lost earnings of the insured (discussed later).

Insurers limit the amount of disability income coverage they will sell to an applicant so that the total of all monthly indemnity does not exceed about 85 percent of earned income for insureds with low annual incomes, and grading downward to about 65 percent or less for those in the highest income brackets. These limits take into account other compensation that may be available to the disabled insured (e.g., employer sick-pay plans, government programs, and other personal or group insurance). Insurers may also reduce these limits for individuals with significant unearned income or for those whose net worth exceeds $3 million.

These limits are intended to minimize the creation of moral hazard in the form of overinsurance, which occurs when benefits equal or exceed a disabled insured's predisability income. Insurers agree that overinsurance provides little incentive for a disabled insured to return to work, and, as a result, recovery often is delayed or does not occur at all. Existing insurance laws in the United States do not provide an effective mechanism for controlling overinsurance at point of claim, so companies must rely almost entirely on issue limits at the time of underwriting in an effort to minimize moral hazard.

Nevertheless, under the regular limits of the leading disability writers for personal insurance, an insured with adequate income in the more favorable risk classifications may acquire up to a maximum of $15,000 to $20,000 in monthly indemnity for total disability. This amount generally is separate from indemnity limits established for special business insurance policies, such as overhead expense insurance.

Basic Benefit Arrangements

The basic benefit arrangement of disability income policies consist of the benefit for total disability and a benefit for waiver of premium. These two components are common to all insurers, regardless of any additional coverages that may be included directly in the policy form. The benefit provision usually describes the circumstances of loss, the way in which the company will pay benefits, and at what point benefits may end.

Total Disability Benefit

The following is typical of the benefit provision for total disability:

When you are totally disabled, we will pay the monthly indemnity as follows:
- You must become totally disabled while this policy is in force.
- You must remain so to the end of the elimination period. No indemnity is payable during that period.

- After that, monthly indemnity will be payable at the end of each month while you are totally disabled.
- Monthly indemnity will stop at the end of the benefit period or, if earlier, on the date you are no longer totally disabled.

Waiver-of-Premium Benefit

The waiver-of-premium benefit under disability income policies characteristically waives (i.e., excuses) any premiums that fall due after the insured has been totally disabled for the shorter of 90 consecutive days or the elimination period, and it allows for refund of any premiums paid during this period. Further premiums are waived while the insured remains disabled, until age 65. Some insurers also waive premiums that fall due within 90 days after recovery. The waiver-of-premium feature invariably terminates when the insured attains age 65.

Other Benefits

The basic provision often contains a number of minor but competitively necessary provisions that are not appropriate as optional benefit riders because they do not carry a significant premium consideration. These supplemental benefit provisions include a transplant benefit, a rehabilitation benefit, a nondisabling injury benefit, and a principal (capital) sum benefit.

The *transplant benefit* provides that, if the insured is totally disabled because of the transplant of an organ from his or her body to the body of another individual, the insurer will deem him or her to be disabled as a result of sickness. This provision also includes cosmetic surgery performed to correct appearance or a disfigurement.

The **rehabilitation benefit** generally allows a specific sum, often 12 times the sum of the monthly indemnity and any supplemental indemnities, to cover costs not paid by other insurance or public funding when the insured enrolls in a formal retraining program that will help him or her return to work.

The **nondisabling injury benefit** pays up to a specific sum, usually one-quarter of the monthly indemnity, to reimburse the insured for medical expenses incurred for treatment of an injury that did not result in total disability.

The **principal sum benefit** is a lump-sum amount payable if the insured dies accidentally. This provision requires that death be caused directly and independently by injury and that it occur within a specified number of days, usually 90 or 180, following the date of the accident.

The principal sum amount benefit also pays a single sum, usually 12 times the sum of the monthly indemnity and any supplemental indemnities, if sickness or injury results in dismemberment or loss of sight and the insured survives the loss for 30 days. The lump sum is in addition to any other indemnity payable under the policy, and it is payable for two such losses in the insured's lifetime. The principal sum benefit usually is limited to the irrecoverable loss of the sight of one eye or the complete loss of a hand or foot through severance above the wrist or ankle.

Supplemental Benefits

Among the leading insurers, the most common optional or supplemental benefits are: (1) a residual disability benefit, (2) a partial disability benefit, (3) a social insurance supplement, (4) an inflation-protection benefit, and (5) provisions for increased future benefit amounts. Although some insurers may include one or more of these benefits in the basic benefit provision, they are more frequently available for an additional premium as optional benefit riders that are attached to the policy. The benefits and the premiums of each optional rider generally are shown on the schedule page.

Residual Disability Benefit

The **residual disability benefit** provides reduced monthly indemnity in proportion to the insured's loss of income when he or she has returned to work at reduced earnings. In policies that provide for a own occupational definition of total disability, the residual benefit is payable only when the insured has returned to work in his or her own occupation. Most insurers allow the insured to be either totally or residually disabled to satisfy the elimination period of the policy and to qualify for waiver of premium.

The most common definition of residual disability employs a time-and-duties test that combines both occupational and income considerations, as follows:

Residual disability means that due to Injuries or Sickness:
1. you are not able to do one or more of your important daily business duties or you are not able to do your usual daily business duties for as much time as it would normally take for you to do them;
2. your Loss of Monthly Income is at least 25 percent of your Prior Monthly Income; and
3. you are under the care and attendance of a physician.

An alternative definition of residual disability is referred to as a pure income test and rests solely on loss of earnings:

Residual disability means that you are engaged in your regular occupation and your Income is reduced due to Accident or Sickness by at least 20 percent of your Prior Income.

The specialty definition of total disability may also be used during residual disability, to avoid ambiguity in the event the insured is deemed totally disabled for his or her professional specialty but is at work and earning reduced income in a general practice. These definitions are commonly restricted to regular occupations to avoid ambiguity when total disability is based on the own occupation provision.

Most insurers do not require that an insured sustain a prior period of total disability before claiming residual benefits. In effect, a residual claim can begin on the incurrence date, and reduced indemnity is payable at the end of the elimination period for the duration of the benefit period. From a practical standpoint, the vast majority of residual claims follow some period of total disability. Residual claims make up only a small portion of all disability claims, whether from incurrence date or as continuation following prior total disability.

The provisions for residual disability resemble those used for total disability, but they are accompanied by a series of technical definitions in order to define prior and current income and to describe the formula employed to compute the proportionate benefits. The customary formula is:

$$\text{Residual Indemnity} = \frac{\text{Loss of Income}}{\text{Prior Income}} \times \text{Monthly Indemnity Benefit}$$

In this formula, *loss of income* means the difference between the insured's prior income and current income. Usually, loss of income in excess of 75 to 80 percent of prior income is considered to be 100 percent loss. In all cases, income refers only to earned income and excludes unearned income from savings, investments, or real property.

Prior income is usually defined as the average monthly income for the tax year, with the highest earnings in the two or three years immediately before the date on which the insured became disabled. Most insurers index prior income at the end of each year of claim to adjust for increases in the cost of living.

Current income means the insured's earned income in each month while he or she is residually disabled. Insurers differ in their treatment of current income, but they calculate it either on the basis of cash actually received or on an accrual method to exclude income that was earned but not collected before disability began.

For example, assume that Jerry, who is residually disabled, is receiving current income of $1,000 per month, but that he had a prior income of $3,000 per month. Assume also that the monthly indemnity is $2,000. Jerry could collect $1,333 under the residual benefit, which is calculated as follows:

$$\text{Residual Indemnity} = \frac{\$3,000 - \$1,000}{\$3,000} \times \$2,000 = \$1,333$$

Some insurers apply the residual benefit formula strictly throughout the benefit period. Several insurers use the exact rate of current income to compute benefits for the first six months of payment and then average current income at six-month intervals for the remainder of the claim. Other insurers guarantee a minimum benefit during the first six months of a residual claim by providing the greater of the residual indemnity from the formula or 50 percent of the monthly indemnity for total disability. The residual benefit is payable for the duration of the policy benefit period or until loss of income is less than 20 or 25 percent of prior income. Insurers usually do not renew residual disability provisions after the insured attains age 65.

Partial Disability Benefit

The residual concept generally has replaced the partial disability benefit for most professional and white-collar occupations. Many insurers, however, provide a partial disability provision as an optional benefit for their less favorable occupational risks. The typical **partial disability benefit** is 50 percent of the monthly indemnity for total disability and is payable for up to six months or, if less, for the remainder of the policy benefit period when the insured has returned to work on a limited basis after a period of compensable total disability. Partial disability customarily is defined in occupational terms with reference to time and duties. The following is typical of this definition:

Partial disability means that you are at work, but because of sickness or injury:
1. you are unable to perform one or more, but not all of the major duties of your occupation; or,
2. you are not able to be present at work for more than one-half of the time required in your usual work week.

Social Insurance Supplement

The **social insurance supplement** (SIS) or **social insurance substitute** evolved as a response to the underwriting problem that is created by the existence of substantial benefits potentially available for disability under workers' compensation or for disability or retirement under the U.S. Social Security Act. Most insurance companies take these substantial benefits into account and, to minimize moral hazard at a later time, sharply limit the amount of conventional disability income insurance that will be issued to applicants with incomes below $35,000, particularly those in their less favorable occupational classes.

However, the insured may not always qualify for the anticipated benefits of the social insurance plans. He or she may suffer a loss that is not covered by workers' compensation or that does not meet the highly restrictive definitions for total and permanent disability under Social Security. If the insurance company has limited the amount of personal insurance, the individual will be underinsured each month by several hundred dollars or more.

The SIS benefit was developed to meet this potential coverage gap. The supplemental benefit provides an amount of monthly indemnity that approximates the amount the insured might reasonably expect to receive from Social Security for total disability. The SIS benefit is paid when the insured meets the policy's definition for total disability but is not receiving benefits from any social service plan. It is payable as a fixed amount of indemnity that ceases when the insured begins to receive any income from a social insurance plan or it may be reduced by a dollar-for-dollar offset of the benefit actually paid under the social insurance plan. If the offset method is used, the insurer usually specifies a minimum amount below which the SIS benefit will not be reduced while total disability continues.

Inflation Protection Benefits

The *cost-of-living-adjustment* (COLA) benefit under disability income policies provides for adjustments of benefits each year during a long-term claim so as to reflect changes in the cost of living from the time that the claim began. Adjustments are computed by the rate of change shown in some price index, such as the U.S. consumer price index. At one time, insurers marketed COLA riders offering fixed-percentage increases. This practice resulted in some benefits outpacing the rate of inflation and led to moral hazard problems.

The method of adjustment is relatively complex, but generally it calls for a comparison of the index for the current claim year with the index for the year in which the claim began. If the index increased or decreased since the start of the claim, benefits for the next 12 months are adjusted by the percentage change in the index. The percentage change is limited to a specified rate of inflation, generally ranging between 5 and 10 percent compounded annually.

The adjusted policy benefits may increase or decrease each year as the index rises or falls, but the benefits cannot be reduced below the level specified in the policy on the date of issue. Some insurers apply a cap to limit increased benefits to a maximum of two or three times the original indemnities. Others place no limit on the maximum increase of adjusted benefits before the insured is age 65.

Provisions for Increased Future Benefit Amounts

Two supplemental provisions allow increases in future benefit amounts: the automatic increase benefit and the guarantee of future insurability. *Automatic increase benefit* provisions provide for scheduled increases in the monthly indemnity, typically in each of five consecutive years at a fixed rate of 5 or 6 percent, with annual premium increases at attained age rates for the portion of increased indemnity. The insured has the right to refuse one or more of the automatic increases during the five-year period and may, at the expiry of the schedule, apply to continue the automatic increases over another five-year period. Some insurers make this provision available without a discernible premium charge as part of the policy on the date of issue, whereas others use a premium-bearing optional benefit rider.

When the insured recovers, the adjusted benefits generally are reduced to the level of those in force on the date of issue. A few insurers allow the recovered insured to retain permanently the adjusted benefits in the last year of claim upon payment of any required premium.

The **guarantee of future insurability** or the **future increase option** allows an insured to purchase additional disability income insurance in future years without evidence of insurability. It is a put option that would be expected to be exercised with greater frequency among those whose insurability is questionable. The total increase that the insured may obtain under this benefit varies among insurers, but most often it cannot exceed twice the monthly indemnity that the insured has in force in all insurers on the original policy's date of issue.

The insured may exercise purchase options once a year, typically until age 50 or 55. The amount of additional monthly indemnity that the insured can purchase each year is subject to the company's limits for insurance in relation to earned income, and, in some insurers, it may be further limited to a specific amount, typically $500. In other insurers, the insured can purchase all or part of the total increase option on any option date before age 45. After that, increases each year may not exceed one-third of the original total.

If the insured is disabled on an option date, he or she can purchase additional monthly indemnity, but the additional amounts at times will not apply to the current claim. Future increase options among the major insurers are now payable immediately for an existing claim, if the insured is disabled on the date he or she may otherwise have exercised the purchase option. Income requirements are based on the earned income at the start of the claim, and immediate benefit payments are subject to an elimination period that begins on the date of issue of the additional insurance coverage.

Comparison of COLA, Automatic Increases, and Future Increase Guarantees

COLA adjusts benefits while the insured is on claim to account for changes in the cost of living from the start of disability, when the claim lasts at least one year. Automatic increases are designed to keep insurance benefits current with changes in earned income or financial needs as a result of modest annual salary increases or the effects of inflation while the insured is not on claim. One insurer combines the automatic increase principle and COLA into a single benefit rider so that consistent adjustments occur annually whether the insured is healthy or disabled.

Future increase guarantees are designed to adjust insurance benefits for individuals who anticipate substantial annual income growth that is above the average national rate for salary changes or who expect periodic substantial changes in income as they mature in their professional or business roles.

Questions

1. Compare and contrast individual and group health insurance coverages with respect to underwriting practices, the impact of adverse selection, administrative costs, and benefits available.
2. How is health insurance a more complicated contractual agreement than life insurance? How is individual health insurance a more complicated contractual agreement than group health insurance?
3. What is a disability and how is it commonly defined in an insurance contract? How does the insurance definition address the potential for moral hazard?
4. How have changing demographics, social customs, and medical technology affected the demand for long-term care insurance?
5. How do the following insurance coverages either complement or overlap each other?
   a. disability income insurance
   b. long-term care insurance
   c. health insurance

CHAPTER

8

ANNUITIES AND OPTIONAL BENEFITS

Objectives

- Describe the purposes and design of annuity products.

- Explain the classification of annuities by (a) number of lives, (b) method of premium payment, (c) time when income payments commence, and (d) disposition of proceeds.

- Differentiate between the various uses for annuities.

- Describe potential tax implications for annuities.

- Explain the purpose of various optional benefits and riders that exist for annuity products.

This chapter closes the five-chapter presentation on individual life and health insurance policies. Here we cover annuities as well as various optional benefits and riders that are commonly included in many of the policies discussed throughout these chapters. As with the preceding chapters in this section, our focus is on individually issued annuities and benefits, even though the majority of annuity-related income to insurers is from group annuities (see chapter 21).

ANNUITIES

Annuities are exceedingly popular as a means of personal savings in the United States and are becoming more prominent in numerous other markets worldwide. This popularity reflects the continuing aging of populations, lagging confidence in government-sponsored retirement programs, and a concomitant desire to increase savings through a tax-favored vehicle in anticipation of retirement financial needs. The chapter 3 discussion about changing demographics, especially in the OECD countries, suggests the possibility of still greater annuity demand as today's baby boom generation (those who will begin retiring around the year 2010) allocates further amounts to retirement savings.

Nature of Annuities

In the broadest sense, an *annuity* is simply a series of periodic payments. An **annuity contract,** then, is an insurance policy that promises to make a series of payments for a fixed period or over a person's lifetime. The person who receives the periodic payment under an annuity is called the **annuitant.** As mentioned in chapter 1, a *life annuity,* also called a **pure life annuity,** is an annuity whose payments are contingent upon the continued existence of one or more lives. In contrast, an **annuity certain** is an annuity whose payments are *not* contingent on the annuitant being alive. A **temporary life annuity** is a life annuity payable for a fixed period or until the death of the annuitant, whichever is earlier. A **whole life annuity** is a life annuity payable for the whole of the annuitant's life.

Purpose of Annuities

Life insurance has as its principal mission the creation of a fund. The annuity, on the contrary, has as its basic function the systematic liquidation of a fund. Of course, most annuities are also accumulation instruments, but this is the mechanism for developing the fund to be liquidated. From a legal viewpoint, therefore, a *whole life annuity* may be defined as a contract whereby for a consideration (the premium), one party (the insurer) agrees to pay the other (the annuitant) a stipulated amount (the annuity) periodically throughout life. In the absence of an explicit provision to the contrary, the understanding is that no portion of the consideration paid for the annuity need be refunded upon the annuitant's death. The purpose of the annuity is to protect against the possibility of outliving one's income—just the opposite purpose of that confronting a person who desires life insurance as protection against the loss of income through premature death.

Each payment under an annuity may be considered to represent a combination of principal and interest income and a survivorship element. Although not completely accurate, one can view the operation of an annuity as follows: If a person exactly lives out his or her life expectancy, he or she would have neither gained nor lost through utilizing an annuity contract. If a person outlives his or her life expectancy under the contract, the additional annuity payments would be derived from the funds contributed by those who failed to survive to their expectancy. Conversely, those annuitants who die before attaining their life expectancies would not have received annuity payments equal to their contributions (plus forgone interest), with the difference between that which they contributed to the insurance pool and that which they received being used to provide continuing income to those who outlive their life expectancies.

As no one knows into which category he or she will fall, the arrangement is equitable and can succeed, from the company's point of view, through the operation of the law of large numbers. In most jurisdictions, only life insurance companies are permitted to sell contracts that guarantee a life income through liquidation of both principal and interest over a person's life.

Despite the difference in function, annuities are simply another type of insurance, and both life insurance policies and annuities are based on the same fundamental principles. Pooling underlies both, and premiums in each case are computed on the basis of probabilities of death and survival as reflected by mortality tables.

Classification of Annuities

Annuities may be classified in numerous ways. We classify them, as shown schematically in Figure 8-1, based on the following:

- number of lives covered
- method of premium payment
- time when income begins
- method of disposing of proceeds
- denomination in which benefits are expressed

Number of Lives Covered   This classification involves the question of whether annuity payments are made with reference to one life or multiple lives. Perhaps most annu-

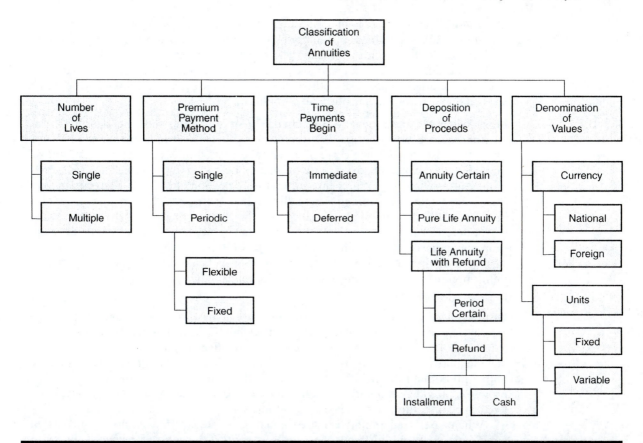

FIGURE 8-1 Basis for Annuity Classification

ities sold worldwide, including in North America, are issued on a single life. That is, payments are made with reference to one life only.

Annuities covering two or more lives are becoming more popular, especially in husband/wife situations. Thus, the **joint and last-survivor annuity** provides income payments for as long as *either* of two or more persons lives. This option is common in employer-sponsored pension plans, as discussed in chapter 21. As this annuity provides for payment until the last death, it will pay to a later date, on the average, than a single-life annuity and, therefore, is more expensive than single-life annuity forms. Stated differently, a given principal sum provides less income under a joint and last-survivor form than under a single-life annuity form at either of the two ages.

The joint and last-survivor annuity continues the same income until the death of the last survivor. A modified form provides (assuming two covered lives) that the income will be reduced following the death of the first annuitant to two-thirds or one-half of the original income. This contract is known as a **joint and two-thirds** (or **joint and one-half**) **annuity.** Naturally, for a given principal, the modified form provides more income initially because of the later reduction.

Another type of multilife annuity, known as a **joint-life annuity,** provides a specified income for two or more named persons, with the income ceasing upon the first death among the covered lives. Such contracts, although relatively inexpensive, have limited markets.

Method of Premium Payment   Annuities may be purchased with single or periodic premiums. Thus, some single-life annuities are purchased with a single payment by beneficiaries under life insurance policies who receive the policy face amount on the death of the insured. Other single-premium payments are accumulated through savings, inheritance, or other means. Most individuals choose to spread the premium payment over a specified period by paying periodic premiums.

Time When Income Payments Commence   Annuities may also be classified as to whether income payments are deferred or immediate. An **immediate annuity** is an annuity purchased with a single premium and the first annuity payment is due (almost) immediately. It would make no sense for the applicant to pay the insurer a large sum of money, just to have the insurer instantly return a portion of it, so the first annuity payment under immediate annuities actually is made one payment interval (e.g., a month or a year) from the date of purchase.

A **deferred annuity,** on the other hand, is an annuity purchased with either a single premium or periodic premiums. The first annuity benefit payment is made after the passage of more than one payment interval. The longer the deferral period, the more flexibility permitted in premium payments. Normally, many years elapse before benefit payments commence.

Disposition of Proceeds   Insurers offer a variety of options as to how annuity proceeds are distributed. The annuitant elects the option that he or she believes is most beneficial to himself or herself; thus, there is some element of adverse selection. Most insurers also include a provision in their contracts to the effect that they will provide any other annuity option that is mutually agreed upon by the insurer and the contract owner. This provision provides flexibility and helps ensure that the contract does not become obsolete or uncompetitive with the passage of time.

When a deferred annuity is issued, a maturity date typically is chosen, such as the annuitant's sixty-fifth birthday. Most insurers contact the contract owner as the maturity date approaches, offering a range of payout options. If the annuitant fails to provide instructions to the insurer, many insurers automatically begin payments under the life-annuity-with-period-certain option. Some insurers allow the cash value to continue to build with no payouts.

Some annuities provide for a so-called "refund" if the annuitant dies before a certain period has elapsed. This subject is discussed in the following section, which deals with the nature of the insurer's obligation before and after income payments commence.

Denomination of Benefits   Historically, annuity benefits have been expressed in fixed currency units, such as dollars. More recently, great interest has been shown in variable annuities (discussed later) in which annuity benefits are expressed in units of ownership in an investment fund. Of course, we also find annuity benefits expressed in various currencies, such as the Swiss franc.

Nature of Insurance Company's Obligation

An annuity can be considered as having an accumulation and a liquidation period. The **accumulation period** is that time during which annuity fund values accumulate, commonly prior to age 65. The **liquidation period** is that time during which annuity fund values are paid to annuitant(s). The annuitant is said to **enter onto the annuity** at the time the accumulation period ends and liquidation via an income option begins.

Figure 8-2 shows a hypothetical deferred annuity on which level premiums of $1,000 per year are paid throughout the accumulation period. For simplicity, we assume a constant interest credit to the annuity cash values, an admittedly unrealistic assumption. The "retirement age" is shown as separating the liquidation and accumulation periods. On

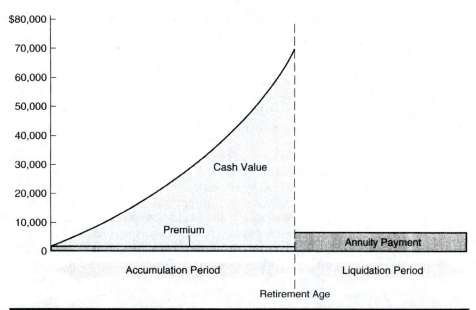

FIGURE 8-2 Illustrative Level-Premium Deferred Annuity

entering onto the annuity at retirement age, the right to the cash value vanishes, replaced by a guarantee of lifetime income. The insurers obligations differ between the accumulation and liquidation periods.

During the Accumulation Period   During the accumulation period of an annuity, the insurer is obligated to return all or a portion of the annuity cash value if the purchaser dies or voluntarily terminates the contract. Otherwise, values accumulate in accordance with contract terms. Minimum cash values are required in many jurisdictions, including all U.S. states. Many insurers provide for a separate surrender charge, as discussed later.

The operation of variable annuities during this period differs from that of traditional fixed-value annuities. As discussed later, the cash values of variable annuities fluctuate with the value of the underlying securities. In any event, the contract owner (or his or her beneficiary) is entitled to the cash surrender value on contract termination.

During the Liquidation Period   The amount of money necessary to provide a given amount and form of income beginning at a set age is the same, other things equal, irrespective of how the funds were accumulated. Consequently, the following discussion of the nature of the insurer's obligation during the liquidation period is applicable to both immediate and deferred annuities, as well as to settlement options (discussed in chapter 10). The discussion also is relevant for both fixed and variable annuities.

Annuities certain.   With annuities certain, amounts are to be paid irrespective of whether the annuitant is alive or dead. Annuities certain contain no element of mortality risk, so on the death of the annuitant, the insurer's obligations are unchanged. The annuitant may terminate the annuity during the liquidation period, often with no penalty, except as may be due because of surrender charges or adjustments in the commuted value of the annuity because of changes in the value of assets backing it (discussed later).

Pure Life Annuities.   Broadly, life insurers offer annuitants two broad classes of *life* annuity payouts: pure and refund. With the pure life annuity, income payments continue for as long as the annuitant lives but terminate on the annuitants death or, with a temporary life annuity, at the end of the designated time period, if earlier. On the death of the annuitant, no matter how soon that may occur after the commencement of income, no further amounts are payable to the annuitants estate or to any beneficiary. With this annuity, the entire purchase price is applied to provide income to the annuitant, no part of it paying for any "refund" benefit. Thus, the pure life annuity provides the maximum income for a given annuity purchase price. Because of the high probability of survival at the younger ages, the difference in income between a pure life annuity and one with a refund feature is small. At older ages, the difference can be great.

Proposed insureds for individually issued life and health insurance policies must qualify for the insurance by demonstrating that they are in good health and are otherwise insurable. Without insurability requirements, adverse selection would be a massive problem for insurers selling individual life and health policies. Those in poor health would be most likely to apply, and rates charged them would not reflect their probabilities of loss or, if they did, those in good health would tend to avoid the insurance. The underwriting process discussed in chapters 25 and 26 exists primarily to deter and detect adverse selection in individual life and health insurance, that is, to deter and detect when those with higher than average probabilities of having claims attempt to enter the insurance pool at an average (and, therefore, "unfairly low") premium rate.

Adverse selection also exists with life annuities. Those with higher than average probabilities of having claims would like to enter the risk pool at an average premium rate. However, "higher than average" losses with annuities translate into people being *healthier* than average, whereas with life and health insurance, this translates into people being less healthy. Adverse selection with life annuities means that those in superstandard physical condition will be more likely to purchase them. Individuals in poor health will automatically shy away from them.

Insurers are aware of this phenomenon and, historically, have priced annuities on the assumption that those who purchase them, as a group, will exhibit mortality superior to the population as a whole and superior to that found under life insurance policies. Experience confirms this tendency, for annuity mortality has been far superior to that under life policies and the population as a whole. An effect of this automatic pricing for adverse selection (i.e., excessive longevity) is that those who believe that their life expectancies will not be "superior" tend to avoid purchasing life annuities; just as those in good health would tend to avoid purchasing life insurance policies that had been priced assuming no underwriting (i.e., priced for adverse selection—excessive mortality).

Thus, by failing to price to risk, life insurers have deprived themselves of many potential life annuity customers and have deprived many potential customers of the opportunity to purchase "fairly" priced life annuities. This fact has limited the growth of the life annuity market and has led many contract owners to withdraw funds from annuities at the maturity date rather than allow the funds to be retained by the insurer and paid out as a life annuity.

So-called impaired health life annuities have been issued as structured settlement annuities for several years (discussed later). Until recently, however, we had witnessed little movement to offer them to the general public, although Professors Murray and Klugman had argued years ago that a market for such annuities should be developed.[1] By 1996, an insurer in the United Kingdom—known for innovativeness in insurance—began selling impaired life annuities, as had one in the United States. The U.K. annuity

---

[1]Michael L. Murray and Stuart Klugman, "Impaired Health Life Annuities," *Journal of the American Society of CLU and ChFC,* Vol. 44 (September 1990).

is underwritten for poor health; the poorer the health the higher the life annuity payout. The U.S. annuity, available only to smokers, allows them to enjoy higher annuity payouts than that typically available in the standard market. Smokers live some 7 to 10 years less than nonsmokers on average, so a fairly priced life annuity for them should be less expensive. To qualify, proposed annuitants must answer "yes" to the question of whether they have smoked an average of at least 10 cigarettes per day for the previous 10 years.

Life annuities with refund features. Regardless of questions of equity and technical soundness, most persons seem to oppose placing a substantial sum of money into a contract that promises little or no return if they should die shortly after income payments commence. Therefore, companies permit annuitants various so-called refund options if death occurs shortly after annuity payments have begun. In contrast to the situation with the pure life annuity, not all of the purchase price of refund annuities is used to provide income payments. Part of the purchase price is applied to meet the cost of guaranteeing a minimum amount of benefits, irrespective of whether the annuitant lives to receive them. Thus, for a given premium outlay, a smaller periodic income payment will be available under a refund life annuity than would be available under an otherwise identical pure life annuity. The minimum benefit guarantee or refund feature may be stated in terms of a guaranteed minimum number of payments or as a refund of the purchase price (or some portion thereof) in the event of the annuitants early death.

With all life annuities that contain a refund feature, any amounts that are payable at the time of the annuitants death can be viewed as a death benefit, the amount of which equals the refund guarantee. Technically, therefore, there is no "refund" but rather a death benefit equal to a set amount payable either as a single sum or periodically.

One class of life annuities with refund features, often named **life annuity certain and continuous** or **life annuity with installments certain,** calls for a guaranteed number of monthly (or annual) payments to be made whether the annuitant lives or dies, with payments to continue for the whole of the annuitants life if he or she should live beyond the guarantee period. Contracts are usually written with payments guaranteed for 5, 10, 15, or 20 years. Of course, the longer the guarantee period, the smaller the income payments, all else being equal.

Two important forms of annuity income promise to "return" all or a portion of the purchase price. The first form, the **installment refund annuity,** promises that, if the annuitant dies before receiving income installments equal to the purchase price, the payments will be continued to a beneficiary until this amount has been paid. The second form, the **cash refund annuity,** promises to pay in a lump-sum amount to the beneficiary the difference, if any, between the purchase price of the annuity and the simple sum of the installment payments made prior to the annuitants death. For a given purchase price, the cash refund annuity provides a somewhat smaller income than the installment refund annuity, as the insurance company loses the interest it would have earned had the balance been liquidated in installments. In both cases, payments to the annuitant continue for as long as he or she lives, even after recovery of the guaranteed minimum benefits.

All refund life annuities can be thought of in two ways. First, we can consider them as a combination of (1) an annuity certain for the length of the guarantee or installment refund period plus (2) a pure life annuity thereafter. Second, we can consider them as being a combination of (1) a pure life annuity for the entire period plus (2) term life insurance whose decreasing face amount is always just enough to provide income payments for the balance of the guarantee period or to provide the amount of the "cash refund." Figure 8-3 illustrates these two concepts, with the solid line representing an annuity certain and the dashed line representing a life annuity.

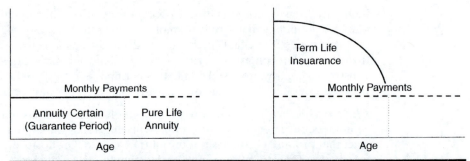

FIGURE 8-3 Two Equally Valid Ways of Considering Annuities with Refund Features

Table 8-1 provides a comparison of the income provided under some of the important forms of annuities for a given principal. The figures are shown on a guaranteed rather than a current basis and utilize the same rate basis. Variations are intended to show the impact that the form of annuity income, the age of the annuitant at the date of commencement of income, and the sex of the annuitant can have on the monthly payment available from a $1,000 principal sum.

It should be apparent from Table 8-1 that the cost of the refund feature is low at the younger ages but becomes quite expensive at the higher ages. Not until about age 60 or 65 is any appreciable difference in income lost to add a refund feature. Consequently, many financial advisors recommend against the purchase of a pure life annuity when one is below age 60 or perhaps age 65.

Of course, at the time the annuity owner is about to enter onto the annuity, he or she could elect to surrender the annuity, withdrawing its full value as a lump sum. These funds could be invested elsewhere, including into another insurers single-premium immediate annuity (SPIA). The first insurer naturally prefers to retain the funds. Some insurers provide an incentive for the owner to annuitize with them. They may offer a one-time bonus or interest rate bonus, thereby increasing the annuitized amount; some offer an annuitization rate greater than that offered under their SPIAs, and most waive surrender charges. In an effort to encourage agents to recommend annuitization, a few insurers pay commissions at annuitization.

For many customers, the preceding choices—although in some ways extensive—seem limiting. Flexibility is lost upon entering onto the annuity. A fixed, guaranteed income stream that is appropriate today may be inappropriate in the future. Of course, sound fi-

| | | **TABLE 8-1** | Immediate Life Annuity Monthly Incomes per $1,000 (Guaranteed Basis, 10 Years Certain) | | | |

Age Last Birthday	**Pure**		**10 Years Certain and Continuous**		**Cash Refund**	
	Male	*Female*	*Male*	*Female*	*Male*	*Female*
50	$ 5.00	$ 4.54	$4.91	$4.51	$4.68	$4.40
55	5.54	4.97	5.37	4.90	5.09	4.75
60	6.26	5.54	5.95	5.41	5.58	5.18
65	7.22	6.34	6.64	6.06	6.19	5.73
70	8.57	7.46	7.40	6.83	6.93	6.42
75	10.47	9.06	8.15	7.68	7.85	7.28
80	13.05	11.35	8.77	8.46	8.96	8.37

nancial planning argues that one should take these facts fully into consideration in deciding upon the liquidation option. A few insurers, however, are now experimenting with some nonconventional means of allowing annuitant flexibility during the liquidation period. For example, a few insurers will allow surrender of a life annuity during the liquidation period provided the annuitant is in good health; in other words, they are protecting themselves against adverse selection. Their annuity rates include a loading for this option.

Types of Annuity Contracts

Only a limited number of different annuity contracts actually exists, although individual insurer variations can be great. Five categories of annuities are discussed next:

- flexible-premium deferred annuity
- single-premium deferred annuity
- single-premium immediate annuity
- variable annuity
- equity-indexed annuity

We recognize that this classification is not internally consistent. Virtually all annuities technically fall within the first three categories listed previously, including variable and equity-indexed annuities. We separate out the latter two annuities for special discussion because they can take the form of any of the three categories and because of their great importance in the annuity markets in North America.

Flexible-Premium Deferred Annuity

Overview The **flexible-premium deferred annuity** (FPDA), one of the most popular individual annuity contracts, permits the contract owner to pay premiums at whatever time and in whatever amount he or she wishes, subject to insurer minimums. It provides for the cash value to be applied at some future time designated by the contract owner to supply an income, if elected, for the annuitant.

Within the United States, Canada, and many other countries, interest credited on the cash values of personally owned annuities is not taxable to the contract owner as long as it remains on deposit with the insurance company. On liquidation, annuity payments are taxable as ordinary income to the extent that each payment represents previously untaxed income. Obviously, the tax-deferred nature of cash accumulations under such annuities represents a significant privilege that is justified as an instrument for encouraging individuals to provide for their retirement needs. As discussed in chapter 13, tax laws impose certain restrictions on annuity withdrawals prior to retirement to ensure that this privilege is not abused.

FPDA contracts permit flexible contributions to be made as and when the owner desires, either monthly, yearly, or, with most companies, as often or as infrequently as the owner desires. There is no set contribution amount or required payment frequency. Although a premium payment is not generally required each year for FPDA contracts, companies usually establish a minimum acceptable payment level (e.g., $25 to $50) if a payment is to be made, and also encourage owners to establish target payment plans.

Within the United States, FPDA contracts have effectively supplanted an earlier product known as the **retirement annuity contract,** which provides for a set schedule of fixed periodic premiums. The product usually is not unbundled, so that its internal functioning is not transparent.

Cash Surrender Values Keen competition for consumer savings among life insurers and between life insurers and other financial institutions continues to result in better-value FPDA contracts. The trend is toward FPDA contracts with little or no front-end loads. Rather, most insurers use a back-end load or *surrender charge* on policy termination, as with some of the cash-value life insurance products discussed earlier. Most contracts permit a *free withdrawal corridor,* meaning that no surrender charge will be assessed on partial surrenders, such as those of less than 10 percent of the cash value.

The surrender charge is usually stated as a percentage of the total accumulation value and commonly decreases with duration. Thus, an insurer may assess a surrender charge of 7 percent on all withdrawals in excess of 10 percent of the fund balance during the first contract year, with this rate decreasing 1 percent per year, thereby grading to zero in the eighth contract year. No surrender charge would be applied thereafter. Surrender charge percentages and durations vary considerably; some first-year charges are as high as 20 percent, but most are within the 5 to 10 percent range. A few policies do not have identifiable back-end or front-end loads.

Interest Rates   FPDA contracts typically guarantee a minimum interest rate, which is often within the 3.0 to 4.5 percent range, depending on economic conditions at the time of issuance. Although this rate may seem low, it must be recognized that the guarantee could easily span three, four, or more decades and, therefore, could prove to be exceedingly valuable. For its part, the insurer would be foolish to guarantee high rates of such long durations. In any event, this type of long-term guarantee is only rarely found in other comparable savings media such as those offered by banks, savings associations, or money management accounts. Box 8-1 offers some cautions about annuity interest rates and other aspects of purchase.

The actual rate of interest credited to the FPDA cash value will be a function of the earnings rate of the insurer and its desired competitive position within the financial services marketplace. Some insurers utilize a **bonus rate** approach wherein first-year considerations receive an extra 1 percent or so over the expected renewal interest rate. All rates are subject to revision by the insurer, although most companies guarantee the current rate for at least the first contract year.

A few insurers are developing equity-indexed FPDAs whose interest rate vary with some underlying securities index (discussed later). Also, note should be taken that the majority of variable annuities (discussed later) are technically FPDAs.

BOX 8-1

CONSIDERATIONS IN PURCHASING A DEFERRED ANNUITY

The purchaser of a deferred annuity can place undue emphasis on the stated current interest rate. Loading charges can be important. Thus, an FPDA crediting 8.5 percent may not develop values as high as one crediting 8.0 percent because of loadings. In any event, prudence should be exercised in interpreting results that show high interest rates (by historical standards) projected for many years or even decades into the future. The wise course of action would suggest examining the insurers past product performance record in an effort to develop a degree of confidence in the illustrated future values.

In some instances, an annuity that performs well during the accumulation phase may not offer equally attractive performance during the liquidation phase, or vice versa. Clearly, the buyer strives to have the best of both situations. Yet the rates used to convert accumulated fund values to monthly payments can vary substantially. For example, one study found that monthly annuity lifetime payments varied between $1,080 and $781 for a male, aged 65, whose cash value was $100,000.

Illustration Table 8-2 illustrates the operation of a hypothetical FPDA during the accumulation phase. This annuity credits 8 percent on the full premium payment—that is, it has no front-end load. It provides for a graded surrender charge of 7 percent in the first year, with a 1 percent per year decrease thereafter. The illustration shows both guaranteed (at 4 percent) and nonguaranteed projected values and the difference between the cash surrender value and the cash value. A variable premium pattern is assumed. Note that the cash values and cash *surrender* values are the same as from the eighth contract year.

The retirement income amount provided by an FPDA is a function of the accumulated cash value, the annuitants sex (where permitted), and the age at which the contract owner elects to have payments commence. The usual range of benefit payout options is available, with each providing both a guaranteed minimum interest rate and a current rate.

Single-Premium Deferred Annuity

Overview The name of the **single-premium deferred annuity** (SPDA) is truly descriptive, as it is a *deferred annuity* contract purchased with a *single premium*. As with the FPDA, a minimum stated rate of interest is guaranteed for the duration of the contract, but most insurers credit competitive market rates. The rate actually credited is a function of the insurers current investment earnings rate and its desired competitive posture in the market, and it is subject to change by the insurer, just as with the FPDA. The current rate may be guaranteed for a single year or for as many as three or more years. Generally, the longer the guarantee period, the lower the rate. Many insurers follow a tiered

TABLE 8-2 Hypothetical Flexible-Premium Deferred Annuity Accumulations

Contract Year	Premium Payment	Year-End Cash Values Based on: Guaranteed Rate (4%)	Current Rate (8%)	Year-End Cash Surrender Values Based on: Guaranteed Rate (4%)	Current Rate (8%)
1	$ 2,000	$ 2,080	$ 2,160	$ 1,934	$ 2,009
2	2,000	4,243	4,493	3,989	4,223
3	1,000	5,453	5,932	5,180	5,636
4	1,000	6,711	7,487	6,443	7,187
5	500	7,499	8,626	7,275	8,367
6	0	7,799	9,316	7,643	9,129
7	0	8,111	10,061	8,030	9,960
8	0	8,436	10,866	8,436	10,866
9	10,000	19,173	22,535	19,173	22,535
10	5,000	25,140	29,738	25,140	29,738
11	0	26,146	32,117	26,146	32,117
12	0	27,192	34,686	27,192	34,686
13	300	28,591	37,785	28,591	37,785
14	493	30,248	41,341	30,248	41,341
15	0	31,458	44,648	31,458	44,648
16	2,000	34,796	50,380	34,796	50,380
17	0	36,188	54,410	36,188	54,410
18	5,000	42,835	64,163	42,835	64,163
19	8,000	52,869	77,936	52,869	77,936
20	15,000	70,583	100,371	70,583	100,371

rate approach wherein the first tier of funds received (e.g., $25,000) is credited with one interest rate, and funds received in excess of this tier are credited with a somewhat higher rate (e.g., 0.25 percent higher). Some companies have as many as four tiers, each of which attracts a higher rate.

The single premium is often unreduced by identifiable front-end loads. Provision is usually made for graded surrender charges, similar to those for the FPDA, and for withdrawal corridors with no surrender charges. SPDA contracts often have **bailout provisions** that stipulate that if the interest rate actually credited to the SPDA cash value falls below a set rate (often set at 1 to 3 percent below the current rate being credited), the contract owner may surrender without incurring any surrender charge. This provision is valuable, but any such withdrawal could result in a tax surcharge, as discussed in chapter 13. Also, if the insurer felt compelled to so reduce its credited interest rate, this probably would occur because overall market interest rates had fallen significantly. Therefore, it might prove difficult for the contract owner to find comparable financial instruments crediting a higher rate.

We discuss two types of SPDAs here. Note should be taken, however, that the equity-indexed annuity discussed later is most commonly sold as an SPDA and that it has gained substantial interest and market share.

Market-Value Annuity   The **market-value annuity** (MVA) (also referred to as a **market-value adjusted annuity**) is a type of SPDA that permits contract owners to lock in a guaranteed interest rate over a specified maturity period, typically from three to ten years. First introduced in the United States in 1984, the MVA is increasingly included as an option with variable annuities. If kept until maturity, its tax-deferred value reaches the amount guaranteed at issue. However, unlike the situation with other fixed-value annuities, if withdrawals occur, the cash value will be subject not only to possible surrender charges but also to a market-value adjustment.

The adjustment may be positive or negative, depending on the interest rate environment at surrender. If interest rates at surrender were higher than those at time of issue, the adjustment would be negative. Conversely, if rates were lower, the adjustment would add to the cash surrender value. The adjustment is intended to reflect the changes in market values of the assets—typically bonds—backing the annuities. Thus, as interest rates rise, the market values of previously purchased bonds decline, and vice versa, all else being equal.

The theory for MVAs is that, if the actual available cash surrender value reflects this market value, the insurer, in effect, shifts much of the risk of market-value changes of assets to the contract owner. Insurers can limit their disintermediation risk (i.e., the tendency to surrender during an increasing interest rate environment) and better match the duration of assets backing the MVA with its corresponding liabilities.

The MVA is less flexible than many other annuities, but it can offer advantages to buyers. For one thing, there is the possibility of a positive adjustment. For another, the typically longer-duration guarantee can afford a greater sense of security. Also, in theory, the MVA should be able to offer higher interest credits than an equivalent-duration SPDA, as the buyer bears more risk.

Certificate of Annuity   Another SPDA variation is the **certificate of annuity** (COA), first offered in the United States in 1983, which provides for a fixed, guaranteed interest rate for a set period of time, typically three to ten years. It is similar to a bank-issued certificate of deposit, except that, as an annuity, interest earnings are tax deferred. The COA differs from other annuities in that no unscheduled withdrawals are ordinarily permitted during the guarantee period. The full cash value is available on death and annuitization.

At the end of the selected guaranteed period, the owner can renew the COA for another period or select any of the standard annuity options. Many insurers' products carry no identifiable front-end or back-end charges.

As the contract does not permit early, unscheduled withdrawals, the interest rate credited to the cash value should be quite competitive, other things being the same. The contract is appealing to individuals who are near retirement, have little prospect of needing the funds during the guarantee period, and are interested in locking in an interest rate.

The SPDA can be an important element in a retirement program. As with all insurance contracts, the contract should suit the needs of the client, and the insurer offering the product should be reliable. The comments offered in Box 8-1 apply here also.

Single-Premium Immediate Annuity

Overview A **single-premium immediate annuity** (SPIA), its name descriptive of its function, provides that payments to the annuitant commence immediately after the insurer has received a single (typically large) premium payment. SPIAs are often used by those who have large sums of money and desire to have the fund liquidated for retirement income purposes. These funds may have been accumulated through personal investments, through savings, or from a lump-sum distribution under a pension or other employer-sponsored retirement plan.

Life insurance death proceeds are often paid out in installments via an SPIA. Commonly, one envisions such installments as being paid under a life insurance policy settlement option provision that itself is an earmarked SPIA. The beneficiary's financial interest, however, may be better served by receiving the death proceeds as a lump sum, then shopping carefully for an SPIA.

Structured Settlement Annuity A contemporary use of SPIAs has evolved from liability insurers efforts to minimize their loss payouts. A **structured settlement annuity** (SSA) is an SPIA contract issued by a life insurer whereby the plaintiff (the injured party) receives periodic payments from the defendant in a personal injury lawsuit. Typically, the defendant and the plaintiff, together with their attorneys and a structured settlement specialist, negotiate a settlement package intended to compensate the plaintiff for his or her losses, including future earnings. Although most personal injury settlements consist of a lump-sum payment, a structured settlement involves periodic payments to the plaintiff. The periodic payments are funded through an SSA purchased by the defendant or the liability insurer from a life insurer that guarantees to make the agreed-upon payments, usually for the life of the injured person (or a designated beneficiary).

In pricing the SSA, the life insurer faces both an investment risk and a mortality risk, as with all annuities. Unlike the situation with most other annuities, underwriters must assist in SSA pricing. Most SSA annuitants can be expected to exhibit substandard mortality experience, as most will have suffered some injury. To be competitive, the insurer must offer the lowest possible price to the liability insurer to win the sale. The greater the assessed likelihood of an early death, the lower the insurer's offered price can be or, stated differently, the higher the benefits can be.

Reverse Annuity Mortgage A **reverse annuity mortgage** involves a (typically) elderly person entering into an agreement with a financial institution, such as a bank, under which the individual who owns a debt-free home receives a lifetime, fixed monthly income in return for gradually giving up ownership of his or her home. At the owner's death, the financial institution gains title to the property, which it can sell for a profit. Such an arrangement can be made between individuals as well. At one time, it was believed that the market for reverse annuities would be huge, but such has not proven to be the case to date.

An interesting variation has recently emerged. The homeowner obtains a loan on the security of his or her home. A portion or all of the loan proceeds is used to purchase an immediate life annuity. When the elderly person's home is sold because of death or otherwise, the loan is repaid from the sale proceeds, and the individual would have enjoyed a lifetime income from the annuity in the interim.

Variable Annuity

Overview   A **variable annuity** is an annuity contract whose cash values and benefit payments vary directly with the experience of assets designated to back the contract. Assets backing variable annuities, as with those backing variable life policies, are maintained in a *separate account,* and the variable annuity values directly reflect the accounts investment results. In contrast, the life insurer's general account assets back the earlier discussed products.

Variable annuities were first offered in the United States in 1952 by the College Retirement Equities Fund, a nonprofit insurer specializing in the educational market. However, it was not until the mid-1960s that life insurers truly can be considered as having entered the market, only after some regulatory issues were resolved.

The rationale for variable annuities is that they should offer, over the long run, protection against the debilitating effects of inflation on fixed incomes—the kind of income provided by fixed annuities. The hope is that *long-run* returns on common stocks and other investments will keep pace with inflation—a reasonable expectation if past results are a reflection of future results. As might be expected, sales of variable annuities tend to rise in rising stock markets and vice versa. Sales of fixed annuities tend to move in the opposite direction of sales of variable annuities.

Cash Surrender Values   The cash surrender value of a variable annuity is its cash value less surrender charges. Most variable annuities have minimal front-end loads but have back-end loads that grade to zero over the first 5 to 10 contract years. The surrender charges are comparable to those for fixed-value FPDAs, as discussed earlier in the chapter.

Variable annuity premiums paid to the insurance company are placed in a special variable annuity account. Each year the premiums, after deduction for expenses, are applied to purchase accumulation units in the account, the number of units depending upon the current unit value. Thus, if each unit, based on current investment results, is valued at $10, a premium of $100 after expenses will purchase 10 units the following year. If the unit value is changed, the $100 premium would purchase more or less than 10 units. This procedure continues until annuity payouts begin. (For constant premium payments, this procedure is the same as dollar cost averaging as an investment strategy.)

Under a traditional FPDA, SPDA, or other fixed-value annuity, the insurance company guarantees a minimum interest rate to be credited to the cash value during the accumulation period. In addition, a minimum annuity payout is guaranteed. Most variable annuities do not contain these interest guarantees. The contract owner typically bears the investment risk and receives the return actually earned on invested assets, less charges assessed by the insurance company, akin to those discussed in chapter 6. No minimum cash value is guaranteed.

The general accounts of insurance companies are restricted as to the kind and quality of investments they may hold. Because these investments support liabilities for products with interest guarantees, they should offer safety of principal and a predictable income stream. In contrast, comparatively few restrictions apply to separate account investments. Income, gains, and losses on separate account assets are credited to or charged against the separate account. Income, gains, and losses on the company's general account business and other separate account business have no effect on the separate account.

Funds of variable annuity contract owners are held in the separate account, and the contract owners participate fully in the investment results. Thus, in theory, the account could fall to zero.

As with the variable life policy, the variable annuity permits simultaneous investment in multiple funds. Transfers among funds are permitted, usually at no charge for up to four transfers per year. Most insurers permit transfers during both the accumulation and liquidation periods. Some insurers even permit a transfer from a variable to a fixed basis.

Minimum Death Benefit   Variable annuities typically promise a **guaranteed minimum death benefit** (GMDB), which often equals the greater of the cash value or the amount invested in the contract, if the annuity owner dies during the accumulation period. Some insurers offer a "ratchet" GMDB wherein a new minimum death benefit is established periodically or the benefit equals the premiums accumulated at a stated interest rate.

Thus, assume the owner pays a premium of $10,000 into the contract, and the cash value escalates to $12,000 over the next two years. Under the traditional GMDB, if the owner dies, his or her beneficiary receives $12,000. If, on the other hand, the cash value declines to $8,000 because of poor investment results, and the owner dies, his or her beneficiary would receive $10,000—the amount invested in the contract.

This guarantee can be important to investors who are concerned about the riskiness inherent in variable annuity investment returns. This benefit has a cost, however, in that the insurer must charge for the guarantee, thus depressing somewhat the effective yield under the policy. Also, most insurers will establish age limits or time limits beyond which the guarantee does not apply.

The feature invites adverse selection in two ways. First, variable annuity owners have an incentive to purchase multiple contracts rather than to seek the identical investments through a single contract. For example, assume that Sam invests $100,000 into a variable annuity and splits the amount between two separate accounts. Assume that one account declines in value to $40,000 while the other appreciates to $65,000. If Sam dies under this scenario, his beneficiary will be entitled to $105,000 ($40,000 + $65,000) because the account values are greater than the original investment.

Assume that Sam's twin, Richard, had purchased two annuities and contributed $50,000 to each. Assume further Richard realized investment results identical to those that Sam realized; that is, one account declined in value to $40,000, while the other increased to $65,000. If Richard dies, his heirs receive $115,000 rather than $105,000. The first annuity will pay $50,000 because the cash value is less than the investment, and the second annuity will pay $65,000 because the cash value is greater than the investment.

By undertaking all investment through a single annuity, Sam, in effect, was penalized because gains in one account can offset losses in another. By purchasing separate annuities, his twin took advantage of his superior knowledge to gain an additional death benefit.

The second way that this feature can invite adverse selection can occur because of the combination of the option to withdraw funds coupled with the wording of some contracts's death benefit promise. Assume that Sam's $100,000 investment declined in value to $71,000. The contract promises to pay *a minimum death benefit equal to the original contribution less withdrawals.* Thus, if Sam died, his heirs would, of course, receive $100,000.

What would they receive if Sam withdrew $70,000 and invested it elsewhere, leaving $1,000 in net cash value? The preceding italicized language would suggest that they should receive $30,000. In other words, he would have a $30,000 death benefit promise supported by a cash value of only $1,000. He has exercised a valuable call option to his benefit and to the insurer's detriment.

Of course, insurers are aware of these possibilities and should price these options accordingly. Alternatively, they could change the option to create less of a financial incentive for the contract owner to select against the company in this way (e.g., use proportional language with respect to withdrawals).

The contract owner may find some disincentives here also. For one, surrender charges may be large. Also, the death benefit does not qualify as life insurance under the U.S. tax code, so it would not enjoy favorable tax treatment on death, as discussed in chapter 13.

Annuity Liquidation   As with other annuities, the owner of a variable annuity may select from many optional modes of payment at time of maturity. Most select some type of life annuity, either with or without a refund feature.

At maturity, the total units accumulated in the cash-value account may be applied, according to actuarial principles and based on current valuation of a unit, to convert accumulation units to annuity units to be valued annually for the annuitants lifetime. The number of annuity units purchased is a function of the assumed interest rate. The **assumed interest rate** (AIR)—also called the **target return**—is the interest rate that, if earned uniformly throughout the liquidation period, would produce a level series of annuity benefit payments. If the separate account earns a rate higher than the AIR, payments will escalate in value. If earnings are less than the AIR, payments will decline in value. Table 8-3 shows annual annuity payments under various fund performance scenarios and assuming an AIR of 5 percent.

Thus, instead of providing for the payment each month of a fixed number of currency units, such as dollars, the variable annuity provides for the payment each month or year of the current value of a fixed number of annuity units. The amount of each payment depends on the value of the annuity unit when the payment is made. The valuation assigned to a unit depends on the investment results of the separate account. For example, if an annuitant were entitled to a payment of 100 annuity units each month (as determined upon entering onto the annuity and using the AIR), and the dollar values of annuity units for three consecutive months were $10.20, $9.90, and $10.10, the annuitant would receive an income for these months of $1,020, $990, and $1,010.

Variable annuities may be purchased on an FPDA, SPDA, or SPIA basis. In all cases, the usual range of payout options is available, and product expenses and charges are identified.

TABLE 8-3	Annual Annuity Payments under Various Performance Scenarios (5 Percent AIR, $1,000 First Payment)				
Time	*1%*	*3%*	*5%*	*7%*	*9%*
0	1,000.00	1,000.00	1,000.00	1,000.00	1,000.00
1	961.90	950.95	1,000.00	1,019.05	1,038.10
2	925.26	962.27	1,000.00	1,038.46	1,077.64
3	890.01	943.94	1,000.00	1,058.24	1,118.69
4	856.11	925.96	1,000.00	1,078.40	1,161.31
5	823.49	908.32	1,000.00	1,098.94	1,205.55
6	792.12	891.02	1,000.00	1,119.87	1,251.48
7	761.95	874.05	1,000.00	1,141.20	1,299.15
8	732.92	857.40	1,000.00	1,162.94	1,348.64
9	705.00	841.07	1,000.00	1,185.09	1,400.02

Source: Reinsurance Reporter (Fourth Quarter, 1994), p. 15.

Regulation of the Variable Annuity   As a security, variable annuities are subject to the same laws as variable life insurance, discussed in chapters 5 and 6. Thus, requirements with respect to disclosure, sales loads, registration and financial standards, and agent licensing as well as other regulations apply to variable annuities.

U.S. laws and regulations on variable annuities are not uniform, although many states have followed the procedures included in the **Model Variable Annuity Regulation** of the NAIC. This regulation provides guidelines for separate account investments and requires that variable annuity contracts state clearly the essential elements of the procedure for determining the amount of the variable benefits. Other policy standards are laid down, including a requirement for mailing annual status reports to contract owners.

Suitability of Variable Annuities   Purchasers of variable annuities should consider that they are undertaking a mutual fund–type investment within an annuity contract. Insurer separate accounts are, in effect, mutual funds and carry similar risk/reward characteristics. The buyer should appreciate this fact. Insurers today typically offer a range of investment options—sometimes from a menu of a dozen or more funds (separate accounts) and often with different investment managers. The investment managers performance record can be a useful guide to possible future performance, although it offers no guarantee of success.

Ideally, the variable annuity will permit the owner to make no-fee asset transfers among the various funds backing the annuity. This affords the buyer flexibility.

Equity-Indexed Annuity

An **equity-indexed annuity** (EIA)—also called simply **indexed annuity**—is a non-variable annuity contract whose interest crediting mechanism is tied directly to some external index, such as the Standard & Poor's 500 Index in the United States.[2] Introduced in 1995 in the United States, EIAs contain elements of both fixed-value and variable annuities but that are not found in either. First, they offer a minimum guaranteed interest rate, typically 3.0 percent. This provides a downside guarantee. Second, they offer the potential for stock-market-like gains by tying the current crediting rate to equity indexes, thus providing upside participation.

Most EIAs are issued as single-premium deferred annuities, although flexible-premium varieties are emerging. Most carry a maturity date of from five to ten years from issuance.

The upside participation generally is stated as a percentage, often called a *participation rate,* of the increase in the index from issue to maturity. A few companies subtract a spread (e.g., 200 basis points) from the increase in the index each year and credit the difference to the contract. Some companies allow contract owners who surrender before the maturity date to participate in a portion of any appreciation, but many do not.

EIAs are particularly attractive to insurers that do not offer variable annuities and to agents who are not licensed to sell variable products. As a general account-based product, it is subject to the same types of marketing and financial regulation as other fixed products. No special licensing, expense and investment management control, or disclosure requirements apply.

As might be suspected, however, the product requires sophisticated design and asset–liability management by the insurer. Design decisions revolve around:

- the choice of equity index and guarantee period
- the indexing method

---

[2]This discussion draws in part from Mel McFall, "The Low-Down on Indexed Annuities," *Reinsurance Reporter* (First Quarter, 1997), pp. 2–6.

- participation percentage or spread
- administration, especially for FPDAs
- how to deal with surrenders and partial withdrawals
- commissions

Asset–liability management, including reinsurance, can be particularly complex with EIAs. The investment to secure that guaranteed rate might be zero-coupon bonds or possibly coupon bonds, depending on cash surrender values. An index option with a strike price equal to the minimum guarantee value could cover the upside participation. It is beyond the scope of this book to delve into the details of this issue, but this introduction should provide the reader with some appreciation for the issues facing insurers with this product.

The EIA is appealing to consumers. One gains upside participation with downside protection. This appeal explains its amazing increase in popularity. Numerous insurers have designed EIAs, with the sales potential said to be enormous, especially in a low-interest environment that enjoys a rising stock market, which was the situation in the United States during the decade of the 1990s.

Simultaneously, EIAs cause some concern. For one thing, the guarantees in the contract carry a cost. For another, the owner does not participate fully in the index, as noted earlier. The great variety of ways for calculating the equity return means that consumers might easily be confused and possibly even misled.

Some have expressed the view that the products' risks and rewards might not be clearly and fully enough explained, thus possibly leading to market conduct difficulties for agents and insurers in the future. Indeed, a few insurers have designed products that qualify as variable annuities, at least in part, to have the products fall under SEC disclosure and other regulation.

Uses and Limitations of Annuities

Annuities can be useful in both the tax-qualified and nonqualified markets. The annuitant has the benefit of the investment management offered by insurers. This can be important for older persons who may desire to be freed of investment cares and management.

Annuitants would enjoy monthly incomes at retirement age that are equal to or higher than those obtainable through the customary channels of conservative investment, if they are willing to have the principal liquidated and enjoy reasonably good health. Each year, the insurer would pay to the annuitant the current income on his or her investment plus a portion of the investment itself. If the buyer exercises care in the purchase decision, the net return on his or her annuity should prove competitive with investments of comparable quality. When tax benefits are considered, the net return often will exceed those of comparable savings media. Of course, with fixed-value annuities, inflation can erode the purchasing power of the annuity payments.

The income is certain; the annuitant may spend it without fear of outliving it. In the absence of an annuity, the danger exists of spending too much or too little. With the annuity, the scale of spending is not only increased but is definite in amount.

Uses in Tax-Qualified Markets

Annuities are popular funding media for retirement plans. In many countries, including the United States, contributions to certain qualified personal retirement plans may be deducted from taxable income. These plans differ greatly, and it is beyond the scope of this section to analyze them. We introduce some of the more common U.S. plans here, with a more thorough treatment contained in chapter 21.

Annuities fund pension and profit-sharing plans qualified under the U.S. Internal Revenue Code (IRC) Section 401 for corporations and self-employed individuals. Annuities are also used with plans qualified under IRC Section 403(b). These plans, commonly referred to as **tax-sheltered annuity** (TSA) plans, are available to employees of public educational institutions and certain tax-exempt organizations. To a specified limit, plan contributions either by the employer or by the employee, through a voluntary salary reduction agreement, are excludable from the employees taxable income. Employees' rights under such plans are nonforfeitable and must be nontransferable. Withdrawals prior to age 59 ½ are subject to a 10 percent surcharge tax in addition to full income taxation.

Annuities are also used to fund **public employee deferred compensation** plans, which are qualified under IRC Section 457 and may be established for persons who perform services for states, political subdivisions of states, agencies or instrumentalities of states or their political subdivisions, and certain rural electric cooperatives.

In the United States, for tax years after 1986, individuals not participating in employer-sponsored retirement plans and those who do participate but whose annual incomes are below certain minimum levels have been able to contribute up to $2,000 of earned compensation to an **individual retirement account** (IRA). Contributions are tax deductible, and interest credited to IRAs accumulates on a tax-deferred basis.

Contributions to an IRA by individuals who do not meet the qualification requirements are not tax deductible, but the earnings are tax deferred. With the so-called **Roth IRA,** withdrawals after age 59½ are completely free of income tax provided the account has been open for at least five years. Annuities can be used to fund IRAs, although such usage may make little financial sense because one is placing a tax-preferred instrument in a tax-preferred plan—often an unwise move.

A **401(k) plan** is a profit-sharing plan established by an employer under which up to three types of contributions are permitted: employer contributions, employee contributions from after-tax income, and employee salary reduction (elective) contributions. Neither employer nor elective contributions are included in the employees taxable income. Furthermore, the employer may deduct both of these contributions from taxable income, up to a limit. Annuities can be used as 401(k) funding vehicles.

Uses in Nonqualified Markets

Each year individuals purchase thousands of annuities unrelated to employment and not qualified under any plan for deductibility of contributions. Unlike the situation with tax-qualified retirement plans, annuity owners face no contribution limitations yet enjoy tax deferral of investment income. Besides deferring tax on investment earnings, they provide contemporary investment returns. Figure 8-4 illustrates this concept.

A $1,000 per year contribution is assumed to be made to an annuity crediting 8 percent on the gross contribution (on a tax-deferred basis) and to another savings instrument earning 8 percent, but on a taxable basis. A marginal tax rate of 31 percent is assumed. The annuity fund builds to more than $122,000 in 30 years whereas the taxable fund grows to about $77,000. For a fair comparison, however, the assumption is made that the annuity value is taken as a single-sum distribution at that time, with the result that all deferred interest earnings would be subject to the 31 percent tax. (Amounts paid on a periodic basis would receive more favorable tax treatment, as discussed in chapter 13.) Even after paying almost $29,000 in taxes, the annuity purchaser would still be $17,000 ahead of the taxable investment.

Even though annuity benefits do not escape taxation entirely, the fact that taxes are deferred for several years means that the contract owner—not the government—has use of the money. The effect is that the power of compounding at before-tax rates yields a significantly larger sum than would otherwise be the case. Moreover, even if that sum were subject to immediate and full taxation later, the net result remains strongly in favor of the tax-deferred instrument.

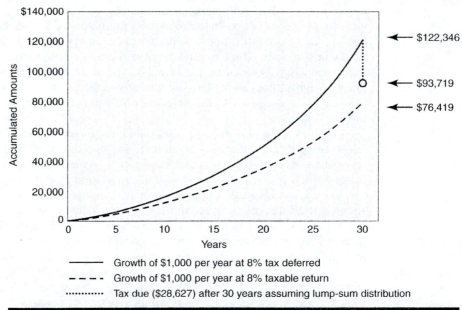

Growth of $1,000 per year at 8% tax deferred
− − − − Growth of $1,000 per year at 8% taxable return
············· Tax due ($28,627) after 30 years assuming lump-sum distribution

FIGURE 8-4 The Benefits of Tax Deferral: An Illustration

Note: Assumes 31 percent marginal tax rate.

OPTIONAL BENEFITS AND RIDERS

The practice of adding supplemental policy benefits to insurance contracts permits flexibility in adapting basic plans to individual needs. Several such common benefits are discussed next.

Disability Benefits

A common practice is to attach riders that provide certain benefits in the event of the insured's disability. The two most common disability benefits are (1) waiver of premium and (2) disability income. The definition of disability, a critically important aspect, usually is the same for both waiver of premium and disability income benefits.

Definition of Disability

Under the disability clauses in life and health insurance policies and annuity contracts, the risk covered pertains to total and permanent disability. Although phraseology varies greatly, the customary wording of the clause declares the policyowner to be entitled to the benefits promised when the insured's illness or injury results in his or her *total and permanent* disability.

As alluded to in chapter 7, the word *total* proved difficult to interpret legally. Regardless of the exact language used, the interpretation given the clause by most insurers today contemplates all cases in which, because of illness or injury, the insured is unable to pursue his or her own occupation or any job for which he or she is reasonably suited by education, training, or experience.

Similarly, some doubt revolves around the meaning of the word *permanent*. The problem, however, is usually settled by the companies themselves, in that the clause specifies that total disability lasting continuously for a stated waiting period shall be presumed to be permanent until recovery.

Waiver of Premium

The **waiver of premium** (WP), also called **premium waiver,** benefit provides that premiums (or mortality and expense charges under universal life and current assumption policies) otherwise due will be waived if the insured becomes totally and permanently disabled before a certain age, typically 65. The contract continues just as if the policyowner were paying the premiums. The waiver-of-premium benefit actually is a disability income payment in an amount exactly equal to the policy's premium (or charges) and, in effect, assigned to the insurance company. It can be seen, therefore, that the benefit does not truly *excuse* premium payments but provides a benefit that makes the payment on behalf of the insured upon his or her disability. Thus, dividends continue to be paid on participating policies, cash values continue to increase, and loans may be secured. Sometimes the price for the benefit is included in the regular premium, but often the waiver-of-premium provision is added to the life or health insurance or annuity contract for a small extra premium.

Most companies require six months of continuous disability before the waiver-of-premium benefit takes effect. As long as disability commences during the period of coverage, all premiums (or charges) are waived while it continues or as otherwise specified in the contract. Many companies provide that premiums are waived only to age 65 if disability begins after age 60 but before age 65. A disability is covered only if it begins prior to a stated age, frequently 65.

All premiums are waived during disability—not just those falling due after the waiting period. This differs from the case in disability income insurance and in most waiver-of-premium provisions in individual health insurance policies.

When incorporated within a term policy, how the WP feature interacts with the conversion feature can be important. Three different provisions are available in the market. First, some contracts provide that if the insured becomes totally disabled, premiums for the term policy will be waived, but if the policyowner wishes to exercise the conversion option during this period, the company will not waive the premiums on the newly converted cash-value policy. In other words, full premiums must be paid by the policyowner for the new policy.

Second, other companies permit the conversion and will waive premiums on the new cash-value policy. Clearly this approach is more valuable to the policyowner than the former.

Third, some companies provide for a waiver of premium on the term policy and on the new policy, but only if the conversion is delayed until the end of the period during which conversion is allowed. At that point, an automatic conversion takes place and premiums on the new policy are waived. This benefit provision falls between the two previously discussed provisions in terms of policyowner value.

Other things being equal, the more liberal the interaction of the WP and conversion features, the higher the additional premium for the WP feature should be, although actual pricing may not reflect this. This interaction can be a significant element of product evaluation.

Disability Income

In the past, many North American insurers offered a *disability income* benefit as a rider to their life insurance policies. This benefit is less commonly offered today.

These riders provide a monthly benefit upon the insured's disability. The amount of the monthly payment often equals 1 percent of the policy's face amount (i.e., $10 per month per $1,000). Many companies limit the maximum monthly income issued to some stated figure, such as $1,000, with a further limit set on the amount the company will participate in with all companies. Most insurers consider six months total disability as permanent and commence payments at the end of the sixth month. This is equivalent to a six-month elimination period with a one-month retroactive payment. Some companies impose a four-month waiting period.

Premiums on both the base policy and the disability income rider are waived during a period of covered disability. Dividends are paid as usual, the policy's death benefit is unaffected, and, in other respects, the basic life contract continues as though no disability had occurred. Should the insured recover, income payments cease and premiums are again due.

Accelerated Death Benefits

The financially debilitating effects of diseases such as AIDS, combined with continuing medical advances and increases in life expectancy, have focused individuals' attention to the possibility of incurring significant end-of-life expenses. The individual may have adequate life insurance, and the life insurance may have cash values. However, the promise to pay the face amount on the insured's death may offer little solace at a time when major expenses are being incurred. The cash surrender value could be helpful because it could serve as collateral for a policy loan, but the total loan will be limited to the policy's surrender value, which itself may be minimal in comparison to the face amount.

If the insured is expected to die within a short time period, the actuarial value of the death benefit promise under the policy will be greater than its cash value, and will be quite close to the face amount if death is expected within a matter of months. Viatical settlement firms, discussed in chapter 10, purchase life insurance policies from individuals who have been diagnosed with terminal illnesses, thereby possibly providing the individual with needed funds. Within the past few years, life insurers themselves have recognized the need to advance a portion or all of what is expected to be a death claim within a short time period. Many life insurance policies issued today allow such an acceleration of death benefits.

Accelerated Death Benefit provisions (or riders) involve the payment of all or a portion of a life insurance policy's face amount prior to the insured's death because of some specified, adverse medical condition of the insured. Such coverage, also referred to as *living insurance,* typically takes one of three forms, as discussed next.

A U.S. insurer is said to have offered the first such coverage as early as 1965. Jackson National Life is believed to be the first U.S. insurer to market the benefit successfully, in 1987, although the Prudential (United States) gets credit for making the benefit popular when, in 1990, it extended the coverage to all of its insureds at no additional cost.[3] The benefit was first introduced in South Africa in 1981 and in the United Kingdom in 1987.[4]

Terminal Illness Coverage

Many insurers offer some type of **terminal illness coverage** that provides that a specified maximum percentage (typically 25 to 50 percent) of the life policy's face amount can be paid if the insured is diagnosed as having a terminal illness. Some companies will permit acceleration of the full policy face amount. Most provisions require that the insured have a maximum of either six months or one year to live. The insurer requires satisfactory evidence that the insured suffers a terminal illness, including (1) certification by a physician, (2) hospital or nursing home records, and, possibly, (3) a medical examination (paid by the insurer).

Many companies make no explicit charge for the coverage because they believe that they can absorb the costs of prepaying a portion of what would be a certain, soon death

---

[3]Iskandar S. Hamwi and Durwood Ruegger, "Past and Present Changes in Living Policy Values," *Journal of the American Society of CLU & ChFC* (November 1994), p. 81.

[4]Ibid., p. 80.

claim anyway. However, some companies assess an administrative expense charge (e.g., up to $200) for processing the request and may reduce the amount payable to reflect lost interest. The benefit may be included in any type of policy.

Insurers typically provide for a maximum total living benefit payout (e.g., $250,000), irrespective of how large the policy's face amount may be. Also, they usually stipulate a minimum proportion (e.g., 25 percent) or amount (e.g., $25,000) that may be accelerated. A concern of many companies is that an unlimited benefit amount may create moral hazard in the form of more fraudulent claims. It is not unusual for the insurer to secure a release from all interested parties (e.g., beneficiary and assignee), not just the policyowner, to avoid any future misunderstanding.

Of course, the decision to exercise the right to accelerate a policy's payments will affect other policy benefits and values. Remaining death benefits, premiums, cash values, and dividends are reduced proportionately. Thus, if a policyowner applies to accelerate 50 percent of the policy's face amount and if the insurer finds that the insured meets the conditions for acceleration, future premiums, cash values, death benefits, and dividends will be reduced by one-half. Table 8-4 shows one insurer's accelerated death benefit illustration, assuming a 50 percent acceleration.

Catastrophic Illness Coverage

Catastrophic illness coverage provides for accelerated death benefit payments on approximately the same terms and conditions as terminal illness coverage, except that the insured must have been diagnosed as having one of several listed catastrophic illnesses. Also referred to as **dread disease coverage,** the provision typically covers stroke, heart attack, cancer, coronary artery surgery, renal failure, and similar catastrophic diseases.

TABLE 8-4 One Insurer's Accelerated Death Benefit Illustration

Relevant Policy and Other Details		
Policy Type	Ordinary Life	
Initial Face Amount	$200,000	
Policy Issue Age	45	
Policy Acceleration Age	55	
Percentage Accelerated	50 percent	
Actuarial Discount	8 percent	
Administrative Fee	$200	

Policy Illustration before Acceleration

Age	Annual Premium	Illustrated Dividends	Payment Net of Dividend	Cash Value	Death Benefits
45	$2,356	$ 0	$2,356	$ 0	$200,000
46	3,822	1,550	2,272	0	200,000
47	3,822	1,550	2,272	650	200,000
48	3,822	1,560	2,262	3,278	200,000
49	3,822	1,602	2,220	6,008	200,000
50	3,822	1,642	2,180	8,844	200,000
51	3,822	1,686	2,136	11,778	200,000
52	3,822	1,730	2,092	14,812	200,000
53	3,822	1,778	2,044	17,942	200,000
54	3,822	1,826	1,996	21,164	200,000
55	3,822	1,876	1,949	24,480	200,000

Policy Illustration after Acceleration

Age	Annual Premium	Illustrated Dividends	Payment Net of Dividend	Cash Value	Death Benefits
56	$1,911	$964	$947	$13,945	$100,000
57	1,911	989	922	15,701	100,000

Effects on Accelerated Proceeds

Accelerated Amount	$100,000
Actuarial Discount	$ (8,000)
Proceeds after Discount	$ 92,000
Administrative Fee	$ (200)
Net Payment Amount	$ 91,800

Both terminal illness and catastrophic illness coverages provide that policy death benefits are reduced on a one-for-one payout basis. Cash values are reduced on either a one-for-one basis or in proportion to the death benefit reduction. According to the NAIC **Accelerated Benefits Guideline for Life Insurance,** prospective buyers of these coverages must be given numerical illustrations that reflect the effects of an accelerated payout on the policy's death benefit, cash values, premium, and policy loans. Additionally, consumers must receive a brief description of the accelerated benefits and definitions of the conditions or occurrences triggering payment. Any separate, identifiable premium charge must be disclosed.

The NAIC and others have been concerned that such benefits, especially the catastrophic illness coverage, could be "oversold." In the 1960s and before, certain dread disease policies with limited coverage fell into regulatory disfavor because of fear-based selling tactics and numerous claim disputes. Allegations of so-called postclaim underwriting were widespread. Clearly, a weakness of these earlier policies and of this latest variation is that other illnesses can be equally devastating, yet no benefit is provided for them. The importance of an adequate health insurance program is underscored.

Long-Term Care Coverage

A third type of accelerated death benefit—*long-term care insurance*—provides that monthly benefits can be paid if the insured is confined because of a medical condition. Of course, LTC insurance is most commonly purchased as a stand-alone policy, as discussed in the preceding chapter, but some is sold as riders to life insurance policies. To qualify for payments, the confinement must be covered, any preconfinement conditions and elimination periods met, and any minimum in-force requirements satisfied. To be covered, the confinement must be medically necessary and in a qualified facility. Although provisions vary, the rider may cover skilled nursing facilities, intermediate care facilities, and custodial care facilities. Some cover home convalescent care.

Many riders are more restrictive than LTC policies and, for example, carry some type of prior confinement requirement in a hospital or other high-care facility to qualify for LTC benefits. Typically, the LTC confinement must have occurred within 30 days after discharge from the hospital (or other facility). Some riders have no prior confinement requirement.

Riders routinely provide for an elimination period. This period may be from two to six months.

Many insurers also require that the contract be in force for a minimum number of years—a so-called *in-force requirement*—before the insured is eligible to collect benefits. This period may range from three to ten years and may vary with issue age. Some contracts have no such requirement.

The monthly benefit typically equals 2 percent of the policy's face amount, subject to some monthly maximum payout and to a total maximum payout (e.g., 50 percent of the policy face amount). Some companies provide a tiered payout of, say, 2.0 percent of the first $150,000 and 0.5 percent of the excess face amount up to $1 million. Thus, a $100,000 policy produces a monthly payment of $2,000. A $500,000 policy yields a $4,750 monthly benefit.

Amounts paid as benefits reduce the total death benefit on a one-for-one basis. Although contract wording varies, the reduction typically affects both the net amount at risk and the cash value proportionately.

Accelerated death benefit coverages are fairly recent to the North American market and, therefore, it is difficult to discern trends. Clearly, however, with the increasing emphasis on insurance for its living benefits, the popularity of this class of coverage can be expected to grow.

Accidental Death Benefit

An **accidental death benefit** (sometimes called **double indemnity**) clause or rider, which may be added to most life insurance contracts, provides that double (or other multiple) of the face amount is payable if the insured dies as a result of an accident. From a financial planning standpoint, there is no reason why double or triple the policy face amount should be paid for an accidental death, as compared with death from other causes. The financial loss to the family is equally great irrespective of the cause of death. Moreover, with respect to most persons, the likelihood of accidental death is less than the likelihood of death from other causes. The clause has value, of course, and its comparatively low premium reflects the relatively low probability of loss. The small premium, coupled with the belief (erroneous for the most part) by most persons that if they die, the cause of death will be an accident, are probably the main reasons for its appeal.

Definition of Accidental Death

A typical clause includes the following definition of accidental death:

Death resulting from bodily injury effected solely through external, violent, and accidental means independently and exclusively of all other causes, with death occurring within 90 days after such injury.

The expression *accidental means* insists that both the *cause* and *result* of the death must be accidental, as discussed in the preceding chapter. The intention of this wording is to limit coverage to deaths that are purely and entirely accidental, although many U.S. courts have ascribed a more liberal interpretation to the terms.

Exclusions

Payments from certain causes of death are explicitly excluded by the accidental death benefit provision. The rather numerous exclusions in the accidental death benefit clause indicate the practical difficulties inherent in this form of coverage. Typically, deaths from the following causes are excluded:

1. certain illegal activities
2. an accident was involved but in which illness, disease, or mental infirmity was also involved
3. certain specified causes in which considerable doubt may exist about the accidental character of the death
4. war
5. aviation, except for passenger travel on scheduled airlines

Time and Age Limit

To be covered, death typically must occur within 90 days of an accident. The purpose of this restriction is to ensure that the accident is the sole cause of death. In general, the time limitations are enforced, although some serious problems can be created, with some courts holding that the 90-day requirement need not be strictly applied.

Accidental death coverage usually expires at age 65 or 70. Most insurers grade premium charges by age at issue, and a number of companies now offer multiple indemnity (two, three, or more times the face amount) coverage.

Guaranteed Insurability Option

One of the problems faced by young people just starting their careers is a combination of limited income and a growing future need for life and health insurance protection as their life cycle evolves. The **guaranteed insurability option** (GIO), also known as the

additional or **guaranteed purchase option,** permits an insured to purchase additional insurance without providing evidence of insurability. We discussed this option in connection with health insurance in the preceding chapter, so the emphasis here is on life insurance.

It was developed to permit young individuals to be certain that they would be able to purchase additional insurance as they grew older, regardless of their insurability. The usual rider gives the insured the option (in finance terms, a *call* option) of purchasing additional insurance at periodic, set intervals (e.g., three years), provided the insured has not attained a specified age, such as age 40. Special option dates may be allowed for such life events as birth or adoption of a child and marriage.

In most cases, the amount of the additional insurance is limited to a multiple of the basic policy face amount or an amount stipulated in the policy for the additional purchase option, whichever is the smaller. Insurers offer up to $100,000 or more per option date. The option requires an extra premium that is based on the company's estimate of the extra mortality that will be experienced on policies issued without evidence of insurability. The premium is payable to the last option date. The premium can be considered as the cost of insuring one's insurability.

We would reasonably expect insureds in poor health to be more likely to exercise their options than insureds who are in good health and otherwise insurable. In economic terms, the option can be viewed as an invitation to adverse selection; buyers use their superior knowledge about their insurability status to secure good deals for themselves. Stated in finance terms, the option holder is more likely to exercise the call option because the options exercise price (the premium for additional life insurance at standard rates) is less than the market price (the premium for additional life insurance at higher than standard rates).

Of course, the insurer is aware that option holders, as a group, will behave in this way. The premium for the option is supposed to be calculated to cover the expected extra mortality incurred. Also, by designing the benefit to limit the age to which and times at which the options may be exercised, the insurer is minimizing opportunities for insureds to select against the company.

For purposes of illustration, assume that the owner/insured purchases a $25,000 ordinary life policy at age 21 and that the guaranteed insurability option is included. Under this option, the company agrees to issue, on the owner/insured's request, an additional policy on his or her life at each option date. No evidence of insurability is required. To minimize adverse selection, option dates customarily occur at set ages, such as 25, 28, 31, 34, 37, and 40. Thus, if the insured desires, he or she could add as much as $150,000 additional coverage. Separate policies need not be issued when the option is included within a universal life or other flexible policy.

Although potentially beneficial, the GIO is not as flexible as one might prefer. It permits the exercise of the option at specified dates only, provides additional protection of relatively low amounts (for most companies), and requires the purchase of an additional insurance policy, with attendant policy fees and front-end loads (although many companies now permit internal policy increases in face amounts via the GIO, such as with universal life policies). Although it would admittedly be complex to devise, price, and administer, insurers could provide a useful service by devising a pure guaranteed insurability rider and policy with greater flexibility. Even so, the rider can prove to be of value, especially to those whose family health history suggests that potentially significant medical problems may develop.

Cost-of-Living Rider

The **cost-of-living-adjustment** (COLA) rider has already been discussed in connection with increasing term life insurance (see chapter 4), flexible-premium life insurance (see chapter 6), and health insurance (see chapter 7). It is, therefore, sufficient merely to recall that this feature can usually be added as a supplemental benefit to most forms of life and disability income insurance. It can be useful when one's needs for insurance are expected to change over time in approximately the same proportion as changes in the cost of living.

Although for many persons the need for life insurance protection may increase, it will not normally increase in proportion to COLA increases. Consequently, this aspect of the rider should be examined carefully.

Additional Insurance Coverage

Insurers have for decades permitted policyowners to attach term riders to basic policies to enhance the total death benefit. Within the past few years, a modified approach of this practice has evolved.

Applicants who today request that insurance riders be added to their base policies may purchase a high-value term life rider or a rider that permits them to make additional premium payments to accelerate cash-value buildup. This buildup may involve no increase in death benefit (as with dump-in premiums under universal life policies) or it may involve the purchase of units of paid-up additional insurance (as with the paid-up additions dividend option).

These riders enhance policy flexibility. Usually, the expenses and commissions associated with the premium for the additional insurance are lower than those for the base policy. Most insurers pass these lower expenses on to policyowners so that the riders can be the means of acquiring additional protection at or close to net rates.

Questions

1. Describe some of the purposes annuities serve. With respect to these purposes, do they retain any advantages over alternative retirement funding vehicles?
2. Describe circumstances for which you would recommend the purchase of each of the following annuities: (1) flexible-premium deferred; (2) single-premium deferred; (3) single-premium immediate; and (4) variable.
3. Compare and contrast the objectives of variable annuities and variable life insurance.
4. Annuities may be classified in numerous ways. Suggest an alternative classification scheme to that presented in this chapter.
5. Adverse selection has arguably led to automatic pricing in the market for annuities. Discuss the impact automatic pricing may have on customers of different types of annuities.
6. Market-value annuities guarantee an interest rate and have surrender charges that vary inversely with the interest rate environment. How does this market-value adjustment of the cash value affect the risks faced by both consumers and life insurers with this product?

CHAPTER

9

LIFE AND HEALTH INSURANCE CONTRACTS: I

Objectives

■ Describe the distinguishing characteristics of life insurance contracts.

■ Explain how a life insurance contract may be formed and how the requirement of insurable interest is satisfied.

■ Identify the provisions in insurance contracts that try to prevent both consumers and insurers from breaching their duty of good faith and fair dealing.

■ Understand agency law as it pertains to the activities of life insurance agents.

■ Describe steps that have been taken to better regulate the market conduct of insurance agents.

INTRODUCTION

As noted in chapter 1, *insurance* can be defined from a legal perspective: For a consideration, one party (the insurer) agrees to pay a defined amount of money or to provide defined services if a covered loss occurs during the policy's term. Behind this simple definition lies generations of legal interpretation. This and the following chapter provide an overview of insurance policies as legal documents. We cover both life and health insurance but emphasize life insurance contracts, as we have already covered many aspects of health contracts in chapter 7. Our emphasis is on U.S. law.

Economics and the Law

Recall also from chapter 1 that insurance markets are imperfect, with information problems abounding for insurers and their customers. For customers, the main problem is that they do not always possess as much information as they might need to be well informed about insurance purchase decisions or about how to ensure that the insurer is performing as required. It is possible for insurers to take unfair advantage of them. This possibility is especially relevant with respect to the legal dimensions of life and health insurance. The vast intricacies of contracts and the law can seem bewildering and almost mysterious to the layperson. Conversely, policyowners and claimants sometimes can take unfair advantage of insurers; that is, moral hazard and adverse selection problems lurk behind numerous customer/insurer interactions.

The laws related to contracts, including life and health insurance contracts, are designed to minimize the possibility of either party taking unfair advantage of the other or of there being any inadvertent misunderstanding. In economic terms, the provisions of insurance contracts as well as the law relating to the contracting process itself exist to minimize information problems for customers and insurers, as we will make clear throughout this and the following chapter. The use of a written document (contract) reduces uncertainty for all interested parties.

Regulatory Control over Policy Provisions

Few statutorily standard policies exist in the United States or in most other countries. Insurance contract provisions, however, are subject to considerable governmental oversight. In the United States and probably most other countries, this control typically involves requirements that (1) no policy form may be used until it is approved by the insurance supervisor and (2) policies must contain certain standard provisions, as specified in the insurance law. The insurance supervisor may disapprove a form if it contains any provision that is judged to be deceptive, inequitable, or misleading. With respect to some health insurance forms, disapproval also may result if the benefits provided seem unfairly low in relation to the premiums charged.

Statutes usually do not prescribe the exact wording for standard provisions; rather, they stipulate that actual policy wording must be at least as favorable to the policyowner as that of the statute. The standard provisions generally required include some or all of the following: (1) the entire contract clause, (2) the incontestable clause, (3) the grace period, (4) reinstatement, (5) nonforfeiture provision, (6) policy loans, (7) annual dividends, (8) misstatement of age, (9) settlement options, and (10) deferment of loan and cash-value payments. Additionally, health insurance policies must contain renewal provisions. These and other provisions are discussed later.

Individual jurisdictions have other regulations that relate to the policy contract or its terms. New York, for example, expressly prohibits any exclusion from liability for death except for war, suicide, aviation, and occupation or residence. Many states require that each policy form be identified by a code number and that a brief description of the policy be placed at the bottom of the first page (e.g., "whole life with premiums payable for life").

Life and health insurance policies are required to be written in simplified language in most U.S. jurisdictions. Most of these laws and regulations are based on the **Life and Health Insurance Policy Language Simplification Model Act** of the NAIC. The laws and regulations require that policy language meet a readability ease test, and that policies be printed in at least a minimum type size, with an accompanying table of contents or index.

As an adjunct to the insurance laws, court decisions have important effects on the way that life and especially health insurance contracts are written. These judicial opinions may give new interpretations to prevailing insurance principles or may restate existing insurance law. Also, the structure of insurance contracts can be influenced by laws on taxes, social insurance programs, human rights, and employment benefits.

Because of the expense of maintaining a different policy form for use throughout Canada and the United States, companies attempt to produce contracts that meet the requirements of all or substantially all states or provinces in which they do business. Occasionally, conflicting requirements or company preferences necessitate the use of special policy forms or modification through endorsements of the regular forms in particular states or provinces.

A host of provisions makes up life and health insurance contracts. Many are included to protect the policyowner (e.g., grace period to prevent inadvertent lapse), that is, to help address potential information asymmetry problems of policyowners. Others are included to make the policy more flexible from the standpoint of the policyowner (e.g., clauses permitting a change of beneficiary), and still others are included to protect the company (e.g., clauses excluding payment if the insured commits suicide within a certain time period), that is, to help address potential adverse selection and moral hazard problems.

Although some provisions can be viewed as protecting both the company and the policyowner, the discussion of contract provisions in this and the following chapter is based on the foregoing organizational pattern. This chapter also includes a brief review of the law as it pertains to the agent.

THE INSURANCE POLICY AS A CONTRACT

An insurance policy is a contract, and it must, therefore, conform to the rules of general contract law. Before examining these basic rules as they apply to life and health insurance contracts, a summary of the characteristics that distinguish insurance contracts from many other contracts is presented. These characteristics underlie the distinctive judicial interpretations accorded insurance contracts.

Distinguishing Characteristics of Insurance Contracts

First, the insurance contract is one of the **utmost good faith**—that is, each party is entitled to rely in good faith upon the representations of the other, and each is under an obligation not to attempt to deceive or withhold material information from the other. In economic terms, each party is supposed to avoid using its superior knowledge to take unfair advantage of the other. The rule of **caveat emptor**—"let the buyer beware"—does *not* generally apply. The company must depend to a great extent on the statements of prospective owners/insureds in assessing their acceptability for insurance, and buyers must rely upon the insurer's good faith because the insurance contract is intricate and highly technical.

The insurance contract is characterized as one of **adhesion,** meaning that its terms and provisions are fixed by one party (the insurer) and, with minor exceptions, must be accepted or rejected *en totale* by the other party (the prospective policyowner). The fact that the contract carries such great information asymmetries because of its highly specialized and technical nature argues against it being a bargaining contract. As a result, the courts hold that any ambiguities or unclear elements in the contract will be construed in favor of the party not participating in the construction of the contract wording—the policyowner.

Life insurance contracts as well as most disability income and long-term care policies are **valued policies,** meaning that the insurer agrees to pay a stated sum of money irrespective of the actual economic loss. Most property and liability and medical expense policies, in contrast, are contracts of indemnity. Under a contract of **indemnity,** insureds suffering a covered loss are entitled to recover an amount not greater than that which would be necessary to place the insured in the same preloss financial position. They cannot recover more than their economic loss. Under a life insurance and some health insurance contracts, the insurer promises to pay a definitive amount of money, which does not purport necessarily to represent a measure of the actual loss.

This fact can easily give rise to moral hazard. If insureds or beneficiaries can recover amounts greater than the economic value of lost incomes or expenses, an incentive is created to bring about the loss or the appearance of the loss. Thus, in determining the amount of insurance that will be issued, insurers carefully consider the extent of the applicant's likely economic loss in the event of the insured's death or incapacity.

The contract also is **conditional** in that the insurer's obligation to pay a claim depends upon the performance of certain acts, such as payment of premiums and furnishing proof of death. This conditionality is designed to protect the insurer from moral hazard.

In addition, the life insurance contract is **unilateral** in nature, meaning that only one party, the insurer, gives a legally enforceable promise. The owner of the contract makes no promise to make premium payments, but if he or she chooses to make them in a timely manner, the insurer is bound to accept them and meet its obligations under the contract. This fact creates some adverse selection in that insureds most in need of insurance will make every effort to pay premiums.

Finally, the life insurance contract is classified as aleatory as opposed to commutative. In a *commutative* contract, an exchange involving approximately equivalent values exists, whereas an **aleatory** contract involves the element of chance, and one party may receive more in value than the other. This important distinction is discussed further later.

Key Definitions

Some key definitions introduced in chapter 1 bear repeating because a clear understanding of them is essential to the material in this and the following chapter. Recall that the *insured* is the person whose life or health is the object of the insurance contract. Except in some health insurance policies, the insured usually has no rights in the policy in his or her capacity as insured.

Rather, the *policyowner,* also called the **policyholder** or simply **owner,** is the person who owns the contract and can exercise all rights under the policy. In most instances, the insured is the owner of the policy, but this usually is not required. Thus, Cathy Lee might own a policy that insures her husband's life. The insurer would deal exclusively with Cathy in all matters pertaining to the execution of the policy such as changing the mode of premiums payment, changing the beneficiary, surrendering the policy, and so on.

The **applicant** is the person who applies for the insurance policy. Most commonly, the applicant is the proposed policyowner and proposed insured. Unless noted otherwise, we will use the term *applicant* to mean proposed owner.

Neither the courts nor legislative bodies use the foregoing terms in a consistent way. The same can be said for insurance agents and employees. For example, more often than not, the term *insured* is used synonymously with the term *policyowner.* For this reason, care should be taken in reading and interpreting court decisions and laws.

Finally, the *beneficiary* is the person to whom life insurance policy death benefits are paid on the death of the insured. In most instances, the beneficiary has no rights in the policy in his or her capacity as beneficiary prior to the death of the insured. If the insured is not also the policyowner, it is common for the policyowner to be the beneficiary. Benefits payable during life under life and health insurance policies are commonly payable to the policyowner.

Formation of Insurance Contracts

The agreement between a life insurance company and a person seeking insurance must meet all requirements prescribed by law for the formation of a contract. For any contract to be valid, four requirements must be met:

- The parties to the contract must be legally capable of making a contract.
- An agreement must exist based on an offer made by one party and an acceptance of that offer by the other party on the same terms.
- There must be a valuable consideration exchanged.
- The purpose of the agreement must be lawful.

Capacity of the Parties

The parties must have the legal capacity to contract. Incompetence in this respect suggests that one party could take unfair advantage, because of information asymmetries, of the other. If the insurance company is licensed to transact business in the jurisdiction under consideration and otherwise complies with its insurance laws, its capacity to contract is clear. Where the insurer is incompetent by reason of noncompliance or incomplete compliance with the requirements of the jurisdiction in which the contract is executed, the question of the validity of the contract and the respective rights of the parties has not been uniformly decided. In some jurisdictions, the contract may be void entirely. In others it may be voidable. A **void** agreement has no legal force or effect, whereas a **voidable** agreement is one that can be made void at the option of the innocent party. In the majority of U.S. jurisdictions, the contract remains binding on both parties.

In connection with the legal capacity of the applicant to contract, no problem ordinarily arises unless the applicant is (1) a minor, (2) intoxicated or under the influence of other drugs, (3) mentally incompetent, or (4) an enemy alien.

Minors   With few exceptions, the minimum age at which a person can enter into contracts (the **age of majority**) in the United States is 18. However, laws are not uniform, especially between countries, and special age limitations may exist in a particular jurisdiction. In some jurisdictions, minors have the legal capacity to enter into contracts if they are married. However, in the absence of contrary law, contracts made by minors are voidable at the option of the minor, except for the reasonable value of necessaries. **Necessaries** include necessities such as food, clothing, and shelter as well as other items appropriate for the person's circumstances.

Meanwhile, the insurance company remains obligated to perform the contract. If the minor decides to void or repudiate the contract, the insurer must return all premiums paid. The competent party—the insurer—is not permitted to use its superior knowledge to take unfair advantage of a person who does not understand fully the meanings of his or her actions. Of course, where the application for insurance on a minor's life is made by a competent adult, no question of capacity arises.

Although life insurance is not a necessary, it has important values to the insured and his or her family. To encourage insurance companies to provide insurance for older minors, but without danger of later repudiation by them, many U.S. jurisdictions have enacted statutes that give minors who are older than a specified age the legal capacity to contract for insurance. The specified ages range from 14 to 18, with 15 being the most frequently stated age. Some of these statutes additionally limit the parties eligible to be named beneficiaries under life insurance policies issued to such minors to spouses or parents.

Intoxicated Persons   A person who is unable to understand the nature of the transaction in which he or she is engaged, because of the influence of intoxicating liquor or drugs, lacks legal capacity. The effect is to make such contracts voidable, and the individual, with some exceptions, may be able to repudiate the contract within a reasonable length of time after he or she recovers sufficiently to understand the consequences of his or her actions. As with minors, the concern here is information asymmetries.

Mental Incompetents   Contracts made by an insane person are voidable and are treated in the same manner as are contracts made by minors, provided no guardian has been appointed. If a person has been declared legally insane and a guardian has been appointed, all agreements made by the ward are void. As in the case of minors, an insane person may be held liable for the reasonable value of necessaries.

Enemy Aliens   Trading with enemy aliens in time of war is illegal, and no valid contract can be entered into during such a period. Contracts already in force between domestic citizens and enemy aliens are either suspended or terminated by declaration of war. Court decisions in regard to life insurance contracts under such conditions are not uniform.

A particularly troubling issue for insurers, especially those in Europe, relates to the holocaust during World War II. Box 9-1 briefly explores this issue.

Mutual Assent

As with other contracts, an offer and an acceptance must exist before an insurance contract is created. However, the process by which an insurance contract comes into being is somewhat different from that for other contracts. Most applicants for individually issued life and health insurance do not approach an insurance company seeking insurance. Instead, the applicant is usually first contacted by an agent, who solicits an application that is submitted to the insurance company.

Premium Not Paid with Application   The insurance contracting process is initiated either by payment of the first premium with the application or by submitting the application without payment. The latter situation is an invitation to the insurance company to make an offer to insure. The insurer can make the offer by issuing the policy. The applicant can accept the insurer's offer by paying the premium at the time the policy is delivered.

Premium Paid with Application   More commonly, a premium is paid with the application. In most instances, a premium receipt is given. Much less frequently, no receipt is issued. In such cases, most jurisdictions hold that no contract is in force until the policy is issued and delivered. Here the applicant is considered to have made an offer that he or she may withdraw at any time before acceptance by the company.

Approval conditional premium receipt.   Three types of premium receipts are found in the United States. Each provides some form of temporary coverage. Thus, the **approval conditional premium receipt** provides that insurance will be effective only after the application has been approved by the company. Thus, the period of protection—from the date of approval until the date the policy is issued or delivered—is typically minimal. The

---

BOX 9-1

LIFE INSURANCE AND THE HOLOCAUST

Many Jewish and other citizens were insured under life insurance policies during World War II. Many were unable to pay premiums because their possessions were confiscated, and they were interred in concentration camps. Surviving beneficiaries of the many thousands who were murdered either did not know of the death or had no means of filing a death claim.

From the insurer's viewpoint at the time, such policies lapsed or went under nonforfeiture options that later expired. Could (and should) death claim payments be denied because of war exclusions; a failure to comply with policy conditions, such as premium payment or claims filing conditions; or prohibitions relating to contracting with enemy aliens?

From the point of view of beneficiaries and their heirs, amounts are due them because many

policies were in force at the time of death, and circumstances beyond their control prevented the timely filing of the death claim. Other policies lapsed because of morally repugnant acts by governments at the time. In many instances, no one having knowledge of the policy survived. Victims of the holocaust and their family members note that they were neither "at war" nor were they "enemy aliens."

However, reconstructing records over 50 years old and tracing families of insureds is exceptionally complex. The issues being addressed more than 50 years after the end of World War II are (1) what should be done to make right this troubling and complex matter; (2) what amount of money should be paid and to whom; and (3) who should pay it?

approval conditional premium receipt has largely been replaced by the insurability conditional premium receipt in the United States.

Insurability conditional premium receipt. The **insurability conditional premium receipt** provides that the insurer is considered to have made an offer conditional upon the proposed insured's insurability, and the applicant accepts the conditional offer by payment of the premium. The insurance becomes effective as of the date of the conditional receipt or, if later, the time of the physical examination, provided that the proposed insured is found insurable. The delivery of the policy itself is not essential. Most U.S. insurers use this type of receipt.

Under this arrangement, if the proposed insured were to die before the application and other information reached the company's home office and the proposed insured otherwise would have been insurable according to the company's usual standards, the claim would be paid. Insurers have paid many such claims. The purpose of this type of receipt is, of course, to provide protection between the date of the conditional receipt (or physical examination, if later) and the time of policy delivery, but only for those proposed insureds who are insurable.

Most U.S. courts interpret the conditional receipt language as written, in the absence of an ambiguity. A minority of courts have adopted the view that this receipt provides unconditional temporary or interim coverage that continues until the insurer takes affirmative action to terminate it.[1] Many of these courts' findings rely on the reasonable expectations doctrine (discussed later) to establish coverage; that is, applicants reasonably expect interim coverage for premiums paid.

Binding premium receipt. The **binding premium receipt** provides insurance that is effective from the date the receipt is given. It provides immediate and, unlike the preceding receipts, unconditional coverage. The agent is instructed to issue the receipt only if the applicant's answers to selected health questions are satisfactory. Usually, both the conditional and binding receipts stipulate a maximum amount payable if death occurs during the period of coverage under the receipt. The coverage is provided for a stipulated, fixed time period or until the insurance company renders an underwriting decision on the application, whichever is sooner. A distinct but growing minority of life insurers use binding receipts.

Policy Effective Date In the absence of complications, the **effective date** of a policy is the date from which insurance protection begins. Ordinarily, it is mutually agreed upon by the company and the applicant. However, complications can arise, the consequences of which can bring the true policy effective date into dispute.

A policy may be backdated to "save age." **Backdating** is the practice by which an insurer calculates premiums under the policy based on an earlier age for the proposed insured. Premiums are thereby lower than they otherwise would be. Backdating beyond six months is sometimes prohibited by law. Although backdating does not alter the effective date of the protection, it does raise two important questions. First, when is the next premium due? Second, from what date do the incontestable and suicide periods run?

A few courts have held that a full year's coverage must be provided for the annual premium. However, the majority of the U.S. court decisions have held that the policy date (i.e., the date appearing on the contract) determines the date on which subsequent premiums are due, even though this means that less than one full year's protection is granted during the first year.

---

[1]See, for example, *Metropolitan Life Ins. Co. v. Wood,* 302 F.2d 802 (9th Cir. 1962).

With regard to the suicide and incontestable clauses, the general rule is that the earlier of the effective date or the policy date establishes the point of measurement. Thus, with a backdated policy, the clauses generally run from the policy date. When the policy date is later than the effective date, the clauses are held to run from the effective date. When the clauses themselves specify a certain date, this date is usually recognized.

Consideration

The consideration by the applicant for the promises of the company consists of the statements in the application and the payment of the first premium. Premium payments subsequent to the first are not part of the legal consideration but are conditions precedent that must be performed to keep the contract in existence.

The insurer may agree to accept a check, note, or, in the absence of a prohibitive statute, services in payment of the first premium. Although a check is customarily considered cash, payment by check is usually accepted only as a conditional payment. This means that if a check is not honored by the bank, no payment is considered to have been made and the insurer's promise is no longer binding, regardless of the policyowner's good faith.

All life and health insurance policies contain a **consideration clause** that summarizes the factors that led the insurer to issue the policy and represents the insured's part of the insurance agreement. It generally is a simple statement that the insured has completed an application and paid a premium in exchange for the company's promise to provide insurance.

Most companies use the consideration clause to make the application a part of the policy. Unless a copy of the application is included in the policy, the insurer cannot at a later time contest the insurance contract because of any misstatements or misrepresentations made in connection with the application. The following example from a disability income policy is typical of the consideration clause:

> We have issued this policy in consideration of the representations in your application and payment of the first-term premium. A copy of your application is attached and is a part of this policy.

Legal Purpose

To be valid, a contract must be for a legal purpose and not contrary to public policy. For example, in many jurisdictions, gambling transactions are illegal and, therefore, unenforceable at law. Gambling transactions and life insurance contracts are both aleatory, as opposed to commutative, in character.

In a commutative agreement, an exchange of approximate equal values is intended. For example, in a real estate sale, the seller relinquishes ownership of property whose value is established mutually by the parties. In return, the buyer pays an amount equal to the agreed value. With aleatory agreements, each party recognizes that one of them may obtain more than the other, but each also recognizes that the outcome is governed by chance. Gambling and wagering arrangements are aleatory.

The distinction between a contract of insurance and a wager is vitally important. One enters a wager in hopes, through chance, of gaining at the expense of others. One enters an insurance contract to avoid a financial loss and transform uncertainty into certainty.[2] The requirement of an insurable interest in insurance takes the agreement out of the gambling category.

In addition to the fact that a life insurance contract will fail when there is no insurable interest on the part of the applicant in the insured, a contract may be illegal and against

---

[2]The law of large numbers removes, to a great extent, speculation on the part of insurance companies. They are not gambling either. Also, when all policyowners are viewed as a group, there is an exchange of approximately equal value between them and the insurer.

public policy for other reasons. As was mentioned earlier, a contract with an enemy alien is held to be against public policy and void. Also, a contract is illegal and void (and the insurer is relieved from paying the death claim) when it is negotiated with intent to murder.

Insurable Interest

An insurance contract must, according to law, be based on an insurable interest. Although this phrase is not subject to precise definition, a person has an **insurable interest** in another's life if he or she can reasonably expect to receive pecuniary gain from that person's continued life, or, conversely, if he or she would suffer financial loss on the person's death. An insurable interest cannot be supported on mere personal interest or affection.

In the absence of a valid insurable interest, life insurance policies are unenforceable at law.[3] The insurance could create a moral hazard of the worst sort; that is, the insured event—death—would be more likely to occur *because* of the existence of the insurance. This moral hazard problem understandably is one that society and, therefore, the law find especially offensive. Consequently, life insurance policies procured without a valid insurable interest are usually held to be illegal and void. Most U.S. jurisdictions, in fact, incorporate this interpretation into statutory law and provide that such contracts are "void unless the benefits are payable to the individual insured or his personal representative or to a person having, at the time of such contract, an insurable interest in the individual insured."[4] This doctrine evolved out of regard for public welfare rather than for the protection of insurance companies.

An insurer has both a strong financial motivation and a legal duty to ascertain that an insurable interest exists. Although the insurer may be relieved from paying the death proceeds under a policy issued with no insurable interest, it nonetheless incurs substantial expenses in such an arrangement and runs the great risk of encouraging early death. The latter problem gives rise to additional mortality costs to the company because not all insurable interest deficiencies will be discovered.

It is perhaps of greater importance that the insurer becomes exposed in tort for a breach of its duty to use reasonable care to avoid creating an incentive for the beneficiary to murder the insured. Thus, in one well-known case, three life insurers issued policies on a child's life, with the child's aunt-in-law as applicant and beneficiary. The jury held that the insurers' failures to ascertain whether, in fact, an insurable interest existed supplied the motive for the aunt-in-law's act of murdering the child. The $100,000 wrongful-death judgment in favor of the child's father against the insurers was substantially greater than the life policies' face amounts.[5]

Insurable Interest in One's Own Life

In analyzing the question of what constitutes a valid insurable interest, we examine it from the standpoint of whether the policy is applied for by the insured on his or her own life or by someone else. A fundamental principle of law is that every person possesses an insurable interest to an unlimited extent in his or her own life, and that he or she, in the absence of a statute to the contrary, may make the insurance payable to whomever he or she wishes.[6] An alternative yet functionally equivalent view is that questions of insurable interest do not arise in such circumstances.

With either view, where the applicant is also the person whose life is to be insured, U.S. courts have refused to require any specific relationship between the amount of insurance

---

[3]*Warnock v. Davis,* 104 U.S. 775, 779 (1881); *Peoples Life Insurance Co. v. Whiteside,* 94 F.2d 409 (1938).

[4]*Georgia Statutes,* 1969 §56-2404.

[5]*Liberty National Life Insurance Co. v. Weldon,* 267 Ala. 171, 100 So.2d (1957).

[6]44 *Am. Jur. 2e, Insurance,* §1729, *Bell v. Phillips et al.,* Tex., 152 F.2d 188 (1946).

and the value of the life on which it is taken. When the contract is taken without collusion and without intent to violate any laws, the natural love of life is held to constitute a sufficient insurable interest and to support a policy for any amount.[7] Although legally there is no limit to the amount of insurance that may be taken out by an individual on his or her own life, in practice life insurance companies limit the amount issued to a sum that is not unreasonably large relative to the insured's financial status and earning capacity.

A few states require that the beneficiary have an insurable interest in the insured's life or be related to him or her in a stated degree of kinship. Beneficiaries not falling within the designated classes are barred from collecting policy proceeds, with the insurer usually required to pay proceeds to the insured's estate. The rationale for this requirement is that the beneficiary who has no insurable interest may be more interested in the insured's early death. Most states, however, apparently disagree with this logic, noting that the insured/owner is highly unlikely to name such a person as beneficiary.

Insurable Interest in Another Person's Life

One person insuring another's life must have an insurable interest in that life. Even in cases in which the interest exists, a policy obtained without the knowledge and consent of the insured is contrary to public policy and void.[8] Insurable interest may arise out of one or more of three classes of relationships.

Family and Marriage Relationships   U.S. courts seem to exhibit some uncertainty as to whether someone has an insurable interest in another's life *solely* because of being related by blood or marriage. Spouses and persons with close blood relationships seem to support an insurable interest, although most cases do not base the decision on the relationship alone. Rather, they have held that, in view of the relationship, it is proper to presume that a pecuniary benefit or gain would have inured to the survivor had the insured lived.

Some jurisdictions have based insurable interest solely on close relationships, such as between husband and wife, parent and child, grandparent and grandchild, and siblings, but have generally refused to extend it further. Regarding other relationships, the courts hold that the interest should be based upon a reasonable expectation of deriving pecuniary benefit from the continuance of the insured's life.

Creditor–Debtor Relationships   The rule is well settled that creditors have an insurable interest in the lives of their debtors, although the important question of an acceptable amount of insurance, as compared with the amount of debt, is not well settled. Where a creditor pays the premiums for a policy insuring the debtor's life, the creditor's insurable interest, arguably, should not be limited solely to the amount of the indebtedness. The creditor should be reimbursed for an amount equal to the debt, the premiums paid, and interest on both. The courts are not uniform concerning the validity of a policy in which the amount of insurance greatly exceeds the debt.

The rule adopted by the U.S. Supreme Court places an indefinite restriction upon the creditor's insurable interest by providing that the relationship between the amount of insurance and the amount of the debt must not be so disproportionate as to make the policy take on the appearance of a wagering contract as distinguished from its legitimate

---

[7]This rule does not apply, therefore, when the proposed insured is the applicant in name only and, in reality, the parties have agreed that the beneficiary is to be the policyowner. In *Dresen v. Metropolitan Life Ins. Co.*, 195 Ill. App. 292 (1915), the proposed insured applied for and had issued a policy on her life, with her paramour named as beneficiary. After she paid the first three premiums, her paramour paid all those remaining. The policy was declared void for lack of insurable interest.

[8]*Am. Jur. 2d, Insurance*, §1741. Some states (e.g., Louisiana) permit either spouse to take insurance on the life of the other without the consent of the insured. But see consequences where the husband took out more than $1 million of term insurance on his wife in *State v. Thompson* (Minn.), 139 N.W.2d 490 (1966).

purpose—security for the indebtedness. In *Cammak v. Lewis,* for example, the court declared that a policy of $3,000 taken out by a creditor to secure a debt of $70 to be "a sheer wagering policy, without any claim to be considered as one meant to secure a debt."[9]

The U.S. Supreme Court has made the relationship between the debt amount and the insurance amount an important factor to be considered, but it has never defined this relationship precisely. Various theories have been used by courts to make the insurance proceeds in excess of the debt payable to the debtor's estate or other beneficiary designated by the debtor. Where the law was not explicit and the terms of the transaction not clear, the most popular theory for making such payments is that the creditor is the trustee for the benefit of the debtor's estate.

Business Relationships   Numerous business relationships, other than that of creditor and debtor, can justify the purchase of insurance by one person on the life of another. Except for corporate-owned life insurance, described in chapter 17, the insurable interest must be based on a substantial pecuniary interest existing between the parties. Thus, an employer may insure the life of an employee and the employee the life of an employer, a partner the life of a copartner and the partnership the life of each partner, and a corporation the life of an officer.

Similarly, a corporation holding a property interest contingent upon another person reaching a certain age may protect itself against the loss of the contingent right through the death of that person before he or she has attained the prescribed age. The courts have even held that those who furnish funds for corporate enterprises have an insurable interest in the lives of the managers and promoters of the corporations. Certain stockholders have purchased life insurance on the lives of prominent financiers who were instrumental in financing and promoting the corporations whose stock they held. In all cases, the person being insured must give his or her consent to the transaction.

The Time and Continuity of Insurable Interest

In property insurance, the general rule is that insurable interest must exist at the time of the loss. In other words, an insurable interest is not necessary at the time the property insurance contract is made. In life insurance, in contrast, insurable interest generally needs to exist only at contract inception, unless the policy itself[10] or statute provides otherwise. The contract will not thereafter be voided if the interest ceases, unless the provisions of the policy are such as to bring about that result. The fact that insurable interest needs to exist only at the inception of the contract is a corollary to the view that life insurance policies are not contracts of indemnity.

This view is also reflected in the fact that when an insured is executed for a crime, the proceeds are payable to the appropriate beneficiary. Similarly, when a beneficiary murders the insured, the proceeds still must be paid, but, of course, to an innocent beneficiary. This assumes that the beneficiary did not procure the policy with the intent of murdering the insured, which would make the contract void from the beginning. Jurisdictions that require an insurable interest between the beneficiary and insured, however, typically require the interest to be a continuing one.

Governing Law

Generally speaking, contract validity is governed by the law and usages of the place where the contract is made. This is held to be where the last and essential acts necessary to formation of the contract took place. Several jurisdictions' laws, including those of

---

[9]*Wall.* 244, 82 U.S. 647.

[10]*Caldwell v. Grand Lodge of United Workmen* (1905), 148 Cal. 195, 82 P 781.

another country, may appear to apply, but in a conflicting manner (conflict of laws), and the general rule becomes subject to special interpretation.

Thus, in a case in which an insured was a citizen of Missouri and made application for insurance in Oklahoma to a Tennessee insurer, the state of domicile was held to have had a more significant relationship to the parties, and, therefore, Missouri law applied.[11] Similarly, assignments and other matters relating to contract performance are governed by the law of the place of performance, regardless of the place where the original contract was made.

The Application and Its Interpretation

An **application** for life or health insurance may be defined as the applicant's proposal to the insurer for protection and may be considered as the beginning of the policy contract. In this document, the proposed insured is required to give accurate answers to questions relating principally to his or her personal and family history, habits, employment, insurance already in force, and other applications for insurance that either are pending or have been postponed or refused. If the application is for disability insurance, additional questions will relate to income and other financial matters.

The policy usually stipulates that insurance is granted in consideration of the application, which is declared to be a part of the policy, and generally contains a clause to the effect that the policy and the application (a copy of which is attached to the policy when it is issued) "constitute the entire contract between the parties." Most laws require that a copy of the application be included as a part of the policy, a failure to do so leading to the insurer being *estopped* (i.e., prevented) from denying the correctness or truth of information in the application.

Insurers place great reliance on information furnished by the proposed insured in deciding whether to issue the requested policy. The company is entitled to have all relevant information that may influence its decision, especially given the natural information advantage that the buyer has over the seller at time of underwriting and the aleatory nature of the life insurance contract. As a result, the applicant should act in good faith, and if the information given is false or incomplete, the insurer may be in a position to rescind or cancel the contract. We take up this important topic next through discussions of concealment, warranties, and misrepresentations.

Concealment

Concealment is the withholding of information. Courts have repeatedly stated that insurance policies are contracts involving the utmost good faith, and in early cases, courts held that with contracts based upon chance, the withholding of any essential facts by either party rendered the risk actually insured different from that intended. The validity of the policy, therefore, depended upon the full disclosure of all material information.

Within most U.S. jurisdictions, as well as in the United Kingdom, the **test of materiality** of a fact concealed (or misrepresented as discussed later) is whether the insurer, had it known the actual facts, would still have issued the insurance, would have issued it with as favorable a premium, or would have issued it on terms as favorable as it did. If the insurer, had it known the truth, would have denied the application, charged a higher premium, or issued a more limited policy, the fact concealed or misrepresented is **material.** In some countries, such as Australia, and in a few U.S. jurisdictions, the law provides

---

[11]V.A.M.S. 375, 420, 376, 620; 36 O.S. 1971, §4024; *Moss v. National Life & Acc. Ins. Co.* (D.C. Mo. 1974), 385 F. Supp. (1921); *Mutual of Omaha Ins. Co. v. Russell* (C.A. Kan.), 402 F.2d 339, 29 A.L.R. 3d 753, certiorari denied 80 S.Ct. 1465, 394 U.S. 973, 22 L.Ed.2d 753 (1968) (flight policy issued to a Kansas citizen in Missouri and court applied Kansas law).

that the test of materiality is whether a "reasonably prudent person" would have believed the information to have been material.

The doctrine of concealment, which was developed in connection with marine insurance, is primarily for the protection of the insurer and, at one time, was applied to all branches of insurance. As the business developed, most U.S. courts concluded that some relaxation of the rule should be made. With respect to life and health insurance, most courts now follow the finding in the case of *Penn Mutual Life Insurance v. Mechanics' Savings Bank and Trust Company.* In this case the court held that "no failure to disclose a fact material to the risk, not inquired about, will void the policy, unless such nondisclosure was with intent to conceal from the insurer a fact believed to be material; that is, unless the nondisclosure was fraudulent."[12] The concealment doctrine still applies in some states and countries such as in the United Kingdom.

Warranties

Closely associated with the common-law doctrine of concealment and representations is the doctrine of **warranty,** which requires that the warranted statement must be absolutely and literally true. The contract can be rescinded or canceled if the falsehood of the statement can be shown, irrespective of its materiality. A company need prove only that a warranted statement is incorrect. Historically, courts assumed that the materiality of the warranty had been established and that all inquiry on the subject was precluded.

Because of the hardship and injustice that the technical enforcement of the common-law rule pertaining to warranties sometimes caused, and also because a few insurance companies took undue advantage of warranties in their policies, many jurisdictions enacted statutes protecting insureds against technical avoidance of life and health insurance contracts because of breach of warranties. These statutes differ widely but, in effect, provide that all statements purporting to be made by the insured shall be deemed representations and not warranties. Effectively, therefore, warranties are of mainly historical interest in North American life and health insurance.

Representations

A **representation** is a statement made to an insurer for the purpose of giving information or inducing it to accept a risk. A **misrepresentation** occurs when the information given is incorrect. Generally, representations are construed liberally in favor of the insured and need be only substantially correct. The tendency in U.S. court decisions has been toward protecting the insured by giving him or her the benefit of the doubt wherever possible.

Perhaps the majority rule in the United States is that a materially false representation renders a policy voidable at the option of the company, even though there was no fraudulent intent on the part of the insured. It has been modified in many jurisdictions, as well as in other countries (such as France and Japan) either by court decision or by statute. Thus, one court stated that "a forfeiture does not follow where there has been no deliberate intent to deceive, and the known falsity of the answer is not affirmatively shown."[13]

Intent is a state of mind and, in effect, French, Japanese, and some U.S. courts require that the insurer show not only that the representations in the application were false but also that they were fraudulently made.[14] In most jurisdictions that provide

---

[12]72 Fed. 413 (C.C.A.), 1986; *Blair v. National Security Insurance Co.,* 126 F.2d 955 (1942); *Haubner v. Aetna Life Ins. Co.,* 256 A.2d 414 (D.C. App. 1969) (insured has affirmative duty to disclose material information).

[13]*Kuhns v. N. Y. Life Ins. Co.,* Appellant, 297 Pa. 418, 423, 147 A.76 (1929); *Travellers Ins. Co. v. Heppenstall Co.,* 61 A.2d 809, 812 (Pa. 1948).

[14]*Russ v. Metropolitan Life Ins. Co.,* 270 A.2d 759, 112 N.J. Super. 265 (1970); *Kizirian v. United Benefit Life Ins. Co.,* 1191 A.2d 47 (1956); *Evans v. Penn Mutual Life Ins. Co. of Philadelphia,* 322 Pa. 547, 186 A. 133 (1946).

that misrepresentations only need to be material, a rescission is permitted without regard to intent or even knowledge.[15] Some jurisdictions provide that the policy will not be invalidated unless the misrepresentation is made with intent to deceive; others provide that the misrepresentation must have contributed to the loss. The general purpose of such laws is to prevent a forfeiture of the policy unless the company has been deceived to its detriment.

Rules of Contract Construction

Insurance contracts are to be interpreted to effectuate the meaning of the parties when they entered into the agreement.[16] The contract language should clearly and unambiguously express the intentions of the parties. The rules of insurance contract construction take into account the distinct relationship between the insurer and the policyowner, which differs substantially from most other contractual relationships. The great information asymmetry existing in insurance creates unequal bargaining power between (1) expert agents, underwriters, and claims and service personnel and (2) relatively unsophisticated, inexperienced applicants, policyowners, insureds, and/or beneficiaries.

Moreover, life and health insurance policies are typically written using standard forms containing much technical language. This contract of adhesion is proposed by the insurer on a take-it-or-leave-it basis with no practical opportunity for the applicant to negotiate modifications. Additionally, the policyowner usually sees the contract for the first time only after paying the premium.

The special nature of this relationship has led jurisdictions to adopt special rules of insurance contract construction that favor the policyowner. We cover three common classes of contract construction rules below. Their presentation here might lead to the inference that each is distinct. In practice, the evolving nature of the law is such that each approach may take elements from the others, and they are not seamless.

Doctrine of *Contra Proferentum*

The *contra proferentum* doctrine emanates from the notion that insurance policies are contracts of adhesion, and, therefore, any ambiguities in contract language are construed strictly in favor of the insured. The corollary of this doctrine is that the contract will be construed precisely as written, in the absence of any ambiguity. This rule still applies in some form in the majority of U.S. courts.

A term or provision susceptible to more than one meaning is *ambiguous*. This long-established principle on contract construction means that the courts will not torture the policy language to find an ambiguity or to ascribe a meaning to the language different from that which is plainly evident, even if the insured suffers hardship based on this interpretation.

Doctrine of Good Faith and Fair Dealing

In the 1970s, California courts were the first in the United States to adopt the principle that insurers owed policyowners an implied covenant of *good faith and fair dealing* that requires each party to the contract to avoid impairing the rights of the other. Today, most U.S. courts apply the doctrine in some form.

Although it has not developed consistently, perhaps it is most commonly applied when an insurer has not dealt fairly with one of its insureds. Thus, in one well-known

---

[15]West's F.S.A., §617.409; *Garwood v. Equitable Life Ass. Soc.*, Fla., 299 So.2d 163 (1974).

[16]This section draws in part from T. Richard Kennedy and Michael A. Knoerzer, "Freedom of Contract and Choice of Law in Insurance," *AIDA Quarterly Update*, Vol. 1, No. 3 (Summer 1995), pp. 12–16.

case involving a time limitation on the right to sue under a disability contract, the court concluded:

> In situations where a layman might give the controlling language of the policy a more restrictive interpretation than the insurer knows the courts have given it and as a result the uninformed insured might be inclined to be quiescent about the disregard or nonpayment of his claim and not to press it in a timely fashion, the company cannot ignore its obligation. It cannot hide behind the insured's ignorance of the law; it cannot conceal its liability. In these circumstances it has the duty to speak and disclose, and to act in accordance with its contractual undertaking.[17]

The duty requires insurers to make prompt and full settlement with insureds and beneficiaries and to consider the insured's interest in settling claims. In some jurisdictions, however, the standard of proof required to impose liability for a breach is so great that plaintiff success is highly unlikely. Breach of the duty is an actionable tort in other jurisdictions and can lead to the offending insurer being liable for compensatory and possibly even punitive damages. Other states do not recognize tort actions but allow broader damages than ordinary contracts, including consequential damages resulting from an insurer acting in "bad faith."

Reasonable Expectations Doctrine

The **reasonable expectations doctrine,** viewed by many legal authorities as an extension of the *contra proferentum* doctrine, was set forth succinctly by Professor Robert Keeton in his famous 1970 article:

> The objectively reasonable expectations of applicants and intended beneficiaries regarding the terms of insurance contracts will be honored even though a painstaking study of the policy provisions would have negated those expectations.[18]

A majority of states recognize the doctrine in some form. Variations range from (1) using it only to resolve ambiguities or to fill gaps created by ambiguities (the majority view) to (2) applying the doctrine to justify contract construction at odds with policy provisions even though no ambiguity exists. The doctrine does not deny an insurer the opportunity to make explicit contract qualifications effective, but to do so, the insurer must call the qualification to the attention of the applicant at the time of contracting. However, the insurer will not be allowed to use contract provisions or clauses to limit coverage in ways that are inconsistent with the reasonable expectations of an insured with an ordinary degree of familiarity with the insurance coverage at issue.

One view of the reasonable expectations doctrine suggests that "marketing patterns and general practices" of an insurer can shape a policyowner's reasonable expectations.[19] Thus,

> An individual can have reasonable expectations of coverage that arise from some source *other* than the policy language itself, and . . . such an extrinsic

---

[17]*Bowler v. Fidelity and Casualty Company of New York,* 53 N.J. 313, 250 A.2d 580 (1969).

[18]Robert Keeton, "Insurance Law Rights at Variance with Policy Provisions," 83 *Harvard Law Review* 961, 967 (part 1), and 1281 (part 2) (1970).

[19]Stephen J. Ware, "A Critique of the Reasonable Expectations Doctrine," 56 *University of Chicago Law Review* 1461, 1463–75 (Fall 1989).

expectation can be powerful enough to override any policy provision no matter how clear.[20]

Some observers contend that insurers help create policyowners' reasonable expectations. Indeed, the insurance industry works diligently to improve its and its agents' images. Advertisements proclaim an insurer's financial soundness, expertise, and professionalism. Prospective applicants are told of the reliability and dependability of the insurer, if only they will submit to the tender ministration of their representatives. Insurers spend enormous sums of money in agent training to support professionalism. Therefore, it should come as no surprise that the courts have taken the insurers at their advertised word.

When we make a payment, we expect to receive something for value given. To suggest that this is not true strikes a discordant note, especially with U.S. courts. They have used strong language to condemn restrictive language in policies, receipts, and other literature given to the applicant as well as aggressive sales promotions to acquire new customers. Thus, in a case dealing with conditional receipts, Judge Learned Hand, said:

> An underwriter might so understand the phrase, when read in its context, but the application was not to be submitted to underwriters: it was to go to persons utterly unacquainted with the niceties of life insurance, who would read it colloquially. It is the understanding of such persons which counts. . . . To demand that persons wholly unfamiliar with insurance shall spell all this out in the very teeth of the language used is unpardonable.[21]

The reasonable expectations doctrine probably arose because the remedies available to insureds and third parties for breach of contract are limited in comparison to those available with respect to products under tort law, which offers an array of possible damages, including punitive damages in many instances. Certainly the distinction between contract and tort law continues to blur, aided by the reasonable expectations doctrine.

Presumption of Death and Disappearance

Life insurance policies understandably require "due proof" of the insured's death before paying the face amount. This is difficult in circumstances in which the insured has disappeared leaving no trace or hint of his or her whereabouts.

A well-settled rule in U.S. law—taken from English common law—is that when a person leaves his or her usual place of residence and is neither heard of nor known to be living for a term of seven years, the person is presumed to be dead. Therefore, if (1) an insured disappears for a period of seven years and (2) the absence is unexplained, the insurance company may be required to pay the policy death proceeds. The issue usually revolves around the second of the two conditions.

Thus, the beneficiary usually seeks to establish that the absence is unexplained by proving that the insured was happy and financially solvent with no reason to leave home. In contrast, the insurer might seek to establish that there were good reasons for the insured to leave home, such as marital or financial difficulties. The burden typically falls on the insurer to rebut the presumption of death.

The only presumption in most jurisdictions, however, is the fact of death; not the time of death within the seven-year period. A minority view is that the insured died on the last day of the seven-year period. However, if evidence is presented that the absent

---

[20]Mark C. Rahdert, "Reasonable Expectations Reconsidered," 18 *Connecticut Law Review* 323, 334 (1986).

[21]*Garnet v. John Hancock Mutual Life Insurance Co.*, Conn., 160 F.2d 599 at 601 (1947), quoted by dissent in *Morgan v. State Farm Life Insurance Co.*, 400 P.2d 223, 240, One. 113 (1965).

person, within the seven years, encountered some specific peril, or within that period came within the range of some impending or immediate danger that might reasonably be expected to destroy life, the court or jury may infer that life ceased before the expiration of the seven years. In such cases, the insurer must pay the face amount of the policy plus interest thereon from the date of *proof* of death.

The policy must be maintained in force if the beneficiary is to collect the proceeds, unless it can be proven that death occurred before the policy terminated or unless a death benefit has remained in force under one of the policy's nonforfeiture options. The time of death may become important if a primary beneficiary dies during the seven-year period and there is a contingent beneficiary. In the absence of an agreement between the parties, a court may have to decide on the distribution of policy proceeds.

Although rare, situations arise in which the insurer has paid the death proceeds to the beneficiary on the presumption that the insured died, and the insured reappears. What rights, if any, does the insurer have to recover proceeds in such instances?

The general rule is that, if the insurer paid the full death proceeds in good faith, the insurer has the right to recover the amount paid on the basis that it was paid under a mistake of fact. If, however, payment by the insurer was less than the full policy amount, as in a compromise settlement, it cannot be recovered.

Insuring Agreement

The insuring clause contains the company's promise to pay benefits. It also may describe the types of losses that the policy will cover, or it may simply tie the promise to all of the terms and limitations of the policy. An illustrative clause of a life insurance policy contains the insurer's promise:

> If the insured dies while this policy is in force, we will pay the sum insured to the beneficiary, when we receive at our home office due proof of the insured's death, subject to the provisions of this policy.

The owner's consideration for this promise is, of course, the application and payment of the initial premium. The promise will continue in effect in accordance with the policy provisions as long as the required condition—payment of renewal premiums—is met.

Over the years, the insuring clause in health policies has evolved from a cumbersome provision, filled with complicated definitions and exclusions, to a reasonably simple and straightforward statement of the company's agreement to provide insurance. The following examples are taken from disability income contracts of three leading insurers, and they display the various forms that the insuring clause may take.

In the first example, the insurer specifies the types of loss against which insurance is provided and defines the two causes from which loss must result:

> Subject to all the provisions of this policy, we insure you against disability or other loss resulting from: sickness, which first makes itself known while this policy is in force; or injury, which is accidental bodily injury that occurs while this policy is in force.

The second insurer includes the same elements as does the first, but it merely identifies the causes of loss, which are then defined elsewhere in the policy:

> We will pay for Total Disability or other covered loss resulting from Injuries or Sickness subject to the definitions, exclusions, and other provisions of this policy. Loss must begin while this policy is in force.

A third insurer uses only a simple sentence to promise insurance for loss that results from two specific causes:

> The company will pay the benefits provided in this Policy for loss due to Injury or Sickness.

Effect of Failure to Read Application and Policy

General contract law imputes to the parties knowledge of the terms and conditions of any contract entered into freely and fairly, in the absence of fraud or mistake, as suggested earlier. As noted earlier, however, this general rule does not seem fully applicable to contracts of adhesion, such as insurance. The information imbalance between the applicant/policyowner and the insurer is significant. As well stated by one authority:

> The insured [applicant] buys protection very much as he would any other commodity. Indeed, in business life, he no more thinks of examining the policy delivered to him by an expert manufacturer of such commodities than he does of taking apart the automobile . . . to discover possible defects in its manufacture. And for the ordinary purchaser it would be easier . . . to detect defects in . . . an automobile . . . than in [an insurance policy]. It is now generally recognized by the public at large, and by some courts as well, that it is only rarely that even careful businessmen [and women] do in fact read insurance polices. . . . The prevailing business custom is for the insured to rely upon the accuracy, skill, and good faith of the person who acts for the insurer in filling out the application, delivering the policy, and collecting the first premium.[22]

To a great degree, neither applicants nor policyowners read the materials or policies presented to them. To suggest that they should know their contents is, at one level, reasonable but, at another level, is simply contrary to fact and perhaps human nature. This reality has led some courts to declare that the policyowner is entitled to assume that the policy provides protection in accordance with his or her reasonable expectations.[23] Other courts exhibit a more traditional view, imputing knowledge of terms, conditions, and limitations. Thus, the question of the responsibilities of the applicant and, later, the policyowner to read relevant material seems confused at this point, with court rulings on both sides of the issue.[24]

Insurer's Liability for Delay, Improper Rejection, or Failure to Act

Many courts have held that when an insurer retains an applicant's premium but has not issued the insurance policy, elementary justice dictates that a contract of insurance is in existence or else the company is liable for damages caused because of its delay or failure to insure. The insurer's liability may derive from the contract because of a receipt or otherwise, or it may be in tort for damages generally. In most cases of the insured's death, these damages will be the face amount of the proposed policy.

The tort (negligence) action is the majority view, but other conduct by the insurer may justify coverage. For example, the failure to return the premium promptly with the

---

[22]Buist M. Anderson, *Anderson on Life Insurance* (Boston, MA: Little, Brown and Company, 1991), pp. 255–257, citations omitted.

[23]*McElroy v. British Am. Assur. Co.,* 94 f. 990 (9th Cir. 1899).

[24]See, for example, *McElroy v. British Am. Assur. Co.,* 94 f. 990 (9th Cir. 1899) and *Globe Life & Acc. Ins. Co. v. Still,* 376 F.2d 611 (5th Cir. 1967).

rejection has been held to be unconscionable and, thus, provides interim coverage.[25] In other cases, the courts have not been concerned with the relationship between the insurance company and its agents. Instead, they have viewed the company and its agent from the standpoint of the applicant; that is, they have applied the reasonable expectations doctrine. The conduct of some insurers has been judged to be in bad faith and coverage reinstated.[26]

The amount of delay that may be involved varies with the circumstances. Often, either the agent or the company, or both, may be aware of circumstances that require an acceptance or rejection within a definite time limit. One example involved a case in which an individual made an application for insurance with the intention of replacing existing insurance. It was clear to the court that the insurer should have recognized the need for a decision before the existing policy lapsed. This was particularly true in the court's view in cases in which the individual insured was no longer insurable.[27]

THE LAW AS IT PERTAINS TO THE AGENT

Life and health insurance companies worldwide rely on agents for product sales and customer advice. Problems sometimes arise in this insurer–agent relationship. If agents are to perform their duties properly, they must be given clear guidance and sufficient authority.

We noted in chapter 1 that one of the four classes of asymmetric information problems is that of *principal–agent*. In that discussion, we made clear that our use of the terms *principal* and *agent* was to be taken in their broadest sense, that is, one person acting for another. The principal–agent problem arises because the interests of the principal and the interests of those whom it engages to act for it do not always align perfectly; in fact, they rarely align perfectly. This misalignment occurs because the incentives that motivate the agent usually differ from those that motivate the principal.

In our discussion here, we take a purely legal view of the principal–agent relationship. The incentive incompatibility mentioned earlier between the principal and agent applies to this subset of principal–agent problems. Indeed, in response to this information problem, an entire body of law has evolved that attempts to establish clear rules of authority and conduct in connection with this relationship. This section covers this law.

Overview

In law, agency is a relationship between two parties against all others. The entity that creates the agency relationship is the **principal.** An **agent** is the principal's representative. In most life and health insurance transactions, the agent is the legal representative of the insurer. In some situations, however, the law considers the agent as serving as the applicant's legal representative. This is particularly true when individuals engage someone—known as a **broker**—to procure insurance on their behalf. Our discussion here, however, examines the more common situation in which the agent serves the interests of the insurer.

Agency law classifies agents in accordance with the type of authority granted by the principal:

- actual or express
- implied
- apparent or perceived

---

[25]*Smith v. Westland Life Ins. Co.,* 115 Cal. Rptr. 750 (1974).

[26]*Life Ins. Co. of Southwest v. Nims,* 512 S.W. 2d 712, Tex. Civ. App. (1974).

[27]*Prince v. Western Empire Life Ins. Co.,* 428 P.2d 163, 19 Utah 174 (1967) (application to replace $80,000 of existing insurance that the insured applicant allowed to lapse; insured was killed in the meantime).

Actual or **express authority** is that granted to an agent by the principal in specific language or terms. It may involve wide or general authority, or it may be limited to a narrow field or even to a specific act. **Implied authority** is that associated with certain duties, such as the cashier's authority to take payment for merchandise at a checkout counter. **Apparent** or **perceived authority** is that which a third person believes the agent possesses because of circumstances made possible by the principal and upon which the third party is justified in relying.

Apparent authority is based on the principle of estoppel. That is, if the principal clothes another with certain vestiges of authority, such as receipt books, application forms, specimen policies, sales literature, and similar items that lead a person to reasonably believe that an agency relationship exists, the principal will be prohibited (i.e., estopped) from declaring later that no agency existed.

Laws require that insurance agents possess certain minimum levels of knowledge about insurance and, in some cases, a certain amount of training before a license will be granted. Agents (and insurers) are further required to observe certain laws and regulations relating to how they conduct themselves in the market. Practices associated with agents' and insurers' sales, counseling, and servicing activities are collectively referred to as **market conduct.** As noted later, insurers and agents in several countries, including the United States, incurred substantial market conduct difficulties in the 1990s.

Besides market conduct rules established by government, insurers have their own rules. Indeed, it is in their own best interest to establish and maintain management policy and practice to ensure that their and their agents' market conduct is consistent with law and regulation. A failure to do so opens them to liability. Beyond rules necessary to comply with the law, however, insurers establish rules to define, limit, and clarify agents' authority and to try to create incentives for agent behavior that are compatible with the insurer's goals and objectives. Unless such rules are known to applicants, however, they may not be binding on them.

Insurers are aware of the powers granted to their agents and of the potential for abuse because of the impossibility of eliminating all incentive incompatibility between them and their agents. Accordingly, they take measures to place applicants on notice of the limitations of the powers granted their agents and to minimize market conduct difficulties. The limitations may appear in special notices or wording in premium receipts, applications, or other documents given to applicants that they should read. Market conduct difficulties also can be minimized by disclosure, but, as discussed more fully in chapter 12, certain affirmative actions are required as well.

Powers of the Agent

Two classes of agents exist in law: (1) general agents and (2) special agents. A **general agent** has powers coextensive with those of his or her principal within the limit of the particular business or territory in which the agent operates. A **special agent** has more limited powers, extending only to acts necessary to accomplish particular transactions for which he or she is engaged to perform.

These terms often have somewhat different meanings in the insurance industry and vary depending on whether they apply to non-life insurance or life insurance. In the former, a general agent often has wide authority to enter into insurance contracts, whereas in the life insurance field, a general agent almost always has limited authority. Thus, the person who may be designated as a general agent for life insurance solicitation purposes is really a special agent under the law. This designation can be even more confusing because the term *special agent* is also used to identify a person who acts as a soliciting agent and who is engaged by a general agent. Such a special agent has even less authority than his or her general agent, but, as with the general agent, he or she legally is considered to be a special agent.

Agents acting within the actual or apparent scope of their authority make their principal liable for their wrongful or fraudulent acts, omissions, and misrepresentations. Provided that the policy or application contains no restrictions on the agent's authority, the acts and knowledge of the agent in relation to anything pertaining to the application or policy generally are held by the courts to be the acts and knowledge of the company. This estops it from taking advantage of applicants or policyowners because of an agent's errors or fraudulent acts.

By placing responsibility for the agent's acts solidly with the insurer, the insurer has a strong incentive to ensure that its agents are well trained and comply fully with all legal and other requirements. Much litigation has arisen, especially during the 1990s, from what may be seen as agents' overenthusiasm and from insurers' failure to establish and enforce clear rules of market conduct to guide agents.

To guard against this, most insurers try to call attention to the limitations of the agent's authority by the use of larger type size or color in receipts or other documents or literature provided to the applicant. They also include various policy-value disclaimers in policy illustrations. If applicants fail to read these warnings, they may have difficulty claiming that they were misled.

Although no unanimity exists on the subject, the weight of authority seems to suggest that, in the absence of restrictions, the company is liable not only for the acts of its agents but also for the acts and knowledge of subagents and employees to whom the agent has delegated authority. In insurance, it is a common practice, and one frequently found necessary, for agents to employ others to assist them in their work. Because authority has been delegated to them, the courts have regarded it as just and reasonable that insurance companies should be held responsible not only for acts of their agents, but also for the acts of the subagents employed within the scope of their agents' authority. Although it may be argued that the company has not authorized its agents to delegate their authority to others and that it would, therefore, be an unreasonable extension of the company's liability, it must be remembered that agents are employed by companies in accordance with the usages and necessities of the business.

In the course of their daily business, agents are frequently asked to express opinions on the reliability of dividend and other nonguaranteed illustrations and on the meaning of policy provisions. It is of the utmost importance that a clear understanding exist between the company and its agents as regards the expression of such opinions.

Early U.S. law was extremely legalistic. A person was required to read and know what he or she had signed. Thus, the mere opinion of an agent could not change the clear meaning of a written document. To suggest such action was to strike at the very heart of contract law, particularly when the actual authority of the agent was limited. This response ignored the realities of insurance practices.

In the field of automobile sales, courts have decided that automobile manufacturers should not be permitted to advertise the virtues of their product and at the same time insist on standing on the terms of the sales contract disclaiming warranties. For the same reason, neither should an insurer be allowed to advertise the expertise of its agency force and then deny these very qualities after the product has been purchased. The concern is that to ignore the disparity of the bargaining positions brought about by information asymmetries between the average insurance purchaser and the relatively knowledgeable insurance agent is to invite overreaching on the part of insurers. Accordingly, when an insurance agent renders an opinion that is contrary to the written contract or marketing materials and the proposed policyowner relies on such an opinion, the insurer may be bound. The courts will, in effect, apply the principles of estoppel, at least implicitly if not explicitly.

Policy Limitations

As a general practice, life insurance companies insert a provision in their policies or application forms prohibiting their agents from altering the contract in any way. Although the wording of such clauses is not uniform, the following may be regarded as representative of the usual provision:

> A change in this policy is valid only if it is approved by an officer of the Company. The Company may require that the policy be sent to it for endorsement to show a change. No agent has the authority to change the policy or to waive any of its terms.

Despite the apparent reasonableness of these policy provisions, court decisions on the matter are by no means in harmony, and, as a result, various rules have been formulated.[28] One such rule provides that policy limitations upon any agent's authority operate as notice to the proposed insured of the limited extent of the agent's powers and, thus, protect the company.[29] In another group of cases, the courts have adopted an attitude that is more favorable to the policyowner/insured by holding that such policy restrictions upon an agent's authority are not conclusive as to those matters involved before the contract is completed, but relate only "to the exercise of the agent's authority in matters concerning the policy after its delivery and acceptance, the theory in the main being that no presumption can reasonably attach that the insured was cognizant of such provisions or could anticipate that they would be incorporated into the policy."[30] Still another rule holds, in effect, that restrictions in the policy relate only to acts before a loss has occurred.[31]

Perhaps the rule having the most support at present is one prohibiting the company from rescinding the insurance in case of policy violation (1) wherein the company or any agent clothed with actual or apparent authority has waived, either orally or in writing, any provision of the policy, or (2) wherein the company, because of some knowledge or acts on its part or on the part of its agent, is estopped from setting up as a defense the violation of the terms of the contract. Courts generally are reluctant to allow parol (oral) evidence to alter the interpretation of a written document. However, whether the courts rely on an oral waiver of policy provisions or upon the doctrine of estoppel, the company is held bound. This holds even though some provision of the contract has been violated and the policy contains a provision limiting the agent's power to make policy changes.

Agent's Liability to Principal for Misconduct

The agent should never further his or her own personal interests by disobeying or exceeding the principal's instructions. Any misconduct of the agent makes him or her personally liable to the principal for resultant damage. This responsibility derives from the law of agency. Any loss or damage to the principal must be indemnified by the agent. Examples of agents' misconduct are exceeding specific authority, binding unacceptable risks, failure to transmit information concerning risks, collusion with the applicant, incorrect statements concerning the proposed insured, failure to transmit funds collected on behalf of the principal, and failure to follow explicit instructions issued by the prin-

---

[28]George James Couch, *Couch Cyclopedia of Insurance Law,* 2nd ed. (Rochester, NY: Lawyers Co-operative Publishing Co., 1959–1968), §26:82.

[29]Ibid., §26:83.

[30]Ibid., §26:86.

[31]Ibid., §26:88.

cipal. In practice, however, most cases involving serious violation of agency agreements are resolved by the agents' discharge and a revocation of license.

MARKET CONDUCT AND THE LAW

The conduct of insurers and agents in marketing life and health insurance is subject to statutory and common-law legal standards. They are subject to various disclosure and related requirements (see chapters 5, 6, and 12) and to Unfair Trade Practices Acts, which prohibit them from engaging in any activities that could mislead consumers (see chapters 12 and 35).

The courts in numerous countries, including the United States, United Kingdom, Australia, and Japan, have been taking a more aggressive position regarding market conduct. Within the United States, allegations of unfair and misleading marketing practices have led to an explosion of litigation focusing mostly on so-called vanishing premiums (see chapter 6).

Background

During the high interest rate environment of the 1980s, life insurance policy sales materials illustrated future premiums and policy values that were predicated on these high interest rates. It was quite common for agents to show applicants that they could pay as few as five to seven annual premiums and their policies would be self-supporting in the sense that internally generated interest (via dividends or excess interest credits) would be more than sufficient to cover all policy charges for the duration of the contract (typically, age 100). Of course, this so-called *vanish premium* or *vanish pay* option did not guarantee that no further premiums would be due, for the scheme's success lay in the insurer being able and willing to continue to credit high interest rates—rates that sometimes were 12 percent or even higher. Many customers replaced older life insurance with the new policies that provided for such high interest rates, after the agent showed the customer how much better off he or she would be under the newer policy—again, all based on illustrated values that relied on the projected high interest rates.

Insurers included the usual disclaimers on their policy illustrations, noting that future values shown were not guaranteed and could vary. In many instances, these caveats printed at the bottom of illustrations, often as footnotes, were ignored, not read, omitted, or considered irrelevant. Agents often pointed out that policy illustrations of past years carried such cautions but that, for the previous three or more decades, life insurers had always paid dividends in excess of those illustrated because the practice was to illustrate conservatively.

By the early 1990s, many policyowners who expected that their policies would be self-sustaining or even paid up ("What's the difference? Isn't this just technical insurance jargon?") found, to their great dismay, that premiums were still due. Interest rates had fallen to their more modest pre-1980s levels, and policy premiums and values reflected this changed reality. Insurers were inundated with consumers complaining that they were misled.

Litigation

The individual lawsuits began, with class action lawsuits soon following. Allegations included deceptive sales practices, fraudulent inducement, intentional misrepresentation, and fraudulent concealment.[32] Insurers responded initially that policyowners were put

---

[32]Richard T. Phillips, "'Vanishing Premium' Litigation: The Plaintiff's Perspective," presentation before the Mississippi Bar Summer School for Lawyers (1996).

on notice about the possibility of declining interest rates through the disclaimer on the policy illustration. They also noted that the illustration was not a part of the contract. Many argued that the problems were isolated, having been caused mainly by a few "rogue" agents.[33]

Insurer defenses have been successful in many instances but less so in others. The courts (and juries) have taken note of the reasonable expectations and other theories to find for the policyowner. Disclaimers often were found to have omitted what juries believed was important information or were ambiguous. In other instances, the disclaimers seemed to be wrong when they stated that "illustrated values reflect the company's current investment experience," when, in fact, the insurer's actual investment return was less than that being illustrated to cause the premium to "vanish."

This important matter is not fully resolved, as litigation continues for many insurers. Thousands of cases have been settled with insurers having paid millions of dollars to date in judgments, fines, and legal fees. This episode should remind insurers of the information problems of its customers and of how the courts seek to rectify this information asymmetry.[34]

PROVISIONS PROTECTING THE POLICYOWNER

We now begin an examination of the actual provisions contained in life and health insurance policies, with particular reference to those sold in the United States. U.S. law and many other countries' laws require the inclusion of certain so-called standard provisions. As noted earlier, the laws do not mandate the actual wording for these provisions; rather, they provide that policies must contain provisions whose language is at least as favorable as that of the statute. Certain other provisions may be included in life and health insurance contracts at the option of the insurer. We cover both required and optional provisions in this and the following sections.

As mentioned at the beginning of this chapter, life and health insurance policy provisions are designed to help address the information problems inherent in these complex financial and legal instruments. Certain provisions can be considered mainly as protecting the policyowner from the lemons problem of the insurer possessing greater knowledge than the policyowner. We cover these provisions in this section. All are required to be included in life and health insurance policies sold in the United States and in several other countries as well. Other provisions, considered mainly as protecting the insurer from adverse selection and moral hazard problems occasioned because the policyowner possesses superior knowledge to the insurer in certain respects, are discussed in the next section.

Entire Contract Clause

The **entire contract clause** provides that the policy itself and the application, if a copy is attached to the policy, constitute the entire contract between the parties. A standard provision, the clause protects the policyowner in that the company cannot, merely by reference, include within the policy its procedural rules or, unless a copy is attached, the application or any statements made to the medical examiner. This clause also protects the company in that the application, if made part of the contract (which it ordinarily is), becomes part of the consideration for the contract, and material misrepresentations

---

[33]For a discussion of possible insurer defenses, see Phillip E. Stano, "Addressing Vanishing Premiums Class Action Litigation," presentation before the Association of Life Insurance Counsel (1996).

[34]Liability issues arising from selling policies over the Internet will undoubtedly be another area in which information asymmetry will be a concern for insurers. The case law is unclear, but such issues will be the wave of the future.

made by the applicant can be used by the company in denying liability (but see following section on the incontestable clause) or seeking reformation or rescission of the contract. See Box 9-2.

Incontestable Clause

The **incontestable clause** provides that the validity of an insurance contract may not be contested after it has been in effect for a certain period of time, such as two years. Now a required provision, it was introduced by life insurance companies on a voluntary basis to provide greater assurance to the public that relatively innocent misstatements by applicants would not be the cause of a claim being denied. Its roots date back to mid-nineteenth-century England when insurers sought to allay public concern through inclusion of an *indisputable clause;* this clause was intended to address the then ultratechnical application of the doctrine of warranties by many insurers. As English insurers sold life insurance in the United States, this innovation and the resulting competition by the British soon forced U.S. life insurers to adopt the same practice. The Manhattan Life, using a five-year time limit, is said to be the first U.S. insurer to have incorporated the clause in its contracts.[35]

The use of the clause spread rapidly because it was perceived as a means of addressing the public's concern about the quality and trustworthiness of U.S. life insurers following a severe post–Civil War depression that precipitated numerous insolvencies. The depressed economic conditions of the 1870s saw insurers seeking new ways of gaining a competitive advantage through contract liberalization. The 1879 adoption of the clause by the Equitable Life Assurance Society gave the clause its greatest impetus.[36]

A typical life insurance policy provision reads as follows:

> Except for accidental death and disability premium payment benefits, we cannot contest this policy after it has been in force for two years while the insured is alive.

The clause is now common worldwide. In the United States, as well as in Japan and several other countries, the maximum period of contestability is two years. In other countries, such as Germany and Spain, the time limit is one year. The clause has been given a broad interpretation in the United States. It prevents a life insurance company from voiding a life or (sometimes) health insurance contract after the passage of the specified time even on grounds of material misrepresentation or fraud in the application for the contract.

---

[35]Luis M. Villaronga, *The Incontestable Clause: An Historical Analysis,* S. S. Huebner Foundation Monograph Series, No. 5 (University of Pennsylvania Press, 1976), p. 7.

[36]Ibid., p. 8.

BOX 9-2

REFORMATION AND RESCISSION

A **reformation** is an equitable remedy wherein a contract is reformed—redrafted—to conform to the original intention of the parties. This remedy is often used when a mistake has been made by one or both of the parties in drafting a contract (e.g., a misspelled name).

A **rescission,** which is an equitable remedy typically involving more serious contentiousness, is a cancellation or avoidance of a contract. This remedy is frequently used when fraud or other material misrepresentation is involved.

The rationale for this broad interpretation is the protection of beneficiaries because they potentially could suffer even greater information asymmetries than the applicant. The clause removes fear and worry about whether the insurance will pay. It removes the fear of lawsuits at a time—namely, at the insured's death—when it may be difficult for the beneficiary successfully to combat an insurer's charge of misrepresentation. The lawsuit could be particularly difficult to contest in view of the fact that the insured individual who made the representations that form the basis of the contract is no longer alive to present his or her side of the case. The clause also is said to benefit society as a whole—that is, it carries some positive externalities—in that it reduces the need for societal support of dependents, which is a statement that applies to life and health insurance policies generally.

From the standpoint of public policy, it is undesirable to have dependents subject to a forfeiture for violations that might remain unknown for many years and, at the death of the insured, leave dependents without protection. Moreover, if a policy is contested, the issue is typically resolved in the courts. This involves delays at the time when the need for speedy payment is greatest. The law typically grants insurers only the first two policy years in which to initiate this process. Thereafter, they are barred from contesting the validity of the contract, unless the insured dies before the time limit has expired; then there is generally no time limit on such a challenge.

The incontestable clause is similar to a short statute of limitations. By inserting the policy provision, the company undertakes to make all necessary investigations concerning the good faith and all other circumstances surrounding the application within the time limit stipulated in the clause. It limits the period of time the insurer can use the defense of fraud, concealment, or material misrepresentation to defeat the contract. The company agrees not to resist claim payment if premiums have been paid, if no violation of the contract has come to light during the stipulated time limit, and if, during the time, the company has taken no action to rescind the contract.[37]

U.S. insurers are permitted to use a somewhat weaker variation of the incontestable clause in their health insurance contracts. The *time-limit-on-certain-defenses clause* bars a challenge to the validity of the contract after a certain time (three years maximum), just as with the incontestable clause, except that it permits a challenge for fraudulent misstatements irrespective of the time elapsed.

Grace Period Provision

The **grace period** provision requires the insurer to accept premium payments for a certain period after their due date, during which period the policy remains in effect. Laws in North America typically require a minimum grace period of 31 days for traditional life and health insurance policies and 60 or 61 days for flexible-premium contracts. During this period the insurer (1) is required to accept the premium payment even though it is technically late (i.e., it is past the due date) and (2) may not require evidence of insurability as a condition of premium acceptance.

If the insured suffers a covered loss through death or loss of health during the grace period, the company must pay the claim but is permitted to deduct the overdue premium plus interest from the payment. The provision's purpose is to protect the policyowner against unintentional lapse. If it were not for this provision and the payment were even one day late, insurers could require evidence of insurability to reinstate the policy.

Although companies are permitted to charge interest on past-due premiums, they rarely do so because of the small amounts involved and the expense of collection. As the

---

[37] A few insurance cases have involved fraud so outrageous that courts allowed contracts to be voided from their inception, even though the period of contestability had expired. See Joseph M. Belth, ed., *The Insurance Forum*, Vol. XII, No. 9 (September 1985), p. 84.

company collects a premium only in the event of claim within the grace period, most policies that lapse pay no share of the cost of insurance for that period. They receive a month's free protection.

Nonforfeiture Provision

The **nonforfeiture provision** stipulates the options available under a cash-value policy if the policyowner elects to terminate the policy and explains the basis or method used to determine these optional values. This provision is relevant only for life insurance policies with cash values and with some long-term care policies.

In the early days, insurance policies had no cash values. If a policy lapsed, the policyowner "forfeited" all contributions in excess of those necessary to cover current and past mortality charges and expenses. Laws in the United States and some other countries now prohibit such forfeitures. In other countries, such as the United Kingdom, cash surrender values are optional with the insurer, although they are commonly included. See Box 9-3.

Under the **Standard Nonforfeiture Laws** in effect in U.S. jurisdictions, cash-value life insurance policies must state the mortality table and rate of interest used in calculating the nonforfeiture values provided by the policy, as well as a description of the method used in calculating the values. In addition, a table is required showing the cash surrender and other nonforfeiture options for each of the first 20 years. (These options are discussed in the next chapter.)

These laws set out the circumstances under which policies must have nonforfeiture values and stipulate the minimum required values. In effect, the laws require cash values under all life insurance policies that involve a substantial prefunding of future mortality charges. For example, under some laws, a policy must contain cash values if premiums are leveled for 20 or more years. Thus, a 10-year level-premium term policy need not have cash values, but a 20-year term policy must have them. We explore the legal and actuarial meaning of the term *substantial* in chapter 29.

Much misunderstanding surrounds cash-value calculations for traditional policies and the stated interest rate. The rate is sometimes mistakenly thought to be a policy's rate of return. This misunderstanding does not apply to the same extent with policies such as universal life (UL) and current assumption whole life (CAWL), wherein cash values are derived using the so-called retrospective approach (see chapter 29 for details). Traditional policies use the prospective approach.

BOX 9-3

CASH SURRENDER VALUES IN THE UNITED KINGDOM

The insurance business is far less regulated in the United Kingdom than in the United States. Unlike U.S. law, U.K. laws impose no requirements for cash surrender values. The question of fair treatment of terminating policyowners has been left to market forces. Because of custom, however, most insurers include in their contracts a provision that grants a terminating policyowner the right to a cash surrender value to be determined by the company at the time of surrender.

Including a cash-value scale in life contracts is not a widely accepted practice. When projections of likely surrender values are made to the customer, they are shown only for the first five years. No minimum values are guaranteed, as in the United States.

Source: Iskandar S. Hamwi and Durwood Ruegger, "Past and Present Changes in Living Policy Values," *Journal of the American Society of CLU & ChFC* (November 1994), p. 78.

The prospective method utilizes a discount approach and derives a present value figure as the cash value. Thus, the higher the interest rate stated in a prospective-based cash-value (i.e., traditional) policy, the lower will be the cash value, other things being the same. Conversely, the lower the interest rate used, the higher will be the policy's cash values, other things remaining equal. Hence, if two traditional whole life policies were identical in every way except that one carried a cash-value interest rate of 3 percent and the other a rate of 5 percent, the policy with the 3 percent rate would have the higher cash values. As a practical matter, of course, things are rarely "identical." Usually—but not always—a policy with a higher cash value has a higher premium, lower dividends, or both. Even if the "identical" assumption is relaxed, one cannot judge the effective rate of return on cash-value policies by reference to this nonforfeiture policy interest provision.

Some persons who do not understand life insurance fundamentals often seize on this low cash-value interest rate and assert that this is the policy's rate of return. This is incorrect. It is merely a conservative discount rate used to derive cash values on a prospective basis.

In contrast to the situation that exists with traditional policies, UL and CAWL policies' stated interest rates—both guaranteed and current rates—are not used to derive cash values on a discount basis. They are simply applied to add amounts to an already (usually) existing cash value—that is, they are used in interest compounding, not discounting. Thus, the higher the interest rate used, the higher are the resultant cash values and vice versa, other things being equal. Again, other things rarely are equal. As illustrated in preceding chapters, one policy may credit a higher interest rate than another, yet have higher loading charges assessed against the cash values, with the result that the total value is less on the higher interest contract.

Reinstatement Clause

Another standard provision, the **reinstatement clause,** gives the policyowner the right to reinstate a previously lapsed policy under certain conditions. The two most important conditions are furnishing of evidence of insurability and paying past-due premiums.

Provide Evidence of Insurability

To deter and prevent adverse selection, insurers require the insured to furnish evidence of insurability that is satisfactory to the company. Otherwise, insureds in poor health would routinely apply for reinstatement, as experience has shown.

Most lapses are unintentional and are followed within a short period of time (two to four weeks) by a reinstatement application. The insurer usually takes a liberal position in such cases, as the likelihood of adverse selection is minimal. Completion of only a short questionnaire is required. Companies have the contractual right to require a medical examination and other detailed evidence of insurability, but, in practice, only limited evidence typically is required for recent lapses. The longer the time period since the lapse, the more closely reinstatement requirements resemble those for new applications.

The term *evidence of insurability* is broader than the term *good health.* Insurability connotes meeting standards with regard to occupation, travel, other insurance, and financial condition, as well as the physical characteristics and health status of the insured. A classic example of the distinction between good health and insurability is the case of a criminal condemned to death—such a person may be in perfect health, but he or she is hardly insurable.

The term *satisfactory to the company* has generally been held to allow the insurer to require evidence that would be satisfactory to a reasonable insurer. An insurer is in business to accept, not to decline, applications, and, if the person is insurable, the presumption is that he or she will be accepted.

An interesting issue in connection with reinstatement relates to how it interacts with the incontestable clause. The law is not entirely clear, but the majority view in the United States is that the incontestable clause is reinstated, making the policy contestable again, but only with respect to statements made in the reinstatement application. A second view is that the original contestable period is effective, whereas a third, and very much a minority, view holds that the original contestable period is effective with respect to the policy as a whole but that the reinstatement itself is a separate agreement that has no incontestable period and can be contested for fraud at any time. In contrast, the courts have been virtually unanimous in holding that the suicide clause does not run again.

Pay Past-Due Premiums

A second condition of reinstatement is the payment of past-due premiums. With traditional cash-value and noncancellable health insurance policies, the usual terms require payment of the overdue amounts, less any dividends that would have been paid, usually with interest at 6 or 8 percent. Any outstanding policy loan also must be either repaid or reinstated through payment of past-due interest.

An argument can be made that nothing should be levied for past-due mortality or morbidity charges, as no coverage was provided during the period of lapse. As a result, some jurisdictions limit the maximum past-due amount that insurers may collect under certain health insurance policies to two months' premiums. Some jurisdictions also limit the collection of past-due amounts under life insurance policies to any increase in reserve between the time of lapse and reinstatement.

The reinstatement provision was originally included voluntarily by companies to safeguard accumulated policy values. Under these older contracts, if the premium was not paid when due, not only did the policy lapse, but accumulated policy values were forfeited. With the inclusion of nonforfeiture options, the value of the reinstatement option has declined.

The standard reinstatement provision does not require that reinstatement be permitted if the policy has been either surrendered or continued as extended term insurance and the full period of coverage has expired. Many companies include this restriction in their contracts. If the extended term period has not expired and has several years to run, insurers often will reinstate the policy with little or no evidence of insurability.

Although company practice is liberal, reinstatement is seldom permitted by companies or required by law more than five years after lapse, due to the high costs involved. At one time, reinstatement was more or less routinely preferred to purchasing a new policy. In today's competitive marketplace, such is no longer necessarily true. The considerations applicable to reinstatement are quite similar to those involved with replacement. See chapter 11.

Misstatement of Age or Sex Provisions

Most U.S. jurisdictions require that life insurance policies include a **misstatement of age** provision stipulating that if the insured's age is found to have been misstated, the amount of insurance will be adjusted to be that which would have been purchased by the premium had the correct age been known. This provision is optional with the insurer in most individual health insurance policies.

For example, consider a $50,000 ordinary life policy issued at age 35 at a $900 annual premium. Assume that, when the death claim was filed, the true issue age was found to be 36, and $50,000 of coverage at this age would have required a premium of $960. The company would pay $46,875 (900/960 × $50,000).

The question arises as to how one measures age. Some companies define age as that of the last birthday. Most companies, however, use the age to the nearest birth-date anniversary. Thus, if a 45-year-old woman is less than six months from her next birth-date anniversary, she will be considered to be age 46.

If the error in age is discovered while the policy is still in force, the procedure followed depends upon whether the age has been understated or overstated. If the age has been understated, the policyowner usually is given the option of paying the difference in premiums with interest or of having the policy reissued for the reduced amount. With an overstatement of age, a refund is usually made by paying the difference in reserves.

This provision, originally included in policies voluntarily by many insurers, is intended to deal contractually with the potential problem of having a misstatement of age being considered a material misrepresentation, and thus being the basis for policy avoidance. By addressing this issue explicitly through a policy provision, insurers, in effect, remove the possibility of a misstatement of age being the basis of their contesting the validity of the contract. Also, as the incontestable clause does not apply to age misstatements, adjustments may be made in policy benefits because of an age misstatement after the period of contestability has expired.

Although not a standard provision, the amount payable would be adjusted in a similar manner if a misstatement of sex had been made on the application. Misstatements of sex are not common and usually occur because of a transcribing error, not because the proposed insured was unsure of his or her sex!

Renewal Provisions

Life insurance policies may be continued by the timely payment of premiums for the length of the policy term. Possibly most, if not all, individually issued life insurance policies in North America stipulate the guaranteed maximum premium that can be charged by the insurer. Of course, some policies carry indeterminate premiums, but a ceiling premium applies here also.

The situation is different for many health insurance policies as mentioned in chapter 7. Each health insurance policy is required to contain a provision that describes its renewal and premium arrangements. Individual health insurance contracts are classified according to their renewal rights, of which the most common are (1) noncancellable, (2) guaranteed renewable, or (3) conditionally renewable.

Renewal rights carry differing costs. Noncancellable policies have guaranteed premiums and are likely to be more expensive than those for which premiums can be changed unilaterally by the insurer. Policies that the company can refuse to renew under certain conditions and in which premiums can change generally are the least expensive forms of individual health insurance. The various insurance laws and regulations are not uniform in defining these renewal categories, but definitions that follow are those in common use for each category in policies offered in North America.

Noncancellable

As noted in chapter 7, a *noncancellable* policy gives the insured the right to renew the policy, typically to age 65, by timely payment of a stipulated premium. A guaranteed premium rate is set forth in the contract and may not be changed by the insurer. During that period, the company cannot cancel the policy or make any unilateral change in its benefits. This renewal category generally is limited to disability income insurance.

Guaranteed Renewable

A *guaranteed renewable* policy also gives the insured the right to renew the policy, typically to age 65, by timely payment of the premium. During that period, however, the company has the right to change the premiums for all insureds of the same class at their original insuring ages, but it cannot cancel the policy or make any unilateral change in its benefits. This renewal category is used for medical expense, long-term care, and disability income insurance.

Conditionally Renewable

A **conditionally renewable** policy gives the insured a limited right to renew the policy to age 65, or some later age, by timely payment of the premium. The insurer has the right to refuse to renew coverage only for reasons stated in the policy by giving written notice to the insured 30 days in advance of the premium due date. The insurer usually retains the right to change premiums and benefits for all insureds of the same class. This renewal category is used for medical expense and disability income insurance.

The stated reasons for nonrenewal vary according to the type of insurance, but the insurer cannot refuse to renew coverage solely because of a change in the insured's health after the policy has been issued. The company may refuse to renew a specific class of insureds or may discontinue a policy series for all insureds in a single jurisdiction. On an individual basis, the insurer may refuse to renew when the insured changes to a more hazardous occupation, when the economic need for the policy ends, or when the insured becomes overinsured through purchase of other insurance that will provide benefits in excess of the expected loss.

This provision is used in most specialized business disability income forms other than overhead expense insurance (see chapter 17). In such policies, the company retains the right not to renew on an individual basis when the covered business risk no longer exists or when other specified events occur. The insurer also may have the right to change benefits, but usually it guarantees that the premium rates will not change.

The conditional renewal provision appears uniformly in noncancellable and guaranteed renewable disability income policies to provide continuous coverage from age 65 to age 75 while the insured remains employed on a full-time basis. During this period, the insured pays a renewal premium at the rates then in effect for persons of the same attained age and class of risk. Monthly indemnity amounts are rarely reduced, but the benefit period usually is limited to two years during the conditional renewal period.

Questions

1. Explain why an insurance contract is considered of utmost good faith and not of caveat emptor.
2. What problems might arise if life policies were contracts of indemnity and property and liability policies were valued contracts?
3. Describe circumstances under which an insurer might consider using each one of the three types of premium receipts.
4. Insurance contracts are aleatory by nature. What common elements in insurance contracts prevent them from becoming vehicles for speculation by either the insured or the insurer?
5. How does recognition by the courts of the doctrines of *contra proferentum*, good faith and fair dealing, and reasonable expectations help put consumers and insurers on an equal footing? Have these doctrines ever led the courts to put insurers in an unfair position?
6. The value of an insurance contract derives to a great extent from the value of information therein. Explain.

CHAPTER

10

LIFE AND HEALTH INSURANCE CONTRACTS: II

Objectives

■ Explain the need for clarity and flexibility in beneficiary clauses.

■ Describe the uses of various life insurance policy settlement options.

■ Give examples that show how nonforfeiture options can provide added flexibility to life insurance policies.

■ Describe the practices of life insurers regarding surplus distribution.

■ Describe various options given to policyowners on the form of surplus distribution.

■ Summarize the legal rights of a policyowner's and a beneficiary's creditors.

This chapter continues our examination of life and health insurance contracts. Here we focus on (1) provisions protecting the insurance company, (2) provisions that supply policyowner flexibility, and (3) creditors' rights in life insurance.

PROVISIONS PROTECTING THE INSURANCE COMPANY

Several life insurance contract provisions primarily protect the life insurance company against adverse selection and other market imperfections. These include the suicide clause, the delay clause, and certain hazard restriction clauses.

Suicide Clause

At one time, life insurance contracts excluded the risk of suicide entirely. This was unfortunate because the very purpose for which the policy was purchased—to protect dependents—could thus be defeated. In addition, it was not necessary to exclude suicide completely to protect the company. Suicide is one of the causes of death that make up the total mortality rate, and such deaths are included in the mortality tables upon which premiums are based.

However, the company must protect itself against cases when insurance is purchased in contemplation of suicide. Adequate protection against this adverse selection and moral hazard possibility can be obtained by excluding the suicide risk for the first one or two policy years.[1] This provision also benefits policyowners generally in that it assures them that their equitable share of mortality charges will not be larger because of their having to cover claims of individuals who purchase insurance in contemplation of suicide.

The clause is intended to protect against adverse selection or moral hazard—not to exclude the risk of suicide as such. Its inclusion is optional, but, because the insurer would not be able to exclude suicide-based death claims were it omitted, virtually every insurer includes it. Most laws permit an exclusion of up to two years, and this is the usual practice. A number of companies use a one-year exclusion. A typical **suicide clause** reads as follows:

> For the first two full years from the original application date, we will not pay
> if the insured commits suicide (while sane or insane). We will terminate the
> policy and give back the premiums paid to us less any loan.

The question of whether a death is suicide or due to other causes is almost always left to a jury in the United States. The legal presumption is that a person will not take his or her own life, so the burden of proof of suicide rests with the insurer. This fact, plus the tendency of courts to seek ways of ruling for dependents, often makes it exceedingly difficult to prove suicide. For example, some courts have held that an "insane" person, by definition, cannot commit "suicide" because suicide requires a knowledge of right and wrong. This result has emerged even in the face of the "while sane or insane" policy language.

Thus, under this interpretation, an insane person who takes his or her own life has not committed suicide, and the company would be required to honor the death claim. Where death is, in fact, determined to be by suicide and within the period of exclusion, the company will refund the premiums paid, with or without interest, depending on the contract.

Delay Clause

Life insurance policies issued in the United States must contain a so-called **delay clause,** which grants the company the right to defer cash-value payment or the making of a policy loan (except for purposes of paying premiums) for up to six months after its request. This provision, which does not apply to the payment of death claims, is intended to protect the company against "runs"—a type of *negative externality* (see chapter 1)—which could cause the failure of an otherwise financially sound company.

The clause had been primarily of historical interest until the recent adverse times for some insurers. As the experience of at least one recent financially troubled insurer revealed, the clause is not always sufficient.

Exclusion and Hazard Restriction Clauses

The great majority of life insurance policies sold in North America and probably elsewhere typically contain only one exclusion—for suicide—and even here, the exclusion is time limited. In contrast, health insurance policies contain several clauses that either exclude or restrict coverage in important ways. This difference is explained to a great degree by the difference in the moral hazard exposure between life and health insurance.

---

[1]The economist might make a distinction between the adverse selection and moral hazard motivations here, although from a legal point of view the distinctions seem irrelevant. Thus, if the proposed insured plans to commit suicide *only* if the policy is issued, the problem is moral hazard; that is, the existence of insurance increases the likelihood of a claim. If the proposed insured plans to commit suicide irrespective of whether the policy is issued, the problem is adverse selection; that is, the individual is using his or her superior knowledge ("I'm going to commit suicide, but the insurer doesn't know it") to procure a good deal for himself or herself (or, rather, the beneficiary).

Moral Hazard in Life and Health Insurance

With life insurance policies, the overwhelming majority of insureds and beneficiaries are not likely to engage in activities the purpose of which is to bring about the insured event. That is, neither the beneficiary nor the insured (!) is keen to bring about the death of the insured! Additionally, the determination of whether the insured event has occurred is relatively simple. It involves answering only two questions: (1) Is the individual dead and (2) is the dead person the insured? Ordinarily, answering these two questions is straightforward. Faking either, although not impossible, is quite difficult.[2]

In contrast, the determination of whether the insured event has occurred under health insurance policies can be quite difficult. This issue is particularly important under disability income and other valued health insurance policies. For example, it can be exceptionally difficult to determine whether, in fact, an insured has injured his or her back. Moreover, even if the back injury is real, determining whether, in fact, it is sufficiently grave to prevent the insured from working can be a challenge. Additionally, insureds bent on collecting under health insurance policies do not have to lose their lives to collect, although they may have to hurt themselves—a not too appealing option either!

As a result of these differences, we observe that insurers only occasionally include special exclusions in life policies. Inclusion of such special exclusions usually is not motivated by moral hazard considerations but by the fact that the insured is exposed to an unusual loss-causing situation or by adverse selection concerns—the two of which can easily overlap. In contrast, exclusions and other restrictions in health insurance policies often are motivated both by moral hazard considerations and by a desire to limit the insurer's exposure. Thus, we discuss life and health insurance policies separately.

Exclusions in Life Insurance Policies

Aviation Exclusion   Occasionally, an underwriter will insist on adding an **aviation exclusion,** which excludes coverage if the insured dies in an aviation accident. It is included in U.S. life insurance contracts today only under certain exceptional circumstances, such as with insureds who are military pilots or fly experimental aircraft. Its inclusion is motivated by concerns about the additional, unusual risk and by possible adverse selection.

All companies cover fare-paying passengers on regularly scheduled airlines. Similarly, anticipated flights on unscheduled airlines usually do not result in any policy restrictions or an increased rate. Even private pilots and the pilots and crews of commercial airlines are insured with standard or with only slightly extra rates. Virtually all coverage restrictions can be eliminated, however, if the insured is willing to pay an extra premium.

War Exclusion   **War exclusion** clauses exclude coverage if the insured's death occurs under certain military conditions. The clauses normally provide for a return of all premiums paid with interest or a refund equal to the policy's reserve. Companies usually insert war clauses in their contracts during periods of impending or actual war, particularly for policies issued to persons of draft age. War clauses are typically canceled at the end of the war period.

The major purpose of war exclusion clauses is to control adverse selection by insurance buyers. Additionally, uncertainty about the additional mortality occasioned by a given military conflict leads insurers to prefer to exclude the exposure altogether rather than to try to price it. Persons about to enter military service are at least vaguely aware of their increased likelihood of death, so they would be more likely to purchase life insurance at standard rates and would be more be inclined to buy larger policies than otherwise.

---

[2]One not so uncommon means of faking a claim involves individuals who purchase life insurance policies, move to another (typically developing) country, and bribe local coroners to certify that they died. If the policy face amount is not too large, the insurer may pay the claim without much investigation.

Exclusion clauses can benefit proposed insureds in that they might be refused coverage altogether if the insurer could not protect itself from an extra military hazard. The experience of many companies after both World War I and World War II showed that they could have covered the war risk without imposing extra premiums. Without such clauses, however, the potential adverse selection involved could have significantly impacted the overall mortality experience.

In general, there are two types of war clauses: (1) the status type and (2) the results type. Under the **status clause,** the insurer need not pay the policy face amount if death results while the insured is in the military service, regardless of the cause of death. Some companies liberalize this clause by excluding only death outside the "home area."

Under the **results clause,** the insurer is excused from paying the face amount only if the death is a *result* of war. The distinction between the clauses resides in the significance of the cause of death: Under the status clause, if the insured is in military service, the cause of death is immaterial, so that even if a person slipped on a bar of soap while taking a bath at home and death resulted, there would be no coverage. Under the results clause, the cause of death would have to be related to military activity.

The validity of war clauses has not been the subject of much litigation, but the clauses' interpretation has given rise to a large volume of cases. Much litigation has revolved around the question of whether a particular clause is a status clause or a results clause. Other litigation has related to the nature of death and the existence of war itself.[3]

Exclusions and Restrictions in Health Insurance Policies

Most limitations in health insurance contracts that relate to moral hazard considerations occur through operation of various definitions related to the benefit provisions. We explored most of these in chapter 7. Also, sometimes it is deemed necessary to attach a rider or waiver to the policy of an individual insured to exclude benefits for a specific health condition. We cover this matter in chapter 26.

All health insurance policies, however, contain several general exclusions. The most common exclusion in disability income contracts provides that the policy will not cover loss that begins in the first two policy years from a preexisting condition. As a general concept, a **preexisting condition** is an undisclosed health condition that was present within a specified number of years before the policy was issued and required medical attention or caused symptoms for which a prudent person would have sought medical care. Long-term care policies also include preexisting conditions clauses, although they usually are more liberal than those found in disability income policies.

The precise definition of a preexisting condition differs from jurisdiction to jurisdiction. Some limit the period of treatment or symptoms to five years before the date of application. In others, it is held to as little as six months. Some jurisdictions do not allow use of the prudent person test.

The preexisting condition exclusion usually applies only to health conditions that the insured did not reveal in the application. Health conditions fully disclosed on the application are usually covered unless the insurer attaches a rider to exclude a condition by specific name or description.

In 1996, the **Health Insurance Portability and Accountability Act** (HIPAA) was enacted, the primary purpose of which was to help ensure that individuals would not lose their medical coverage or be subject to new preexisting condition periods when they changed or lost their jobs.

Virtually all health insurance policies exclude any loss caused by war or act of war. Health insurance policies also automatically exclude losses caused by intentionally

---

[3]See *Berley v. Pennsylvania Mutual Life Insurance Company,* 373 Pa. 231, 95 A.2d 202 (Pa. 1953), and *Stucker v. College Life Insurance Co. of America,* 208 N.E.2d 731 (Ind. 1965).

self-inflicted injury. Until recent years, all individual disability income contracts used an exclusion for normal uncomplicated pregnancy and childbirth. The major companies now omit the pregnancy exclusion in disability income policies intended for their most favorable occupational classes. Individual medical expense policies contain more numerous exclusions, similar to those of group insurance.

A final important limitation, which is not part of the exclusion provision, appears in the general provisions of the policy and calls for the suspension of coverage while the insured is on active duty in the military service of any country or international authority. This *military suspense provision* allows the insured to place the policy back in force without evidence of good health when active duty ends.

PROVISIONS PROVIDING POLICYOWNER FLEXIBILITY

We now examine provisions in life and health insurance policies that provide policy-owners with greater flexibility. In effect, these provisions provide owners with a package of options, thus enhancing the value of the contract. This discussion necessarily relates more to life than to health contracts because of their third-party nature and their prematurity values.

The Beneficiary Clause

The **beneficiary clause** in a life insurance contract typically permits the policyowner to have policy death proceeds distributed to whomever and in whatever form he or she wishes. The policyowner can prepare a plan of distribution in advance that accomplishes his or her personal objectives by allowing appropriately for future contingencies.

In some countries, such as the United Kingdom, the application for insurance does not provide for a beneficiary designation. In such instances, death proceeds are usually distributed according to the decedent's will.

Nature of Designation

Primary and Contingent Designations   The person named as the first to receive policy death proceeds is called the **primary beneficiary.** More than one person can be designated as the primary beneficiary.

The time between when the primary beneficiary is designated and the insured dies may be many years. If no primary beneficiary is alive at the time of the insured's death, proceeds ordinarily would be payable to the insured's estate in the absence of contrary instructions in the beneficiary designation itself. This result may not be the most desirable because it would subject the proceeds to additional costs (see chapter 16) and may not be consistent with the policyowner's wishes.

A solution to this potential problem is to name a **contingent beneficiary,** also called a **secondary beneficiary,** whereby a person is named to receive death proceeds if the primary beneficiary is not alive at the insured's death. Also, a contingent beneficiary could be named to receive any payments still to be made under a settlement option (see later) after the death of a primary beneficiary who had outlived the insured. More than one contingent beneficiary may be named.

Any contingent or later (called *tertiary beneficiary*) designation typically is made at the same time that the primary beneficiary is designated. A beneficiary designation with both primary and contingent beneficiaries might read:

> Proceeds to be paid to Christine B. Gill, wife of the insured, if living; otherwise to Bart Simpson, nephew of the insured.

Revocable and Irrevocable Designations The partition of rights between the policy-owner and the beneficiary depends upon whether the beneficiary designation is revocable. A **revocable designation** is a beneficiary designation that may be changed by the policyowner without the beneficiary's consent. In contrast, an **irrevocable designation** is one that can be changed only with the beneficiary's express consent. Irrevocable designations are used in situations in which a policyowner does not want to or cannot retain the right to change beneficiaries, such as with divorce settlements. Irrevocably named beneficiaries have a vested right in the policy that is so complete that neither the policyowner nor his or her creditors can impair it without the beneficiary's consent.[4]

Thus, with an irrevocable beneficiary designation, the policyowner may not take any action that diminishes or affects the beneficiary's right to receive the full amount of insurance at the insured's death, unless some specific policy provision authorizes the policyowner alone to make policy loans, surrender the policy, or exercise other specific prematurity rights or privileges. In the usual case, the practical effect is as if the beneficiary and the policyowner were joint owners of the policy. The policyowner cannot act without the consent of the irrevocable beneficiary and, of course, the beneficiary has no rights to effect any policy changes.

Most policies contain a provision reserving to the policyowner the power to change the beneficiary or beneficiaries while the policy is in force. When this right is reserved—in other words, if the designation is revocable—the named beneficiary obtains no vested rights in the policy or in its proceeds. The beneficiary possesses a "mere expectancy until after the maturity of the contract." Thus, when the policyowner reserves the right to change the beneficiary, he or she is regarded, in the absence of any other assignment of policy rights, as the complete owner of the policy.

Clarity in Designating the Beneficiary

The importance of exercising care in the beneficiary designation cannot be overemphasized. If the policyowner's intentions are to be carried out effectively, the language must be precise and unambiguous.

Numerous examples may be cited to illustrate the need for care in describing beneficiaries. Consider some class designations. "To my children" is a designation that invites misunderstanding and possibly litigation. The policyowner who designates "my minor children" may not be thinking about the fact that eventually children will reach adulthood. When a husband's policy was payable to "the insured's children," this was judged to include those from a former wife but not his wife's children by a former husband.

Adopted children are included in the term *children,* whereas stepchildren may not be included. Illegitimate children, if they are acknowledged by the policyowner, are generally included in the designation. However, if the policyowner fails to legitimize them, generally they will not be considered. The term *dependents* is limited to those actually dependent upon the policyowner for support.

The term *relative* has been held to include those by marriage as well as by blood, but not an illegitimate child; the term *heirs* refers to those who take under the status of descent and distribution. Even if the intended persons finally receive the policy proceeds, litigation and delay can erode proceeds, and the sheer human aggravation can foster ill will and invites family discord. Too often, the construction of the beneficiary designation receives far too little care and attention.

Insurers wish to avoid disputes involving beneficiary designations. The issue ordinarily is not whether policy proceeds are due but rather to whom they are to be paid. In

---

[4]*Condon v. New York Life,* Iowa 658, 166 N.W. 452 (1983).

situations in which the insurer faces multiple claims for policy proceeds, because of ambiguity in the beneficiary designation or otherwise, it will often **interplead** them—that is, pay the proceeds to a court for it to decide the rightful recipient.

A Minor as Beneficiary

The designation of a minor as beneficiary presents unique problems. For example, if a minor beneficiary is named irrevocably, the policyowner is prevented from exercising virtually any options under the policy, as the minor must consent to any action, yet he or she lacks the capability to do so. A guardian must be appointed, and even then the guardian would most likely not have the authority to provide the necessary consent to a change because the change would, in all likelihood, tend to diminish the minor's estate without any offsetting advantage. A guardian is committed to conserving the minor's estate.

Minor beneficiaries also raise the question of how payment of the proceeds is to be accomplished if the policy matures and becomes payable before the beneficiary has reached the age of majority. A minor is not legally competent to receive payment and cannot give a valid release for it. To avoid the possibility of having to pay a second time, insurers generally will not make payment of any substantial amount directly to minor beneficiaries but instead require the appointment of a guardian. This process is time-consuming and can be expensive.

Change of Beneficiary

The policyowner usually may change the designation whenever and to whomever he or she wishes, provided the original designation is *not* irrevocable. Of course, any legal (see chapter 9 discussion on insurable interest) and contractual restrictions on designating the beneficiary must be respected. The policy typically provides the method for accomplishing the change. Although companies usually require that the procedure be followed carefully, in the majority of cases a beneficiary change is a routine matter.

If the policyowner has done all that he or she can to effect a beneficiary change but did not follow the procedure because of factors beyond his or her control, a beneficiary change will be deemed to have been accomplished, notwithstanding the failure to comply fully with the policy requirements. The courts reached this result by using the **doctrine of substantial compliance.** Thus, for example, when a policyowner/insured signed a change of beneficiary form and sent it to his wife to deliver to the company agent but was killed before delivery to the agent, the change of beneficiary was held effective.[5] In another case, the policyowner/insured requested change of beneficiary forms, signed them, but delayed forwarding them to the company, although there was ample time and opportunity. The forms were mailed after the death of the insured, but this was held to be an ineffective change of beneficiary.[6]

Some policyowners have attempted a beneficiary change through their wills. If the contract fails to specify the manner for changing the beneficiary (a rarity today) or if the procedure is not the exclusive method (also a rarity), a beneficiary change by will is held valid. In general, however, U.S. courts will not recognize a change via one's will if the policy sets forth an exclusive procedure for effecting a change.

Common Disaster

The beneficiary's right to receive life insurance policy proceeds is usually conditioned on his or her surviving the insured. Usually, survivorship poses no problem, but if the insured and the beneficiary die in the same accident and no evidence shows who

---

[5]*Pabst v. Hesse,* 173 N.W.2d 925, 286 Minn. 33 (1970).

[6]*Magruder v. Northwestern Mut. Life Ins. Co.,* 512 F.2d 507, C.A. Tenn. (1975).

died first, the question arises as to whom to pay the proceeds. No common-law presumption based on age or sex exists as to who died first. With much diversity in the decisions, U.S. courts in states that have not adopted the Uniform Simultaneous Death Act (discussed next) have awarded the proceeds to the insured's estate, in the absence of a contingent beneficiary, particularly where the insured had reserved the right to change the beneficiary.

Most states, however, have enacted the **Uniform Simultaneous Death Act,** which provides in a section on insurance that "where the insured and beneficiary in a policy of life or accident insurance have died and there is not sufficient evidence that they have died otherwise than simultaneously, the proceeds of the policy shall be distributed as if the insured had survived the beneficiary." This, of course, resolves the question of survival in those states in which the act is effective, but it fails to solve the main problems facing policyowners and insurance companies. Specifically, if the proceeds are payable in a lump sum and no contingent beneficiary is named, no matter who is determined to have survived, the proceeds will be paid into the probate estate of the insured or the beneficiary. This possibly will subject the proceeds to depletion through potentially unnecessary probate and related costs, additional taxes, and the claims of creditors.

Related to this issue is the more frequent short-term survivorship situation in which the beneficiary survives the insured by a short period of time. Here survivorship is not questioned, but similar problems exist. In addition, shrinkage in the proceeds is a possibility because of prior election of a life income settlement option, under which the entire proceeds are considered fully earned even though the beneficiary lived to receive only one or a few installments.

In approaching this problem, many companies use a **survivorship clause** (also called a *time clause*), which provides that the beneficiary must survive the insured by a fixed period after the insured's death to be entitled to the proceeds. This clause, in conjunction with the naming of contingent beneficiaries, can prevent the proceeds from falling into the probate estate of either an owner/insured or the original beneficiary. Another provision sometimes utilized is a direction that the proceeds are to be paid to the beneficiary only if he or she is alive at the time of payment. The latter provision, with the proper use of the income settlement options, will also avoid most of the problems mentioned earlier.[7]

Settlement Options

The value of life insurance is never more evident, and financial decisions are never more difficult, than at the time of a death. Thus, policyowners should carefully consider the manner in which death proceeds will be paid. Failure to arrange for the proper payment of proceeds may defeat the very purpose for which the insurance was intended.

Greater than 90 percent of all life insurance death proceeds are paid to beneficiaries as a single sum of money shortly after the insured's death. Beneficiaries often are ill prepared emotionally and otherwise to make decisions concerning the disposition of what may be large sums. Poor investment and purchase decisions are too easily made during periods of great stress. Would it often not be wiser to permit the insurer to retain the proceeds for a while before decisions are made?

The following section discusses the policy provisions—the **settlement options**—that grant policyowners (and beneficiaries) options as to how death proceeds will be paid. Most insurers also permit cash surrender values and matured endowments to be paid under settlement options. These can be particularly valuable options at retirement.

---

[7]Also, some insurers include a *turnaround provision* within their contracts, which permits the policyowner, if he or she is other than the insured, to change the beneficiary for up to 60 days following the insured's death. This provision is used primarily for policies purchased for business purposes.

The Legal Nature of Settlement Options

Following the insured's death, a contractual relationship is created between the insurance company and the beneficiary, whether the proceeds are payable in a lump sum or under a settlement option. If, during the insured's lifetime, the policyowner set up a settlement arrangement, performance of that agreement after the insured's death is regarded merely as a continuation of the third-party beneficiary arrangement. If, on the other hand, a beneficiary elects to receive the proceeds under one of the settlement options, some courts have held that a new direct contractual relationship is established between the company and the beneficiary. In either case, however, as a party to a direct contractual relationship or as a third-party beneficiary, the beneficiary may enforce his or her rights under the life insurance contract or subsequent settlement agreement.

Types of Settlement Options

Settlement options are usually designated in the contract, and most contracts provide a choice from among the options discussed here. Although most companies permit arrangements not specifically granted by contract, virtually all companies are more liberal respecting income settlement plans adopted by the policyowner before death than in regard to those requested by the beneficiary.

The policyowner may give the beneficiary as much or as little flexibility in designating the settlement option as the policyowner desires. Thus, a policyowner could fix absolutely the manner in which proceeds are to be paid, with the beneficiary having no right to alter the arrangement at the insured's death. Alternatively, the policyowner could design a settlement agreement that gave the beneficiary total freedom to alter its terms but, in the absence of a change by the beneficiary, the policyowner's wishes would be followed by the company. Of course, a flexibility continuum exists between these two extremes. Insurers work closely with policyowners to provide for the desired degree of flexibility.

Cash As mentioned previously, most death proceeds are paid as a lump sum of cash (check or bank draft) as a single sum. In a strict sense, this is not an "option" because life insurance contracts usually stipulate a cash settlement in the absence of any other direction by the policyowner or beneficiary.

Many policies provide for interest to be paid from the date of death, even if a settlement option had not been elected. Indeed, several jurisdictions require the payment of such interest. Although lump-sum settlements may be indicated, the interest option (discussed next) is flexible and permits adjustments to be made in light of changing economic, health, and other circumstances.

Interest Option Under the **interest option,** the proceeds remain with the company and only the interest earned thereon is paid to the beneficiary. A minimum interest rate is guaranteed in the contract, although companies routinely credit a higher rate. In most companies, the interest cannot be left to accumulate and compound but must be paid out monthly, quarterly, semiannually, or annually. As legal limits restrict the length of time a principal sum may be kept intact (discussed later), companies frequently limit the time that they will hold funds under this option to the lifetime of the primary beneficiary or 30 years, whichever is longer.

The interest option is one of the most popular options. Its main advantage is that it assures the beneficiary freedom from immediate investment worries, while guaranteeing both principal and a minimum rate of return. The right of withdrawal and the right to change to another option provide flexibility in the interest option, and this option is often the foundation upon which most comprehensive settlement agreements are formulated. Depending upon individual company rules and law, the primary beneficiary may be given:

- The right to name who is to receive any balance at his or her death, or the right to change the contingent beneficiaries previously designated by the policyowner.
- The right to make withdrawals of all or part of the principal, subject to any limitations prescribed by the policyowner in the settlement agreement. Most companies permit any reasonable combination of limiting factors (so much money per year, distribution at certain ages, and so forth), or the proceeds may be held without any withdrawal privileges.
- The right to change to another settlement option at a later time when circumstances may have changed. For example, the proceeds may be left under the interest option, with the right of the primary beneficiary to change to any other option, including the life income option (discussed later), at a later date.
- Protection from most creditors, if a spendthrift clause is included in the policy.

Fixed-Period Option   The **fixed-period option,** as its name indicates, provides for the payment of proceeds as an annuity certain over a definite period of months or years, usually not longer than 25 or 30 years. This is one of the two options based on the concept of systematically liquidating principal and interest over a period of years, without reference to life contingencies. The other is the fixed-amount option (discussed next).

If the primary beneficiary dies during the fixed period, the remaining installments (or their commuted value) are paid to the contingent beneficiary. The amount of proceeds, the period of time, the guaranteed minimum rate of interest, and the frequency of payments determine the amount of each installment. Any interest in excess of the guaranteed rate is usually paid at the end of each year.

The fixed-period option is valuable when the most important consideration is providing income for a definite period, as in the case of a readjustment period following the insured's death or while children are in school. Most companies permit policyowners to give the beneficiary the right to receive the present value of all remaining installments in a lump sum; this is referred to as the **right to commute.** Some companies permit the beneficiary to select the date when payments are to begin. However, aside from these options, the fixed-period option is not very flexible.

As the basic characteristic of this option is the period of time selected, outstanding policy loans at the insured's death reduce the amount of each installment but do not affect the number of installments. For the same reason, any dividend accumulations, paid-up additions, or other additional death benefit payments increase the beneficiary's income while the number of installments remains the same.

Fixed-Amount Option   The **fixed-amount option** is also an annuity certain but with the income amount rather than the time period fixed. A specified amount of income is designated, such as $2,000 per month, and payments continue until the principal and interest thereon are exhausted.

Fixed-amount options can be more advantageous than fixed-period options because they are more flexible. Most companies permit policyowners to specify varying amounts of income at different times, and beneficiaries may be given the right of withdrawal, in whole or in part, or the right to withdraw up to a certain sum in any one year on a cumulative or noncumulative basis. With both fixed-period and fixed-amount options, the commencement of installments can be deferred to a future time by holding the proceeds under the interest option until that time.

As the amount of each installment is the controlling factor under this option, dividend accumulations, additions payable, or additional death proceeds, together with any excess interest earned while installments are being paid, increase the number of installments but do not affect the installment amount. Conversely, loans outstanding at the insured's death or withdrawals of principal by the beneficiary decrease the number of installments.

A special rule often governs minimum installments under the fixed-amount option. Usually, at least $50 per year or a minimum of a stated amount per month is required to be paid out for each $1,000 of proceeds. The rule is in keeping with the purpose of the option—that is, to exhaust the principal and interest within some reasonable length of time.

The fixed-amount and fixed-period options represent the same idea expressed in different ways. For this reason, the guaranteed interest factor is usually the same for both options in a given contract. Both are annuities certain; that is, each systematically liquidates principal and interest over a period of years, without reference to life contingencies.

Single Life Income Option   The several forms of single life income options represent the other broad class of settlement options—those that liquidate principal and interest *with* reference to life contingencies. Single life income options, of course, are single-premium immediate life annuities and, thus, serve the same economic functions, as discussed in chapter 8.

The amount of each installment depends on the type of life income selected, the amount of the proceeds, the rate of interest being credited, the age of the beneficiary when the income commences, and the sex of the beneficiary (where permitted). The most common forms of life income options (annuities) are (1) the pure life income option, (2) the refund life income option, and (3) the life income option with period certain.

With the **pure life income option,** installments are payable only for as long as the primary beneficiary (the income recipient) lives. In other words, no further payments are due to anyone when the primary beneficiary dies. As no refunds or further payments are made at the beneficiary's death, the pure life income option provides the largest life income per $1,000 of proceeds. As with other pure life annuities, most persons hesitate to risk forfeiting a large part of the principal on early death, particularly if there are relatives to whom they wish to leave funds. For example, this form probably is inappropriate for many widows and widowers with young children, as it affords no protection to the children in the case of early death.

The refund life income option may take the form of a **cash refund annuity** or an **installment refund annuity.** As discussed in chapter 8, both annuities guarantee the return of an amount equal to the principal sum, less the total payments already made. The difference in the two forms is that, under the cash refund option, a lump-sum settlement is made following the primary beneficiary's death instead of the installment payments being continued.

Under the **life income option with period certain,** the most widely used life income option, installments are payable for as long as the primary beneficiary lives, but should this beneficiary die before a predetermined number of years, installments continue to a second beneficiary until the end of the designated period. The usual contract contains two or three alternative periods, the most popular ones being 10 and 20 years, but others may be obtained on request. This option is frequently useful where a widow or widower and minor children are concerned, as it assures the desired income for life while still guaranteeing that the income will last until the children are grown, regardless of the parent's date of death.

Table 8-1 in chapter 8 shows three forms of single life income options. Observe that the longer the guarantee period, the less the monthly proceeds. Moreover, as expected, the older the beneficiary, the greater the life income. A drawback of the life income option is that the income amount to be received by the beneficiary cannot be ascertained prior to the death of the insured, as it depends on the beneficiary's age. The amounts shown in Table 8-1 are calculated on the basis of the insurer's guaranteed minimum rate of interest. Normally, the actual amounts paid are higher than the minimums guaranteed.

Joint and Survivorship Life Income Option Under the **joint and survivorship life income option,** life income payments continue for as long as at least one of two beneficiaries (annuitants) is alive. As this option is a joint and survivorship annuity, it may continue payments of the same income to the surviving beneficiary or reduce the installments to two-thirds ("joint and two-thirds"), three-fourths ("joint and three-fourths"), or one-half ("joint and one-half") of the original amount and continue the payment of this reduced amount for the surviving beneficiary's lifetime. Some companies grant joint and survivorship options with a period certain of 10 to 20 years.

The joint and survivorship option can be particularly useful in providing retirement income for a husband and wife. The proceeds of a matured endowment or annuity or the cash values of any policy can be applied under this option.

Other Settlement Arrangements In many instances, policyowners find that they can best provide for beneficiaries by selecting combinations of settlement options. Virtually any desired income pattern may be obtained by using the options either singly or in combination. Options can operate concurrently, successively, or both.

Some companies provide options designed to meet a specific need or serve a particular purpose. These special options are usually a combination of the basic options to fit a particular situation with an attractive sales title applied to them. For example, a so-called **educational plan** option provides a fixed income during 9 or 10 months of each college year, with a modest "graduation present" in cash after the final installment. This is really a combination of the fixed-amount and interest options with appropriate limitations placed on them to produce the desired effect.

In an effort to provide better service to beneficiaries and to retain more of the policy proceeds within the insurer corporate family, many insurers provide beneficiaries with the option of having proceeds paid into an insurer-sponsored **flexible spending account,** which is an interest-bearing account on which drafts may be written. Some insurers automatically establish such an account for beneficiaries, subject to a minimum death benefit (e.g., $10,000). The beneficiary is free to leave proceeds in this account or to write checks to withdraw any portion or all of the proceeds. This option meets the objective of providing the beneficiary with time to decide about the disposition to be made of the funds.

Notwithstanding the wide variety of settlement plans offered by the various options and combinations of options, situations arise when the standard options do not fit exactly. Upon submission of the facts, the company usually is willing to develop a special settlement plan within reasonable limits. Where an individual desires still greater flexibility than the insurance company will permit, consideration should be given to the use of an individual trustee or the services of a trust company. This is particularly to be considered if discretionary powers are indicated. A life insurance company normally will not accept any arrangement whereby it must exercise discretion in carrying out the terms of the agreement.

Assignment Provision

Although insurance policies possess some unique characteristics, they are property and, therefore, subject to the law on property. Box 10-1 reviews the nature of property ownership, including insurance policies.

Ownership rights in life insurance policies, like other types of property, can be transferred by the current owner to another person. Such transfers are referred to as **assignments.** Assignments are of two types: absolute and collateral.

BOX 10-1

THE LEGAL NATURE OF PROPERTY

The term **property,** as used in the law, refers not to the object itself but to the ownership rights associated with the property—that is, rights of possession, control, and disposition. If the ownership rights are associated with land and objects permanently attached to land, such as buildings, the property is referred to as **real property.** If the ownership rights concern movable property, such as automobiles, furniture, stocks, and insurance policies, the property is classified as **personal property.**

There are two types of personal property: (1) choses in possession and (2) choses in action. **Choses in possession** are tangible objects (e.g., jewels). **Choses in action,** in contrast, refer to ownership rights evidenced by something tangible but which itself does not have value. Thus, an insurance policy is a chose in action as the contract itself has no value; it evidences an intangible of value. To recover value from a chose in action, legal action may be necessary.

Absolute Assignments

An **absolute assignment** is the complete transfer by the existing policyowner of all of his or her rights in the policy to another person. In other words, it is a change of ownership. In the case of a gift, the assignment is a voluntary property transfer involving no monetary consideration. Gifts of life insurance policies are frequently made among family members for both personal and tax reasons.

From time to time, a life insurance policy is sold for a valuable consideration. For example, a policy owned by a corporation on the life of a key employee may be sold for an amount equal to its cash surrender value to the employee upon employment termination. As with a gift, these transactions are accomplished through an absolute assignment of policy rights, typically by using an absolute assignment form furnished by the insurer.

One of the most common circumstances in which absolute assignments are used is with viatical settlements. These are discussed in Box 10-2.

As pointed out earlier, an irrevocable beneficiary must consent to an assignment of the policy, as he or she is, in effect, a joint owner. Of course, a revocable beneficiary has no rights respecting the transfer. The question arises, however, whether an absolute assignment, by itself, changes the beneficiary. Many courts have held that they do, whereas other courts have held the opposite.[8] The new owner, of course, can change the beneficiary by following the customary procedures.

Collateral Assignments

A **collateral assignment** is a temporary transfer of only some policy ownership rights to another person. Collateral assignments are ordinarily used in connection with loans from banks or other lending institutions (and persons). Such assignments are partial in that only some (not all as in an absolute assignment) policy rights are transferred. They are temporary in that the transferred partial rights revert to the policyowner upon debt repayment.

The vast majority of life insurance policy collateral assignments in the United States use the American Bankers Association (ABA) Collateral Assignment Form No. 10. The

---

[8]*Continental Assur. Co. v. Connoy,* 209 F.2d 539 (3rd Cir. 1954), and *Rountree v. Frazee,* 282 Ala. 142, 209 So.2d 424 (1968).

BOX 10-2

VIATICAL SETTLEMENTS

Individuals with relatively short life expectancies often face unemployment and large medical and hospice bills. Many have no health insurance. If they are insured under life insurance policies, they may be able to sell their policies for a substantial percentage of the face amount via a so-called **viatical settlement** to a **viatical settlement firm**—a specialized company (or group of investors) that purchases life insurance policies from terminally ill individuals. Viatical settlements provide an alternative to surrendering the policy for its cash value, enabling the person to preserve financial security. In the United States, some 90 percent of viatical settlements cover AIDS victims.

Individuals, agents, and financial planners typically bring potential sellers to the viatical firm. The firm then makes a purchase offer to the policyowner. The offer amount depends primarily on the policy face amount and the insured's life expectancy but also takes into consideration likely future premium payments, outstanding policy loans, and prevailing interest rates. Any life insurance policy or certificate can be used. Of course, the viatical settlement firm requires certification from a physician that the individual's condition can reasonably be expected to result in death within a certain time period.

If the offer is accepted, the policyowner transfers ownership to the viatical settlement firm via an absolute assignment. The firm names itself as beneficiary. Upon the death of the insured, it collects the policy proceeds. Its hope is to garner a profit for the investors.

Because of concerns over possible abuse, the NAIC promulgated the **Viatical Settlements Model Act** and a companion regulation that require certain disclosures to be made to the **viator**—the person who sells his or her policy. These include the impact of the transaction on eligibility for government benefits, possible tax implications, rescission rights, and alternatives to viatical settlements, such as accelerated death benefits. The models also cover the licensing of viatical firms and brokers, as well as offer guidelines that establish minimum prices as a percentage of the policy death benefit. These guidelines range from 50 percent for life expectancies of 24 months or longer to 80 percent for life expectancies of less than six months.

About one-half of the states have adopted some version of the models, although many have altered the minimum pricing requirements, especially for life expectancies of greater than 24 months. They recognize that the 50 percent standard was set when the only terminal illness covered was AIDS, which at the time typically involved a two-year life expectancy.

All proceeds of a viatical settlement are income tax free if the viator meets a definition of being terminally ill. The law's definition of **terminally ill** is that the individual must be certified by a physician as having an illness or physical condition that can reasonably be expected to result in death within 24 months or less.

Sources: D. A. Sommer, S. G. Gustavson, and J. S. Trieschmann, "Viatical Settlements: Perspectives of Investors, Regulators, and Insureds," *Journal of the American Society of CLU & ChFC* (March 1997), pp. 54–60; and Gregg M. Schneider, "Viatical Settlement Industry Comes of Age," *Contingencies* (November/December 1997), pp. 62–65.

form was developed jointly by the American Bankers Association and the Association of Life Insurance Counsel. The ABA Form 10 attempts to provide adequate protection to the lender and, at the same time, permits the policyowner to retain certain rights under the policy. Thus, the assignee (e.g., the lending institution) obtains the right to:

1. collect the proceeds at maturity
2. surrender the policy pursuant to its terms
3. obtain policy loans

4. receive dividends
5. exercise and receive benefits of nonforfeiture rights

On the other hand, the policyowner retains the right to:

- collect any disability benefits
- change the beneficiary (subject to the assignment)
- elect optional modes of settlement (subject to the assignment)

Under the form, the assignee agrees

1. to pay to the beneficiary any proceeds in excess of the policyowner's debt;
2. not to surrender or obtain a loan from the insurance company (except for paying premiums) unless there is default on the debt or premium payments, and then not until 20 days after notification to the policyowner; and
3. to forward the policy to the insurer for endorsement of any change of beneficiary or election of settlement option.

Policy Assignment Provision

Although most policies are assignable in the absence of policy assignment provisions, North American life insurance companies usually include such provisions in their policies. Although much variation exists in the wording, one company's provision reads:

You can assign this policy. We will not be responsible for the validity of an assignment. We will not be liable for any payments we make or actions we take before notice to us of an assignment.

Assignment provisions of life insurance policies do not prohibit an assignment without the company's consent but simply provide that the company need not recognize the assignment until it has received written notice of it, and that it assumes no responsibility as to its validity. The company's major concern is to avoid paying the claim twice.

Change of Plan Provision

Many policies contain a **change of plan provision** granting the policyowner the right to change the policy form. The conversion feature discussed in chapter 4 is an example of a change of plan provision. Most companies limit the change to plans of insurance involving a higher premium rate, although some permit a change to a lower premium rate plan but only with satisfactory evidence of insurability. Flexible-premium policies, in essence, contain a broad change of plan provision.

In connection with a change to a higher-premium plan of fixed-premium life insurance, the policyowner usually must pay the difference between the policy reserve on the new form and the policy reserve under the original policy. Changes to plans with higher premium rates do not necessitate evidence of insurability. Companies that do not grant changes to lower-premium plans as a matter of contract right usually will do so as a matter of practice. As evidence of insurability is required, the incontestability clause is reinstated in the same manner as for a reinstatement. If a change to a lower-premium form is requested, any decrease in reserve or cash surrender value occasioned by the change would be paid by the company to the policyowner.

To deter and detect adverse selection, insurers will, as a general rule, attempt to reserve the right to underwrite any policy change involving an increase in a policy's net amount at risk or other policy benefit. Conversely, changes involving a decrease in a policy's net amount at risk or other policy benefit do not require evidence of insurability. Thus, a change from a lower-premium policy form to a higher-premium form—being a change to a higher-reserved policy (and, therefore, to a lower net amount at risk), all else being equal, requires no evidence of insurability.

Change of Insured Provision

Some companies include a **change of insured provision** permitting a change of insureds under the policy. This provision can be particularly useful for business life insurance. In the past, when an employee whose life was insured for the benefit of the corporation either retired or otherwise terminated employment, the life insurance had to be surrendered (or sold) and new insurance purchased on the life of the replacement employee. The change of insured provision, which is subject to insurability requirements, eliminates this necessity and, in effect, also eliminates the front-end load that otherwise would be payable on a newly purchased contract.

Nonforfeiture Options

The **nonforfeiture options** afford policyowners who choose to terminate their cash-value insurance policies the option of utilizing the cash surrender value in several ways. Only a few cash-value health insurance policies exist (see chapter 7), so the focus in this discussion is on life policies. They typically stipulate that the surrender value may be taken in one of three forms:

1. cash
2. a reduced amount of paid-up insurance of the same kind as the original policy
3. extended term insurance for the full face amount

Cash

Cash-value policies may be surrendered for their net surrender value. Of course, when this option is elected, the protection ceases and the company has no further obligations under the policy. Consequently, even though this option can provide a ready source of cash for emergencies and other needs, it should be elected only after careful consideration. Almost the same amount of cash may be obtained through a policy loan (discussed later), and this may be a better alternative than surrendering the policy.

The available net surrender value is the gross cash value shown in the policy, decreased by any surrender charges (which are common in universal life policies) and the amount of any policy loans outstanding, and increased by the cash value of any paid-up additions, any dividends accumulated at interest, and any prepaid premiums.

Some policies provide for partial surrenders. As noted in chapter 6, this is a common feature in universal life (UL) policies. Additionally, many policies provide living benefits riders that can prove useful in certain family emergencies (see chapter 8). Traditional participating whole life and endowment policies as well as policies with paid-up additions riders provide that paid-up additions (discussed later) may be surrendered, in whole or in part. Furthermore, as a matter of practice (not by contract), many companies permit a partial surrender of traditional cash-value policies. However, unlike the situation with a UL policy, the face amount is typically reduced by an amount equal to the proportion by which the cash value is reduced. For example, if $6,000 of a $10,000 cash value is surrendered on a $50,000 ordinary life policy, the face amount may be reduced by 60 percent. This reduction is intended to minimize adverse selection.

Reduced Paid-Up Insurance

The **reduced paid-up insurance** nonforfeiture option permits the policyowner to use the cash surrender value as a net single premium to purchase a reduced amount of paid-up insurance of the same type as the original basic policy, exclusive of any term or other riders. All riders and supplementary benefits, such as for disability and accidental death, are terminated, and no further premiums are payable. The exchange is made at net rates, so it is based on mortality and interest only, net of expenses.

Table 10-1 shows that, after 10 years, each $56 of cash value could be exchanged for $344 of paid-up whole life insurance. This option would be appropriate when a smaller amount of whole life insurance would be satisfactory and it was desirable to discontinue premium payments. It could be attractive, for example, to the policyowner/insured who is approaching retirement, when typically an individual's income and need for life insurance are reduced.

Extended Term Insurance

The **extended term insurance** (ETI) nonforfeiture option gives the policyowner the right to use the net surrender value to purchase paid-up term insurance for the full face amount of the policy. The length of the ETI period is determined by applying the net surrender value as a single premium, to provide level term insurance for whatever duration the funds will carry the policy. Policy loans reduce both the net surrender value and the face amount. Paid-up additions increase both.

Referring again to Table 10-1, note that the tenth-year cash surrender value of $56 per $1,000 face amount can be used as a single premium to purchase $1,000 term insurance coverage (the full face amount), to remain in effect for 10 years and 64 days at which time the policy expires. If the policyowner fails to make a specific election to the contrary, this option is usually the automatic one. The ETI option would be appropriate if the need for the full amount of insurance protection continued but the financial capacity or desire to meet premium payments had diminished.

If a UL policyowner ceases to pay premiums, the policy's face amount is maintained in force for as long as the cash value plus interest is sufficient to pay monthly mortality and expense charges. This constitutes the normal operation of the UL policy and, therefore, need not be viewed as a nonforfeiture option. This runoff is mathematically identical to that found under the conventional ETI option. Therefore, in effect, ETI is the automatic UL option.

TABLE 10-1 Minimum Nonforfeiture Values, per $1,000 (*1980 CSO Mortality Table*, 7½% Interest, Ordinary Life, Male, Age 35)

End of Year	Cash Value	Paid-Up Insurance	Extended Term Insurance[a]	
			Year	Days
1	$ 0	$ 0	—	—
5	14	112	3	295
10	56	344	10	64
15	108	517	13	28
20	171	646	13	343

[a]Based on the 1980 *Commissioners Extended Term Table.*

Policy Loan Clause

All U.S. jurisdictions require inclusion of a **policy loan provision** in cash-value life insurance policies, under which insurers must make requested loans to policyowners, subject to certain limitations. The provision usually contains these key elements:

1. The insurer will lend to the policyowner an amount not to exceed the policy's cash surrender value less interest to the next policy anniversary.
2. Interest on the loan is payable annually at a rate specified in the policy.
3. Any due and unpaid interest will be paid automatically by a further loan against the policy's cash value.
4. If the total indebtedness equals or exceeds the cash surrender value, the policy will terminate, subject to 31 days' notice to the policyowner.
5. The policyowner may repay the loan either in whole or in part at any time.

Policy loans can be a source of flexibility for the policyowner. No one need approve the loan, and it is confidential. The loan interest rate is favorable and contractually set (discussed later). The amount available for loan usually is predicated on the policy's cash value, including the cash value of any paid-up additions. There is no fixed repayment schedule, although, of course, it ultimately will be repaid if the policy is surrendered, when the policy matures as a death claim, or if the total indebtedness, including unpaid interest, equals or exceeds the cash value. The automatic continuation of the loan is one of the unique features of policy loans.

From the insurer's point of view, the loan is fully secured. If the policyowner surrenders the policy, the loan is repaid from the policy's surrender proceeds, the difference between the cash surrender value and the loan amount being paid to the policyowner. If the insured dies, the loan is repaid by deducting the loan balance from the policy's death proceeds.

Policy Loan Interest Rate

The policy loan interest rate or the procedure for determining it is stated in the policy. In the past, U.S. law limited the maximum interest rate that insurers could charge. When market rates are above the contractual policy loan rate, a natural economic incentive is created to borrow at the favorable policy loan interest rate and to invest the proceeds at the higher market interest rate. The practice, known as **disintermediation,** occurs periodically, especially on older policies that carry fixed policy loan rates of 5 to 8 percent. To rectify the imbalance, the NAIC adopted a **Model Policy Loan Interest Rate Bill** that permits variable interest rates. All states have enacted this or a comparable law.

Under the law, insurers can change the policy loan interest rate up to four times each year. Companies are required to evaluate the need for a policy loan interest rate change at least once each year. The rate is not permitted to exceed the greater of Moody's Composite Yield on seasoned corporate bonds two months prior to the determination date or the interest rate credited on cash values plus 1 percent. The insurance company is not permitted to increase the applicable interest rate unless the defined ceiling permits a change of at least one-half of 1 percent upward.

The bill does not require the insurance company to increase the policy loan rate whenever it would be permissible, nor does it prohibit insurers from using fixed rates. On the other hand, when interest rates decline, the law requires that the insurance company reduce the interest rate whenever the ceiling rate has declined to at least one-half of 1 percent below the rate currently being charged on policy loans. This requirement generally assures that the applicable interest rate will decline as market interest rates decline.

Enactment of the NAIC model does not make variable interest rates applicable to policy loans on existing policies. It is applicable only to new contracts issued with the variable interest rate provision. As discussed in chapter 5, several companies have offered their policyowners the variable loan interest rate provision in exchange for more liberal dividends.

Automatic Premium Loan

Although not usually required, many companies include the **automatic premium loan** (APL) provision, which provides that, if a premium is unpaid at the end of the grace period and if the policy has a sufficient net cash value, the amount of the premium due will be advanced automatically as a loan against the policy. UL policies, because of their nature, do not have APL provisions.

In some jurisdictions, the policyowner must specifically elect to make the provision operative. The purpose of the APL provision is to protect against unintentional lapse, as when a premium payment is overlooked. If the policy lapsed, the nonforfeiture options would be effective, but if the policyowner wanted to reinstate the policy, he or she might have to furnish evidence of insurability. With the APL, the policyowner needs only to repay the loan and the original policy death benefit continues. A disadvantage of the APL is that it may encourage laxity in payment of premiums and can result in indebtedness exceeding the cash value. This problem will be recognized as the same type of concern as that existing with UL policies, wherein mortality and expense charges are deducted from the cash value.

Borrowing Your Own Money?

The policy loan feature of cash-value insurance policies has been the subject of considerable misunderstanding and misinformation. Some persons contend that the insurance company should not charge interest on policy loans, as "you're borrowing your own money." This view is incorrect and demonstrates a lack of understanding of life insurance fundamentals.

Policy loan interest should be charged for two reasons. First, in calculating the premiums to charge the public, life insurers assume in their computations that the assets generated by the total net cash inflows from the policies will be invested and will earn interest. As noted in chapter 2, the company discounts (lowers) premiums in advance in anticipation of these interest earnings. If the policyowner removes (via a policy loan) his or her proportionate share of these assets, and if the insurer charged no interest on this loan, then the company's assumptions regarding future earnings on these assets would not be realized. If the insurer did not charge interest for loans, it logically also should not discount premiums in anticipation of future investment earnings. The net result would be that premiums would be significantly higher, but policyowners would not have to pay interest.

The second reason for charging policy loan interest is the same reason that other loans carry such charges. Although many persons (and sometimes even insurance laws and regulations) refer erroneously to a policyowner's right to "borrow the policy's cash value," this phraseology is both misleading and wrong. Policyowners cannot borrow their cash values. Rather, they have a contractual right (option) to borrow money from the life insurance company by using their policy's cash values as security for the loan. The transaction is analogous to the owner of a certificate of deposit (CD) securing a loan from a bank for an amount equal to the CD and pledging the CD as collateral security. The bank would certainly charge interest on the loan even though it might be fully collateralized, just as the life insurer charges interest on fully secured policy loans.

Provision Regarding Surplus Distribution

Participating (with profits) life and health insurance policies are common worldwide. Of course, the distinguishing characteristic of participating policies is that they carry the right to share in distributable surplus. The mechanism by which par policies participate is via dividends in some countries, including the United States, and via bonuses in other countries, such as the United Kingdom and other Commonwealth countries. Box 10-3 lists the common methods of allocating bonuses.

Virtually all U.S. jurisdictions require that divisible surplus accumulated on behalf of participating policies be distributed annually to policyowners. States increasingly are requiring somewhat similar treatment with respect to excess interest and other earnings on UL and the interest-sensitive types of policies. Both participating and interest-sensitive policies are required to have policy provisions relative to distribution of these excess amounts. The functioning of these provisions, as applied to the interest-sensitive types of policies, was discussed in chapter 6, so their treatment here will be brief. We focus chiefly on fixed-premium participating policies.

Nature of Surplus Distribution

An insurance company's board of directors determines, in the aggregate, the amount of surplus to be distributed each year to policyowners. This decision is made considering the company's financial position, profitability objectives, and other factors. Actuarial advice is provided to management and the board to assist in making this decision. Management, with board approval, decides how to apportion the divisible surplus among the various blocks of policies. Insurance policies are silent as to the proportion of total surplus that is to be distributed among policies.

Many governments, including those of some U.S. states, France, the United Kingdom, Singapore, and many other countries, limit the proportion of profits flowing from participating business sold by stock insurers that may be paid to stockholders. Limits of 5 or 10 percent are common worldwide. Many governments, including those of some U.S. states, also limit the amount of surplus that a mutual life insurer can accumulate to a stated percentage of policy reserves (e.g., 10 percent in New York). However, most U.S. insurance codes are silent on these matters.

BOX 10-3

COMMON METHODS OF ALLOCATING BONUSES IN THE UNITED KINGDOM

Participating or with-profits life insurance policies in the United Kingdom (and many other countries) share in distributable surplus through **bonuses.** Common methods of allocating these bonuses include the following:

- **Simple reversionary bonus**—This bonus is declared periodically as a percentage addition to the sum assured (face amount). The bonus percentage does not vary by the insured's age or the length of time that the policy has been in force.

- **Compound reversionary bonus**—This bonus is similar to the simple bonus except that the percentage addition is of the sum assured and previously declared bonuses.

- **Terminal (or capital) bonus**—This bonus is paid as an additional benefit on the insured's death and is in addition to the reversionary bonuses. It allows the policy to share more fully and equitably in accumulated surplus.

Source: Consumers and Life Insurance (Paris: OECD, 1987), p. 30.

Direct Recognition

As discussed in chapter 6, many life insurance policies include a **direct recognition provision** that permits the company to recognize directly in its excess interest or dividend formula the extent of policy loan activity within the policies. These provisions can increase the effective cost of policy loans and result in higher dividends or excess interest paid under nonborrowing policies. Such provisions link the policy loan and surplus distribution or excess interest provisions, whereas without the provisions they are not directly related. This linkage makes loan decisions more complex. Traditional planning techniques must be modified to evaluate policy loan economics.

Dividend Options

The options available to policyowners for receiving their policies' share of distributable surplus—the dividends—provide another potentially important source of flexibility. With interest-sensitive policies, excess interest earnings are earmarked to increase the policy's cash value or to reduce the level of future premiums, or both. The five most common dividend options under participating cash-value life insurance policies are:

1. pay in cash
2. offset the premium payment
3. purchase paid-up additional insurance
4. accumulate at interest
5. purchase one-year term insurance

The policyowner elects the desired option at the time the policy is purchased. The option can be changed at any time under most policies, although evidence of insurability may be required if the effect of the requested change is to increase the policy's net amount at risk. The options to purchase paid-up additional insurance and one-year term insurance are not offered with par term policies. Typically only the first two dividend options are available under participating health insurance policies.

Cash   Most jurisdictions require that the dividend be made available in cash. Under this option, the insurer mails a check for the dividend to the policyowner each year. Policyowners usually find one of the other options more attractive. This option is costly for the company to administer.

Apply toward Premium Payment   Although applying the dividend toward payment of the next premium due under the policy is the economic equivalent of cash, many policyowners elect this option to reduce their current outlay. They could, of course, take the dividend in cash and remit the full premium, obtaining the same economic effect.

Purchase Paid-Up Additions   The policyowner may have the dividend applied to purchase units of paid-up additional insurance under the policy. With this option, the dividend is applied as a net single premium at the insured's attained age to purchase as much paid-up insurance as it will provide of the same type as the basic policy. (Note that, in operation, this option resembles the reduced paid-up nonforfeiture option.)

The right to purchase a series of paid-up additions at net rates can be attractive, especially for an insured whose health has become impaired. No evidence of insurability is required at the purchase of each additional insurance amount.

Paid-up additions themselves may be participating or nonparticipating. If they are participating, the annual dividends on the paid-up additions further enhance the policy's total cash value and death benefit. Most companies permit changes to this option after issue, often without evidence of insurability.

Some individuals do not wish to purchase single-premium life insurance, and paid-up additions, although small in amount, are a type of single-premium life insurance.

Some consider it wiser to use dividends to reduce current premiums to permit the purchase of additional insurance. Even so, purchasing paid-up additions can be a worthwhile approach to increasing insurance protection. The additions offer further flexibility because of their cash value. This cash value can be obtained, in whole or in part, by selective surrender of the paid-up additions, without disturbing the basic policy.

Accumulate at Interest   Dividends may be allowed to accumulate at interest under the contract. The insurer guarantees a minimum rate of interest, although companies typically credit higher rates. Accumulations can be withdrawn at will by the policyowner. If death occurs, the policy's face amount plus dividend accumulations are paid, and, in the event of surrender, the cash surrender value plus dividend accumulations are paid.

Purchase One-Year Term   Some companies make available an option to apply the dividend to purchase one-year term insurance. The option takes one of two forms. One form applies the dividend as a net single premium to purchase as much one-year term insurance protection as it will buy. The other form purchases one-year term insurance in an amount equal to the policy's cash value with the excess dividend portion applied under one of the other dividend options. The latter form is often used in connection with split-dollar insurance (see chapter 17). The object is to assure the beneficiary payment of an amount equal to the policy's face amount if the insured dies, even though the cash value may be fully pledged.

Other Options   Companies often permit dividends to be used in other ways. One is the so-called *vanish pay option* discussed in chapters 5 and 9. Recall that, under this option, a cash-value policy can be made self-sustaining at the time when the total policy cash value equals or exceeds the net single premium for the insured's attained age for an amount of insurance equal to the policy's face amount.

Another dividend option, the **add-to-cash-value option,** is similar to the paid-up additions option in that it permits the dividend to accumulate as additional cash value but, unlike the additions option, involves no additional pure insurance protection. In other words, the option generates exactly a unit of additional death benefit for each unit of additional cash value. This option permits companies selling whole life insurance to match the UL cash value and death benefit growth.

CREDITOR RIGHTS IN LIFE INSURANCE

Treatment of debtors in early times was often harsh. Governments increasingly found such harsh treatment objectionable, recognizing that it resulted in negative spillovers (externalities) to families and society as a whole. Thus, laws were enacted to provide for an equitable distribution of the assets of debtors, while giving them an opportunity for rehabilitation. These laws came to have particular relevance for life insurance because of its special relationship to family economic security.

This section explores the rights of creditors (and, therefore, debtors) in life insurance policies. We first examine the rights of the policyowner's creditors, then the rights of the beneficiary's creditors. The focus is on U.S. law.

Rights of the Policyowner's Creditors

The *Bankruptcy Reform Act* permits states the option of avoiding the bankruptcy protection under the federal law and relying on their own state law. Most states, in fact, have chosen this option, so that only in about a dozen states does the bankrupt person have a choice of electing the state exemption or the Bankruptcy Reform Act's exemption.

The Federal Bankruptcy Law

Insolvency is not the same as bankruptcy. Insolvency is the inability to pay one's debts. **Bankruptcy** is the application of bankruptcy laws to a debtor who may not be insolvent. One becomes bankrupt when one comes under the protection of the bankruptcy laws.

Title to a bankrupt person's property vests in a trustee appointed by the bankruptcy court to manage the bankrupt's financial affairs. The estate may include so-called exempt property at the beginning of the proceedings. *Exempt property* is property excluded from the bankrupt's creditor's claims. The debtor has the choice of either state or federal exemptions. The act provides for, among other things, a modest homestead exemption. To avoid discrimination against nonhomeowners, the act provides an equivalent exemption of other property if the homestead exemption and certain other exemptions are not used.

Under the law, creditors of the insured/policyowner have no interest in insurance policy proceeds if:

- the beneficiary is other than the insured/owner, his or her estate, or his or her legal representatives and
- the beneficiary is named irrevocably.[9]

If the policy is made payable to the insured/policyowner, his or her estate, or legal representatives, it is subject to the claims of creditors in case of bankruptcy, except for any other exemptions. If the insured/policyowner names a beneficiary not in the classes just listed but reserves the unqualified right to change the beneficiary, the policy will pass to the trustee in bankruptcy if it has a cash surrender value, and to the extent of such value. Except for the application of either federal or state exemption statutes, the courts can be expected to interpret a revocable beneficiary designation as giving the trustee in bankruptcy the power to distribute a policy's cash surrender value among creditors.

The courts have held that the trustee has no interest in policies without cash values. In *Morris v. Dobb, trustee,* a husband took out a policy payable to his legal representatives and subsequently transferred it to his wife four months prior to filing a bankruptcy petition. The policy had no cash value, and the court ruled that the trustee had no interest in the policy.[10]

Cases arise wherein, shortly following the filing of the petition in bankruptcy, a policy payable to the insured/policyowner or his or her representatives matures through the death of the insured/bankrupt. In this instance, are the creditors entitled to the policy proceeds? The question was decided by the Supreme Court and incorporated into the Bankruptcy Reform Act.[11] According to current law, the trustee in bankruptcy obtains title only to the net cash surrender value of the policy at the time of the filing of the bankruptcy petition. The trustee's interest does not extend to any other policy values, such as life insurance death proceeds.

The Bankruptcy Reform Act also reserves to the bankrupt an aggregate interest (originally $4,000) in life insurance policies on his or her life. Amounts in excess of this are payable to creditors unless they are exempted by state laws.

As relates to protection from creditors, whether one should retain the right to change beneficiaries depends largely on the state exemption laws and the federal bankruptcy law. Although an irrevocable beneficiary designation protects policy proceeds and cash

---

[9]*Central National Bank of Washington v. Hume,* 128 U.S. 195 (1888); *Morse v. Commissioner of Internal Revenue,* 100 F.2d 593 (1939).

[10]110 Ga. 606, quoted *In Re Buelow,* 98 Fed. 86 (1900); *Burlingham v. Crouse,* 228 U.S. 459 (1913).

[11]See, for example, *Burlingham v. Crouse,* 228 U.S. 459 (1913); *United States v. Binham,* 76 F.2d 573 (1935).

values from creditors, it greatly limits the insurance policy's usefulness. The free use of an insurance policy might outweigh the benefit of it being secured from creditors. When life insurance is only a modest part of a developing estate, the right to change beneficiaries often should be reserved, so that the policy can be available as an asset with free assignability. As the insured/policyowner begins to expand his or her business activity, the desirability of retaining this feature of the policies can be reviewed. In any event, a change of ownership may be preferred to an irrevocable beneficiary designation.

State Exemption Statutes

From earliest times, the U.S. Congress has deferred to state exemption statutes. State exemption statutes protect policy values from the claims of the insured's creditors even if he or she is not bankrupt, although the bulk of litigation has involved bankruptcy. Such statutes vary substantially from state to state, so generalizations are limited.

Almost all states provide protection for a policy's cash values, with many of the statutes modeled after that of New York. Previously, many statutes limited protection to the spouse and children, but most states no longer follow this practice.

The right to procure a policy's cash surrender value has been held to be a right that is purely personal to the policyowner. It is a condition precedent in the insurance contract whereby the insurance company does not develop any obligations until certain procedures are observed. Accordingly, no amounts are due the policyowner from the insurer until the policyowner exercises his or her call option.[12] Similarly, the cash surrender value of an endowment insurance policy is not a vested interest and thus not an asset of the bankrupt debtor.[13] Any payments made to the policyowner, such as cash surrender values or dividends that have been deposited to the debtor's account, typically are not exempt.

Many statutes are quite brief. For example, Nebraska provides that "all and every benefit accruing under any annuity contract or any other policy . . . shall be exempt from attachment and all claims of creditors and of beneficiary if related by blood or marriage."[14]

Under the laws of most states, endowment policies are included in the exemptions granted to the debtor. Many states also exempt annuity cash values.

Some of the laws providing exemption are applicable only if the named beneficiary is in a certain class, such as the individual's spouse or children or a dependent relative. Some provide the exemption to any beneficiary who has an insurable interest in the insured's life. Few require an irrevocable beneficiary designation.

Most are broad in scope, providing that the values are exempt unless the beneficiary is the insured or a third-party owner. A few laws limit the amount of the annual premiums payable for exempt insurance. Under other statutes, the limitation is based on the total amount of insurance proceeds, although such policy amount limitations are becoming less common.

Many states exempt payments made under disability income insurance policies from the claims of the insured's creditors. Even payments in possession of the insured may be exempt.

Rights of the Beneficiary's Creditors

We now examine the rights of the beneficiary's creditors. As we will see, beneficiaries enjoy much protection.

---

[12]R.C.W.A. 48.18.410. *In re Elliott,* 446 P.2d 347, 72 Wash.2d 600 (1968).

[13]*In re Privett,* C.A. Okla., 435 F.2d 261 (1970).

[14]Law of 1933, amended 1941, §44-37.

Prior to Maturity

In the absence of a statute exempting the proceeds or cash values of life insurance from the claims of the beneficiary's creditors, the question of whether creditors can reach the cash value depends upon whether the beneficiary possesses any property rights in the policy. In most instances, the beneficiary possesses no such rights.

If the beneficiary does not possess such a right in the policy, his or her creditors cannot reach the cash values. Remember that a revocable beneficiary has a mere expectancy and, consequently, no property right exists to be attached. Even with an irrevocably named beneficiary, creditors cannot reach the cash value of the policy, as the beneficiary does not possess the right to obtain the cash value without the consent of the owner.

At Maturity

The rights of a beneficiary, whether designated revocably or irrevocably, vest absolutely at the insured's death. In the absence of an exempting statutory provision, the beneficiary's creditors are entitled to the insurance proceeds as soon as that right vests in the beneficiary.[15]

Some of the state laws exempting life insurance proceeds and avails from claims of creditors expressly refer only to creditors of the policyowner/insured. However, most states have broad statutes that exempt insurance proceeds, even in the possession of the beneficiary, against the creditors of both the insured and the beneficiary. Several statutes extend this protection to proceeds payable to the insured's estate provided the proceeds inure to the benefit of certain designated relatives or dependents.

Most such statutes limit the exempt insurance to a stated amount, and a few apply the beneficiary's exemption only to group life insurance proceeds. State statutes frequently provide that proceeds payable to beneficiaries under fraternal benefit policies are exempt from claims of creditors.

Many statutes also protect annuity income from the claims of creditors. Some afford this protection only to annuities purchased by someone other than the annuitant, but many apply the protection to annuities owned and purchased by the annuitant. These statutes, sometimes but not always, limit the amount of exempt annuity income to a stated monthly amount, such as $300.

Special Priorities and Constraints

The preceding rules about creditors' rights do not apply to federal tax liens and situations involving misappropriated funds. Also, most states will permit the use of special clauses to protect life insurance proceeds from creditors of the beneficiary. We cover each next.

Tax Liens

The tax collector takes a dim view of anyone, dead or alive, who fails to pay taxes due. Under a federal government tax lien, the government need not prove that the debtor or taxpayer is insolvent when it places levies on the taxpayer's assets. If the policyowner/insured retains certain rights under a policy, these rights can be reached by the government,[16] in spite of state exemption statutes. Under federal tax lien law, life insurance companies are required to pay to the federal government the net surrender values of policies as of the time of judgment.

---

[15]*Murray v. Wells,* 53 Iowa 256 (1880), §640; 57 A.L.R. 692. In the case of *Holmes, appellant v. Marshall,* 145 Cal. 777 (1905), the court held that under certain conditions, the exemption extends "not only against the debts of the person whose life was insured, and who paid the premiums, but also to the debts of the beneficiary to whom it is payable after the death of the insured." See also S. Dak. L. Ch. 58-12-4 (1966).

[16]26 U.S.C.A. (I.R.C. 1954), §7403; *U.S. v. Sterkowica,* 266 F.Supp. 703 (1967); *Appleman, Insurance Law and Practice,* §10905.

Misappropriation of Funds

Although beneficiaries' rights in life insurance proceeds have been greatly enlarged by legislation, it is contrary to public policy to permit life insurance to shelter assets that equitably belong to another. Thus, when premiums are paid from misappropriated funds or with the intent to defraud creditors, the right to follow the funds is not lost merely because the money was used to buy life insurance.

In general, the aggrieved party can follow the wrongfully acquired funds and enforce its rights against the proceeds under the constructive or resulting trust theory. Under this theory, the person holding the funds does so as a trustee for the other party.

Little uniformity exists as to the amount of recovery. In some cases, the premiums paid from misappropriated funds were obtainable by the aggrieved party. In other instances, the aggrieved obtained proceeds in the proportion that the premiums paid from misappropriated funds bore to all premiums paid. Thus, when a policyowner's clear intention is to defraud his or her creditors by taking out insurance or by assigning it, the beneficiary is not protected against claims of the policyowner's creditors.

Spendthrift Trust Clause

In addition to the broad statutes that exempt life insurance proceeds from creditors' claims, most states allow policyowners to include in the policy settlement provisions a clause that provides further protection to the proceeds from claims of the beneficiary's creditors. The somewhat offensively named **spendthrift trust clause** may provide that the beneficiary has no power to assign, transfer, or otherwise encumber the installment payments to which he or she is entitled under the settlement option. The clause can be attached to a policy in the form of an endorsement or rider and becomes a part of the policy. Installment payments made under a settlement option that contains such a clause are not subject to any legal process, execution, garnishment, or attachment. In many cases, creditors have been unsuccessful in reaching the funds held by the insurer even where the beneficiary had an unlimited right to withdraw the entire proceeds.[17]

In most states, the provisions extend only to beneficiaries other than the policyowner. Otherwise, such a device could be used by a policyowner to defraud creditors.

If the mode of settlement is selected by the beneficiary, the payments received may not be secure from the claims of the beneficiary's creditors. The spendthrift clause protects only the money being held by the insurance company. Once money is paid to the beneficiary, it loses its distinction as unpaid life insurance proceeds.

The outstanding characteristic of spendthrift statutes is the permissive nature of the exemption. The company and the policyowner must agree on the exemption before it can become operative. Practically, this means that the policyowner must insert the clause in the policy's installment settlement provisions. Such clauses often severely restrict the beneficiary's prerogatives. The spendthrift trust clause should be used only after appropriate consideration of other planning objectives.

In most states in which no statute exists, the courts have upheld the use of spendthrift clauses. In only a few states are the clauses not valid, and even in these a discretionary trust may be used to accomplish the same thing.

Questions

1. If the beneficiary clause is not drafted with care, its intended purpose may not be fulfilled. How can unexpected circumstances or ambiguity in the beneficiary clause complicate the settlement of life insurance proceeds?

---

[17]*Genesee Valley Tr. Co. v. Glazer,* 295 N.Y. 219, 66 N.E.2d 169, 164 A.L.R. 911 (1946).

2. Evaluate the following statement: "When you take out a policy loan, you should not have to pay interest because you are borrowing your own money."

3. Four women have each taken out $1 million life insurance policies on themselves to protect their children and husbands. None of their husbands are competent money managers. The first woman has one child in elementary school, the second has one child in high school, the third has one child in college, and the fourth one has an adult child who is an investment manager. Assume you are to advise the women how to arrange the settlement options under their life insurance policies. What settlement options would you recommend for each woman, and why?

4. Why might a policyowner elect to receive his or her share of distributable surplus in a form other than cash?

5. How do U.S. laws protect the rights of beneficiaries' and policyowners' creditors?

CHAPTER

11

INSURANCE ADVISOR AND COMPANY EVALUATION

Objectives

- Describe the responsibilities that are placed upon insurance advisors.

- Explain how a consumer can benefit from the assistance of an insurance advisor.

- Describe the various types of organizations that offer life and health insurance.

- Identify sources that provide useful information for the evaluation of life insurers.

- Describe one way to evaluate a life insurance company.

Insurance purchasers want high-quality insurance that offers good value; stated differently, they want well-suited, low-cost insurance with favorable contractual terms, from a financially secure, well-managed insurer. The preceding two chapters covered various contractual aspects of life and health insurance evaluation. This chapter continues the evaluation theme with an examination of insurance suppliers and advisors. All of these elements together define high quality and good value.

THE INSURANCE PURCHASE DECISION

Some individuals shop carefully before deciding on the types and amounts of insurance to buy and from whom to buy it. However, the majority of buyers do little or no comparison shopping and may make unsound decisions regarding the particular type and amount of insurance to buy or the insurance company from which to buy it.

Making a wise life or health insurance purchase decision is not easy. One must first decide whether any insurance is needed. If some is appropriate, the amount must be decided upon next. These two issues are analyzed in chapter 14.

Questions also must be answered as to the type of insurance to buy (see chapters 7 and 12) and from whom to buy it. This latter issue can be the most important, for a poor-quality insurer or poor advice can wreck what might be otherwise sound decisions.

INSURANCE ADVISOR EVALUATION

Importance of an Advisor

Although some insurance purchasers do not need the services of an insurance agent or other advisor, most probably do. Insurance products today are more complex than ever, and most persons are not well enough informed to make wise purchase decisions without some advice. Stated differently, use of an advisor helps rectify the information imbalance that exists for purchasers.

Many individuals offer this advice—some for a fee and most for a commission. A competent, informed, trustworthy insurance advisor is perhaps a consumer's best assurance against making an unwise purchase decision.

Persons Providing Life and Health Insurance Advice

For most individuals, an insurance agent is the source of both advice and the policy. To become an agent, applicants usually must secure a license by passing a qualifying examination and meeting certain character and residence requirements. In many jurisdictions, they must undertake certain minimum continuing education activities to renew the license. In addition, agents in the United States who sell variable products must be registered with the National Association of Securities Dealers (NASD) and have additional state licenses.

Personal financial planners also offer advice on insurance. Most planners also sell insurance for a commission—that is, they are licensed agents. Some planners do not sell insurance but instead offer advice on a fee-only basis.

Many accountants offer insurance advice, most of them for a fee and some of them on a commission basis—that is, they are licensed agents. Attorneys often are involved in more complex insurance cases and offer their services as insurance advisors from a legal and tax viewpoint. Bank employees increasingly are a source of life and health insurance advice, with many holding agent licenses.

Evaluation of Advisors

From the buyer's standpoint, a good agent or other advisor is one who does the following:

- places the interest of the client first
- has up-to-date knowledge of the business
- gives the client continuing service

It is not easy to find such an advisor. Helpful sources of information can include local business and professional persons, current clients of the prospective advisor, and insurance advisors themselves, although this word-of-mouth approach is far from foolproof. The value of the opinions of business and professional persons depends on their insurance knowledge and their experience with a prospective advisor. The advisor's clients may be limited in their perspective by lack of experience with other advisors; they may not know what services to expect. On the other hand, if an individual is pleased with an advisor and his or her service, this can be important.

A proxy for client satisfaction with agents in the United States is whether the agent has qualified for the National Quality Award (NQA) of the National Association of Life Underwriters (NALU), an insurance trade association of agents. The NQA is awarded each year only to those agents who experience low lapse (voluntary policy termination) rates on the business they wrote in the previous two years. Preferably, the agent would have qualified for the NQA for many consecutive years. Low lapse rates suggest that clients are pleased. LIMRA International, an insurance-industry-sponsored marketing research organization, offers a parallel award for the agents of its member insurers outside the United States. The qualifications for its International Quality Award (IQA) are similar to those of NALU's NQA.

Most individuals do not have the opportunity or inclination to investigate a prospective advisor carefully. There are, however, several inquiries that can be made with relatively little effort.

First, what is the advisor's education and training? The greater the education and professional training, the better. Of course, lack of a college degree or specialized professional training should not be a determinative criterion. One might prefer to deal with advisors who hold recognized professional designations. See Box 11-1.

BOX 11-1

THE CLU, ChFC, CFP, AND RHU PROFESSIONAL DESIGNATIONS

Many insurance and related professional designations exist. Some are highly specialized and may not be relevant to life or health insurance advising. Other professional certifications have yet to prove themselves as to durability or professional substance. Three designations worthy of consideration are (1) chartered life underwriter (CLU), (2) chartered financial consultant (ChFC), and (3) certified financial planner (CFP).

The CLU program is the oldest of the three. To obtain and use the CLU designation, the student must pass 10 examinations, meet certain ethical and experience requirements, and agree to comply with a code of ethics and certain continuing education requirements. The examinations relate to economics, finance, and accounting, as well as to insurance law, employee benefit planning, understanding of life products and markets, business, estate, and personal uses of life and health insurance, and investments.

The ChFC and CFP professional designations are broader in scope than the CLU designation. The CFP program, which predates the ChFC program, requires candidates to meet certain educational requirements that consist of more than 100 topics determined by the CFP Board to constitute a core curriculum for financial planner practitioners. The CFP candidate must pass 10 hours of examinations over a two-day period.

The ChFC program requires the student to pass 10 examinations, some of which are waived if the student already holds the CLU designation. Both CFP and ChFC examinations test students'

understanding of the broad concepts and applications of personal financial planning. The successful candidate in each program must meet certain ethical and experience requirements, agree to comply with codes of ethics, and meet continuing educational requirements. Students taking ChFC courses can take a five-course CFP module within the ChFC curriculum and qualify to sit for the CFP certification examination.

Another designation applicable to the sale and service of disability income and other health insurance products is the Registered Health Underwriter (RHU). To earn the RHU designation, students must complete three courses, meet specified experience requirements, maintain ethical standards, and agree to comply with a code of ethical conduct and applicable continuing education requirements.

Although only the CLU designation is oriented specifically toward life and health insurance, both the CFP and ChFC programs are designed to help ensure that the individual is well versed in insurance and insurance applications. Individuals who hold one or more of these professional designations should be presumed to be knowledgeable professionals. Of course, many capable advisors hold no professional designation. Furthermore, no professional designation is a guarantee of competence or trustworthiness.

Web sites for the preceding organizations are as follows:

CLU, ChFC, and RHU: www.amercoll.edu
CFP: www.cfp-board.org

Second, the advisor should have been involved in the life and health insurance business long enough to acquire the knowledge and skills needed to provide quality advice and service. Some writers recommend a minimum experience of five years. Even a relatively new advisor, however, may have support services that provide reasonable assurance that his or her relative lack of experience will not be detrimental to the client. Also, not every individual situation requires the most highly trained advisor, such as one who might specialize in intricate estate planning or tax work. Relatively new, younger advisors frequently relate well to young men and women who are just beginning their families and careers. Moreover, there is something to be said for having an advisor of approximately the same age as the client so that their working life spans closely coincide.

Third, it would be helpful to know how the agent or advisor maintains current knowledge in his or her field. When was the last time he or she attended an advanced education or training program or seminar? Is the person working toward a professional designation? What professional certification exams have been passed?

Fourth, if the advisor is an agent, the extent to which business can be placed with more than one insurer and whether all types of insurance are sold can be important. An agent who does not hold a securities license cannot offer variable products. Some agents represent a single insurer and cannot place business with other companies. In some markets, this limitation may not be a problem, depending on the quality of the company represented and its products. For more specialized needs, this could pose difficulty for the client, as no single company is best in everything.

Fifth, irrespective of the advisor's competence, professional designations, and the like, does he or she seem to be the type of person in whom one can place complete trust? The buyer often discloses much confidential information and can render himself or herself vulnerable in both a practical and emotional sense. Intuition plays an important and worthy role here.

Advisor Responsibilities

Ethical, Professional, and Legal

Insurance advisors have ethical, professional, and legal responsibilities to their clients. Ethical responsibilities are the ones that flow from society's unwritten standards of moral conduct. One test of ethical behavior is whether the advisor's peers would find his or her conduct above reproach if they were fully aware of all aspects of that conduct.

Advisors holding certain certifications or memberships may have responsibilities to their professional organizations, such as the Society of Certified Public Accountants, the American Bar Association, the International Board of Certified Financial Planners, the Society of Financial Services Professionals, and others. These societies' rules attempt to establish minimum levels of acceptable ethical and professional conduct, and continuing society membership is conditioned on compliance with those rules. The common theme running through these and other such professional societies is that members pledge themselves to consider the client's interest above all others, especially their own.

Finally, responsibilities are imposed on advisors by the law. Thus, for example, laws prohibit agents from replacing an existing life insurance policy through misrepresentation, from commingling of customer funds with their own, and from making any false or misleading statements to consumers. Additionally, certain disclosure requirements must be followed (see chapter 12).

An increasingly important aspect of an advisor's legal responsibilities stems from common-law standards of conduct, as discussed in chapter 9. Generally, advisors must exercise at least the degree of care as that exhibited by a reasonably prudent person of their peer group. Thus, the conduct of an attorney expert in tax law will be judged against that of other tax attorneys. Similarly, a life insurance agent's conduct will be judged against that of other, reasonably prudent insurance agents.

The situation, however, can become complex. An agent professing no particular expertise other than that required of a licensed agent will not ordinarily be held to as high a standard of conduct as agents who hold themselves out as experts. The courts have been quite willing to judge agents' responsibilities and conduct on the degree of expertise that they themselves profess to have. Thus, in one case, an agent was found negligent in failing to arrange properly the ownership of a life insurance policy to fund a business continuation agreement, the consequence of which was unanticipated state and federal estate taxation.[1] In another case, a life insurance agent was held liable for selling a policy unsuitable to the insured's needs.[2] A particularly important contemporary concern of U.S. life insurance agents and advisors is the potential for liability resulting from certain marketing practices.

The Exercise of Due Care by Advisors

The term **due care** means the process through which an insurance advisor investigates the quality and value of the insurance program recommended to the client. As applied to variable products and other securities in the United States, the roughly equivalent term is **due diligence**—the process by which a broker-dealer ensures that an investment is as represented. The terms carry different legal connotations, with the latter carrying greater consequences for abridgement.

Due care can be considered as comprising three elements. First, the advisor should take care to ensure that the insurance recommended is appropriate for the specific needs and circumstances of the client. Second, the advisor should take care to ensure that the recommended insurance is credibly illustrated, offers good value, and contains appropriate policy provisions. We cover these two elements in the next chapter except for contractual provisions, which have already been covered. Finally, the advisor should take care to ensure that the recommended insurer is financially sound and operationally efficient. The balance of this chapter focuses on the last item.

ORGANIZATIONS PROVIDING LIFE AND HEALTH INSURANCE

Several types of organizations offer life and health insurance, five of which are presented here. Their relative importance in terms of life insurance in force, premiums written, and assets is shown in Figure 11-1. We focus here principally on organizations providing life insurance, as health insurance organizations are covered extensively in chapter 19. Recall from chapter 1, however, that most life insurance companies sell health insurance. Government-provided life and health insurance coverage under social insurance programs are discussed in chapter 22.

Commercial Life Insurance Companies

Commercial life insurers are organized as either stock or mutual life insurance companies. A **stock life insurance company** is a corporation authorized to sell life and (usually) health insurance, which is owned by its stockholders and is organized and incorporated for the purpose of making a profit for its stockholders. The shares of stock can be owned

---

[1] *State Farm Life v. Fort Wayne National Bank,* 474 N.E.2d 524 (Ind. 1985).

[2] *Knox v. Anderson,* 159 F.Supp. 795, 162 F.Supp. 338 (D. Haw. 1958), 297 F.2d 702 (9th Cir. 1961) cert. denied, 370 U.S. 915 (1962).

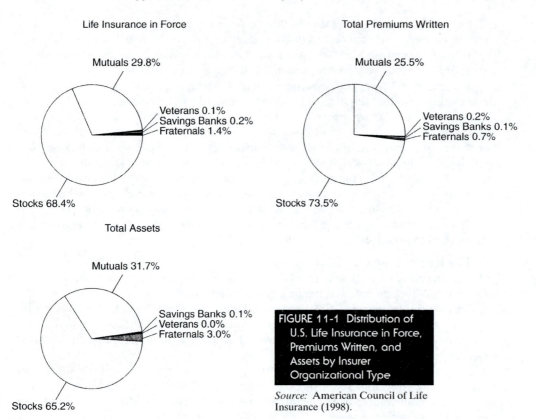

Life Insurance in Force

Mutuals 29.8%

Veterans 0.1%
Savings Banks 0.2%
Fraternals 1.4%

Stocks 68.4%

Total Premiums Written

Mutuals 25.5%

Veterans 0.2%
Savings Banks 0.1%
Fraternals 0.7%

Stocks 73.5%

Total Assets

Mutuals 31.7%

Savings Banks 0.1%
Veterans 0.0%
Fraternals 3.0%

Stocks 65.2%

FIGURE 11-1 Distribution of U.S. Life Insurance in Force, Premiums Written, and Assets by Insurer Organizational Type

Source: American Council of Life Insurance (1998).

by individuals, other stock insurers, mutual insurers, or companies or entities outside the insurance industry. Policyowners have no ownership interest in stock companies.

A **mutual life insurance company** is a corporation authorized to sell life and (usually) health insurance, which is owned by and operated for the benefit of its policyowners. It has no stockholders and, generally, cannot be owned by other insurers or anyone other than policyowners. Policyowners share in corporate profits through dividends paid on their policies.

Almost 1,700 commercial life insurance companies are domiciled in the United States. Together these stock and mutual insurers dominate the United States life insurance market, writing about 98 percent of total life insurance. Stock insurers are the most numerous worldwide, although mutual insurers dominate many markets, including, for example, Japan and Korea as well as the United States at one time. Many life insurers are affiliated with other life and non-life insurers in fleets with a single owner.

Stock insurers comprise 95 percent of the total, with mutuals accounting for the balance. This figure potentially is a little misleading because about 7 percent of stock insurers are owned by mutuals. On a fleet basis, the number of stock fleet companies is 1,491, falling to 88 percent of the total, with mutual fleet companies numbering 204 or about 12 percent. Mutual companies are generally older and larger than the stock companies. Several mutual companies have converted to stock insurers recently (see chapter 23).

Comparisons are often made between stock and mutual insurers. A few of the arguments for each are examined here.

Control

As a stock insurer is owned by shareholders, the directors and officers answer to them and not directly to the policyowners. Control legally lies with the holders of the majority of the stock. Just as with other large corporations, however, a stock insurance company with a large number of widely scattered stockholders typically is controlled by its management group through proxy arrangements. The likelihood that management of a substantial and well-established stock life company will ignore the interests of policyowners is, however, slim because of competition and insurance regulatory oversight. Limited management participation by policyowners is permitted by many stock insurers and is required in some countries. For example, policyowners may be given the right to elect several directors, although only a minority of them.

In a mutual insurer, policyowners theoretically own the company and control management. In practice, this is true only to a limited extent. The limited effectiveness of policyowners' control of a mutual company is due to (1) policyowners generally not perceiving themselves as owners of the company but rather as customers, (2) policyowners being numerous and widely scattered geographically, (3) policyowners having little capacity or inclination for intercommunication, (4) the stake of each policyowner in the insurer being proportionally small, and (5) many policyowners not understanding the nature of a mutual company nor knowing or caring that they have a right to vote in elections of directors. As a practical matter, mutual companies typically are controlled more by their management group through proxy arrangements than by policyowners. This principal–agent problem is explored in more detail in chapter 23.

Security

Another long-debated aspect of the stock versus mutual issue relates to which is the more secure financially. Proponents of the stock form sometimes argue that, in a stock company's initial development period, its capital and surplus can be larger than the initial surplus of a mutual insurer and that, therefore, the stock insurer could be considered more secure. Even in jurisdictions in which this may be true, this element of security becomes much less important with time.

Proponents of the mutual form often note that an additional margin of security is available to policyowners through the conservatism built into participating policy premiums. If necessary, mutual insurers could absorb adverse experience through reduced dividend payments. Increasingly, however, stock insurers are afforded the equivalent option through the nonguaranteed elements of their nonparticipating policies.

The relative security of stock and mutual companies is largely an academic question. The basic issues underlying financial security are sound and efficient management and adequate supervision and control by government authorities. Moreover, the individual purchaser would be interested in the financial security of the particular insurer or insurers under consideration, not whether mutuals or stocks as a group are more financially secure.

Cost

Another dimension of the stock versus mutual debate has been the question of relative product cost. Proponents of mutual companies have argued that, because profits flow to policyowners, their policies will be less costly than those sold by stock companies, as stockholders benefit from favored financial results.

Generalizations on the question of cost are not very helpful. Some mutual companies are more efficiently run than some stock companies, and vice versa. Even if a given insurer is efficiently operated, there remains no guarantee that policyowners—either in a mutual or stock company—will receive the benefit. Stock companies may pay out substantial dividends to stockholders. Mutual companies may elect to restrict policy-owner dividend payments in order to build surplus.

Whether a particular policy is low cost usually is not a function of organizational form but rather of insurer efficiency and the extent to which the insurer passes on to policy-owners resulting efficiency gains. As was clear from earlier chapters, variations are great.

Fraternal Benefit Societies

A **fraternal benefit society** is an organization operating under a lodge system that provides social and insurance benefits to members and family dependents. Fraternals account only for about 1 percent of the total U.S. life insurance market, but they are quite important in some geographical areas. Fraternal benefit societies have several features that distinguish them from commercial insurance companies. As fraternals are not covered elsewhere in this volume, their operations will be covered here in some detail.

Background

Fraternal benefit societies had their genesis in North America during the late 1800s and the early 1900s, at the time of the immigration influx into the United States and Canada. Many ethnic and nationality groups sought means of preserving their cultural heritages and providing a modicum of life insurance protection for their families as they struggled to gain economic freedom in their new country. The fraternal benefit system was born in that environment, and many societies now operating trace their origins to that time.

More than 100 fraternal benefit societies operate in the United States and Canada. About one-half of them are small societies operating in a single jurisdiction only. Other small or medium-sized societies are licensed in several jurisdictions, with a few licensed in all.

Structure

Fraternal benefit societies are organized and regulated under an entirely different set of laws than are commercial insurers in both the United States and Canada. To be called a fraternal benefit society, the organization must have a representative form of government, operate under a lodge system, and provide fraternal and insurance benefits to members and family dependents. Societies must be organized and must operate for one or more social, intellectual, educational, charitable, benevolent, moral, fraternal, patriotic, or religious purposes for the benefit of members.

Membership in many societies is based on the particular background of the individual society and the purpose for which it was formed. A society may serve persons of a particular ethnic or nationality group, a particular religious denomination or sect, or a particular occupational background.

A society must have a representative form of government. This means that the supreme governing body of a society must be elected either directly by the members or by delegates from the local lodges or intermediate bodies chosen in accordance with a society's constitution and bylaws. Proxy voting is prohibited, thus precluding the use of this device as a means of perpetuating a management group. The supreme governing body of a society must be elected and meet at least once every four years and elect a board of directors to conduct the business of the society between meetings.

Operating under the lodge system requirement means that a society must organize local lodges into which members are admitted in accordance with a society's bylaws, rules, and ritual. Lodges are generally required to have monthly or, in a few jurisdictions, at least quarterly meetings. Licensed fraternal benefit societies have more than 40,000 lodges.

In addition to the requirement of providing insurance benefits to their members, fraternal benefit societies provide numerous and varied volunteer, charitable, institutional, recreational, health, educational, religious, and membership activities and benefits through local lodges. Society members perform countless fraternal service acts annually for the benefit of their fellow members and the general public.

Because of their lodge system of operation and performance of benevolent, charitable, and volunteer activities for members and the general public, fraternal benefit societies are exempt from income taxation in the United States. The laws of every jurisdiction declare fraternal benefit societies to be "charitable and benevolent" institutions, and exempt them from premium taxation. Although acknowledging the charitable and benevolent work of many fraternals, critics of their tax-exempt status note that (1) the extent of this type of work varies among fraternals, and (2) more importantly, tax neutrality principles (see chapter 35) argue for government showing no tax favoritism among competitors.

The Fraternal Insurance Contract

Fraternal benefit societies provide insurance benefits through what are called fraternal certificates to differentiate them from commercial insurance policies. The fraternal insurance product typically contains the same or similar provisions as those found in a commercial insurance policy because the laws of most jurisdictions either prescribe standard and prohibited provisions akin to those required for commercial policies or require that the fraternal certificates meet the standard contract provisions required for commercial life and health policies.

A fraternal insurance certificate must contain two significant, unique provisions. One is the **open contract** provision that requires the certificate to state that the society's constitution and bylaws, and any future changes therein, are a part of the contract with the member/insured. Furthermore, any such changes shall bind the insured member and his or her beneficiaries, as though such changes had been made prior to the time of the application for insurance. No change may destroy or diminish the insurance benefits provided by the certificate. Under the closed contracts of commercial insurers, in contrast, the terms of the contract and the application constitute the entire agreement between the insurer and the policyowner.

The other unique provision is the **maintenance of solvency** provision. Statutes require that a society provide in its bylaws that, if the reserves for any or all classes of insurance become impaired, the board of directors may require insured members to pay an amount equal to an equitable portion of the deficiency. If such payment is not made, it either (1) must stand as an indebtedness against the certificate, with interest, or (2) the insured member may accept a proportionate reduction in benefits under the certificate. Because of this feature, fraternal benefit societies are exempt from state guaranty fund laws.

Pricing and Products

The laws of all North American jurisdictions require fraternal insurance certificates to be valued annually on specified tables of mortality. Some jurisdictions permit societies to value their newly issued certificates on any modern table authorized for commercial life insurers. Most societies value their current certificates on the *1980 CSO Table*.

In the early days of fraternal benefit societies, many operated on a pure assessment system. The system is historically interesting, as it provides insight into the need for risk-based pricing. Under the **pure assessment system,** premium payments from members were required only when a member of the insured group died. These payments were used to provide the death benefits promised to the insured. No advance payments were collected and no advance funding was involved. Fundamental to the assessment system was the assumption that an annual influx of new, younger members would tend to maintain the same age distribution (and, therefore, mortality risk) for the whole group, which would prevent the cost of insurance from increasing. The inequity of equal assessments, irrespective of members' ages, eventually became apparent and adversely affected the ability to secure and retain new members at the younger ages.

The defects of the pure assessment system led to the adoption of the **graded assessment system,** under which assessments were graded upward by age at entry. This modification still failed to recognize that the cost of insurance on a year-to-year basis depends on the current age. A few of the societies, realizing this fact, followed the yearly renewable term (YRT) plan for assessments. This was a financially sound plan, but as commercial companies had discovered, prohibitive costs developed at the older ages.

Gradually, the societies realized that life insurance pricing should be based either on the YRT plan or, if whole life insurance was to be provided, on the level-premium plan with attendant reserves. The ultimate transition to a sound actuarial basis, which has been accomplished by all fraternal societies of consequence, was aided by legislation initiated by the fraternals themselves through the National Fraternal Congress of America and the Associated Fraternities of America.

Fraternal benefit societies in most states and Canada are permitted to issue death, endowment, annuity, temporary or permanent disability, hospital, medical, and nursing coverage. Some societies have chosen to limit their insurance operations to life, endowment, and annuity benefits, whereas others confine their insurance operations to health or accident only benefits.

Model Fraternal Code

The National Fraternal Congress, in conjunction with the National Association of Insurance Commissioners, adopted a Uniform Fraternal Code model bill in 1962 that has been enacted in more than one-half of the states. Portions of it have been enacted in other states.

In 1983, the National Fraternal Congress drafted and adopted a Model Fraternal Code for the organization and supervision of fraternal benefit societies. That code, enacted in more than 20 states, modernizes the law relating to fraternal benefit societies. It authorizes societies to issue such benefits as are now authorized, or may in the future be authorized by statute or administrative regulation for life insurers, but that are not inconsistent with the membership and other requirements of the laws governing fraternal benefit societies. The Model Fraternal Code also permits fraternal benefit societies to establish separate accounts for writing variable products and to carry out their stated purposes indirectly through subsidiary corporations or affiliated organizations.

Savings Banks

Three states—Connecticut, Massachusetts, and New York—permit savings banks to sell life insurance. Although the business and assets of mutual savings bank life insurance are substantial, they are relatively insignificant when compared with the aggregate figures for commercial life insurance companies, as Figure 11-1 illustrates. Just as with fraternal life insurance, a somewhat detailed discussion is presented here on mutual savings bank life insurance because it is not covered elsewhere in this volume.

Background

Massachusetts, in 1907, became the first state to empower its mutual savings banks to establish life insurance departments for the purpose of providing life insurance and annuity benefits to residents and those working in the state. Similar laws were enacted in New York in 1938 and in Connecticut in 1941.

The Massachusetts law was the result of proposals made by Louis D. Brandeis following the Armstrong investigation in New York (see chapter 3). The testimony taken in the investigation had emphasized the excessive amounts spent by some insurers at that time for commissions on new business and also had brought out the comparatively high cost of weekly premium industrial insurance and its high rates of lapse.

The purpose of the Massachusetts law was to provide low-cost, over-the-counter insurance to all residents of the commonwealth who wanted it. The reduction in cost under the savings bank system depended primarily on the elimination of the sales costs incurred by commercial companies, chiefly through eliminating commissions to soliciting agents, and the benefit of a lower rate of lapse.

Bills for the establishment of savings bank life insurance have been introduced in a number of other states where savings banks are not as strong and numerous, but, since the Connecticut bill in 1941, no new enabling legislation has passed. The most active opposition to savings bank life insurance has come from life insurance agents who consider savings bank life insurance an unfair threat to their means of livelihood. In the past, commercial life insurance companies opposed such bills mainly on the ground that they were discriminatory, in that the insurance departments of the banks were not made subject to the same conditions and requirements as those to which the commercial insurance companies were subject. Recent legislation has generally provided for the same requirements and conditions as those that apply to commercial companies.

Nature

Savings bank life insurance is transacted on an over-the-counter basis or by mail and without the use of soliciting agents. This is a type of direct-response marketing (see chapter 24). This approach can result in considerable savings in expenses, fewer lapses, and a low cost to policyowners.

Some economies of scale are achieved because of the centralization in each state of certain actuarial, medical, and other services. In this way, it is unnecessary for each savings bank to deal with many of the technical details of life insurance administration. The central organization computes premium rates, which are the same for all issuing banks in a given state, and also prepares policy forms, application blanks, and so on. Thus, in some ways, the savings bank life insurance system is similar to a single life insurance company, with the central organization serving as the home office and the individual banks as branches. Each issuing bank, however, is an independent unit, issues its own contracts, maintains records, and retains and invests the assets of its own insurance department.

The surplus funds of the insurance department of a bank are available only to the policyowners of that bank. In addition, the assets and liabilities of the banking and insurance departments of a given issuing bank are segregated. Furthermore, an equitable allocation of expenses between the banking department and life insurance department is required. The central organization, however, maintains a contingency or guaranty fund (established by the contributions of the insurance banks) that is available to protect policyowners of all participating banks in the event of financial difficulty.

An important feature of savings bank life insurance, which lends stability to the system, is the so-called **unification of mortality** under which the mortality experience of the banks in a state is pooled. Because relatively small amounts of insurance are issued and in force in many of the banks, the mortality experience of individual banks is subject to relatively large yearly fluctuations. Pooling increases the financial stability of the individual banks. Each bank then shares proportionately in the pooled mortality cost.

The banks have authority to sell the usual types of ordinary policies, annuities, and group insurance. Sales of term insurance—especially decreasing term insurance to cover the unpaid balance of a mortgage—have been proportionately higher than in commercial companies. Waiver of premium benefits are available in all three states. Disability income benefits are not available under the ordinary forms of policies issued, and only New York permits accidental death benefits to be issued on ordinary policies.

The terms of the contracts are similar to those of commercial insurers, and all contracts are participating. Cash and loan values and nonforfeiture options are available after one year and, in the early years, are more liberal than in the usual commercial company contracts. These favorable values reflect the lower first-year expense, due to the absence of agents' commissions and other agency expenses and low overhead costs.

The amount of insurance obtainable by any one applicant is limited by law in each state. The limit in Massachusetts is $500,000. The New York limit is $50,000 for individual coverage and $250,000 for group coverage. In Connecticut the limit of insurance obtainable by one applicant is $100,000 for individual coverage and $200,000 for group coverage, indexed to the consumer price index. Savings bank life insurance is available only to residents of or workers in the state, but of course, it remains in force if the policyowner leaves the state.

Government

Governments often provide certain types of individually issued life and health insurance. Most often, the insurance is sold through a government-owned insurer, a diminishing number of which occupy monopoly positions in their markets. Within the United States, the state of Wisconsin is the only state-run life insurance operation. See Box 11-2.

Governments also often provide optional life and health insurance for military and, sometimes, other government personnel. Within the United States, insurance for military personnel is the principal form of government-provided life and health insurance. Again, because these programs are not covered elsewhere in this volume, they will be discussed here in some detail. We cover four major programs.

United States Government Life Insurance

The oldest of the United States government life insurance programs, **United States Government Life Insurance** (USGLI), was established by Congress in 1919 and granted renewable term insurance, to a maximum of $10,000, to those in the military and naval services, for the benefit of selected beneficiaries only. Later, the right of conversion to cash-value policies was accorded. In 1928, a special disability income rider was made available.

Sales of USGLI were terminated in 1951, and today the total amount in force under this program is small. All USGLI policies were declared paid up as of 1983.

BOX 11-2

THE WISCONSIN STATE LIFE FUND

Wisconsin is the only U.S. state wherein the government is authorized to sell life insurance. The Wisconsin State (Life) Fund, established in 1911, permits certain designated government officials and state banks to sell life insurance coverage through the state fund but only within the state.

All applications are processed and supervised through the insurance commissioner's office and administered by the state treasury department.

The fund engages in no advertising and employs no agents, so the insurance costs are low. The total amount of insurance in force is small.

National Service Life Insurance

The second of these programs, **National Service Life Insurance** (NSLI), was established by the National Service Life Insurance Act of 1940. After passage of this act, USGLI could only be obtained by individuals entering service between 1921 and 1940 or upon their reenlistment. During World War II, the NSLI program became the largest single life insurance operation in history at that time, with a peak of over $121 billion of life insurance in force. Following World War II, only a small percentage of insureds renewed their term insurance or converted to cash-value forms of life insurance made available to them.

Under NSLI, the face amount of the insurance issued ranged from a minimum of $1,000 to a maximum of $10,000, in multiples of $500. The maximum government life insurance permitted under all plans combined is $10,000. In addition to a five-year term policy, NSLI made available five whole life policy forms and three endowment forms.

NSLI dividends have been liberal, and the net cost of these policies has been exceedingly favorable. The United States government absorbs all administrative expenses and reimburses the NSLI Trust Fund for certain service-connected deaths.

In view of the far-reaching extent of this government insurance program, many feared that NSLI would seriously interfere with commercial insurance. These fears proved largely unfounded. The government's system seems to have made the younger generation more life insurance–minded. Moreover, a maximum of only $10,000 insurance was available, and only a small proportion of service personnel retained their government insurance after discharge.

Gratuitous-Indemnity Program

The Servicemen's Indemnity Act of 1950, passed after a long series of investigations into the operation, cost, and justification of the entire government life insurance program, essentially ended the sale of new NSLI to those in the service. It automatically insured persons on active duty between 1950 and 1956 for $10,000, less the amount of any NSLI and USGLI maintained in force.

The **gratuitous-indemnity benefit** was payable only in monthly installments for 10 years, and only to a restricted group of beneficiaries. Following discharge from service, the veteran had the right to apply for NSLI if he or she applied within the stipulated time period. Owners of regular NSLI and USGLI in active service were permitted either to cancel their old policies and come under the gratuitous-indemnity plan (reacquiring them after discharge) or to continue NSLI or USGLI in force, with the pure insurance risk part of the premium waived by the government.

The Servicemen's and Veterans' Survivor Benefit Act of 1956 made sweeping changes in the entire program. Among other things, the act terminated the gratuitous-indemnity program. Social Security benefits were extended to service members and dependents on a full contributory basis. With this action, the extension of government life insurance benefits to new personnel was terminated. A considerable amount of government life insurance remains in force, particularly under the NSLI program.

Servicemen's and Veterans' Insurance

Members of the U.S. uniformed services and veterans might be able to qualify for several insurance programs today. These programs are (1) Servicemen's Group Life Insurance (SGLI), (2) Veterans Group Life Insurance (VGLI), (3) Service-Disabled Veterans Insurance (RH), and (4) Veterans Mortgage Life Insurance. We discuss each next.

Servicemen's Group Life Insurance Established in 1956, SGLI provides members of the uniformed services on active duty with group insurance written by commercial life insurance companies. Similar in concept to the federal employees group life insurance plan, the program is administered through a primary insurer licensed in all states. Other insurers participate as reinsurers even though they are not so widely licensed, subject to Veterans Administration approval of the criteria for selecting such companies. Approved companies may elect to participate in converting SGLI to individual policies, irrespective of whether they act as reinsurers of the group plan.

Premiums paid by service personnel cover normal peacetime mortality costs and administration expenses. All costs attributable to the extra hazards of military service are paid by the federal government. Insurance is provided automatically to full-time, active-duty persons in the uniformed services. The insurance remains in effect during active duty and for 120 days after separation from service, unless it is terminated earlier at the insured's request, and unless the insured is totally disabled at the time of separation or release from active duty. Coverage of up to $100,000 is automatic upon entry into a period of active duty or reserve status with an option available to purchase an additional $100,000.

Veterans Group Life Insurance   The Veterans Insurance Act of 1974, amended in 1981, established a postseparation insurance program that provides for conversion of SGLI, at reasonable rates, to a five-year, nonrenewable term policy known as Veterans Group Life Insurance. At the end of the term period, the insured has the right to convert the insurance to an individual cash-value policy with any of the participating insurers. A list of eligible companies is furnished by the office of SGLI. The new policy is issued at standard rates regardless of the insured's health and for not more than the amount of VGLI. The conversion privilege is identical to that which existed under the prior law and applies to all VGLI coverage.

Service-Disabled Veterans Insurance   Under Service-Disabled Veterans Insurance (RH), eligible veterans may receive a $10,000 life insurance policy. All RH policies provide for waiver of premiums, at no extra cost, if the insured is determined to be totally disabled for at least six months and total disability begins before age 65. Policyowners eligible for waiver of premiums may purchase up to $20,000 additional coverage under the Supplemental Service-Disabled Veterans Insurance (SSDVI) program. Premiums for this additional SSDVI may not be waived.

Veterans Mortgage Life Insurance   Under Veterans Mortgage Life Insurance, eligible veterans can be issued up to $90,000, which is payable to the mortgage holder upon their death.

LIFE INSURANCE COMPANY EVALUATION

Many organizations provide life insurance, although stock and mutual insurance companies dominate the North American market as well as virtually every other market. Further discussion will, therefore, focus on these insurers.

Importance of Insurer Selection

Life and health insurance involves long-term financial guarantees. The insurance guarantee differs from guarantees on other consumer products in at least three important respects. First, in insurance, the guarantee *is* the product. There is no inherent value in the pieces of paper called an insurance policy. Only the guarantee embodied in the policy has value. Second, the duration of the guarantee is potentially much longer than most others. The insurer states, essentially, that it intends to fulfill all of its obligations under an insurance policy whenever it is called upon to do so—tomorrow or 50 years hence. Third, because of the great information asymmetry that exists between buyers and sellers, buyers cannot easily assess the integrity of the insurer and, hence, the value of its guarantee.

For these three basic reasons, the financial strength and integrity of a life insurance company are more vital to its customers than is true of most other enterprises.

The issue of financial strength has become far more important than in past times. In the past, life insurer financial difficulty was comparatively rare. Today, however, we have witnessed important insurer insolvencies in most of the world's major insurance markets, including the United States, Canada, Japan, the United Kingdom, and others. Thus, it is more important than ever that insurer selection be made on the basis of an informed, unbiased evaluation.

In addition to the issue of financial strength, life insurance purchasers are interested in product value. Efficiently operated insurers are in a better position to continue to offer their customers good product value.

Criteria for Insurer Evaluation

Insurer evaluation should be formed around at least four general criteria:

- financial soundness and performance
- product availability
- service quality
- ethical behavior

We discuss each of these next.

Financial Soundness and Performance

The most important element of insurer evaluation is its financial soundness. If an insurer is of questionable financial strength, all other evaluation aspects can be meaningless.

It is difficult to establish general rules as to what makes a company safe. Many insurers point to their large amounts of insurance in force, implying that this connotes safety. Others might focus on their total assets or policy reserves; they may suggest that high levels mean correspondingly high security.

Yet an insurer's size in terms of assets has little to do with safety, even though the relative conservatism of the valuation basis often has a direct relationship to security. Assets are accumulated from premiums and investment income and stand behind policy liabilities that represent the insurer's present estimate of the amount necessary, with future premiums and earnings, to meet its contractual obligations as they fall due. Laws usually mandate minimum reserves, but most well-established insurers maintain reserves in excess of these minimums. The extent to which an insurer maintains reserves in excess of the minimum is a function of management philosophy and can be influenced by tax laws.

Although the entire financial picture, as measured by assets, liabilities, insurance in force, level of premiums, mortality and morbidity experience, and so on, can be informative in appraising a life insurance company, much more information is needed to conduct an adequate appraisal. Even then, because of the complexities involved, it is exceedingly difficult for someone working only with published data and information to make an informed assessment of insurer strength, although obvious problems sometimes can be identified through a financial analysis based on published data. Greater reliance, however, is placed on the evaluation of specialty rating services. Later sections of this chapter delve more deeply into these matters.

Product Availability

The range and quality of products offered by insurers have obvious relevance to insurer evaluation. Most insurers do not attempt to serve all markets; many specialize in one or a few areas only. Organizational structure, service facilities, and cost of operation differ widely, depending on the insurer's target markets and management efficiency and effectiveness. As discussed in chapters 1 and 23, insurers may enjoy economies of scale and of scope, with one type of operation affecting the cost of another.

Individual insurers vary considerably in the quality and types of policies made available. For example, some high-quality companies choose not to offer a full range of individual life and health insurance products to all markets. Thus, even if a given company were judged to be otherwise acceptable, its product offerings might eliminate it from consideration.

Another significant factor relates to the insurer's underwriting practices. Many insurers will issue insurance to individuals expected to exhibit higher than standard mortality or morbidity, and companies differ as to what constitutes a standard risk. Some insurers are more liberal than others in the flexibility permitted in utilizing settlement options. Agents and other financial advisors typically are well informed about individual insurer product availability. In some instances, access to specialty brokers may prove necessary.

Service Quality

Service is a term with a variety of meanings. Good service can be thought of as service that meets or exceeds the customer's expectations. Variations in service are more a matter of management efficiency and philosophy than of insurer type. Some insurers handle a request for information, a policy loan, the processing of a claim for benefits, and other aspects of life insurance service much more efficiently and courteously than do other companies. The service aspect of health insurance policies has always been greater than that for life policies. However, this dimension has become much more important with life insurance with the advent of more flexible policies and the greater emphasis nationally and worldwide on improving service.

There is great variation in the level of service rendered by agents and other financial advisors. Some insurers place great emphasis on agent training and spend large sums to keep agents informed about legal and tax changes, as well as other changes that vitally impinge on the service an agent can render. The agent's willingness and desire to provide quality service often is a separate issue altogether and is influenced by incentives built (or not) into the agent compensation package.

The quality of service rendered by an insurer depends totally on the quality of its employees. An insurer that invests heavily in its human capital and hires highly qualified employees has an edge over insurers that do not. This dimension of insurer evaluation is difficult to assess, but consumer instinct often is a good guide. Additionally, insurers routinely "benchmark" themselves in terms of service efficiency. As discussed later, an insurer's lapse rates are a useful measure of service quality differences among otherwise similar insurers.

Ethical Behavior

A buyer will want to purchase insurance from, and the conscientious agent will want to sell insurance for, only those insurers whose conduct is consistent with high ethical standards. Ethical behavior extends to all aspects of insurance company operations, from marketing, underwriting and pricing, to service and claims.

A key ethical element is that of fairness. Most life and health insurance policies sold today permit the insurer to make periodic adjustments to premiums or policy values consistent with past or expected future experience. These policies entail an insurer's actual or implicit promise to permit policyowners to share equitably in the insurer's favorable experience. As illustrated in chapter 4 and elsewhere, this does not always happen, although the majority of life insurers probably strive for fairness.

Determining whether a particular insurer will deal ethically with its policyowners is not easy. To an extent, regulatory oversight is meant to ensure a certain minimum level of ethical behavior, but ethics encompasses more than compliance with the law.

One particularly daunting ethical problem that insurers (and agents) have faced recently relates to their conduct in the marketplace. Indeed, the many lawsuits and fines faced by North American life insurers during the 1990s (see chapter 9) stemming from poor market conduct have galvanized the industry's attention. Indirect consequences, such as reduction in the industry's image, potentially more rigorous regulation, and ever more insurer and executive liability, have been noted. One result was the creation of the Insurance Marketplace Standards Association (IMSA) in 1996.

This voluntary association encourages life insurers to maintain high standards of ethical behavior in the sale and marketing of individual life insurance and annuities by becoming members. The association's standards do not apply to other areas of insurer operation. The core of IMSA's program are the *Principles of Ethical Market Conduct* and the *Code of Life Insurance Ethical Market Conduct.* See Box 11-3. The *Code* embodies 27 interpretative standards, which themselves have operative parts.

Under the program, life insurers voluntarily adopt the *Principles* and *Code* and then create and apply practices assuring companywide compliance with them. Assessments are a key element of the program. Insurers are to conduct a self-assessment, making changes in procedures and practices as required to comply. In addition, the company must secure a favorable opinion by an independent assessor of the insurer's policies and procedures. Upon successful completion of these requirements, companies may advertise their membership in IMSA. The hope is that membership will connote adherence to high ethical standards by the insurer in connection with the sale of individual life products.

The program has garnered support from several large insurers, but many express concern about it, particularly related to the potential for plaintiff attorneys to use the program against the very insurers that participate in it. For example, the self-assessment could uncover unacceptable past behavior, which would be discoverable in lawsuits.

Another issue of ethical behavior relates to the credibility of illustrations given to prospective policyowners by insurers and agents. We will explore this issue in the next chapter. Here it is sufficient to note that knowledge of insurers' overall operating performance can provide a basis for evaluating policy illustrations.

BOX 11-3

THE *PRINCIPLES OF ETHICAL MARKET CONDUCT* OF THE INSURANCE MARKETPLACE STANDARDS ASSOCIATION (IMSA)

Each IMSA member pledges to comply with the following principles in all matters affecting the marketing and sale of individually issued life insurance and annuity products:

- To conduct business according to high standards of honesty and fairness and to render that service to its customers, which, in the same circumstances, it would apply to or demand for itself.

- To provide competent and customer-focused sales and service.

- To engage in active and fair competition.

- To provide advertising and sales materials that are clear as to purpose and honest and fair as to content.

- To provide fair and expeditious handling of customer complaints and disputes.

- To maintain a system of supervision and review that is reasonably designed to achieve compliance with these *Principles of Ethical Market Conduct.*

Sources of Information about Life Insurers

Sources of information about particular life insurers include (1) rating agencies, (2) governmental associations and agencies, (3) insurance companies and their trade associations, (4) agents and other insurance advisors, and (5) publications and other public sources. Each is discussed next.

Rating Agencies

As alluded to earlier, it is virtually impossible for the average person, on his or her own, to assess an insurer's financial position.[3] Yet insurance buyers need this type of information if they are to make informed purchase decisions.

Several rating agencies specialize in financial evaluations of insurers. Their activities have become increasingly prominent since the recent financial difficulties experienced by some insurers. The ratings issued by these agencies represent their opinions of the insurers' financial condition and their ability to meet their obligations to policyowners. Rating downgrades are watched closely.

Nature of Ratings   Ratings provide a means by which consumers can differentiate among various companies. Stockbrokers and other financial analysts use rating agency evaluations as a means of understanding more about stock insurance companies. Rating agency evaluations are subjective and are not a guarantee as to future performance by the insurer. Nonetheless, they do provide important information that enhances the public's knowledge about and perspective on insurers.

Not all insurers receive a rating from each rating agency. Some agencies rate most insurers whereas others rate only selected companies. Not having a rating from a specific rating agency does not necessarily imply that something is wrong with a company. It may mean that the management of the company believes that the expenditure of time, money, and other resources involved in obtaining a rating is not warranted, that it is not necessary to have a rating from a particular agency, or that the company's lines of business are outside the scope of what an agency evaluates.

A rating for a given insurer is only an indicator of relative financial strength. Different agencies have different portrayals of the financial and other operations of the same company. Subjectivity of ratings is reflected in the different ratings that are assigned an insurer by different rating agencies.

Most agencies use a wide variety of information in developing their ratings. Some ratings rely solely on statistical data. Sources of information include publicly filed forms with the insurance regulatory, special requests to insurers for information, visits to the company, visits of the company's management to the rating agencies, written and verbal communication between the two, and combinations of some or all of these methods. Types of information used in the rating process may include a review of historical information and trends, an assessment of the quality of the insurer's management, a review of current operations, an analysis of different types of financial information, and a review of management's future plans and aspirations.

Risks Faced by Insurers   All ratings involve a subjective evaluation of the risks associated with a life insurance company. The evaluation by the rating agency is an attempt to categorize the relative risk (contingencies) of an insurer in relation to other insurers. Each agency publishes a rating scale to facilitate this comparison.

According to the Society of Actuaries, life insurers face four types of risks. An examination of these risks is a key part of evaluating the overall risk profile of a life insurance company. The **asset depreciation (C-1) risk** is the risk of losses in bonds, mortgages,

---

[3]This section draws partly from *Insurance Company Rating Agencies: A Description of Their Methods and Procedures* (Kansas City, MO: NAIC, 1992) and *Life Insurance Industry Rating Agencies.*

stocks, real estate, and other investments through either default on payment of interest or principal or through loss of market value. **Pricing inadequacy (C-2) risk** is the risk that premium rates will be unable to cover unfavorable changes in mortality, morbidity, health care inflation, and so on.

   Interest rate change (C-3) risk is the risk of unexpected cash outflows or cash inflows during periods of rising or falling interest rates, with negative disinvestment or investment implications for the life insurer. **General business (C-4) risk** derives from such factors as expansion into new geographic areas or lines of business, changes in the tax law, fraud, lawsuits, contingent liabilities, and other environmental sources of risk that do not fit into the C-1 through C-3 categories. Runs on life insurer assets by policyowners fit into this category of risk. Many life insurer insolvencies derive primarily from C-4 risks that involve management fraud or a misallocation of assets.

Differences in Ratings and Rating Scales   Table 11-1 shows the rating scales used by the leading rating agencies. The rating systems in the table cannot be compared absolutely because of differences in the meanings of different rating categories among the agencies. For example, an A– rating from A.M. Best may not mean the same thing as an AA– rating from Duff & Phelps. Additionally, Weiss Research ratings rely on statistical analysis alone whereas the ratings from the other services incorporate more than statistical analysis.[4]

Factors in the Rating Process   The most important information in the rating process is probably the life insurer's surplus (also called capital). The primary question involves whether the insurer's surplus is adequate to cover its financial obligations under adverse

---

[4]Standard & Poor's rating service also offers ratings based on statistical analysis alone, although they are not shown in Table 11-1.

TABLE 11-1   Rating Scales for Five Insurance Rating Agencies [With Web Addresses]

A.M. Best [www.ambest.com]	Standard & Poor's [www.standardandpoors.com/ratings]	Moody's [www.moodys.com]	Duff & Phelps [www.dcrco.com]	Weiss [www.weissratings.com]
A++/A+ (superior)	AAA (superior)	Aaa (exceptional)	AAA (highest)	A+/A/A– (excellent)
A/A– (excellent)	AA+/AA/AA– (excellent)	Aa1/Aa2 (excellent)	AA+/AA/AA– (very high)	B+/B/B– (good)
B++/B+ (very good)	A+/A/A– (good)	A1/A2/A3 (good)	A/A+/A– (high)	C+/C/C– (fair)
B/B– (fair)	BBB+/BBB/BBB– (adequate)	Baa1/Baa2/Baa3 (adequate)	BBB+/BBB/BBB– (below average)	D+/D/D– (weak)
C++/C+ (marginal)	BB+/BB/BB– (may be vulnerable)	Ba1/Ba2/Ba3 (questionable)	BB+/BB/BB–	E+/E/E– (very weak)
C/C– (weak)	B+/B/B– (vulnerable)	B1/B2/B3 (poor)	B+/B/B–	F (failed)
D (poor)	CCC+/CCC/CCC– (extremely vulnerable)	Caa	CCC+/CCC/CCC–	U (unrated)
E (under regulatory supervision)	CC	Ca		
F (in liquidation)	C	C		
S (rating suspended)	D (liquidation)			

Note: Scales are not comparable.

economic conditions and other circumstances. Rating agencies use their own risk-based capital methodologies in evaluating surplus adequacy.

Besides the perceived required surplus, other quantitative factors may be reviewed and may guide the agency in determining its ultimate rating. These factors may be revealed in reports on individual companies published by an agency. Some agencies also provide a generic discussion of these factors, listing and describing them in a general report to interested audiences.

A critical aspect in a rating agency evaluation is an analysis of the composition of the insurer's investment portfolio. There are many levels of investment quality within the categories of corporate securities, mortgages, and real estate.

An important aspect of the rating process for many agencies is a review of the insurer's asset–liability management process. This review may identify a potential mismatching of asset and liability cash flows and the resulting potential investment risk. The rating agency wants to understand the insurer's risk with regard to its asset–liability management practices.

Rating agencies use many qualitative factors in analyzing an insurer. These factors provide the evaluator with an intuitive feeling about the company's strategic direction, the competence of its management, and related factors.

Governmental Agencies

The Insurance Regulator The insurance department of the state, province, or other jurisdiction can be a potential source of insurer information. Each department can advise whether a given insurer is licensed and in good standing within the jurisdiction. Additionally, insurers must file detailed annual financial statements with each jurisdiction in which they are licensed. Within the United States, these financial statements are prepared in accordance with statutory accounting principles and contain the insurer's balance sheet, income statement, and numerous supporting exhibits and schedules (see chapters 34 and 35). These publicly available statements contain a wealth of information on insurers. Many jurisdictions require that insurers file abbreviated financial statements on a quarterly basis.

Within the United States, each state's insurance supervisor is charged with conducting periodic (e.g., every three years) on-site financial examinations of its domestic insurers (see chapter 35). Examinations also may be conducted whenever the insurance regulator deems necessary. Examination reports contain the opinion of the examiner team as to whether the insurer is fully in compliance with state law, and any variances are noted. Many insurer operational aspects are noted, along with verification of the financial statement information. Insurer examination reports, available for public review, can be a source of useful information. Regrettably, many of these reports are outdated by the time they become available.

Insurance regulators receive and dispose of complaints about insurers. The nature of the complaints against specific insurers may be available. Insurers against whom many complaints are lodged relative to their total business within a jurisdiction often are found to be in financial difficulty.

The Insurance Regulatory Information System Either state insurance departments or the NAIC may be a source of information from the NAIC's Insurance Regulatory Information System (IRIS). IRIS assists state insurance departments in overseeing the financial condition of insurers. IRIS has two phases: a statistical phase and an analytical phase.

The **statistical phase** involves the calculation of 12 financial ratios based on data extracted from each insurer's annual statement that is filed with the NAIC. Insurers with four or more ratios outside of a prescribed "usual range" may be earmarked for further review—the so-called **analytical phase.** Typically, about one-fifth of all U.S. life insurers have four or more ratios outside the usual range. Box 11-4 describes the 12 IRIS life/health ratios and gives their usual ranges.

During the analytical phase, a team of examiners from various state insurance departments meets to review the outlier insurers' and selected other insurers' annual statements. The team assigns a first, second, third, or no priority to each insurer. These designations are meant to establish the order in which the insurers should be reviewed by their domiciliary state. Insurers within the no-priority designation can be put into the state's normal review process.

The information from the statistical phase of IRIS is available to the public. Information from the analytical phase is not available.

The fact that an insurer has four or more ratios outside the usual range does not necessarily indicate that it is facing financial adversity, but the information can be significant. Explanations for this fact ideally should be sought from the state insurance commissioner's office or from the insurer itself, although the insurer may not provide an unbiased assessment.

The Securities and Exchange Commission Information about stock insurers may be available through the filings required of the Securities and Exchange Commission (SEC). So-called 10-K forms contain insurer financial information prepared in accordance with generally accepted accounting principles (GAAP) (see chapter 34). This and related disclosure information can provide more insight into insurer operations.

BOX 11-4

THE NAIC'S IRIS RATIOS AND THE RANGES OF USUAL VALUES

Ratio 1: Net Change in Capital and Surplus
Greater than –10 percent and less than 50 percent

Ratio 1A: Gross Change in Capital and Surplus
Greater than –10 percent and less than 50 percent

Ratio 2: Net Gain to Total Income
Greater than 0 percent

Ratio 3: Commissions and Expenses to Premiums and Deposits
Less than 60 percent

Ratio 4: Adequacy of Investment Income
Greater than 125 percent and less than 900 percent

Ratio 5: Nonadmitted to Admitted Assets
Less than 10 percent

Ratio 6: Real Estate to Capital and Surplus
Less than 200 percent for companies with capital and surplus greater than $5 million; less than 100 percent for companies with capital and surplus equal to or less than $5 million

Ratio 7: Investments in Affiliates to Capital and Surplus
Less than 100 percent

Ratio 8: Surplus Relief
Greater than –99 percent and less than 30 percent for companies with capital and surplus greater than $5 million; greater than –10 percent and less than 10 percent for companies with capital and surplus equal to or less than $5 million

Ratio 9: Change in Premium
Greater than –10 percent and less than 50 percent

Ratio 10: Change in Product Mix
Less than 5.0 percent

Ratio 11: Change in Asset Mix
Less than 5.0 percent

Insurance Companies and Trade Associations

The insurance companies from which one considers purchasing a product are themselves obvious sources of information. Certainly they can give information of the type they provide to state regulators and the SEC. They also can reveal their ratings and provide their explanation for them.

Insurers can be asked for any information that would permit one to assess the company's level and quality of service and how they treat existing policyowners in relation to matters of equity and fairness. Insurers can be asked whether they have been identified as a priority company through the NAIC's IRIS evaluation. If unusual IRIS ratios are exhibited or if any other aspect of company operation or management raises questions, the insurer itself can be asked to provide explanations. Of course, one must be aware that insurer responses may not be free of bias.

Insurer trade associations sometimes are asked to provide limited information on their members, especially if a member insurer has received adverse publicity. The major U.S. life and health insurance trade associations include the American Council of Life Insurance (ACLI) in Washington, DC (whose members account for more than 90 percent of U.S. life insurance in force), the National Fraternal Congress of America in Naperville, Illinois (whose members are fraternal insurers), the Health Insurance Association of America (HIAA) in Washington, DC (whose members account for the great majority of health insurance written by commercial life insurers), and the Blue Cross/Blue Shield Association of America in Chicago (whose members are Blue Cross/Blue Shield organizations).

Publications and Services

For most consumers and advisors, insurance and related publications as well as the general business press usually are the first sources of adverse information on insurers. Reporters who delve into details of insurer operation and management have often provided early warnings of impending insurer difficulty. Another publication of potential value is *Best's Key Rating Guide.* Published annually by A.M. Best Company, this volume gives five-year financial summaries in the form of financial ratios and related information.

Much information is available through Web sites and other electronic media such as compact disks. These sites and services, often available through libraries and vendors, can provide up-to-date, detailed financial information and other information about many insurers, extracted from news articles and magazines as well as from insurer annual reports.

Insurance Advisors

It is important for agents and other financial advisors to keep abreast of developments within the financial services community. Indeed, insurance advisors are the sole source of insurer information for the majority of insurance purchasers.

Of course, advisors obtain their information from the sources discussed earlier and also from an informal network of "street talk." For example, many agents and other advisors, because of their own solvency concerns, were not recommending that their clients purchase insurance from Executive Life, even when major rating services gave the now-failed insurer high ratings.

If two or more agents are competing for a customer's business, each may have an additional incentive to secure information on the financial condition of its competitor insurers. The client can thereby become better informed but must exercise care in evaluating the competitors' claims.

For most life and health insurance buyers, the agent is the most important source of insurer information. For this reason, the care with which the advisor is selected is even more critical.

Elements of a Life Insurer Evaluation

With the preceding discussion in mind, the elements of one approach to insurer evaluation may be laid out. Whatever approach is followed, the objective should be to maximize the chances of a consumer doing business with a financially strong insurer with impressive performance characteristics.

Overview of Insurer

Any evaluation should begin with a complete identification of the insurer, including its full name and address. The insurer's history, including its age and its management, can provide insight. Whether the insurer is organized as a stock, mutual, or fraternal ordinarily is noted, as is any fleet or other affiliation. A committed, strong parent company can be a source of additional financial strength for the insurer. A less than committed parent company can view the insurer as a ready source of cash.

The size of the insurer as measured by assets, premium income, life insurance in force, surplus, or all four of these usually is noted, although size is no guarantee of solidity. Larger insurers can have a greater spread of risk via number and diversification of insureds and assets. On the other hand, smaller insurers often focus on particular market segments and can obtain risk spread through reinsurance and appropriate investment management. The insurer's mix of business by major line (individual, group and credit life, health, and annuity) and mix of assets often are noted.

Licenses

An insurer should be licensed and in good standing to sell insurance in the prospective policyowner's jurisdiction. Large insurers usually are licensed in more jurisdictions than are smaller insurers, thus permitting a better geographical risk spread, although, again, reinsurance can achieve the same effective result for smaller insurers. Also, some insurers believe that they can operate more efficiently and effectively by avoiding some jurisdictions.

The state of New York has long been recognized as a leader in insurance regulatory vigilance. Unlike the situation in other states, life insurers licensed to conduct business in New York are subject to key portions of New York law in all states in which they do business. This extraterritorial aspect of New York law makes its regulation all the more important. Many authorities believe, therefore, that the fact of being licensed in New York can itself be considered as a positive factor in determining insurer solidity.

Rating Agency Evaluations

The ratings and accompanying commentary by the major rating services should, of course, be included as a key element of life insurer evaluation. Obviously, the higher the ratings, the better. Rating agencies issue reasoned, independent evaluations of insurers' financial conditions and operating results. How the ratings are used is an individual decision. One long-time observer of the life insurance business has suggested that, as a conservative approach to selection, an insurer should meet two criteria:

- it should be in the top two rating categories of at least two of the major rating firms and
- it should not fall below the fourth category of any of the major rating firms.[5]

---

[5]Joseph M. Belth, "The Quandary of the Life Insurance Agent in a Time of Uncertainty," *Journal of the American Society of CLU & ChFC,* Vol. 46 (May 1992), p. 76.

Financial Analysis

Even with the complexities involved in evaluating insurers' financial condition, many individuals—advisors, consumers, and others—will, nonetheless, wish to conduct their own evaluations, ordinarily as a supplement to rating agency evaluations. Regrettably, such evaluations typically must rely on publicly available financial and other information. Publicly available financial data are, for the most part, based on statutory accounting principles (SAP). Limited financial data based on generally accepted accounting principles (GAAP) might also be available.

As discussed in chapter 34, both SAP and GAAP provide static, historical insurer data. Neither reflects the risks inherent in company operations, and neither captures the embedded value inherent in a going concern. Use of SAP, in particular, can be inadvertently misleading. For example, a growing, vibrant insurer might show low SAP profitability because SAP requires that expenses be written off in the year they are incurred, whereas GAAP seeks to match the incurred expenses with the expected revenue flows. In contrast, a struggling insurer in decline might show high profitability under SAP because its low new business writings did not produce a high first-year expense drain whereas GAAP would reveal a more accurate trend.

Even with these and other deficiencies, the analyst typically has no choice but to rely heavily on SAP-based data. In doing so, care should be exercised, however. No finding should be viewed by itself as necessarily determinative. Rather, the collection of information should be used to form an overall impression.

The traditional elements of financial analysis include (1) surplus adequacy, (2) asset quality, (3) profitability, (4) liquidity, and (5) leverage. We use ratio analysis exclusively. Of course, the problem with ratio analysis is that it fails to reveal interrelationships among the variables, so it possibly omits important information. Until workable, easy-to-use, multivariate approaches to financial analysis are available, however, univariate ratio analysis must suffice.

No attempt is made here to suggest acceptable values for the ratios. Each ratio must be considered against prevailing industry values at the time of evaluation. The NAIC as well as the rating agencies discussed earlier provide this information.

Surplus Adequacy   The relative level of an insurer's surplus is perhaps the most useful item in assessing financial condition. Surplus is the excess of assets over liabilities. Insurers need surplus to absorb unanticipated fluctuations in asset values and in operational results—that is, to cover C-1 to C-4 risks. The greater the surplus relative to an insurer's obligations, the more secure it is, other things being the same.

In evaluating the adequacy of a U.S. insurer's surplus, it is necessary to make certain adjustments in SAP surplus and liabilities. SAP requires the establishment of certain liabilities to minimize fluctuations in insurer surplus. These liabilities, which are discussed in chapter 34, are the asset valuation reserve (AVR) and the interest maintenance reserve (IMR). They are not, in fact, true liabilities, as they do not represent amounts actually owed to anyone. As such, they should be excluded from all SAP liability values and added to SAP capital and surplus figures.

Thus, here and elsewhere, by *surplus* we will mean statutory surplus plus the AVR and IMR. By *liabilities* we will mean statutory liabilities less the AVR and IMR.[6]

---

[6]Other refinements of SAP values are sometimes made, for example, to account for any voluntary reserves, redundancy in policy reserves, any surplus notes, and separate account business.

As an absolute figure, the amount of surplus has relatively little meaning. Two surplus ratios, however—*surplus adequacy* and *rate of surplus formation*—can prove instructive. The first ratio is:

$$\text{Surplus Adequacy} = \text{Surplus} \div \text{Liabilities} \tag{1}$$

The higher the ratio, the greater the indication of financial strength, although surplus and reserve levels can vary substantially, depending on an insurer's mix and age of business. The ratio ignores the degree of conservatism inherent in one insurer's reserves versus that of another. For this reason, it should be interpreted with care, and preferably only with similarly situated insurers.

A second useful measure of surplus adequacy is the rate of surplus formation:

$$\begin{matrix}\text{Rate of} \\ \text{Surplus Formation}\end{matrix} = \begin{matrix}\text{Growth Rate} \\ \text{of Surplus}\end{matrix} \div \begin{matrix}\text{Growth Rate} \\ \text{of Liabilities}\end{matrix} \tag{2}$$

Calculated over a reasonable time period, such as five years, this ratio ideally should be positive. A consistent, substantial increase in surplus relative to liabilities suggests that the insurer's financial security is likewise increasing. The higher the ratio, the better, all else being equal. Other measures of surplus adequacy are sometimes used.[7] Most are variations or refinements on the foregoing two ratios.

Asset Quality   The lower the quality of an insurer's assets, the greater the surplus needed to absorb adverse fluctuations, all else being equal. Indeed, an insurer can appear to be in a strong surplus position yet, because of the riskiness of its assets, actually may be vulnerable.

Assets back an insurer's liabilities. **Admitted assets** are those that may be included in determining an insurer's statutory solvency, that is, those counted in measuring the excess of assets over liabilities. **Nonadmitted assets** are not recognized by regulatory authorities in assessing solvency and include items such as furniture, certain equipment, and agents' balances.

Invested assets are the income-producing assets of an insurer. The composition of invested assets varies from company to company. By diversifying their investments, companies minimize the volatility of their portfolio (see chapter 33).

A bond is a debt instrument that promises to pay a set amount after a fixed period of time. It may also generate annual interest income. Because a life insurance company guarantees the payment of certain amounts to policyowners in the future, bonds are a popular investment medium. Performance in this area may have a substantial impact on product performance.

---

[7]Another measure of an insurer's surplus position is surplus per $1,000 of insurance in force, but this ratio is not very meaningful. It gives too much weight to group insurance and no weight to annuities, supplementary contracts, health insurance, and the minor types of liabilities, all of which need surplus held for them.

Two other ratios used at times as measures of company strength involve the substitution of assets for surplus. These ratios are (1) assets as a percentage of liabilities and (2) assets per $1,000 of insurance in force. As assets equal liabilities plus surplus, the ratio for assets as a percentage of liabilities is simply 100 percent plus the figure for the surplus as a percentage of liabilities. Therefore, a comparison of insurers on the ratio of surplus to liabilities or the ratio of assets to liabilities will produce identical results.

The amount of assets per $1,000 of insurance in force is almost completely meaningless as a measure of insurer strength. Rather than measuring financial strength, this figure reflects the age and composition of the insurer's business. A company with large reserves for annuities and supplementary contracts could conceivably have assets of greater than $1,000 per $1,000 insurance in force and yet be in financial difficulty.

Bonds of average or below-average quality (so-called non-investment-grade bonds) can yield higher returns, but the principal and payment of interest may also be at risk. Some portion of the insurer's bond portfolio can also be in or near default, thus risking loss of both principal and interest. Investment prudence is the key. Limited investment in bonds of average or below-average quality should not be considered imprudent.

The ratio of non-investment-grade bonds to surplus reveals the extent to which the insurer's surplus could cover those bonds in the event that a severe economic downturn affected their performance. Therefore, the first asset quality ratio is:

$$\text{Investment in Junk Bonds Ratio} = \text{Non-Investment-Grade Bonds} \div \text{Surplus} \qquad (3)$$

Non-investment-grade bonds is taken here to mean the sum of an insurer's investments in below-investment grade (ineloquently called "junk") bonds and bonds in or near default. Obviously, the lower the investment in junk bonds the better, all else being equal.

Next to bonds, mortgages often are an insurer's most popular investment. The trend in recent years has been to commercial mortgages. In adverse economic times, insurers may experience adverse mortgage performance. The ratio of mortgages in default to surplus indicates the extent to which an insurer's surplus can cover mortgage defaults. Thus:

$$\text{Mortgage Default Ratio} = \text{Mortgages in Default} \div \text{Surplus} \qquad (4)$$

Mortgages in default is taken here to be the sum of an insurer's mortgages on which interest is overdue by more than three months, mortgages in the process of foreclosure, and properties acquired in satisfaction of debt. The lower the mortgage default ratio, the better.

Another potentially important asset quality ratio is:

$$\text{Investment in Common Stock Ratio} = \text{Investment in Common Stock} \div \text{Surplus} \qquad (5)$$

Common stock value can fluctuate greatly from year to year. This ratio is an indication of the extent to which an insurer's surplus could be affected by these fluctuations.

Profitability Profit is essential for an enduring, strong insurer. It reflects the ability and competence of management. Insurers with comparable product mixes provide a more relevant basis for comparison. Results of insurers with substantially dissimilar life product mixes are subject to misinterpretation; for example, an insurer specializing in individual term life insurance would most likely show a higher expense ratio than one specializing in group term life insurance.

More than a single year should be examined to detect unusual trends and variations because many factors may distort results. In particular, reinsurance can cause great fluctuations in premiums and reserves. Also, ratios based on SAP data, over a longer time period, are more meaningful.

Four profitability ratios are potentially important. The first is:

$$\text{Return on Equity} = \text{Net Gain from Operations} \div \text{Surplus} \qquad (6)$$

This ratio reflects the return on an insurer's capital and surplus from insurance operations and investments. **Net gain from operations** is the approximate SAP equivalent of net income under GAAP. The higher an insurer's return on equity, the more effectively it uses owner funds.

An insurer's investment yield is a potentially important profitability factor as well as an indicator of product performance. The ratio is:

$$\text{Yield on Investments} = \text{Net Investment Income} \div \text{Invested Assets} \qquad (7)$$

This ratio reflects how well investments are being managed. The higher the yield, the better, other things being the same. Unfortunately, other things rarely are the same. A higher yield may reflect higher risk. This is another reason why the asset quality evaluation is important.

The rough insurer counterpart to return on sales is measured by the ratio of net operating gain to total income. That is:

$$\text{Net Operating Gain Ratio} = \frac{\text{Net Gain from Operations}}{} \div \text{Total Operating Income} \qquad \textbf{(8)}$$

Total operating income basically is the sum of premium and investment income. This ratio is a measure of the average profitability within each dollar of revenue. Clearly, the higher the ratio the better. Again, however, results should be interpreted with caution and only over time because of the use of SAP data.

Liquidity Adequate liquidity should be maintained to meet an insurer's expected and unexpected cash needs. Otherwise, assets may have to be sold at disadvantageous prices. One useful measure of liquidity is:

$$\text{Current Liquidity} = \text{Unaffiliated Investments} \div \text{Liabilities} \qquad \textbf{(9)}$$

Unaffiliated investments refers to the assets of an insurer made up of investments other than bonds, stock, and other investments held in affiliated enterprises, less property occupied by the insurer, typically its home office. The current liquidity ratio, therefore, measures the proportion of net liabilities covered by cash and unaffiliated investments. The lower the ratio, the more vulnerable the insurer to the uncollectible premium balances or the marketability of affiliate investments.

Three other useful liquidity ratios of importance are:

$$\text{Investment in Real Estate Ratio} = \text{Investment in Real Estate} \div \text{Surplus} \qquad \textbf{(10)}$$
$$\text{Investment in Affiliates Ratio} = \text{Investment in Affiliates} \div \text{Surplus} \qquad \textbf{(11)}$$
$$\text{Nonadmitted Assets Ratio} = \text{Nonadmitted Assets} \div \text{Surplus} \qquad \textbf{(12)}$$

The ratios of investments in real estate,[8] in subsidiaries,[9] and in nonadmitted assets[10] to surplus each measure the extent to which an insurer's investment portfolio may be illiquid. Also, these asset classes often produce no income, and excessive investment in them may result in financial difficulty. The lower these ratios, the better, all else being equal.

Leverage Leverage is a measure of how intensively a company uses its equity. Leverage increases return on equity, but it also increases risk. In the context of insurance, three measures of leverage are commonly used. The first is the ratio of liabilities to surplus. This ratio is the reciprocal of the surplus adequacy test discussed previously, and, therefore, it is simply another way of viewing the same thing. Either ratio may be used in a financial evaluation.

The second ratio measures the intensity of surplus use in premium writings:

$$\text{Net Premiums Written Ratio} = \text{Net Premiums Written} \div \text{Surplus} \qquad \textbf{(13)}$$

The ratio measures the insurer's exposure to pricing errors. The higher the ratio, the greater the exposure, all else being equal. Ideally, this ratio should be used to compare insurers of comparable product mixes.

---

[8] This is IRIS ratio 6.
[9] This is IRIS ratio 7.
[10] This is IRIS ratio 5.

A final leverage measure reveals the extent to which an insurer relies on reinsurance. All insurers purchase reinsurance to reduce claims fluctuations. Some insurers rely on reinsurance, not for claim fluctuation purposes but to reduce the strain on their surplus caused by the insufficiency of funds collected to cover liabilities established under SAP. Financial problems can arise from undue reliance on such reinsurance.

If the surplus strain were to continue for many years, the insurer's solvency could be jeopardized. If the insurer continued to rely heavily on reinsurance to relieve the strain, its profitability could be expected to suffer. After all, reinsurers themselves must make a profit.

Finally, excessive reliance on reinsurance may introduce an additional solvency risk for the direct-writing insurer. If the reinsurer were to default on its obligations, the direct-writing insurer's solvency could be undermined.

A commonly used measure of the extent to which the insurer relies on surplus relief reinsurance is:

$$\text{Surplus Relief} = \frac{\text{Reinsurance Commissions}}{\text{and Expense Allowances}} \div \text{Surplus} \qquad \textbf{(14)}$$

Reinsurance commissions and expense allowances include all commissions and expense allowances paid to the direct-writing insurer by its reinsurers, less reinsurance commissions and expense allowances that the direct-writing insurer paid on any assumed reinsurance. The ratio reflects the extent to which an insurer's surplus is dependent on payments from reinsurers. The lower the ratio, the better, other things being the same.

Product Performance Indicators

Most of the preceding ratios reflect an insurer's financial condition. Emphasis is on solvency with insurer performance being relevant to the extent that it might affect solvency.

Although insurance purchasers report that they are primarily concerned with the solvency of their insurer, they also value product performance. Regrettably, as discussed in chapter 12, there is no foolproof means of prospectively evaluating insurer product performance. Some insurer performance measures, however, can be helpful in gaining insight into the product performance potential of an insurer. The four major components comprising insurance product cost are discussed next.

Lapse Rates   **Lapse rates** measure the proportion of policyowners who voluntarily terminate their insurance during a year. Lapse rates are generally higher in the first policy year than they are in subsequent years. Lapse rates vary by the socioeconomic and demographic characteristics of an insurer's policyowners and with overall economic conditions. Comparatively high lapse rates are expected for some target markets and product types.

Lapse rates can be viewed as a proxy for policyowner satisfaction. Insurers with low lapse rates must be providing their customers with the quality of products and services they desire. High lapse rates may be inherent in an insurer's selected market, or they may reflect policyowner dissatisfaction.

Excessive lapses can have a negative impact on:

- Expenses—the insurer will be unable fully to recover initial expenses; thus they must be passed on to persisting policyowners, raising their costs.
- Investments—the insurer may lose planned investment cash flows; this may result in forced sales of investments at a loss in order to meet surrender demands.

- Mortality or morbidity adverse selection—in general, insureds who have adverse health or other insurability problems tend not to lapse, causing the insurer to experience a greater proportion of claims than expected if the lapse rate is high.

Thus, lapses can negatively affect each of the three other major pricing factors. Because of this fact and because it is a proxy measure for policyowner satisfaction, if one had to select but a single proxy for product performance, it probably would be the lapse rate.

Comparable product sale mixes produce more comparable and relevant bases for comparison. Comparisons between insurers with substantially dissimilar life product mixes should be avoided.

Investment Yield   As noted earlier, the yield on an insurer's investments can be an important factor in assessing insurer profitability. Investment yield is also important to customers because a strong insurer investment return should translate into a superior return to policyowners.

The net rate of investment return before income taxes is a sound basis on which to compare insurers, provided differences in asset risk are considered. From the policyowner's perspective, the spread between the actual return and the interest credited on a particular product line is the more critical performance measure.

Expenses   The insurance customer desires quality service at the lowest possible cost. The ratio of ordinary life general expenses to premiums provides a measure of how much of each premium dollar received is needed to cover an insurer's expenses. The lower the ratio, the better, all else being equal.

Comparisons between insurers with substantially dissimilar product mixes probably should be avoided, as expenses naturally vary by product type. Moreover, insurers with large blocks of new business relative to renewal business can be expected to exhibit a higher ordinary expense ratio because of the higher first-year expenses of new business.

Mortality/Morbidity   A low ratio of actual to expected mortality or morbidity suggests favorable experience. This is important because these savings can be passed to policyowners. Although many factors can distort this ratio, it is the only available measure for comparing mortality experience between companies. The A.M. Best Co. uses this ratio when reviewing company mortality experience, and it renders a comment about the extent to which the insurer's ratio is favorable. When using this ratio to determine its comments, Best takes into consideration the age of the company's business and types of business.

Conclusion

It is clear, therefore, that there are no completely satisfactory means for comparing the financial condition and operational performance of insurers. As a consequence, substantial reliance continues to be placed on rating agencies' evaluations of insurers. One might also be able to glean much from comparing a few, simple financial ratios with national norms and those of competing insurers. With all of this done, however, the fact remains that insurance customers still must rely in good faith on the integrity and trustworthiness of insurance company management.

Questions

1. A prospective customer asks you, an insurance advisor, how you will meet the criteria of due care in your work. How do you respond?
2. A prospective customer has collected statistical and rating information on life insurers as well as product information on a wide variety of life insurance products. What can you, as an insurance advisor, offer this customer?

3. Compare and contrast fraternal benefit societies and commercial life insurers.
4. What competitive advantages in the life insurance market are gained by each of the following entities from their institutional and organizational characteristics?
   a. commercial life insurers
   b. fraternal benefit societies
   c. savings banks
   d. government
5. How is the ownership and control of stock and a mutual life insurer different, from both a *de jure* and a *de facto* perspective? Of what importance are these two differences to potential policyowners?
6. The adequacy of a given amount of surplus is commonly determined through the use of two ratios. Compare and contrast these two ratios. Explain how they can best be used to obtain a measure of the financial strength of the insurer.

CHAPTER

12

LIFE INSURANCE POLICY EVALUATION

Objectives

■ Understand aspects of customer evaluation.

■ Compare and contrast various methods for comparing life insurance policies on a cost basis.

■ Outline steps that can be taken to assess the credibility of an illustration.

■ Describe NAIC cost and benefit disclosure requirements.

■ Explain how the replacement of life insurance policies is regulated.

INTRODUCTION

As explained in chapter 11, insurance advisors should exercise due care in policy advisement. This means ensuring that the insurance recommended is (1) appropriate for the specific needs and circumstances of the client; (2) credibly illustrated, offers good value, and contains appropriate policy provisions; and (3) from a financially sound and operationally efficient insurer. The preceding chapters covered the third item as well as appropriate policy provisions. This chapter continues the policy evaluation theme, focusing on the first and second points.

CUSTOMER EVALUATION

The advisor and consumer should ensure that the contemplated insurance is **suitable,** that is, a policy that is appropriate for the specific needs and circumstances of the consumer. To ensure suitability, the advisor must *know the customer,* which means developing an understanding of the buyer's circumstances, including his or her age, family status and related obligations, job status, income, wealth, inheritances, investment objectives, risk tolerance, tax status, health, and any other relevant factors. Many of these elements are explored in chapter 14.

One element that has become especially relevant within the past few years is risk tolerance—that is, the degree to which a consumer is comfortable taking financial risk. Suitability includes a determination of the person's risk-taking style, and matching prospective insurance products to this style. One commentator on the life insurance

277

industry has suggested that risk styles can be classified as falling into four general categories. Descriptions of these four categories, along with possible matching cash-value insurance policies, are shown in Box 12-1.

No regulatory mandated life or health suitability standards exist in the United States for nonvariable products, although many companies and agents have their own approaches. Standards do exist for variable life products, within other segments of the U.S. financial services business, and for life insurance in certain other countries. For example, within the United Kingdom, agents are required to understand each customer's situation and determine the suitability of specific products for that customer. They must give their "best advice," including recommending the best product for the need, or decline the sale. This means that there must be no other policy offered by the agent that satisfies the customer's needs better. An elaborate and costly compliance mechanism has grown up around these and other requirements of the U.K. Financial Services Act.

Within the U.S. securities industry, the National Association of Securities Dealers (NASD) has established explicit guidelines and policies regarding the entire securities distribution process. These rules apply to the sale of variable life and annuity products but not other insurance policies. Thus, a salesperson has a "fundamental responsibility

---

BOX 12-1

FOUR CATEGORIES OF RISK STYLES

Prospective life insurance purchasers can be classified in numerous ways in terms of their risk-taking propensities. We list here four categories, along with life insurance policies that seem to fit each. To simplify the discussion, we assume that some form of cash-value policy has been determined to be appropriate.

- *Risk averse*—individuals who expect nothing but positive returns with virtually no possibility of loss. These individuals prefer bank savings accounts, certificates of deposit, and government securities. Such persons want absolute certainty that premiums can never be increased and that the death benefit is guaranteed for life. Traditional whole life policies seem appropriate. Variable life policies seem inappropriate.

- *Low risk*—individuals who will take on some additional risk but prefer reasonable certainty with only modest volatility. These individuals prefer "blue chip" stocks and high-grade corporate bonds. Such persons are willing to forgo absolute guarantees to secure a better value, but the likelihood of having to pay premiums beyond those illustrated should be minimal. Whole life or universal life may be appropriate but with premium

payments scheduled to continue for at least 80 percent of the policy's duration.

- *Moderate risk*—individuals willing to take on moderate financial risk and willing to accept corresponding volatility in return for higher investment returns. These individuals prefer growth stocks and high-yield, moderate-grade corporate bonds. Such persons need few guarantees and are willing to take the chance of having to inject more money into their policies. Whole life, universal life, and variable life policies containing up to 40 percent term blend with premium payment periods of as little as one-half of the policy duration might be appropriate.

- *High risk/speculative*—individuals willing to take on substantial financial risk in exchange for the possibility of high returns. These individuals prefer aggressive-growth securities, highly leveraged real estate, and high-yield junk bonds. Such persons are comfortable with few or no guarantees and are willing to take the chance of having to inject substantial additional money into their policies if results prove poor. Whole life, universal life, and variable life policies containing as much as 80 percent term blend with premium payment periods of as little as 20 percent of the policy duration might be appropriate.

Source: This box draws, in part, from James G. Powers, "Risky Business: One Size Does Not Fit All," *Best's Review,* Life/Health edition (December 1996), pp. 84–86.

for fair dealings" with customers. This responsibility requires the NASD member to have reasonable grounds to believe that the recommendation being made is suitable for the customer. This means that the salesperson must obtain basic information concerning the customer's financial and tax status, investment objectives, and other facts needed to support a recommendation. The representative must reasonably believe that the customer has sufficient knowledge and experience to evaluate the merits and risks of the recommended product. In other words, the representative must "know the customer" and recommend products appropriate for that customer's individual circumstances.

Banks offer another example of suitability standards. Guidelines issued by the American Bankers Association (ABA) require that sales personnel develop "reasonable grounds" on which to conclude that a product is suitable, based on information disclosed by the customer. The Office of the Comptroller of the Currency (OCC) also has issued an Advisory Letter on this subject, suggesting that national banks should investigate the appropriateness of recommended insurance and annuity purchases by their customers. ABA guidelines also establish needs-based selling standards and know-the-customer standards for information gathering. These standards apply to life insurance products sold by banks.

POLICY EVALUATION

After addressing the suitability issue, the prospective buyer often will want to conduct or have conducted on his or her behalf an evaluation of the recommended policy(ies). This evaluation typically involves an illustration of policy values developed by the agent or insurer. The buyer should not necessarily seek that mirage called "the best buy." Rather, the buyer should seek a policy that seems to offer good value in relation to other policies available from other sound life insurance companies.

Policy Illustrations

A **policy illustration** shows key policy information and values usually on a guaranteed as well as a nonguaranteed, current basis. Policy illustrations show how a life insurance policy is structured and how it might perform in the future. Thus, they show patterns of changes in premium outlays, cash-value accumulation, and death benefits that can evolve with different policies and with different configurations of the same policy. Using different assumptions, they also can convey some sense of the sensitivity of illustrated values to different scenarios. They can be altered to reflect different tax and other circumstances specific to the consumer.

Policy illustrations also are used in comparisons of one policy with another, although not without some difficulty (discussed later). Policy illustrations are not projections of expected future performance. Rather, as discussed in earlier chapters, they show how policy values could emerge *if* current insurer performance and philosophy remained unchanged. Policy illustrations containing nonguaranteed policy elements should not be confused with the actual policy. Illustrations contain some values that are contractually guaranteed, but they also typically contain values that do not appear in the contract itself and that are not guaranteed.

Assessing Illustration Credibility

We know that actual policy values are almost certain to differ from illustrated values for policies containing nonguaranteed elements. Ordinarily, we do not and cannot know the amount by which actual values will differ, nor do we know whether any difference will be favorable to the policyowner. In other words, we face uncertainty as to the reliability or credibility of the illustration.

General Factors Affecting Credibility

This uncertainty has two dimensions. First, factors wholly external to the insurer will shape future values to a great extent. Thus, future market investment yields will be higher or lower than they were at the time the policy was illustrated. Inflation will be higher or lower, and epidemics and other mortal calamities will occur or not. All will affect insurer operational results and, therefore, policy values. Insurance management can do little except to try to anticipate how best to manage through such exogenous factors.

Second, factors internal with the insurer will influence future policy values. The quality of the insurer's underwriting will influence mortality experience. The quality of agent advice and insurer service and the competitiveness of the insurer's policies will influence lapse rates. Expenses and investment returns, although shaped by external factors, also are within the insurer's control to a certain degree. These elements were explored in the previous chapter.

Also, the insurer controls the basis on which the policy was illustrated at the time of sale. Was the illustration based on reasonable and credible pricing assumptions or were values "pushed" using various techniques to make the illustration appear more attractive than justified by the insurer's experience? We explore this question here.

Company-Specific Factors Affecting Credibility

As explored in earlier chapters, four key areas affect life insurance policy pricing: (1) mortality, (2) interest, (3) loading, and (4) lapse rates. A policy illustration is a composite reflection of assumptions in each area, with actual policy values being determined by experience deviations from the assumptions. We explore the issue of company-specific factors affecting illustration credibility by reference to these four areas.

Mortality   Ordinarily, we expect insurers to base their illustrations on their actual, recent mortality experience. As we know, mortality rates have generally been declining for many years. Some insurers have included projected mortality improvements in their illustrated values. To the extent that illustrative pricing relies on mortality better than current experience, the insurer effectively is passing much of the mortality price risk to the customer, makes the policy appear more attractive from a cost standpoint than it may be, and makes its illustrations less comparable to those of other insurers. Ideally, the mortality rates underlying a policy's illustrated values reflect actual recent historical insurer experience.

Interest   As with mortality, we expect insurers to base illustrated values on interest rates that are supportable in light of the insurer's actual investment yields. If this is not the case, the insurer's illustrations can be misleading and are not comparable with those of other insurers.

Also, some insurers use the portfolio average method of investment income allocation whereas others use the investment generation method. Knowledge of which approach is followed is necessary to evaluating illustration credibility, as we have discussed in earlier chapters.

Loading   Provisions for expenses, taxes, and profits are important elements in illustrated values. As with mortality and interest, loadings should be adequate to cover expected expenses and taxes and to provide a reasonable profit margin. If this is not the case, the insurer might be guilty of attempting to make the illustration appear better than justified. Also, loadings can vary by generation of policyholders, with older policies, in effect, subsidizing newer ones. Whether this is occurring should be known.

Lapse Rates   We know that high lapse rates are normally associated with higher-priced insurance. Insurers should use reasonable lapse rates, based on their recent experience. If they use lower lapse rates, the effect can be that actual policy values will not grow as fast even if all other pricing factors were as originally illustrated.

At the other extreme, some lapse-supported pricing (see chapter 6) has been observed. If actual policy results would be negatively affected by persistency being better than that assumed in the illustration, the policy is lapse supported. This imposes an additional risk on the customer and makes the policy illustration less comparable with others.

The NAIC Illustration Model Regulation

Because of the great concern over market conduct difficulties (see chapter 9) stemming directly from policy illustrations, in 1995, the NAIC promulgated the Life Insurance Policy Illustration Model Regulation, now in effect in more than one-half of the states. The regulation goals are "to ensure that illustrations do not mislead purchasers of life insurance and to make illustrations more understandable." The standards established by the regulation demand sweeping changes in the way policy illustrations are calculated, prepared, and presented to customers.

Illustration Requirements The model does not require the use of policy illustrations in sales, but, if the insurer uses an illustration with a particular policy, prospective policyowners must be given an illustration and it must comply with the model's standards. The illustration must be clearly labeled as a "life insurance illustration" and must contain such basic information as the name of the insurer; the name and address of the agent; the name, age, sex, and underwriting class for the proposed insured; the initial death benefit; and the dividend option or other nonguaranteed elements applied.

The so-called **Basic Illustration** must follow a specified format. It must include a table of values based on the insurer's current pricing factors. Values must be shown to policy maturity, although not every year need be shown beyond the first 10 policy years. The Basic Illustration contains both a Narrative Summary and a Numeric Summary. The **Narrative Summary** provides a description of how the policy functions. For flexible-premium policies, the Narrative Summary must explain the premium required to be paid to guarantee coverage for the term of the contract.

The **Numeric Summary** must show values based on (1) guarantees alone, (2) current assumptions, and (3) a midpoint set of assumptions, all at specified years. Both the agent and the customer must sign this summary indicating that they have discussed and understand that nonguaranteed elements are subject to change and can be higher or lower than those illustrated. This signed summary must be retained by the insurer for the life of the policy plus three years.

Reporting Requirements The insurer is to provide a report annually to the policyowner showing the status of the policy. Previous year and current values must be shown. The report must disclose if the policy would lapse, based on guaranteed values, during the next reporting period.

The policyowner must be notified of any change in pricing elements that negatively affects policy values. The insurer must either provide an updated illustration or notify the policyowner of the availability of such an illustration.

Prohibitions The regulation proscribes a number of practices. Thus, insurers and agents may not represent the policy as other than life insurance or describe nonguaranteed elements in a misleading manner, such as suggesting that they are guaranteed. They cannot represent that premium payments will not be required unless factual and are prohibited from using the terms *vanish* and *vanishing premium*.

Insurers may not project mortality gains in their illustrations, and they may not illustrate a lapse-supported policy. All illustrated values must be supportable based on the insurer's existing experience.

The Illustration Actuary One of the most important elements of the model regulation is the requirement that life insurers must appoint an **illustration actuary** who must make certain annual certifications to the insurance regulator regarding the insurer's practices and compliance. The practical effect of this requirement is to place much of the responsibility for ensuring reasonable illustration practices on the actuarial profession—a logical place. The actuarial profession has received its share of criticism in connection with insurers' market conduct difficulties.

Thus, the actuary must certify that illustrations rely on a **Disciplined Current Scale** (DCS), meaning that each set of assumptions implicit in an illustration is based on the insurer's actual recent experience, defined by the Actuarial Standards Board as "current, determinable and credible." Additionally, the actuary must disclose:

- Whether nonguaranteed elements illustrated for both new and in-force policies are inconsistent with nonguaranteed elements actually being paid.
- Whether, since the last certification, a currently payable scale, issued within the previous five years, has been reduced for reasons other than changes in the experience factors underlying the DCS.
- Whether nonguaranteed elements illustrated for new policies are inconsistent with those illustrated for similar in-force policies.

The ultimate impact of this NAIC regulation is unknown. Many proponents believe that it will bring much needed discipline to an important area of insurance pricing and marketing. Others see the regulation as being in part regulatory overkill and in part having omitted some key elements. For example, the regulation focuses on the ability of an insurer's portfolio of products to maintain its current nonguaranteed element scale rather than on the intent of the insurer to do so.

Comparing Illustrated Policy Values

As mentioned previously, one use of policy illustrations is in comparing policies. As should be clear from the foregoing explanations and as explained more fully at the end of this section, such comparisons carry important limitations. Even so, they have value, especially for two or more comparable policies illustrated on the same bases.

The Need for Comparisons

Life insurance policy costs can vary greatly. Variations can result from differences in company operational efficiency, investment performance, underwriting policy, profit objectives, the costs associated with marketing, and a host of other variables. A higher-cost policy may reflect either better value or simply an expensive policy with little or no justifiably offsetting benefits.

Although insurance awareness is rising, so is product complexity. Chapters 9 and 10 highlighted how information asymmetries between the policyowner and the insurer continue to influence the evolution of the law in favor of the policyowner. Consumers often erroneously equate a policy's premium with its cost. The premium is a measure of the annual outlay for a policy, not its cost. Cost includes all elements of a policy (premiums, death benefits, cash values, and dividends), not just premiums.

Because many consumers are unaware of cost and quality differences or are bewildered by the seeming complexity of the purchase decision, they engage in little or no comparison shopping. They may trust that their insurance agent or other advisor will guide them safely through the insurance jungle. This failure to shop carefully and completely trusting advisors often result in a dissatisfied customer who lapses or replaces his or her insurance or, worse, sues alleging that he or she was misled or provided poor or incomplete advice.

Objectives of Comparisons

The objective of any method used to compare two insurance policies is to guide the customer to policies offering good value. The cost of life insurance to any individual is dependent on that particular individual's unique circumstances and the actual cash flows experienced under the policy. This can be determined only after the contract terminates by death, maturity, or surrender. For this reason, many experts contend that life insurance policy cost comparisons have little or no meaning and should not be conducted. Others contend that the best means of estimating future policy performance should include an evaluation of the past performance of the insurer's policies.

Past performance is often a useful indication of likely future performance, and any evaluation of a potential policy ideally should include an examination of the insurer's historical record with respect to older policies. Unfortunately, relevant historical policy information is not always available, for a variety of reasons: The particular policy under review may have been sold for only a short time period; the insurer itself may be relatively new; or the data are not published. Even if available, the data may be irrelevant because the insurer's philosophy or performance characteristics may have changed.

Common Cost Comparison Methods

No method of comparing life insurance costs takes into consideration all possible purchase decision factors. Cost information should be supplemented with benefit and other information. However, we can start with an appreciation of seven cost comparison methods. With one exception, the methods can be useful in appropriate circumstances as an aid in life insurance policy evaluation. The careful reader will observe that most cost comparison methods either derive a cost of insurance by assuming an interest rate or derive an interest rate by assuming a cost of insurance. A summary table at the end of this section highlights the main characteristics of each method.

Traditional Net Cost Method   The **traditional net cost** (TNC) method, in use for years, is the easiest cost comparison method to understand and calculate, but it also can be the most misleading. To derive cost estimates under the TNC method, one adds the illustrated premiums over a selected time period (usually 10 or 20 years) and subtracts from this figure the sum of the policy's illustrated dividends, if any, taken to the end of the period. From this result is subtracted the policy's illustrated cash surrender value (and terminal dividends, if any) at the end of the chosen period. Dividing by the face amount (in thousands) and by the number of years in the time period yields the TNC per thousand per year. The formula for the TNC method, as well as the others discussed in this chapter, is shown in the chapter appendix.

Although this method can be helpful for determining income tax liabilities under a life insurance policy (see chapter 13), its results are misleading when used to estimate policy costs. By ignoring the time value of money, it fails to weight fairly life insurance policy cash flows. Moreover, the TNC can be manipulated easily by lowering dividends or cash values on policies in their early years and increasing them in later years, thus appearing to lower policy costs. Use of this method for comparing policy costs is illegal in most U.S. jurisdictions.

Interest-Adjusted Net Cost Method   The **interest-adjusted net cost** (IANC) method was developed to correct for the omission of the time value of money within the TNC method. The IANC analysis, like the TNC analysis, is conducted over set time periods (typically, 10 and 20 years) and considers a policy's estimated premiums, death benefits, cash values, and dividends in much the same manner as the TNC method, except that interest is recognized.

To calculate a policy's IANC (also called the **surrender cost comparison index**), the premiums and illustrated dividends are accumulated at some assumed interest rate over the selected time period. The accumulated dividends are subtracted from the accumulated premiums. From this figure is subtracted the cash value (and illustrated terminal dividend, if any) at the end of the time period. The result of this calculation is then divided by the value of one accumulated per year for the time period at the assumed interest rate and by the face amount in thousands. If the interest rate assumed in the IANC analysis were zero, the policy's TNC would be obtained. The formula for the IANC is given in the chapter appendix.

The NAIC Life Insurance Disclosure Model Regulation (discussed later) requires the calculation of two interest-adjusted cost indices for a policy: a surrender cost index and a net payment cost index. The **net payment cost comparison index** is an estimate of the average annual net outlay (premium less illustrated annual dividend), adjusted by interest to reflect the time when premiums and dividends are paid during a 10- or 20-year period. The *surrender cost index* is the payment index less the annualized equivalent of the cash value available to the policyowner at the end of the 10- or 20-year period, adjusted for interest. Interest-adjusted indices can be of value in showing the relative estimated costs of two or more similar policies.

The IANC method can be used to compare similar policies only because a fair comparison requires approximately equal outlays.[1] The IANC method has other limitations. The method is subject to manipulation in much the same way as, although to a lesser extent than, the TNC method. As with other methods, it provides a valid measure of cost only over the time period chosen and then only if all assumptions proved to be fact and if actual future policy values equaled exactly those illustrated, both of which are highly unlikely.

IANC indices (both surrender and net payment) are often shown on both a guaranteed and an illustrated (or projected) basis. As mentioned later, this is required under the latest NAIC model disclosure regulation. The previous NAIC model regulation effectively required the same thing.[2]

Table 12-1 shows IANC figures at 5 percent for policies whose gross premiums per $1,000 appeared in Table 5-2. Observe that (1) little relationship exists between premiums charged and projected net costs, and (2) net costs vary greatly among these similar policies.

Policy A's gross premium is $11.83 per $1,000 of insurance, and its projected 20-year IANC is $1.36 per $1,000. This $1.36 index can be interpreted as follows. If a 35-year-old male bought this ordinary life policy and paid the stipulated premium for 20 years and, at that time, surrendered the policy, the policyowner's average annual cost per $1,000 of insurance would have been $1.36, *assuming* that (1) dividends were paid exactly as illustrated and (2) the policyowner valued money at 5 percent per year (the interest rate specified by most states' disclosure regulations). Cost here means the average annual amount estimated to be retained by the insurer for its benefit payments and loadings.

---

[1] If outlays were held approximately equal for two policies, one of which had a significantly lower premium than the other (i.e., they were dissimilar), some form of "side fund" accumulation arrangement would be necessary under the lower-premium policy. If a fair comparison were to be made, this in turn would necessitate an adjustment downward in the lower-premium policy's face amount to maintain approximately equal total death benefits under each plan. For further details, see the discussion later in this chapter on the cash accumulation method.

[2] It mandates that an **equivalent level annual dividend** (ELAD) be shown. The ELAD is interpreted as that portion of the pricing of a participating policy that is not guaranteed. It represents the average annual illustrated dividend, weighted for the time value of money. It is calculated by accumulating the annual illustrated dividends at interest and dividing the result by the appropriate interest factor to obtain a level annual equivalent to the (nonlevel) illustrated dividends.

TABLE 12-1	Interest-Adjusted Net Cost Figures for Selected Ordinary Life Policies (From Table 5-1, Age 35, Male, $25,000)		
Type of Policy	*Company*	*Gross Premium per $1,000*	*20-Year IANC per $1,000*
Participating	A	$11.83	$1.36
	B	13.95	1.28
	C	14.20	0.34
	D	15.66	1.20
	E	16.01	2.76
	F	21.68	5.49
Nonparticipating	G	10.70	3.99
	H	11.37	1.47
	I	12.22	6.63
	J	14.04	6.06
	K	17.00	9.45
	L	18.60	8.98

Source: A.M. Best Co.

An understanding of the interest-adjusted method is important because many insurers routinely provide the indices on their policy illustrations. The method is not commonly used by agents and financial consultants when they prepare their own cost comparisons between two or more policies. Other methods are usually more suitable, especially when dissimilar policies are being compared.

Equal Outlay Method   One method used by some planners to compare the costs of two or more policies is what the authors have named the **equal outlay method** (EOM). This method assumes that equal amounts of money are expended under each of two or more proposed insurance arrangements. It can be used to compare both similar and dissimilar policies, although not without some problems.

Comparisons of flexible-premium policies.   When two policies have flexible-premium payments, both premiums and face amounts can be set at the same levels, thereby permitting the comparison to focus on the competing policies' surrender values at specific future points. Other things being the same, the policy with the larger illustrated future values is preferred.

Table 12-2 illustrates this approach. Cash surrender values on two universal life (UL) policies are shown on two bases: guaranteed and current. The planned annual outlay for both policies is illustrated as $1,000 per year and death benefits are set at $100,000 per year. Both policies guarantee a minimum interest rate of 4.0 percent and currently credit 9.0 percent. On both bases, policy B illustrates greater values at every duration. Thus, other things being the same (e.g., credibility of illustrations, contract provisions, agent service, company quality, etc.), policy B would be preferred to policy A.

Comparisons involving fixed-premium policies.   The EOM is also used to compare the illustrated values of two or more policies when one policy is a fixed-premium contract. The premiums for the flexible-premium policy are set equal to those for the fixed policy. The flexible premium could be assumed to track exactly either the fixed-premium policy gross premium or premium net of illustrated dividend. Future cash surrender values then can be compared as they were under the previous example.

As a practical matter, such comparisons are only rarely made on the basis that both future premium and death benefit patterns are equalized. The usual way is to hold outlays

TABLE 12-2   Equal Outlay Method: Two Universal Life Policies (For 35-Year-Old, Nonsmoking Male)

| | *Policies A and B* | | *Cash Surrender Values* | | | |
| | | | *Guaranteed Basis* | | *Current Basis* | |
YEAR	PLANNED ANNUAL PREMIUM	ANNUAL DEATH BENEFITS	POLICY A (4%)	POLICY B (4%)	POLICY A (9%)	POLICY B (9%)
1	$1,000	$100,000	$ 123	$ 718	$ 125	$ 789
2	1,000	100,000	798	1,493	950	1,714
3	1,000	100,000	1,485	2,249	1,844	2,720
4	1,000	100,000	2,181	3,018	2,813	3,807
5	1,000	100,000	2,888	3,796	3,862	4,988
6	1,000	100,000	3,588	4,581	4,996	6,253
7	1,000	100,000	4,294	5,367	6,221	7,686
8	1,000	100,000	4,999	6,157	7,543	9,116
9	1,000	100,000	5,700	6,944	8,971	10,788
10	1,000	100,000	6,396	7,739	10,513	12,479
11	1,000	100,000	7,098	8,510	12,179	14,359
12	1,000	100,000	7,755	9,882	13,982	16,394
13	1,000	100,000	8,409	10,038	15,936	18,595
14	1,000	100,000	9,039	10,778	18,058	20,979
15	1,000	100,000	9,638	11,488	20,349	23,548
16	1,000	100,000	10,201	12,159	22,839	26,338
17	1,000	100,000	10,719	12,795	25,542	29,361
18	1,000	100,000	11,185	13,385	28,479	32,644
19	1,000	100,000	11,590	13,922	31,671	36,807
20	1,000	100,000	11,926	14,396	35,141	40,079

constant and set only initial policy death benefits approximately equal. One would normally attempt to obtain only a close match of subsequent death benefit amounts.

The equal outlay method also can be used to compare two or more fixed-premium policies or a flexible-premium and a fixed-premium contract wherein the fixed contract's premium is below the minimum required for the flexible contract. The procedure is often used in making buy-term-and-invest-the-difference (BTID) comparisons. The method can be used for any two policies in which one has a higher premium than the other. It can be simpler than techniques discussed later, but it also can result in unfair comparisons, as will be explained.

Illustration.   To illustrate, assume that our trusty 35-year-old male nonsmoker is interested in comparing a yearly renewable term (YRT) policy with an ordinary life policy. The aggregate YRT premiums shown in Table 4-2 and the ordinary life premiums and values from Table 5-3 are used. The equal outlay procedure requires that the outlays for the two plans be equal. This is accomplished by assuming that annual differences between the higher-premium policy and the lower-premium policy are accumulated each year at some reasonable after-tax rate of return. The outlays for the two arrangements are, thus, held equal.

Table 12-3 illustrates this procedure by assuming that dividends on the ordinary life policy are used to purchase paid-up additional insurance. The ordinary life's annual premium is $1,533, and the initial premium for the YRT policy is $145. The difference is $1,388. The difference in the second year's premiums is $1,385. This difference is added to that of the previous year's fund balance ($1,388 plus interest of $83) to yield a begin-

TABLE 12-3   Equal Outlay Method: Ordinary Life and YRT (From Tables 4-2 and 5-2)

(1)	(2)	(3)	(4)	(5)	(6)	(7)	(8)
				Plan Values		*Death Benefits*	
END OF YEAR	ORDINARY LIFE PREMIUM	YRT PREMIUM	DIFFERENCE BETWEEN PREMIUMS	DIFFERENCE COMPOUNDED AT 6 PERCENT	ORDINARY LIFE CASH SURRENDER VALUE[a]	YRT PLUS SIDE FUND[b]	ORDINARY LIFE AND PAID-UP ADDITIONS
1	$1,533	$145	$1,388	$ 1,471	$ 15	$101,471	$100,078
2	1,533	148	1,385	3,028	1,195	103,028	100,550
3	1,533	154	1,379	4,671	2,515	104,671	101,410
4	1,533	162	1,371	6,405	3,991	106,405	102,655
5	1,533	172	1,361	8,232	5,634	108,232	104,285
6	1,533	185	1,348	10,154	7,456	110,154	106,286
7	1,533	200	1,333	12,177	9,476	112,177	108,661
8	1,533	219	1,314	14,300	11,704	114,300	111,393
9	1,533	242	1,291	16,526	14,163	116,526	114,491
10	1,533	268	1,265	18,859	16,870	118,859	117,938
11	1,533	288	1,245	21,310	19,843	121,310	121,743
12	1,533	333	1,200	23,861	23,100	123,861	125,869
13	1,533	373	1,160	26,522	26,664	126,522	130,325
14	1,533	417	1,116	29,296	30,534	129,296	135,033
15	1,533	466	1,067	32,185	34,733	132,185	139,997
16	1,533	521	1,012	35,189	39,287	135,189	145,215
17	1,533	581	952	38,309	44,224	138,309	150,700
18	1,533	646	887	41,509	49,571	141,548	156,454
19	1,533	716	817	44,907	55,359	144,907	162,486
20	1,533	791	742	48,388	61,621	148,388	168,807

[a]Guaranteed cash surrender value plus illustrated cash surrender value of paid-up additional insurance.
[b]$100,000 YRT face amount plus column 5.

ning fund balance for policy year 2 of $2,856 (not shown). This procedure is continued for several more years.

Table 12-3 shows that side fund values are projected to be greater than those of the whole life policy through policy year 12. From policy year 13 onward, the whole life's illustrated cash values are greater than the side fund's projected balance.

The analysis is not unbiased because the YRT arrangement provides a higher death benefit in the early years for the same outlay. To have a fairer comparison, total death benefits should be held equal. If this were done, either the face amount of the higher-premium policy should be increased to that of the term-plus-side-fund death benefit or the term policy face amount should be decreased. Either approach results in slightly more money being credited to the side fund.[3] An attempt, however, is made to maintain only approximate equality of death benefits.

The term policy arrangement's total projected death benefits exceed those of the ordinary life policy through policy year 10 and, as with the side fund balance, exceeds the

[3]In the first instance, the whole life premium would need to be raised to support the higher face amount, which would mean more money for the side fund. In the second instance, the term premium would be lowered to support the lower face amount, thus resulting in the premium savings being available for the side fund.

ordinary life figures by substantial amounts in the early policy years. The ordinary life's illustrated death benefits become substantially greater than those under the YRT arrangement in later years.

Where does this analysis leave us? First, if the need for insurance is, say, for 10 years or less, the YRT arrangement seems superior based on illustrated values and the stated assumptions. This result is expected and would be found with most forms of whole life versus term comparisons. On the other hand, this ordinary life policy's relative position appears to improve continuously from a cost standpoint (based on these assumptions) as time passes. However, an unequivocal endorsement of the ordinary life policy could not be made, even if future values were fixed and the planning horizon were longer than 10 or so years, because the equal outlay method is incapable of rendering a fair analysis if total death benefits cross at any point in the analysis.

Cash Accumulation Method   The **cash accumulation method** (CAM) is a more sophisticated cost comparison method than the equal outlay method.[4] The CAM functions in the same way as the EOM in that (1) outlays for two plans being compared are set at equal levels, (2) annual premium differences are accumulated at some assumed interest rate, and (3) one simply observes the cash-value/side-fund differences over time in an effort to draw meaningful cost-based conclusions. The CAM corrects for the unequal death benefit bias of the equal outlay method. The face amount of the lower-premium (e.g., term) policy is hypothetically adjusted each year so that the sum of the side fund and the new face amount of the term policy exactly equals the face amount of the higher-premium (e.g., whole life) policy. In the early policy years, this often means that the lower-premium policy's face amount will be declining.

Illustration.   Table 12-4 illustrates the CAM applied to the same two policies as in Table 12-3. The 6 percent after-tax interest assumption is maintained. The outlays are held at the same level by accumulating the annual differences at interest, as are the total illustrated death benefits (columns 8 and 9). This eliminates the bias in Table 12-3 against the YRT plan that existed in the early policy years.[5] As a result of a lower YRT face amount and, thereby, a lower YRT premium in early years, the accumulated differences are larger than with the EOM comparison.

Under this CAM comparison, one observes that the illustrated cash surrender value of the ordinary life policy first exceeds the projected side-fund balance in policy year 13, and that by policy year 20 the projected difference between the two values has widened, reaching $13,826 ($61,621 less $47,795). Although not shown here, differences past year 20 track a similar pattern.

In the early policy years, there appears to be a clear cost advantage for the term arrangement, and, as expected, the advantage is even greater than that which existed under the equal outlay method. Because the death benefits under each plan are held equal, one can focus on the fund versus cash-value differences.

Which plan is the better buy? The best answer is: "It depends." If the prospective purchaser is more interested in short- to medium-term results, the term arrangement appears superior, based on the stated assumptions and with other things being the same. If a longer-term view is taken, the ordinary life plan may be the preferred approach, based on the stated assumptions and with other things being equal.

---

[4]See Michael L. Murray, "Analyzing the Investment Value of Cash Value Life Insurance," *The Journal of Risk and Insurance,* Vol. XLIII (March 1976), pp. 121–128.

[5]Although not a problem with this analysis (because dividends are earmarked to purchase paid-up additional insurance), any dividends paid in cash or accumulated at interest should be included as a part of the total death benefit if the insurer pays such dividends on death. Similarly, terminal dividends paid on death should be included. Any regular or terminal dividends paid on policy surrender should be included as a part of the surrender value.

TABLE 12-4 Cash Accumulation Method: Ordinary Life and YRT (From Tables 4-2 and 5-2)

				Plan Values			Death Benefits	
(1)	(2)	(3)	(4)	(5)	(6)	(7)	(8)	(9)
END OF YEAR	ORDINARY LIFE PREMIUM	YRT PREMIUM	DIFFERENCE BETWEEN PREMIUMS	DIFFERENCE COMPOUNDED AT 6 PERCENT[a]	ORDINARY LIFE CASH SURRENDER VALUE[b]	YRT FACE AMOUNT	YRT FACE AMOUNT PLUS SIDE FUND[c]	ORDINARY LIFE AND PAID-UP ADDITIONS FACE AMOUNTS
1	$1,533	$143	$1,390	$ 1,473	$ 15	$ 98,605	$100,078	$100,078
2	1,533	144	1,389	3,034	1,195	97,516	100,550	100,550
3	1,533	149	1,384	4,683	2,515	96,727	101,410	101,410
4	1,533	156	1,377	6,423	3,991	96,231	102,654	102,654
5	1,533	165	1,368	8,259	5,634	96,026	104,285	104,285
6	1,533	178	1,355	10,191	7,456	96,095	106,286	106,286
7	1,533	193	1,340	12,223	9,476	96,438	108,661	108,661
8	1,533	213	1,320	14,355	11,704	97,037	111,392	111,392
9	1,533	237	1,296	16,590	14,163	97,900	114,490	114,490
10	1,533	265	1,268	18,930	16,870	99,007	117,937	117,937
11	1,533	289	1,244	21,384	19,843	100,358	121,742	121,742
12	1,533	339	1,194	23,933	23,100	101,936	125,869	125,869
13	1,533	387	1,146	26,583	26,664	103,741	130,324	130,324
14	1,533	441	1,092	29,336	30,534	105,696	135,032	135,032
15	1,533	502	1,031	32,189	34,733	107,807	139,996	139,996
16	1,533	574	959	35,137	39,287	110,077	145,214	145,214
17	1,533	654	879	38,177	44,224	112,522	150,699	150,699
18	1,533	744	789	41,304	49,571	115,149	156,453	156,453
19	1,533	845	688	44,511	55,359	117,973	162,484	162,484
20	1,533	957	576	47,793	61,621	121,012	168,805	168,805

[a](Column 4 plus column 5 for the previous year) × 1.06.
[b]Guaranteed cash surrender value plus illustrated cash surrender value of paid-up additional insurance.
[c]Column 5 plus column 7.

289

Importance of assumptions. The interest rate assumed in the analysis can be of crucial importance. Table 12-5 shows 10- and 20-year figures for the column 5 (accumulated differences) and column 6 (ordinary life cash surrender) values in Table 12-4 at various interest rates. The variations in values can be great. At an after-tax interest rate between 7 and 8 percent over the 20-year period, the benefit swings in favor of the term arrangement.

A comment should be made about the process of equalizing death benefits. In effect, few purchasers of term insurance actually would cancel (or add) portions of term coverage each year to match exactly the side-fund change. This would not only be inconvenient, but it could result in the policy face amount falling below required company minimums. The CAM does not actually require that the term policy's face amount be changed. Neither the CAM nor any other cost comparison method is intended to dictate how an insurance program should be structured. This is a separate decision. Its utility is in showing how relative costs and values vary by imposing a hypothetical equality requirement over outlays and death benefits.[6]

Comparative Interest Rate Method   Another popular method used to compare the relative costs of two policies is the **comparative interest rate** (CIR) method, perhaps more commonly known as the **Linton yield** method after M. A. Linton of the Provident Mutual Life Insurance Company, who derived the method.[7] The CIR method is a special case of the CAM. It differs only in that it solves for the interest rate that causes the ac-

TABLE 12-5   Cash Accumulation Method: Effect of Changing Interest Assumptions (Table 12-4 Policy Values)

(1)	*(2)*	*(3)*	*(4)*	*(5)*
Duration (Years)	*After-Tax Interest Rate Assumed (%)*	*Accumulated Premium Differences*	*Ordinary Life Surrender Value*	*Excess of (3) over (4)*
10	3	$15,936	$16,870	$ −934
	4	16,874	16,870	4
	5	17,871	16,870	1,001
	6	18,931	16,870	2,061
	7	20,056	16,870	3,186
	8	21,252	16,870	4,382
	9	22,522	16,870	5,652
	10	23,871	16,870	7,001
20	3	32,392	61,621	−29,229
	4	36,841	61,621	−24,780
	5	41,943	61,621	−19,678
	6	47,795	61,621	−13,826
	7	54,507	61,621	−7,114
	8	62,207	61,621	586
	9	71,041	61,621	9,420
	10	81,174	61,621	19,553

[6]The CAM used here equalizes end-of-year death benefits. Beginning-of-year death benefits could have been used. Ideally, midyear figures should be used, but this adjustment complicates the analysis and adds little to precision.

[7]See Joseph M. Belth, "The Rate of Return on the Savings Element in Cash-Value Life Insurance," *The Journal of Risk and Insurance,* Vol. XXXV (December 1968), pp. 569–581, and Stuart Schwarzschild, "Rates of Return on the Investment Differentials between Life Insurance Policies," *The Journal of Risk and Insurance,* Vol. XXXV (December 1968), pp. 583–595.

cumulated value of the annual differences in policy premiums (the side fund) to be equal to the higher-premium policy's cash surrender value at the end of the period of analysis. Stated differently, the CIR is the rate of return that must be earned on a hypothetical side fund in a BTID plan, so that the value of the side fund will exactly equal the illustrated cash surrender value of the higher-premium policy at a designated point in time. The higher the CIR, the less expensive the higher-premium (e.g., whole life) policy relative to the alternative plan (e.g., term plus side fund).

As with the CAM, outlays and death benefits are held equal. The CIR method requires the use of a computer because the solution interest rate is found by an iterative trial-and-error process.

Illustration. Table 12-5 showed that at some interest rate between 7 and 8 percent, the 20-year figures switched from favoring the ordinary life plan to favoring the YRT arrangement. In fact, at 7.93 percent, the 20-year accumulated differences exactly equal the 20-year illustrated surrender value. Thus, 7.93 percent is the 20-year comparative interest rate for the illustrated ordinary life policy, compared to the YRT policy and based on the stated assumptions.

CIR results for this ordinary life policy/YRT combination are uniformly lower for durations of under 20 years. For example, the five-year CIR is –6.65 percent; this suggests that the consumer would have to *lose* 6.65 percent per year for five years for the YRT/side-fund arrangement to equal the ordinary life performance. The 10-year CIR is 4.00 percent. These low, early CIRs are consistent with the observation that most whole life policies do not perform well if kept for periods of less than 10 or so years. Figure 12-1 shows the progression of the CIRs by duration in this policy.

Importance of assumptions. The CIR method can be used to compare any two dissimilar policies, and if a standard set of term rates is used, CIRs of similar policies can be compared easily. Rankings of similar policies based on the IANC method are highly correlated with rankings based on the CIR method.

The CIR figure is sensitive to the level of the rates used for the lower-premium policy, just as the IANC method is sensitive to the interest rate used. If one wanted to make a cash-value policy appear more attractive relative to a term policy, one need only select a high-cost term policy to use in the analysis to develop an attractive CIR. The opposite result could be obtained by reversing the bias.

A comparative interest rate has meaning as an interest rate that can be imputed to a policy. The CIR can be contrasted with the rate earned on other financial instruments, although the shortcomings in doing so should be understood. Cash values and other

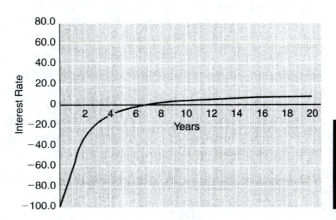

FIGURE 12-1 Comparative Interest Rates by Duration: Ordinary Life versus Yearly Renewable Term, Using Table 5-2 and Table 4-2 Values

savings are not the same. For example, cash-value life insurance policies may enjoy certain advantages (e.g., favorable tax treatment, premium waiver features, etc.) not found in other financial instruments. Evaluations of two financial instruments are rarely made solely on the basis of interest rates. The CIR is an imputed rate of return and, although analogous to an internal rate of return as that concept is understood in finance, it is not identical to it. It does not represent the actual rate of return that the company is crediting to the policy.

Internal Rate of Return   The **internal rate of return** (IRR) method is similar to the CIR method in that it solves for a rate of return, but it differs in that it makes no allowance for the policy's internal mortality charges. Two internal rates of return are typically shown with this method: a surrender-based IRR and a death-based IRR.

The **surrender-based IRR** is derived by solving for the interest rate that causes the accumulated premiums (net of dividends, if appropriate) at selected durations to equal that duration's cash surrender value. No allowance is made in the calculation for the value to the death benefit promise (i.e., mortality charges).

In the early policy years, a policy's surrender-based IRR typically is negative. For policies without cash values, the IRR equals minus 100 percent for all durations; this suggests, erroneously, that the premium payment has purchased nothing. This result occurs because the method ignores the value of the death benefit promise. With cash-value policies, this IRR typically increases yearly.

The **death-based IRR** is derived by solving for the interest rate that causes the accumulated premiums (net of dividends, if appropriate) at selected durations to equal the duration's death benefit. No allowance is made in this IRR for the fact that portions of premiums under cash-value policies build cash values. In the early policy years, a policy's death-based IRR typically is quite large, but it declines steadily with time. It is particularly high for term policies because of their low initial premiums.

The IRR figures can be interpreted as representing the yield that the policyowner, with the surrender-based IRR, or the beneficiary, with the death-based IRR, will have received if the policy is terminated by surrender or death. The implication of the method is that all premiums paid are properly allocated toward building the cash value, with the surrender-based IRR, or toward the death benefit, with the death-based IRR, neither of which is actuarially correct.

Table 12-6 illustrates both IRR calculations for the Table 5-2 ordinary life policy. Thus, if the policy is surrendered at policy year 5, the surrender-based IRR is projected to be –10.09 percent. If the policy death benefit were paid in policy year 5, the death-based IRR is projected to be 104.49 percent.

The two-pronged IRR method has shortcomings, yet no more so than the combination of the surrender cost index and the net payment index, which also are intended to reflect a measure of policy value on surrender and on death. The IRR method is commonly used in evaluation of life insurance policies purchased for business purposes. Other things being equal, the policy with the higher IRR figures is preferred.

Yearly Rate of Return Method   The **yearly rate of return (YROR) method** can be especially useful in analyzing cash-value policies.[8] It involves solving for the rate of return to make *benefits* available for a particular policy year equal to the *investment* in the policy for that year. The *benefits* under a cash-value life insurance policy are the cash value and dividend (if any) at the end of the policy year being analyzed, plus the expected value

---

[8]See Joseph M. Belth, *Life Insurance: A Consumer's Handbook,* 2nd ed. (Bloomington, IN: Indiana University Press, 1985), pp. 89–91.

TABLE 12-6	Internal Rate of Return Method: Ordinary Life (From Table 5-2: Dividends Purchase Paid-Up Additional Insurance)				
(1)	*(2)*	*(3)*	*(4)*	*(5)*	*(6)*
Year	*Ordinary Life Premium*	*Ordinary Life Surrender Value*[a]	*IRR on Surrender Value (%)*	*Total Death Benefit (Year-End)*[b]	*IRR on Death (%)*
1	$1,533	$ 15	−99.02	$100,078	6,428.22
2	1,533	1,195	−48.54	100,550	661.42
3	1,533	2,515	−27.29	101,410	266.14
4	1,533	3,991	−16.46	102,655	153.96
5	1,533	5,634	−10.09	104,285	104.49
6	1,533	7,456	−5.97	106,286	77.50
7	1,533	9,476	−3.11	108,661	60.80
8	1,533	11,704	−1.04	111,393	49.60
9	1,533	14,163	−0.52	114,491	41.65
10	1,533	16,870	1.73	117,938	35.76
11	1,533	19,843	2.69	121,743	31.25
12	1,533	23,100	3.46	125,869	27.70
13	1,533	26,664	4.08	130,325	24.86
14	1,533	30,534	4.59	135,033	22.53
15	1,533	34,733	5.00	139,997	20.60
16	1,533	39,287	5.34	145,215	18.97
17	1,533	44,224	5.63	150,700	17.58
18	1,533	49,571	5.87	156,454	16.40
19	1,533	55,359	6.08	162,486	15.37
20	1,533	61,621	6.26	168,807	14.47

[a]Guaranteed cash value plus cash value of paid-up addition.
[b]$100,000 face amount plus face amount of paid-up addition.

of the net death benefit for that year. The *investment* in a policy for a particular year is made up of the premiums paid that year plus the cash value at the beginning of the year. The YROR is derived by dividing the annual policy benefits by the corresponding year's investment and subtracting 1 from the quotient. The formula is:

Yearly Rate of Return = (Policy Benefits ÷ Policy Investment) − 1

An analogy. An analogy might prove helpful. Assume that £1,000 was invested in a no-load unit trust (mutual fund) that developed a value (benefit) of £1,080 at the end of the first year. Assume that another £1,000 was invested at the beginning of the second year and that the total fund value at the end of the second year was £2,330. The first year's rate of return would be calculated as follows:

Yearly Rate of Return$_1$ = (Benefits ÷ Investment) − 1 = (£1,080 ÷ £1,000) − 1 = 0.08

The second year's return would be:

Yearly Rate of Return$_2$ = [£2,330 ÷ (£1,000 + £1,080)] − 1 = 0.12

In other words, the effective first-year return on the fund was 8.0 percent. The second year's return was 12.0 percent. Note that the second year's investment includes the £1,080 together with the additional payment of £1,000 because leaving the £1,080 value intact is the economic equivalent to investing £1,080.

Illustration. A similar procedure is followed for life insurance YROR computations. A key difference is that cash-value life insurance policies provide savings and death protection. The value of this death protection benefit must be included in the calculations. The YROR formula is shown in the chapter appendix.

Table 12-7 illustrates a YROR calculation using the YRT premiums of Table 4-2 and the lower-cost UL policy of Table 12-2. Values shown are based on current assumptions only.

The YROR gives a year-by-year rate of return for a cash-value policy whereas the CIR and the IRR give an average rate of return. Yearly values for mortality charges (as measured, for example, by YRT premiums) are needed for both the CIR and YROR methods.

The YROR can be helpful in deciding whether to retain a policy for another year and in assessing a policy's year-to-year performance.[9] It will reveal unusual discontinuities in the progression of policy values, which could indicate insurer manipulation. This method should be used only for policies with cash values, and the results should be interpreted cautiously when cash values are small.

Cost Analysis in Replacements

The preceding cost comparison methods, when adjusted, can be used to compare an existing policy with a proposed new one. Such comparisons are often necessary to help determine whether an existing policy should be replaced with a new one.

---

[9]A complementary method to the YROR is the **yearly price of protection** method. It involves assuming yearly rates of return and deriving yearly prices—the complement to the YROR. The formula for this method is obtained by solving the YROR formula for the yearly price of protection.

TABLE 12-7 Yearly Rate of Return Method: Universal Life $100,000 Face Amount (Using Table 4-2 YRT Rates as Price of Protection)

(1) Policy Year	(2) Planned Premium	(3) Beginning-of-Year Investment [(2) + (4) previous]	(4) Year-End Surrender Value	(5) Price of Protection per $1,000	(6) Total Price of Protection[a]	(7) Yearly Rate of Return (%)
1	$1,000	$ 1,000	$ 789	$1.45	$144	−6.71
2	1,000	1,789	1,714	1.48	145	3.94
3	1,000	2,714	2,720	1.54	150	5.74
4	1,000	3,720	3,807	1.62	156	6.53
5	1,000	4,807	4,988	1.72	163	7.16
6	1,000	5,988	6,253	1.85	173	7.32
7	1,000	7,253	7,636	2.00	185	8.52
8	1,000	8,686	9,116	2.19	199	7.24
9	1,000	10,116	10,788	2.42	216	8.78
10	1,000	11,788	12,479	2.68	235	7.85
11	1,000	13,479	14,359	2.88	247	8.36
12	1,000	15,359	16,394	3.33	278	8.55
13	1,000	17,394	18,595	3.73	304	8.65
14	1,000	19,595	20,979	4.17	330	8.74
15	1,000	21,979	23,548	4.66	356	8.76
16	1,000	24,548	26,338	5.21	384	8.86
17	1,000	27,338	29,361	5.81	410	8.90
18	1,000	30,361	32,644	6.46	435	8.95
19	1,000	33,644	36,807	7.16	452	10.75
20	1,000	37,807	40,079	7.91	474	7.26

[a]($100,000 − col. 4) × (col. 5) × (0.001)

The *interest-adjusted method* can be used to compare an existing policy with a proposed one, provided they are of the same type. Adjustments, however, are necessary in the calculation, and they can cause more confusion than clarity. These adjustments involve altering the death benefit and outlays of either the existing or proposed arrangement to recognize any value realized from termination of the existing policy. For example, if a $100,000 existing policy carries a cash surrender value of $30,000, this amount would be realized on policy termination and would be available to augment the death benefit under the proposed arrangement and to offset its premium payments. In any event, the method is rarely used in replacement evaluations.

The *equal outlay method* is often used in comparing an existing to a proposed policy. If the proposed policy is a flexible-premium contract, the analysis is simple. The only needed change is to assume some appropriate disposition of the existing policy's cash value. This potential surrender value could be paid into the proposed policy or it could be maintained outside the insurance program. If the cash value is assumed to be paid into the new policy, no other special adjustments are necessary for a reasonably fair analysis, assuming the death benefits of the two policies are held roughly equal. One simply illustrates future values of the two policies and compares results. If, however, the released cash value is not paid into the new policy and if the amount is not inconsequential, two adjustments should be made for a reasonably fair analysis. First, the death benefits should be made approximately equal, and second, the time value of money associated with the released cash value should be recognized.

A comparison between two fixed-premium policies can be made using the equal outlay method if adjustments are made to minimize bias. Results, however, are frequently ambiguous. A cost-based decision can be made using these results if the policy against which the method is biased proves superior.

In exploring the replacement alternative under this approach, the cash surrender value realized under the existing insurance must be recognized. This can be done in either of two ways. First, it can be assumed that the released surrender value is invested. Thus, the total death benefit of the proposed arrangement would be the proposed policy's face amount plus a side fund composed of the released surrender value. To compare similar death benefits, the face amount for the proposed policy is set equal to the net amount at risk of the existing policy. The released cash value also should be shown, at interest, as being available to augment the total value available on surrender under the proposed arrangement. One then equalizes outlays by accumulating the differences, as before.

The second approach is to assume that a maximum policy loan is obtained from the existing policy. In essence, this enables the analysis to ignore the cash surrender value of the existing policy because it would be available for outside investment under either the existing or the proposed arrangement. Also, it results in an automatic adjustment within the existing policy to permit a fairer comparison. The net death benefit of the existing arrangement would be the face amount less the loan. The death benefit of the proposed plan should be set at this same level. This, of course, results in a lower outlay for the proposed policy than would otherwise be the case. Also, the existing policy's future net surrender values should be lowered by the loan amount, and the policy loan interest payment should be included as a part of the existing policy's yearly outlay.

The latter approach is easier to follow and implicitly takes into consideration the possible advantage accruing to the existing policy from a low policy loan interest rate. After making the necessary adjustments, one then proceeds as before, equalizing outlays under the two arrangements by accumulating the differences.

The ambiguous results of the equal outlay method, as a technique for comparing existing and proposed policies, can usually be avoided through use of the *cash accumulation* or *comparative interest rate* methods. An essential adjustment in using either of these methods, however, is to treat the cash surrender value of the existing policy as an additional first-year payment under that policy or to recalculate its outlays and values assuming a maximum policy loan. This permits a fair analysis. Aside from this adjustment, the analysis is conducted as before and interpreted accordingly.

The *internal rate of return* method is not commonly used in replacement evaluations. IRR figures for an existing and a proposed policy often yield ambiguous results.

The *YROR* method can be particularly instructive in replacement evaluations if the existing policy has cash values and is proposed to be replaced by a term policy. YROR figures are derived directly, using the term rates as the yearly prices of protection. If the YROR figures are low, a replacement may be in order.

Comparison Limitations

Cost comparison methods yield precise figures. This precision can lend an unwarranted aura of authenticity and credibility to results. All cost comparison methods have limitations, many of which were discussed earlier. Other potential limitations include the fact that some cost comparison methods can be used fairly to compare similar policies only. Furthermore, some methods focus on one or two policy years only, possibly ignoring other equally important years. All methods must make some arbitrary assumptions to derive costs. The appropriateness of these assumptions for the buyer should be explored. A most important limitation to note is that no method is capable of factoring into the cost formula the quality and integrity of the advisor and insurer. Other limitations are discussed next.

Reliance on Illustrated Values   One particularly important limitation is that all methods rely on illustrated policy values. When cost comparison methodologies were originally developed, they were arguably more useful than they are today. Policies issued at that time had fixed-premium patterns with fairly consistent design features and profit margins. The only nonguaranteed policy elements were dividends, and, as discussed later, they were typically illustrated conservatively. Economic conditions were more stable with interest rates showing little volatility. Thus, the likely variation of actual values from illustrated policy values was less then than now. Correspondingly, cost comparisons based on illustrated values usually more closely reflected actual policy results then than they do now.

Historically, U.S. dividend illustrations were based on the company's portfolio average investment rate of return. Companies were loath to pay lower dividends than those originally illustrated. As a result, illustrations were conservative. In effect, the purchaser of such a policy had reason to believe that these nonguaranteed illustrated dividends would, in fact, be paid and probably at higher levels than illustrated.

During the late 1970s and 1980s, many North American insurers selling participating insurance shifted to new-money approaches of investment income allocation within their dividend formulas. Other insurers introduced nonpar UL and CAWL policies with one or more nonguaranteed policy elements. Usually, cash values were predicated on new-money rates.

This was done at a time of rapidly rising interest rates, so the result was that dividends and nonguaranteed cash values illustrated at new-money rates were naturally higher than those illustrated on portfolio rates because the portfolio rate is a weighted average of old and new investment returns. At this point, the two types of illustrations became far less comparable.

Many new nonparticipating products used not only current investment returns but also contained an element of anticipated favorable future results. This put further competitive pressure on illustrations. It was no longer sufficient, in such a competitive environment, in the judgment of many companies, to illustrate dividends based solely on current and immediate past actual results, let alone portfolio results. They perceived that it was necessary to build into dividend illustrations an element of anticipated future results, not dissimilar from the approach being followed in many new-money nonparticipating products. What had been *illustrations* of past results increasingly became *projections* of future results.

The likelihood of actual results being as favorable as those illustrated or projected depends on current interest rate trends. What is clear, however, is that the portfolio-based products' values should fluctuate the least, whereas the new-money-product values can be expected to experience the greatest fluctuation, all else being equal.

The wide potential variation of actual values from illustrated values coupled with the different bases for illustrating values has led many persons to conclude that cost comparisons of many contemporary products may be fundamentally inappropriate. Whether variations inherent in policy illustrations today are so great as to warrant the abandonment of comparative performance measures remains an unsettled issue. In fact, comparisons are being made, and with the implicit endorsement of the U.S. insurance regulators. In view of this reality, greater discipline has been incorporated into product design, especially as it relates to nonguaranteed policy elements, as discussed earlier. Certainly, a meaningful understanding of the assumptions underpinning illustrated values is a necessary prerequisite for cost comparisons.

As values illustrated for many years into the future are highly uncertain, the use of shorter planning horizons is probably more appropriate today. On the other hand, the long range should not be ignored, particularly when major differences exist.

Tax and Creditor Considerations   As discussed in chapter 13, life policy benefits and those from other sources might not be taxed the same. The cost analyses shown here do not explicitly consider any income, estate, or other taxes that might be due on policy benefits.[10] For example, many states exempt life insurance death proceeds paid to certain specified beneficiaries (e.g., family members) from inheritance taxes. The tax, however, is imposed on other assets that pass at death. Thus, this (usually) 6 percent tax would mean that a $94,000 life insurance policy would be equivalent to $100,000 of other assets.

Also, life insurance death proceeds may enjoy certain protection from creditors' claims (see chapter 10). These and other considerations should enter into any analysis when insurance is being compared with noninsurance financial instruments.

Premium Payment Mode   Another limitation of cost comparison methods is that they usually are predicated on annual premiums. However, only about 20 percent of policyowners pay premiums annually. Insurers incur extra expenses on policies for which premiums are paid monthly, quarterly, or semiannually, and they also lose the use of the funds for the full year. Additionally, lapse rates vary by premium payment mode.

Insurers load nonannual premiums for these factors, plus, in some instances, for higher profits. This means that policy costs can vary considerably as between annual and nonannual premiums. A consumer could be misled into purchasing a policy whose cost is relatively low when illustrated using annual premiums but whose cost is uncompetitive when the actual mode of premium payment is considered. Implicit carrying charges associated with nonannual premiums can be estimated by the formulas in Box 12-2, and the results factored into the purchase decision.

---

[10]Thus, the cash surrender values shown throughout this chapter are on a before-income-tax basis. The assumption implicit in this approach is that the relevant policies are held until death, in which case any gain is exempt from income tax, or that taxation of gains is avoided via a qualified policy exchange. If one were interested in the surrender of policies and the possibility of incurring income taxes on any gain, after-tax cash surrender values should be used. These values are found by subtracting any expected taxes due on surrender from the policy's cash surrender value. See chapter 13.

BOX 12-2

CALCULATION OF CARRYING CHARGES FOR NONANNUAL PREMIUM MODES

The carrying charges for nonannual premium payment modes can be estimated from the following formulas where:

C_k = Carrying Charge for Mode k
M = Monthly Premium
Q = Quarterly Premium

S = Semiannual Premium
A = Annual Premium

$$C_M = [36(12M - A)] / (13A + 42M)$$
$$C_Q = [12(4Q - A)] / (5A - 2Q)$$
$$C_S = [2(2S - A)] / (A - S)$$

Source: Joseph M. Belth, "A Note on the Cost of Fractional Premiums," *The Journal of Risk and Insurance,* Vol. XLV (December 1978).

As an example, assume that a $1,000 annual-premium policy has a monthly premium of $90. The reader can verify that the implicit carrying charge from the monthly formula is 17.2 percent.

Special Benefits and Supplementary Coverages   Another shortcoming of the foregoing cost comparisons is that they are incapable of valuing policy provisions that do not relate directly to the factors that enter the formulas. Thus, one policy may have more favorable wording for its incontestable, grace period, reinstatement or other clauses, yet this fact is not valued appropriately.

The methods also ignore supplementary benefits that may be included in the policy, such as waiver of premium or family coverage. This omission is appropriate if the benefit is not included in both policies. Otherwise, the policy comparisons should be based on the entire package. An insurer may have a reasonably attractive basic life policy but may charge excessively for the options. Some insurers include supplementary coverages of little actuarial value purposefully to make their policies more difficult to compare and thereby to mask an expensive policy.

Table 12-8 provides a summary of the key characteristics of the cost comparison methods discussed in this chapter. The table is intended only to highlight points, and, as with all such summaries, is subject to numerous qualifications.

ANNUITY COST ANALYSIS

As discussed in chapter 8, annuities are gaining in popularity. During their accumulation phases, annuities have little or no element of pure life insurance protection. Annuity cost comparisons are, therefore, simpler than life insurance cost comparisons.

Although less complex, annuity cost comparisons are no less essential. If an annuity provides for a front-end load, a back-end load, or both, one must take care in assessing its competitiveness. The advertised rate of return can be a poor guide to value. Rather, the effective yield based on gross contributions should be calculated.

The calculation is the same as that of the IRR method. It is the interest rate that causes a stream of payments to equal a stipulated future value. It should be based on gross contributions and on the contract cash *surrender* value (i.e., net of all surrender charges).

Table 12-9 provides an illustration. The purchaser is assumed to contribute $1,000 per year to a flexible-premium deferred annuity. The insurer currently credits 8.25 percent to the net cash value. Projected cash surrender values for selected future years are

TABLE 12-8 Summary of Key Points of Common Cost Comparison Methods

	Traditional Net Cost	Interest-Adjusted Net Cost	Equal Outlay	Cash Accumulation	Comparative Interest Rate	Internal Rate of Return	Yearly Rate of Return	Yearly Price
Technique	Sum premiums less cash value and dividends; ignores interest	Sum premiums at interest less sum dividends at interest and cash value	Accumulate premium differences at interest	Accumulate premium differences at interest while holding death benefits constant	Accumulate premium differences at interest rate that causes premiums to equal surrender value and to equal death benefits	Accumulate premiums at interest rate that causes premiums to equal surrender value and to equal death benefit	Ratio of policy "benefits" to "investment"	Policy "investment" less "benefits"
Solves for	Net cost	Average net cost	Surrender value and death benefit differences	Surrender value differences	Average rate of return that causes equality	Internal rate of return on surrender and on death	Yearly rate of return	Yearly price of protection
Assumptions Needed	Money has no time value	Rate of return	1. Rate of return 2. Equal outlay	1. Rate of return 2. Equal outlay 3. Equal death benefits	1. YRT rates 2. Equal outlay 3. Equal death benefits	Full premium needed to develop cash value and to develop death benefit	YRT rates	Rate of return
Compares Similar Policies?	No	Yes	Yes, but results often ambiguous	Yes	Yes, if common YRT rates used	Yes	Yes, if common YRT rates are used	Yes
Compares Dissimilar Policies?	No	No	Yes, but results often ambiguous	Yes, with care	Yes, with care	No	Yes	Yes
Requires Computer?	No	No, but time-consuming	No, but time-consuming	Yes	Yes	Yes	No	No
Useful for Replacement Evaluation?	No	No	Yes, with modification	Yes, with modification	Yes, with modification	No	Yes, but results often ambiguous	Yes, but results often ambiguous

YRT denotes yearly renewable term.

TABLE 12-9	Illustrative Annuity Yields			
(1)	(2)	(3)	(4)	(5)
Year	Annual Contribution	Cash Surrender Value	Advertised Yield (%) (Based on Net Contribution)	Effective Yield[a] (%) (Based on Gross Contribution)
1	$1,000	$ 866	8.25	–13.48
2	1,000	1,717	8.25	–9.76
3	1,000	2,647	8.25	–6.12
4	1,000	3,750	8.25	–2.57
5	1,000	4,988	8.25	–0.08
10	1,000	13,796	8.25	5.78
15	1,000	26,889	8.25	7.00
20	1,000	46,350	8.25	7.46
25	1,000	75,278	8.25	7.69
30	1,000	118,277	8.25	7.82

[a]From date of issue to year indicated.

shown in the third column. The purchaser might be shown these values and advised that the current accumulation rate was 8.25 percent. This rate is based on contributions net of expenses and is not representative of the annuity's effective yield.

The final column gives the effective average yields for selected time periods. The impact of the loads is obvious. If the insurer credited 8.25 percent to the net contribution, and if the annuity were terminated at the end of the tenth year, the effective yield would be 5.78 percent, not 8.25 percent.

As with the life policies discussed previously, illustrations are of projected values and should be taken as such. Annuity projections may be based on portfolio rates or new-money rates, which can complicate analysis. Most of the other limitations discussed previously with life policies apply also to annuities.

COST AND BENEFIT DISCLOSURE

Most U.S. and many other jurisdictions require that certain information disclosures be made to prospective policyowners. Special disclosure requirements apply to policies when a replacement is proposed. Additional disclosure often is required in connection with flexible-premium and variable policies. These disclosures are intended to help the consumer become better informed, thereby rectifying, to some extent, the information imbalance between buyer and seller. The hope is that the buyer will make better purchase decisions.

Of course, insurers have natural incentives to provide information beyond that mandated by regulation. Additional disclosure is provided through annual statement filings and via certain voluntary guidelines of The Society of Financial Service Professionals (formerly The American Society of CLU & ChFC).

Background of Disclosure Issue

Although recommendations for improving life insurance disclosure were made as early as 1906 via the Armstrong Investigation in New York and in 1908 by the Wisconsin insurance commissioner, significant activity on the issue did not occur until the 1960s. Following a threat of federal legislation, the NAIC adopted an interim model life insurance disclosure regulation in 1973 and a final version in 1976. A still later version was adopted, the details of which are discussed later.

Important U.S. congressional subcommittee hearings on life insurance marketing and disclosure were held in 1973 and 1978, both of which raised questions about existing disclosure and marketing practices.[11] The Federal Trade Commission (FTC) staff also investigated life insurance marketing and released a report in 1979.[12] The report identified several consumer problems and offered detailed recommendations as to how to solve the problems. The FTC staff believed significant changes should be made in the NAIC approach to disclosure, and its report caused much turmoil within the U.S. life insurance industry. The industry testified vigorously against the report.

Since then, except for congressional hearings related to life insurer market conduct, relatively little activity has occurred at the federal level. The NAIC's recent efforts have been directed less toward disclosure than toward discipline in whatever disclosures were made, as discussed previously.

NAIC Disclosure Requirements

About 40 U.S. jurisdictions require disclosures to prospective life insurance purchasers as recommended in the NAIC **Life Insurance Disclosure Model Regulation** or its predecessors. The regulation does not apply to annuities, credit life insurance, group life insurance, variable life insurance, and life insurance policies issued in connection with pension and welfare plans. The regulations require that a prospective purchaser be supplied with:

- a **Buyer's Guide** that contains an explanation of life insurance products and how to shop for them, and
- a **Policy Summary** containing pertinent data about the particular policy the prospect is considering.

Disclosure Requirements

The insurance company is required to ensure that all prospective purchasers receive a Buyer's Guide and a Policy Summary prior to accepting the applicant's initial premium, *unless* the policy for which application is being made or the Policy Summary contains an unconditional refund provision of at least 10 days' duration. In these cases, the Buyer's Guide and Policy Summary may be delivered with or prior to delivery of the policy. Most states mandate a 10-day "free look" requirement, and many insurers allow a 30-day period. A Buyer's Guide and a Policy Summary are also to be provided to any prospective purchaser who requests them.

The disclosure regulation requires agents to inform prospective purchasers of the full name of the company that they are representing. Terms such as *financial planner, investment advisor, financial consultant,* and *financial counseling* may not be used in such a way as to imply that the agent is generally engaged in a fee-for-service advisory business, unless that is actually the case. The use of the TNC method of cost comparison is prohibited except to show a policy's cash flow pattern.

Several provisions in the latest model regulation are not found in most states' actual regulations. Thus, the latest model regulation requires that the method of investment income allocation (i.e., new-money or portfolio average) be shown in the Policy Summary issued, and that, if an insurer fails to follow the contribution principle, a statement to that effect must also be included. Under the model regulation (but not in most

---

[11] *The Life Insurance Industry—Parts 1, 2, and 3* (Washington, DC: U.S. Government Printing Office, 1973) and *Part 4* (1974); and *Life Insurance Marketing and Cost Disclosure* (Washington, DC: U.S. Government Printing Office, 1978).

[12] *Life Insurance Cost Disclosure* (Washington, DC: Federal Trade Commission, 1979).

states' regulations), any change from one investment income allocation method to another requires that affected policyowners be notified.

Additionally, the model regulation, but not most states' regulations, gives existing policyowners the right to receive updated Policy Summaries. Also, insurers must calculate (but need not provide to the consumer) a discontinuity index that would detect policies with manipulated values. Also, the latest model provides for modified disclosure requirements for certain special life insurance plans, such as universal life and enhanced ordinary life as well as preneed funeral contracts.

A further modification of the disclosure regulation, which is not in effect in any state, would substitute a **life insurance yield comparison index** for the surrender cost comparison index. This yield index is calculated by using a standard, prescribed set of term (mortality) rates that are applied to the policy's net amount at risk (rather than to the difference between the policy's death benefit and a hypothetical side fund, as in the CIR method).

The Buyer's Guide

The Buyer's Guide is intended to help prospective purchasers (1) decide how much life insurance to buy, (2) decide what kind of policy to buy, and (3) compare the costs of similar life insurance policies. The language of the guide is mandated by the regulation.

The suggestion in the Buyer's Guide for choosing an appropriate amount of life insurance to buy is general; it advises the consumer to figure out how much cash and income would be needed if the insured died. The guide explains briefly the principal types of life insurance—term, whole life, universal life, and variations—and points out positive and negative aspects of each. The consumer is advised that "cost comparison index numbers can point the way to better buys" and is admonished that "a policy with smaller index numbers is generally a better buy than a similar policy with larger index numbers. . . ." These index numbers are contained in the Policy Summary.

The Buyer's Guides used in most jurisdictions contain an explanation of the distinction between participating and nonparticipating life insurance, although the newer Buyer's Guide in the latest model regulation focuses more on guaranteed and nonguaranteed values. The Buyer's Guide includes a general description of the surrender cost comparison index and the net payment cost comparison index, and advice on how to use them. These indices are to be computed on both guaranteed and illustrative bases.

The Policy Summary

The Policy Summary contains information and data on the specific policy being considered by the consumer. The name and address of the insurance agent (if any) and the insurance company must appear on the summary, along with the generic name of the insurance policy (e.g., whole life insurance).

The Policy Summary must contain certain policy data (premiums, death benefits, cash surrender values, and dividends) for the first five policy years, and for representative policy years thereafter, in sufficient number to illustrate clearly the pattern of premiums and benefits. These years must include the tenth and twentieth years and for "at least one age from 60 through 65 and policy maturity."

In addition to the preceding policy data, the effective policy loan interest rate must be stated and 10- and 20-year surrender cost and net payment cost indices provided. The procedure with which to calculate the indices is mandated by the regulation—a 5 percent interest assumption is to be used.

Universal Life Disclosure Regulation

The NAIC also adopted a **Universal Life Insurance Model Regulation.** This regulation establishes minimum valuation and nonforfeiture standards for UL and CAWL policies, and mandates certain policy provisions. It also supplements disclosure requirements of the foregoing disclosure regulation. For example, it requires that a policyowner must receive, at least annually, a report that summarizes the recent activity in the policy, including full policy values. About one-quarter of the states have adopted this regulation or some variation of it, and other states impose some of the regulation's requirements. As a practical matter, most companies voluntarily comply with the regulation.

Annuity Disclosure Regulation

The NAIC **Model Annuity and Deposit Fund Disclosure Regulation** applies to individual deferred annuities, selected group annuities, and deposit funds accepted in connection with life insurance and annuity contracts. The regulation's purpose is to help the prospect select an appropriate annuity and to understand its features. About one-half of the states have adopted the regulation.

The regulation requires that prospective purchasers be provided a prescribed Buyer's Guide to Annuities and a Contract Summary. The Buyer's Guide explains annuities and the types of annuity contracts. General annuity features, typical charges, and benefits are summarized. The guide points out that a yield on gross premiums at the end of 10 years and at the time income payments are scheduled to begin is provided in the Contract Summary. This yield figure should be used to compare annuity contracts, as it takes into account both illustrated interest credits and all charges.

The Contract Summary provides the same generic type of information for an annuity that the Policy Summary does for life insurance policies. In addition to the two yield figures, the summary provides relevant data on all policy elements for each of the first 10 years and for representative contract years thereafter to illustrate clearly the pattern of considerations and benefits.

Disclosure for Variable Contracts

As discussed in earlier chapters, variable life and annuity contracts are subject to both federal and state regulation disclosure requirements. The intent of these requirements is to allow the prudent investor to be able to make an informed decision about whether to purchase the security (variable product), that is, to try to rectify some of the information asymmetry between buyer and seller.

State-Mandated Disclosure

Disclosure in connection with the sale of variable products typically follows the provisions the NAIC's Variable Life Insurance Model Regulation or an earlier or similar version of the regulation, in effect in most states. The regulation requires insurers to provide the following information to the applicant for a variable life policy:

- A summary explanation of the principal features of the policy, including a description of the manner in which the variable benefits will reflect the separate account investment experience and factors that affect the variation.
- A statement of the investment policy of the separate account.
- A statement of the net investment return of the separate account for the lesser of each of the last 10 years or each year the account has been in existence.
- A statement of the charges levied against the separate account during the previous year.
- A summary of the method to be used in valuing assets held by the separate account.
- A summary of the federal income tax aspects of the policy applicable to the insured, the policyowner, and the beneficiary.
- Illustrations of benefits payable under the contract, which may not include projections of past experience but may use hypothetical assumed rates of return to illustrate possible levels of death benefits.

The regulation does not require disclosure of agent commissions. Compliance with the regulation can be achieved by delivery to the applicant of a prospectus containing effectively the same information as that previously. In addition to this initial disclosure, the regulation mandates that insurers provide annual policy status reports to policyowners that summarize policy and separate account activity for the preceding year.

Federal-Mandated Disclosure

Federally mandated disclosure follows the requirements of the Securities Exchange Act of 1993. Applicable to both variable annuity and life contracts, disclosure, which must be full and accurate, is accomplished through two mechanisms. First, the securities issuer must file a registration statement with the Securities and Exchange Commission (SEC), which contains detailed information on the security, the issuer, the officers, and security holdings. Details of the underwriting arrangement and financial statements also must be included.

Second, the act requires that each potential buyer must be given a prospectus. This booklet includes the identity and nature of the insurer's business, the use to which the insurer will put the premiums, financial information on the insurer, the fees and expenses to be charged, and policyowner rights. It contains most other information included in the registration statement. The prospectus is to be highly readable, easily understandable, and kept current.

Annual Statement Disclosure

Insurers are required to file detailed financial statements annually in each jurisdiction in which they are licensed. These statements, as explained in chapter 33, contain the insurer's balance sheet, income statement, and a host of schedules and exhibits that relate to the insurer's investments and operations.

Two aspects of these annual statements provide information that can be helpful in evaluating life insurance policy performance. First, Schedule M requires that the insurer describe in detail the precise methods and assumptions used to calculate policy dividends. Although insurer compliance with this requirement is uneven, the interested person nonetheless could use this information to learn more about the assumptions underpinning an insurer's dividend illustrations.

Second, Exhibit 8 of the annual statement can be a particularly fruitful source of information about insurers' pricing practices. The insurer first identifies whether it issues policies that contain nonguaranteed elements, whether via surplus participation or other means, and then the nature of the nonguaranteed elements. Insurers that issue participating insurance must disclose whether they follow the contribution principle in surplus distribution, and, if not, they are required to explain their practices.

For nonparticipating contracts containing nonguaranteed elements, the insurer is to state its practice with respect to the determination and redetermination of the contracts' nonguaranteed elements. Finally, and of potentially great importance, the insurer is to state whether any of the experience factors (mortality, interest, loadings, and lapse rates) included in its policy illustrations differ from its actual current experience, and if so, how. If a substantial probability exists that current policy illustrations cannot be supported by the insurer's current or anticipated experience, this fact is to be disclosed. A prospective purchaser would be keenly interested in knowing if an insurer's policy illustrations were not supportable by the insurer's actual operational results.

The Society of Financial Service Professionals Questionnaires

The Society of Financial Service Professionals provides two questionnaires to life insurers to solicit information about the nonguaranteed performance assumptions underlying their policy illustrations. Completion of the questionnaires is voluntary. Answers are made available to agents and other advisors. The hope is that insurers will answer fully, thus providing advisors and their customers insight into insurers' pricing practices. Two questionnaires exist: the *Life Insurance Illustration Questionnaire* (IQ) for nonvariable life insurance policies and the *Variable Life Insurance Illustration Questionnaire* (VIQ) for variable life products.

Under both questionnaires, insurers selling participating life insurance are to specify whether the contribution principle is followed and, if not, to explain how its surplus distribution practices differ. Insurers also are requested to disclose whether the underlying experience factors for any nonguaranteed policy element differ from current experience and, if so, to describe the differences. The insurer is asked to indicate whether there is a substantial probability that currently illustrated values will change if current experience continues unchanged. These queries are similar to those in the NAIC Exhibit 8 interrogatory.

There follows a series of questions about underlying mortality assumptions. Thus, the insurer is asked to indicate whether mortality charges are lower than actual company experience would justify and whether some element of future mortality improvement is included in the illustrated charges. A "yes" answer would indicate that the insurer is using or projecting mortality rates in its illustrated policy values that are not currently supported.

Another section of the questionnaires deals with interest rate assumptions. Under the IQ, the insurer is to describe the basis (investment generation, portfolio average, or other) of the interest rate used in any nonguaranteed pricing elements, including whether the company's actual investment earning rates on the assets backing the policy's liabilities exceed the rates being credited to the policy. This information is helpful in evaluating the volatility of illustrated values in light of contemporary investment returns. This question has no meaning for variable products. The VIQ, however, does inquire whether the policyowner assumes all investment risk and whether the initial death benefit is guaranteed regardless of investment performance.

The final two sections of each questionnaire seek information about expense charges and company persistency, similar to that mentioned previously. One important question is whether policy values would be negatively affected if actual persistency were better than that assumed—in other words, if the policy is lapse supported.

The intent of these and the other questions is to develop information useful in assessing (1) whether the insurer's policy illustration is predicated on realistic, current company experience and (2) the extent to which actual policy values may be subject to fluctuations.

The society also provides a *Replacement Questionnaire* (RQ). Unlike the IQ and VIQ, the RQ is designed for use by agents in assisting clients in deciding whether to replace existing insurance.

Neither these questionnaires nor any professional practice standard or regulation in the United States requires disclosure to prospective purchasers of the fact and extent of agents' commissions. Many persons believe that consumer disclosure should include information on commission payments to alert the prospective buyer as to the nature and extent of the agent's interest in the sales transactions. Commission disclosure is required in several countries, including Australia, Norway, and the United Kingdom.

LIFE INSURANCE POLICY REPLACEMENT REGULATION

The very mention of the word *replacement* evokes strong opinions and emotions from many within the U.S. life insurance business. As its name suggests, **replacement** is the exchange (termination) of one policy for another. Many insurance executives, agents, and regulators have expressed alarm over the extent of replacement activity, arguing that life insurance consumers are losing vast sums by switching policies. Others argue that replacement is usually in the consumer's interest, that an existing life insurance policy should be no more sacred or immune to replacement than any other consumer purchase, and that today's products are superior to older policies.

The issue is complex because the replacement decision often revolves around nonguaranteed, illustrated values for both existing and proposed policies. Use of these values as an important factor in the decision whether to replace can lead to mistakes. Such values are not guaranteed and the basis upon which they are derived often differ, as noted previously and in earlier chapters.

Some agents and insurers have a marketing strategy that is based on replacement of existing insurance. Some agents have been accused of engaging in **churning,** which involves the systematic and indiscriminate replacement of existing insurance for purposes of securing new, higher commissions.

The 1970 and 1979 NAIC Model Replacement Regulations

In 1970, the NAIC adopted its first model life insurance replacement regulation. This regulation had a clear antireplacement bias. The notice required to be provided to the consumer contemplating replacement pointed out that "as a general rule, it is not advantageous to drop or change existing life insurance in favor of a new policy."

The NAIC adopted a revised replacement regulation in 1978 that represented an improvement over the previous regulation. Several states' replacement regulations are patterned after this version. Under this regulation, the agent who proposes a replacement must provide the policyowner with a Replacement Notice and a completed Comparative Information Form. The agent is to leave copies of all sales materials used with the applicant and to send to the replacing insurer signed copies of the notice and the Comparative Information Form, plus copies of all sales proposals. An agent who attempts to conserve the existing policy must leave with the consumer copies of all materials used in connection with that effort, and must submit to his or her own insurer copies of the same material.

The replacing insurer is to send to the existing insurer a verified copy of the Comparative Information Form within three days of receipt of the insurance application. Furthermore, the replacing insurer must either delay issuance of the new policy for 20 days or provide a 20-day unconditional refund offer with the replacing policy.

If the existing insurer undertakes a conservation effort, it must either complete, correct, and send to the consumer the Comparative Information Form it received from the replacing insurer or send the consumer a Policy Summary completed in compliance with the disclosure regulation. Cost comparison information need not be included in the Policy Summary. The existing insurer is, in turn, to provide the replacing insurer with a copy of the materials it sent to the consumer in its efforts to conserve the policy.

Both the older and newer versions of the regulations have shortcomings. Critics claimed that the regulations constituted a road map as to how to replace. On the other hand, claims were made that the regulations discouraged many justifiable replacements because of the time-consuming task of compliance. Others pointed out that the disclosure form provided much policy data, the usefulness of which was at best questionable and at worst counterproductive.

The 1984 NAIC Model Replacement Regulation

In 1984, the NAIC adopted its latest replacement regulation. This model is patterned, in key parts, after the replacement regulation adopted by Virginia in 1982. Several states' regulations are similar to this latest model. The new regulation retains much from its predecessors, but it eliminates the requirement that a comparison form be used. The applicant is to be provided with a notice, but it is far simpler than earlier notices and puts more of the burden on the consumer to protect his or her own interest. Other differences in procedure are required.

Although acknowledged to be an improvement over earlier model regulations, the 1984 model is still considered by some to be inadequate in protecting consumers. The NAIC is considering revisions to this model regulation.

The Replacement Debate

Arguments as to whether replacements are "good" or "bad" provide the individual buyer little guidance. The question is whether a particular proposed replacement is in the policyowner's best interest. Generalizations are of no help in attempting to answer this question.

Many replacements are, no doubt, contrary to the policyowner's best interests. No less doubtful is it that many other replacements are justified. The policyowner considering replacement should weigh several factors. Box 12-3 highlights the more common

---

BOX 12-3

CONSIDERATIONS IN LIFE INSURANCE REPLACEMENT

Replacement of one life insurance policy with another involves consideration of several factors. Potential reasons why replacement might not be in the consumer's best interest include the following:

- The existing policy may have a lower premium rate per $1,000 because it may have been issued at a younger age.
- The incontestable period of the existing policy may have expired or be closer to expiration.
- The suicide period of the existing policy may have expired or be closer to expiration.
- The insured may be uninsurable or insurable only at higher than standard rates.
- The owner usually will incur front-end loads again on the purchase of a new policy, whereas these amounts may have already been paid under the existing policy.
- Cash-value increases under new policies usually are less than those found with older policies.
- The existing policy may contain more liberal provisions (e.g., lower policy loan rate or more attractive settlement option rates) than those found in new policies.
- The insurer for the existing policy may be disposed to make alterations in the policy to make it more suitable or attractive.

On the other hand, the preceding arguments could prove to be unpersuasive for one or more of the following reasons:

- The proposed policy may, in fact, have a lower premium rate per $1,000 even at a higher issue age because competition has driven rates to new lows.
- Unless the individual intends to misrepresent information, that a new period of contestability may be incurred probably is of little importance.
- Unless the individual intends to commit or has tendencies toward committing suicide, that a new suicide period may be incurred is of little importance.
- Some policies today have low or no front-end loads, and, even with the payment of a new front-end load, a new policy may be superior, from a cost standpoint, to the existing policy.
- Cash-value increases on a new policy could be equal to or greater than those of the existing policy, especially when the released cash value from the existing policy is invested.
- The newer policy may contain more liberal provisions (e.g., premium payment flexibility or greater participation in the insurer's investment experience) than those in the existing policy.

Therefore, as is often the case in life insurance, no clear-cut, generalized answer exists as to whether policyowners are better off financially by replacing an older policy with a new one. If the existing policy is a guaranteed-cost, nonparticipating cash-value contract that was issued some years ago, replacement frequently is advantageous if the individual is insurable at standard rates.

considerations. Thus, most cash-value life insurance policies have their initial costs charged, one way or another, against early cash values. These initial high costs would have already been met under an older policy. However, a cost analysis can help determine whether this argument is persuasive, just as a cost analysis can help reveal whether a higher premium rate for a new policy seems justified financially.

It should always be considered that incontestable and suicide clauses begin anew under new policies, but this fact is rarely persuasive enough by itself to forestall a replacement. Moreover, some companies will waive these clauses on new policies to the extent that they had elapsed under the older policy.

It is often said that existing policies may have more favorable provisions than new policies and that a cost analysis alone fails to reveal this. This can be correct; however, the opposite can also be true. In any event, the importance of evaluating contractual provisions should again be mentioned as a key element in policy evaluation.

If an older policy is not perceived as serving the consumer's needs, the existing insurer may be willing to make an internal exchange on more beneficial terms than those that a new insurer may be willing to offer. Also, older policies sometimes can be adjusted to meet new circumstances through changes in dividend options or through policy loans and other alterations.

A proposed policy replacement should be approached with no prejudices either for or against replacement. Replacement is neither good nor evil. It is a neutral financial activity and a sound, fair analysis will help determine whether, in a given situation, it should be undertaken. As a general rule, if results of the analysis do not provide a reasonably clear decision in favor of replacement, the policyowner probably should not replace. In any event, a policyowner should never discontinue existing coverage before the new coverage is approved for issuance by the replacing company and is in effect.

Questions

1. Describe a number of financial risks that may come with the purchase of a life insurance policy.
2. All cost comparison methods have limitations. Describe some of these limitations and the restrictions they place on the use of cost comparison methods.
3. Explain how the following policy evaluation methods can provide useful information to the consumer provided careful attention is paid to their restrictive assumptions and limitations:
   a. comparative interest rate method
   b. yearly rate of return method
   c. interest-adjusted net cost method
4. The National Association of Insurance Commissioners (NAIC) has adopted two regulations, the NAIC Model Life Insurance Replacement Regulation (1979), and the NAIC Model Replacement Regulation (1984), whose purposes are to assist the consumer in making a wise life insurance purchase decision.
   a. Describe briefly the requirements of each of these regulations and how these requirements are intended to assist the consumer.
   b. Critique each of the regulations.
   c. Outline the factors that consumers should weigh when considering replacement.
5. If you could assess what an individual's tolerance for financial risks is (see Box 12-1, categories of risk styles), how would you use this information to advise individuals interested in purchasing life insurance?
6. How do cost and benefit disclosure requirements benefit the life insurance industry and the consumer?

Appendix

FORMULAS FOR SELECTED COST COMPARISON METHODS

Symbols used in the following formulas are:

n = Number of years
P_t = Illustrated premium at beginning of policy year t
D_t = Illustrated dividend at the end of policy year t
CV_n = Illustrated cash value plus terminal dividend at the end of policy year n
F_t = Illustrated death benefit at end of policy year t
i = Assumed interest rate
YP_t = Assumed yearly price of insurance per \$1,000
DB_t = Illustrated death benefit at the beginning of policy year t

TRADITIONAL NET COST METHOD

The formula for the traditional net cost for a period of n years is

$$TNC_n = \frac{\sum_{t=1}^{n} P_t - \sum_{t=1}^{n} D_t - CV_n}{(F_n)(0.001)(n)} \tag{1}$$

INTEREST-ADJUSTED NET COST METHOD

The formula for the interest-adjusted net cost for a period of n years is

$$IANC_n = \frac{\sum_{t=1}^{n} P_t(1 + i)^{n-t+1} - \sum_{t=1}^{n} D_t(1 + i)^{n-t} - CV_n}{(F_n)(0.001)\left[\sum_{t=1}^{n} (1 + i)^t\right]} \tag{2}$$

If the policy death benefit is not level over the period of evaluation, and *equivalent level death benefit* (*ELDB*) may be calculated as follows and substituted for F_n in the preceding equations:

$$ELDB_n = \frac{\sum_{t=1}^{n} DB_t(1 + i)^{n-t+1}}{\sum_{t=1}^{n} (1 + i)^t} \tag{3}$$

The net payment index formula is identical to equation (2) except the cash-value (CV_n) term is omitted.

EQUIVALENT LEVEL ANNUAL DIVIDEND

The formula for the equivalent level annual dividend (ELAD) for a period of n years is

$$ELAD_n = \frac{\displaystyle\sum_{t=1}^{n} D_t(1 + i)^{n-t}}{(F_n)(0.001)\left[\displaystyle\sum_{t=1}^{n} (1 + i)^t\right]} \tag{4}$$

YEARLY RATE OF RETURN METHOD

The formula for the yearly rate of return method for policy year t is

$$YROR_t = \frac{CV_t + D_t + (YP_t)(F_t - CV_t)(0.001)}{P_t + CV_{t-a_1}} - 1 \tag{5}$$

YEARLY PRICE OF PROTECTION METHOD

The formula for the yearly price of protection method for policy year t is

$$YPP_t = \frac{(1 + i)(P_t + CV_{t-1}) - (CV_t + D_t)}{(F_t - CV_t)(0.001)} \tag{6}$$

CHAPTER

13

LIFE AND HEALTH INSURANCE TAXATION

Objectives

- Describe tax provisions affecting life and health insurance.

- Outline tests used by the federal government to determine if a policy meets the definition of life insurance.

- Distinguish between the tax treatment of death proceeds and living proceeds.

- Outline the steps that can be taken to assess the taxable share of an individual's estate.

- Describe situations in which making gifts through life insurance policies may be advisable.

B ecause of their socially worthwhile role, life insurance and annuity contracts are accorded favorable tax treatment in the vast majority of countries, including the United States. This chapter introduces the U.S. federal income, estate, and gift tax treatment of life and health insurance and annuities as contained in the Internal Revenue Code (IRC).

INCOME TAX TREATMENT

In examining the income taxation of life and health insurance and annuities, it will prove convenient to examine the tax treatment by contract component.

Premiums

Premiums paid in the United States for individual disability income and life insurance policies and for individually issued annuities are considered a personal expense and are not deductible for income tax purposes. (In contrast, some tax relief is provided in connection with premiums paid for qualifying life insurance in most countries.) Contributions to tax-qualified retirement arrangements funded by annuities may be tax deductible, but this deduction attaches to the arrangement, not the product (see chapter 21). Premiums paid for medical expense and qualified long-term care (LTC) insurance are deductible to the extent that they and family medical expenses exceed 7.5 percent of the taxpayer's adjusted gross income, a high hurdle. LTC premiums are subject to further limitations, which are indexed for inflation and which increase with the insured's attained age. For example, a deduction limitation of $375 applies to LTC premiums for a 50-year-old and a limitation of $2,500 applies to premiums for individuals over the age of 70.

Of course, premiums paid to fund life insurance payable to a charity may be deductible as charitable contributions, and premiums paid for life and health insurance and annuities under an alimony agreement may be deductible as alimony payments. Moreover, premiums paid by employers for life and health insurance protection and for annuities that benefit employees are generally deductible as a business expense.

Death Proceeds

Section 101(a)(1) Treatment

IRC Section 101(a)(1) establishes the general rule that life insurance death proceeds are exempt from federal income tax. Proceeds must be paid "by reason of the death of the insured," which means that the insured's death must have caused the maturity of the contract. Other amounts paid at the time of death, such as annuity cash values or other proceeds that would have been payable during the insured's lifetime, do not qualify as "death proceeds."

Thus, if an insured under a $100,000 life insurance policy died after premiums of $3,000 had been paid, the entire $100,000 would be received income tax free by the beneficiary. With the exceptions noted later, this result applies irrespective of the cash value or the amount of premiums paid, and irrespective of who was the policyowner, insured, beneficiary, or premium payor. **Death proceeds** include the policy face amount and any additional insurance amounts paid by reason of the insured's death, such as accidental death benefits and the face amount of any paid-up additional insurance or any term rider.

Exceptions to Section 101(a)(1) Treatment

The general rule is simple, but it has complicating exceptions. These exceptions are discussed next.

Transfer for Value Rule   If a life insurance policy or any interest in a policy is transferred to another person for a valuable consideration, death proceeds can lose their tax-exempt status [IRC §101(a)(2)], in whole or in part. The excess of (1) the gross death proceeds over (2) the consideration paid plus net premiums paid would be taxable to the beneficiary as ordinary income. The amount of the consideration paid plus all net premiums paid by the transferee (the person to whom the policy or interest was transferred) may be recovered income tax free on death. Thus, if Barbara sold (i.e., changed ownership) her $100,000 policy to Mabel for $3,000 and if Barbara died 10 years later with Mabel having paid $12,000 in premiums (net of dividends), the beneficiary would receive $15,000 tax free ($3,000 consideration plus $12,000 premiums paid), but the $85,000 balance is taxable.

The **transfer for value rule** applies to any transfer for a valuable consideration of a right to receive all or a part of the death proceeds of a life insurance policy. The most common situation in which the rule is invoked involves sales of policies. Thus, death proceeds collected by a viatical settlement firm are subject to this rule. The rule, however, is not limited to sales; it applies to any transfer involving a valuable consideration.

The following transactions are exempt from the transfer for value rule:

1. When the transfer is to the insured. (For example, a corporation sells its key person policy to the insured/key employee who resigns.)
2. When the transfer is to
   a. a partner of the insured,
   b. a partnership in which the insured is a partner, or
   c. a corporation in which the insured is an officer or shareholder.

3. Transfers that do not involve a tax basis change, including
   a. a tax-free corporate organization or reorganization or
   b. a bona fide gift.

Thus, irrespective of any earlier transfers for value, if ownership of the policy is acquired by the insured, death proceeds are income tax exempt (item 1 in the preceding list). Similarly, any transfer in connection with the business applications noted in items 2 and 3(a) results in death proceeds being income tax exempt. Finally, when a policy is transferred as a gift and not for a valuable consideration, death proceeds remain income tax exempt. Thus, a gift of a policy on one spouse's life to the other spouse through an absolute assignment falls outside the transfer for value rule.

Failure to Meet IRC Definition of Life Insurance IRC Section 7702 contains a definition of life insurance for purposes of determining whether a policy qualifies for favorable tax treatment. This definition is important for many reasons.

Background. As noted in earlier chapters, the design of life insurance policies in the United States underwent substantial change during the late 1970s and early 1980s. Sales presentations emphasized the high potential tax-deferred savings that individuals could accumulate through their life insurance policies, using illustrations predicated on the then high current interest rates. These new products raised significant questions as to the appropriateness of certain tax benefits that had been provided to traditional types of life insurance policies. In response, the Tax Equity and Fiscal Responsibility Act of 1982 (TEFRA) provided a definition of life insurance for flexible-premium products. Moreover, the taxation of annuities was modified to reduce incentives for their use as short-term investment vehicles.

The Deficit Reduction Act of 1984 greatly expanded and refined the provisions enacted by TEFRA. Specifically, the new law added Section 7702 to the IRC, which provided, for the first time, a federal, statutory definition of life insurance. It also modified the annuity taxation rules enacted by TEFRA to inhibit further the use of annuities as short-term investment vehicles. Failure of a policy to meet the definition results in the policy being treated as a combination of term insurance and a taxable side fund.

Traditional whole life policies generally contain an established actuarial relationship among premiums, cash values, and death benefits. With the development of flexible-premium policies, these relationships became more complex. Most early universal life policies were designed simply with a corridor of pure life insurance protection between the policy's cash value and the face amount, rather than incorporating a specific actuarial relationship. As a result, some universal life policies were established with cash values substantially in excess of the amount actuarially required to fund future policy charges, making them more like investments than life insurance.

Descriptions of alternative tests. To address this situation, Congress mandated that life insurance policies must be considered life insurance under applicable state law and meet one of two quantitative tests. Whichever test is chosen, that test must be met for the entire life of the contract.

The first test applies mainly to traditional cash-value policies. This **cash-value accumulation test** requires that the cash surrender value cannot at any time exceed the net single premium required to fund future contract benefits. The net single premium is calculated using interest at the greater of 4 percent or the rate guaranteed in the contract. The mortality charges are based on those specified in the contract, or, if not specified, the mortality charges used in determining the contract's statutory reserves. For contracts issued after October 20, 1988, the mortality charges must be reasonable and cannot exceed those of the prevailing mortality table required by the state insurance regulators.

The second test, intended for universal life and related policies, requires the policy to meet both a guideline premium and a cash-value corridor requirement. The **guideline premium requirement** is met if the cumulative premiums paid under the contract do not at any time exceed the greater of the guideline single premiums or the sum of the guideline level premiums at that time. The **guideline single premium** is computed using interest at the greater rate of 6 percent or the rate guaranteed in the contract. Mortality charges are based on the same standard as applies in the cash-value accumulation test. The **guideline level premium** is computed in a manner similar to the guideline single premium, except that the minimum interest rate is 4 percent rather than 6 percent.

The **cash-value corridor requirement** is met if the policy's death benefit at all times is at least equal to certain percentage multiples of the cash value. These percentages range from 250 percent for insureds of attained ages up to 40, grading to 100 percent for attained age 95. Table 13-1 shows applicable percentages for various ages. Thus, if a 35-year-old owns a policy whose cash value is $10,000, the policy death benefit must be at least $25,000 ($10,000 × 250 percent) for the policy to meet the corridor requirement.

The law requires that the policy maturity age must be assumed to be between ages 95 and 100. Thus, policies endowing before age 95 do not qualify as life insurance under the IRC. This requirement effectively killed endowment sales in the United States. The law generally applies to policies issued after December 31, 1984.

Consequences of failing to meet the definition. Failure to meet the IRC definition excludes the cash-value portion of a life insurance policy from the favorable IRC Section 101(a)(1) treatment—that is, the cash-value portion is not treated as death proceeds. The net amount at risk in such policies does, however, qualify for Section 101(a)(1) treatment. As explained later, "living proceeds" also incur adverse tax consequences from a failure to meet the definition.

Miscellaneous Other highly specific reasons can cause life insurance death proceeds to be taxed, wholly or partly. It appears that a lack of insurable interest at the time of policy issuance will cause the contract to be considered a wager, and, therefore, death proceeds received in excess of net premiums paid would be taxable as ordinary income. Whether an insurable interest existed would be determined under the applicable state law (see chapter 9). Also, state law would determine whether any proceeds would be paid.

TABLE 13-1 IRC Section 7702 Corridor Requirements at Selected Ages			
Insured's Attained Age at Beginning of Contract Year		**Percentage Decreases Ratably**	
Greater Than	**Not More Than**	**From**	**To**
0	40	250	250
40	45	250	215
45	50	215	185
50	55	185	150
55	60	150	130
60	65	130	120
65	70	120	115
70	75	115	105
75	90	105	105
90	95	105	100

Other situations that can invite income taxation include the following:

- proceeds received under a qualified pension or profit-sharing plan
- proceeds received by a creditor from life insurance on the debtor/insured's life
- proceeds received as corporate dividends or compensation
- proceeds received as alimony
- proceeds received as restitution of embezzled funds

Finally, death proceeds payable to a corporation may attract ordinary income tax treatment via the corporate **alternative minimum tax** (AMT), a tax that is intended to ensure that no taxpayer with substantial economic income avoids tax liability. Whether the tax is due hinges on so-called tax preference items. Tax preference items are, in general, amounts that accrue to the corporation but are not included in its regular taxable income. In effect, certain tax preference items that may escape inclusion in a taxpayer's regular taxable income are added to that regular income to derive an *alternative minimum taxable income* (AMTI). The AMT tax rate of 20 percent and exemption applied to the AMTI yield the AMT. Any positive difference between the AMT and the tax due on the regular taxable income must be paid in addition to the normal tax.

Life insurance death proceeds received by a corporation and increases in policy cash values are tax preference items and, thus, could give rise to an AMT situation. The AMT could apply when (1) a policy's yearly cash-value increase exceeds that year's net premium or (2) death proceeds paid exceed the policy's cash-value. If life insurance death proceeds or cash values are expected to provoke the AMT, consideration should be given to having the insurance owned outside the corporation.

Tax Treatment of Settlement Options

The favorable income tax treatment of life insurance death proceeds is unaffected by election of a settlement option, although income taxes may be due on any interest paid on the death proceeds. Thus, under the interest option, interest received by the beneficiary is taxable as ordinary income. Interest retained by the insurer also is taxable unless the beneficiary cannot withdraw either principal or interest for a stated time period. At the end of the time period, all accrued untaxed interest is taxable.

Under the installment and life income settlement options, each payment is deemed to be composed of part principal and part interest. The portion deemed to be a return of principal is not taxed. The procedure for deriving this portion is to calculate an *amount held by the insurer* (usually, the single-sum amount payable at the insured's death) and prorate this amount over the actual or expected payment period. Amounts in excess of the annual prorated principal are treated as interest and are taxable income to the recipient.

To derive the prorated amount excludable as a return of principal under the fixed-period option, the amount held by the insurer is divided by the number of installments within the fixed period. The excess of each payment over this amount is deemed interest income. Thus, if $100,000 of death proceeds is paid over a 10-year fixed period and the payments are $15,000 per year, $10,000 ($100,000 divided by 10 years) is excluded from yearly taxable income as being a return of principal.

The procedure to derive the excludable amount of each payment under the fixed-amount option entails dividing the amount held by the insurer by the number of payments required to exhaust the principal at the guaranteed interest rate. The amount of each payment in excess of this figure is deemed to be interest. Payments made beyond the guaranteed period are considered to be interest only and, therefore, fully taxable.

Under the life income settlement options, the amount held by the insurer is divided by the recipient's life expectancy, as determined by IRS-prescribed mortality tables, to derive the excludable portion of each payment. If the life income option contains a refund feature or guaranteed minimum number of installments, the amount held by the insurer is reduced by a factor intended to represent the actuarial value of the refund or guarantee feature. The insurer furnishes this figure.

For example, assume $100,000 of death proceeds is paid under the life income option with a 10-year period certain. The beneficiary is a 60-year-old male with a life expectancy, according to the IRS's mortality table, of 24.2 years. The insurer advises that the actuarial value of the 10-year, period-certain feature is 8 percent of the amount held by the insurer. Stated differently, the contingent beneficiary's interest in the payments is valued at 8 percent of the total because there is a chance that the primary beneficiary might die during the 10-year period. Thus, the $100,000 proceeds would be reduced by 8 percent to $92,000, which, when divided by the 24.2-year life expectancy, yields $3,802, the amount excludable annually as return of principal. The same exclusion amounts apply for as long as the payments are made to the primary beneficiary, even beyond the individual's life expectancy.

Living Proceeds

Of course, proceeds payable by reason of the death of the insured apply exclusively to life insurance policies. Life, health, and annuity contracts can involve payments during the insured's lifetime. We discuss each type of insurance separately.

Payments under Life Insurance Policies

Living proceeds payable under life insurance policies can include dividends, cash values, matured endowments, policy loans, and accelerated death benefits. We cover each here, but first we need introduce another important IRC definition.

The Definition of Modified Endowment Contracts   A **modified endowment contract** (MEC) is a life insurance policy entered into after June 20, 1988, which meets the IRC Section 7702 definition of life insurance as discussed earlier, but that fails to meet the so-called seven-pay test. A MEC is subject to tax rules that differ from non-MEC life insurance policies. The IRC was amended to include this differential tax treatment because of the practice of many insurers selling single-premium whole life policies more as tax-deferred savings instruments than as policies providing protection against the financial consequences of premature death.

A life insurance policy fails to satisfy the **seven-pay test** if the cumulative amount paid under the contract at any time during the first seven contract years exceeds the cumulative amount that would have been paid had the policy's annual premium equaled the net level premium for a seven-pay life policy. The seven level premiums are determined at policy issuance, and the policy death benefit is taken to be that of the first contract year, irrespective of any scheduled benefit decreases.

Certain living benefits payable under a MEC are taxed more as an annuity (discussed later) than as otherwise qualifying life insurance. The tax treatment of death benefits is unaffected by whether a policy is a MEC. We now employ this definition to examine the tax treatment of life policy components.

Dividends   Dividends are normally considered a nontaxable return of excess premiums. This result is unaffected by the dividend option selected. If dividends are left to accumulate at interest, the interest credited on the accumulation is, of course, taxable.

Two exceptions exist to this general rule. First, if the policy is a MEC or fails to meet the IRC definition of life insurance, dividends are taxable, unless they are used to purchase paid-up additional insurance. Also, dividends payable under a MEC may be subject to an additional 10 percent penalty tax. Second, if the total of the dividends received under a non-MEC policy exceeds the total of the premiums paid, all dividend amounts received in excess of the sum of premiums paid constitute ordinary income.

Cash Values   Tax consequences attach to a policy's cash value. We discuss three consequences next.

Interest on cash value.   The interest credited to a life insurance policy's cash value is not currently taxable if the policy meets the IRC definition of life insurance. This favorable tax treatment applies also to MECs. If a policy fails to meet the IRC definition, a portion of the year's cash-value increase will be subject to ordinary income taxation if the year's benefits under the policy exceed the premiums paid during that year. "Benefits" are the sum of (1) the year's cash-value increase, (2) the value of pure life insurance protection, and (3) dividends received. The value of the pure life insurance protection is determined by multiplying the net amount at risk by the lesser of (1) the applicable IRS uniform premium rate or (2) the mortality charge, if any, stated in the contract.

If a life insurance policy meets the test originally but later fails to do so, all prior years' deferred income is included in the taxpayer's/policyowner's gross income in the year when the policy first fails to meet the test. The policyowner relies on the life insurance company to ensure that this does not occur.

Debate continues over whether sound public policy should permit the tax-advantaged inside interest buildup within life insurance policies. Critics claim that this favorable tax treatment is unjustified as it distorts the savings market, making life insurance products artificially more attractive than other savings instruments. They also note that the government loses tax revenues because of this tax favoritism and that "corrective" measures must be regularly adopted in an effort to minimize life insurance purchasers taking undue advantage of this tax favoritism.

Proponents of the status quo point to the socially worthwhile benefits of life insurance, arguing that the current tax treatment provides reasonable safeguards against abuse while encouraging families to make provisions for their financial security. They also note that the income may not actually be received by the policyowner unless the policy is surrendered, much as the homeowner does not actually receive his or her home's appreciated value without selling the home. (Tax economists would counter that this value should also be taxed.)

The U.S. General Accounting Office (GAO) concluded that the tax preference may encourage savings and long-term capital formation via life insurance companies but not for the entire economy.[1] The GAO concluded that only one argument for maintaining the current tax preference had potential merit—that of providing for one's dependents.

Cash surrender payments.   The general rule for taxation of lump-sum cash surrender value payments on life insurance policies is the **cost recovery rule** under which the amount included in the policyowner's gross income upon policy surrender is the excess of the gross proceeds received over the cost basis. The **cost basis** of a life insurance contract normally is the sum of the premiums paid less the sum of any dividends received in cash or credited against the premiums. **Gross proceeds** are the amounts paid on surrender, including the cash value of any paid-up additions and the value of dividends accumulated at interest.

For example, assume that Rebecca's $100,000 ordinary life policy, issued 20 years ago, carries an annual premium of $1,300 and has a cash surrender value of $30,000. The

---

[1] *Tax Treatment of Life Insurance and Annuity Accrued Interest* (Washington, DC: GAO, 1990), pp. 38–43.

sum of all dividends over the 20-year period is $19,000. If Rebecca surrendered the policy, the amount subject to ordinary income tax treatment would be calculated as follows:

	Sum of premiums paid	$26,000
Less:	Sum of dividends received	−19,000
Equals:	Cost basis	$ 7,000
	Gross proceeds	$30,000 (cash surrender value)
Less:	Cost basis	−7,000
Equals:	Taxable gain	$23,000

Premiums paid for supplementary benefits such as the waiver of premium and accidental death benefit features are not a part of the basis. Premiums waived under a waiver-of-premium feature, logically, should be included in the cost basis as the benefit is economically equivalent to disability income benefits. (Apparently the tax court disagrees.[2]) If policy loans are outstanding on surrender, the net surrender value (cash surrender value less loan) constitutes the gross proceeds, but the cost basis is lowered by the loan amounts previously received.

The cost basis of a life insurance policy includes the pure cost of insurance. Theoretically, yearly mortality charges, which exist with every life insurance policy, should be excluded from the basis as representing current expenditure and not an investment. Thus, taxable income to the policyowner technically is understated by the value of these mortality charges.

Losses on surrender of a life insurance policy normally cannot be recognized for income tax purposes. The rationale for disallowing a deductible loss is that the method for computing taxable gain (and loss) makes no allowance for mortality charges. Therefore, any loss is assumed to be composed, in whole or in part, of such mortality costs.

The cost recovery rule generally applies to life insurance cash-value withdrawals and partial surrenders. Thus, using our previous example about Rebecca, assume that she withdraws $5,000 in cash value from her policy while continuing the policy. As the cost basis is $7,000, the entire $5,000 is received income tax free. The withdrawal lowers her basis to $2,000.

Exceptions occur for cash distributions under MECs and as a result of certain policyowner-initiated reductions in policy benefits or withdrawals. In these latter situations, the distribution can be taxed as ordinary income to the extent untaxed income exists in the contract. Distributions under a MEC (and also under annuities, discussed later) are subject to the *interest first rule* meaning that they are taxable as income to the extent that the cash value of the contract immediately before the payment exceeds the contract's cost basis. Additionally, a 10 percent penalty tax may apply to distributions prior to age 59½.

Policy exchanges. The policyowner undertaking a replacement can avoid what otherwise would be a taxable gain if the replacement qualifies as an IRC Section 1035 policy exchange. To qualify, the exchange must be of

- a life insurance policy for another life insurance policy or endowment or annuity contract;
- an endowment for an annuity contract or another endowment of no greater maturity date than the replaced endowment; or
- an annuity for another annuity.

In such situations, any gain is rolled into the new contract and no gain need be recognized on replacement. The new policy's cost basis is adjusted to include the basis of

---

[2] *Estate of Wong Wing Non v. Comm.,* 18 TC 205 (1952).

the old policy. The distinction between (1) an exchange and (2) a surrender and purchase is not always clear. Several IRS private letter rulings suggest that, in general, the contract to be replaced should be assigned to the replacing insurance company, without the policyowner actually receiving any surrender value proceeds.

Matured Endowments   Living proceeds received from a matured endowment are taxed the same as proceeds received on policy surrender, that is, the cost recovery rule—assuming, of course, that the policy meets the IRC definition (or is grandfathered) and is not a MEC. The cost basis is subtracted from the gross proceeds to derive taxable income.

Policy Loans   Policyowners can secure policy loans on the security of the policy's cash value. The interest rate charged or the method used to derive the interest rate is stated in the contract.

Interest payments.   Policy loan interest paid by individuals, as with other personal loans, is not tax deductible. Policy loan interest paid on policies owned by a business and covering the lives of **key persons,** defined as officers and 20 percent owners, may be deductible, subject to certain conditions. Deductions are allowed only for loans on policies covering key persons and for loan amounts of less than $50,000 per individual insured. The $50,000 limitation does not apply to policies purchased prior to June 21, 1986. The total number of key persons within a business for whom policy loan interest can be deductible may not exceed the greater of (1) five or (2) the lesser of 5 percent of the total officers or 20 individuals.

This business-related deduction does not hold when policy loans are used to finance life insurance under a systematic plan of borrowing. This rule applies only to contracts purchased after August 6, 1963, and contains four exceptions. The most important exception is the **four-in-seven exception,** under which a deduction is allowed if no part of at least four of the first seven annual premiums due on a policy is paid through borrowing, either from the policy or elsewhere. If borrowing in any year exceeds the premium for that year, the excess is considered to be borrowing used to finance the previous year's premium. Thus, the four-in-seven test is violated if policyowner borrowing during the seven-year period exceeds an amount equal to three years' premiums, irrespective of when the borrowing takes place during the period. The four premiums can be paid in any order. It appears that, once the seven-year requirement has been satisfied, borrowing beyond that period can be at any level.

The loan payment.   The general rule is that taking a loan under a life insurance policy does not, in itself, constitute a taxable distribution. If the contract is a MEC (or an annuity), however, policy loans are themselves taxable as income to the extent that the cash value of the contract immediately before the payment exceeds the contract's costs basis. The 10 percent penalty tax may also apply if the loan is taken out before the insured reaches age 59½.

A potential tax trap.   A non-MEC life insurance policy under which substantial loans are outstanding can constitute a tax trap for the ill-informed. Recall that policy loans reduce a policy's cost basis. For policies carrying large loans, the net cash surrender value (cash surrender value less loan) can be quite small. Upon surrender, the owner would receive a check for the small net cash value. At the same time, the owner could face a monumental tax bill because of the negative cost basis. This pitfall can be especially cruel if the surrender occurs because of financial reverses.

Accelerated Death Benefits   As discussed in chapter 8, some life insurance policies allow payment of a portion or all of the death benefit if the insured is terminally or chronically ill. The general rule is that accelerated death benefits payable in connection with a *terminally* ill insured will be treated as amounts paid "by reason of the death of the insured" and, therefore, received income tax free. To qualify, a physician must certify that the insured's illness or physical condition can reasonably be expected to result in death within 24 months. This same tax treatment and conditions apply to amounts received *from* a viatical settlement firm in connection with its purchasing a policy on a terminally ill insured.

Payments under Health Insurance Policies

The income tax treatment of amounts paid under individual health insurance policies is reasonably straightforward. Generally, amounts received under such policies are amounts received for personal injuries and sickness and are treated as reimbursement for expenses incurred.

The income tax treatment of long-term care benefits, including accelerated death benefits payable under a life insurance policy because of an insured's chronic illness, is more complex. Generally, fixed amounts received in excess of a per diem limitation are included in taxable income. The per diem limitation is the *greater* of $175 (indexed) or the actual costs incurred for qualified long-term care. A chronically ill person is one who is not terminally ill and has been certified by a licensed health care practitioner as being unable to perform at least two activities of daily living for at least 90 days. A person suffering a severe cognitive impairment also can qualify.

Payments under Annuities

Annuity tax rules have become more stringent over the years in an effort to discourage the use of annuities as short-term, tax-deferred investments rather than as long-term, retirement-funding vehicles. Tax law defines an annuity as any periodic payment resulting from the systematic liquidation of a principal sum. Both annuities certain and life annuities are included in this definition. Tax treatment varies depending on whether living proceeds are paid during the accumulation or liquidation period.

Tax Treatment during the Accumulation Period   In general, interest credited to the cash values of personally owned annuities accumulates tax deferred. This means that, with the exceptions noted later, the contract owner need not include this interest income in his or her gross income until such time as annuity liquidation begins.

Dividends paid, cash-value withdrawals, loans, and amounts received on partial surrender of an annuity, however, are taxable as ordinary income to the extent that the contract cash value exceeds the cost basis; that is, the interest first rule applies, as with MECS. The balance is received as a recovery of investment and is tax free.

Not only must post-1982 annuities and contributions follow this rule, but a further 10 percent penalty tax is imposed on taxable payments. The penalty does not apply in certain circumstances, including but not limited to (1) a series of substantially equal lifetime periodic payments, (2) any payments made to the taxpayer who is at least 59½ years old, (3) any payments under tax-qualified retirement plans, and (4) any payment attributable to the taxpayer's disability or death.

Tax Treatment during the Liquidation Period   The rules for taxation of annuity payments are identical in principle to those discussed earlier with respect to life insurance settlement options. Therefore, emphasis will be placed here only on the differences.

An exclusion ratio must be derived. The **exclusion ratio** is the ratio of the investment in the contract to the expected return under the contract. The ratio is multiplied by the amount of each guaranteed payment to yield the amount of each annuity payment excluded from gross income. The **investment in the contract** normally is the premiums paid net of dividends received and not previously taxed. Under settlement options, the death proceeds constitute the contract investment. The **expected return** of the contract is, in general, the total amount that the annuitant can expect to receive under the contract.

The tax treatment of the fixed-period and fixed-amount annuity options is the same as that of the equivalent settlement option. The tax treatment of the life income options is the equivalent of that of the life income settlement options.

FEDERAL ESTATE TAX TREATMENT

Besides income taxes, insurance proceeds can be subject to death-related taxes, the most important of which in the United States is the federal estate tax. Thus, we must ensure an understanding of federal estate tax law, the provisions of which often are unfamiliar to many individuals. Chapter 16 builds on this information as it examines how life insurance is useful in estate planning.

Overview of Federal Estate Tax

The federal estate tax is a tax on a person's right to transfer property on his or her death. Although not a tax on the property itself, it is calculated on the value of such property. The tax, introduced at a modest level in 1916, can be of great importance in large estates. Generally, a federal estate tax return must be filed and any estate taxes paid within nine months of the death of any U.S. citizen or resident who leaves a gross estate of more than a specified exempted amount. The exempted amount, which had been $600,000 for many years, increases in an erratic way to $1 million for deaths occurring in the year 2006 and later, as shown in Figure 13-1. An extension of up to 10 years for payment of the taxes may

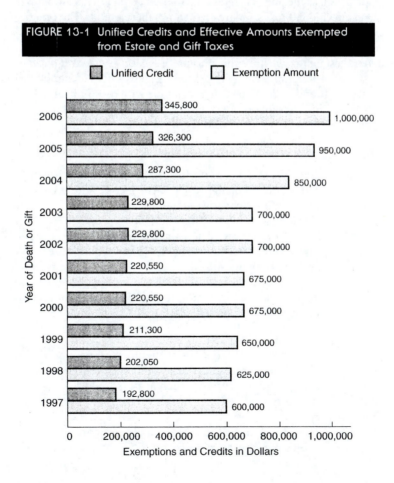

FIGURE 13-1 Unified Credits and Effective Amounts Exempted from Estate and Gift Taxes

be granted by the IRS for "reasonable cause," including taxes associated with certain closely held businesses.

The federal estate tax is a graduated tax, starting at 18 percent and building to a 55 percent marginal rate for taxable amounts over $3.0 million. An additional 5 percent tax applies to estates in the $10,000,000 to $21,040,000 range as representing a phase-out of the graduated rates and the exempted amount.

The first step in calculating the federal estate tax is to measure the value of the decedent's gross estate. The **gross estate** is, roughly, the value of all property or interests in property owned or controlled by the deceased person.

Next, allowable deductions are subtracted from the gross estate, resulting in the *taxable estate*. *Allowable deductions* include funeral and administration expenses, debts of the decedent, as well as bequests to charities and the surviving spouse. The gross estate less all allowable deductions except bequests to the surviving spouse and to charities is referred to as the **adjusted gross estate.**

To the taxable estate is added adjusted taxable gifts, which are taxable gifts made after 1976, to yield the *tentative tax base*. The reason for this addition is that the estate tax law is part of a so-called unified transfer tax law that applies to transfers made at death and during life. It is necessary to add the value of lifetime taxable transfers (gifts) back to the tax base to derive the appropriate marginal tax bracket.

The appropriate tax rate is then applied to the tentative tax base to derive the *tentative federal estate tax*. From this tentative tax is subtracted certain credits for gift and other taxes paid as well as the unified credit. The **unified credit** is a tax credit that can be applied to offset estate and gift taxes. Figure 13-1 shows these credits. The practical effect of the unified credit is to eliminate transfer taxes on total lifetime and testamentary transfers in the amounts shown in Figure 13-1. After applying all applicable credits against the tentative federal estate tax, we have the amount of *federal estate taxes owed*.

Table 13-2 summarizes the preceding steps. The relevant items that compose the category are found under each category, along with the applicable IRC section. The balance of this section presents more detailed information regarding the federal estate tax, beginning with an elaboration of the gross estate.

The Gross Estate

The gross estate, the starting point for estate tax computation, is composed of the value of the decedent's interest in all property. The gross estate is derived by summing the values of each of the categories shown under the heading "Gross Estate" in Table 13-2. Some are reviewed briefly here. Outright ownership of property is not required for its value to be included in the gross estate. The value for estate tax purposes is the fair market value of the property at the date of death or, if a lower estate value would result (e.g., because of investment losses), six months after death—the so-called **alternate valuation date.** A penalty of from 10 to 30 percent of the amount of tax owed can be imposed by the IRS for undervaluation. Special valuation rules are available for real property used for farming and other business purposes.

Property Owned by the Decedent

Property owned by the decedent includes all property of the decedent passing by will or by the state's intestacy laws if the decedent died without a valid will. Thus, the value of all personal property, such as personal effects, automobiles, and jewelry, and of real property, such as one's home, vacant land, and business, are included within this category.

For most persons, this is the largest single category of the gross estate. If the decedent had owned a life insurance policy on someone else's life (i.e., the decedent was *not*

TABLE 13-2 Federal Estate Tax Computation

Gross Estate	−	Allowable Deductions	=	Taxable Estate	+	Adjusted Taxable Gifts	=	Tentative Tax Base	×	Tax Rate	=	Tentative FET	−	Credits	=	Federal Estate Tax
Owned property (Sec. 2033)		Funeral expenses [Sec. 2053 (a)(1)]				Gifts made after 1976 that are not other- wise includable in the gross estate, net of annual exclu- sions taken [Sec. 2001(b)]				See Table 13-3 [Sec. 2001(c)]				Unified credit (Sec. 2010)		
Dower and courtesy interests (Sec. 2034)		Administration expenses [Sec. 2053(a)(2)]												State death taxes paid (Sec. 2011) See Table 13-4		
Gifts within three years of death (Sec. 2035)		Claims against estate [Sec. 2053(a)(3)]												Gift taxes paid (Sec. 2012)		
Gifts with life interest retained (Sec. 2036)		Mortgages and other debts [Sec. 2053(a)(4)]												Federal estate taxes on previous transfers (Sec. 2013)		
Gifts taking effect at death (Sec. 2037)		Unreimbursed casualty and theft losses (Sec. 2054)												Foreign death taxes paid (Sec. 2014)		
Revocable gifts (Sec. 2038)		Charitable, public, and religious bequests (Sec. 2055)														
Annuities (Sec. 2039)		Bequests to surviving spouse (Sec. 2056)														
Joint interests (Sec. 2040)																
Powers of appointment (Sec. 2041)																
Life insurance death proceeds (Sec. 2042)																
Transfers for insuffi- cient consideration (Sec. 2043)																
Certain marital deduction property (Sec. 2044)																

the insured), its interpolated terminal reserve plus any unearned premiums for the policy would be included in the decedent's gross estate.

Certain Gifts

The IRC provides that the value of certain classes of gifts also must be included in the gross estate. They fall into four categories.

First, the value of certain gifts (Section 2035) made by the decedent within three years of his or her death is added back to the gross estate. These include transfers in which the donor/decedent had retained certain interest in or power over the gifted property and gifts of life insurance policies. Gift taxation is discussed later.

Second, the value of gifts with a life interest retained (Section 2036) is added back to the gross estate. Such gifts are those in which the decedent gifted property to someone but retained for life the right to receive income from the property, the right to use the property, or the right to designate who ultimately receives the property or income. For example, if Sarah gave her house to Blake but retained the right to live in the house for the rest of her life, this IRC section requires that the value of the house be included in Sarah's gross estate.

Third, the value of gifts taking effect at death (Section 2037) may be included in the gross estate. A gift-taking effect at death occurs when property is given to someone (in trust or otherwise) but with the stipulation that he or she may take possession or enjoyment of it only upon the donor's death. If the likelihood of the gift reverting to the donor immediately before death is greater than 5 percent, the entire value is included in the gross estate. For example, assume that John established a trust for his granddaughter, Kay, with the trust corpus (assets) to be paid to her on his death, but if she predeceased him, the corpus is to revert to him. If the chance that he would survive Kay were greater than 5 percent, the value of the entire gift would be included in his gross estate.

Fourth, gifts wherein the decedent retained the power to alter, amend, revoke, or terminate the gift are revocable gifts (Section 203) and their value is included in the gross estate.

Annuities

If a decedent was receiving annuity payments at his or her death—either from purchase of an annuity or under a life insurance policy settlement option—and if those payments ceased at the annuitant's death, no property interest exists to include in the gross estate. However, as we know, annuity and settlement option payments often provide a guaranteed income feature. If income (or other) payments are to be made to another person on the annuitant's death, the present value of those survivor benefits might be included in the estate.

Survivor benefits are included in a decedent's gross estate to the extent that the decedent paid for the contract. Thus, if the decedent paid *no* part of the contract purchase price, the entire value of the survivor benefits is *excluded* from the gross estate. If the decedent paid the full contract purchase price, the opposite result occurs. If the decedent paid only a portion of the purchase price, that proportionate share of the survivor benefit is included in the gross estate.

For example, if Martin contributed the full $50,000 toward the purchase of a joint and last survivor annuity and the value of the survivor benefit on his death was determined to be $40,000, the entire $40,000 is included in his estate. If Martin had paid one-fourth of the purchase price, $10,000 is included, and so on.

The cash value of an annuity during its accumulation period is included in the decedent's estate under this code section if, and to the extent that, the decedent made contributions toward its purchase.

Joint Interest Property

Property owned jointly during lifetime by the deceased person and someone else, referred to as *joint interest property* under the IRC, is included, in whole or in part, in the decedent's gross estate. The extent to which this property is included is a function of the nature of the ownership interest. Although state variations exist, four types of joint ownership are commonly found.

Property is held in **joint tenancy with right of survivorship** when it is owned by two or more persons and, on the death of any owner, his or her ownership interest passes automatically to the survivors. Ownership is not vested in the individuals but in the owners as a group. As such, 100 percent of the property's value is included in the decedent's gross estate, except to the extent that the survivors contributed to the property's purchase. Thus, if Inbum's estate, on whom the burden rests, can prove survivors contributed $80,000 toward a $100,000 property purchase price, only 20 percent of the property's current value would be included in his estate. Under a joint tenancy, the decedent's heirs have no claims against the property; the surviving owners continue to be the sole owners, but as a group. Ownership interest arising from a joint tenancy cannot be passed by will.

A **tenancy by the entirety** is a joint ownership of property created between spouses only. As with the joint tenancy, it provides a right of survivorship. Unlike the joint tenancy, however, the property is deemed to be owned 50 percent by each spouse, irrespective of who contributed the purchase price. Thus, 50 percent of the then property value is included in the gross estate of the first spouse to die. Ownership interest does not pass by will but by the nature of the ownership.

A **tenancy in common** is a joint-ownership arrangement wherein each member owns his or her share outright. Ownership interest can be passed to heirs by will. On the death of a member of a tenancy in common, his or her proportionate share is included in the gross estate.

The fourth form of joint ownership, **community property,** establishes that property acquired during marriage is the property of the marriage community. On the death of one spouse, one-half of the property value is included automatically in the decedent's estate, irrespective of the proportion of the purchase price paid by the decedent. Rules pertaining to community property law vary greatly from state to state. Eight U.S. states (Arizona, California, Idaho, Louisiana, Nevada, New Mexico, Texas, and Washington) have community property laws. Wisconsin adopted a marital property system in 1986 that is similar to community property in many respects.

Power of Appointment

If a decedent held a general power of appointment over property on his or her death, the value of the property is included in the gross estate. A **general power of appointment** exists when an individual has the right to dispose of property that he or she does not own, including giving it to himself or herself. For example, Daniel may be receiving a lifetime income under a trust and have the power to withdraw all or a portion of the trust corpus during his lifetime. This right to invade the trust corpus is a general power of appointment and will cause the entire value of the trust to be included in Daniel's gross estate on death, even though he may never have actually exercised the withdrawal right.

Property over which an individual has a general power of appointment will not be included in the gross estate if the holder's right to consume or invade the property is limited by certain defined standards, such as those relating to his or her health, maintenance, education, or support. Also, a **special power of appointment,** wherein the individual has the power to appoint anyone other than himself or herself or his or her estate or creditors to receive property, does not cause property to be included in the gross estate.

Life Insurance

IRC Section 2042 provides that life insurance death proceeds are included in a decedent's gross estate for federal estate tax purposes if either of these two conditions applies:

- the proceeds are payable to or for the benefit of the insured's estate or
- the insured possessed, at death, any incidents of ownership in the policy.

Thus, even if the insured did not own the policy, death proceeds are included in the gross estate if the estate is the beneficiary. Also, proceeds payable not "to," but "for" the benefit of the decedent's estate are included in the gross estate. For example, if Glen, as the owner and beneficiary of a $250,000 policy on Thelma's life, collaterally assigns the policy to a bank to cover her loan of $100,000, the $100,000 death proceeds utilized to extinguish the estate's debt is included in Thelma's estate even though Glen was both owner and beneficiary of the policy.

If the deceased insured possessed no incidents of ownership in the policy and if proceeds are not payable to or for the benefit of the estate, proceeds escape inclusion in the gross estate under this IRC section (although other sections occasionally result in their inclusion). Incidents of ownership include the right to change the beneficiary, the right to surrender or otherwise terminate the policy, the right to assign the policy, the right to obtain a policy loan, and, in general, the ability to exercise any important right of the policy. Complete policy ownership certainly will cause death proceeds to be included in the estate, but possession of only one important policy right causes the entire proceeds to be included in the gross estate.

A policy can be removed from the gross estate, even though the insured was the owner, if it is given or sold to someone else via absolute assignment (and provided proceeds are not payable to or for the benefit of the estate). If the ownership transfer is via gift and occurs within three years of the date of death, however, the policy proceeds will be included in the gross estate as a gift made within three years of death (IRC Section 2035).

Miscellaneous

Certain other interests are included in the gross estate: (1) dower and courtesy interests (Section 2034) and (2) certain marital deduction property (Section 2044). A dower (for the wife) or a curtesy (for the husband) is a statutory requirement directing that a surviving spouse must receive at least a certain minimum proportion of the estate of the deceased spouse.

Transfers for insufficient considerations (Section 2043) are included in the gross estate. They are transfers wherein the amount paid for property was below fair market value (e.g., deAnn sold her business to Bettie, her daughter, for below fair market value). The excess of the fair market value over the consideration received is included.

The Taxable Estate

After deriving the gross estate value, the next step is to derive the taxable estate—the gross estate less deductions. IRC Sections 2053 to 2056 define these deductions. Each of these sections is discussed later.

Expenses, Debts, and Claims

Deductions are permitted for the cost of the decedent's funeral and for the expenses associated with the administration of the estate. These latter expenses include items such as appraisal fees, attorney's fees, and executor's commissions.

Claims against the estate—such as those arising from unpaid property, income, and other taxes owed prior to death—are deductible. Indebtedness of the decedent can be deducted provided the asset, if any, to which the indebtedness applies is included in the estate. Thus, mortgage and auto loan balances at the time of death are deductible. Other debts such as those arising from consumer loans and credit card balances are also deductible provided the decedent is legally responsible for their payment.

Unreimbursed Losses

Casualty and theft losses incurred during estate settlement are deductible from the gross estate. If the loss is indemnified by insurance or otherwise, only the net loss is deductible.

Charitable and Related Transfers

Property left to qualified religious, charitable, scientific, literary, and educational organizations as well as property left to foster amateur sports competition and the prevention of cruelty to children or animals is deductible. Additionally, bequests to qualified veterans' organizations are deductible.

Family-Owned Business Interests

A recent addition to the IRC eases the estate tax burden for qualified family-owned businesses, making it easier to keep the business in the family. To qualify for this special deduction, the decedent must have materially participated and owned the business and a family member must do likewise afterward. Certain minimum time periods apply. The executor must elect the additional deduction. The estate may exclude the lesser of (1) the value of the business interest or (2) the excess of $1.3 million over the usual exemption amount. For example, for deaths occurring in the year 2000, the executor could exclude up to $625,000 of the business interest plus the $675,000 exemption amount.

To qualify, the business interest must comprise at least 50 percent of the adjusted gross estate. A *qualified family-owned business interest* is defined as any trade or business with its principal place of business in the United States, which is owned at least 50 percent by one family, 70 percent by two families, or 90 percent by three families provided the decedent's family owned at least 30 percent.

Transfers to Surviving Spouse

The value of property left to a surviving spouse may be deducted as a **marital deduction.** If all property is left to the surviving spouse, the taxable estate is zero. For most marriages, this deduction is the most important.

Generally, only property that would be included in the surviving spouse's estate qualifies for the marital deduction. This requirement means that certain terminable interests in property left to the spouse will not qualify, such as a life-only interest in property. The IRC, however, in Section 2056, provides certain exceptions to the terminable interest rule. Perhaps the most important exception relates to **qualified terminable interest property** (QTIP), which is property passing from the decedent that meets these conditions:

- the surviving spouse is entitled to a lifetime income payable at least annually from the property,
- no one can appoint (e.g., by gift) any part of the property to anyone except the spouse during the spouse's lifetime, and
- the executor makes an irrevocable election to have the marital deduction apply.

Thus, a surviving spouse can be given a lifetime-only interest in property and have the value of the property taken as a deduction from the gross estate if these conditions are met. The spouse must receive income at least annually from the property and no one must be able to divert property ownership away from the spouse during his or her lifetime.

Tentative Tax Base

To the taxable estate is then added the value of adjusted taxable gifts to derive a tentative tax base. *Adjusted taxable gifts* are gifts made after 1976 (1) for which a gift tax return was filed, (2) which are not otherwise included in the decedent's gross estate, and (3) which are net of permitted annual gift exclusions.

The U.S. estate tax law is part of a transfer tax law that applies to both living and testamentary (i.e., death) transfers. This unified approach means that it is necessary to add back, for estate tax purposes, the value of property gifted during life that did not qualify for the annual exclusion. This permits the calculation of a transfer tax based on all taxable transfers, both living and testamentary. A credit is permitted (as discussed later) for previous gift taxes paid. This recalculation is necessary because transfer tax rates are progressive.

Individuals are permitted to give away annually up to $10,000 per donee (gift recipient) and not pay any gift tax or even file a return. If a spouse joins in the gift, up to $20,000 per donee annually may be given without incurring any gift tax. These figures are indexed for gifts made after 1998. Moreover, one spouse may give the other any amount and incur no transfer tax liability, as the unlimited marital deduction is available for such gifts.

The value of adjusted taxable gifts is the sum of all post-1976 gifts, net of exclusions and deductions. Also, unlike the taxes on incomplete gifts included in the gross estate, gift taxes paid on these adjusted gifts may be excluded from the gross estate. The value included in the tentative tax base is the property value at the time of the gift, not its fair market value at date of death.

Tentative Federal Estate Tax

To the tentative tax base is applied the appropriate federal estate tax rate to derive the tentative federal estate tax. Table 13-3 gives these transfer tax rates by bracket. If the tentative tax base is more than $10,000,000, an additional 5 percent marginal tax rate is applied up to a value of $21,040,000. This additional tax is intended to phase out the benefits of a graduated tax rate and of the unified credit.

Federal Estate Tax Owed

The actual federal estate tax owed is obtained by netting certain permissible credits against the tentative federal estate tax. The credits are discussed here.

Unified Transfer Tax Credit

U.S. tax law permits a substantial unified credit to be applied against estate (and gift) taxes otherwise due. This unified credit is applied on a cumulative basis to all lifetime and testamentary transfers. It applies as a dollar-for-dollar offset against the tax. Historically, the credit has been sufficient to avoid all estate taxes on a computational tax base of $600,000 or less. The credit will increase in the future to allow estate tax exemption in accordance with the amounts shown in Figure 13-1.

Credit for State Death Taxes Paid

States levy their own forms of death taxes. Federal law permits a credit to be taken against the federal estate tax for death taxes paid to states, subject to a maximum.

Table 13-4 shows maximum permissible credits. Some states do not levy taxes as high as the permissible federal credit. Such states typically utilize a *credit estate tax* which

TABLE 13-3 Federal Unified Transfer Tax Rates

If the Amount Is:		Tentative Tax			
Over	*But Not Over*	*Base Amount*	*+*	*Percent*	*On Excess Over*
$ 0	$ 10,000	$ 0		18%	$ 0
10,000	20,000	1,800		20%	10,000
20,000	40,000	3,800		22%	20,000
40,000	60,000	8,200		24%	40,000
60,000	80,000	13,000		26%	60,000
80,000	100,000	18,200		28%	80,000
100,000	150,000	23,800		30%	100,000
150,000	250,000	38,800		32%	150,000
250,000	500,000	70,800		34%	250,000
500,000	750,000	155,800		37%	500,000
750,000	1,000,000	248,300		39%	750,000
1,000,000	1,250,000	345,800		41%	1,000,000
1,250,000	1,500,000	448,300		43%	1,250,000
1,500,000	2,000,000	555,800		45%	1,500,000
2,000,000	2,500,000	780,800		49%	2,000,000
2,500,000	3,000,000	1,025,800		53%	2,500,000
3,000,000	10,000,000	1,290,800		55%	3,000,000
10,000,000	21,040,000	5,140,800		60%[a]	10,000,000
21,040,000		11,761,800		55%	21,040,000

[a]For post-1987 transfers between $10,000 and $21,040,000 there is a 5 percent surcharge.

TABLE 13-4	Maximum Credits for State Death Taxes		
If Tentative Tax Base:			
Is More Than	**But Does Not Exceed**	**The Maximum Credit Is**	
$ 0	$ 100,000		$ 0
100,000	150,000	$0 plus 0.8% of the excess over	100,000
150,000	200,000	$400 plus 1.6% of the excess over	150,000
200,000	300,000	$1,200 plus 2.4% of the excess over	200,000
300,000	500,000	$3,600 plus 3.2% of the excess over	300,000
500,000	700,000	$10,000 plus 4% of the excess over	500,000
700,000	900,000	$18,000 plus 4.8% of the excess over	700,000
900,000	1,100,000	$27,600 plus 5.6% of the excess over	900,000
1,100,000	1,600,000	$38,800 plus 6.4% of the excess over	1,100,000
1,600,000	2,100,000	$70,800 plus 7.2% of the excess over	1,600,000
2,100,000	2,600,000	$106,800 plus 8% of the excess over	2,100,000
2,600,000	3,100,000	$146,800 plus 8.8% of the excess over	2,600,000
3,100,000	3,600,000	$190,800 plus 9.6% of the excess over	3,100,000
3,600,000	4,100,000	$238,800 plus 10.4% of the excess over	3,600,000
4,100,000	5,100,000	$290,800 plus 11.2% of the excess over	4,100,000
5,100,000	6,100,000	$402,800 plus 12% of the excess over	5,100,000
6,100,000	7,100,000	$522,800 plus 12.8% of the excess over	6,100,000
7,100,000	8,100,000	$650,800 plus 13.6% of the excess over	7,100,000
8,100,000	9,100,000	$786,800 plus 14.4% of the excess over	8,100,000
9,100,000	10,100,000	$930,800 plus 15.2% of the excess over	9,100,000
10,100,000	No limit	$1,082,800 plus 16% of the excess over	10,100,000

stipulates that the state death tax is the greater of (1) the tax developed by applying the state's computational tax rules or (2) the maximum federal credit permitted.

Credit for Gift Taxes Paid

Taxes paid on previous gifts can be taken as a credit against the estate tax. This treatment is appropriate as the value of previous gifts is added back into the estate.

Other Credits

Two final credits are permitted. First, to prevent double taxation, a credit is allowed for death taxes paid to another country or U.S. possession if (1) the value of the property is included in the gross estate and (2) the property is situated in that other country or possession.

Second, occasionally a decedent leaves property and the heir dies within a short time of the first person's death. If estate taxes were paid on the property left to the heir, a part or all of that tax may be available as a credit against the estate tax bill of the second decedent. The permissible credit is a decreasing percentage of the estate tax paid on the first death transfer; thus,

- 100 percent if deaths occur within two years
- 80 percent if deaths occur within three or four years
- 60 percent if deaths occur within five or six years
- 40 percent if deaths occur within seven or eight years
- 20 percent if deaths occur within nine or ten years
- 0 percent if deaths occur ten or more years apart

Illustration

An illustration will help solidify the preceding points. Assume that Mike Magnus, aged 48 and a resident of the U.S. state of Georgia, dies in 2001, leaving behind his wife, Dawn, and their two children, Yoko and Cary, both adults. Table 13-5 shows the personal balance sheet for Mike and Dawn, including the nature of the ownership interests. Dawn is beneficiary under the annuity.

In addition to the assets shown in Table 13-5, Mike is the insured and owner of $100,000 of group life insurance. Dawn is beneficiary. Only two years earlier, Mike had transferred ownership of a $500,000 term life policy to Yoko, and she promptly named herself as beneficiary. Mike continued to pay premiums on the policy. Four years ago, Mike and Dawn had given $200,000 to Cary to help him start a landscaping business.

Mike's will provides that Dawn is to receive the common stock, the autos, and Mike's personal effects. It also provides (perhaps unwisely) that the mortgage loan is to be paid off. The real estate investment (a $1 million office complex) is to be held in trust for the children, with Dawn receiving the income from the investment for her lifetime. She is given no rights to alter this trust arrangement. Mike stipulated that Georgia State University is to receive $10,000 for its risk management and insurance program. The balance of the estate is to be divided equally between the two children. The values included in Mike's gross estate are summarized in Table 13-6, and allowable deductions are shown in Table 13-7.

Subtracting the value of the deductions ($1,100,000) from the gross estate ($2,610,000) reveals a taxable estate of $1,510,000. We must add the value of adjusted taxable gifts to this figure. The $500,000 term policy given to Yoko does not fall within this category because no gift tax return was required to be filed, the value of the gift being less than $10,000. The $200,000 given jointly by Mike and Dawn to Cary is an adjusted taxable gift,

TABLE 13-5   Illustration: Personal Balance Sheet of Mike and Dawn Magnus

	Market Value	Nature of Ownership/Liability
Assets		
Residence	$ 200,000	Tenants by the entirety
Common stock	300,000	Mike
Corporate bonds	200,000	Mike
Vacant land	300,000	Dawn
Real estate investments	1,000,000	Mike
Annuity cash values	300,000	Mike
Personal effects	50,000	Dawn
Personal effects	50,000	Mike
Checking and savings account	40,000	Tenants by the entirety
Autos	40,000	Mike
Total assets	$2,480,000	
Liabilities		
Home mortgage	$ 100,000	Tenants by the entirety
Credit card balance	5,000	Dawn
Credit card balance	5,000	Mike
Auto loans	20,000	Mike
Total liabilities	130,000	
Net worth (assets less liabilities)	$2,350,000	

TABLE 13-6 Values Comprising Mike's Gross Estate

Item	Fair Market Value	Justification for Inclusion in Gross Estate
Residence	$ 100,000	Section 2040 (Dawn considered as owning half)
Common stock	300,000	Section 2033 (Ownership)
Corporate bonds	200,000	Section 2033 (Ownership)
Real estate investment	1,000,000	Section 2033 (Ownership)
Annuity cash value	300,000	Section 2039 (Annuity)
Personal effects	50,000	Section 2033 (Ownership)
Checking/savings account	20,000	Section 2040 (Dawn considered as owning half)
Automobiles	40,000	Section 2033 (Ownership)
Group life insurance	100,000	Section 2042 (Incidents of ownership)
Personal life insurance	500,000	Section 2035 (Gift made within three years of death)
Gross Estate	**$2,610,000**	

TABLE 13-7 Allowable Deductions in Mike's Estate

Item	Value		Justification for Deduction
Funeral expenses	$ 5,000		Section 2053(a)(1)
Administration expenses	90,000		Section 2053(a)(2)
Claims against estate	10,000		Section 2053(a)(3) (Income and property taxes)
Debts		$50,000	One-half of mortgage loan
		5,000	Mike's credit card balance
		20,000	Automobile loan
	75,000		Section 2053(a)(4) total
Charitable bequests	10,000		Section 2055
Marital deduction		$100,000	His share of residence
		300,000	Common stock
		300,000	Annuity cash value
		50,000	Personal effects
		20,000	His share of checking/savings
		40,000	Automobiles
		100,000	Group life insurance
	910,000		Section 2056 total
Total Deductions	**$1,100,000**		

but only to the extent of one-half of the value of the gift (because it was a joint gift) and only after taking the $10,000 annual gift exclusion.

Thus, the computational tax base is as follows:

	Taxable estate	$1,510,000
Plus:	Adjusted taxable gifts	90,000
Equals:	Computational tax base	$1,600,000

By referring to the $1.5 to 2.0 million bracket of Table 13-3, it can be seen that the tentative federal estate tax is (1) $555,800 plus (2) 45 percent of the excess of $1,500,000 ($100,000) or $45,000, for a total of $600,800.

Credits available to offset the tentative tax are (1) the unified transfer credit and (2) the state death tax credit. No gift tax credit is available, as no gift taxes actually were paid on the earlier gifts. The unified credit is $220,550. Note that the maximum state death tax credit given in Table 13-4 is $70,800 (for $1.6 million).

Thus, the federal estate tax actually owed would be calculated as follows:

	Tentative federal estate tax	$600,800
Less:	Unified credit	−220,550
Less:	State death tax credit	− 70,800
	Federal estate tax owed	$309,450

It is instructive, at this point, to summarize the cash needs of Mike's estate. They derive from amounts needed to:

Pay mortgage	$100,000
Pay Mike's credit card balance	5,000
Pay auto loan	20,000
Pay funeral expenses	5,000
Pay administration expenses	90,000
Settle estate claims	10,000
Make charitable bequests	10,000
Pay state death taxes	70,800
Pay federal estate taxes	309,150
Total liquid needs	$755,250

This amount must be paid by Mike's executor from estate resources. Even though the estate net worth is considerable, it is relatively illiquid. Assuming that the property distribution directed by Mike's will is to be followed, the only remaining liquid assets are the corporate bonds of $200,000. This means that other assets must be sold to settle the estate's obligations, and the estate's obligations must be met before distribution of property to the heirs.

Note that the entire estate tax obligation could have been eliminated had Mike's will directed optimum use of the marital deduction. This oversight, plus a lack of consideration of other planning techniques, is an example of poor planning. This and other problems are discussed more fully in chapter 16.

GIFT TAX TREATMENT

As with the federal estate tax, the federal gift tax is imposed upon the right to transfer property to another person. The estate tax reaches those transfers that take place when a property owner dies, whereas the gift tax reaches those transfers that take place during the property owner's lifetime.

Despite the imposition of this tax, there can be advantages to making gifts. To understand these, we first examine the general provisions of the gift tax law. Next we consider the gift tax treatment of life insurance and annuities. Chapter 16 explores the planning aspects of gifts.

Overview of Federal Gift Tax Law

A lifetime gift to an individual incurs a federal gift tax generally at the same rate as the federal estate tax. The unified rate schedule in Table 13-3 shows the tentative tax relating to both estate and lifetime transfers. As in the estate tax situation, the unified credit is applied directly to reduce the tentative gift tax.

The amount of gift tax payable in a specific taxable period is determined by a three-step process:

1. Add all of the donor's lifetime taxable gifts, including prior gifts and current gifts. [Taxable gifts do not include the $10,000 per year (indexed) per donee exclusion for present interest gifts.]
2. Apply the unified rate schedule to the total taxable gifts to derive the tentative tax.
3. Subtract the unified tax credit to yield the gift tax payable in the current period.

Gift Tax Exclusion

The federal gift tax law is not aimed at the usual exchange of gifts associated with birthdays, holidays, and similar occasions. The law permits the donor to make this type of gift without tax by excluding the first $10,000 of outright gifts in any one year to any one recipient. This annual $10,000 exclusion applies to gifts made to each recipient, irrespective of the number. Moreover, it is available year after year. This means that an individual could give $10,000 to each of a large number of recipients each year without incurring any gift tax liability.

The exclusion is indexed for inflation with respect to gifts made after 1998. The IRC provides that the indexed exclusion is rounded to the next lowest multiple of $1,000. Because the inflation adjustment occurs in multiples of $1,000, it can be several years between adjustments.

The exclusion is applied to each donee individually, and if a donee receives less than $10,000, the exclusion is limited to the actual amount of the gift. If Bill gives $9,000 to Joan and $11,000 to Nancy, Bill can exclude only $19,000 ($9,000 for Joan and $10,000 for Nancy). He would have $1,000 in taxable gifts for the year.

The annual exclusion is available only when the gift is one of a present interest. A **present interest** is one wherein the donee must have possession or enjoyment of the property immediately rather than at some future date. The exclusion is not available for gifts of **future interest** in property, that is, any interest in property that does not pass into the donee's possession or enjoyment until some future date.

The Gift-Splitting Privilege

When a married individual makes a gift to someone other than a spouse, it may be regarded as made one-half by each spouse. This privilege of splitting a gift when made to a third party is extended only to property given away by a husband or wife. The taxpayer is given the advantage of doubling the annual exclusion. Therefore, a married individual can make gifts of $20,000 (indexed) per year to each beneficiary without incurring any gift tax liability, if the spouse consents to splitting the gift.

Deductions

As with the federal estate tax marital deduction, the **gift tax marital deduction** permits tax-free transfers between spouses. This deduction is available without limit.

The IRC permits full deduction for gifts to qualified charities of the same types as those mentioned in the discussion of the estate tax charitable deduction. Gifts to private individuals can never qualify for the charitable deduction, no matter how needy or deserving the beneficiaries may be.

Gifts of Life Insurance and Annuities

A life insurance policy is especially well suited as a gift. Gifts are also made of annuities. Gifts of life insurance and annuities include gifts of the contract itself, gifts of premium payments, and gifts of policy proceeds. Each of these is dealt with individually, as the valuation of each differs.

Gifts of Insurance Contracts

If an insured irrevocably assigns all of his or her rights in an existing insurance contract for less than an adequate consideration, he or she has made a gift of the contract and gift taxes may be due. Of course, if the owner receives an adequate consideration for the transfer, it is not a gift. If the owner gives an existing contract upon which premiums remain to be paid, the value of the gift is the policy's **fair market value,** which is its replacement cost. If a comparable contract is not ascertainable, the fair market value equals the **interpolated terminal reserve** (an amount equal to the policy reserve interpolated to the date of the gift) plus the value of unearned premiums and any accumulated dividends, and less any policy indebtedness. The reserve value, not the cash surrender value, is considered, although the difference often is negligible except in the early policy years. If the policyowner gives a single-premium or paid-up life insurance policy or annuity, the value of the gift equals the **replacement cost** of the contract, which is the single premium that an insurance company would charge for a comparable contract issued at the insured's/annuitant's attained age. A comparable contract is one providing payments of the same amount.

The following example illustrates the computation of a contract's fair market value using its interpolated terminal reserve. Assume that a gift is made today of a contract issued ten years and eight months ago. This year's annual premium of $1,800 was paid on its due date, eight months ago. The tenth and eleventh year's terminal reserves follow along with the amount of the year's increase in reserve.

	Eleventh-year terminal reserve	$16,000
Less:	Tenth-year terminal reserve	−13,900
Equals:	Increase in reserve	$ 2,100

The value of the gift is composed of the reserve at the time of the gift plus the unearned premium. The reserve at the time of the gift equals the reserve at the beginning of the year ($13,900) plus the pro rata increase in the reserve ($8/12$ of $2,100 or $1,400) for a total of $15,300. The unearned premium is $600 ($4/12$ of $1,800), that portion of the premium paid that is applicable to insurance protection *not* already provided. The value of the gift, therefore, is $15,900.

Gifts of Premiums

When an individual makes the premium payments on a life insurance policy or annuity contract that he or she does not own, the individual has made a taxable gift to the owner in an amount equal to the premium paid, subject to the $10,000 annual exclusion. Thus, if Larry makes a premium payment on a policy owned by Kelley on her own life and under which Jay is the beneficiary, Larry has made a gift to Kelley in the amount of the premium payment.

Similarly, premiums paid by an insured are gifts, if the insured has no incidents of ownership in the policy and proceeds of the policy are payable to a beneficiary other than his or her estate. Premiums paid by a beneficiary on a policy that he or she owns are not gifts.

Gifts of Insurance Proceeds

Under ordinary circumstances, life insurance death proceeds are not gifts. In some extraordinary instances, however, there may be a taxable gift. When one person owns a policy, a second is the insured, and a third is the beneficiary, a gift can be considered as occurring from the policyowner to the beneficiary at the insured's death. The amount of the gift equals the full amount of the insurance proceeds.

Thus, if Jan owns a policy of life insurance on her husband's life, with their children named as revocable beneficiaries, Jan will be deemed to have made a gift to the children in the full amount of the proceeds when they are paid at her husband's death. There is no intent to make a gift in the literal sense, but a taxable gift has been made nevertheless.

A gift of endowment insurance proceeds likewise occurs when, upon the maturity of an endowment policy, the proceeds are paid to a revocable beneficiary of the policy who is not the owner.

GENERATION-SKIPPING TRANSFER TAX

The IRC provides for a **generation-skipping transfer (GST) tax** to be levied when a property interest is transferred to persons who are two or more generations younger than the transferor. The *transferor* for property subject to the federal estate tax is the decedent and, for property subject to the gift tax, the transferor is the donor. The GST tax is intended to ensure that transfer taxes are paid by wealthy persons who might otherwise avoid a generation of transfer taxes by passing their property to heirs (so-called **skip persons**) beyond those of the immediately following generation. The tax is in addition to any federal estate or gift taxes owed because of the transfer.

For example, a grandmother may gift property directly to her granddaughter rather than to her son. In the absence of the GST, this gift could avoid all transfer taxes that otherwise might have been incurred if the transfer were first to her son, and then by the son to the granddaughter.

The amount of the GST tax is a function of the property value transferred and the applicable tax rate. Each person may transfer up to $1.0 million during his or her lifetime free of the GST tax. If the spouse joins in the transfer, a $2.0 million lifetime exemption applies. These exemption amounts are indexed for inflation for transfers taking place after 1998, with revised exemptions rounded to the next lowest $10,000.

The value of transferred property in excess of the exemption is subject to the maximum prevailing transfer tax rate, currently 55 percent. The GST tax is of little importance to persons of modest wealth, but those with greater wealth could incur substantial taxes under this provision.

Life insurance death proceeds, irrespective of the manner in which they are paid, can attract the GST tax if they are paid to a skip person. This unpleasant result can be avoided by avoiding inclusion of the death proceeds in the insured's estate and through appropriate use of life insurance trusts, as discussed in chapter 16.

Questions

1. Summarize the U.S. federal tax treatment of life insurance premiums, living proceeds, and death proceeds. Argue the merits of this treatment from a public policy perspective.
2. Explain the income tax consequences to the policyowner if a policy fails to meet the definitional tests under IRC Section 7702. How do these tests reflect a stance taken by the U.S. government regarding the tax treatment of life insurance?
3. Stan, aged 78, and his wife bought land in an industrial park five years ago for $240,000. It has appreciated in value to $400,000 and it is expected to appreciate greatly in the years to come. They are considering giving this land to their three adult children. Discuss the pros and cons of the proposed gift from an estate planner's point of view.
4. Outline the steps that need to be taken to derive the gross estate value and, subsequently, the taxable estate.
5. What factors need to be considered when estimating probable estate administration expenses?

CHAPTER

14

LIFE AND HEALTH INSURANCE IN PERSONAL FINANCIAL PLANNING

Objectives

- Explain the nature and purpose of financial planning.
- Describe the steps by which a financial plan can be made thorough and sensitive to an individual's objectives.
- Explain how a financial plan can be given a greater chance to succeed.
- Understand the roles that life and health insurance can take in a financial plan.
- Appreciate the uses and limitations of dynamic and static analyses for predicting the ability of life and health insurance products to meet future financial needs.

INTRODUCTION

Life insurance and health insurance have long been recognized as necessary and essential elements in individuals' and families' financial programs. With the continuing decline in informal security mechanisms in virtually all societies and a parallel decline in government-provided security in many OECD countries, we can reasonably expect life and health insurance to become even more important in individual and family financial plans in the future.

At the same time, we should recognize that life and health insurance, while of great importance, must reinforce and complement individuals' broader financial planning objectives. In this sense, family units should be run on a sound business basis, the underpinning of which is the financial planning process. This chapter first provides an introduction to this process and highlights the general means by which life and health insurance can assist in accomplishing one's financial plans. We then narrow our focus to the planning process as applied exclusively to life and health insurance.

PERSONAL FINANCIAL PLANNING

Nature and Purpose of Financial Planning

Although no universally accepted definition of **personal financial planning** exists, we can consider it as the process whereby an individual's or a family's overall financial objectives are used to develop and implement an integrated plan to accomplish the objectives.[1] The essential elements of this financial planning concept are the *identification* of overall financial goals and objectives and then the *development* and *implementation* of an integrated plan to accomplish the objectives taking into consideration the individual's circumstances. The idea is to focus on the individual's (or family's) objectives as the starting point rather than starting with a particular financial instrument and determining how it may fit into a financial plan.

Financial planning in the past was far simpler than today—earn a little, save a little, educate the children, and then retire with reasonable comfort. Planning today is more complex because of three factors: (1) greater economic uncertainty (e.g., greater fluctuations in interest rates and inflation), (2) constantly changing rules (e.g., frequent tax law changes), and (3) a proliferation of new financial instruments (e.g., futures and variable universal life products). These factors combine to render sound planning more of a necessity than in past times.

Most persons use a variety of financial instruments to achieve their financial objectives. Thus, such basic financial tools as life insurance, property and liability insurance, mutual funds, common stocks, bonds, annuities, savings accounts, wills, trusts, and real estate prove to be essential elements of many soundly conceived financial plans.

Within the financial planning process, life and health insurance can prove to be valuable and flexible financial instruments. Moreover, for many persons, the life insurance agent is the initiator of the financial planning process and may join other professionals, such as accountants, attorneys, tax consultants, and trust officers, in participating in or leading the financial planning process.

The Financial Planning Process

The personal financial planning process offers a road map for accomplishing an individual's financial objectives. It provides an orderly, systematic approach to planning. The process itself involves six interrelated steps, which together should readily meet due care standards discussed in chapter 12. Although the steps are presented here as discrete actions to be taken, each step in fact blends into and complements those steps that precede and follow it. Figure 14-1 illustrates this process.

Gather Information

The first step in the financial planning process is to assemble relevant quantitative and qualitative information. Relevant financial information varies from situation to situation but usually includes a listing of the individual's assets and liabilities as well as information regarding the person's income and expenditures. Additionally, information is usually needed concerning the nature of the person's investments; life, health, and other insurance protection; employee benefits; tax situation; relevant estate planning documents such as wills and trusts; and inheritance prospects. This gathering of information about the client is usually accomplished with the aid of a fact-finding questionnaire.

In addition to the preceding quantitative information, qualitative information is sought concerning the individual's interests, lifestyle, attitudes and desires, family situation, risk tolerance, and health and related information that will underlie the individual's goals and objectives. In fact, often at this stage the financial advisor assists the individual in establishing his or her objectives—the second step in the financial planning process.

---

[1] This and the following sections draw on G. Victor Hallman and Jerry S. Rosenbloom, *Personal Financial Planning,* 3rd ed. (New York: McGraw-Hill Book Company, 1983), Chaps. 1 and 2 and C. Arthur Williams, Jr., and Richard M. Heins, *Risk Management and Insurance,* 5th ed. (New York: McGraw-Hill Book Company, 1985), Chaps. 1 and 9.

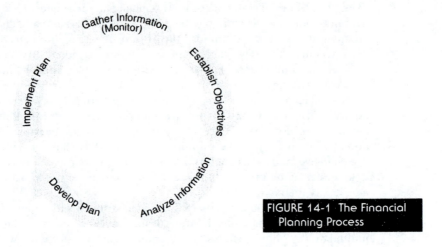

FIGURE 14-1 The Financial Planning Process

Establish Objectives

The process of setting goals and objectives is the most important and challenging. The competent financial planner is most helpful at this stage, for if an individual's goals and objectives are poorly conceived and formulated, any ensuing financial plan is likely to be faulty. To aid the client in this endeavor, the advisor often must probe into aspects of the client's business and personal affairs and relationships that can be among an individual's most sensitive and confidential. This requires establishing a keen bond of trust and ensuring that this trust bond is never broken. It also involves the ability of the advisor to communicate and probe effectively and professionally.

Analyze Information

The third step in the personal financial planning process is to analyze the quantitative and qualitative information gathered, in light of the client's objectives. Life and health insurance needs would be determined (see later in this chapter). Insurance policies would be reviewed carefully, as would all other financial, tax, and legal documents that the planner was competent to examine. Other financial and legal advisors may need to be consulted and advice sought from them at this stage. Deficiencies in the client's existing financial arrangement would be revealed by this analysis and the groundwork laid for the next stage in the process.

Develop the Plan

As the planner analyzes the information gathered, probably in consultation with the client and other advisors, he or she probably already is mentally formulating the elements of a proposed financial plan. The plan should represent a coordinated, integrated effort to resolve problems and to help the client achieve his or her objectives in light of current financial, tax, and other constraints and limitations, with appropriate consideration concerning future possibilities.

Implement the Plan

With the financial plan now available, the advisor holds further discussions with the client to help him or her understand how the plan can be implemented and how present financial and other constraints may affect the complete achievement of objectives. An outline plan showing implementation dates and types of actions to be taken and products to be purchased is often used. The proposal may be modified in light of further goal clarification resulting from continuing discussion.

Implementation normally requires the services of other professionals, especially those in the legal and tax areas, if the planner is not professionally qualified in them. Appropriate involvement of these professionals in the planning process smooths the implementation process.

Monitor and Revise the Plan

After the plan is implemented, results should be monitored to ascertain the extent to which they are compatible with initial expectations. If they are not, changes may be needed. In addition to the need for revisions occasioned by results deviating from expectations, revisions also will be necessitated by tax and other environmental changes and by the client's changing financial fortunes, family situation, and goals and objectives.

No plan is foolproof. Changes will occur and should be expected. Too often, the need for the planner to stress this simple yet important fact to the client is overlooked in the planning process.

Elements of a Personal Financial Plan

Personal financial plans should be *personal*. They should be tailored to the individual, with no two plans being exactly alike. Even so, almost all financial plans have certain elements in common. This section presents an overview of the five common elements (see Figure 14-2) as well as an introduction as to how life and health insurance can be useful in helping to accomplish an individual's objectives.

Establish the Risk Management Plan

Nature of Personal Risk Management   Most financial planning experts agree that the most basic element of each individual's financial plan is the establishment and maintenance of a sound program of personal risk management. The practice of **risk management** can be defined as the identification, measurement, and treatment of exposures to potential losses. Risk management is concerned with losses that arise from damage to or destruction of property, from liability, and from loss of income or additional expenses occasioned by death, incapacity, unemployment, retirement, and loss of health. Historically the business enterprise has been the chief focus of risk management attention, but the individual and family also should practice risk management.

The practice of risk management is not an option. Individuals and families need merely to exist to face exposures to loss. Such exposures can be ignored altogether, but this is tantamount to selecting a risk management approach by default, and the approach selected often is unlikely to be the best one. By properly managing one's exposures to loss, more acceptable results can be accomplished at minimum long-run costs.

Risk Management Process   Risk management involves the identification, measurement, and treatment of property, liability, and personal loss exposures. The risk management process tracks the six-step personal financial planning process.

Gather information.   One must first gather information to permit loss exposure identification. Individuals, families, and businesses face three classes of losses: property, liability, and personal. **Direct property loss exposures** are those that exist because of the possibility of damage to, destruction of, or disappearance of personal or real property. **Indirect property loss exposures** exist when an individual, family, or business can suffer a reduction in income (revenues less expenses) from the loss of use of property or when the value of property that is not damaged is lessened because of direct damage to other property. To

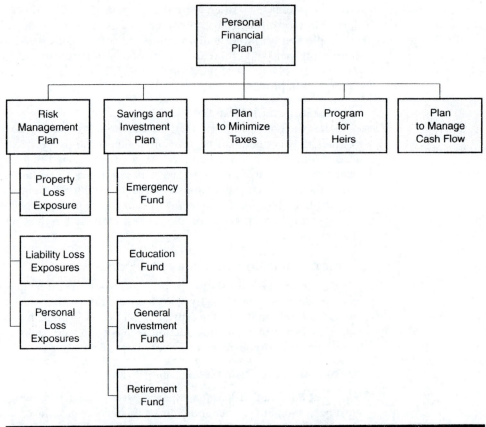

FIGURE 14-2 Elements of a Personal Financial Plan

illustrate: A family might have to live in a hotel until fire damage to their home is repaired. The possibility of extra living expenses would constitute an indirect property loss exposure to the family.

Liability loss exposures arise from an individual's intentional actions or failure to exercise a sufficient degree of care such that another person or property is harmed. One can be sued for numerous reasons, the most common cause being lawsuits from automobile accidents.

Personal loss exposures arise from the possibilities of death, incapacity, illness or injury, retirement, and unemployment. (The retirement exposure is of such importance as to warrant separate treatment. See later in this chapter and chapter 16.) Such losses are associated with families, but businesses can and do suffer personal losses as well. For example, the death of a key employee in a small business could have a severe adverse financial impact on the business. Of course, of the three classes of loss exposures—property, liability, and personal—this book deals only with the personal category.

Establish risk management objectives. The second step in the risk management process is to establish objectives. These objectives should be consistent with and complement those established in connection with one's overall personal financial plan. In fact, the goals associated with the personal risk management program should already have been developed as a part of the establishment of the personal financial goals. Often the overall goal may be stated simply as the family's avoiding financial catastrophe as a result of any of the three loss exposure classifications.

Analyze information. The third step in the risk management process is to analyze the information gathered to permit estimation of the potential financial consequences of losses. This important step technically involves an estimation of the chance that a particular loss will occur and the impact that such a loss would have upon the financial affairs of the individual, family, or business.

The likelihood of death within one year for persons during their working years is small. However, the likelihood of death prior to age 65 is not insignificant. Indeed, approximately one in six persons now between the ages of 20 and 40 will die prior to age 65. Also, for many persons, death occurring after age 65 can create significant financial hardships, and death probabilities after age 65 are high. The key to planning for the death contingency is to focus on its financial consequences to the family or business, irrespective of its probability of occurring. We explore this item later in this chapter.

Poor health, like death, may cause two types of losses: (1) loss of earnings and (2) extra expenses. The value of earnings lost because of a total disability may be estimated in a manner similar to that used in estimating the economic loss occasioned by death.

Unexpected extra expenses accompanying an injury, a sickness, or an impairment can take the form of hospital bills, surgical fees, drugs, or other medical expenses. Estimating the probability that a person will suffer a "morbidity condition" and the extent to which that condition will be disabling is difficult because (1) morbidity, unlike mortality, cannot be defined exactly, (2) morbidity varies in severity as well as frequency, and (3) morbidity conditions are not reported on a regular basis to public authorities. Even so, we have some information, as given in chapter 7.

Involuntary unemployment caused by economic factors, including company downsizing, is another threat to a person's earning power. The potential loss can be estimated in a manner similar to that used for disability. Unemployment rates of 4 to 7 percent have prevailed in the United States in recent years, with rates in excess of 10 percent common in many European and especially developing countries. Unemployment rates vary greatly over time and across countries.

One measure of the magnitude of unemployment loss is the duration of the unemployment. As one would expect, the average duration is related to the general state of the economy, but particular industries, areas, or persons can suffer substantial losses even when the economy is performing satisfactorily.

Develop the risk management plan. Once exposures have been identified and measured, the various tools of risk management should be considered and a decision made with respect to the best combination of tools to be used. The tools include primarily:

1. **risk avoidance**—avoiding the risk altogether
2. **risk reduction**—reducing the chance that a loss will occur or reducing the magnitude of a loss if it does occur
3. **risk transfer**—transferring the financial consequences of any loss to some other party
4. **risk retention**—retaining or bearing the risk personally

Examples of each category include: (1) not purchasing a car for a college student, thus avoiding the liability and other exposures of auto ownership; (2) wellness programs adopted by employers or, from an individual's viewpoint, exercising regularly and adopting proper eating habits, thus reducing the risk of having a heart attack; (3) purchasing a medical expense policy from an insurance company, thereby transferring the financial consequences of incurring medical expenses because of loss of health; and (4) retaining any income losses that would result from a disability lasting three months or less.

Implement the risk management plan. The fifth step in the risk management process is to implement the risk management plan. For the average family, implementation may entail simply purchasing an insurance policy. If the personal risk management program involves things such as risk reduction through better eating and exercise habits, however, a major personal commitment is required from the individuals concerned.

Monitor and revise the risk management plan. The sixth and final step in the risk management process involves monitoring the entire risk management plan and revising it as circumstances dictate. This means that the family should be aware that possible exposures to loss can be eliminated (e.g., by selling the beach house and eliminating the financial consequences to the family of its possible destruction), created (e.g., by buying a ski condominium unit), and altered (e.g., leasing the newly acquired condo unit creates new possibilities for incurring liability). This step in the risk management process can be viewed as "completing the circle" in the sense that it represents a linkage with the first step in the process.

Uses of Life and Health Insurance in Personal Risk Management Life and health insurance has little relevance to the property and liability risk exposures of an individual, family, or business. However, its uses will usually prove to be an element of the risk management program of the average individual and family.

Among private-sector financial instruments, life insurance alone guarantees that, for a relatively modest outlay, an individual's dependents or business will not have to suffer financially because of the individual's death. As discussed later, life insurance can be useful in other elements of a given individual's personal financial plan, although its providing of protection against the adverse financial consequences of death undoubtedly is its best-known function.

As the elimination of the possibility of a major sickness or injury is not possible, other means are required for dealing with the financial consequences that arise from loss of earnings and expenses caused by incapacity and loss of health. In the majority of cases, health insurance is the method chosen and is essential in an individual's risk management plan.

This protection usually is provided by one's employer, with some protection provided through government plans. Even with such coverage, however, many persons discover upon close examination that they and their families remain unduly exposed to adverse financial risk from possible loss of health because employer and government-provided coverages leave major protection gaps.

Establish a Savings and Investment Program

The second element of most persons' financial plans involves the establishment of a savings and investment program. As with other elements, this one cannot be separated completely from the others. For example, the establishment of a family emergency fund (discussed later) actually is a mechanism to manage risk and could be considered there.

For some persons, especially those just entering the work force, the concept of establishing a savings and investment plan can seem distant or even illusory. Some families' incomes are such that all income must be spent on current living expenses, with no surplus available for savings. Other persons, for various reasons (usually lack of discipline), spend all of their disposable income on current consumption, even though their total current needs could be met reasonably within their current income level and, at the same time, leave sufficient funds to establish a savings and investment program. Individuals want to accumulate wealth for a number of reasons; some of the more important reasons are discussed later.

Emergency Fund An emergency fund is usually needed to meet unexpected expenses such as lost income because of short-term disability or unemployment or property losses not covered by insurance. The size of the needed emergency fund varies greatly and depends upon factors such as family income, number of income earners, stability of employment, assets, debts, insurance deductibles, uncovered health and property insurance exposures, and the family's attitudes toward risk and security. The size of the emergency fund often is expressed as a certain number of months (such as three to six) of a family income.

By its nature, the emergency fund should be invested conservatively. There should be almost complete security of principal, marketability, and liquidity, although, of course, a reasonable rate of return is a desired objective. Within these constraints, logical investment outlets for emergency funds have included regular savings accounts in banks and other savings institutions, certain types of government securities, and life insurance policy cash values.

Education Fund The cost of higher education has increased dramatically over the last few years in most countries, particularly at private colleges and universities, but also for grade school. These high costs can result in a tremendous financial drain for a family with college-age children, and, as a predictable drain, it can be prepared for in advance.

An educational investment fund, a relatively long-term objective, is set up with the hope that the fund will not be needed in the meantime. Therefore, wider investment latitude is justified than in the case of the emergency fund, with the result that a more attractive investment yield often can be obtained.

Life insurance can be used as a vehicle for funding educational needs, at least in part. The cash-value buildup in any cash-value insurance policy can be tapped at the time of the need. In addition, a life insurance policy can ensure that the educational fund is completed even if the principal wage earner of the family dies prematurely. Finally, some life insurance companies sell specific educational insurance policies, the purpose of which is to provide funds at the time the child reaches college age.

General Investment Fund Many persons desire to accumulate capital for general investment purposes. They want to obtain a better future standard of living, a second income in addition to the earnings from their employment or profession, greater financial security or a sense of personal self-reliance, the ability to retire early, or a capital fund to pass on to their children or grandchildren, or they may simply enjoy the investment process. In any event, individuals normally invest with the view of maximizing their after-tax rates of return, consistent with their risk tolerances, and the investment constraints under which they must operate.

A wide variety of fixed-value and variable investments exists. Fixed-value investments are those whose principal and/or income are contractually set in advance in terms of a specified or determinable value. Variable investments are those for which neither the principal nor the income is contractually set in advance.

Common fixed-value investments include bonds, savings accounts, certificates of deposit, treasury bills and notes, preferred stock, and most life insurance and annuity cash values. Variable investments include home ownership, common stocks, mutual funds, business interests, commodities, fine artwork, precious metals, as well as variable annuities and variable life insurance.

Retirement Fund   Another aspect of most persons' investment programs is the provision for retirement. Establishment of a retirement fund is typically of less concern to young working persons, but its importance increases directly with proximity to retirement. Although a subset of the general investment program, its importance argues for its being segregated, especially as several funding instruments and laws are oriented exclusively toward this specific purpose. For this reason, we take it up as a separate matter in chapter 16.

Minimize Taxes

Because most families pay taxes of various sorts, the desire to minimize taxes is logical and a laudable element of personal financial planning. Thus, the tax implications of most financial transactions should be considered.

Citizens of virtually every country are subject to a variety of taxes. These may include sales taxes, property taxes, social insurance taxes, income taxes, local taxes, estate and gift taxes, value-added taxes, and others. The relative importance of these taxes varies considerably from country to country and from individual to individual within a given country. When engaging in tax planning, however, most persons are concerned primarily with income taxes, death taxes, and perhaps gift taxes.

That anyone would purchase life insurance or annuities solely to gain tax advantages is doubtful. Nonetheless, there can be little doubt but that the tax advantages enjoyed by these products enhance their attractiveness. We introduced this tax treatment in the preceding chapter so need not repeat it here.

Establish a Program for Heirs

Whether by design or default, all individuals have a plan as to how their assets will be distributed on their deaths. Either the individual prepares the plan or, failing that, the law imposes a plan. A sound personal financial plan does not leave this element to chance or to law. It includes a conscientiously formulated and implemented program that comes into being upon the death of the individual, if not prior thereto, as we discuss in chapter 15. The orderly and efficient transfer of property and the meeting of the objectives established for one's heirs constitute the heart of this plan element.

This element of financial planning must be coordinated with the personal loss exposures identified and incorporated in the risk management plan. In fact, it is impossible actually to separate fully the death-related portions of the personal risk management plan from the establishment of a program for one's heirs.

Manage Family Cash Flow

The last element of the typical personal financial plan is management of cash flow. This element permeates all others and, therefore, logically should not be viewed as the final element but rather as providing the broad scheme that permits the accomplishment of all other elements.

Managing family cash flow means establishing a budget wherein periodic (e.g., monthly) income and expenditure patterns are projected, together with a system for tracking and analyzing actual income and expenditures. Clearly, all of the earlier elements of a person's financial plan would fit into the budget and analysis process.

As one would suspect, life and health insurance can assist in the cash flow management process only indirectly. For example, premium payment modes often can be varied to suit an individual's special income pattern, or policy loans or cash-value withdrawals can be used to overcome temporary cash flow shortages. Cash-value life insurance policies can be arranged so that premiums can be paid through policy loans or cash values when the need arises.

Business and Personal Financial Planning

The distinction between business financial planning and personal financial planning is essentially one of convenience, the chief difference being the entity for which the planning is performed. Even so, the principles, if not all of the details, are identical.

For many persons, moreover, a close relationship exists between the home and the business or vocation in which they are engaged. Indeed, the owner of a business, generally speaking, conducts the business primarily for the purpose of supporting a household, thus showing that the welfare of the home and the business can be so intimately related as to be inseparable. Therefore, it should be understood that references to personal financial planning extend to business financial planning, to the extent that an individual's personal financial affairs are influenced by or are derived from his or her business or vocation. We take up this important topic in chapter 17.

Common Mistakes in Financial Planning

It is clear from the preceding discussion that consumers have innumerable opportunities to make mistakes in financial planning. Many persons fail to plan or do not follow a consistent, logical pattern in carrying out their financial plans. Failure to plan is not only foolish but often costly. It is easy, however, for busy persons to procrastinate. Many believe that their assets or incomes are not sufficient to justify a financial plan, or they believe that the costs of planning services will be too high relative to benefits. Others either fail to plan or follow seemingly erratic patterns in accomplishing financial objectives because planning involves consideration of such unpleasant events as death, disability, unemployment, old age, destruction of property, and being sued.

These reasons, either alone or in combination, do not constitute valid objections to financial planning. This is not to suggest that the family earning $25,000 per year will utilize the same financial instruments or seek advice from the same financial advisors as a family earning $250,000 per year. However, each family should make plans to deal with death, disability, savings, and so on. Details vary, but the need for planning does not.

In spite of this logic, many consumers fail to plan or make mistakes in planning. Ask any financial planner to recite the many serious consumer mistakes that he or she has witnessed, and the questioner should be prepared for a lengthy monologue. In fact, from surveys of certified financial planners, we know of the most frequently encountered mistakes. Table 14-1 shows the nine most frequently cited mistakes.

TABLE 14-1	The Nine Most Frequent Mistakes in Financial Planning
Rank	*Mistake*
1	Failure to set measurable financial goals
2	Making a financial decision without understanding its effect on other financial issues
3	Confusing financial planning with investing
4	Neglecting to reevaluate financial plan periodically
5	Believing that financial planning is for the wealthy only
6	Believing that financial planning is for the elderly only
7	Confusing financial planning with retirement planning
8	Waiting until a monetary crisis to undertake financial planning
9	Expecting unrealistic returns on investments

Source: CFP Board Licensee Survey, March 1997.

SOME SOCIAL DIMENSIONS OF LIFE AND HEALTH INSURANCE PLANNING

Life and health insurance planning takes place in a complex environment in which demographic, economic, political, social, and a host of other factors influence perceptions and decision making. Chapter 1 explored the economics underpinning this decision making. Additionally, the more important factors influencing perceptions and decision making were examined in chapter 3 in the discussion on life and health insurance consumption. The material in those chapters may be in need of review, as they are fundamental to this chapter's subject matter.

An important area not well covered in chapters 1 or 3 relates to how the social sciences, other than economics, view certain dimensions of life and health insurance. This section focuses on these aspects of uncertainty, attempting to draw inferences that may promote further understanding of the life and health insurance purchase decision. The treatment is unavoidably incomplete, for the subject matter touches on some of the most complex of human motivations and emotions, those related to physical and mental incapacity, loss of health, and death.

Of course, the way a society and a family view death—whether it is, in effect, celebrated, dreaded, or somewhere between the two extremes—influences why an individual would consider purchasing life insurance. In many instances, individuals act as if they consider themselves immortal; they seem psychologically unwilling or unable to face their own mortality. The same sentiments seem often to apply, but to a somewhat lesser extent, to health.

The subject of how one deals with incapacity and death is intertwined with one's culture, including religious beliefs and convictions. In postagricultural societies, money has been closely associated with all personal loss exposures, so life and health insurance itself is viewed through cultural lenses. Box 14-1 offers a sociologist's insights, for example, on the relationship between money and death.

The sometimes intimate relationship between religious commitment and security reinforces the view that we are not dealing with a logical, economic problem alone. The issue has anthropological, sociological, and psychological dimensions. As such, until these sciences can provide a complete explanation for human decision making (which most likely is never), any presentation on these aspects of life and health insurance purchases will itself remain incomplete.

Anxiety

We noted in chapter 1 that humans throughout history have exhibited a desire to reduce uncertainty. Uncertainty can cause anxiety.[2] *Anxiety* may be defined as a collection of fears resulting in an unpleasant uneasiness, stress, generalized pessimism, or various risk-aversion attitudes. Psychologists consider that an individual's capacity to tolerate and manage anxiety is a sensitive measure of the healthy integration of his or her personality.

Sociologists, taking a somewhat different approach, consider the individual's roles (e.g., child, parent, etc.) and related responsibilities through life. These responsibilities also can create anxiety.

Anxiety is not an absolute condition. It ranges from extreme neurotic anxiety with an overreaction to a perceived threat to a range of normal anxiety with a reaction that

---

[2]This and the following sections draw in part on Irving Pfeffer and David R. Klock, *Perspectives on Insurance* (Upper Saddle River, NJ: Prentice Hall, 1974), Chap. 14.

BOX 14-1

THE RELATIONSHIP BETWEEN DEATH AND MONEY

With agricultural and other preindustrial societies, the *economic* consequences of the death of a family member were often less urgent than in industrialized societies. The family still had its land, the extended family ensured adequate security, and voluntary or reciprocal associations provided assistance. With industrialization came new death-related businesses. Simple "last requests" and traditional family distribution gave way to highly formalized systems of wills and estate planning.

Although industrialization meant that families could enjoy greater income, it also made them more vulnerable because of the disability, unemployment, or death of the breadwinner. A secure income stream—money—became more important. Life and health insurance became part of the general movement to formalize the management of death.

Sociology has been criticized for perpetuating a secular and rational image of money without paying due attention to its symbolic and sacred functions. In most societies today, money has both a practical and symbolic relationship with death. The widespread practice of spending large sums of money at times of death testifies to the existence of a powerful and legitimate symbolic association between money and death.

The abhorrence of pauper burials in many Western societies is another indicator of money's importance at the time of death. It explains, for instance, the popularity of industrial life insurance in the late nineteenth century in the United States and other Western countries.

This dual relationship between money and death—actual and symbolic—is essential to the understanding of the development of life insurance. Its intimacy with death has made life insurance vulnerable to objections based on magical and religious grounds. Many see speculating with the solemn event of death to be a degrading sacrilegious wager, which God would resent and punish as crime. By insuring his life, a man was not only "betting against his God" but, even worse, usurping His divine functions of protection. Because the ultimate function of life insurance is to compensate the widow and orphans for the loss of a husband and father, critics object that this turned man's sacred life into an "article of merchandise."

In many societies, a secret fear is the relationship between insuring one's life and losing one's life. The fear of precipitating death was once among the most common objections to the purchase of life insurance. It remains in many societies today. Thus, because of its involvement with death, life insurance has been tied to religion, magic, and superstition.

Source: Harold D. Skipper, Jr., and Tara Skipper, "The Sociocultural Environment for Risk and Insurance," in *International Risk and Insurance: An Environmental-Managerial Approach* (Boston: Irwin/McGraw-Hill, 1998) as adapted from V.A.R. Zelizer, *Morals and Markets: The Development of Life Insurance in the United States* (New York: Columbia University Press, 1979), pp. 43–73.

is proportionate to the threat. Normal anxiety can be dealt with constructively at the level of conscious awareness or it can be relieved by various risk management techniques.

Insurance is a device that can reduce psychological uncertainty. In this respect, it can be akin in its effect to psychiatry, education, religion, and other anxiety-reducing mechanisms. Life and health insurance enhances peace of mind and financial security and can provide a partial relief from anxiety.

Anxiety is often fostered, sometimes inadvertently, through the financial planning process. In establishing objectives for the family, consideration is given to events that are among life's most stressful—death, loss of health, retirement, and divorce—and to the anxiety that they create due to transitions into new roles (e.g., widowhood, retirement, etc.).

A scale to measure the relative degrees of life change inherent in various life events has been developed. Table 14-2 lists several life event changes commonly associated with financial planning and shows their relative ranking and their so-called life change unit (LCU) value (with 100 being the greatest value). Life changes induce stress. Note that the death of a spouse is potentially the most stressful of life's events.

Financial planners and insurance salespersons sometimes use the possibility of these life events and transitions into different stages in life (roles) to arouse anxiety within their clients—to motivate them to reflect on the possible financial consequences of the occurrence of the events. The advisor can then paint a picture of freedom from or at least reduction in anxiety. If this is done properly and with sensitivity, the individual may be motivated to act. If it is done crudely, the reaction may be one of distaste and may lead to inaction or even hostility. The prospect's willingness to buy or follow advice is a function of his or her informational set, emotional condition, trust, and the manner in which the subject matter has been presented by the advisor.

Anxiety is an inhibitor. The healthy response is to deal with it constructively. This can be done in some instances through mechanisms such as insurance that, instead of repressing the fears, threats, or conflicts, transfers the source of insecurity and permits the individual to make a better adjustment to his or her environment.[3]

Emotions

Emotions are a primary determinant of behavior. This is particularly true of the life insurance purchase decision. *Emotions* are learned reactions to a set of experiences or perceptions that has been either very favorable or very distressing. Contact with events or thoughts

TABLE 14-2	Rankings and Relative Degrees of Life Change in Selected Life Events	
Rank	**Life Event**	**LCU Score**
1	Death of spouse	100
2	Divorce	73
4	Death of a close family member	63
6	Personal injury or illness	53
9	Retirement	45
11	Major change in health of a family member	44
16	Major change in financial state	38
17	Death of a close friend	37

Source: Richard H. Rahe, "Life Change and Subsequent Illness Reports," in *Life Stress and Illness,* E. K. Eric Gunderson and Richard H. Rahe, eds. (Springfield, IL: Charles C. Thomas, 1974), pp. 60–61.

---

[3]This explanation does not account for the phenomenon of gambling, also indulged in by insurance-minded individuals. The rational economic person might engage in betting for its thrill and excitement but would never engage in systematic gambling in practice, as the expected value would be less than the cost of playing the game. The standard economic argument is that gambling is economically disadvantageous whereas insurance is advantageous because of diminishing marginal utility.

Research on economic behavior has described theoretical reasons based on psychology and economics for why an individual might both gamble and purchase insurance. See D. Kahneman and A. Tversky, "Prospect Theory: An Analysis of Decisions under Risk," *Econometrica,* Vol. 47 (March 1979), pp. 263–291, and Mach Maching, "Choices under Uncertainty: Problems Solved and Unsolved," *Journal of Economic Perspective,* Vol. 1 (1987), pp. 121–154.

BOX 14-2

DEATH AND THE FIVE STAGES OF GRIEF

The death of a loved one, especially a child, can cause such overwhelming grief we might doubt whether we will survive ourselves. In fact, for elderly couples who have lived together for many years, the death of one of them seems to reduce the life expectancy of the survivor. Sudden, unexpected deaths are acknowledged to be the most difficult with which to come to terms.

Many psychiatrists contend that grief has five distinct stages and that we proceed through them in order, although little agreement exists about the length of each stage. The five stages are as follows:

Stage	Emotion
1	Shock and denial
2	Anger
3	Bargaining
4	Depression
5	Acceptance

that recall these experiences can stimulate a desire to remove or satisfy the resulting emotions. For example, individuals who have experienced severe financial difficulty as children because of the death or permanent disability of a parent might be strongly motivated to avoid recurrence of that status for their families through the purchase of insurance.

Emotions can be learned from the experiences of others. Because emotions can be generalized from one set of circumstances to another, many insurance advisors are successful in communicating to a client the emotional consequences of failing to obtain insurance protection. The purchase of insurance can provide the individual with an overt and constructive outlet for his or her emotional concern.

Stuart Schwarzschild made this most fundamental point in an article titled simply "The Love Theory."[4] He noted that, irrespective of the economic basis for life insurance, the underlying motivation for the vast majority of purchasers revolves around the emotions of love and affection that the insured holds for those in some way dependent upon him or her.

Life insurance death proceeds undoubtedly help dependents and loved ones from a financial point of view. In doing so, anxiety caused by financial concern is reduced. The agent or planner can point this out. Perhaps life insurance death proceeds also enhance a feeling among dependents and loved ones of the extent to which the deceased person cared for them, and this too can be emphasized.

However, our understanding of the psychological and sociological effects on dependents and loved ones of insurance death proceeds is exceptionally poor. For example, many psychiatrists contend that we experience five stages of grief on the death of a loved one (see Box 14-2). It is not clear that death proceeds soften or shorten or have any effect whatsoever on any of these stages. (It is also unclear whether and, if so, how the financial planning process can affect these stages.) Agents and planners must take great care in treading on this raw emotional ground.

LIFE AND HEALTH INSURANCE PLANNING

We now shift our focus to life and health insurance planning. Perhaps the biggest mistake made by individuals in connection with life and health insurance planning is one that cannot be corrected after incapacity or death: not having enough life or health insurance.

---

[4]Stuart Schwarzschild, "The Love Theory—New Rationale for the Purchase of Life Insurance," *Best's Review,* Life/Health ed., Vol. 73 (September 1972), pp. 46–48.

Uses of Life and Health Insurance

Most of the uses of life and health insurance have been highlighted throughout the previous chapters. We introduce some additional uses here and examine other uses in more detail. Most life insurance is purchased for one or more of the following reasons:

- *Income replacement*—to replace some or all of the income lost by the premature death of an income earner.
- *Debt repayment*—to pay off an outstanding debt, such as a home mortgage loan or automobile loan, on the death of the person (usually the debtor) who is repaying the debt.
- *Savings creation*—to create a savings, such as an education fund for children or an emergency fund for the family, on the death of the person who otherwise would have created it had he or she lived.
- *Wealth replacement*—to replace the value for one's heirs of assets consumed or given away during life. Two types of wealth replacement in connection with qualified retirement plans are introduced in Box 14-3. We cover the issue of wealth replacement in connection with gifts in chapter 15.
- *Pay death taxes*—to pay estate and other death taxes that arise from a person's death. We cover this topic in chapter 15.
- *Business purposes*—to provide funding for special business needs such as business buyouts, key employee indemnification, or compensation packages for key employees and executives. We cover this topic in chapter 17.

In general, health insurance policies are purchased for more specialized uses. Disability income insurance is designed to replace income lost because of inability to earn an income. We covered this topic in chapter 7. Some disability income policies are designed for business purposes akin to those for life insurance. These are discussed in chapter 17.

Of course, medical expense insurance and long-term care insurance provide expense reimbursement. These insurance policies and their uses were covered in chapter 7, with additional coverage in chapters 19 and 20. Thus, although this chapter covers both life and health insurance, our emphasis is on life insurance. Of the categories of uses for life insurance, we focus on income replacement, debt repayment, and savings creation.

The Life and Health Insurance Planning Process

The financial consequences of loss of health and of premature death constitute key personal loss exposures faced by all individuals. As such, the risk management (or financial planning) process provides an excellent framework for analysis of these exposures. The term **insurance programming** also has been used for decades to describe the risk management process applied to personal insurance planning.

Other approaches are sometimes followed to estimate the consequences of personal loss exposures and, thereby, the need for insurance. Unless the approach incorporates all steps of the risk management process, any resulting plan may be faulty. For example, life insurance equal to five, six, or seven times the breadwinner's annual salary is sometimes suggested as appropriate for the average family. These and other such simple approaches ignore potentially vital aspects of sound risk management.

The risk management process helps determine whether any insurance is needed and, if some is needed, the amount. A judgment as to the most suitable types of insurance and as to the insurer from which to purchase them also should result from the process. The process, ideally, should not take a static view of an individual's needs but rather should be capable of factoring into the analysis the possibility of changing financial requirements over time. Our presentation here tracks the process as described earlier.

BOX 14-3

WEALTH REPLACEMENT USES OF LIFE INSURANCE: PENSIONS

Life insurance is sometimes used in connection with pure life annuities. Many annuitants, especially participants in qualified retirement plans (see chapter 21), elect to receive payment in the form of a joint and last survivor annuity. The annuity provides income for as long as either the employee or his or her spouse is alive, with no further income paid to anyone after both deaths. Amounts accumulated in qualified retirement plans can be quite large, representing a significant share of some individuals' wealth. The retiree may wish to bequest much of this wealth to his or her heirs, but annuitization may preclude or curtail this possibility. To provide both a lifetime income *and* the desired bequest, the pensioner can convert the retirement account into an annuity *and* purchase life insurance in an amount sufficient to replace some or all of the retirement account value.

A related use of life insurance is the so-called **pension maximization** strategy wherein the participant in a qualified retirement plan who otherwise would receive income in the form of a joint and last survivor annuity (1) chooses instead to receive income under the single life annuity option, which provides a greater income than does the survivor annuity, and (2) purchases life insurance to replace the value of the survivor annuity to the spouse. This concept makes financial sense only if the premium for the needed life insurance can be funded by the additional income arising from having selected the single life annuity in favor of the joint and last survivor annuity.

Gather Information

The first step is the gathering of relevant quantitative and qualitative information to permit a sound identification of financial loss exposures arising from the individual's death or loss of health. As mentioned earlier, this involves identification and valuation of the individual's assets and liabilities, as well as information on the person's income and expenditures. The information is often gathered through a fact-finding questionnaire.

Assets Assets normally are considered either liquid or illiquid. **Liquid assets** are those assets available to be liquidated with reasonable price certainty. These would be available to meet income or other monetary needs on an individual's death, loss of health, or incapacity. They normally include stocks, bonds, money market and savings accounts, mutual funds, and amounts available in pension, profit-sharing, or individual retirement accounts. All assets should be assessed at their market value. If real estate is to be sold, its value should be included, as would any interest to be sold in a closely held business. The latter assets, however, may be difficult to sell quickly at their market value. (See chapter 17.)

Illiquid assets are those assets not available to meet income or other monetary needs because they cannot or will not be liquidated. They might include the family's house, automobiles, personal effects such as clothing and jewelry, and household goods. These assets are usually passed to heirs intact. The realizable value of any of these items to be sold on death should be included as liquid assets.

The death benefit of any life insurance payable to or for the benefit of the family should be included as a liquid asset for life insurance planning purposes. This is appropriate because one is attempting to estimate the resources and liabilities of an individual assuming he or she dies today.

Life insurance cash values are not normally shown as separate assets for death planning purposes. Cash values are subsumed in life insurance death proceeds. If an important part of one's savings program is funded via insurance cash values, it can be more revealing and helpful to list cash values as assets available on death. An advantage of this approach is that the personal balance sheet can be used for death, incapacity, retirement, and other savings and investment planning programs. If this is done, only the net amount at risk of life insurance should be shown for death planning purposes.

Liabilities   A review of the individual's liabilities will show which ones are to be paid at death or transferred to heirs. Most liabilities must be paid at death. Some liabilities may be assumable by others (e.g., some mortgage loans), or they may be in more than one person's name. For non–death planning purposes, liabilities ordinarily would not be paid in full.

Typical liabilities to be paid on death include outstanding balances on credit cards, tax obligations, personal loans and notes, and auto loans. If the home mortgage loan is to be paid, its outstanding balance would be included. If it is not to be paid off at death or at incapacity (the usual situation), it should be excluded but mortgage loan payments included as an income need (discussed later).[5]

Income   The current and likely future income of the individual or family is an important driver in estimating future resources and needs. Information on income will be developed in the information-gathering process. The importance and security of future income typically vary depending on the individual's family status.

Single-parent family.   For a single-parent family, income usually is derived primarily or solely from the parent's salary. A single-parent family unit is more likely than a two-parent family to have income from outside the unit. Thus, a divorced individual may be receiving alimony or child support payments. A divorced person sometimes receives financial support from parents or grandparents, and a widowed spouse may be receiving income from the deceased spouse's investments, employer, or insurance, or from government sources.

As the single parent's salary is usually the most important income source, the parent's death or incapacity could have a financially devastating impact on those dependent on the wage earner. This potential income loss should be clearly recognized and dealt with through life insurance and disability income insurance.

The divorced single parent also could have his or her income disrupted by the death or incapacity of the former spouse who provides child support or other financial assistance. Similarly, a relative's voluntary financial support to a single-parent family could cease on the donor's death or incapacity. Both situations should be identified as potential loss exposures and addressed.

Two-parent, single-income family.   The two-parent family in which only one parent earns an income may, in many ways, be similar to the single-parent family in terms of vulnerability to income loss because of death or incapacity of the wage earner. As a result, similar considerations apply.

Often overlooked is that the family may also suffer financially on the death or incapacity of the non-wage-earning parent. This spouse usually provides valuable household services and, increasingly, assists in various ways when a family-owned business is involved. No monetary wage may be paid for either class of service. Death or incapacity could result in major increases in family expenses.

If the surviving spouse and children are unable to perform the necessary household functions, the family may be forced to secure outside household services (e.g., a housekeeper) and rely on service businesses (e.g., dry cleaners, restaurants, auto service firms,

---

[5]Of course, it is often unwise to pay off a home mortgage loan. The interest rate usually is low in comparison to available long-term investment returns and interest payments usually are tax deductible.

and child-care providers). Similarly, any uncompensated business services must be replicated by someone who most likely will expect wages. Additionally, incapacity could result in long-term care and other expenses. Total expenses could rise significantly. Also, final expenses (discussed later) can be significant.

Two-parent, dual-income family. The income of a two-parent, dual-wage-earner family could be materially affected by the death or incapacity of either wage earner. Such a family often is at less risk than the family unit dependent on a single income, as the death or incapacity of one wage earner will not leave the family without any income—however reduced it may be.

If the dual-income family is financially dependent on both incomes, consideration must be given to the impact on the family of the loss of income from one or both wage earners. Both life and disability insurance and possibly long-term care insurance often will prove a necessity on both lives.

Single individual. Single-person households are becoming more common. Such persons often must rely exclusively on their own incomes. Typically, the greatest personal risk revolves around loss of health and incapacity. The death risk may pose little financial concern unless there are nonresident dependents or unless bequest or estate planning considerations suggest otherwise.

The foregoing family situations are presented simply. In fact, complications are increasingly common. We see more remarriages, blended families, lifetime partners, households of unrelated individuals, and families with two or more sets of children, often of vastly different ages. With increasing life expectancy and increasing proportions of elderly, we also see more elderly widow and widower households. Although the basic planning principles remain the same irrespective of household type, the way the principles are applied differs substantially.

Savings and Investment Programs The death or incapacity of a parent causes a disruption in savings. Perhaps the most common concern in this respect is disruption of saving to fund college education for children. An otherwise soundly conceived plan to accumulate funds to finance education can be completely disrupted by the death or incapacity of a parent. As a result, most parents consider the contingency of disruption of planned savings and investment programs as falling properly in the loss exposure category.

Final Expenses Death itself creates expenses and taxes—so-called **final** or **post-mortem expenses.** For example, probate costs will be incurred. As discussed in chapter 15, **probate** is the process of filing, validating, and executing a will by a court. Probate costs vary significantly by jurisdiction and as a function of the estate size. Such costs in the United States commonly range from 2 to 5 percent of the gross estate, but they can be higher. Executor fees also may be incurred.

Postmortem expenses include estimated final illness expenses. Of course, a well-designed and implemented financial plan should provide for health insurance or other means for meeting these expenses. Also, funeral expenses, which today average around $5,000 in the United States, should be recognized in the financial plan.

Death-related taxes can constitute a major final expense for those whose net worth is large (see chapter 16). These taxes can equal 50 percent or more of an estate and should be estimated and included as a postmortem expense to be met on death.

Establish Objectives

A family should establish not only overall financial objectives but specific subobjectives as well. For personal insurance planning purposes, this usually means that the individual must—often with his or her spouse—determine the income levels needed on the death or incapacity of either spouse. These decisions are personal and, although subject to precise-appearing quantitative analysis, they remain subjective. There is no correct answer.

A commonly stated objective is to allow the family to maintain its current living standard on an individual's death or incapacity. This may translate into a survivor income need of at least 60 percent of the predeath family income. The amount typically would be less than the current total family income, as the deceased spouse's self-maintenance expenses would end. For a family with children, self-maintenance expenses normally are considerably less than one-half of the total family income.

This objective may translate into an income need of 75 percent or more in the case of disability. Employment-related expenses and taxes usually are reduced on disability. On the other hand, health care expenses often will rise, thus highlighting again the need for sound medical expense coverage. The objective may translate into long-term care needs that could be greater or less than the current family income, depending on its level.

Income objectives are often predicated on the human life value concept. The idea is to estimate the financial impact on income recipients of the death or incapacity of the main income earner and to replace that amount of lost income—in other words, to replace (financially) the person as a source of earnings. This is the same as maintaining the current living standard. However, the individual may adopt an objective of providing an amount that is greater or less than his or her human life value. For example, if the individual is enjoying exceptionally high earnings, a rational decision might be to replace only that amount necessary to ensure the family a comfortable life but not to continue an elaborate lifestyle.

One should also establish objectives regarding such things as:

- liabilities to be paid off on death or incapacity
- amounts necessary to cover final expenses
- amounts necessary to cover long-term care expenses
- amounts (if any) to establish a family emergency fund
- amounts (if any) to establish a fund to finance education
- bequests to friends and relatives and to charitable or other institutions

It is not sufficient merely to conclude that a certain amount of money would be desirable for a particular purpose. One must also decide how to provide the money and over what time period. For example, if an education fund is to be established, this goal-setting exercise should address the issue of how the money will be paid (e.g., as a lump sum, annually, or monthly).

The objective-setting process usually takes place as part of information gathering. The advisor leads the client through a loss exposure identification/objective-setting exercise, providing guidance yet being careful not to impose his or her own values.

Objectives often are changed or adjusted as the costs of their implementation become clearer. These costs emerge from the next two steps in the process.

Analyze Information   The third step in the process is to analyze the relevant data and loss exposures in light of the individual's stated objectives. In risk management terms, this step involves an attempt to measure the financial consequences of the losses.

Loss analysis has two dimensions: frequency and severity. For personal insurance planning purposes, loss frequency information (e.g., probabilities of death and incapacity) often has little utility to the individual. The individual will either live or die, suffer a disability or not, and so on. Sound risk management analysis presumes that the potential loss could occur and attempts to measure its likely financial consequences. A plan of action is then developed (see next step) to deal with the potential loss if it occurs.

Applied to insurance planning for an individual, this means that the analysis of the financial consequences of a personal loss should assume that it is about to occur. The analysis yields a measure of the potential loss severity (e.g., the consequences of death) from a financial point of view. Thus, this step's function really is to estimate loss severity only.

The needed analysis often is neither simple nor precise. This is because the analysis necessarily involves assumptions concerning the future, and actual results will invariably differ from assumptions. Even so, the exercise has merit. If done properly, it provides an idea of the possible range of the family's financial loss as well as the extent of disruption to present plans that would occur. Although this and the next step (plan development) are presented here separately, they often are accomplished together.

Several approaches can be followed in measuring the financial consequences to a family (or a business or others) of the death or incapacity of one of its members. In all cases, however, the basic approach is the same. The family (or others) will have certain resources from which to meet its objectives (in whole or in part). To the extent that existing resources do not meet the objectives fully or fail to provide a good match, the individual will be faced with three choices:

1. revise the financial objectives downward,
2. ensure that additional resources will be available, or
3. a combination of options 1 and 2.

The financial objectives established by individuals usually fall into two categories: (1) cash and (2) income.

Cash objectives. Cash objectives (or needs) require a single-sum cash amount to fulfill. They are the easiest to estimate. Typical cash objectives arise from the need or desire to pay outstanding liabilities such as auto and personal loans, credit card balances, and incurred income tax liabilities. If an objective is to pay an outstanding mortgage loan balance, this too would be included.

Cash needs also might arise from a desire to establish or augment an educational fund. Final expenses, for the most part, also fall into this category. Each of these cash needs will have been identified in the information-gathering/objective-setting stages.

Medical expenses typically also fall into this category. Of course, it is exceptionally difficult to estimate such future expenses. With a comprehensive health insurance plan, these expenses will be effectively covered, so they need not be estimated.

Income objectives. Quantifying income objectives (needs) requires assumptions that render approximations only. Deriving a measure of a family's (or other's) income needs involves, first, a determination of the annual net amount needed, taking into consideration all important variables such as likely income resources (e.g., government benefits), changing family responsibilities, and inflation. Second, for life insurance planning purposes these annual net income amounts typically are converted to a single-sum (present value) equivalent. This involves assumptions as to future interest rates. For disability income and long-term care needs, the net amounts need not be taken to present values because such policies usually are denominated in monthly income.

The life insurance planning process is simple in concept. Needed assumptions, however, as to future inflation and interest rates render the analysis more complex. In addition, several methods can be used to derive the needed figure. Some aspects of these important elements are reviewed next.

Available methods. Several methods can be used to analyze death-related income needs. The two most common ones are (1) the capital liquidation and (2) the capital retention approaches. The **capital liquidation approach** assumes that both principal (capital) and interest are liquidated over the relevant time period to provide the desired income. The **capital retention approach** assumes that the desired income is provided from investment earnings on the principal and that no part of the desired income is from capital. In other words, the capital is retained undiminished, even after death.

Each method has advantages and drawbacks. The liquidation approach requires a smaller capital sum to provide a given income level than does the retention approach. The retention approach permits a capital sum to be passed on to the family's next generation (or to whomever is designated). It is considered more conservative, because in an emergency, capital could be invaded.

When the need for income is for the whole of life, the capital liquidation method can be approached in one of two ways. First, the future desired lifetime income can be funded through the purchase of a life annuity. The annuitant cannot outlive the income, but, for reasons examined in chapter 8, the purchase probably should not be made before age 65 or 70. Income needed prior to this time could be provided from life insurance through the fixed-period settlement option or from other sources.

The second way of funding lifetime income is to assume a maximum age beyond which the income recipient is unlikely to live and to provide for the complete liquidation of principal and interest between the present and that age. Some analysts suggest age 90 as the terminal age. This approach to funding "lifetime" income can be achieved through the fixed-period settlement option or through other means.

Each of these capital liquidation approaches has advantages and drawbacks. The critical decision variable in the second approach is the maximum age. If the terminal age is set too low, the income recipient may outlive the income—a disastrous result. The higher the age, the higher the principal sum required to fund the income.

Other things being the same, the life annuity will generate a higher income than the other liquidation approach (assuming a high terminal age), as each payment contains an element of survivorship benefit. Moreover, with the life annuity, the income recipient cannot outlive the income.

The decision to follow the capital retention or one of the capital liquidation methods is not an all-or-nothing proposition. One need not either pay out all capital or retain all capital. There is a continuum between the two extremes.

Inflation assumptions. The effects of inflation on anticipated future income needs and resources and other relevant areas should be factored into the analysis. Future inflation rates are impossible to predict. For example, annual changes in the U.S. consumer price index since the 1960s have ranged from 1 to 14 percent. Inflation rates in many other countries have exhibited even more volatility.

The best approach to factoring inflation into any analysis often is to select a range of inflation rates and determine the sensitivity of results to changing inflation assumptions. Unless presented in a clear, simple manner, however, this type of sensitivity analysis can obscure the broader purpose of the analysis. Care must be taken to avoid this result.

Interest assumptions. The interest rate selected for discounting can greatly influence results, especially when sums are discounted over many years. The interest rate chosen affects both needs and resources.

The selected interest rate ordinarily is that which can be earned after taxes in the present economic environment on secure, fairly liquid investments—that is, a conservative rate. Speculative investments are not generally advised for family financial planning.

Prevailing interest rates are referred to as **nominal interest rates.** Nominal interest rates are influenced by consumer inflation expectations. The difference between the nominal interest rate and the inflation rate is referred to as the **real interest rate.** The real interest rate typically will be positive in a healthy economy, and most economists anticipate that the real rate will be around 2 or 4 percent in the United States. Viewed historically, the U.S. real interest rate has actually varied from a low of –6 percent to as much as +6 percent. Such extremes are considered temporary anomalies.

As with inflation, a range of interest rates ideally should be applied to the analysis to determine results under changing assumptions. To simplify tax considerations, the interest rate selected should be an after-tax rate. If investment returns are expected to be tax exempt, the gross return will be the same as the after-tax return. If not, an estimation of the income recipient's marginal income tax bracket is required. Thus, if a gross taxable investment return of 9 percent is expected and if the income recipient is expected to be in the 30 percent marginal tax bracket, the effective after-tax return is 6.3 percent. The formula for the effective after-tax return is:

After-Tax Rate of Return = (Gross Rate of Return) × (1.0 – Marginal Tax Rate)

The interaction of inflation and interest. The interaction between the assumed inflation rate and the assumed discount (interest) rate should be understood. Consider, for example, that a $10,000 per-year income is desired for five years and that an after-tax discount rate of 8 percent is judged reasonable. If inflation is ignored, the present value of five $10,000 payments at 8 percent interest, with the first payment made now, is $43,120.[6]

A non-level payment stream (such as that developed if inflation is considered) requires a different approach. Assume the same five $10,000 payments and 8 percent after-tax interest rate as before. Assume now that inflation is estimated to be 5 percent annually over the payout period and that it is desired to provide the equivalent purchasing power of today's $10,000 for each payment.

Table 14-3 illustrates the calculation for this inflation-adjusted income stream. It shows that $47,298 invested to earn 8 percent after taxes will just be sufficient to provide a yearly income whose purchasing power remains constant in the face of a 5 percent inflation rate. As expected, this sum is greater than that needed if one ignores inflation.

An approximation of the present value of an inflated income series can be obtained by discounting at the real interest rate, that is, the difference between the nominal interest rate and the assumed inflation rate. For example, the present value of the five $10,000 annual payments at 3 percent (8 percent – 5 percent) is $47,171 rather than $47,298. If the time period involved is not great and if only a good approximation is

TABLE 14-3 Present Value of $10,000 per Year with Inflation of 5 Percent (First Payment Now)

(1)	*(2)*	*(3)*	*(4)*	*(5)*
Year	*Annual Payment in Today's Dollars*	*Annual Payment in Inflated (5%) Dollars [(2) × (1.05)^t]*	*Present Value Factor at 8%*	*Present Value at 8% of Inflated Payments*
0 (Now)	$10,000	$10,000	1.000	$10,000
1	10,000	10,500	0.9259	9,722
2	10,000	11,025	0.8573	9,452
3	10,000	11,576	0.7938	9,190
4	10,000	12,155	0.7350	8,934
				$47,298

[6] $PV = (\$10,000) \times \left[\sum_{t=1}^{5} \left(\frac{1}{1+i} \right)^{t-1} \right] = \$10,000 \times 4.312 = \$43,120$

sought—which is usually the case in such planning—this approach can suffice. The true present value, however, will always be understated when both the nominal and real rates are positive—the usual situation.

The preceding example assumed capital liquidation over a fixed period. What if a lifetime income is needed? To derive the needed present value, one can calculate the present value of income payments to a certain advanced age and then add to that figure the present value of the purchase price at that time of a life annuity.

An example will illustrate the concepts involved. Assume that a $10,000 after-tax annual income is desired for the full lifetime of a 35-year-old. Assume 8 percent to be a reasonable after-tax return and inflation to be 5 percent.

The problem can be approached in stages. First, assume that a life annuity will be purchased at age 70 to fund the post-70 lifetime income need, and that income prior to then will be provided from a fund established for that purpose, such as the fixed-period annuity option. The amount of money needed to fund the inflated payments from age 35 to age 70 is $225,510, derived using the procedure illustrated in Table 14-3. To determine the value today of the purchase price of the annuity that begins at age 70, the amount of the (inflated) annual income at age 70 must be known. Although the purchasing power is to be $10,000, the nominal value would be $55,160.[7] In other words, at 5 percent inflation, $55,160 in 35 years would have the same purchasing power as $10,000 today.

At age 70, a decision would be required as to the best type of annuity to be purchased. An analysis of the pros and cons of variable annuities, indexed annuities, and flexible-premium deferred annuities could be conducted at present under various payout assumptions designed to hedge the inflation risk. Realistically, however, annuity (and other investment) products available many years from now may bear little resemblance to products that exist today. Thus, unless the income recipient were now within a short time period of purchasing a life annuity, any detailed analysis as to the most appropriate annuity type and how best to structure the annuity payout might be largely wasted effort.

Hence, for long-term income planning, one probably should merely estimate an annuity purchase price for the projected (inflated) income. This price should be based on current guaranteed purchase rates. These long-term guaranteed rates typically will be based on a 2½ to 4 percent interest assumption, with the insurer actually crediting contemporary rates of return. By using the guaranteed rates, however, implicit allowance is made for inflation and perhaps for higher annuity purchase prices occasioned by increased longevity.

An insurance company would charge a 70-year-old between $600 and $900 for each $100 of annual income desired, with the income starting at age 70. Thus, for an income of over $55,000, the purchase price at age 70 might be (with rounding) between $330,000 and $500,000. Using the lower figure, one has but to calculate the value at age 35 of the $330,000 sum needed at age 70. Discounting at 8 percent yields a present value of $22,308.[8] Stated differently, $22,308 today will grow to $330,000 in 35 years at an after-tax earnings rate of 8 percent.

Therefore, the total amount of money estimated to be needed now (at the income recipient's age 35) to provide $10,000 annually for life in constant purchasing power is $247,818; the sum of the two present value figures ($225,510 + $22,308 = $247,818).

This precise-appearing number should be recognized for what it is: our best guess. It is based on numerous assumptions, a change in any one of which could affect results significantly. For example, if all other assumptions remained the same but the actual after-

---

[7]$(\$10,000) \times (1.05)^{35} = \$10,000 \times 5.516 = \$55,160$

[8]$PV = (\$330,000) \times (1/1.08)^{35} = (\$330,000) \times (0.0676) = \$22,308$

tax return were 7 percent instead of 8 percent, the sum needed today to fund the $10,000 income stream would be increased to $289,527. In cases such as those investigated here, liberal rounding should be normal practice. Thus, the $247,818 figure might become $250,000 (a typical premium banding amount) and $289,527 might become $300,000.

If a lifetime income is desired, but without using a life annuity, one can utilize either (1) the capital liquidation approach that requires the establishment of a maximum age beyond which the income recipient would be highly unlikely to live or (2) the capital retention approach. The capital liquidation approach not involving a life annuity follows the procedure used to derive present values in Table 14-3. Continuing the same example, assume that income was desired to age 85; that is, $10,000 of real income would be needed for 50 years. The present value of this stream is $242,112. This figure can be found by use of the shortcut formula shown in Box 14-4.

Under the capital retention approach and using the same interest and other assumptions as before, but ignoring inflation for now, one would ask this question: What amount of money must be available now, the income alone from which would provide $10,000 per year? The answer is obtained by dividing the interest rate into the desired annual income. The result, $125,000, is easily verified by multiplying $125,000 by the 8 percent earnings assumption, to show that it produces the needed $10,000.[9]

To ignore inflation in the capital retention approach is as foolish as doing so under the capital liquidation approach. The income recipient would want to receive $10,000 this year, $10,500 next year, and so on. The capital sum necessary to provide these inflated income payments is calculated to be $360,000, using the formula shown in Box 14-5. In deriving a measure of the financial consequences of death, it often proves more convenient to net expected future income resources against future expected income needs, and then to derive a present value for the annual differences.

Difference between Objectives and Resources The final step in the analysis is to net the resources available against the established needs for cash and net income to derive a figure for the shortfall (or overage) of resources to meet needs. This figure represents a measure of the net financial consequences of death to the family, based on the objectives identified earlier. Ideally, a range of figures would be developed based on various interest, inflation, and other relevant assumptions to provide an idea as to the sensitivity of the results to the assumptions.

---

[9]Note, however, that the $125,000 would generate the $10,000 at the end of the year. If it were desired to have the first payment made now, $10,000 should be added to the $125,000 principal, to yield a needed amount of $135,000.

BOX 14-4

FORMULA FOR PRESENT VALUE OF INCOME STREAM CHANGING AT A CONSTANT RATE

The present value of an income stream that either steadily increases or decreases can be found by the following formula:

$$A = P[(1 - e^n)/(1 - e)]$$

where

A = present value figure sought
P = initial payment
$e = [(1 + r)/(1 + i)]$
r = assumed inflation rate
i = assumed discount rate

BOX 14-5

FORMULA FOR THE CAPITAL SUM NECESSARY TO PROVIDE AN INCREASING PERPETUITY

The formula for the capital sum needed to provide a steadily increasing income stream in perpetuity is as follows:

$$C = P/(1 - e)$$

where C is the capital sum figure sought, P, e, r, and i are as defined in Box 14-4, and e is between 0 and 1. For e equal to or greater than 1, results are invalid.

Static versus Dynamic Analysis   The range of values developed previously for the financial consequences of death is valid for the year of analysis only. That is, the measure represents the financial consequences of death assuming death occurs at the present. The financial analysis is incomplete, however, unless some idea can be obtained as to probable future figures. The financial consequences of death can be expected to vary with time. It may either increase or decrease.

If net needs are estimated to decrease over time, the death benefit of any policy purchased to fill the gap should also decrease. If needs are expected to increase, the policy purchased to help meet the needs should be flexible enough to track future anticipated increases.

The traditional static approach to planning answers the question: "What if I were to die today?" The purpose of the question is to derive a quantitative measure for the adverse financial consequences of death. The procedure to convert from the traditional static planning approach to a dynamic approach is conceptually simple. The dynamic approach asks the same question as does the static approach, but it is repeated for each succeeding year; thus:

"What if I were to die today?"
"What if I were to die next year?"
"What if I were to die two years from now?"
"What if I were to die three years from now?"
And so on.

To answer each question, future resources must be estimated. The future needs already would have been estimated, but a revised present value calculation would be necessary. The estimation of future resources and needs is not easy. It requires assumptions as to future savings and investment habits, future earnings, as well as a host of other items. The process can be exceedingly complex. The objective is to obtain some idea of the likely pattern of future resources and needs.

If a broad, integrated financial plan of the type discussed earlier in the chapter has been developed, it will contain projections as to future savings, investments, earnings, and other aspects of resources. These figures can be used to estimate the financial consequences were death to occur in some future year. If no overall financial plan is available from which to draw these estimates, figures should be developed.

Because of the highly subjective nature of the needed assumptions, one should not be too concerned with precision. As future investment, savings, or other goals sometimes are not met, the projections should be conservative.

Plan Development

The next step in the risk management process is to develop a plan to accomplish the stated objectives, based on the analysis of the financial consequences of death and incapacity. This plan should evolve only after the various alternative means of treating the loss exposures have been explored. The plan usually emerges as the relevant information is being analyzed in light of objectives.

In considering alternatives, the planning time frame can be separated into short-run and long-run periods. The viable alternatives available to the individual over the short run usually are exceedingly limited, with more emerging over the long run.

Viable short-run alternatives are those that can be adopted now and in the near future to fill the financial gap created by death or incapacity. In the short run, there is insufficient time to increase savings or investments meaningfully, and there is little or no control over the level of other resources (e.g., government benefits).

The longer term affords more alternatives. Sufficient time exists to implement an enhanced savings and investment program to fill a financial void. One may choose to enhance savings through life insurance policy cash values, an annuity, or savings outside the insurance mechanism. Insurance-funded savings programs can offer some advantages over other savings media, although the benefits of diversification should be kept in mind and many insurance products are heavily loaded.

The dynamic analysis results should suggest a pattern of future needs. An increasing, decreasing, constant, or fluctuating future need pattern will be revealed. Ideally, the insurance purchased to fill this need should be capable of tracking the estimated future pattern. Also, as actual results rarely follow estimations exactly, the plan (insurance) should be sufficiently flexible to adapt to unanticipated changes.

The prior information analysis step should include a review of existing life and health insurance policies and annuities from a cost as well as a structure viewpoint. If existing policies are not well suited to current needs or not competitively priced, replacement should be considered. If replacement is justified, alternatives to existing policies should emerge at this stage. If existing policies are judged suitable and cost-effective, any recommended change in the beneficiary designation, ownership, settlement option, or other area is a part of plan development.

In developing a plan, one or more low-cost life and health insurance policies from high-quality companies that are suitable in light of the client's characteristics, objectives, and current financial condition should be identified. How any needed policies are structured in terms of beneficiary designations, ownership, premium payment frequency, and other important provisions should be included in the plan.

Ideally, the plan should not evolve in isolation from other personal planning needs, such as establishment or revision of wills and trusts. A comprehensive plan includes more than taking care of legal necessities. A clearly established predeath plan, for example, should guide survivors (and the executor) through this most traumatic of life's events. Most agents and financial planners are not qualified to develop and implement all aspects of a plan. A team approach is needed, as suggested earlier in this chapter.

Plan Implementation

Once a plan has been developed and agreed to by the individual, the program must be implemented. Plan implementation usually means, among other things, completing any necessary insurance applications and providing funds to pay the first premiums. If changes are needed in existing policies or if policies are to be replaced, the necessary forms must be secured, completed, and furnished to the appropriate insurers. The insurance dimensions of the plan are not fully implemented until needed policies are issued on an acceptable basis and structured in line with earlier established goals.

Plan Monitoring and Revision

If the individual's future were to evolve exactly as had been estimated, if assumptions as to future inflation rates, interest rates, and other areas proved to be fact, if no important tax law or other environmental changes were made, and if no better life or health insurance or other financial products became available in the future marketplace, plan revision would be unnecessary. Clearly, this will not happen. Deviations of actual from estimated results should be expected.

Important life events such as marriage, divorce, important business undertakings, home buying, birth of children, children attaining financial independence, change in employment status, and the like should trigger an automatic reevaluation of the program. In general, program evaluation should take place every one to three years, irrespective of the happening of important life events.

Any significant changes in environmental factors should also trigger reevaluation. Changes in government security benefits, inflation rates, interest rates, employee benefit programs, tax laws, and a host of other variables can cause a program to go off its mark. New insurance and other financial products can render older products obsolete.

Both the individual and the advisor should be attuned to environmental and personal changes that can affect the program. Ideally, the insurance products selected to implement the program would be sufficiently flexible to be able to adapt to changes. A policy that provides for experience participation contains an automatic mechanism for at least partially adapting to changing economic conditions. The guaranteed right to purchase additional insurance without evidence of insurability, either by increasing the existing policy's benefit amount or by purchase of a new policy, can be another mechanism permitting flexibility. Universal life and other policies that permit premium payment flexibility and policy death benefit adjustability can be particularly well adapted to changing life cycle needs.

Life Insurance Planning Illustration

An illustration should be helpful in bringing together the concepts discussed previously. For reasons of space, the presentation focuses only on death planning and, then, only on the analysis and plan design steps.

Relevant Information and Objectives

Steven and Gwen McCorquodate, both age 35, have two children, Philip, age 7, and Debbie, age 2. Steven is the manager of a clothing store and Gwen is a grammar school teacher. The total annual before-tax family income is $100,000, which translates to $70,000 after taxes. Steven earns $63,000 ($45,000 after taxes); Gwen earns $37,000 ($25,000 after taxes). Other relevant financial information is shown in Table 14-4.

Steven and Gwen, with the counsel of their agent, have determined that their overall objective is for each to be able to maintain his or her standard of living if the other dies. This objective requires an estimated annual income of about $45,000 per year after taxes while both children are at home, $43,000 while only Debbie was at home, and $40,000 thereafter. These income objectives assume that the mortgage loan and other debts are paid (an objective). They also desire to establish a fund of $50,000 for the children's education and to have an emergency fund of $20,000.

Static Analysis

In conducting a static analysis, several assumptions are necessary. The key ones here are:

- A reasonable after-tax earnings (discount) rate will be 7 percent.
- The average annual inflation rate will be 4 percent.
- Their wages will increase at the rate of 5 percent per year on average.

Moreover, it is assumed that a life annuity will be purchased at age 70 to fund needed lifetime income from that age, and that the annual income objective as well as Social Security benefits increase each year with the inflation rate.

TABLE 14-4 Steven and Gwen's Financial Situation

	If Steven Dies First	If Gwen Dies First
Nonliquid Assets		
Home	$130,000	$130,000
Autos	13,000	13,000
Household/personal effects	37,000	37,000
	$180,000	$180,000
Liquid Assets Available on Death		
Individual life insurance	$ 50,000	$ 0
Group life insurance	25,000	50,000
Pension plan death benefits	10,000	0
Savings/investment	20,000	20,000
Checking account balance	2,000	2,000
	$107,000	$ 72,000
Cash Needs on Death Based on Objectives		
Mortgage loan balance	$110,000	$110,000
Auto loan balance	10,000	10,000
Establish emergency fund	20,000	20,000
Establish educational fund	50,000	50,000
Credit card balances	3,000	3,000
Funeral expenses	5,000	5,000
Probate/administration expenses	3,000	3,000
	$201,000	$201,000
Annual Income Objectives/Resources		
Desired after-tax family income on death	$ 45,000	$ 45,000
• with both children at home/in college	43,000	43,000
• with one child at home/in college	40,000	40,000
• with no child at home/in college		
Social Security Survivor Benefits[a]	$ 13,050	$ 9,360
• both children under 18 or, if in college, under 22	6,525	4,680
• one child under 18 or, if in college, under 22	8,700	6,420
• at survivor's age 65		

[a]Social Security survivor benefits are based on the insured status and past earnings records of the worker (see chapter 22).

Assuming Steven Dies First   Table 14-5 illustrates the derivation of the present value of net income needs, assuming Steven dies first. Column 2 shows the annual income objective in today's dollars and column 3 shows the equivalent in inflated dollars. Column 4 shows the estimated annual Social Security survivor (children's) benefit (inflated at 4 percent) that would be payable. Gwen's annual income is shown in column 5. These figures are increased by 5 percent per year. The column 6 figures are the amounts by which Social Security and Gwen's income fall short of the desired objective.

The amounts become significant, but the purchasing power is the relevant concern, not the absolute size of the numbers. Thus, if inflation averaged 4 percent, a $101,518 income at age 65 would have the same purchasing power as $31,300 today [the $31,300 being the difference between the income objective ($40,000) and the uninflated Social Security benefit ($8,700)].

The present value of each column 6 figure is shown in column 7. The discount rate used is 7 percent. Summing the column 7 figures yields $193,144, the present value of the

TABLE 14-5 Present Value of Net Income Needs

	(1)	(2)	(3)	(4)	(5)	(6)	(7)
Year	Gwen's Age	Annual Income Objective	Annual Income Objective (at 4%) −	Annual Social Security Benefit (at 4%) −	Gwen's Annual Earnings (at 5%) =	Annual Income Shortage	Value Today of Inflated Income Shortages
1	35	$45,000	$ 45,000	$13,050	$ 25,000	$ 6,950	$ 6,950
2	36	45,000	46,800	13,572	26,250	6,978	6,521
3	37	45,000	48,672	14,115	27,562	6,995	6,109
4	38	45,000	50,619	14,679	28,941	6,999	5,713
5	39	45,000	52,644	15,267	30,388	6,989	5,332
6	40	45,000	54,749	15,877	31,907	6,965	4,966
7	41	45,000	56,939	16,512	33,502	6,925	4,614
8	42	45,000	59,217	17,173	35,177	6,867	4,276
9	43	45,000	61,586	17,860	36,936	6,789	3,951
10	44	45,000	64,049	18,574	38,783	6,692	3,640
11	45	45,000	66,611	19,317	40,722	6,571	3,341
12	46	45,000	69,275	20,090	42,758	6,427	3,053
13	47	45,000	72,046	21,729	44,896	6,257	2,778
14	48	45,000	74,928	22,598	47,141	6,058	2,514
15	49	45,000	77,925	11,751	49,498	5,829	2,261
16	50	43,000	77,441	12,221	51,973	13,716	4,971
17	51	43,000	80,538	12,710	54,572	13,745	4,656
18	52	43,000	83,760	13,218	57,300	13,749	4,353
19	53	43,000	87,110	13,747	60,165	13,726	4,061
20	54	43,000	90,594	0	63,174	13,674	3,781
21	55	40,000	87,645	0	66,332	21,313	5,508
22	56	40,000	91,151	0	69,649	21,502	5,193
23	57	40,000	94,797	0	73,131	21,665	4,890
24	58	40,000	98,589	0	76,788	21,801	4,599
25	59	40,000	102,532	0	80,627	21,905	4,318
26	60	40,000	106,633	0	84,659	21,975	4,049
27	61	40,000	110,899	0	88,892	22,007	3,790
28	62	40,000	115,335	0	93,336	21,998	3,540
29	63	40,000	119,948	0	98,003	21,945	3,301
30	64	40,000	124,746	0	102,903	21,843	3,070
31	65	40,000	129,736	28,218	0	101,518	13,336
32	66	40,000	134,925	29,346	0	105,579	12,962
33	67	40,000	140,322	30,520	0	109,802	12,599
34	68	40,000	145,935	31,741	0	114,194	12,246
35	69	40,000	151,773	33,011	0	118,762	11,902
					Present value of column 7		$193,144

entire income stream to age 70. In other words, if all assumptions actually materialized as fact in the future, $193,144 would provide an annual (inflated) income to precisely fill the income gap revealed in column 6.

The preceding calculation allows for income only through age 69. Provision should be made for income beyond this period. At age 70, the needed (real) income of $40,000 would require a nominal income then of $157,840. Social Security benefits are estimated to be $34,330, thus leaving a shortfall at age 70 of $123,510. If the capital liquidation approach is used wherein an annuity would be purchased at age 70 to fund this and future income shortfalls, its estimated purchase price at age 70 would be $741,060, using an annuity purchase price of $600 per each $100 of annual income. The value today of this needed amount is about $70,000.[10]

The following is a summary of the net life insurance needed today on Steven's life:

+	Present value of income stream to age 70	$193,144
+	Present value of annuity for age 70 and later	70,000
+	Cash needs objectives	201,000
=	Total needed to fulfill objectives	$464,114
−	Existing resources	107,000
=	Shortage	$357,144

The analysis reveals that, if the stated objectives are not modified and are to be met, an additional $357,000 of life insurance is needed on Steven's life.

The result is influenced by the interest and inflation assumptions. Table 14-6 shows how the net result can vary significantly under different inflation and interest rate assumptions. As results are so sensitive to the assumptions, resulting net figures over such long time periods are, at best, educated guesses. The appearance of scientific precision should not obscure this simple truth.

Assuming Gwen Dies First The same analysis should be conducted assuming Gwen dies first. Recall that the family's income and other objectives apply irrespective of who dies first and that the same financial and income information applies as before. The only exceptions are that Steven's life insurance (total of $75,000) and pension death benefit ($10,000) must be excluded as liquid resources and the Social Security survivor benefit, based on Gwen's lower earnings, would be lower. Also, Gwen's employer provides $50,000 of group term coverage.

The cash needs are the same as for the analysis with Steven—that is, $201,000. Existing resources are $72,000, showing a net deficit of $129,000.

Steven earns more than the desired income objective. The present value of the excess of his after-tax income plus Social Security over the desired income is more than the $129,000 deficit. If, therefore, it were decided not to pay the mortgage loan and other

TABLE 14-6 Variability of Results with Changing Inflation and Interest Assumptions (Assumes Steven Dies First—Static Analysis)

Interest Assumption %	Inflation Assumption (%)				
	0	2	4	6	8
0	$1,184,000	$1,399,000	$1,772,000	$2,414,000	$3,522,000
1	896,000	1,059,000	1,339,000	1,819,000	2,643,000
3	543,000	639,000	800,000	1,073,000	1,536,000
5	360,000	418,000	513,000	672,000	938,000
7	261,000	298,000	357,000	451,000	608,000
9	207,000	231,000	268,000	327,000	421,000
11	176,000	192,000	216,000	254,000	313,000

[10]$PV = \$741{,}060 \times (1/1.07)^{35} = \$69{,}437$

debts but rather to continue to make payments from current income, there probably would be no need for additional life insurance on Gwen's life. If it is desired to pay the mortgage loan in full, the amount of life insurance needed would be about $129,000.

Dynamic Analysis

The preceding analysis developed a life insurance figure assuming death occurred at present. However, would $357,000 be adequate if Steven survived the current year and died in the following year? How would the result change if Steven survived both the current and the following year and died during the third year from now? What about death during the fourth year? The fifth year, and so on? The answers to this series of questions can be exceedingly important. At $357,000, Steven could be either grossly overinsured or underinsured in later years.

The dynamic approach requires assumptions as to future liquid assets and cash needs. Thus, the declining outstanding mortgage loan balance will lessen future cash needs. Inflation, however, most likely will drive up credit card balances and probable funeral and probate costs. If the emergency fund is to maintain its purchasing power, it also must increase with inflation. The value of savings and investments is expected to rise, as is employer-provided pension plan death benefits. Indeed, all elements of Steven and Gwen's pro forma financial situation are dynamic over time. Accumulated resources, income sources, and cash and income needs all change as Steven and Gwen move through their family life cycle.

To illustrate this process, assume that the pension plan death benefit increases 15 percent annually and that the value of savings and investments increases 10 percent annually. These rates of increase are assumed to include both reinvestment of earnings and additional contributions. Checking account balances, charge card balances, final expenses, and desired emergency fund balances are assumed to increase with the inflation rate.

Tables 14-7 and 14-8 summarize these figures, over time, based on the same assumptions and information used in the static analysis plus the additional stated assumptions. Estimated future liquid asset values available if Steven were to die in each year are shown in Table 14-7. For example, the total liquid asset value, if Steven were to die in year 7, is estimated at about $136,092, composed of a $23,131 pension plan death benefit, $35,431 in then current investments and savings, a $2,531 checking account balance, and the $75,000 of life insurance. No change is assumed in the life insurance because this is the value sought.

Table 14-8 follows the same approach, but it is based on liabilities and objectives. Thus, if Steven were to die six years from the present (i.e., in year 7), the then outstanding mortgage loan balance would be $104,764. Credit card and personal loan balances, estimated to grow at the inflation rate, might be around $16,449. At that time, $25,306 would be required to maintain the same $20,000 emergency-fund purchasing power, based on the inflation rate assumption of 4 percent.

The next column of the table shows that the value needed to fund the college education then would be $75,037. This figure deserves comment. Steven and Gwen desire to establish a $50,000 educational fund if either Steven or Gwen were to die now. At a 7 percent assumed earnings rate, this means that they believe they will need $98,358 by year 11 (when Philip is age 17). Thus, the amounts necessary in the intervening years must be such as to grow to $98,358 by year 11.

The simplifying assumption is made that one-half the fund balance is paid to Philip at his age 18, and the balance, accumulated at interest, is paid five years later when Debbie enters college at her age 18. Thus, no educational fund is shown as needed beyond her age 18. If, in fact, both Steven and Gwen survived to this point, they should have already made provision for financing their children's educations.

TABLE 14-7	Estimated Annual Values of Future Liquid Assets				
Assuming Death Occurred in Year	Pension Plan Death Benefits (at 15%) +	Savings and Investment Balances +	Checking Account Balances (at 4%) +	Total Life Insurance Assuming No Change =	Annual Projected Liquid Asset Values
1	$ 10,000	$ 20,000	$2,000	$75,000	$ 107,000
2	11,500	22,000	2,080	75,000	110,580
3	13,225	24,200	2,163	75,000	114,588
4	15,209	26,620	2,250	75,000	119,078
5	17,490	29,282	2,340	75,000	124,112
6	20,114	32,210	2,433	75,000	129,757
7	23,131	35,431	2,531	75,000	136,092
8	26,600	38,974	2,632	75,000	143,206
9	30,590	42,872	2,737	75,000	151,199
10	35,179	47,159	2,847	75,000	160,184
11	40,456	51,875	2,960	75,000	170,291
12	46,524	57,062	3,079	75,000	181,665
13	53,503	62,769	3,202	75,000	194,476
14	61,528	69,045	3,330	75,000	208,903
15	70,757	75,950	3,463	75,000	225,170
16	81,371	83,545	3,602	75,000	243,517
17	93,576	91,899	3,746	75,000	264,222
18	107,613	101,089	3,896	75,000	287,598
19	123,755	111,198	4,052	75,000	314,005
20	143,318	122,318	4,214	75,000	343,850
21	163,665	134,550	4,385	75,000	377,598
22	188,215	148,005	4,558	75,000	415,778
23	216,447	162,806	4,740	75,000	458,993
24	248,915	179,086	4,929	75,000	507,930
25	286,252	196,995	5,127	75,000	563,373
26	329,190	216,694	5,332	75,000	626,215
27	378,568	238,364	5,545	75,000	697,477
28	435,353	262,200	5,767	75,000	778,320
29	500,656	288,420	5,997	75,000	870,074
30	575,755	317,262	6,237	75,000	974,254
31	662,118	248,988	6,487	75,000	1,092,593
32	761,436	383,887	6,746	75,000	1,227,069
33	876,651	422,276	7,016	75,000	1,379,943
34	1,006,998	464,503	7,297	75,000	1,553,798
35	1,158,048	510,954	7,589	75,000	1,751,590

Continuing across the table at year 7, it is seen that an estimated $10,123 would be needed at that time to cover final expenses. Column 7 shows the estimated cash amount needed, $105,051 in year 7, to fund the purchase, at age 70, of the life annuity referred to earlier.

Column 8 is the simple sum of columns 2 through 7. It shows the amount required to fund all cash needs each year, assuming death occurred in that year. Hence, if death were to occur in year 7, an estimated $336,730 would be required to fund fully all of the needs shown in columns 2 through 7.

TABLE 14-8   An Illustration of Dynamic Needs Analysis

(1)	(2)		(3)		(4)		(5)		(6)
Assuming Death Occurred in Year	Annual Mortgage Loan Balance	+	Annual Balance on Other Debts (at 4%)	+	Annual Emergency Fund (at 4%)	+	Annual Educational Fund Balances (at 7%)	=	Annual Postmortem Expenses (at 4%)
1	$110,000		$13,000		$20,000		$50,000		$ 8,000
2	109,366		13,520		20,800		53,500		8,320
3	108,651		14,061		21,632		57,245		8,653
4	107,846		14,623		22,497		61,252		8,999
5	106,939		15,208		23,397		65,540		9,359
6	105,916		15,816		24,333		70,128		9,733
7	104,764		16,449		25,306		75,037		10,123
8	103,466		17,107		26,319		80,289		10,527
9	102,003		17,791		27,371		85,909		10,949
10	100,355		18,506		28,466		91,923		11,386
11	98,498		19,243		29,605		98,358		11,842
12	96,405		20,013		30,789		52,621		12,316
13	94,047		20,813		32,021		56,305		12,808
14	91,389		21,646		33,301		60,246		13,321
15	88,395		22,512		34,634		64,463		13,853
16	85,020		23,412		36,019		68,976		14,408
17	81,218		24,349		37,460		0		14,984
18	76,934		25,323		38,958		0		15,583
19	72,106		26,336		40,516		0		16,207
20	66,666		27,389		42,137		0		16,855
21	60,536		28,485		43,822		0		17,529
22	53,629		29,624		45,575		0		18,230
23	45,845		30,809		47,398		0		18,959
24	37,075		32,041		49,294		0		19,718
25	27,192		33,323		51,266		0		20,506
26	16,056		34,656		53,317		0		21,327
27	3,507		36,042		55,449		0		22,180
28	0		37,484		57,667		0		23,067
29	0		38,983		59,974		0		23,990
30	0		40,542		62,373		0		24,949
31	0		42,164		64,868		0		25,947
32	0		43,851		67,463		0		26,985
33	0		45,605		70,161		0		28,064
34	0		47,429		72,968		0		29,187
35	0		49,326		75,886		0		30,355

The present value of the income stream necessary to fill the income gap to age 70 appears in column 9. The yearly shortage figures were shown in Table 14-5. Their present value was $193,144—the figure shown for the first year in column 9. If death occurs in year 2, not in year 1, the amount needed to fund the income shortages as of year 2 is estimated to be $199,228; as of year 3, $205,707, and so on. Thus, if Steven were to die in year 7, an estimated $236,443 would be required at that time to fund the Table 14-5 income shortages from the seventh year to age 70.

(7)		(8)		(9)		(10)		(11)
Cash Needed in Year of Death to Purchase Annuity at Age 70	=	Annual Total Cash Needs	+	Present Value in Year of Death of Income Shortage to Age 70	−	Total Estimated Resources	=	Additional Life Insurance Needed in Year of Death
$ 70,000		$271,000		$193,144		$ 107,000		$357,144
74,900		280,406		199,228		110,580		369,054
80,143		290,385		205,707		114,588		381,504
85,753		300,971		212,622		119,078		394,515
91,756		312,199		220,017		124,112		408,104
98,179		324,105		227,940		129,757		422,288
105,051		336,730		236,443		136,092		437,081
112,405		350,113		245,585		143,206		452,482
120,273		364,297		255,429		151,199		468,527
128,692		379,326		266,044		160,184		485,186
137,701		395,246		277,507		170,291		502,462
147,340		359,484		289,901		181,665		467,720
157,654		373,647		303,317		194,473		482,492
168,689		388,592		317,855		208,903		497,544
180,498		404,354		333,623		225,170		512,807
193,132		420,967		350,740		243,517		528,190
206,652		364,662		360,615		264,222		461,056
221,117		377,915		371,151		287,598		461,468
236,595		391,760		382,420		314,005		460,175
253,157		406,204		394,502		343,850		456,857
270,878		421,250		407,487		377,598		451,139
289,840		436,898		413,206		415,778		434,326
310,128		453,140		419,124		458,993		413,272
331,837		469,966		425,281		507,930		387,316
355,066		487,353		431,724		563,373		355,704
379,921		505,276		438,507		626,215		317,567
406,515		523,693		445,689		697,477		271,906
434,971		553,189		453,340		778,320		228,209
465,419		588,366		461,535		870,074		179,828
497,999		625,863		470,362		974,254		121,971
532,859		665,838		479,915		1,092,593		53,160
570,159		708,457		404,885		1,227,369		−113,727
610,070		753,900		320,257		1,379,943		−305,785
652,775		802,358		225,187		1,553,798		−526,253
698,469		854,036		118,762		1,751,590		−778,792

Total projected annual resources (column 10) are then netted against the sum of yearly cash and income needs to derive yearly figures that represent the total projected annual shortages of resources to meet needs (column 11). If the assumptions used to derive these figures actually materialized as fact in the future, the column 11 figures would represent the amounts of life insurance that should be carried on Steven's life in each year.

As shown in Figure 14-3, the needed amounts increase through year 11. The needed amount then decreases because one child (Philip) is considered no longer financially

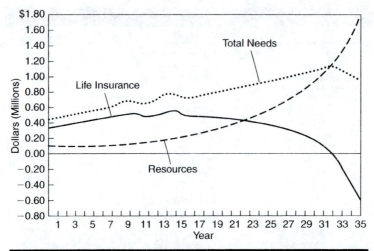

FIGURE 14-3 Projection of Life Insurance Needs ($i = 4\%$, $r = 7\%$)

dependent. Projected needs begin to increase again but then decline in year 17, when Debbie becomes financially independent. Amounts thereafter remain around $400,000 for several years and then drop precipitously as total estimated resources reach high levels. If all assumptions proved to be fact, the need for life insurance protection on Steven's life is estimated to cease at about his age 65. This assumes a constant savings pattern as well as large employer-provided funding. Whether these will be realized in fact is always questionable and, therefore, a financial plan should be flexible enough to adapt to unrealized hopes.

A note of caution is in order. The precise-appearing numbers can lend an unwarranted aura of authenticity to this type of analysis. In Table 14-8, column 11 figures shown for many years into the future should be regarded more as educated guesses than as established needs. Credence should be given to the general level of the first five or perhaps ten years' values, but, beyond that, one would be well advised to seek general trends only. The intent of this exercise is to show how future death patterns can be estimated and to highlight the great importance of selecting a policy that can adjust to the future pattern.

Computer-Assisted Planning

Dozens of computer software programs are available to assist individuals as well as agents and financial planners in determining life and health insurance needs. Such software often is part of a broader personal financial planning package, thus allowing an integrated approach. These programs can facilitate analysis of different scenarios and assist greatly in periodic plan revision.

In addition, several life insurance companies, life insurance quote services, accounting firms, financial planning firms, and others maintain Web sites that contain life insurance needs analysis engines. Although many of these sites are too elementary, some offer a sound, if basic, analysis with hyperlinks to numerous other information and analysis sources.

Questions

1. Describe both qualitative and quantitative factors that help form a thorough and sound financial plan.
2. How might the passage of time influence initial assessments made in creating a financial plan? Refer to changes that may be needed in both qualitative and quantitative factors initially used.
3. Life insurance policies can serve many purposes. Describe six different purposes for a life policy maintained by the primary income earner of the household over his or her life span.
4. Evaluate this statement: "There are so many unknowns, that planning now for the future would be impractical." How would you support or criticize this approach to planning?
5. What are some potential consequences of committing each of the nine most common mistakes in financial planning?

CHAPTER

15

ESTATE PLANNING

Objectives

- Understand the tools available to assist in planning an orderly estate.

- Explain the impact that death can have on taxes, court costs, and other obligations arising at the time of death.

- Describe the ways that trusts can reduce or defer tax liabilities on an estate.

- Describe the flexibility afforded by both wills and trusts for directing the timing and quantity of estate share distribution.

P revious chapters suggested some of the ways that life insurance can be useful as an instrument for individual and family economic security. This chapter builds on those discussions, including the chapter 13 explanation of estate taxation, to examine how life insurance can be helpful in estate planning. We include in this examination discussions of the general nature of estate planning, the nature of the estate planning team, and some common estate planning tools. Our focus is on the situation in the United States.

THE ESTATE PLANNING PROCESS

The purpose of estate planning is to develop a plan that will enhance and maintain the financial security of individuals and their families. Estate planning is concerned with the distribution of property at death, but it is intimately and unavoidably intertwined with lifetime financial planning.

Most individuals believe that estate planning is relevant only for the wealthy. This is not correct. Individuals with only modest wealth should be concerned with the appropriate and least costly distribution of their property at death.

The estate planning process is identical in principle to the financial planning process.[1] First, data must be obtained and objectives established. This normally is done as a part of the fact-finding for the overall personal financial plan. Any existing estate plan should be evaluated for inadequacies. A plan is then designed for, presented to, and approved by the individual. After review and approval, the plan must be implemented, in-

---

[1]This and the next section draws heavily on *Readings in Estate and Gift Tax Planning*, 2nd ed. Copyright © 1983 by The American College. Used with permission.

cluding the execution of necessary legal documents and transfers of property. Finally, the individual should be made aware that a periodic review of the plan is desirable to determine if changes in financial positions, family relationships, goals, laws, or other circumstances necessitate changes in the plan.

The creation of a comprehensive and creative estate plan is a highly rewarding experience for the estate planning practitioner. Although the emphasis placed on certain aspects of estate plans varies depending on the knowledge and background of the practitioner, the primary objective of a good planner should be to effectuate and implement the desires and objectives of the individual for whom the plan is created in an efficient and effective manner. An estate plan reflects the values of the individual. It may evidence his or her cares and concerns for other human beings as well as for himself or herself. The plan also may reflect his or her own self-interest, grievances, and grudges. Much will be revealed about the individual's character, philosophy of life, and attitudes by the types of planning options selected and the reasons for which he or she selects them.

THE ESTATE PLANNING TEAM

Individuals from more than one professional discipline are qualified to assist clients in estate planning. The best results usually are obtained from enlisting a variety of advisors to assist in total financial planning, including estate planning.

The estate planning team has traditionally consisted of an attorney, an insurance specialist, a bank trust officer, an accountant, and an investment counselor. A financial planner also often is involved. Most financial planners had specialized in one of the disciplines noted previously but have now chosen to take a more holistic approach to advising. Frequently, the financial planner or the insurance specialist makes the first contact with the client, sensitizes him or her to the need for estate planning, and motivates him or her to become involved in the process. This person often acts as coordinator for the entire plan, although any capable member of the team might fill this role.

The accountant is the advisor most likely to have annual contact with the client through preparation of the client's tax returns. This gives him or her the opportunity to be familiar with the size, amount, and nature of the individual's estate. The accountant may be the person who can most easily provide a valuation for any asset in the estate when it is not easily ascertainable. Valuation is particularly crucial if the estate plan includes a buy-sell agreement to provide for a transfer of the business interest upon death or disability (see chapter 17). The accountant also may help prepare the estate tax return.

The trust officer may be the person to whom the individual initially turned for information and for estate planning services if professional management was desired in the administration of trusts. A competent trust officer will be familiar with estate planning and the various estate planning tools. The long-term nature of the relationship between the trustee and the beneficiaries argues for great care to be exercised in trustee selection. Bank trust departments are often trustees.

The life insurance specialist plays an important role on the estate planning team because he or she can provide products that will supply the estate with the necessary cash to pay the estate tax and other liabilities as well as to fund income needs of surviving family members. Life insurance is the primary asset of many estates, and, consequently, a major source of family income after an estate owner dies.

The attorney is a crucial member because plans usually cannot be executed properly without knowledge of the law. Furthermore, only attorneys may practice law. The attorney is responsible for legal advice and for preparing documents assuring that the individual's intentions are expressed in legally enforceable language that serves as the basis for carrying out the plan. These documents virtually always include wills, and many include trusts, buy-sell agreements, and other documents if a sophisticated estate plan is necessary.

Estate planning has become vastly more complicated and challenging as a field of practice. The effective estate planner is familiar with applicable local and federal law and has a good working knowledge of matters pertaining to property, probate, wills and trusts, taxation, corporations, partnerships, business, insurance, and divorce. An estate planner must be able to explain relevant portions of these subjects in plain language.

HOW PROPERTY PASSES AT DEATH

Before we explore the tools used in estate planning, we should understand how property passes at death. When a person dies, all real and personal property that he or she owns or controls and all property to which he, she, or the family is entitled passes to someone. Such property passes, however, in different modes, depending on the nature of the property. For purposes of settling a deceased person's affairs, four modes exist.

First, for most individuals, the most important mode of property distribution on death is **probate,** which is the judicial process by which the will of a deceased person is presented to a court, and the court appoints someone to administer the affairs of the estate, including distribution of the property in accordance with the terms of the will. Property that passes by will (or state intestacy laws, discussed later) is sometimes referred to as **probate property.** The probate process plus estate administration can be expensive, often costing 3 to 5 percent of the value of the deceased person's property.

Second, property passes at death via the nature of property ownership. For example, a joint tenancy with the right of survivorship means that, at the death of one of the owners, title (ownership) vests automatically in the survivor. Such property cannot be passed by will so is not subject to probate but may be included in the gross estate, as discussed in chapter 13.

Third, property can pass by right of contract. Contracts established prior to death that call for payments at or after death pass outside the probate estate. Certain trusts (discussed later) and life insurance contracts are perhaps the best known such contracts. Their value will be included in the taxable estate if the decedent held any incidents of ownership or if the proceeds were payable to or for the benefit of the estate.

Finally, property can pass by right of law. Social Security survivor benefits are perhaps the best known. Such property is not subject to probate and is not included in the gross estate.

ESTATE PLANNING TOOLS

Tools available for estate planning should be used to ensure that (1) assets are sufficient to meet objectives, (2) beneficiaries receive assets in the proportion and manner desired, (3) the minimum in income, estate, gift, and state death taxes and other transfer costs is paid, subject to accomplishing the desired objectives, and (4) sufficient liquidity exists to cover transfer costs. Several estate planning tools are examined next with the preceding objectives in mind.[2]

---

[2]This section draws in part on Fred A. Tillman and Jack Rice, *Who's Next Please?* (Indianapolis, IN: Russell R. Muller Retail Hardware Research Foundation, 1982), Chap. 9.

Wills

A **will** is a legal declaration of an individual's wishes as to the disposition to be made of his or her property on death. It is the principal means by which most estate plans are implemented. A person who dies without a valid will or without having made a complete disposition of his or her property is said to have died **intestate.** In such instances, the state prescribes to whom and how the decedent's property is to be distributed through so-called **intestate succession statutes.** The distribution is based on the degree of individuals' **consanguinity**—blood relationship—to the decedent rather than on the decedent's intentions. Without a will, property cannot be left to charity or to a friend. The state, rather than the individual, appoints the person to administer the decedents' estate—called an **administrator**—and the state, not the individual, chooses guardians for any minor children. If no relatives exist, all of the decedent's property goes to the state, in which case it is said to **escheat.** For these and many other reasons, a will is an essential element of an estate plan.

A will affords the opportunity to declare beneficiaries and to name an **executor,** a person to administer the estate settlement process. The typical will calls for the payment of the deceased person's debts and all estate expenses. The will can provide for gifts to charities and other persons who are objects of the deceased's bounty. Wills can cause the creation of trusts and allow for the naming of trustees and of guardians for minor children. Wills permit the implementation of plans to save income, estate, and gift taxes and to minimize estate expenses. As with the overall estate plan, the will should be reviewed frequently and revised as needed so that objectives are met. If family circumstances or laws have changed since the will was written, it may fail to reflect faithfully the property owner's current wishes, but the existing will is the one that will be followed.

Wills are particularly important tools for owners of closely held businesses. The will can authorize the executor to continue the business, so as to avoid a forced sale, or it can direct its sale. Children or others with an interest or aptitude for the business can inherit the business directly, thereby possibly avoiding family discord.

A will is an **ambulatory instrument,** meaning that it does not take effect until the death of the **testator,** the person making the will. Therefore, it can be changed at any time during life. A new will can expressly revoke any prior wills. A **codicil** changes the part of the will with which it is inconsistent. A will also can be revoked by physically destroying or mutilating it. Individual state law must be carefully followed in revoking a will and in crafting a new one to ensure its validity.

Wills also may be modified by state law. For example, a bequest to a former spouse, which is executed prior to divorce, typically is invalid. Some states even declare the entire will invalid upon divorce. Children born or adopted after a will is executed might be permitted to share in the estate, even though they were not mentioned in the will.

As only the original will is valid, it is important that it be kept in a safe place and that others know its location. Generally, a safe deposit box is not a good place to keep a will. Invariably, so it seems, when a safebox is used, the testator dies on Friday night, and it may be impossible to obtain the will until Monday. There might be a need to read the will immediately to be certain that all the testator's instructions are carried out.

A will must meet technical and legal requirements. First, the testator must be of proper age. In most states this is the age of majority; some states allow a younger person to make a will, although such wills invite legal challenges. The testator must be competent to make a valid will. Competency means that the testator understands that he or she is making a will, knows the extent and nature of the property being disposed of, and knows the natural objects of his or her bounty. The will must be free from fraud, duress, and undue influence.

The will also must be in writing and properly executed, according to applicable state law. Oral wills generally are not valid with some exceptions. The will must be signed, indicating intent to make a will, and generally attested to by the appropriate number of witnesses (which varies from state to state).

In many states, a surviving spouse is entitled to what is called a statutory or forced-heir share of the deceased spouse's property—usually a one-third share. If the decedent's will leaves a lesser amount to the surviving spouse, the survivor can elect against the will and receive the same amount that would have been received had the testator died without a will. In some states, the right to elect against the will extends to children as well.

Living Wills

An estate's value can be substantially reduced because of extraordinary, end-of-life medical measures intended to extend life. Indeed, an average of about 15 percent of *lifetime* medical expenses is incurred in the last six months of life. In response to this potential situation, an increasing number of individuals execute living wills. A **living will** is a legal instrument setting forth the individual's wishes as to the use of life-sustaining measures in case of terminal illness, prolonged coma, or serious incapacitation. Older people with a living will spend only about one-third as much on their final hospital stay as those without one.

State requirements for living wills vary but most statutes require the inclusion of an express statement that the individual is "of sound mind," is voluntarily making the declaration, and desires no artificial prolongation of the dying process. State laws typically define key terms, such as *life-sustaining procedure* and *terminal illness,* and require that the living will be signed, dated, and witnessed in the manner of a testamentary will. No witness may have any interest in the individual's estate.

Living wills offer some clear advantages in this age of impressive life-prolonging technology, which may, unfortunately, not translate into improving the quality of life. A living will ensures that the individual's (as opposed to some well-intentioned family member's) wishes are being carried out. A living will also can ease the anguish that family members may suffer in making what probably could be an excruciating life-or-death decision. A related, companion financial planning tool is the durable power of attorney, highlighted in Box 15-1.

BOX 15-1

THE DURABLE POWER OF ATTORNEY

The **durable power of attorney** is a legal instrument allowing individuals to protect themselves when they have become incapacitated or have been declared incompetent to conduct their own affairs. Many financial planning experts consider this instrument to be among the most important in connection with planning for the elderly. It allows the holder of the power to complete and sign tax returns, pay bills, and generally make and execute other financial decisions on behalf of the incapacitated or incompetent individual.

Obviously, the person named to hold the power should be one in whom the individual has the utmost trust. In most instances, a child holds the power. Upon recovery by the individual, full legal control reverts to him or her. Upon death, the power is terminated.

Gifts

A **gift** is the transfer of property ownership for less than an adequate price. The difference between the property's fair market value and its sales price, if any, is the value of the gift and defines a gift. For a gift to be complete, the **donor** (gift giver) and **donee** (gift recipient) both must be competent, and the donor must have a clear intent to make a gift. Furthermore, the donor must give up ownership and control, and the gift must be delivered and accepted by the donee. A gift is not considered complete for tax purposes if it is delivered and then borrowed back for an indefinite period of time.

As mentioned in chapter 13, $10,000 (indexed) can be given away in property or cash each year to any one person, regardless of relationship, without incurring gift tax liability. A gift can be split between husband and wife, irrespective of which one owns the property. With a split gift, up to $20,000 (indexed) per year per donee can be given without gift tax consequences.

By making gifts (in property or cash) within the annual exclusion, the value is removed from the estate for tax purposes. In other words, $10,000 ($20,000 if a split gift) per year can be given to any one person, with no gift tax liability incurred, and the gifted property will be removed from the estate. If a gifting program is started early and continued, a series of annual exclusion gifts can substantially reduce estate taxes.

If a gift of more than $10,000 ($20,000) is made to any one person during the calendar year, a *taxable* gift has been made. A federal gift tax return should be filed and gift tax assessed according to the tax rate schedule. It is not necessary actually to pay tax until the unified tax credit has been exhausted.

There are many advantages from making taxable gifts. Box 15-2 lists some of the common nontax reasons to make gifts. Some of the tax-based reasons for making gifts are as follows:

- Individual gifts, up to the amount of the annual exclusion, are not added back to the estate for purposes of calculating federal estate tax. Thus, the estate is reduced by the amount of the annual exclusion.
- A credit is allowed against any federal estate tax due, equal to the amount of any gift tax paid during lifetime. That is, taxes are not paid twice on the same transfer.
- The gift tax is tax exclusive whereas the estate tax is tax inclusive. In other words, the assets used to pay gift taxes are not themselves subject to tax, yet assets used to pay estate taxes are included in calculating that tax. Box 15-3 illustrates the potential importance of this advantage.
- No federal estate tax is due on the appreciation of the value of the gift from the date of gift to the date of death.
- If a gift is made to someone other than the spouse, federal income tax can be saved if the property transferred would have otherwise produced taxable income to the donor.

A life insurance policy often is an excellent type of property to gift. The value of the gift is the replacement cost, as discussed in chapter 13. Were the policy included in the estate at the time of death, the estate tax value would be the amount of the death proceeds. If the face amount of the policy were $100,000 and the value for gift purposes were no more than $10,000, the policy could be transferred by gift within the annual exclusion, and there would be no gift tax consequences. Of course, the donor must live for more than three years from the date of the gift to avoid inclusion of the policy proceeds in his or her estate under IRC Section 2035.

Greatly appreciated property may make an appropriate gift. If sale of the property is anticipated, a gift to a person who is in a lower income tax bracket can make good

BOX 15-2

NONTAX REASONS FOR MAKING GIFTS

Motivations for making gifts often are either unrelated or only indirectly related to saving on estate or income taxes. Nontax reasons for making gifts include the following:

- Individuals derive satisfaction from giving to others.
- The expense of administration and other costs associated with processing the estate can be minimized or avoided by giving the property away during lifetime.
- Anyone can review the public records of a probate court. By making a gift, the property is removed from probate and privacy is retained.
- By giving the property away, management responsibilities are shifted to the new owners.

- Should a person believe that he or she is no longer able to manage assets properly, the assets might be given away to protect their value. (Unfortunately, most persons are unable to recognize when they are no longer competent to make this decision.)
- Making gifts to children can provide them with the opportunity to learn how to manage money or property.
- If an individual has assets that he or she wishes to pass to a particular individual and anticipates the possibility of family disharmony, making a gift during life can be important to meet the objective. If a will does not exist or is declared invalid because of a will contest, property that passes through the estate could ultimately be passed to unintended individuals. By giving the property away, this risk is eliminated.

financial sense. The donee would then sell the property and pay less taxes on the gain. The gift tax consequences should be compared with the income (or capital gains) tax consequences to determine whether taxes in the overall transactions are lessened.

If the property will be sold after death, it often should be retained rather than given away. This is because appreciated property receives a stepped-up tax basis if included in the estate, whereas property that is given away carries over the donor's tax basis. If property is given away and the donee sells it, income tax must be paid on any difference between the amount received on sale and the donor's tax basis. If the property is retained and its value included in the estate, an estate tax must be paid on the fair market value of the property. The value of the property included in the gross estate, however, becomes the new basis to be used by the beneficiaries or the estate for income or capital gains tax purposes.

Thus, suppose Larry owns only one piece of property. He paid $10,000 for it, and it is now worth $200,000. If he gives the property away and the donee sells it, the donee must pay income or capital gains tax on the $190,000 gain. If he does not give away the property but retains it until his death, naming the person to whom he would have given it during lifetime as the beneficiary, the value of the property ($200,000) will be included in his estate for estate tax purposes. The $200,000 value becomes the new tax basis for the beneficiary. If the property is then sold for its $200,000 fair market value, there is no gain, and no income or capital gains tax has to be paid by the beneficiary.

As can be seen, it might be better for tax purposes to keep property rather than to give it away. One should determine in each case which approach renders the least taxes. The additional costs associated with probate should not be overlooked. These costs might offset any tax savings.

There are other potential disadvantages to making taxable gifts in excess of the equivalent exemption amount. One disadvantage, of course, is the loss of control. Moreover, the transfer tax is paid earlier than would otherwise be the case if the assets were held until death.

BOX 15-3

AN IMPORTANT TAX ADVANTAGE OF GIFTS: TAX EXCLUSIVENESS

The U.S. federal transfer tax system generally is tax *inclusive*. This means that estate taxes are levied on the total value of property in an individual's taxable estate, including the property used to pay estate taxes. Property transferred during life, however, is generally tax *exclusive*. That is, transfer taxes do not apply to the taxes themselves. This difference can profoundly affect the total transfer taxes paid.

For example, Manfred wishes to transfer property valued at $3.0 million to his daughter, Dagmar. Assume that he is in the 55 percent marginal transfer tax bracket, so gift taxes would be

about $1.65 million ($3.0 million × 0.55). Thus, Manfred needs $4.65 million to transfer $3.0 million to his daughter via gifting.

If Manfred chose to retain the property and transfer it to Dagmar at his death, however, the estate would need $6.67 million. The estate taxes on $6.67 million would be $3.67 million (at the 55 percent rate), netting the $3.0 million to Dagmar. Thus, Manfred would require some 43 percent more property to achieve his objective at death than during life. Of course, this treatment ignores the fact that transfer tax payment is made earlier with a lifetime rather than a testamentary transfer.

Joint Ownership of Property

The various types of joint ownerships, presented earlier, need not be discussed again except to point out that joint ownership can be a means of bypassing the probate estate and, thus, avoiding probate costs. This can be helpful in some situations.

A potential disadvantage of joint ownership should be noted. Under a tenancy by the entirety (right of survivorship between husband and wife), the tax law requires that 50 percent of the fair market value of the property be included in the gross estate of the first joint tenant to die. Although this form of ownership avoids estate tax on one-half of the total property value in the first estate, 100 percent of the fair market value at the time of the death of the surviving spouse would be included in his or her estate. This is true because he or she would receive the first decedent's interest through survivor's rights. (This, of course, assumes that the surviving spouse does not sell or give away the property during his or her lifetime.)

As only 50 percent of the value of the property was included in the first spouse's estate, the stepped-up basis for income tax purposes would apply only to that part of the total value. The excluded 50 percent would not receive a stepped-up basis. If the property might be sold during the surviving spouse's lifetime, this area should be examined carefully. It might be better if the entire property value were included in the gross estate to obtain a stepped-up basis on the total value of the property.

Trusts

A **trust** is a legal arrangement whereby one party transfers property to someone else who holds the legal title and manages the trust property for the benefit of others. The person who establishes the trust is the **grantor** (or **settlor**). The person who receives the legal title and manages the property is the **trustee,** and the person for whose benefit the property is held is the **beneficiary.** As the word *trust* implies, faith and confidence are placed in the trustee to act solely on the beneficiary's behalf. Legally, the trustee has a fiduciary responsibility to act in accordance with the law and the provisions of the trust instrument.

Trusts are effective estate planning tools. They often supply elements that are impossible to obtain through a direct gift. Income, estate, and gift tax savings also can be effected through the use of trusts. Trusts can eliminate the need for guardianship of property. They can provide financial support for a disabled child or other family member. One can provide a life income for family members, with the principal of the trust distributed to charity. Assets can be protected from creditors through the use of a trust.

Generic Types of Trusts

Many types of trusts exist, each designed to meet specific objectives. A trust created during life is referred to as an **inter vivos** or **living trust.** With an inter vivos trust, a living person creates the trust and transfers property to it.

A trust created at death through a person's will is referred to as a **testamentary trust.** With a testamentary trust, property is transferred at death. It allows a testator to "control property from the grave" in that he or she can specify the postdeath form and timing of distributions to children and others. This type of control can be useful in terms of protecting property from being squandered and to ensure effective property management.

A living trust can be revocable or irrevocable. With a **revocable trust,** the grantor can terminate or alter the trust as he or she wishes and regain ownership of the property. With an **irrevocable trust,** he or she permanently relinquishes ownership and control.

A revocable trust might be desirable as a device for transferring assets directly to beneficiaries outside of the probate estate. This avoids probate costs in estate settlement. Because the property is outside of probate, the business of the trust can continue on an uninterrupted, confidential basis, or the trust can be terminated and assets distributed to the beneficiaries confidentially and without administrative delay.

A revocable trust is not without disadvantages. No income, estate, or gift tax savings exist under a revocable trust. The transfer to the trust does not constitute a completed gift; therefore, no gift tax is assessed. As a complete gift is not made, effective ownership of the property is retained by the grantor for tax purposes. Thus, the trust property will be included in the taxable estate, and trust income is taxable to the grantor. Administration and management charges in many cases must be paid under a trust arrangement. These charges offset savings in probate generated from the use of a trust.

Control and ownership are relinquished over property placed in an irrevocable trust. This loss of flexibility could be a high price to pay should conditions change. When property is placed in an irrevocable trust, generally a complete gift has been made that may have gift tax consequences. Of course, income and estate tax savings applicable to any gift of property or cash may result.

Marital Deduction and Credit Shelter Trusts

The marital deduction can be an important estate planning device. The marital deduction provisions of the IRC provide for an unlimited deduction for property left to the surviving spouse. It is, therefore, possible to leave everything to the surviving spouse and incur no federal estate tax. To do so, however, might actually result in a higher total estate tax liability when the taxes on the estates of both spouses are taken into consideration. Box 15-4 offers an example of this situation.

Trust arrangements typically are used to effect the plan explained in Box 15-4 through what are known as two-trust wills. Testamentary trusts are established to permit the surviving spouse to have substantial enjoyment of all of the estate owner's property during his or her lifetime, to bypass the surviving spouse's estate as to the property that will eventually go to others, and to qualify an optimal amount of the assets for the estate tax marital deduction.

BOX 15-4

ESTATE PLANNING FOR LEN AND BECKY

After deductions for expenses, debts, and losses, Len's estate has a value of $3 million. The year of death is assumed to be 2006 or later. If the entire value were left to his surviving spouse, Becky, and not dissipated or given away under the annual exclusion during her lifetime, an estate tax of $740,300 would be imposed upon Becky's subsequent death (provided death occurs in 2006 or later) and probate cost probably would be at least $90,000 (3 percent of probate estate). This would result in $2,169,700 being left ultimately to the children ($3,000,000 – $740,400 – $90,000).

There are better ways to provide for the surviving spouse. Assuming Len died in 2006 or later, he could have left Becky $2 million under the marital deduction. This amount would not be taxed in Len's estate. The $1 million balance, which could be left to the children or others, is equal to the exemption equivalent, and the unified credit would equal the amount of tentative tax based on the taxable estate. Thus, no estate tax would be payable.

Assuming that Becky owns no other assets and does not dissipate or give away the $2 million received from Len, her estate would pay estate taxes of $322,400, after application of the unified credit (and estimated final expenses of $60,000). The other $1 million escapes all estate taxation on Becky's death.

The Marital Trust   First, a **marital trust** is established to receive property that qualifies for the marital deduction when the first spouse dies. When the surviving spouse dies, any amounts not consumed or given to others will be taxed in his or her estate. Although the establishment of a trust for the marital deduction property is not essential, it may prove convenient for investment management and administration purposes.

Generally, the marital trust must provide that the surviving spouse has the right to consume or give away the principal of the trust. This general power of appointment gives the spouse the right to invade principal whenever desired and permits the trust to qualify for the marital deduction. The trust must provide for the distribution of income to the spouse at least annually. If the trust remains intact and the surviving spouse does not exercise the power of appointment, either during lifetime or through his or her will, the property of the trust can be distributed to beneficiaries as designated in the will of the first spouse to die.

Generally, a property interest will not qualify for the marital deduction unless it is included in the surviving spouse's gross estate. Certain terminable interest property passing to a surviving spouse does not qualify for the marital deduction. As discussed in chapter 13, however, the law allows *qualified terminable interest property* (QTIP) to qualify for the marital deduction if certain conditions are met.

The QTIP election can be of great importance in estate planning. It permits a decedent to provide for the surviving spouse during his or her lifetime, yet allows the decedent to direct property to others—for example, the children—without loss of the marital deduction. A trust is commonly used. Thus, a QTIP trust can offer the same tax advantages as other approaches while retaining assets under terms that have been established upon the first spouse's death. The spouse may be given the power to invade the trust corpus for reasons of health, education, maintenance, and support. In addition, the spouse may be given the right to take the greater of $5,000 or 5 percent of the trust corpus per year (a so-called **5-by-5 power**). The QTIP trust is commonly used to ensure that, on the death of one spouse, the remarriage of the surviving spouse will not result in the children of the first marriage being left nothing.

The Credit Shelter Trust Property that is not left to the surviving spouse outright, in the marital (or QTIP) trust, or not used to meet expenses, taxes, and other bequests is placed in a second trust known as a **credit shelter trust** (also known by several other terms, including a **bypass trust,** a **nonmarital trust,** and a **residuary trust**). The surviving spouse often has the right to the income for life from the credit shelter trust property. The income from the trust could supplement the income provided by the marital trust and the principal could also be available, if needed, in accordance with the 5-by-5 power and the right to invade for health, education, and support reasons. On the death of the surviving spouse, all right to income from the residuary trust is terminated, and the trust property would not be taxed in his or her estate. This gives the surviving spouse the effective use of all the decedent's property during his or her lifetime, without having the residual trust included in that spouse's estate for federal estate tax purposes.

An Illustration Figure 15-1 compares (1) the simple will approach, in which Len's $2 million net estate is left outright to Becky, and (2) the two-trust arrangement in which the $2 million estate is divided between the marital and residuary trusts. The residuary trust receives property equivalent in value to that necessary to utilize fully the unified credit.

Because trust corpus passes outside the probate estate, no probate costs are assessed against its value on the beneficiary's death. Also, because the beneficiary does not own

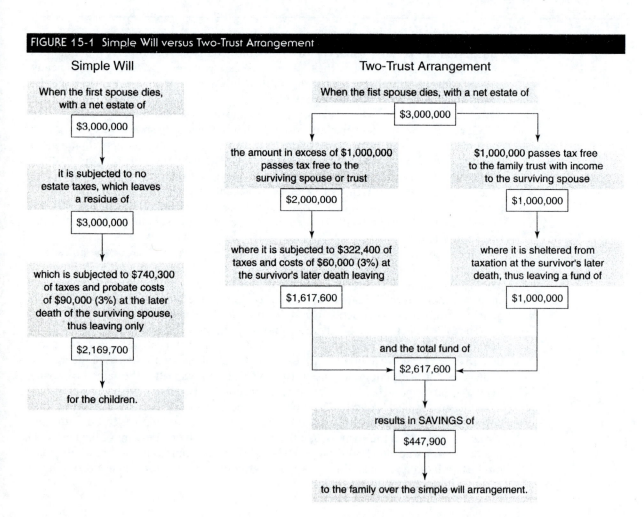

FIGURE 15-1 Simple Will versus Two-Trust Arrangement

Simple Will

When the first spouse dies, with a net estate of

$3,000,000

it is subjected to no estate taxes, which leaves a residue of

$3,000,000

which is subjected to $740,300 of taxes and probate costs of $90,000 (3%) at the later death of the surviving spouse, thus leaving only

$2,169,700

for the children.

Two-Trust Arrangement

When the fist spouse dies, with a net estate of

$3,000,000

the amount in excess of $1,000,000 passes tax free to the surviving spouse or trust

$2,000,000

where it is subjected to $322,400 of taxes and costs of $60,000 (3%) at the survivor's later death leaving

$1,617,600

$1,000,000 passes tax free to the family trust with income to the surviving spouse

$1,000,000

where it is sheltered from taxation at the survivor's later death, thus leaving a fund of

$1,000,000

and the total fund of

$2,617,600

results in SAVINGS of

$447,900

to the family over the simple will arrangement.

or control the trust, it is excluded from her estate. These two sources constitute the savings of $447,900 of the trust arrangement over the simple will arrangement. As a result of the use of the marital deduction and the two-trust will, the deceased couple's children (or other beneficiaries) would receive a significantly larger share of the estate than if it were necessary to pay estate tax.

Trusts for Minor Children

Many persons make gifts from time to time to their minor children to accumulate a substantial fund for education or other use when they are old enough to handle the responsibility. A trust can be useful in such situations.

As noted in chapter 13, the annual exclusion is available only for gifts of present interest. Unless the beneficiary has the right to the present possession and enjoyment of the property, the annual exclusion will not be allowed. Thus, the annual exclusion would not be available for a gift to a minor in trust if the funds were not presently available to that minor.

One way to avoid this problem is to establish the trust for minors known as a **Section 2503(c)** trust. By meeting the requirements for this trust, a gift can be made to minors without the loss of the $10,000 annual gift tax exclusion. To qualify for the annual exclusion, the trust must provide that:

1. The trustee has the discretion to distribute both principal and income.
2. The beneficiaries are entitled to receive the principal of the trust when they reach age 21.
3. Should any of the beneficiaries die before reaching maturity, his or her share of the assets would pass through his or her estate.

By meeting these requirements, income can be accumulated until the minor reaches age 21, and the $10,000 annual exclusion per beneficiary can be used. This type of trust is a popular device. Grandparents who wish to establish an educational fund for their grandchildren often use it. A provision could be included in the trust allowing it to continue beyond age 21, provided the beneficiaries agree to this continuation. A generation-skipping transfer tax could be imposed in such situations if the amounts involved were substantial (see chapter 13).

With a Section 2503(c) trust, gifts of life insurance policies in trust for minors should qualify as those of a present interest if (1) any policy value may be used for their benefit, (2) policy ownership vests at age 21, and (3) the policy proceeds or value would be included in the child's gross estate were he or she to die prior to age 21. Any premiums paid by the grantor should also qualify as present interest gifts.

Gifts also can be made to minors under the **Uniform Gifts to Minors Act** or under the more recent **Uniform Transfers to Minors Act.** Under these acts, an adult is named custodian for the minor and manages the property through a custodian account. The property is distributed to the minor at age 18 or 21, depending on state law.

Crummey Trusts

In spite of its name (which is a successful litigant's name), the Crummey trust is a useful device. With the **Crummey trust,** the annual exclusion is available for gifts made to such a trust, provided the beneficiaries have a reasonable opportunity to demand distribution of amounts contributed to the trust. A Crummey provision ordinarily works as follows. The grantor makes a gift to an irrevocable, living trust. The trust beneficiaries often are the grantor's children, grandchildren, or both.[3] The beneficiaries are notified

---

[3]If the grandchildren are beneficiaries, a generation-skipping transfer tax may be incurred if substantial amounts are involved. See chapter 13.

by the trustee that they have the power for a defined period (typically 15 to 60 days) after receiving notification to withdraw some portion of the transferred property. The simultaneous acts of the grantor transferring property to the trust and the beneficiaries being permitted to withdraw the same property from the trust is tantamount to the grantor giving the property to the beneficiaries outright, thus qualifying for the $10,000 annual exclusion.

Of course, it is not anticipated that the beneficiaries will, in fact, withdraw any property from the trust during the defined period. In effect, each beneficiary is given a short-term general power of appointment. By not executing their powers, the beneficiaries permit their powers to lapse. The lapse of a general power is a gift-taxable transfer, unless the property is subject to a 5-by-5 power. As a consequence, limiting each beneficiary's Crummey power to $5,000 guarantees that the lapse will not be treated as a taxable gift from each beneficiary to all other beneficiaries.

Irrevocable Life Insurance Trusts

Overview   As noted earlier, the value of a life insurance policy for gift tax purposes is the interpolated terminal reserve plus any unearned premium rather than the policy face amount. This makes the gift of a life insurance policy a popular tax-saving device. Many persons use a trust. Under an **irrevocable life insurance trust** (ILIT), an insurance policy on the grantor's life is owned by an irrevocable inter vivos trust, with the policy proceeds payable to the trust as beneficiary. Generally, should the grantor live more than three years from the date the trust is established, and if all incidents of ownership in the policy are relinquished, the proceeds will not be a part of the grantor's taxable estate. If the policy is applied for and owned by the trustee from its inception, the policy death proceeds should be excluded from the gross estate even if death occurs within the first three years, provided the purchase of the insurance was at the discretion of the trustee.

The trustee pays policy premiums from either the trust corpus or from annual gifts to the trust from the grantor. The latter is the more common case, although the gifts should not be designated as premium payments. The trustee will have been given the authority (at his or her discretion) but not required to purchase insurance and, if desired, to use trust funds—including those gifted annually by the grantor—to pay premiums.

An Illustration   Figure 15-2 illustrates the functioning of an ILIT. In this example, the widow's estate, composed almost exclusively of land that has long been in the family, is valued at $5.1 million. Estate taxes are $2.7 million. Of course, the marital deduction is not available, hence, the high taxes.

The widow's will provides that her three children are to share equally in her estate. She had wisely and accurately estimated her estate settlement costs at $2.7 million and had created an ILIT, which was the owner and beneficiary of a $2.7 million policy insuring her life. On her death, the life insurance company paid the $2.7 million death proceeds to the trust.

The trust agreement authorized the trustee to purchase property from the estate, which the trustee elected to do, thus acquiring family land valued at that amount and simultaneously providing the executor with the needed cash to pay estate taxes. The trustee distributed the land valued at $2.7 million to the three children in equal proportions. After paying the IRS, the executor distributed the remaining $2.4 million of family land equally to the children, thus providing each with a one-third total ownership in the land, valued at $1.7 million. We can see, therefore, that the life insurance—which was not included in the gross estate thanks to sound estate planning—has enabled the family to retain ownership of the land and to meet estate settlement obligations.

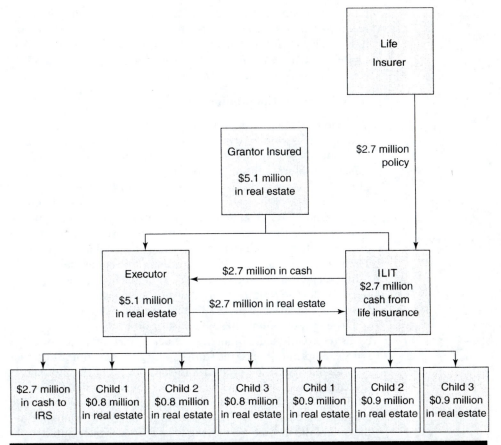

FIGURE 15-2 Operation of the Irrevocable Life Insurance Trust at Grantor's Death

Considerations in Using an ILIT   The funds gifted to the trust by the grantor/insured should qualify as gifts of a present interest if the trust contains a Crummey provision. To avoid the donor incurring gift taxation, the gifts should not exceed $10,000 ($20,000 if a split gift) per trust beneficiary. To avoid the beneficiaries incurring gift taxation from allowing their short-term general power of appointment to lapse, the donor's annual gifts should not exceed the product of the number of trust beneficiaries times $5,000 (or 5 percent of trust corpus, if this is greater).

Death proceeds can be invested or distributed to trust beneficiaries through arrangements that are not available under life insurance policy settlement options. Therefore, it generally is more desirable to have policy proceeds paid in a single sum to the trust rather than have the insurance company pay the proceeds on an installment basis. Of course, there is no guarantee that the trustee will make wise investments, and there are no guarantees with the trust as there are under an insurance contract.

The need for an insurance trust rather than the outright gift of life insurance should be carefully considered. The $10,000 annual exclusion can be made available for the outright gift of a life insurance policy, as well as for the premiums paid on a policy by the donor. When a policy is assigned to such a trust or when premiums are paid on policies held in such a trust, the $10,000 annual exclusion may not be available unless a Crummey provision is included in the trust instrument. Therefore, the gift of a policy in trust and the future premium payments can be fully taxable gifts that are later added back to the estate for estate tax purposes. Also, there are no income tax savings for an insurance trust if the policy insures either the donor or his or her spouse. If the trust were sufficiently funded so that the income to the trust were adequate to pay the premiums, the trust income would still be taxed to the grantor.

Charitable Remainder Trusts

Overview   A **charitable remainder trust** (CRT) is a living, irrevocable, tax-exempt trust in which the donor contributes property to the trust, reserving to himself or herself (or someone else) an income stream from the trust, with the residual trust corpus, called the **remainder interest,** ultimately passing to a charity. The CRT can be an effective means of helping a charity and of saving on transfer taxes. Many estate planners consider the CRT to be one of the best and most underutilized estate planning tools.

A typical CRT arrangement is as follows. First, an individual with highly appreciated assets, such as stock, real estate, or interests in a closely held business, transfers the property to the trust. Often the property has provided a low income in relation to its value. The trustee promises to make a stream of income payments to the trust beneficiary (often the grantor), which is called a **retained interest** in the trust, either over the beneficiary's lifetime (and possibly that of the spouse also) or for a term not to exceed 20 years. This income usually is subject to income taxation.

The trustee often will sell a part or all of the donated property, investing the proceeds to provide some or all of the needed income to the beneficiary. Because the trust is tax exempt, any sale is free from capital gains taxation. Thus, considerably more money is available than if the grantor had sold the property and paid taxes, as Figure 15-3 illustrates (based on an asset whose market value is $3 million and tax basis is $360,000). Under a CRT, the grantor avoids capital gains on the sale of the highly appreciated property and effectively converts low-yield property into an important source of income. At the end of the income period, the trust corpus is distributed to the charity.

Because a charity is entitled to the remainder interest, the grantor is entitled to an income tax deduction immediately in an amount equal to that interest. The amount of the deduction is determined actuarially in accordance with IRS procedures. In general, the more distant the remainder interest and the higher the retained interest, the less the deduction, and vice versa.

Figure 15-4 illustrates the CRT process, assuming the same $3 million highly appreciated asset as in Figure 15-3. Here, Manfred is the grantor and income beneficiary. He is to receive a lifetime annual income of 6 percent of the initial trust value or $180,000 per year. The remainder interest is valued at $990,000 by IRS procedures and, therefore,

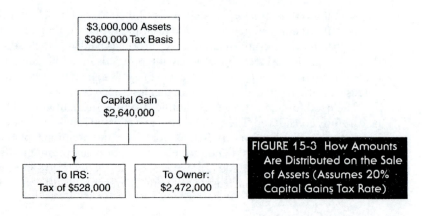

FIGURE 15-3 How Amounts Are Distributed on the Sale of Assets (Assumes 20% Capital Gains Tax Rate)

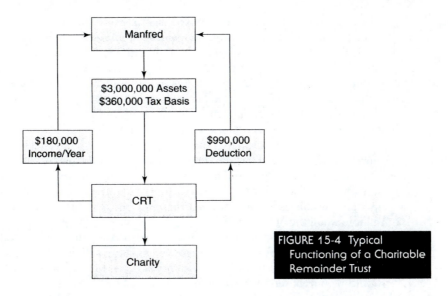

FIGURE 15-4 Typical Functioning of a Charitable Remainder Trust

this amount is deductible as a charitable contribution for tax purposes. The trustee might have sold the asset to realize $3 million but the capital gain escapes all taxation.

Types of CRTs   CRTs are of two types. A **charitable remainder annuity trust** (CRAT) pays a fixed amount to the income beneficiary at least annually and this amount is not changed during the life of the trust. No additional assets may be contributed to a CRAT.

A **charitable remainder unitrust** (CRUT) pays a fixed percentage of the fair market value of its assets to the income beneficiary at least annually. Trust assets are revalued each year, so the income will vary each year. A CRUT may accept additional contributions.

Use of Life Insurance with a CRT   Of course, the grantor loses ownership and control of the property transferred to the CRT. The CRT, thus, saves estate taxes but the transfer deprives heirs of the value of the property, a dissatisfying result for many individuals.

Many donors will, therefore, establish what are called **wealth replacement trusts,** which are simply irrevocable life insurance trusts containing insurance whose death benefit roughly equals the value of the property transferred to the CRT. The life insurance premium might range from perhaps 5 percent of the face amount for 70-year-old individuals to less than 1 percent for individuals under age 40, amounts almost certainly well below the income from the CRT. Moreover, if structured properly, death proceeds will not be included in the grantor's gross estate.

Thus, for example, Manfred might create a wealth replacement trust with Dagmar as trust beneficiary. The trust would purchase a $3.0 million life insurance policy on Manfred's life. Manfred would make annual gifts to the trust in the amount of the policy premium, funded from the CRT income stream.

LIFE INSURANCE FOR ESTATE LIQUIDITY

Life insurance is often the best way to provide the liquidity needed for estate clearance. For example, consider the individual who dies, leaving property valued at $3.0 million. Assume estate settlement costs, mostly in the form of federal estate taxes, of $1.0 million.

Of course, the state and federal governments, as well as attorneys and others working on behalf of the estate, expect to be paid without undue delay and to be paid in cash.

If the $3.0 million in property is illiquid, the executor could be forced to sell some of it at disadvantageous prices. Even if the property is liquid, the estate owner may have preferred that the property pass to his or her heirs intact, such as often is the situation with real estate and closely held businesses (see chapter 17). In such cases, life insurance that itself is not included in the estate—for example, owned by an ILIT—can be used to meet estate settlement costs while accomplishing the individual's wishes.

Moreover, life insurance is unique among financial products in that the event that causes the cash obligation—death—can concomitantly generate the cash. We can think of the life insurance premium in this sense as being the price or premium for a call option. Thus, for a premium of perhaps 1 to 3 percent of the total estate obligation, the individual purchases an option equal in value to the contingent obligation and that is callable when the obligation falls due. The individual, thereby, can be assured that his or her estate can be passed to heirs intact without concern about forced sales, about having to liquidate family property, or about having to sell high-income-generating assets.

Even so, several questions remain to be answered. In particular, what products should be purchased? Who should own the policy? How should the beneficiary designation be structured? How can the insurance be structured to have the funds available for the person who must pay estate costs?[4]

For married couples, the marital deduction coupled with the unified credit may eliminate or greatly reduce estate taxes at the death of the first spouse, focusing on the need for liquidity to meet estate taxes on the second spouse's death. Assuming that life insurance is the best means to provide this liquidity, several ways are available for providing the cash economically. One way is to use individual policies that insure both lives in a sufficient amount to meet the projected need. A second approach is to use a joint life policy that provides for payment of the face amount at the first death. A third approach is to use a second-to-die policy that pays the face amount when the second insured dies, rather than the first.

Finally, only one spouse might be insured. If the insured is the first to die, the proceeds can be retained for ultimate liquidity needs. This may be the only solution if one spouse is uninsurable, and it may be reasonable even if both are insurable if the surviving spouse could invest the proceeds to supplement income.

Formerly, cross ownership of life insurance between spouses was not uncommon. The obvious reason was to avoid the inclusion of insurance proceeds in the estate of the insured. Now, with the unlimited marital deduction, less need exists for insurance to be owned by the spouse of the decedent insured.

In large estates and with large amounts of insurance, it may be appropriate to have the insurance owned by a party other than the insured or spouse. A trust is one alternative. A child may be another. Use of an ILIT as owner may be especially wise if the insurance is not to be used at the first death but instead retained for meeting estate liquidity needs on the second death. As noted earlier, gifts to the trust (which can be used by the trust to pay life insurance premiums) can qualify for the annual gift tax exclusion if the trust contains a Crummey provision.

Special care should be taken in designating ownership of joint policies. If the surviving spouse/insured is owner of a second-to-die policy, the proceeds will be included in the estate of the second to die. With a first-death policy, the survivor may be able to gift the proceeds before being subjected to tax, although if the survivor is elderly, this possibility may be remote.

---

[4]This section draws in part on *Personal Estate & Retirement Planning Course,* The Life Underwriter Training Council.

It cannot be assumed that, if insurance is payable to the surviving spouse or to the children of the estate owner, it will somehow help the executor pay estate clearance costs. Common alternatives include:

- having the insurance payable to the estate
- relying on the beneficiary to lend money to the estate
- relying on the beneficiary to buy assets from the estate

The first alternative has several disadvantages:

- Proceeds will be included in the estate and subject to tax, although the marital deduction could negate this tax. (Note, however, that the marital deduction is not available for assets used to pay estate taxes.)
- In most states, administration costs will be increased, as they are a percentage of probate assets.
- Proceeds become subject to the claims of estate creditors.
- State death tax exemption for insurance proceeds may be lost.

The likelihood of the second or third alternative functioning as planned depends on who is named beneficiary. The likelihood of the estate owner's plans being carried out is greatest when the insurance is payable to a trust, with the trustee authorized to either lend money to the estate or purchase assets from the estate. Trust provisions cannot require the trustee to loan money or purchase assets from the estate without jeopardizing the estate tax advantages of using a trust. As mentioned earlier, they merely give the trustee the power to do so at the trustee's discretion. In most instances, a trustee could be expected to loan money or purchase assets should the need arise and the trust instrument has authorized (but not required) such action.

Insurance purchased for estate liquidity is commonly owned by and payable to an irrevocable, inter vivos trust, with trust income payable to the spouse for life and corpus payable to the children at the spouse's death. This follows the two-trust arrangement discussed earlier. In fact, the will of the insured estate owner often pours the nonmarital share of the estate into the irrevocable insurance trust.

Unmarried persons do not have benefit of the unlimited marital deduction, instead having to settle for the unified credit only and other estate planning tools to minimize estate settlement costs. Options as to the types of insurance to purchase to cover these costs are more limited for unmarried people. However, all other elements of the preceding discussion apply equally to them.

LIFE INSURANCE AND THE GENERATION-SKIPPING TRANSFER TAX

Life insurance can become involved in a generation-skipping transfer (GST) and, thereby, provoke a GST tax. As discussed in chapter 13, a GST tax may be levied when property is transferred to a person who is two or more generations younger than the transferor. The transferee is referred to as the *skip person.* In general, a GST can evolve from (1) the payment of premiums, (2) the transfer of policies, and (3) the payment of death proceeds.[5]

Transfers of Funds to Pay Premiums

Generally, funds transferred to a skip person to pay premiums on a life insurance policy or an annuity are considered a GST. Additionally, transfer to a trust for which a skip person is beneficiary may result in a GST when the property is transferred to the trust, such as amounts to pay premiums on a policy owned by an irrevocable life insurance trust.

---

[5]This section draws on "Generation-Skipping Transfer Tax," *Advanced Sales Reference Service,* Sec. 56 (Cincinnati, OH: The National Underwriter Company, 1999).

The $10,000 annual gift tax exclusion ($20,000 if a split gift) and the $1 million lifetime GST exemption ($2 million if a spouse joins in the transfer) may be available to reduce or eliminate any GST tax.

Thus, present interest gifts of funds of $10,000 or less to cover premiums on life insurance—in trust or otherwise—would not ordinarily invoke any GST tax. Nontaxable gifts are not subject to the GST tax.

Transfer of Policies

A GST generally occurs when a life insurance or annuity contract is transferred to a skip person. Additionally, such an insurance contract transferred to a trust with a skip person as beneficiary may result in a GST. Again, the $10,000 annual exclusion and $1 million lifetime exemption would be available.

Policy Death Proceeds

Regardless of the manner of payment of life insurance or annuity proceeds, a GST will have been made if policy benefits are transferred from an insured or annuitant to a skip person. Thus, if a grandparent is the insured and owner of a $3 million life insurance policy and a grandchild is beneficiary, a GST will have occurred on the grandparent's death, and $1.1 million of GST tax [($3 million – $1 million) × 0.55] would be due on the transfer.

Leveraging the $1.0 Million Exemption

As already noted, a transferor is allowed a $1.0 million (indexed) lifetime exemption ($2.0 million if the spouse joins in the transfer). Thus, an insured/transferor may transfer a policy or funds to pay premiums on a policy to a skip person and, through use of the lifetime exemption, possibly avoid any GST tax. Death proceeds received also would be free of any GST tax.

Leveraging of the $1.0 million GST lifetime exemption can be accomplished by allocating the exemption against the premium dollars (or against the value of the policy on transfer) versus the higher ultimate value of the death proceeds. Leveraging of the $1.0 million exemption can also be accomplished for premiums on policies in an ILIT or for policy transfer to such a trust. Allocation of the $1.0 million exemption is, however, postponed.

For example, assume that Richard creates an irrevocable life insurance trust for the benefit of his children and grandchildren. Each year he transfers $50,000 to the trust to be used (at the trustee's discretion) to make premium payments on a $2.0 million policy on his life. Each year he allocates $50,000 of his $1.0 million GST exemption to each transfer.

Assuming Richard makes no other allocations of his $1.0 million exemption, the trust will not be subject to any GST tax during its first 20 years ($50,000 × 20). At the end of 20 years, Richard will have exhausted his $1.0 million GST exemption, and additional amounts contributed to the trust will be subject to the GST tax.

If Richard died during the 20-year period, no GST tax would be due on the $2.0 million death proceeds. If he died after the first 20 years, a pro rata share of the death proceeds might be subject to the GST tax. Of course, to ensure that no GST tax ever would be payable, one ideally would use a policy that became paid up before the transfers to the trust exceeded the $1.0 million GST exemption.

CONCLUSION

Individuals of all levels of wealth should make plans for orderly distribution of their property at their death. If they do not do it, the government will do it for them! One of the biggest obstacles to making plans rests in the unpleasantness inherent in the subject of death and the awkwardness of discussing it.

As a subject of financial planning, estate planning provides the structure of implementing one's postdeath wishes at minimal costs. We might routinely think of life insurance as an effective, efficient mechanism for providing financial support to families. However, many people seem surprised to learn of the important role that life insurance can and does play in providing the liquidity necessary to settle estate obligations. As noted earlier, life insurance is unique among financial service products in that the event that creates the obligation can simultaneously cause generation of the funds to meet the obligation. As long as death itself causes additional expenses and taxes, life insurance can be expected to pay this vital role.

Questions

1. What are some of the potential consequences of not creating a will and a living will?
2. What three considerations are especially important when assessing liquidity needs in estate planning?
3. Describe some approaches by which trusts can be used to deflect or defer taxes on shares of estates being passed on to spouses and children.
4. Describe some appropriate uses for revocable and irrevocable trusts.

CHAPTER

16

RETIREMENT PLANNING

Objectives

- Understand how longer life spans, increasing retiree costs, and uncertain Social Security benefits may affect estimated retirement needs.

- Summarize the retirement planning process, including the estimation of retirement needs and related savings requirements.

- Describe the tax treatment of nonqualified retirement plans.

- Explain how various nonqualified plans can be used for retirement planning.

A key element of personal financial planning is that of providing for one's retirement. Products and services offered by life insurers and their agents have always played an important role in the provision of economic security in retirement. This chapter examines retirement planning generally and explores how selected individually issued insurance products fit into such planning.

INTRODUCTION

Perhaps the most essential step in the retirement planning process is a recognition of the need to plan. Surveys confirm that most U.S. workers fail to estimate their retirement needs, in large measure because they are intimidated by the process. Figure 16-1 shows results from one such survey.

Moreover, it seems that most U.S. workers do not save enough to provide for their retirement. In a survey by Merrill Lynch, less than 50 percent of respondents aged 45 to 64 stated that they were saving anything for retirement and only 35 percent of those aged 25 to 44 were saving for retirement. Moreover, both groups said that they save at less than one-third the rate at which they should be saving for retirement. Whether similar results apply internationally is not known. However, as the benefits provided by public pension programs worldwide are reduced, we could speculate that a similar trend, if not the order of magnitude, might exist elsewhere.

In most countries, economic security systems in general and retirement systems in particular have been described as being like a three-legged stool. (See Figure 16-2.) One leg is retirement income security provided through government schemes, such as the Social Security program in the United States. We explore this system in chapter 22. Another leg is employer-sponsored, tax-qualified, retirement plans, which we take up in chapter 21. The third leg is the individual's private initiative.

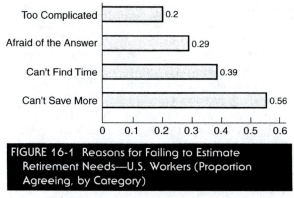

FIGURE 16-1 Reasons for Failing to Estimate Retirement Needs—U.S. Workers (Proportion Agreeing, by Category)

Source: 1997 Retirement Confidence Survey.

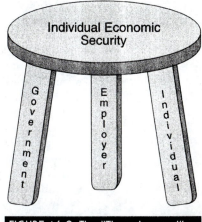

FIGURE 16-2 The "Three-Legged" Stool of Economic Security

This chapter focuses primarily on this third leg and also examines employer-sponsored, nonqualified retirement benefits. An individual's initiative may take the form of personal savings or postretirement employment. Reliance on employment is a dubious choice, as we cannot know whether our health will permit it or whether the opportunity will present itself. In contrast, a well-designed and implemented plan of personal savings can provide greater assurance. We begin our examination by exploring the environment in which planning takes place. We then present the steps of the retirement planning process, with particular reference to private individual savings. We close the chapter with an examination of several types of nonqualified retirement benefit arrangements.

THE ENVIRONMENT FOR RETIREMENT PLANNING

Retirement planning, as a subset of financial planning, can be rationally conducted only with an understanding of relevant environmental factors. An overview of some of these factors is presented here.

Longevity

Individuals today live longer than at any time in history. When Germany, under Chancellor Otto von Bismarck, established the world's first formal public retirement program in the 1880s, age 65 was set as that country's national retirement age. With a life expectancy of 45 years at that time, very few Germans actually lived long enough to collect anything. (It is perhaps surprising that more than a century later, age 65 remains synonymous with retirement.) At the beginning of the twentieth century in the United States, life expectancy was about 50 years. People typically worked until they died, with few living long enough to retire! As a consequence, the notion of "retirement" was foreign to most citizens.

In the much less distant past, the average person retired at age 67 and died at age 72. Provision needed to be made for only five years' retirement income on average. Today, the average 65-year-old U.S. woman with at least a ninth grade education can expect to live to age 90, and a man can expect to live to age 82. Indeed, in the year 2000, more than one in four 65-year-old U.S. men and women can expect to live to age 90. The proportion attaining age 90 in 1960 was only about 14 percent. Because of these facts, substantially increased funds are needed to provide for retirement security.

Moreover, despite longer life spans, better health, and changes in laws to encourage employment, individuals have been retiring earlier than they did formerly. The average retirement age in the United States has declined from 67 to 63 since the 1950s. This fact can lead to erroneous conclusions for today's workers who are years away from retirement. Their parents, with memories of the 1930s' economic depression, often were determined savers in contrast to many of today's baby boomers. Additionally, their parents' timing was fortuitous: They worked during economically robust years when employers were generous with benefits. Investments in homes yielded returns substantially in excess of inflation and overall investments performed well. Social Security benefits were and remain relatively more generous for them than for following generations. Prospects that such favorable circumstances will be repeated in the next few decades seem remote, with the result that today's workers probably would be well advised not to count on an early retirement under such favorable conditions.

Increasing longevity also affects the composition of families, with a concomitant need for special planning. For example, we know that death rates for men are higher than those for women. Additionally, men tend to marry women younger than themselves. This combination means that older persons are more likely to be widows than widowers. Thus, at age 75 and older, two-thirds of men but only one-quarter of women live with a spouse. At age 65, there are 100 men for every 150 women. At age 85, the ratio becomes 100 men to 260 women.

Inflation

Inflation remains the archenemy of retirement planning. Although a 4 percent inflation rate may seem reasonable or even low in many countries, the result is a doubling of prices in 18 years. Figure 16-3 illustrates the long-term debilitating effects of inflation on retirement income. It shows the nominal amounts needed in the future to maintain $10,000 in real income in the face of various inflation rates. Thus, if inflation were to average 6 percent, the retiree would need $32,071 in income in year 20 to have the same purchasing power as $10,000 today.

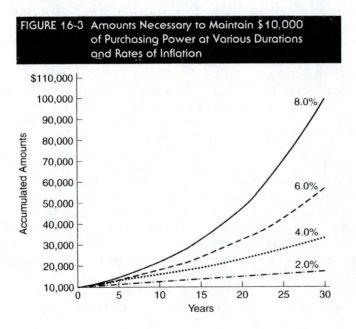

FIGURE 16-3 Amounts Necessary to Maintain $10,000 of Purchasing Power at Various Durations and Rates of Inflation

Thus, if one wishes to establish a retirement income whose purchasing power does not diminish with inflation, provision must be made for a constantly rising nominal retirement income. This fact complicates the retirement planning process in the same way that it complicates the life insurance planning process, as discussed in chapter 14.

Retiree Health

Most retirees enjoy relatively good health, and prospects are bright that tomorrow's retirees will be even healthier. Fully one-half of persons who are 75 to 84 years old are free of health problems that require special care or that curb activities. Even among those aged 85 and over, one-third report no limitations on their overall health.

Even so, the aging process takes its toll, and, in general, the older a person becomes, the greater will be his or her likely need for health care services. Often, the most financially debilitating health-related retiree expense relates to long-term care costs. An estimated one in four U.S. citizens over age 65 will spend some time in a nursing home, at an annual cost of from $25,000 to $70,000. The Brookings Institution estimates that by the year 2020, costs could be $158,000 per year. Such unanticipated costs can quickly wreck an otherwise soundly conceived retirement plan.

With increasing age, we are more likely to require assistance with the activities of daily living, even if we are healthy. For example, whereas 6 percent of those aged 65 to 74 in the United States require assistance with bathing, this percentage increases to 31 percent for those aged 85 and greater. Such care can be expensive in terms of the compensation for caregivers or in terms of the time of helpful friends or relatives. As noted in chapter 7, contrary to the views of most persons, the U.S. federal government covers only a minor portion of such bills and the state-based Medicaid program covers such costs only for the financially destitute.

Of course, for some persons, it may be rational for them to give away their assets to qualify for Medicaid, but this approach can be problematic because of legal requirements. Also, losing control of one's finances and becoming dependent on welfare are not attractive prospects for most people. Adequate retirement savings can be the answer for many persons, often coupled with long-term care insurance, as discussed in chapter 7.

Social Security

As discussed in chapter 22, government social insurance programs in general and the U.S. Social Security program in particular provide benefits that are skewed in favor of lower-income workers. Those with moderate to high incomes, therefore, cannot depend on Social Security retirement benefits to provide a significant share of their retirement income.

This fact is illustrated in Figure 16-4. It shows the results of a Georgia State University study of retiree income replacement ratios in the United States. The figure shows the percentage of preretirement salary necessary for retirees to maintain their standard of living. These percentages are derived by taking into consideration changes in a person's postretirement taxes, expenditures, and savings. Conventional wisdom suggests that retirees need a retirement income of about 70 percent of their preretirement wages to maintain a standard of living in retirement that is equivalent to the one enjoyed before retirement. Obviously, individual circumstances could greatly influence this percentage, but it is a useful point of departure.

As Figure 16-4 illustrates, the 70 percent figure is a reasonable gross estimate for all but the low-income segments. Note that for the lower-income groups, the preponderance of retirement income is derived from Social Security retirement benefits. With increasing income, the relative importance of Social Security diminishes. Note also that the

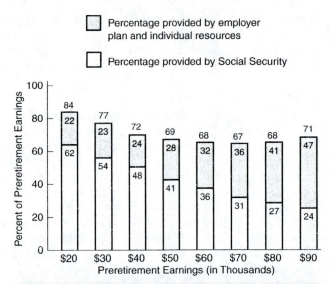

FIGURE 16-4 Income Replacement Ratios in the United States (Married Couple, One Wage Earner, Age 65 Worker, Age 62 Spouse)

Source: Bruce A. Palmer, *1997 GSU/Aon RETIRE* Project Report,* Center for Risk Management and Insurance Research, Georgia State University (1997), p. 12.

income replacement ratios actually increase for higher incomes primarily because of taxes on Social Security benefits.

Thus, if similar results can be projected for future retirees, middle- to upper-income persons can count on Social Security providing a maximum of 40 percent of their retirement income. The balance must come from personal savings and employer-sponsored retirement plans.

Whether similar results can be realistically expected for the future is questionable. Already the U.S. Congress taxes Social Security benefits for higher-earning retirees (see chapter 22), in effect applying a modified means test. Moreover, as of the year 2000, the lowest age at which the full retirement benefit can be collected began gradually increasing from the traditional retirement age 65.

Further cost-reduction measures may be reasonably expected. Currently, the ratio of tax-paying workers to retirees is about 3.3 to 1. By the year 2029 (the year that the last of the baby boomers reaches age 65), the ratio will have dropped to less than 2 to 1. Although much of the current and future Social Security taxes are intended to be reserved to cover the projected shortfall of the then benefit payments over the then Social Security tax revenues, it is less than obvious that the system will function as hoped. For one thing, if no changes are made in the system, the surpluses are projected to be exhausted in the 2030s. Furthermore, current surpluses are being used to cover current U.S. federal budget deficits. The Social Security Trust Fund is lending the surpluses for other federal uses; the trust fund, in effect, holds IOUs from other parts of the government.

The question arises as to who will repay the loans at the time the baby boomers begin retiring in large numbers. The only groups with funds to meet these obligations are workers and retirees. Some estimate that, by 2040, workers could find Social Security taxes taking as much as 40 percent of their pay if benefits remain roughly at today's levels. Any result even close to such a figure could be expected to create substantial intergenerational conflict. The alternative is to provide retirees with relatively lower retirement benefits. Realistically, the most feasible scenario would seem to be some combination of higher worker taxes and lower retiree benefits, coupled with some privatization of the system, as discussed in chapter 22. The net effect of the foregoing analysis suggests that today's workers are wise to place less reliance on the Social Security system providing as generous retirement benefits as those provided to past retirees.

Irrespective of the degree of faith one has in the level of the Social Security retirement benefits, it is wise periodically to request updated information on the likely benefit level that would be available on retirement. The needed information can be requested from a local Social Security office and it can be obtained through the Social Security Administration's Web site (www.ssa.gov).

Employer-Provided Benefits

About one-half of all U.S. employees are covered by employer-sponsored retirement plans. The larger the employer, the greater the likelihood that a retirement plan is available. Employees without this coverage must rely exclusively on Social Security benefits, on their personal assets, and on postretirement employment for retirement income.

Most employed individuals might be surprised to discover the relatively low levels of likely future employer-sponsored retirement benefits. Figure 16-5 shows the breakdown of income for those aged 65 and over by broad category. Note that, for the average person, only 16 percent of total income was provided by an occupational pension. Of course, this ratio is only an average figure, with wide variations depending on industry grouping, size of firm, and a host of other factors.

The situation can be even worse for highly compensated employees. Although Social Security typically replaces 50 percent of the preretirement wages of workers earning $25,000 per year, it replaces less than 20 percent of the preretirement wages of workers earning $90,000 and only 3 percent of the preretirement wages of workers earning $350,000 per year.

Additionally, U.S. law (see chapter 21) effectively limits the tax-qualified retirement benefits that can be provided to highly compensated employees. Thus, lower wage earners within a business often are entitled to *proportionately* higher retirement benefits

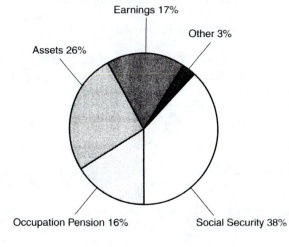

FIGURE 16-5 Percentages of Aggregate Income of U.S. Population Age 65 and Over

Source: Susan Grad, "Income of the Population 55 and older," SSA Publication, No. 13-11871 (June 1988), Table 47.

(i.e., a higher wage replacement ratio) than higher wage earners.[1] The combination of lower wage replacement ratios from both Social Security and employer-sponsored qualified retirement plans means that individual initiative and possibly employer-sponsored *nonqualified* retirement plans are relatively more important for high wage earners than for low wage earners.

Moreover, the current generation of workers changes jobs more frequently than did past generations—an average of five times during the working lifetime. The Congressional Research Service estimated that the effect of five job changes would leave a person with one-half the pension amount of the individual who did not change jobs.

Additionally, many employers have discontinued their retirement plans altogether or shifted away from defined benefit plans to defined contribution plans. **Defined benefit plans** guarantee a monthly retirement benefit based on some combination of salary and length of service (see chapter 21). The employer is responsible for ensuring that adequate funds exist to provide the promised benefit.

With **defined contribution plans,** which include profit-sharing and 401(k) plans, the employer contributes a certain amount annually to each participant's account. With 401(k) plans (see chapter 21), the employer typically matches some portion or all of the amounts contributed by employees. The failure of many employees to participate plus a reasonable matching percentage mean that the typical 401(k) plan costs the employer perhaps only 1 to 2 percent of payroll. With profit-sharing plans, the employer need not make any contribution in unprofitable years. In contrast, employer contributions to defined benefit plans average some 7 percent of payroll. In effect, therefore, the trend in employer-sponsored plans is to shift the risk from the employer to the employee.

Even so, defined contribution plans offer advantages. The employee usually has some discretion in his or her account investments and, with wise decisions, can accumulate substantial sums. Additionally, these plans are more portable than defined benefit plans, thus resulting in less loss with job changes.

In summary, the typical employee probably is well advised not to be overly optimistic about the proportion of retirement income that might be provided through occupational plans. Employer-sponsored plans are founded on what the employer perceives it can afford to provide, not on what the employee may need in the future.

Psychological Dimensions of Retirement

The foregoing environmental factors relate more to the retirement planning process than to retirement itself. However, we should consider in this process that the psychological dimensions of retirement will determine whether we are content with the financial aspects of retirement.

An important aspect here relates to the seeming paradoxes exhibited by many older people.[2] The first element of this paradox concerns their perceptions of the adequacy of their financial resources in meeting their financial needs. The majority of older Americans consider their incomes sufficient to meet their needs. They express high levels of satisfaction with their financial resources; indeed, they express greater satisfaction than

---

[1]Of course, as a group, low wage earners are less likely to qualify for any employer-sponsored retirement benefits. The focus here is at the level of the individual business and typical retirement benefits rather than across all wage earners.

[2]This discussion draws from Linda K. George, *Financial Security in Later Life: The Subjective Side* (Boettner Institute of Financial Gerontology, University of Pennsylvania, 1993).

do middle-aged workers. Yet, older Americans have less than one-half of the income of middle-aged Americans.

Additionally, the correlation between objective levels of financial resources and satisfaction is weaker among the elderly than among other adults. Low-income elderly are almost as likely to be satisfied as their more financially advantaged peers. In statistical terms, income and wealth explain about 50 percent of the perception of financial well-being for all adults, but only 25 percent for older adults. Older adults seem to view financial well-being differently from their younger peers.

Social psychologists suggest that levels of satisfaction tend to be high when objective circumstances are (1) congruent with one's aspirations or (2) perceived as equitable and fair. Thus, an important reason for the reported high levels of satisfaction with financial resources in later life is that financial aspirations tend to diminish in later life. Older adults simply do not aspire to the levels of financial resources desired by their younger peers and are, thus, more satisfied. Also, the elderly seem to view the world as more equitable and fairer than their younger peers. This too contributes to their higher reported levels of satisfaction.

All is not positive, however. Linda K. George notes that a majority of older adults report that they are afraid that their financial resources will be insufficient to meet their future financial needs.[3] This perception seems largely to be unrelated to objective levels of financial resources, with high-income retirees being as likely as low-income retirees to be worried about the adequacy of their resources.

Thus, with regard to the *present,* the majority of older adults are satisfied with their financial resources, regardless of their objective wealth levels. In contrast, with regard to the *future,* most older adults are worried about the adequacy of their financial resources, again regardless of their objective wealth levels. Moreover, these fears seem to be as prevalent among the young-old as among the oldest-old. We might have expected fear of the future to decline among the very old, as they view a future that is, realistically, quite short, but such is not the case.

Fear of the future explains several otherwise confusing behaviors. Thus, older adults may delay seeking needed medical care, refuse to purchase services that would make their lives easier, and generally deprive themselves of needed products and services. They deprive themselves of legitimate expenditures today because the money may be needed for more serious problems in the future. This pattern is especially prevalent among older couples when economic resources may be perceived as inadequate to meet possible long-term care needs for two persons whose life expectancies may be quite different.

According to George, underlying this fear is the issue of personal control.[4] Americans particularly hold strong beliefs relative to personal control—the desire to be in control of the major parameters of our lives and, for events that we cannot control, the desire to be in control of how they are handled. Financial assets are a control-enhancing and control-preserving resource. The emotional intensity associated with the fear that financial assets will be inadequate for future needs is more than concern about money; it is concern that we will lose control, personal autonomy, and ultimately independence. An understanding of these and other psychological dimensions of retirement and retirement planning will aid both the individual and his or her counselor in making better-suited decisions.

---

[3]Ibid., p. 16.
[4]Ibid., pp. 19–20.

The preceding discussion of the environment in which contemporary retirement planning takes place should serve to emphasize the growing importance and role of private initiative in the provision of retirement income. The earlier a retirement savings plan is established, the less painful it is financially. The "magic of compounding" truly is an important ally of the saver.

THE RETIREMENT PLANNING PROCESS

The retirement planning process is conceptually identical to and a subset of the personal financial planning process. Thus, the following discussion is structured around that process.

Gather Information

Both death-related and retirement-related information typically would be gathered at the same time. The needed information includes existing liquid assets that could be used to provide retirement income and information concerning employer-sponsored retirement plans and other such sources of retirement income.

Information regarding probable retirement benefits provided under any government program, such as Social Security, also should be obtained. Estimates are necessary in most cases. If the time to retirement is long, estimates will be gross approximations only.

Establish Objectives

Retirement objectives usually are couched in general terms, such as being able to maintain one's current standard of living during retirement. As mentioned earlier, many experts suggest a retirement income objective of 70 percent of preretirement wages. For low wage earners, this percentage may provide an unacceptably low standard of living; for high wage earners, it may be too ambitious a goal. Irrespective of the ultimate target wage replacement ratio, consideration should be given to the fact that work-related expenses will cease and that Social Security, federal income, and state and local taxes might cease or diminish on retirement. Additionally, the proportion of income devoted to preretirement savings will cease as the individual enters the "dissavings" period of life. In setting objectives, consideration should be given to long-term care and its financing.

Analyze Information

With objectives established, the relevant information gathered earlier must be analyzed to measure the financial consequences of retirement. Our discussion here will focus on income needs during retirement, although we should recognize that long-term care and medical expenses (see chapter 7) are important elements of retirement planning. Additionally, intergenerational transfers also are a source of retirement benefits, particularly in countries where the extended family remains a potent force. Box 16-1 highlights the main categories of such transfers.

Computer-assisted retirement planning is routine today. Sophisticated programs are available from commercial software vendors and from some Web sites of financial institutions, accounting firms, and consultants. Financial advisors as well as consumers rely on these programs, both to guide them through the process and to conduct the analysis. Nonetheless, an understanding of the actual analysis process is important.

Thus, to derive the sought-after figure, the present value of future income needs is netted against the present value of future estimated resources. The result is a measure of the net present value of the shortage of resources to meet the desired income objective.

BOX 16-1

THE "CURRENCIES" OF INTERGENERATIONAL TRANSFERS

The term *intergenerational transfer* refers to any flow of resources between different generations of the same nuclear or extended family. Thus, it encompasses flows from parents to children and vice versa. Intergenerational transfers occur in one or more of three "currencies":

- space—usually in the form of coresidence
- time—usually in the form of services (e.g., assistance with the activities of daily living)
- money—in the form of money or goods

In many families and societies, the value of intergeneration transfers easily exceeds the value of retirement income from former employers, government, and personal initiative. Such transfers redistribute wealth within families and can have profound effects on the economic security needs of individuals.

Interest rates used should be reasonable in light of historical and current trends, as should projected inflation rates. Utilizing the assumed inflation rate, we can determine the (inflated) level of income desired at retirement age, based on a projection of the current-day equivalent. Next, the expected annual income resources are netted against the desired annual income needs. Three common classes of resources are (1) employer-sponsored income, (2) government-provided income, and (3) income from individual resources.

The uncertainties associated with the Social Security system were presented earlier. The system's future benefits may be relatively less generous than those provided today or in the past. An estimate of future benefits can be obtained from the Social Security office, and those figures may then be either factored into the analysis as given or reduced by some amount and then factored into the analysis.

The same Social Security estimation quandary exists for retirement planning and predeath planning, although it is more complex here. No resolution will be perfect. The additional complexity comes about because the Social Security survivor benefit is a known, calculable product, and near-term projections probably are reasonable. For persons who are not near retirement, however, projecting Social Security retirement benefit levels several decades from the present is speculative. As a result, these calculations should be viewed as providing gross estimates only. In any event, Social Security retirement benefits should be netted against the retirement income need to derive annual deficit figures.

Employer-sponsored retirement benefits can be equally, if not more, troublesome to estimate. Individuals change employers. Even if one remained with the same employer until retirement, there is no guarantee that the benefit plan would remain the same. Plans are changed. Even if neither the employer nor the plan were changed, obtaining reliable estimates for future benefits can be difficult. As discussed in chapter 21, retirement benefits provided under an employer-sponsored pension, profit-sharing, or other such plan are a function of the plan benefit formula and future employer funding levels.

Even so, an attempt should be made to establish a conservative estimate for retirement income from employer-sponsored sources. One approach is to determine from the employer the employee's projected benefit level and then to determine an expected wage replacement ratio at retirement. The wage replacement ratio is the fraction found by dividing (1) the postretirement, employer-sponsored retirement income by (2) the preretirement annual wage.

Thus, if the employer-sponsored retirement income is expected to be 40 percent of the preretirement wage level, and if the retirement income need is 70 percent of the preretirement wage level, one need examine only a 30 percent net retirement income level from nonemployer sources. Projected personal savings and investments also should be netted against the retirement income need.

Using either the capital retention or one of the two capital liquidation approaches discussed in chapter 14, one then derives an inflation- and interest-adjusted figure for the present value of the future income stream as of the planned retirement age. For example, assume that Helen, aged 45, earns $75,000 today and anticipates that her future raises will average 6 percent per year. She anticipates retiring at age 65 on an amount equal to 70 percent of her then preretirement income.

Her anticipated income just before retirement is found by accumulating her current $75,000 salary at 6 percent for 20 years, to yield about $240,000.[5] In other words, Helen expects to be earning $240,000 per year just prior to retirement. (This amount seems large, but if inflation were to average 4 percent over the 20-year period, the actual purchasing power of the $240,000 in today's dollars would be about $110,000.[6])

Assume that Helen's Social Security benefit is estimated to provide an inflation-adjusted retirement income equal to 20 percent of her preretirement salary. Assume further that Helen estimates that her employer-sponsored plan will provide a retirement income of an additional 30 percent of her preretirement salary. Thus, Helen believes that the combination of Social Security and her employer's retirement plan will meet 50 percent of her 70 percent retirement goal. She need only provide for the additional 20 percent, or $48,000 ($240,000 × 0.20), from personal resources.[7]

If Helen wishes to maintain purchasing power throughout her retirement years, the $48,000 figure should increase yearly by the inflation rate.[8] Thus, with a 4 percent inflation assumption, Helen will need $49,920 the following year, $51,917 the year after that, and so on, to maintain a real income of $48,000.

If she wanted to purchase an annuity to provide this amount, the probable cost at age 65 might be $700 to $1,100 for each $100 of annual income desired. Using the higher figure to implicitly account for inflation, Helen should aim to have accumulated about $528,000 ($48,000 × $1,100/$100) by age 65.

To accumulate this sum through level contributions to an annuity or other savings vehicle, Helen must make annual payments of about $12,000, if the savings medium earns 7 percent.[9] If Helen would like her annual retirement savings to grow with her expected 6 percent salary increases, she could begin saving about $5,500 and increase it by 6 percent per year.[10] This steadily increasing contribution would also grow to the needed $528,000 amount if all assumptions were realized.

---

[5]$75,000 × (1.06)^{20} = $75,000 × 3.2071 = $240,532

[6]$75,000 × (1.06/1.04)^{20} = $75,000 × (1.01923)^{20} = $109,775

[7]Technically, if the $240,000 figure were her income at age 64, her first-year retirement income should be increased by one year's inflation rates to maintain the purchasing power. Given the uncertainty inherent in results of this type, this degree of precision can be ignored.

[8]This analysis assumes that the Social Security retirement benefit and the employer-provided benefit will each also increase with the inflation rates. This assumption probably is reasonable for Social Security, but perhaps not as reasonable for the employer plan. If Helen wished to allow for a constant employer benefit in the calculation, needed future income should be increased by an additional amount equal to the employer-provided benefit ($240,000 × 0.40) times the compounded inflation rate.

[9]$528,000 ÷ $\left[\sum_{t=1}^{20}(1.07)^t\right]$ = $528,000 ÷ 43.865 = $12,037

[10]The first-year savings amount would be found as follows:

$528,000 ÷ $\left[\sum_{t=1}^{20}(1.07)^t(1.06)^t\right]$ = $528,000 ÷ $\sum(1.1342)^t$ = $528,000 ÷ 96.44 = $5,476

Develop a Plan

Next, the alternative means of accumulating the needed sum should be explored. For example, one could establish a tax-qualified individual retirement account (IRA) and begin making level, increasing, or some other pattern of annual contributions. Table 16-1 highlights three types of IRAs in the United States. Other means for accumulating the amount might include:

- Purchasing a non-tax-qualified, flexible-premium deferred annuity (see chapter 8).
- Establishing a non-tax-qualified savings or investment program.
- Establishing a nonqualified retirement plan with the employer, if feasible (discussed later).
- Having the employer establish a 401(k) arrangement or begin contributing to such an arrangement, if feasible (see chapter 21).

TABLE 16-1 Types of Retirement-Based IRAs in the United States

Type	Functioning	Who Qualifies?	Withdrawal Provisions	Other Considerations
Tax-deductible IRA	Permits tax-deductible contributions of up to $2,000 per year ($4,000 for qualifying married couples) and tax deferral on investment income until withdrawal, usually not before age 59½.	Individuals not covered by an employer's retirement plan or who are eligible for such coverage and have incomes below certain threshold levels (e.g., $60,000 for married couples in 1998, indexed).	Withdrawals at age 59½ are subject to ordinary income taxation. Earlier withdrawals generally are subject to an additional 10 percent penalty tax. Withdrawals must begin not later than age 70½.	Withdrawals prior to age 59½ are not subject to the 10 percent penalty tax if the distribution is in the form of an annuity because of death or disability, for high medical expenses, for medical insurance premiums for the unemployed, for college tuition, or for purchase of first home.
Non-tax-deductible IRA	Permits contributions of up to $2,000 per year ($4,000 for qualifying married couples) and tax deferral on investment income until withdrawal, usually not before age 59½. Contributions are not tax deductible.	Individuals who cannot or do not make contributions to a tax-deductible IRA or a Roth IRA.	Same as tax-deductible IRA except the individual can recover contributions tax free.	Same as tax-deductible IRA.
Roth IRA	Permits contributions of up to $2,000 per year ($4,000 for qualifying married couples) and tax-free investment income. Contributions are not tax-deductible.	Individuals whose incomes are below certain relatively high threshold levels (e.g., $160,000 for married couples in 1998, indexed).	Withdrawals are income tax free, including all investment income, if made not less than five years after the account is established and after age 59½ or because of death, disability, education expenses, or first home purchase. Withdrawals of contributions before age 59½ are tax free but earnings withdrawals are taxable.	Regular IRAs can be "rolled over" into Roth IRAs for persons with incomes below certain levels ($100,000 in 1998, indexed) without tax penalty, but the value of all previously untaxed amounts will be subject to taxation.

- Having the employer establish a tax-sheltered annuity plan, if feasible (see chapter 21).
- Making sufficient premium payments to a needed life insurance policy to develop higher cash values.
- Finding a rich, generous friend or relative.
- Combinations of the foregoing items.

One or several of these arrangements usually prove feasible. Ideally, contributions would be income tax deductible, earnings would accumulate on a tax-deferred basis, and withdrawal incomes would be tax free. The advantages and disadvantages of annuities and life insurance cash values in this regard were noted in earlier chapters.

One aspect of plan development that often emerges just prior to retirement revolves around decisions as to whether employer-sponsored (and other retirement) income amounts should be paid as a life annuity, and if so, whether the single-life or joint and last survivor life annuity seems more attractive. If a joint-life annuity payout seems desirable, the prospective retiree may find that a larger effective payout can be achieved by using a combination of the single-life option and life insurance on the annuitant's life. The decision as to which approach is superior turns on whether the additional income realized from electing the single-life annuity over the joint-life annuity is sufficient to pay the premiums on a life insurance policy whose face amount would provide an income to the other person (e.g., a spouse) that is at least equal to that which would have been provided under the joint and last survivor annuity (see Box 14-3).

Implement the Plan

After plan alternatives have been considered and a plan developed and agreed upon, the plan should be implemented. This may entail applying for an annuity, following through with the paperwork to establish an IRA or other tax-qualified plan, or making other commitments, such as purchasing long-term care insurance.

The key to sound plan implementation is less the paperwork mechanics and more a firm commitment by the individual to make the necessary contributions regularly. More individually crafted retirement plans fail from lack of commitment than for any other reason.

A part of plan implementation involves decisions about when to retire. Of course, these decisions were implicit in the foregoing discussions, but they warrant some elaboration. Many people are fearful of making the wrong retirement decision. They are concerned that their savings will be insufficient to provide for an adequate retirement (as one commentator put it: "They will run out of money before they run out of life") or that they are not prepared mentally for the adjustment to retirement.

Financial considerations will always play an important role in retirement decisions. However, as suggested earlier, we should also be attuned to the social, health, and psychological dimensions. When workers see their peers retiring, they may feel that it is time to do likewise. Also, many people retire because of health considerations, especially at the younger retirement ages. Moreover, the degree of satisfaction one feels from his or her job and the demand for his or her services influence the timing of retirement. These types of influences on decisions about when to retire are not easily estimated in earlier life.

Many employees are not truly prepared for retirement emotionally, especially if they retire because of corporate restructuring and accompanying early retirement packages. Outplacement firms have found a market niche in assisting employers and employees in this process. Even when retirement is unrelated to corporate restructuring, some seven in ten employers offer retirement counseling and preparation services at some level to employees.

Even so, most workers state that they need additional help from a financial advisor in making retirement-related financial decisions, according to Merrill Lynch surveys.

Also, estate planning (see next chapter) receives much more attention in the retirement years, as people seek to arrange their financial affairs.

Retirement remains one of life's most difficult transitions. A Roper Starch survey revealed that 41 percent of retirees experience a difficult adjustment. In contrast, only 12 percent of newly married and 23 percent of new parents find the adjustment to be difficult. Younger retirees experience the most difficult transition.

Monitor and Revise the Plan

As with predeath planning, actual results under one's retirement plan are highly unlikely to track precisely those assumed for the future. This necessitates periodic fine-tuning and, occasionally, a complete overhaul. Important life events and environmental changes can materially affect results.

NONQUALIFIED RETIREMENT BENEFITS

As discussed in the preceding section on the environment for retirement planning, highly compensated employees often are entitled to proportionately lower Social Security and employer-sponsored retirement benefits than are other workers. Also, many owners of small businesses do not offer extensive retirement benefits to their rank-and-file employees, but they would like to provide for themselves, for their families, and often for particularly valuable employees. These facts have led increasing numbers of businesses to offer special retirement benefits either instead of or as a supplement to a qualified retirement plan. The objective is to attract and retain talented employees by rewarding them in special ways and/or to provide benefits for the firm owners.

These plans are typically *nonqualified,* meaning that the employer makes no effort to meet the qualification requirements under the Internal Revenue Code (IRC) or the Employee Retirement Income Security Act (ERISA) for tax-favored treatment of the plan costs or benefits. A qualified plan must meet certain nondiscrimination and a host of other requirements, as discussed in chapter 21. However, the employer's contributions are immediately tax deductible, and the employee enjoys certain tax advantages as well.

Types of Nonqualified Retirement Plans

Nonqualified executive benefit plans can be structured to provide virtually any package of benefits and can provide them to whomever the business wishes. Indeed, the very purpose of nonqualified benefit plans is to discriminate in favor of a few select employees. As such, contributions usually are not immediately deductible by the business for income tax purposes.

We explore nonqualified executive benefit plans in this and the following chapter. Here, we explore three types of nonqualified retirement plans:

- nonqualified deferred compensation plans
- supplemental executive retirement plans
- incentive compensation plans

Nonqualified Deferred Compensation Plans

A **nonqualified deferred compensation plan** is a contractual arrangement under which compensation for services rendered is postponed, usually until retirement. If the plan is properly arranged, the employee will not pay tax on these deferred amounts until they are actually received (e.g., subsequent to retirement), when the individual may be in a lower marginal income tax bracket. The employer does not obtain an income tax deduction for these payments until such time as they actually are made available to the employee.

The plan may be either employer or employee initiated. In either instance, however, the idea is to postpone some portion of present compensation or raises or bonuses, in return for which the employer agrees to pay a deferred income, usually at a rate augmented by interest, at some future time. The employee may desire to avoid additional current income (which presumably is not presently needed) and current taxation on that income and/or the employer may wish to use the plan to encourage the employee to remain with the firm for some minimum period of time.

Under a variation of deferred compensation plans—called **death benefit only (DBO) plans**—the employer promises to pay an income benefit to the employee's survivor upon the employee's death. No retirement benefit is involved in DBO plans, often because the employee will have an adequate retirement income from a qualified plan. DBO plans are less costly than other forms of deferred compensation plans and may help retain employees by providing them with a heightened sense of family security.

Supplemental Executive Retirement Plans

A **supplemental executive retirement plan** (SERP) is a nonqualified retirement plan that provides retirement benefits to selected employees only. Because the plan purposefully is not qualified under the IRC or ERISA, the business has great flexibility as to whom to include (and exclude) as well as the benefit arrangements. Benefits can be set at any level desired and can be paid for life or for a set number of years.

Thus, some SERPs provide a flat amount per year to participating employees. Other SERPs—called **excess SERPs**—seek to replace the retirement benefits that highly compensated employees lose because of IRC or ERISA limitations. Thus, the employer would provide a benefit amount equal to the difference between (1) the full amount under its qualified retirement benefit formula, ignoring any IRC- or ERISA-imposed limits, and (2) the actual qualified plan and Social Security retirement benefits.

Another popular SERP—called a **target SERP**—seeks to replace retirement benefits lost by ERISA-imposed limits *and* counteract the Social Security benefit bias in favor of low-income workers. Thus, the employer may promise to provide selected executives with a total retirement benefit of a set percentage of their final pay, such as 75 percent. The employer would pay an amount equal to the difference between (1) the target retirement benefit (i.e., the stated percentage times the final pay) and (2) the qualified plan and Social Security retirement benefits.

Incentive Compensation Plans

A final means of providing nonqualified retirement benefits is through incentive compensation arrangements. **Incentive compensation** is a means of compensating executives to try to better align their and the business's interests. In economic terms, such compensation is an attempt to address the principal–agent problem.

Perhaps the best-known incentive compensation scheme is the **stock option plan,** which offers executives the option of purchasing the corporation's shares at fixed, typically below-market prices. The idea is that, by offering executives such options, they have an incentive to enhance the market value of the firm's shares, thereby allowing themselves a greater profit when they exercise the options.

Stock option plans have some drawbacks, however. The exercise of the option requires substantial cash. Also, once exercised, taxes are due on the gain. Finally, if share prices fluctuate greatly, the option may be worth little or nothing.

Another, related incentive compensation scheme is the phantom stock plan. Under the **phantom stock plan,** the executive is granted a set number of hypothetical units in the business and receives an income, at the end of a specified period, which is based on the appreciation in value over the period of those hypothetical units. The appreciation often is not based on the market value of the business but, instead, on some formula or other method designed as an incentive for specific financial results. The income may equal the appreciation only or may equal both the initial share value plus appreciation. Taxes are due at the time the income is paid, but the plan requires no other cash outlay by the executive and typically is not directly related to market vagaries.

Funding Nonqualified Retirement Plans

Nonqualified retirement plans may be funded or unfunded. A plan is **funded** if the employer establishes and maintains assets in an escrow account or trust fund as security for its promise to make future payments. The employee is said to have a beneficial interest in such plan assets.

An **unfunded** nonqualified plan exists when the employer has not formally earmarked assets to fund the plan, or, stated differently, when the employee must rely exclusively on the employer's unsecured promise to make payments. A plan is not considered funded merely because the employer establishes a reserve fund to meet future obligation under the plan, provided the fund is not formally linked to the obligation and remains a general asset of the business subject to attachment by its general creditors. The establishment of such reserve funds often is referred to as **informal funding.**

Employer contributions to a funded nonqualified plan are taxable to the employee, unless the employee's rights in the funds are subject to a "substantial risk of forfeiture." Whether a substantial risk of forfeiture exists is not easily determinable. Because of these and other tax uncertainties, nonqualified funded plans are used only in exceptional circumstances.

Tax Treatment of Nonqualified Retirement Plans

Income Taxation

Nonqualified retirement plans have income tax implications for both employers and employees. Generally, the employer is not entitled to an income tax deduction until such time as amounts are actually or constructively received by the employee. Thus, premium payments or other contributions to fund a nonqualified retirement plan informally are not deductible currently by the employer. When payments are made to the employee, upon retirement (or otherwise) or to his or her heirs in the case of death, the employer may take a deduction for the payments to the extent that they are deemed reasonable compensation.[11]

A properly drafted deferred compensation, SERP, or incentive compensation agreement should result in no income tax obligations to the employee during the deferral period. Payments will be treated as ordinary income to the employee when they are actually or constructively received by the employee. Income is considered **constructively received** if it is made available to the employee or if he or she could have taken it but chose not to. Income is not constructively received if it is subject to a substantial risk of forfeiture. Moreover, even if the employee's rights are nonforfeitable, there will be no constructive receipt provided (1) the agreement was entered into before the compensation was earned and (2) the employer's promise to pay is unsecured.

If the promise to pay is secured in any way, such as the employee being given an interest in assets or other media (e.g., life insurance) used to fund the agreement, the employee will be taxed on the economic benefit of the security interest. To minimize the

---

[11]Generally, unreasonable compensation is not a problem. It can be a problem when the employee is also a substantial stockholder. In such cases, the IRS often argues that the compensation really is a disguised dividend and, therefore, not tax deductible to the corporation.

chance of taxation under the economic benefits doctrine, these agreements are made with provisions that rights to payments will be nonassignable and nontransferable.

Contributions by an employer to an appropriately established irrevocable trust to hold assets from which deferred compensation payments will eventually be made are not taxable to the employees at the time the contributions are made. Under these so-called **rabbi trusts,** trust assets remain subject to the claims of the employer's general creditors if the employer becomes insolvent, but in the absence of such claims, trust assets must be used solely to provide deferred compensation benefits. Named after the first such arrangement established for a rabbi, these trusts are intended to provide some psychological security to participating employees that they will receive benefits even when there has been a management change or a hostile takeover.

Under another type of trust, the so-called **secular trust,** trust assets are not subject to the claims of the employer's general creditors. Thus, employees enjoy an even greater degree of security. However, trust contributions would be taxable to employees as a substantial forfeiture risk does not exist. These trusts are typically used when the employee is in a lower tax bracket or otherwise wants to recognize income currently.

Estate Taxation

If an employee was receiving or was entitled to receive payments at his or her death, and if the agreement provided that these payments were to continue after death, the present value of the remaining payments normally would be included in the decedent's gross estate. If payments were continued to the employee's spouse, they might qualify for the marital deduction. If payments ceased on death, there obviously would be nothing to include in the gross estate.

If death occurred during the deferral period, the present value of the future payments would be included in the decedent's gross estate if the deceased employee had an enforceable right in the future to receive postemployment benefits. If the plan did not provide such postemployment benefits, any payments made to the named beneficiary might not be included in the gross estate. Also, if the payment of survivor benefits is optional on the part of the employer, they escape inclusion in the gross estate.

Life Insurance in Nonqualified Retirement Plans

Informal funding through life insurance is especially attractive when the plan provides for the payment of death benefits.[12] When a reserve is established through investment in assets other than life insurance, and the employee dies shortly after the plan is begun, the size of the fund may be inadequate to meet the employer's obligation. When life insurance is used as an informal funding device, the premature death of the employee not only gives rise to the employer's obligation to pay death benefits but also creates the funds with which to meet that obligation. The employer is the applicant, policyowner, premium payor, and beneficiary of the policy on the employee's life.

Another factor that enhances the attractiveness of life insurance as an informal funding device is the income-tax-deferred status of the cash-value buildup in the policy during the accumulation period. Earnings on most other forms of assets that might be used to accumulate a reserve would be currently taxable to the employer.

Life insurance used to informally fund a nonqualified deferred compensation plan can involve an alternative minimum tax problem for the corporation. This situation, however, should be less crucial than that with many other forms of corporate-owned life

---

[12]This section draws from Edwin H. White and Herbert Chasman, *Business Insurance,* 5th ed. (Englewood Cliffs, NJ: Prentice-Hall, 1980), pp. 553–555.

insurance. An additional offsetting item—compensation expense—can be netted against cash-value increases and any death proceeds received. Although not tax deductible, such expenses are valid for book purposes.

The employer may either use the policy's values to provide the promised benefits or retain the policy until the employee dies, recovering costs at that time. The first approach involves policy loans or surrender proceeds to make payments. Policy loans often are available at favorable interest rates and may be tax deductible, as discussed in chapter 13.

Benefits may also be met by surrendering portions (e.g., paid-up additions) or all of the policy. The disadvantage of this approach is that the employer forgoes tax-free death proceeds to secure surrender proceeds that are taxable to the extent that they exceed the employer's cost basis.

Many small employers follow what might be labeled as an *individual cost recovery method* in connection with informally funding nonqualified retirement benefits. With this method, the employer purchases the life insurance with the clear intention of keeping it in force until the employee's death, whenever that may occur. The employer, therefore, is less concerned about the adequacy of the cash-value buildup than about purchasing an amount of life insurance that is adequate to allow it to recover the amount of employee benefit payments (either on an after-tax or a before-tax basis), the premiums paid, and the opportunity cost of the funds. Implicit in this approach is the assumption that the employer can meet employee payments from its cash flows.

Another informal funding method sometimes followed by larger companies might be called an *aggregate cost recovery method.* Under this method, the corporation purchases several, perhaps even hundreds, of life insurance policies insuring the lives of the employees for whom postretirement benefits are to be provided. The benefits need not and usually are not limited to retirement income but often include postretirement medical or life insurance coverage. The corporation is the owner and beneficiary of the policies. With the tax-free recovery of death benefits, the hope is that total death benefit payments will cover most or all of the postretirement benefits promised.

Unlike the situation under the individual cost recovery method, no attempt is made actually to pair the benefits promised to particular individuals to specific policies insuring their lives. Policies purchased in this fashion are commonly called **corporate-owned life insurance** (COLI), although the original connotation of the term related more to life insurance purchased by closely held businesses (see chapter 17).

The Financial Accounting Standards Board (FASB) requires that employers accrue postretirement benefits as a charge to earnings and as a balance sheet liability as the benefits are earned rather than as they are paid (which was the situation formerly). The existence of a balance sheet liability has prompted employers to provide either fully funded plans or other earmarked financing tools, such as life insurance.

Informal funding via COLI does not reduce the balance sheet liability. Rather, it creates a dedicated asset from which benefits ultimately can be financed. COLI cash values are assets that meet the accrued liability. Some have argued that a further asset equal to the present expected value of future death benefits should also be booked.

COLI death proceeds ordinarily should be received by the corporation free of income tax. Similarly, cash values ordinarily should accrue income tax free. Premium payments cannot be deducted from taxable income, although benefit payments made by the employer to the employee (whether from policy values or elsewhere) are tax deductible.

Many companies have purchased COLI with a view to financing the premiums through tax-qualified policy loans. Under these financing plans, interest on all policy loans of up to $50,000 was tax deductible, thus tax leveraging the tax-deferred inside interest buildup. Changes in the tax law now severely limit this technique.

CONCLUSION

The analogy of retirement (and other economic security needs) to a three-legged stool offers a helpful metaphor in considering how we should make financial plans for our retirement years. Government will remain an important source of retirement income for low-income persons, but it seems destined to become increasingly less important for middle-income and especially high-income persons. Individuals in these latter groups must look to their employers and to themselves for meaningful retirement income. The low U.S. savings rate suggests that, among other things, U.S. citizens might not be providing for their retirement to the extent to which they should.

It also seems likely that government will remain an important financing source for medical expenses during retirement, although here too we observe retrenchment (see chapter 22). Supplement medical expense insurance could become more relevant in retirement in the United States and other countries (see chapter 7). The financing of long-term care will almost certainly become a more critical component of individual retirement planning, with long-term care insurance playing an ever-expanding role (see chapter 7).

Life insurance companies and their representatives have an important role to play in the provision of retirement security. Indeed, in most countries with aging populations, we are already witnessing a shift in personal insurance demand away from mortality-based products to accumulation-based ones. This shift corresponds with what Gentaro Kawase, former chairman of the Nippon Life Insurance Company, observed was a trend toward life insurance and other financial services products that were more "for me" and less "for others" because the emphasis has shifted from "for death" to "for life" products.

Questions

1. Why is it that retirement planning should be conducted only with an understanding of the relevant environmental factors?
2. How do the various steps in retirement planning described in this chapter help one achieve a well-constructed retirement plan?
3. How are issues related to health, employment, and value systems important in retirement planning?
4. What objectives are usually behind the use of nonqualified retirement plans? How can the use of life insurance enhance the compensation provided under nonqualified retirement plans?

CHAPTER

17

BUSINESS PLANNING

Objectives

■ Describe dimensions along which the death or disability of a key individual may impact the financial position of a firm.

■ Describe ways that life and disability insurance can address problems arising from the death or disability of:
   a. the sole proprietor of a firm
   b. a partner in a firm
   c. a majority shareholder in a firm

■ Explain the benefits available to both employees and employers from the use of split-dollar life insurance plans as a form of compensation.

■ Discuss the tax consequences of split-dollar plans.

L ife and health insurance is most often purchased for family or other personal reasons. The preceding chapters emphasized this fact. However, individually issued life and health insurance can serve important business purposes as well, as the discussion in the preceding chapter on nonqualified retirement benefits emphasized.

In this chapter we explore other business uses of life and health insurance. As we will discover, their beneficial uses extend over a range of special business applications. Here we cover three applications:

- key employee indemnification
- business continuation arrangements
- nonqualified executive benefits

KEY EMPLOYEE INDEMNIFICATION

Rationale and Definition

Many business firms have been built around a single individual whose capital, energy, technical knowledge, experience, or power to plan and execute make him or her a particularly valuable asset of the organization and a necessity to its successful operation. Numerous examples illustrate the dependence of a successful business upon the personal equation. Thus, a corporation may be greatly dependent on one of its officers whose financial worth as an endorser, or ability as an executive, may be the basis of the firm's good credit rating.

A manufacturing or mining enterprise may be dependent upon someone who possesses the chemical or engineering knowledge necessary to the operation's success. The sales manager of a large business establishment may have made herself indispensable through her ability to organize an efficient body of salespeople, to employ the most effective methods of selling, and to develop profitable markets.

Innumerable examples illustrate the importance of a human life (as an asset) to the successful operation of a business. In each instance, the death or disability of the key employee could have profoundly adverse financial effects on the firm. As with the potential loss of any other firm asset, insurance can be used to indemnify the business, making it whole in the event of such a loss. Thus, **key employee insurance,** also called **key person** (and **key man**) **insurance,** is purchased to indemnify a business for the decrease in earnings brought about by the death or disability of a key employee.

The importance of key person life insurance was recognized in a well-known 1951 tax court case. The court stated:

> What business purpose could be considered more essential than key man [or woman] insurance? The business that insures its buildings and machinery and automobiles from every possible hazard can hardly be expected to exercise less care in protecting itself against the loss of two of its most vital assets—managerial skill and experience.[1]

Economic losses and business instability due to death or disability may be guarded against by making the business itself the owner and beneficiary of appropriate policies on the lives of key employees. In the event of death or disability, the business will be indemnified promptly for the loss of the services of the deceased or disabled employee, and the proceeds received will aid in bridging the period necessary to secure the services of a worthy successor or substitute or to provide general business stability.

Anything that stabilizes the financial position of a firm enhances its value and, thereby, improves its general credit rating. Insuring the lives of key persons assures banks and other lending institutions as well as suppliers that the business will have a financial cushion if one or more key personnel die or becomes disabled. In addition, if a cash-value form of life insurance is used, the firm's liquidity is enhanced through the accumulation of cash values that are available at all times. The cash values are balance sheet assets. Similarly, if prospective lenders or other creditors are assured of the firm's continuation as a going concern in the event of the death or disability of the owner(s), the firm will not only be able to obtain a larger line of credit but usually will be able to obtain it on better terms.

In addition to its role in the general improvement of a firm's credit rating, a life insurance contract is useful because it may be pledged as collateral via a collateral assignment or a policy loan secured from the insurer. The basic security for such loans lies in the contract's savings element with the loan amount covered fully by the policy's cash value.

A policy also may be pledged as collateral with a different purpose in mind: to protect the lender against loss arising only out of the death of a key person or the borrower. Thus, life and health insurance may be used advantageously in those instances when an already established businessperson may need more credit for the business's proper development, but the banker does not believe that the business itself warrants further loans. To the banker, the individual at the head of the business is the important asset. The banker may believe that, although the business itself does not warrant another loan, the business plus the individual who manages it would justify the extension of further credit. The contingency of early death or disability, however, must be provided for. In other words, a life or health insurance policy in favor of the creditor is a hedge against the con-

---

[1] *The Emeloid Co. v. Comm.,* 189 F.2d 230 (3rd Cir. 1951).

tingency of the loss of the value of the life upon which the repayment of the loan is primarily dependent.

In addition to its use in short-term credit situations, life insurance may be used as collateral in connection with bond issues. For example, assume that a firm raises $500,000 in bonds that mature in 20 years, and that the nature and organization of the business are such as to make it chiefly dependent for its credit and successful operation upon Robert. Under these circumstances, Robert's death might impair the concern to such an extent that the liquidation of its assets might prove insufficient for the full redemption of the bonds. Thus, life insurance can be the means of assuring creditors that the bonds will be redeemed upon maturity, thereby helping to reduce the use of any severe restrictions and the interest rate charged.

Estimating the Amount of Potential Loss

As with estimating the amount of potential loss to a family from the death or disability of the principal income earner, so too is it difficult to determine accurately the economic loss that would be suffered by a business concern on a key person's death or disability. However, the same approach conceptually is followed. We seek to answer the question of how much money would be needed to ensure that the business (family) can continue as before.

Businesses purchase all types of insurance to stabilize their financial position. Usually, we think of stabilization in terms of protecting the value of the firm. We know that the value of a business is the present value of current and future profits. The market establishes this value for businesses whose stock is publically traded. The market will penalize the stock price if it perceives that any major operational, property, liability, or personnel loss negatively affects profits. Property, liability, business interruption, key person, and other insurance can be thought of as the business having hedged this possibility, such that any loss will be indemnified, thus shoring up share prices. The firm might establish the risk management objective that no loss to the firm—whether it be a property, liability, business interruption, or personnel loss—will cause the share price to fall by more than a certain amount or perhaps not at all.

Establishing value for businesses whose stock is not publically traded on an organized exchange poses more of a challenge. Although the value of such a business is the present value of all current and future profits, this value is not established by a market and must be estimated. Some advisors will estimate this figure by taking some multiple of the business's net worth as shown on its balance sheet or by estimating the present value of future profits. Thus, a closely held business might want to ensure that no loss to the firm would cause the net worth or future profits to fall by more than a certain amount or perhaps not at all.

As applied to key person insurance, consideration must be given to questions such as how to estimate the actual impact on the firm's finances of a key person's death or disability, whether the loss would be temporary or permanent, and the appropriate discount rate to use. The degree of accuracy inherent in these and other factors used to estimate the value of the economic loss produced by the death or disability of a key person varies according to the type of business, particular function of the key person, and other circumstances. Box 17-1 offers an example of how one business approached the problem.

Procedures

Procedurally, the business entity (be it a corporation, partnership, or sole proprietorship) applies for the policy and is the owner and beneficiary. It also pays the premiums. Of course, key employee insurance is not a type of policy but, rather, a special application

BOX 17-1

ESTIMATING KEY PERSON ECONOMIC LOSS: AN EXAMPLE

Younghee and her husband, Doocheol, are co-owners of a Korean restaurant that has achieved regional fame since it opened 10 years ago, garnering many favorable reviews for the quality of its food and service. Both Younghee's talents as the restaurant's master chef and Doocheol's meticulous attention to the details of service are indispensable elements of the business's success.

The restaurant's annual gross revenue has grown to be $2 million from which the family nets $200,000 before taxes. The book value of the restaurant is $300,000. Because of Younghee's established reputation, if she were to die or become disabled to the degree that she could no longer perform her duties as chef, the business would suffer a substantial decline. In fact, it is estimated that total revenue would fall by 50 percent, with the result that total income to the family would decline by 75 percent, to $50,000—a $150,000 per-year decline.

Were Doocheol to die or be unable to work because of disability, it is estimated that total revenues would suffer a more gradual, but progressively steeper decline, with the result that net family income would fall by one-fourth (i.e., $50,000) during the year following death or disability, with further declines thereafter, ultimately reaching 75 percent.

The problem may be approached by estimating the present value of lost earnings or by estimating the additional compensation necessary to secure a replacement of comparable talent and skill. The likelihood of securing a replacement chef of the equivalent talent of Younghee is slim. The likelihood of engaging someone with Doocheol's managerial talents is high, but it would be necessary to pay a substantial wage.

Thus, if Younghee were to die or become disabled and the intention was that the business maintain its approximate before-tax income level, life insurance and disability insurance on Younghee could be purchased equal to the present value of the projected lost earnings (i.e., $150,000 per year). If a 10-year time period and a 12 percent discount rate were judged reasonable, then about $850,000 of life and disability insurance on Younghee would meet the need.[a]

A competent replacement for Doocheol would require an estimated salary of $120,000 per year—some $70,000 per year more than the business currently pays Doocheol. If the same 10-year planning horizon and 12 percent interest rate are used, the business would need about $400,000 of life and disability insurance on Doocheol's life to meet the goal.[b]

---

[a] $150,000 \times \left[\sum_{t=1}^{10}(1/1.12)^t \right] = \$150,000 \times 5.560 = \$847,500$. The 12 percent discount rate is the firm's internal cost of capital. The appropriate time period is a matter of business judgment, based on factors such as age, nature of the business, and personal and business objectives.

[b] $70,000 \times \left[\sum_{t=1}^{10}(1/1.12)^t \right] = \$70,000 \times 5.560 = \$395,500$

---

of the usual types of insurance. Thus, the policy type should be selected based on the expected need duration and on the possible desire to have cash values available for other purposes (e.g., as loan collateral or to informally fund a deferred compensation arrangement). On the death or disability of the key employee, insurance proceeds are paid to the business. Figure 17-1 illustrates this procedure.

Whole life and universal life policies are most often used for key employee indemnification. If the need is short term or if funds can be put to better use outside the life insurance policy, term life insurance policies may be preferable. Specialized disability income policies are available to provide key person disability income insurance and to cover business overhead expenses. Boxes 17-2 and 17-3 discuss these two types of business-related health insurance.

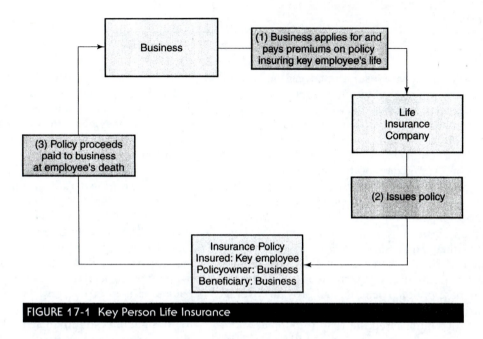

FIGURE 17-1 Key Person Life Insurance

BOX 17-2

KEY EMPLOYEE DISABILITY INCOME INSURANCE

Key employee disability insurance provides for payment of a monthly indemnity to a business entity during the total disability of an essential employee who is the named insured under the policy. Benefits begin after a specified period of disability—the elimination period—and they continue while the insured is disabled for up to 12 or 24 months.

The amount of indemnity is typically high to reflect the value of the employee to the business, and generally it is and should be issued independently of any limits that the insurance company may have set for personal insurance. Although the payment of benefits depends on the disabled status of the insured, the policy itself is owned by the business entity and all benefits are paid directly to the business. The maximum limits vary but can reach in excess of $15,000 a month.

Key employee insurance is offered by only a few specialty companies such as Lloyds of London and the American International Group. Few, if any, standard commercial companies offer a policy with these characteristics.

Tax Treatment of Key Person Insurance

The income tax treatment of key employee insurance is straightforward, being similar to that for personally owned insurance (see chapter 13). Unless the business would be subject to the alternative minimum tax (discussed later), no income tax is attributable to either cash-value increases or receipt of policy death or disability proceeds. Premiums paid are not tax deductible, although an economic argument can be made that the actuarial value of the death protection to the firm (but not amounts paid to build cash values) should be deductible for the same reasons that a business can deduct premiums paid for property and liability insurance protection.

BOX 17-3

OVERHEAD EXPENSE INSURANCE

Overhead expense insurance covers the monthly business expenses of business owners and professionals in private practice when they are disabled. A reimbursement-type benefit is paid during total disability that is uniformly defined in occupational terms. The policies usually begin benefits at the end of 30 or 60 days of disability and pay up to a specified amount of benefit each month while disability continues, until an aggregate benefit amount has been paid. The aggregate amount generally is a multiple of 12, 18, or 24 times the monthly benefit, rather than a specifically limited duration of months. The basic policy waives any premium due during disability. Most insurers allow insureds to purchase optional benefits that provide coverage during periods of partial or residual disability or that give the insured the right to purchase additional insurance at a future time without evidence of good health.

Covered expenses usually are those that the U.S. IRS accepts as deductible business expenses for federal income tax purposes. They include rent or mortgage payments for the business premises, employee salaries, installment payments for equipment (but usually not inventory), utility and laundry costs, business insurance premiums that are not waived during disability, and any other recurring expenses that the insured normally incurs in the conduct of his or her business or professional practice. The major insurers pay benefits on a cumulative basis, so that if the full monthly benefit has not been paid in a given month because of lower than expected covered expenses, any unpaid benefit is carried forward and is available to be paid in any month in which expenses exceed the designated monthly benefit. Benefits generally are available to insure up to $10,000 a month of covered expenses.

Policy death proceeds will be excluded in the key employee/insured's gross estate for federal estate tax purposes if the insured possessed no incidents of ownership in the policy and if the proceeds are not payable to or for the benefit of the insured's estate. If the insured had an ownership interest in the business, however, the death proceeds payable to the business would be considered in deriving the value of the business for estate tax purposes. Presumably, the loss of the key person would be an offsetting factor in the evaluation.

BUSINESS CONTINUATION ARRANGEMENTS

Businesses whose ownership interests have no ready market are referred to as **closely held businesses.** The problems of business continuation are particularly acute for such firms. These problems stem from the typical characteristics of such businesses:

- *Unity of ownership and management.* The owners typically manage the firm, receiving a salary.
- *Small number of owners.* The great majority of closely held businesses are owned by less than 10 individuals.
- *Ownership interest not readily marketable.* Because the ownership interest of the closely held business is not traded on organized exchanges, there is typically not a ready market for that interest. The only persons typically interested in purchasing such an interest are the other owners or possibly competitors.

Closely held businesses are a major source of U.S. economic activity and employment. Some 18 percent of financial assets held by U.S. households is invested in privately held, mostly family-run businesses—a larger proportion than that which households hold in shares of public corporations. Although the majority of closely held firms are small, at least 41,000 family-held businesses nationwide have annual sales of more than $25 million.[2]

Problems of business succession are, by definition, particularly acute for privately held firms, yet owner-managers more often than not fail to address them. In one survey, only 45 percent of family business owners had identified a successor, and only one in three had prepared a succession plan.[3]

Moreover, as *The Wall Street Journal* notes, even business owners who plan for succession often overlook critically important issues. The publication reported that survivors often find themselves facing creditors who doubt their business abilities and, therefore, reduce credit lines and call loans. Many customers try to take advantage of successors, as do many employees.[4] Every ownership transfer involves some difficulty, with fewer than one in three family businesses reported as surviving without major difficulties into the second generation.[5] Clearly, the greater the care and thought exercised in business continuation planning, the greater the likelihood of business survival for the benefit of all stakeholders. Yet, too often, those who built and control the business refuse to plan; to do so is to face their own mortality.

The problems of business stability and continuation following the death or disability of one or more of the owners of a closely held business are critically important to both the family of the deceased owner and the surviving owners and employees. Life and health insurance can play especially vital roles in this regard. To understand this role, it is necessary to review briefly the effects that the death or disability of an owner can have on the stability and continuation of each of the three business forms.

Sole Proprietorships

A **sole proprietorship** is an unincorporated business owned by a single person who usually also manages it. No legal distinction exists between the proprietor's personal and business assets and liabilities. It is the simplest form of business to establish and operate. In the absence of work in professions or trades that themselves require licensing or other documentation, the sole proprietor may establish himself or herself in business by the mere declaration that he or she is in business.

More than 13 million sole proprietorships exist in the United States, with thousands more formed each year (and with thousands dissolved each year). The great majority of sole proprietorships are small with about one-third being one-person operations and more than 95 percent having fewer than 10 employees.

A sole proprietorship is a fragile business enterprise because of its dependence on a single individual. Upon the death of the proprietor, the proprietor's personal representative generally is obligated to liquidate the business, thus possibly losing the business going-concern value for the proprietor's heirs. A properly funded advance agreement whereby the sole proprietor agrees to sell and another party agrees to purchase the business interest on the proprietor's death or disability could preserve the firm's going-concern value.

---

[2]Terence P. Paré, "Passing on the Family Business," *Fortune* (May 7, 1990), p. 81.

[3]Barbara Marsh, "When Owners of Family Businesses Die, Survivors Often Feel Unsuited to Fill Void," *The Wall Street Journal* (May 7, 1990), p. 81.

[4]Ibid.

[5]Paré, "Passing on the Family Business," p. 81.

Prospective buyers might include a friendly competitor or one or more key employees. A binding buy-and-sell agreement between the proprietor and a friendly competitor could be negotiated and funded by life and/or disability income insurance purchased by the competitor or a trust on the proprietor's life. Premiums would be paid by the competitor.

Alternatively, one or more key employees, dependent perhaps on the business for their livelihood, might find the prospects of acquiring the business to be attractive. A buy-and-sell agreement funded by insurance on the proprietor's life could guarantee their eventual ownership while acting as an inducement for the key employee(s) to remain with the business. The policy could be owned by and payable to the employee or owned by and payable to a trust that collects the proceeds and supervises execution of the agreement.

Premiums for this insurance are not tax deductible, but policy proceeds ordinarily would be received income tax free. If the key employee(s) do not have sufficient funds to pay the required premiums, the proprietor could assist the employee(s) through a split-dollar arrangement (see later in this chapter).

Partnerships

A **partnership** is a voluntary association of two or more individuals for the purpose of conducting a business for profit as co-owners. More than 1.5 million partnerships exist in the United States, with most engaging in commercial activities, in contrast with professional activities such as law or medicine.

There are two basic types of partnerships. A **general partnership** is one in which each partner is actively involved in the management of the firm and is fully liable for partnership obligations. A **limited partnership** is one having at least one general partner and one or more limited partners who are not actively engaged in partnership management and who are liable for partnership obligations only to the extent of their investment in the partnership.

Potential Problems Flowing from the Partnership Form

The partnership form of business organization has a number of advantages, but it is subject to the general rule of law that any change in the membership of the partnership causes its dissolution. The law provides that upon the death of a general partner, the partnership is dissolved and, in the absence of arrangements to the contrary, the surviving partners become liquidating trustees. They are charged with the responsibility of winding up the business and paying to the estate of the deceased a fair share of the liquidated value of the business.

Liquidation of a business, which involves the forced sale of assets, almost invariably results in severe asset shrinkage. Under these conditions, accounts receivable might bring only a fraction of their normal value; inventory and plant must be disposed of, often at sacrifice prices; and goodwill is completely lost. From the viewpoint of the survivors, liquidation not only produces losses to them by shrinkage in asset values but, more important, destroys their very means of earning a living.

The seriousness of the consequences often leads survivors to attempt to continue the business by buying out the interest of the deceased partner and reorganizing the partnership. This procedure usually is not practicable, however, for two reasons. First, in most cases, it is not possible to raise the necessary cash. Second, even if the surviving partners can raise the cash to purchase the interest of the deceased, they must prove that the price paid for the interest is fair. Their fiduciary status makes this impracticable. In fact, in some states, they are not permitted to purchase the interest, as this involves a trustee purchasing trust property.

In the usual case, it also is impracticable for an heir who has not already been involved in the business to become a member of the reorganized partnership or to purchase the interests of the surviving partners. The record of litigation clearly indicates that, in the absence of advance agreement among the partners, attempts to continue the business are fraught with legal and practical complications.

Another set of problems can occur when a general partner becomes disabled. His or her special talents, knowledge, and ability may no longer be available to the partnership. Instead, the disabled partner becomes a drain on the business financially, and the nondisabled partner(s) must assume the disabled partner's responsibilities and duties but with inadequate compensation. The nondisabled partners face the problem of earning sufficient money to provide for their usual shares of partnership profits as well as those of the disabled partner. If they hire a capable replacement for the disabled partner, it is even more difficult to maintain the disabled partner's salary. On the other hand, if a replacement is not hired, the burden on the nondisabled partners may become unbearable, particularly if the disability lasts a long time.

As in the case of death, the alternative of taking in family members who are not already active in the business is fraught with dangers and problems. Similarly, liquidation is not ordinarily a desirable solution. Beyond the possible losses brought about by the forced sale of the business, the nondisabled partners must start building their careers again.

Partnership Buy-and-Sell Agreements

As a means of avoiding the foregoing difficulties, it is increasingly common for the members of a partnership to enter into a buy-and-sell agreement. This agreement binds the surviving partners to purchase the partnership interest of the first partner to die or become disabled at a prearranged price set by the agreement and obligates the deceased partner and his or her estate to sell this interest to the other partners. The value of the partnership interest is determined at the time the agreement is entered into and periodically revalued, or a formula for value determination is included in the agreement.

Buy-and-sell agreements are of two types: entity and cross-purchase. Under an **entity buy-and-sell agreement,** the business itself is obligated to buy out the ownership interest of any deceased or disabled partner, with each partner having bound his or her estate to sell if he or she is the first to die.

Under a **cross-purchase buy-and-sell agreement,** each owner binds his or her estate to sell his or her business interest to the surviving owners, and each surviving owner binds himself or herself via the agreement to buy the interest of the deceased owner. In other words, the agreement is among the business owners themselves, not between the business enterprise and its owners.

The business continuation arrangement of a professional partnership (e.g., for attorneys or physicians) usually differs from that discussed previously. Provision usually is made for a continuation of income to the deceased partner's estate or heirs for a specified time period, with the income amount possibly based on a profit-sharing agreement. A separate agreement might provide for the purchase and sale of the deceased partner's tangible business assets.

Use of Life Insurance

Life insurance commonly is used to fund such agreements. Under the entity approach, the partnership itself applies for, owns, and is beneficiary of a life insurance policy on each partner's life. The face amount of each policy usually equals the value of the insured partner's ownership interest. Under the cross-purchase approach, each partner applies for, owns, and is beneficiary of a life insurance policy on each of the other partners' lives. The face amount of each policy usually equals the agreed-upon value of the interest that the surviving partner/policyowner would purchase from the deceased partner's estate. Figures 17-2 and 17-3 illustrate both approaches.

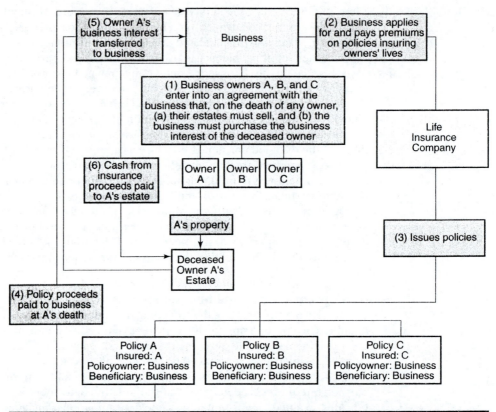

FIGURE 17-2 Entity Buy-and-Sell Agreement: Assumes Owner A Dies

Upon the first death among the partners, the operation of the plan is simple. The life insurance proceeds are used by the partnership or surviving partners, as the case may be, to purchase the interest of the deceased from his or her estate. The partnership is reorganized by the surviving partners and continues in operation, and the heirs of the deceased receive in cash the going-concern value of the involved partnership interest. All parties benefit by the arrangement, and the problems of liquidation are obviated. The surviving partners can enter into a new buy-and-sell agreement or amend the original agreement to account for changes in the value of their respective interests.

Use of Disability Income Insurance

The preceding discussion focused on buyouts occasioned by the death of a partner. The same principles apply with respect to disability buyouts, although the policy options are more limited. Such insurance is offered by a few major insurers only.

Disability income insurance to fund business continuation arrangements (cross-purchase or entity plans) is the second most common use of business disability income insurance. The policies provide cash funds to a business or professional partnership or small corporation to purchase the business interests of a totally disabled partner or shareholder. Policies are arranged so that benefits are not payable until after 12, 24, or 36 months of disability. The duration is chosen to correspond to a "trigger point," which is the date designated in the formal buy-and-sell agreement at which the healthy persons must buy out the totally disabled insured/owner.

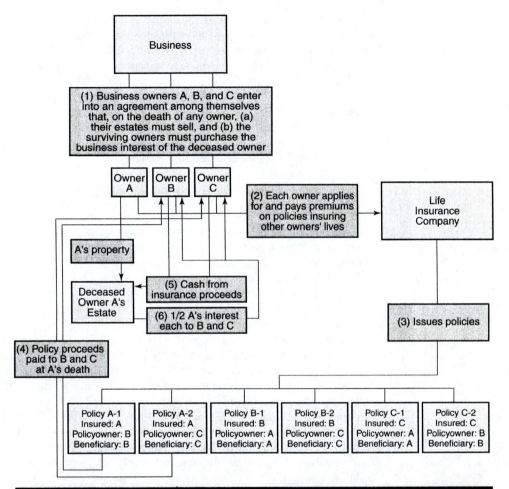

FIGURE 17-3 Cross-Purchase Buy-and-Sell Agreement: Assumes Owner A Dies

Insureds generally are considered totally disabled if, because of sickness or injury, they are unable to perform the major duties of their regular occupations and are not actively at work on behalf of the business or practice with which they are associated. Benefits may be paid as monthly indemnity to a trustee, who then releases the total payment at the trigger point. More commonly, benefits are paid as a lump sum or under a periodic settlement arrangement in reimbursement for the actual amount paid by the buyers to purchase the disabled insured's interest.

The maximum benefits of buyout policies are established at the time of underwriting and are based on the value of the business entity as determined by one or more generally accepted accounting methods. The maximum insurable percentage of an individual's worth in a business is about 80 percent for a lump-sum benefit. This insurable percentage reduces rapidly after age 60 (e.g., 50 percent at age 61 and 25 percent at age 62), as it is logical for business partners to begin planning for transition at the insured's retirement and concern about heightened moral hazard. Policies that provide monthly payments for three or five years in lieu of a lump sum also reduce the benefit substantially for ages near retirement. The maximum underwriting limit usually increases with the length of the elimination period.

Under **indemnity disability income policies,** insurers must pay the maximum amount specified in the policy regardless of the actual value of the business at the time of the claim. Under **reimbursement disability income policies,** on the other hand, insurers pay the lesser of the policy benefit amount or the actual value of the business at the time the buyout occurs. For this reason, indemnity policies rarely provide a maximum of more than $350,000 for any one insured, although reimbursement policies may be available with maximums of $1 million on any one individual.

A **future buyout expense** option is usually available. This provides the owner/insured with the option of increasing the maximum buyout expense benefit without evidence of insurability on specified option dates.

The Tax Aspects of Partnership Buy-and-Sell Agreements

Life Insurance   The income tax treatment of partnership buy-and-sell life insurance is the same as that for personal insurance. Premiums are not deductible whether paid by the partnership or a partner. Death proceeds receive IRC section 101(a) treatment; that is, normally income tax free. The cost basis of each surviving partner is increased by the proceeds received by the partnership in the case of the entity plan and by the amount paid for the deceased partner's interest under the cross-purchase plan.

Life insurance death proceeds are excluded from the gross estate of the insured unless the insured possesses any incidents of ownership or the proceeds are payable to or for the benefit of the insured's estate. Any death proceeds payable to the partnership normally would increase the value of the partnership for estate tax purposes.

In the past, the purchase price established by a buy-and-sell agreement would fix the value of the business for estate tax valuation purposes if certain conditions were met, even if the fixed value were substantially less than the fair market value. For buy-and-sell agreements entered into or substantially modified after October 8, 1990, the value of a closely held business interest (both partnership and corporation) is to be determined without regard to any agreement exercisable at less than fair market value. This general rule does not apply (i.e., an agreement's value *will* control) if the agreement:

- is a bona fide business arrangement;
- is not a device to transfer property to members of the decedent's family for less than an adequate consideration; and
- has terms comparable to those entered into through an arm's-length transaction.[6]

Disability Income Insurance   The income tax treatment of key employee disability income insurance and disability buyout insurance is the same as that for personal coverage—that is, premiums are not deductible and benefits are received income tax free. Premiums paid for overhead expense insurance ordinarily are deductible by the business as a necessary business expense. Benefits received are all considered ordinary income, but they may be offset in whole or in part by the business expenses that the policy benefits are designed to cover.

---

[6]IRC §3703. In addition, case law has established the following four conditions: (1) The estate of the deceased must be obligated to sell the business interest on death, (2) the deceased owner must have been prohibited during life from selling his or her business interest without first offering to sell it to the other party or parties at no more than the contract price, (3) the sale price must have been fair and adequate at the time the agreement was made, and (4) the price must be fixed by the terms of the agreement or by a formula or method set out in the agreement.

Closely Held Corporations

A **closely held corporation,** also referred to as a **close corporation** and as a **closed corporation,** is a closely held business (discussed earlier) in corporate form. Therefore, such corporations are typically owned by a small number of persons who manage the firm's operations. The stock is not listed on any organized exchange, is seldom sold, and, when sold, is typically purchased because of death, disability, retirement, or major corporate restructuring.

Potential Problems Flowing from the Corporate Form

Although the death of a shareholder does not legally dissolve a corporation, the nature of a closely held corporation leads to practical problems that often make retirement of the deceased's interest desirable. As alluded to earlier, the practical difficulties encountered in attempting to continue operation of such a business following the death of a shareholder stem from these facts:

- The shareholders of a close corporation typically are also its officers.
- Owners have an incentive to pay corporate profits to themselves in the form of salaries rather than as dividends because salaries are tax deductible and dividends are not.
- There is no ready market for the stock.

Close corporations are so similar to partnerships in their basic operation that they have been described as "incorporated partnerships." Often they are operated more like partnerships or even sole proprietorships. Consequently, a prearranged plan to retire a shareholder's interest following death or total disability can be as vital for its shareholders as for the owners of the other two business forms.

The Majority Shareholder Situation   Upon the death or total and permanent disability of a majority shareholder in a closed corporation, the other shareholders face four alternatives:

- to accept an adult heir of the deceased into management of the firm;
- to pay dividends that are approximately equivalent to the salary of the deceased/disabled shareholder, to the heir or heirs;
- to admit into active management of the firm outside interests to whom the stock of the deceased may have been sold; or
- to purchase the stock from the disabled owner or from his or her estate.

All of these measures may prove undesirable or impracticable. In the first case, an heir who has not had a previous meaningful involvement in the business normally would be unable to contribute much to the management of the business, and might be a source of disruption in its operation.

The second alternative probably would be unpalatable to the other owners, as they would be bearing all the burdens of management but would be sharing the fruits of their labor equally with someone who was contributing nothing but capital to the firm. If the minority owners chose to pay less in dividends than the approximate salary of their former associate, this could lead to dissatisfaction on the part of heirs.

The entrance of outsiders into the management of the firm could prove highly unsatisfactory. Associates in a close corporation, as in a partnership, typically join forces because they work well together and each has a certain contribution that, taken together, produces a vigorous, profitable combination. In many cases, the outsiders may be unacceptable, and they may lead to a disruption of the business or, in extreme cases, even to liquidation of the firm. More important, if the outsiders' stock constitutes a majority interest, the minority owners would be at the mercy of the new majority owners, who would control such matters as compensation and dividend policy.

The final alternative may be impracticable because the minority owners may be unable to raise the cash or agreement may not be possible as to a fair price. Indeed, the heirs may simply refuse to sell.

The disabled majority shareholder or his or her heirs also could be in an unenviable position. They face the possibility of trying to sell their stock either to the minority shareholders or to outsiders, neither of whom may be predisposed to offer a reasonable price. Indeed, the minority shareholder/officers most likely would not have the resources to buy out the majority interest, and, even if they did, they might prefer to take this amount of money and start a new business.

Outsiders would purchase a majority interest only with the greatest of caution, as the principal value of the business often is in the remaining employees, who could resign. Alternatively, heirs could demand an active role in the business or demand cash dividends, and either course could lead to ruin.

The Minority and 50/50 Shareholder Situations   The minority shareholder situation poses potential problems that are no less formidable. The minority shareholder's heirs, although they may not be able to exercise control, they may be able to render life miserable for the survivors. All shareholders have rights, such as being entitled to a proportionate share of dividends, to examine the corporate records (with legitimate reason), and generally to participate in all shareholder activities. Lawsuits by disgruntled minority shareholders are not uncommon.

The majority shareholder's beneficiaries can enforce their wills on the surviving shareholders; minority shareholder's beneficiaries generally cannot. This distinction, however, might be more apparent than real. In the first instance, the minority shareholders may decide to abandon the business altogether and start out afresh on their own. The disabled majority shareholder or his or her heirs may be at the mercy of the minority shareholders, as they may be the ones who understand the business best and are most likely to continue it as a successful going concern.

Clearly, however, the disabled minority shareholder or his or her heirs are in a most unenviable position. They own stock that was possibly subject to substantial federal and state death taxes yet may have little or no marketability. Who would rationally purchase a minority interest in a closely held corporation? Additionally, they receive no income from their investment, as closely held corporations rarely pay dividends.

Corporate Buy-and-Sell Agreements

These and other difficulties can be avoided by a properly drawn buy-and-sell agreement. Such agreements may be of the entity (usually called **stock-redemption**) or cross-purchase type, each of the same genre as discussed earlier with respect to partnership buyouts. Figures 17-2 and 17-3 are equally applicable to both partnership and corporate buy-and-sell agreements.

The agreement binds the surviving shareholders (cross purchase) or corporation (stock redemption) to purchase the stock of the deceased/disabled shareholder at a price set by the agreement, and it obligates the shareholder and/or his or her estate to sell his or her stock to the surviving shareholders (cross purchase) or the corporation (stock redemption). As in the case of the partnership agreement, each shareholder's interest is valued at the time the agreement is drafted, and it should be revalued periodically and the agreement amended to incorporate the new values. Funding instruments should be reviewed and changed when necessary.

Use of Life and Health Insurance

These agreements are most commonly funded with life insurance policies. Each shareholder is insured for the value of the stock interest owned, the insurance being owned by either the corporation or the other shareholders. Upon the first death among the shareholders, the life insurance proceeds are used by the corporation or surviving shareholders, as the case may be, to purchase the stock of the deceased person from his or her estate. The business future of the survivors is assured, and the estate beneficiaries receive cash instead of a speculative interest.

The shareholders of a closely held corporation who are active in the business are in a position similar to that of partners in a partnership. Consequently, the possibility of a working owner becoming disabled is a serious risk for the business. The best available solution lies in funding a properly drawn buy-and-sell agreement with appropriate amounts of disability insurance, as discussed earlier.

The Tax Aspects of Corporate Buy-and-Sell Agreements

Premiums paid for life and health insurance to fund corporate buy-and-sell agreements are not income tax deductible under either the stock-redemption or cross-purchase approaches. Neither death proceeds nor disability income payments ordinarily give rise to taxable income in the absence of an alternative minimum tax situation (discussed later). Cash-value increases similarly do not usually generate taxable income.

It is possible to run afoul of the transfer for value rule (see chapter 13) with life insurance purchased to fund a stock-redemption buyout agreement. If life insurance is owned by a corporation to fund an entity buyout agreement and it is decided later to change to a cross-purchase agreement, the corporate-owned policies could not be transferred directly to the relevant shareholder (i.e., to someone other than the insured) without activating the transfer for value rule (and its value possibly being treated as a dividend). The rule allows exceptions for transfers between partners and the partnership but not for transfers from corporations to shareholders. Some authorities have suggested that this problem can be avoided if the stockholders are also partners in a bona fide partnership because a transfer to partners is a transfer for value exception.

As with the partnership entity buy-and-sell agreement, life insurance policy death proceeds will not be included in a deceased shareholder's estate unless the shareholder held one or more incidents of ownership or unless the proceeds were payable to or for the benefit of the shareholder's estate. Death proceeds payable to the corporation may, however, cause the deceased shareholder's stock value to rise.

Another consideration in using life insurance to fund entity agreements is whether life insurance cash-value increases or policy death proceed payments would invoke the alternative minimum tax (AMT). As mentioned in chapter 13, this tax may be imposed on tax preference items. The AMT could apply when (1) a policy's yearly cash-value increase exceeds that year's net premium or (2) death proceeds paid exceed the policy's cash value.

Under most cash-value life insurance contracts sold today, the yearly cash-value increases, after the first few policy years, exceed the net annual premium. Also, death proceeds will exceed a policy's cash value (i.e., policies will have a positive net amount at risk). Either or both instances could trigger the AMT, depending upon the details of the particular corporation. For the majority of corporations, cash-value increases are unlikely to cause an AMT problem.

If corporate ownership of a life insurance policy would trigger the AMT, consideration should be given to the cross-purchase approach wherein the corporation is neither the owner nor the beneficiary of the policies. Note also that the AMT could be triggered by key person life insurance as well as other instances involving corporate-owned life insurance (discussed later).

Factors to Consider When Choosing a Buy-and-Sell Agreement

Many factors—both financial and otherwise—should be considered when choosing the type of corporate buy-and-sell agreement. Several factors are summarized next.[7]

Taxation   The relative tax brackets of the corporation and the shareholders may influence whether the cross-purchase or stock-redemption approach is preferred. If the corporation is in a lower tax bracket than the shareholders, a redemption plan may be preferred. This is because premium payments would take a smaller share of the corporation's after-tax income than it would of the shareholders' after-tax income. Conversely, if the shareholders are in a lower bracket than the corporation, a cross-purchase plan may be preferable. This is because premium payments would take relatively less of the shareholders' after-tax income than of the corporation's after-tax income. Also, if the life insurance would cause the corporation to be in an AMT situation, a cross-purchase arrangement may be preferred.

If other factors suggest the use of a cross-purchase plan, even though the corporation is in a lower tax bracket than the shareholders, consideration can be given to funding the insurance through a split-dollar arrangement with the corporation (discussed later). This approach can utilize the corporation's lower bracket.

Ease of Administration   With only two shareholders, there is little difference in the ease of administration with either a stock-redemption or a cross-purchase plan. Each requires the purchase of only two insurance policies—either by the corporation for a redemption or the shareholders themselves for a cross purchase.

As the number of involved shareholders increases, the situation becomes more complicated. Under a stock-redemption plan, the corporation need purchase only one policy per shareholder. Under a cross-purchase plan, however, each shareholder generally would purchase a policy on each of the other shareholders' lives. The total number of policies needed for a cross-purchase arrangement is $n(n-1)$, where n is the number of shareholders. Thus, with five shareholders, 20 policies would be needed.

Effect upon Cost Basis   With a stock-redemption plan, the corporation purchases stock from the selling shareholder or estate. The purchased stock becomes treasury stock and is no longer considered to be outstanding. The other shareholders retain their original stock with no increase in cost basis, even though they will now own a larger percentage of the shares outstanding and, thus, a larger percentage of the corporation. As their cost basis has remained the same while their control and ownership have increased, upon subsequent sale these two factors will increase their taxable gain.

With a cross-purchase plan, the remaining shareholders purchase stock with their own funds, thereby acquiring an increase in basis that is equal to the purchase price of the new shares. Upon any subsequent sale, this new basis reduces the amount of any taxable gain realized by the selling shareholder. This effect is illustrated in Box 17-4.

This outcome can be an important consideration if one or more shareholders are likely to sell their shares during life. If the shareholder is likely to retain the stock until death, the stock will obtain a stepped-up cost basis to its then fair market value on the death of the shareholder. The result, therefore, would be the same, irrespective of whether the ownership interest had increased through a cross-purchase or entity agreement.

Accumulated Earnings Problem   The IRC imposes an accumulated earnings penalty tax on corporations that accumulate earnings and profits beyond that needed for legitimate business purposes to prevent the amounts from being taxed to shareholders. The tax is in addition to the corporation's regular tax liability and is applied at a 28 percent

---

[7]This section draws from *Advanced Business Planning Course,* The Life Underwriter Training Council.

BOX 17-4

AN ILLUSTRATION OF THE DIFFERENCE IN TAX RESULTS BETWEEN CROSS-PURCHASE AND STOCK-REDEMPTION BUYOUTS

The ABC Corporation, with a fair market value of $1.5 million is owned equally by Alain, Bruce, and Claude. Each originally invested $100,000 in the business, which remains the cost basis. Each owner is insured for the value of his ownership interest (i.e., $500,000). Alain dies and the business continuation agreement is effected. Subsequently, Bruce retires and sells his ownership interest to Claude, outlined as follows.

IMPACT OF DEATH AND LATER SALE UNDER A STOCK-REDEMPTION PLAN

- At Alain's death, the corporation collects $500,000 in death proceeds and redeems his stock.

- The business value remains $1.5 million.

- Bruce's ownership interest value equals $750,000 and the cost basis remains $100,000.

- Claude's ownership interest value equals $750,000 and the cost basis remains $100,000.

- When Bruce subsequently retires and sells his ownership interest to Claude (a living buyout), the result is a $650,000 capital gain for Bruce ($750,000 – $100,000), assuming no change in the value of that interest.

- If the capital gains tax rate is 20 percent, taxes of $130,000 would be due on the $650,000 gain.

IMPACT OF DEATH AND LATER SALE UNDER A CROSS-PURCHASE PLAN

- At Alain's death, Bruce and Claude each collect $250,000 in death proceeds and buy Alain's stock from his estate.

- The business value remains $1.5 million.

- Bruce's ownership interest value equals $750,000 but the cost basis is $100,000 + $250,000 = $350,000.

- Claude's ownership interest value equals $750,000 but the cost basis is $100,000 + $250,000 = $350,000

- When Bruce subsequently retires and sells his ownership interest to Claude (a living buyout), the result is a $400,000 capital gain for Bruce ($750,000 – $350,000), assuming no change in the value of that interest. The result is found as follows:

$$\text{Sale Price} = \$750,000$$
$$\text{Less: Cost Basis} = \underline{-350,000}$$
$$\text{Equals: Capital Gain} = \$400,000$$

- If the capital gain tax rate is 20 percent, taxes of $80,000 would be due on the $400,000 gain.

rate. In general, however, an aggregate of $250,000 may be accumulated for any reason without danger of incurring the tax.

Several cases have recognized as a legitimate business purpose the accumulation of funds for the buyout of a minority shareholder to eliminate dissent or to promote management efficiency.[8] The courts disagree, however, as to whether an accumulation to redeem a majority interest serves a legitimate business purpose.[9]

A cross-purchase plan avoids the accumulated earnings concern altogether as the policies are not owned by the corporation. If other concerns suggest the need for a stock-redemption plan, even in the face of an otherwise potential accumulated earnings problem, consideration can be given to not obligating the corporation to carry life insurance

---

[8]*Mountain State Steel Foundries, Inc. v. Comm.*, 284 F. 2d 737 (4th Cir. 1960); *Oman Construction Co. v. Comm.*, TC Memo 1965-325; *Dill Mfg. Co. v. Comm.*, 39 BTA 1023 (1939); *Gazette Publishing Co. v. Self,* 103 F. Supp. 779 (E.D. Ark. 1952); and *Farmers Merchant Investment Co. v. Comm.*, 29 TC Memo (CCH) 705 (1970).

[9]*John B. Lambert & Asso. v. U.S.*, 76-1 USTC (CCH) 84, 271 (Ct. Cl. 1976) and *Cadillac Textiles, Inc. v. Comm.*, 34 TC Memo (CCH) 295 (1975).

and using the proceeds to purchase the decedent's stock. Instead, the corporation's liquidity need can be met by carrying key person life insurance on the shareholder. Life insurance purchased to indemnify the corporation for loss of a key person's service has been held to be a reasonable business need, and earnings used for such a purpose should avoid attracting the penalty tax.[10] Similarly, earnings accumulated to meet a corporation's obligations under a nonqualified retirement agreement (see chapter 16) should be considered a reasonable business need.[11]

Corporate Creditors Under a stock-redemption plan, the corporation is the owner and beneficiary of the life insurance policies funding the arrangement. Any policy cash values and death proceeds are, therefore, subject to attachment by the creditors of the corporation because the policy values are general corporate assets. This problem is not encountered under a cross-purchase plan.

State Law Restrictions The laws of most states provide that corporate redemptions can be made only from available corporate surplus; thus, no surplus—no redemption. Insurance proceeds and contributions to capital can help alleviate this problem under a stock-redemption plan. The problem is not faced under cross-purchase buyouts.

Loan Limitations Many close corporations operate on credit. In the normal course of business, this fact presents no problems. The loan agreements used by most banks, however, contain a restriction prohibiting the payment of dividends or redemption of stock without the bank's prior consent. If credit is likely to be an important element in business operations, a stock-redemption agreement could fail unless it were fully funded and the indebtedness satisfied, so that creditors would not object to a redemption. This issue does not arise with a cross-purchase agreement.

Attribution Rules As a general rule, a complete redemption of a shareholder's stock by a corporation will result in capital gains treatment. A redemption of only a portion of a shareholder's stock, however, generally will invoke dividend treatment—an undesirable result. Hence, most stock-redemption plans involve the complete redemption of stock.

A problem can arise, however, in certain family-owned and other corporations because of the IRC's *attribution rules,* the effect of which can be to attribute the stock owned by family members or estate beneficiaries to a decedent. Thus, if Nancy owns 100 shares of stock in Nancy's Fancy Books and her husband, Carlos, also owns 100 shares, Carlos's ownership interest will be attributed to Nancy on her death. In this instance, a complete redemption of Nancy's 100 shares would be deemed only a partial redemption and, thereby, would invoke unfavorable dividend treatment. The family attribution rules can be waived provided the shareholder from whom the stock is redeemed:

- retains no interest in the corporation, except as a creditor, immediately after the redemption;
- does not acquire any interest in the corporation, except by bequest or inheritance, within 10 years of the redemption; and
- files an agreement to notify the IRS if he or she obtains a forbidden interest within the 10-year period.

The waiver of family attribution is not allowed if certain interfamily transfers occurred within the 10-year period preceding the redemption. If a disallowed transfer did

---

[10]*Harry A. Koch Co. v. Vinal*, 228 F. Supp. 782 (D. Neb. 1964); *Vuono-Lione, Inc. v. Comm.*, TC Memo 1965-96; and *Emeloid Co. v. Comm.*, 189 F.2d 230 (3rd Cir. 1951).

[11]*John P. Scripps Newspapers v. Comm.*, 44 TC 453 (1965) and *Okla. Press Publ. Co. v. U.S.*, 437 F.2d 1275 (10th Cir. 1971) on remand, 28 AFTR 2d 71-5722 (E.D. Okla. 1971).

occur but income tax avoidance was not its principal purpose, the waiver will be permitted nonetheless.

Section 303 Stock Redemptions

Many estates are composed largely of stock in a closely held business. Such estates often have liquidity problems. These problems can cause a forced, disadvantageous sale of estate assets or even business liquidation. The U.S. Congress enacted IRC Section 303 to help alleviate these problems. A so-called **Section 303 redemption** is an income-tax-free stock redemption allowed qualifying estates, in an amount to cover federal and state death taxes, funeral expenses, and estate administration expenses. This redemption can be important because normally a partial redemption of stock is treated as a taxable dividend to the redeeming shareholder or his or her estate.

To qualify for a Section 303 redemption, the value of the stock must be included in the decedent's gross estate and must represent more than 35 percent of the decedent's adjusted gross estate. The redemption must be made within three years and 90 days of the filing of the estate tax return.

This technique clearly can be useful when the shareholder's business ownership represents a major portion of the total estate assets. Life insurance is a natural funding vehicle for Section 303 redemptions. The corporation applies for, owns, and is the beneficiary of a policy whose face amount is sufficient to provide the corporate funds needed to effect the redemption. Figure 17-4 illustrates the process. The income tax

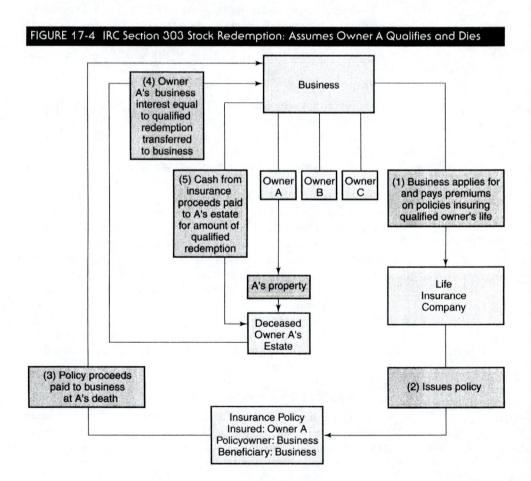

FIGURE 17-4 IRC Section 303 Stock Redemption: Assumes Owner A Qualifies and Dies

treatment of this insurance is essentially that of key employee insurance, although the life insurance might be subject to any accumulated earnings taxation of the corporation. Additionally, an AMT situation can exist.

Use of ESOPs in Business Continuation Arrangements

An **employee stock ownership plan** (ESOP) is a qualified employee benefit plan that is designed to purchase the employer's stock. We discuss ESOPs more fully in chapter 21. As a qualified plan, ESOPs must comply with the requirements of ERISA and must operate for the exclusive benefit of the firm's employees generally.

However, ESOPs must purchase shares of the employer's stock from someone, and why not from the estate of a deceased owner? Under this arrangement, the ESOP would enter into a buy-and-sell arrangement with one or more of the business owners. This arrangement would provide that the ESOP would purchase and the estate would be bound to sell some or all of the decedent's shares. To fund the arrangement, the ESOP could purchase life insurance on the owner's life, with the ESOP being policyowner and beneficiary.

NONQUALIFIED EXECUTIVE BENEFITS

Individually issued life and health insurance policies often are used to provide supplementary benefits to selected employees. The employees typically are those whose skills, talents, and experience make them particularly valuable to the business.

Chapter 16 introduced the concept of nonqualified compensation arrangements, including a discussion of the motivation for their use and an examination of such arrangements in the context of retirement benefits and planning. Our focus here is on two other types of executive benefit plans: executive bonus arrangements and split-dollar insurance.

Executive Bonus Plans

An **executive bonus plan** is an arrangement under which the employer pays for individually issued life insurance for selected executives. It is a simple arrangement. The employer agrees to pay the premiums for a policy that is owned by the employee. The employer is free to discriminate among employees benefitted by this plan.

The premium payments by the business are compensation and, therefore, tax deductible (unless total compensation is judged to be "unreasonable" by the IRS, which does arise occasionally if the executive is also the business owner). To claim this deduction, the death proceeds cannot be payable to the business. This latter requirement is found in IRC Section 162, so these plans are sometimes called *Section 162 plans.*

The executive must include the amount of the premium payment in his or her taxable income. Because the plan provides nonqualified life insurance, the executive cannot exclude any of the payment from taxable income. Some employers pay an additional bonus to the executive to cover this income tax obligation. Figure 17-5 illustrates the executive bonus plan.

As the owner of the policy, the executive may name the beneficiary and exercise all other policy rights. Of course, the death proceeds will be included in the executive's gross estate if he or she retains any ownership interest or if proceeds are payable to or for the benefit of the estate.

Split-Dollar Life Insurance Plans

Split-dollar life insurance is an arrangement for providing funding for individually issued, cash-value life insurance. It is a funding method, not a type of policy. The arrangement divides or splits the death benefit, the living benefits, and possibly the premium between two parties—hence, the name *split-dollar insurance.*

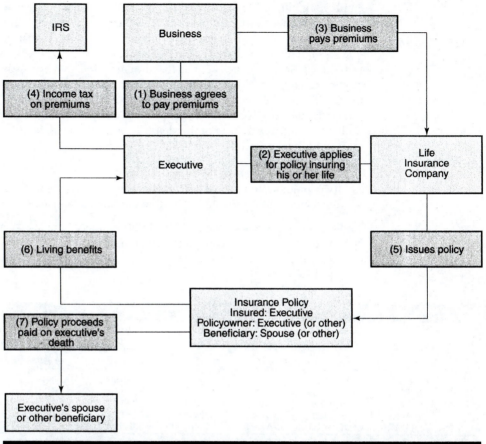

FIGURE 17-5 The Executive Bonus Plan

The objective of split-dollar plans is to join together the needs of one person with the premium-paying ability of another. Often this means cooperation between an employee and his or her employer, but the concept can be applied to an infinite variety of other relationships: child–parent, shareholder–corporation, buyer–seller, and so on.

The split-dollar plan may provide employees with substantial amounts of life insurance protection, generally at a current outlay well below that which they would pay for the same policy purchased individually. The employee also can be allowed to purchase the policy from the employer at termination or retirement, and this can provide the employee with a supplemental retirement benefit.

When used as a fringe benefit, split-dollar insurance proceeds are usually intended (1) as a death benefit to the employee's beneficiary and (2) as a reimbursement to the employer for its share of premiums paid. The same concept has gained added significance for the shareholder-employee in recent years.

The Classical Split-Dollar Plan

An understanding of the so-called classical split-dollar plan will be helpful, although few such plans actually are structured precisely this way. Under this arrangement, the employer and employee join in the purchase of a cash-value insurance contract on the employee's life. The employer provides the funds to pay that part of each annual premium that is equal to the annual increase in the cash value. The employee pays the balance. The employer is entitled to receive death proceeds from the policy equal to the cash value, or at least a sufficient part thereof to equal its total premium payments. The employee names the beneficiary for the balance of any proceeds. Table 17-1 illustrates such a policy.

Although the employee's share of annual premiums may be substantial in the early years, it will decrease each year as the annual increases in cash value grow progressively larger. In many cases, the employee's share reaches zero after a relatively short time. As the employer takes over more of the obligation to pay premiums, its share of the death proceeds increases. Nevertheless, through the appropriate use of dividends or other options, the employee's share of the death benefit often can be maintained at an approximately constant amount.

Split-Dollar Systems

Two major systems have been developed for the establishment of a split-dollar life insurance plan: the endorsement system and the collateral assignment system.

Endorsement System When a split-dollar plan is established under the **endorsement system,** insurance on the employee's life is applied for and owned by the employer. The employer is primarily responsible for premium payments. In the classical split-dollar

TABLE 17-1 Illustration of Classical Split-Dollar Plan ($250,000 Ordinary Life)

| | Male, Nonsmoker, Age 45 $4,660 Annual Premium | | | | Dividends Applied to Purchase One-Year Term For 20 Years Balance Applies to Paid-Up Additions | | | |
| | Corporation | | | | Insured/Employee | | | |
YEAR	ANNUAL BEFORE-TAX EXPEN-DITURE	ANNUAL AFTER-TAX EXPEN-DITURE[a]	NET CASH VALUE	NET DEATH BENEFIT	ANNUAL BEFORE-TAX EXPEN-DITURE	ANNUAL AFTER-TAX EXPEN-DITURE[b]	NET CASH VALUE	NET DEATH BENEFIT
1	$ 0	$ 0	$ 0	$ 0	$4,660	$4,660	$ 0	$250,000
2	125	125	125	125	4,535	4,535	0	250,000
3	4,660	4,660	4,785	4,785	0	97	4,039	254,296
4	4,660	4,660	9,445	9,445	0	109	4,466	255,206
5	4,660	4,660	14,105	14,105	0	124	5,347	257,553
6	4,660	4,660	18,765	18,765	0	141	6,846	261,495
7	4,660	4,660	23,425	23,425	0	162	9,087	266,761
8	4,660	4,660	28,085	28,085	0	185	11,957	273,395
9	4,660	4,660	32,745	32,745	0	212	15,486	281,015
10	4,660	4,660	37,405	37,405	0	243	19,451	289,365
11	4,660	4,660	42,065	42,065	0	292	24,118	298,665
12	4,660	4,660	46,725	46,725	0	336	29,613	309,865
13	4,660	4,660	51,385	51,385	0	386	35,711	321,794
14	4,660	4,660	56,045	56,045	0	442	42,405	334,344
15	4,660	4,660	60,750	60,750	0	508	49,696	347,427
16	4,660	4,660	65,365	65,365	0	590	57,587	360,970
17	4,660	4,660	70,025	70,025	0	681	66,090	374,930
18	4,660	4,660	74,685	74,685	0	783	75,473	389,533
19	4,660	4,660	79,345	79,345	0	895	85,498	404,520
20	4,660	4,660	84,005	84,005	0	1,053	95,921	419,639

[a] Assuming a corporate tax bracket of 25 percent.

[b] Assuming a 28 percent tax bracket for 20 years. Includes economic benefit value.

arrangement, the employee agrees to reimburse the employer for the portion of each premium payment that exceeds the annual increase in the policy's cash value. The employer is named the beneficiary for that portion of the proceeds that is equal to the cash value—the exact amount of its cumulative premium payments. The employee designates a personal beneficiary to receive the remainder of the proceeds.

The employee's rights are protected by an endorsement on the policy that modifies the employer's rights as policyowner. This endorsement provides that the designation of the employee's personal beneficiary to receive the proceeds in excess of the cash value cannot be changed without the insured employee's consent.

Some life insurers have adopted a slightly different approach to the split-dollar endorsement system. These companies permit the ownership of policy rights to be split, with the insured employee designated as owner of the portion of the death proceeds in excess of the cash value and the employer designated as owner of all the other rights and benefits under the policy.

If the split-dollar plan is terminated prior to the death of the insured employee, the employer recovers its premium outlay directly from the cash value that it controls as owner of the policy. This may be accomplished by surrendering the policy or giving the insured employee the option to purchase it for an amount equal to its cash surrender value.

Collateral Assignment System   When a classical split-dollar insurance plan is established under the **collateral assignment system,** the insured employee applies for and owns the policy. He or she then designates his or her own personal beneficiary. The insured employee is primarily liable for premium payment. In a separate agreement, the employer obligates itself to lend the employee an amount equal to the annual increases in the cash value. Generally, this loan is made interest free. Thus, the employee's out-of-pocket cost is limited to that portion of each annual premium that exceeds the annual increase in cash value. To protect the employer, the employee collaterally assigns the policy to the employer as security for the amount of the loan. At the insured employee's death, the employer recovers the amount of its loan from the death proceeds, not as a beneficiary of the policy, but as a collateral assignee.

Factors Bearing on Choice of Split-Dollar Systems   Several factors help suggest which split-dollar system should be used. One factor to consider is whether the employer wants the cash value available for use in its business during the term of the split-dollar plan. If it does, the endorsement system or split ownership variation is preferable. Under the collateral assignment system, the policy cash value generally is not available to the employer. Under the endorsement system, the employer as policyowner is free to borrow from the policy at any time and for any reason. If the employee is not an officer or shareholder, the endorsement method may be preferable to the employer as a means of retaining key employees because the policy and its protection would be lost in the event of employment termination.

When the parties intend to use the policy to fund a nonqualified retirement arrangement, the endorsement method should be used. This is especially true when the insured employee is not a shareholder or officer of the corporation. At the retirement of the insured employee, the employer can elect to take out a policy loan or to receive the cash value under a settlement option or continue to pay the premiums on the policy until the employee's death.

If the collateral assignment system is used, the insured employee is owner of the policy. If the policy is to be used to fund a nonqualified retirement plan, it will have to be transferred to the corporation. This would involve a transfer for value, subjecting a portion of the death proceeds to income taxation unless the insured employee was a shareholder or officer of the corporation.

If a policy already in force and personally owned by the insured employee is to be used to establish a split-dollar plan, it is simpler to adopt the collateral assignment system. If the policy is a key person policy owned by the employer, however, the simpler approach is to utilize the endorsement system.

If it is desirable to have the employee accumulate some savings through the policy, the collateral assignment method ordinarily would be preferred. Under equity split-dollar plans (discussed later), the employer's interest in the cash value equals the sum of its premium contributions. With most single-life cash-value policies, the annual cash-value increases exceed the premium after a few years. Under an equity split-dollar plan, title to the excess of the gross policy cash value over that portion of the cash-value due the employer because of its premium payments rests with the employee.

Income Tax Consequences of Split-Dollar Plans

Split-dollar plans give rise to income tax consequences to both employees and employers.

Income Tax Treatment of Employees   The typical split-dollar plan is considered to result in a taxable *economic benefit* to the employee, represented by the amount of the annual premium cost that the employee should bear and of which he or she is relieved. The value of the benefit, to be included annually in the employee's taxable income, is an amount equal to the one-year term cost of the life insurance protection to which the employee is entitled, less any portion of the premium paid by the employee. If the premium paid by the employee exceeds the economic benefit, there is no taxable income to the employee. However, no carryover is allowed of any excess premium. In deriving the annual economic benefit to the employee, the one-year term insurance rates contained in the government's PS-58 Rate Table or the term rates of the insurer may be used. Table 17-2 gives the PS-58 rates.

TABLE 17-2 PS-58 Rate Table					
Age	*Premium*	*Age*	*Premium*	*Age*	*Premium*
15	$1.27	37	$ 3.63	59	$ 19.08
16	1.38	38	3.87	60	20.73
17	1.48	39	4.14	61	22.53
18	1.52	40	4.42	62	24.50
19	1.56	41	4.73	63	26.63
20	1.61	42	5.07	64	28.98
21	1.67	43	5.44	65	31.51
22	1.73	44	5.85	66	34.28
23	1.79	45	6.30	67	37.31
24	1.86	46	6.78	68	40.59
25	1.93	47	7.32	69	44.17
26	2.02	48	7.89	70	48.06
27	2.11	49	8.53	71	52.29
28	2.20	50	9.22	72	56.89
29	2.31	51	9.97	73	61.89
30	2.43	52	10.79	74	67.33
31	2.57	53	11.69	75	73.23
32	2.70	54	12.67	76	79.63
33	2.86	55	13.74	77	86.57
34	3.02	56	14.91	78	94.09
35	3.21	57	16.18	79	102.23
36	3.41	58	17.56	80	111.04

If the insurer publishes rates for individual, initial issue, one-year term policies that are available to all standard risks, these rates may be used in place of the PS-58 rates. Many insurers' term rates are significantly lower than the PS-58 rates. Using the lower rates decreases the amount of taxable income imputed to the employee. Box 17-5 offers an example of how the economic benefit is determined.

Many split-dollar plans today involve second-to-die policies. The economic benefit imputed to such policies is calculated by using the one-year term rates as given in U.S. Life Table 38 for joint and last survivor mortality. These rates are substantially lower than the PS-58 rates—typically only 1 to 10 percent of the PS-58 rates, depending on age.

The value of any policy dividends used to benefit the employee also is included in his or her taxable income. As with the economic benefit treatment, the tax implications of any additional benefits received by the employee on account of policy dividends under a split-dollar plan will be the same whether the endorsement system or the collateral assignment system is used.

Income Tax Treatment of Employer Premiums paid by an employer on insurance covering the life of an employee when the employer is directly or indirectly a beneficiary under the policy are not deductible. As a result, the employer is not allowed a tax deduction for its share of premiums under a split-dollar plan.

Income Tax Treatment of Death Proceeds The income tax treatment of any death proceeds payable under a split-dollar plan will be governed by IRC Section 101(a). Thus, in the absence of IRC Section 7702 (definition of life insurance) or transfer for value problems, both the employer and the personal beneficiary of the employee will receive their share of the proceeds income tax free.

Estate Tax Treatment of Split-Dollar Plans

The IRC provides that death proceeds of insurance are included in the gross estate of a decedent/insured if he or she possessed any incidents of policy ownership or if proceeds are payable to or for the benefit of the insured's estate. Under the usual endorsement system, the employer is the sole owner of the life insurance policy. To protect the

---

BOX 17-5

AN EXAMPLE OF THE DETERMINATION OF THE ECONOMIC BENEFIT UNDER SPLIT-DOLLAR INSURANCE

Jack is the insured/employee under a $100,000 ordinary life policy under a classical split-dollar arrangement. The annual premium is $2,000. In the year in question, the annual increase in cash value and, thus, the employer's contribution toward the premium is $1,800. Jack must, therefore, pay $200 ($2,000 – $1,800). If Jack were to die during the year, the portion of the death proceeds payable to the employer is $10,000 (the total of its premium contributions), with the remaining $90,000 of death proceeds payable to Jack's personal beneficiary.

To determine the amount of the taxable economic benefit to Jack, the first step is to calculate the term cost of the insurance protection provided

to his or her personal beneficiary. We need Jack's age to calculate this figure. He is 42. Based on the PS-58 Rate Table, the term cost of insurance protection is $5.07 per $1,000. Because $90,000 would be payable to Jack's beneficiary, the value of the insurance protection is $456 ($90,000 × $5.07/$1,000).

Jack contributed $200 toward the premium payment. Hence, the value of the net economic benefit and the amount included in his taxable income is $256 ($456 – $200). Each year the amount included in Jack's taxable income will vary because the term rate and protection amount will be different.

insured employee's rights under the agreement, the ownership rights of the employer are modified by endorsement that provides that the insured employee's personal beneficiary cannot be changed without the insured employee's consent. This is an incident of ownership. This ownership right might be avoided if the agreement provides that the beneficiary cannot be changed without the consent of the beneficiary, rather than of the insured. Even if the death proceeds are included in the insured's gross estate, they should qualify for the unlimited marital deduction if they are paid to the surviving spouse.

Under the collateral assignment system, the insured employee generally is the policyowner. As such, he or she can exercise all of the incidents of ownership, and the death proceeds should be included in his or her gross estate. The estate tax value of the proceeds should be the full proceeds, less the amount paid to the employer in satisfaction of the debt owed to it under the split-dollar agreement.

When the collateral assignment system is used and the insured employee wishes to avoid inclusion of the proceeds in his or her gross estate, the beneficiary for the insured/employee's share of the proceeds should initially apply for and own the life insurance policy. The owner/beneficiary may be a trust, the insured's spouse, or any other third party. The policyowner should then enter into the collateral assignment split-dollar agreement with the insured's employer. Under this arrangement, the insured employee arguably has no incidents of ownership in the policy, and the proceeds should be excluded from his or her gross estate.

If a third party, such as an irrevocable trust, owns the policy, the insured employee is deemed to be making gifts of the economic benefit to the third party. Of course, any gift tax consequences can be offset by using the $10,000-per-donee annual exclusion for present interest gifts. It is advisable to have a Crummey withdrawal power with trusts. (See chapter 15.)

When a split-dollar plan (regardless of the system) is instituted between a corporation and a majority shareholder-employee, the portion of the proceeds payable to a beneficiary other than the corporation may be included in the gross estate of the insured majority shareholder-employee, even when the necessary steps have been taken to eliminate the possession of any incidents of ownership in the policy held directly by the insured. This result is based on an estate tax regulation that imputes the incidents of ownership possessed by a corporation in an insurance policy on the life of a majority shareholder to the shareholder to the extent that the proceeds are not payable to or for the benefit of the corporation. Proceeds payable to the corporation are not included in the shareholder's estate but are considered in establishing the value of the decedent's stock.

To avoid inclusion of these policy proceeds in the estate of a controlling shareholder, the corporation must be relegated to the status of a secured lender. To so qualify, the corporation must not have the right to terminate the policy in any way or to borrow against the policy. An alternative is for an irrevocable trust to own the policy and to have the split-dollar agreement provide that the trustee will name the corporation as a revocable, creditor beneficiary without any ability to borrow or pledge. The corporation would have no rights in the policy under this approach.

Variations of the Classical Split-Dollar Plan

Under the classical split-dollar plan, the employer makes annual contributions of an amount equal to the increases in cash value, and the insured employee contributes the balance of the annual premium due, if any. In the first few years of the plan, the financial burden on the insured employee could be substantial. Also, when the employee's premium contribution exceeds the economic benefit, no carryover of the excess contribution to future years is allowed. As a result of these difficulties and other planning opportunities, several variations of the classical split-dollar approach have evolved, a few of which are discussed next.

Reverse Split-Dollar If it is desirable for the employee, instead of the employer, to have rights to the cash value and for the employer, instead of the employee, to control the disposition of the death proceeds, a reverse split-dollar plan may be appropriate. Under **reverse split-dollar** (RSD), the traditional roles of employer and employee are reversed, with the pure death protection payable to the corporation and death proceeds equal to the cash value payable to the employee's beneficiary. The employee owns the policy, including the cash value, and endorses to the employer the right to name the beneficiary for a portion of the death proceeds.

The employee is responsible for the entire premium, with the employer paying the portion of the premium that reflects the value of its economic benefit. As one of the goals of RSD may be to transfer employer wealth to the employee, the economic benefit value paid by the corporation ordinarily would be the PS-58 rate rather than the insurer's lower term rate. By doing so, the corporation is subsidizing the purchase of the employee's life insurance. The employee will, thereby, pay less than the annual cash-value increase.

When the arrangement is terminated, the employer simply ceases to make further premium payments and relinquishes its right to a portion of the death benefits. The idea is that the employee obtains full policy control without tax consequences.

RSD has strong advocates and equally strong opponents. No IRS rulings on RSD have been made, so potentially important tax issues cannot be addressed with certainty. RSD can be useful when the employer desires key person protection or informal funding for a DBO plan or when death proceeds would be useful for a stock redemption. RSD can be of substantial value to the employee as a subsidized savings mechanism, and ultimately as meaningful death protection.

Figure 17-6 illustrates how an RSD plan's initial $500,000 death benefit can be split between employer and employee. The illustration assumes that the corporation ceases its premium payments and policy involvement when the employee becomes 65.

Equity Split-Dollar In a classic split-dollar plan, the employer's interest in the policy equals the greater of the policy's cash value or the aggregate of its premium payments. Under **equity split-dollar,** the employee obtains ownership of the excess of the cash value over any premium payments.

The IRS has ruled that certain equity split-dollar plans give rise to taxable employee income on the excess. As mentioned earlier, the collateral assignment method conceptually should avoid this possibility, but the issue is not completely clear.

Alternative Premium Payment Arrangements Besides the premium payment approach of the classical, RSD, and equity split-dollar plans, several other alternative payment approaches are possible. For example, under the *averaging approach,* the employer pays a level amount each year that is equal to a specified fraction of the policy's cash

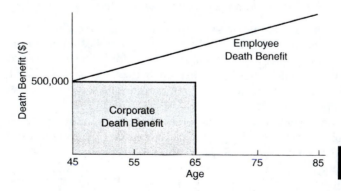

FIGURE 17-6 Reverse Split-Dollar Illustration

value after a specified number of years. For example, each year the employer might pay one-twentieth of the twentieth-year cash value. The employee pays the balance of each premium. Thus, the employee's contribution is leveled to ease his or her burden in the early policy years. Over the specified period, aggregate contributions by both the employer and the employee are the same as under the classical plan.

Under the *PS-58 cost approach,* each year the employee pays an amount that is equal to that year's PS-58 cost. Depending on the use of dividends, the death benefit may vary from year to year. The employer pays the balance, if any, of each premium. A policy issued at a young age eventually may generate PS-58 costs substantially greater than the gross annual premium.

Under the **employer-pay-all approach,** the employer pays the full premium each year. The employee makes no contribution to the premium and merely reports taxable income on the value of the economic benefit received each year.

The so-called *bonus plan* is a minor adaptation that combines aspects of the PS-58 and employer-pay-all approaches. The employer is willing to pay the entire cost of the plan. Cognizant of the fact that its expenditure on behalf of the employee's economic benefit is not deductible, the employer adopts a PS-58 cost plan and pays the employee a bonus sufficient to enable the employee to pay the PS-58 costs. The employer's expenditure is precisely the same as with the employer-pay-all approach, but a portion of it (equal to the PS-58 measured bonus) is presumably deductible as compensation. The employee now pays tax on the bonus rather than on PS-58 costs.

The classical split-dollar plan allocates a death benefit to the employer equal to the greater of the sum of its aggregate contributions or the cash value. Another approach is to allocate to the employer a portion of the death proceeds equal to the employer's contributions accumulated at some specified rate of interest. This reflects the time value of money.

"Unsplitting" the Policy

Split-dollar plans are not designed to last forever. At some point, the economic benefit charges can become particularly burdensome, the employee will retire or resign, or business or personal reasons may necessitate the termination of the plan. Upon plan termination (other than by death), the policy often is made available to the employee. Three alternatives for "unsplitting" split-dollar plans are: (1) conversion to key person insurance; (2) a sale or rollout; and (3) a spinout.

Conversion to Key Person Insurance   Under this approach, the insured (or third-party owner) releases his or her interest in the policy to the corporation. This normally is an undesirable solution unless the insured is an officer or shareholder of the corporation because it would appear to constitute a transfer for value. If the insured is a principal shareholder, he or she may prefer to have the corporation retain the policy death proceeds to be used in a Section 303 redemption or a postdeath total liquidation of the corporation.

Sale or Rollout   A sale or a **rollout** occurs, respectively, when the corporation sells the policy to the insured for its full cash value or makes a maximum policy loan or withdrawal or surrender of paid-up additions, followed by a transfer of its remaining ownership rights in the policy to the insured. In the latter case, the employer probably would sell the policy to the insured for the difference between the gross cash surrender value and the policy loan, if any.

Under an endorsement split-dollar plan, a sale to the insured should not give rise to a taxable event if the sales price equals the policy's fair market value. It also will not invoke income taxation of the death proceeds as the transfer for value is to the insured—one of the exceptions.

The transfer of the policy to the insured via the policy loan approach—the rollout—can give rise to taxable income to the employee. The position of the IRS is that the transfer is taxable income to the extent that the net policy cash value (cash value less loan amount) exceeds the aggregate premiums paid by the employee.

This adverse tax effect can be avoided by a rollout when the cash value is about equal to or less than the cumulative premiums contributed by the employer. Alternatively, the collateral assignment method can be used, thereby presumably avoiding a policy transfer altogether and, hence, avoiding attendant taxable income.

The insured would have a continuing interest obligation on the policy loan. As the corporation has recovered an amount equal to the cash value and no longer has any commitment under the split-dollar agreement, it can (if it wishes) give the insured employee annual bonuses that are equal to the gross interest payable.

Spinout   Another approach is referred to as a **spinout** under which the corporation merely transfers its interest in the policy as a bonus to the insured. Any transfer to a third-party owner should be a separate subsequent event, with the insured gifting the policy to the third-party owner to avoid a transfer for value.

Under a spinout, the insured is taxed on the value of the policy. If the insured chose to do so, he or she could borrow against the policy to pay the tax. This leaves the insured with a considerably smaller policy loan than he or she would have with the rollout. Again, the corporation may give the insured employee annual bonuses equal to the gross interest payable on this (smaller) loan.

Caveat   Each of the foregoing unsplitting techniques works nicely for a classical split-dollar plan. Under such a plan, the corporation's contributions are no more than the policy's cash value. However, with more ambitious plans (i.e., plans in which the corporate contributions have exceeded the increase in cash value), it is necessary to reckon with the excess of total corporate contributions over total cash value. This excess was, presumably, in the nature of a loan to the employee. A release or discharge of this indebtedness generates taxable income to the individual so enriched. The solution may be to undertake unsplitting only in a policy year when the cash value is as large as (or, at least, not much smaller than) the corporation's cumulative contributions. This approach will eliminate (or at least minimize) the problem of discharge of an indebtedness.

Other Uses of Split-Dollar Insurance Plans

In the typical employer–employee split-dollar plan, insurance is purchased on the life of the employee. An employee, however, may need insurance protection on the life of someone else. Split-dollar plans can be useful in these cases also.

Sole Proprietor Buyout   A sole proprietor may not have any family members to whom he or she wants to leave the business at death. It may be difficult to sell the business to an outsider at a fair price. In such a situation, it is not unusual for the business owner to offer to sell the business to an interested employee at the business owner's death.

Although the employee may be eager to accept the offer, one major stumbling block often is the lack of funds with which to make the purchase. An obvious solution would be insurance owned by the employee on the life of the sole proprietor. To solve the problem of the employee not having sufficient funds, the employer may enter into a split-dollar insurance plan with the employee. In this case, the insurance is on the life of the employer rather than on the employee.

Split-Dollar in a Cross-Purchase Buy-and-Sell Agreement   One drawback to the use of a cross-purchase buy-and-sell agreement is that the shareholders are personally responsible for the payment of premiums on insurance used to fund the plan. The corporation can help finance the purchase of the needed insurance through the use of a split-dollar plan. When a split-dollar plan is entered into for this purpose, the collateral assignment system generally is used. Each shareholder applies for and owns a policy on the life of his or her coshareholder(s). Each shareholder then collaterally assigns the policy he or she owns on his or her coshareholder's life to the corporation as security for the corporation's premium payments.

If a split-dollar plan used to fund a cross-purchase buy-and-sell agreement is arranged under the endorsement system, it could result in a transfer for value problem. Under this system, normally the corporation applies for and owns the life insurance. It then transfers the right to receive a portion of the policy proceeds on the life of each shareholder to his or her coshareholder. This is a transfer for value (the consideration being services rendered to the corporation) to a coshareholder of the insured. Such a transfer does not come within any of the exceptions to the transfer for value rule and would, thus, subject the proceeds to income taxation. Some companies believe this potential problem can be avoided by setting up the ownership and beneficiary arrangement at policy inception, thereby avoiding any transfer.

When one of the parties to the cross-purchase buy-and-sell agreement is a majority shareholder-employee, the use of a split-dollar plan to help fund the agreement could create a serious estate tax trap. This is because the incidents of ownership in the life insurance policy on his or her life possessed by the corporation will be attributed to the majority shareholder-insured if the ownership incidents extend to the proceeds of the policy not payable to the corporation. The result could be that the value of the stock in the corporation and the insurance proceeds received by the coshareholder and used to purchase the stock will both be included in his or her gross estate.

Split-Dollar in a Nonqualified Retirement Plan   A split-dollar arrangement can provide the mechanism for informally funding a nonqualified retirement plan. The employer's access to policy cash values provides the means from which payments are ultimately made.

Family Split-Dollar   An employer–employee relationship is not necessary to take advantage of the benefits of a split-dollar insurance plan. For example, parents may be concerned about the lack of life insurance protection for their married child. They may be willing to assist the child's spouse financially in the purchase of insurance on his or her life, but they might not wish to do so at the expense of reducing the share of their estate to be passed on to others. In this circumstance, the parents can enter into a split-dollar plan with their child's spouse by the terms of which the parents will receive from the proceeds an amount equal to the premiums they paid. The child will then be protected by insurance on his or her spouse's life at a minimal outlay to them. As this is not an employer–employee arrangement, there should be no taxable income. The value of the economic benefit received as a result of the arrangement, however, may be treated as a taxable gift from the parents. In most cases, however, a gift tax will not be payable because the economic benefit will not exceed the $10,000 annual exclusion.

CONCLUSION

As this chapter and the final portion of the preceding chapter have shown, individually issued life and health insurance can prove to be exceptionally beneficial to businesses, especially closely held ones. Table 17-3 provides a summary of the uses discussed in this and the preceding chapter. The challenge for agents and other financial advisors is less the legal, tax, and other technical aspects of business uses of life and health insurance and more how to inform and motivate those who would benefit from such uses.

TABLE 17-3 Summary of Business Uses of Life and Health Insurance

Plan	*Objective*	*How Insurance Can Be Used*	*Policyowner and Beneficiary*	*Premium Payor*	*Income Tax Treatment*	*Estate Tax Treatment*
Deferred Compensation	Attract or retain selected employees by deferring current taxable income and providing extra retirement income	Business purchases life insurance, with the death benefit or cash values providing the promised income	Business	Business, but the employee might take salary reduction	Premiums are not deductible to business nor taxable income to the executive. Death proceeds are not taxable income. Benefit payments are tax deductible to employer and taxable income to executive	Present value of promised benefits included in employee's gross estate
Supplemental Executive Retirement	Attract or retain selected employees by providing extra retirement income	Business purchases life insurance, with the death benefit or cash values providing the promised income	Business	Business	Premiums are not deductible to business nor taxable income to the executive. Death proceeds are not taxable income. Benefit payments are tax deductible to employer and taxable income to executive	Present value of promised benefits included in employee's gross estate
Incentive Compensation	Provide executives incentives to achieve financial goals for the business	Business purchases life insurance, with the death benefit or cash values providing the promised benefits	Business	Business	Premiums are not deductible to business nor taxable income to the executive. Death proceeds are not taxable income. Compensation is tax deductible to employer and taxable income to executive	Any earned compensation is included in the executive's gross estate
Key Person	Provide financial protection to the business on death or disability of particularly valuable employee(s)	Business purchases life and/or disability income insurance, the benefits from which help stabilize financial results or used to hire replacement	Business	Business	Premiums are not tax deductible to the business nor taxable income to the insured. Benefits ordinarily received free of income taxes	No implications for the insured/executive unless he or she is the business owner, in which case the value of the business included in the estate could be enhanced

TABLE 17-3 *(continued)*

Plan	Objective	How Insurance Can Be Used	Policyowner and Beneficiary	Premium Payor	Income Tax Treatment	Estate Tax Treatment
Business Continuation	Ensure the orderly and fair transfer of the ownership interest in a closely held business	Business (entity buy-and-sell plan) or other interested party(ies) (cross-purchase plan) agrees to buy the interest of any deceased or disabled owner and owner agrees to sell. Life and/or disability income insurance is used to fund the plan	Business with entity buyout or interested party(ies) with cross-purchase buyout	Business with entity buyout or interested party(ies) with cross-purchase buyout	Premiums are not tax deductible by nor taxable income to anyone. Death proceeds are received income tax free. With cross-purchase plan, the purchased business interest receives an increased cost basis	Properly arranged, the life insurance should not be included in the gross estate of the deceased owner
Executive Bonus	Attract or retain selected employees by providing additional life insurance	The business arranges for the executive to purchase a life insurance policy	Executive or third party if the executive wishes	Business	Premium payments are tax deductible to the business and taxable income to the executive. Death proceeds are income tax free	Death proceeds are included in the executive's gross estate unless a third party owns the policy
Split Dollar	Attract or retain selected employees by providing additional life insurance on a split-funded basis	Business (endorsement method) or employee (collateral assignment method) purchases life insurance, the death benefit and premium payments of which are split between the employee and business	Business, with the endorsement method, or employee (or designated third party) with the collateral assignment method	Business typically pays an amount equal to or greater than the annual increase in cash value and employee pays the balance	Premiums are not tax deductible to the business. Employee taxed on economic benefit less employee's premium payment. Death proceeds not taxable to business or employee's beneficiary	Death proceeds payable to the employee's beneficiary are included in the employee's gross estate unless a third party owns the policy. If employee is majority owner of business, any ownership rights by the business can cause proceeds to be included

Questions

1. Jane, Sheila, and Tim each own one-third of ABC Corporation, which is valued at $10 million. Each owner is married and has children. The corporation is the primary source of income for each family. No contingency plans have been made to handle the possible death of any of the stockholders. Inform the owners about the alternative arrangements available to them and make a recommendation.

2. Caroline and Jessie are partners in a brewery.
   a. Upon the death of one of the partners, what circumstances might cause the liquidation of the business?
   b. What problems may arise out of a forced liquidation?

3. Who besides the owners are stakeholders in a publicly traded firm? For our purposes, we will define stakeholders as all those who have some interest in the performance of the firm. How can their interests be protected by key person life insurance?

4. Choose a number of tax provisions relating to split-dollar plans, and explain what is likely to be the federal government's rationale behind this tax treatment.

5. Describe the essential features of split-dollar plans and the purposes for which they are used.

CHAPTER

18

GROUP INSURANCE

Objectives

■ Explain the circumstances that have given impetus to the growth and persistence of employee benefit plans.

■ Explain how group and individual insurance underwriting differ.

■ Describe the advantages that group insurance enjoys over individual insurance.

■ Review the nature of coverage and the typical approaches used to define benefits for group life insurance.

■ Identify the important elements in group life insurance marketing.

■ Describe the tax treatment of group life insurance.

T his chapter begins a five-chapter discussion of employee benefit plans with an emphasis on insured plans. A brief overview of employee benefit plans is first presented, followed by a discussion of group insurance. Chapters 19 and 20 cover medical care costs and benefits and chapter 21 is devoted to retirement plans. Chapter 22 provides a discussion of the various social insurance programs in the United States, completing the employee benefit plan presentation.

INTRODUCTION TO EMPLOYEE BENEFIT PLANS

Government, employers, and individuals all play a role in the economic security of families and individuals. Employee benefit plans have an important place in this process. **Employee benefit plans** are employer-sponsored plans that provide benefits to employees as part of their total compensation. These benefits are an important part of the system of total compensation provided by U.S. employers and employers in other developed countries. Along with other elements of a company's compensation system, these employee benefits should be effectively planned, coordinated, and balanced to help meet the objectives of both employees and the employer.

Rationale for Employee Benefit Plans

The term *employee benefits* has many definitions. In a broad sense all forms of compensation (other than direct wages and cash bonuses) provided or made available by an employer, including government-mandated benefits, employee-pay-all plans, and perquisites provided to high-ranking executives and managers, can be classified as employee benefits.

The rationale for employee benefits includes both business and economic reasons.[1] For example, to achieve a smoother income/consumption stream over their entire life cycle, some employees could have a preference for future retirement income over some portion of current wages—a preference consistent with life cycle utility maximization models as defined in chapter 1. The **deferred age theory** holds that retirement benefits should be thought of as employee agreement to defer current wages in favor of payments during retirement when income is presumably lower (see chapter 21). Such concepts assume that individuals can be expected to maximize their utility over their entire lifetimes, that is, to arrange their affairs as best they can to derive maximum enjoyment (and minimum discomfort) throughout their lives.

A more pragmatic reason for employee benefit plans is to meet competition for employees. The direct compensation and the company's benefit package must be competitive with those offered by competitors for employees' services. This can be particularly critical in hiring or retaining senior management employees. In countries where labor is scarce, the marginal utility of making employee benefits available can be competitively critical.

The decision to install a pension or other benefit plan entails comparing the economic value arising from its installation against the cost of the program. Governments often provide tax advantages to encourage employers to adopt pension and other benefit programs. Such tax advantages have been a significant factor in the growth of benefit plans in the United States and other countries.

The presence of employer-provided medical benefits may also reduce turnover, thereby contributing to increased productivity. Retirement income programs in which employer contributions are tied directly to profitability frequently lead to enhanced productivity (see chapter 21). In such cases in which better performance by employees leads to greater profits and, in turn, greater contributions to the retirement plan, employers and employees have a shared interest in profitability.

Organized labor has also played an influential role in the development and expansion of employee benefits. In addition to the direct results of collective bargaining, the outcome of the negotiations indirectly affects the employee benefits commonly provided nonunion employees. Furthermore, companies may decide to offer or expand their benefit plans to dissuade employees from joining a union and discourage the establishment of a union in the first place.

All developed countries (and to a lesser extent, developing countries) have seen significant development and growth in employee benefit plans. Many of today's largest corporations have extensive global employee benefit plans. Each country's rules and regulations must be adhered to for operations in that country. Local customs, traditional benefit design, and the availability of adequate insurance in each local market have made designing, implementing, and maintaining an equitable benefit package throughout all operations a complex task. It also has made the administration of multinational programs more complex. As a result, the role of employee benefit specialists in the overall risk management of multinational companies has been enhanced significantly.

---

[1]This section draws on Bruce A. Palmer, "Employee Benefits," in Harold D. Skipper, Jr., ed., *International Risk and Insurance* (Boston, MA: Irwin/McGraw-Hill, 1998), Chapter 24, pp. 647–683.

Of course, other factors also play an important role in the growth and development of employee benefit plans. We discuss them in the other chapters in this section.

Growth in Employee Benefit Plans

U.S. Benefit Plans

According to a 1996 study of 802 companies, the average payment for employee benefits was 41.3 percent of payroll in 1996, down from 42.0 percent the previous year.[2] The average payment in 1996 was $14,086 per year per employee. Table 18-1 shows the distribution of employer costs of employee benefits in 1994, 1995, and 1996.

This study also estimated that employee benefits for all employees in the United States in 1996 amounted to slightly more than $1.5 trillion, an increase of more than $93 billion from 1995. Since 1975, benefits have grown from 30 percent to 41.3 percent of payroll. Almost one-half of the increase is due to the expansion of mandated benefits. The remainder of the increase resulted from an escalation in insurance costs (mainly health insurance), and an increase in vacations and holidays granted by employers. Clearly, employee benefits have become a major cost of doing business and a major resource in support of U.S. employees and their families.

International Benefit Plans

An international benefits policy requires considerable planning both at the corporate level and in relation to the local environments in which a company operates. The creation of such a policy calls for a clear understanding of a company's basic benefit philosophy. U.S. multinational companies generally manage benefits in their international subsidiaries closely and usually have consistent benefit programs worldwide as a goal. In practice, too many benefit decisions are made at corporate headquarters by managements unfamiliar with the details of the specific non-U.S. environments involved.[3]

TABLE 18-1   Employee Benefits as a Percentage of Payroll, 1994, 1995, and 1996

Types of Benefits	Benefit as a Percentage of Payroll All Employees		
	1994	*1995*	*1996*
Legally required payments[a]	8.9%	8.9%	8.8%
Retirement and savings	7.2	7.5	6.3
Life insurance and death benefits	0.4	0.4	0.4
Medical and medically related benefits	10.4	10.5	9.6
Paid rest periods, lunch periods, etc.	2.2	2.2	3.7
Payment for vacations, holidays, sick leave, etc.	9.7	10.2	10.2
Miscellaneous benefits	1.9	2.2	2.3
Total	40.7	42.0	41.3

[a]Includes OASDHI, railroad retirement, unemployment compensation, workers' compensation, and statutory disability benefits.

Source: Chamber of Commerce of the United States, *Employee Benefits 1997.*

---

[2]Chamber of Commerce of the United States, *Employee Benefits 1997.* This study is updated annually.

[3]Jim McKay, "International Benefits Policy: A U.S. Multinationals' Perspective," *Employee Benefits Journal,* Vol. 19, No. 4 (December 1994), pp. 22–25.

The ability of corporate headquarters to impact overseas benefit programs varies by country. Indeed, even in a given country, it can vary depending on the size of the subsidiary, the power or influence that subsidiary wields (usually based on profitability), and whether the multinational is opening a completely new operation or inheriting an existing benefit program through an acquisition. It is essential that both corporate and local advisors work together to steer management away from inappropriate decisions that benefit neither the corporation as a whole nor the local subsidiary in particular. Regardless of the benefit philosophy of the multinational, a company needs to have proper management infrastructure and communication channels in place to support effectively the implementation of any policy.

In implementing their international benefit programs, multinational companies utilize international benefit networks, working arrangements among insurers through which companies with employees in multiple foreign countries can obtain various employee benefit coverages. Multinational pooling facilitates implementation of a global corporate benefits policy. It permits the corporate benefits manager to implement a global benefits policy according to a written worldwide benefits philosophy. The advantages of multinational pooling to international organizations may be summarized as follows:

- reduced cost of providing employee benefits through receipt of an international dividend based on experience rating of all the employers plans
- reduced underwriting requirements
- consolidated summary of global benefits
- detailed financial information
- enhanced control and coordination of benefits
- increased negotiating power with insurers

The underlying concept of multinational pooling is simple. It involves the implementation of host-country benefit plans of a multinational corporation, according to local laws and practices, with a superimposed umbrella contract that attempts to treat the different local units as if they were a single entity. Multinational pooling is, thus, a system under which insurance coverages in various countries are brought together into one pool. The purpose of establishing such an arrangement is to permit a reduction in the administration expenses and risk charges of insurers through experience rating of the pool, whereas groups of employees in different countries are assessed as a single group in underwriting terms.

Each network is coordinated by one insurance company or secretariat. In a given individual network, the local insurer can be wholly or partially owned by the coordinating network partner. In addition, the local insurance company can be an independent insurer with an affiliate arrangement to the network coordinating entity. A single network may also be made up of both owned and affiliated local insurers.

All of these major networks operate on a worldwide basis, providing insurance facilities in up to 140 countries. Each major network currently underwrites somewhere between 50 and 460 multinational contracts. The total number of multinationals using network facilities is, of course, smaller than the addition of these network contracts would suggest because many multinationals use the facilities of more than one insurance network. According to some estimates, the total premium volume generated with these networks from multinational business is more than $2 billion. More than 20 consulting and brokerage firms are actively engaged in international benefits consulting. These figures not only indicate the volume of business being transacted on a multinational basis, but they also demonstrate the acceptance of the multinational pooling concept that has occurred since its introduction more than 30 years ago. During this period, it has become an effective risk management tool not only in terms of cost savings but also as an efficient means of obtaining information on benefit plans in other countries.

As discussed later, experience rating is an accounting system under which the costs ultimately charged to a group contractholder are determined largely by the group's own experience. For multinational pooling, this technique is applied to contracts issued by a network of insurers in different countries that is linked in a common pool. This adaptation is necessary because, in many countries, local insurance companies are strictly regulated by supervisory authorities or by cartel arrangements that inhibit local experience rating of group contracts. In addition, in countries with keen competition and where insurance companies are free to determine their own investment policies, premiums, reserve levels, and dividend formulas, local contracts are often issued on the basis of lowest possible premium rates without dividends or other experience participation.

Different networks have somewhat different requirements for installing standard pooling arrangements. In general, however, the minimum conditions may include:

1. implementation of local group contracts in at least two countries
2. minimum size of the pool in terms of a certain minimum number of lives (e.g., 100 or 300) or a certain minimum volume of annual premium (e.g., $20,000)

To reduce costs, many large employers are paring down the number of international benefit networks with which they will deal. Today benefit networks are competing for shares of a shrinking market. As a consequence, some of the networks have developed small group programs. Under these programs, multinationals are pooled with other small multinationals and gain or lose with the experience of the pool as a whole regardless of a particular multinational's experience for the year and contribution to the pool. A variation is a "time" pool in which, for groups smaller than the standard size, pooling is offered over an extended length of time, such as three or five years, instead of on an annual basis.

Originating in the early years of the twentieth century to provide life insurance benefits, the group approach has been applied to an increasing variety and number of groups and is now utilized to provide a wide range of employee benefits. Group insurance is the youngest branch of the life insurance business. The remainder of this chapter is devoted to group insurance.

GROUP INSURANCE FUNDAMENTALS

Group insurance is a means through which a group of persons who usually have a business or professional relationship to the contract owner are provided insurance coverage under a single contract. The accepted meaning of group insurance is not as elementary as this definition might suggest. What is considered group insurance today might not have been considered group insurance several decades ago. Over time, innovative underwriting techniques of group insurers and liberalized regulatory actions have broadened the definition.

A sound understanding of group insurance and the scope of group products can be acquired only through a discussion of its distinguishing characteristics, its differences from and similarities to other forms of insurance, and a reasonably detailed examination of each of its components.

Distinguishing Characteristics

In a comparison of group insurance with other forms of insurance written by life insurance companies, several distinguishing features are evident: (1) the substitution of group underwriting for individual underwriting, (2) the use of a master contract, (3) lower administrative cost, (4) flexibility in contract design, and (5) the use of experience rating.

Group Underwriting

Probably the most significant distinguishing characteristic of group insurance is the substitution of group underwriting for individual underwriting. In group cases, no individual evidence of insurability is usually required, and benefit levels can be substantial, with few, if any, important limitations.[4]

Group underwriting normally is not concerned with the health or other insurability aspects of any particular individual. Instead, it aims to obtain a group of individual lives or, what is even more important, an aggregation of such groups of lives that will yield a predictable rate of mortality or morbidity. If a sufficient number of groups of lives is obtained, and if these groups are reasonably homogeneous in nature, then the mortality or morbidity rate will be predictable. The point is that the group becomes the unit of underwriting, and insurance principles may be applied to it just as in the case of the individual. To assure that the groups obtained will be reasonably homogeneous, the underwriting process in group insurance aims to control adverse selection by individuals within a given group.

In underwriting group insurance, then, certain important features should be present that either are inherent in the nature of the group itself or may be applied in a positive way to avoid serious adverse selection. These are reviewed next.

Insurance Incidental to Group   The insurance should be incidental to the group; that is, the members of the group should have come together for some purpose other than to obtain insurance. For example, the group insurance furnished to the employees of a given employer must not be the feature that motivates the formation and existence of the group.

Flow of Persons through the Group   There should be a steady flow of persons through the group; that is, there must be an influx of new young lives into the group and an outflow from the group of the older and impaired lives. With groups of actively working employees, it may be assumed that they are in average health.

Automatic Determination of Benefits   Group insurance underwriting commonly requires an automatic basis for determining the amount of benefits on individual lives, which is beyond the control of the employer or employees. If the amount of benefits taken were completely optional, it would be possible to select against the insurer because those in poor health would tend to insure heavily and the healthy ones might tend to elect minimum coverage.

As the group mechanism has evolved, however, insurers have responded to demands from the marketplace, particularly large employers, for more flexibility in the selection of benefits. This flexibility typically is expressed in optional amounts of life and health insurance in excess of basic coverage provided by the employer and in more health care financing choices.

Also, increasingly popular **cafeteria plans** allow participating employees to select among an array of benefits using a predetermined allowance of employer funds. Individuals select, subject to certain basic coverages being required, a combination of benefits that best meets his or her individual needs.

Minimum Participation by the Group   Another underwriting control is the requirement that substantially all eligible persons in a given group be covered by insurance. In plans in which the employee pays a portion of the premium (contributory), generally

---

[4]In recent years, there has been a trend in the United States toward large amounts of group life coverage on individual lives with a consequent increase in utilization of evidence of insurability, as in the case of ordinary insurance. Another exception is the underwriting of small groups (fewer than 10 lives). Some form of individual evidence of insurability usually is required for these groups. (These cases are treated later in this chapter.)

at least 75 percent of the eligible employees must join the plan if coverage is to be effective. In the case of noncontributory plans, 100 percent participation is required. By covering a large proportion of a given group, the insurance company gains a safeguard against an undue proportion of substandard lives. In cases in which employees refuse the insurance for religious or other reasons that do not involve any elements of selection, this rule is relaxed.

Third-Party Sharing of Cost   A portion of the cost of a group plan ideally should be borne by the employer or some other third party, such as a labor union or trade association. The noncontributory employer-pay-all plan is simple, and it gives the employer full control over the plan. It provides for insurance of all eligible employees and, thus, eliminates any difficulties involved in connection with obtaining the consent of a sufficient number of employees to meet minimum participation requirements. Also, there is no problem of distributing the cost among the various employees, as in the contributory plan.

Contributory plans usually are less costly to the employer. Hence, with employee contributions, the employer is likely to arrange for more adequate protection for the employees. It can also be argued that, if the employee contributes toward his or her insurance, he or she will be more impressed with its value and will appreciate it more. On the other hand, the contributory plan has a number of disadvantages. Its operation is more complicated, and this, at times, increases administrative costs considerably. Each employee must consent to contribute toward his or her insurance, and, as stated before, a minimum percentage of the eligible group must consent to enter the arrangement. New employees entering the business must be informed of their insurance privilege.

If the plan is contributory, employees may not be entitled to the insurance until they have been with the company for a period of time (e.g., one month). If they do not agree to be covered by the plan within a period of 31 days, they may be required to provide satisfactory evidence of insurability to become eligible. Some noncontributory plans also have these probationary periods.

Efficient Administrative Organization   A single administrative organization should be able and willing to act on behalf of the insured group. In the usual case, this is the employer. In the case of a contributory plan, there must be a reasonably simple method, such as payroll deduction, by which the master policyowner can collect premiums. An automatic method is desirable from both an administrative and an underwriting standpoint.

A number of miscellaneous controls of underwriting significance are typically used in group insurance plans, but the preceding discussion permits an appreciation of the group underwriting theory. The discussion applies to groups with a large number of employees. A majority of the groups, however, are not large. The group size is a significant factor in the underwriting process. In smaller plans, more restrictive underwriting practices relating to adverse selection are used. These may include less liberal contract provisions, simple health status questions, and, in some cases, detailed individual underwriting of group members.

Group Policy

A second characteristic of group insurance is the use of a group policy (contract) held by the owner as group policyholder and booklet-certificates or other summary evidence of insurance held by participants. Certificates provide information on the plan provisions and the steps required to file claims. The use of certificates and a master contract constitutes one of the sources of economy under the group approach. The master contract is a detailed document setting forth the contractual relationship between the group contract owner and the insurance company. The insured persons under the contract, usually employees and their beneficiaries, are not actually parties to the contract, although they may enforce their rights as third-party beneficiaries.[5] The four-party relationship (employer, insurer, employee, and dependents) found in a group insurance plan can create a number of interesting and unusual problems that are common only to group insurance.

Lower Cost

A third feature of group insurance is that it is usually lower-cost protection than that which is available in individual insurance. The nature of the group approach permits the use of mass-distribution and mass-administration methods that afford economies of operation not available in individual insurance. These economies are more significant in larger cases. In some smaller-group cases, administrative unit expenses could conceivably exceed those of individual insurance. Also, because group insurance is not usually underwritten on an individual basis, the premiums are based upon an actuarial assessment of the group as a whole, so a given healthy individual can perhaps buy individual term life insurance at a lower cost. Employer subsidization of the cost is a critical factor in group insurance plan design.

Probably the most significant savings in the cost of marketing group life insurance lies in the fact that group commissions absorb a much smaller proportion of total premiums than commissions for individual contracts. The marketing system relieves the agent or broker of many of the duties, responsibilities, and expenses normally connected with selling and servicing of individual insurance. Because of the large premiums involved in many group insurance cases, the commission rates are considerably lower than for individual contracts and are usually graded downward as the premium increases.

Some large-group insurance buyers deal directly with insurance companies and commissions are eliminated. In these cases, however, fees frequently are paid to the consultants involved.

The nature of the administrative procedures permits simplified accounting techniques. The mechanics of premium collection are less involved, and experience refund procedures are much simplified because there is only one party with whom to deal—the group policyowner. Of course, the issuance of a large number of individual contracts is avoided and, because of the nature of group selection, the cost of medical examinations and inspection reports is minimized. Also, regulatory filings and other requirements are minimized.

In the early days of group life insurance, administration was simple. That is no longer true. Even with group term life insurance, for which there is no cash value, the push for accelerated death benefits, assignment to viatical companies, and estate or business planning record keeping means that the administration of coverage may be as complex as with an individual policy.

Flexibility

In contrast to individual contracts that must be taken as written, the larger employer usually has options in the design and preparation of the group insurance contract. Although the contracts follow a pattern and include certain standard provisions, there is considerably more flexibility here than in the case of individual contracts. The degree of flexibility permitted is, of course, a function of the size of the group involved. The group insurance program usually is an integral part of an employee benefit program and, in

---

[5]The issue of whether the participants are "parties to the contract 'or merely' third-party beneficiaries" is under litigation in the United States.

most cases, the contract can be molded to meet the objectives of the contract owner, as long as the requests do not entail complicated administrative procedures, open the way to possibly serious adverse selection, or violate legal requirements.

Experience Rating

Another special feature of group insurance is that premiums often are subject to experience rating. The experience of the individual group may have an important bearing on dividends or premium-rate adjustments. The larger and, hence, the more reliable the experience of the particular group, the greater is the weight attached to its own experience in any single year. The knowledge that premiums net of dividends or premium-rate adjustments will be based on the employer's own experience gives the employer a vested interest in maintaining a favorable loss and expense record. For the largest employers, insurers may agree to complicated procedures to satisfy the employer's objectives because most such cases are experience rated and reflect the increased cost.

Some insurers experience rate based on the class or type of industry, or even based on the type of contract. For small groups, most insurance companies use **pooled rates** under which a uniform rate is applied to all such groups, although it is becoming more common to apply separate pooled rates for groups with significantly better or worse experience than that of the total class. The point at which a group is large enough to be eligible for experience rating varies from company to company, based on that insurer's book of business and experience. The size and frequency of medical claims vary considerably across countries and among geographic regions within a country and must be considered in determining a group insurance rate. The composition (age, sex, and income level) of a group will also affect the experience of the group and, similarly, will be an important underwriting consideration.

Advantages and Limitations of the Group Mechanism

Advantages

The group insurance mechanism has proved to be a remarkably effective solution to the need for employee benefits for a number of reasons. The utilization of mass-distribution techniques has extended protection to large numbers of persons with little or no life or health insurance. The increasing complexity of industrial/service economies has brought increasingly large numbers of persons together, and the group mechanism has enabled life insurance companies to reach vast numbers of individuals within a relatively short period and at low cost. Group insurance also has extended protection to a large number of uninsurable persons. Equally important has been the fact that the employer usually pays a large share of the cost. Moreover, in most countries, including the United States, the deductibility of employer contributions and the favorable tax treatment of the benefits to employees make it a tax-effective vehicle with which to provide benefits.

Another significant factor, and one of the more cogent motivations for the rapid development of group insurance, has been the continuing governmental role in the security benefits area. Within the United States, the Old-Age, Survivors, Disability, and Health Insurance program has expanded rapidly, but many observers believe that, had not group insurance provided substantial sums of life insurance, health insurance, and retirement protection, social insurance would have developed even more rapidly. As economies worldwide continue to reduce the size and scope of social insurance programs, we can expect the demand for group-based security to grow even more.

Limitations

From the viewpoint of the employee, group insurance has one great limitation—the temporary nature of the coverage. Unless an employee converts his or her coverage to an individual policy (which usually is more expensive and provides less liberal coverage), the employee loses his or her insurance protection if the group plan is terminated and often also at retirement because employment is terminated.[6]

Group life and health protection is continued after retirement in a significant proportion of cases today in the United States, but often at reduced levels. Recently, with the introduction of a new U.S. accounting standard (FAS 106) requiring that the cost of such benefits be accrued and reflected in financial statements, an increasing number of employers have discontinued postretirement life and health benefits entirely. When such continued protection is not available, the temporary nature of the coverage is a serious limitation. Retiree group health insurance often is provided as a supplement to Medicare (see chapter 22).

Another problem of potential significance involves individuals who may be lulled into complacency by having large amounts of group life insurance during their working years. Many of these persons fail to recognize the need for, or are unwilling to face the cost of, individual life insurance. Perhaps of even greater significance is the fact that the flexibility of the group approach is limited to the design of the master policy and does not extend to the individual covered employees. Furthermore, group plans typically fail to provide the mechanism for any analysis of the financial needs of the individual—a service that is normally furnished by the agent or other advisor. Many agents, however, discuss group insurance coverage with individuals as a foundation for discussing the need for additional amounts of individual life and health insurance.

Eligible Groups

The types of groups eligible for group insurance coverage have broadened significantly over the years. This wider eligibility is reflected in both regulations and the underwriting philosophy of group writing insurers. Group insurance is permitted today for types of groups that did not exist in the early days of its development, and it is written on some types of groups whose applications would not have even been given consideration when the product was first introduced. Within the United States, the NAIC *Model Group Insurance Bill* permits coverage on four specific categories of groups. Many states permit coverage on additional types of groups not identified in the NAIC model bill.

Employees of a Single Employer

The employees of a single employer comprise the first category mentioned in the NAIC model bill. An employer may be a sole proprietorship, a partnership, or a corporation. Also, employees may include not only the immediate employees of the employer, but several other categories as well. The single-employer group is by far the dominant type of group that is provided group insurance coverage.

Debtor–Creditor Groups

Group credit insurance (life and disability income) has grown rapidly in the United States, reflecting a credit-oriented society. The contract owner in these plans is the creditor, such as a bank, a small-loan company, a credit union, or any business that has significant accounts receivable, including those that rely heavily on credit card customers. If the debtor dies or becomes disabled, the insurance proceeds are generally paid to the credi-

---

[6]In the United States, the 1985 Consolidated Omnibus Reconciliation Act (COBRA) requires group health coverage to be extended for up to 36 months for certain "qualifying events." Termination of employment is a qualifying event, but termination of the group plan typically is not. See chapter 19.

tor to liquidate the indebtedness that provided the basis for the coverage rather than to the individuals who are insured or their beneficiaries. Debtors usually must be under a binding, irrevocable obligation to repay the indebtedness for coverage to be effected.

Labor Union Groups

Members of labor unions may be covered under a group contract issued to the union itself. The insurance must be for the benefit of persons other than the union or its officials. Generally, the entire premium may not be paid directly by member contributions. It is common, however, for payment to be made from funds partially contributed to the union by members specifically for their insurance and partially by the union from its own funds. In some cases, the union pays the total premium from its own funds.

Group contracts often are written on multiemployer groups and issued to the trustees of a fund created through collective bargaining processes. This arrangement is typically established by two or more employers in the same or a related industry, by one or more labor unions, or even jointly by employers and labor unions. The Taft-Hartley Act prohibits U.S. employers from turning over funds for employee welfare plans directly to a union—hence, the need for a separate trust and its trustees to serve as the group contract owner and decision maker.

Multiple-Employer Trusts

Multiple-employer trusts (METs), a subset of **multiple-employer welfare arrangements** (MEWAs),[7] market group benefits to employers that have a small number of employees. METs may be sponsored by life insurance companies, independent administrators, or two or more employers in the same industry. The sponsor designs the plan, selects the employers (or other groups) permitted to participate, and usually handles the administration. Most trustees function in a passive role and are used mainly as the nominal group policyholder for insurance held by or on behalf of a MET.

All financial transactions flow through and are accounted for by the trust. The member employers pay premiums to the sponsoring organization, which uses the money to purchase a group contract. The entire group of employers is experience rated, thereby permitting greater credibility to be given the group's own experience.

Self-insured METs assume the responsibility of making claim payments through a third-party administrator. They should assess adequate premiums (contributions) and maintain appropriate reserves. In the early development of METs, this was not always done properly.

METs have proven to be a source of regulatory confusion, enforcement problems, and even fraud. A U.S. General Accounting Office (GAO) report showed that from January 1988 to June 1991, METs left some 398,000 participants and their beneficiaries with over $129 million in unpaid claims and many other participants without insurance.[8] More than 600 METs failed to comply with state insurance laws, and some violated criminal statutes.

The GAO report confirmed that state efforts to regulate METs, enforce state laws, and recover unpaid claims were hindered because the states could not identify METs operating within their jurisdictions. Furthermore, when complaints did come to the attention of state regulators, they were frequently frustrated because METs asserted that they were exempt under the Employee Retirement Income Security Act (ERISA). As a result, in 1992 the U.S. Congress enacted legislation that requires self-insured METs to meet state insurance regulations concerning the adequacies of contributions and

---

[7]*MEWA* is a generic term arising under the Employee Retirement Income Security Act (ERISA) for any multiple-employer arrangement regardless of whether trusteed.

[8]Employee Benefits: MEWA Regulation: GAO HRD-92–40 (March 1992).

BOX 18-1

MISCELLANEOUS GROUP COVERAGES

Larger companies sometimes arrange for payroll deduction with a nonlife company for group automobile or group homeowners' coverage. Some plans provide for an individual policy. Usually the employer does not subsidize the premium.

Prepaid legal expense plans are paid in full or part by the employer. Two types of plans are commonly offered. The first is an access plan in which participants can obtain telephone consultation through a toll-free number, limited to a certain number of hours per month or year. Services covered include preparation of a will, writing letters, and discounts for other legal services.

The other type of plan commonly offered is comprehensive, covering many legal services. Such plans provide for many common legal services, such as will preparation, adoptions, estate closings, leases, and home improvement contract review. Benefits are typically scheduled with limits on the frequency of covered services. Although the scheduled benefit will be paid to any providers who accept the scheduled benefits, a panel of preferred providers is often established to provide the legal services.

reserve levels. There has been a significant reduction in the number of self-funded METs since the legislation was adopted.

Miscellaneous Groups

As suggested earlier, many other types of groups not specifically identified in the NAIC model bill are eligible for group insurance through company underwriting practice and enabling state laws. These include trade associations, professional associations, college alumni associations, veteran associations, religious groups, customers of large retail chains, and savings account depositors, among many others.

Although not discussed here, in addition to life, health, and retirement benefits, the group approach has been used with a number of other benefits. See Box 18-1.

GROUP LIFE INSURANCE

Group life insurance is one of the most common forms of employee benefit plans. Almost 40 percent of all life insurance in force (by face amount) in the United States is on a group basis. Other countries' percentages are generally lower. The average amount of group life insurance in force per certificate is more than $32,000. More than 89 percent of group life coverage is accounted for by employer–employee groups.

Nature of Coverage

In addition to the eligibility of the group itself, other criteria are involved in coverage under a group life insurance contract. Because the single-employer group is the most prevalent type, the remainder of this discussion is directed principally toward this type of group.

Minimum Size and Proportion

Many years ago, insurers believed that a minimum of 50 lives was necessary to qualify for group life coverage and state law reflected this belief. Moreover, individual life insurance agents had great antipathy to group life insurance as a threat to their livelihood, and they lobbied very effectively to impose minima on group size and participation. Today states permit groups to be insured with 10 or fewer lives. State laws also stipulate the minimum proportion of eligible employees that should be insured under a group life contract.

Requirements of this nature assure the maintenance of a reasonable average age, with a view to preventing a rise in total premiums from year to year. They also protect the insurance company against the group becoming substandard through adverse selection. Economies of scale mean that the larger the group, the less the expense per person insured. For these reasons, insurance companies usually prescribe a minimum number of employees to be covered for group life insurance. In general, for employer-pay-all (noncontributory) plans, insurers usually require that all employees or all of any class thereof, as determined by the conditions of employment, must be insured. When employees contribute a portion of the premium (i.e., a contributory plan), at least 75 percent of the employees usually must be included under the plan.[9]

Individual Eligibility Requirements

In general, only regular, active, full-time employees are eligible for group life insurance. All such employees or all employees in certain classes determined by conditions pertaining to their employment (e.g., "all salaried employees" or "all hourly paid employees") must be included in the group as eligibles.

Another individual eligibility requirement is that an employee must be actively at work and must work no fewer than the normal number of hours in a workweek at his or her job on the date when he or she becomes eligible for coverage. The requirement assures a reasonable minimum of health and physical well-being and protects the insurer against serious adverse selection.

A waiting or **probationary period** often is applied to new employees (usually one to six months) before they become eligible for insurance. The probationary period minimizes the administrative expenses involved in setting up records for employees who remain with the employer for a short period; although with the widespread use of computers, this consideration is less important than formerly.

After the completion of the probationary period, under a noncontributory plan, the employee automatically is covered. Under a contributory plan, the employee is given a period of time, known as the **eligibility period,** during which he or she is entitled to apply for insurance without submitting evidence of insurability. This period is limited, usually to 31 days, to minimize adverse selection. For the same reason, it is customary to require evidence of insurability from employees who have discontinued their coverage and desire to rejoin the plan. If the plan is written on a noncontributory basis, these rules do not apply because all employees (or all employees within the designated classes) automatically are covered unless they specifically decline coverage.

Duration of Coverage

Once the insurance becomes effective for a particular employee, the protection continues for as long as he or she remains in the service of the employer (assuming, of course, that the employer maintains the plan in force and the employee continues to pay any contributory premium required). The master contract usually gives the employer the right to continue premium payments for employees who are temporarily off the job, provided that the employer does so on a basis that precludes individual selection. Upon permanent termination of service, the employee's coverage continues for 31 days be-

---

[9]As the types and sizes of groups covered have expanded, the minimum participation requirements have become a function of size, legal requirement, and rate basis. So-called association cases commonly insure less than 75 percent of the eligible group, reflecting a somewhat higher rate basis than normally used on employer groups. Similarly, in the 10 to 25 life range, many companies require a participation of 85 percent. Participation levels below 75 percent are often allowed with simplified short-form health questionnaires on each individual.

yond the date of termination. This extension of coverage gives the employee an opportunity to replace the expiring protection with individual insurance, to obtain employment with another firm with group insurance, or to convert the expiring term insurance to a cash-value form of insurance.

Many plans continue coverage after retirement providing at least enough life insurance to cover the employee's last illness and funeral expenses. In the past, many plans continued full benefits on retired lives with no special provision for prefunding the rapidly rising costs as the number of covered retired employees increased. The cost of providing this life insurance coverage can be very high, and new accounting standards require employers to accrue these expenses yearly instead of expensing them on a pay-as-you-go basis. (See discussion under "Postretirement Coverage" later.)

Benefits

Approaches to Benefit Amounts

To minimize adverse selection, the amount of group life insurance for which an employee is eligible usually is determined by a system that precludes the employee from selecting the coverage amount. Traditionally, this system used one or more of four bases for determining the amount of group coverage: (1) a set amount for all employees; (2) a function of employee compensation; (3) a function of employees' positions; or (4) a function of each employee's length of service. Any life insurance benefit schedule that tends to discriminate in favor of highly compensated or executive employees can cause the loss of important tax benefits in the United States.

Fixed Amount   The use of a fixed-amount benefits plan places all employees in one category. It has the advantage of simplicity, but it also has the potentially important disadvantage of placing all employees on an equal level. If group insurance is to serve as a means of rewarding workers in the interest of less turnover (and this is one of the strong arguments for it), it seems neither wise nor fair that low-paid or new employees should obtain the same benefits as those who are skilled or have served the employer for years. However, the fixed-amount plan greatly minimizes adverse selection and stabilizes cost. In the United States, this type of benefit has been used principally in conjunction with union welfare funds.

Amount of Compensation   Most U.S. group life plans base the amount of insurance on employees' earnings. The plan could be based on any common earnings unit. Most plans utilize a benefit formula that is a multiple of earnings, usually rounded to the nearest $1,000. Multiples of 1, 1.5, and 2 times earnings are common. The trend is to higher amounts, and multiples of 3, 4, and 5 times salary are not uncommon among plans offered by large employers, particularly when some choice is involved, such as under cafeteria plans.

Position   When the salary or wage is difficult to determine in advance, as in the case of pieceworkers or salespersons, the insurance may be set according to the position held by the employee. Thus, officers, superintendents, and managers may receive $50,000 each; supervisors and salespersons $30,000 each; and all other employees $20,000 each. This approach tends to reflect need and ability to pay.

Service   Under the so-called service plan, the amount of protection is increased in accordance with the length of time that the employee has been in the employer's service. Because the plan provides increasing amounts of insurance based on length of service, it tends to result in progressively higher premium costs. Such plans are becoming rare, however.

Combination To benefit its most valuable employees, an employer may adopt a plan in which amounts of group term life insurance are determined on the basis of both salary and length of service. Such a plan would determine the amount of insurance to which an employee is entitled by multiplying the employee's annual salary by the product of the appropriate salary and years of service factors. For the reasons mentioned earlier, this approach is seldom used today.

Minimum and Maximum Amounts

Regardless of the plan used, some provision always is made to keep the amounts of insurance extended to executives and others with high salaries in line with the total amount of protection extended to the whole group. Thus, although some insurers will not write less than $2,000 on any one insured, most require at least $5,000 or $10,000—and even more on small groups. In addition, insurers will not write more than a certain maximum amount, which is determined by both the number of persons insured and the average amount of insurance per employee. In the past, state-mandated maximums were common.

Underwriting limitations on amounts are used in smaller groups to minimize adverse selection. In larger groups in which the group's individual experience has a strong effect on the level of dividends or premium-rate adjustments, a maximum is often desirable to avoid undue fluctuations in cost from year to year.[10]

Virtually any company will write $100,000 on an individual life under proper underwriting circumstances, and, in some cases, $1 million or more. Many insurance companies permit individual amounts in excess of their normal maximums provided that evidence of insurability is submitted for the excess amounts or that other safeguards are established to protect against severe adverse selection.[11] The willingness of some insurance companies to superimpose a schedule of life insurance benefits on an already existing plan provided by another insurer has led to the writing of amounts of group life insurance on a single life that are far beyond what one insurer's underwriting rules will permit.

Conversion Privilege

An insured employee has the privilege of converting his or her group life insurance protection to an individual policy of cash-value insurance under certain conditions. Normally, the employee may convert, within 31 days after termination of employment or cessation of membership in an eligible classification, to one of the insurer's regular cash-value forms at standard rates for his or her attained age. The most significant advantage to the employee lies in the fact that no evidence of insurability is required.[12]

The death benefit provided under a group life insurance contract is continued during the conversion period (usually 31 days) after an employee withdraws from the eligible group. If the employee dies during this period, a death benefit is paid under the group policy, and any premiums that may have been paid on a conversion policy are returned.

---

[10]In many cases, companies will place a maximum on the amount of coverage on a single life that will be charged to the experience of the individual case, with any excess coverage being pooled among cases.

[11]Other safeguards include consumer reports on one or more individuals, extra premiums charged on the case, excess amounts reinsured, special reserves built for the case, and excess-amount risks pooled for experience purposes.

[12]A conversion privilege also is available on the termination of the master contract but under far more restrictive conditions. In view of the importance of group insurance as a factor in the security of most employees, some liberalization of the conversion privilege upon termination of the master contract would seem desirable. Although adverse selection could be a problem, the improved service to insured employees would appear to justify a continuing effort to liberalize the conversion privilege.

Waiver-of-Premium Benefits

A waiver-of-premium clause commonly is used in group life contracts. This clause provides that coverage will continue indefinitely with no payment of premium from the employer or, if the plan is contributory, from the employee, as long as the insured proves his or her disability periodically.

Larger employers often eliminate the waiver-of-premium provision and substitute the employer's continuing premium payments. This provides the employer the advantage of paying ongoing premiums instead of incurring a claim charge (typically 75 percent of the face amount, which would impact the plan's experience). Of course, if the employer changes insurers, it will need to be assured that the new insurer accepts the disabled lives, as the new company would normally not accept these risks. In addition, waiver typically applies only when disability occurs prior to the employee's sixtieth (or sixty-fifth) birthday, and the amount of insurance continued under waiver is sometimes reduced as the disabled person attains specified ages such as 65 or 70. Some plans even reduce continued amounts to zero at specified ages.

Plans of Insurance

Yearly Renewable Term Insurance

The basic plan of insurance under which group life insurance is provided is yearly renewable term insurance—the same coverage that is provided through individual policies. With respect to any covered employees, the protection technically expires at the end of each year, but it is renewed automatically without evidence of insurability. As in the case of individual coverage, the premium rate per $1,000 of protection increases at an increasing rate from year to year. Despite this, the employee's contribution (if the plan is contributory) usually remains at the same level regardless of his or her attained age. The level contribution by the employee is practicable because the employer absorbs the portion of the cost in excess of the employee's annual contribution. Thus, the employer's contribution for any individual participant usually increases year by year. On the other hand, the employer's total contribution to the plan may well remain stable or even decline, depending upon the benefit formula, the age and sex composition of the group, and the experience of the plan.

Table 18-2 presents the calculation of the monthly premium for a hypothetical group. The expected difference in male and female mortality is reflected in the calculation as is the use of a 10 percent industry loading, a $10 contract expense loading, and a 5 percent discount for size. The monthly premium rate per $1,000 ($0.27) remains in effect during the rating period, and each month that rate is multiplied by that month's volume of life insurance to determine the monthly premium payable. In addition to the factors used in this example to load or reduce rates, insurers may also adjust rates based on the average amount of insurance involved and whether the insurance is noncontributory.

If the experience under a pooling arrangement of small-size employers is favorable, the dividend or retroactive rate adjustment will reduce the employer's cost. Under some plans, the dividend might equal and occasionally exceed the employer's contribution. In the latter instance, the excess of the dividend is at times applied in some manner for the benefit of the employees. This is required by law in some jurisdictions.

Group insurance premiums are paid monthly by the employer. Other premium modes are possible, but quarterly premiums are used only with small groups. All adjustments in the amount of insurance during the year—arising out of new employees, terminations, and reclassifications—are made on the basis of the average monthly premium rate, regardless of the actual ages of the employees involved. At the end of each policy year, a new average monthly premium is computed. With small groups, however, age-

TABLE 18-2   Calculation of Group Term Life Insurance Premium

	(1)		×	*(2)*		=	*(3)*	
	Volume of Insurance			**Monthly Rate per $1,000**			**Monthly Premium**	
AGE	MALE	FEMALE		MALE	FEMALE		MALE	FEMALE
20	$ 300,000	$ 400,000		$0.12	$ 0.07		$ 36.00	$ 28.00
30	1,200,000	1,100,000		0.14	0.08		168.00	88.00
40	800,000	600,000		0.30	0.18		240.00	108.00
50	400,000	200,000		0.84	0.59		336.00	118.00
60	60,000	30,000		2.13	1.70		127.80	51.00
	$2,760,000	$2,330,000					$907.80	$393.00

Male + female monthly premium	$1,300.80
Monthly premium after 10% industry loading	
($1,300.80 × 1.10)	1,430.88
Monthly premium after $10 constant expense loading	10.00
	$1,440.88
Monthly premium after size discount	
($1,440.88 × 0.95)	$1,368.84
Monthly premium rate per $1,000	
(1,368 divided by 5,090[a])	0.27
Final monthly premium	
(5,090 × 0.27)	$1,374.30

[a]Total volume of insurance is $5,090,000 ($2,760,000 + $2,330,000).

Source: HIAA, *Group Life and Health Insurance,* Part A, p. 164.

graded rates are commonly used to reflect changes in the age distribution on a month-to-month basis and to avoid the possibility of substantial average rate changes at renewal.

Group term insurance rates are usually guaranteed for one year only, but this point now has become the subject of competitive pressure and negotiations. Rate guarantees for longer than one year are offered frequently, particularly to large groups. From a practical standpoint, insurers try to avoid rate increases because they are disturbing to the contract owner, and, whenever possible, they prefer to make adjustments in cost through the experience-rating process.

For contributory group term life plans, employee contributions frequently are at a uniform rate per $1,000, regardless of age. In regard to setting the level of contributions, an important principle is that the cost to the employees is such that the insurance is an attractive buy in comparison with insurance available to them under individual policies.

Most states require that the employer pay at least a portion of the premium for group term insurance, and a few states impose limitations on the amounts that may be paid by any employee. The most common restriction limits the contribution to the greater of 60 cents per month per $1,000 of coverage or 75 percent of the premium rate for that employee.

Cash-value life insurance and other products can be offered through the group mechanism. Group paid-up, group ordinary, and group universal life products are discussed later in connection with postretirement group life coverage.

Supplemental Life Insurance

To provide flexibility to employees in tailoring group life insurance protection to their needs, supplemental life insurance sometimes is made available as part of a group life insurance plan. The supplemental coverage normally is contributory and may have age-banded rates with the number of options available based on the underwriting requirements of the life insurance company, the wishes of the employer, and applicable statutory requirements. The term **voluntary life insurance** is frequently used to denominate plans in which each employee can choose an amount of additional insurance in increments up to a maximum that is based on the employee's earnings (e.g., three times salary).

Credit Life Insurance

A variation on group life insurance is group credit life insurance, which provides a death benefit equal to the unpaid consumer debt of the insured. The creditor (usually a bank) is both the group policyholder and the beneficiary of the policy. The amount of insurance protection is tied directly to the debtor's account balance. The premiums are usually paid by the debtor, as a component of the cost of servicing the debt. However, dividends payable under the policy are paid to the creditor—the group policyholder. This feature can make group credit life insurance very profitable to the creditor and has led to some marketing abuses.

As a result, there is considerable regulation of group credit life insurance in the United States. Many states have promulgated maximum rates in order to avoid excessive charges being made, the purpose of which is to maximize dividends to the creditor at the expense of the debtors.

Accelerated Death Benefit

The accelerated death benefit, discussed in chapter 8 in connection with individual life insurance policies, is also available under group life contracts. It is intended to provide to an insured who is terminally ill an advance payment of a portion of the face amount. The purpose of this type of benefit is to help relieve some of the financial burden associated with a terminal illness.

Taxation of Group Term Life Insurance in the United States

Although the tax treatment of group insurance premiums paid by an employer is relatively straightforward, the income tax treatment to covered employees is more complex. In general, premiums paid for employees' group insurance are deductible by the employer in the United States and most countries. Premiums paid by sole proprietors and partners for group insurance on their own lives, however, are not generally deductible, because they are not considered employees.

Employee Income Taxation

Under U.S. law, the value of the first $50,000 of employer-provided group term life coverage is income tax exempt to the employee. Amounts in excess of $50,000 may invoke taxable income. If the employee contributes toward the cost of the insurance, all of his or her contributions are allocable to the coverage provided in excess of $50,000. This is advantageous because it reduces or even eliminates any income tax consequences to the employee for having group coverage in excess of $50,000.

The economic benefit flowing to employees who enjoy coverage in excess of $50,000 is calculated on a monthly basis. The following procedural outline illustrates both the calculation of the amount taxable to the employee and the offset of any employee contributions:

1. Find the total amount of group term life insurance coverage for the employee in each calendar month of a taxable year.
2. Subtract $50,000 from each month's coverage.

TABLE 18-3 Uniform Premium Table I ($1,000 of Group Term Life Insurance Protection) Provided after June 30, 1999

Age	Value
Under 25	$0.05
25–29	0.06
30–34	0.08
35–39	0.09
40–44	0.10
45–49	0.15
50–54	0.23
55–59	0.43
60–64	0.66
65–69	1.27
70 and above	2.06

The employee's age for purposes of the Uniform Premium Table is his or her attained age on the last day of the taxable year.

Source: IRC §79.

3. Apply the appropriate rate from the Uniform Premium Table (Table 18-3) to any balance for each month.
4. From the sum of the monthly cost, subtract total employee contributions for the year.

An example will illustrate this approach. Assume that José, age 56, is provided $150,000 of group term life insurance coverage throughout the year by his employer, and that he contributes $15 per month ($0.10 per $1,000) toward this coverage. The procedure to derive José's taxable income from the employer providing this protection would be as follows:

	Amount of coverage	$150,000
Less:	Exempt amount	– 50,000
Equals:	Excess over exempt amount	$100,000
	Excess over exempt amount	$100,000
Times:	Uniform Premium Table rate	× 0.43
	Tentative monthly taxable income	43.00
Times:	Months of coverage	× 12
Equals:	Tentative yearly taxable income	$516.00
	Tentative yearly taxable income	$516.00
Less:	Employee contributions ($15/month × 12 months)	– 180.00
Equals:	Taxable economic benefit	$336.00

The preceding tax treatment assumes that certain conditions specified by U.S. tax code and related regulations (discussed later) have been met. In designing a plan to meet these requirements, two areas are of special concern: (1) groups covering fewer than 10 employees and (2) the nondiscrimination rules of Code Section 79(d).

Number of Lives

When a group has fewer than 10 lives, underwriting and amounts of insurance are both limited by IRS Regulation 1.70–1(c), which requires that all full-time employees who provide required satisfactory evidence of insurability must be included, unless they explicitly state their intention not to participate. The formula for determining the amount of life insurance is prescribed, and underwriting is restricted to a medical questionnaire. No physical examination is permitted. Where 10 or more lives are involved, the basic rule is that regular underwriting is permissible and the amount of insurance for each employee can be computed under any formula that precludes individual selection.

Nondiscrimination Rules

Under the U.S. Tax Equity and Fiscal Responsibility Act of 1982 (TEFRA), the exemption from income taxation of the cost of the first $50,000 of group term life insurance is not available to key employees if the plan discriminates in their favor as to either eligibility or type and amount of benefit. The law and accompanying regulations provide detailed definitions of what constitutes a key employee and discrimination.

Benefits are not considered discriminatory if all benefits available to key employees are also available to all participants. Furthermore, benefits will not be considered discriminatory merely because they bear a uniform relationship to total compensation or the basic rate of compensation of each employee.

Other Tax Aspects

As with individual coverages, death proceeds payable under group life insurance are received income tax free in the United States and most other countries, whether they are received from term or cash-value group insurance.[13] The general rules for including life insurance proceeds in the gross estate for U.S. estate tax purposes apply.[14] An employee can assign all incidents of ownership in group life insurance, as long as both the master policy and applicable state law permit it.

Postretirement Coverage

Three general approaches have been used to provide life insurance protection to retired employees: (1) continuation of a portion of the term life insurance; (2) cash-value life insurance; and (3) retired lives reserve (RLR). Continuation of a portion of the group term life insurance is straightforward. Unless the original amount of coverage is modest, the coverage to be continued often is a flat amount, such as $5,000 or $10,000, or it varies from 25 to 50 percent of the former coverage. The other two approaches deserve further consideration.

Cash-Value Life Insurance

Group life insurance that continues after retirement is available through three categories of products. Group paid-up insurance and group ordinary insurance have been available for a number of years, although neither is widely sold. A new product, group universal life insurance, which can also provide postretirement life insurance coverage, has been well received.

Group Paid-Up Insurance   At one time, the group term plus paid-up approach was the most popular U.S. plan for providing postretirement life insurance coverage. This plan is a combination of accumulating units of single-premium whole life insurance and de-

---

[13]IRC §101(a). See chapter 13.

[14]See chapter 13.

creasing units of group term life insurance. The combination provides the same death benefits as do regular employer group term plans. Each paid premium consists of the individual employee's contribution and the employer's contribution. Employee contributions usually are applied to purchase increments of paid-up, single-premium whole life insurance, the amount of which is determined by the individual employee's attained age and the contribution amount. The employer's contribution is applied to provide an amount of decreasing term insurance, which, when added to the accumulated face amounts of the paid-up whole life insurance purchased by the employee, equals the total amount for which he or she is eligible.

Ordinarily, at retirement the portion of the insurance that is still on a term basis is discontinued, and the paid-up insurance remains in force for the balance of the employee's lifetime. The employee may have the right to convert the term portion. When employees terminate employment prior to retirement, similar provisions apply. They may surrender the policy for cash if they wish to terminate the insurance entirely. There is relatively little interest in this coverage today.

Group Ordinary Insurance   There is no typical group ordinary insurance product. Rather, the terminology is used to describe any traditional product (except group paid-up insurance) that provides cash-value life insurance to a group of employees and that will qualify for favorable income tax treatment under IRC Section 79. The cost of the term portion of the coverage is paid by the employer, and the cash-value portion, which the employee may be able to decline, generally is paid by the employee.

In general, federal income tax treatment of the term life insurance portion of group paid-up insurance and group ordinary insurance is essentially the same as it is for group term life insurance. The portion of any employer contributions paid for the cash-value portion of the insurance is taxable to the employee as additional compensation. The sale of this type of coverage has been minimal in recent years.

Group Universal Life Insurance   Today, numerous U.S. insurers market a group universal life product (GULP). These products include the typical guaranteed interest rate, fixed death benefit and loan options, plus the flexibility and potential returns associated with new life products. Universal life is particularly attractive in light of the new U.S. Financial Accounting Standard No. 106, which requires that plan sponsors report the liability of future postretirement life insurance benefits on an accrual accounting basis. Employers wishing to prefund their liability on a more favorable tax basis may consider the use of life insurance products.

Overall, GULP works much the same way as individual universal life (see chapter 6). As a group program, however, it differs in certain ways.

- Coverage generally is issued up to some limit without evidence of insurability. Although limits vary (depending on specific plan provisions, the size of the participating group, and the insurer's underwriting standards), such coverage usually is high enough to meet most employees' needs.
- Policies typically are available on a low or no-commission basis.
- Administrative charges should be lower than those assessed for individual coverage.
- Plans are typically employee-pay-all plans.

Another (less positive) difference is that the use of group underwriting standards to limit adverse selection may cut into GULP's flexibility to some extent. Active employment, for example, is likely to be a prerequisite for participation, and minimum and maximum amounts of coverage (e.g., from one to four times pay) usually are prescribed.

Some proof of insurability also may be required for large amounts. Nevertheless, the overall plan design remains highly flexible.

GULP can be an inexpensive, convenient way to purchase portable cash-value life insurance. Employees have a chance to invest—at attractive interest rates—in a tax-favored vehicle. As other forms of capital accumulation have been limited by recent U.S. tax law changes, GULP has become more popular.

Retired Lives Reserve

A **retired lives reserve** (RLR) is a group reserve accumulated prior to retirement to be used to pay premiums on term insurance after retirement. Under a properly designed plan, an employer can make tax-deductible contributions to the fund on behalf of employees and the contributions are not taxable income to the employees. The fund may be administered through a trust or by a life insurance company. As long as any employees under the plan are alive, the reserve cannot revert to the employer. If an employee dies or quits before retirement, the reserve value is used to fund future costs for others in the plan.

The employer may deduct the portion of the premium credited to any retired lives reserve fund (discussed later) for continuing coverage on retired employees. However, the amount added to the retired lives reserve must be no greater than the amount required to allocate the cost over the working lives of the employees, and the contract owner must have no right to capture any portion of the reserve so long as any active or retired employees remain alive. Similarly, a corporation's nonrefundable contributions to an employees' trust to provide group health and group term life insurance for both active and retired employees are deductible under Code Section 162. Contributions by the employer that are applied toward the savings portions of group cash-value plans are deductible by the employer but taxable currently to the employee.

The U.S. Tax Reform Act of 1984 introduced additional constraints on the use of retired lives reserves that have materially reduced its utilization. For example, the law made deductions for contributions on behalf of key employees contingent on the plan being nondiscriminatory under Section 79 (see foregoing taxation discussion) and generally limited the amount of coverage to $50,000.

Provisions of Contracts and Certificates

Various important features of group life insurance policies have already been discussed. In connection with the term of the contract and renewal, when the policy is a group term life plan, the insurance companies in the United States cannot refuse to renew each year if the employer wishes to continue the contract and pay the premiums. The premium rates, however, may be increased to such an extent that, for practical purposes, the right to renew may be of no value.

The master policy also provides that, if at any time the number of employees is less than the required number (e.g., 10), or if the plan is contributory and the required minimum percentage (e.g., 75 percent) of employees is not covered under the plan, the contract may be canceled.

Also, U.S. laws require certain standard provisions. Thus, the employer must deliver to the employee a certificate showing the amount of insurance and the name of the beneficiary and containing a conversion clause. Another required clause provides for an adjustment of premiums and insurance if the age of an employee has been misstated. If the age has been overstated, the employer will receive a refund. If the age has been understated, the employer will be required to pay the amount by which past premiums have been deficient. Note that this method of adjusting policies for misstated ages differs from the adjustment made in individual life policies.

Group life insurance policies also contain an incontestable clause, although it is of less significance than in individual insurance. In addition, the policy usually provides for (1) a grace period of 31 days in connection with premium payments; (2) a right to have death proceeds paid in installments; (3) the necessity of making claims within one year following the last premium payment for the employee in question; (4) continued insurance for the period provided by the contract on laid-off employees, provided the employer continues to pay the necessary premium; (5) waiver of premium for an employee with disability commencing prior to age 60; and (6) extension of the insurance to employees who are eligible but have been erroneously reported ineligible.

Supplemental Coverages

Supplemental benefits may be added to group term life insurance contracts through the use of riders. These riders may include (1) accidental death and dismemberment insurance, (2) survivor income benefits, and (3) dependent life insurance. These coverages also may be written as separate contracts.

Accidental Death and Dismemberment Insurance

Many group life insurance contracts provide accidental death and dismemberment (AD&D) coverage. AD&D insurance provides a benefit if an employee dies, loses the sight of one or both eyes, or loses a hand or a foot directly and solely as a result of an accidental bodily injury. Although it can be written on a nonoccupational basis only, AD&D insurance usually is written as 24-hour coverage, particularly for small groups.

The benefit structure of AD&D coverage is based on an amount called the **principal sum benefit,** which is typically equal to the coverage under the basic group life insurance contract. In the event of accidental death, the benefit equals the principal sum. In addition to this accidental death benefit, a benefit schedule is provided in the contract that relates types of injuries to the principal sum. Thus, for example, in the case of loss of both hands, both feet, or both eyes, the principal sum is payable. One-half the principal sum is payable for the loss of one hand, foot, or eye.

The accidental death benefit usually is payable in a lump sum (although installment payments may be requested) to the designated beneficiary. For other losses, payment is made to the employee. Accidental death and dismemberment benefits normally cease at retirement, even if the basic life insurance coverage continues.

Under some plans, an elective benefit, called **voluntary AD&D,** that is not part of a regular group life insurance program is available. Employees usually pay all or almost all of the premium, and the employer's payroll deduction facilities are used for collecting employee contributions. The benefits of voluntary AD&D are essentially the same as those of basic AD&D, the most significant differences being in the substantial amounts of coverage available and the employee's privilege of selecting the amount of coverage.

Survivor Income Benefits

Survivor income benefits are a form of monthly income that becomes payable upon the death of an employee who may be covered under either a pension plan or a group life insurance plan. Three characteristics distinguish true survivor income benefits from the more traditional types of group life insurance: (1) The proceeds are payable in the form of monthly income only; (2) the covered employee does not name his or her beneficiary because benefits are payable only to specified beneficiaries; and (3) benefits usually are payable only as long as there is a living survivor beneficiary and, in some cases, may cease on remarriage.

The survivor income benefit is seldom offered today in the United States. Group survivor benefit was a conceptually attractive product with a direct approach to a perceived need. It had two problems, however. It was complicated both to understand and to administer. Also, group life insurance with settlement options can provide many of the important features of the survivor benefit product.

Dependent Life Insurance

Group life insurance contracts commonly provide coverage on the lives of employees' dependents. U.S. law permits employers to extend group term life insurance to the employee's spouse and eligible children. The amounts of dependent life insurance usually are small in relation to the amount of insurance on employees. The definition of dependents usually includes an employee's unmarried dependent children over, say, 14 days of age but under some specified age, such as 19. The employee is automatically the beneficiary under the coverage.

Many states limit life insurance benefits on dependents. These limits usually restrict the amount of insurance on the spouse to a maximum amount and frequently provide that in no event can the spousal benefit be more than 50 percent of the benefit provided the employee. Spousal benefits of $1,000, $2,000, and $5,000 are common. Children's benefits also are restricted in many jurisdictions.

GROUP DISABILITY INCOME INSURANCE

Group insurance can be written to provide virtually any combination of benefits, although life, health, and retirement benefits are the most common. As with individual policies, group health insurance benefits may be broadly classified as (1) disability income and (2) medical expense. Because medical expense benefits are discussed in detail in the next two chapters and disability contract provisions were covered in chapters 7, 9, and 10, this discussion can be brief and it relates to disability income benefits. There are two approaches to providing group disability income benefits: short-term disability and long-term disability.

Short-Term Disability

In general, disability income plans are designed to provide a level of benefits that replaces between 50 percent and 70 percent of an employee's gross income. Many short-term disability income plans and the majority of long-term plans base benefits on a single percentage of earnings excluding bonuses and overtime.

In short-term plans, it is common to place a maximum dollar amount on the benefit that will be provided regardless of earnings. For example, a plan covering hourly paid employees may have a benefit equal to 70 percent of earnings that might be subject to a maximum of $250 week. If earnings vary widely, a benefit schedule will reflect this fact and the maximum benefit will be graded by classes of income.

Short-term plans usually contain an *elimination period* (waiting period). In the typical plan, there is no elimination period for disabilities resulting from accidents, but a waiting period varying from one to seven days is used for disabilities resulting from sicknesses. Other combinations of elimination periods are also utilized.

Benefits for both accident and sickness are usually payable for up to 13 to 52 weeks, with 26 weeks being the most common *benefit period*. U.S. federal law requires that pregnancy be treated the same as a sickness under all fringe benefit plans for employers with 15 or more employees. Many states have stricter requirements than the federal requirement. The cost impact of these laws can be substantial.

Long-Term Disability

Long-term disability income benefits are provided in recognition of the continuing need for income for the duration of a long-term disability arising from either accident or sickness, and without regard to whether it is job connected. The definition of disability usually requires total disability. However, some companies include a residual disability benefit and a presumptive disability clause in their contracts, as defined in chapter 7. Under the residual benefit clause, the insured does not have to be totally disabled to qualify for benefits. For example, if disability reduces an insured's income by at least 20 percent in the first two years, the plan pays a proportionate benefit. This residual disability benefit is consistent with the increasing emphasis on rehabilitation services as part of plan benefits. Under the presumptive benefit provision, the total loss of sight, speech, hearing, or two or more limbs automatically qualifies the individual for long-term disability benefits. The usual elimination period is waived.

An elimination period of from 7 days to 12 months is included. It is often designed to provide long-term disability income protection upon cessation of the short-term disability benefit coverage. With continuous disability, benefits usually continue until age 65, but alternative approaches, such as two or five year's coverage, or lifetime accident coverage, are not uncommon.[15]

The size of the group is a most important underwriting consideration. Large groups allow considerable latitude in underwriting. Another important underwriting consideration is the nature of work performed by the group. Blue-collar groups are underwritten with considerable caution.

Taxation of Disability Income Benefits

As with all types of health insurance benefits, premiums (or other employer contributions) paid by an employer for disability income insurance for employees are generally tax deductible by the employer and are not taxable income to the employee for income tax purposes in the United States and most other countries. Employee contributions, on the other hand, are not tax deductible by the employee. It is consistent with these two rules that the payment of benefits under an insured plan or a noninsured salary continuation plan are treated as taxable income by the employee to the extent the benefits received are attributable to employer contributions. Thus, if the employer pays 75 percent of the monthly premium and the employee pays 25 percent, 25 percent of any benefits received will be tax free and 75 percent taxable.

MARKETING GROUP INSURANCE

The Group Insurance Market

Although the product designs and the various aspects of service are important, the sale and renewal of group insurance products is very price sensitive. The group insurance market is highly segmented and this must be considered in developing premium rates. Although varying somewhat by company, the market can be segmented by (1) size of group, (2) type of group, and (3) funding method (discussed later).

---

[15]U.S. plans must meet the requirements of the Age Discrimination in Employment Act of 1978 (ADEA) and the 1986 amendments thereto. This law abolished mandatory retirement due to age for most workers and reserves certain references to "Age 70" under ADEA.

For premium determination purposes, companies may use community rates for groups of less than 25 lives, use manual rates for groups of 25 to 100 lives, and involve the employer's own experience for groups of over 100 lives (see chapter 20). Different splits, varying by product, may be used for retrospective experience-rating purposes.[16]

Group Insurance Distribution

The group department of a typical insurer markets its products through its general agencies or branch offices and through brokers and employee benefit consultants. The sales department is typically headed by an executive officer (group sales vice president) who is responsible for sales and service. Although some group insurance (usually the smaller-sized cases) is sold by an insurer's own career agents, group sales more commonly follow the brokerage model with group representatives calling on independent benefit consultants, national brokerage houses, independent property and liability agencies, and agents of other insurers. Sales to the larger-case employer–employee and association markets tend to be made through specialized brokers or, in some instances, written directly with the employer. Many of the recent developments in distribution systems reflect a continuing effort to find more effective ways to deliver insurance products to larger numbers of customers. Chapter 24 offers a more comprehensive discussion of insurance marketing.

In addition to group insurance as such, various forms of **mass marketing** and work-site marketing have developed, frequently involving an agent. Association group, credit card solicitations, and payroll deduction efforts are examples of mass marketing. Although association group and credit card solicitations are direct-response techniques, generally an agent is involved in the association group business. Supplementary coverage such as payroll deduction (salary allotment) is a form of mass marketing sponsored by the employer. Just as innovations in products continue (leveraged by the financial environment and changing technology), marketing distribution systems must respond interactively to all present and evolving systems. This process should become even more innovative to the extent that distribution is separated from manufacturing and made a specific profit center.

As the foregoing discussion makes clear, U.S. distribution networks are organizationally diverse. Banks have long sought to participate in the U.S. insurance market. Historically, banks have been prohibited from doing so, but this is changing. U.S. banks generally appear to be gaining ground in their argument that globalization of financial services requires large-sized, financially diversified firms. Proposals of major reforms of the U.S. financial system would permit considerably greater banking participation in the U.S. insurance markets. Most observers believe that banks and other financial institutions ultimately will be permitted to participate fully in the U.S. insurance market. In Europe and other OECD countries, banks are already major players.

Group Insurance Pricing

The pricing (rate-making) process in group insurance is essentially the same as pricing in other industries. The insurance company must generate enough revenue to cover the costs of its claims and expenses and contribute to the surplus of the company. It differs in that the price of a group insurance product is initially determined on the basis of expected future events and also may be subject to experience rating so that the final price

---

[16]Frank Reynolds, "Introduction to Actuarial Aspects of Group Insurance," *Study Note,* Society of Actuaries (1994), pp. 6–7.

to the contractholder can be determined only after the coverage period has ended. Group insurance pricing consists of two steps:

1. the determination of a unit price, referred to as a rate or premium rate for each unit of benefit (e.g., $1,000 of life insurance, $1 of daily hospital benefit, or $1 of monthly income disability benefit)
2. the determination of the total price or premium that will be paid by the contract-holder for all of the coverage purchased

The approach to group insurance rate making differs depending on whether manual rating or experience rating is used. In the case of **manual rating,** the premium rate is determined independently of a particular group's claims experience. When **experience rating** is used, the past claims experience of a group is considered in determining future premiums for the group and/or adjusting past premiums after a coverage period has ended. As in all rate making, the primary objective for all types of group insurance is to develop premium rates that are adequate, reasonable, and equitable.

Manual Rating

In the manual-rating process, premium rates are established for broad classes of group insurance business. Manual rating is used with small groups for which no credible individual loss experience is available. This lack of credibility exists because the size of the group is such that it is impossible to determine whether the experience is due to random chance or is truly reflective of the risk exposure. Manual rating is also used to establish the initial premiums for larger groups that are subject to experience rating, particularly when a group is being written for the first time. In all but the largest groups, experience rating is used to combine manual rates and the actual experience of a given group to determine the final premium. The relative weights depend on the credibility of the group's own experience.

Manual premium rates (also called tabular rates) are quoted in a company's rate manual. As pointed out earlier, these manual rates are applied to a specific group insurance case in order to determine the average premium rate for the case that will then be multiplied by the number of benefit units to obtain a premium for the group. The rating process involves the determination of the net premium rate, which is the amount necessary to meet the cost of expected claims. For any given classification, this is calculated by multiplying the probability (frequency) of a claim occurring by the expected amount (severity) of the claim. The second step in the development of manual premium rates is the adjustment of the net premium rates for expenses, a risk charge, and a contribution to profit or surplus.

The term **retention,** frequently used in connection with group insurance, usually is defined as the excess of premiums over claims payments and dividends. It consists of charges for (1) the stop-loss coverage, (2) expenses, (3) a risk charge, and (4) a contribution to the insurer's surplus. The sum of these changes usually is reduced by the interest credited to certain reserves (e.g., the claim reserve and any contingency reserves) the insurer holds to pay future claims under the group contract. For large groups, a formula is usually applied that is based on the insurer's average experience. The formula varies by the size of a group and the type of coverage involved.

Insurance companies that write a large volume of any given type of group insurance rely on their own experience in determining the frequency and severity of future claims. Where the benefit is a fixed sum, as in life insurance, the expected claim is the amount of insurance. For most group health benefits, the expected claim is a variable that depends on such factors as the expected length of disability, the expected duration of a hospital confinement, or the expected amount of reimbursable expense. Companies that do not have enough past data for reliable future projections can use industrywide sources. The major source for such U.S. industrywide data is the Society of Actuaries.

Insurers must also consider whether to establish a single manual rate level or develop select or substandard rate classifications. Typically, insurers base select or substandard rate classifications on objective standards related to risk characteristics of the group such as occupation and type of industry. These standards are largely independent of the group's past experience.

The adjustment of the net premium rate to provide reasonable equity is complex. Some factors such as premium taxes and commissions vary with the premium charge. At the same time, the premium tax rate is not affected by the size of the group, whereas commission rates decrease as the size of a group increases. Claim expenses tend to vary with the number, not the size of claims. Allocating indirect expenses is always a difficult process as is the determination of the risk charge. Community-rating systems, developed originally by Blue Cross/Blue Shield, are often defined to limit the demographic and other risk factors being recognized. They typically ignore most or all of the factors necessary for rate equity and may be as simple as one rate applicable to all single employees and another rate applicable to those with families. There is little actuarial rationale for charging all groups the same rate regardless of the expected morbidity. Community rating has been mandated in some jurisdictions. This makes it a matter of public policy rather than an actuarial pricing question.

Experience Rating

Experience rating is the process whereby a contractholder is given the financial benefit or held financially accountable for its past claims experience in insurance-rating calculations.[17] Probably the major reason for using experience rating is competition. Charging identical rates for all groups regardless of their experience would lead to adverse selection with employers with good experience seeking out insurance companies that offered lower rates, or they would turn to self-funding as a way to reduce costs. The insurance company that did not consider claims experience would, therefore, be left with only the poor risks. This is why Blue Cross/Blue Shield had to abandon community rating for group insurance cases above a certain size.

The starting point for prospective experience rating is the past claim experience for a group.[18] The incurred claims for a given period include those claims that have been paid and those in process of being paid. In evaluating the amount of incurred claims, provision is usually made for catastrophic claim pooling. Both *individual and aggregate stop-loss limits* are established in which exceptionally large claims (above these limits) are not charged to the group's experience. The "excess" portions of claims are pooled for all groups and an average charge is accounted for in the pricing process. The approach is to give weight to the individual group's own experience to the extent that it is credible. In determining the claims charge, a credibility factor, usually based on the size of the group (determined by the number of lives insured) and the type of coverage involved, is used. This factor can vary from zero to one depending on the actuarial estimates of experience credibility and other considerations such as the adequacy of the contingency reserve developed by the group.

In effect, the claims charge is a *weighted average* of (1) the incurred claims subject to experience rating and (2) the expected claims, with the incurred claims being assigned

---

[17]This section draws on William F. Bluhm, "Experience Rating and Funding Methods," in William F. Bluhm, principal editor, *Group Insurance,* 3rd ed. (Winsted, CT: ACTEX Publications, 1999), Chapter 24.

[18]Because premium rates must be known in advance of the policy anniversary, it follows that the experience of the immediately preceding policy year will not be available at the time of the rating process. The experience year used will usually end a few months in advance of the renewal date or the rerating date.

BOX 18-2

FORMULA FOR CALCULATING CASE CLAIMS CHARGE UNDER EXPERIENCE RATING

Case Incurred Claims = Paid Claims + Change in Claim Reserve for Experience Period
Credibility Factor = C (based on number of lives insured)
Case Claims Charge = C × Case Incurred Claims + $(1 - C)$ × Average Incurred Claims

a weight equal to the credibility factor and the expected claims being assigned a weight equal to one minus the credibility factor (see Box 18-2). The incurred claims subject to experience rating are after consideration of any stop-loss provisions. Where the credibility factor is one, the incurred claims subject to experience rating will be the same as the claims charge. In such cases, the expected claims (average experience) underlying the prospective rates will not be considered.

Thus, when companies insure a group of substantial size, experience rating reflects the claim levels resulting from that group's own unique risk characteristics. It has become common practice to give to the group the financial benefit of good experience and hold them financially responsible for bad experience at the end of each policy period. When experience turns out to be better than was expected in prospective rating assumptions, the excess can either be accumulated in an account, the account generally called a **premium stabilization reserve, claim fluctuation reserve** or **contingency reserve,** or the excess (or some portion thereof) can be refunded. The refund is either called a **dividend** (mutual company) or an **experience-rating refund** (stock company). A generic experience-rating refund formula would include some or all of the following elements:

Premium Stabilization Reserve = Prior Balance Carried Forward
+ Premiums
+ Investment Earnings on Money Held
– Claims Charged
– Expenses Charged
– Risk Charge
– Premium Stabilization Reserve Addition
– Profit

The net result of the experience rating process is usually called the contractholder account balance, representing the final balance attributed to the individual contractholder. As pointed out earlier, this balance or a portion of the balance can be refunded to the contractholder. The adequacy of the group's premium stabilization reserve influences dividend or rate adjustment decisions. The derivation of prospective gross premiums is discussed further in chapter 30.

ALTERNATIVES FOR GROUP BENEFIT PLAN FUNDING

Introduction

During the 1960s, with rare exceptions, the arrangement under which U.S. group benefit plans were funded was the traditional group insurance contract. In the 1970s and 1980s many corporations experienced reduced profits and cash flow problems. At the same time, benefits programs became more liberal with accompanying premium increases.

Escalating health care inflation and greater utilization increased the cost of providing health insurance benefits. During the same time period, the cost of borrowing money for corporate purposes rose to historic highs. These developments gave risk managers and other financial officers a reason to investigate alternate financing mechanisms for their benefit programs.

Generally, employers were (and are) interested in examining alternative methods of financing benefit programs for one or more of the following reasons:

1. to control and use reserve funds that would normally be available to the insurance company under a conventional insured plan
2. to reduce or eliminate payment of premium taxes and insurer risk, profit, and contingency charges that normally are part of the cost of a conventional insured plan
3. to exercise more control over their plan design by avoiding state insurance mandates and requirements
4. to participate more fully in their own favorable experience
5. to enjoy improved cash flow via more immediate recognition of their own experience

In response to these developments, a number of techniques have been developed by insurers that modify conventional methods of funding group insurance but offer a reasonable guarantee of comparable benefits.

Fully Insured Plan Variations

Retrospective Premium Arrangements

Under a **retrospective premium arrangement,** premiums are set realistically to cover expected claims and expenses without the margin for contingencies usually included to cover higher than expected levels of either. In lieu of the premium margin, there is an agreement under which the insurer reserves the right to collect additional premiums at the end of the contract year if claims and expenses are higher than the premiums paid. The additional premium usually is limited so that the amount paid will not be greater than that which would have been required under the insurer's premium schedule had the margin been included.

Cost-Plus Funding

Cost-plus funding offers an employer another funding alternative for group benefits by the employer assuming a portion of the risk normally assumed by an insurer. The employer may achieve lower charges with the insurer remaining the guarantor of benefits. The reserves normally held by the insurer (less than one-third for claims-reporting lag) can be held by the employer, and this increases the options for the use of money. Money that in a conventionally insured plan would have been returned as a dividend is never paid out by the employer.

Through a cost-plus plan the employer assumes the cost of the benefit payments and administrative expenses of the plan on a month-to-month basis up to specified annual deferred and stop-loss limits. In using this funding method, certain values of a conventionally insured plan are lost. Monthly budgeting is more difficult with the loss of a fixed, level premium, and cash flow will be less predictable in the short run. Upward claim fluctuations may mean a greater plan cost in some years than would have been the case with an insured, guaranteed plan. Also, financial responsibility for terminal (runoff) claim liability beyond a minimum established reserve is assumed by the employer.

Extended Grace Period

Another way of increasing the funds available to the contract owner is to extend the usual 31-day grace period for the payment of premiums by an additional 30 to 60 days. This permits the contract owner to retain the use of two or three months' premium, thus permitting the employer effectively to retain a substantial portion of the reserves normally held by the insurer.

Release of Reserves

An insurer, on request, may agree to release the reserves it is holding on the employer's contracts. Because liability for benefits due after termination of the contract remains with the insurer, the insurer usually will require a letter of credit for the amount of the reserves released or audited acceptable financial statements from the contract owner.

Flexible-Funding Life Insurance

Flexible funding is a cost-plus approach to funding life insurance. Under this arrangement, the contract owner's monthly premium is equal to the claims paid in the previous month plus reserve adjustments, premium taxes, and the insurer's expense charges. The contract owner may accept liability for all claims or the plan may limit the contract owner's liability to what the premium would have been under a conventional fully insured arrangement.

Alternatives to Fully Insured Plans

The concept of an employer self-funding a benefit plan as an alternative to an insured plan is not new. Health benefit programs initially were self-funded, and self-funding has been a vehicle commonly used by employers for workers' compensation benefits.

In evaluating whether to adopt self-funding, it is of primary importance to consider the size of the group. In considering the cost of self-funding versus insurance, the financial manager weighs the advantages against the cost of additional management and administrative resources required and, if an outside claims administrator is used, loss of insurance company expertise in such areas as claims payment and cost containment. Also, the importance of current cash flow to the employer, the additional risk under some cash flow arrangements, and employee reaction to self-funding all must be factored into the analysis.

Minimum Premium Plans

Under a **minimum premium plan** (MPP), the contract owner assumes liability for all but the largest claims or very unfavorable total experience of the plan. MPPs create a partially self-funded arrangement that has premium tax savings for the employer as one of its primary objectives.

Under an MPP, the employer/contract owner deposits funds, as needed, to a special bank account to cover claims funded by the contract owner. The insurer, acting as agent of the contract owner, pays claims from the special account first. The insurer continues to provide the same services, assumes the same risks, and, unless some special arrangement is made, holds essentially the same claim reserves as those under a conventional fully insured plan. The reserves must be maintained because on termination of the group plan the insurer is still responsible, as under a fully insured plan, to pay all covered outstanding claims. In some minimum premium plans, however, the contract owner agrees to assume responsibility for all outstanding claims upon discontinuance of the plan. In such cases, the need for the insurer to maintain reserves is removed, although the insurer can be at risk upon contract owner bankruptcy.

An individual stop-loss arrangement, which is part of such plans, limits the contract owner's liability for any insured individual's claims within a specific time period to a predetermined maximum. Amounts over this maximum (the individual or specific stop-loss limit) do not count toward claims funded by the contract owner. Also, an aggregate stop-loss limit applies to the aggregate of all claims during the plan year. It is typically calculated at between 100 to 120 percent of the projected claims level that the insurer would have used had it computed a premium for a conventionally fully insured plan. Claims over the aggregate stop-loss limit are paid from insurer funds. Premiums to cover losses over the stop-loss limits, to maintain reserves, and to cover operating costs are paid to the insurer.

Most states assess premium taxes only on premiums received by the insurance company for payment of claims under an insurance contract. Thus, by channeling most of the claim funds directly from the contract owner to the covered individuals, an MPP makes it possible to avoid premium taxes on approximately 80 to 90 percent of claims costs.

Administrative Services Only

Under an **administrative services only** (ASO) self-insurance arrangement, the employer purchases specific administrative services from an insurance company or from an independent third-party administrator. These services will normally include reviewing claims, making payment from the employer's funds, and related administration services. In the usual case, full administrative, underwriting, and actuarial services are provided as well. There is, however, no insurance and, therefore, no insurance contract is involved. The ASO agreement is a service contract between the insurer as administrator and the employer as buyer. It specifies the services to be provided by the insurer, the rights and obligations of both parties, and the administrative fees involved.

The employer that chooses ASO frequently purchases stop-loss insurance on medical care expenses from an insurer as protection against the risk of catastrophic losses. As with minimum premium plans, stop-loss insurance purchased with an ASO contract can take the form of either individual or aggregate stop-loss insurance or both (aggregate insurance is typically calculated at 115 to 130 percent of projected claims).

Letters of Credit

Although a letter of credit is not itself a cash flow option, it is sometimes required as a security measure to protect the insurance company because of the risk inherent in several alternate funding arrangements. It is a document issued by a bank to the insurer to guarantee the contract owner's promise to pay monies due under such funding arrangements. The bank receives a fee for this credit-guarantee service.

Table 18-4 shows various funding methods available and summarizes the handling of the key cost components under each.

Questions

1. How have circumstances related to labor markets, the general business environment, and the federal tax treatment of employee benefits greatly helped promote the establishment of employee benefit plans?
2. How is it that group underwriting can diminish adverse selection and lower underwriting costs? What features do insurers look for in a group to achieve these benefits of group underwriting?
3. How do insurers take additional measures, as reflected in the nature of coverage and benefits extended, to increase the benefits of group underwriting?
4. How do the practices of marketing and rating differ between group and individual insurance?

TABLE 18-4 Group Benefit Funding Methods				
	Premium Rates	*Reserves*	*Risk*	*Insurer Retention*
Insured conventional	Established and guaranteed for a stated period (usually 12 months)	Established and held until plan ceases	Assumed by insurer above premium income	Commissions, administrative expense, risk charge, and taxes
Insured retrospective premium rating	Established at a level lower than conventional, with provision for lump-sum additional payment	Established and held until plan ceases	Assumed by insurer above premium income, including retro-spective limit	Commissions, administrative expense, risk charge, interest loss, and taxes
Insured cost-plus funding	None or only for first year; premium is equal to paid claims plus insurer charges	Partially estab-lished, perhaps in the form of a de-posit, and held until plan ceases	Assumed by in-surer in excess of a generally conserva-tive stop-loss point	Commissions, administrative expense, lower risk charge, interest loss, and taxes
Partially self-funded minimum premium plan	Covers all charges by the insurer; includes amounts needed to fund the insured part of the risk, reserve charges, insurer administrative expense, taxes on premiums received by the insurer, and stop-loss rates	Established on both the insured and self-funded portions of the plan; these reserves are held by either the insurer or the contract owner until the plan ceases	Assumed by in-surer for amount in excess of predeter-mined premium and plan contribu-tions; in event of termination of the plan, the runout claims are insured by the insurer or self-funded by the contract owner	Commissions, administrative ex-pense, risk charge, and taxes on only the premium received by the insurer where per-mitted by state law
Self-insurance with administrative services only	None or used only for cost analysis and any stop-loss rates	None or used en-tirely by employer for cost accounting and tax purposes	Assumed by employer	Administrative ex-pense; consultant fees may be borne separately by employer

CHAPTER

19

HEALTH CARE PLANS: I

Objectives

■ Identify market imperfections that affect the demand and supply of health insurance.

■ Describe the circumstances that have led to particularly high health care costs in the United States.

■ Explain how health care providers and insurers in the United States have responded to control health care costs.

■ Describe the types of organizations set up for delivery of health insurance and health care in the United States.

■ Elaborate on the following aspects of the health care and health insurance markets in the United States:
  a. the level of health expenditures in the United States relative to other countries
  b. the differences between traditional and managed care
  c. the prevalence of self-funding by employer

INTRODUCTION

Although most individuals do not need acute medical services frequently, when care is needed, the cost can be burdensome unless services are paid for by private insurance or another third-party payor such as the government. Provision of affordable medical care is important to society at large because basic medical services, such as vaccinations, protect society through the reduction in the incidence, severity, or spread of certain diseases.

The financial risk to an individual or to society at large for provision of medical services is a risk that is managed in a variety of ways worldwide. The health care delivery and financing system in a given country reflects the cultural, economic, and political character of that nation and points up the difficult choices made in allocating scarce health resources across the population. For example, many industrialized countries place great value on equal access to health care by individuals, even if it means that some must wait for or be denied certain specialized medical services. Most provide basic universal coverage to all, although certain high-technology procedures and treatments may not be readily available. To those who are well insured, the United States provides nearly instantaneous access to state-of-the-art technology, but those with no medical insurance find expensive treatment less accessible. The U.S. culture generally places relatively less value on social equity (equal access) and relatively greater value on private market solutions to financing health care.

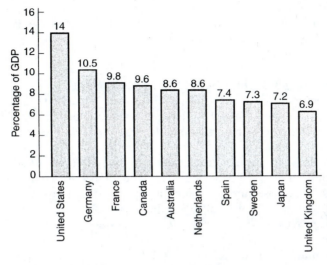

FIGURE 19-1 Health Care Expenditures as a Percentage of GDP for 10 Countries

Source: OECD (1996).

The level of health care services provided within a nation corresponds to the stage of economic development within the country. Typically, developed market economy countries or industrialized countries with relatively high per capita income have modern health care services available to most of the population. A country may finance services for certain portions of the population differently from the way it finances services for other portions. In 1996, the average percentage of gross domestic product (GDP) devoted to health care among 29 OECD countries was about 7.8 percent. As Figure 19-1 shows, spending was 14.0 percent of GDP in the United States, followed by 10.5 percent of GDP in Germany, and 9.8 percent of GDP in France.

THE ECONOMICS OF HEALTH CARE

In a perfectly competitive market, buyers decide what to purchase based on full information about the quality and price of goods and services.[1] Buyers, not sellers, determine the demand for goods and services, and demand for normal goods or services decreases with an increase in price, other things being equal. Price rationing occurs because buyers base purchasing decisions on the relative quality and price of the good as well as on their willingness and ability to pay. In a perfectly competitive market, no barriers to entry exist. In the real world, of course, the health care market has imperfections, and these imperfections help shape health care financing.

Services may be financed (1) out of general tax revenues, (2) under a social insurance model, (3) through a voluntary private insurance system, or (4) a combination of these. Chapter 22 provides a discussion of social insurance, with particular emphasis on the U.S. approach to health care financing, which involves social insurance, use of general tax revenues, and voluntary private insurance.

Health Care Market Imperfections

The comparison of the health care market with a perfectly competitive market provides insight into how cost and quality problems arise, and facilitates identifying potential

---

[1]This section draws on Helen I. Doerpinghaus, "Health Care Financing Worldwide," in Harold D. Skipper, Jr., ed., *International Risk and Insurance* (Boston, MA: Irwin/McGraw-Hill, 1998), Chapter 22.

inefficiencies that can lead to service quality or pricing problems that negatively affect patients, providers, and insurers within the health care system. Examination of market imperfections also helps explain the difficulty of reforming health care financing and delivery systems.

Measuring Marginal Benefit of Medical Care

Measurement of the marginal benefit of medical services on health status is difficult. Individuals cannot purchase health per se from providers but instead purchase medical services to improve or maintain health. From the standpoint of society, preventative medical services such as vaccinations provide a much greater marginal benefit than do more expensive, more technologically intensive interventions. Once vaccination and basic health services are provided, overall health is positively affected more by factors such as diet, exercise, and smoking than by the advancement of sophisticated technological procedures. Public policy relating to the optimal amount of medical care that should be provided to individuals is a complex question.

Information Asymmetries

Information asymmetry exists between buyers and sellers in the medical care market. Providers are well informed about the services they deliver, but consumers often find it difficult to secure information about particular medical services. For physicians, hospitals, and other providers to provide full information to consumers is costly, and providers tend to provide only essential information relative to a particular medical treatment. Consumers, without medical training, find it difficult to understand or evaluate various alternatives even when information on alternative treatments is available. Evaluating alternatives includes consideration of service quality, measured by criteria such as the success rate of the treatment, the degree of invasiveness of the procedure, or the length of recovery time. In addition, the need to gather and analyze information usually occurs when the buyer is ill, putting the consumer even more at an informational disadvantage. A partial solution to this is found in the general practitioner who serves as an advisor to patients determined to need nonroutine medical treatment.

Information asymmetries also exist with respect to the price of medical services. Consumers generally have limited incentives to be well informed about the price of medical services because third parties (government, employers, or private insurers) pay for most medical services. Even when consumers attempt to price and compare services, it is often difficult to determine in advance the total cost of services. Physicians themselves may not have financial incentives to be well informed about prices if their income is unaffected by the quantity or quality of services delivered (e.g., salaried physicians). Information asymmetries, associated with understanding the nature of the medical treatment and comparing prices of alternative treatments, all constrain price rationing and efficient purchase of medical care.

Private health insurance markets are particularly vulnerable to adverse selection. Individuals have a great deal more information about their individual health status and likely need for medical services than do insurers. This informational disadvantage to insurers frequently results in adverse selection. Information on individual health status is relatively expensive to obtain. As noted in chapter 1, *adverse selection* occurs when individuals with higher than average health risks seek insurance and insurers, unaware of their risk levels, fail to charge an adequate premium by classifying them inaccurately. As a result, adverse selection leads to individuals with lower risks subsidizing those with higher risks. Ultimately, low-risk individuals buy less than full insurance coverage or withdraw from the insurance pool entirely because coverage is too expensive given their good health status. Minimizing the impact of adverse selection underlies basic contract design and company underwriting processes relating to health insurance coverage.[2]

Moral Hazard

Third-party payment for medical services not only reduces incentives for consumers to seek price information but also increases the potential for moral hazard. Insureds are not paying market prices for services directly but rather view the care as free or pay an amount significantly less than full price (such as the deductible or copayment amount) for services. When the consumer's perception of cost is less than his or her perception of the price of services provided, consumers tend to demand more services than they would otherwise. In theory, as price decreases, demand increases, other things being equal. Because insureds do not bear the full cost of medical care, insureds may be less careful about their health or well-being or engage in activities that can compromise their health status. This *moral hazard problem* inflates the demand for medical services relative to the demand for services when buyers pay the full price for care.

To minimize the impact of moral hazard, insurers design contracts that transfer at least some cost of losses back to the policyowner by using deductibles, coinsurance clauses, and benefit limits. These provisions are included in an effort to make the marginal benefit of being careful positive. These efforts are also intended to minimize the tendency to "overservice" because the provider knows that the patient will have to bear part of the cost.

Supplier-Induced Demand

Another important characteristic of the health care market lies in the fact that providers treating insured patients have an incentive to recommend and perform more health services than they would in the absence of insurance—another element of moral hazard in health insurance. Medical professionals frequently disagree on the beginning or end of a particular episode of illness and on the health services needed to alleviate the condition. This incentive is enhanced as practitioners face the increasing likelihood of malpractice suits under the U.S. legal system (discussed later). Recommending use of services that may be unnecessary but that benefit the provider economically can even result in medical fraud (e.g., recommendations for services not needed and directing patients to a laboratory or other service facility in which a physician has an ownership interest).

Barriers to Entry

Unlike perfectly competitive markets, the medical services market often has barriers to entry. Providers must meet stringent capital, licensing, or other regulatory requirements that limit the number of market entrants. For example, hospitals require large capital expenditures for facilities and equipment. Physicians are required to obtain medical degrees, certifications, or other licensing to practice medicine. Barriers to entry contribute to monopoly power among providers, which can increase price and lower the quality of services provided.

---

[2]Adverse selection is an important concern in the medical expense insurance market in which society may value universal, affordable, and available coverage (i.e., everyone is insured). Many industrialized countries mandate universal coverage to minimize adverse selection problems. Mandating universal coverage implies cross-subsidization across health status or income levels when medical care is funded through an income tax. However, a given society may conclude that cross-subsidization is preferable to having uninsured individuals with limited access to health care.

Other Economic Considerations

Cultural Beliefs

Cultural beliefs about the nature of health care—whether it is a right or a privilege or falls on a continuum between the two—are important factors that shape the health care financing system of a given country. Many people believe that access to medical care is a universal right rather than a privilege for those who can afford care. For those who consider health care as a right, everyone, in theory, is entitled to all services equally at no cost to the individual. Medical care is costly, however, and some trade-offs in coverage are inevitable due to resource constraints; that is, rationing must occur in some form. Thus, certain subgroups of citizens may be uninsured (such as the poor or the unemployed), waiting times to receive care may be long (rationing through one's price of time), or access to state-of-the-art technology or certain procedures may be restricted, especially for persons of advanced age.

Growth of Medical Technology

The health care market is characterized by rapid and continuing advances in medical technology requiring continuous capital expenditures. Although the price of new technology declines over time, in the medical industry, the constant invention of new products and the capital expenditures required to remain up-to-date and competitive are especially pronounced.

Cost/benefit analysis of medical technology can be difficult. Estimating the benefits of new technology requires consideration of factors such as improved morbidity and mortality rates, decreased lengths of hospitalization, and decreased recovery times. Estimation of the economic value of human life is also required. Cultural beliefs on prolonging life and quality of life also complicate benefit analysis. Despite these difficulties, most agree that the aggregate benefits of the development and use of rapidly advancing medical technology far outweigh the costs.

Medical Malpractice Costs

Medical malpractice suits have become an important factor in rising health care costs, particularly in the United States. Patients have become increasingly likely to resolve disappointment with treatment outcomes through litigation. The litigious nature of the U.S. culture reinforces this avenue for conflict resolution. Malpractice litigation and settlement, however, are inefficient ways to compensate victims because they also include payments for such losses as pain and suffering and attorney fees. The increased incidence of medical malpractice claims has caused physician malpractice insurance costs to rise, and these costs are ultimately passed on to consumers. An increasing number of established physicians have opted out of practicing medicine as a result of the litigious environment.

The increased willingness to sue is driven in part by a change in patient–physician relationships. Traditionally, a family practitioner treated a broad range of needs over an extended time, fostering a relationship of trust between physician and patient. Today, specialists outnumber general practitioners, and patients are less likely to know and trust these providers. When treatment fails or even when unrealistic expectations are not met, patients, encouraged by attorneys or even greed, are more likely to sue providers.

As pointed out earlier, physicians may practice defensive medicine in an effort to avoid medical malpractice liability. They order tests and procedures that may not be necessary in an effort to reduce their liability in case of suit. These additional diagnostic procedures and treatments also drive up the total cost of health care.

Economies of Scale

It can be argued that the production of health care services has large economies of scale. As a result, it is less costly to society to produce these services using a public utility model rather than a competitive market model. The concept of economies of scale in health care may seem puzzling given the sheer number of physicians, hospitals, and other health care providers within most developed countries. However, the market for health care services is a local, not a national, one in all but the very smallest countries. Thus, the markets for health care services usually encompass a relatively small geographic area. As a result, competition in all but the largest cities may not be sufficient for a workable competitive market. The question of scale economies is one of the factors underlying the continuing debate between those who believe that government is the most efficient provider and those that believe that the private market is the appropriate approach for the efficient financing and delivery of health care.

THE HEALTH CARE ENVIRONMENT

Rising health care costs are a global phenomenon, constituting a major problem in both social insurance and voluntary employer-provided health plans, especially in developed countries. Many governments are exploring the possibility of shifting more medical expense costs to employers and individuals.

In contrast to the United States, most other developed countries have some broad national health insurance scheme for individuals of all ages. In these countries, employers commonly offer supplemental medical expense plans to provide employees with higher-quality medical care than that available from the normal health insurance providers. Table 19-1 presents an overview of health care benefits in selected countries.

Medical Care Cost Trends

In the United States, the rate of increase in health care expenditures throughout the 1980s and early 1990s was significantly higher than the increases in general inflation, population growth, and the overall increase in GDP. During much of this period, increases in health care costs were at rates two times that of inflation. Health care costs accounted for about 14 percent of U.S. GDP. Other countries, even those with universal health care systems, spend less on health care than the United States.

Although all indications point to demand and costs continuing to increase in the future, employees, employers, providers, and politicians have all become concerned with doing something about controlling costs. Indeed, from 1993 to 1996, there was minimal price inflation for medical goods and services, reflecting the overall reduction in inflation generally in the United States. There is mounting evidence, however, that health care inflation is again growing.

Causes of Health Care Inflation

As individuals live longer, they consume more and more medical services. Across all demographic groups, demand has increased for quality health care and state-of-the-art treatment. The U.S. population age 75 and older is projected to increase four times faster than that of persons under age 65. Many of the elderly have chronic, disabling illnesses. Institutional care is anticipated to increase, and hospital and nursing home care is expected to consume an even larger share of personal health care spending.

As discussed earlier, the rapid advances in sophisticated, expensive diagnostic and therapeutic technology have helped fuel the growth in health care expenditures. Also, dramatic increases in the price per episode of inpatient care, despite a continuing reduction in the amount of inpatient care, have contributed to medical inflation. As overall hospital utilization continues to decline, fewer patients must carry the load of a greater portion of each hospital's total overhead.

TABLE 19-1	Overview of Health Care Benefits in Selected Countries
Country	**Benefits Provided**
Brazil	Basic health care benefits are provided by the government. Supplemental coverage typically is provided through prepaid groups (clinics, cooperatives, and preferred provider organizations, or PPOs), with insured plans growing in popularity.
Germany	Universal, comprehensive health care benefits are provided by the government. High wage earners may opt out and select private insurance (employer must pay one-half of the insurance premiums) and/or may be provided supplementary insurance for high-quality care (e.g., private accommodations).
Japan	Universal, comprehensive health care benefits are provided by the government. Large employers with more than 700 employees may opt out and form their own private health insurance society.
Norway	Universal, comprehensive health care benefits are provided by the government. Private plans are essentially nonexistent.
South Korea	Universal, comprehensive health care benefits are mandated by the government and are provided through either government facilities or government-authorized health care groups ("societies"). The government plan includes copayments (from 20 to 55 percent) and deductibles that may be financed through private insurance.
Thailand	Comprehensive health care benefits are provided by the government, although coverage is not universal. Employers commonly sponsor insured plans that cover basic health care. Employees do not contribute to the basic coverage but often purchase supplemental coverage through the same contracts.
United Kingdom	Universal, comprehensive health care benefits are provided by the government. Redundant insured plans provided by employers are growing in popularity because of improved service over the government system.
United States	A wide variety of nongovernment arrangements is offered by employers with the government generally providing coverage only for the elderly and the very poor. Employer plans range from basic to comprehensive coverage as well as the possibility of no coverage (the United States is one of only a few countries that does not have universal coverage through the government or employers). Employees typically share in the costs.
Zimbabwe	Virtually no health care benefits are provided by the government or through employers.

Sources: Bruce A. Palmer, "Employee Benefits" in Harold D. Skipper, Jr., ed., *International Risk and Insurance* (Boston, MA: Irwin/McGraw Hill, 1997), p. 692.

Both the utilization and the cost of ambulatory care (hospital outpatient and physician's office) are increasing at a rapid pace. In the United States, most surgery that should be done on an ambulatory basis is done that way. The number of visits to physicians' offices and of tests taken with expensive equipment has risen. The shift to outpatient surgery has been accompanied by a dramatic increase in the volume of these procedures. More individuals are having outpatient operations than was the case when such operations were available on an inpatient basis only.

Another source of the cost increase stems from the nature of supply and demand for medical services. As mentioned earlier, the demand for services is frequently controlled by the provider. Research indicates typically abused procedures in the United States include C-sections, hysterectomies, heart bypass surgery, and imaging diagnostic procedures.

Cost shifting, another component of increased cost in employer-sponsored health plans, is the result of other payors not reimbursing providers at levels sufficient to recover cost and make a profit. Medicare, the federal insurance program, limits the amount it will pay to hospitals and other providers for the elderly, for the disabled, and for patients with end-stage renal disease. Hospitals and physicians tend to make up for the lost revenue by increasing fees to others. Any person or organization that is actually paying charges ends up with a higher bill. Bad debts, indigent care, inadequate Medicaid reimbursement, and discounted rates for contracting health maintenance organizations (HMOs) and preferred provider organizations (PPOs) also add to the cost shifts of the noncontracting plans. As a result, there have been dramatic rate increases to nonnegotiated hospital rates. This is why some plans experience 20 percent inflation whereas others experience single-digit or low double-digit increases. Other factors increasing costs include excess hospital capacity, varying medical practice standards, overuse of specialist physicians, a focus on acute care versus preventive care, and fraud. According to a May 1992 report to Congress by the General Accounting Office (GAO), health care fraud and abuse cost the U.S. economy as much as 10 percent of the money spent on health care annually. Figure 19-2 presents the annual change in total health benefit cost in the United States in recent years.

Employer Responses to Rising Costs

Until recently, employer responses to rapidly increasing costs were to raise the share of costs paid by employees or efforts to cap the employer's contribution (cost). These efforts included:

- increased employee contributions
- increased employee copayments (e.g., increased deductibles, raised coinsurance percentages, and greater use of internal limits on certain types of benefits)
- introduction of flexible benefit plans (discussed later) in which the employee chooses from a variety of life insurance, medical care, and other benefits provided by a fixed employer contribution
- termination of the plan itself

All of these responses can be considered passive in the sense of managing an important human resources problem. Most larger employers are approaching the problem positively by attempting to manage the medical care benefits provided their employees as part of their overall employee benefit program. Employers have responded to increases in plan costs by initiating some or all of the following actions related to their health benefit plans:

- reduce coverage through increased deductibles, out-of-pocket limits, and maximum amounts, including maximums for coverages such as mental health and chemical dependency

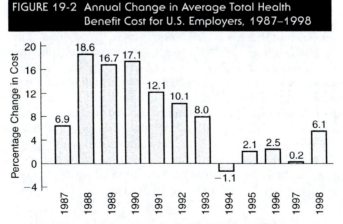

FIGURE 19-2 Annual Change in Average Total Health Benefit Cost for U.S. Employers, 1987–1998

Source: William M. Mercer Companies, LLC, *National Survey of Employer-Sponsored Health Plans* (1999), New York.

- redesigning benefits to create incentives for more efficient utilization of health care resources
- improving the administration and financing of the plan
- use of alternative delivery and reimbursement systems such as health maintenance organizations (HMOs), preferred provider organizations (PPOs), and point-of-service plans (POSs)

Although all of these activities have contributed to more effective management of employer health care cost, to date the greatest attention has been placed on benefit redesign. As changes have taken place, the concept of managed care has evolved.

Development of Managed Care

As health care costs have escalated and cost containment efforts have been emphasized, benefit redesign, alternative delivery systems, self-insurance, and other developments have led to the emergence of the concept of managed care with a profound impact on health insurance. During the early 1990s, the health care delivery and financing system has evolved at a pace few anticipated, largely responding to the acute concern about the ever-rising cost of care. The most visible change has been explosive development of managed care delivery systems of which health maintenance organizations (HMOs), preferred provider organizations (PPOs), exclusive provider organizations (EPOs), and various forms of provider-sponsored organizations (PSOs) are the best-known examples.

Characteristics of Managed Care

The concept of managed care embodies a direct relationship and interdependence between the provision of and payment for health care.[3] **Managed care** involves a population orientation and the organization of care-providing groups or networks that accept responsibility and usually share financial risk with the insurer for a population's medical care and health maintenance. The provider network is the single most important feature distinguishing a managed care plan from an indemnity (fee-for-service) plan. This feature is key to enabling the insurer to exert influence over the delivery, use, and costs of services.

Linking the insurance of and delivery of services, managed care in effect reverses the financial incentives of providers that are prevalent in the traditional indemnity (fee-for-service) plan. In essence, fee-for-service is essentially a piecework, pay-as-you-go system in which the care provider is financially rewarded for high utilization. Managed care, however, uses the concept of prepayment in which care providers are paid in advance a preset amount for all the services their insured population is projected to need in a given time period. **Capitation,** a method by which providers are paid for services on a per member, per month basis, is a common form of prepayment. The provider (e.g., a physician) receives payment whether or not services are used, assuming a share of the financial risk involved in delivering services. Fee-for-service plans may withhold a portion of the customary fee (usually 15 to 20 percent), which may be returned based on the services provided to a defined population, relative to a targeted amount of resources, established in advance on an annual basis. The impact of these methods reverses the financial incentives, controlling rather than promoting utilization. Such payment systems can be used with all types of individual and institutional providers.

The use of financial incentives to control utilization is not without problems. The arrangements have altered both the fundamental way physicians are compensated and how health care services are delivered to, and paid for, by the consumer. Under some pay-

---

[3]This discussion draws from Harry A. Sultz and Kristina M. Young, *Health Care USA: Understanding Its Organization and Delivery* (Gaithersburg, MD: Aspen Publishers, Inc., 1997), Chapter 8.

ment agreements, physicians may be penalized financially if they order a hospital stay, give a referral to a specialist, or order expensive tests. Managed care can place physicians in an adversarial relationship with their patients. The physician–patient relationship, which has been sacred to the medical community, has been significantly altered, perhaps forever. This is a serious problem that will have to be resolved as the delivery of health care continues to evolve.

Table 19-2 summarizes the differences between the objectives and operations of traditional indemnity insurance and managed care. Although managed care arrangements continue to evolve, several key factors are common to all arrangements. These include:

- management of both the financing and delivery of health care
- institution of cost control techniques
- some sharing of financial risk between providers and payors
- management of the utilization of services

There is a continuum of managed care models that moves from the least control by the managed care organization to the most control (Figure 19-3). The least controlled programs, such as traditional indemnity insurance with managed care features, allow unlimited access to providers but at higher cost to the payor and the enrollee. Programs with the most control, such as the staff model HMO (discussed later), strictly limit access to system providers but at a lower cost to payors and enrollees.

Growth in Managed Care

HMOs enroll more than 20 percent of the U.S. population. Large HMOs (more than 100,000 members) are growing at a rapid pace. Although 89 HMOs in the United States have more than 100,000 members, 82 percent of all HMOs have fewer than 100,000 enrollees.[4]

HMO plans are becoming hybrid and more diversified. Among plans more than three years old, over one-half have added PPOs, traditional indemnity options, or employee assistance programs to assist individuals with substance abuse or mental health problems. PPOs, EPOs, and POSs (discussed later), which are primarily a development

TABLE 19-2 Differences between Traditional Insurance and Managed Care

Characteristic	*Traditional Insurance*	*Managed Care*
1. Choice of provider	Plans restrictions on choice of providers	Encourages or requires use of selected providers
2. Provider payment	Offers fee-for-service reimbursement of providers	Pays negotiated rates to providers
3. Relation to health care delivery system	Functions apart from the health care delivery system	Integrates the finance and delivery system
4. Financial risk	Assumes all financial risk	Shares risk with providers
5. Cost control measures	Offers few financial incentives to control costs	Creates financial incentives for providers and enrollees to control costs
6. Relation to service quality	Takes little interest in measuring quality and appropriateness of services	Participates actively in methods to measure quality and monitor appropriateness of care
7. Financial focus	Has no real budget for cost of services, simply "pay as you go"	Establishes budget for cost of services; prepayment of a fixed premium in most cases

---

[4]*1996 Source Book of Health Insurance Data,* p. 34.

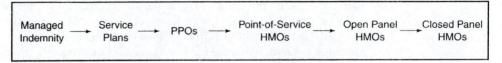

Increasing Control of Cost and Quality of Care

FIGURE 19-3 Continuum of Managed Care Plans

Reprinted/adapted with permission from Eric R. Wagner, "Types of Managed Care Organizations," in Peter R. Kongstvedt, ed., *The Managed Health Care Handbook,* 3rd ed., p. 35, © 1996, Aspen Publishers, Inc.

of the 1980s, also are growing rapidly. The percentage of employers offering a PPO plan has increased from 36 percent in 1993 to 59 percent in 1996.[5]

The rapid growth of managed care plans reflects the recognition by major employers and insurers that ways must be found to reduce costs while assuring that patients get appropriate care. Insurers increasingly have recognized that traditional fee-for-service indemnity plans do not provide mechanisms to contain costs. As a consequence, many insurers have made major commitments to develop and sustain comprehensive managed care systems.

Federal Regulation

Many aspects of federal regulation have affected the establishment and character of group insurance plans. The most important of these include the Social Security Act, discussed in chapter 22, and certain nondiscrimination rules discussed throughout chapters 18, 19, 20, and 21. Other important U.S. laws include the Age Discrimination in Employment Act, the Employee Retirement Income Security Act (ERISA), the Americans with Disabilities Act, the Family Medical and Leave Act, and the Health Insurance Portability and Accountability Act, all discussed here.

The **Age Discrimination in Employment Act,** enacted in 1967, prohibited age discrimination for most workers. The law was amended in 1986 to eliminate the upper age limitation, effectively eliminating compulsory retirement, except for senior executives. In 1990, Congress explicitly brought employee benefits under the provisions of the Age Discrimination in Employment Act, requiring benefits to be continued for older employees. The act permits a reduction in the level of some benefits for older workers, provided the cost of providing older employees with the specific benefits is no greater than the cost of providing similar benefits for younger employees. Medical expense coverage, however, cannot be reduced. These restrictions apply only to benefits for active employees; there are no requirements under the act that any benefits be continued for retired workers. In contrast to other benefits, employees over age 65 cannot be required to pay any more for their medical expense coverage than is paid by employees under age 65.

A 1978 amendment to the Civil Rights Act, known as the **Pregnancy Discrimination Act,** requires for all employment-related purposes that pregnancy be treated the same as any illness. The amendment applies only to the benefit plans (both insured and self-funded) of employers with 15 or more employees. Although employers with fewer employees are not subject to the provisions of the amendment, they may be subject to comparable state laws.

The **Employee Retirement Income Security Act** (ERISA) was enacted to protect the interests of participants in employee benefit plans as well as the interests of the ben-

---

[5]A. Foster Higgins & Co. (now William M. Mercer Companies, LLC), *National Survey of Employer-Sponsored Health Plans,* New York (1996) p. 20.

eficiaries. ERISA clarified and reserved to the federal government the authority to regulate employee benefit plans. Although ERISA's provisions primarily address the activities and responsibilities of employer-sponsored pension plans, the law also establishes federal authority over employee welfare plans—including health insurance benefits. ERISA defines a **welfare benefit plan** as any plan, fund, or program established or maintained by an employer (or by an employee organization) for the purpose of providing employee benefits through the purchase of insurance or otherwise. ERISA's most important provisions relating to employer-sponsored health insurance plans include the preemption of all state laws regulating employee benefit plans. This situation is a principal attraction of self-funding. As amended, other provisions of ERISA exclude employer welfare plans from the funding and coverage provisions that govern pensions and require that employer-sponsored health insurance plans allow employees and their dependents whose coverage is terminated under most circumstances to continue coverage from the employer plan. As discussed in chapter 21, ERISA also gives to the states regulatory authority to impose and enforce financial standards for multiple-employer welfare arrangements including multiple-employer trusts.

For employers with 20 or more employees, the **Consolidated Omnibus Budget Reconciliation Acts of 1985, 1986, and 1990** (COBRA) require that group health plans allow employees and certain beneficiaries to elect to have their current health insurance coverage extended, at group rates, for up to 36 months following a qualifying event that results in the loss of coverage. Failure to comply with the act will result in an employer losing the income tax deduction for the cost of the health plan. Also, the employer may be subject to civil penalties and highly compensated employees will be taxed on employer contributions made in their behalf.

The following are **qualifying events** if loss of coverage by an employee or the employee's spouse or dependent child results:

- the death of the covered employee
- the termination of the employee except for gross misconduct
- a reduction of the employee's hours so that the employee or dependent is ineligible for coverage
- the divorce or legal separation of the covered employee and his or her spouse
- the employee's eligibility for Medicare (for spouse and children)
- a child's ceasing to be an eligible dependent under the plan

Under the act, any employee, spouse, or dependent child who loses coverage because of any of these events is entitled to elect continued coverage without providing evidence of insurability. The beneficiary must be allowed to continue coverage that is identical to that provided to employees and dependents to whom a qualifying event has not occurred.

The cost of the continued coverage may be passed on to the qualifying beneficiary but cannot exceed 102 percent of the total cost to the plan for the period of coverage for a similarly situated active employee to whom a qualifying event has not occurred. The continuation of coverage is not automatic but must be elected by a qualifying beneficiary. COBRA does not apply to group life insurance.

The 1990 **Americans with Disabilities Act** is having a major impact on employment practices, but employee benefits are largely exempt from its provisions. The act, however, does impose some restrictions on employers with respect to employee benefits. For example, a person with a disability who does not pose increased risks cannot be denied coverage or be subject to different terms based on the disability alone. It appears, however, that employers can deny coverage or require higher employee contributions based on medical underwriting.

The main focus of the **Health Insurance Portability and Accountability Act of 1996** (HIPAA) is to make health insurance coverage portable and continuous for workers in small businesses (2 to 50 lives). Employees who change or lose jobs and meet eligibility conditions must either be accepted into a group plan or offered an individual policy. The act restricts the ability of insurers to refuse coverage for individuals with preexisting conditions, and introduced the concept of medical savings accounts on a limited basis as a test (see chapter 20). The act also increased the deduction for health insurance expenses incurred as self-employed individuals.

The **Family Medical and Leave Act of 1993** requires employers of more than five persons to allow eligible employees up to 12 weeks of leave during any 12-month period for personal illness, birth, adoption, or illness of spouse, child, or parent. Employers must provide the same health insurance coverage as during active employment.

Postretirement Welfare Costs

After a long study, the Financial Accounting Standards Board (FASB) issued FAS 106. This standard effectively ended the pay-as-you-go *accounting* for nonpension benefits retirees. This rule does not change the actual cost of providing welfare benefits for retirees. At the same time, it has had a significant adverse effect on earnings for many companies. Employers must calculate the cost of providing coverage to all active and retired employees as a current lump-sum value and begin expensing a designated portion of that amount over employees' working years. Although the financial impact varies from company to company (depending on factors such as employee demographics and benefit plan provisions), many employers have seen as much as a tenfold increase in current accounting expense for medical benefits. This change in accounting treatment has forced employers to recognize that retiree medical coverage is an expensive benefit.

FAS 106 rules have resulted in two major changes by employers. First, many employers have lowered or eliminated retiree health care benefits or are considering such a change. Due to legal uncertainty as to the ability to eliminate or reduce benefits that have been promised to retirees, most employers are making changes in benefits available to future retirees only. Second, employers have increasingly explored methods to prefund retiree medical benefits.

The change in accounting treatment does not directly affect funding decisions. There is, as yet, no legal requirement or fully tax-qualified vehicle available to prefund retiree welfare plans. Employers have generally chosen to maintain pay-as-you-go financing while moving ahead to accrual-based accounting. Assuming the employer wishes to consider advance funding, a number of vehicles are available. In selecting one of them, employers must consider three key questions:

- Can employers take a tax deduction on contributions to the plan?
- Does the income from plan investments accumulate tax free?
- Are plan participants taxed on their benefits when received?

Using these criteria, none of the available funding vehicles meets all of an employer's needs. The available funding vehicles include (1) 501(c)(9) Voluntary Employees Beneficiary Association (VEBA) (a trust established to provide sickness and accident benefits to employees); (2) 401(k) Pension Plan Trust (a special account established within a company's defined benefit pension plan to pay for medical and life insurance benefits); and (3) corporate-owned life insurance. Although all three may be tax effective to an extent under current law, recent tax rule changes have significantly limited their attractiveness. HIPAA placed new, significant restrictions on the deductibility of interest paid with respect to loans against corporate-owned, leveraged life insurance (COLI) policies.

A *leveraged COLI program,* usually adopted by a large public corporation, involves the purchase of life insurance on the lives of a large number of employees (e.g., all employees over 55) as a corporate investment or as a means to finance indirectly the employer's obligation to provide postemployment life or health insurance benefits. The arrangement represents a major expansion of the concept of key person life insurance (see chapter 17).

Although effectively eliminating the ability to deduct policy loan interest under leveraged programs, key person life insurance policies and life insurance policies used to fund the buy-and-sell agreements of smaller businesses are largely unaffected by the changes.

State of the U.S. Health Care System

Despite devoting a larger share of its GDP to health care (see Figure 19-1) than any other nation, the United States is one of the few developed countries that does not provide universal coverage to its citizens. The U.S. health care system is characterized by increasing costs in a competition-based market, questions about quality of care, and lack of access to health care by millions of U.S. citizens.[6]

Competition in health care has become widespread since the mid-1980s. In the last few years, all of the stakeholders in health care have been scrambling to find the right approach, in terms of size and service, to remain competitive in the rapidly changing health care marketplace. The pervasive influence of managed care, the reductions in state and federal financial support, and the ever-increasing sophistication of health care technology have combined to offer remarkable opportunities to break away from outdated traditions and take venturesome risks. The result has been better monitoring and control of costs, but legislators seem far more concerned with quality of care in managed care plans than they do in the cost of plans or access to care for the 40 million uninsured Americans.

The most significant issue facing the U.S. health care system is lack of health insurance and, as a result, access to health care. Estimated at some 40 million, the uninsured are among the country's most economically and politically vulnerable citizens. Most are poor; two-thirds are in families with incomes less than twice the federal poverty level. Three-fourths of the uninsured are workers and their dependents. Many uninsured workers are employed only part-time, a growing segment of U.S. employment. These groups generally are in poorer health than those persons with health insurance.

Health care resources are scarce relative to needs. The appetite for health care is virtually infinitely expandable. Furthermore, even if the United States increased the total resources devoted to health care (at the state or national level), there is a point at which other societal goals would force a limit to the allocation. In this context of scarcity, fair access must mean universal access to a basic level of health care or a basic benefits plan. There is a growing consensus that this question of access to health care services by all must be resolved.

In sum, the public and the other stakeholders in the health care system have a general dissatisfaction with the manner in which health care has been delivered—the inexplicable variation in how patients are treated, the resultant costs, and the increasing number of people without access to at least a minimum level of basic care. Similar dissatisfaction exists among health care providers but for quite different reasons. Although the causes of the problems are easily identifiable, they do not lend themselves to simple, uncomplicated solutions. The vested interests in the traditional modes of health care delivery have repeatedly demonstrated their ability to generate political opposition to serious legislative challenges to the health care status quo. However, these same interests,

---

[6]This section draws from Sultz and Young, *Health Care USA,* Chapter 3.

including health care political lobbies, seem ineffectual in the face of overwhelming market forces. Rather than change occurring as a result of carefully crafted public policy, economic forces are driving a health care system reformation that is altering the roles of many traditional health care institutions. That some aspects of market-driven reform are painful and unpopular is simply a consequence of shifting the power from providers to purchasers and limiting consumer options. The end result, however, is expected to be a more comprehensive, coordinated, and cost-efficient system.

HEALTH INSURANCE PROVIDERS

Health insurance in the United States is available from five principal sources: (1) commercial insurers, (2) Blue Cross and Blue Shield organizations, (3) managed care organizations, (4) self-insured plans, and (5) federal or state governments. Each is discussed briefly here.

Commercial Insurance Companies

Approximately 1,000 U.S. commercial insurers write some form of health insurance.[7] These stock and mutual corporations are organized as life, property and casualty, or health insurance companies to provide medical expense and disability income insurance on a group or individual basis. The health insurance policies of commercial insurers generally provide for payment of benefits directly to the insured, unless the insured assigns payment to the medical services provider.

Although approximately 700 insurers write group insurance, virtually all group health insurance coverage is written by fewer than 100 companies. The 20 leading writers account for 63 percent of total group health insurance premiums and 78 percent of total individual health insurance premiums. At the end of 1995, more than 185 million persons were covered under policies issued by private health insurers.[8]

Blue Cross and Blue Shield Plans

The Blue Cross and Blue Shield Association coordinates the 58 Blue Cross/Blue Shield plans that operate statewide or regionally across the nation, mostly as nonprofit hospital and medical service corporations. These plans have tended to dominate the market for basic medical coverage in many geographic areas because of lower premiums from a favored tax status with the majority of states, and because of close ties to the hospitals and organized medical societies in the localities that they serve. Major medical and group dental insurance is also often available from Blue Cross/Blue Shield plans. At the end of 1996, more than 67 million persons were covered under Blue Cross and Blue Shield plans.

Blue Cross plans are nonprofit hospital expense prepayment plans. Most plans were organized by hospitals in the area served by the plan. Historically, member hospitals usually elected the board of directors, which normally included members from the public and the medical profession, as well as hospital administrators. Today, the composition of the boards has changed significantly to reflect more business and consumer representation.

The plans provide for hospital care on a service-type basis, by which Blue Cross enters into contracts separately with member hospitals for certain types and amounts of hospital services and then reimburses the hospital directly for those covered services rendered to plan subscribers. The subscriber, the Blues' term for the insured, is billed only for those services not covered by Blue Cross and, unlike commercial health insurance, there usually is no direct payment to the covered person.

---

[7]Because of the more detailed treatment of commercial insurers in chapters 11 and 23, this discussion is brief.

[8]HIAA, *1998 Source Book of Health Insurance Data*, p. 39.

The majority of Blue Cross plans are coordinated with Blue Shield plans. **Blue Shield** plans are nonprofit organizations offering prepayment coverage for surgical and medical services performed by a physician. Independently organized on a state or regional basis within a state, these plans are members of the National Association of Blue Cross and Blue Shield Plans and are now commonly controlled locally by a board of directors representing both the consumer and the medical profession. As in the case of Blue Cross, each plan operates autonomously, but the National Association's comprehensive contract definitions assure common administration from plan to plan for subscribers in large national or multistate groups.

The typical Blue Shield plan provides benefits similar to those provided under the surgical and physicians' expense benefit provisions of commercial health insurance policies. Blue Cross/Blue Shield major medical coverage is available on both a group and an individual basis. The major medical plans resemble those of commercial insurers. A deductible is involved and the subscriber usually must pay a 20 percent coinsurance until copayment expenses reach a certain amount, after which no coinsurance applies. The benefit maximum for major medical expense may be $250,000 or more. Many, if not most, Blue Cross/Blue Shield plans offer comprehensive major medical (discussed later) for their local groups.

The distinct advantage enjoyed by Blue Cross/Blue Shield has been the favorable tax treatment given these organizations. Although commercial insurers have long been subjected to federal income taxes, a variety of state taxes—including a significant tax on premiums received—and even certain local taxes, Blue Cross/Blue Shield organizations traditionally have been virtually immune to significant state taxes and are afforded relatively favorable treatment under the federal income tax laws. The trend at the state level, however, seems to be to tax the Blues as any other health insurer, and the Tax Reform Act of 1986 eliminated their complete exemption from federal income tax. Although the tax act eliminated complete exemption, various deductions result in an average effective tax rate for Blue Cross and Blue Shield plans that is below the average tax rate for insurance companies.

The Blues historically have been among the largest indemnity insurers in the United States and they collectively make up the largest health care entity in the country. They have responded to market demand for managed care products and services. Today, Blue Cross and Blue Shield plans collectively comprise one of the largest providers of managed health care in the United States. More than 44 million people are enrolled in a Blue Cross and Blue Shield managed care network. From 1986 to 1998, enrollment in such managed care plans increased from 13 percent to 64 percent of total, collective Blue Cross and Blue Shield enrollment (see Figure 19-4).[9]

In the 1970s and the 1980s, there was a consolidation of most Blue Cross and Blue Shield plans. In nearly all cases, this involved a complete merger; in a few instances, the consolidation was partial, resulting in a single staff but separate governing boards. To compete with organizations with large amounts of capital or direct access to capital markets to fund future growth, some plans have converted to for-profit status. Others have demutualized, and still others are consolidating or affiliating to form regional organizations. Although consolidation will provide the capital resources and economies necessary for geographic expansion and may relieve some of the pressure on profit margins, the Blue Cross and Blue Shield plans will need to continue to increase enrollment to compete successfully.

---

[9]*Fact Book: All About the Blue Cross and Blue Shield Organization,* Blue Cross and Blue Shield Associations, p. 4, and http://www.bluecares.com/know/factssystem.html.

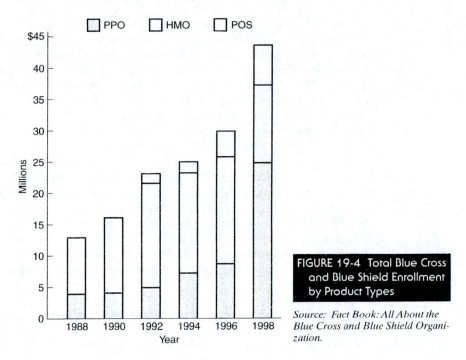

FIGURE 19-4 Total Blue Cross and Blue Shield Enrollment by Product Types

Source: Fact Book: All About the Blue Cross and Blue Shield Organization.

Managed Care Organizations

More than two-thirds of the U.S. population is enrolled in some form of managed care plan. The proportion of workers covered by managed care plans climbed from 58 percent in 1993 to more than 80 percent today. Clearly, managed care plans have become a major factor in the health care marketplace.[10]

Health Maintenance Organizations

Health maintenance organizations (HMOs) are legally organized entities that share the common characteristics of responsibility for both financing and delivering comprehensive health care services to a defined group of members for a prepaid, fixed fee.[11] HMOs differ from traditional insurance indemnity plans in that they are both the financing *and* servicing mechanism. They emphasize preventive medicine and early treatment through prepaid routine physical examinations and diagnostic screening techniques. At the same time, they provide complete hospital and medical care for sickness and injury.

The 1973 federal legislation and later amendments in 1976 essentially provided for substantial government funding through grant arrangements to encourage the establishment of health maintenance organizations. The most important support for development of HMOs came from the law's requirement that certain employers must offer their employees the option of coverage by an HMO as an alternative to traditional forms of insurance. This requirement ceased on October 1, 1995.

HMOs are the largest of the managed care approaches in terms of enrollment. About one-fourth of the nation's population is enrolled in HMOs.

---

[10]HIAA, *1997–98 Source Book of Health Insurance Data*, pp. 55–56.

[11]This discussion draws from Eric R. Wagner, "Types of Managed Care Organizations," in Peter R. Kongstvedt, ed., *The Managed Health Care Handbook*, 3rd ed. (Gaithersburg, MD: Aspen Publishers, Inc., 1996), Chapter 3.

The five commonly recognized HMO models are staff, group, network, individual practice association, and direct contract. The major differences among these models pertain to the relationship between the HMO and its participating physicians.

In a **staff model,** the physicians who serve the HMO members are employed by the HMO and typically are paid on a salaried basis but may also receive bonus or incentive payments that are based on their performance and productivity. At times, the staff model is referred to as a "closed panel" plan because participants are required to obtain all services from a staff employee. In the staff model, the HMO also operates the facilities in which its physicians practice, providing on-site ancillary support services such as radiology, laboratory, and pharmacy services. Hospital care and other services usually are purchased by the HMO through fee-for-service or prepaid contractual arrangements.

In a **group model,** the HMO contracts with a multispecialty physician group practice to provide all physician services to its members. The physicians in the group practice are employed by the group practice and not by the HMO. Physicians in a group practice share facilities, equipment, medical records, and support staff. The group may contract with the HMO on an all-inclusive capitation basis or on a cost basis.

In the **network model,** the HMO contracts with more than one group practice to provide physician services. These groups can be either multispecialty or small groups of primary care physicians (i.e., family practice, internal medicine, pediatrics, and obstetrics/gynecology). Network model HMOs may be either open or closed panel plans.

The **individual practice association** (IPA) involves physicians' organizations comprised of community-based independent physicians, in either solo or group practices, who provide ambulatory services to HMO members. Like the staff model HMO, hospital care and specialty services not available through IPA-participating physicians may be purchased by the HMO from other area providers, either on a prepaid or fee-for-service basis. HMO relationships with an IPA may be established on an exclusive or nonexclusive basis.

The **direct contract model** HMOs maintain contractual relationships with individual physicians in contrast to physician groups as in the IPA and network models. Unlike IPA models, direct contract model HMOs retain most of the financial risk for providing physician services.

Thus, HMOs are basically prepaid group practice plans that have an agreement with one or more hospitals for admission of enrolled members on a service-type basis, and a group of physicians organized into a cooperative to provide complete office and hospital care. Most HMOs are organized as group models.

HMOs typically accept enrollment only from clearly designated groups, such as employees of any of several employers, or residents of a particular locality, although some may permit enrollment from the general population on an individual basis. The plans are designed to provide an economic incentive to accept focused access to health care providers. HMOs also facilitated the development of managed care as a significant cost containment concept.

Until recent years, most HMOs operated as nonprofit organizations. The majority of new HMOs, however, are for-profit organizations. Although many subscribers are covered by HMOs that have been sponsored by consumer groups, a sizable and growing portion is covered by plans sponsored by insurance companies or Blue Cross/Blue Shield organizations. Physicians, hospitals, and labor unions also sponsor such plans.

Some insurers view HMOs as competitors and disagree with their sponsorship by insurance companies. Others view them as a viable alternative method of financing and delivering health care that can be offered to employers as one of the products in their portfolio. A few insurers and Blue Cross/Blue Shield plans provide multiple-option plans (i.e., HMO or an indemnity plan with a PPO) under a single medical expense contract. These simplify plan administration and, normally, the entire contract is subject to experience rating.

Preferred Provider Organizations

Preferred provider organizations (PPOs) are groups of health care providers that contract with employers, insurance companies, union trust funds, or others to provide medical care services at a reduced, negotiated fee. Like HMOs, they may take the form of group practices or separate individual practices. PPOs typically differ from HMOs in two aspects. First, they provide benefits on a fee-for-service basis as their services are used. Fees are usually subject to a schedule that is the same for all participants in the PPO. Second, plan participants have financial incentives to use the preferred provider network. A participant's access to specialists is not controlled by a primary care physician, as is the case in most HMO plans and all POS plans (discussed later). The proportion of employers offering PPOs increased from 36 percent in 1993 to 59 percent in 1996.[12]

Exclusive Provider Organizations

Exclusive provider organizations (EPOs) are similar to PPOs in their organization and purpose, but, unlike PPOs, EPOs limit their participants to participating providers. In general, individuals covered by an EPO are required to receive all their covered health care services from providers that participate with the EPO. Because of the severe restriction on choice of provider, only a few large employers have been willing to convert their entire health benefits program to an EPO format.

Point-of-Service Plans

Although not really a health care provider per se, a **point-of-service plan** (POS) is a hybrid arrangement that combines aspects of a traditional medical expense plan with an HMO or a PPO. In a POS plan, a participant's access to a provider network (usually an HMO) is controlled by a primary care physician. Participants retain the option to seek care outside the network but at reduced coverage levels. POS plans are sometimes referred to as "open-ended HMOs."

The POS plan is the fastest-growing health plan in the United States. In 1996, 36 percent of employers offered a POS plan, up from 28 percent the year before. Although POS plans remain most common among the largest employers, dramatic growth is characteristic of all size groups.[13] Figure 19-5 shows employee enrollment by type of health plan.

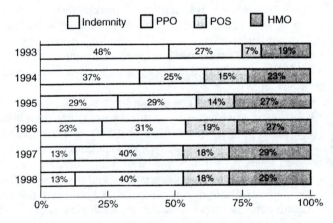

FIGURE 19-5 U.S. Employee Enrollment, 1993–1998

Source: William M. Mercer Companies, LLC, *National Survey of Employer-Sponsored Health Plans,* p. 12.

---

[12]Foster Higgins (now William M. Mercer Companies, LLC), *National Survey of Employer-Sponsored Health Plans,* p. 20.

[13]Ibid., p. 23.

Other Managed Care Organizations

Physician-hospital organizations (PHOs) are organizations that are jointly owned and operated by hospitals and their affiliated physicians and typically are developed to provide a vehicle for hospitals and physicians to contract together with other managed care organizations to provide both physician and hospital services. **Carve-out plans** are health care programs managed separately from an employer's general health care plan by HMOs or PPOs that specialize in a particular type of care. An HMO or PPO that specializes in a particular type of care may be more successful at controlling costs for that type of care than a general-purpose medical care network. Mental health, substance abuse, prescription drugs, and dental care are some of the more common types of care approached in this manner.

Self-Insured Plans

As discussed in chapter 18, employers have increasingly adopted funding methods that are alternatives to the traditional group insurance contract. Both medical expense and disability income insurance are made available through self-insured or self-funded plans of employers, labor unions, and fraternal or cooperative groups. These plans may require enrolled members to share in the funding through dues or contributions. The benefits provided under these plans are similar to those of commercial group insurance contracts but usually are the amount desired and affordable by a specific group of individuals.

Larger employers, particularly those with employees in more than one state, are likely to provide benefits through a trust governed by ERISA. Because ERISA preempts state insurance laws under certain conditions, employers that use a trust or self-funding arrangement do not have to provide the specific insurance benefits mandated in a number of states. The additional costs of providing mandatory benefits (see Box 19-1), which often differ from state to state, have led to an increase in self-insured groups. Insurance companies may service these groups under administrative service only (ASO) arrangements or by minimum premium plans (MPP), as discussed in chapter 18.

The continuing rise in health care costs is causing more and more employers to move to self-insurance. In general, the vast majority of large employers moved to some form of self-insurance in the 1970s and early 1980s. But as health insurance premiums have continued to rise, small- and medium-size employers have also turned increasingly to self-insurance.

The percentage of employers self-funding their health benefit programs varies by type of plan. Table 19-3 summarizes the use of self-funding by type of health benefit plan.

BOX 19-1

MANDATED BENEFITS IN THE UNITED STATES

U.S. state laws increasingly mandate specific types and levels of benefits that must be contained in medical expense contracts. There are more than 1,000 specific benefits mandated by state laws and regulations; at least 200 of these apply to HMOs. Recently, bills setting minimum requirements for coverage of hospital length-of-stay and bills requiring payment for emergency department services, even in nonurgent circumstances, have been adopted in a number of states. To the extent that these laws and regulations apply only to benefits that are included in insurance contracts, employers can avoid providing these mandated benefits by using alternative funding methods that do not involve insurance contracts (e.g., self-funding).

Source: Peter R. Kongstvedt, ed., *The Managed Health Care Handbook,* 3rd ed. (Gaithersburg, MD: Aspen Publishing Company, 1996), p. 831.

TABLE 19-3	Percentage of Large U.S. Employers Using Self-Funding by Type of Health Benefit Plan
Type of Plan	**Percentage of Employers Self-Funding**
Indemnity	68%
PPO	73
POS	55
HMO	10

Source: William M. Mercer Companies, LLC, *National Survey of Employer-Sponsored Health Plans* (1998), pp. 21, 25, 29, and 33.

As might be expected, large employers are most likely to self-fund their health benefit plans. For example, with indemnity plans, 59 percent of employees with 500 to 999 employees self-fund compared with 97 percent of firms with 20,000 or more employees. Similarly, with PPO plans, the corresponding percentages are 65 and 91 percent. Three-quarters of all employer-sponsored HMO plans are community rated and 19 percent are experience rated. Only 5 percent of all HMO plans are self-funded. Most self-insured plans purchase some form of stop-loss coverage.[14]

U.S. Federal and State Governments

Over 44 percent of U.S. health care expenditures is spent at all levels of government for health and medical programs, including funding for research projects and construction of medical facilities. Expenditures of the federal government were more than double those at the state and local levels.

The majority of federal spending for health services is directed to six major groups: persons eligible for Medicaid, persons eligible for Medicare, military personnel and their dependents, veterans, federal civilian employees, and Native Americans. The major part of state spending for health services is paid toward workers' compensation medical expenses, state contributions to Medicaid, and the public health programs of the nation's 53 official state health agencies.

Although most of the government programs are directed toward the indigent or to selectively defined groups, several important programs apply to the general public. These programs, discussed in chapter 22, are the benefits available from Medicare for medical expenses, from Social Security for disability, from workers' compensation, and, in five states and Puerto Rico, from temporary disability plans.

Questions

1. Compare and contrast market inperfections in life and health insurance. Are the economics of life insurance and health insurance the same?
2. What do you think are some of the advantages and disadvantages of the current health insurance system in the United States?
3. Support and/or criticize some of the steps being taken in the United States to control health care costs.
4. What advantages can employers expect by switching to self-insured health care plans?

---

[14]Ibid., pp. 16–30.

CHAPTER

20

HEALTH CARE PLANS: II

Objectives

■ Describe the benefits available under medical expense insurance plans.

■ Describe important features of major medical expense insurance.

■ Describe a variety of health care cost control techniques.

■ Explain the advantages offered by cafeteria plans and medical savings accounts.

■ Describe the benefits commonly offered by group dental and vision plans.

MEDICAL EXPENSE INSURANCE BENEFITS

Health insurance provides full or partial reimbursement for a wide range of health care expenses incurred by employees and their eligible dependents.[1] The particular coverages offered by plans continue to change and expand in response to changes in health services demand and technology. Basic benefits, plan components, and coverage arrangements are discussed here.

Hospital Expense Benefits

As with individual insurance, group coverage for hospital expenses normally distinguishes between the room and board charges and expenses for other hospital services. The **room and board charges** typically include the cost of a room, meals, and nursing services routinely provided to all inpatients. This benefit may be expressed as a daily payment for each day of confinement up to a maximum or as a service benefit with the benefit payment based on charges for a semiprivate room. Most hospital expense insurance plans have a special provision increasing the room and board benefit when use of an intensive care unit is necessary. The daily room and board benefit and charges for other necessary services and supplies resulting from a single confinement are payable under basic health insurance plans up to a maximum number of days per year, such as 31, 70, 120, or 365.

Coverage of **other hospital services**—sometimes referred to as miscellaneous expense, other charges, or ancillary services—provides reimbursement for hospital charges such as drugs and medicines, diagnostic X-rays and laboratory tests, and use of an operating room

[1]This discussion draws on Burton T. Beam, Jr., and John J. McFadden, *Employee Benefits* (Homewood, IL: Dearborn Financial Publishing, Inc., 1996) and HIAA, *A Course in Group Life and Health Insurance*, Part A, Part B, and Part C (Chicago: Health Insurance Association of America, 1994).

and ambulance service. The hospital miscellaneous expense benefit may be written on an unscheduled basis for up to some multiple of the daily room and board rate. Some plans pay in full up to a dollar maximum (e.g., $500) with coinsurance (e.g., 75 percent) for expenses in excess of the maximum. Other plans provide full reimbursement for miscellaneous hospital expenses.

Surgical Expense Benefits

Surgical coverage provides reimbursement for physician charges for surgical procedures. Surgical expense benefits may be provided on a scheduled or nonscheduled basis. Under a **scheduled plan,** a specific payment maximum is allotted for each surgical procedure. A typical published schedule may include 100 different operations that cover each of the important categories of surgical procedures. Reimbursement for unlisted procedures is based on a scale proportionate to the listed procedures.

Differences among company schedules are based on (1) the amount that they allow for each procedure; (2) the overall maximum benefit for multiple procedures; and (3) the relative or proportionate value of the procedures listed in the schedule to each other.

Schedules, referred to as **relative value schedules,** are sometimes denominated in units rather than in dollars. A factor that reflects the level of charges in a geographic area multiplied by the number of units provided for each procedure determines the maximum amount the plan will pay.

Under a **nonscheduled plan,** instead of a specific allowance, reimbursement of the surgeon's fees, and usually the anesthetist's fee, are based on the usual and customary charge for the procedure performed. A **usual and customary charge** is one based on the charges normally made for the service provided by physicians in the given geographic area. In the case of multiple operations, the benefit paid may vary depending upon whether the two or more operations involve separate incisions, are in different operative fields, or are separated in time.

Extended Care Services

Skilled Nursing Expense Benefits

Skilled nursing facility expense coverage provides reimbursement for medical expenses incurred when an insured individual is confined in an extended care facility and requires ongoing active medical and skilled nursing care. The definition of an extended care facility is important because the coverage is not intended to provide custodial care in institutions with little or no medical care facilities. Insurers either specify the services that must be provided or restrict coverage to those institutions approved by Medicare as skilled nursing facilities.

The amount and extent of benefits available vary. Thus, there may be a total dollar limit of each day of confinement in an extended care facility or a specific dollar limit for room and board and for necessary services and supplies. A daily limit expressed as a percentage (usually 50 percent) of the hospital room and board benefit available under hospital or major medical expense insurance coverage is used by some plans. Plans usually provide for a maximum of 30 to 200 days per confinement in an extended care facility.

Coverage is limited to those individuals (1) requiring supervised medical treatment, (2) confined in an extended care facility at the recommendation of a physician, and (3) under a physician's care while confined. It is common to require hospitalization for a minimum period (e.g., three to five days) prior to confinement in an extended care facility. In addition, many plans require that confinement in the extended care facility begin within a specific period (e.g., 7 to 14 days) from the date of discharge from the hospital.

Home Health Care Expense Benefits

Home health care benefits are similar to skilled nursing expense benefits but designed for those situations in which the necessary part-time skilled care ordered by a physician following hospitalization can be provided in the patient's home. The purpose of the coverage is to minimize institutional confinement when more comfortable and less expensive services can be provided in the patient's home.

Home health care coverage typically includes care by a physical, occupational, or speech therapist; periodic home nursing care; periodic services of a home health aide; medical social services; and care provided by a hospital intern or resident under an approved hospital teaching program. These services may be provided by a hospital or by a home health care agency.

Payment of home health benefits may require prior hospitalization or confinement in an extended care facility for the same or a related disability. In this case, covered home health care services must begin within a specified number of days following hospital or nursing home discharge.

Home health care coverage usually is limited to a maximum number of covered visits by a licensed health care professional. Thus, services rendered by a person who ordinarily resides in the individual's home or who is a member of his or her immediate family typically are not covered. Expenses for custodial care, meals, and general housekeeping services are usually excluded.

Hospice Care Expense Benefits

A **hospice** is a program of care for the terminally ill patient and his or her family with a focus on palliative care and social support services. Trained medical personnel, homemakers, and counselors (who make up a hospice team) help the patient and the family cope with the social, psychological, and physical stresses of death and bereavement. Most hospice care benefits may pay for additional home care and respite care for family caregivers, as well as hospice facility care, palliative drugs, and therapy and family counseling.

Hospice care expense benefits coverage typically pays usual and customary charges made by a hospice. The benefit period starts when an attending physician certifies that the patient is expected to live six months or less. Hospice coverage ends when the patient dies or at the end of a specified period (such as 6 or 12 months), whichever occurs first. A new benefit period may be established by recertification if the patient is still living at the end of a benefit period.

Other Medical Expense Benefits

A variety of coverages is available to finance other types of health expenses. For example, most plans cover the cost of diagnostic X-ray examinations and laboratory tests when these services are rendered in a physician's office or in a hospital outpatient department.

Most plans provide reimbursement for physicians' nonsurgical fees for acute or preventive care. Inpatient physician visits are often covered in full; outpatient or office visits (for nonpreventive care) typically are subject to cost sharing.

Coverage for mental and alcohol/substance abuse health benefits has increased during the past decade. In fact, they are commonly mandated by state law.

Typical reductions and limitations placed on inpatient and outpatient mental and alcohol/substance abuse health benefits include (1) limits on the duration of a hospital stay (e.g., 30 to 60 days as opposed to 120 to 365 days for other medical care), (2) reductions in the in-year maximum or lifetime maximum ($250,000 lifetime versus $1 million in some plans), (3) ceilings on the number of outpatient health services to be covered, and (4) lower coinsurance for mental and alcohol/substance abuse versus other medical services. The

Mental Health Parity Act, effective January 1, 1998, requires some plans to have the same benefit maximums for mental health benefits as for all other benefits.

GROUP MEDICAL EXPENSE COVERAGES

Group health insurance refers to arrangements in which coverage is provided for groups of individuals under a single master contract issued to a group contract owner. The contract owner may be an employer, an association, a labor union, a trust, or any other legitimate entity that was not organized solely for the purpose of obtaining insurance. Members of larger groups generally obtain coverage without having to furnish evidence of insurability, but such evidence usually is required for groups of fewer than 10 lives. Group health insurance plans generally cover the group member, his or her spouse, and any dependent children.

In the past, the basic hospital-surgical plans consisted of separate benefits for hospital expenses, surgical expenses, and physicians' charges. Coverage was limited and many types of medical expenses were not covered. Over time, basic coverages for other types of medical expenses were developed and employers began to provide more extensive benefits to employees. These basic coverages offered by private insurers (commercial insurers and Blue Cross and Blue Shield Associations) were gradually augmented by supplemental major medical plans and today have been almost supplanted by comprehensive major medical plans. Dental insurance, vision insurance, and prescription drug coverage have, for the most part, continued to be offered as separate coverage.

Major Medical Expense Plans

Major medical expense insurance plans provide broad coverage and significant protection from large, unpredictable, and, therefore, unbudgetable medical care expenses. From the beginning, most such plans covered a wide range of medical care charges with few internal limits and a high overall maximum benefit. Although born as a supplement to basic health insurance plans, there now is a stand-alone package known as a comprehensive major medical plan.

Supplemental Major Medical Plans

A **supplemental major medical plan** is a plan superimposed on a basic plan provided by an insurer or another company such as Blue Cross and Blue Shield. An insured individual is reimbursed for the charges covered under the reimbursement formulas in the basic plan as if the supplemental plan did not exist. All covered expenses not reimbursed under the basic plan are subject to a so-called corridor deductible before the supplemental major medical plan will begin reimbursement. After this corridor deductible amount has been satisfied, the supplemental major medical plan usually pays a percentage, such as 80 percent, of the remaining covered expenses. Thus, the claimant shares in the claim cost to the extent of the deductible plus the percentage of expenses not reimbursed as a result of the coinsurance provision.

Comprehensive Major Medical Plans

Comprehensive major medical expense insurance covers virtually all types of medical care services and supplies. The reimbursement formula applies to the total covered expenses subject to a deductible. Thus, a simple comprehensive plan could provide for the reimbursement of 80 percent of all combined covered expenses in a calendar year after a deductible of $300, up to a lifetime maximum of $1 million. The main advantages of comprehensive major medical plans are simple plan design, fewer first-dollar benefits to help control costs and utilization, and avoidance of duplicate coverage and frequent plan revisions.

A variety of modified comprehensive designs has been developed providing some first-dollar coverage. In some plans, certain types of expenses, such as hospital expenses, are not subject to a deductible, and no coinsurance is applied on the initial hospital expenses, such as the first $2,000 or $5,000. Surgeons' fees may be treated similarly, subject to a usual and customary fee limitation. It is possible to waive or modify the deductible and coinsurance features for other services, such as physicians' hospital visits and diagnostic tests, thus further matching the basic plus supplemental major medical concept. Most plans today provide a $1,000 or $2,000 maximum annual out-of-pocket cap on employee-paid expenses—a stop-loss provision. The elements of a particular plan reflect both the desires of the contract owner and the underwriting practices of the insurer. Figure 20-1 illustrates a comprehensive plan both with and without first-dollar coverage on initial hospital expenses.

Features of Major Medical Plans

Supplemental and comprehensive major medical plans have common provisions, such as covered expenses, deductibles, coinsurance, coordination of benefits, and overall maximums.

Covered Expenses

Major medical plans cover usual and customary charges incurred for most medical care services, supplies, and treatments prescribed as necessary. Exact eligible charges and their description vary from plan to plan. Coverage for confinements in skilled nursing facilities as well as home health care services and hospice care expense benefits are also covered.

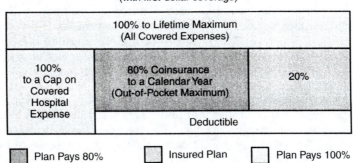

FIGURE 20-1 Typical Comprehensive Major Medical Plan Designs

Comprehensive Medical Policy
(without first-dollar coverage)

100% to Lifetime Maximum

80% Coinsurance to a Calendar Year
(Out-of-Pocket Maximum) — 20%

Deductible

Comprehensive Medical Policy
(with first-dollar coverage)

100% to Lifetime Maximum
(All Covered Expenses)

100% to a Cap on Covered Hospital Expense — 80% Coinsurance to a Calendar Year (Out-of-Pocket Maximum) — 20%

Deductible

Plan Pays 80%   Insured Plan   Plan Pays 100%

Deductibles

A **deductible** is a specified amount of initial medical costs that the participant must pay before any costs are paid by the plan. Thus, in a plan with a $300 deductible, the participant must pay the first $300 in expenses for covered health care services. The deductible provision usually has a family limit equal to two or three times the individual limit. After the deductible has been satisfied, the plan pays for additional health care expenses according to other plan provisions. In the past, a number of plans offered first-dollar coverage with no deductible or coinsurance required. Such plans have declined significantly in number in recent years. In meeting the deductible amount, an accumulation period feature recognizes the fact that small, frequent medical expenditures can accumulate to a significant amount in some cases. The **accumulation period provision** defines the period of time during which incurred medical care expenses may be accumulated to satisfy the deductible.

A variety of deductible provisions exists. The type and amount of the deductible and the way it operates, as with all design aspects of a plan, reflect the policyowner's desires and the underwriting requirements of the insurer.

Deductibles can be classified as all cause, per cause, corridor, and integrated. Under the **all cause deductible,** all expenses incurred are accumulated to satisfy the deductible regardless of the number of illnesses or accidents giving rise to the expenses. Under the **per cause deductible,** all expenses incurred because of the same or related causes are accumulated to satisfy the deductible. Benefits are paid, following the satisfaction of the deductible, for expenses incurred during the remainder of the **benefit period.** The calendar year is almost universally used for both the deductible accumulation period and the benefit period. It is also usual to include a **carryover provision.** Under such a provision, expenses incurred in the last three months of a calendar year (which are applied toward satisfaction of the deductible for that year) may be carried over to be used in satisfying the deductible for the next calendar year. A **family deductible provision** is usually included that waives the deductible for all family members after any two or three of them individually have satisfied their deductibles in the same year.

A **corridor deductible,** used in connection with supplemental major medical plans, reflects the fact that it applies after the basic plan benefits have been exhausted. The corridor deductible must be satisfied by additional incurred expenses before the supplemental major medical benefits are payable.

Supplemental plans also may use an **integrated deductible.** This deductible is defined as the greater of (1) a fairly high amount, such as $500, or (2) the basic plan benefits. For example, if the basic plan paid $625 and the stated value of the deductible was $500, the deductible would be deemed to have been met and supplemental major medical benefits would be payable.

Coinsurance

The term **coinsurance** refers to the percentage of covered expenses paid by a medical expense plan. Thus, a plan with 80 percent coinsurance will pay 80 percent of covered expenses while a person who receives benefits under the plan must pay the remaining 20 percent. The term **percentage participation** is used in some plans. Many plans apply a cap to the coinsurance and deductible amount to be borne by the insured (e.g., $1,000) by eliminating coinsurance for the balance of the calendar year.

Maximum Benefit

Except for specifically identified coverage limitations, usual and customary charges for all eligible expenses are covered by the plan provisions up to the overall **maximum benefit** of the plan. The overall maximum benefit may be written on a lifetime or a per cause basis. In this connection, a **reinstatement provision** is usually included. Because it is not uncommon to find maximums as high as $1 million and even unlimited benefits, the reinstatement provision has lost much of its significance. Box 20-1 shows the application of basic cost control features on a given claim.

Coordination of Benefits

With the increase in dual-income families, it is common for individuals to be covered under two group insurance plans, providing the potential for an individual to receive dual or double payments for the same medical bills. **Coordination of benefits** (COB) is used in virtually all group plans to prevent the recovery of more than 100 percent of actual health care expenses. COB requires two affected insurance plans to work together so that the bills are paid but the covered individual does not profit by receiving duplicate payments. Employee medical care plans coordinate benefits not only with other group medical insurance plans and health maintenance organization plans but also may do so with at least the mandatory benefits under state no-fault automobile laws and Medicare.

Retiree medical expense plans typically include more restrictive integration methods to deal with Medicare coverage situations. A method called **carve-out** or *maintenance of benefit* limits the total reimbursement to the largest benefit of the plans by first calculating the plan's normal benefit then subtracting to determine the employer's final payment. A second method, called *exclusion,* or *modified carve-out,* subtracts Medicare's payment from eligible expenses before plan benefits are calculated. These integration methods are rarely used with plans for active employees.

Subrogation

In general, **subrogation** means the substitution of another party (in this case the employer or the insurer) in place of a party (the employee or a dependent) that has a legal claim against a third party. Thus, an employee benefit plan that includes subrogation provides the employer or insurer that pays a claim, for which a third party is liable, with the rights that a covered employee or dependent might have against the third party. Such claims might arise out of workers' compensation accidents, and the employer's insurer could receive reimbursement if the employee or the dependent received benefits under a workers' compensation statute. The time delays involved in settling claims have historically caused some insurers to be reluctant to include specific subrogation provisions

---

BOX 20-1

DETERMINATION OF MAJOR MEDICAL CLAIM AMOUNT PAYABLE

SUPPLEMENTAL PLAN		COMPREHENSIVE PLAN	
Covered expenses	$4,000	Covered expenses	$4,000
Less expenses payable under basic plan	2,500	Less deductible	300
	$1,500		$3,700
Less deductible	300	Less 20% coinsurance	740
	$1,200	Benefit payable	$2,960
Less 20% coinsurance	240		
Benefit payable	$ 960		

in group insurance contracts, but the need for cost control has increasingly caused this provision to be included.

Major medical plans are offered by both life insurers and Blue Cross and Blue Shield. HMOs offer coverage at least equal to that provided under major medical expense plans, and often their coverage is more comprehensive. HMOs are more likely to offer a range of preventative care services such as periodic examinations, immunizations, and health education.

Comprehensive Medical Expense Plans

Comprehensive medical expense coverage is an adaptation of the major medical approach. Essentially, the structural approach of up-front deductibles and coinsurance is applied not only to supplemental medical services but to basic services as well. In addition to deductibles and coinsurance, other cost controlling features are included requiring second surgical opinions, full coverage for certain diagnostic tests, preadmission certification requirements for hospitalizations, utilization reviews by the insured or a third-party administrator, and enhanced reimbursements if procedures were performed at an outpatient facility. Comprehensive plans, as with major medical plans, have a maximum copayment (e.g., $10.00) after which the plan reimburses 100 percent of the usual, customary, and reasonable (UCR) fee. Special daily limitations and annual maximum and lifetime caps also apply. These and other cost control techniques incorporated in both major medical and comprehensive medical plans are discussed next. As these coverages have evolved, the comprehensive medical and comprehensive medical expense plans have become essentially the same.

COST CONTROL COMPONENTS

Comprehensive major medical benefit plans are rapidly replacing basic-plus supplemental major medical plans.[2] Compared to other types of traditional group insurance plans, a comprehensive plan is simpler to understand and easier to communicate to employees because it applies one overall reimbursement formula to covered expenses. Even though comprehensive plans differ in detail, most have provisions that encourage the use of outpatient treatment settings and encourage more effective use of health care services through various incentives. In designing a comprehensive health care plan, a large number of possible components is considered. These cost-containment techniques and components are considered here.

Basic Cost Controls

Cost control is a key issue in medical benefit plan design. Virtually all group medical expense insurance plans have traditionally incorporated certain basic provisions intended to contain costs: deductibles, coinsurance, internal benefit limits, coordination of benefits, and subrogation. These basic provisions were discussed earlier. As managed care has evolved, other approaches to control cost developed, some of which are discussed next.

Many experts believe employees who share in health care costs should do so at the point of service (i.e., by utilizing deductibles, coinsurance, and internal benefit limits) rather than through increased premium contributions (cost sharing) by employees. The increased premium contribution lowers the employer's health insurance premiums but does not affect the overall cost of health care.

---

[2]This analysis draws from Jerry S. Rosenbloom, ed., *The Handbook of Employee Benefits,* 4th ed. (Homewood, IL: Richard D. Irwin, 1996) and Peter R. Kongstvedt, ed., *Essentials of Managed Health Care,* 2nd ed. (Gaithersburg, MD: Aspen Publishers, Inc., 1997).

Various cost-sharing methods have become common components of health benefit plans but they should be reviewed regularly to reflect medical trends if participant incentives to control costs are not to diminish. A carefully designed and implemented utilization review program (discussed later) can help reduce the need to increase deductibles and coinsurance levels. Although maintaining cost sharing at a constant proportion of total costs is necessary to help control participants' overuse of health care services, it is often not well received by employees.

Second Surgical Opinions

Another utilization control that has been widely adopted involves obtaining a **second opinion** before surgery is to be performed. Second surgical opinions may be voluntary or mandatory. Voluntary second surgical opinion programs are less effective than programs requiring second surgical opinions for specified procedures. The purpose of a second surgical opinion program is to eliminate unnecessary surgery and to encourage plan participants to make a more informed decision regarding surgery.

Most plans with second surgical opinion programs provide 100 percent reimbursement for the consultation fee of the physician from whom the second opinion is obtained. Under such plans, payment is usually also made for any "tie-breaking" third surgical consultations and for related diagnostic X-rays and lab work.

Although a second surgical opinion program can be useful, most studies of such programs have found few savings. Many professionals believe that the real value of a second surgical opinion lies in educating participants to be better consumers of health care services and reducing providers' unnecessary surgery requests as a result of knowing the review process exists.

Preadmission Testing

The first day or two of hospital confinements, particularly for surgical procedures, are often devoted to necessary diagnostic tests and X-rays. **Preadmission testing** involves performing these tests on an outpatient basis, avoiding unnecessary hospitalization. Such testing has been widely adopted.

Utilization Review

Utilization review programs are a vehicle for coordinating a series of cost control innovations developed separately. Utilization review programs are concerned primarily with the appropriateness of care delivered in hospital settings. Most programs contain five components: (1) preadmission certification, (2) concurrent review, (3) discharge planning, (4) catastrophic case management, and (5) retrospective review including hospital bill audits.

Preadmission Certification

Preadmission certification programs require prior review of a hospital admission for nonemergency conditions and often outpatient surgery as well. Emergency admissions usually must be certified within 24 hours after admission. The purpose of preadmission review is to determine the appropriateness of care and to discourage admission of patients for testing and treatment that can be performed safely and less expensively in another setting.

Concurrent Review

Concurrent review is an ongoing monitoring of a patient's hospital stay to determine whether the patient is in need of continuing inpatient treatment. A variant of concurrent review, known as chart audit, is an on-site concurrent review. This approach seems to be gaining acceptance.

Discharge Planning

Discharge planning identifies the appropriate level of care a patient may need when a hospital setting is no longer necessary. The purpose of discharge planning is to enable patients to be released from inpatient care as soon as appropriate. As part of the review, special equipment and nursing services to care for the patient outside of the hospital are identified.

Case Management Programs

Case management programs involve professionals assessing a case, taking into account the patient's needs and treatment plan, managing the use of available resources, and evaluating the work environment situation. They are often included as part of utilization review programs or are available to employers from independent review organizations and many insurers. The initial stage of a serious illness (e.g., severe stroke or multiple sclerosis) or injury (e.g., major head trauma, spinal cord injury, or severe burns) is the point at which the final outcome can be changed most dramatically. With about 10 percent of claimants causing 70 percent of claim payments, it is essential to identify potentially large claims early. Such programs utilize case managers (usually nurses) and consulting physicians to manage large claims carefully, including the possible use of alternate care.

Firms specializing in medical case management work with medical care providers to implement alternatives if and when they are appropriate. The patient and his or her attending physician always have final control over the plan of treatment.

Mandatory preadmission certification and concurrent review are rapidly becoming general practice. Employers' plan designs often establish a schedule of penalties to motivate individuals to participate in the preadmission and concurrent review programs. Some employers impose a moderate penalty for noncompliance (e.g., an additional $100 deductible) whereas others decrease the employer's coinsurance share to 50 percent.

Retrospective Review

Many utilization review plans include a component involving retrospective review of large claims. **Retrospective review** involves a review of large claims enabling employers and health insurance providers to evaluate the utilization review process itself as well as the effectiveness of the professionals involved. Such reviews also include hospital bill audits.

The purpose of a **hospital bill audit** is to verify that a patient received all of the hospital services and items for which he or she was billed. Most errors during an audit are found among ancillary charges and intensive care services.

Increasingly, data management is an integral part of the managed care process. Claims data are analyzed carefully to determine a given plan's utilization rates, which in turn can be compared with average or target levels of utilization. This data analysis also can determine if particular health care providers are showing efficient and cost-effective practice patterns.

Other Cost Control Programs

Preferred provider, exclusive provider organizations, and point-of-service managed care plans, discussed in chapter 19, are viewed by employers and insurers as a significant factor in their efforts to control medical care costs. We discuss next a number of other programs designed to control costs and improve the quality of care.

Prescription Drug Copayment Plans

One method used to manage prescription drug costs is to encourage the use of less expensive generic drugs instead of brand-name drugs, subject to physician approval. The average cost of generic drugs can be as much as 40 to 50 percent less than the average cost of a corresponding brand name. Employers are encouraged to obtain a listing of generic substitutes for brand-name drugs and to share this list with employees.

Most prescription drug plans provide the covered employee an economic incentive to use generic prescription drugs by using a lower copayment (e.g., $5 for generic and $10 otherwise). Also, the arrangement with the pharmacy may also provide incentive to the pharmacy to dispense generic drugs.

A mail-order prescription drug plan is a convenient and reasonable arrangement for long-term and maintenance drugs. A six-month supply of drugs can be dispensed by a mail-order drug program, thus saving five dispensing fees and five deductibles. Although mail-order drug programs can save time and money, savings may be negated if medication is changed or discontinued soon after a large supply has been delivered to the patient.

Outpatient Surgery

Outpatient or **ambulatory surgery** is a program under which a patient has surgery performed and is released on the same day to recuperate at home. Outpatient surgery can be performed in a hospital outpatient surgery facility, a freestanding ambulatory surgery center (surgi-center), or for minor surgery, in a primary care center or physician's office. Surgical procedures that can be completed on an outpatient basis avoid the additional cost of hospitalization.

Health Education and Screening Programs

Helping employees improve their health status and reduce the probability of preventable risks is the single most significant approach to reducing the number and severity of health problems. Health promotion and disease prevention activities such as smoking cessation, high blood pressure detection and control, nutrition counseling, weight management, exercise, back injury prevention, and stress management can all be instrumental in managing health care costs.

Although promotion of healthful employee habits does not necessarily require extensive company resources for the program to be effective, it does require the commitment and encouragement of top management. Some low-cost yet potentially effective activities include such efforts as encouraging exercise and weight control by establishing company running or walking teams, providing space for before or after work aerobics classes, providing low-fat, low-salt foods in the company cafeteria and vending machines, and holding periodic health education and screening programs to teach about and detect serious illnesses.

Savings associated with health promotion activities are not often immediate and are smaller the higher the employee turnover rate. Many researchers are convinced, however, that such activities should facilitate a healthier work force and lower total health care expenditures.

Employee Assistance Programs

Employee assistance programs (EAPs) provide a broad range of services including counseling for marital and family problems, job-related problems, and emotional disturbances as well as alcohol and drug abuse problems. To implement such programs, larger employers frequently employ full- or part-time personnel for in-house counseling and referral of employees to local services. Smaller employers may establish such programs by contracting with an outside consulting service. In lieu of a formal employee assistance program, employers can also encourage self-referral by providing a community resource guide to employees.

Maternal and Well-Baby Care Programs

As an increasing number of women of childbearing age have entered the work force, greater emphasis has been given to maternity and children assistance programs as part of corporate health insurance plans. This interest was enhanced by the 1978 Pregnancy Disability Amendments to the 1964 Civil Rights Act requiring that health care benefits for maternity be the same as health care benefits for other conditions.[3]

Corporate prenatal programs include expense associated with prenatal/obstetrical, "well-baby" and "well-child" care. Medical costs for low birth-weight and preterm babies can range from $15,000 to over $100,000, compared with roughly $3,000 for the birth of a normal weight baby. In view of the costs involved, corporate prenatal programs can be cost-effective. In addition, sick babies may also delay or prevent a female employee from returning to work. Such services include physical visits, immunizations, well-newborn care, health education, developing screening, clinical, laboratory, and radiological testing.

Birthing Centers

Maternity care is one of the most frequent reasons for hospitalization. The birthing center concept (or hospital short-stay program for maternity) is an effective means of minimizing costs associated with routine maternity care. Birthing centers are usually freestanding facilities separate from a hospital. These facilities, intended for *low-risk pregnancies,* provide midwifery or maternity services generally delivered by a physician. The mother and child are discharged within 24 hours of delivery in most cases.

FLEXIBLE BENEFIT PLANS

Flexible benefit plans can provide a variety of benefits, one of which can be an effective cost containment tool. Cafeteria plans, including flexible spending accounts, and medical savings accounts are discussed next.

Cafeteria Plans

The term **cafeteria plan** refers to an employee benefit plan in which choices can be made among several different types of benefits. Section 125 of the Internal Revenue Code provides favorable tax treatment to a cafeteria plan under which all participants are employees who may choose among two or more benefits consisting of cash and qualified benefits. Qualified benefits include most welfare benefits ordinarily resulting in no taxable income to employees if provided outside of a cafeteria plan. Employees have taxable income only to the extent that they elect normally taxable benefits—cash and employer-paid group term life insurance in excess of $50,000. In general, a cafeteria plan cannot include retirement benefits except for a 401(k) plan (see chapter 21). Some benefits cannot be provided under a cafeteria plan, for example, scholarships and fellowships, transportation benefits, educational assistance, no-additional-cost services, and employee discounts.

A common type of cafeteria plan is one that offers a basic core of benefits to all employees, plus a second layer of optional benefits that permits an employee to choose benefits beyond those of the basic package. These optional benefits can be purchased with additional contributions or dollar/credits given to the employee as part of the benefit package.

Another cafeteria plan is one in which an employee has a choice among a limited number of predesigned benefit packages. The predesigned packages may have signifi-

---

[3]Many states have adopted laws that affect insured employers of as few as one worker but most often four or six.

cant differences or they may be virtually identical, with the major difference being in the option selected for the medical expense coverage. For example, the plan may offer two traditional insured plans, two HMOs, and a PPO. The increased choices provided covered employees naturally lead to some adverse selection. As a result, more and more employers are integrating flexible benefits and managed care to maximize employee incentives to elect and use cost-effective managed care programs.

Flexible Spending Accounts

In addition to normal cafeteria plans, Section 125 also allows employees to purchase certain benefits on a before-tax basis through the use of a flexible spending account. A **flexible spending account** (FSA) allows an employee to fund certain benefits on a before-tax basis by electing to take a salary reduction, which can then be used to fund the cost of any qualified benefits included in the plan. FSAs are used for medical and dental expenses not covered by the employer's plan and for dependent care expenses. FSAs can be used by themselves or incorporated into a more comprehensive cafeteria plan. The cafeteria plans of most large employers are designed with an FSA as an integral part of the plan.

The amount of the salary reduction must be determined prior to the beginning of the plan year. If the monies in the FSA are not used during the plan year, they are forfeited and belong to the *employer*.

The growing interest in cafeteria plans on the part of employers can be traced generally to a belief that (1) employees better perceive the value, nature, and relative costs of the benefits being provided; (2) a flexible benefit structure meets the varying and changing needs of individual employees; (3) because cafeteria plans may involve a limiting of employer contributions, this approach provides opportunities to control escalating benefit levels and costs; and (4) it is an effective way to direct employees into managed care with limited access to providers.

Medical Savings Accounts

A **medical savings account** is a tax-exempt, custodial account established for the purpose of paying medical expenses in conjunction with a high-deductible ($1,500 to $2,250 for single individuals and from $3,000 to $4,500 for families) major medical policy (see Box 7-2, chapter 7). The account is a savings account into which the insured (or an employer) can deposit money to be used for medical expenses not covered by insurance such as deductibles, eye glasses, or routine office visits. In contrast to FSAs, funds not used are allowed to accumulate and grow to help offset future expenses. Any funds not spent from the MSA eventually revert to the *insured*. This provides an incentive for the insured to spend carefully because the MSA funds are, in effect, his or her own money.

MSAs may be established by self-employed individuals or any employees of businesses with 50 or fewer employees who are covered under an employer-sponsored high-deductible health insurance plan. This program, established by the Health Insurance Portability and Accountability Act of 1996 (HIPAA), is a four-year "pilot" program ending on December 31, 2000, at which time Congress will evaluate the success of the program.

Some believe that MSAs may make sense when used with traditional indemnity plans but not with managed care plans. An argument against MSAs is that employees will focus on receiving cash at the end of the year by minimizing treatment for minor medical expenses and preventative care. This could lead to major expenses that could have been avoided or minimized with earlier treatment. Proponents argue that any technique that lowers costs for employers will encourage some small employers to provide coverage that would have previously been unaffordable. The most significant unresolved issue regarding MSAs is the challenge of incorporating them into a managed care environment.

OTHER HEALTH INSURANCE PLANS

Comprehensive health insurance plans are the standard approach. Although they have eliminated the need for many coverages formerly introduced as separate plans, dental insurance, vision insurance, and prescription drug coverages have, for the most part, continued to be offered as separate plans. In addition, a relatively new coverage, long-term care insurance, is also offered as a separate product.

Dental Insurance Plans

Group dental insurance has been one of the fastest-growing employee benefit plans. A **group dental insurance plan** provides coverages for almost all dental expenses. A unique characteristic of dental insurance is the inclusion of benefits for both routine diagnostic procedures (e.g., oral examinations and X-rays) and preventative dental treatment (e.g., teeth cleaning and fluoride treatment).

Benefits may be provided on a scheduled basis, on a nonscheduled basis, or on some combination of the two. A scheduled dental plan provides benefits up to the amount specified in the fee schedule. Most scheduled dental plans provide benefits on a first-dollar basis and contain no deductibles or specified coinsurance percentage. Benefit maximums are often lower than reasonable and customary charges leading to a cost savings by the employer.

Nonscheduled plans, often called comprehensive dental plans, resemble major medical expense contracts because dental expenses are paid on a reasonable and customary basis, subject to any exclusions, limitations, or copayments in the contract.

They usually include both deductibles and coinsurance provisions, but the provisions may vary for different classes of dental services. The typical plan classifies dental services into broad categories:

- diagnostic services
- basic services (e.g., fillings, oral surgery, peridontics, and endodontics)
- major services (e.g., inlays, crowns, dentures, and orthodontics)

Diagnostic and preventative services are typically not subject to a deductible or coinsurance. The other two categories are generally subject to an annual deductible (e.g., between $50 and $100 per person) and a coinsurance provision (e.g., 50 to 80 percent). The cost of basic services may be reimbursed at a high percentage (e.g., 80 percent) in contrast to major services, which are subject to a lower percentage (often 50 percent). There is also a maximum for benefits payable to any one person.

Vision Care Insurance Plans

Medical expense coverages long have covered expenses for diagnosis and treatment of an illness or injury of the eye. **Vision care expense plans,** on the other hand, provide reimbursement for the cost of eye examinations to determine whether the individual needs glasses and, if so, for the cost of required frames and lenses. Single vision, bifocal, and trifocal lenses usually are covered, as are contact lenses and other aids for subnormal vision.

To minimize overutilization, coverage usually is limited to only one examination and one pair of lenses or contacts in any 24 consecutive months. Medical or surgical treatment, sunglasses, safety glasses, and duplication of existing lenses or frames because of breakage or loss are commonly excluded. Dental and vision care plans are really not insurance but prepayment plans.

Long-Term Care Plans

Long-term care (LTC) is a relatively new addition to the insurance industry, and its products are still evolving to meet consumer needs. The growth of group LTC insurance can be described as slow and cautious. Adequate actuarial data needed to design and price coverage have not been available. Also, until recently, the tax status of group LTC coverage has been uncertain. Finally, participation in group plans has been modest because older employees who believe that they need the coverage often found it too expensive. In general, employers have been reluctant to contribute toward the cost of LTC programs.

Most of the early group LTC policies were designed for specific large employers, and much variation existed. Today, most insurers have a standard group LTC contract, which in virtually all cases is consistent with the provisions in the NAIC **Long-Term Care Insurance Model Act**. Group LTC policies tend to be comparable to the broader policies sold in the individual market discussed in chapter 7.

The primary purpose of the **Health Insurance Portability and Accountability Act of 1996 (HIPAA)** was to help ensure that individuals would not lose their medical coverage or be subject to new preexisting condition periods when they changed or lost their jobs. The bill included an increased health insurance premium tax deduction for the self-employed and provisions to reduce fraud and to simplify administrative systems. The bill also included LTC insurance consumer protection standards and provisions clarifying the federal tax treatment of the long-term care policies.

TAXATION OF GROUP HEALTH INSURANCE

Medical Expense Insurance Benefits

In the case of employer-provided medical expense insurance benefits, employer contributions are deductible by the employer and are generally not taxable income to the employee. Benefits received by an employee are not taxable to an employee unless they exceed the medical expenses incurred. In self-insured medical expense reimbursement plans, benefits to highly compensated employees may be taxable if the plan discriminates in favor of such individuals.

Because health insurance benefits realistically are not available for other types of consumption or for savings, it is logical that they should not be subject to a tax levied on net income. Another important policy justification for the health benefit exclusion is to encourage the purchase of private insurance to minimize the role of government in bearing the burden of health care costs.

Disability Income Benefits

As with all types of health insurance benefits, premiums (or other employer contributions) paid by an employer for disability income insurance for employees are generally tax deductible by the employer and are not taxable income to the employee. Employee contributions, on the other hand, are not tax deductible by the employee.

Consistent with these two rules, the payment of benefits under an insured plan or a noninsured salary continuation plan result in taxable income to the employee to the extent that benefits received are attributable to employer contributions. Thus, under a noncontributory plan, the benefits are included in an employee's gross income. Under a partially contributory plan, benefits attributable to employee contributions are received free of federal income taxation and benefits attributable to employer contributions are includable in gross income (employees are eligible for a tax credit, however).

A tax credit is available to persons who are totally and permanently disabled. This credit is taken on the employee's federal income tax return. The maximum credit is $750 for a single person and $1,125 for a married person filing jointly.

Long-Term Care Plans

It is easy to conclude that health insurance benefits utilized to pay for an operation or a physician's examination should, as a matter of public and tax policy, be excludable from income.[4] However, uncertainty has existed about the tax treatment of LTC mainly because LTC involves a combination of services, some of which are health care and others of which appear more like personal items (e.g., room and board in an assisted living facility). This uncertainty was resolved for certain types of policies with enactment of HIPAA. The legislation clarified that *qualified* LTC costs and benefits generally will be treated the same as other health costs and benefits.

If policies and insurers follow the consumer protection standards included in the law, such policies receive the following tax treatment:

- In general, benefits are excluded from taxable income. Benefits paid by per diem-based policies are tax free up to $175 a day, indexed for inflation. Insurers must report to the IRS the amount of LTC insurance benefits paid.
- Insurance premiums and out-of-pocket spending for LTC services qualify as medical expense deductions subject to the standard limitation. There are limits on the premium deduction based on age.
- Self-employed individuals can deduct LTC insurance premiums from their income, beginning with 40 percent in 1997 and ultimately reaching 80 percent of the premium in 2006.
- Employer contributions to an employee's LTC premium are excluded from taxable income of the employee. LTC insurance cannot be offered, however, as part of a cafeteria plan.

Passage of HIPAA is expected to increase interest in LTC insurance through the tax changes. Additionally, many consumers will learn about LTC insurance for the first time as a result of learning about the new tax treatment.

Questions

1. Explain the difference between the roles of a deductible and a coinsurance arrangement in a health insurance contract.
2. Speculate on the impact that the use of deductibles and coinsurance arrangements might have on the degree of moral hazard displayed by an individual insured. Would the impact on an insured's behavior likely be the same from both?
3. Existing incentives built into the U.S. health care system may promote inefficiency and unnecessary expenditures. How are utilization review programs trying to control these undesirable consequences?
4. Differentiate between cost control methods that increase the insured's share of costs at the point of service and those that do so through utilization review programs.
5. How are medical savings plans expected to improve the performance of traditional indemnity plans in comparison with managed care plans?

---

[4]This discussion draws on Health Insurance Association of America, *Long-Term Care: Knowing the Risk, Paying the Price* (Washington, DC: HIAA, 1997), pp. 104–108.

CHAPTER

21

RETIREMENT PLANS

Objectives

■ Understand how federal legislation supports as well as regulates the use of private pension plans.

■ Describe the common features of a pension plan, including eligibility, normal retirement age, and benefit formula.

■ Describe the limitations imposed upon the otherwise favorable federal tax treatment of pension fund contributions and buildup.

■ Describe methods used to finance private pension funds.

■ Describe the risks associated with pension plans that insurers underwrite.

INTRODUCTION

Each person has primary responsibility for his or her own welfare, or so individualistic societies such as the United States decree. Personal thrift has played and probably always will play a major role in providing for old-age security. Government efforts, for the most part, have been directed toward providing a basic minimum benefit, as a matter of right, through various forms of social insurance. With assurance of a minimum benefit, the employee, through individual effort, supplemented by any benefits an employer may provide, can seek to raise his or her old-age income to an adequate level. Tax-favored treatment has facilitated these efforts.

Private Pension Plans

One of private industry's most significant contributions to old-age security lies in the development of private pension plans. Every established firm eventually must face the problem of superannuated workers, and at that point it must choose among three alternatives:

- discharge them without a retirement income
- leave them on the payroll
- grant them a retirement income

For business, ethical, and legal reasons, the first choice is questionable and the second obscures retirement costs in the payroll and fails to provide a fair and efficient means of rewarding employees from the payroll. Because its flexibility permits the private pension system to meet the particular needs of various industries, a well-planned retirement

515

program of an employer for a company's employees usually proves to be the most efficient and cost-effective way to deal with superannuated workers.

In making the decision to install a retirement program, an employer naturally considers its competitive position within its industry and the value of the increased efficiency and production arising from its installation against the cost of the program (see chapter 18). Because of favorable tax treatment for qualified plans, the cost of a retirement program to employers has been relatively low. This fact has been a significant factor in the rapid development of private pension plans in the United States.

The rapid growth of private pension plans serves as evidence not only of the employer's interest in, but also of industry's acceptance of, the desirability of a planned retirement program. As would be expected, there is a variation in retirement programs worldwide. For most countries, employers are required by the government or it is their customary practice to provide both pension and lump-sum severance plans. In contrast to the United States, with its extensive collection of nondiscrimination requirements, other countries permit a pension plan design that favors highly paid employees. Some countries emphasize pension plans (e.g., United States) whereas others (e.g., Brazil) emphasize lump-sum severance benefits. See Table 21-1 for an overview of retirement plans in selected countries. As of 1992, the Department of Labor reported that there are over 700,000 defined benefit and defined contribution plans in existence covering almost 82 million participants.[1] As of 1996, approximately 65 million individuals were participants in private pension plans with life insurance companies in the United States.[2]

Emerging Pension Issues

Despite the past growth of private pension plans, the United States faces the major challenge of providing for the economic security of its elderly population without placing unreasonable tax burdens on future generations.[3] Public retirement systems, already burdened by the rising life expectancy and a trend toward earlier retirement, will experience a sharp rise in its retired population and the retiree–worker ratio when the "baby boom" generation begins to retire. Saving for retirement is insufficient to meet the income requirements of future U.S. retirees. This can be seen in the overall decline in contributions to retirement plans, the underfunding of many private and public plans, and low saving rates.

There are six primary sources of retirement income, the funding of which will determine whether retirees' incomes meet expectations. Box 21-1 highlights these. To the degree that funding falls short, either retirees' entitlements and aspirations will have to be curtailed (by delay of retirement or by reduced living standards during retirement years), or the intergenerational transfer of purchasing power from the working generation must be increased primarily through higher payroll taxes.

In recent years, there has been a gradual shift in coverage, especially among small employers, from employer-funded retirement plans to more discretionary saving vehicles. Many life insurance products have shifted the responsibility for investment decisions to policyowners (e.g., variable life and annuity products), leading to an important need for greater understanding of investment management.

---

[1]U.S. Department of Labor, Pension and Welfare Benefits Administration, *Private Pension Plan Bulletin* (Winter 1996), p. 59.

[2]*1997 Life Insurance Fact Book* (Washington, DC: American Council of Life Insurance, 1997), p. 24.

[3]This section draws on The ERISA Industry Committee, *Getting the Job Done—A White Paper on Emerging Pension Issues* (Washington, DC), July 1996 and Committee for Economic Development, *Who Will Pay for Your Retirement?—The Looming Crisis* (New York: CED, 1995).

TABLE 21-1 Overview of Retirement Plans (Pension and Severance) in Selected Countries

Country	Benefits Provided
Brazil	There are some private defined benefit plans, but defined contribution plans are growing in popularity. Severance plans resemble a defined contribution retirement plan with an 8 percent annual employer contribution.
Germany	Employers are permitted to establish tax-deductible book reserves without establishing a separate trust for pension schemes. Separate trusts and insured schemes are also common.
Japan	Lump-sum severance plans are universal, using tax-deductible book reserves as the funding mechanism. Separate pension trusts are allowable only for employers with more than 100 employees. Insured pension schemes are available for smaller employers. Pension trusts are subject to an annual tax of approximately 1.2 percent on the assets. No vesting is required. Employers with more than 5,000 employees may contract out of government-provided pensions.
Norway	Pension schemes are common only in medium-size and large companies. Nearly all plans consist of insurance contracts rather than separate trusts.
South Korea	Employer-provided defined benefit pension schemes do not exist. Lump-sum severance plans with low benefit levels are nearly universal. Individual defined contribution plans with employer contributions are becoming popular.
Thailand	Employer-sponsored pension plans are not mandatory but, where provided, the employees must contribute at least 3 percent of salary. Employers contribute at least as much as the employees and may contribute up to a tax-deductible limit of 15 percent. Invested assets are not in an irrevocable trust, thereby allowing the employer to capture some of the investment income as income to the company. This is equivalent to the book reserve method in other countries.
United Kingdom	A wide range of defined contribution and defined benefit plans is available. If the benefits provided are substantial, the employer can contract out of the government-provided pension benefits. Lump-sum payments at retirement are common, resulting in many arrangements that mimic the severance plans found in other countries. The United Kingdom is one of only a few countries that does not require a minimum recognition of accrued liabilities through separate funding or book reserves.
United States	With less than one-half of the work force covered, employer-provided retirement plans are not as common as in most other countries where there is nearly universal coverage of employees. A wide variety of defined benefit and defined contribution plans using tax-exempt trusts or insurance contracts is used. Non-tax-deductible book reserves, with no separate funding, are common for benefits provided to executives. Mandatory employee contributions are allowable but are not common. When employee contributions are mandatory or otherwise allowed, their tax status is dependent on the particular type of plan established by the employer.
Zimbabwe	Employees contribute 5.0 to 7.5 percent of salary into employer-sponsored defined benefit plans. Employers typically contribute an additional 10 to 12 percent of employee salaries. Funds must be in a separate trust with one-half of the trustees representing employee interests. Some 55 percent of all trust fund assets must be invested in government securities.

Source: Bruce A. Palmer, "Employee Benefits," in Harold D. Skipper, Jr., ed., *International Risk and Insurance: An Environmental-Managerial Approach* (Boston, MA: Irwin/McGraw Hill, 1998), p. 689.

BOX 21-1

SOURCES OF RETIREMENT INCOME

There are six primary sources of retirement income:

1. *Social Security.* About 90 percent of all U.S. workers participate in the Social Security system whose role is to guarantee at least a minimum level of retirement income for every eligible retiree. This government program has greatly reduced poverty in the United States, although 12 percent of older people are still below the poverty level. In 1994, the median benefit for an individual was about $9,972. The maximum annual benefit for a couple is now $20,646.

2. *Defined Benefit Plans.* The largest accumulation of private-sector retirement funds is in defined benefit plans, which promise specific benefits and are typically sponsored by large employers. Approximately 15 percent of U.S. workers are enrolled in such plans, although there has been a tendency for small employers to discontinue the plans because of excessive regulatory burdens and costs. These plans, in combination with Social Security, generally replace about 60 percent of preretirement earnings for those who have worked at least 30 years. Workers who change jobs frequently or work part-time often fail to qualify or accumulate adequate vested benefits from these plans. (Those who do become vested may receive benefits from more than one plan.) Government workers are generally covered by defined benefit plans, many of which are underfunded and frequently have made overly generous promises.

3. *Defined Contribution Plans.* These plans promise no specific retirement benefit; instead, employers make specific contributions (often according to a formula related to income or profits) to an employee's retirement account. Such plans are often favored by smaller firms because they are less regulated and have lower administrative costs and more certain contribution requirements. An important advantage of defined contribution plans is no public liability for inadequate funding. However, these plans often produce a lesser final benefit than a defined benefit plan. There are five times as many defined contribution plans in the United States as defined benefit plans, but many are small, and only about 26 percent of U.S. workers are active participants in a defined contribution plan that is their primary retirement plan.

4. *Personal Savings.* An important source of retirement income is personal savings, which has been traditionally relatively low in the United States. Personal savings has fallen from 9 percent of personal income in 1981 to 4.5 percent through the first six months of 1996. Nevertheless, personal savings is a significant source of retirement income.

5. *Postretirement Employment.* For many, jobs (usually part-time) provide meaningful opportunities and often a necessary retirement supplement. About 22 percent of U.S. retirees had income from earnings (in 1990). Under Social Security rules, for those under 65 and below 70 benefits are reduced for earnings in excess of certain limits. Social Security benefits are not reduced for workers who are 70 or older.

6. *Private Intergenerational Transfers.* The transfer of savings from deceased parents to children is an important source of income that for many could serve as a partial offset to shortfalls in their own retirement funding.

Source: The ERISA Industry Committee, Washington, DC (1996), p. 17.

Prompt changes in retirement policies are needed. To compensate for the rise in life expectancy, both business and government should encourage workers to take retirement at a later age. Many countries are examining ways to reduce their government pension schemes and shift retirement benefit costs to the private sector. In addition, gradual retirement or phased retirement, in which individuals move to a part-time employment plan, is being strongly encouraged (see Box 21-2). Policies should also be instituted that encourage savings and funding of pension promises.

Proposals to reform private pensions in order to improve retirement income security are under consideration. Debate continues concerning appropriate ways to meet the challenges posed by current economic and societal changes as well as the impending re-

BOX 21-2

GRADUAL OR PHASED RETIREMENT IN OECD COUNTRIES

Throughout many OECD countries, **gradual retirement,** or **phased retirement,** in which individuals move to a part-time employment status before retiring fully, is being strongly encouraged, commensurate with the increase in pensionable age. Gradual retirement may become a necessity in the future in developed countries faced with aging populations and threats to the financial security of their social insurance (retirement) schemes. Indeed, part-time earnings, resulting from some employment activity beyond the pension entitlement age, may become so significant in some countries that it will constitute a fourth pillar underpinning old-age financial security—in addition to social insurance, employee benefit plans, and individual savings for retirement.

Source: Lei Delsen and Genevieve Reday-Mulvey, "Gradual Retirement in the OECD Countries: Macro and Micro Issues and Policies (A Summary)," *The Four Pillars,* No. 18 (Geneva: Geneva Association, November 1995).

tirement of the baby boom generation. It is beyond the scope of this text to analyze and discuss the evolving national pension policy debate, although chapter 22 offers a short discussion of public pensions. The remainder of this chapter is devoted to current principles and practices in the private pension field.

CONCEPTS OF PENSION PLAN DESIGN AND OPERATION

Impact of Legislation

Income Tax Law

The U.S. federal income tax law is quite favorable to the establishment of qualified pension programs. This is because (1) employer contributions are deductible from corporate taxable income as ordinary and necessary business expenses in determining the income tax; (2) investment earnings of a qualified pension plan are exempt from income taxation until benefits are paid out; and (3) employer contributions are not taxable to employees as income in the years in which they are contributed, but rather at such time as they are received in the form of benefits (usually after retirement, at a lower tax rate). If the full benefit is received in a single year, it may be eligible for favorable lump-sum income taxation. As a practical matter, few funded plans are not qualified within the meaning of the tax law.

The requirements for a plan to be qualified are summarized in Box 21-3.

Employee Retirement Income Security Act

In addition to the federal income tax law, the **Employee Retirement Income Security Act** (ERISA) of 1974 is exceedingly important for retirement plan design and operation. The provisions of ERISA pertaining to participation, vesting, and funding influence virtually every aspect of retirement plan design in the United States.

Limitations on Contributions and Benefits Contributions to and benefits received under qualified plans are limited by ERISA. With respect to defined benefit plans—generally a plan whose benefits are fixed and the contributions vary (discussed later)—the plan must provide that the annual benefit (1999) may not exceed the lesser of (1) $130,000 (adjusted annually for cost-of-living changes) or (2) 100 percent of the

BOX 21-3

KEY REQUIREMENTS OF QUALIFIED PLANS

For a pension or other retirement plan to be recognized as a **qualified plan** under U.S. law, it must meet the following general requirements:

- *A written, legally binding arrangement* must exist and must be *communicated* to the employees.
- The plan must be established with the intent that it be a permanent and continuing arrangement and must be for the *exclusive* benefit of employees or their beneficiaries.
- It must be impossible for the principal or income of the plan to be *diverted* from these benefits to any other purpose until all liabilities have been satisfied.
- The plan must benefit a broad class of employees and *not discriminate* in favor of officers, stockholders, or highly compensated employees.
- The plan must meet certain *minimum requirements of participation and vesting.*
- The plan must provide that, in the event of a plan merger, each participant's *benefit under the resulting plan will be at least equal to the benefit* to which he or she would have been entitled had the plan terminated prior to the merger.

- The plan must provide that a participant's benefits under the plan *may not be assigned or alienated* except as required under a qualified domestic relations order.
- The plan must stipulate *when benefit payments will commence* (and this time is subject to certain stipulated maximums) and provide for the minimum distribution requirements.
- If the participant is married, the plan must, under certain circumstances, provide for a joint and survivor or survivor annuity.
- The plan must provide for *limitations on compensation recognized for plan benefit determination purposes and on maximum benefits to be provided.*
- The plan must provide that benefits to a participant or beneficiary *may not be decreased by reason of increases in Social Security benefits* following the earlier of the termination of employment or the commencement of receipt of benefits under the plan.
- The plan must provide for a *claims review procedure* if the claim of a participant or beneficiary is disallowed.

participant's highest average compensation for three consecutive years. Notwithstanding this limitation, however, ERISA permits an annual benefit of at least $10,000 for an employee if he or she has not participated in a defined contribution plan—generally a plan in which contributions are fixed and benefits vary—of the employer (discussed later). If a participant has less than 10 years of plan participation or 10 years of service or retires prior to attaining Social Security normal retirement age, reductions in the amount of the maximum allowable benefits and the percentage of compensation limits under the plan must be made. Reductions must also be made if benefits are paid in a form other than a life annuity or a qualified joint and survivor annuity.

With respect to defined contribution plans, the annual addition to a participant's account may not exceed the lesser of (1) $30,000 (adjusted annually for cost-of-living changes) or (2) 25 percent of the participant's covered compensation for the year. For purposes of the limitation, annual additions to an employee's account include employer contributions, forfeitures, and 100 percent of after-tax employee contributions. For this purpose, pretax employee contributions are treated as employer contributions.

Prohibited Transactions and Fiduciary Responsibility   Plan assets must be legally separated from those of the employer or other sponsoring organization. This is to comply with ERISA's fiduciary requirements as well as the IRS code mandate that the plan be operated for the exclusive benefit of participants and their beneficiaries. This segregation of assets can be accomplished by having them held in trust or held by a life insurance company under a contract. A trust may be used for convenience or control even when an insurer holds and manages the assets with the insurance or annuity contract treated as part of trust assets.

ERISA imposes certain excise taxes on prohibited transactions between the trust and disqualified persons. **Prohibited transactions** include the sale, exchange, leasing, lending (except for certain loans to the participant), and furnishing of goods or services between the plan and a disqualified person. A *disqualified person* includes, among others, the employer, any fiduciary of the plan, a service provider, an employee organization, the trustee, and substantial owners of the organization. The tax is initially 15 percent of the amount involved in the transaction and is imposed on the disqualified person. The failure of the disqualified person to correct the transaction within a prescribed time could result in an additional penalty tax of 100 percent of the amount involved. The Department of Labor, however, is authorized to provide exemptions from the prohibited transaction restrictions and has done so in many cases.

ERISA also requires that a plan fiduciary discharge its duties solely in the interest of the plan participants and their beneficiaries. In regard to its conduct, the fiduciary is held to a strict **prudent-person standard** that requires the fiduciary to act with the care, skill, prudence, and diligence under the prevailing circumstances that a prudent person acting in a like capacity and familiar with such matters would use. In addition, a fiduciary can be personally liable for breaches by a cofiduciary. ERISA also provides limitations and requirements with respect to (1) the investment of fund assets in employer securities or employer real property, (2) plan termination insurance, and (3) reporting and disclosure. The Internal Revenue Service (IRS) with respect to a plan qualification also makes provision for judicial review of an adverse decision.

The legal and tax details of pension plans are complex, and a complete discussion is beyond the scope of this text.[4] Because these laws and regulations play such a major role in every aspect of the creation, design, and operation of a pension plan, several general aspects are nonetheless covered next.

Private Pensions: The Employee Perspective

Private pension and profit-sharing plans and products are marketed more to plan sponsors/employers than they are to the employees/beneficiaries. As a result, the employer's needs are given priority in designing and financing a given plan. Thus, issues such as the desire to attract and retain employees, budget constraints, tax reduction and tax shelter advantages, efficient administration, and superior investment returns are generally among the key considerations and make up the primary issues from an employer's perspective. Although the needs of the average employee are considered by human resources managers, the decision-making process does not always give adequate consideration to the retirement needs and concerns of the covered employees. As noted elsewhere in this volume, the market has seen, however, the emergence of retirement security for individuals as a significant issue. Therefore, the design of effective retirement programs that will stand the test of time and be fully appreciated and utilized by employees/beneficiaries requires consideration of the employee's perspective.

As discussed in chapter 16, the purpose of a retirement program (whether it involves a defined benefit plan, a defined contribution plan, or both) is to provide retirees a reasonable degree of financial security. Employee concerns about the impact of inflation, the security and adequacy of Social Security benefits, the cost of postretirement medical

---

[4]See Dan M. McGill, Kyle N. Brown, John J. Haley, and Sylvester J. Scheiber, *Fundamentals of Private Pensions,* 7th ed. (Philadelphia, PA: University of Pennsylvania Press, 1996) for a detailed treatment of private pensions. This chapter draws heavily on this volume.

care, the financial solidity of insurers' promises, and the employer's willingness and ability to maintain its retirement benefit program are factors that should be considered in the decisions relating to pension plan design and funding. Insurers should also keep the employees' perspective in mind in developing products and services for the private pension market.

Pension Plan Design

Coverage Requirements

A qualified pension plan must set forth rules to determine who will be covered by the plan. Relatively few plans cover all employees of an employer. Coverage may be restricted based on an age and/or service criteria. For example, employees who always work fewer than 1,000 hours per year are frequently excluded from coverage. Coverage also may be restricted based on a reasonable classification, such as to employees of a given plant or division or to employees covered by a collective bargaining agreement. IRS regulations require that noncollectively bargained plans must cover at least 70 percent of all nonhighly compensated employees, or the percentage of the nonhighly compensated employees covered must be at least 70 percent of the percentage of highly compensated employees benefiting under the plan, or the plan benefits a nondiscriminatory classification of employees and passes an average benefits test. IRC §401(a)(26) requires that such defined benefit plans cover at least the lesser of 50 employees or 40 percent of all employees of the employer.

Pension plans may make coverage for the individual employee contingent upon a minimum length of service (eligibility period) or attainment of a certain minimum age or both. A plan may not require, as a condition of participation, a minimum period of service longer than one year or a minimum age of more than 21 years. However, it may require two years of service if it provides for the full and immediate vesting of all participants upon entry into the plan. **Vesting** refers to the employee's nonforfeitable rights in employer contributions (discussed later).

For coverage testing purposes, employees of all corporations, partnerships, and other businesses who are members of a controlled group are treated as if they were employees of a single employer. A qualified plan cannot exclude from eligibility employees who are hired after a specified age (such as age 60), but it can defer the normal retirement age to the fifth anniversary of participation. Such eligibility requirements are intended to reduce the cost of the plan by eliminating certain groups of employees who show a record of high turnover, by deferring the retirement benefits for those hired who are close to retirement, and by simplifying the administration of the plan.[5] In any case, the eligibility provisions must be drawn carefully to meet the objectives intended, taking into account the nondiscrimination requirements of the Internal Revenue Code; the Civil Rights Act of 1964, which has been interpreted to require nondiscriminatory provisions for male and female employees; and the Age Discrimination in Employment Act.[6]

Normal Retirement Age

Every pension plan must define a **normal retirement age,** which is the youngest age for which an employee is entitled to retire with full benefits. This cannot be later than age 65 (or the fifth anniversary of plan participation if later). This is necessary because a fixed

---

[5]The purpose of deferring the retirement age for employees who are hired when they are close to retirement is to minimize the cost of a defined benefit pension program. The cost of providing a defined benefit pension increases with the age of the employee. In addition, an employer normally feels less responsibility for the retirement needs of a person who was in his or her service for only a few years before retirement.

[6]Generally, the Age Discrimination in Employment Act does not prohibit age provisions normally included in a qualified retirement plan, although there are some exceptions.

age or schedule of ages for retirement is fundamental in estimating costs, in determining the appropriate rate of accumulating funds for retirement benefits, and, most important, in permitting organizations and employees to plan for retirement. Virtually all pension plans also make provision for early or deferred retirement, subject to certain conditions.

It is possible, of course, to establish a range of ages at which employees are permitted to retire, such as 55 to 65. In such cases, an assumption is made, in estimating costs, as to the distribution of employees retiring at each age. Many negotiated pension plans do not explicitly state one specific early retirement age; instead they base it on years of service. This, of course, is applicable only to defined benefit plans. Defined contribution plans, by their nature, do not face the same issues, although normal retirement age must be defined by the plan.

Benefit Formulas

Because an employee's standard of living normally is related to his or her earnings, it is important that retirement benefits bear a reasonable relationship to those earnings.[7] For an employee to have an adequate income at the time he or she retires, it generally has been considered necessary to have an income, including Social Security, that is approximately 70 to 75 percent of his or her average compensation in the years immediately preceding retirement. The target retirement benefit, of course, varies by income level. Table 21-2 presents a study of gross and net (of Social Security benefits) replacement ratios for retirees.[8]

Because of inflation and the fixed nature of most pension arrangements, a problem that also receives attention is maintaining the adequacy of income after retirement. Some possible approaches to this problem are (1) cost-of-living or wage-indexed benefits,

TABLE 21-2	Comparison of Gross and Net (of Social Security Benefits) Income Replacement Ratios	
Preretirement Salary	**Replacement Ratios[a]**	
	Gross Ratios	**Net Ratios**
$20,000	84%	22%
$30,000	77%	23%
$40,000	72%	24%
$50,000	69%	28%
$60,000	67%	32%
$70,000	67%	36%
$80,000	68%	41%
$90,000	71%	47%

[a]Assumptions: Married couple; one wage earner; worker, age 65; spouse, age 62.

Source: 1997 *Georgia State University/AON RETIRE Project Report.*

---

[7]Historically, the great majority of union-negotiated plans provide benefits that are tied to length of service rather than to earnings and it is typically assumed that the duration of employment within the collective bargaining unit is such that the average employee will have a retirement benefit, including Social Security, that is comparable (as a percentage of earnings) to that of salaried employees. Additionally, if a union group has less variation in pay, such a formula can provide retirement income that is a reasonable percentage of the employee's pay.

[8]See Bruce A. Palmer, Georgia State University/AON, *RETIRE Project Report* (The Center for Risk Management and Insurance Research, 1997).

(2) periodic increases in benefits for retired employees on an ad hoc basis, and (3) encouraging employees to save during working years the amount they expect they will need to cover the increased cost of living in retirement years.

Traditionally, benefit formulas have been placed into two broad categories: (1) defined benefit and (2) defined contribution. Under a **defined benefit plan,** a fixed benefit payable at retirement is developed by a formula, and the cost of the plan will depend on the age, earnings distribution of eligible employees, and the operating experience (i.e., mortality, turnover, salary increases, investment return, and expenses) of the plan. A **defined contribution plan** establishes a rate or amount of annual contributions to be made by the employer only (noncontributory plans) or employee and employer jointly (contributory plans), and the amount of benefit provided at retirement for each employee depends on the amount accumulated in the employee's account, which varies depending on the age, contribution amounts, investment return earned on the accumulated contributions, and length of time covered under the plan. Thus, in defined benefit formulas, the benefit is fixed and the contribution varies, whereas in a defined contribution approach, the employer's contribution is defined by formula (or may be determined annually in the case of a profit sharing or stock bonus plan) and the benefit amount varies.

A defined contribution plan provides an individual account for each participant and bases the employee's benefits solely on the amount contributed to the participant's account and on any expense, investment return, and forfeitures allocated to the participant's account. Because the definition of the basis for contribution(s) is completely flexible, several variations of defined contribution plans have evolved with the dual objectives of provision of retirement income and deferral of current taxable income, as discussed later. When a participant becomes eligible to receive a benefit, his or her benefit equals a lump-sum distribution or, in some plans, an annuity equal to the amount that can be provided by the fund balance.

In addition to the defined benefit and defined contribution formulas, there are also hybrid plans. One such plan is referred to as a target-benefit plan. The **target-benefit plan** is a defined contribution plan that targets benefit levels like a defined benefit plan. Under a target-benefit plan, the employer chooses a target level of retirement benefit using a benefit-formula approach similar to that used in designing a defined benefit plan. The contributions necessary to fund this target are then determined, based on assumed interest and mortality factors. Once the amount of the contribution (stated as a percentage of the participant's compensation) is determined, the plan then operates as a defined contribution plan. The participant is entitled, upon his or her retirement, to the equivalent annuity benefits that can be purchased by the amount in his or her account, rather than the target benefit used to establish the amount of the employer's contribution to be made on the employee's behalf.

Another hybrid plan, known as a **cash-balance plan,** is a form of defined benefit plan that operates like a defined contribution plan. It combines some of the features of defined benefit plans with some features of defined contribution plans. Employer contributions are based on age at entry, but ultimate benefits are based on actual investment returns. Under a cash balance plan, employer contributions are actual benefit credits based on compensation, and sometimes age and/or service, and the ultimate benefit (account balance) is subject to the accumulation of these credits at a guaranteed rate of return. Each participant has an "individual account" (not a true accounting separate account) that increases at least annually to reflect new benefit credits and credited interest. This account balance is recorded in a memorandum account. Employer contributions may or may not actually be deposited annually into the plan for each participant according to a benefit formula (e.g., 5 percent of compensation). The account is credited with interest as specified in the plan (e.g., a flexible rate such as the average rate on one-year Treasury bills or a fixed rate). Because the benefit is defined by a formula that is based on compensation (e.g., career average or final average compensation), the employer has funding flexibility and is responsible for the actual investment risk as in a defined-benefit plan.

When a participant leaves or retires, the vested portion of the account balance can typically be taken in cash or in the form of an annuity. This use of liberal vesting provisions makes the plan benefits portable, and naturally this is viewed favorably by participants. Also, cash-balance plans are considered easier for employees to understand than other types of defined benefit plans. Accelerated vesting schedules may increase the employer's costs, although employers often adopt this type of a formula in conjunction with other changes. The use of individual accounts, cash distribution upon termination of employment, and easier communication with participants are typical features of defined contribution plans. A variety of other hybrid plans also combine features of both defined benefit and defined contribution plans.

Because of the increasing popularity of benefit formulas based on account balances, the fixed-benefit nature of a defined benefit plan has lost some of its popularity (see Figure 21-1). Although the defined benefit formula may produce a fixed benefit for a given year of service, the final retirement benefit is often a function of the employee's compensation in his or her final years of service prior to retirement. Thus, the defined benefit is not really definite as to amount until it has been recomputed based on the employee's final years of pay—frequently the average of his or her last three to five years of credited service prior to retirement. (This feature serves to protect the individual's retirement benefits from inflation during his or her working career but makes the benefit more difficult to predict.)

Many collective bargaining agreements involve defined contributions but with distinct characteristics. These so-called **Taft-Hartley plans** really are not defined contribution plans; the benefit is defined as well as the contribution. This is an actuarial anomaly because only by sheer coincidence could these two fixed functions remain in balance over any time period. Practically, the anomaly is resolved through periodic adjustments of the benefit scale, the contribution rate, or both. These plans are considered defined benefit plans for purposes of ERISA.

Defined benefit formulas may be a flat amount, or they may be related to earnings, to service, or to a combination of earnings and service. Thus, a given formula may provide a retirement benefit of $300 a month regardless of earnings or service, 30 percent of final average pay, 1.5 percent of annual pay for each year of credited service, or other formulas. In any case, where appropriate, earnings and service are specifically defined.

Defined benefit formulas based upon earnings are frequently integrated with Social Security benefits. There are two approaches: (1) the offset approach and (2) the integration-level approach.

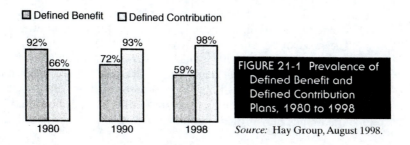

Percentage of Employers Offering

□ Defined Benefit   □ Defined Contribution

92%	93%	98%
66%	72%	59%
1980	1990	1998

FIGURE 21-1 Prevalence of Defined Benefit and Defined Contribution Plans, 1980 to 1998

Source: Hay Group, August 1998.

Under the offset approach, an integrated benefit provides an offset to the plan benefit for the actual or estimated Social Security benefit. In the case of the integration-level approach, a larger benefit is provided based on earnings in excess of the Social Security wage base per annum is provided. This latter integration method recognizes the fact that the employer pays taxes on wages up to the Social Security wage base and that Social Security benefit formulas are weighted in favor of the lower-income amounts.

Defined benefit formulas based on service frequently give credit for both **past service**—that is, service prior to the installation of the plan—and **future service**—that is, after the installation of the plan. Generally, the total cost of the credits granted for past service represents the **initial past-service liability** at the date of plan installation. Credit for past service is sometimes limited by counting service after a given age only, such as 35 or 40, or by limiting the number of years' credit for past service to, say, 15 or 20. The resulting benefit must not discriminate in favor of highly compensated employees. In any case, an employee's retirement benefit is the total of past- and future-service credits under the pension plan at retirement.

Maximum Benefits

Before ERISA, it was not customary for plans to impose an upper limit on benefits payable (other than that implicit in a flat benefit formula). ERISA and later amendments imposed a limit on the benefits that can be provided under a qualified defined benefit plan and a limit on the contributions under a defined contribution plan. In addition, there is a maximum limit on compensation that can be recognized in the benefit formula under all qualified plans.

No qualified plans may take into account compensation in excess of $160,000 in determining benefits or contributions. This $160,000 limit is subject to cost-of-living adjustments in the same manner as the dollar limits on benefits discussed earlier. Additional requirements apply to contributions and benefits under a top-heavy plan. A **top-heavy plan** is one under which the value of accrued benefits for key employees (certain officers and owners) and their beneficiaries exceeds 60 percent of the value of accrued benefits for all employees and their beneficiaries. Many small plans are top-heavy. Whether a plan is top-heavy is determined each plan year.

If a plan is top-heavy, it is subject to more rapid vesting, and, for nonkey employees, minimum benefits or contributions. As a practical matter, when the requirement applies, most plans usually apply it to all employees.

Supplemental Benefits

In addition to a retirement income, many pension programs include death, disability, or other supplemental benefits during the preretirement period. Naturally, which supplemental benefits are provided will depend on the personnel policy, finances, and other individual circumstances of the employer. Supplemental death and disability benefits are subject to requirements and limitations imposed by IRS regulations.

The Retirement Equity Act of 1984 provides for automatic death benefits payable to qualified spouses for all vested participants—whether they are active, terminated, or retired—under defined benefit pension plans. Both the participant and the spouse may waive a death benefit in the form of a joint and survivor annuity in writing.

The survivor benefit can be provided directly from a trust or by the purchase of an annuity. Normally, the plan provides these benefits directly from an unallocated trust fund. The design should be simple and easy for the employee to understand.

Employers should carefully coordinate the portions of supplemental benefits to be provided under the retirement plan and under a separate group insurance program. Qualified plans may provide supplemental benefits that are only incidental to retirement benefits. Management has come to recognize that, to the maximum extent possible, there must be a coordination of all sources of income available to the employee. Historically, coordination of all forms of employee benefits including government benefits has been a challenge.

Employee Contributions

Defined benefit pension plans may be contributory or noncontributory. Under a **contributory plan,** the employee provides part of the funds necessary to purchase his or her benefits with the employer assuming the remaining cost. Under a **noncontributory plan,** the employer bears the total cost of the program. At least 90 percent of all non-savings U.S. plans are noncontributory. Before ERISA, the majority of plans that were not the result of collective bargaining were contributory.

Recent laws and government regulations have made the administration of contributory plans exceedingly complex in the United States and, therefore, the current trend in pension plans is toward noncontributory plans. In addition, the theoretical case for noncontributory plans rests largely on the deferred-wage concept. If retirement benefits can be regarded as deferred wages, the argument that the employer should assume the total cost of these benefits is logical. On the other hand, if they are not considered deferred wages, the rationale for unilateral financing is less compelling.

Apart from the philosophical aspects of the question, strong practical arguments favor a noncontributory approach to financing. For example, employer contributions to a qualified pension plan are deductible for income tax purposes. Employees' contributions generally (discussed later) must be made from after-tax income.

Vesting

A well-established principle of pension planning is that employees must be permitted to recover their own contributions with interest (or adjusted for earning experience) if they terminate employment. Employees' rights in that portion of accrued benefits derived from their own contributions are nonforfeitable. However, employees do not necessarily have such rights in the contributions of employers made on behalf of employees. The employee's nonforfeitable—that is, vested—percentage of the employer contributions may vary from 0 to 100 percent. The employee's vested interest is shown in the plan's **vesting schedule,** which usually bases vesting on length of service and, in some cases, age of the participant (e.g., full vesting after 5 years of service or upon the attainment of age 65, whichever is earlier).

The vesting provisions of pension plans can be classified on at least four different bases:

- the *types* of benefits vested
- the point in *time* when the eligible benefits vest
- the *rate* at which the accrued benefits vest
- the *form* in which the benefits may be taken

As to the *types* of benefits vested, retirement, death, and total disability are all vested when the employee enters payment status. For benefits not in pay status, however, the traditional approach has been to vest the basic retirement benefit only. As to *time,* employers may grant immediate vesting in the employer contributions, or, as usually is the case, the vesting may be deferred until certain service requirements have been met.

As to the *rate* at which benefits vest, the employer's contributions may vest in full or only in part, although eventually it will have to be 100 percent. A graded vesting provision, which provides an increasing percentage of vesting based on service up to 100 percent, is in reality partly a time and partly an amount classification. Benefits derived from employer contributions must be fully vested at normal retirement age and also must meet either one of two minimum standards: (1) complete vesting of all accrued benefits after five years of recognized service or (2) a so-called three-to-seven-year standard under which accrued benefits must be at least 20 percent vested after three years of recognized service, and an additional 20 percent each year during the following four years.

The *form* of the vested benefits depends to some extent on the contractual instrument used to fund the benefits. If the plan is funded through a trust, the vested terminated employee generally retains a deferred claim against the trust fund in the amount of his or her vested annuity benefits, although, with spousal consent, some plans also provide for a lump-sum settlement. If the plan is funded through a contract with a life insurance company, the vested benefits may take the form of a paid-up insurance or annuity contract or a deferred claim against the plan.

The term **portable pensions** has found some acceptance in the U.S. pension literature to describe vested pension benefits that would follow the employee and be put into any new plan under which he or she is covered, or vested benefits that would be transferred to some central pension clearinghouse. Portability of pensions is, at least to a limited extent, a reality in that ERISA provides for rollover contributions to an individual retirement account and to other qualified retirement plans.

Under ERISA, an individual may avoid taxation on an early distribution of money or property from an individual retirement account (IRA) or qualified plan by reinvesting the money or property received, within 60 days, in another qualified IRA or plan for his or her benefit.

Methods of Distribution

A pension plan may be required to distribute benefits in the form of a joint and survivor annuity or a life annuity. Other common methods of distribution for defined contribution plans are payments in equal periodic installments for a certain term (i.e., monthly for 10 years) or for life with a period certain, or in a lump sum. Lump-sum distributions received by individuals at least age 50 in 1986 usually are eligible for favorable 10-year income averaging treatment, or they can be rolled over into an IRA or another qualified plan to defer income taxes. Lump-sum distributions made from an IRA before age 59½ are generally subject to a 10 percent excise tax unless they are rolled over. In a defined benefit plan, all forms of distribution other than a qualified joint and survivor annuity require spousal consent.

The Small Business Job Protection Act of 1996 modified the required beginning date for minimum distribution requirements to allow individuals other than 5 percent owners, who are still working at age 70½ to delay distributions from qualified plans and tax-sheltered annuities. The act repealed the special five-year forward averaging mentioned earlier.

METHODS OF FINANCING

Funding Procedure

Once the basic benefit features of a pension plan have been determined, consideration must be given to the various techniques used to calculate the contribution requirements and measure plan liabilities—so-called actuarial cost methods. The methods, of course, apply only to defined benefit plans because defined contribution plan liabilities are by definition a simple accumulation of the contributions made and investment earnings thereon.

An **actuarial cost method** is a particular technique for establishing the amount and incidence of the annual contributions required to provide pension plan benefits and expenses, and the related actuarial liability. The legal instruments, such as pension contracts issued by insurance companies are referred to as **funding media** or **funding vehicles.** Trust agreements under the direction of trustees and pension contracts issued by insurance companies may incorporate both the rules for the accumulation, investment, and disbursement of plan assets and the pension provision. A given pension plan might have one document relating to the plan benefits provided and a separate legal instrument under which the asset accumulation operates, the plan being incorporated only by reference. With separate documents, it is possible to amend the plan and not alter in any way the funding method being employed. The essence of the funding process is the accumulation of assets to offset the liabilities arising under the pension plan as measured by the actuarial method utilized.

Prior to the enactment of ERISA, a few plans operated on the pay-as-you-go basis.[9] Under this arrangement, retirement benefits were paid as a supplementary payroll. Payments were taken from current operating revenues.[10] No funds were set aside in advance for the payment of pension obligations even at retirement. This type of arrangement furnished the smallest degree of security to the employee because neither active nor retired employees could look to a segregated fund or a third-party guarantee for satisfaction of pension claims.

In contrast, ERISA requires advance funding of qualified pension plans. The acceptable methods of advanced funding may be broadly classified as (1) benefit allocation and (2) cost allocation methods. **Benefit allocation cost methods** are those that allocate benefits and then derive the actuarial present value of benefits. **Cost allocation cost methods** are those that compute the actuarial present value of total benefits to be paid and then assign a portion of that value (or cost) to each plan year.

Under any actuarial cost method, the **normal cost** is the cost that would be attributable to the current year of a plan's operation if from the earliest date of credited service, the plan had been in effect and costs had been accrued in accordance with a particular actuarial cost method. Some actuarial cost methods separate past-service benefits from future-service benefits and establish a **supplemental liability** for past-service benefits, which is funded separately. Although given pension benefits can be funded by several methods, usually one or the other will be more appropriate, depending upon the benefit formula and other characteristics of the plan and the plan sponsor's funding objective.

Benefit Allocation

The benefit allocation cost method of funding, also known as the **accrued benefit** or **single-premium method,** involves setting aside, in one sum, an amount needed to fund one unit of benefit. In practice, this unit of benefit is almost always related to a year of service—that is, the benefit earned during one year of service. Thus, if an employee currently earns an annual benefit at age 65 of $35, a paid-up annuity in that amount would be funded for that employee. Thereafter, this particular employee would have a paid-up annuity in the appropriate amount funded each year at an increasing cost per dollar of benefit based on his or her attained age at the time of each contribution. At retirement, this employee's income would be the total of each of these annual increments of benefits.

---

[9]Under *Opinion 8,* issued in 1966 by the Accounting Principles Board of the American Institute of Certified Public Accountants, neither pay-as-you-go nor terminal funding was an accepted principle of accounting for the cost of pension plans in financial statements during this period.

[10]Social Security benefits are generally funded this way, as are employer-provided pension plans in several countries.

The benefit allocation method assumes that the normal cost of a pension plan for any particular year is precisely equal to the present value of the benefits credited to the employee participants for service during that year. Thus, a funding policy geared to this cost method funds future-service benefits fully as they accrue. Past-service benefits are funded according to a schedule adopted by the employer in accordance with various schedules laid down in ERISA, usually over a period of years. The benefit allocation method of funding is virtually always used in connection with group deferred-annuity contracts and may be used with other types of plans.

Two popular funding methods are the unit credit and the projected unit credit methods. Both of these methods are individual calculation methods with past-service liabilities. In the **unit credit method,** the normal cost is the present value of benefits expected to accrue in the current year, and the past-service liability is the present value of all benefits earned by the participant as of the calculation date. This method is often used in plans in which the pension benefit is not related to the participant's pay.

The projected unit cost method is similar to the unit credit method, except that it considers projected instead of accrued benefits. In the **projected unit credit method,** the normal cost is the present value of the participant's projected benefit attributable to the current year's service, and the past-service liability is the present value of the participant's projected retirement benefit attributable to service earned prior to the calculation date. This method is required for pension expense determination on companies' financial statements and may be appropriate for pay-based pension plans.

Cost Allocation

The other category of funding methods, the cost allocation method, can be used with any type of benefit formula but is especially adaptable to the type of formula that provides a composite benefit as opposed to a series of unit benefits. Cost allocation methods may be classified as *individual* and *aggregate* level-cost methods. Individual level-cost methods include those *without supplemental liability* and those *with supplemental liability.*

Individual level-cost methods   Under the **individual level-cost method without supplemental liability,** the total benefits to be paid to an employee are estimated and the sum required to provide the benefits is accumulated through level amounts contributed over the remaining years of service. The most familiar form of the individual level-cost method is the individual level-premium method, which is employed in connection with individual and group cash-value insurance contracts. This funding method provides the benefits that would be payable to the employee if his or her rate of compensation remained unchanged to normal retirement age. The premium is a function of the entering age of the employee.

If the rate of compensation or benefits increases, an adjustment in the amount of insurance is made, and the funding of the increase in benefits is accomplished by a separate and additional level premium, payable from the date of increase and based on the age at that time. Contracts funded by this method are written in amounts designed to provide benefits for the entire period of credited service and, consequently, no distinction is made between past- and current-service costs—that is, the supplemental liability for past service is not separately determined and handled.

The **individual level-cost method with supplemental liability** (past-service liability determined separately) serves as the funding guide for many trust fund plans and deposit administration contracts. The rationale here is that benefits are funded on a level-amount basis or as a level percentage of pay over the employee participant's *entire* working lifetime. The supplemental liability for past-service benefits is separately ascertained. It may be viewed as the accumulated value (with the benefit of both interest and survivorship in service) of the normal cost contributions assumed to have been made with respect to all participants with credited past service at the time the plan is installed. Widely known as the **entry-age normal method,** this funding method permits a flexible policy with regard to funding the past-service liability.

Aggregate level-cost methods   The aggregate level-cost methods are analogous to the individual level-cost methods, except the calculation of costs and contributions are made on a collective rather than individual basis. As in the case of the individual level-cost methods, the annual cost accruals may be determined with or without past-service supplemental liability being determined separately.

Under the **aggregate level-cost method without supplemental liability,** the total employer cost of all future benefits for present employees, less employer funds on hand, is expressed as a level percentage of future payroll of present employees. Each year, as new employees enter, the level percentage must be recalculated. The actual calculation is made by dividing the present value of future payroll into the excess of the present value of future estimated benefits over plan assets to yield what is generally called the **accrual rate** or **aggregate-cost ratio.** The cost is determined by multiplying the compensation, or appropriate portion thereof, paid during the year to employees entering into the funding calculations by the accrual rate. In the case of the **aggregate level-cost method with supplemental liability,** the actuary determines a supplemental liability separately to provide greater funding flexibility. Aggregate-cost methods are most widely used in trusteed (noninsured) plans, although they are equally adaptable to group deposit administration and immediate participation guarantee contracts (discussed later).

Funding Requirements

ERISA imposes certain funding requirements that are generally limited to defined benefit pension plans. With respect to money-purchase plans, which are defined contribution plans, an employer is required to make contributions in accordance with the plan's contribution formula. The determination of required contributions under defined benefit plans is more complex, but basically contributions must be sufficient to cover normal costs and to amortize past-service costs and experience gains and losses over a specified time. Separately, amortization schedules apply for experience gains and losses and for liabilities created by a plan amendment or change in actuarial assumptions.

In addition, if the plan is not fully funded with respect to current liability (the present value of benefits earned to date based on mandated interest rates), a deficit reduction contribution may be required to amortize more quickly unfunded past-service liabilities. Minimum contributions are required to be deposited quarterly. Notwithstanding the foregoing rules, the employer's deductible contribution is limited to the amount necessary to make the plan fully funded—that is, the contribution necessary to make the value of the plan assets equal to the accrued liabilities under the plan, calculated on a going-concern basis or, if less, 155 percent grading to 170 percent of its current liability by 2005 over the value of plan assets.

An employer's failure to meet the minimum funding requirements will result in the imposition of a nondeductible excise tax of 10 percent. This tax is imposed annually on the accumulated funding deficiency. Furthermore, failure to fund the deficiency within 90 days, plus extensions, after the mailing of the deficiency notice with respect to the excise tax (10 percent for single-employer plans and 5 percent for multiple-employer plans) will result in an additional tax of 100 percent of the funding deficiency.

The **Pension Benefit Guarantee Corporation** (PBGC) is a government corporation set up by ERISA in 1974 to provide plan termination insurance to protect participants in qualified defined benefit plans up to certain limits. In carrying out this responsibility, the PBGC regulates plan terminations and imposes certain reporting requirements on covered plans that are in financial difficulty or in a state of contraction.

Failure to make required contributions within 30 days of the due date is a PBGC reportable event and requires PBGC notification. Failure to make required contributions within 60 days of the due date triggers required participant notices. Furthermore, if an accumulated funding deficiency exceeds $1 million, the PBGC can place a lien on the employer for the unpaid amount.

Pension Costs

Advance funding involves funding for the payment of pension benefits in advance of their due date. With defined benefit plans, the cost of providing the benefits must be estimated years in advance. In estimating pension costs, some of the factors that may be taken into account include (1) mortality, (2) interest, (3) expense of operations, (4) turnover, (5) disability, (6) age of retirement, and (7) changes in compensation. These factors vary considerably over time, so the use of the word *estimating* is appropriate.

The ultimate cost of a pension plan equals the benefits paid out, plus the cost of administration, less the earnings on any funds set aside for the payment of benefits. This is not, however, the true cost to the employer. For the true cost of a plan to be obtained, the actual cost should be reduced for such cost-saving factors as reduced labor turnover, retirement of inefficient employees, improved morale, and other less easily quantifiable benefits. Because these factors are difficult to evaluate, the net financial outlay generally is assumed to represent the cost of the plan. Because a pension plan is a long-range venture, ultimate costs cannot be accurately determined in advance. This is true even in an insured pension plan because most contracts are experience rated, and the employer's own experience will have a marked effect on the level of dividends or experience-rating credits.

The term *pension costs* is often used to refer to financial accounting pension expense. Funding and financial accounting expense requirements for pension costs are determined under separate rules and, therefore, are usually different amounts. Financial Accounting Standard No. 87 dictates the determination of pension expense for companies subject to generally accepted accounting principles, whereas the Internal Revenue Code dictates pension funding requirements.

Virtually all U.S. life insurance companies now use the investment year or new-money method of crediting investment income to pension plans. Under the **investment year** or **new-money** approach, assets acquired during each calendar year are treated as a separate cell with the net investment income (including realized capital gains and losses) derived from these assets credited to the cell. The asset composition of the cell changes annually because of maturities, repayments, redemptions, sales, and exchanges. Naturally, this affects the rate of return credited to the cell. In the past, it was standard practice to credit the account with the net rate of interest earned on the insurer's total investment portfolio—the **average** or **portfolio rate.** The investment year method was adopted by life insurers to meet the competition of banks for pension funds and to maintain equity between contractholders.

Pension Financing Vehicles

With regard to financing, pension plans may be classified on three bases: (1) fully insured plans, (2) noninsured plans, and (3) split-funded plans. As the name suggests, **fully insured pension plans** rely exclusively on insurance contracts as the funding media. **Noninsured plans**—also called self-administered or **trusteed pension plans**—in contrast, involve no element of insurance and require the creation of a trust with the trustee or investment manager being responsible for plan investment management. A split-funded pension plan relies partially on insurance.

Noninsured Plans

Under the **noninsured plan,** there are no guarantees—the employer assumes all the risks—investment, mortality, and expense. Noninsured plans involve the establishment of a trust for the benefit of the employees. Under defined benefit plans, an **enrolled actuary**[11] is employed to apply IRC Section 412 to determine the minimum and maximum contributions that should be made to the trust. A bank or insurance company invests the funds so deposited and when an employee retires, the bank or insurance company makes a monthly or lump-sum payment to the retired employee on the direction of the employer. Under a trusteed defined benefit plan, the enrolled actuary takes no responsibility for investment and mortality results but uses reasonable actuarial assumptions in estimating pension costs. Similarly, the trustee takes no responsibility except to invest the money in accordance with the law and its best judgment or at the direction of the employer or its investment advisors (depending on the trust indenture).

The employer is in a sense a self-insurer. The employer or, in the event of employer insolvency, the employee assumes risks that may be assumed by the insurance company under an insured plan. The plan provisions usually limit the insolvent employer's liability to whatever monies are in the trust. The benefits promised by a defined benefit pension plan usually are insured at least in part by the PBGC. Because the noninsured plan is a self-insured plan, this approach carries the least risk for large companies (or groups of companies) with sufficient spread of risk to permit predictable results (i.e., law of large numbers) and to keep administrative costs reasonable. Further protection is provided to participants by the minimum-funding requirements under ERISA, which were discussed earlier.

The trusteed approach may have advantages for those corporations large enough to self-insure the pension risk including (1) economy of operation, (2) greater flexibility in both funding and plan provisions, and (3) the possibility of better investment results because of greater investment freedom. Although trusteed plans are noninsured in that no guarantees are provided to covered individuals, the use of insurance company services is not precluded. Several insurance companies offer investment, administrative, and actuarial services, which do not involve guarantees to individuals. Investment of funds with insurance companies at a minimum guaranteed rate of return via guaranteed investment contracts is also quite popular. Even though such contracts do not fall within the traditional definition of insured pension plans, these arrangements have proven to be an important source of business for insurance companies.

Split-Funded Plans

Split-funded plans are pension programs in which two or more types of contracts are combined or an employer makes use of an insurance contract in conjunction with a noninsured arrangement. All these variations are called **split-funding contracts.** Frequently, a bank holds and invests a portion of the **active life fund,** that is, funds accumulated on behalf of plan participants not yet retired. As employees retire, funds may be moved to a life insurance company to provide guaranteed annuities. If the life insurance company holds no funds prior to retirement and receives money to purchase the guaranteed annuities only as employees retire, the arrangement is called a **maturity funding contract.** In another version, a portion of the contribution is invested in cash-value life insurance policies with the remainder of the fund held and invested by the trustee.

Noninsured pension arrangements are worthy of more comprehensive treatment, but in view of the nature of this text, the remaining discussion is concerned primarily with insured pension plans.

---

[11]An enrolled actuary must sign the actuarial report required by ERISA. Such individuals must have met the standard and qualifications set by the Joint Board for the Enrollment of Actuaries established by the secretaries of Labor and the Treasury.

INSURED PENSION CONTRACTS

Life insurance companies offer considerable flexibility in tailoring a funding vehicle to meet individual employer needs. In this discussion, names are attached to various types of insured pension arrangements, but it should be understood that the contracts can be modified to fit particular requirements.

Life insurance companies are in the business of accepting risks, so they are willing to underwrite several different risks associated with pension plans, and to underwrite them in varying degrees, depending upon the employer's wishes. Some of these risks are:

1. More individuals may live to retire than the mortality tables used anticipated.
2. Those who retire may live longer than the mortality tables used anticipated.
3. The rate of interest earned on investments may fall below the anticipated level.
4. There may be defaults in the investment portfolio, or it may be necessary to sell particular investments at a loss.
5. Plan expenses may be higher than anticipated.

In a well-designed employee benefit program that provides death, disability, and retirement benefits with reasonably comparable values, the actuarial experience will not be significantly different whether more employees become disabled, more die, or more live and retire. If just one function such as death is isolated, obviously a higher or lower rate than expected can significantly change the experience with respect to that one plan. As companies develop more sophisticated benefit programs, the effect of risk becomes less significant. This is because adverse experience under one plan (e.g., higher mortality under the death benefit plan) may result in more favorable experience under another plan (e.g., high mortality under the retirement plan) results in lower payouts.

Life insurance companies provide a variety of services, many of which may be varied to suit the employer's wishes. Except for certain benefit guarantees, the services provided by a life insurance company also can be provided by consultants and other organizations specializing in pension services.

Single-Premium Annuity Contracts

The insurance company probably rises to its maximum usefulness in the rather unusual situation in which the employer determines the benefit that will ultimately be payable to each of its employees and makes a single payment to an insurance company to guarantee that all these benefits will be paid as they become due—a **single-premium group annuity contract.** This arrangement is frequently used for a body of employees who have already retired and in the situation in which an uninsured trusteed arrangement is terminated for one reason or another, and the monies in the trust are used to purchase immediate or deferred annuities for the employees covered by the plan. For an ongoing plan, an annuity settlement of retired life obligations may result in favorable accounting treatment for the plan sponsor. It is unusual with respect to employees who are still working and covered by an ongoing plan.

Level-Premium Annuity Contracts

Sometimes an employer estimates the pension that will be payable when each employee reaches his or her normal retirement age, and an insurance company is asked to quote a *level payment* that is guaranteed to provide the estimated pension. The insurance company guarantees to pay the indicated amount of benefit if the indicated premium is paid each year until the employee retires.

Under an **individual policy pension** trust, benefits are funded by separate, individual policies issued on the lives of employees, the policies generally being issued to and held by a trustee. Under a **group permanent** contract, a **level-premium group annuity** contract, or a **level-premium contract with lifetime guarantees,** benefits are funded by a master group annuity contract issued to the employer with certificates of coverage given to the employees. In either event, a life insurance feature is commonly provided prior to retirement. Under these types of arrangements, the insurance company assumes all the risks and provides all the services, and, in particular, it guarantees a price structure.

Single-Premium Deferred Annuities

Under **group deferred annuity** contracts, employer contributions are used to purchase single-premium deferred annuities for employees based on the amount of annuity benefit accrued by the participant each year. The employee's pension is separated into pieces that are associated with years of employment. Thus, for each year of service, the employee might be entitled to an annual pension of 2 percent of salary, or of a flat monthly amount, such as $50, for each year's service. Each year, the employer then purchases a single premium unit of deferred annuity, which becomes payable when the employee reaches normal retirement age. The employee's pension is the sum of the units purchased for him or her. Once the annuity has been purchased, the insurance company assumes all the risks and provides all the services. Although the company's risk with respect to any individual may extend for 40, 50, or 60 years with respect to the premium it *has received,* the life insurance company has not guaranteed the price it will charge for additional units *to be purchased* several years in the future. Customarily, however, insurers guarantee their rate structures for the first five contract years.

A basic characteristic of all the previously described insurance arrangements is that each employee can be told with certainty that a benefit has been purchased or is being purchased for him or her, and the insurer guarantees that it will be paid. The employer is in the secure position of knowing that it is not placing on future management the risk that the promised benefits will turn out to have been inadequately funded, and the responsibility for making up a deficiency or incurring employee dissatisfaction by reducing the promised benefits.

With this type of arrangement, monies are set aside to provide pensions for all qualified employees. Yet many will not stay with the employer until they have satisfied the vesting provisions. Many employers want to discount their payments in advance for the probability that some employees will not persist in employment. For these and other reasons, both level-premium and single-premium deferred annuities are less popular today, and the deposit administration contract concept has been developed in response to these shortcomings.

Deposit Administration Contracts

Under the **deposit administration contract,** the life insurance company takes all the risks and provides all services, but *only with respect to employees who have retired.* With respect to employees who have not yet reached their retirement dates, the life insurer provides no direct guarantees regarding employer contributions, except that pensions will be provided to the extent that monies are available at the time the employees retire. An enrolled actuary supplies the employer with estimates of the amount of money that should be set aside each year to make reasonably certain that sufficient funds will be available to purchase annuities for employees as they retire. These monies are given to the life insurance company for safekeeping and investment. The insurer guarantees that there will be no capital impairment and that at least a specified minimum rate of interest will be earned on the funds. It also guarantees a particular price structure to purchase annuities for the employees as they retire.

The deposit administration contract sets out a schedule of annuity purchase rates and a rate of interest (both conservative) at which the monies in the active life fund will be accumulated, both being guaranteed, usually, for the first five contract years. After the period, these guarantees can be changed from year to year as to future contributions. The minimum rate of interest and the rate schedules in effect at the time monies are paid to the insurer apply to these funds, regardless of when they are withdrawn from the active life fund to provide an annuity. Some companies guarantee purchase rates for five to ten years of *retirement,* with a right to change the annuity purchase basis for new retirees after that. Following the change, another five- or ten-year period may be applicable. The volatility of investment results has caused many companies to avoid long-term guarantees.

The life insurance company has not assumed the risk of the number of persons who will stay with the employer until retirement, but it has assumed all the other risks listed earlier. The insurer may not provide all services because the employer or its consultant may maintain employee records, determine the amounts to be paid into the plan, and evaluate the adequacy of funds to provide for future retirements.

Immediate Participation Guarantee Contracts

The **immediate participation guarantee contract (IPG)** is similar to the deposit administration contract in that the employer's contributions are placed in an unallocated fund and the life insurance company guarantees that the annuities for retired employees will be paid in full. They differ from deposit administration contracts in the extent to which and the time at which the insurance company assumes mortality, investment, and expense risks with respect to retired lives.

The IPG contract may be said to have two stages. The first or active stage continues for as long as the employer makes sufficient contributions to keep the amount in the fund *above* the amount required to meet the life insurance company's price to provide guaranteed annuities for employees who have retired. The contract enters its second stage if the amount in the fund falls to the required amount, the so-called critical level.

In the active stage, the contract fund is charged directly with the contract's share of the life insurance company's expenses and all retired benefits in pay status and credited directly with its share of investment income (minus a small risk charge). The fund is also credited or charged directly with the contract's share of the insurer's capital gains and losses and the investment and expense experience with respect to retired employees. If the employer allows the fund to fall to the critical level and the contract enters the second stage, the amount in the fund is used to establish fully guaranteed annuities for all benefit commitments, and the fund itself ceases to exist.

As long as the employer's contributions are sufficient to maintain the contract in active status, the insurer is relieved of investment, mortality, and expense risks with respect to all active employees and mortality risk for retired employees. If and when the contract enters the second stage, all these risks are assumed by it. Of course, the insurer is under a substantial risk during the active status of the contract because it has provided a guaranteed price structure that the employer can unilaterally decide to use at any time that it believes the probable future course of investment, mortality, and expense risks to be such that it will be to its advantage to shift the risk to the insurer; in other words, the contract provides a call option to the employer.

Recently, some IPG contracts have been modified, eliminating the guaranteed annuity rates; instead, they provide a certificate stating that nonguaranteed payments will be made until the fund is exhausted under an "investment only" contract. Under this arrangement the employer is responsible for the adequacy of funding, and employees have no assurance from the insurer that their benefit payments will continue until death.

All of the preceding arrangements are general account obligations of the insurer. In contrast to the special investment arrangements discussed next, all assets of the insurer stand behind these obligations.

Special Investment Arrangements

Separate Accounts

Separate accounts are held separately from the general account assets of insurers and are not subject to the usual insurer investment restrictions. Insurers issue contracts whose liabilities are backed by separate account assets. These contracts are credited directly with the investment results of the separate account.

During the 1970s, the most common form of separate account was one in which the funds of many contractholders were pooled for investment in common stocks. Today, however, insurance companies have pooled accounts invested in stocks, bonds, mortgages, real estate, and other assets. Also, a contractholder with a large account, who does not wish to participate in a pooled separate account, may request the creation of a separate account for its exclusive use.

Separate accounts also are used to provide variable annuity benefits. Amounts placed in the account usually are converted into units, and the amount of each employee's benefit is measured in terms of units. Each monthly annuity payment equals the product of the number of units to which the employee is entitled and the unit value for the month. (See chapter 8 for more details on variable annuities.)

Guaranteed Investment Contracts

Under **guaranteed investment contracts** (GICs), the insurance company accepts a specific amount of money, usually $100,000 or more, and agrees to return the money at a fixed date (1 to 15 years) in the future. Interest is guaranteed for the life of the contract, usually at rates that are competitive with other long-term, fixed-income investments. The interest may be paid at fixed intervals or held to compound until the termination date of the contract.

Because the fixed term of the contract is one of its key features, substantial penalties usually are imposed for premature withdrawal (if it is allowed at all). Expenses of the insurance company often are expressed as a small subtraction from the gross interest rate quoted in arriving at the contract guaranteed rate.

There are two types of GICs: the bullet GIC and the window GIC. The **bullet GIC** is structured to accept a single-sum deposit (generally $100,000 or more) for a specified period of time (usually three to seven years). The bullet GIC guarantees principal and interest at a stipulated rate, and it is agreed that the principal and interest will be returned at a specified date or dates. Both the amount of money deposited and the lock-in period are a function of the pension fund manager's investment strategy. Bullet GICs are usually marketed to defined benefit plans because they fit well with the timing of contributions from these plans, which are generally quarterly. The relative inflexibility associated with making contributions to a bullet GIC led to the creation of the other basic GIC type, known as a window GIC.

The **window GIC** is designed to meet the need for periodic contributions inherent in some defined contribution plans, which credit an employee's account balance with the plan contribution (frequently monthly or semimonthly) as salaries are paid. To accommodate periodic variable contributions, a window period is established. When a window GIC is used, the interest guarantees are locked in immediately, but the timing of contributions is usually left open for up to a year. The amounts contributed and the withdrawal amounts are not known. Under defined contribution plans, the exact yearly contribution is known only at the end of the plan year. The window GIC provides flexibility to accommodate periodic contributions, typically within a specified corridor. The bullet GIC, on the other hand, suits a defined benefit plan because, under these plans, the precise plan contribution is actuarially determined once a year.

Each basic GIC (bullet or window) can be modified to meet specific needs of a given pension plan. For example, it is not unusual to design a window GIC to guarantee the first-year rate but to leave years 2 through 5 open during the first year. Another variation of the window GIC is the provision that allows the insurance company to accept contributions up to a certain amount rather than for a window period. Similarly, the basic design of a bullet GIC can be modified to allow the plan sponsor to lock in current rates for a deposit to be made on an agreed-upon future date. Other design adjustments are possible.

In general, GICs have been a significant investment vehicle for pension and 401(k) plans over the last 20 years. In the early 1990s, confidence in GICs was seriously shaken by the financial troubles of some insurance companies that were affected by defaults of junk bonds they purchased in the 1980s and poor mortgage loan results. GICs do not generally enjoy the status of "insurance" and, therefore, they are not entitled to state guarantee fund coverage in the event of defaults.

OTHER RETIREMENT PLANS

Profit-Sharing Plans

Profit-sharing plans are a type of defined contribution plan in which employer contributions are typically based in some manner on the employer's profits. Annually, each employee is allocated a share of the profits contributed to the profit-sharing plan. Although relatively rare, money made available each year may be used as single premiums to purchase whatever amounts of annuity can be provided on the basis of a price structure guaranteed by an insurance company.

Profit-sharing plans were originally introduced to share profits with employees with the goal of improving productivity. They were adapted to provide retirement benefits in order to avoid the cash flow problems that a qualified defined benefit pension plan creates by virtue of mandatory annual contributions. The employer retains a certain amount of control over the level of annual contributions made to the plan and the allocation formula used. Plans may also be designed to allow employees to withdraw funds from participant accounts, but they must allow this flexibility to all participants. Allocation formulas cannot favor highly compensated employees except as permitted under regulations. Employers are not required to make a contribution each year but must contribute recurring and substantial contributions. Profit-sharing plans are not required to have current or accumulated profits for the employer to be able to make a profit-sharing contribution in a given year.

Although profit-sharing plans fall under the defined contribution category and share all the defined contribution characteristics, IRS regulations are somewhat more liberal in certain areas. The deduction for employer contributions to a profit-sharing plan is limited to 15 percent of the aggregate participant payroll. Any one participant is eligible to receive a contribution up to the defined contribution limit of 25 percent of salary or $30,000, whichever is lower.

Profit-sharing plans are frequently installed with other defined benefit or money-purchase pension plans. For example, an employer might institute a 15 percent profit-sharing plan and a 10 percent money-purchase pension plan. This approach retains some flexibility while assuring a minimum level of benefits for participants.

If the contributions allocated to each employee are placed in individual accounts for them under noninsured trusts, their accumulation at retirement may be used to purchase a guaranteed annuity under an arrangement similar to that of the maturity funding contract described earlier. Many insurance companies have developed both group and individual contracts that function during the accumulation phase somewhat like the noninsured trust and at retirement like a maturity funding contract.

Stock Bonus Plan

The **stock bonus plan** is a plan established and maintained by an employer to provide benefits similar to a profit-sharing plan except that the benefits can be distributed in the form of stock of the employer. The typical contribution formula under a stock bonus plan is expressed as a flat percentage of covered payroll or requires the employer to contribute a set percentage of profits but not less than a fixed amount each year. Stock bonus plans are intended specifically to give employees an ownership interest in the company at a relatively low cost to the employer. Stock bonus plans are often used by closely held companies to help create a market for stock of the employer.

Employee Stock Ownership Plan

The term **employee stock ownership plan** (ESOP) describes a wide variety of defined contribution plans that invest primarily in employer stock. In addition to providing a benefit plan with stock ownership for employees, ESOPs have been used to meet a wide variety of financial and other objectives of the employer. In essence, the ESOP is a stock bonus plan with the additional feature that, if certain requirements are met, the plan can be used as a means of raising funds on a tax-favored basis. Under a qualified ESOP, an employer can indirectly borrow money from a bank and repay the loan with fully deductible repayment amounts. The repayments are deductible in full because they are structured as contributions to an ESOP. This is accomplished by first having the plan trustee borrow money from a bank (guaranteed by the employer). The borrowed money is then used to purchase a block of stock from the employer. Shares of this stock will subsequently be allocated to participants' accounts in the ESOP as plan contributions are made by the employer. These contributions are tax deductible by the employer with the contributions designed to be enough to enable the plan trustee to gradually repay the loan to the bank. The net result of the arrangement is that the employer immediately receives the full proceeds of the bank loan and, in effect, pays off the loan through tax-deductible contributions to the plan on behalf of plan participants.

In small companies, it is often important for shareholders to locate a market for financial and estate planning purposes. An ESOP can be helpful in creating a market for an owner's shares during lifetime or at death, generally with favorable tax consequences. Although these are complex transactions, which must be crafted carefully, the benefits can be substantial.

Employee Savings Plans

In recent years, many U.S. employers have introduced one or more types of employee savings plans to supplement other existing retirement plans. A **savings plan** is a defined contribution plan under which employees have separate accounts. Usually, qualified savings plans are designed as profit-sharing plans because only a profit-sharing plan permits account withdrawals during employment, and this is an important feature if the plan is to be a flexible savings medium for employees. Thus, in general, a savings plan can be viewed as a contributory profit-sharing plan. Thrift plans and 401(k) plans are two forms of such employee savings arrangements.

Thrift Plans

Traditionally, a **thrift plan** is a contributory profit-sharing plan designed to encourage employees to save from after-tax income. An employee, for example, might be permitted to contribute up to 10 percent of his or her salary to the plan. All investment earnings accumulate tax free until distribution, although the employee contribution itself is not tax deductible. Withdrawals from thrift plans are permitted under conditions specified in the plan by the employer. These conditions usually reflect the employer's view of the plan as a long-term savings program. Premature withdrawal of the interest earned on the employee's contributions and any employer contributions may be subject to a 10 percent premature distribution tax.

Most thrift plans provide for partial matching of employee contributions by employers. The employer usually contributes 50 cents for each dollar of employee contributions, although other matching arrangements are used. Most plans, however, will not provide for matching of contributions in excess of 6 percent of an employee's salary. Employees frequently are given some choice about how the funds in their thrift plan accounts are invested; usually they allocate their contributions among various investment funds (e.g., money market, corporate bonds, or stock). Many traditional thrift plans have been changed to 401(k) plans to permit employee pretax salary reductions (discussed later).

401(k) Plans

A **401(k) plan** is an employee savings plan that allows for employee contributions on a pretax basis and for partial employer matching of employee contributions. However, a 401(k) plan provides *current* as well as future tax savings for employees. Under a 401(k) plan, employees agree to defer a percentage of *pretax* income. The money arising from this decision reduces current (taxable) salary and is placed directly in the 401(k) plan by the employer. The 401(k) contribution is considered to have been made by the employer and is, therefore, generally not treated as part of an employee's taxable income for federal income tax purposes.[12]

The maximum reduction in salary permitted under 401(k) plans is indexed (and was $10,000 in 1999). All employee contributions are 100 percent vested, regardless of the vesting schedule applicable to any employer contributions. All investment income accumulates tax free until distributed. The employee may decrease or even eliminate future contributions simply by changing his or her salary reduction agreement.

To encourage employees (especially those who are lower paid) to participate in the plan, many companies match a portion of the employee's elective deferrals. Usually, the employer will match from 25 cents to a dollar for every dollar the employee defers.

The 401(k) arrangement is a very popular employee benefit. Employees gain tax and other advantages, and employers save on unemployment taxes and workers' compensation insurance premiums because of the reduction in their employees' salaries. On the other hand, the IRS has established strict rules for 401(k) plans; the nondiscrimination and the withdrawal provisions, in particular, are very stringent. No withdrawals from 401(k) plans are allowed before age 59½, except for participants who die, become disabled, retire, change jobs, or suffer financial hardship. Withdrawals may also be permitted in the case of certain plan terminations and certain sales or disposition of corporate assets. Some 401(k) plans permit loans to employees; loans are limited to the lesser of $50,000 or 50 percent of the vested value of an employee's account.

Participants are generally permitted to direct the investment of their account among offered alternatives. Some employers even allow employees to make the individual in-

---

[12]Although 401(k) contributions are not subject to federal income taxes, a few states and municipalities tax them and they are subject to Social Security taxes.

vestment choices for their 401(k) money—a self-directed 401(k) plan. They can trade individual stocks and bonds and select from a wide range of mutual funds through open-ended 401(k) brokerage accounts. An increasing number of employers offer a self-directed option to their employees.

Simplified Employee Pension Plans

The **simplified employee pension plan** (SEP) is an expanded version of an employer-sponsored IRA with features similar to a qualified plan. In contrast to the employer-sponsored IRA, the deduction limits under the SEP are much higher.

Basically, the SEP is a written plan that requires the employer to make contributions, based on a formula contained in the plan, for all employees who have attained the age of 21 and who have performed service [and earned at least $400 (in 1999 as indexed) in compensation] for the employer during at least three of the preceding five calendar years. Funds contributed to the SEP by the employer are allocated directly into IRAs maintained for each plan participant.

The contribution for each covered employee may not exceed the lesser of 15 percent of the employee's covered compensation or $30,000, compared to a maximum of $2,000 with an IRA. In addition, the plan may be integrated with Social Security, although the method of integration is slightly different from a profit-sharing or money-purchase plan. SEPs were developed with the intention of simplifying the administration and reporting requirements for the employer. As a result, SEPs have been widely used by self-employed persons.

Typically, the employer funds the SEP, but a salary-reduction SEP is possible also. Under a **salary-reduction SEP,** an employee may agree with his or her employer to have a reduction in his or her salary to fund the SEP. If a salary-reduction SEP is used, the maximum by which an employee can reduce his or her salary to fund the SEP is the lesser of 25 percent of compensation or $10,000 (in 1999 as indexed). The SEP can be designed to use both employer contributions and salary-reduction employee contributions. As a result of the Small Business Job Protection Act of 1996, no new salary-reduction SEPs may be established after December 31, 1996, but existing plans may remain in place. After that date, however, salary-reduction arrangements can be part of a SIMPLE IRA (see discussion later in this chapter).

Tax-Sheltered Annuities

Employees of a charitable organization (described in Section 501(c)(3) of the Internal Revenue Code), which is exempt from tax under Section 501(a), and employees of a public educational institution and certain other public bodies are entitled to special tax treatment on monies used by their employer to purchase an annuity for them. Under a **403(b) annuity,** employees may agree with their employer to have a portion of the money that would otherwise be part of their pay set aside by the employer in an annuity contract for them. These funds eventually will be subject to tax, but not until the money, with accumulated interest, is actually received, either as a cash withdrawal or as annuity payments. The funds are commonly called **403(b) annuities** (from the applicable section of the Internal Revenue Code) or **tax-sheltered annuities (TSAs).**

The regulations governing the maximum amount that may be set aside each year on behalf of an employee are complex. In general, however, the maximum contribution equals 20 percent of the employee's current year's total compensation (after salary reductions), times the total period of employment with his or her employer (expressed in years and fractions thereof), less the sum of prior contributions and certain other tax-deferred employer contributions on the employee's behalf. An overall contribution limit of $10,000 applies (in 1999 as indexed). Tax-deferred annuities are also subject to nondiscrimination rules. Various types of insurance contracts (individual and group) are used as the funding vehicles for these annuities, which are a substantial source of business for many insurance companies.

Employees of other public bodies such as states, counties, or municipalities and tax-exempt organizations enjoy a similar device, albeit with somewhat different deferral limits. Under a **Section 457 deferred compensation** arrangement, the employer agrees with each employee to reduce his or her pay by a specified amount and to invest the deferrals in one or more investment outlets that may include insurance products. The amounts so deferred, plus investment earnings, will be distributed to the employee on death, retirement, or other termination of employment. Deferred annuities, which may be fixed or variable, are popular in these deferred compensation plans.

Self-Employed Pension Plans

For many years there were restrictions on the participation of partners and proprietors in qualified retirement programs. Special plans called **Keogh** or **HR-10 plans** were used to cover partners or proprietors—that is, self-employed individuals. After 20 years of the campaign for parity between self-employed and corporate retirement plans, the Tax Equity and Fiscal Responsibility Act of 1982 (TEFRA) finally granted this parity to all new and old retirement plans established by self-employed businesses. With that parity came the ability of self-employed businesses to maintain the same types of defined benefit and defined contribution plans as were available previously only to corporations.

Individual Retirement Accounts

Individual retirement accounts and annuities (IRAs) are plans adopted by individuals that provide tax-deferred benefits somewhat similar to those available from an employer plan. IRAs were first created by ERISA to encourage retirement savings by persons who were not actually participating in qualified pension, profit-sharing, or Keogh plans. Anyone can set up an IRA, irrespective of whether he or she is covered by a qualified plan. IRA contributions, however, are deductible from current taxable income only if the person making them is not covered by a qualified plan. If the person is covered by a qualified plan, a portion of the contribution may be deductible, depending on the individual's earnings level and marital status. Investment earnings on all contributions (irrespective of whether they are deductible) accumulate tax free until distributed. The source of the funds contributed to an IRA does not determine eligibility or deductibility, so long as the contributing individual has includable compensation that is at least equal to the amount of the contribution (discussed later).

There is considerable interest in strengthening the role of some types of IRAs in response to the desire to encourage long-term savings to meet the retirement and long-term care needs of the aging U.S. population.

Types of IRAs

A **regular IRA** is one established by an individual to provide retirement income for himself or herself. Any person can contribute 100 percent of annual *earned* income to a regular IRA up to a maximum contribution of $2,000 per year. Because the primary purpose of IRAs is to provide income during retirement, there are significant penalties for withdrawal of funds prior to that time. The minimum age at which distribution can be made without a 10 percent penalty is 59½. If death or disability or other significant health costs are incurred prior to that age, however, the IRA can be distributed to the survivors or individuals without the 10 percent tax penalty for early withdrawal. Early distribution in the form of substantially equal payments over the life expectancy may also be exempt from the 10 percent penalty tax.

The Taxpayer Relief Act of 1997 (TRA97) added an exception to the 10 percent penalty tax for early distributions from IRAs for distributions made after December 31, 1997 with respect to qualified higher education expenses. TRA97 also permits penalty-free early withdrawals for the first-time purchase of a principal residence, subject to a maximum of $10,000.

Working employees who are eligible for regular IRAs are allowed to establish **spousal IRAs** for their *nonworking spouses.* The limit of $2,000 applies, as in the case of the regular IRA. If an individual establishes *both* a regular and a spousal IRA, the total *combined* contribution is limited to the lesser of $4,000 per year or the annual earned income of the spouse. Although contributions can be apportioned between the regular and the spousal IRAs in any proportion desired, no more than $2,000 a year can be placed in any one account.

Deductible contributions are restricted for employees covered under qualified plans if their income exceeds specified limits. If the adjusted gross income (AGI) of an individual (or married couple if a joint return is filed) exceeds the $31,000 ($51,000) limit under the law, the $2,000 IRA limit is reduced in increments of $200 per $1,000 of additional adjusted gross income, becoming zero at $41,000 ($61,000). See Figure 21-2. The Taxpayer Relief Act of 1997 increased these pay limits, grading from $30,000 ($50,000) for 1998 up to $50,000 ($80,000) for 2007 and later. TRA97 also amended the code to

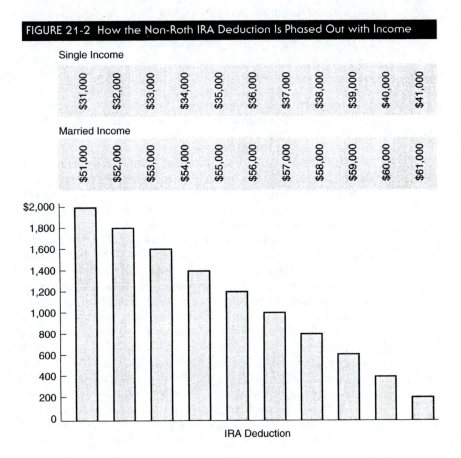

FIGURE 21-2 How the Non-Roth IRA Deduction Is Phased Out with Income

provide that an individual's spouse's participation in a qualified plan would *not* be attributed to the nonactive participant spouse. The maximum deductible IRA contribution for an individual, who is not an active participant but whose spouse is, is phased out for taxpayers filing a joint return with AGI between $150,000 and $160,000.

Under a **Roth IRA** (effective January 1, 1998) contributions are not deductible, but qualified distributions are tax free. Individuals making contributions to a Roth IRA can still make contributions to a deductible IRA. The maximum annual contributions to all IRAs, however, are limited to $2,000. A nonworking spouse may contribute up to $2,000, as long as the couple's combined earnings are at least equal to both spouses' contributed amounts.

Eligibility for a Roth IRA is phased out for single taxpayers with AGI between $95,000 and $110,000 and for joint filers with AGI between $150,000 and $160,000. Unlike traditional IRAs, contributions may be made to Roth IRAs even after an individual reaches age 70½.

Qualified distributions from Roth IRAs may be taken after a five-year period that begins with the first tax year in which a contribution was made. These specific situations count as qualified distributions:

- after age 59½
- upon death, to designated beneficiaries or the estate
- upon disability
- to pay for first-time homebuyer expenses subject to a $10,000 lifetime cap

Nonqualified withdrawals are subject to the 10 percent withdrawal tax.

In addition to these traditional IRAs, beginning in 1998, individuals can contribute up to $500 per beneficiary (until the beneficiary reaches the age of 18) to an **education IRA,** a tax-favored trust or custodial account (discussed later) created to pay the cost of a beneficiary's education. Contributions are not deductible but withdrawals (contributions *and* earnings) to pay the cost of a beneficiary's postsecondary school tuition and room and board are tax free. Eligibility is phased out for single taxpayers with AGI between $95,000 and $110,000 and for married taxpayers with AGI between $150,000 and $160,000.

IRA Funding Instruments

ERISA authorized three different funding instruments for IRAs: (1) individual retirement accounts, (2) individual retirement annuities, and (3) individual U.S. retirement bonds. The third type (the IRA bond) was based on a special issue of government savings bonds originally authorized but not offered since April 30, 1982. The bonds were discontinued, primarily due to a lack of interest on the part of investors.

Of the two presently available types of IRA funding instruments, individual retirement accounts are the more popular. More than 90 percent of all IRAs are invested in some form of individual retirement account. This particular type of IRA takes one of three distinct forms. One form is a **bank trust** or **custodial account,** whereby contributions usually are invested in one or more of a bank's interest-bearing instruments or, in some cases, self-directed accounts. Commercial banks, mutual savings banks, credit unions, and savings and loan associations generally offer this form of IRA. A second form also involves a trust or custodial account, whereby investments generally are made exclusively in **mutual fund** shares, usually within a specific family of funds. The third form is a trust arrangement offered by stockbrokers, called a **self-directed account.** Under this form of IRA, the owner is permitted to select and manage his or her own individual investments from a wide range of available stocks, bonds, mutual funds, and direct participation programs. Mutual fund and broker accounts technically use a bank as a trustee, but the bank's role is purely custodial and the investor views the fund or broker as the sponsor of the IRA.

The other type of authorized IRA is the **individual retirement annuity.** Individual retirement annuities generally are either fixed- or variable-annuity contracts that are issued by insurance companies. These contracts are flexible-premium deferred annuities. That means that a series of equal or differing contributions may be made periodically under the contract.

Because these insurance contracts are restricted and nontransferable to meet the necessary IRA requirements, no trustee or custodian is required. When the participant or beneficiary reaches retirement age, the contract may then be used to provide a regular income payment by one of several settlement options (see chapter 8). Because the laws governing IRAs specifically prohibit IRA investment in life insurance, such policies may not be used for any type of IRA.

Rollovers

In order to increase the amount of investment flexibility available to participants in IRAs and qualified plans, the code permits the use of IRAs as vehicles for investment *rollovers.* Thus, it is possible to roll over from one IRA to another and roll over distributions from qualified plans. The annual contribution limits for regular and spousal IRAs do not apply to rollover IRAs, but to avoid taxation as a premature withdrawal, the rollover must be completed within 60 days of the withdrawal.

Simple Plans

A simplified retirement plan for small business, called the **savings incentive match plan for employers** (SIMPLE), is available to eligible employers as a tax-favored means of providing a retirement option for employees that does not have to satisfy many of the qualified plan requirements. Such a plan allows employees to make contributions by salary reduction of up to $6,000 per year, and it requires employers to make contributions of either 2 percent of pay or 100 percent of the first 3 percent of salary reductions. Employer contributions are tax deductible whereas assets in a SIMPLE account are not taxed until distributed to the employee. In addition, SIMPLE plans need not satisfy nondiscrimination requirements (including top-heavy rules), or many other qualified plan rules.

An employer can maintain a SIMPLE plan if it employs no more than 100 employees who received at least $5,000 in compensation from the employer for the preceding year. In addition, the employer must not maintain another employer-sponsored retirement plan to which contributions were made or benefits accrued. SIMPLE plans may be structured as an IRA or as a 401(k) qualified cash or deferred arrangement.

Questions

1. U.S. federal income tax laws encourage the use of private pension plans. There are a number of restrictions placed on this favorable tax treatment, however. What are these restrictions and what is their intended impact on the use of pension plans?
2. What are the fundamental features that go into the design of a private pension plan?
3. Life insurers underwrite a number of risks associated with pension plans. What are these risks, and how do life insurance products address them?
4. Discuss the merits of each of the following methods used to fund defined benefits: (a) benefit allocation method; (b) individual level-cost method; and (c) aggregate level-cost method.

CHAPTER 22

SOCIAL INSURANCE

Objectives

- Explain the rationale behind the implementation of a social insurance scheme.

- Describe the eligibility requirements for various OASDHI benefits.

- Describe the nature of benefits available under OASDHI.

- Explain the formulas used for calculating benefits under OASDI.

- Describe the nature of coverage available under U.S. unemployment insurance and workers' compensation insurance.

Governments play an important role in providing economic security to families and individuals. Social insurance programs develop primarily in response to a perceived need by society for certain types of economic security measures for which neither individuals themselves nor private insurers can (or will) provide adequate coverage.[1]

Although there are many definitions of social insurance, for purposes of this discussion, social insurance is considered to be a program that meets the following three criteria:

1. Income security is provided for well-defined risks.
2. Participation is compulsory for the target population.
3. Contributions are not fully adjusted for probability of loss.

This definition includes government-mandated private programs and those programs that partially reflect the probability of loss, such as some workers' compensation programs. It does not include means-tested social assistance programs intended to alleviate poverty.

SOCIAL INSURANCE PROGRAMS

Social insurance programs typically are financed through payroll taxes, general revenues, or both. In some countries, the target populations are required to participate in private plans that provide social benefits. In France, for example, all workers are compelled to participate in their employers' private pension plans.

---

[1]This discussion draws on William S. Custer, "Social Insurance Worldwide," in Harold D. Skipper, Jr., ed., *International Risk and Insurance* (Homewood, IL: Richard D. Irwin, 1998), Chapter 21.

Social insurance contributions, whether in the form of taxes or contributions, vary by income or wealth but not on the basis of individual exposure to risk of loss. Given compulsory participation and contributions unrelated to risk, redistribution of income or wealth occurs commonly in social insurance programs. In the case of retirement income security, this redistribution occurs both within and between generations.

Rationale for Social Insurance

A country's decision to utilize a social insurance mechanism for providing security benefits depends upon a number of economic issues and the country's cultural response to those issues. In a competitive market, social insurance usually is a response to some type of market failure, coupled with a society's desire to promote social equity or to protect certain vulnerable segments of its population.

The risks generally covered by social insurance usually do not lend themselves to market-based approaches. The most important departure from competitive market assumptions is that coverage for these risks may be perceived as a *public good* (i.e., benefits to society are external to the individual). For example, the provision of health care benefits may lower the overall incidence of disease in a country through preventive care. It may also increase the productivity of workers directly through better health and indirectly by reducing the need for family members to forgo participation in the work force.

Because the total benefits to society can exceed those inuring exclusively to the individual, economic theory suggests that individuals making up a society will consume too little insurance (in society's view) if they face the true cost of that insurance. Subsidizing the costs of these risks effectively lowers its price, thereby encouraging more consumption.

Arguably, however, the most important motivation to society to provide these coverages is the desire to reduce the inequality that arises in a modern, capitalistic system. Societies vary in the extent to which they tolerate inequality, but most are uncomfortable with gross inequality, particularly when it is caused by factors beyond the individual's control. As a result, almost all developed and developing countries provide some level of social insurance coverage.

In those cases in which consumers are likely to demand less of the coverage than society would like them to purchase, private insurers are also likely to supply too little of them. As we note in chapter 1, insurance markets are characterized by *adverse selection*. Those with the greatest risk are most likely to seek coverage. As a result, insurers do not provide coverage for all exposures. Social insurance overcomes this problem by making insurance mandatory.

In the case of health insurance, society may value and social insurance programs may promote an increased consumption of health services. In addition, society may value increased risk taking as a means of increasing productivity. Private insurers, confronted by *moral hazard* (see chapter 1), may not offer coverage generous or widespread enough to meet these societal goals.

Where administrative, financing, or marketing economies of scale exist, a large, mandatory program will have market power and may be able to exploit them and achieve savings that private insurers may be unable to attain. Social insurance programs may exploit economies of scale either by creating regulated private monopolies or administering a public program.

Figure 22-1 illustrates the effects of providing insurance coverage through a social insurance mechanism. If individuals' consumption of certain insurance coverage carries pervasive positive externalities for society (i.e., it is a public good), individuals' consumption

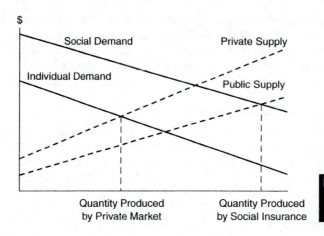

FIGURE 22-1 The Simple Economics of Social Insurance

of this coverage in a private market will be less than society desires. In Figure 22-1, society demands more insurance at every price than do individuals. As suggested earlier, governments attempt to resolve this issue, in part, by increasing the demand for this coverage by making participation compulsory.

Also, as private insurers face adverse selection and moral hazard, they will supply less than optimal coverage. By reducing or eliminating individual risk selection, government alleviates the problem of adverse selection. Moral hazard, however, remains an issue in social insurance programs. As increased consumption of certain covered services is often a goal, moral hazard is tolerated or even encouraged in ways that a private market could not permit. Governments thereby can supply more of this coverage at any given price, as shown by the public supply curve in Figure 22-1. As a result, the quantity demanded and supplied at each price is increased, yielding greater consumption of the goods and services society values, as illustrated by the social insurance equilibrium.

International Social Insurance Programs

Economic security is, of course, a problem for all countries and societies. Every developed country and most developing countries have social security programs that respond to the needs government perceives to be inadequately met by individuals or private insurers (see Table 22-1). What is a proper and adequate social security system for one country is obviously not necessarily satisfactory for another country. Much depends on economic, demographic, social, and even philosophical conditions.

Coverage may be universal, based on labor force attachment, or limited in other ways (e.g., self-employed and high-salaried employees may be excluded). In some coun-

TABLE 22-1	Number of Countries with Social Insurance Programs by Type of Program				
Type of Program	**1940**	**1958**	**1977**	**1987**	**1997**
Any type of program	57	80	129	141	172
Old-age, disability, survivors	33	58	114	130	166
Sickness and maternity	24	59	72	84	111
Work injury	57	77	129	136	164
Unemployment	21	26	38	40	68
Family allowance	7	38	65	63	86

Source: Social Security Programs throughout the World—1997, p. xiv.

tries, separate plans were developed for white-collar and manual workers although they eventually were combined. It is a common practice to have a separate system for government employees, but in some countries the general program covers these workers.

The provision of medical care through social security systems may be much more necessary in economically poor countries than in well-developed countries. The demography of a country can also have a significant effect on the character of a country's social security system. For example, when there is a high mortality rate in a country, the accompanying conditions lead to relatively low retirement ages for old-age pensions. A country with low earnings levels, with most people at bare subsistence levels, and with little personal savings may have a benefit level that is relatively higher (in relation to wages) than that required in economically more developed countries.

In many developing countries, the extended family still plays an important role as a source of economic security. The younger, active members of the family take care of the elderly and disabled. Any social benefits provided in these nations are often large lump-sum payments under a so-called provident fund plan rather than periodic payments. However, with growing industrialization and urbanization, these countries may well need the more usual type of social security benefit programs.

In most countries, the first form of social security was workers' compensation because of employers' legal responsibilities in many of these cases. Today, all developed countries and many other countries have systems that provide more social security programs (benefits) than does the United States. This is particularly the case in regard to medical care benefits, cash sickness payments, and maternity benefits and family allowances. On the other hand, unemployment insurance is not widespread outside economically developed countries. In a growing number of economically advanced countries, provision is made for automatically increasing the benefit level in accordance with changes in the price level or other economic conditions.

In most countries, social insurance systems are financed by taxes or contributions (which are not necessarily equal) from three parties: the worker, the employer, and the government. In some countries, the social insurance system has difficulty in getting the government to pay its required contribution. The combined level of contributions to systems with a broad span of benefits at high levels runs up to as much as 40 percent or more of payroll. In some cases, the government's share can be quite significant, with the funds coming from general taxation.

U.S. Social Insurance Programs

Since the introduction of the U.S. Social Security program in 1935, most U.S. nationals have come to expect the government to provide at least a minimum level of protection for workers against the financial consequences of premature death, old age, disability, and unemployment.

For the majority of U.S. nationals, the most important form of household wealth is the anticipated Social Security retirement benefits. The introduction of Medicare has enhanced the significance of this source of wealth. A host of public policy issues has been debated since the start of Social Security.

Most systems are based more on social adequacy than on individual equity concepts.[2] **Social adequacy** means that benefits paid provide a certain minimum standard

---

[2]The classic paper on the issue of social adequacy is Reinhard A. Hohaus, "Equity, Adequacy and Related Actions in Old-Age Security," in William Haber and Wilbur J. Cohen, eds., *Social Security: Program, Problems and Policies* (Homewood, IL: Richard D. Irwin, 1960), pp. 61–63. For an excellent historical review of the development of Social Security in the United States, see Edward D. Berkowitz, "The Historical Development of Social Security in the United States," in Eric R. Kingson and James H. Schulz, eds., *Social Security in the 21st Century* (New York: Oxford University Press, 1997), pp. 22-38.

of living to all contributors. **Individual equity** means that contributors receive benefits directly related to their contributions. The present U.S. system provides benefits on a basis that falls between these two definitions but with an emphasis on the former. Thus, benefits are heavily weighted in favor of lower-income groups, individuals with spouses and large families, and persons who were near retirement when they were first covered by Social Security. The purpose of the social adequacy principle is to provide a minimum floor of benefits to all groups.

Because private insurance operates on the individual equity principle, the issue of providing retirement and other benefits through either public or private means has been an ongoing debate. Disagreements over the impact of Social Security on the U.S. savings rate continue. In central and eastern Europe, where social security systems first developed, proposals are under consideration to abolish the extensive governmental retirement systems, replacing them with private security systems. In the United States, there has been a debate over making OASDI voluntary, or else partially or fully privatizing it. Others have argued that in light of the greater longevity of people, the increasing divorce rate, and the aging of the population generally, the adequacy of the combined public and private approach is questionable. Other issues include intergenerational equity and concern over the ability of the government system to pay promised benefits when this generation of workers retires.[3]

The Report of the U.S. 1994–1996 Advisory Council on Social Security addresses these questions.[4] It contains three proposals to evaluate the Social Security system's unfunded liability. Two of the three propose the partial privatization of Social Security through mandatory individual retirement accounts, a controversial new concept. One of the plans would also change the basic structure of Social Security. These proposals will be considered further in the later discussion of the current financial condition of Social Security and Medicare.

Social insurance programs in the United States may be put into four categories:

1. old-age, survivors, disability, and health insurance
2. unemployment insurance
3. workers' compensation insurance
4. temporary disability insurance

These social insurance programs play a significant role in employee benefit planning. The largest insurance expenditure for most employees is their contribution to Social Security. Furthermore, almost 25 percent spent by U.S. employers on benefits for their employees is used for legally required payments to social insurance programs. Finally, these programs form the foundation on which many individual insurance plans and employee benefit plans are built.

The emphasis in this text is on private employee benefit programs. Social Security, however, is so significant, both in terms of its own benefit structure and its impact on private plan design, that a reasonably detailed overview of this program seems essential. A brief overview of the other social insurance programs also is included.

---

[3]For an excellent review of all aspects of Social Security and issues relating thereto, see Eric R. Kingson and James H. Schulz, eds., *Social Security in the 21st Century.*

[4]Report of the 1994–1996 Advisory Council on Social Security, Vols. I and II, *Findings and Recommendations* (January 1997). See also, Joseph F. Quinn, "Social Security Reform: Marginal or Fundamental Change?" *Journal of the American Society of CLU & ChFC,* Vol. LI, No. 4 (July 1997), pp. 44–53.

OLD-AGE, SURVIVORS, DISABILITY, AND HEALTH INSURANCE PROGRAM

The Social Security Act of 1935, inspired largely by the severe business depression of 1930 to 1936, gave the United States an old-age benefit system for the first time.[5] This depression highlighted the reasons such a government plan of protection was needed: (1) the national economy had gradually been transformed from an extended family, self-sufficiency basis, in which the aged contributed to family support, to a complex urban system under which the self-sufficiency of the nuclear family largely ceased; (2) there was an increasing need, under the new urban system, for the old to have money for room and board without their having the opportunity to earn a living; (3) the increasing specialization and efficiency of industrial establishments made it difficult for the old to retain their jobs and to secure new jobs if the old ones were lost; and (4) there was a rapid increase, both absolutely and relatively, in the number of old persons in the population. At first, benefits were available only to the worker, but in 1939 the system was enlarged to provide insurance protection to the worker's family also. The new enlarged system then assumed the name of Old-Age and Survivors Insurance (OASI).

Several amendments were made in the 1940s and 1950s, the effects of which were to expand the system and increase benefits. Amendments in 1956 made disability income part of the bundle of benefits provided in the act, changing the name to Old-Age, Survivors, and Disability Insurance (OASDI).

Further amendments and benefit increases were made throughout the 1960s and 1970s. The 1965 amendments introduced, among other things, a new Title XVIII to the Social Security Act. This title initiated a health insurance program for the aged, popularly referred to as Medicare, thus changing the name to the Old-Age, Survivors, Disability, and Health Insurance (OASDHI) program—its current name.

The U.S. Social Security program seems regularly to undergo legislative change. Additionally, certain benefit values change automatically each year. Our discussion, therefore, certainly will be outdated with respect to certain values and likely will be outdated with respect to certain legislative matters. For these reasons, information in this section should be read for its general benefit rather than specifics. The reader interested in up-to-date information should check the Social Security's Web site at http://www.ssa.gov.

Coverage

Coverage for old-age, survivors, and disability insurance is conditioned on attachment to the labor market. Unlike many social insurance programs in other countries, the U.S. program is not based on the principle of universal coverage of all nationals but rather only of those who are employed (or self-employed).

Virtually all occupations are covered, although certain occupations are subject to special eligibility rules because of administrative or constitutional reasons. Covered on an elective basis are ministers and state and local government employees who are covered under a comparable retirement system. All states have entered into agreements with the Secretary of Health and Human Services. Some states have provided coverage for most employees whereas other states have provided coverage for only a few employees.

---

[5]The 1935 Social Security Act was a broad attack on the problems of financial insecurity. In addition to old-age insurance benefits, the act covered areas such as aid to the blind, orphans, and aged and unemployment insurance. This discussion is concerned with the present system only. For an extensive study of Social Security, see Robert J. Myers, *Social Security* (Philadelphia, PA: University of Pennsylvania Press, 1993).

Groups composed of employees whose positions are not under a state or local retirement system may be mandatorily covered. Presently, about 95 percent of the employed in the country are covered under OASDI and must pay Social Security taxes.

Eligibility for Benefits

The benefits derived from OASDI depend upon the insured status of the individual worker. There are three types of insured status: (1) fully insured, (2) currently insured, and (3) disability insured. Determination of an individual's insured status depends upon his or her number of quarters of coverage and, in some instances, when they were earned.

For 1999, a **quarter of coverage** is given for each full $740 unit of annual earnings on which Social Security taxes are paid, up to a maximum of four quarters for the year. This earnings amount is adjusted annually according to changes in the national average wage level.

Fully Insured Status

An individual can attain **fully insured** status by being credited with either (1) 40 quarters of coverage earned at any time after 1936 or (2) at least one quarter of coverage (whenever earned) for every calendar year elapsing after 1950 (or after the year in which the worker attains age 21, if later) up to the year in which he or she reaches age 62, or, if earlier, dies or becomes disabled. A worker who fulfills the first requirement remains fully insured even if he or she spends no future time in covered employment. A minimum of six quarters of coverage is required in any case. Subject to certain requirements set forth in law, a year during which a worker is disabled does not adversely affect his or her eligibility for fully insured status.

Currently Insured Status

An individual can attain **currently insured** status by being credited with a minimum of six quarters of coverage during the 13-quarter period ending with the quarter in which he or she dies. Fully insured status is related to the length of attachment and currently insured status to the recency of attachment to the related labor market.

Disability Insured Status

An individual worker is eligible for cash disability benefits if he or she (1) is fully insured; (2) has at least 20 quarters of coverage out of the last 40 quarters prior to disability; and (3) has been disabled for at least five months by an impairment that is so serious that it prevents him or her from engaging in "any substantial gainful activity" and has lasted or may be expected to last at least 12 months or to result in death. For persons disabled before age 31, the coverage requirements are reduced. For blind persons, the second requirement need not be met. The disabled individual also must be willing to accept state vocational rehabilitation services.

Benefit Amounts

To understand the Social Security benefit structure, one must understand certain key concepts and terms in the law that determine benefit amounts.

Primary Insurance Amount

All monthly income benefits are based on the worker's **primary insurance amount** (PIA), which is the monthly amount paid to a retired worker at normal retirement age

(age 65 for workers born before 1938) or to a disabled worker. The primary insurance amount, in turn, is based on the worker's average indexed monthly earnings.[6]

Average Indexed Monthly Earnings

The **average indexed monthly earnings** (AIME) method is designed to ensure that monthly cash benefits reflect changes in wage levels over the worker's lifetime so that the benefits paid will have a relatively constant relationship to the worker's earnings before retirement, disability, or death. The result is that workers who retire today and workers who will be retiring in the future at normal retirement age will have about the same proportion of their earnings replaced by Social Security retirement benefits.

Earnings for years after 1950 are indexed by multiplying the actual earnings subject to Social Security taxation for the year being indexed by the ratio of (1) average national wage for the second year[7] before the worker reaches age 62, or, if earlier, becomes disabled or dies, to (2) average national wage for the year being indexed (see Table 22-2). For example, assume that George retired at age 62 in 1996. The significant year for setting the index factor is the second year before he attained age 62 (1996). If George's actual taxable wages were $10,000 in 1956, this amount is multiplied by the ratio of the average national wage ($25,913.90) in 1996 to the average national wage ($3,532.36) in 1956. Thus, George's indexed earnings for 1956 would be calculated as follows:

$$\text{Actual Earnings in 1956} \cdot \frac{\text{Average Annual Wages in 1996}}{\text{Average Annual Wages in 1956}} = \text{Indexed Earnings for 1956}$$

and

$$\$10{,}000.00 \cdot \frac{\$25{,}913.90}{\$3{,}532.36} = \$73{,}361$$

TABLE 22-2	Maximum Family Benefit for Selected Average Indexed Monthly Earnings (AIME) for Persons Who Reach Age 62 in 1999 or Who Die before Age 62 in 1999
AIME	*Maximum Family Benefit*
$5,000	$2,730
4,500	2,599
4,000	2,467
3,500	2,336
3,000	2,192
2,500	1,962
2,000	1,747

---

[6]Prior to the 1977 amendments to the Social Security Act, there was a technical flaw in the provision for computing benefits. As a result of the flaw, covered workers could benefit unduly during certain types of inflationary conditions. First, the benefit scale was adjusted upward to reflect price inflation. Second, as wages tended to increase during inflationary periods, higher normal wages also would produce still higher future benefits. The gist of the problem was that future benefits were *overpriced* for inflation. The AIME computation method was introduced to correct the problem.

[7]The two-year lag is due to data availability.

A similar calculation is carried out for each year in the measuring period except that earnings for and after the indexing year are counted in actual dollar amounts. The adjusted earnings then are used to determine the worker's AIME, which in turn is used to determine the primary insurance amount.[8]

To obtain the AIME, one must first calculate the number of years elapsing between (1) the first day of the year in which the insured reached age 22 or January 1, 1951, if later, and (2) the year before the insured becomes 62, or, if earlier, dies or becomes disabled. Five is arbitrarily subtracted from this result and this yields the computation years, n.[9] This further result is converted from years into months.

The worker's indexed covered earnings are then calculated for the relevant time period (all years from 1951 on), following the procedure illustrated previously. These earnings, prior to indexing, are subject to year-by-year maximums, moving from $3,600 in 1951 to $72,600 in 1999. The n years with the highest indexed earnings are used, but if the individual does not have as many years with earnings as must be used, zeros must be used for the remaining years. Those periods during which an insured individual is disabled are omitted in the calculation of the number of years used in determining the average indexed monthly earnings. The effect of the drop-out and disability freeze provisions is to increase the average indexed monthly earnings and, consequently, the benefits to be provided. Earnings in any years after 1950 can be used, including years before age 22 and years after age 61.

PIA Formula

After the worker's AIME is established, a weighted formula is used to determine the primary insurance amount. Based on the benefit formula that is applicable to the cohorts of persons who attain age 62 in 1999 (or workers under age 62 who die or become disabled in 1999), the PIA is determined as follows:

90% of the First $505 of AIME

+

32% of the Next $2,538 of AIME

+

15% of the AIME in Excess of $3,043

The formula break points are adjusted annually, for subsequent cohorts, to reflect changes in average wages in the national economy. In addition, the benefit amount resulting from application of the formula is subject to the automatic cost-of-living adjustment provisions (discussed later) starting with the year of attainment of age 62 (or prior death or disability).

The PIA formula is intended to implement a major goal of the Social Security Program, the redistribution of income to provide a floor of security for lower-paid workers. This, of course, results in a lower income replacement rate and "rate of return" for higher earners. Until relatively recently, the vast majority of Social Security recipients have received more in the form of the value of their benefits than the accumulated value of what they paid in premiums (taxes), taking into account the time value of money. This

---

[8]Earnings before 1951 are not used in the AIME benefit computation method but rather can be used in a different special procedure if it produces more favorable results (which, currently, will rarely—if ever—be the case).

[9]For persons disabled before age 47, the number of drop-out years is generally four for ages 42 to 46, three for ages 37 to 41, two for ages 32 to 36, one for ages 27 to 31, and none for ages under 27 (ignoring the seldom used "child-care" drop-out years).

is no longer true and the fact underlies many of the issues that are part of the ongoing policy debates relative to the future of Social Security.

Automatic Cost-of-Living Adjustment (COLA)

Monthly cash benefits are adjusted automatically each December for specified changes whenever the consumer price index for all urban wage earners and clerical workers (CPI) increases during the measured period. Benefits are increased by the same percentage (rounded to one-tenth of 1 percent) as the percentage by which the CPI for the cost-of-living computation quarter (the third quarter of the calendar year) exceeds the CPI for the most recent calendar quarter in which a general benefit increase became effective. If the cost-of-living adjustment is made, the taxable earnings base and earnings test exempt amounts (discussed later) also are automatically adjusted.[10]

The cost-of-living provision is valuable because, with its use, the real purchasing power of the cash benefits is maintained during inflationary periods. In view of the political sensitivity of Social Security benefits, it is not surprising that if the CPI declines during the measuring period, benefits are not changed (but subsequent increases are then based on the CPI level before the decline).

Maximum Family Benefits

There is a limit on the maximum monthly benefits that can be paid to a family based on the earnings record of one person (see Table 22-2). For persons disabled in 1981 and later, the maximum family benefit is the lower of (1) 85 percent of the worker's AIME (or actual PIA if higher) or (2) 150 percent of the PIA. The maximum family benefit for persons who reach age 62 in 1999 or who die before age 62 in 1999 is based on the following formula (subject to the COLA provisions):

150% of the first $645 of PIA

+

272% of the next $286

+

134% of the next $283

+

175% of the PIA in excess of $1,214

Whenever the total monthly benefits payable to all beneficiaries on the basis of a worker's earnings record exceed the maximum allowed, each family member's benefit is reduced proportionately (but not the worker's benefit), to bring the total within the maximum.

Nature of Benefits

The OASDI program provides retirement, survivor, and disability benefits. As pointed out earlier, all benefits are based on the insured worker's primary insurance amount.

Retirement Benefits

The insured worker's monthly retirement benefit, a life annuity, is referred to as the **old-age insurance benefit** and equals 100 percent of the worker's PIA for retirement at the **normal retirement age (NRA),** which is 65 for workers born before 1938. It slowly

---

[10]In general, these items are adjusted annually based on changes in average wages in the national economy.

increases then until it is 67 for those born after 1959.[11] The spouse of a retired worker is entitled to a benefit **(wife's/husband's benefit)** equal to 50 percent of the worker's PIA if he or she is at the NRA or older at the time of claim,[12] or, regardless of age, if the spouse has under his or her care a dependent and unmarried child of the worker under age 16, or, regardless of age, if the child has been disabled since before age 22.

In addition, each unmarried child under 18 (or under 19 if the child is attending a primary or secondary educational institution on a full-time basis) or disabled before age 22 is entitled to a benefit **(child's benefit)** equal to 50 percent of the worker's PIA. The total benefits payable to a retired individual and his or her family members are subject to the overall family maximums. Retirement benefits are available only to fully insured workers.

Survivor Benefits

The unremarried spouse of a deceased, fully insured worker can be entitled to survivor benefits as early as age 60 **(widow's/widower's benefits)**. He or she is entitled to 100 percent of the deceased worker's PIA if he or she waits until the NRA or later to receive benefits, or to 71.5 percent of the PIA if the benefit is claimed at age 60, or proportionately more when claimed after age 60 and before the NRA. However, the widow's/widower's benefit cannot, if the worker retired before the NRA, exceed the larger of (1) the worker's benefit or (2) 82.5 percent of the PIA.

The NRA for widows and widowers increases beyond age 65 for those attaining age 60 in and after 2000 and gradually rises to 67 for those attaining age 60 in 2022 (i.e., becoming 67 in 2029). When this occurs, the benefit rate for initial claim at age 60 remains at 71.5 percent of the PIA, with proportionate amounts for initial claims between age 60 and the NRA. If the widow/widower is aged 50 to 59 and also disabled, she or he can be entitled to a disability benefit, which equals 71.5 percent of the PIA. Regardless of age, if a widow/widower has under her or his care a dependent and unmarried child under age 16 of a worker or a child who has been disabled since before age 22, he or she can be entitled to a benefit **(mother's/father's benefit)** equal to 75 percent of the PIA.

In addition, a dependent and unmarried child under age 18 (or under 19 if the child is attending a primary or secondary educational institution on a full-time basis) or regardless of age, if disabled before age 22, is entitled to a benefit **(child's benefit)** equal to 75 percent of the primary insurance amount. Dependent parents who are 62 and over are each entitled to a benefit equal to 75 percent of the PIA **(parent's benefit).**[13] The same maximum family benefit applies as in retirement cases. In addition to the income benefits, a lump-sum benefit of $255 **(death benefit)** is paid on the death of the worker who was living with a spouse or who leaves a spouse or child entitled to monthly benefits.

All of these survivorship benefits are available to the family members of a fully insured worker. The family members of a currently insured worker are eligible only for (1) the mother's/father's benefits; (2) the survivor child's benefit; and (3) the lump-sum death benefit.

---

[11] A man or woman worker with NRA of 65 can elect to retire at age 62 with a permanently reduced benefit equal to 80 percent of his or her full benefit (PIA). When the NRA increases to above 65, the reduction for early retirement increases (and the factor for age 62 is 70 percent when the NRA is 67). Benefits are reduced for retirement between ages 62 and the NRA.

[12] The spouse of a retired worker, when the NRA is 65, may qualify for benefits as early as age 62 but with a reduced benefit; 75 percent of the full benefit is payable at age 62, and proportionately more if benefits are first claimed between ages 62 and 65. When the NRA increases above 65, the reduction for early retirement increases (and the factor for age 62 is 65 percent when the NRA is 67).

[13] If only one parent is entitled to this benefit, the amount is 82½ percent of the deceased's primary insurance amount.

Disability Benefits

The disability income benefit equals 100 percent of the primary insurance amount and continues only during disability or until the NRA is reached, when it becomes a retirement benefit. The initial determination of disability is made by state agencies, with the Social Security Administration having the right of review. **Disability** is defined as the inability to engage in any substantial gainful activity by reason of any medically determinable physical or mental impairment that can be expected to result in death or that has lasted or can be expected to last for a continuous period of not less than 12 months. The determination of continuance of disability is made by the state agencies.

Monthly payments are made to family members of persons receiving disability insurance benefits. The family members eligible for these benefits are the same as the ones who would qualify as family members of persons receiving retirement benefits. A lower family maximum benefit applies in disability cases than in retirement and survivor cases (namely, the lower of 150 percent of PIA or 85 percent of AIME, but not less than the PIA).

Rehabilitation is a part of the disability program. Thus, a disabled beneficiary who performs services despite severe handicaps can continue to receive benefits for nine months. In addition, the law provides a three-month period of adjustment for beneficiaries who medically recover from their disabilities.

An unmarried child of a deceased, disabled, or retired covered worker who has been disabled since before age 22 is eligible for a cash disability benefit at age 18 or after. The child's disability benefits are payable for as long as the disability continues and are the same as the benefit received by a nondisabled, dependent child of a disabled, retired, or deceased worker. Also, a mother's/father's benefit is payable to the parent who has in his or her care a disabled child receiving benefits. This applies if he or she is a spouse of a disabled, retired, or deceased worker. The rehabilitation features of the disability program also apply to a disabled child.

Reductions and Other Benefit Changes

A Social Security beneficiary can be subject to a total or partial reduction in benefits under certain situations in addition to being reduced for initially claiming benefits before the NRA in some circumstances.

Earnings Test

From the inception of the OASDI program, there has been some form of restriction on benefits provided to persons who have substantial earnings from employment. This provision, referred to as the retirement earnings test, does not apply to investment income, pensions, or other nonearned income. The underlying principle is that retirement benefits should be paid only to persons who are substantially retired.

Today benefits are reduced for Social Security beneficiaries under the age of 70 if they have earnings from work that exceed a specified level. If an eligible person is, in 1999, aged 65 through 69, and receives earnings of more than $15,500 a year from covered or noncovered employment, some or all benefits will be lost for that year. Earnings of $15,500 or less cause no loss of benefits. There is a loss of $1 in benefits for every $3 of earnings on the portion of earnings over $15,500 (for persons under age 65, the loss is $1 of benefits for every $2 of earnings over $9,600[14]). However, no benefits are lost for any month in the first year of retirement in which the individual neither earns more than one-twelfth of the annual exempt amount in wages nor renders substantial services

---

[14]This amount for persons aged 65 through 69 is scheduled to increase to $17,000 in 2000, $25,000 in 2001, and $30,000 in 2002 and thereafter. For persons under age 65, the amount increases automatically each future year in accordance with changes in the general level of wages.

in self-employment. The earnings test applies to all beneficiaries under age 70 except disabled beneficiaries, who have a stricter test.

The earnings of a person who is receiving benefits as a family member or as a survivor affect only his or her own benefits and not payments to other members of his or her family. Thus, if the wife of a deceased worker loses her benefit because of the earnings test, her children (if they are under age 18, disabled since age 18, or until they are age 19 if they meet the school-attendance requirement) will continue to receive their benefits.

Dual Eligibility

A person eligible for more than one benefit will receive, in effect, the highest benefit for which he or she is eligible. Thus, a wife, eligible in her own right as an insured worker, can draw benefits under her husband's insured status only to the extent that they exceed the amount of her old-age benefit. Also, the benefits for a spouse or widow(er) of a retired, disabled, or deceased insured worker are reduced by two-thirds of the amount of any pension that such spouse earned from a retirement system for government employees that was not coordinated with Social Security on the last day of service.

Delayed Retirement

A worker receives an increase in his or her old-age benefits for each month that he or she delays retirement between the NRA and age 70 (but not in the auxiliary benefits for his or her family members). The increase is 4 percent for 1992 and 1993 attainments, 4½ percent for 1994 and 1995 attainments, 5 percent for 1996 and 1997 attainments, and so on, and eventually 8 percent for attainments of the NRA in 2009 (then age 66) and after. Work beyond retirement age frequently results in a higher AIME. Years worked after age 61 can be selected as years of highest earnings. The delayed retirement credit is passed along in the benefit for the surviving widow or widower.

The size of the delayed retirement credit (DRC) plays a key role in encouraging or discouraging workers to retire after age 62. When the DRC reaches 8 percent, the present rules will be close to being the actuarial equivalent of retirement at NRA.

Changes in Family Status

Social Security benefits are terminated when changes in family status, such as marriage or divorce, alter the conditions under which payments are made. For example, payments to a nondisabled child stop when he or she reaches age 18, or 19 if the child is attending high school full-time, and payments to a widow or widower generally stop if she or he remarries (but not if the beneficiary is age 60 or over).

Other

Failure to file for benefits after eligibility may deprive a person of benefits for a period of time. The act generally grants monthly benefits retroactively for a period of 6 months (12 months for disability cases). The individual also has a responsibility, periodically, to check into the accuracy of the Social Security Administration's records relating to his or her account. Benefits also may be lost because an individual is convicted of certain subversive crimes.

Taxation of Social Security Benefits

As a result of 1983 amendments, part of Social Security benefits may be subject to federal income taxation. Beginning in 1994, up to 85 percent of Social Security benefits is included in the gross income of beneficiaries whose modified adjusted gross income (which is the adjusted gross income, plus tax-exempt interest income, plus 50 percent of Social Security benefits) exceeds certain base amounts. The base amounts are $34,000 for a single taxpayer, and $44,000 for married taxpayers filing jointly, and zero for married taxpayers filing separately who lived together at any time during the year. Because these amounts are not indexed, more and more people reach "taxable status" over time.

Medicare Program

The 1965 amendments in the Social Security Act added Title XVIII, thereby initiating a health insurance program for the aged. Medicare represented one of the most sweeping changes ever made in the Social Security system.[15]

Medicare is, in general, a two-part program of federal health insurance. Under **Part A,** the Hospital Insurance Plan, essentially all persons aged 65 or over and all persons who have been receiving Social Security disability benefits for at least two years are covered for extensive hospitalization benefits.

Part B, which is optional, provides a supplementary program for surgical and physician's care, and certain other benefits, for persons aged 65 or over and all persons who have been receiving Social Security disability benefits for at least two years. Eligible persons must pay a monthly premium of $45.50 in 1999 for this coverage—approximately 25 percent of the cost for Part B benefits. The remainder comes from general revenue. The premium changes yearly.

Medicare is secondary in payment to private group health insurance or liability insurance in some cases [e.g., to liability insurance under automobile policies, to group health insurance for chronic renal disease for the first 36 months, and to group health insurance for persons actively at work (and their spouses) for employers with 20 or more employees].

Hospital Insurance

The basic hospital plan benefits include the following:

1. *Inpatient hospital services* for up to 90 days in each *benefit period.* There also is a provision for a lifetime reserve of 60 days that can be used after the 90 days in a *spell of illness.* In 1999, the patient pays a deductible amount of $768 for the first 60 days, plus coinsurance of $192 a day for the next 30 days for each spell of illness, plus coinsurance of $384 a day for the lifetime-reserve days. Hospital services include all those ordinarily furnished by a hospital to its inpatients. However, payment is not made for private-duty nursing or for the hospital services of physicians except by medical or dental interns or residents in training under approved teaching programs. Inpatient psychiatric hospital service is included, but a lifetime limitation of 190 days is imposed.

2. *Posthospital skilled nursing care* (in a facility having an arrangement with a hospital for the timely transfer of patients and for furnishing medical information about patients) after a patient is transferred from a hospital (after at least a three-day stay) for up to 100 days in a benefit period. In 1999, after the first 20 days, patients pay coinsurance of $96 a day for the remaining days of care in a spell of illness.

3. *Home health services* on an unlimited-visit basis without a requirement of prior hospitalization. The recipient must be in the care of a physician and under a plan established by a physician. These services include intermittent nursing care, therapy, and the part-time services of a home health aide. The patient must be homebound, except that when certain equipment is used, the individual can be taken to a hospital, extended care facility, or rehabilitation center to receive some of these covered home health services in order to get the advantage of the necessary

---

[15]The 1972 amendments extended Medicare to persons under 65 who receive Social Security or railroad retirements benefits based on long-term disability for at least 24 months or who have chronic renal disease and require hemodialysis or a kidney transplant.

equipment. In and after 2003, some of these services will be provided under Supplementary Medical Insurance, with phasing-in of this basis from 1998 to 2002. This change will affect only the accounting and financing for these benefits, and the beneficiaries will, in the aggregate, have the same benefit protection.

4. *Hospice care* for terminally ill patients.

A *benefit period* is considered to begin when the individual enters a hospital, and it ends when he or she has not been an inpatient of a hospital or skilled nursing facility (including rehabilitation services) for 60 consecutive days. The deductible amounts for inpatient hospital care are increased to keep pace with increases in hospital costs. The daily coinsurance amounts for long hospital stays and skilled nursing care benefits are correspondingly adjusted.

In 1983, in order to provide financial incentives to hospitals to contain costs, a case payment system was adopted that radically changed hospital reimbursement under Medicare shifting from a retrospective to a prospective mode. This new reimbursement system was based on preset payments for services rendered to patients with similar diagnoses rather than on costs incurred. The **diagnosis related group (DRG)** payment system based hospital payments on established fees for services required to treat a specific diagnosis rather than discrete units of services. Thus, if the optimal patient care outcome could be achieved at a resource cost lower than the preset payment, the hospital realized an excess payment for the case. The principle of case-based prospective payment has been adopted in varying forms by numerous states and private third-party payors.

Supplementary Medical Insurance

Subject to a $100 annual deductible and a 20 percent participation (coinsurance) of covered expenses (subject to a maximum of the standard charges recognized by Medicare) above the deductible, the supplementary plan provides the following benefits:

1. *Physicians' and surgeons' services,* whether furnished in a hospital, clinic, office, home, or elsewhere.
2. *Home health services* are available without limit (identical to those covered under hospital insurance) and are not subject to cost-sharing provisions.
3. *Medical and health services,* including diagnostic X-ray, laboratory, and other tests; X-ray, radium, and radioactive-isotope therapy; ambulance services; surgical dressings and splints, casts, and other devices for reduction of fractures and dislocations; rental of durable medical equipment, such as iron lungs, oxygen tents, hospital beds, and wheelchairs used in the patient's home; prosthetic devices (other than dental) that replace all or part of an internal body organ; braces and artificial legs, arms, and eyes; physical therapy treatments; influenza and pneumococcal shots; pap smears and pelvic exams for cancer; colorectal screening tests; diabetes self-management training; bone mass measurement procedures; and so on. In some instances, certain services are not subject to the deductible and/or coinsurance provisions (e.g., diagnostic laboratory tests).
4. *Psychiatric care,* subject to a special limitation on outside-the-hospital treatment of mental, psychoneurotic, and personality disorders. Payment for such treatment during any calendar year is limited, in effect, to 50 percent of the expenses.

The program recognizes only the so-called "reasonable charges" for services. Thus, not all physician charges may be reimbursable under the program. If any of the services outlined previously are covered under the basic hospital plan, they are excluded from coverage under the supplementary plan. The law provides for special rules regarding enrollment periods and the time when coverage commences. Tables 22-3 and 22-4 summarize Medicare benefits as of January 1, 1999.

TABLE 22-3 Summary of Medicare Benefits (Part A)

Table of Medicare Benefits (Part A)
Effective for 1999

Service	Benefit	Medicare Pays	A Person Pays
Hospitalization	First 60 days	All but $768	$768
Semiprivate room and board,	61st to 90th day	All but $192 a day	$192 a day
general nursing, and other	91st to 150th day[a]	All but $384 a day	$384 a day
hospital services and supplies	Beyond 150 days	Nothing	All costs
Skilled Nursing Facility Care	First 20 days	100% of approved amount	Nothing
Semiprivate room and board,	Additional 80 days	All but $96.00 a day	$96.00 a day
skilled nursing and rehabilita-	Beyond 100 days	Nothing	All costs
tive services, and other services and supplies[b]			
Home Health Care[c]	First 100 days in	100% of approved amount;	Nothing for services;
Part-time or intermittent	spell of illness	80% of approved amount	20% of approved
skilled care, home health aid		for durable medical	amount for durable
services, durable medical		equipment	medical equipment
equipment and supplies, and other services			
Hospice Care	For as long as the	All but limited costs for	Limited costs for
Pain relief, symptom manage-	doctor certifies	outpatient drugs and	outpatient drugs and
ment, and support services for	need	inpatient respite care	inpatient respite care
the terminally ill			
Blood	Unlimited if med-	All but first 3 pints per	For first 3 pints[d]
When furnished by a hospital	ically necessary	calendar year	
or skilled nursing facility during covered stay			

[a]Up to 60 reserve days may be used only once in a lifetime.

[b]Neither Medicare nor private Medigap insurance will pay for most nursing home care.

[c]Home health care benefits moved to Part B under the 1997 budget agreement.

[d]Blood paid for or replaced under Part B of Medicare during the calendar year does not have to be paid for or replaced under Part A.

Medicare + Choice Program

As a result of legislation in 1997, beneficiaries can, beginning generally in 1998, opt out of the traditional Medicare program described earlier insofar as benefit coverage is concerned and go into a so-called Medicare + Choice plan. Medicare + Choice is designed to allow beneficiaries to have access to a wide array of private health plan choices in addition to traditional fee-for-service Medicare. These choices include:

- traditional fee-for-service Medicare
- private-fee-for-service Medicare + Choice
- coordinated care plans that provide health care service, including:
  1. HMO plans
  2. plans offered by provider sponsored organizations (PSOs)
  3. preferred provider organization (PPOs) plans
  4. a Medicare + Choice medical savings account (MSA)

Medicare + Choice plans must provide all current Medicare-covered items and services. They may incorporate extra benefits in a basic package or they may offer supplemental benefits priced separately from the basic package. A Medicare + Choice plan is a secondary payor to any employer-provided health coverage.

TABLE 22-4 Summary of Medicare Benefits (Part B)

Table of Medicare Benefits (Part B)
Effective for 1999

Service	Benefit	Medicare Pays	A Person Pays
Doctors' services, inpatient and outpatient medical and surgical services and supplies, physical and speech therapy, diagnostic	Unlimited if medically necessary	80% of approved amount (after $100 deductible); reduced to 50% for most outpatient mental health services	$100 deductible[a] plus 20% of approved amount and limited charges above approved amount[b]
Clinical Laboratory Services Blood tests, urinalyses, and more	Unlimited if medically necessary	Generally 100% of approved amount	Nothing for services
Home Health Care[c] Part-time or intermittent skilled care, home health aid services, durable medical equipment and supplies, and other services	Unlimited but covers only basic health care not covered by Hospital Insurance (Part A)	100% of approved amount; 80% of approved amount for durable medical equipment	Nothing for services; 20% of approved amount for durable medical equipment
Outpatient Hospital Treatment Services for the diagnosis or treatment of illness or injury	Unlimited if medically necessary	Medicare payment to hospital based on hospital cost	20% of hospital (whatever the charges) (after $100 deductible)[a]
Blood	Unlimited if medically necessary	80% of approved amount (after $100 deductible and starting with fourth pint)	For first 3 pints plus 20% of approved amount for additional pints (after $100 deductible)[c]
Ambulatory Surgical Services	Unlimited if medically necessary	80% of predetermined amount (after $100 deductible)	$100 deductible, plus 20% of predetermined amount

[a]Once a person has had $100 of expense for covered services in 1999, the Part B deductible does not apply to any further covered services received for the rest of the year.

[b]A person pays for charges higher than the amount approved by Medicare unless the doctor or supplier agrees to accept Medicare's approved amount as the total charge for services rendered.

[c]Blood paid for or replaced under Part A of Medicare during the calendar year does not have to be paid for or replaced under Part B.

Managed Care and Medicare/Medicaid

Medicare and Medicaid[16] have increasingly relied on managed care. HMOs enter into contracts with the Medicare program (using capitation arrangements) as part of their business strategy. Market penetration to date has been limited relative to the working-age population. By the beginning of 1997, more that 4.9 million Medicare beneficiaries were enrolled in HMOs having Medicare risk contracts, representing 13 percent of total beneficiaries. Since 1993, Medicare managed care enrollment has increased 108 percent.

State Medicaid programs also have turned to managed care. Total enrollment has been rising dramatically with total enrollment in 1996 at 40 percent of Medicaid recipients as compared with 9.5 percent in 1991. Forty-nine states offer some type of Medicaid managed care plans.[17]

---

[16]Medicaid is a mandatory joint federal/state program that provides basic medical care services to the economically indigent population.

[17]Harry A. Sultz and Kristina M. Young, *Health Care USA—Understanding Its Organization and Delivery*, 2nd ed. (Gaithersburg, MD: Aspen Publishers, Inc., 1999), pp. 267–268.

Financing OASDI and Medicare

OASDI

The Old-Age, Survivors, and Disability Insurance system is financed on a contributory basis, shared equally by employee and employer.[18] The employee pays a tax on the wages he or she receives, and the employer pays a tax on its payroll. The 1999 rate of contribution is 6.2 percent of covered wages and of payroll for a total contribution of 12.4 percent of covered payroll (present law schedules no change in this rate in the future). The tax in 1999 for OASDI is calculated on the first $72,600 of wages paid to an employee. The maximum taxable earnings rise with earnings trends. The employer withholds the employee's tax from his or her pay and remits the employee's tax and its own tax to the U.S. District Director of Internal Revenue.

The tax pattern is somewhat different for the self-employed persons covered under the act. To finance this phase of the program, the self-employed pay a tax equal to the combined employer/employee rate, but with a special deduction of 50 percent of the Social Security self-employment tax from their income when computing their federal income tax. This tax, 12.4 percent in 1999, is imposed on 92.35 percent of net earnings from self-employment up to the same maximum amount as in the employer/employee tax. The self-employed person pays his or her tax on the basis of a special schedule attached to the federal income tax return.

Over the years, both the tax rates and wage bases have been dramatically increased to finance increased benefit levels and new benefits that have been added to the overall Social Security program. Table 22-5 shows the magnitude of these increases for selected years.

Medicare

The basic Hospital Insurance Plan (Part A) is financed by a separate Hospital Insurance (HI) tax imposed upon employers, employees, and self-employed persons. No maximum earnings base is applicable in 1999 in contrast to the maximum of $72,600 for

TABLE 22-5 Changes in Tax Rates for OASDI and Medicare Part A (HI) for Selected Years

Year	Earnings OASDI	Earnings HI	Tax Rate Employer and Employee Each OASDI	Tax Rate Employer and Employee Each HI	Maximum Employee Tax OASDI	Maximum Employee Tax HI
1950	$ 3,000		1.5%	—	$ 45.00	—
1970	7,800	$ 7,800	4.20	0.6%	327.60	$ 46.80
1980	25,900	25,900	5.08	1.05	1,315.72	271.95
1986	42,000	42,000	5.70	1.45	2,394.00	609.00
1990	51,300	51,300	6.20	1.45	3,180.60	743.85
1991	53,400	125,000	6.20	1.45	3,310.80	1,812.50
1994	60,600	All earnings	6.20	1.45	3,757.20	Unlimited
1995	61,200	All earnings	6.20	1.45	3,794.40	Unlimited
1996	62,700	All earnings	6.20	1.45	3,887.40	Unlimited
1997	65,400	All earnings	6.20	1.45	3,054.80	Unlimited
1998	68,400	All earnings	6.20	1.45	4,240.80	Unlimited
1999	72,600	All earnings	6.20	1.45	4,501.20	Unlimited

---

[18] The Federal Insurance Contributions Act (FICA), Chapter 21, Internal Revenue Code.

OASDI. For 1999 (and after), the rates of the Hospital Insurance tax are 1.45 percent for employees and 1.45 percent for employers and 2.9 percent for self-employed persons. As in the case of the OASDI tax, there is a special federal income tax deduction of 50 percent of the Hospital Insurance self-employment tax. This income tax deduction is designed to treat the self-employed in much the same manner as employees and employers are treated for Social Security and income tax purposes under present law.

Supplementary Medical Insurance (Part B) is voluntary and is financed through premiums paid by individuals who enroll and through funds from the federal government. For 1999, each person who enrolls must pay a basic premium of $45.50 per month, and the federal government pays about three times as much as a matching amount from general revenues. The monthly premiums are, of course, in addition to the deductible and coinsurance amounts paid by the patient.

When paid, the funds collected for the several programs are allocated to the Old-Age and Survivors Insurance Trust Fund, the Disability Insurance Trust Fund, the Hospital Insurance Trust Fund, and the Supplementary Medical Insurance Trust Fund. They are managed by boards of trustees consisting of the secretaries of the Treasury, of Labor, of Health and Human Services, the Commissioner of Social Security, and two public trustees. The Secretary of the Treasury is the managing trustee of the trust funds. The funds must be invested in securities that are the direct obligation of or guaranteed by the U.S. government. Funds are disbursed from these accounts to cover benefit payments and administrative expenses.

The Social Security program is essentially a partially funded system. Current payroll taxes and other contributions received by the program are used to pay the current benefits of persons who, for the most part, are no longer paying Social Security taxes because of disability or retirement, and the excess of income over expenditures is invested in government bonds. Private-sector insurance retirement plans are based on considerably more advance funding whereby assets are accumulated from current contributions to pay the future benefits of those making the contributions.

The Social Security program does have limited reserves to serve as emergency funds in periods when current benefit expenditures exceed current contributions, such as in times of recession. However, these reserves are currently relatively small although large in absolute amounts—$762 billion at the end of 1998 (they are enough to cover one and one-half year's expenditures, but estimated to be larger in the future—about 3.6 year's expenditures some 15 years hence according to the intermediate-cost estimate) and could pay benefits for only a limited time if contributions to a trust fund ceased.

Current Financial Condition of Social Security and Medicare

A serious short-range financing crisis confronted the OASDI program in the early 1980s, largely as a result of the adverse economic conditions then (and the financing under the 1977 act being based on moderately optimistic economic assumptions).[19] The 1983 amendments (which were based largely on the recommendations of the bipartisan National Commission on Social Security Reform) attempted to establish the program on a sound financial basis at least for the 1980s, and it was hoped for the next 70 years as well. Furthermore, the objective was to provide anticipated long-range financing (up to the mid-2000s). These amendments made many changes to accomplish this result: extending coverage to almost all categories of workers previously not covered, delaying cost-of-living adjustments of benefits for six months each year, making up to 50 percent of benefits subject to income tax for high-income recipients and returning the revenue

---

[19]Robert J. Myers, "Social Security and the Federal Budget: Some Mirages, Myths, and Solutions," *Journal of the American Society of CLU & ChFC* (March 1989), pp. 58–63.

to the trust funds, raising the normal retirement age on a deferred gradual basis (equivalent to an across-the-board benefit cut), and advancing some of the previously scheduled increases in the tax rates.

The actual experience of the OASDI program after 1983 was even more favorable than had been projected, and a fund balance of almost $762 billion was accumulated by the end of 1998. However, primarily because of changed assumptions, the long-range financing picture is less favorable now than it was projected to be when the legislation was enacted.

According to the intermediate-cost estimate in the 1999 Trustees Report, the OASDI fund balance will build up to a peak in 2020 and will then steadily decrease until becoming exhausted in 2034. After then, if the income provisions are not changed, benefits would have to be reduced by 29 percent for the program to remain in balance.

This situation has resulted in many different proposals for change, such as: (1) increasing the normal retirement beyond the age 67 now scheduled (such as to age 70, on a gradual, deferred basis or indexing the normal retirement age to U.S. longevity at the retirement ages); (2) gradually lowering the benefit level, especially for high-paid workers; (3) reducing the COLAs (e.g., by basing them on the CPI increase, minus 1 percent); (4) means testing or income testing the benefits; and (5) investing part of the trust fund assets in equities (so as to obtain more investment income). The solution to the financing problem could, of course, be through a combination of these changes, including increasing the contribution rates.

More drastic proposals for change have been made in the direction of privatizing the program, in whole or in part, by directing some or all of the contributions to private-sector investments like mutual funds. The proponents of this approach assert that the higher investment returns will more than offset the elimination or diminution of the social adequacy element and the greater reliance on individual equity procedures. A major difficulty involved with privatization is how to finance the mammoth transition costs in taking adequate and equitable care of the existing benefit roll and those near retirement age (as well as providing reasonable disability and young survivor benefits protection over the long run). Proponents of the present program believe that privatization, whether partial or total, really means destruction, either gradually or immediately.

Social Security in the Future

The dramatic changing age distribution in the United States is the primary cause of the funding imbalance of the Old-Age, Survivors, and Disability Insurance program. From a Social Security funding perspective, the key ratio of Social Security contributors to beneficiaries, already down from 5 to 1 in 1960 to 3.3 to 1 today, will decline further to only 2 to 1 in 2030 and slightly lower thereafter.[20] This primary engine of growth, the expanding wage base, is slowing down both because of the aging of the baby boomers and the decline in the growth in real wages.

In 1994, a Social Security Advisory Council was appointed, as was done every four years in recent decades. Reflecting the diverse views of its members and the nation, its 1996 report proposed three very different proposals mentioned earlier.[21] The first is termed the *Maintenance of Benefits Plan*. It follows past tradition by raising revenues to meet current benefit obligations within the system's current structure. It does, however, suggest that up to 40 percent of trust fund reserves could be invested in private capital.

---

[20] *1997 Annual Report of the Board of Trustees of the Federal Old-Age and Survivors Insurance and Disability Insurance Trust Funds*, Table II F19 (April 1997).

[21] Report of the 1994–1996 Advisory Council on Social Security, Vols. I and II: *Findings and Recommendations* (January 1997).

The second proposal, called the *Individual Accounts Plan,* trims benefits and adds revenue. It also adds a controversial new component—modest individual defined contribution accounts within the federal government, funded by an increase in the payroll tax, over which participants would have limited investment discretion.

The third option, labeled the *Personal Security Account Plan,* would replace the current Social Security system with a very different one, with flat benefits independent of earnings and large mandatory personal retirement accounts funded by a diversion of part of the current payroll tax. These retirement accounts would be held and managed by individuals. The two individual account plans would create a two-tier system, with a lower tier focusing on income adequacy (and resultant redistribution of income) and an upper tier generating benefits directly related to contributions. With privatization, the Social Security objectives (income adequacy and individual equity) would be separated and become explicit.

It is beyond the scope of this text to discuss in detail these proposals and the issues involved. However, they are very important public policy questions.[22]

It is very likely that the Hospital Insurance portion of Medicare will be confronted by a financing crisis within the next decade. At the beginning of 1999, the HI trust fund held $120.9 billion in assets, which represented 85 percent of the outgo for the year (as compared with 100 percent for 1996). Under intermediate assumptions, the fund is depleted in mid 2015.

Whatever direction is taken in connection with health care proposals and other recommended modifications of the overall Social Security program, the Social Security Act marks a milestone in the evolution of U.S. history. Its influence on the economic security of the people of the United States is significant and pervasive.

OTHER U.S. SOCIAL INSURANCE PROGRAMS

This section provides an overview of (1) unemployment insurance, (2) workers' compensation insurance, and (3) temporary disability insurance. Unemployment insurance is a joint federal-state program, and workers' compensation insurance and temporary disability laws are individual state programs.

Unemployment Insurance

In contrast with OASDHI, **unemployment insurance** (payment of periodic cash income to workers during periods of involuntary unemployment) is financed and administered primarily by the states, with some federal participation. The Social Security Act of 1935 provided for a payroll tax to be levied on covered employers in all states. The act was intended to motivate the individual states to establish unemployment insurance programs under guidelines issued by the federal government. This was accomplished by granting a credit against up to 90 percent of the federal tax if a state established an acceptable program based on the federal guidelines. All states now have such unemployment insurance programs.

Unemployment insurance programs have several objectives: (1) to provide weekly cash income to workers during temporary periods of involuntary unemployment; (2) to help stabilize the economy during recessionary periods; (3) to encourage employers to stabilize employment; and (4) to help the unemployed find jobs.

[22]For a discussion of the long-range financing problems of Social Security and possible structural and other changes to resolve these problems, see Robert J. Myers, "How to Resolve the Long-Range Financing Problems of Social Security," Yung-Ping Chen, "A New Social Security: An Alternative to the Moynihan Plan," and Mark Shemtob, "Social Security for the Next Century," *Contingencies* (November/December 1998). See also Robert C. Atchley, "Doomsday 2029? Social Security Projections Don't Tell the Whole Story," *Journal of the American Society of CLU & ChFC* (July 1998), pp. 30–35.

Coverage and Benefits

Although the detailed requirements vary from state to state, the pattern of requirements that must be met to be eligible to receive unemployment benefits includes: (1) having a recent, prior attachment to the labor force (usually 52 weeks or four quarters); (2) being able to work and being available for work; (3) actively seeking work; (4) satisfying any prescribed waiting period (usually one week); and (5) being free from disqualification (e.g., discharge for misconduct). Unemployed workers are required to register at local unemployment offices, and officials of the U.S. Employment Service provide assistance in finding suitable jobs.

In most states, regular unemployment insurance benefits are paid for a maximum of 26 weeks. The basis for determining the amount of the weekly benefit payment varies, but in one way or the other it reflects the individual compensation during a base period just prior to unemployment. Benefits in all states are subject to minimum and maximum amounts. The 1999 minimum weekly benefits range from $5 in Hawaii to $87 in Michigan and Washington, while the maximum weekly benefits range from $190 in Alabama and Mississippi to $573 in Massachusetts.[23]

During periods of high unemployment, some workers exhaust their regular unemployment benefits. A federal-state program of *extended benefits* has been established that pays additional benefits to such workers. The state must extend the benefit duration by 50 percent up to a maximum of 13 weeks. The costs of the extended benefits are shared equally by the federal government and the states.

Financing of Benefits

State unemployment insurance programs are financed largely by payroll taxes paid by employers on the covered wages of employees.[24] All tax contributions are deposited into a Federal Unemployment Trust Fund administered by the Secretary of the Treasury. Each state's separate account is credited with its unemployment tax contributions and the state's share of investment income. Unemployment benefits are paid from each state's account.

As of June 1998, each covered employer had to pay a federal payroll tax of 6.2 percent on the first $7,000 of annual wages paid to each covered employee. Employers can apply as a credit toward the federal tax any state contributions paid under an approved unemployment insurance program and any tax savings under an approved experience-rating plan. The maximum credit is 5.4 percent, leaving 0.8 percent to be paid to the federal government. Many jurisdictions use a taxable wage base in excess of the $7,000 federal standard and have a higher tax rate.

All states use a method of **experience rating** whereby an employer whose employment record is volatile has a higher tax rate than an employer whose employment record has been stable. The theoretical basis for using experience rating is to provide a financial incentive to employers to stabilize their employment. Many cyclical and seasonal firms, however, have little control over their employment and see little financial incentive for them to stabilize employment. It is worth noting that all experience-rating plans have a cap. Once the cap is reached, there is no marginal cost to the employer for additional unemployment.

Workers' Compensation Insurance

Workers' compensation laws require employers to provide employee benefits for losses resulting from work-related accidents or diseases. Based on the principle of liability without fault, the employer is held absolutely liable for the occupational injuries or

---

[23]www.itsc.state.md.us

[24]In four states—Alabama, Alaska, New Jersey, and Pennsylvania—employees must also contribute.

diseases suffered by the workers, regardless of who is at fault. Disabled workers are paid for their injuries according to a schedule of benefits established by law. Employees are not required to sue their employers to collect benefits. The full cost of providing workers' compensation benefits ordinarily is borne by the employer. The political hope was that this cost would be included in the cost of production and passed on to the consumer. In practice, the ultimate burden of the cost will be borne by the employees (through lower wages), the firm's owners (through lower returns), or the firm's customers (through higher prices), depending on the demand and supply characteristics (elasticity) of each.

Coverage and Benefits

The key criterion for coverage under workers' compensation laws is that accidental occupational injuries or death must arise out of, and be in the course of, covered employment. Self-inflicted injuries and accidents resulting from an employee's intoxication or willful disregard of safety rules usually are excluded. Illnesses resulting from occupational diseases are covered in all states. Some states, however, cover only those diseases specifically listed in the law. Workers' compensation laws provide (1) medical care reimbursement, (2) disability income, (3) death benefits, and (4) rehabilitation benefits. Benefit levels vary significantly from state to state.

Financing of Benefits

Employers can comply with the law by purchasing a workers' compensation policy, by self-insuring, or by obtaining insurance from a monopolistic or competitive state fund. Most employers purchase workers' compensation policies from private insurance companies. The policy guarantees the benefits that must be legally provided to workers who are occupationally disabled.

Self-insurance is allowed in most states. Many large firms prefer to self-insure their workers' compensation losses, in the hope of avoiding some of the administrative costs associated with workers' compensation contracts. In such cases, the employer must obtain administrative approval and usually is required to post a bond or other security.

Workers' compensation insurance can be purchased from a state fund in 19 states. In six of these states, covered employers must purchase the workers' compensation insurance from a monopolistic state fund. In the other 13 states, the insurance may be purchased from a state fund or private insurers.

Workers' compensation premiums are calculated as a percentage of payroll and are based upon the occupational classes of workers. Larger employers with workers' compensation premiums above a specified amount are subject to experience rating. Under experience rating, employers are encouraged to take an active interest in employee safety because injuries and fatalities directly impact their workers' compensation premiums.

Temporary Disability Insurance

Five states—California, Hawaii, New Jersey, New York, and Rhode Island—and Puerto Rico have temporary disability benefit plans. Under these laws, employees can collect disability income benefits regardless of whether their disability begins while they are employed. These benefits are not provided for disabilities covered under workers' compensation laws. From a benefit standpoint, these laws (except in New York) generally are patterned after the state unemployment insurance law.

Employees contribute to the cost of the plans in all six jurisdictions. In two of them, California and Rhode Island, only employees contribute. Except for Rhode Island, which has a monopolistic state fund, an employee may obtain coverage from either a competitive state fund or private insurers. The laws require that private coverage must provide benefits that are at least as liberal as those prescribed under the law. In effect, these plans are compulsory group health plans similar to the voluntary plans in effect in many businesses. Self-insurance generally is permitted.

Current Developments

Powerful demographic, fiscal, economic, and social forces are placing increasingly severe strains on social security systems worldwide. For example, the worker-to-retiree ratios around the world have been declining steadily, particularly in developed countries. By the year 2020 ratios for selected OECD countries are projected to fall, on average, 73 percent from their 1990 levels (see Table 22-6). These support ratios reflect the increasing life expectancy, medical and economic advances, and declining fertility rates. The world's population is aging and will age even more rapidly in the next century.

The aging of the population and a low birth rate are the most important challenges to social insurance programs worldwide. Although the rationale for creating and maintaining social insurance programs has not changed, the costs of maintaining them are increasing and are expected to increase dramatically in the coming decades. Many

TABLE 22-6 Support Ratios OECD Countries Number of People Aged 25 to 59 for Each Person Aged 65 and Over			
	1960	*1990*	*2020*
Canada	5.5	4.2	2.7
Japan	7.4	4.2	1.8
United States	4.6	3.7	2.8
EU Countries[a]			
Belgium	3.9	3.2	2.3
Denmark	4.2	3.0	2.2
France	3.8	3.3	2.3
Germany	4.0	3.4	2.5
Ireland	3.5	3.6	2.6
Italy	5.0	3.3	2.2
Netherlands	4.7	4.7	2.5
Portugal	5.4	5.4	2.7
Spain	5.5	5.5	2.6
United Kingdom	4.0	4.0	2.5
Australia	5.1	4.1	3.7
Austria	3.8	4.1	3.0
Finland	6.0	3.7	2.1
Hungary	5.1	3.6	2.7
Iceland	4.9	4.2	3.0
New Zealand	4.7	4.1	3.1
Norway	4.0	2.7	2.5
Poland	7.4	4.6	3.1
Sweden	3.9	2.6	2.1
Switzerland	4.6	3.3	2.3
Turkey	10.2	8.6	6.4
Total OECD Countries[b]	**4.5**	**3.4**	**2.5**

[a] Member countries as of 1991. Luxembourg is not included.

[b] Arithmetic average.

Source: United Nations, *World Population Prospects* (1992 ed.).

countries face the unpleasant choice of reducing benefits or increasing taxes (contributions) to finance their social insurance programs. Another approach under consideration is privatization of government social security programs and increased reliance on individual savings. For many countries, the long-term solution may be a shift to the private sector, whether through an explicit privatization (as seen in Chile and the United Kingdom) or through a more gradual shift as public programs are progressively deemphasized and incentives supporting private savings are gradually enhanced.

In some countries, the individual retirement savings market (see chapter 21) is developing even more rapidly than the employer-provided sector, even before any reductions in social security benefits. As a result of media coverage suggesting an impending crisis, people are becoming increasingly anxious over the security of public pension funds. For example, in France these concerns spawned a booming new market for retirement-related insurance. In the United States individual annuities are supported by $693 billion in assets. Privatization initiatives have been underway for some time in many countries.

Public policy relating to **gradual retirement** (often called **phased, partial** or **part-time** retirement) is the idea of providing a transition period between a full-time career and complete rest. Many formulas for workload downsizing exist and the transition periods during which this occurs can run anywhere from one to ten years. Approximately five years is the transition period most commonly encountered in OECD countries.[25] Regardless of the approach followed in developed economies, the coordination and integration of public- and private-sector policies is crucial to a given policy's effectiveness. A properly coordinated public-private approach to gradual retirement can ease reforms under consideration in Social Security pensions (e.g., increasing the eligibility age for such benefits). Although it is beyond the scope of this volume to consider the multiple changes and innovations in social insurance programs worldwide, such public policy issues are likely to be one of the most important domestic political issues in the early decades of the twenty-first century.

Although the details differ, much can be learned from cross-country comparisons. The Social Security Administration conducts periodic surveys on developing world trends.[26] Other important sources of information along with their Web sites are shown in Box 22-1.

---

[25] Yung Ping Chen, "Partial Pensions for Partial Retirement: Need for Coordinating Social Security Policy with Employment Policy," Mini-White House Conference on Aging, National Council of Senior Citizens Report to European Commission, September 1994.

[26] Social Security Administration, *Social Security Programs Throughout the World* (updated periodically).

BOX 22-1

SOCIAL INSURANCE INFORMATION SOURCES

International Social Security Association	http://www.aiss.org
International Labour Organization	http://www.ILO.org
Organization of American States	http://www.oas.org
Organization for Economic Cooperation and Development	http://www.oecd.org
European Union	http://www.EUROPA.EU.INT
The World Health Organization	http://www.who.CH
Information about specific countries	http://www.aiss.org/othersites

Questions

1. Explain how OASDI meets some of the objectives of a social insurance program.
2. How do the eligibility requirements for old-age and disability insurance in the United States influence OASDI's position with regard to the objectives of a social insurance program?
3. Explain the term *average indexed monthly earnings (AIME)*.
4. The primary insurance amount (PIA) is calculated with a weighted formula that incorporates breakpoints. What is the purpose and significance of the weights and breakpoints?
5. Explain the following statement: "The ultimate burden of the cost of workers' compensation insurance is a function of the elasticity of demand for the employer's product or service."

CHAPTER 23

LIFE INSURANCE COMPANY ORGANIZATION AND MANAGEMENT

Objectives

■ Summarize the issues associated with stock and mutual insurers.

■ Describe the organizational structures common to stock and mutual life insurers.

■ Identify the motivations behind demutualization.

■ Explain the functions of life insurance company departments.

■ Identify trends in life insurance company management.

INTRODUCTION

The majority of the life and health insurance in force in the private sector worldwide is issued by commercial life insurance companies, several aspects of which were discussed in chapter 11.[1] As with other parts of this volume, this chapter is devoted primarily to commercial life insurance companies.

Commercial life insurance companies commonly are classified as stock or mutual companies. The distinguishing characteristic of a stock life insurance company is its ownership by stockholders. If a company has stockholders, it is a stock company. In some countries, the government may be the sole stockholder of an insurer that competes with proprietary insurers. Mutual life insurance companies are "owned" by policyowners.

Worldwide stock insurers outnumber mutuals by a wide margin.[2] Chapter 11 and Figure 11-1 showed that U.S. mutual insurers generally are larger than stock life insurers. In the past, mutuals were dominant with respect to life insurance in force, but their share has

---

[1]Chapter 11 also discusses fraternals, savings banks, and various government plans as providers of life insurance. Chapters 19 and 20 discuss Blue Cross/Blue Shield and health maintenance organizations, and chapter 22 discusses government as a provider of social insurance benefits.

[2]Unless otherwise noted, all statistical aggregates used in this chapter are taken from *1998 Life Insurance Fact Book* (Washington, DC: American Council of Life Insurance, 1998).

declined to less than 40 percent today from 62 percent in 1960. During this time period, the number of stock insurers increased from 1,273 in 1960 to a peak of 2,225 in 1988. At the end of 1997, Table 23-1 shows that the number of stock life insurers stood at 1,511, the rate of decline reflecting the consolidation activity taking place. The number of mutual life insurers similarly declined from a peak of 163 in 1953 to the present 100 companies.

A similar trend is underway in the United Kingdom, Australia, and Canada. The number of mutual life companies in the United Kingdom has declined by one-third in recent years. As a result, the mutual sector's market share has fallen from 45 percent to 30 percent.[3] In Australia, the three largest companies have either demutualized or announced intentions to do so. Collectively, their market share is about 50 percent of the Australian market. Demutualizations are under way in Canada, as well, with all major mutuals. In Japan, on the other hand, mutual insurers continue to dominate the market reflecting the fact that holding companies have been illegal since World War II. Nevertheless, the move toward the stock form of organization is continuing in most countries.

In terms of market share, the shift from mutual to stock insurers has changed the life insurance industry's ability to respond to the deregulation of the financial services marketplace. Stock life insurance companies can be owned by other stock life insurance companies, by mutual life insurance companies, or by companies outside the life insurance industry. A mutual company is owned by its policyowners and cannot be owned by any other entity.

Many life insurers are affiliated with other life insurance and nonlife companies in fleets with a single owner. Of the 1,511 U.S. stock companies shown in Table 23-1, 113 were actually owned by mutual parents. Therefore, on a fleet basis, the number of stock fleet companies is 1,491, and the number of mutual fleet companies (including both mutual parents and stock subsidiaries) is 204.

Together stock and mutual life insurers provide over 98 percent of the total life insurance underwritten by U.S. organizations. The remainder is provided by fraternal societies, savings banks, and the Veterans Administration (see chapter 11).

TABLE 23-1 Change in Number of U.S. Life Insurance Companies in Business in the United States

	1987	1996	1997	Annual Change % 1986–1996	Annual Change % 1995–1996
In Business Year End					
Stock	2,212	1,577	1,511	3.3	–4.2
Mutual[a]	125	102	100	–2.0	–2.0
Other[b]	NA	NA	9	NA	NA
Total	2,337	1,679	1,620	–3.3	–3.5

[a]Includes mutual holding company data.

[b]Includes hospital, medical, dental, and indemnity companies.

Source: 1998 Life Insurance Fact Book (Washington, DC: American Council of Life Insurance, 1998), p. 56.

---

[3]Peter Needleman and Ian B. Farr, "Mutuality Under the Microscope," *Emphasis,* No. 3 (1997), pp. 18–21.

ORGANIZATIONAL FORM IN LIFE AND HEALTH INSURERS

Principal–Agent Relationships

In organizations in which there is a separation of ownership and control, principal–agent relationships lead to conflict and the need for resolution of incentive problems as alluded to in chapter 1. The operation of the life insurance industry involves three primary parties: the company owners, the company managers, and the policyowners. Agency theory applied to insurance has focused on the incentive conflicts among the three parties and the manner in which these conflicts can be controlled. The differing abilities of stock and mutual insurers to control owner–policyowner and owner–management conflicts have significant implications for the comparative advantage of the two ownership structures in various insurance activities.

The size of large, open organizations forces them to seek agents with specialized knowledge and skills. Operating under delegated authority, agents are expected to increase the owner's wealth. Residual claims to common stock (e.g., dividends and appreciation) are rewards for bearing the residual risk of the corporation. Large companies typically have many owners, permitting them to diffuse their residual claims broadly.

Several control mechanisms are available to help assure that management actions will not impose too much cost on the shareholders. The board of directors, competition among managers seeking executive positions, and the threat of an outside takeover all help reduce the costs that managers can impose on the stockholders and policyowners.

The board of directors, as representatives of the shareholders for a company, play an important role in protecting the interests of shareholders and policyowners. Recent insolvencies of life insurers because of excessive risk taking have resulted in a significant increase in the risk management responsibilities of the board of directors. These responsibilities have been further enhanced by a litigation-prone environment in which boards are being sued for alleged lack of proper oversight.

The possibility of a takeover is an external constraint that helps control agency problems in large corporations. As a result of the unrestricted nature of the common stock residual claims, capital markets develop. These markets function to price residual claims, enable shareholders to transfer these claims at a low cost, and improve the potential for takeovers. Thus, capital markets and boards of directors serve as mechanisms to discipline management. Managers are also motivated to minimize agency costs to foster a favorable performance evaluation of their organizations in the capital markets.

In general, agency theory suggests that stock companies should be more prevalent in activities that involve significant managerial discretion (e.g., group insurance and health insurance) whereas mutual companies should be more prevalent in lines of insurance characterized by good actuarial tables and long-term contracting (e.g., whole life contracts).[4] The stockholder–policyowner incentive conflict is more severe with long-term policies because long-term contracts carry greater opportunities to change dividend, investment, and financing policies to the detriment of policyowners.

The separation of the managerial and ownership/risk-bearing functions in the stock company means that the managers of such a company do not bear personally the full financial effects of their decisions. Managers logically make decisions and take actions to

---

[4]Steven W. Pottier and David W. Sommer, "Agency Theory and Life Insurance Ownership Structure," *The Journal of Risk and Insurance,* Vol. 64, No. 3 (1997), pp. 529–543.

maximize their own utility (actions that increase their power, prestige, or income) that may be inconsistent with the best interests of the stockholders. The managers will generally not have interests that are perfectly aligned with those of the shareholders or the policyowners.

Separation of the policyowner and ownership/risk-bearing functions also creates incentive conflicts. Stockholders have incentives to increase the value of their claims at the expense of the policyowners after policies are sold. For example, a decision to lower crediting rates to maintain a spread would lower the value of policyowners' contracts and increase the profits of the company. The relative difficulty of a policyowner changing to another insurer, without incurring again front-end expenses, strengthens the stockholders' and managers' incentive conflict with policyowners. The recent emphasis on stock-based compensation for managers also tends to align better the interests of the managers and shareholders relative to the policyowners.

In a mutual company, the ownership function is merged with the policyowners' function of minimizing the incentive conflicts between owners and policyowners. The rights of mutual policyowners (as owners) usually are more restricted than the rights of common stockholders. Mutual policyowners have the right to vote to elect directors (the rights of policyowners cannot be accumulated) and to share in the value of the company if it is liquidated or demutualized. These rights expire with the policy. Upon termination of a policy, the policyowner usually has no rights to capital (except for cash values in life insurance products).

The elimination of the stockholder group reduces potential costs imposed on mutual policyowners from decisions relating to dividends, financing, and investment over the lives of their policies. The potential advantage mutuals have in controlling the incentive problem between policyowners and stockholders is offset by a worsened incentive problem between the owners and managers of the company as compared with the stock company. The difficulty of accumulating mutual owners' votes virtually eliminates the constraint provided by the threat of an outside takeover. The cost of controlling management in mutual companies is higher than in stock companies.

As pointed out previously, stock insurers early on dominated the market, but following the Armstrong Investigation in 1905, many major companies mutualized (discussed later) and the mutual segment of the business became dominant until the 1960s when the stock companies' market share began to grow again at an increasing rate. For reasons discussed later, a number of mutual companies have demutualized. These same forces have caused a new concept, the mutual holding company, to become a significant factor in determining life insurance ownership structure. Given the new interest in evaluating organizational form and in using subsidiaries of different forms for specific purposes, it is clear that the choice of organizational form is a significant decision for managers who seek the most efficient method of meeting their goals.

Life Insurance Company Formation

Although it is theoretically possible for the life insurance business to be undertaken by an individual or by a partnership, the form of organization should be one that provides both permanence and a high degree of security of payment. A corporation meets these requirements and, under many countries' laws (including the United States), it is the only form of business organization permitted to undertake a life insurance business. Thus, from a practical and legal viewpoint, the operation of a life insurance business requires the formation of a corporation. Both stock and mutual insurers are organized as corporations.

Stock Life Insurers

A stock life insurance company is one that is organized for the purpose of making profits for its stockholders. Traditionally, stock insurers have issued guaranteed-cost, nonparticipating policies, in which the policyowners share neither in any savings or profits nor in any losses that might arise in the operation of the business. Every policy element is fixed at issue. Stock insurers, especially in Canada and Europe, also issue participating policies without voting rights on which dividends are paid to policyowners. Many jurisdictions impose limitations on the extent to which the stockholders of the company may benefit from the participating business.[5] The majority of U.S. states, however, impose no special regulation on the participating insurance sold by stock insurers.

With the introduction of participating policies by stock companies, the distinction between stock and mutual companies on the basis of participation became less relevant. Most individual cash-value policies sold today in developed countries "participate" in the insurer's operational performance in one way or another. Group insurance products of stock companies also have been indistinguishable from those of mutual companies for some time.

The life insurance business is highly specialized and is subject in every country to special laws. Under these laws, a company must have a minimum amount of capital and surplus before it can secure a certificate of authority to operate as a life insurance company.

For instance, under New York state law, a stock life insurance company must have a minimum of $2 million capital and a paid-in initial surplus of the greater of $4 million or 200 percent of its capital. Every such company must at all times maintain a minimum capital of $2 million. The minimum capital required after formation of the company is regulated by the risk-based capital (RBC) formula developed by the NAIC. As discussed later in this volume, the formula establishes target surplus amounts required above baseline requirements and reflects the risks inherent in an insurer's contractual obligations and asset portfolio. Minimum capital and surplus requirements are intended to ensure that any insurer can make the deposits required to become licensed, has sufficient funds for normal operations, and has a contingency fund to meet adverse fluctuations in experience that might occur during the initial development period. Once the stock has been subscribed and the various legal requirements met, the insurer can be organized by the stockholders and begin business.

Mutual Life Insurers

A mutual life insurance company also is a corporation, but it usually has no capital stock and no stockholders (but see Box 23-1). The policyowner in a mutual company is both a customer *and*, in a limited sense, an owner of the insurer, in contrast to the policyowner in a stock company, who usually is a customer only.

Technically, the assets and income of a mutual insurer are owned by the company. The policyowners usually are considered to be contractual creditors with the right to vote for directors as provided for by law. The insurer is administered and its assets are held for the benefit and protection of the policyowners and beneficiaries as reserves, surplus, or contingency funds, or they are distributed to them as dividends to the extent that the board of directors (trustees) deems such action warranted. Thus, in a mutual

---

[5]For example, the state of New York provides that profits on participating policies and contracts be limited to the larger of (1) 10 percent of gains on such policies or (2) 50 cents per year per $1,000 of participating business. See §216, *New York Insurance Law.* Illinois requires at least 90 percent of the profits on participating business to inure to the benefit of participating policyowners. See Illinois Insurance Code, Section 233. Similar limitations exist in Canada, Singapore, the United Kingdom, and other countries.

BOX 23-1

CANADIAN PARTICIPATING SHARES

Canadian mutual life insurers have recently been authorized to issue "participating shares" and, since 1992, they have had authority to issue preferred shares. Participating shares may provide voting rights and the right to receive remaining property if the company is wound up. See Canadian Insurance Companies Act.

insurer, the policyowner pays a typically fixed premium stated in his or her policy (usually higher than the premium for a similar guaranteed-cost contract), but the actual or net cost to the policyowner will depend on the dividends or other credits allocated to his or her policy each year by the board of directors. The fixed premium stated in the contract is the initial and maximum outlay, but the final actual net outlay is less by the amount of dividends paid or interest credited on the contract.

Mutual insurers mostly issue participating policies. Sometimes they also issue nonparticipating policies, but these policyowners, as with policyowners of stock companies, are simply customers of the mutual company. As mentioned earlier, the traditional emphasis on participation versus nonparticipation as a characteristic distinguishing a mutual from a stock insurer is no longer valid.

The organization of a new mutual insurer presents some serious practical problems. As in the case of a stock company, funds are needed to cover the expenses of operation, make the required deposits with the insurance regulatory authorities, and provide a surplus or contingency fund to meet any unusual fluctuations in experience before the insurer has had time to accumulate such funds from its operations.

In the case of a stock insurer, funds for all these purposes are obtained from the sale of stock, but in a mutual insurer, the only sources of funds at the beginning are the first premiums paid in by the original-member policyowners or funds borrowed to establish the insurer. The lack of profit incentive is undoubtedly a significant factor in explaining why relatively few mutual insurers are formed, but, in addition, the statutory requirements for the formation of a new mutual life insurance company may be exceedingly stringent. For instance, the state of New York does not permit a mutual company to begin operation as a going concern unless it has applications for not less than $1,000 each from 1,000 persons, accompanied by the full amount of one annual premium for an aggregate amount of $25,000, plus an initial surplus of $150,000 in cash. It should be apparent that there would be great difficulty in finding a large number of individuals who are insurable and who are willing to apply for insurance in, and to pay the first premium to, an insurer that is not yet in existence and not yet able to issue policies.

These difficulties of organization of a new mutual life insurance company are so great that none has been organized in the United States, Japan, the United Kingdom, or most other countries for many years, and no new mutual life insurer is likely to be formed. The only practical way of organizing a new life insurance company in the United States is on a stock basis. After it has been fully established and has attained adequate financial stability, a stock insurer can be converted into a mutual company.[6]

---

[6]Many of the large U.S. mutual companies were, in fact, originally stock companies that were mutualized. At one time, some states provided for a guaranty capital put up temporarily by the persons interested in forming a mutual insurer. This guaranty capital was to be retired as soon as the mutual insurer's operations stabilized financially. Sometimes the stock remained outstanding for some period while the company operated on the mutual basis.

ORGANIZATIONAL STRUCTURE

Holding Companies

In recent years in Europe and North America, the use of holding companies has been a central part of intercorporate reorganizations in managements' attempts to help their organizations improve their earnings and long-term growth possibilities through diversification. Financial services deregulation has enhanced this development. For the most part, **holding companies** are financial corporations that own or control one or more insurers, broker-dealer organizations, investment companies, consumer finance companies, and other financial services corporations.[7] Some stock life insurance companies are owned or controlled by nonfinancial holding companies and conglomerates that group together in unrelated fields.

The relationship of mutual insurance companies to the holding company device is different from that of the stock insurance company. A holding company formed by one or more stock companies is commonly called an **upstream holding company** because the holding company sits at the top of the intercorporate structure. It is owned by the stockholders, and, in turn, it owns subsidiaries. A **downstream holding company** is usually formed by a mutual insurance company and sits in the middle of the intercorporate structure. It is owned wholly or in part by the mutual that sits at the top, and it owns subsidiaries.

The significance of the distinction is that the downstream holding company presents few problems to insurance regulators because the parent mutual is directly subject to insurance regulations. As a consequence, a downstream holding company has been a viable device only if the parent mutual has a strong surplus position. Even the large mutual life insurance company with a significant surplus position has limited ability to acquire other companies.

Other companies can only be acquired as subsidiaries by a mutual life insurer, a structure that limits the size of acquisitions because subsidiaries are subject to a 30 percent risk-based-capital factor (see chapter 35). Statutory accounting requires write-off of the goodwill element of the purchase price, and legal investment laws may limit the amount an insurer may invest in subsidiaries. Also, as a practical matter, mutual life insurers can only offer to pay in cash—a very expensive way to transact business.

Until recently, use of an upstream mutual holding company was not a viable option because of the absence of statutory authority. In 1995, Iowa adopted a law making a mutual insurance holding company (MIHC) a feasible approach to gain many of the capital market advantages available to stock companies. Under the act, a mutual insurer can form a mutual holding company with an active stock subsidiary. Policyowners become members of the mutual insurance holding company and have their policy relationship with the stock insurer subsidiary of the new holding company. Initial shares of the subsidiary's capital stock are issued and held by the mutual holding company. Then the mutual holding company, acting through the stock subsidiary, can access the public markets, although the statute stipulates that it must maintain a voting-share majority in the subsidiary. Through use of two (or more) classes of shares, it is possible to sell a majority of the economic value of a converted company to public shareholders so long as the MIHC retains a majority of the voting rights.

Although the ultimate outcomes of a real demutualization and the MIHC (a de facto demutualization) are similar—capital is raised by issuing stock to outside investors—

---

[7]Holding companies had been illegal in Japan until recently, although various forms of cooperation had been achieved among financial services firms through other means.

some believe that policyowner rights, control, and protections are not adequate under the MIHC approach (see Box 23-2).[8]

Although both policyowners and stockholders are interested in a strong and viable company, their ultimate goals are different. Policyowners are interested in the provision of high-quality policies at the lowest cost whereas stockholders want the highest possible rate of return. This agency conflict of interest lies at the heart of the need for careful regulatory oversight.

The MIHC approach has attracted considerable interest among some U.S. mutual life insurers. A number of U.S. states have enacted MIHC conversion authority and legislation is under consideration in several others. To date, six mutuals have converted to an MIHC structure.

The development of the MIHC concept has generated a major industry debate between proponents and those who feel the approach does not treat policyowners

---

[8]Jason B. Adkins, "The Policyholder Perspective on Mutual Holding Company Conversions," *Journal of Insurance Regulation* (Fall 1997), pp. 5–15.

BOX 23-2

ISSUES RELATING TO THE MUTUAL INSURANCE HOLDING COMPANY (MIHC)

1. *The Fundamental Flaw*
   If the implications of an MIHC reorganization were disclosed to and understood by the policyowners, most of them would vote against the reorganization. On the other hand, if strong safeguards were added to protect the interests of the policyowner, prospective shareholders would be reluctant to invest in the reorganized enterprise.

2. *Dilution of Policyowner Interests*
   The surplus of a mutual company is held for the exclusive benefit of the policyowners. The effect of an MIHC reorganization is to terminate or dilute the exclusive ownership interests of the policyowners without compensation.

3. *The Enrichment Issue*
   Making stock available to officers and directors creates a conflict-of-interest situation because those individuals then have personal financial incentives to take actions that favor shareholders at the expense of policyowners.

4. *The Income Tax Issue*
   The organization may receive more favorable tax treatment through the creation of a mutual holding company.

5. *The Closed Block*
   A closed block is not appropriate in a reorganization under a mutual holding company law because the ownership rights of the policyowners are not bought out.

6. *SEC No-Action Letter*
   An SEC no-action letter says in essence that the SEC staff does not intend to treat the policyowners' membership interests in the mutual holding company as securities for the purpose of the federal securities laws.

7. *The Burden Issue*
   The company should be required to show that the plan is in the best interests of the policyowners.

8. *Confidentiality Provision*
   If a company, in connection with a reorganization, files material that does not fit under one of the exemptions in the state's open records law, the material should be available to the public.

Source: Joseph M. Belth, "The Mutual Holding Company—A Flawed Concept," *The Insurance Forum,* Vol. 24, No. 12 (December 1997).

fairly.[9] States making this option available to their domestic companies contend that provisions are in place that assure that the insurance regulator has adequate regulatory control to protect policyowners. Although the move away from mutual ownership is a worldwide trend, the United States seems to be the only major market in which the mutual holding company concept is being implemented.

Affiliations and Outsourcing

The rapidly changing financial services business has enhanced insurer interest in corporate restructuring and affiliations. The purpose of such activities is to increase efficiency and profitability and to survive the challenges of new competitors entering into traditional insurance areas. Such transactions include acquisitions (friendly and unfriendly), demutualization, holding company formation, and mergers. Although acquisition and merger activity has increased steadily as consolidation has taken place in the industry, strategic alliances (joint ventures and cooperation agreements) have long been a key element in insurer strategy. Through such alliances, a life insurer can gain access to resources of other firms but still remain independent.

In the drive to focus on their core competencies, improve customer service, and reduce operating expenses, **outsourcing** has become an important strategic tool for many life insurers. Insurers have brand labeled another insurer's product with claims handled by a third-party administrator. Also, investment management can be provided by an investment banking firm or other asset management organization, and data processing and network management can be handled by a service bureau. Finally, distribution can be conducted through a combination of direct and third-party arrangements. Virtual banking has become a reality in the United States, the United Kingdom, Canada, Australia, and other countries. The insurance industry is starting down a similar path. One of the major benefits of using the virtual company approach is to reverse the typical insurance company cost structure from 80 percent fixed/20 percent variable to 20 percent fixed/80 percent variable cost mix. To date the movement toward the virtual insurance company (see Box 23-3) has been sporadic. Taking outsourcing to its practical limits means that the insurer will have become a general contractor that obtains the required skills and expertise from a competitive field of subcontractors. Monitoring the performance of one or more subcontractors that have direct management control, of course, creates incentive conflict problems for senior management. Affiliations and outsourcing will continue to play a significant role as industry consolidation continues.

---

[9]See Steven Sullivan, " The Debate Over Mutual Holding Companies," *Contingencies* (November/December 1998), pp. 50–55.

BOX 23-3

THE VIRTUAL INSURANCE COMPANY

The virtual insurance company is one that delivers products and services to the customer by coordinating the unique contributions of multiple suppliers. From the customer's perspective, the virtual insurance company provides a full range of insurance and related financial service products. Risk management, retirement and tax planning, claims processing, underwriting, distribution, and asset management are all viewed by the customer as occurring within the structure and control of the insurance company.

Corporate Governance

In view of the incentive conflict between managers and shareholders, and the need to minimize information asymmetries, governments have a significant influence on corporate governance. The U.S. Securities and Exchange Commission (SEC) has a major influence on corporate governance of U.S. companies, including insurers. Other countries have similar regulatory agencies. U.S. corporate governance is regulated primarily through the SEC's proxy rules. These rules require disclosure to shareholders concerning the structure, composition, and function of corporate boards of directors and their committees. In particular, companies are required to disclose sufficient details concerning director and nominee relationships with the company and its customers and suppliers to enable shareholders to assess meaningfully director independence.

Disclosure is required concerning

- standing audit, compensation, and nominating committees
- director attendance at meetings
- director resignations
- shareholder proposals
- settlement of election contests

The purpose of these rules is to make appropriate information available to shareholders, enabling them to assess the performance of their directors and to facilitate informed voting in economic terms—to rectify to some degree inherent information asymmetry problems. The SEC has recently expanded the rules relating to the disclosure of senior management compensation.

Although the actions of the SEC directly affect both stock and mutual life insurance companies that file reports with the SEC or that market equity products through registered separate accounts, other initiatives in the corporate governance arena have been directed specifically at mutual life insurance companies. A number of difficult, sensitive issues concerning mutual companies have surfaced at hearings, including, for example, whether policyowners have proprietary interests in the company and whether disclosure of dividend distribution policies should be required.

CORPORATE REORGANIZATION

Mutualization of Stock Insurers

Although today only of historical interest, some stock insurers have been converted from stock form into mutual form through a procedure called **mutualization,** which involves the retirement of the outstanding capital stock of the insurer, coupled with the transfer of control of the insurer from the stockholders to the policyowners.[10] The motivations for such a move vary widely, including, for example, a desire to prevent control of the company from falling into undesirable hands through a change in stock ownership.

The officers of the insurer usually initiate mutualization proceedings by submitting a proposal to the board of directors. The key factor is the price to be paid for each share of stock and the manner of payment. The price must be attractive enough from the

---

[10]In the past 25 years, two U.S. stock companies have converted to mutuals, *1996 Life Insurance Fact Book,* p. 109.

viewpoint of the stockholders to induce them to relinquish their rights of ownership and control. On the other hand, from an insurer's viewpoint, the price must be limited practically by the fact that the remaining surplus, after mutualization, must be adequate to permit sound operation. Sometimes it is quite important that the payment for the shares be spread over a long period of time so as to avoid an undue burden on current surplus.

If the plan (including the price to be offered to the stockholders) is approved by the board of directors, it usually must be submitted to the insurance regulatory authorities for approval. Upon approval, the plan is then submitted to the policyowners and stockholders in accordance with the applicable insurance law.

In executing a mutualization plan approved by the necessary majorities, the company takes up the stock to the extent that it is feasible to do so. Some of the stockholders may object to the plan for one reason or another, and the process of taking up stock usually will require some time. As the stock is bought up, it is not canceled but transferred to trustees for the policyowners, who vote the stock on their behalf. Normally, a substantial majority of the total stock can be purchased immediately, so that effective ownership and control are obtained by the policyowners. Ultimately, when all the shares of stock have been purchased, the stock may be canceled and the insurer becomes fully mutualized.

Demutualization of Mutual Insurers

In recent years, a number of major mutual life insurers have converted from mutual to stock companies. As a result of the growing interest in demutualization, a task force of the U.S. Society of Actuaries studied issues involved in demutualization. The task force concentrated on three principal aspects of demutualization: (1) maintenance of reasonable policyowner dividend expectations, (2) the aggregate amount of compensation to policyowners in exchange for their membership rights, and (3) the allocation of this aggregate amount of compensation among participating policyowners.[11]

Following this report, legislation was adopted in New York in 1988 to allow a mutual insurer to convert to a stock company. Since then additional states have adopted permissive legislation. In 1988, the Maccabees Mutual Life Insurance Company converted to stock form pursuant to the Michigan statute. Union Mutual successfully completed its demutualization and legally became a stock company in 1989 as did the Equitable Life Assurance Society in 1992.[12] State Mutual Life Assurance Company of America was the first Massachusetts-domiciled life insurance company to pursue a demutualization under the new legislation, a conversion that was completed in 1995. The Prudential Insurance Company of America, John Hancock, Metropolitan Life, and the Mutual of New York have also announced their intention to demutualize.

Motives for Conversion

The primary reason why a mutual life insurance company would consider demutualization is to obtain access to equity capital and related financing alternatives (convertible debentures, warrants, and preferred stock). The reason is becoming increasingly

---

[11]*Report of the Task Force on Mutual Life Insurance Company Conversion* (Itasca, IL: July 1987). This report is in the process of being updated by the American Academy of Actuaries.

[12]The Equitable, in completing its demutualization process, raised $450 million in its initial public offering. A French insurer, AXA, also invested $1 billion in the Equitable in exchange for notes, which were subsequently converted into stock, giving AXA 49 percent ownership.

important. As the integration of the financial services industry accelerates, the requirements for capital growth and capital investments multiply. Besides a possible desire to enhance the firm's margin of solvency through an influx of new capital, there is also the need to make major capital investments in (1) computer systems, equipment, and facilities; (2) the growth of sales and distribution capabilities; and (3) acquisitions that broaden product offerings, increase scale, bring access to new customers and new markets, and so on.

For mutual and stock life insurance companies, the main source of equity capital has been and will continue to be retained earnings from their insurance operations. To the extent that retained earnings cannot provide all of the capital required (and today's competitive markets place limits on the amount of retained earnings available from existing business), insurers must access the capital markets for new equity or debt funds. For example, new business may initially create net cash outflows and create a strain on surplus due to high distribution costs. In response to this and other capital needs, stock companies have available the full range of public market financing options. Mutual companies can obtain capital funds through debt but have only limited access to equity capital. For some mutual insurers, this limited access may not be sufficient.

A second interest in demutualization could stem from the enhanced corporate structure flexibility it would permit. A basic structural advantage of the stock life insurance company form is that it permits formation of an upstream holding company. Through this mechanism the company can (1) limit the impact of insurance regulatory controls and restrictions on noninsurance operations, and (2) permit acquisitions to be made without diminution of statutory surplus.

The latter benefit, which may be particularly important in the present industry consolidation phase, requires a brief explanation. If a U.S. life insurance company acquires another insurance company, the excess of the purchase price over the acquired company's statutory surplus must be charged immediately to the statutory surplus of the acquiring company. If the acquisition is made by an upstream holding corporation, however, there is no charge to the statutory capital of either insurance company. Because the market values of most stock life insurance companies are well in excess of their respective statutory book values, this requirement places severe limitations on the ability of mutual life insurance companies to make necessary acquisitions of stock insurance companies (both of the life as well as the property and liability type).

These are the two key reasons for a mutual company to consider demutualization. There are two other reasons mentioned, which for most insurers will be less important. The present U.S. federal income tax law for life insurance companies includes for mutual life insurance companies an add-on tax element that can constitute a major share of the company's total tax. Although the federal tax savings from conversion could be significant, the converted insurer most likely will have to pay cash dividends to shareholders that could consume all or a major part of these tax savings. Also, the availability of common stock increases compensation flexibility for managers and permits acquisitions to be done for stock (and without tax consequences to the seller).

Demutualization changes the relationships and incentive conflicts among owners, policyowners, and management. The typical conversion statute does not recognize management and employees.[13] Management has no incentive to demutualize and dilute its

---

[13]The discussion draws on Richard A. Hemmings and Robert S. Seiler, "An Economically Viable Model for Insurers to Demutualize," *Best's Review,* L/H (November 1995), pp. 45–49.

corporate control by creating a group of shareholders who could be expected to be less docile than mutual company policyowners. Employees have no means to participate in the conversion aside from their positions as policyowners. Traditionally, the policyowners of a mutual company have been regarded by regulators and insurers alike as the owners of the mutual insurer. This view had its origin in statutes granting the mutual policyowner the right to elect directors, to share in the profits of the insurer through dividends, and in most states, the right to receive a distribution in the event that the company is liquidated while solvent or goes through a statutory demutualization. The courts, however, have recognized that the membership rights of policyowners are contractual rights arising from the insurer's policies and not an actual equity stake that policyowners purchased in the company.

The Conversion Process
In a traditional conversion, the mutual life insurance company literally is transformed into a shareholder-owned enterprise through a process in which policyowner membership rights are exchanged for valuable consideration (i.e., cash, premium credits, additional benefits, or possibly common stock in the resulting stock company). If the company wishes to raise new equity capital (which is one of the principal reasons for conversion), that step may be taken at the time of conversion or at some later date. If new capital is raised on the conversion date, ownership of the insurer will be shared between the policyowners and the new shareholders. If no new capital is raised, the policyowners initially may own all of the shares of the company.

In some cases, the conversion may be taken so that the converted mutual insurer may be acquired by another company, a so-called **sponsored demutualization.** In this case, the consideration to policyowners usually will be in the form of cash or additional benefits.

The converting mutual company may wish to go through a restructuring in which an upstream holding company is created. The parent holding company would own all of the shares of the converted insurance company, the policyowners would receive shares of the holding company, and the shares sold to the public also would be shares of the holding company.

The demutualization process in the United States involves three distinct approval phases. The first is the decision by the insurer's board of directors (trustees) that a conversion is important to the company's future progress, and that the conversion plan is in the interest of policyowners. Although legal requirements vary, the board's action usually requires approval of a supermajority of the directors.

The second approval required usually will be that of the insurance regulator of the insurer's domiciliary jurisdiction. The purpose is to assure that the proposed conversion plan meets

- the various legal requirements, including, but not limited to, the provision for future policyowner dividends
- the fairness of the total consideration to policyowners in exchange for their membership rights
- the allocation of that amount among policyowners, the fairness of the amounts paid by nonpolicyowner shareholders (particularly in the case of a proposed acquisition of the insurer by another entity)
- limitations on acquisitions of stock by officers and directors

The insurance regulator most likely will employ actuarial, legal, investment banking, and accounting consultants to render opinions as to its appropriateness. Almost always there will be a public hearing to permit interested parties to present concurring and opposing views. After the hearing, the regulator either approves the conversion plan as submitted, approves the plan with amendments, or rejects the plan. Approval or, at least, a "nonobjection" position by insurance regulatory authorities in other jurisdictions in which the insurer is licensed also may be required.

Once the insurer and the insurance regulator have agreed on a conversion plan, it is submitted to policyowners for their approval. The degree of support required varies, but a typical U.S. requirement is that two-thirds of those voting must approve the conversion plan. Before voting, all policyowners receive a comprehensive set of materials describing the conversion plan and presenting the specific amount of consideration or the number of shares (or the basis on which this number would be determined) that the policyowner will receive in exchange for the surrender of his or her membership rights. If a favorable vote is received, the mutual life insurance company can then proceed with the conversion.

A key and complex question concerning demutualization is how it will affect the insurance coverages of persons with participating policies. The conversion should not have a materially adverse impact on the insurer's ability either to meet the policy guarantees or to pay policyowner dividends on a scale that is comparable to the dividends that would have been paid in the absence of demutualization.

In most U.S. demutualizations, a closed block of policies (see Box 23-4) is established for present policyowners constructed to protect the reasonable dividend expectations of individual participating policyowners of the former mutual company and certain other comparable business. The funding of the closed block and the allocation of policyowner considerations involve substantial value for which different policyowners have competing interests.

Current Developments

As the need for capital has grown, alternative approaches to demutualization have been developing.[14] In 1995, Illinois adopted a statute that facilitates the process by using subscription rights to balance the interests of all stockholders including management and employees.[15] All stockholders are required to execute subscription contracts and remit funds for the amount of shares they wish to purchase. The money is placed in escrow and the total number of shares subscribed is then calculated. Under the statute, there are restrictions on the rights available to each group to assure an equitable distribution of the subscription rights. If there is an oversubscription, the shares are allocated on a fair and equitable basis among all eligible subscribers who elected to purchase. The estimated market value of the converted stock company is established by a qualified independent party, usually a securities underwriter. The entire process must be approved by the insurance regulator. The net effect is to convert the insurer into a stock company with an influx of capital from the purchased shares.

Having legislation on the books is one thing; deciding to demutualize is quite another. The determination as to whether an insurer should seek to convert will be an in-

---

[14]See Michael A. Cohen, Larry G. Mayewski, and Michael L. Albanese, "End of an Era?" *Best's Review*, L/H (August 1998), pp. 39–45.

[15]Michigan and Pennsylvania have adopted legislation similar to the Illinois law.

BOX 23-4

THE CLOSED BLOCK ACCOUNTING STRUCTURE

The closed block is an accounting structure that helps determine dividends on policies within the block. Commonly it covers all the traditional participating, individual life insurance policies with experience-based dividend scales in force at the time of conversion. It doesn't affect the company's liability for benefits guaranteed by those policies; these are still ultimately backed by the entire company. But by isolating a block of policies, funding for the appropriate amount, and preventing any transfer of funds to or from the closed block (except under defined circumstances), the total dividends distributed to the policies in the block are ultimately determined by its experience rather than the discretion of management. The fair allocation of these dividends is still a management responsibility, however, and to some extent so is the timing.

The closed block accounting structure records on a memorandum basis the assets allocated to the closed block policies. These assets are increased by the block's premium and investment income and decreased by benefits paid (death benefits, surrender benefits, and dividends) on the block's policies. These assets are also decreased by any expenses and taxes charged to the closed block according to

the conversion plan. None of the closed block assets may be transferred to the shareholders.

The amount of initial assets is determined so that, if current experience continues, there are just enough assets, together with anticipated premium and investment income, to provide for:

- the anticipated benefits under the closed block policies
- the anticipated expenses and taxes to be charged to the closed block according to the conversion plan
- the anticipated dividends on the policies according to the current dividend scale

Because no assets may be removed from the closed block except as provided by the conversion plan, no assets may revert to benefit the shareholders. If future experience is better than the current experience anticipated in the initial funding, additional assets will build up on the closed block and will have to be used to increase dividends accordingly. Conversely, deteriorating experience will reduce dividends. Thus, the policyholders' expectations that their dividends will reflect emerging experience are protected by the closed block mechanism.

Source: Dale Hagstrom and Godfrey Perrott, "Change of Ownership: Actuarial Aspects of Demutualization," *Contingencies* (January/February 1998), (Copyright © 1998, American Academy of Actuaries), p. 43.

dividual insurer decision based on the insurer's position in the market, its business goals, its capital position and needs, and the likelihood and ability to achieve these goals without undertaking the wrenching course of demutualization. The analysis required for such a decision is burdensome and ordinarily will not be undertaken unless it is believed to be necessary. These considerations will undoubtedly lead to considerable interest in the holding company concepts underlying the Iowa and Illinois approaches to facilitating mutual company access to the capital markets. Box 23-5 lists U.S. jurisdictions that allow mutual conversions as of 1999.

As competition has tightened in the financial services marketplace, margins have declined and demand for capital has increased; mutual life insurance companies will be required to consider seriously whether conversion represents a necessary strategic action. The globalization of financial services and investment also will be a significant consideration.

BOX 23-5

U.S. JURISDICTIONS THAT ALLOW MUTUAL CONVERSIONS (AS OF 1999)

DEMUTUALIZATION

Alabama	Nebraska
Arizona	Nevada
Arkansas	New Hampshire
California	New Jersey
Colorado	New Mexico
Delaware	New York
District of Columbia	Ohio
Florida	Oklahoma
Georgia	Oregon
Idaho	Pennsylvania
Illinois	Rhode Island
Indiana	South Carolina
Iowa	South Dakota
Kansas	Texas
Kentucky	Utah
Louisiana	Vermont
Maine	Virginia
Maryland	Washington
Massachusetts	West Virginia
Michigan	Wisconsin
Minnesota	Wyoming
Montana	Puerto Rico

MUTUAL HOLDING COMPANY

California	Missouri
District of Columbia	Nebraska
Florida	North Dakota
Idaho	Ohio
Illinois	Oregon
Iowa	Pennsylvania
Kansas	Rhode Island
Kentucky	South Carolina
Louisiana	Texas
Massachusetts	Vermont
Minnesota	Wisconsin
Mississippi	

Source: http://www.insurance-finance.com/demu.htm.

HOME OFFICE ORGANIZATION AND ADMINISTRATION

Fundamentally, the organization of a life insurance company home office follows the pattern of other corporations that are concerned with the collection, investment, and disbursement of funds. Organization in general has three main elements: (1) levels of authority, (2) departmentalization, and (3) functionalization. Each of these elements plays an important role in establishing an efficient organizational structure and in ensuring efficient coordination of effort within that structure.

The organization of a life insurance company is no different in its possession of these elements. Life insurance companies are most frequently line-staff-functional organizations. Individual segments of a life insurance company, however, may be organized on a line basis with all operations placed directly under the control of the manager. The agency department, on the other hand, normally is organized on a line and staff basis, whereby the agency vice president is supported by line assistants (e.g., directors of agencies) and also staff assistants (e.g., directors of research and training).

Insurers differ widely by size, objectives, fields of operation, and other factors. Their actual organizational patterns also differ because many insurers' organizational patterns have developed as a matter of evolution. Subject to this limitation, it is the purpose of this section to outline the more important official positions, committees, and departments of the average, well-established life insurance company and to describe briefly their respective functions and duties.

Levels of Authority

There usually are four levels of authority in a life insurance organization. The board of directors and its various committees are, of course, the top or directorial level of authority. The chief executive officer (CEO) and other senior officers of the company are found at the executive level. In addition to serving as part of the executive management team, the senior executive officers are given authority and responsibility for particular functions. Each of the vice presidents has subordinates at the managerial level who are responsible for the day-to-day functions of their departments. These subordinate managers, who may serve in line, staff, or functional relationships, make decisions on all matters within the limits of authority delegated to them. Finally, the supervisors in charge of subdivisions of the departments are found at the supervisory level of authority.

The Board of Directors

The board of directors and the several committees of the board constitute the top level of authority in a life insurance company. In a mutual company, the directors typically are elected by the policyowners from among their own number, whereas in a stock company, they are elected by the shareholders. Whatever the method of election, the board possesses complete supervisory powers over those who manage the insurer. It is empowered not only to select the president and other principal officers but to delegate to them such powers as it sees fit. It also meets at stated intervals to approve or disapprove the recommendations of officials and the findings of committees and to consider and pass judgment upon all important matters concerning the general business conduct of the insurer. Because the transactions of a life insurance company assume a great variety of forms, it usually is considered desirable that the board be composed of individuals who possess varying, wide experience.

To expedite the proper fulfillment of its functions and to bring its members into close touch with the business affairs of the insurer, the board divides itself into a number of standing committees. In many companies, the president and other officers are members of the board of directors and, hence, are entitled to membership on important committees. If the executive officers are not directors, they are invited to various meetings in an advisory capacity. These committees vary in different insurers but usually they include an executive or insurance committee, a finance committee, a claims committee, an audit committee, and a compensation committee. The executive committee, consisting of the president and certain members of the board, considers such matters as bear a vital relation to the general business policy of the insurer. For example, the committee determines the kinds of insurance contracts the company will sell, the provisions of the contracts, the premium rates, the territory in which the company will operate, and so on.

The finance committee—consisting of the chief executive officer, the chief investment officer, the treasurer of the company, and a certain number of the outside directors—exercises supervisory control over the company's investment policy and practices. In larger companies, a separate committee may deal with real estate and mortgage loans. The claims committee has general control over the payment of claims, and, in particular, it determines policy regarding doubtful or contestable claims. The audit committee, usually made up of nonemployee directors, maintains general supervision over the company's accounting system and records. Its objective is to give additional assurance regarding the integrity of (1) financial information used by the board in making decisions and (2) financial information distributed to outsiders. In the case of stock companies, it has become a widespread practice also to establish a compensation committee of nonemployee directors to oversee the insurer's compensation policies and to approve specifically the compensation of senior management.

In general, the officers of the company who carry on its active management initiate action, the function of the directors being to approve or disapprove the recommendations made. For the most part, directors' committees are guided by the recommendations of the officers of the insurer who are directly concerned. This is particularly true in the case of committees that deal with technical details of the business.

Executive Officers

The executive officers are responsible for carrying out the policies determined by the board of directors and for the general management of the business. These officers usually include the CEO and the president (these can be the same individual), one or more vice presidents, and the treasurer. The CEO usually is entrusted by the board of directors with broad executive powers and ideally should be well versed in financial matters and have broad financial services experience, so as to interpret properly the results attained in the respective departments of the company, advise the board of directors in supervising the general business conduct of the company, determine the best policy for it to pursue, and direct the work of the subordinate officials. He or she also is entrusted with the duty of selecting subordinate officials and department heads. The several vice presidents, each of whom usually has charge of a department, also must keep up with the general business operations of the company, so as to be in a position to assist the president in his or her duties, assume the president's responsibilities (or those of a ranking vice president) during his or her absence, and be prepared to assume the office in the event of promotion.

Departmentalization

The operations of life insurance companies involve three basic functions: to sell, to service, and to invest. For an insurer to carry out these functions properly, it must have high-quality professional actuarial, legal, underwriting, and accounting advice. Consequently, most insurers operate within seven major functional areas: actuarial, marketing, accounting and auditing, investments, law, underwriting, and administration.

Departmentalization simply means the division of work to be performed into logical sections or assignments. Business organizations normally are departmentalized on either a functional, a geographical, or a product basis. Examples of all three types of departmentalization are found in many life insurance companies. Thus, the actuarial department is established on the basis of function, a southern department follows from a geographical viewpoint, and the ordinary or group departments are established on the basis of product. In any case, a given insurer usually will follow its own unique pattern. The following discussion of functional departmentalization illustrates the internal organization and activities of a life insurance company.

Actuarial

The *actuarial department* establishes the insurer's premium rates, establishes reserve liabilities and nonforfeiture values, and generally handles all the mathematical operations of the insurer. This department also is responsible for analyzing earnings and furnishing the data from which annual dividend scales and excess interest and other credits are established. The actuarial staff, with assistance from the legal department, designs new policies and forms and is responsible for filing them with the various regulatory officials. The department also makes mortality and morbidity studies and often supervises the underwriting practices. It works closely with the marketing department in considering policy design and other factors that affect the insurer's competitive position. Because of the importance of the technical actuarial element in group insurance and group annuities, this department frequently handles the administration of this business or exercises a considerable degree of functional responsibility over it.

In recent years, globalization of the world's markets has led to increased complexity and volatility. As a result, there is a need for a comprehensive risk management system to address today's range and magnitude of business risks. Financial instruments, including derivatives, synthetics, and structured products, play a key role in today's risk management strategies. In this environment, actuaries have become deeply involved in asset–liability management processes as well as other aspects of financial management. The role of the actuary is vital to the operation of a life insurance company. In many smaller companies, the actuary in effect serves as executive vice president and exercises considerable influence over all areas of operations.

Marketing

The *marketing department* is responsible for the sale of new business, the conservation of existing business, and certain types of service to policyowners. This department supervises the activities of the company's agents and also is responsible for advertising; sales promotion; market analysis; recruiting, selection and training of agents; and controlling agency costs. (See chapter 24.)

Accounting

The *accounting and auditing department,* under the direction of the vice president and comptroller, is responsible for establishing and supervising the insurer's accounting and control procedures. Auditing, at both the agent and home office levels, is done by an independent unit of this department that usually has direct access to the audit committee of the board. The preparation of the company's financial statements is handled here, although the actuarial department exercises considerable functional control in this regard. The accounting department is, of course, responsible for matters concerning tax laws and regulations. Also, it is responsible for expense analysis and other operational statistics not handled by the actuarial department. (See chapter 34.)

Investment

The *investment department,* usually under the direction of an investment vice president, handles the company's investment program under policies laid down by the board of directors. Besides passing on the merits of the company's investments prior to presenting them to the finance committee for final approval, the department usually is the custodian of the insurer's bonds, stocks, and other investments, and is entrusted with the duty of collecting the interest and dividends earned on them.

To invest the company's money in securities that are safe and yet will yield a higher return than the rate assumed for premium and reserve computation requires skill and a wide knowledge of the various classes of investments in which life insurance companies are permitted to place their funds. The volatile interest rates experienced in recent years, coupled with innovative new products and increased competition, have enhanced the importance of highly competent investment management. (See chapters 32 to 34.)

Legal

The *legal department* is charged with the responsibility of handling all the company's legal matters. These include, among other things, regulatory compliance matters (see chapter 35), the conduct of court cases growing out of contested claims (see chapters 9 and 10), foreclosure proceedings and imperfect titles; the sufficiency and correctness of policy forms, agency contracts, bonds, and notes; the inspection of titles to property purchased by the company or upon which it has granted loans; and the analysis and interpretation for the benefit of the company of the statutory and court law governing life insurance in the jurisdictions in which the company operates.

Underwriting

The *underwriting department* is responsible for establishing standards of selection and for passing judgment on applicants for insurance. (See chapters 25 and 26.) In some insurers, the *medical department* is given separate status. The medical director supervises the company's medical examiners and may be the final authority to pass upon the insurability and classification of proposed insureds. In some instances, however, general underwriting control may rest with a vice president who is not a physician. The department makes use of many underwriting specialists who are not physicians. Many underwriting decisions do not depend upon a physician's opinion because insurability connotes more than good health.

Administration

The *administrative departments* are responsible for providing home office service to the company's agents and policyowners. Administrative departments also are responsible for human resources, home office planning, and other staff functions. The secretary of the company has charge of the insurer's correspondence, the minutes of the board of directors, and its various committees and the company's records.

Some of the significant areas of administration that are not dealt with directly in other chapters are discussed here, including policyowner service, claims administration, information systems, and human resources.[16]

Policyowner Service   The policyowner service (POS) function is usually organized as a department under the supervision of a vice president. As competition has increased in recent years, quality service to customers has become an increasingly important aspect of effective life insurance company operations.

Policyowner service departments administer the insurance contract from the time of issuance until termination. In addition to responding to requests for information by policyowners, beneficiaries and agents, the POS department is responsible for administering contract values, maintaining policy records, informing policyowners of developments that affect their contracts, and processing any changes requested by policyowners. The POS department also may be responsible for policy issue, premium billing and collection, agent or broker compensation, and at times claims administration.

The quality of service provided by the POS department is critically important in building and maintaining effective relationships between the insurer and the agent and policyowner—an important marketing goal. In addition to policyowners and agents, beneficiaries and account holders also are served by the POS department. In contrast to the usual situation with the cash-value policy, owners of IRAs, mutual funds, and pensions need periodic investment reports and frequently request information about transferring funds between accounts, the tax treatment of transactions, and so on. This makes it necessary for POS specialists to be knowledgeable about the insurer's financial products as well as its basic individual life insurance contracts.

POS departments can be organized by function (e.g., coverage changes, reinstatements, policy values, policy loans, replacements); by product (e.g., individual insurance, group insurance, health insurance, pensions); or by customer (a specific member of the

---

[16]This section is adapted from *Operations of Life and Health Insurance Companies*, Chapters 10–11, 15–16, copyright ©1986, LOMA.

department provides all the service needs of a specific customer assigned to that individual). Some insurers organize the POS function regionally.

Claims Administration   The claims administration function is usually organized according to the types of products (e.g., individual life, group life, individual health, group health, pensions) sold by the insurer. A claim unit or department may be established for each line of business. Regional claim offices are usually given authority to process and pay certain types of claims up to a specified monetary limit varying by product line. Different limits are also established for individual claims personnel based on the size and type of claim.

Life and health insurance claim procedures involve (1) gathering information about the claim, the claimant, and any beneficiary; (2) investigating instances of invalid claims or possible fraud; and (3) processing the claim for payment. In addition to administrative procedures, claims personnel must be well trained in all aspects of the insurer's product(s) including the medical and legal aspects affecting claims administration.[17]

Claim administration is an important function both in terms of providing quality service to claimants and beneficiaries and in terms of good business practice. The vast majority of all claims are paid promptly. In cases in which a claim must be denied because it is invalid or fraud is involved, the present litigious nature of U.S. society makes it essential to have well-trained personnel in all aspects of the claim administration process.

Information Systems   Information systems have become essential to a successful financial services organization. As technology and computer applications have increased in sophistication and utility, the role of the information systems department has grown in importance. The department develops and manages the company's computer information system including a database, a data communication network, and decision support applications. The department is responsible for office automation, word processing services, electronic mail, facsimile transmission, electronic filing, teleconferencing, and other technology-based activities. It assists other departments in developing or purchasing the computers and software they need to carry out their responsibilities.

Insurers need two types of information if they are to manage effectively: management information and operational information. *Management information* is information that managers need to formulate objectives, monitor progress toward these objectives, and generally to support the decision-making process. These are broadly referred to as decision support systems. *Operational information* is information that employees need in all functions and departments to perform their work. Both types of information are important and should be available on a timely and accurate basis.

New-product development is critically dependent on the systems capability of the insurer. Every part of the insurer is dependent on the availability of effective computer support and software applications. The systems include database management, word processing, and office automation systems.

Human Resources   Today's human resources department has moved beyond its traditional administrative role to that of an integral partner in helping a company achieve its important business objectives by using people's skills and talents to the best advantage. The availability of competent, effective human resources in an organization is critical to its operation. Their creativity, intelligence, resourcefulness, and diligence are essential to a company's success, regardless of the availability of other resources such as money, technology, and information.

---

[17]The International Claim Association has an extensive education program that includes courses in these areas.

The human resources department is responsible for assuring an appropriate supply of qualified personnel to manage the company effectively in light of its philosophy and objectives. This includes activities such as job analysis, job structuring, human resources planning, recruitment, selection, placement, training and professional development, performance appraisal and compensation, and succession planning and administration. The human resources department also administers all employee benefits and other services provided to employees.

The steady growth in the legal and regulatory rules in all areas of human resources activity has made the management of human resources more complicated. This complexity is enhanced considerably for those companies doing business internationally.

Many companies also departmentalize on the basis of product—that is, they have separate departments for ordinary, health, and group insurance, depending upon the lines they write. Still others use profit centers as a basis of organization. The organization of any specific company is unique, a function of the company's history, its leadership over time, and changes in the economic and regulatory environment.

Trends in Life Insurer Organization

Life insurer organization structures are changing in response to technological developments, the need for profitability, and the increasing demand for better customer service. In effect, the traditional hierarchical organization is evolving into a network organization.[18] This new organizational concept that is emerging, although not entirely eliminating hierarchy, emphasizes task accomplishments, making use of networks of relationships involving employees and outside resources. This includes the use of strategic alliances and outsourcing communication systems that extend beyond the traditional corporate structure. Network organizations by definition are learning organizations in which employees continuously upgrade their knowledge bases and skill sets as part of their ongoing responsibilities to each other.

Characteristics reflecting the network organization include:

- fewer layers of management
- wider spans of control
- organization of small work groups and work teams
- reliance upon outsourcing, strategic alliances, and external communication systems in business operations

Fewer Layers of Management

It is common for senior and middle managers to overmanage and mismanage the activities of their subordinates. One author suggests that age, prosperity, and size contribute to overlayered organizations. Mergers, acquisitions, and diversification into a new business also can lead to overlayering. Planning staffs frequently overlap line management, resulting in slow decision making as well as excess overhead. Today technological developments are leading to a reduction in the number of layers of management. This is so because:

- Accountability and responsibility can now be downloaded because the information needed for decision making is on the employee's computer.
- Computers are doing the work of organizing, assembling, and analyzing data once done by middle managers.
- Computers allow errors to be corrected at the source, reducing the need for data checks by management.

---

[18]This section draws on Stephen W. Forbes, "The Insurance Organization: Then and Now," *Resource* (June 1996), pp. 46–49.

- Widespread use of management-by-exception reporting on the computer decreases the amount of time that managers need to spend reviewing the work of their subordinates.

Fewer layers of management can result in

- elimination of redundant functions and responsibilities
- an increased individual sense of self-esteem as employees are given more knowledge and freedom to make decisions
- more timely responses to customers
- enhanced responsiveness to changing market and product needs

Wider Spans of Control

The ability of the life insurance manager to obtain computerized information regarding the work of subordinates has permitted the expansion of spans of control. This reduces the need for meetings between a supervisor and individual employees.

Wider spans of control also give employees a greater feeling of independence because they have less direct supervision. This organizational environment permits managers to focus on strategic issues and improving operations rather than on tactical matters because these are now part of everyone's knowledge base on the computer.

Wider spans of control will not automatically result in increased productivity. To gain improved productivity, managers in such an environment must be able to handle the significantly increased responsibilities arising from their increased reliance upon technology to obtain management information. Managing greater numbers of employees requires managers to enhance their leadership and participative management skills.

Work Groups and Work Teams

In the network organization, responsibility and accountability are delegated lower in the organization through creating strategic business units and small work groups that are responsible for specific products, markets, customers, or distribution systems. Many insurers have created separate businesses to provide investment and information system services in competition with outside suppliers. Work teams are frequently found in such areas as new business processing, customer service, and claims payments. The formation of smaller work teams and business units improves responsiveness to customer service needs, helps clarify accountability, and facilitates tracking results through performance measurement and capital management systems and the development of appropriate incentive compensation plans. They also facilitate the allocation of capital resources to meet return on capital objectives and product line-specific asset–liability management. Perhaps most important, work teams and smaller business units help attract, develop, and retain capable individuals by giving them assignments with a wide range of responsibility, autonomy, and accountability.[19]

Strategic Alliances, Outsourcing, and External Communications Network

Strategic alliances may be formed with customers, suppliers, and competitors to help each party attain its objectives. Common alliances in the life insurance industry include:

- domestic and foreign insurers (e.g., to enter foreign markets)
- life insurers and banks (e.g., marketing insurance and annuity products)
- life insurers and technological firms (e.g., software development)
- life insurers and health care organizations (e.g., HMOs)

---

[19]Instituting work teams to improve productivity, quality, and customer service does not always produce good results. See Life Office Management Association, *Work Teams in the Life Insurance Industry* (Atlanta, GA: LOMA, 1996).

Outsourcing of business can control costs, allow management to concentrate on its core competencies, and facilitate an organizational restructuring, a merger, or an acquisition. *External communications networks* such as the Internet are becoming important management tools in gaining competitive intelligence and marketing insurance products. Life insurers are in various stages of using these additional management tools in delayering their organizations, increasing managements' spans of control, and generally facilitating organizational change.

LIFE INSURER MANAGEMENT

Planning along with decision making is a primary function of management. The first step in providing a foundation for guiding decision making and goal setting is for senior management and the board of directors to define an overall corporate mission.

Strategic Management

The *strategic planning process* involves a systematic approach to analyzing the environment, assessing the organization's strengths and weaknesses, and identifying opportunities in which the organization could have a competitive advantage. Strategic planning is intended to allow managers to forecast the future and to develop courses of action that will result in maximizing the chance of a successful future for a company.

The first step in strategic planning is for management and the board of directors to define the overall objectives of the company—its mission. A *mission* is the fundamental, unique purpose that sets a business apart from other firms of its type and identifies the scope of its operations in product and market terms.

Once the mission statement has been crafted, the next step in the strategic planning process is to establish *long-term objectives* that collectively appear to assure accomplishment of the company's mission. The primary objective ordinarily would be the maximization of shareholder value in a stock insurer and policyowner value in a mutual company.

Strategic planning can be contrasted with *operational planning* designed to guide an organization's day-to-day activities. Operational planning is tactical; it describes methods to be used at various levels in the organization to achieve lower-level objectives and ultimately to accomplish major corporate objectives.

If an organization produced only a single product or service, managers could develop a single strategic plan that covered everything it did, but most financial services organizations are in diverse lines of business. Therefore, an organization needs corporate-level strategy (determines the roles that a business unit in the organization will play), business-level strategy (each division will have its own strategy that defines the products or services it will offer and the markets it wants to target), and functional-level strategy (support for the business-level strategy).

Planning and Control Cycle

All well-managed companies utilize a planning and control cycle made up of four stages: (1) strategic planning, (2) tactical planning, (3) performance monitoring, and (4) control and readjustment.[20]

---

[20]This section draws on Stephen W. Forbes, "The Planning and Control Cycle," *Resource* (January/February 1989).

These stages describe a management process without any particular time frame. The *strategic planning stage* defines the target markets, products (and services), and distribution systems that are coordinated to achieve the company's profitability and solvency objectives in light of the established overall corporate mission. These objectives must be achieved within solvency constraints defined by management in regard to cash flow and capital adequacy.

Everything in the management of a life insurer affects everything else. The effective manager must be able to see the logical interrelationships among micro decisions as they affect each other and the company's macro performance. In a financial context, a life insurer can be viewed as an aggregate of individual products and associated cash flows. The financial criteria employed to measure profitability can vary, but return on equity and value added are two widely used measures. These profitability criteria are often measured for strategic business units for purposes of determining relative performance, investment strategies, resource allocations, and incentive compensation.

Capital adequacy (both short and long term) is an important consideration in individual product design and the portfolio of products offered by a life insurance company. If required surplus is impaired, the insurer will face regulatory intervention. Rating services also pay close attention to surplus levels. Thus, cash flow and surplus management are important financial considerations, often serving as constraints on product design.

Once the target markets, distribution systems, and product mix meet the profitability and capital (surplus) criteria, the next stage of the planning cycle, *tactical planning,* can begin to provide the implementation of the strategic plan. The tactical plan involves the development and maintenance of all of the managerial and distribution components required to carry out the strategic plan within the timetables and cost constraints assumed in the product profitability and solvency models. Timely, efficient implementation is as important as good strategic planning. Realistic, achievable tactical plans must be developed for the product portfolio selected.

The third stage of the planning and control cycle is *performance monitoring.* The purpose, of course, is to determine if the insurer's strategic and tactical plans are being carried out so as to meet profitability and solvency objectives. Effective performance monitoring systems involve a limited number of meaningful reports generated for each strategic business unit and for the company as a whole. The timing of the reports and the amount of detail depend upon the use to which the reports are put. Senior management reports are likely to take a summary form to facilitate management by exception, enabling executives to concentrate on correcting variances from planned objectives. Obviously, the quality and integrity of the data are critically important.

Effective performance monitoring permits *control and readjustment,* the fourth stage of the planning and control cycle. Performance monitoring will lead to control and readjustment of tactics to achieve a given strategic plan, or readjustment of the strategic plan itself if it appears to be unattainable even after feasible adjustments have been made. This completes the cycle, in which strategic plans involving products, markets, and distribution systems are modified as experience unfolds and ideas for new products and strategies evolve as a natural part of the management process.

It is important to remember that creativity and imagination are critical to successful life insurance company management. There are always a number of ways to attack a problem strategically and tactically. The effective executive-manager will examine a number of alternative approaches, applying the technical tools at his or her disposal and at times even inventing new ones. Management is a dynamic process in which creativity is a critically important resource.

Value-Based Planning

The management of a life insurer's capital resources is central to the successful fulfillment of its mission. Key questions that every company faces include:

- How will corporate capital be allocated among many possible applications?
- What market segments and products represent the most attractive opportunities for investing in the company's future?
- What constitutes an adequate rate of return for the company's investments?
- How will management performance be evaluated?

Value-based planning is increasingly used in the life insurance industry as a tool for analyzing these issues and establishing long-range strategy. **Value-based planning,** also called **embedded-value analysis,** focuses on the economic net worth of a company and its relative increase from planning period to planning period.

The value of a company comprises three elements: (1) current capital and surplus together with nonbenefit contingency reserves; (2) the value of expected future net cash flows from existing business; and (3) expected future net cash flows from future business. These values are defined as the present value of future cash flows discounted at a specified hurdle rate of return for alternative investments with similar risk characteristics. The discount rate is determined by reference to the company's cost of capital in the capital markets, and it may be adjusted to reflect the different risks associated with different products or ventures.

A product or business venture creates value if discounted cash flows exceed the initial investment. Four broad strategies are generally available to management with respect to existing product lines and businesses:

- The product or venture can be discontinued and market share surrendered.
- Additional investment can be discontinued and market share harvested as it declines.
- Sufficient investment can be made to maintain existing market share.
- Significant investment can be made to build market share.

To determine whether value is created by the adoption of these strategies, the cash flows associated with the investment required for each strategy are discounted at the selected rate. The investment required for each strategy is the sum of the value that might be received through divesting the product or venture by sale or reinsurance agreement and the additional capital required to adopt the strategy. When discounted cash flows exceed the required investment, value is created and adoption of the strategy is indicated. New products, ventures, and acquisitions can be tested similarly for value creation. As discussed in chapter 34, aggregate value added during any planning or measurement period is the difference in beginning and ending values, adjusted for surplus paid out in dividends and paid in through capital injections during the period.

Value-based planning is a standard for strategic and capital allocation decision making. It serves as a rational basis for establishing the critical long-term policies that guide successful pursuit of the corporate mission. These include:

- Establishing a long-term financial strategy that satisfies the requirements of the various constituencies (primarily customers, investors, employees, regulators, and rating agencies) that management serves.
- Determining a capital structure that is consistent with corporate policies regarding operational (benchmark capital, uncommitted capital, and risk-based capital targets) and financial (debt–equity) leverage.

- Allocating capital to ventures, products, and acquisitions that will create future value for policyowners and stockholders.
- Identifying performance standards by which the success or failure of management action may be evaluated.

In competitive businesses, the financial results depend ultimately on the success of the company in achieving a unique or predominant position in the segments of the market that it chooses to serve. This position may stem from a low-cost structure, a unique sales operation, a special underwriting or investment skill, and so on; each of these elements is important in enhancing profit. The key to the success for the company is to assure that these unique positions continue and that changes in other elements of the cost or pricing structure do not negate these positions.

In all areas of organization there are no simple answers, only different choices, each with its own advantages and disadvantages. The choice will often depend more on the company's history, its current circumstances, or sometimes on the easy availability of information than on the merits one can determine on balance of a particular approach.

Questions

1. What do the differing abilities of stock and mutual insurers to control the owner–policyowner and owner–management incentive conflicts suggest about the advantages and disadvantages of these corporate forms?
2. What might motivate the management of a mutual life insurance company to consider demutualization?
3. What are some of the disadvantages of demutualization?
4. How are functions of the home office underwriting and actuarial departments coordinated? How might shoddy performance in one of these departments affect the effectiveness with which the other department carries out its duties?

MARKETING LIFE
AND HEALTH INSURANCE

Objectives

- Describe the variety of channels that exist for the distribution of life and health insurance.

- Discuss international trends in the distribution of insurance and the roles of multinational insurers.

- Identify practices used for compensating both management and intermediaries involved in marketing life insurance.

- Describe the life and health insurance product development process.

- Identify challenges and opportunities facing the future of life and health insurance marketing.

A life insurance company's success reflects the consolidated effort of all of its activities. As pointed out in chapter 23, these activities may be arranged into three major functional classifications—marketing, investments, and administration. Of these three areas, marketing is the largest in terms of both personnel requirements and costs and is critical to success.

Life insurers historically considered marketing to be synonymous with selling, and most insurers considered their customers to be their agents. By the middle of the twentieth century, a customer-oriented philosophy began to emerge in business generally, coming to some national markets later than others. As this new marketing concept was adopted by more and more companies, it began to spread to services industries generally and the life insurance industry specifically. The concept involves:

- focusing on consumer needs
- integrating all activities of the organization, including production, to satisfy these needs
- achieving long-term profits through satisfaction of consumer needs

Although life insurers were late in adopting this concept, the recent intense competition within the life insurance business and the growing competition from other financial services organizations substantially heightened its importance. To be successful today, a life insurer must create a satisfied customer and then turn that customer into a client. Historically, this was done by the agent. Today insurers seek ways to augment and enhance the service provided by the agent.

DEVELOPING AND MAINTAINING A MARKETING PROGRAM

We define **marketing** as the provision of products well suited to consumers' needs through effective, appropriate distribution channels. A **distribution channel** is the means by which products or services are provided to customers and encompasses the entirety of a company's marketing network. Distribution channels are also called **distribution systems** or **marketing channels.**

A **marketing program** is a tactical plan that deals primarily with the product, price, distribution, and promotion strategies that a company will follow to reach its target markets and to satisfy their needs. The development and maintenance of a realistic marketing program is the primary responsibility of senior marketing executives. The elements of a marketing program include an analysis of the markets available to or desired by the insurer, identification of the nature of the perceived competition, and determination of the distribution techniques to be used. Use of sophisticated data warehousing, data mining, and database management techniques can materially increase a marketing program's effectiveness. A marketing plan must also include the design of a sales compensation system, a basic pricing strategy, and the special administrative systems and support needed by particular market segments or products. The marketing plan is then utilized to develop a product portfolio and project future production by product and amount.

Once the insurer's marketing plan is initially documented, management evaluates its growth and profit goals, and the capabilities and core competencies of the home office and marketing operations. The marketing plan should reflect a realistic assessment of the company's strengths and weaknesses in relation to factors considered critical to the plan's success. This assessment leads to broad or narrow product portfolios, different distribution channel structures, geographic concentration, and so on, that is, the search for a competitive advantage. It should be noted that, with the competitive emphasis on rates of return for interest-sensitive products and for separate-account business such as variable life and annuities, a close coordination with the investment function is essential.

The results of this planning and development activity will be a quantification of what the company wants to achieve, reflecting a balance between long-term and short-term goals. With priorities established, specific goals set down, and a product portfolio established, the stage is set for selecting and utilizing one or more distribution channels to deliver products to the markets selected. Typically, however, the distribution channel comes first, and the tentative decisions regarding distribution significantly influence the process of developing a product portfolio.

DISTRIBUTION CHANNELS

An insurer that considers itself to be truly market driven (in contrast to product or distribution driven) would use distribution channels that reflected the ways that its customers wanted to interact with the insurer. Of course, for most insurers, there are practical limits to the implementation of this philosophy. Even so, the great variety of distribution systems found in life insurance suggests that insurers continue to strive toward this elusive goal.

In this section, we present the major distribution channels found in life insurance. As will be seen, life insurers have evolved an almost bewildering array of distribution systems. To simplify this complexity, we structure our discussion around three broad categories of distribution channels:

- marketing intermediaries
- financial institutions
- direct response

Marketing intermediaries are individuals who sell an insurer's products, typically on a face-to-face basis with customers and usually for a commission on each sale. Agents and brokers are marketing intermediaries. Most life insurance worldwide is sold through marketing intermediaries. In North America, they account for more than 90 percent of new individual life insurance sales and for majority shares of other life and health insurance sales.

Financial institutions are deposit-taking, investment, and other financial firms that sell insurers' products. They include commercial banks, investment banks, thrifts, credit unions, mutual fund organizations, and other insurers. Banks are important distribution channels in some markets, especially in Europe, but less so in Asia and North America. Banks' share of the overall U.S. life insurance market is less than 5 percent, although their share of new individual annuity sales exceeds 20 percent. Securities firms write a significant share of variable products, with other financial institutions having small shares.

With the **direct-response** distribution channel, the customer deals directly with the insurer without benefit of any intervening intermediary or firm. No face-to-face contact ordinarily is involved with the customer responding to some type of solicitation directly from the insurer, such as through the mail, television, or telephone. This distribution channel accounts for about 2 percent of total U.S. life insurance sales.

These three categories of distribution systems are distinguishable based on the life insurer's relationship with the customer. Thus, with marketing intermediaries, the customer's relationship with the insurer is direct but often closely identified with the insurer. With financial institutions, the relationship also is indirect but usually with the customer identifying more with the institution than with the insurer. With direct response, of course, the relationship is direct. Insurers often use many distribution channels, as we discuss throughout this section. Figure 24-1 shows the three categories of distribution channels.

The following discussion classifies all life insurance distribution into one of these three categories. Our orientation is the United States. As a practical matter, however, much overlap exists between the systems. Additionally, the distinctions between the various channels are not always crisp because marketing evolution has blurred formerly distinct demarcation lines.

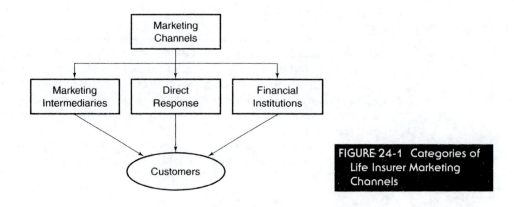

FIGURE 24-1 Categories of Life Insurer Marketing Channels

Distribution through Marketing Intermediaries

We can divide marketing intermediaries into two broad classes, depending on whether the insurer is attempting to build its own agency sales force. Thus, many insurers have an **agency-building distribution** strategy under which they recruit, train, finance, house, and supervise their agents. Such insurers are heavily involved in recruiting individuals new to the insurance business.

Other insurers follow a **non-agency-building distribution** strategy under which they do not seek to build their own agency sales force. Instead, they rely on established agents for their sales. Under this strategy, the insurer seeks experienced salespersons and avoids expenses associated with training, financing, and providing office facilities.

Figure 24-2 shows the various divisions of agency-building and non-agency-building distribution channels. We cover each next, relying on this agency-building distinction. Of course, an insurer may use several distribution channels. The reason for multiple distribution strategies is to serve several markets effectively. A market-driven strategy calls for an optimal market-product-distribution linkage.

Agency-Building Distribution

Most students of the industry agree that life insurers utilizing the agency-building distribution strategy have been responsible for the widespread acceptance of life insurance. These insurers have provided the initial training essential to successful intermediary marketing. Four types of agency-building distribution channels exist:

1. career agency
2. multiple-line exclusive

FIGURE 24-2 Life Insurer Distribution Channels: Marketing Intermediaries

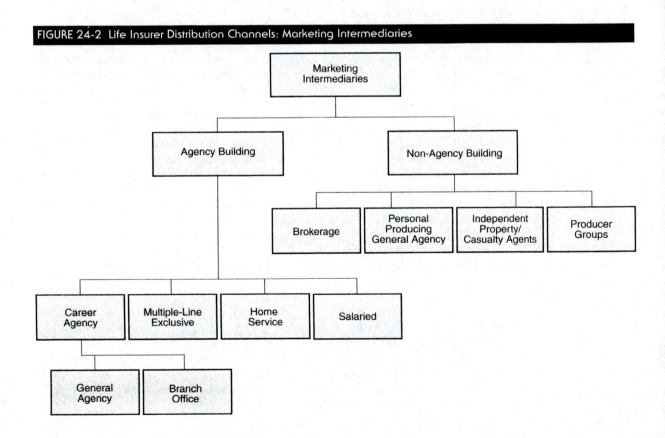

3. home service
4. salaried

Each of these channels relies on **agents** who are commissioned or salaried salespeople who hold full-time contracts to represent the insurer. Most of these agents are **exclusive agents** (also called **tied** or **captive agents**), meaning that they represent a single insurer only.

Career Agency   **Career agents** are commissioned life insurance agents who primarily sell one company's products. They are probably the most commonly known life insurance agents. Well-known U.S. life insurers using the career agency distribution channel include Metropolitan Life, Northwestern Mutual Life, and New York Life.

Two approaches to career agency distribution are found: branch offices and general agencies. We discuss each next.

The branch office system.   Under the **branch office system,** also called the **managerial system,** the insurer establishes agencies in various locations, each headed by an **agency manager** who is an employee of the insurer. The largest life insurers worldwide tend to use the branch office system. The agency manager is charged with the responsibility of recruiting new agents within a given territory and training and otherwise helping and encouraging them in their work as solicitors.

Agency managers may be assisted by an office manager, assistant managers, supervisors, specialist unit managers, or district managers. Assistants are responsible for specific functions or for units of agents, or they may provide overall assistance to the head of the agency. The office manager is particularly important in the branch office system. He or she is expected to keep all office records; look after all correspondence in connection with applications and policies; assist in filing proofs of loss, applications for policy loans, and payment of cash values on surrenders; answer all communications from policyowners not sufficiently important to be referred to the home office; and supervise the clerical staff.

Agency-building systems (either general agency or managerial) also are used by *fraternal* organizations that offer life and health insurance to their members. The agents of these religious and social groups may sell policies only to members of the fraternal society.

The general agency system.   The **general agency system,** which, in its pure form, is only theoretical today in the United States, is the older of the two career agency systems and aims to accomplish through general agents what the branch office system accomplishes through agency managers. The company-appointed **general agent** (GA) typically represents the company within a designated territory over which he or she is given control. The general agent's contract requires that the insurer pay a stipulated commission on the first year's premiums plus a renewal on subsequent premiums. In return, the general agent agrees to build the company's business in that territory.

The GA is responsible for agent recruitment, training, and supervision, as with the agency manager. Agents contract with the insurer through the GA and are paid a commission by the insurer for their sales. The GA also receives a commission on agents' sales, called an **override** or **overriding commission.**

In the past, the GA operated more or less as an independent entrepreneur, managing his or her agency and meeting all operational expenses from override commissions. Routine administrative matters today usually are handled by a separate group of persons located in the general agent's office or in separate offices throughout the country and are directly responsible to the home office. It is also now common for the insurer to pay the office rent directly. This is done to discourage the closing of the office, which would leave the insurer without representation. In addition, companies now make substantial expense reimbursements allowances.

Multiple-Line Exclusive Agency   The second major agency-building life insurance distribution channel is the multiple-line exclusive agency. **Multiple-line exclusive agents** (MLEAs) are commissioned exclusive agents who sell the life and health and property and liability insurance products of a single group of affiliated insurers. In the United States, well-known insurers using the multiple-line exclusive distribution channel include State Farm and Allstate.

As contrasted with other agency-building distribution systems, MLEAs often are not all housed in the same office. Rather each agent has his or her own office with clerical support that services clients and supplements the agent's personal sales efforts.

Although other agency-building systems are stagnant or declining, multiple-line companies have been growing. The number of MLEAs grew by 16 percent over the period from 1981 to 1996. One reason for this growth is the economies realized through multiproduct distribution and through higher customer loyalty.

Home Service   A third agency-building life insurance distribution channel is the **home service distribution system,** also known as the **combination** or **debit distribution system,** which relies on exclusive agents who are assigned a geographic territory. The target market for home service distribution is lower-income consumers. At one time, agents collected renewal premiums on business in force in their territory (called their **debit**), but the collection aspect has been deemphasized by many companies.

Originally, much of the business consisted of industrial insurance with weekly collections of premium. Today almost all of the new sales consist of ordinary insurance with premiums collected on a monthly basis or billed through the mail. The assigned territory is becoming a sales region, as less of the business requires collection of premiums by the agent.

The home service distribution system at one time was the largest and was used by the largest life insurers, including Prudential and Metropolitan. Many insurers have since abandoned this distribution system as being too costly. The number of home service agents has fallen by 76 percent during the past 15 years.

Salaried   The fourth agency-building life insurance distribution channel is use of salaried insurer employees. Even though most life insurance is sold by commissioned salespeople, a small share is sold by agents who are paid mostly or exclusively by salary. For example, savings bank life insurance (see chapter 11) is sold in the states of Connecticut, Massachusetts, and New York through salaried bank employee-agents, although the trend is for the savings banks to use more conventional approaches. The most important salaried distribution, however, occurs in group insurance.

Group insurance actually involves three very distinct product lines—retirement, group life, and group health products. The insurer typically markets through **group sales representatives** who are salaried employees of the insurer charged with promoting and possibly servicing the insurer's group business. Group sales representatives usually are also paid incentive bonuses based on achievement of production goals.

The group representative's responsibilities may be to sell group products directly to customers or to promote the insurer's group sales through its own or other insurers' marketing intermediaries to whom commissions are paid. Thus, group sales representatives call on their own career agents, independent benefit consultants, third-party administrators, national brokerage organizations, independent property and liability agents, and agents of other companies.

Most of the smaller-sized cases are sold through career agents, either the insurer's own career agents or agents of other companies. Sales to larger employer–employee cases and association groups tend to be made through specialized brokers or, in some instances, written directly with the employer. Many of the recent developments in

BOX 24-1

WORKSITE MARKETING

Some employers offer their employees individual insurance through payroll deduction, called **worksite marketing.** Originally, such coverage was designed for employers that were ineligible for group insurance because of their small number of employees. As group insurance coverage is now available for most small groups, the increased interest in worksite marketing is primarily due to employer attempts to contain rising costs of employee benefits. Most plans are employee-pay-all plans. Nevertheless, the ease of payroll deduction and liberal underwriting make such plans attractive. In addition, coverage portability is also appealing.

distribution systems reflect a continuing effort to find more effective ways to deliver insurance products and service larger numbers of customers.

In addition to group insurance as such, various forms of mass marketing have developed, frequently involving an agent. Association group, credit card solicitations, and worksite marketing are examples. See Box 24-1.

Agency Management   Effective field management is essential to the success of agency-building distribution systems.[1] An agency head's responsibility is to manage resources to achieve the common objectives of the agency and the company. In terms of activities, these duties consist of

- manpower development, including product and sales skills training
- supervision of agents
- motivation of agents and staff
- business management activities (e.g., office duties, public relations activities, interpreting insurer policy, and expense management)
- personal production

Personal production by the agency head has a low priority in agency-building companies. Although it is usually permitted, the need for growth and the design of the agency manager's or GA's compensation formula both mitigate against significant activity of this type.

Agent recruiting usually is the agency manager's or GA's most important responsibility. The turnover rate of agents in many markets is 25 percent per year, so the agency head has to replace a fourth of the agency's sales force each year just to maintain the agency's size. Recruiting is not one activity but a process, the steps of which include

1. finding sources of prospective agents
2. determining acceptable qualifications
3. approaching prospective agents
4. using selection tools
5. interviewing candidates
6. contracting with qualified individuals

The manager may attempt to locate several (three to five) prospective agents at one time. As there is always fallout in the selection process, the group techniques usually allow some recruits to be added to the agency from each recruiting effort. Recruiting a group rather than one agent at a time also is a more efficient use of a field manager's time.

---

[1]This section is adapted from Dennis W. Goodwin, *Life and Health Insurance Marketing* (Atlanta, GA: LOMA, 1989).

Considerable effort has been made in raising the standards for new agents and in increasing their productivity. One strategy that has proven helpful is precontract or preappointment training. It refers to a period of time before the prospective agent is contracted, during which licensing, training, and field work may take place. Only after this period is a full-time contract offered. Most insurers have become increasingly careful in their selection of new agents. They also devote much attention to the training of their agents in the nature and uses of life and health insurance and sales methods.

In view of the broad range of interest-sensitive and traditional products on the market today, the agency head has a significant challenge in adequately training an agency force. Agency managers and GAs do, however, have access to a wealth of training materials. In addition to those made available by the company, a wide array of material is available from industry associations and commercial publishers. The agency head also must maintain an appropriate and effective continuing education program for all agents, those recently established as well as experienced professionals. One-half the U.S. states require that agents pursue some form of continuing education to maintain their licenses.

The level of supervision provided for agents is a function of the agent's experience and length of service. Close supervision is particularly helpful to a new agent until he or she develops good work habits and feels comfortable in the working relationship with the supervisor. Experience has shown that agents react positively to supervision in which they (1) are told what to expect at the outset, (2) view the supervision as helpful in improving their performance, and (3) help set the objectives against which they will be measured. Most agency managers and GAs have some form of daily communication with their agents. The relationship that develops between an agent and the agency head is an important factor in the success or failure of a new agent.

In the sales management process, an agency head provides the stimulus to make an agent feel motivated to take action that results in sales and related goals. Agency heads demonstrate personal interest in each agent, use formal in-depth reviews and group meetings, encourage attendance at industry organization meetings, provide special office privileges, and conduct sales contests, all to create an environment in which agents will feel motivated. Each of these motivational activities is intended to demonstrate to each agent the concern of the agency head for the agent's welfare and thus stimulate the agent to higher production.

In addition to these basic activities, the agency head also must carry out many normal business management activities including expense management, managing the office, public relations activities, and interpreting company policy. As the agency grows, the agency manager or GA must develop second-line management and must delegate the functions for which his or her personal involvement is not essential. Otherwise, he or she will be unable to give adequate personal attention to matters that are critical to the success of the agency.

As the field office administers a broad range of financial products, the agency head must provide increasing management support and expertise as the agency grows. To provide this support, some agencies have added functional specialists. Thus, an agency might have a brokerage specialist, specialists in various product lines, or technical support persons in specialized areas.

Non-Agency-Building Distribution

The other major classification of life insurance marketing channels relying on marketing intermediaries is called non-agency-building distribution, as noted earlier. Four common non-agency-building distribution channels are

- brokerage
- personal-producing general agents

- independent property and casualty agents
- producer groups

Agents selling through these channels are always nonexclusive; they sell for more than one insurer. Not all of these channels exist in every country, with some countries having no parallel to the non-agency-building system. In markets where they exist, terminology may differ; for example, the U.K. concept of independent financial advisors (IFAs) is akin to U.S. brokerage.

Insurers that market through nonexclusive agent strategies provide products or services to agents who are already engaged in life and health insurance selling. Thus, the key to this strategy is to gain access to the producer. The producer's loyalty is retained by quality service, good compensation, and sound personal relationships.

Brokerage Brokerage insurers gain access to agents through a company employee, often called a **brokerage representative** or **supervisor,** who acts as the insurer's representative, or through an independent **brokerage general agent** who performs the same function. Both of these individuals are authorized to appoint brokers on behalf of the insurer. Direct contracting in response to trade press advertising also is used.

The term **broker,** as used in the U.S. lexicon of life insurance distribution, refers to a commissioned salesperson who works independently of the insurer with whom the brokerage business is placed and who has no minimum production requirements with that insurer. In property and casualty insurance, a broker usually represents the client rather than the insurer. In most U.S. jurisdictions, a life broker actually is an agent for the insurer but subject to less supervision and control than that found with career agents. In other countries, the term *broker* in life insurance refers to a full-time intermediary who offers policies from several, if not all, life insurers in the market and who usually is the legal representative of the applicant, not the insurer.

The U.S. situation can be still more complex. The term *broker* can refer to at least three different distribution channels. First, most career agents *broker* business. As used as a verb in this way, it refers to the practice of full-time agents of one company occasionally selling the policies of other insurers. Career agents may sell for other insurers because (1) their primary insurer does not offer the policy or coverage needed by the customer, (2) their primary insurer has declined or offered highly rated coverage, or (3) the customer wants quotes from more than one insurer.

Second, the term *broker* refers to independent life insurance producers who have primary affiliation with no particular insurer and who specialize in particular products or (typically) high-end target markets. These brokers usually are former career agents who have become independent producers, meeting their own office and other expenses. Often they are among the most knowledgeable marketing intermediaries.

Third, the term *broker* refers to a salesperson whose primary product is not insurance but who sells insurance as an ancillary service to his or her customers. This category can include real estate agents, automobile dealers, accountants, lawyers, and financial consultants.

At one time, insurers that utilized a brokerage strategy and sold through independent life agents and representatives of other companies specialized in term and substandard business. Today the range of products for which companies using the brokerage strategy compete has broadened to include almost all lines of insurance. Innovative products, pricing, commissions, and service are the competitive tools involved.

Companies seeking economic efficiencies through spreading their fixed costs have increasingly looked at supplementing their traditional channels of distribution with additional distribution outlets. Many insurers that traditionally have been career agent "shops" exclusively are now aggressively pushing their brokerage business.

Personal-Producing General Agents   A second type of marketing intermediary falling within the non-agency-building category is the personal-producing general agent. **Personal-producing general agents** (PPGAs) are independent, commissioned agents who typically work alone and focus on personal production. Some PPGAs appoint subagents, although most do not. PPGA insurers gain access to producers through an organizational structure that is similar to the one used by brokerage insurers: (1) company-employed regional directors of PPGAs, (2) independent contractors—managing general agents, and (3) direct contracting with individuals identified through trade press advertising. Both regional directors and managing general agents are authorized to appoint PPGAs.

The PPGA strategy has two variations. In the more traditional regional director approach, experienced life agents are hired under contracts that provide both direct and override commissions plus some type of expense allowance. For this, the PPGAs supply their own office facilities and receive technical assistance in the form of computer services and advanced sales support. Although personal-producing general agents usually have contracts with more than one insurer, companies using the traditional approach try to be the PPGA's primary carrier. The managing general agent approach typically specializes in single products, such as universal life or disability income, and is essentially franchised to appoint PPGAs for the company in a territory.

Although there are philosophical differences in approach, a clear difference at the producer level between the brokerage and the PPGA strategy is in the commission schedule. The former resembles a career agent contract and the latter has elements of a general agent contract. Another difference is that brokerage business from a single agent often is sporadic, whereas PPGA business is intended to be continuing. Both strategies can operate simultaneously in the same insurer, along with others.

Independent Property and Casualty Agents   A third type of marketing intermediary using the non-agency-building approach is the independent property and casualty agent. **Independent property and casualty agents** are commissioned agents whose primary business is the sale of property and casualty insurance for several insurers. Often the property and casualty insurers that the agent represents will have life insurer affiliates, and they encourage the agent to take advantage of his or her customer relationships to sell life insurance for them. Additionally, unaffiliated life insurers often seek independent property and casualty agents as salespeople.

Technically, independent property and casualty agents who sell life insurance usually do so either as brokers or PPGAs. However, because of their importance and uniqueness, and as a contrast with the MLEA, we present them as a separate distribution channel.

Producer Groups   A fourth variation of the non-agency-building distribution strategy has been the development of **producer groups,** which are independent marketing organizations that specialize in the high-end market. Producer groups are distinguished by three characteristics:

1. Membership is composed of independent life agents who specialize in high-end markets.
2. The group is self-supporting, having negotiated special commission rates with several insurance companies.
3. Minimum production requirements apply to members.

Under its contracts with insurers, it receives maximum compensation with virtually no market support services. Producer groups provide the necessary sales and marketing support systems to the member agents. Specialized software and other strong computer and research support are hallmarks of producer groups, often affording their members a competitive advantage.

The marketing organization typically provides its own continuing education program, administration, illustration services, presubmission underwriting, and case management (after submission) to the producer. It also provides market-specific or sales-concept support. Most producer groups have created their own reinsurance companies—an additional source of profitability. With such producer groups, part of the negotiation with direct-writing insurers focuses on terms and conditions under which the insurer cedes business to its reinsurance company.

The M Financial Group is the oldest and largest producer group. Others include The Partners Group, the Hemisphere Group, First Financial Resources, and Forth Financial Resources.

Financial Institution Distribution

As discussed in chapter 35, the U.S. financial services business has traditionally been segmented, principally because of legal restrictions. Today regulatory barriers are being dismantled, with insurance and banking experiencing waves of change. This is a result of the inexorable influence of economic forces in market economies as the global economy has evolved.

Today commercial and investment banks and other financial institutions have become important marketing channels for annuities and some life and health insurance products in the United States. More than 4,000 U.S. commercial financial institutions holding 70 percent of all U.S. deposits are engaged in marketing insurance products.

We classify life insurance distribution via financial institutions into three categories as follows:

- deposit-taking institutions'
- investment banks
- other financial institutions

Figure 24-3 shows these three categories. By **deposit-taking institutions,** we mean any financial intermediary engaged in accepting deposits from and making loans to the public. This category includes commercial banks, which are by far the most important such institution in terms of assets, but it also includes thrifts, credit unions, and any other specialized deposit-taking arrangement. By **investment banks,** we mean a financial intermediary engaged in bringing together investors and issuers of securities. This category includes marketing intermediaries whose primary business is the sale of securities. **Other financial institutions** include mutual fund organizations, pension funds, and insurers.

Deposit-Taking Institutions

U.S. deposit-taking institutions have been active in marketing annuity products since the mid-1980s, producing significant growth in the last decade. The Supreme

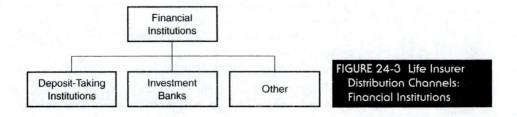

FIGURE 24-3 Life Insurer Distribution Channels: Financial Institutions

Court's unanimous decision in 1995 that annuities are financial products, not insurance products, and can be sold by commercial banks stimulated their marketing efforts. New individual annuity sales by banks are estimated to be at least 20 percent of total sales. More than one-half of the largest U.S. banks market annuities, and the proportion is growing. According to the Association of Banks-in-Insurance, 86 percent of those who purchased annuities through financial institutions and 91 percent of those who live in rural areas were *first-time* buyers.

U.S. deposit-taking institutions' efforts to sell life and health insurance policies have not been as successful as with annuities, with the exception of credit life and health insurance. Banks indicate, however, that with the changing regulatory environment they will strengthen marketing efforts related to term life insurance, cash-value life insurance, long-term care insurance, and disability income insurance.

Annuities and life and health products are distributed primarily by agents employed by commercial banks or subsidiaries and by bank staff (e.g., branch managers and customer service representatives). Many banks rely on various direct-response techniques (see next section), often in addition to agents. **Third-party marketers**—sales representatives employed by an outside marketing company—also are involved in bank annuity, life, and health insurance product sales.

Investment Banks

Investment banks and their retail marketing divisions are important distribution channels for variable and fixed annuities as well as some life and health insurance. Stockbrokers often are classified and treated as insurance brokers because their primary sales activity is other than insurance and they may often sell for multiple companies.

It is estimated that they account for approximately one-third of new variable annuity sales and 5 percent of variable life sales. One stockbroker firm already is the second largest writer of single-premium variable life insurance in the United States.

Other Financial Institutions

We are witnessing the evolution of mutual fund organizations as a life insurance distribution channel. Already, several no-load mutual fund organizations offer life and health insurance with, for example, one such organization already being licensed to sell life insurance in almost all states. Their Web sites invite inquiries regarding insurance purchases, and we can expect sales transactions via the Internet soon.

This classification also includes insurers. An increasing number of companies have discovered that it is not economical for them to manufacture all the products that their agents believe they need, or that they cannot be competitive in all areas. They have sought to import certain products developed by other companies. The result has been increased interest and activity in manufacturer–distributor relationships. In one study, one-half of the U.S. life insurance companies surveyed stated that they distribute one or more products manufactured by other companies. These arrangements are mostly to fill out a product line, as sales account for only 5 percent of new premiums. Disability income insurance is the most commonly imported product. Such manufacturer–distribution relationships are less common in other markets worldwide.

Financial institutions are gaining market share as more and more institutions develop relationships with life insurance companies and strengthen their own distribution system. Over time, as sectoral barriers continue to fall, more financial institutions will undoubtedly develop or acquire life insurance companies and operate them as subsidiaries (and vice versa).

Direct-Response Distribution

Of the three major categories of distribution channels in life insurance, direct response is the least important as measured by premiums written. *Direct-response marketing* can take many forms, but in a broad sense it means that the sale is made from the company direct to the customer without involving a face-to-face meeting between buyer and seller. In a direct-response sale, no commissions generally are paid, as the buyer responds directly to the company because of solicitation via mail, broadcast media, the Internet, and so on.

There is growing interest in direct-response marketing of life and health insurance because some companies that specialize in direct-response sales have been able to sell as many new policies as the largest career agent companies with thousands of agents. Also, an upsurge in telemarketing of life insurance products in the United Kingdom has peaked the interest in the United States and elsewhere.

Direct marketing offers the consumer some of the same coverages available from marketing intermediaries. The principal differences to the consumer are usually cost and service. The same level of coverage sold through an agent may sometimes cost more than when sold through an efficient direct-response marketing program, but, of course, the potential exists for greater personal service if an agent is involved in the transaction.

At one time, life and health insurance sold by direct-response marketing was primarily supplemental coverage (i.e., it helped to fill the gaps in basic coverages). The products were simple. They were easy to understand, required relatively small premium outlays, and were serviced through the economies of computerized solicitation, issuance, and administration. This approach favors the sale of a large number of small policies.

More recently, companies have begun to offer comprehensive life and health insurance protection, annuities, estate planning, and other products through direct-response marketing methods. Where direct-response marketing is targeted to a select group of consumers, and the insurer has an affinity agreement with the consumer, it can offer a broader range of relatively complex products. At least one successful insurer sells automobile insurance, cash-value life insurance, and annuities to its customer base and does it effectively. It utilizes professional, salaried salespersons in a telemarketing arrangement.

Regardless of how the sale has been completed—by an agent or direct-response marketing—from that point on, the client frequently deals with the insurer on a direct basis. Premium notices are sent by mail. Premiums are paid by mail or automatic bank draft and at times claims are filed and benefit checks are delivered by mail. In this sense, the direct-response concept—whereby the insurer deals directly with the consumer—is not restricted to a few direct-response specialty companies, but is a concept that is common to all elements of the insurance business.

Direct-response marketing can be accomplished through several media. Figure 24-4 shows the more common ones.

Direct mail is the oldest method of direct-response marketing. It depends on the availability of mailing lists that may be obtained from many sources. Today lists can be created that are specific as to the economic, demographic, and other characteristics of individuals on the lists. A **sponsored arrangement**—under which the insurer arranges with an association or similar group to offer products to its membership—can be very effective for direct-response marketing. The association membership is mailed solicitations, or advertisements are placed in the association's magazine or newsletter.

Newspapers, magazines, and other print media reach large numbers of consumers but only on a broad basis. In terms of total numbers reached, broadcast surpasses all other media. The direct-response marketing use of television, utilizing well-known per-

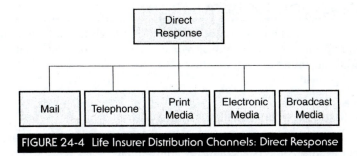

FIGURE 24-4 Life Insurer Distribution Channels: Direct Response

sonalities as sponsors, is popular for two reasons. First, the size of the audience is staggering in its potential. Second, direct-response specialists have learned how to reach specialized groups of viewers efficiently. However, the use of such "stars" to sell insurance products has come under attack. Opponents claim that the material often is misleading and the products are high in price.

The National Association of Insurance Commissioners (NAIC) identified three broad types or categories of advertisements: (1) institutional advertisement, (2) invitation to inquire, and (3) invitation to contract. The NAIC model advertising regulation provides detailed stipulations as to the content of advertisements, particularly those that are invitations to contract. Limitations and exclusions must be clearly set forth, and deceptive words and phrases may not be used. Some U.S. states require approval of every advertisement prior to use.

The prevalent direct-response media in use today (direct mail, print media, and broadcast media) have begun to be combined with telemarketing—the use of the telephone to solicit life and health insurance sales. The importance of this medium is evidenced by the proliferation of toll-free numbers. Telemarketing is a high unit-cost medium, but justification for this higher cost is found in relatively high response rates. Telemarketing also is personal once a consumer makes the initial telephone call. Personalization and mass marketing are combined in telemarketing, thus improving marketing effectiveness.

Much discussion centers on the concept of shopping for financial products and services using electronic media. Commercial on-line networks and the Internet are now utilized by all forms of marketing intermediaries as well as by financial institutions to promote themselves and their products and services. Some insurance companies and many marketing intermediaries and financial institutions provide on-line premium quotations and accept applications for coverage. Most have created sites on the Internet's World Wide Web that perform some or all of these functions.

Making and accepting payments cause concerns from the standpoint of security—particularly on the Internet. Most knowledgeable observers believe that network users will be content to make payments and receive delivery of products and file claims electronically. As in other industries, the time lag between introduction and widespread adoption of innovations in insurance tends to be long. The process of adopting automated teller machines required more than a decade after their appearance.

Electronic banking and securities transactions already are a reality with most large firms, although usage is not yet widespread. Electronic sales of any but simple life and health insurance products should not be expected to make significant competitive inroads against other means of distribution in the near future. Meanwhile, networks will play a significant role as sources for communication and information. The effects will be felt in the other distribution channels through customers being better informed.

THE INTERNATIONAL DIMENSIONS OF DISTRIBUTION

Having discussed life insurance marketing channels in the United States and their relative importance, it is instructive to examine such marketing in selected other countries. In addition, multinational insurers continue to be prominent in life insurance distribution worldwide.

Life Insurance Distribution Worldwide

In Canada, about 60 percent of life insurance premium income is generated by full-time career agents. Brokers account for approximately one-third of premium income, independent marketing organizations for 4 percent, and multiple-line agents 3 percent. As is true in almost all developed markets, brokers and independents are taking market share from career agents.

Distribution channels in the United Kingdom have been in a state of flux since the late 1980s because of regulatory changes. The Financial Services Act of 1986 resulted in a clear distinction between independent financial advisors (IFAs) and appointed and company representatives. IFAs (insurance brokers, banks, building societies, lawyers, and accountants) are required by law to survey the market to find the best product to meet the needs of their clients. Appointed and company representatives sell only their company's products. Brokers have traditionally been stronger than in other European countries, but they too are losing market share to banks and building societies. As a result of fines, disclosure regulations, and adverse publicity, the traditional tied agent sales force has been decimated, with the number of career agents having fallen by more than 50 percent. Most insurers have switched to IFAs. There also has been a significant increase in the use of the direct-response channel, particularly in personal lines.

In France, market shares have changed dramatically with the development of *bancassurance*. Today, more than 50 percent of life insurance policies were sold at banks, the post office, or the Treasury compared with 19 percent in 1983.

Swiss and German life insurers rely primarily on exclusive agents for distribution. In these markets, it is difficult for a new entrant to gain a significant market presence because there are relatively few independent distribution networks. This has led to an acceleration in the number of megamergers and acquisitions within Europe among insurance companies as well as between insurance companies and banks.

Distribution in Japan remains dominated by the industry's large network of female exclusive agents. Because agent commissions traditionally were set by the Ministry of Finance (MOF), agents almost never left one company for another, although this is changing. Several companies recruit full-time university graduates and have been modestly successful.

In most Latin American countries, career agents have been the traditional distribution channel. In recent years, however, independent agents, brokers, marketing organizations, and international brokers have developed. Distribution practices vary widely.

In the Pacific Rim countries, as in Japan, there is widespread use of exclusive agents. Both Taiwan and Korea recently have opened their markets to foreign insurers. Nevertheless, the largest domestic insurers still dominate the market (e.g., in Taiwan the three largest domestic companies maintain most of their 80 percent market share).

Although the 1990s witnessed a decline in the hiring of career agents in several developed market economy countries, several emerging markets have experienced strong growth in career agents. This is particularly true for China and Indonesia and many Latin American and Eastern European countries.

The Role of Multinational Insurers

Mergers, acquisitions, strategic alliances, and new entrants are changing the face of the life insurance industry. Until the late 1970s and 1980s, life insurance markets in North America and Europe were the world leaders in terms of premium volume, assets, and growth. As these markets matured, however, life insurance growth surged in Japan and other Asian countries. Also, new markets emerged in Latin America and Eastern Europe. This shift resulted in increasing interest by life insurers from traditional markets in the possibility of expanding operations internationally.

European insurers have invested enormous sums buying into insurance markets worldwide. Many have positioned themselves well within the European Union (EU) via mergers, acquisitions, and joint ventures. Several major U.S. insurers are moving into Europe; most U.S. insurers' activity, however, has been in the Pacific Basin and Latin America. In Europe, insurance subsidiaries of banks are among the largest producers of new life insurance premiums. Prominent companies in developing countries such as Korea, Singapore, and Taiwan are beginning to expand outside their own borders. Table 24-1 presents a representative listing of international insurers under their home countries.

TABLE 24-1 Representative International Insurers

Australia	*The Netherlands*	*United States*
AMP	ING (Nationale Nederlanden)	Aetna
Colonial	AEGON	AFLAC
National Mutual	Fortis (AMEV)	AIG
Canada	*Republic of China*	Allstate
Crown Life	Cathay Life	American General
MANULIFE	Shin Kong Life	AON
Canada Life	*Spain*	Chubb
Sun Life	MAPFRE	CIGNA
Great-West Life	*Sweden*	CNA
Denmark	Skandia	G. E. Capital
Baltica	Trygg Hansa	Hartford
France	*Switzerland*	John Hancock
AGF	Winterthur	Liberty Mutual
AXA	Zurich	Lincoln
Victoire	Baloise	Metropolitan
Germany	Swiss Reinsurance	New York Life
Allianz	Swiss Life	Principal
Gerling-Konzem	*United Kingdom*	Prudential (U.S.)
Munich Reinsurance	BAT	St. Paul
Italy	Commercial Union	Transamerica Travelers
Generali	General Accident	UNUM
Japan	Guardian Royal Exchange	
Dai-ichi Mutual	Legal & General	
Meiji Mutual	Norwich Union	
Nippon Life	Prudential (U.K.)	
Korea	Standard Life	
Samsung	Royal and Sun Alliance	
Mexico		
Provincial		

As a world economy emerged over the years, the relative stability of the U.S. economy and growth of the U.S. financial markets made them attractive to international investors. For some time, international insurers (mostly European companies) have had significant investments in the U.S. life and health industry. In view of the size of the U.S. market, which represents about one-quarter of the world's life premiums, an insurer cannot be a true multinational insurer without a U.S. presence. The U.S. market is relatively easy to enter and interest in doing so has intensified. In recent years, favorable exchange rates have created attractive opportunities for international investors. Table 24-2 presents a representative list of foreign-owned insurers active in the United States.

International insurers may choose to enter the United States by acquiring a company directly, through a joint venture, or as a reinsurer. Entering the U.S. market as a reinsurer is not attractive to many non-U.S. firms because of the virtual absence of a capacity problem for the life and health insurance industry. Although there have been a few examples of mutual insurers being acquired, acquisition of a stock insurer is generally more feasible. There is a trend toward demutualization.

It is widely agreed that many small- and medium-size U.S. insurers will not be able to survive the competitive U.S. environment. It seems reasonable to assume that international insurers will continue to find a supply of available companies and that interest in entering the U.S. market will continue.

TABLE 24-2 Representative Foreign-Owned Life Insurers Active in the U.S. Market

AEGON—*The Netherlands*
  Monumental Life
  Western Reserve Life
  Bankers United Life
  Iowa Fidelity Life
  Life Investors of America

Allianz—*Germany*
  Fidelity Union
  Fireman's Fund

AXA—*France*
  Equitable Life Assurance
    Society
  Provinces Unies (Canada)

Fortis Group—*The Netherlands*
  Fortis Benefits
  Time Insurance
  United Family

Generali—*Italy*
  Business Men's Assurance
    (BMA)

ING (International Nederlanden
Group)—*The Netherlands*
  Life of Georgia
  Security Life of Denver
  Southland Life

Manufacturers Life—*Canada*
  Manufacturers Life (U.S.)

Meiji Mutual—*Japan*
  Pacific Guardian

Nippon Life—*Japan*
  Nippon Life

Prudential—*United Kingdom*
  Jackson National Life

Royal Sun Alliance—*United Kingdom*
  Royal Life
  Royal Maccabees Life

Sun Life Assurance—*Canada*
  Sun Life Assurance (U.S.)
  Sun Life and Annuity
    of New York

Zurich Insurance—*Switzerland*
  Zurich American
  Kemper

Only a handful of U.S. insurers is truly multinational. Currently, there may be no more than 200 U.S. insurance companies (out of more than 4,000) with any type of international operation at all. Furthermore, participation in the Canadian insurance market accounts for the great majority of these companies' international market environment.

The primary reason that many U.S. insurers are not participating in international markets is that U.S. insurers have long enjoyed a large, expanding domestic market, so that relatively few companies have felt a need to establish a presence abroad. Other reasons may include the historical insularity of the United States, a centralized management organization of many large U.S. insurers, lack of capital, and the tendency of U.S. companies generally to be overly concerned with short-term results. Recently, several major life insurers have established operations in Europe and the Far East, but the move of U.S. insurers into world markets is expected to continue to be limited to a relative handful of insurers.

COMPENSATION IN MARKETING

Management Compensation

Basic Approach

The agency manager is compensated for services according to the terms and conditions of a written compensation contract.[2] In general agency insurers, the typical agreement provides for a scale of override commissions based on the first-year premiums for new business and a separate scale or scales of override commissions for renewal premiums. In addition, the general agent receives expense allowances based on first-year commissions or premiums and, in many cases, a renewal expense allowance. Bonuses are paid for a variety of reasons—persistency, growth, agent retention and productivity, and low loan activity—that are not too different in motivational purpose from those seen in managerial company contracts.

In managerial companies, the compensation typically is an annual salary based on an incentive compensation formula applied to the previous (sometimes current) year's agency production. Most insurers design their formula to achieve specific objectives. Thus, for example, some companies pay extra compensation to the agency manager based on the production of each new career agent for that agent's first two or three years; others pay a bonus for new gains in personnel. Some companies pay a bonus when annual production exceeds that of the previous years. Still others offer bonuses based on persistency targets or improvements in agency persistency. Regardless of the particular contract that an insurer may offer to an agency manager, the job of building a "career shop" is such that the contracts differ only in the emphasis that is placed on individual elements of the job. Expense control is often reflected specifically as an aspect of performance measurement for managerial compensation.

Current Developments

A number of interesting developments are taking place in management compensation.[3] First, a minimum agency size, or the ability to attain some optimum or cost-effective stage, is becoming a standard requirement. This is vital to a successful career agency operation, but arriving at that effective stage depends on a number of unrelated events.

---

[2]This section is adapted from Goodwin, *Life and Health Insurance Marketing.*

[3]This section draws on John M. Wellborn, "Compensation Trends for the 1990s," *MarketFacts* (March/April 1991), pp. 18–23; and E. William Weeks, "Career Compensation: Where It's At and Where It's Headed," *MarketFacts* (May/June 1997), pp. 9–13.

It is important to recognize, however, that size by itself will not ensure agency success. An adequate amount of production per agent, regardless of agency size, is critical. Sufficient capitalization and sound business judgment and management also are significant factors in agency success.

The margins available to provide management compensation and expense absorption are shrinking in most developed countries, including the United States. The per-unit payment on products delivered has been steadily declining in these markets, and this can be offset only by increasing agent productivity. There also is a need to invest in technology to improve agent productivity, control costs, and provide needed agent support. High utilization is essential to permit recovery of technology costs.

Managerial insurers often control expenses through an expense management formula. This formula credits or charges the manager based on the relationship between actual costs and a standard tied to production and sometimes additional factors, such as the number of agents, mix of business, and business in force. These are often limited, but the net impact on the manager's income can be significant. Some insurers try to link compensation directly to agency profitability (e.g., they penalize agency head compensation for poor persistency or for excessive loans on in-force business).

A few insurers are substituting customer-oriented and household-performance measures in assessing agency performance. These measures often align more closely with the insurer's marketing strategy than do the more traditional measures such as those discussed previously.

Traditionally, a distinguishing characteristic of a general agency operation has been the value of future renewal commissions built up as deferred compensation either as a retirement program or as a factor contributing toward a retirement program. This feature of a general agent's contract has been almost sacred, but now it is being reconsidered in light of changing conditions. Renewals can be eliminated by the replacement of existing business either now, with newer products paying less or nothing, or later, when nothing can be done to offset their disappearance. In the long run, the answer may be a formal retirement program.

Marketing Intermediary Compensation

Compensation in Agency-Building Distribution Channels

Career Agents   A significant portion of the career agent's contract is devoted to the compensation he or she is to receive. Agent compensation ordinarily is on a commission basis. It usually calls for a high commission on the first year's premium (e.g., 55 percent) and a smaller commission on renewal premiums (e.g., 5 percent), although pressures exist to alter this traditional approach as discussed later in this chapter. Common practice is to **annualize first-year commissions,** meaning that, regardless of the mode of premium payment, the insurer pays a commission assuming that all or most of the year's premium is received at the time the policy is issued. If a 55 percent commission rate is assumed, then 55 percent of the full year's premium will be paid to the agent as soon as the policy is issued.

Most contracts provide for the vesting of renewal commissions if the agent achieves certain levels of production or completes a minimum period of service, such as 5, 10, 15, or perhaps 20 years. **Vesting** refers to the ownership of the renewals. From a practical standpoint, vesting means that the agent's renewals will continue to be paid even if he or she terminates his or her connection with the insurer. Vesting is more common with the general agency distribution channel than with others.

In recognition of the service an agent is called on to give long after the renewal commissions have expired, many companies pay a service fee that continues as long as the agent remains with the company and the policy stays in force. The service fee is a small percentage, usually 2 or 3 percent, and almost never vests in the agent.

Many insurers also pay additional commissions or bonuses based on satisfactory production (e.g., premiums, volume, or number of lives sold) or persistency, or a combination of both. The presence and nature of this additional compensation vary widely and are functions of the insurer's philosophy. In addition to direct compensation, fringe benefits such as retirement, life, health, and disability insurance benefits are provided by many insurers.

Under a straight-commission contract, the agent earns nothing until he or she makes sales. As a result, a new agent has to draw on other sources of income until his or her commissions build to a reasonable level. Insurers commonly finance a new agent's first years in the business. Losses are generally shared between the insurer and the general agent or branch manager. Financing income usually consists of earned commissions plus supplemental payments (often called training allowances).

Financing plans differ widely but may be illustrated in general terms. For example, a variable training allowance plan (TAP) pays earned commissions plus an additional percentage of commissions. This type of plan is production driven. The higher the agent's production, the more training allowance he or she receives. Drawbacks include unstable income for the agent and financial difficulties during low production time. To help alleviate such problems, some plans pay a percentage of the average of commissions earned in previous months. Another alternative is a fixed TAP that provides a predetermined schedule of fixed monthly payments with payments decreasing as the agent gains more experience. For an agent to maintain a stable income with fixed TAPs, commissions must increase as training allowances decrease.

Another variation is a line-of-credit plan. An account is established for the agent, which is credited with commissions and fixed or variable training allowances. Each month the agent receives an amount equal to a predetermined financing level. As long as the account is replenished with new sales, the agent receives relatively stable income. If the agent has a debit balance in the account at the end of the program, some companies require the agent to repay them, usually by withholding commissions.

A few companies have salary plans that provide the agent with a stable, level income. These plans withhold commissions for the duration of the plan. The salary plan presents the greatest risk to the company because commissions withheld may not be sufficient to offset the salary.

Companies require agents to produce certain amounts of business—to *validate*—before they will pay the monthly income stated in their financing plans. Generally, the requirements are proportional to the amount of the monthly income provided. Companies invest substantial amounts of money into developing new agents through subsidies during the financing plan. The subsidy is the difference between income earned under the financing plan and income that would have been earned under the straight contract without any subsidy.

Historically, U.S. life insurance companies licensed to do business in New York have been barred from paying agents' compensation any greater than the present value of 55 percent of the first year and 5 percent in years 2 to 10 of a level annual premium. Because of the extraterritorial aspect of New York law, an insurer licensed in New York had to comply with this commission limitation in all states in which it did business. Insurers not licensed in New York typically paid higher commission rates.

Effective in 1998, the New York expense limitations were changed and are more flexible, although many limitations remain. Additionally, the legislation retains the branch office and general agency distinctions. These distinctions are deeply ingrained in company structures and practices.

The old Section 4228 of the New York insurance code effectively required high first-year and low renewal commissions. This section was enacted in response to expense and other excesses by life insurers that were uncovered in the famous 1906 Armstrong Investigation. The section's purpose was to protect consumers from insurers' spending too great a proportion of premium dollars in agent compensation. With a changing marketplace, the limitations effectively prevented insurers from adopting what could be more pro-consumer compensation practices. The old law contained a complicated array of limits on first-year commissions, renewal commissions, training allowances, expense allowances, agency conferences, and agents' security benefits. Table 24-3 highlights some of the differences between the old and new law.

Multiple-Line Exclusive Agents   Multiple-line exclusive agents are compensated under a contract which covers compensation (commissions and expense allowances) for all lines of insurance offered by the group. Compensation arrangements, including financing plans, for MLEAs do not differ greatly from those for career agents, although commission rates for MLEAs are sometimes lower than those of career agents. Additionally, vesting usually is nonexistent or less generous.

Home Service Agents   Compensation for home service agents basically tracks that for career agents, unless the agent collects premiums for the insurer. In these instances, the agent receives a percentage of the amounts collected as a servicing fee. These fees usually are greater than renewal commissions and can represent a substantial proportion of the home service agent's total compensation.

Salaried   Group representatives specialize in selling and servicing his or her company's group insurance products. Group representatives work with agents, brokers, and consultants in selling and servicing their group business. There are significant variations in the details of group representative compensation plans, but almost always they are compensated by salary and most are eligible for bonuses based on performance.

As for the agents with whom they work, commission rates paid to agents are considerably lower than commission rates for individual insurance. In general, this reflects the facts that the average premium on a group insurance contract is usually much larger than the premium on the average-sized individual policy and that, for all but the smallest cases, a group representative performs many of the sales and service activities involved in a group insurance case.

Commissions are normally determined by either graded or level commission schedules, as illustrated in Table 24-4. Over a period of time, the compensation paid for a given

TABLE 24-3   Commission Limits for Life Insurance in New York (by Policy Year and Distribution Channel)

	Branch Office		**General Agent**	
Policy Year	*Old Law*	*New Law*	*Old Law*	*New Law*
1	55.0%	55.0%	60.0%	63.0%
2	6.5	22.0	9.0	27.0
3	6.5	20.0	9.0	23.0
4	6.5	18.0	9.0	20.0
5–10	6.5	No limit	9.0	No limit
11–15	4.5	No limit	6.5	No limit
16+	2.0	No limit	2.0	No limit

Source: Paul W. Laporte, "Compensation Breaks Loose—The Modernization of New York's Section 4228," *MarketFacts* (September/October 1997).

TABLE 24-4	Group Insurance Commission Schedules		
Level		**Graded Premium Scale**	
Case Size	*Flat Percent*	*Premium*	*Percent*
Under 50 lives	10.0%	First $50,000	10.0%
50–99 lives	5.0	Next 100,000	5.0
100–499 lives	3.0	Next 150,000	3.0
500–999 lives	2.0	Next 200,000	1.0
1,000–2,999 lives	1.0	Next 500,000	0.5
3,000 lives and over	0.5	Thereafter	0.3

Source: William F. Bluhm, Principal Editor, *Group Insurance,* 2nd ed. (Winsted, CT: ACTEX Publications, 1996), p. 465.

amount of premium is essentially equivalent under either schedule. Under either approach, commission scales for large cases will generally not vary between first and renewal years. With small cases, there are sometimes higher first-year commissions and production bonuses.

The majority of large group insurance buyers retain a broker or employee benefit consultant to advise them on their benefit plans and in dealing with insurance companies. In group insurance, brokers and consultants are legally agents of the buyer and owe their allegiance to the buyer rather than to the insurers through which they place their clients' coverages. The commission schedules used for brokers and consultants are usually the same as those used for agents. For large cases, however, it is common for the compensation to be a negotiated amount.

Compensation in Non-Agency-Building Distribution Channels

Brokers and PPGAs   Compensation in the non-agency-building distribution channels can vary greatly, but some general observations can be offered. For brokers, compensation often resembles that provided to career agents. For PPGAs, first-year overrides and expense allowances equal to an additional 30 to 40 percent may be paid. Companies also pay overrides on renewal commissions. In addition to these commissions, general agents and brokers also may be eligible for production bonuses and be invited to sales conferences.

Brokerage companies do not have the close relationship that exists with career agents. As a result, some do not annualize commissions because it is sometimes difficult to retrieve unearned commissions if contracts lapse. Brokers who infrequently do business with a given company receive few extra benefits or bonuses. On the other hand, large brokerage producers may be treated as well as career agents, and this treatment can even include a full range of employee benefits. Most agents receive no service fee allowance on brokered business.

Independent Property and Casualty Agents   The intense competition for the life production of independent property and casualty agents has caused the total compensation package typically made available to independent agents to be similar to that granted career agents. The independent agent normally is provided the opportunity to qualify for sales contests, trips, awards, and other special prizes. The agreement between the company and the agent or agency may also provide for persistency or production bonuses, fully vested renewal commissions, service fees payable after expiration of renewal commissions, and commission overrides if the agency possesses a general agent (usually PPGA) contract.

A significant difference between the contracts offered to independent agents and those offered to MLEAs pertains to agent financing plans, which are not made available to independent agents. A major reason for this is that property and casualty agents usually begin their careers with a book of business.

Financial Institution Compensation

Commissions are the primary method insurers use to compensate financial institutions for insurance sales. Other methods include lease fees, service fees, expense reimbursement, and percentage of commissions.

Producers are most often compensated on a salary-plus-incentive basis for selling life and health products. For annuity sales, they are compensated either by commissions with a draw or on a salary-plus-incentive basis. Some commercial banks rely on commissions exclusively, with a few relying exclusively on salary.

PRODUCT DEVELOPMENT

Product development in a life insurance company must reflect and integrate many related elements.[4] Products are created to facilitate the achievement of the life insurer's goals, and the product line should reflect the company's character, its culture, and its long-range strategic plans. Obviously, the insurer's goals should be built around its perception of the needs of its customers. In addition, products must be designed and developed with concern for the needs of the marketing personnel, shareholders, and the public.

Product development is a continuous process. It includes the evolution of an idea, its refinement, and ultimately the implementation of a marketable product. Even then, the process is incomplete until the actual experience in marketing and managing the product has been reviewed and analyzed so that any necessary modifications can be made in a timely manner. This monitoring and analysis may lead to revisions of existing products or to other new products or marketing concepts.

Product development typically is organized by project. Such projects may range from the establishment of a new line of business to the creation of a portfolio of products, or to the design of a single product to augment an existing product line. When developing any product or group of products, the company must give careful attention to the integration of the ultimate product array, so that it properly and consistently serves the needs of the market in which the insurer operates.

The product development process includes both product design and product implementation. Constraints imposed on development or activities from both inside and outside of the company must be recognized and either eliminated or managed. **Product design** includes the generation and evaluation of a product idea, the clarification of the idea, and the assessment of its marketability. **Product implementation** includes the final determination of rates, values, and dividends; the design of policy and application forms; the filing of these forms with regulatory authorities; the creation of supporting marketing materials and administrative systems that facilitate effective distribution and administration of the product; and the actual introduction of the product.

Approximate evaluations of profitability and marketability are made periodically throughout the product development process. A fine-tuning of design and pricing takes place during the implementation phase. The schematic presented in Figure 24-5 provides a visual overview of the concepts involved in the product development process.

Only after a life and health insurance company has developed a marketing plan should it consider the products it will develop to meet the needs of its chosen markets.

---

[4]Adapted from Robert D. Shapiro, "The Process of Premium Formulation," *SOA Part 7 Study Note.* Copyright ©1982 by the Society of Actuaries, Schaumburg, Illinois.

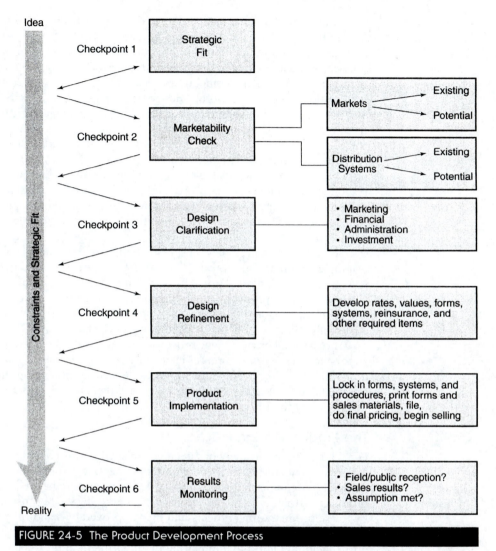

FIGURE 24-5 The Product Development Process

Source: Allen D. Booth and Robert D. Shapiro, "The Product Development Program for Insurance Companies," *SOA Part 9L Study Note* (Shaumburg, IL: Society of Actuaries, 1982), p. 3. Reprinted with permission.

In practice, of course, this order—define a target market and determine its needs, design products, and then consider how best to market them—is often reversed. With established companies, a process of constantly evaluating and upgrading the product portfolio is necessary to respond to a changing external environment and revised company objectives.

Assessing the External Environment

Product development should reflect the changing demographic, social, economic, legal, and competitive environment. Chapters 3, 14, and 16 offer discussions of many environmental influences. Ideally, an insurer's market research function monitors the external environment continuously and forecasts trends, so that the company can develop products to take advantage of new opportunities and to make needed adjustments to its current portfolio.

Competition in life and health insurance comes from both other insurance companies and other financial institutions. Competition from other insurers can have a significant impact on product design. It may relate to competition for agents and brokers or to price, product features, underwriting, or policyowner service. An insurer must respond to the actions of its major competitors when they develop products that threaten its market position. Pressure on product designers also is created when a competitor develops an exciting new product, thus creating an innovative image for itself. An insurer's sales force may demand a similar product, and the product designers may have to respond with a product so that the insurer does not appear to be falling behind.

One critical management decision in product development has to do with evaluating whether to respond quickly to competition or wait to determine how the market will respond to a competitor's new product. In particular, where high start-up costs or development expenses for administrative systems are involved, an insurer may decide to wait and assess the response to a competitor's product before committing resources to such a product.

Some major insurers have a specific philosophy of always staying just behind the leading edge on any new product introduction. They let another company introduce a new product, obtain regulatory approval, and educate agents and the public about the virtues of the new product. Where the product is successful, these insurers then bring out an improved version of it as quickly as possible. This strategy is feasible because insurers usually cannot patent or copyright new products.

The external environment provides a complex, difficult array of influences. Many factors in that environment interact and are synergistic, but all impinge on the product design process. Despite the uncertainties and the complexity of monitoring the environment and forecasting trends, the process of product design is critically dependent on the quality of this effort.

The Product Design Process

Once a marketing strategy has been established that is consistent with the company's corporate objectives and its perception of the external environment, then the broad guidelines are in place for the product design process to begin and decisions about the product portfolio to be made. The insurer's marketing strategy usually will be developed by the senior marketing officers and then approved by senior management. Establishing product design objectives that are consistent with the marketing strategy is a joint effort including not only the marketing department and product design actuaries but also other functional areas such as underwriting, investment, and policyowner service.

Changes in the product mix may be essential if the insurer is to survive. Particular lines of business may have to be eliminated because they are no longer growing and profitable. These decisions are best initiated by staff who have no vested interest (as line personnel might have) in continuing to offer unprofitable, existing products. In addition, the design of innovative products usually requires extensive research, which is best performed as a staff function. For these reasons, the product design function usually is a staff function.

The Implementation Process

After the basic product proposal has been approved, the staff must implement the proposal. Implementation includes establishing the administrative procedures and processes necessary to introduce the product to the market. The process includes:

- pricing the final product
- designing the policy contract and application forms

- filing and obtaining legal approval from all appropriate jurisdictions
- developing promotion and training materials
- developing and putting in place all information and other (e.g., underwriting) systems necessary to market and administer the product

Initial product pricing will have begun in the design phase with final determination reserved for the implementation stage. In practice, premium rates cannot be set simply by building in profit along with the other assumptions as to mortality, morbidity, persistency, expenses, and other expected characteristics of the business. Instead, premium rates must be established to balance the various, often conflicting, requirements of management, stockholders (if any), agents, and present and future policyowners, within the overall constraints resulting from the need to preserve company solvency.

Sophisticated forward planning is a critical element of the premium formulation process. The nature of the business environment demands the ability to react quickly to changes and new opportunities. Actuaries, as managers of the pricing process, must develop detailed forecasts and evaluate anticipated and future scenarios while at the same time work with stochastic values. Although the particular procedural details of premium formulation may vary from company to company and from one line of business to another, the general process includes (1) defining a pricing plan, (2) establishing actuarial assumptions, (3) determining products and prices, and (4) operating and managing results. The process of premium formulation is a continuous and circular process; the experience from one round of pricing is used as the basis for the next round of pricing.

Most companies develop their rates on best-estimate actuarial assumptions, building in a specific profit margin. By developing the premium scale utilizing realistic actuarial assumptions, management of the results is easier. The assumptions underlying asset share and other studies can then function as performance standards for the company.

Price Management

Price management requires systematic comparison of actual with expected results and taking action to rectify any significant deviations from expected results. Thus, a rate increase on an individual health block of business, a revision in a dividend scale, or new rates might be indicated. The projections described previously provide a basis for creating the expected results.

The reason for any significant deviations should be determined. Once the deviations have been defined and appropriate corrective action has been implemented, the process can continue to its next sequence. It is a dynamic circle of planning, product review, and experience analysis. Findings may suggest that existing products or services have entered into the maturity or even decline stages of the product life cycle (discussed next). If needed changes might create undesirable or even unacceptable results (e.g., required premium increase could price the insurer out of particular critical markets), a complete reassessment of the insurer's basic pricing plan may be indicated.

The Product Life Cycle

In marketing theory, the **product life cycle** is a theoretical construct that attempts to describe the key turning points and stages in the life of an industry product from introduction to decline. Like any generalization, it does not perfectly describe every product's life; however, it does represent a powerful analytical tool that marketers use to set strategy.

The four stages of the product life cycle are introduction, growth, maturity, and decline. These stages are represented in Figure 24-6, a graph that displays the values of hypothetical sales and profits throughout the four stages.

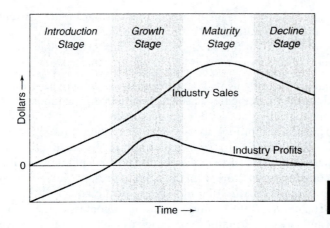

FIGURE 24-6 Product Life Cycle

During the **introduction stage** for a new product, sales are low and profits are negative because of the investment in start-up costs. In this stage, the typical promotion strategy is to convince consumers of the utility and value of the product itself rather than focusing on a particular brand or make. Pricing is not a major concern at this stage, as there are usually few competitors.

As the product moves into the **growth stage,** sales and profits increase dramatically. Eventually, profit per unit sold declines. This is because new competitors enter the market and offer lower prices or superior products. Promotion focuses on distinguishing the advantages of one brand over another (i.e., product differentiation).

In the **maturity stage,** sales level off and total profits decline. There are few new entrants because existing competitors keep profit margins low. Some competitors withdraw because of the limited profit potential.

In the **decline stage,** sales and profits continue to slide. There is a general shakeout of the market. Unprofitable distribution channels are eliminated. Competitors generally sacrifice market share to maintain profit margins.

The product life cycle is a useful concept because it can help predict how the market is likely to work in different phases. For example, a company entering the market during the growth stage would be well advised to build unique, valuable features into its version of the product because consumers will begin to make choices based on individual features once the value of the generic product is well established.

With a couple of key additions, the product life cycle can be adapted as a useful tool for describing the evolution of many life insurance products. One key addition is the regulatory environment for the new product. Another key addition is tax law. Because many products are so dependent on tax efficiencies for their marketability, changes in tax rulings and laws can have a major impact on their development.

THE FUTURE OF LIFE INSURANCE MARKETING

The marketing scene continues to change at an unprecedented rate. The financial services evolution has masked the remarkable changes taking place in the provision of insurance services themselves. Distribution systems in developed countries have been influenced significantly by the cost pressures that continue to drive much of the merger and acquisition activity. As Figure 24-7 shows, there are significant differences in marketing costs for different distribution channels. Companies are trying either to significantly reduce the cost of their distribution system or are looking for other lower-cost methods of distribution.

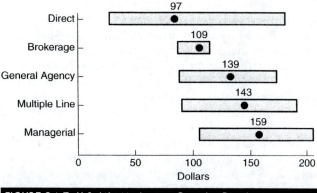

FIGURE 24-7 U.S. Life Marketing Costs by Distribution Channel (Range and Average per $100 of Weighted New Life Premium)

Source: LIMRA.

The Production Challenge

Surveys of life insurance executives consistently rank the need to improve distribution productivity and to reduce distribution costs as among the greatest challenges they face.[5] Marketplace dynamics are shaping the current distribution difficulties. Changing demographics are creating a greater demand for asset accumulation products. Consumers want more information, which heightens price sensitivity. Competition for consumers' savings is also intensifying, primarily from outside the mainstream of the life industry. All of these factors have contributed to greater cost transparency and a more informed and demanding consumer.

Additionally, insurance executives report that distribution costs are too high and productivity too low. This is unsurprising because distribution-related costs may account for two-thirds to three-fourths of an insurer's total expenses. Additionally, the typical agent in the United States averages less than one policy sale per week.

Executives also complain about agent recruiting and retention. Public trust of the life insurance business and its agents is low, harmed by the negative publicity associated with the many market conduct problems insurers have faced. This makes recruiting more difficult. Agent retention is low. The typical insurer must hire five to seven agents to yield one productive agent four years later. Insurer investment in a new career agent can easily exceed $100,000. This low retention rate puts enormous cost pressure on the system. Moreover, even those who survive to their fourth year often leave as their value to other insurers, especially those relying on a non-agency-building distribution strategy, rises enormously.

The size of a company's investment in new agents and the period of time to recover it depend on several factors such as agent productivity, persistency, inflation, and most importantly, retention. Although improving agent retention is more difficult than improving persistency and productivity, capital spent in this area has the potential for much higher returns.

An even greater distribution issue relates to the appropriate alignment of customer, agent, and insurer interests. The traditional heaped first-year commission arrangement has been the norm for decades. Its rationale stems from the belief that life insurance has

---

[5]This section draws from Richard A. Goldman and John M. Fenton, "Trends in Agent Compensation," *Emphasis* (1997/1), pp. 6–9; and Patricia L. Guinn, "Distribution: The Time to Act Is Now," *Emphasis* (1998/1), p. 24.

to be sold—it is not bought (voluntarily) by consumers—and the concomitant belief that a high initial commission is essential if agents are to have sufficient motivation to sell.

The belief that consumers will not purchase life insurance on their own volition or, as a variation of this theme, except through a commissioned agent, is today open to question. It is probably true that the great majority of consumers need prodding by someone to purchase life insurance, but that person need not be a commissioned agent, and if the person is an agent, he or she need not necessarily be compensated through a heaped commission structure. Moreover, it is not self-evident that the only way to motivate agents to sell life insurance is through the heaped commission approach.

This emphasis on new sales can encourage a short-run perspective—one that many executives believe is incompatible with building long-term customer relations (and trust) for the insurer and the agent. Ill-advised replacements and churning are the unfortunate but not unexpected consequences.

Possible Compensation Solutions

Many life companies have turned to compensation-based solutions rather than making more fundamental and, therefore, more difficult changes in their distribution systems. Many others are exploring the use of alternative distribution channels consistent with a market-driven marketing philosophy. Some insurers will use alternative approaches to complement existing distribution channels, either to generate leads or to provide product to market segments not reached by agents. Other insurers may take more drastic actions, spurred on by financial institution and direct-response distribution successes.

Agent commissions are perhaps the most visible form of distribution costs and, thus, receive the most attention. Yet other distribution costs often exceed the cost of agent commissions. These include but are not limited to field manager income and agency expenses, marketing support, and field benefits.

Current efforts in compensation, however, still aim at reducing the more visible agent commission. Ultimately, total product margins are driven by the perceived value of the product to the consumer. This includes the value of services provided by the agent. Increased sophistication of both consumers and insurers should produce a closer alignment of agent compensation with the value of services delivered.

Insurers and distributors of life insurance are exploring the following nontraditional approaches to agent and manager compensation:

- level commissions
- assets under management
- salary plus bonus
- partnering

These alternatives relate mostly to agency-building distribution systems because companies selling through non-agency-building distribution channels have less leverage to affect agent compensation. However, other channels will inevitably be affected.

Level Commissions

Many insurers are considering adoption of levelized commissions, which can minimize the loss incurred on business not in force for a long enough period to recover initial expenses. Level commissions also can achieve a better alignment of the insurer's, agent's, and consumer's interests. The trend toward level commissions is well under way in Canada, with interest in it growing worldwide.

Whether levelized commission plans actually lead to increased value to the company or to the consumer will depend on the way they are implemented. Transition from the traditional to a level commission approach is not easy. Moreover, if the discounted value of the levelized commission scale is the same as the value of the heaped scale, the change will release little value.

Improved policy persistency could enhance value, allowing for a decrease in commissions that could be shared between the company and the consumer. This may be offset by lower sales (as agents have less immediate incentive), which would increase distribution costs. Levelized commissions, in themselves, do not offer huge financial benefits, so long as the total value of the commission paid is the same as under the traditional scale.

Assets under Management

Traditional life and annuity commissions are based on premium. A growing number of annuity contracts offer an asset-based commission option to the retail distributor. However, aside from the financial institution distribution channel, most distributors seem to prefer up-front commissions. Lately, however, agents have come to see that asset-based payments can be quite attractive if the block of business grows with sustained high investment returns.

Some insurers are now considering an assets under management (AUM) approach for certain types of life insurance products. Their rationale is that the most profitable business is that wherein the underlying assets remain with the insurer. Under an AUM plan, agents and managers are paid to align their goals with those of the company by gathering and preserving more money under management. This requires more of a total customer approach than is implicit in traditional compensation approaches, which have more of a transactional orientation. Although similar to levelized commissions, an AUM approach offers greater potential for veteran agents. It may also be more suitable for a multiproduct distribution. Future pay plans could combine levelized commissions with an AUM design.

Salary Plus Bonus

Under salary plus bonus plans, individuals responsible for the sale of life insurance receive a salary with an incentive bonus tied to performance. Several commercial banks consider this approach desirable. Even though such plans are probably more applicable to home office direct sales personnel than to field agents, more organizations are considering this approach.

In situations in which the organization generates leads (e.g., bank annuity marketing to customers with maturing CDs), the overall payout is reduced to reflect the value created through lead generation. Incentive bonuses can be based on multiple factors, including gross revenue, net or gross profit, cross selling, and client acquisition and retention.

Partnering

Some agencies and producer groups have adopted the concept of *partnering.* In such an arrangement, senior members of the group receive percentages of cases or percentages of profits. Although compensation still tends to be variable, these plans recognize that much of the revenue generated by a marketing organization (such as a financial services boutique) is attributable to the marketing effort and infrastructure support of the organization as a whole. Thus, more of the revenue is allocated for these purposes. This approach lends itself to the division of labor, as specialty roles within a selling and planning organization.

Choosing the Right Distribution Model

An effective life company distribution model should be customer focused. It should also reflect both company goals and customer needs. That is, it should be consistent with the company strategy, supportive of its values, and economically viable, while satisfying customer demands for value. The model should provide the company adequate control of sales activities to ensure they are consistent with company goals and objectives and meet compliance standards. It should also include appropriate incentives to produce desired behaviors. Most importantly, it should be cost-effective.

The marketplace eventually determines what amounts will be paid for products and services. As consumers become better informed, their purchasing decisions regarding financial products and services will be increasingly influenced by the level and pattern of sales compensation priced into products. Low-load mutual funds have demonstrated that buyers will discriminate on product loads. However, many life insurance products are less transparent, which somewhat disguises the loads for distribution costs.

The Life Insurance Market of the Future

One fact with which insurers must deal is a decline in the households owning individual life insurance in many developed markets, including the United States. Although the number of U.S. households owning some form of life insurance has grown, the proportion of insured households has dropped. This overall decline in the percentage of insureds is entirely due to a dramatic drop in ownership of individual life insurance. In 1960, almost three in four U.S. households owned agent-sold individual life insurance; today, less than one-half do. During this same period, the percentage of households with group life insurance grew dramatically.

The primary mission of the life insurance industry is changing in most developed nations. The focus of support and, thus, customer service has shifted from the insureds' heirs to the insureds themselves. Life insurers are increasingly being called on to support an aging customer. The relatively recent practice of early payment of death benefits to those with terminal diseases underlines how much the focus has shifted.

It is clear that the public's evolving security needs differ structurally from those of previous decades. There is a clear trend toward increasing growth in spending to guard against the risks associated with poor health and, as suggested in chapter 15, outliving one's assets in retirement in contrast to protection against premature death.

The public sector provides more than 60 percent of the expenditure for personal economic security in the United States and even higher percentages in many other countries. Although concerns for retirement security, health, and long-term care will continue to grow, the ability of governments to pay for them at current levels is questioned. Increasing pressure for financial security can be expected if needs are to be met through private-sector spending.

The U.S. public continues to believe that life insurance is the most appropriate vehicle for the protection of the family in the event of the breadwinner's death. Life insurance, however, has lost ground in terms of its recognition by the public as a suitable means of accumulating funds for children's education and for retirement. Many life insurers have responded to these shifts in public perceptions and preferences by establishing broker-dealers to facilitate their marketing of investment products such as mutual funds, variable annuities, variable life, and variable universal life products. Approximately 40 percent of all U.S. agents are licensed to sell variable products. More than one-half of individual annuity premiums are from variable contracts sales.

The retirement and health care side of the life insurance industry is expected to grow because a natural set of consumer needs remains unfulfilled. In fact, the real rate of growth in market potential is expected to increase for several reasons:

1. Governments' reduced inclinations to assume full responsibility for individual security have caused individuals to become more concerned about providing independently for their personal financial security.

2. Growing proportions of the populations will be senior citizens. They are the most security-conscious demographic segment.

3. Corporations will continue to be more active in assisting employees in achieving a measure of financial security at the employees' expense. One reason is that corporations will continue to seek ways to reduce their own employee benefit cost increases.

In the context of a growing market, there are reasons why the providers of services could change, either in identity or in methodology. First, as noted earlier, the industry is considered by many to be inefficient in its delivery of products. Second, because of basic inefficiencies, many new products' profit margins are believed by many to be inadequate by historical standards. Third, many companies have focused their efforts on the high-end markets. These markets may be oversold while unmet needs exist in less upscale areas.

As a result, it is likely that the successful insurer of the future will be larger, more market focused, and more efficient. This means it is likely that some middle-tier insurers will rise to the top via growth coupled with mergers or acquisitions; that many fringe companies will disappear; and that traditional agency insurers can remain competitive only in defined niches. Furthermore, insurers are likely to make more use of variable-expense, non-agency-building distribution channels.

With respect to the upscale market—with a focus on planning and tax implications—relatively little change is expected to occur in terms of the nature of services demanded. This market will remain an agent-served market, and it will continue to use a range of life insurance and other financial products. Agents may move to greater fee-based compensation as they emphasize advice and service more than the actual sale of products. Its growth rate probably will not change materially (unless taxed away). The new distribution model will likely be built around the concept that life insurance is part of a broader plan integrating multiple financial products.

The size of the U.S. mid-scale market will probably grow materially for many of the reasons indicated. Successful competitors will focus on needs and will supplement and support their distribution systems effectively, using the Internet, telemarketing, financial institutions, and other third-party intermediaries. Multiline insurers that can effectively cross-sell multiple products will have a cost advantage in this market. Current assumption and variable products should be featured, along with basic term insurance and cash-value products with traditional guarantees. Annuities supported by continued favorable tax treatment should continue to grow.

Downscale markets will probably be served by simple security products, worksite marketing, possibly multiple-line exclusive agents, perhaps financial institution marketing, and government programs. The home service business will probably survive, but it will be in a continuing state of contraction. Direct-response marketing is expected to play a more important role in the future, especially as relates to the Internet as an information and advertising source and possibly as a source of sales.

It is believed that corporate markets will grow at a rate exceeded only by that of the mid-scale market. There are an estimated 5 to 6 million firms in the United States with less than 100 employees. Many have unmet needs for group insurance, retirement plans, and business insurance. Many small firms do not offer their employees any group products, and many business owners have no individual business life or disability income insurance to insure business continuation in the event of death or disability. Small business is served predominately by career agents.

Large corporations can be served directly by insurers. Their experience with cost-plus and administrative-services-only group plans taught them that direct contact is possible and cost-effective. An extension of direct corporate purchase could be the negotiation of rates and products for distribution directly to corporate employees. Most of these buyers will come from the mid-scale segment. Advisors and consultants could play a new, important role because of this major trend.

To address effectively the many productivity issues faced by life insurance executives, consideration must be given to both agent and field management compensation. Without alignment between the insurer's goals and its compensation package, it risks getting more of what it may not want, while paying a great deal for it. In addition to the introduction and effective management of newer distribution channels, alignment will be the most important force shaping future trends in compensation and distribution.

Questions

1. Discuss the strengths and weaknesses of various types of agency-building, non-agency-building, and financial institution distribution systems. What competitive advantages might each of these distributions possess in the marketing of specific life and health products?
2. Describe a number of compensation practices used for management and intermediaries involved in the marketing of life insurance. How do different compensation practices seek a balance between the interests of both the owners and employees of a life insurer?
3. Describe the number of product design decisions that contribute to the development of a successful life insurance product. What input can the actuarial, underwriting, and marketing departments have in the design of a product?
4. Review the growing pressures on the traditional agency systems used by the life and health insurance industry and the possible adjustments under consideration that can improve the systems' productivity.

CHAPTER

25

LIFE AND HEALTH INSURANCE UNDERWRITING: I

Objectives

■ Explain why it is necessary to go through a selection process in life and health insurance.

■ Describe the adverse selection problem as it affects life and health insurers.

■ Identify the principles that guide life insurers in the practice of underwriting.

■ Describe the tension that exists between attempts to achieve actuarial equity and the inevitablity of cross-subsidization.

■ List the key factors affecting insurability for life and health coverages.

INTRODUCTION

Underwriting is the process by which an insurance company decides whether to issue requested insurance and, if it decides to issue it, on what terms and conditions and at what price. The employees who practice underwriting are called **underwriters.** They can be considered as the "gatekeepers" for insurers. They are responsible for assessing the loss potential of each proposed insured, using information gathered for that purpose. They are then responsible for ensuring that the proposed insured is assigned via the premium charged (and less frequently via policy conditions) to the class of insureds whose loss potentials align most closely with that of the proposed insured.

The definition of underwriting, thus, implicitly incorporates two elements: (1) selection and (2) classification. **Selection** is the process whereby an insurer evaluates individual applications for insurance to determine the degree of risk represented by the proposed insured. **Classification** is the process of assigning a proposed insured to a group of insureds of approximately the same expected loss probabilities as the proposed. *The purpose of underwriting is to ensure that those applying for insurance are assessed and appropriately classified.*

Underwriting deals with probabilities rather than with certainties. This most fundamental point is lost on some critics of the business. Underwriters rely on statistical studies that associate certain characteristics or traits with the likelihood (probability) of death and loss of health. For example, underwriters inquire about each proposed insured's weight relative to his or her height because we know that in a group of otherwise identical individuals the life expectancy of overweight individuals is shorter than that of average-weight persons. A sufficiently overweight individual, therefore, will pay higher premiums, all else being equal, than an average-weight person because that individual belongs to a classification of insureds whose life expectancies are shorter, not because the underwriter expects that particular individual to live a shortened life.

For the great majority of loss-causing insured events, it is impossible for underwriters to state whether a given individual will suffer an insured loss within a given time period. If they could predict with such accuracy, there would be no need for the pooling of risks. Each insured simply would be charged a premium equal to precisely the amount of the known claim payment (perhaps adjusted for interest and expenses) rather than one reflecting the *expected* value of claims.

THE NEED FOR UNDERWRITING

Underwriting is fundamental to all types of insurance whose purchase is voluntary and is written in a private market. Without it, either government must provide (or subsidize) the insurance or only simple, low-value types of insurance would be sold. This section explores the reason for this truism.

Risk Pooling and Fair Prices

In any insurance plan, each insured person contributes to a common fund or pool from which amounts are paid to or on behalf of the insureds who suffer covered losses. If the plan is to function smoothly on a voluntary basis, each insured's contribution to the pool should be based on the *expected* loss potential that he or she transfers to it; in other words, each insured should pay an **actuarially fair price.**

Underwriting seeks to determine the expected loss potential and select the price that most closely aligns with it. In this way, insureds with approximately equal expected loss potential are classified equally and charged the same rates. Conversely, those whose expected loss potentials are different are classified differently and charged different rates. This process allows us to achieve **actuarial equity**—charging proposed insureds rates that reflect their expected loss potentials and having no intentional subsidy between rates classes.

Group versus Individual Insurance

With group insurance, the group as a whole is the insured unit, so each group must contribute an amount sufficient to cover its expected loss potential. With individually issued insurance, each individual should contribute an amount sufficient to cover the expected value of his or her losses. This chapter's focus is individually issued life and health insurance.

Because the insured unit differs between group and individual insurance, underwriting similarly differs between them. With group insurance, as discussed in chapter 18, the insurer is concerned with characteristics of the group as a whole, not with the characteristics of the individuals who compose the group. No *individual* underwriting is conducted or necessary unless the group is composed of a few persons only. Thus, individuals covered under their employers' group life and health insurance plans are not typically underwritten. They qualify for the group coverages by virtue of the group itself having qualified.

Mandatory versus Voluntary Insurance

If participation in an insurance pool is mandated by government for a given cohort of individuals and the pool must accept all such individuals, contributions to the pool need not reflect each insured's expected loss potential. Government simply mandates participation and requires contributions based on whatever criteria it deems appropriate. Insureds cannot exercise discretion as to whether they will participate in the pool, nor can they influence the premium they pay by altering their loss characteristics. Of course, this is the essence of social insurance, as we discuss in chapter 22.

Underwriting is both unnecessary and irrelevant for social insurance. All that is necessary for the pool to function smoothly is that contributions at least equal benefit payments. There need be no relationship between a given individual's contributions and his or her expected benefit payments. Indeed, one of the purposes of social insurance usually is to redistribute income from the relatively wealthy in a society to the less wealthy. A voluntary insurance arrangement could not accomplish this goal because participation by the wealthy could not be assured. In fact, we could be almost certain that such an arrangement would fail (except for any charitable motivation, which ordinarily is realized through charitable contributions and good works rather than through the insurance mechanism).

This distinction between voluntary private insurance markets and mandatory social insurance is crucial to understanding why underwriting is necessary in private insurance markets and not for social insurance and why private markets can fail if the pool (insurer) is prohibited from pricing for risk.

Fair Prices and Subsidization

In a voluntary insurance market, if some insureds pay premiums that are insufficient to cover adequately the expected value of their losses (and expenses), other insureds must make good the deficit. In other words, insureds with low loss propensities would be subsidizing those with higher loss propensities. When we are dealing with hundreds and thousands of other insureds, each of whom is anonymous to us, we are not keen voluntarily and knowingly to subsidize any of them. Indeed, it is *we* who would want a subsidy if we can get it. Stated differently, who among us would insist that an insurer charge us higher premiums if we believe that it is charging too low a premium given our loss propensities? Human nature being what it is, we are content to accept a subsidy from anonymous people (i.e., paying a price lower than the cost of production), but we are not happy about providing one to anonymous people (i.e., purposefully paying a price greater than the cost of production). Box 25-1 provides an example of how the insuring process can break down if such subsidization is knowingly allowed to occur.

Of course, insureds who do not suffer losses always "subsidize" those who do. However, this type of after-the-fact subsidy is fair in the absence of a moral hazard problem and assuming fair pricing because its occurrence is random. Each insured's likelihood of receiving this loss-payment subsidy from the insurance pool *is* the likelihood of his or her suffering a loss. This being true, contributions (premiums) from pool participants (insureds) should logically vary from participant to participant to reflect each participant's likelihood of collecting. Otherwise, those participants who have a small likelihood of collecting from the pool might refuse to participate. This same problem does not occur with mandatory social insurance programs, of course, because government has the power to require participation even with actuarially unfair contributions.

The Importance of Information

In any group of individuals of the same age, some are near death, some have impaired health, some are exposed to unusual risks of death or ill health because of occupation or other activity, the great majority are in good health, and a few are free of even the slightest impairment. Knowledge and understanding of the way the various factors influence mortality and morbidity enable the company to classify insureds into groups that will

BOX 25-1

AN EXAMPLE OF THE NECESSITY OF EQUITABLE PRICING

One hundred boat owners voluntarily agree to form an insurance pool that will pay if anyone's boat is destroyed. Each boat owner is known to be a skilled, safe operator who maintains his or her boat impeccably. The group expects an average of one boat per year to be destroyed, suggesting a loss probability of 1 percent for each owner. Each boat is valued at $10,000, so each person contributes $100 (0.01 × $10,000) to the pool.

David Zealous learns of the group and wants to participate. The underwriting investigation reveals that David has a history of unsafe operation. The underwriter reckons that David will wreck his boat about every third year, suggesting a loss likelihood of 33 percent per year. Thus, if they admit him to the group, the average annual loss payment would rise to $13,333—$10,000 (0.01 × $10,000 × 100) to cover average losses from the original group and $3,333 (0.33 × $10,000 × 1) to cover the average of David's annual losses. The pool should charge David a premium of $3,333 per year, if his participation is to be fair to the others. If the underwriter ignored his higher likelihood of loss, premiums would have to rise to $132 ($13,333 ÷ 101) if the pool were to remain solvent. David would effectively receive a subsidy from the group of $3,201 ($3,333 – $132) per year.

It would be a marvelous deal for David if he could pay $132 per year and receive $10,000 every third year on average. In fact, the many other boat owners whose skill level equaled David's also would be keen to join the group. If the group admitted a total of 100 other "Davids," average premiums would have to rise to $1,717 per boat owner if the pool were to remain solvent.

If a government regulation barred the group from denying David's (and others') entry into the group at the average premium, the safe boat owners over time would discontinue their participation in the pool. Premiums would then rise, causing other, less reckless boat owners to withdraw, necessitating still another round of premium increases. This process could continue until the entire pool collapsed from having only the worse boat owners trying to insure each other.

give relative mortality and morbidity rates close to those that are anticipated. Groups subject to a higher than average mortality or morbidity are unflatteringly said to be **substandard.**

If complete information were available to the underwriter on each proposed insured, underwriting would be a straightforward process. However, it is impractical and too costly for the insurer to acquire all possible information about each person's insurability. Moreover, it is not necessary to have such complete information. In fact, the pooling mechanism can function smoothly using even grossly incomplete information *if* insureds do not possess important information about their insurability not also possessed by insurers.

Thus, using our boat owner example from Box 25-1, if neither the group nor David knew that he was reckless, the group would have no reason to refuse his admission. He would be admitted to the group and charged an average premium. Of course, over time, the group and David presumably would come to recognize that he was being heavily subsidized, and they would either refuse to renew his coverage, charge a premium that was commensurate with his loss propensities, or disband.

The Adverse Selection Problem

Insurers cannot assume a natural symmetry of information between them and their proposed insureds. Usually, the buyer knows more about his or her health and other items affecting his or her loss potential than does the insurance company (although the insurer, after having secured underwriting information, usually can interpret it with more accuracy than can the insured). Proposed insureds have an incentive to withhold some of what they may know about their insurability status. In this way, they might be able to contribute to the risk pool an amount less than their expected collections from it. It is only natural that we want to procure insurance (and most everything else in life) on a basis that is most favorable to ourselves (i.e., at the lowest price, even if that involves a loss to the supplier).

Thus, in a voluntary insurance market, a natural information asymmetry exists between buyer and seller in the absence of underwriting. Even with underwriting, some insureds do not reveal knowledge that would affect their underwriting classification. This failure to reveal relevant information may be because the insurer did not ask the right questions or because of applicant forgetfulness or misrepresentation (see chapter 9).

This information asymmetry encourages adverse selection. As we have noted elsewhere in the volume, *adverse selection* (also called *antiselection)* exists whenever an individual has the freedom to buy or not to buy, to choose the amount or plan of insurance, and to persist or to discontinue as an insured. An important corollary to the general purpose of underwriting as discussed at the beginning of this chapter is that *underwriting is necessary to deter and detect adverse selection.*

The Adverse Selection Spiral

Note, however, that adverse selection is not limited to the buying process, although that is the focus of this chapter. It occurs also when existing insureds perceive that their premiums are too high relative to their loss potential, and they have the option of discontinuing their insurance at little or no penalty. The accuracy of this statement is illustrated, for example, by the failure of the assessment form of life insurance in which premiums were *not* graded according to age (see chapter 3). The younger members of the pool withdrew, ultimately causing the entire scheme to fail because of an **adverse selection spiral**—the tendency of insureds who are charged premiums sufficiently greater than the expected value of their losses to withdraw from the insurance pool, thereby precipitating premium increases for the remaining insureds, from among whom another round of withdrawals occurs, leading to still higher premiums, and so on, leading to a continuing spiral of withdrawals and premium increases that can result in the pool collapsing. This type of adverse selection is exacerbated by pricing and underwriting practices that fail to consider the major risk factors as understood by insureds.

If individuals know that an insurer will insure them without undertaking any underwriting, those in poor health and who otherwise can be expected to exhibit mortality (or morbidity) higher than average will tend to apply for the coverage, hoping to secure a more favorable rate. Numerous studies can be sited to support this observation.

For example, consider the mortality experience under group term conversions. As discussed in chapter 18, insureds under group term life insurance plans typically have the right to convert this insurance to individual policies at standard rates if they cease to be eligible for the group insurance (e.g., because they lost their jobs). Individuals in good health tend not to convert, whereas those in poor health tend to exercise this call option (because the option's strike price is less than its market price). Figure 25-1 shows the mortality experience as reported in a study of group term conversions. The effects of adverse selection are obvious.

Conversely, if individuals know that the insurer will undertake an investigation of their insurability status, those in poor health (or otherwise substandard) might not apply at all or might be more forthright in answering underwriting queries—for they know that the insurer will check on the veracity of their responses. Also, agents themselves

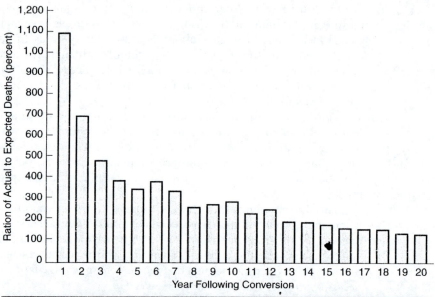

FIGURE 25-1 Ratio of Actual Mortality for Group Life Conversions to Expected Mortality, by Year Following Conversion, All Ages Combined

Source: Society of Actuaries.

engage in selection by seeking customers who are most likely to be insurable. Most have little interest in trying to sell life or health insurance to someone whom they suspect will be declined by the underwriters.

It is for these reasons that 90 percent of individuals who apply for life insurance in the United States are accepted at preferred or standard rates and only 5 percent are declined.[1] This high percentage of acceptances is not representative of the insurability status of the U.S. population as a whole. Rather, it suggests that underwriting generally functions as we expect and want it to function to both deter and detect adverse selection. By deterring and detecting adverse selection, insurance premiums are kept within a reasonable range, thereby preserving a private market. Without underwriting, the adverse selection spiral could, in the worst case, cause the complete collapse of an insurance market or, in the best case, cause such an escalation in premiums that all but the riskiest individuals would refuse to purchase insurance and would withdraw from the market.

In a British study, for example, it was found that premiums for term life insurance would be about twice as high if insurer mortality experience were the same as that for the population as a whole.[2] Stated differently, because of underwriting, premiums for the average U.K. purchaser of term insurance were at least one-half that which they would have been without underwriting. Of course, it is wrong to assume that an insurer's mortality or morbidity experience would mirror that of the population as a whole, if un-

---

[1] *1998 Life Insurance Fact Book* (Washington, DC: American Council of Life Insurance, 1998), p. 15.

[2] Association of British Insurers, as cited in André Chuffart, *Private Life Insurance: The End of an Era?* (Zurich: Swiss Reinsurance Company, 1995).

derwriting did not exist. Without this gatekeeping function, adverse selection would ensure that the insured population would exhibit mortality experience far worse than that experienced for the population as a whole.

The Role of Competition

Clearly, voluntary private insurance markets cannot function at peak efficiency and often not at all without underwriting to deter and detect adverse selection. However, even if adverse selection were no problem, insurers still would have to underwrite for competitive reasons.

Competition drives businesses in general and insurers in particular constantly to seek advantages over rivals. These advantages may be in the form of new policies, special provisions in policies, new ways of marketing, lower premiums, and hundreds of other, less visible means. One means of securing an advantage is through the application of superior information via the underwriting process. Thus, an insurer might be able to secure more complete information about its proposed insureds at little cost, enabling it to make better classification decisions.

Another means of securing a competitive advantage has been through mortality and morbidity studies and research, which enable actuaries and underwriters to gain a better understanding of the factors influencing mortality and morbidity. The stronger this understanding, the more precise can be the insurer's pricing and underwriting. Precision requires greater classification refinement.

Consider, for example, how life insurers priced and underwrote life insurance prior to the introduction of separate rates for smokers and nonsmokers in the 1970s. Figure 25-2 is a stylistic portrayal of expected mortality experience at that time for insureds of the same age and sex. Average mortality is represented by 100 percent. Generally, insureds whose anticipated mortality was 125 percent or less of the average mortality were classified as standard and charged the same premium rate. Those whose anticipated mortality was greater than 125 percent of average were substandard and charged accordingly.

Although actuaries had known for many years that smoking materially increased one's risk of dying, they had not incorporated this fact into their pricing. As a consequence, underwriters generally did not assign smokers to less favorable classifications,

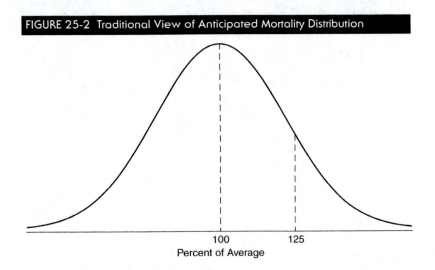

FIGURE 25-2 Traditional View of Anticipated Mortality Distribution

100   125
Percent of Average

and the rates for smokers and nonsmokers were the same. This situation changed in the 1970s when one life insurer, in seeking a competitive advantage over its rivals in the high-income market, began charging separate rates for smokers and nonsmokers. By doing so, it was able to offer significantly lower rates for nonsmokers, thereby under-pricing its competitors in this market segment.

In employing its knowledge of the adverse effects of smoking, it effectively split the traditional standard group into two groups. Thereby, it began to "cream" the market—agents placed their nonsmoking clientele with this insurer and their smoking clients with other insurers. Smokers tended to seek insurance from the insurers that continued to use traditional pricing, as these smokers (more often, their agents) now understood that they were effectively being subsidized by the nonsmokers.

If the other insurers had *not* moved to differentiate between smokers and non-smokers, the proportion of smokers in their insured group would have grown as more smokers sought insurance from them while nonsmokers sought insurance from the in-surers that recognized their more favorable loss propensities by offering lower rates. Thus, to compete successfully, other insurers had to adopt separate pricing and under-writing standards for smokers and nonsmokers. Separate pricing for smokers and non-smokers is now commonplace in the United States and many other markets.

Figure 25-3 offers a stylized view of this split of the traditional standard group into smokers and nonsmokers. It reveals that the traditional distribution actually had masked two other, distinct mortality distributions. The traditional distribution, of course, always included both smoker and nonsmoker mortality, as is evident by noting that the sum of the smoker and nonsmoker mortality curves precisely equals the traditional curve.

Many companies have now moved beyond the smoker–nonsmoker dichotomy. Some have further split the smoker and nonsmoker classifications into preferred and standard categories, thus having four categories that they consider as falling within the standard range. Figure 25-4 illustrates this further refinement in classification. Other in-surers have even more refined categorization.

Reliance on the traditional distribution and its attendant pricing and underwriting could have persisted (and does in some markets internationally) had competitors been content with the status quo. However, the very reason why we prefer competitive mar-kets is this unrelenting drive toward product and pricing innovation. Competitive in-

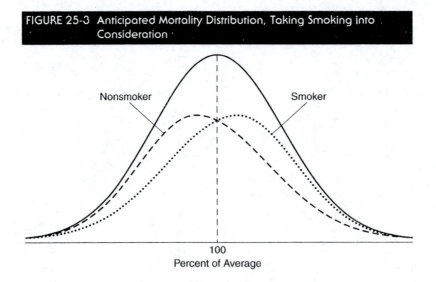

FIGURE 25-3 Anticipated Mortality Distribution, Taking Smoking into Consideration

Nonsmoker

Smoker

100
Percent of Average

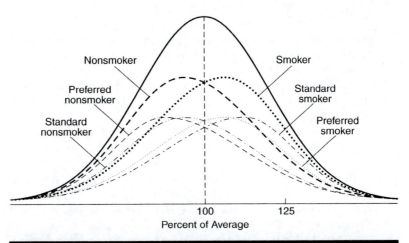

Percent of Average

FIGURE 25-4 Anticipated Mortality Distribution, Taking Smoking and Preferred Status into Consideration

surance markets continuously drive insurers to refine their pricing and underwriting, thus offering the possibility of greater consumer choice and value.

Conclusion

The preceding discussion has demonstrated the need for and importance of underwriting in private, voluntary insurance markets. Underwriting promotes market efficiency and, therefore, better consumer choice and value in the long run. As discussed in this chapter and elsewhere in the volume (see chapters 1, 20, 22, and 35), however, markets do not always function as well as we might like. Additionally, although efficiency is important, it is never a society's only goal. In the absence of conflicting social goals or severe market imperfections, however, we should want minimal government interference with the choices that private insurers make in how they underwrite and the factors they use.

In 1980, the American Academy of Actuaries (AAA) issued a Risk Classification Statement of Principles dealing with underwriting, the goals of which succinctly summarize much of the foregoing discussion. According to the AAA, a risk classification system should seek to accomplish these three goals:

- protect the insurer's financial soundness,
- be fair, and
- permit economic incentives to operate, thus encouraging the widespread availability of insurance.[3]

GUIDING PRINCIPLES IN UNDERWRITING

Each insurer establishes its own underwriting policies and practices, often with the guidance of its reinsurers. These policies and practices reflect certain widely accepted underwriting principles. Some principles conflict with others, with an insurer's policies and practices reflecting the resultant balance among them and other considerations.

---

[3]American Academy of Actuaries Committee on Risk Classification (June 1980), p. 2.

Large Standard Group

In establishing their underwriting policies and practices, most insurers strive to establish classification standards that ensure that a large percentage of insureds will fall into the standard group. The justification for this guideline lies in the desire to have a group large enough to assure stable, predictable mortality (morbidity) experience and to minimize the administrative costs of having multiple classes. It also is implicit recognition that underwriting is not an exact science.

Evidence of this in practice is the fact that typically greater than 90 percent of the applications for ordinary insurance are accepted at standard or preferred rates in most national markets. For example, within the United States, about one in every eight applications is accepted at preferred rates and four in five applications are accepted at standard rates. It is interesting to note that, although preferred risks account for around 12 percent of applications, they account for almost 30 percent of insurance by amount issued.

Although our understanding of the factors influencing mortality and morbidity continues to improve, the fact remains that the appraisal of one's insurability status is imprecise. For this reason, overexacting standards and procedures cannot be justified. Also, they could cause an excessive number of rejections and rated cases, which could undermine the morale of salespersons and increase the cost of operation. Additionally, excessive rejections could lead to poor public relations and even a call for government-provided insurance, which, of course, need not rely on individual risk classification. Apart from these considerations, the broader the base, the more stable will be the mortality and morbidity experience. The extension of this principle is limited by considerations of equity and competition.

Although an important underwriting guideline is to have the majority of insureds fall within the standard and preferred groups, competition is continuing to provoke more refined risk classification, resulting in further splitting of these groups, as illustrated in Figure 25-4. Some companies offer as many as seven subdivisions.

Balancing the Size of Substandard Groups

The substandard classes or gradations of risk to be recognized in a company's premium rate structure are a function of the balance between the need, on the one hand, to minimize the number of classifications for the purposes of stability in mortality and morbidity experience and administrative efficiencies and, on the other, to maximize the number of classifications to avoid competitive disadvantages and to achieve reasonable equity.

Naturally, the size of the company, its marketing objectives, product type, and other company policies are involved in the decision to provide substandard insurance and in the classifications to be established. When a sufficiently large portion of insureds possess a factor that calls for higher premiums, such as smokers, many insurers will subdivide the standard group into two (or more) classifications.

Balance within Each Class

Having defined its risk classifications, a company should maintain a reasonable balance among the insureds accepted in each classification. If the overall loss experience within each classification is to approximate the predicted average for the group, every insured within that class whose loss experience is expected to be higher than average should be offset by one whose experience is expected to be lower than average.

Maintaining the proper balance within the classifications is particularly difficult. In considering borderline applications, home office underwriters are tempted, because of agency pressures, desire for business, and human nature, to approve them for the lowest possible rating. This is evidenced by the fact that studies consistently show that the distribution of risks within each substandard classification is skewed toward the top limit of the class. This fact is considered, of course, in establishing the premium rate for the class, but it demonstrates the human element in the underwriting process.

Equity among Insureds

The manner in which insureds are rated should be built on the principle of actuarial equity. Some grouping of insureds is desirable to yield a reasonable volume of experience within a given classification and because of expense considerations. On the other hand, to be satisfactory to the proposed insured and the company, the spread between the worst and best risks within a classification should not be so broad as to produce significant inequity or hinder a company in competition. In practice, the width of rating classes tends to vary directly with the degree of substandard rating, with which, in turn, the accuracy of predicted extra mortality also varies. Hence, the width of each class is a function of the dependability of the available data on impaired lives and of competition. Differences between companies, in practice, are the result of different judgments as to what is the best overall policy.

Risk classification is a process of differentiating among groups of individuals so that each insured contributes in proportion to the anticipated loss exposure that he or she brings to the group. Actuarial equity calls for equivalent treatment (classification) of equivalent risks. This requires not only that equal classes be treated equally but also that unequal classes not be treated equally.

In the case of social insurance, in which coverage and participation are mandatory, adverse selection is not a problem and the issue of individual equity is far less important. With private insurance, however, reasonable individual equity is necessary to the successful operation of the insurance mechanism. Risk classification is absolutely essential in private insurance.

Social Acceptability

Classification factors used by insurers should be socially acceptable. This principle often has little or nothing to do with underlying risk characteristics and, therefore, can prove inconsistent with the principle of actuarial equity. Historically, the practice of charging individuals according to their relative risks of dying or becoming disabled has been viewed as fair. This is because the actuarial (and economic) definition of fairness has been itself generally accepted; that is, rates are fair if they reflect the expected value of each insured's losses.

Public acceptance of the actuarial definition of fairness has been waning, especially regarding socially sensitive classification factors. For example, a U.S. survey showed that although 49 percent of those surveyed believed it is fair to price life insurance according to one's risk of dying, fully 38 percent viewed it as unfair.[4]

Recent studies of public attitudes toward risk classification show that the U.S. public tends to accept as fair the use of those risk factors over which individuals have some degree of choice (e.g., hazardous hobbies and smoking). In contrast, the public tends to perceive as unfair the use of risk factors over which we have no real control (e.g., heart attack history or cancer). Figure 25-5 shows results from one survey of the U.S. public.

This result is disturbing for insurers, for many, perhaps most diseases, are beyond individuals' control. Yet, they can have a profound effect on mortality and morbidity. It

---

[4]*MAP 1994* (Washington, DC: American Council of Life Insurance, 1994), p. 68.

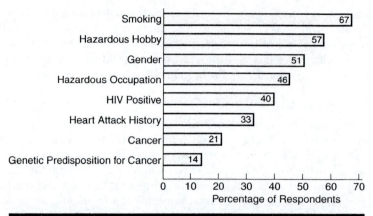

FIGURE 25-5 Attitudes about Underwriting Factors (Percent Agreeing That Use of Factor Is Fair)

Source: MAP 1990 (Washington, DC: American Council of Life Insurance, 1990).

also raises the important question as to how we determine what is within an individual's control (see discussion later on genetics).

The public seems also to believe that insurers make some adverse decisions with insufficient actuarial or medical justification.[5] This concern arose in public debates about the use of blindness as a classification factor and finds voice also in the genetic-testing debate (discussed later). To the extent that the concern is valid, better research can mitigate it. To the extent that it is invalid, perhaps better explanations for underwriting decisions would help.

At the same time, insurers realize that some past practices were, in fact, flawed and actually penalized both buyers and insurers. For example, many years ago, U.S. life insurers routinely charged higher life insurance rates to black than to white persons. The justification for this differential was that blacks as a group did not live as long as whites of the same age and sex. Population and insured mortality statistics were cited in support of this practice—that is, the practice was "actuarially justified" (even if distinguishing a "black" from a "white" person was fraught with problems).

At about the same time that U.S. society concluded that the use of race in any context as a decision factor was offensive, insurers realized that the observed differences in mortality between blacks and whites was driven not so much by race but by socioeconomic and other factors. For example, we know that poor people do not live as long as wealthier people, and that more blacks than whites are poor. We should recognize that merely establishing a statistical relationship between a factor and mortality or morbidity does not also establish causation. Relevance can be important. Thus, it is wrong to consider the socially acceptable principle as being always in conflict with actuarial fairness—it can result in a more efficient insurance mechanism. However, it seems that such a happy alignment does not materialize very often.

Insurers have faced a range of concerns by various interest groups historically about the social acceptability of certain underwriting practices. The discussion later on genetic testing as well as some discussions in the following chapter build on the issue of social acceptability.

---

[5]D. Case, "Arguments Against Risk Classification in Life Insurance," *Medical Section Report,* Vol. XVIII, No. 1 (Spring 1994), p. 5.

Recognition of Underlying Loss Assumptions

Risk classification reflects the mortality (morbidity) levels assumed in determining the premium rate applied. If the proposed insured is to be considered at standard rates, the expected loss experience must be comparable to that used in determining these rates.

In practice, some companies (especially large ones) continually study their morbidity and mortality experience and evaluate their classification rules. They review their experience on lives accepted as standard and compare their experience on impaired lives with the standard experience. Based on this study and analysis, each company adjusts its classification rules where indicated. The objective is to assure reasonable homogeneity within a given classification.

As insured experience is made up of selected lives, the underwriting that is to be exercised in the future should at least be as effective as that used in the past, if experience is to be similar to that provided for in the premium rate structure. A situation of generally improving mortality or morbidity, however, might permit acceptance of some impaired lives without exceeding that assumed in the premium calculations. Such action, however, would adversely affect the company's competitive position if other companies continued to accept only standard risks at their standard rates.

FACTORS AFFECTING INSURABILITY

In deciding whether to issue insurance (selection), and if so, on what terms and conditions and at what price (classification), life insurance companies examine several factors to ensure that insureds are treated equitably and to guard against them being charged either excessive or inadequate rates for the insurance coverage. Underwriting is the essential link through which insurers seek to operationalize the three objectives that rates should be adequate, equitable, and not excessive. This section reviews the chief factors examined by life insurers in underwriting life and health insurance.

Life Insurance Underwriting Factors

Age

Expected future mortality is highly correlated with age. The older a person, other things being the same, the greater the likelihood of death. We know, of course, that chronological age actually is a proxy for biological age. Regrettably, science does not as yet offer sufficiently accurate, low-cost means of determining one's biological age, so one's chronological age is used as a convenient proxy.

Age is a key factor in determining the rate an individual is to be charged for life insurance. Age is rarely a selection factor, however, except for individuals who are of advanced age or, with some types of insurance, very young. Some insurers may use age alone to deny some types of insurance to older persons (e.g., those who are past age 75). This may occur because the insurer believes its statistical base to be too small to permit proper rating, has insufficient confidence in its underwriting process for advanced ages, or believes the premium rate it would charge is too high for marketing purposes.

The applicant is not required to furnish proof of age at the time he or she applies for insurance, as (1) such a requirement could cause delay, (2) few persons misstate their age, (3) proof is usually easily obtained if needed, and (4) the misstatement of age clause handles those situations in which a problem arises. In the case of an immediate annuity, under which it would be impractical to adjust the amount of the benefits if a misstatement of age is discovered at the time of the annuitant's death, proof of age usually is required at the time of annuity purchase.

Sex

The sex of proposed insureds, like their age, is rarely used as a selection factor, but it is routinely used as a classification (rate-setting) factor with respect to individual life insurance. Yearly probabilities of death of females are less than the yearly probabilities of death of similarly situated males. As a result, the majority of insurers worldwide charge lower life insurance premium rates and higher annuity rates for females than for males. This was not always true. Several decades ago insurers charged men and women the same rates because of the "frailty" of women and the "hazards of childbirth." Increasingly accurate statistics, competition, and a widening mortality gap between the two sexes caused insurers to alter this practice.

Although mortality statistics clearly show a difference in death rates between men and women and, therefore, can be used *actuarially* to justify charging different rates for men and women, other important considerations have arisen. The question now being debated is: Is it *socially* acceptable to charge men and women different rates for life insurance (and annuities)?

Medical Aspects

Physical Condition   The physical condition of a proposed insured is of basic significance in underwriting. One of the determinants of physical condition is build. Build includes height, weight, and distribution of the weight. Experience has shown that being overweight increases the likelihood of death at all ages. Although being moderately overweight may not, in and of itself, have a ratable effect, it can magnify the significance of other physical ailments, such as cardiac conditions.

Most companies use a table showing average weights according to height, age, and sex. The table is then extended to other weights, and expected extra mortality is shown as a percentage of standard. At the best weights—less than the average—the tables indicate a better than average expected mortality rate.

Other aspects of a proposed insured's physical condition also are important. Companies know from experience that future mortality experience will depend, in varying degrees, upon abnormalities in one or more of the important systems of the body—that is, the nervous, digestive, cardiovascular, respiratory, or genitourinary systems, and glands of internal secretion. The defects and disabilities that may be found in the organs of the body and the methods of ascertaining them are necessarily medical in character. It is beyond the scope of this book to explore them, but a few of the common ones that usually increase the risk may be mentioned.

Thus, an examination of the circulatory system may reveal elevated blood pressure, a heart murmur, or a high or irregular heart rate. An analysis of the urine may disclose the presence of albumin, sugar, or red blood cells. Indications of any of these or similar conditions necessitate further examination before the application can be accepted on terms satisfactory to both parties. Coronary risk factors are used by many companies in their overall assessment of expected mortality. Factors such as low blood cholesterol, optimal blood pressure, and non–cigarette smoking contribute significantly to improved mortality from heart disease.

Acquired immune deficiency syndrome (AIDS) is important to life and health insurers because of its rapid spread and fatal effect. Insurers desire to treat AIDS as any other medical condition for individual underwriting purposes. This means being able to have proposed insureds tested for the presence of the AIDS virus antibodies, which would indicate exposure to the virus. The right to test persons applying for individual life and disability income insurance for exposure to the AIDS virus has been generally accepted. Issues that previously existed about unfair discrimination and test result confidentiality have largely been resolved. Insurers test solely on the basis of age, amount of insurance, and medical history, and they have established procedures to safeguard confidentially. The right of insurers to test persons applying for individual or group medical expense coverage for exposure to the AIDS virus remains a controversial issue, and some jurisdictions prohibit this testing.

Personal History   Insurance companies inquire into facets of the proposed insured's background that could have a bearing on his or her expected mortality. This investigation may include the individual's health record, habits, driving violations, and amount of insurance already owned.

The health record is usually the most important of the personal history factors. If the individual has in the past suffered a serious illness or accident, an appraisal of its probable effects on future life will be made. The appraisal frequently will require that, in addition to the medical history given by the proposed insured, reports be obtained from personal physicians and hospitals.

Insurance history is important. The proposed insured may have been refused life insurance by some insurer or offered insurance under special terms. If so, this fact may imply an extra hazard that existed formerly and may still be present and should be investigated. In some jurisdictions, legal restrictions prohibit the basing of an adverse action solely on information of any previous such action by another company. In any event, sound underwriting practice dictates that the company make every effort to establish for itself the proposed insured's insurability. Also, the individual may have such a large amount of insurance already in force on his or her life that a request for more may be indicative of moral hazard, if not justified by present income and finances.

Family History   Family history is considered important by most companies because of the transmission of certain characteristics by heredity. Family health history is influenced by inherited genetics.

If the history shows that most members of the family have lived to old age without incurring heart disease, cancer, diabetes, and other serious diseases, it may be inferred that the proposed insured will be less susceptible to these diseases. In many companies, however, family history is not used directly in classification unless it reveals a characteristic that also appears in some form in the proposed insured. For example, two or more deaths below age 60 because of cardiovascular disease in the family may be viewed negatively.

Tobacco Use   Whether an individual uses tobacco in any form, whether chewing, dipping, or smoking cigarettes, cigars, or a pipe, is an important risk factor by itself. In the past, smoking or other tobacco use was considered in underwriting, but only rarely as a factor of importance by itself. For example, if a person had a respiratory problem and smoked, the underwriting decision might be less favorable than for an otherwise similarly situated nonsmoker. Smoking unaccompanied by any other negative factor, however, was not a cause for a less favorable rating and continues to be ignored as a factor in many markets worldwide.

Insurers now understand that smoking and other tobacco use, even in the absence of any other negative factor, causes expected future mortality to be worse than the average, and the degree of variation is of such significance as to warrant separate classification. So important is this factor that the average female smoker can be expected to exhibit higher mortality than the average nonsmoking male of the same age. Smoking aggravates many other health problems.

Information regarding tobacco usage is elicited on the application and verified through medical and nonmedical sources. Verification has proven difficult, with many persons misrepresenting the fact that they smoke. In persons applying for large amounts, tobacco use is verified by testing urine for the presence of nicotine.

Most insurers subdivide the standard group into about 75 percent nonsmokers, who experience about 85 percent relative mortality, and 25 percent smokers, who experience about 150 percent relative mortality. This differential varies by age; in the 40–49 age group, cigarette smokers experience twice the mortality rates of nonsmokers.

A few companies still call their nonsmoker class "preferred" and require that additional criteria such as build be met. The nonsmoker group, however, is not a "super-standard" group. Assuming a continuing decline in the proportion of the smoking population, the nonsmoker will effectively become standard, with smoking becoming a risk factor leading to a substandard classification.

Alcohol and Drugs

Information is usually sought regarding the proposed insured's use of habit-forming drugs and intoxicating beverages. Excessive alcohol use is associated with higher than standard mortality. If the individual uses alcoholic beverages in large amounts, he or she may be declined or offered substandard insurance, depending upon the degree of use. Use of alcohol in moderation is considered normal.

Use of drugs not prescribed by a physician or drug abuse may call for a declination, depending upon the type of drug. A history of misuse or unsupervised use may require an extra rating, depending upon the length of time since the drug or drugs were used, the nature of the treatment given, and whether there has been participation in a continuing support program (e.g., Alcoholics Anonymous).

Occupation

Occupational hazards are not as important today as they were in the past, although in certain cases they can be. They may increase the risk in at least three different ways. First, the occupation may present an environmental hazard, such as exposure to violence, irregular living, or a temptation to experiment with drugs or overindulge in alcohol. Second, the physical conditions surrounding an occupation can have a decided bearing upon health and longevity, as in the case of persons who work in close, dusty, or poorly ventilated quarters or are exposed to chemical toxins. Finally, there is the risk from accident, such as is faced by professional automobile racers, crop dusters, and professional divers.

An individual who has recently changed from a hazardous occupation to a safer form of employment must be underwritten carefully, as he or she may still retain ill effects from the earlier employment or because the change may have been prompted by a health factor. Also, such a person is more likely than a person without such a history to return to the former occupation. The usual practice is to ignore prior occupation if the individual has been removed from it for a period of one or more years. Because of increased attention to job safety and working conditions, ratings have been reduced or eliminated for many occupations.

Hazardous Sports and Avocations

Persons with a high standard of living and searching for new ways to spend their leisure time often resort to hobbies and avocations. Such activities as scuba diving, mountain climbing, competitive racing, hang gliding, and skydiving clearly can involve a significant additional hazard to be considered in the underwriting process. If a hazard causes increased expected mortality and the individual is insurable on some basis, he or she usually is charged a flat extra premium commensurate with the risk. A rider excluding death resulting from participation in the hazardous activity may be employed occasionally.

Aviation

Flights as a fare-paying passenger on regularly scheduled airlines are not sufficiently hazardous to affect risk. Where there may be a definite aviation hazard involving commercial, private, or military flying, the proposed insured may be requested to complete a supplementary questionnaire devoted entirely to this subject. The company may then charge an extra premium to compensate for the aviation hazard, or, infrequently, this cause of death may be excluded from the policy entirely.

If the risk is excluded and if death occurs because of aviation activities, the company is liable only for a return of premiums paid or the reserve accumulated on the policy, or, sometimes, whichever of the two produces the larger figure. Most scheduled airline and private pilots are issued standard insurance without aviation restrictions.

Military Service

In the absence of hostilities, contracts are issued to U.S. military personnel with no exclusions or limitations. The adverse selection involved when individuals are engaged in or facing military service during a period of armed conflict can constitute an underwriting problem. Underwriting action taken in the past included outright declination, a limitation on the amount of insurance issued, or the attachment of a war exclusion clause (see chapter 10) that limits the insurer's obligation to the refund of premiums paid with interest, depending on the cause of death.

War clauses were used extensively during World War II in policies issued to military personnel. They were also used by U.S. insurers during the Korean conflict, primarily for military personnel going to Korea or for members of particularly hazardous combat forces. War clauses generally were not used by U.S. insurers during the Vietnam War. In any event, when hostilities cease, war clauses are routinely canceled and cannot be reactivated.

Residence

The mortality rate in most developing countries is higher than in most developed countries, primarily because of general living conditions. Individuals moving to a developed country from a developing country may already have been adversely affected by these conditions. When the proposed insured resides in a developing country, the possible increased hazards of climate, general living conditions, and political unrest will be included in the insurer's premium rate structure.

A concern for insurers located in one country and underwriting individuals residing or who have resided in other countries can be the inability to develop the full extent of underwriting information. It can be difficult to obtain investigative reports, attending physicians' statements, and other underwriting information on a timely basis.

An additional problem with foreign residents is that restrictions on claims investigations may be such that, for all practical purposes, both the contestable and suicide provisions may have been essentially waived at the time of issue. Moral hazard problems are exacerbated, with an increased incidence of fraudulent claims having been experienced by several insurers. Also, currency restrictions may make it difficult for the insured to pay premiums.

Financial Status and Speculation

No doubt, the great majority of applicants respond fully and accurately to insurers' underwriting inquiries. Unfortunately, insurers do not know a priori which ones are responding in this fashion and which ones are not. A few individuals withhold or misrepresent information when they apply for insurance. Others seek insurance while knowing or suspecting the existence of an adverse condition that the company does not know about in the hope that the condition will not be discovered. Therefore, for larger amounts of insurance, companies make independent investigations about all aspects of insurability, including not only those previously discussed but also character and financial standing.

Information sought about character includes business as well as personal activities. The applicant's reputation for meeting obligations and for fairness in dealings may indicate the type of moral risk that is involved in his or her insurance. Financial status, as represented by personal net worth, size and sources of income, and permanency of the income, is probably as important as any factor. Even when the amount of insurance applied for is not large, if the applicant appears to have sufficient protection already, the case will bear close investigation.

Determining the motivation for the proposed insurance is a primary element in financial underwriting. This is best demonstrated by a well-established purpose, logical beneficiary, and reasonable amount in relation to the insured's (and if different from the insured, the policyowner's) financial status. When the motivation is questionable, it is essential to resolve any doubts and establish that the purchase is not speculative (discussed later).

Perhaps the most common underwriting guideline is a simple formula with which the underwriter estimates the maximum amount of life insurance that would be appropriate under ordinary circumstances. This amount is determined by multiplying the proposed insured's annual income by a multiple that is a function of age. Table 25-1 presents typical multiples. Thus, this guideline suggests that a 40-year-old making $100,000 per year could justifiably have as much as $1,300,000 of life insurance in force on her life. This is a guideline, not an absolute standard. All facts surrounding the case should be considered in establishing an acceptable level of insurance.

Speculation must be avoided, not only when the insured takes out insurance on his or her own life, but when one person wishes to insure the life of another. Although the law gives an individual an unlimited insurable interest in his or her own life, the need for insurance, as determined from such factors as financial status and dependents, largely governs the maximum amount the company will sell to an individual. If the insurance is applied for by one person on the life of another, companies also want to know about the insurable interest and the extent of the economic loss that the death of the insured would cause the applicant. Applications for life insurance for speculative purposes are rare when compared with the total insurance sold, but the cases are frequent enough to be of importance. Individual cases have involved millions of dollars. Also, a company has a legal responsibility to protect against speculation by an individual who does not have an insurable interest in the life of another because it could be held liable for damages if the insurance itself was a contributing factor in the insured's death. Underwriting for financial status is concerned more with avoiding the creation of moral hazard, whereas the earlier underwriting factors were concerned more with deterring and detecting adverse selection.

Table 25-1	Underwriting Guidelines for Maximum Insurance Amounts		
Age	*Income Multiple*	*Age*	*Income Multiple*
25 and less	18	46–50	10
26–30	16	51–55	9
31–35	14	56–60	7
36–40	13	61–65	5
41–45	12	Over 65	4

Today most companies will insure children at birth. The mortality experience for this class of business has been excellent. Some companies will issue whatever amounts are reasonable on a child's life, provided that the parents (if they are insurable) have a suitable insurance program and provided that all children in the family are insured for comparable amounts. The underwriting problem is to guard against one child being selected for insurance.

Comparatively few persons at advanced ages can qualify as good risks. The earning power of such individuals usually has decreased or ceased, thus reducing the insurable value and the need for protection. Companies insure older persons only after careful underwriting, and then usually to provide liquidity to meet estate taxes and other cash needs following the death of a person with substantial assets. Whether intentional or not, insurance of older persons by those on whom they are dependent is often speculative and is, therefore, approached with caution by insurers.

Health Insurance Underwriting Factors

In underwriting individual health insurance—just as with life insurance—the hazards that affect the probability of loss must be evaluated. In contrast to life insurance, the multiplicity of health insurance benefit types has an important bearing on the evaluation of the hazards. The claim rates and the average severity of the claims are affected by many of the same factors as those discussed for the life risk, but their significance varies. To avoid duplication, the following discussion on selection and classification in health insurance attempts to concentrate on the unique aspects of individual health insurance underwriting.

Age

Age affects annual claim costs differently, depending on the type of benefit involved, although both frequency and severity generally increase with advancing age for all types of benefits. In the case of long-term care insurance and long-duration disability income insurance, the increase in risk can be as rapid as that found in death rates. For medical expense coverages and short-term disability income contracts, the increase is not marked until about age 55. Thus, guaranteed-renewable and noncancellable long-term care (LTC) policies, disability income policies, and life insurance disability riders are usually issued with premiums graded according to age of issue. Other types of policies, such as those that are optionally renewable by the insurance company, sometimes utilize a flat premium from, say, ages 18 to 55, with sharply higher rates utilized for renewals or new issues at higher ages.

In the past, policies have not been available at ages much beyond 60, although in recent years LTC and medical care expense coverage has been extended increasingly to older ages. Normally, little need exists for income-replacement coverage at advanced ages, as some form of retirement income is available to most insureds. Some disability policies provide for continuance to age 75 or even for the insured's lifetime, subject only to full-time employment. In contrast with disability income insurance, the need for long-term care policies typically increases with increasing age.

Adverse selection and moral hazard can be a severe problem at older ages, but considerable medical expense protection is provided for retiring persons under group policies and under government schemes. Most individual medical expense policies are limited as to amount and type of coverage after a certain age, such as 65 or 70, although some companies have made lifetime coverage available. In the United States, many companies offer Medicare supplemental policies that pay expenses not covered by Medicare.

Sex

As with life insurance, a person's sex is of considerable significance in health insurance underwriting. Females show higher disability rates than males at all but the upper ages (e.g., 55 and older) in most studies. This is true even for policies that exclude or limit coverage of pregnancy, miscarriage, abortion, and similar occurrences.

In the past, underwriters believed that these higher rates were due to greater moral hazard in connection with women, as they were not normally the primary breadwinners. Also, companies were reluctant to issue disability income coverage to working women because their employment was often considered temporary and intermittent. Wherever issued, such coverage frequently provided shorter and lower income benefits than those issued to men. Life insurance disability income riders and long-term noncancellable disability income policies were seldom issued to women. For all types of policies, women were usually charged a higher rate than men, even if the maternity risk was excluded. When such coverage was included, rates for the childbearing ages were even higher. These practices, based on the higher rates of disability actually experienced, were almost universal.

Currently, however, as a result of a more enlightened view by insurers resulting from greater competition and because of legislation and regulation in the area of civil rights, sex has virtually ceased to be a selection determinant in North America. Many companies now offer the same policy benefits and provisions to men and to women at a unisex rate, and often with an exclusion or limitation for normal pregnancy. Some companies, however, charge sex-distinct rates.

Medical Aspects

To evaluate a proposed insured for health insurance, it is necessary to consider both his or her health history and current physical condition. This evaluation is done primarily by estimating the probable influence of current impairments and previous medical histories on future claims.

Medical History   The importance that the underwriter attaches to a history of past illness or accident will vary, depending upon the nature of the condition and its severity, the frequency of attacks, the degree of permanent impairment, and the length of time that has elapsed since recovery. This is important for both accidental injury and sickness coverages. For example, a history of epilepsy or vertigo would increase the probability of accidents, and diabetes, obesity, or cardiovascular conditions would increase the duration of incapacity from injury or sickness.

Particular attention is paid to chronic conditions in which the probability of recurrence is high. Less attention is necessary for acute conditions, even if they are quite serious, recovery has been good, permanent impairment is not evident, and a reasonable time has elapsed without recurrence. Thus, a chronic condition such as asthma will be regarded more seriously than a history of kidney stones or gall bladder trouble. Naturally, conditions that are both chronic and serious, such as heart disease, poorly controlled hypertension, and cancer, will be underwritten quite carefully and may require declination if coverage on an extra premium basis cannot be offered.

Physical Condition   Obviously, the present and potential physical condition of the proposed insured is important. The present physical condition and past health record must be evaluated to predict the probability of future incapacity. Naturally, an individual who is currently incapacitated or undergoing medical treatment for a significant ailment at the time of application is not eligible for insurance against losses resulting from the currently existing impairment.

Fitness, as evidenced by blood pressure and pulse as well as weight, is of considerable significance. Thus, although obesity and elevated blood pressure are not disabling in and of themselves, they are considered indicators of a higher future incidence of cardiovascular impairment. Obesity can also complicate any future surgical procedures or incapacity due to any cause and can increase the time needed for recovery. As in the case of life insurance, tobacco usage also is recognized as a significant underwriting factor. Many companies use separate health insurance premium rates for tobacco users and nonusers.

Fitness takes on another dimension with regard to underwriting long-term care insurance. Here the underwriter is concerned about the physical ability of the applicant to undertake the essential activities of daily living such as bathing, eating, moving about, and so on. A person can be in reasonably good health, yet, because of conditions such as severe arthritis or dementia, be considered uninsurable for LTC insurance. Thus, the underwriter will seek lifestyle information that incorporates the ability of the applicant to undertake activities of daily living.

Underweight, especially if marked, is also an underwriting consideration that should be viewed in the light of the proposed insured's history—as in the case of ulcer, bronchitis, frequently recurring colds or pneumonia, and colitis. It could also be an indication of an undiagnosed condition that would call for a medical examination by the company. Underweight in and of itself, however, usually is insignificant.

Mental Factors   Both health and life underwriters are concerned about the mental state of applicants. This factor is particular relevant with LTC insurance. In general, persons whose mental facilities have deteriorated because of age or otherwise might not be insurable in the private voluntary market. Insurers do not have good statistical information on the effect of, say, dementia or Alzheimer's disease, on LTC claims. Clearly, persons who are unable to take care of themselves fully because of substantial cognitive impairments can be expected to result in high LTC claims.

Family History   The application may request information on the age and health status of living parents, brothers, and sisters, and on age at death and cause of death for those who are deceased. Although family history usually is not of great significance in underwriting health insurance, it is sometimes taken into account, especially when evaluating an applicant who shows early signs of cardiovascular disease or diabetes.

Financial Status

The financial status of the proposed insured can be a prime underwriting consideration for individual health insurance coverages.

Plan of Insurance   It may seem strange at first, but one of the most important factors affecting actual claim rates is the type of policy and amount of benefit. In this regard, the definition of disability itself is important (e.g., "own occupation" or "any occupation," or whether the disability must be total or can be partial, as discussed in chapter 7). In medical expense coverages, the definition of claim eligibility may be in terms of admission to a hospital, treatment by a physician, or the incurring of an expense. The length of the elimination period, the benefit period, the amount of the deductible, and the extent of percentage participation (coinsurance) can be major factors in determining claim rates for disabilities of short duration.

In contrast to the differences in rates due to different definitions of covered events, differences in types and amounts of benefits will produce different claim rates. This can be a reflection of moral hazard. Under exactly the same definition of disability and elimination period, for example, higher claim rates result for a disability income benefit than for a waiver-of-premium benefit. In general, the greater the prospective benefit in terms of both amount and duration, the greater will be the claim rate, other things being equal. Naturally, when the potential benefit exceeds the loss, particular difficulties arise. In such a case, the insurance becomes almost an invitation to moral hazard because the insured can make a profit from disability. The motivation for malingering and a slow recovery will be great.

The underwriter's primary concern with differences in disability definition is to be careful in applying appropriate criteria to specific types of insurance. When a policy or life insurance disability rider is noncancellable, stricter standards are usually applied in initial underwriting. There can be no renewal underwriting or premium adjustment, as is possible with individual health policies with other renewal provisions. More conservative standards must also be applied to contracts providing high benefits in regard to amount or duration, or both. Similarly, stricter standards are applied to policies covering sickness than to those covering accidental injury only.

In practice, the strictest underwriting standards are applied to the long-term, noncancellable disability income policies and to life insurance disability riders. Similar high standards may be applied with long-term care and major medical expense contracts. Disability income contracts and medical expense contracts renewable at the option of the company are underwritten more liberally. The most lenient underwriting standards are applied to industrial and limited policies in which benefit amounts are small and durations are short.

There is growing conviction in the industry that more exacting standards should be applied to all plans regardless of renewability provisions because the main claim problem is the large continuing claim rather than repeat claims. Once an insured is on claim status, it really does not matter if the contract is noncancellable or optionally renewable. Also, many health insurers have found themselves having to defend their more lenient underwriting practices against charges of **postclaim underwriting**—that is, charges that the insurer purposefully issues insurance with minimal underwriting investigation so as to save money but then underwrites at the time of any claims, thereby allowing insureds to believe falsely that they had coverage when they, in fact, did not.

Relation of Insurance to Loss   The most significant underwriting safeguard against moral hazard is a reasonable relationship between the insurance benefit and the amount of potential loss. Underwriters believe and economic theory supports the view that the insured should share in the loss to some extent. This may be accomplished by limited benefit periods, limitations on the amount of insurance issued, and policy provisions limiting the amount that may be collected in relation to the loss.

In long-term care insurance policies, payments are limited to the actual amount expended or to a contractually stated amount designed to avoid creation of moral hazard. Moreover, not all expenses associated with incapacity are subject to reimbursement. In medical expense coverages, the amount of benefit for each type of expense usually is limited and stated in the contract. Also, some policies exclude such expenses as nurses' fees and the cost of drugs, appliances, prosthetics, and blood plasma.

In major medical expense policies, such items as dental services, services in government hospitals, and services primarily for rest or diagnosis usually are not covered. These contracts also commonly include deductible and coinsurance provisions. The deductible serves mainly to hold down costs, but the coinsurance provision causes the insured to participate directly (to the extent of 20 to 25 percent) in loss payments above the deductible.

Disability income contracts rely mainly on limiting the amount of benefit in relation to earned income. Companies will not issue coverage for more than a portion of the proposed insured's earned income. This portion may be a straight percentage of earned income or a percentage plus or minus a stated amount. It was not uncommon in the past to insure as much as 75 or 80 percent of the insured's earned income, but with disability benefits being included in social insurance programs, this percentage has rapidly decreased.

In addition to setting an amount limit based on percentage of income, most life insurance companies establish a maximum issue and participation limit—the overall maximum amount of disability coverage they will participate in writing on any one individual regardless of income. This amount usually varies by class. Many companies have a maximum limit that is as high as $20,000 per month on the best class of risks, and a few will consider even higher amounts.

Most companies also will test the need and incentive to return to work by scrutinizing the individual's unearned income and net worth. This financial analysis can be important when application is made for sizable amounts of disability insurance.

For those with higher incomes and coverages involving long benefit durations, noncancellable or guaranteed-renewable features, and life insurance disability income riders, even stricter standards are applied. In noncancellable policies, the average earnings clause is occasionally used, particularly when the benefit duration is long. The **average earning clause** provides that, if the total benefits under all valid disability income policies exceed the average monthly earnings of the insured over the previous two years or his or her current monthly earnings, whichever is greater, then the company will pay only such a portion of the amount of benefit due as the amount of such earnings bears to the total benefits under all such policies.

Most companies do not use the clause. As it takes no account of take-home pay, it is of limited value anyway. Benefit prorating provisions are rarely found in medical expense or long-term care policies, and there may be no protection against duplication of benefits in the usual policy. In the United States, state laws sometimes prohibit individually issued medical expense policies from having coordination-of-benefit clauses. Rising health insurance claims and the rising level of disability claims under social insurance programs have directed attention to the underwriting problems in these areas, and safeguards against these situations are being sought.

Occupation

The probability of disablement is materially affected by occupation, particularly as regards the perils of accidental injury. Certain occupations, such as heavy construction, logging, and mining, are usually considered uninsurable on an individual basis. The duties of an occupation will also affect a claimant's ability to work, and this, as well as the accident peril, is a basis for classifying and rating occupations. For example, after becoming disabled by a lower back condition, it would be easier for a desk clerk than, say, a construction worker to return to work. Experience has indicated that the incentive to malinger is greater among certain lower-paid occupations in which the work is repetitive and unchallenging than among business owners and professionals. This factor is of significance mostly in connection with disability income coverage.

For disability income, insurable occupations are classified into broad groups of about the same average claim cost, with appropriate scales of premium rates applying to each class. The number of classes may vary from four to six, depending on the company and the types of coverage provided. There is some diversity among companies in this regard.

The complexity of occupational classifications is greatest in the noncancellable policies. Limited and industrial contracts are usually sold at a uniform rate for all occupations, with some being excluded by policy provisions. Some companies restrict sales of noncancellable policies to occupations with relatively favorable experiences. Most companies have limitations as to benefit periods and amounts available to the less favorable occupations.

Occupation is not ordinarily a rating factor in individually issued medical expense insurance, in part because occupational injuries are excluded. Occupation is not a factor in long-term care insurance rating either.

Other Moral Hazard and Adverse Selection Problems

Moral hazard (speculation) presents particularly serious problems in health insurance. The subjective nature of the disability status and the difficulties in defining the insured events complicate the problem considerably. In underwriting a disability application, the underwriter must make subjective evaluations that take into consideration such nebulous factors as motivation to work, occupational stability, and the financial situation of the proposed insured. For example, the owner of a small profitable business who knows that continued profitability depends on his or her being on the job every day may have a much stronger motivation to return to work than an individual whose business may be on the verge of collapse. The underwriter must make a subjective evaluation as to which individual will be disabled longer in the event of an accident or sickness, and which one will be more inclined to malinger and take unfair advantage of any benefit provisions.

The character of the insured is one of the important determinants of claim rates. Insurers must contend with such conditions as psychosomatic illness, accident proneness, and hypochondria, as well as deliberate malingering. The underwriter must be careful to avoid overinsurance. In addition to the basic safeguard of limiting the amount of benefit to something less than the insured's take-home pay and avoiding duplicate coverages, companies scrutinize all aspects of the underwriting process for evidence of moral hazard.

An applicant who voluntarily approaches a company for insurance requires careful consideration. Experience has indicated that there is a better than average chance that he or she has knowledge of some condition that will make the insurance particularly valuable to him or her—that is, adverse selection exists. In most cases in which the occupation is characterized by unstable earnings, irregular and seasonable work, or any connection with illegal or dubious activities, underwriters hesitate to approve the application. Such activities as dishonest or questionable business practices or ethics, questionable associates, criminal activity, and poor personal habits all present danger signals. Poor personal habits include gambling, excessive drinking, and use of addictive drugs. Any evidence of fraud or misrepresentation in the application is also considered significant.

Other Factors

Other factors that affect physical hazards to some degree include foreign travel or residence, habits, and avocations. Foreign travel or residence is considered in underwriting health risks because of the difficulty in claim administration and in obtaining underwriting data. Habits of drug addiction or excessive use of alcohol are, of course, quite significant. These affect both the physical and moral hazard and normally lead to rejection.

Exclusion riders are usually used for individuals who participate in particularly hazardous sports. Private aviation activities are excluded by policy wording from some disability contracts in which an accidental death benefit is included in the contract. For those companies granting unrestricted aviation coverage, such activities, including the type and frequency of flying, become an underwriting consideration.

Underwriting and Genes

Either directly or indirectly, genetic processes underlie perhaps the majority of the factors that affect insurability in individually issued life and health insurance.[6] Advances in our understanding of these processes continue to provide innovative ways of treating diseases. These same advances can be used by insurers to further refine insurance pricing and risk classification. However, many individuals and organizations consider the use of certain genetic information by insurers as socially unacceptable.

New genetic information can be potentially of enormous benefit to underwriters and actuaries. Its use ultimately could alter underwriting processes in fundamental ways. At the same time, prohibitions on its use also could fundamentally alter underwriting processes. In other words, however the issue is resolved, underwriting in individually issued life and health insurance is likely to be changed in important ways. Because of this view, we examine here both the fundamentals of genetics and the issues associated with the current debate.

Background

Several years ago, it became possible to analyze an individual's DNA (the molecule that contains all genetic information) and to identify specific genes in the DNA. A gene is the basic unit of heredity. Humans have some 100,000 genes that are grouped together into packets called chromosomes. We inherit 23 pairs of these chromosomes from each of our parents.

The discovery of DNA has produced an explosion of research into the genetic structures fundamental to life and heredity. The most ambitious is the 20-year Human Genome Project, funded by the U.S. government and begun in 1984. This multibillion-dollar project's purpose is to identify the complete makeup of all 100,000 genes. Such a mapping of the human genome already has begun to allow an unprecedented understanding of diseases and the development of innovative means of treating them. The promise for the future is a far greater understanding, allowing for specific tests (and, ideally, specific treatments) for gene abnormalities that cause or influence disease.

Science seems to be moving toward the belief that gene abnormalities cause all disease or they strongly influence the ability of the body to recover from disease or injury. Gene abnormalities can be broadly classified as inherited (from our parents) or acquired (resulting from mutations caused by aging or the environment). Thus, some diseases stem from inherited genes only, such as Huntington's disease and sickle cell anemia. Most diseases stem from a combination of inherited and acquired gene abnormalities. This class, which includes coronary artery disease, diabetes, hypertension, a tendency to obesity, and cancer, are of particular interest to underwriters because they are associated with the more common mortality and morbidity risks.

Genetics and Underwriting

Public Concerns   The possibility of testing for abnormal genes has raised fears about insurance and insurability. Insureds who learn that they carry genes linked to medical conditions worry that their coverage may be canceled or their premiums raised. Potential applicants for insurance fear that they may be forced to take genetic tests, receive

---

[6]This section draws from Patrick L. Brockett, "Genetic Testing, Insurance Economics and Societal Responsibility," *North American Actuarial Journal,* Society of Actuaries (January 1999); Charles S. Jones, Jr., "The Current State of Genetic Testing: An Insurance Industry Perspective on the Rush to Legislate," *North American Actuarial Journal,* Society of Actuaries (January 1999); "Genetic Information and Voluntary Life Insurance," *Issue Brief,* American Academy of Actuaries (Spring 1998); and *The Need for Genetic Information in Risk Classification,* American Council of Life Insurance (1994).

unwanted information about their health status, and perhaps be denied access to coverage now and in the future. Individuals are also concerned about the privacy of genetic information and the implications such information may have for their families—after all, if one family member has the gene abnormality, others may have it also. Researchers worry that fears about use of genetic information will deter volunteers from participating in research projects.

Many medical personnel argue that this genetic revolution is moving so quickly that most uses of genetic testing information by insurers is likely to be either unsupported statistically or misused because medical research is inadequate to allow meaningful application to insureds. Finally, there is concern that insurers will use genetic tests to select only low-risk individuals to insure, leaving a "genetic underclass" of individuals who cannot procure coverage.

These concerns have led some to believe that insurers should not be permitted to take into account genetic information in underwriting some or all types of life and health insurance. They believe, in summary, that use of this type of genetic information simply is socially unacceptable irrespective of its relevance and potential usefulness to insurers.

Fundamental to this view is that genetic test information is different from other types of medical information. One authority's reasons justifying this difference are shown in Box 25-2.

BOX 25-2

HOW GENETIC TEST INFORMATION DIFFERS FROM OTHER MEDICAL INFORMATION

In a thought-provoking paper given at the 1998 Thomas P. Bowles Symposium on Genetic Testing at Georgia State University, Donald C. Chambers, Chief Medical Director of Lincoln National Reinsurance Company, cites with approval a paper by Gould who suggests that genetic information differs in seven fundamental ways from other medical information. Gould states that genetic testing information, unlike other medical information, is:

1. *Personal*—What could be more individual than one's DNA?

2. *Predictive*—Unlike most medical tests, genetic tests give healthy people information about potential future risk.

3. *Powerful*—The information has the power to change the course of lives, plans, and behaviors.

4. *Private*—It remains uncertain how and from whom to shield genetic information. Who should have access to the information? Employers? Future marital partners? Insurance companies?

5. *Pedigree-sensitive*—The information affects not just the individual being tested but also that person's relatives.

6. *Permanent*—Until gene therapy can make a lasting change in one's genome, the results are permanent.

7. *Prejudicial*—Even a whiff of potential disease could create discrimination or stigma.

Chambers notes that, although some may regard the foregoing list as somewhat contrived, it remains a fact that the majority of people view genetic information as being different and unique. "Given that 'perception is reality,' those who attempt to argue that genetic information is not special, but rather that it is like all other medical information, are swimming up a swiftly moving stream."

Sources: Donald C. Chambers, "The Future of Risk Classification in the Age of Predictive DNA-based Testing," *North American Actuarial Journal,* Society of Actuaries (January 1999) and R. Gould, *Cancer and Genetics: Answering Your Patient's Questions,* American Cancer Society (1997).

Insurer Responses Insurance companies, unsurprisingly, oppose restrictions on their use of any genetic information. They note that they have a long history of using genetic information in underwriting. Underwriters have sought information on family history, cholesterol, hypertension, coronary heart disease, cancer, diabetes, and many other diseases that likely have a genetic basis. Many proposed insureds are requested to undergo blood and other tests for conditions or diseases that may have a genetic component. Insurers' right to underwrite on the basis of this information is essential to risk classification.

Some advocates of prohibiting insurer use of genetic information would limit their bans to genetic *testing* information. Insurers note that, with few exceptions, a positive genetic test will indicate only an increased probability of developing a disease, not a certainty of developing it. Concerns about cancellation or premium increases for individually issued life insurance and for noncancellable disability income insurance are largely unfounded, they observe, because insurers generally cannot cancel or raise the rates on policies already in force. For other individually issued health insurance, insurers cannot raise rates except on a class basis, and they cannot cancel a person's insurance policy because of his or her actual or potential claims.

Moreover, most health insurance and much life insurance are issued on a group basis, which typically does not require individual underwriting. In such situations, genetic information ordinarily is irrelevant to the insurer.

Insurers note that much misconception exists about genetic testing. For example, many people assume that genetics applies only to inherited genes. As noted earlier, gene disorders can be inherited or acquired, and insurers generally are more interested in the latter.

Regarding the concern about creating a genetic underclass, certainly the widespread use of such test results would cause some people who formerly could have procured insurance at standard rates to be rated substandard or even denied insurance. This result, however, is no different than that which has applied with every scientific innovation found relevant for underwriting. More knowledge inevitably leads to more refined classification, and, as noted earlier in this chapter, this is good, on balance, for a competitive market. The proportion of individuals who qualify for insurance at standard or preferred rates has hovered above 90 percent for many years. Also, negative test results could lead to even lower rates for many insureds, as it has for nonsmokers. Additionally, with greater knowledge about one's propensities, one can control disease progression or even onset, thus possibly allowing the person to become insurable. For example, if a genetic test reveals a genetic predisposition for hemochromatosis (iron-rich blood), the individual might be able to secure early treatment, thereby qualifying for standard life insurance.

Life versus Health Insurance Several states prohibit insurers from using genetic test results in connection with the issuance of medical expense insurance. The sentiment for prohibitions in this area seems stronger than that found with disability income or life insurance. We examine possible reasons for this next.

Medical expense insurance as a public good. Access to adequate health care is considered by many U.S. citizens as an extension of the right to "life, liberty, and the pursuit of happiness." It is viewed more in the nature of a public good (see chapters 1 and 19); that is, society as a whole derives benefits from its citizens having better health. A right to adequate health care is meaningless if the individuals needing it cannot afford it.

Hence, if society believes in a right to adequate health care, it must also support a right to health care financing. Anything that materially interferes with this right would, therefore, be inconsistent with the public-good nature of health care financing. This includes the potential of denying individuals medical expense insurance because of genetic test results. This logic provides the rationale for banning use of genetic information with respect to medical expense insurance.

The same logic does not apply, or does not apply with as much force, with respect to individually issued disability income and life insurance policies. Social insurance programs already provide basic levels of disability income and life insurance (survivor) benefits for most U.S. citizens. No compelling case has been made that disability income or life insurance, beyond these basic government benefits, should be treated as public goods.

Adverse selection differences.   There is a more practical dimension to insurers having greater concern about governmental interference with life and disability income underwriting standards than with medical expense underwriting. For several reasons, the opportunity for and consequences of adverse selection are greater in these lines than in medical expense insurance.

First, most medical expense coverage is issued on a group basis, thereby affording less opportunity for adverse selection than for disability income and life insurance, much greater proportions of which are issued on an individual basis. Second, premiums for individually issued life insurance policies and noncancellable disability income policies already in force cannot be raised by the insurer if adverse experience materializes. Individual medical expense insurance policies allow the insurer to raise premiums on existing policies, on a class basis.

Third, medical expense benefits typically are payable only on an indemnity basis. Disability income (generally) and life insurance benefits are payable on a valued basis (see chapter 9). Thus, it is much more difficult to collect benefits that are greater than the economic loss under medical expense insurance than under disability income or life insurance. In fact, the financial consequences of adverse selection in life insurance can be quite large.

Fourth, consistent with the perceived public-good nature of medical expense insurance, it is viewed more of a necessity than is disability income or life insurance. Products whose purchase is considered more discretionary are prone to greater adverse selection.

Finally, individually issued disability income and life insurance policies typically remain in effect for much longer periods than do individually issued medical expense insurance policies. This means that underwriting considerations with the former insurance must take into consideration a longer time horizon, and the effects of any adverse selection remain for similarly long periods. For these reasons, insurers have greater concern about possible genetic-related underwriting limitations in the individually issued life and disability income insurance lines than in other lines.

The Outlook for Use of Genetic Test Information

At the time this book was going to press, no insurers were requiring genetic tests for any lines of insurance. For one thing, they are expensive and can be difficult to interpret. Industry representatives seem to believe that insurer-initiated testing will occur only many years into the future, with a few believing that insurers will never initiate such tests (which seems questionable as long as insurers seek a competitive advantage over rivals).

Insurers draw a clear distinction between tests that they initiate and those that have already been conducted with results given to the individual. Their concern, of course, is the proposed insured who possesses genetic test information when they do not and the potential for this information asymmetry to lead to adverse selection. It appears that, so long as the proposed insured does not possess this information, insurers are content not to seek it currently.

Questions

1. What undesirable consequences might follow if underwriting were not permitted in the private, voluntary markets for life and health insurance? How does society benefit from the practice of underwriting?

2. In their Risk Classification Statement of Principles dealing with underwriting, the American Academy of Actuaries suggested that a risk classification system should seek to: (1) protect the insurer's financial soundness; (2) be fair; and (3) permit economic incentives to operate, thus encouraging the widespread availability of insurance. How are insurers forced to make trade-offs between these goals in practice?

3. What are the principal factors that affect the life risk from an underwriting standpoint? How are advances in technology changing the importance and use of these factors in underwriting?

4. Ken and his wife have three children ages 7, 3, and one week. Ken applied for a $250,000 life insurance policy on the one-week-old child. What information would you require in order to guard against speculation?

LIFE AND HEALTH INSURANCE UNDERWRITING: II

Objectives

- Identify sources of information used by life and health insurers for underwriting.

- Describe the methods used by life insurers to classify standard and substandard risks.

- Describe special underwriting practices as they relate to nonmedical life insurance, guaranteed issue insurance, and highly impaired risks.

- Explain the dimensions along which U.S. legislation restricts the practice of underwriting.

- Explain the purpose and use of reinsurance by life and health insurers.

This chapter continues our examination of underwriting in life and health insurance. Here we explore the sources of insurer underwriting information and how that information is used. We also examine some special underwriting practices. Underwriting is influenced by laws and regulations, so we also examine those most relevant to underwriting. We close our discussion on underwriting with an explanation of the role, importance, and functioning of reinsurance. Reinsurance is directly relevant to underwriting because it influences insurers' decisions as to how much insurance to issue and because reinsurers are important sources of underwriting and pricing guidance for primary insurers.

SOURCES OF INFORMATION CONCERNING LIFE AND HEALTH INSURANCE RISKS

Insurers obtain information about proposed insureds from several sources, including (1) applications, (2) physical examinations, (3) laboratory testing, (4) agents, (5) attending physicians, (6) inspection companies, and (7) industry-sponsored databases. Not all sources are necessarily used in connection with a given application. Also, the information from these sources often overlaps. Experience has proven this overlap to be beneficial. In many countries, especially in Europe and North America, laws establish procedures to ensure fair and equitable treatment of the consumer with regard to information confidentiality, accuracy, disclosure, and proper use.

The Application

Although application forms are by no means uniform in their content or arrangement, they often consist of two parts. Part I of *life insurance* applications contains questions requesting information regarding name, present and past home and business addresses, occupation, sex, date of birth, name and relationship of beneficiary, amount and kind of insurance for which application is being made, amount of life insurance already carried, driving record, past modifications or refusal to issue insurance, past and contemplated aviation activities, avocations, and plans for foreign residence or travel. In addition, the company will ask if the life insurance applied for is intended to replace insurance.

Part I of the *health insurance* application consists of certain information about the proposed insured and members of his or her family. It reveals whether a family policy is being applied for and has a description of the policy for which application is being made. The application form is usually quite detailed and complete for noncancellable, guaranteed renewable, and optionally renewable insurance, but less so for industrial and limited policies. In its most complete form, it will include the individual's name, address, sex, occupation, business, and employer.

Normally, it will also call for information as to present earnings and health insurance carried in all companies, including the one to which application is being made as well as replacement intentions, if any. Any life insurance in force must be listed, particularly if any disability income riders are involved. Such coverages must, in many cases, be described completely, including any applicable waiting periods and deductibles. The applicant is required to state whether any life or health company has ever rejected or modified his or her application, canceled or refused to renew a policy, or refused payment of a claim, as well as the reason for any such treatment.

Part II of both life and health insurance applications consists of medical history, furnished by the proposed insured to the medical or paramedical examiner or, if the policy is applied for on a nonmedical basis, to the agent, in response to questions that the latter is instructed to ask. Thus, questions are asked regarding the illnesses, diseases, injuries, and surgical operations experienced in the last 10 years, and regarding every physician or practitioner whom the proposed insured has consulted in the past five years (or some other period of time). Other questions relate to the present physical condition. All companies ask questions relating to the proposed insured's use of alcohol, tobacco, and drugs. Finally, questions may be asked about the individual's parents and siblings, including the number who are living, their present health condition, and the date and cause of any deaths that have occurred.

Applications for long-term care (LTC) insurance often will include questions designed to assess whether the applicant suffers from any cognitive impairment. In many instances, a separate test, such as the Short Portable Mental Status Questionnaire or the Mini Mental Status Examination, will be required for this assessment. Other, indirect information may be indicative of cognitive or physical impairment, such as no longer operating an automobile. LTC applications also elicit information about the individual's capacity to undertake the activities of daily living. These questions focus on the individual's marital status, extent of social activity, and general exercise level.

Some companies use simplified underwriting for younger applicants and for smaller amounts that have a lesser mortality or morbidity risk; in these cases, in order to save time, only a few questions of a nonmedical nature are asked. This process is similar to that of a regular Part I application, but the medical history questions, which usually make up Part II, are condensed into only a few, less detailed questions. This can be done because medical history at younger ages is generally not extensive or significant.

Physical Examination

If a physical examination is necessary, the proposed insured's answers to the Part II medical history questions are recorded by the physician or paramedic. Insurance companies routinely use paramedical personnel in lieu of physicians. Paramedical centers operate in many countries, although the majority of paramedical examinations are undertaken in the proposed insured's home or office.

The physician or paramedic reports the findings on the current medical examination. The examination by a paramedic might include height and weight measurements, chest and abdomen measurements, a blood profile, a blood test (that includes exposure to the AIDS virus), and a urinalysis that includes testing for nonprescription drug use and possible tobacco usage. A regular medical exam might include all of these items plus an examination of the condition of the heart, lungs, and nervous system. For larger life and disability policies, more detailed information involving complete blood and urine testing, electrocardiograms, pulmonary functions tests, and chest X-rays may be requested.

The medical examination is not foolproof. Many serious medical conditions can be detected only through sophisticated tests or invasive procedures that are inappropriate for insurance underwriting and, therefore, can pass undetected. Also, some individuals go to considerable effort to appear at their best through rest and diet, and may deliberately or unintentionally not disclose important items of health history. Through the use of available information from all sources, the underwriter hopes to achieve an accurate assessment of the individual and arrive at a fair decision.

Paramedical facilities are increasingly popular because of a combination of cost savings and a shortage of physicians to administer insurance exams. Most insurance companies use this service for policies whose requested benefit amount is greater than the insurer's nonmedical issue limits but less than a certain size, or in lieu of a second medical exam (when one is required).

In health insurance, a medical examination is used regularly in applications for large and disability income policies and sometimes for LTC and major medical policies at the older ages. In other types of health insurance, it may be used in doubtful cases. It is virtually never used with limited policies. In general, the frequency of medical examination use and the detail involved are not as great for health insurance applications as for life cases because of expense considerations.

Laboratory Testing

The scope of blood and urine testing for life and health insurance has increased dramatically in recent years, principally because of concern over excess claim exposure due to AIDS and illegal drug use. Insurers have found that this testing is cost justified, even at low levels of coverage in some cases. A side effect of this increased testing has been the increased availability of other useful information for risk selection purposes such as liver enzymes, lipids, and glucose levels.

A menu approach to testing offered by testing laboratories allows insurers to customize the testing of the blood and urine. The options for a venous blood draw range from a complete profile with 20 or more chemistries to a "mini-profile" that provides chemistries in key areas only, such as AIDS antibody testing, glucose tolerance, liver function, and lipids. More limited testing is also available with finger stick methods of collection such as the "micro-profile" or dried blood spot testing.

Urine specimens are routinely collected at the same time as the blood specimen, and traditional urine tests have been expanded to include testing for controlled substances, medications, and nicotine. Additionally, urine testing is now available for the AIDS virus and is being utilized by some companies. Saliva testing is being investigated as a possible testing vehicle. The newer testing methods are not approved for use in all jurisdictions and tend to be used more frequently at lower limits to expand insurers' testing programs.

Advances in genetic research mean that new information is becoming available on a variety of genetic illnesses. As noted in the preceding chapter, the life insurance industry's position is to treat genetic tests used by medical professionals in diagnostics, treatment, and preventive medicine no differently from any other medical tests used in clinical medicine. Presently, insurers do not order genetic tests.

The Agent's Report

Most insurers request a report about the proposed insured from the agent. Companies will usually ask the agent how long he or she has known the proposed insured and whether he or she knows of any adverse information. The agent may also be asked to express an opinion about his or her knowledge of the individual's financial standing, character, and environment. With LTC insurance, agents may be asked for impressions about applicants' cognitive abilities.

When a company does not require an agent's report, it relies on its general instructions to its agents to prevent them from writing applications on persons who are unacceptable risks. If the agent believes the risk is doubtful, he or she may be instructed to submit a preliminary inquiry. If the individual has ever been refused insurance by any company, the agent may be instructed to report this fact to the company.

Insurers know that agents have financial incentives to make the sale and, therefore, to present proposed insureds favorably. Reporting adverse information can harm the sale, but agents' ethical and legal duty call for them to report fully and accurately. This problem of incentive conflict is another example of the principal–agent problem discussed in chapter 1 and elsewhere in this volume.

Attending Physicians' Statements

The attending physician statement (APS) is used when the individual application or the medical examiner's report reveals conditions or situations, past or present, about which more information is desired. It may reveal additional health conditions or the names of additional physicians not reported in the application.

Because legal considerations prevent a physician from divulging information without the consent of the patient, this consent is always obtained. The applicant or proposed insured signs an authorization at the time of application, and a copy of this authorization is sent to the physician with the request for information. Standards exist in some jurisdictions for these authorizations, as well as restrictions as to the extent to which information obtained with them may be disclosed to others. The APS is considered by many to be the most important source of underwriting information.

Inspection Companies

Life insurance companies often obtain consumer reports on all persons who apply for relatively large amounts of insurance. In the case of modest amounts (say $100,000 and less) and at the younger ages, many companies do not routinely obtain such reports. The reports can provide information bearing on the insurability of the proposed insured. Most insurers obtain these reports from an **inspection company** that collects and sells information about individuals' employment history, financial situation, creditworthiness, character, personal characteristics, mode of living, and other possibly relevant, personally identifiable information. Within the United States, inspection companies are called **consumer reporting agencies** and their reports are called consumer reports.

A **consumer report** is defined by the U.S. Fair Credit Reporting Act (FCRA) as a written, oral, or other communication of any information by a consumer reporting agency that has a bearing on the consumer's creditworthiness, credit standing, credit capacity, character, general reputation, personal characteristics, or mode of living, and which is used or expected to be used in whole or in part to establish eligibility for credit, *personal insurance,* employment, or certain other purposes. An **investigative consumer report** is a consumer report in which information on a consumer's character, general reputation, personal characteristics, or mode of living is obtained from personal interviews with the consumer's neighbors, friends or associates.

When the insurer receives an application, if its rules call for an inspection report, one is promptly ordered, giving the applicant's name, age, sex, occupation, and places of residence and business. The request for the report is made at the field level in some insurers. The completed report is sent directly to the home office. The laws of several countries, including the United States, require that the consumer be notified in writing if an investigative consumer report is to be requested.

When the amount of insurance is not particularly large, the inspection company employee will make a rather general inquiry into the habits, character, financial condition, occupation, avocations, and health of the applicant, relying primarily on public records and the applicant. If the amount of insurance is large or if there is concern about possible adverse selection or moral hazard, a more careful and detailed report (in the United States, an investigative consumer report) may be obtained, particularly regarding financial information, and more informants may be contacted. To obtain the necessary information for a more thorough report, the investigator may interview the applicant's employer, neighbors, banker, accountant, business associates, others who may be able to contribute the information desired, and often also the applicant. The investigator will also examine public records.

Insurers also rely on inspection companies for conducting interviews with applicants for long-term care insurance. In these interviews, the investigator may administer tests and make personal observations to assess whether any cognitive impairment seems present. For example, delayed word recall is said to be of great value in this regard. Inquiries also will focus on the applicant's ability to undertake the activities of daily living. Many insurers rely on their agents to conduct these interviews.

In lieu of inspection reports from outside investigative agencies, many insurers rely on personal interviews. During these interviews, which are conducted by personnel of the insurer directly with the applicant, the interviewer completes a questionnaire that elicits information from the applicant akin to that which would be obtained in inspection reports. As companies are becoming more comfortable with the results of these interviews, this format is being used for increasingly larger amounts. The interview technique is used by the majority of insurers writing LTC insurance.

Industry-Sponsored Databases

Another source of information regarding insurability in some countries is an industry-sponsored database of personal information. For example, within the United States, the Medical Information Bureau (MIB) is a membership association of virtually all U.S. life insurance companies (at www.MIB.com). Its purpose is to assist its member companies in detecting adverse selection. The MIB is a repository for confidential data, primarily of a medical nature, on several million individuals who have applied for life or health insurance to member companies.

Member companies are required to code and report to the MIB certain medical impairments that they discover about their proposed insureds at the time of underwriting.

Only data obtained from a medical source or directly from the applicant are to be reported as medical codes. A limited number of nonmedical codes exist, such as adverse driving record, aviation, hazardous sport activities, or known or suggested association with criminal activities, which are reportable because they may be considered significant by home office underwriters. Member companies do not indicate their underwriting decisions in their reports to the MIB, nor do they state the amount or type of insurance applied for.

Member companies screen proposed insureds against MIB computer data files. If an impairment code is found for a proposed insured, the company attempts to substantiate the code through its own investigation. If it fails to substantiate the recorded condition, it can submit a request for details through the MIB to the original reporting company. The original reporting company furnishes whatever details (if any) it wishes. MIB rules and many state laws stipulate that a member may not take any unfavorable underwriting action wholly or in part on the basis of MIB information. Such information is to serve only as an "alert" to the member. Using other sources, the member is expected to substantiate any unfavorable underwriting action by corroborating data regarding a particular condition. The MIB also provides the dates of database inquiries. This alerts companies to the possibility that the proposed insured may be avoiding certain underwriting requirements by applying for smaller amounts in several companies rather than for a large amount in one company.

A service provided by MIB that is of special interest to health insurers is the disability income record system (DIRS). The purpose of this system is to provide information about applications for disability income insurance that will assist insurers in recognizing situations involving potential overinsurance that creates moral hazard.

The DIRS employs a central file that records certain nonmedical information about disability applications processed by the subscribing companies. When a member receives an application for disability income insurance involving a monthly disability income benefit of $300 or more with a benefit period of at least 12 months, it sends this information to the DIRS file. This information, retained in the file for five years, is made available to any other member company to which an individual may apply for disability income insurance.

MIB procedures and some state privacy laws require that an individual be informed in writing before completing an application for insurance that the company may report information to the MIB. The applicant is also advised how to obtain disclosure of his or her MIB file and dispute its accuracy. The same authorization form that is signed by the applicant and used to obtain information from attending physicians also authorizes the MIB to release information to the insurer. MIB disclosure and disputed accuracy procedures are set forth in the U.S. Fair Credit Reporting Act and state privacy requirements.

METHODS OF RISK CLASSIFICATION

Once underwriting information about a proposed insured has been assembled from various sources, it must be evaluated and a decision reached as to whether the individual is to be accepted at one of the preferred or standard rate classes, treated as a substandard but acceptable risk, or rejected entirely. Occasionally, a risk is postponed for a period of time until the effect of a condition or impairment is resolved. For instance, if the proposed insured is expecting to undergo imminent surgery, a decision could be postponed until after the surgery.

Ideally, the selection and classification system used by a company should (1) measure accurately the effect of each factor affecting the risk; (2) assess the combined impact of interrelated factors including the conflicting ones; (3) produce equitable results; and (4) be relatively simple and inexpensive to operate. Two basic systems have evolved to accommodate these concerns: the judgment method and the numerical rating system.

The Judgment Method

Originally, and for many years, companies used the judgment method in life insurance underwriting. The method still finds applicability in health insurance underwriting. Under this method, the company depends upon the combined judgment of those in the medical, actuarial, and other areas who are qualified for this work to make underwriting decisions.

The judgment method of rating functions effectively when there is only one unfavorable factor to consider or when the decision to be made is simply whether to accept the proposed insured at standard rates or to reject him or her entirely. Where multiple factors (some possibly in conflict) are involved or a proper substandard classification is needed, it leaves something to be desired. Moreover, it requires the use of highly skilled personnel to achieve proper risk appraisal with consistency of treatment. To overcome the weakness of the judgment method of rating, the life insurance business developed the numerical rating system.

The Numerical Rating System

The numerical rating system is based on the principle that a large number of factors enters into the composition of a risk and that the impact of each of these factors on longevity can be determined by a statistical study of lives possessing that factor. Under this plan, 100 percent represents a normal or standard risk, one that is physically and financially sound and has a need for the insurance.

Each of the factors that might influence a risk in an unusual way is considered a debit or a credit. Values are assigned to the individual factors. For example, if the mortality of a group of insured lives reflecting a certain degree of overweight, or a certain degree of elevated blood pressure, has been found to be 150 percent of standard risks, a debit (addition) of 50 percentage points will be assigned to this degree of overweight or blood pressure.

Judgment still enters into the operation of the numerical system, primarily in the assignment of numerical values to each factor and, when it occurs, in determining the effect of two or more factors that are related to each other in some way. When two factors are so related that one affects the other, judgment and past experience may dictate an addition that is greater or smaller than the mere sum of the numerical factors. For example, if family history shows several early deaths from heart disease, this adverse factor may be nullified somewhat by good physical condition, good build, normal electrocardiograms, and similar favorable factors. On the other hand, this type of family history plus findings of obesity or elevated blood pressure will probably warrant a larger addition than the sum of the two adverse factors.

The system in practice is applied with common sense and has the advantages of greater consistency of treatment and of permitting lay underwriters to process all applications other than those requiring detailed medical analysis. This reduced reliance on physicians in underwriting helps minimize the expense of the underwriting process.

Numerical ratings range in most companies from 75 or less to a high of 500 or more. In most companies, ratings below 125 are considered preferred or standard. Proposed insureds who produce a rate in excess of the standard limit are either assigned to appropriate substandard classes or declined.

The scale of ratings produced by the numerical rating system might be classified in a particular company as follows:

Preferred / Standard / Substandard ••• / Uninsurable

75 85   100   115   130   150   180 •••   500   600

The illustration shown in Box 26-1 should help make clear the operation of the numerical rating system. Some companies' ratings extend to as high as 1,000 percent. Generally, ratings of more than 500 percent are classified as experimental underwriting.

There can be wide differences in underwriting decisions among competing life insurance companies, and these can be explained in two ways. First, the size of the numerical debits in their impairment manuals may differ. Second, their judgment in assessing debits and credits may differ. In addition, some numerical measures of impairments or variations of impairments do not appear in the manuals.

Use of Computers in Underwriting

Life insurance underwriting departments have utilized computers for many years to relieve underwriters of many clerical operations associated with application screening. Certain application data, including answers to underwriting questions, can be input by personnel at agency offices or by home office personnel. The computer can identify answers that raise possible underwriting problems. The computer, in effect, underwrites the application and eliminates the need for a normal underwriting review unless problems are identified.

BOX 26-1

ILLUSTRATION OF THE NUMERICAL RATING SYSTEM

Jim Carman, age 35, applies for a universal life policy. Information obtained by the company reveals the following:

Height—5 feet, 9 inches

Weight—205 pounds

Family history—better than average

Habits—good

Personal history—medical attention for slightly elevated blood pressure

A paramedical examination is requested and Jim's blood pressure is found to be 150/90. An attending physician's report is obtained to provide details on the extent of the elevation and the response to treatment.

The insurer first ascertains the basic rating for Jim, which depends on his build. According to the company's build table, Jim is overweight for his height, and the expected mortality for such overweight persons will be 25 percent higher than average mortality. According to the insurer's blood pressure table, Jim also has elevated blood pressure, which means that his expected mortality will be 75 percent higher than average. On the other hand, a credit of 10 is allowed for a favorable family history. The facts are summarized in the following table.

Factor	Debits	Credits
Build: overweight	25	
Personal history: blood pressure	75	
Family history		10
Total	**100**	**10**

Thus, to the average mortality of 100, we add the debits (100) and subtract the credits (10) to yield a numerical rating for Jim of 190. This puts him in the substandard category.

The percentage of applications that can be computer rated depends on the computer database and the sophistication of the computer program in identifying and rating adverse data. At a minimum, the computer identifies "yes" or "no" answers. If the answers are all "no," the application can be approved. At the other extreme, the computer can calculate the mortality debits for build, blood pressure, and other numerical measurements, and show on a screen the details to a "yes" answer, so that the underwriter does not need to await receipt of the written application before completing underwriting action.

The electronic underwriting manual is also a new procedure that assists in the underwriting process. Data from a typical paper underwriting manual are transferred to a disk format for use on a personal computer. The underwriter typically inputs either the full name of or an abbreviation for an impairment, and all information pertaining to that impairment appears on the monitor. The typical screen provides a description of the disorder, a list of suggested requirements necessary for evaluating the disorder, positive and negative risk factors, and a range of ratings that the underwriter uses to develop a mortality assessment. Updating is quick, simple, and inexpensive.

Also available are expert system programs that calculate specific mortality ratings for the underwriter after particular data from medical exams, attending physicians' statements, blood profile results, EKG interpretations, and the like have been coded and inputted. These programs also suggest additional requirements that should be secured and the positive and negative risk factors that the underwriter should be cognizant of when deriving the final assessment.

Systems such as these develop a judgment base so that the program can remember different situations and act accordingly. Most of them do not have the authority to reject an application; for the time being, this is the exclusive province of the underwriter. Expert systems are intended to provide consistency, cost savings, and quick turnaround time.

CLASSIFYING SUBSTANDARD RISKS

In the classification of substandard life and health insurance, provision must be made for higher than standard mortality and morbidity. This may be done by charging an extra premium or by other methods. The methods are discussed here, first with reference to life insurance and then health insurance.

Life Insurance on Substandard Risks

Statistical information on past experience is essential to develop a credible and equitable basis for providing insurance on lives subject to different impairments. Companies have accumulated considerable statistics on impairments that aid them in estimating their influence on mortality. Similarly, the wide experience of reinsurers, especially with substandard risk appraisal, has assisted direct-writing companies in establishing sound underwriting systems.

Companies use two types of statistics on past experience. Experience under life insurance policies is useful, but often it is not available in sufficient quantity, particularly for impairments that occur infrequently, whose effects are poorly understood, and that are associated with mortality so high that insurance is unobtainable at a reasonable price. Articles in medical journals are useful to underwriters in that they provide data on impairments for which insurance is unavailable or for which insurance experience is not sufficiently current to reflect the results of new medical developments.

Some companies use reinsurance extensively to seek standard insurance on risks that are substandard by their own underwriting standards. Some reinsurance companies pursue this business aggressively. They are willing to assume risks that a direct-writing company, concerned about maintaining competitive pricing for standard risks, is not willing to assume.

Incidence of Extra Mortality

Many factors may cause a proposed insured to be declined or rated substandard. About three-fourths of all declined U.S. applicants have serious health impairments. Almost 90 percent of substandard ratings in the United States are related to various physical impairments such as heart murmurs, obesity, diabetes, and elevated blood pressure.[1] However, rating systems for substandard insurance do not precisely follow over time the pattern of extra mortality of each impairment. This would be difficult and probably impracticable because knowledge of substandard mortality is insufficiently developed. Absolute equity is an objective to be sought; it is not attainable.

The majority of companies, therefore, categorize substandard insureds into three broad groups:

- those in which the number of extra deaths is expected to remain at approximately the same level in all years following policy issuance
- those in which the number of extra deaths is expected to increase as insureds grow older
- those in which the number of extra deaths is expected to decrease with time

Examples of the constant type of extra deaths would be persons with a hazardous avocation or occupation. An example of increasing extra mortality would be persons with diabetes, whereas individuals who had just undergone successful operations would be representative of the decreasing category. Such a classification permits companies to assess premiums according to the incidence of the extra deaths. If companies expect the same number of extra deaths to occur in two groups over a particular period of time but also expect the timing to be different, different types of extra premiums will be needed for the extra mortality in the group in which the extra deaths occur early (decreasing) compared to those needed for the group in which the deaths occur later (increasing).

Methods of Rating

Several methods exist for rating impaired lives. In general, an effort is made to adapt the method to the type of exposure represented by the impaired individual, but departures from theoretically correct treatment are made for practical reasons. The objectives in establishing an extra-premium structure are that it be:

- equitable between impairments and between classes
- easy to administer
- easily understood by agents and the public

Several of these premium structures are discussed next.

Multiple Table Extra By far the most common method used for substandard life insurance is the multiple table extra method. Substandard risks are divided into broad groups according to their numerical ratings. Premium rates or mortality charges are based on mortality experience that correspond to the average numerical ratings in each class. Most companies use the same nonforfeiture values and dividends as they do for standard risks. Some companies do not permit the extended term insurance option on highly rated cases.

---

[1]The reasons for extra ratings in a sample of U.S. insurers include cardiovascular renal disease or its symptoms, 19 percent; weight problem, 27 percent; other medical reasons, 47 percent; and occupation and other reasons, 7 percent. *1998 Life Insurance Fact Book* (Washington, DC: American Council of Life Insurance, 1998), p. 16.

Generally, numerical ratings of up to approximately 125 are considered preferred or standard, and insureds with these ratings pay the lowest premiums. The procedures for establishing a substandard class are identical, except that the average rating of each additional substandard class is progressively higher than that for the preferred or standard class. Companies usually provide for at least four and sometimes as many as six or seven substandard classes when special nonforfeiture values are used, and as many as 16 classifications when standard values are used.

Proposed insureds are then placed in the appropriate class in accordance with their numerical ratings. The average numerical rating within these classes may range from about 125 to 500, or even higher. An example of a scale of substandard classifications is shown in Table 26-1.

Under this method, a special mortality table is developed for each substandard classification that reflects the experience of each, and a set of gross-premium rates is computed for the classification. Table 26-2 shows illustrative gross-premium rates for an ordinary life contract under different scales of substandard mortality classifications. The standard rates are also shown for purposes of comparison.

Companies also vary premium rates for substandard risks by plan with the extra charges being lower for the higher cash-value plans, other things being equal. The substandard premiums are lower for high cash-value plans because of the decreasing net amount at risk over the life of the policy. Also, except for level term plans, substandard premiums do not increase in proportion to the degree of extra mortality involved because, for cash-value products, the loading does not increase in proportion to the degree of extra mortality involved. Universal life extra premiums are based on the net amount at risk and, depending on plan design, could either be equivalent to term or to ordinary life extra premiums.

Multiple table extra ratings do not differentiate among the various types of substandard risks with different incidences of extra mortality (i.e., increasing, decreasing, or constant). The assumption of a constant percentage of the standard mortality rates implies a number of extra deaths per thousand that increases with age for all types of cases rated on this basis. Although this method theoretically may not exactly reflect the incidence of extra risk, the method is justified on an expense basis and, on the average, it is reasonably accurate. Many companies use the multiple table extra method for some impairments and flat (usually temporary) extras for others.

TABLE 26-1	Illustrative Scale of Substandard Mortality Classifications	
Table	**Mortality (%)**	**Numerical Rating**
1	125	120–135
2	150	140–160
3	175	165–185
4	200	190–210
5	225	215–235
6	150	240–260
7	275	265–285
8	300	290–325
10	350	330–380
12	400	385–450
16	500	455–550
Uninsurable	–	Over 550

TABLE 26-2 Illustrative Participating Gross-Premium Rates (Ordinary Life, Male, Nonsmoker)

Age	Rates for Standard Risks	Table 1 120%–135%	Table 2 140%–160%	Table 3 165%–185%	Table 4 180%–210%
15	$ 8.19	$ 8.94	$ 9.69	$10.44	$11.19
20	9.12	10.02	10.92	11.81	12.72
25	10.46	11.49	12.51	13.54	14.56
30	12.45	13.75	15.15	16.45	17.65
35	14.82	16.45	18.07	19.70	21.32
40	18.08	20.01	21.93	23.86	25.78
45	22.25	24.70	27.15	29.60	32.05
50	28.43	31.46	34.48	37.51	40.53
55	36.48	40.23	43.98	47.73	51.48
60	47.22	51.80	56.37	60.95	65.52
65	62.05	67.25	72.45	77.65	82.85

Notwithstanding the fact that many companies write insurance on persons subject to 500 percent of standard mortality, there is a point beyond which the degree of extra mortality is so high and the number of similar risks so limited that companies do not wish to insure those persons even when they have reasonable reinsurance facilities. Also, as the ratings increase, fewer applicants are willing to pay the necessarily higher premiums (or mortality charges). The ones who are willing to pay the higher amounts may know, somehow, that they are even worse risks than the company has estimated. As the premium is increased for a policy of individual insurance, the likelihood of adverse selection increases markedly.

Flat Extra Premium This method is used when the extra mortality, measured in additional deaths per thousand, is expected to be constant, either for a temporary period or permanently, and when it is largely independent of age. Under this method, a regular policy is issued, but a constant extra premium is charged to provide for the additional expected mortality. The policy is treated as standard for the purpose of dividends and nonforfeiture values.

The method is appropriate for most hazardous occupations and avocations, as much of the extra mortality is of an accidental nature and independent of age. It is also appropriate for covering temporary extra mortality (for a specified period) as when most of the extra risk falls in the early years after an operation or when there is a particular event such as a coronary thrombosis. Coronary ratings are typically made up of a table rating plus a temporary flat extra premium.

Other Methods Another method of treating substandard insureds is to provide a limited death benefit equal to a refund of premiums if death occurs in the first few (typically the first two) years. This limited death benefit, together with a higher standard premium, is used by some companies that offer insurance by mail, with little or no underwriting, usually to older age groups (over 50). Another common form of limited death benefit contract is a graded death benefit, with the amount payable increasing in each of the first three to five years, after which the full death benefit is payable.

Companies sometimes have been willing to treat proposed insureds who would have been substandard as standard risks, if the policy applied for is of a relatively high-premium variety. Such a policy would have a higher reserve than lower-premium forms, thus lessening the risk assumed by the insurer. It is assumed that there is less adverse selection with high-premium plans. Some companies refuse to issue term plans at high ratings, such as ratings above 250 or 300 percent, primarily because of concern about adverse selection, particularly at each premium due date, when the better risks have less incentive to continue the policy.

Improvement in Expected Mortality

After a policy has been issued substandard under the permanent flat extra premium or multiple table extra method, the insured may become eligible to purchase insurance at standard rates or under better terms than those governing the rated policy. Under such circumstances, insureds expect reconsideration. Many ratings are automatic in the sense that the rating is reduced in conjunction with the new underwriting evidence on a repeat sale that has a lower or no rating. Many companies enclose a notice with the policy informing the insured that they will consider reducing or removing the rating on or after a specific anniversary, and some also send a reminder on that anniversary. Most reconsiderations are noncompetitive, but some may be triggered by an offer of standard insurance made by another company.

To prevent insured persons from withdrawing, companies generally make some provision for handling these improvements. For the company to remove the extra charge without loss to itself, the extra charge in the first instance should have been computed with data from which the improved lives were eliminated at the point at which their ratings were removed. If the extra premium for the impairment was calculated from data that included lives that had improved, the company theoretically should not remove the extra charge. In this latter case, some of the insureds would no doubt improve, but others will grow worse. As the company could not increase the charges against those that deteriorate, it should not reduce charges for those who improve. As a practical matter, competitive considerations mean that most companies will reduce or remove a rating if they receive evidence that the risk has improved.

When an apparent reduction in expected mortality is due to a change in residence, occupation, or avocation, some companies require a probationary period of one or two years prior to rating removal. At the end of this period, the company makes a retroactive refund of the extra premium dating from the time the change occurred. This protects the company against the possibility that the insured will return to the former occupation, avocation, or residence. For practical reasons, however, some companies make the change without such a probationary period.

Health Insurance on Substandard Risks

As in the case of life insurance, the insurance company can either reject an application, accept it at standard rates on a regular policy form, accept it on a higher-premium plan, or accept it on a regular policy form with an extra premium. In recent years, there have been significant advances in the underwriting of impaired risks for health insurance, so that today only a small proportion of these risks is ineligible for insurance on some basis. In addition to those used in life insurance, techniques for handling impaired risks include the use of exclusion riders and limitations on policy benefits.

Exclusions

In contrast with life insurance, exclusions are a common method of handling physical impairments in health insurance. An exclusion rider is an endorsement attached to a policy that excludes from coverage any loss arising from the named disease or physical impairment. After such losses have been excluded and other aspects of the case have been deemed normal, full coverage can be issued for other types of losses at standard rates. The exclusion may be somewhat broader than the condition that leads to its use. For example, a proposed insured with a history of kidney stones might be offered a policy excluding all diseases of the kidneys or genitourinary tract. Such an approach is considered essential because a kidney stone condition might aggravate another related disease, and it also avoids possible problems if a claim based on a slightly different manifestation of the same condition is filed.

Although a broad exclusion rider impairs the value of the coverage, it is usually preferable to the alternative. The only alternative often is declination if the condition is one that would be impossible to price accurately (such as a highly subjective condition). Furthermore, from the company's standpoint, the existence of the impairment can often produce disability, even from unrelated ailments. Conditions that commonly require waivers include back injuries, appendicitis, hernias, and elective surgical procedures. If, however, in the case of disability insurance, a long elimination period is requested, many conditions such as hernias and appendicitis may not require waivers.

Extra Premiums

Most companies offer full coverage to certain impaired risks at an extra premium. Some companies offer coverage only on selected impairments or selected plans; others offer on all bases. Some reduce benefits, increase the elimination period for certain impairments, charge an extra premium, or utilize one or more of these features in combination. Companies void the preexisting condition exclusion in the policy with respect to an impairment for which an extra premium is charged.

There are a multitude of problems in obtaining morbidity statistics that accurately reflect increased expected morbidity. Yet the prospect of offering broad coverage for preexisting conditions that could cause disability or hospitalization has encouraged many companies to change their underwriting practices and grant more complete coverage for an extra premium. Many impairments that could not be satisfactorily covered in the past because they either were too broad in scope or had too many systemic complications (such as many heart conditions or diabetes) can now be covered for a price. The use of the extra-premium approach, however, does not eliminate the need for exclusions. Although exclusions are probably resorted to less frequently, there are still problems in granting unrestricted coverage in all instances.

Modification of Type of Coverage

The third major method of handling impaired health risks is to modify the type of policy. In the case of borderline applications, health insurance underwriters frequently settle the problem by offering a different and more limited form of coverage. This limitation may be a lower amount, a shorter benefit period, or a longer elimination period. This last device is particularly useful for cases in which the medical history involves short-term disabilities only.

Renewal Underwriting

Renewal underwriting is concerned with the health history of the insured and also changes in occupation, income, residence, or habits, all of which may have made him or her a less desirable risk. With optionally renewable policies, the company has an opportunity to reevaluate its insureds periodically. Some companies do not avail themselves of their right to reunderwrite optionally renewable policies unless or until the loss ratio for that particular group of policies reaches a point at which action must be taken.

Cancellation and reunderwriting seem unfair to some persons. It is said that the insured often does not fully understand the terms of the contract or, if he or she understands them, does not appreciate their full importance. This is one reason so many insurers charge more and guarantee renewal of their policies to a specified age, rather than emphasizing one-year term plans.

SPECIAL UNDERWRITING PRACTICES

Usual underwriting practices are relaxed in several areas. In the process, special underwriting concerns are created. The following discussion is intended to explain how reasonable results can be obtained in these areas.

Nonmedical Life Insurance

A substantial proportion of all new ordinary insurance is written without the benefit of a medical or paramedical examination—so-called **nonmedical life insurance.** In one sense, the use of the term is unfortunate because it sometimes conveys the erroneous idea that the insurance is issued without any medical information. Of course, this is not true. Medical information is still sought, but it is gathered from the proposed insured by the agent who asks medically related questions from the application (and possibly from attending physician statements and other sources). The term *nonmedical* should be understood to be synonymous with *no physical examination ordinarily required.*

For many years, a medical examination was considered a necessity. Toward the end of the nineteenth century, life insurance companies in England began to experiment with nonmedical underwriting on a limited basis. Not until 1921, however, did several Canadian companies begin to experiment with nonmedical underwriting as it is practiced today. The motivation for the development was a shortage of medical examiners, particularly in the rural areas, and the desire to reduce the expense rate on the predominantly small policies issued at that time. The practice spread to U.S. companies about four years later and is firmly entrenched today in Canada, the United States, Japan, Europe, and elsewhere.

Although nonmedical underwriting lessens the demands on the medical profession and facilitates the sale and processing of an application, the primary justification for it lies in expense saving. As long as the expenses saved by eliminating the insurer's having to pay for a medical examination are greater than the cost of any extra mortality incurred because of its elimination, the process is economically sound. Actuarial studies underlie the nonmedical rules utilized by life insurance companies. Modifications are made in these rules from time to time as indicated by emerging experience, including the increasing costs of medical examinations in recent years.

Perhaps the most important safeguard built into the nonmedical underwriting rules is a limit on the amount available on any one insured. In the early days, this limit was $1,000. When experience proved to be more favorable than anticipated, the limits were gradually raised. During the 1970s, many companies provided up to $100,000 or higher on a nonmedical basis (subject to age limitations), and virtually all issued $50,000 on that basis.

In the 1980s, nonmedical limits exploded. Some companies had limits as high as $500,000 at the younger ages (through age 30) and at least one company had a $1 million maximum. The maximum age generally held at 40 or 45. The reasons for this dramatic change were the effects of inflation on underwriting expenses, continuing reduction in deaths from natural causes at the younger ages, and high interest rates that decreased substantially the present value of the extra mortality from not obtaining a medical exam.

Usually, these large amounts of nonmedical insurance were underwritten without blood testing. Today the situation has changed. The impact of AIDS and lower interest rates has led to significantly lower blood testing limits. Currently, most companies require a blood test for amounts of $100,000 or more and many companies have a lower limit. Also, nonmedical limits have been reduced at the younger ages.

A second safeguard built into nonmedical rules is a limit on the ages at which the insurance will be issued. Nonmedical insurance is not regularly available beyond age 50 or 60, except in special situations, such as a salary savings group for which the age limits might be higher. Most companies impose no lower age limit, offering it down to age zero.

Other safeguards include the general limitation of nonmedical insurance to medically standard risks. Companies will usually consider occupations in which the extra hazard is largely accidental as well as all aviation and avocation exposure on a nonmedical basis. Some companies offer nonmedical coverage to higher ages or for larger amounts if the proposed insured has completed a comprehensive physical within the past six months or one year and the results are available from the attending physician. In addition to the expansion of nonmedical underwriting, there has also been expanded use of simplified underwriting in which only a few medical history questions are asked.

The application form used for nonmedical insurance contains the questions that would normally be asked by a medical examiner as well as the usual questions completed by the agent under a medical application. In the cases in which adverse medical information is developed from these or other sources, the company may request a paramedical examination or attending physicians' statements and, at times, it may require a complete medical examination. This occurs with an estimated 10 percent of nonmedical applications.

Guaranteed Issue Insurance

One of the important contractual arrangements under which retirement benefits are provided to employees is the individual contract pension trust. Under this arrangement, benefits are provided through retirement annuity or retirement income contracts purchased by the employer, through a trustee, for each of the employees eligible to participate in the pension plan. Traditionally, when retirement income contracts were used, each employee had to furnish evidence of insurability in the form of a satisfactory medical examination.

Many companies today underwrite such plans on a guaranteed issue basis, meaning that if the *group* is acceptable, the insurance company dispenses with individual underwriting and agrees in advance to accept applications for insurance on all employees who are actively at work. With this arrangement, there is no underwriting of individuals' lives; being actively at work is the only requirement.

The mortality experience on these arrangements is higher than usual mortality, as would be expected. To offset the anticipated extra mortality under guaranteed issue plans, many companies pay lower commissions, and either charge a higher premium or classify the policies separately for dividend purposes.

Reinstatements and Policy Changes

When a life insurance policy lapses for nonpayment of premium, the policyowner has the contractual right to apply for policy reinstatement. The owner must pay past-due premiums, plus provide evidence of insurability that is satisfactory to the insurer. Evidence of insurability is typically provided via a reinstatement application. This application is a shortened version of the original application, designed to be completed with minimal effort and time. Underwriting requirements commonly are less strict for recently lapsed policies and the entire process is streamlined. For policies that have been lapsed for a longer time and for which reinstatement is sought, the underwriting procedure more closely resembles that for a new insurance policy.

Underwriting also may be required in connection with certain policy changes. In general, an insurer will require evidence of insurability on any policy change that increases the policy's net amount at risk except, of course, when the change is one guaranteed by the contract (e.g., automatic face amount increases under a cost-of-living-adjustment rider). Thus, if a policyowner wishes to increase the policy face amount under a universal life or other policy, evidence of insurability ordinarily will be required.

Also, if it is desired to add additional benefits—such as waiver of premium, accidental death benefit, or guaranteed insurability option—to an existing policy, the insurer typically will require evidence of insurability. Similarly, underwriting and additional requirements are necessary to reduce or remove the extra premium on a rated policy. In each case, the essential purpose is to avoid adverse selection.

Highly Impaired Risks

In some cases, individuals with significant impairments have opportunities to obtain insurance at a cost that they can afford even though the original application may have been declined by one or more companies. These opportunities can be found with companies that specialize in this market.

Specialist brokers often have arrangements with a large number of these specialist companies and can readily identify the company likely to make the best offer for a specific impairment. Insurers often have a business arrangement with substandard specialist companies or brokers to assist their agents in obtaining coverage through an alternate source. A proposed insured should not be unduly discouraged by a declination from one company, as considerable variation in underwriting judgment can exist even among the companies specializing in highly impaired risks.

LAWS AFFECTING UNDERWRITING

As discussed previously, the underwriting process can involve the collection and use of information that is highly personal. This fact has led to public concern about how insurers use this information, as well as about the confidentiality with which it is maintained. Within the United States, the Fair Credit Reporting Act (FCRA) was one of the first federal laws that addressed these concerns. Other federal and state laws and regulations place limits on insurers' freedoms with respect to the collection, maintenance, use, and disclosure of personally identifiable information. Other countries, especially in Europe, have similar and sometimes more inclusive laws, but those of the United States will be used as representative of governmental concern about the uses of personally identifiable information in the underwriting process.

The Fair Credit Reporting Act

The FCRA was one of the first important U.S. laws to affect life insurance companies' information-gathering practices. Several of its requirements already have been mentioned. It requires users of investigative consumer reports to notify subject individuals that reports will be or have been requested. The user—in this case, the insurer—also must advise the consumer that he or she has the right to request disclosure of the nature and scope of the investigation.

Every consumer reporting agency (CRA), when it is requested to do so, must disclose to the consumer all information in the consumer's file as well as the sources of the information. Sources of information used exclusively to prepare an investigative consumer report need not be revealed. The CRA must also identify all persons who have procured a consumer report on the individual during the previous year (two years for employment purposes). Finally, the CRA is to provide the consumer with a written summary of the consumer's rights under the FCRA. The disclosure may take place in person, by telephone, by electronic means, or by any other reasonable means. The choice of disclosure mode is the consumer's.

If an insurer makes an adverse underwriting decision on the basis of information in a consumer report, it is required to notify the consumer of the decision and that the report affected the decision. The insurer is to provide the individual with the name, address, and telephone number of the CRA furnishing the report. Finally, the insurer is to inform the consumer of his or her right to obtain a free copy of the report from the CRA and to dispute the accuracy or completeness of any information in the report.

If the consumer disputes the completeness or accuracy of an item of information in his or her file or report, the CRA must reinvestigate at no charge to the consumer and record the current status of the disputed information. This reinvestigation must be completed within 30 days of the time the CRA receives notification of the dispute. If the reinvestigation proves the file information to be inaccurate or if it cannot be substantiated, the disputed data must be corrected or deleted. If, on the other hand, the reinvestigation fails to resolve the dispute, the consumer has the right to file a statement of up to 100 words presenting his or her side of the contested matter. Thereafter, the statement or a clear summary thereof must accompany the consumer report.

Several U.S. states have their own Fair Credit Reporting Acts. Generally, they track the federal law, except for extending certain additional rights to consumers or for limiting the CRA's actions in some ways.

The NAIC Model Privacy Act

The National Association of Insurance Commissioners' Insurance Information and Privacy Protection Model Act (NAIC Model Privacy Act) has been adopted by about 15 states. However, its importance extends beyond these states' borders because most insurers comply with the act's requirements, even in those states that have not enacted the law.

The NAIC Model Privacy Act is both a lengthy and a complex document. The act clearly and purposely is patterned after the insurance recommendations contained in the Privacy Protection Study Commission (PPSC) Report,[2] although it does not afford privacy protections at the level of those recommended by the PPSC. The act prohibits the use of pretext interviews (an investigator pretending to be someone that he or she is not in order to secure information) except in certain claim situations. The act also requires that a notice of an insurer's information practices be given to applicants and to certain policyowners. In general, the act's protections are applicable to personal insurance only.

The act mandates that insurers and agents specify clearly to an individual those inquiries that elicit information desired solely for marketing, research, or other purposes that are not directly related to the insurance transaction at hand. It also mandates minimum standards for disclosure authorization forms used by insurance institutions, agents, and insurance-support organizations.

Individuals are given the right under the act to be interviewed in connection with the preparation of any investigative consumer report. Certain persons are given a right of access to personal information on them maintained by insurers, agents, and insurance-support organizations. A corresponding right to request correction is provided.

The act requires insurers to advise individuals applying for personal (but not business-related) purposes of the reasons for any adverse underwriting decision affecting them and,

---

[2]Privacy Protection Study Commission, *Personal Privacy in an Information Society* (Washington, DC: G.P.O., 1977), pp. 188–222.

if it is requested, to provide them with the information upon which the decision was based. The model act further stipulates that no insurer or agent may base an adverse underwriting decision on the mere fact of a previous adverse underwriting decision. It also provides that no insurer should base an adverse underwriting decision on personal information received from an insurance-support organization whose primary source of information is insurance institutions (e.g., the MIB).

The disclosure section of the act is the most complex. It specifies the circumstances under which insurers, agents, and insurance-support organizations may disclose information about an individual without the individual's consent.

Unfair Discrimination Laws and Regulations

In addition to the limitations on U.S. life insurance companies' freedom to contract discussed earlier, various state laws and regulations prohibit insurers from using certain information to discriminate among individuals applying for insurance. All states' insurance codes contain unfair trade practices acts. These laws prohibit insurers from discriminating unfairly in premiums charged, policy terms, or benefits provided between individuals of the same class and with "equal expectation of life . . . in any contract of life insurance or of life annuity . . . [and] essentially same hazard in . . . any policy or contract of health insurance. . . ." These laws form the basis upon which insurance regulators have promulgated regulations addressing unfair discrimination based on several characteristics, as discussed next, including a person's sex, marital status, race, religion, and national origin.

Unfair Sex Discrimination

The issue of unfair discrimination based on sex continues to be important to the insurance business. The U.S. Supreme Court decision in the 1983 *Norris* case prohibits consideration of a person's sex in the determination of employment-related retirement benefits.[3] Insurance trade associations argued against the plaintiffs in this case, basing their support for sex-distinct employee benefits on actuarial fairness precepts. The Court found the employment nondiscrimination provisions of the Civil Rights Act to supercede actuarial considerations. The situation is generally different with use of a person's sex as a classification factor in individually issued life insurance. To date, only the state of Montana has barred the use of sex-distinct rating in such insurance.

The argument by opponents of sex-based pricing is that, irrespective of statistics, use of a person's sex as a rating factor is socially unacceptable. The insurance industry contends, of course, that use of sex-based pricing is not only justified (actuarially, women as a group live longer than men as a group) but that to fail to recognize sex-based price differences would itself be unfair discrimination.

The NAIC's Model Regulation to Eliminate Unfair Sex Discrimination or similar regulation has been adopted by the majority of states. The regulation does not prohibit use of sex-based pricing; rather, it prohibits the denial of insurance coverage or benefits on the basis of sex or marital status.

Unfair Discrimination Based on Physical or Mental Impairment

The NAIC also adopted a Model Regulation on Unfair Discrimination in Life and Health Insurance on the Basis of Physical or Mental Impairment. The regulation prohibits refusal or limitation of coverage or rate differentials based solely on physical or mental impairment unless the refusal, limitation, or rate differential "is based on sound actuarial principles or is related to actual or reasonably anticipated experience." In other

---

[3] *Arizona Governing Committee . . . v. Norris,* 77 L.Ed.2d 1236 (July 1983).

words, if an actuarial relationship is established between the impairment and the insurer's classification, the impairment itself may be used as a factor.

A companion regulation, the NAIC Model Regulation on Unfair Discrimination on the Basis of Blindness or Partial Blindness, has been adopted, in one form or another, in most states. The regulation stipulates that the refusal to insure or to continue to insure, or the limitation on the amount, extent, or kind of coverage available to an individual, or the charging of a different rate solely on the basis of blindness or partial blindness constitutes an unfair discrimination under the state's Unfair Trade Practices Act. This regulation omits the actuarial relationship exception, so blindness itself cannot be used as a factor in underwriting. The model does, however, allow the underlying cause of one's blindness to be considered. The regulation enjoys strong insurance industry support.

Unfair Discrimination in AIDS and Sexual Preference

There was substantial opposition in the 1980s to insurers' use of tests to detect AIDS antibodies. In fact, several jurisdictions passed laws prohibiting such usage in connection with some lines of health insurance or life insurance or both. Ultimately, these laws were repealed as being overly broad or modified to address medical expense insurance only.[4]

In debate about use of testing, it was found that many insurers used a person's sexual preference or information that was considered suggestive of a person's sexual preference in the underwriting process. In response, the NAIC developed a model bulletin called the *Medical/Lifestyle Questions and Underwriting Guidelines.* The guidelines prohibit insurers from inquiring about or using a person's sexual orientation in connection with life or health insurance underwriting. The guidelines have been promulgated in almost all states.

Unfair Discrimination in Domestic Abuse

The issue of whether it is fair to charge a higher rate or deny life or health insurance to a victim of domestic abuse has proven difficult to resolve. Advocates of proscriptions on use of this information contend that it is socially unacceptable to do so and that it punishes the victim. Insurers note that domestic violence increases the likelihood of the victim being injured or even killed and, therefore, is relevant as a classification factor in individually issued life and health insurance.

The NAIC has adopted three model laws relating to domestic abuse in life and health insurance. One relates to medical expense insurance, another to life insurance, and the third to disability income insurance. Each would prohibit insurers from using the fact of domestic abuse as a classification factor. To date, about one-half of the states have similar or identical laws.

Unfair Discrimination in Health Status and Availability

The purpose of the **Health Insurance Portability and Accountability Act** of 1996 (HIPAA)[5] was to increase access and portability of health care insurance. The act increases availability through changes in access, portability, and renewability of group health plans. This increased availability is achieved by:

- prohibiting discrimination of insureds and dependents due to health status
- placing limitations on what can be included in preexisting conditions
- guaranteeing availability and renewability for certain employers in the small-group market.

---

[4]Washington, DC was among the jurisdictions enacting such a ban. Because of the high incidence of AIDS in Washington, most life insurers ceased writing business there—an example of how a market can fail because of concerns about adverse selection.

[5]Pub. L. No. 164-191, 110 Stat. 1936 (1996).

Under HIPAA, the preexisting condition exclusion is permissible only if treatment, advice, or diagnosis for the condition is received within the six months prior to an employee's attempt to enter a new group health plan. Previously undiagnosed genetic disorders are not considered preexisting conditions. Furthermore, and arguably most significant, maternity cannot be considered a preexisting condition. Newborns and adopted children are exempt from *any* preexisting condition exclusions as long as they are added to coverage within 30 days of birth or adoption, respectively.

Under HIPAA, preexisting exclusions must be reduced by the length of the "aggregate period of prior creditable coverage."[6] Creditable coverage includes coverage under:

- a group health plan
- an individual health plan
- Medicare
- Medicaid
- a military-sponsored health plan
- a program of the Indian Health Service
- a state health benefit risk pool
- the Peace Corps[7]

HIPAA requires that employers must provide "certificates" to employees when they cease coverage. The changes that make coverage more portable are intended to decrease "job lock," that is, the fear of changing jobs because of loss of employee and dependent insurance coverage.

HIPAA also requires that each health insurance insurer that offers health insurance coverage in the small-group market (employer with between 2 and 50 employees) in a state accept every small employer group in the state that applies for coverage. Insurers in the large- and small-group markets are required under HIPAA to renew or continue in-force coverage at the option of the plan sponsor except for the following reasons:

- nonpayment of premiums
- fraud
- a violation of participation or contribution rules
- termination of coverage in the market
- a group of enrollees in a network plan who do not live, reside, or work in the network service area or no longer have an affiliation with an association plan

Availability is further increased by clarification of certain COBRA regulations.

HIPAA also provides for the establishment of medical savings accounts and defines long-term care as accident and health insurance contracts providing long-term care plans with the tax-favored status that other health insurance coverages have long enjoyed (see chapter 20).

Unfair Genetic Discrimination

The debate concerning the use of genetic information in underwriting was set out in the preceding chapter. It is sufficient here to note that most states have enacted laws restricting insurers' use of genetic information in some way. Consideration is being given to proscriptive legislation at the federal level.

---

[6]29 U.S.C. §1181 (a)(3).
[7]29 U.S.C. §1181 (c)(1).

Most state laws apply to medical expense insurance, although some apply also to disability income and life insurance.[8] The scope of the laws varies. Some restrict insurers' use of any type of genetic information and from any source (i.e., from family history, medical treatment, or genetic testing). Other laws are applicable only to information derived from genetic tests, and still others apply only to specified genetic conditions such as Tay Sachs disease, sickle cell anemia, and hemophilia.

Most laws prevent insurers from refusing coverage or varying premiums based on the designated information. Other laws allow such adverse classification decisions if there is actuarial justification.

Unfair Discrimination and the Future of Voluntary Insurance Markets

As discussed in chapter 25, the right to distinguish between low- and high-risk applicants for individually issued, voluntarily purchased life and disability income insurance is critical to the viability of the private market for such policies. It is also important to individually issued medical expense insurance, although somewhat less so.

Classification factors used by insurers must be socially acceptable. What is socially acceptable can be expected to continue to evolve over time. To date, most laws and regulations restricting insurers' use of socially sensitive information have not seriously threatened the viability of the voluntary private insurance market in life and disability income insurance. The same cannot be said of medical expense insurance, which is more and more considered as a public good and, therefore, outside that market.

The public often neither makes nor appreciates the distinction between group and individually issued insurance or between life and medical expense insurance. Indeed, the word *insurance* typically is associated more with automobile and homeowners' insurance than with life and health insurance. The public is not well informed about the conditions under which insurance can be canceled or premiums increased. The underwriting process is sometimes seen as a means simply to charge higher premiums or to set up insureds for later denials of their insurance claims. Concerns persist about whether insurers will protect their customers' privacy adequately, especially in an era of computerization and medical sophistication.

Some of the insurance industry's terminology does not foster public understanding. We use the term *discrimination* in a clinical, nonjudgmental sense to mean distinguishing between two persons. The public associates nefarious and unfair dealing with this most critical term. Clearly, if the voluntary private insurance market is to flourish, we need better communications between the insurance-buying public and insurance companies.

REINSURANCE OF LIFE AND HEALTH INSURANCE RISKS

Reinsurance is the transfer of all or a portion of an insurer's loss exposure under an insurance policy to another insurance company. It is insurance for the insurer. The company that issued the policy originally is known as the **direct-writing or ceding company.** The company to which the risk is transferred is the **reinsurer or assuming company.**

Probably all life insurance companies worldwide rely on reinsurance, which is probably the most international of all insurance lines. It is not unusual for reinsurers in Europe, Asia, and North America to provide coverage on large exposures. We cover both life and health reinsurance.

---

[8]Information in this section is drawn from Mark A. Hall, "Restricting Insurers' Use of Genetic Information: A Guide to Public Policy," *North American Actuarial Journal* (January 1999).

Reinsurance is underwritten by specialized insurers whose exclusive business is reinsurance, called **professional reinsurers,** and by the reinsurance departments of direct-writing companies. The purpose for which reinsurance is purchased as well as the technical details of the reinsurance are the same irrespective of the source of the reinsurance capacity.

Purpose of Reinsurance

Although the primary purpose of reinsurance is to avoid too large a risk concentration within one company, it also may be used to take advantage of the underwriting judgment of the reinsurer, to transfer all or certain classes of substandard business (see Box 26-2), to reduce the strain on surplus caused by writing new business, to stabilize the overall mortality or morbidity experience of the ceding company, or, in the case of newly organized or smaller companies, to obtain advice and counsel on underwriting procedures, rates, and forms. A company also must provide its agency force with competitive facilities and needs reinsurance to permit acceptance of the cases written by its agents, regardless of the amounts involved.

BOX 26-2

BULK REINSURANCE ARRANGEMENTS

Life reinsurance—known as **assumption reinsurance**—may be undertaken to transfer all or a specific portion of a company's existing liabilities to the reinsuring company, including the administration of these policies directly with policyowners. Assumption reinsurance might be utilized when a company wishes to withdraw from business entirely or from a particular territory. Alternatively, specified blocks of business may be reinsured under **portfolio reinsurance.** Questions have arisen as to whether direct-writing companies should be able to make such transfers without policyowner consent.

To address these concerns, assumption reinsurance transactions are governed and regulated in many states by statutes, most of which are patterned after the NAIC Model Assumption Reinsurance Act. The model act requires approval of the transaction by the insurance commissioner of each state in which risk being transferred resides, and affirmative consent to or rejection of the transfer by the owner of the policy being transferred.

In this connection, the transferring or ceding company must deliver a notice of transfer to the policyowner, which provides the owner with the option to reject the transfer. Under the model act, the notice may remain outstanding for 24 months. If the ceding company has not received the policyowner's consent or rejection to the transfer within the 24-month period, the ceding company must mail a second notice to the policyowner. This second notice may remain outstanding for a period of one month. Therefore, under the model act, a policyowner has an effective right to consent to or reject the transfer of his or her policy for a 25-month period.

Some states, however, have legislated abbreviated notice periods. Georgia requires a 90-day notice period (60-day first notice, 30-day second notice); Missouri requires a 24-month notice period (12-month first notice, 12-month second notice); and Washington requires only a one-time, 30-day notice period.

Once the notices of transfer are delivered to policyowners, the model act provides that consent shall be obtained through (1) affirmative response from the policyowner approving the transfer, (2) silence and no response from the policyowner after expiration of all notice periods, or (3) upon payment of premiums to the assuming company.

Source: Steven B. Jajjar, "Regulatory Approvals for Assumption and Bulk Reinsurance Transactions," *Insurance/Healthcare Review,* (Spring 1998), p. 3.

Reinsurance also is used regularly by most companies as a means of obtaining better underwriting offers for proposed insureds who do not qualify for a standard or a moderately substandard offer under their own underwriting standards. Some reinsurers with liberal underwriting philosophies aggressively seek this type of business. Typically, the ceding company will retain only a small or no portion of the risk. Some reinsurers require a ceding company to maintain a portion of the risk on facultative cases (discussed later).

Health reinsurance is one of the fastest-growing reinsurance lines. Reinsurers have played a constructive role in not only providing capacity for innovative health-related coverages, such as long-term care insurance, but they also have been instrumental in helping direct-writing insurers design and price such products.

Some health insurance coverages (e.g., major medical, long-term care, and disability income plans) involve substantial liability. As in the case of life insurance, reinsurance is utilized to avoid disruptive fluctuations in experience and company operating results. Reinsurance is also used for experimental coverages or for the writing of unusual lines with an inadequate spread of risk.

The Concept of Retention

An insurer's **retention** is the amount of primary insurance that it retains for its own account. A life insurance company deals with a type of risk that, in the aggregate, may be measured and predicted with a remarkable degree of accuracy, the closeness of the approximation depending on the number and homogeneity of the individuals in the group. On the other hand, the exposure of one individual may be $1 million and the exposure of another only $25,000. The probability of death for each may be the same, but the impact on the surplus of a company because of death clearly would be much greater with the $1 million policy.

With a recently organized or small company, a maximum limit on the amount of insurance it will retain for its own account on any individual is deemed necessary. In companies with a relatively small total number of insureds, mortality and morbidity experience can fluctuate widely from year to year. In such companies, the surplus funds available to absorb unusual losses usually are small, and a single large claim or several significant claims might have a marked adverse effect on operations for the year. As a company increases in size because of an increasing total volume of insurance in force and increasing surplus funds, the chance of significant fluctuations in its overall experience will decrease (thanks to the law of large numbers), and the company's ability to absorb unusual losses will increase. Thus, it can gradually and safely increase its maximum retention on any one life.

There is no simple formula for fixing a retention limit because it depends on a number of factors that are peculiar to a company's economic position and manner of operation. Such factors include (1) the size of the company's unallocated surplus, (2) the quality of its agency force, (3) the quality of the home office underwriting staff, (4) the distribution of insurance in force (by amount, number of policies, sex and age, proportion of substandard, etc.), and (5) the probable distribution of new business and average amount per policy.[9] More subjectively, retention is a function of the degree of management's (and the board's) tolerance for variability in anticipated operational results.

---

[9]A study by Kwangbong Lee, Bruce A. Palmer, and Harold D. Skipper, Jr., "An Analysis of Life Insurer Retention Limits," *The Journal of Risk and Insurance,* Vol. LIX (June 1992), found insurer size to be the most important determinant of insurer retention limits for life insurance. Other factors included the insurer form (stock or mutual), the insurer's relative new business emphasis, average policy size, and the insurer's relative emphasis on term life insurance.

In general, the smaller the group of units exposed to loss and the less homogeneous they are, the sharper and more sudden can be the fluctuations and, therefore, the lower would be a company's limit of retention. Life retention limits range from $25,000 in small, recently established companies to $20 million or more in the largest U.S. companies. With disability income and LTC insurance, retention limits usually are stated as monthly indemnity amounts, such as $2,000. There are usually various limits within a given company, depending upon age at issue, substandard classification, and, sometimes, plan.

Reinsurance Arrangements

The traditional plans of reinsurance developed to deal with individual risks may be broadly classified as proportional reinsurance and nonproportional reinsurance plans. Under **proportional reinsurance** plans, the reinsurer and the ceding company share both premiums and claims on a given risk in a specified proportion. In contrast, **nonproportional reinsurance** provides for the reinsurer to pay a claim only when the amount of loss exceeds a specified limit (excess of loss coverage). Nonproportional reinsurance plans have the objective of stabilizing the overall claims experience of the ceding company. Nonproportional life reinsurance usually takes one of three forms: stop-loss reinsurance, catastrophe reinsurance, or spread-loss reinsurance, each discussed briefly in Box 26-3.

The characteristic that differentiates nonproportional plans from traditional proportional reinsurance plans is that they relate the reinsurer's liability to some measure of overall experience on all or specified blocks of the ceding companies' business rather than to individual or specified policies of insurance. In addition, the proportion in which the ceding company and the reinsurer will share losses under nonproportional reinsurance is not determinable in advance. These forms are adaptations of property and liability reinsurance and are not widely utilized in life reinsurance, with them being more common in health reinsurance.

Agreements

Reinsurance may be arranged on a facultative or an automatic basis. With **facultative reinsurance,** each application is underwritten separately by the reinsurer. When the direct-writing company receives an application for a policy for more than the amount it wishes to assume, it negotiates with one or more reinsurers for a transfer of that part of the insurance that is in excess of the amount the company wishes to retain. Copies of the ceding company's application materials are sent to the reinsurer(s) for evaluation. The reinsurer (or reinsurers) then makes its own underwriting judgment and advises the ceding company.

The facultative method has certain advantages. It is flexible, and questions about the underwriting information can be discussed in the reinsurance negotiations. The orig-

---

BOX 26-3

FORMS OF NONPROPORTIONAL REINSURANCE

Stop-loss reinsurance becomes payable if and when aggregate claims experienced by the ceding company in a year exceed some predetermined level. **Catastrophic reinsurance** covers multiple insured losses arising from a single accident or other occurrence. Under **spread-loss reinsurance,** excess claims in a year are covered by the reinsurer, which are then, in effect, reimbursed over a period of time, thus allowing the ceding company to spread its loss over several years.

inal insurer also obtains the advice of the reinsurer with which it negotiates. The major disadvantages are the additional time required for completing the transaction, which may result in loss of business to competitors, and a higher cost per unit for such coverage.

With **automatic** (also called **treaty**) **reinsurance,** the direct-writing company *must* transfer an amount in excess of its retention of each applicable insurance policy to the reinsuring company immediately upon payment of premium and the issuance of the policy, and the reinsurer *must* accept the transfer that falls within the scope of the agreement. The treaty always provides that not more than a certain amount per policy may be transferred to the reinsurance company, and the agreement may provide for a distribution of the excess to more than one reinsuring company. A "split account" system may be based on percentage shares of each reinsured policy or on the first letter of the insured's surname (e.g., reinsurer 1 gets letters A through K and reinsurer 2 gets L through Z). When an application exceeds the limits of automatic treaties, facultative reinsurance is secured.

With reinsurance arrangements, the original insured is not a legal party to any reinsurance contracts that may result. He or she must look solely to the direct-writing company for any payments to which he or she is entitled under the policy, and the direct-writing company is liable for such payments, regardless of the existence and terms of any reinsurance contracts to which it may be a party.

Life Reinsurance Plans

Three life reinsurance plans are in general use under both facultative and automatic agreements. We cover each here.

Coinsurance Plan   Under the **coinsurance plan,** the reinsurer assumes a proportionate share of the risk according to the terms that govern the original policy. The reinsurer is liable for an amount determined by the size of the insurance assumed in relation to the original insurance amount.

Thus, if the reinsurer has accepted one-half of the original insurance, it becomes liable for one-half of any loss. In return for this guarantee, the reinsurer receives a pro rata share of the original premium less a ceding commission and allowance. These payments reimburse the direct-writing company for an appropriate share of the agent's commissions, premium taxes paid, and a portion of the other expenses attributable to the reinsured policy. Also, the reinsurer reimburses for a proportionate share of any dividends paid. In general, the reinsurance contract is a duplicate of that entered into between the direct-writing company and the policyowner. The ceding company and the reinsurer share a risk (premiums and claims) according to agreed proportions, with the reinsurance rates derived from the original rates charged the policyowner.

Yearly Renewable Term Plan   Another reinsurance plan is the **yearly renewable term plan** under which the reinsurer assumes the reinsured policy's net amount at risk in excess of the ceding company's retention. The ceding company pays premiums on a yearly renewable term basis. This plan is particularly appropriate for smaller ceding companies because it results in larger assets for these companies and is simpler to administer than the coinsurance plan. Thus, for policies with declining net amounts at risk, a decreasing amount of reinsurance is purchased each year.

If a loss occurs, the reinsurer is liable for the amount that it assumed that year, and the ceding insurer is liable for its retention plus the full reserve on the reinsured portion of the policy. Premium rates for yearly renewable term reinsurance are established independently of the premium charged the policyowner.

Modified Coinsurance Plan   In the interest of permitting a company to retain control over the funds arising out of its own policies, a **modified coinsurance plan** has been developed. Under this arrangement, the ceding company pays the reinsurer a proportionate part of the gross premium, as under the conventional coinsurance plan, less commissions and other allowances, premium taxes, and overhead allocable to reinsured policies. At the end of each policy year, the reinsurer pays to the ceding company a reserve adjustment that is equal to the net increase in the reserve during the year, less one year's interest on the total reserve held at the beginning of the year. The net effect of the plan is to return to the ceding company the bulk of the funds developed by its policies.

Modified coinsurance can be considered as yearly renewable term on a calendar-year basis because the reinsurer, after paying the reserve adjustment, cash surrender values, and commissions and allowances, is left with only a risk premium. Aside from the reserve adjustment, the modified coinsurance plan follows that of the regular coinsurance plan. Table 26-3 provides a comparative analysis of the three basic life reinsurance plans.

TABLE 26-3 Comparative Analysis of Reinsurance Plans

Plan	Amount of Reinsurer's Liability in Case of Death	Responsibilities of Reinsurer	Allocation of Premium	Advantages
Yearly renewable term	Net amount at risk on portion of original policy reinsured[a] (reinsured amount tracks policy's net amount at risk above retention)	Reserves: yearly renewable term reserves only Nonforfeiture value: none Dividends: none	Premium to reinsurer equals net amount at risk times yearly renewable term rate for attained age (first-year rate may be 50% of renewal or less, to recognize insurer's high, first-year expenses)	Preferred by majority of companies; allows greater amount of asset retention and more premium for investment simplicity; inexpensive to administer
Coinsurance	Face amount on portion of original policy reinsured[a] (reinsured amount tracks policy's face amount in excess of retention)	Reserves: pro rata share Nonforfeiture values: pro rata share (reinsurer usually does not participate in policy loans) Dividends: pro rata share	Premium to reinsurer equals pro rata share of gross premium less allowances	Preferred by companies with high acquisition costs for term plans Reinsurer shares in surplus drain of new business by absorbing a proportion of the initial expense and reserve liability
Modified coinsurance	Same as coinsurance	Reserves: none. However, at end of policy year, reinsurer pays to ceding company net amount of increase in reserves during year, less growth due to required interest Nonforfeiture values: none because reserves are held by ceding company Dividends: pro rata share	Premium to reinsurer equals pro rata share of gross premium less allowances	Same as coinsurance but also cash-value plans, plus return to ceding company of bulk of funds developed by policies Original insurer's assets not diminished

[a]In most cases, the portion of the original policy reinsured equals the face amount of the original policy minus the ceding company's retention limit. In some cases under facultative agreements, however, the ceding company might retain less than its usual retention limit.

Illustration of Sources of Funds   Table 26-4 includes an example of the distribution of liability between a direct-writing company and a reinsurer with respect to a $100,000 ordinary life policy issued to a 35-year-old male reinsured under the coinsurance, yearly renewable term, and modified coinsurance plans. In each case, a retention of $25,000 is assumed. The column labeled "surplus" equals the amount that each company would have to draw from its surplus to pay a death claim. The balance effectively is paid by release of the reserve.

Thus, under the coinsurance plan, it can be seen that the direct writer would always provide $25,000 and the reinsurer would always provide $75,000 of any death claim. Each establishes full reserves for its proportion of the reinsured policy. In contrast, it can be seen that, under the yearly renewable term plan, the reinsurer maintains none of the reserve, with the full amount established by the direct-writing company. Note also

	Direct Writer		Reinsurer		
TABLE 26-4					
Year	**Reserve**	**Surplus**	**Reserve**	**Surplus**	**Total**
			Coinsurance		
1	$ 228.50	$24,771.50	$ 685.50	$74,314.50	$100,000
2	466.25	24,533.75	1,398.75	73,601.25	$100,000
3	712.25	24,287.75	2,136.75	72,863.25	$100,000
4	966.75	24,033.25	2,900.25	72,099.75	$100,000
5	1,230.00	23,770.00	3,690.00	71,310.00	$100,000
10	2,672.50	22,327.50	8,017.50	66,982.50	$100,000
20	6,229.50	18,770.50	18,688.50	56,311.50	$100,000
			Yearly Renewable Term		
1	$ 914.00	$24,771.50	$ 0.00	$74,314.50	$100,000
2	1,865.00	24,533.75	0.00	73,601.25	$100,000
3	2,849.00	24,287.75	0.00	72,863.25	$100,000
4	3,867.00	24,033.25	0.00	72,099.75	$100,000
5	4,920.00	23,770.00	0.00	71,310.00	$100,000
10	10,690.00	22,327.50	0.00	66,982.50	$100,000
20	24,918.00	18,770.50	0.00	56,311.50	$100,000
			Modified Coinsurance		
1	$ 258.50	$24,771.50	$ 685.50	$74,314.50	$100,000
2	1,186.02	24,533.75	678.98	73,601.25	$100,000
3	2,180.94	24,287.75	668.06	72,863.25	$100,000
4	3,210.34	24,033.25	656.66	72,099.75	$100,000
5	4,275.25	23,770.00	644.74	71,310.00	$100,000
10	10,127.76	22,327.50	562.24	66,982.50	$100,000
20	24,612.90	18,770.50	305.10	56,311.00	$100,000

TABLE 26-4   Source of Funds for Paying a Death Claim under the Coinsurance, Yearly Renewable Term, and Modified Coinsurance Plans (Ordinary Life, Male, Aged 35, Policy Amount $100,000, $25,000 Retention)[a]

[a]Assumes the *1980 CSO Table,* 5%, NLP reserve method, and claim paid on last day of policy year prior to any reserve payment from the reinsurer to the direct writer.

that the reinsured amount tracks precisely the surplus (or net amount at risk) shown for the coinsurance plan.

Finally, observe that the reserve held by the reinsurer under the modified coinsurance plan equals the change in reserve under the coinsurance plan less a year's interest on the reserve held at the beginning of the policy year. Thus, in the first year, the reinsurer does not assess any interest charge because the beginning reserve is zero.

Health Reinsurance Plans

As pointed out earlier, reinsurance methods involve sharing the risk on either a proportional or nonproportional basis.[10]

Proportional Plans   Proportional reinsurance can be expressed either as quota share or surplus share. Under **quota-share reinsurance,** the insurer and the reinsurer share in a predetermined proportion of every risk underwritten in a specified category. Thus, a company might reinsure 40 percent of every risk written on a certain policy form, regardless of the size of the risk. This basis also could apply to the company's entire health insurance portfolio or to one specific benefit among several benefits offered. In certain cases (e.g., experimental coverage), the ceding company might want the reinsurer to participate in a relatively large share of the risk.

In **surplus-share reinsurance,** the reinsurer assumes the liability above the ceding company's retention. Once the retention is selected, the reinsurer shares proportionately in the risk. Thus, if a disability policy is issued for $4,000 a month and the retention is $2,000 a month, 50 percent of all payments are reinsured. Similarly, if the policy is for $8,000 a month, 75 percent of all payments would be reinsured. This method of reinsurance perhaps is the best means of leveling out marked or chance fluctuations in experience, especially when an insurer does not have the proper spread of risk on large cases.

A relatively small portion of an insurer's health business typically is reinsured, with this portion made up of the large risks that are potentially less desirable, especially for disability income and accidental death. In such cases involving greater potential adverse selection and moral hazard, underwriters exercise greater care in selection and greater care is also exercised in handling such claims.

Excess-of-Loss Reinsurance   With **excess-of-loss reinsurance,** a reinsurer reimburses a portion of the claim payments of the ceding insurer, but only after the ceding insurer has made payments for a specified number of months of incapacity or after its retention is exceeded. In **excess-of-time (extended elimination) reinsurance,** the extended-wait period extends beyond the elimination period found in the policy itself. The extended-wait period can be one, two, five, or even ten years under this plan before the reinsurer becomes responsible for payment. The reinsurer's share of such claim payments after the extended-wait period may be 70 to 80 percent of the monthly benefit. This reinsurance covers total disability benefits only and does not cover any other benefit of the policy, such as partial disability. It is not unusual to combine extended-wait with other types of reinsurance, such as surplus-share reinsurance.

As in the case of life reinsurance, an automatic reinsurance agreement is often used, or it may be combined with automatic and facultative segments. The latter is more common. A facultative arrangement would have no automatic provision, and each case would be underwritten by the reinsurer.

---

[10]This and the following section are based upon *Individual Health Insurance, Part A* (Washington, DC: Health Insurance Association of America, 1992), pp. 149–154.

The Future of Reinsurance

With continued consolidation of the life insurance market in the United States and other major markets, insurer retention levels will continue to increase. Reinsurer's traditional role of augmenting direct-writing insurer capacity certainly will remain important to both primary insurers and reinsurers. However, we can reasonably expect that the role of reinsurers will continue to evolve beyond that of providing much-needed capacity. Reinsurers increasingly are providing additional value in their relationships with their clients by assisting in market research, product development, legal and financial advice, and consultations on mergers and acquisitions, in addition to providing support in the traditional areas of underwriting and product pricing.

Reinsurers can be expected to continue their move into nontraditional life and health insurance markets. For example, they increasingly provide capacity, advice, and support for self-funded employee benefit plans. Their role in helping banks in their move into insurance distribution and even underwriting is a further example. Reinsurance, especially coinsurance, is increasingly seen as a financial resource to the firm rather than exclusively as a cost.

Innovative life and health insurance products expose insurers to new types of mortality and morbidity risks. Perhaps of greater importance, they also expose insurers to risks associated with asset–liability mismatch, with interest rate variability, and with a host of other financial risks that require sophisticated financial risk management tools. Many reinsurers are responding to the challenge by offering these new risk management services as they seek to form closer alliances with their clients.

Questions

1. Explain how information sources, methods of risk classification, and marketing pressures can lead competing life insurers to arrive at widely different underwriting decisions for the same individual.
2. Explain the theory behind nonmedical life insurance and indicate which underwriting safeguards are used with this type of insurance.
3. How do the Fair Credit Reporting Act (FCRA) and NAIC's model laws on unfair discrimination protect the rights of consumers?
4. Explain how reinsurance is applied in establishing the underwriting policies of a life insurance company.

CHAPTER

27

LIFE AND HEALTH INSURANCE ACTUARIAL PRINCIPLES

Objectives

- Explain how the laws of probability facilitate the pricing of life and health insurance products.

- Describe the process of constructing mortality tables.

- Identify different types of mortality tables.

- Explain the use of mortality tables in life insurance rate making.

- Explain the use of interest rate assumptions in life insurance rate making.

The student cannot truly understand life and health insurance until he or she has developed a sound appreciation for the underlying mathematics of life and health insurance. Chapter 2 provided an overview of the subject. This chapter begins a more detailed treatment. It presents a discussion of the raw materials—probability, mortality, and interest concepts—of life insurance mathematics and applicable principles. Chapter 28 applies these principles to develop net premiums. Assuming an understanding of net premiums, chapter 29 examines the concepts and regulations regarding life insurance reserves and surrender values. Chapter 30 then examines the computation of a gross-premium rate structure and delves into nonguaranteed life insurance policy pricing and benefit elements. Finally, chapter 31 presents various aspects of rate making, reserving, and surplus distribution as related to health insurance.

MEASUREMENT OF RISK IN LIFE INSURANCE

Some means of scientifically measuring risk is necessary if insurance is to be priced properly. This measurement of risk lies at the foundation of any system of insurance and is possible through the application of the laws of probability.

The Laws of Probability

Three probability laws are used in life and health insurance: (1) the law of certainty, (2) the law of simple probability, and (3) the law of compound probability. The use of these principles facilitates the mathematical description of risk. The three laws may be stated as follows:

1. Certainty may be expressed by unity, or 1.
2. Simple probability, or the probability or chance that an event will occur, may be expressed by a fraction, which may take a value of from 0 to 1.
3. Compound probability, or the chance that two independent events will occur, is the product of the separate probabilities that the events, taken separately, will occur.[1]

A general statement of the method for determining **simple probability** is that the *denominator* equals the total number of equally likely possible events or exposures (e.g., lives) and the *numerator* is composed of only those instances that satisfy some stipulated condition (e.g., deaths).

The corollary that *the sum of all the separate probabilities equals 1* is based on the assumption that the events are mutually exclusive and exhaustive. Events are **mutually exclusive** if the occurrence of one of the events precludes the possibility of the occurrence of the other. For example, if a person dies at age 35, he or she clearly cannot die at age 36 or any other age. *Exhaustive* means the events under consideration cover all possibilities.

The **compound probability** that two independent events will occur equals the product of the simple probabilities that the events taken separately will happen. Suppose that two coins are tossed, and one wants to know the chance that both will fall heads up. Because the chance that each separate coin will fall heads up is one-half, the probability that *both* will fall heads up is one-quarter ($1/2 \times 1/2$).

$$\text{One Coin:} \quad \frac{\text{Desired Outcome}}{\text{All Outcomes}} = \frac{H}{H+T} = \frac{1}{2}$$

$$\text{Two Coins:} \quad \frac{\text{Desired Outcome}}{\text{All Outcomes}} = \frac{HH}{HH+HT+TH+TT} = \frac{1}{4}$$

According to the law of compound probabilities, only when two events are independent will the product of simple probabilities equal the probability that both events will occur. For the two events to be **independent,** the happening of the one must be unrelated to the occurrence of the other.

THE USE OF PROBABILITY TO FORECAST FUTURE EVENTS

These three laws of probability are useful in estimating the likelihood of future events. Future events can be foretold in one of two ways: (1) by **deductive reasoning** and (2) by **inductive reasoning.** The validity of the deductive reasoning depends on the completeness with which all the causes at work in the determination of any phenomenon are known. In the above coin-toss example, we knew by our powers of observation that the chance of a coin falling heads up was one-half. We *deduced* this. Deductive reasoning does not furnish a sound basis for insurance purposes. We cannot yet estimate loss probabilities (e.g., probabilities of death) deductively.

We can, however, estimate such probabilities inductively. This logic flows from the assumption that what has occurred in the past will occur again in the future, if the same conditions are present. Reasoning inductively does not require an analysis of the causes of phenomena to be able to predict future events.

Inductive reasoning is applied in life and health insurance. Thus, from data showing ages at death in the past, probabilities of death and of survival in the future are estimated. This prediction is based on the assumption that a *law of mortality* exists. This law

---

[1]Laws of compound probability in which the separate events are dependent do not enter into the present discussion.

holds that certain causes are in operation that determine that, out of a large group of persons, a certain proportion will die each year until all have died. It is assumed that the impact of the law of mortality would be subject to precise measurement if only the causes at work were known. It is not necessary, however, to know all the operating causes to predict fairly accurately the rate of mortality in a group of persons. By studying the rate of death within any group (if the group is sufficiently large) and noting all the circumstances that might, according to our best knowledge, affect that rate, it is possible to anticipate that any future group of persons with approximately the same set of circumstances will experience approximately the same rate of death. Thus, a working basis is available for predicting future rates of death. Mortality statistics are necessary to develop a scientific plan of life insurance.

The Law of Large Numbers

The accuracy with which the theoretical estimates approximate actual experience has important bearings on the success of any method of insuring lives. This accuracy depends on two factors: (1) the accuracy of the statistics underlying the estimates and (2) the number of units or trials taken.

With reference to the first factor, it should be obvious that accurate data are a fundamental requirement if an accurate measure of the law of mortality is to be obtained. Mortality statistics, from whatever source, should be scrutinized carefully to detect inaccuracies in the original data. Another dimension of accuracy is the presumption that future mortality experience can be reasonably approximated by past mortality experience—this is not always correct.

The second factor that determines accuracy of the estimates is the number of units or trials taken. As the number of trials is increased, the variation of actual from the probable experience decreases, and, if a very great number of trials is taken, actual and probable experience will coincide. This generalization is called the **law of large numbers.**[2] For example, if a coin were flipped 10 million times and there was exactly one-half chance that each flip would produce heads, the actual results would be so near 50 percent heads that the relative difference would be negligible. The law of large numbers is fundamental to insurance and relies on the independence assumption.

Premium rates are based on estimates of future probabilities of loss. These estimates are not valid representations of future experience unless a sufficiently large number of cases exists to guarantee that large fluctuations in results will be minimized. Prediction of future mortality rates in life insurance based on what has happened in the past can be made for a large group of persons. It cannot be made for a single individual or even a relatively small number of persons (such as 1,000). When a mortality table shows that persons of a certain age die at the rate of seven per 1,000 per year, that does not mean that out of a group of 1,000 exactly seven will die within a year, but, rather that out of a large group, containing many thousands, the deaths will occur approximately at the rate of seven per 1,000.

With reference to the prediction of future mortality rates, the law of large numbers has a double application: (1) to the database from which the statistics were drawn and (2) to the population to which the rates will be applied. Future mortality is estimated on the basis of past mortality data. The statistics used for this purpose, however, must include a sufficiently large group of representative individuals to ensure the operation of the law of large numbers. Assuming that the collected data are accurate and based on a large enough sample, they may be used to estimate future mortality. Then, in applying

---

[2]See also the discussion in chapter 2. In mathematical terminology, this statistical principle is known as *Bernoulli's theorem.*

these mortality rates, a large enough number of individuals must be involved if the actual experience in the future is to be reasonably close to the anticipated experience.

Distribution of Life Insurance Claims

Suppose that a hypothetical life insurance company insures the lives of a certain number of persons in a single year and that the probability that any one of the insureds will die that year is two in 100. The insurer expects a certain number of claims (2 percent of all the insureds), but its actual claims may be more or less than the expected number. According to the law of large numbers, if the number of insureds is large enough, the actual claims will likely show only a small relative deviation from the expected claims. Using probability theory, one can calculate the probabilities of various deviations from the expected claims, depending on the number of insureds.

Figure 27-1 shows the probability of various deviations for which the number of lives insured is 1,000, 5,000, 25,000, and 50,000. In particular, the figure shows that the probability of actual claims being within 5 percent of expected claims is 18.2 percent if 1,000 lives are insured, 39.0 percent if 5,000 lives are insured, 74.2 percent if 25,000 lives are insured, and 89.0 percent if 50,000 lives are insured. Although not shown in the chart, the probability of actual claims being within 5 percent of expected claims is greater than 99.99 percent if 1 million lives are insured.

Mortality Statistics

The establishment of any plan of insuring against death requires some means of giving mathematical values to the probabilities of death. The preceding discussion of the laws of probability demonstrated that this can be accomplished through the application of the laws of probability to mortality statistics. Mortality tables are presentations of such data organized in a form to be usable in estimating the course of future deaths.

The two basic sources of mortality statistics are:

1. population statistics derived from census enumerations and the returns of deaths from registration offices
2. statistics derived from insured lives

Both census enumerations and death registration records can contain significant error. Census data, collected by a large number of individuals through personal interviews, are particularly susceptible to error. Frequently there is misclassification of information, inaccurate information is provided by the respondents either willfully or inadvertently, tabulation errors creep in, and, not infrequently, ages are reported as unknown. Public records of death are frequently incomplete and inaccurate.

On the other hand, the mortality statistics of insured lives tend to be quite accurate. The nature of the insurance process leads to a careful recording of the date of birth, sex, and date of death of insured individuals. This facilitates derivation of accurate death rates for the various age and sex classifications.

The mortality experience among insured lives is significantly different from that of the general population because most insured lives have been subjected to an insurer's underwriting process. Virtually all mortality tables used today by life insurers are based on the experience of insured lives.

Mortality Table Construction

The theory of probability is applied in life insurance through the use of a mathematical model known as a mortality table. A **mortality table** represents a record of mortality observed in the past and is arranged so as to show the probabilities of death and survival at each separate age. It shows a hypothetical group of individuals beginning with a cer-

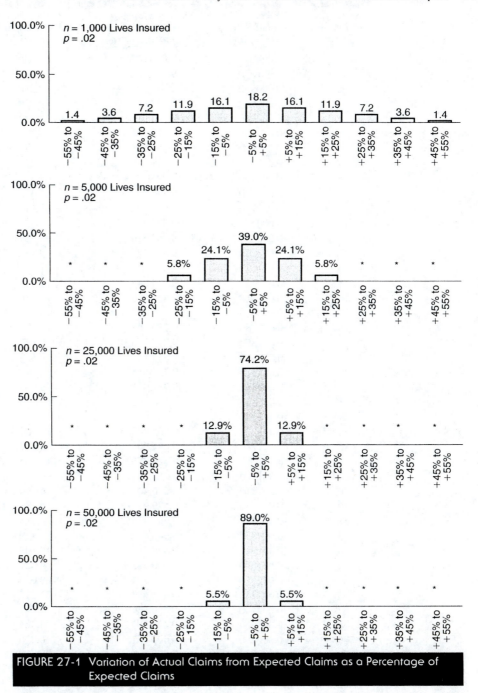

FIGURE 27-1 Variation of Actual Claims from Expected Claims as a Percentage of Expected Claims

*Probabilities are less than 1 percent.

tain age and traces the history of the entire group year by year until all have died. Because any description will best be understood by reference to an actual table, the U.S. *Commissioners 1980 Standard Ordinary Table of Mortality* (*1980 CSO Table*) for males is presented in Table 27-1.

Age (x) at Beginning of Year	Yearly Probability of Dying (q_x)	Number Living at Beginning of Designated Year (l_x)	Number Dying during Designated Year (d_x)	Yearly Probability of Surviving (p_x)
0	0.004180	10,000,000	41,800	0.995820
1	0.001070	9,958,200	10,655	0.998930
2	0.000990	9,947,545	9,848	0.999010
3	0.000980	9,937,697	9,739	0.999020
4	0.000950	9,927,958	9,432	0.999050
5	0.000900	9,918,526	8,927	0.999100
6	0.000860	9,909,599	8,522	0.999140
7	0.000800	9,901,077	7,921	0.999200
8	0.000760	9,893,156	7,519	0.999240
9	0.000740	9,885,637	7,315	0.999260
10	0.000730	9,878,322	7,211	0.999270
11	0.000770	9,871,111	7,601	0.999230
12	0.000850	9,863,510	8,384	0.999150
13	0.000990	9,855,126	9,757	0.999010
14	0.001150	9,845,369	11,322	0.998850
15	0.001330	9,834,047	13,079	0.998670
16	0.001510	9,820,968	14,830	0.998490
17	0.001670	9,806,138	16,376	0.998330
18	0.001780	9,789,762	17,426	0.998220
19	0.001860	9,772,336	18,177	0.998140
20	0.001900	9,754,159	18,533	0.998100
21	0.001910	9,735,626	18,595	0.998090
22	0.001890	9,717,031	18,365	0.998110
23	0.001860	9,698,666	18,040	0.998140
24	0.001820	9,680,626	17,619	0.998180
25	0.001770	9,663,007	17,104	0.998230
26	0.001730	9,645,903	16,687	0.998270
27	0.001710	9,629,216	16,466	0.998290
28	0.001700	9,612,750	16,342	0.998300
29	0.001710	9,596,408	16,410	0.998290
30	0.001730	9,579,998	16,573	0.998270
31	0.001780	9,563,425	17,023	0.998220
32	0.001830	9,546,402	17,470	0.998170
33	0.001910	9,528,932	18,200	0.998090
34	0.002000	9,510,732	19,021	0.998000
35	0.002110	9,491,711	20,028	0.997890
36	0.002240	9,471,683	21,217	0.997760
37	0.002400	9,450,466	22,681	0.997600
38	0.002580	9,427,785	24,324	0.997420
39	0.002790	9,403,461	26,236	0.997210
40	0.003020	9,377,225	28,319	0.996980
41	0.003290	9,348,906	30,758	0.996710
42	0.003560	9,318,148	33,173	0.996440
43	0.003870	9,284,975	35,933	0.996130
44	0.004190	9,249,042	38,753	0.995810
45	0.004550	9,210,289	41,907	0.995450
46	0.004920	9,168,382	45,108	0.995080
47	0.005320	9,123,274	48,536	0.994680
48	0.005740	9,074,738	52,089	0.994260
49	0.006210	9,022,649	56,031	0.993790

TABLE 27-1 *(cont.)*

Age (x) at Beginning of Year	Yearly Probability of Dying (q_x)	Number Living at Beginning of Designated Year (l_x)	Number Dying during Designated Year (d_x)	Yearly Probability of Surviving (p_x)
50	0.006710	8,966,618	60,166	0.993290
51	0.007300	8,906,452	65,017	0.992700
52	0.007960	8,841,435	70,378	0.992040
53	0.008710	8,771,057	76,396	0.991290
54	0.009560	8,694,661	83,121	0.990440
55	0.010470	8,611,540	90,163	0.989530
56	0.011460	8,521,377	97,655	0.988540
57	0.012490	8,423,722	105,212	0.987510
58	0.013590	8,318,510	113,049	0.986410
59	0.014770	8,205,461	121,195	0.985230
60	0.016080	8,084,266	129,995	0.983920
61	0.017540	7,954,271	139,518	0.982460
62	0.019190	7,814,753	149,965	0.980810
63	0.021060	7,664,788	161,420	0.978940
64	0.023140	7,503,368	173,628	0.976860
65	0.025420	7,329,740	186,322	0.974580
66	0.027850	7,143,418	198,944	0.972150
67	0.030440	6,944,474	211,390	0.969560
68	0.033190	6,773,084	223,471	0.966810
69	0.036170	6,509,613	235,453	0.963830
70	0.039510	6,274,160	247,892	0.960490
71	0.043300	6,026,268	260,937	0.956700
72	0.047650	5,765,331	274,718	0.952350
73	0.052640	5,490,613	289,026	0.947360
74	0.058190	5,201,587	302,680	0.941810
75	0.064190	4,898,907	314,461	0.935810
76	0.070530	4,584,446	323,341	0.929470
77	0.077120	4,261,105	328,616	0.922880
78	0.083900	3,932,489	329,936	0.916100
79	0.091050	3,602,553	328,012	0.908950
80	0.098840	3,274,541	323,656	0.901160
81	0.107480	2,950,885	317,161	0.892520
82	0.117250	2,633,724	308,804	0.882750
83	0.128260	2,324,920	298,194	0.871740
84	0.140250	2,026,726	284,248	0.859750
85	0.152950	1,742,478	266,512	0.847050
86	0.166090	1,475,966	245,143	0.833910
87	0.179550	1,230,823	220,994	0.820450
88	0.193270	1,009,829	195,170	0.806730
89	0.207290	814,659	168,871	0.792710
90	0.221770	645,788	143,216	0.778230
91	0.236980	502,572	119,100	0.763020
92	0.253450	383,472	97,191	0.746550
93	0.272110	286,281	77,900	0.727890
94	0.295900	208,381	61,660	0.704100
95	0.329960	146,721	48,412	0.670040
96	0.384550	98,309	37,805	0.615450
97	0.480200	60,504	29,054	0.519800
98	0.657980	31,450	20,693	0.342020
99	1.000000	10,757	10,757	0.000000

Overview

The heart of the mortality table is the column "Yearly Probability of Dying," with the yearly probability of surviving being simply 1 minus the probability of dying. The other essential features of a mortality table are the two columns of the "Number Living" and the "Number Dying" at designated ages.

It will prove helpful to introduce some standard actuarial notation to simplify later discussion. These include:

$$x = \text{age}$$
$$l_x = \text{number living at age } x$$
$$d_x = \text{number of individuals age } x \text{ dying within one year}$$
$$= l_x - l_{x+1}$$
$$q_x = \text{probability of individuals age } x \text{ dying within one year}$$
$$= d_x \div l_x$$
$$p_x = \text{probability of individuals age } x \text{ surviving one year}$$
$$= l_{x+1} \div l_x$$

A person of any age will either die or survive that year. Thus, it can be seen for any age,

$$q_x + p_x = 1 \tag{1}$$

Moreover, it should be noted that each d_x and l_x is related as follows:

$$l_{x+1} = l_x - d_x \tag{2}$$

In other words, the number of persons living at any age $x + 1$ (l_{x+1}) can be found simply by subtracting the number dying (d_x) in the previous year from the number who were alive at the beginning of the previous year (l_x).

In the case of the *1980 CSO Table,* it is assumed that a group of 10 million males (l_0) come under observation at exactly the same moment as they begin the first year of life (age 0).[3] Of this group, 41,800 die ($d_0 = 10,000,000 \times 0.00418$) during the year, leaving 9,958,200 lives (l_1) to begin the second year. (Applying formula 2, $l_0 - d_0 = l_1$ or 10,000,000 − 41,800 = 9,958,200.) The table proceeds in this manner to record the number dying in each year of life and the number living at the beginning of each succeeding year, until only 10,757 of the original group are found to be alive by age 99, and these 10,757 die during that year.

Derivation of Death Rates

It is impossible for any insurance company to insure a group of several million persons of exactly the same age and sex and at exactly the same time. It would also be impossible to keep any such group under observation until all died because some persons would voluntarily terminate their policies. Insurance policies are written at all times of the year and on lives at various ages. It is possible, however, for one insurer or a group of insurers to keep a record of all insured lives, showing at each age the number of persons under observation and the number who die. If a sufficient volume of data is collected showing (1) the ages at which persons come under observation and (2) the number of each sex dying at each age, a mortality table may be constructed.

---

[3]The *1980 CSO Table* has separate tables for male and female lives. The illustrations throughout this mathematical discussion are based on male lives, but the reader should note that a distinction by sex and smokers is made in the actuarial processes employed by most companies. There are also composite tables, and some companies adjust the rates to an age-last birthday or age-nearest birthday basis.

Suppose, for illustration, that the following data have been collected for female lives:

Age	Number of Life-Years Observed	Number of Dying during Year
0 to 1	10,000	80
1 to 2	30,000	90
2 to 3	150,000	600
3 to 4	80,000	360

From these figures, death rates may be computed for the respective ages in the following manner:[4]

Age	Rate of Death Expressed as a Fraction	Rate of Death Expressed as a Decimal
0	80/10,000	0.0080
1	90/30,000	0.0030
2	600/150,000	0.0040
3	360/80,000	0.0045

The rate of mortality (q_x) at any given age is the quotient of the number of deaths by the end of one year (d_x) and the corresponding exposure at the beginning of the year (l_x).[5] The rate represents the probability that a person who has just attained a given age will die before he or she attains the next age. The rate of mortality is usually expressed in terms of the number of deaths per thousand.

A mortality table may be constructed by using an arbitrary number of persons, known as the **radix,** assumed to be alive at a given age, usually the youngest age for which death rates are available, and successively applying the mortality rates at each higher age. Applying the death rates developed previously to an arbitrary radix of 10 million will illustrate the process:

(1) Age (x)	(2) Number Living at Given Age (l_x)	(3) Mortality Rate for Given Age (q_x)	(4) Number of Deaths before Next Age [(2) × (3)] (d_x)	(5) Number Living at Next Age [(2) – (4)] (l_{x+1})
0	10,000,000	0.0080	80,000	9,920,000
1	9,920,000	0.0030	29,760	9,890,240
2	9,890,240	0.0040	39,561	9,850,679
3	9,850,679	0.0045	44,328	9,806,351

---

[4] If the period of observation is more than one year, which it usually is, the number under observation is adjusted to reflect this fact. Thus, if the period of observation were five years, one individual under observation would be observed at five successive ages, unless he or she died or the policy lapsed during the period. The deaths occurring at each age are compared with the total "exposure" at that age.

[5] The distinction between *mortality rates*, as the rates here are called, and *probabilities of death* is one of preciseness of attained age. For purposes of simplification here, death rates and probabilities of death are assumed to be identical. For the construction of a mortality table, probabilities of death are necessary; they refer to rates of dying among a group of persons who have just attained a certain age of life. See Robert W. Batten, *Mortality Table Construction* (Englewood Cliffs, NJ: Prentice-Hall, Inc., 1978).

Because the probability of dying at age 0 is assumed to be 0.0080, 80,000 deaths are expected during the year among the 10 million starting at age 0. This leaves 9,920,000 of the group to begin age 1. These die at the rate of three per thousand (0.0030), yielding 29,760 deaths during the year. In this way, the original 10 million are reduced in number by deaths year after year until all have died. This is the basis for the statement that the mortality table represents "a (hypothetical) generation of individuals passing through time."

Because the radix of the table is arbitrary, the numbers in the columns headed "Number Living" and "Number of Deaths" are not significant in and of themselves.[6] They simply reflect the series of death rates (q_x), the real heart of a mortality table.

Sometimes a mortality table has an additional column showing the "expectation of life" or "life expectancy" at each age. The figure in this column opposite any age is the average number of full years of life lived after attaining that age by all who reach that age, and is calculated from the following formula:

$$e_x = \sum_{t=1}^{w-x-1} \frac{l_{x+t}}{l_x}$$

where

e_x = life expectancy for an individual age x

w = terminal age of the mortality table being used

Expectation of life can be a misleading term, as it has no significance for any individual. The probable future lifetime of any person depends on many factors, including his or her state of health, and may be longer or shorter than average. It is commonly supposed that life insurance companies base premium rate calculations on the assumption that everyone will live for the period of his or her life expectancy. This is not the case, as explained later in chapters 28 and 30.[7]

Adjustments to Mortality Data

The mortality tables used by life insurers in calculating premium rates, reserves, and cash values often do not reflect the precise mortality rates developed from the basic mortality data. Because the volume of experience is not uniform at all ages and is insufficient to provide completely creditable or reliable statistics, two types of adjustments may be made to the derived rates: (1) In a process called **graduation** the rates are smoothed into a curve, and (2) a margin may be added to the rates in the derived curve.

Graduation is performed to eliminate the irregularities in the observed data that are believed not to be true characteristics of the universe from which the sample experience was extracted. One of several methods of graduation is used, depending upon the data involved and the purpose of the computation. The objective in all cases, however, is to introduce smoothness and regularity, while preserving the basic characteristics of the observed values.

---

[6]For the *American Experience Table,* the radix was 100,000 at age 10; for the *1941 CSO Table,* it was 1 million at age 1; for the *1958 CSO Table,* 10 million at age 0; and for the *1980 CSO Table,* it is 10 million at age 0.

[7]This discussion relates to the curtate expectation of life (e_x), which counts only full years of future lifetime. There is also a complete expectation of life, approximately one-half year longer, that recognizes the final fractional year of life.

When derived rates will be used as a valuation mortality table, a *margin* may be added to them; it is added in the interest of conservatism (see chapter 29). In a mortality table used to value life policy liabilities, this means showing higher death rates than those actually expected. In an annuity valuation table, it means showing lower rates of mortality than those expected. Thus, the *1980 CSO Table* as a life insurance valuation table had margins added to the underlying mortality rates. Margins may also be provided by adjusting the underlying data prior to the derivation of the basic rates themselves. The insertion of these margins enhances the security of life insurance contracts and is considered a sound practice.

Types of Mortality Tables

Valuation versus Basic Tables

A **valuation mortality table** is used as the basis for calculating minimum reserves and cash surrender values. As noted earlier, these tables usually contain margins that render them conservative. The use of such tables is prescribed by law.

Valuation tables may also be used for gross-premium calculation for participating, indeterminate premium, and current assumption policies. In such cases, the dividend scale or current mortality charges are based on a basic table.

A **basic mortality table** reflects the actual experience of the population from which it was drawn. No margins are added to such tables. Basic tables are commonly used for:

1. calculation of gross-premium rates
2. development of current mortality charges for universal life and other current assumption policies
3. development of dividend scales and actual dividend payments on participating policies
4. mortality studies of the insurer's own experience, especially in identifying trends
5. financial statements prepared under generally accepted accounting principles (see chapter 34)
6. asset share, model office, and other financial studies and projections

Select, Ultimate, and Aggregate Tables

Mortality tables may be classified as *select*, *ultimate*, and *aggregate*. These terms relate to the extent to which the data used have been affected by the underwriting process. As discussed in chapter 4, insured lives, having passed the necessary requirements before becoming insured, show a lower rate of mortality than lives not subject to such scrutiny. Thus, the number of deaths occurring among 10,000 insureds aged 40 who have just passed a medical examination can be expected to be lower than among 10,000 persons aged 40 who were first insured at age 30 and have been insured for 10 years. It is important, therefore, for an insurer in estimating the probable mortality to know whether it has a large number of newly selected lives.

A **select mortality table** is based on data of newly insured lives only. An **ultimate mortality table** excludes these early data—usually the first 5 to 15 years following entry—and is based on the ultimate mortality among insured lives in later policy years. The *1980 CSO Table* shown in Table 27-1 is an ultimate table. Because insurers and their regulators are usually interested in establishing conservative reserve estimates, it is generally considered safer for an insurer to compute reserve liabilities on the basis of the mortality among risks for whom the benefits of fresh medical selection have passed. An **aggregate mortality table** includes all the mortality data, the early years following entry as well as the later ones.

A select mortality table shows rates of mortality by both age and duration of insurance. Because the greatest effect of selection generally wears off in 5 to 15 years, the mortality rates are usually differentiated by duration only for such a period. An example of a select mortality table (not based on the *1980 CSO Table*) is presented in Table 27-2. The blocked ages show how the mortality rates vary by duration even though each is aged 30. The rates shown in column "6 and Over" constitute the ultimate mortality level and could be used in the development of an ultimate mortality table.

Select tables are used for purposes of analysis and comparison. The basic tables prepared and published by the Mortality Committee of the Society of Actuaries from data supplied by a group of established insurers are constructed to show both select and ultimate mortality because their primary purpose is to reflect mortality trends.

The mortality tables used in determining participating life insurance premiums usually are ultimate tables. Select mortality is frequently used in asset-share calculations, in dividend and other nonguaranteed element calculations, and in the calculation of nonparticipating gross premiums.

Mortality Tables for Annuities

A mortality table based on life insurance experience is not suitable for use in connection with annuities for several reasons. One reason is that annuities generally are not purchased by individuals in poor health. At the higher ages (particularly in the case of annuity contracts purchased by single premiums for immediate income), the rates of mortality experienced among annuitants generally are lower than among insureds under life insurance policies. A life insurance mortality table would overstate expected mortality rates.

Another important reason is that the constant improvement in mortality rates (offset periodically by developments such as AIDS) provides a gradually increasing margin of safety for life insurance but has the opposite result for annuities. In fact, it is recognized that no annuity mortality table based on past experience can be used safely. What is needed is a table that shows the (lower) rates of mortality anticipated in the future rather than the rates that have been experienced in the past. Such a table is known as a **table with projection.**

Static Tables versus Tables with Projection

Historically, most life insurance mortality tables used were **static tables** in that they did not provide for changes in their rates depending on the calendar year to which they applied. As the secular trend toward mortality improvement has continued, these static

TABLE 27-2	Select and Ultimate Mortality Table Rates Per (1,000)						
			Year of Insurance				
Age at Issue	1	2	3	4	5	6 and Over	Attained Age
25	0.71	0.82	0.88	0.93	0.97	1.01	30
26	0.72	0.82	0.89	0.96	1.00	1.06	31
27	0.73	0.83	0.92	0.99	1.05	1.12	32
28	0.74	0.84	0.93	1.03	1.11	1.21	33
29	0.74	0.84	0.97	1.08	1.20	1.32	34
30	0.74	0.86	1.02	1.16	1.31	1.44	35

tables have periodically been replaced by other static tables based on more recent experience. In recent years, many companies made some provision for their expectation that underlying mortality improves with time and are not using static tables. The improvement in mortality has led to increasing margins in life insurance premiums because the postponement in death payments enables insurers to earn additional interest on their invested funds and to collect additional premiums. In participating policies as well as indeterminate premium and current assumption nonparticipating policies, these gains can be credited to policyowners via enhanced dividends or other nonguaranteed payments or benefits.

The situation has been just the reverse in connection with annuity contracts, in which improving mortality has led to smaller margins. Postponement of death has led to additional annuity payments. To avoid the large expense of frequently constructing new static tables, the traditional practice was to make an allowance for the decrease in mortality rates by using age setbacks; that is, the static table was still used, but the rates shown in the table were assumed to be those that apply to lower actual ages. For example, a 65-year-old person may be assumed to be subject to the mortality rates of a person of 64 or 63, thus increasing the premium for a given amount of annuity income. Setbacks of from one to four years are used by many annuity companies.

Annuity tables used today usually contain projection factors on different bases that can be applied to the basic table to make allowance for future reductions in mortality rates. For example, suppose that the mortality rate for 65-year-olds is expected to improve at the rate of 1 percent per calendar year. The projected mortality rate for 65-year-olds in some future calendar year, say, $CY + N$, can be calculated from the mortality rate in an earlier calendar year, CY, by the following formula:

$$q_{65}^{CY+N} = q_{65}^{CY}(1 - 0.01)^N$$

The importance of providing for mortality improvement in annuity mortality tables can be seen in the fact that annuity business constitutes a majority and growing proportion of most life insurance companies' total business. (Annuity business includes, in addition to individual annuities, group annuities and settlement option arrangements.) The need is particularly critical in the case of variable annuity products both because of the growing proportion of such business, and the fact that there is no interest margin to help offset mortality losses that develop.

Smoker versus Nonsmoker Tables

Separate basic and valuation mortality tables have been developed for smokers and nonsmokers in recognition of the substantial mortality differences between the two groups. Figure 27-2 illustrates the relative mortality differences between smokers and nonsmokers for one large U.S. reinsurer. It also shows the life expectancy for each category of smoker. (Conversely, a company recently announced that it has an annuity product with higher benefit payments for smokers than for nonsmokers.)

Published Tables in Use Today

A multitude of mortality tables are used today. The ones discussed next are used chiefly for purposes of valuing U.S. insurers' policy liabilities and establishing minimum acceptable surrender values but not for rate making.

Life Insurance Tables   The *Commissioners 1941 Standard Ordinary Table of Mortality* (*1941 CSO Table*) was used extensively for U.S. policies issued between 1948 and 1966. The *1941 CSO Table* is still important because much outstanding insurance is based on

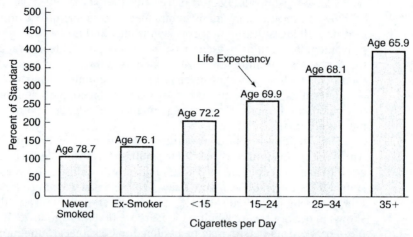

FIGURE 27-2 Mortality and Life Expectancy Comparisons of Smokers and Nonsmokers

Source: Lincoln National Reinsurance Company.

this table. For many years prior to the advent of the *1941 CSO Table,* the *American Experience Table of Mortality* was widely used.[8]

The *Commissioners 1958 Standard Ordinary Mortality Table* (*1958 CSO Table*) was developed by the U.S. Society of Actuaries from the combined ultimate mortality experience of 15 large insurers between 1950 and 1954. At one time it was required that the *1958 CSO Table* be used as the basis for minimum reserves and nonforfeiture values in all states. In the mid-1980s, the *1980 CSO Table* (discussed later) replaced the *1958 CSO Table* as the mandatory table.

The latest U.S. ordinary life tables are the *Commissioners 1980 Standard Ordinary Mortality Tables (1980 CSO Tables)*, with separate versions for males and females.[9] These tables reflect a decline in mortality rates at most ages from those in the *1958 CSO Table.* The *1980 CSO Table,* however, reflects a slight increase in male mortality rates in the late teenage years. This increase results in higher 1980 male mortality rates at some ages, relative to the 1958 rates. The increases in male mortality rates during the late teenage years result in *declining* male mortality rates between ages 21 and 28 in the *1980 CSO Table.* By contrast, the 1980 female mortality rates always increase with age after about age 10, as is true in most other mortality tables.

The latest U.S. mortality table for industrial insurance is the *1961 Commissioners Standard Industrial (CSI) Mortality Table.* Use of the *1961 CSI Table* was mandatory for

---

[8]Although of little practical significance, it is historically interesting to note that the *Actuaries'* or *Seventeen Offices Table,* which in large measure preceded the *American Experience Table*, was of British origin and introduced into the United States by Elizur Wright as the standard for the valuation of policies in Massachusetts.

[9]Other *1980 CSO Tables* exist. Because of the interest in some states in gender-neutral rating and reserving, there are various merged-gender tables. Also, a 10-year select *1980 CSO Table* exists as well as a table for extended term insurance (the *1980 CET Table*). The CSO select table is based on the same ultimate data as underlie the regular *1980 CSO Tables.* The mortality rates vary not only with age and sex, but also with the number of elapsed years since the policy was issued. Finally, there is a set of nonsmoker/smoker *1980 CSO Tables.* These tables can be used in states that permit reserving and surrender value differences between smokers and nonsmokers.

computing minimum reserves and nonforfeiture values for industrial policies issued after 1967. There also is a table for use with group life insurance—the *Commissioners 1960 Standard Group Mortality Table.*

Annuity tables The *1937 Standard Annuity Table* formerly was used extensively for U.S. individual annuity business. The steady improvement in mortality led to the development of the *Annuity Table for 1949*, which introduced projection factors to reflect continued improvement in mortality rates. The *1955 American Annuity Table* was developed to provide reasonable rates for annual-premium deferred annuities and life income settlement options. The *Group Annuity Table for 1951* was the first table based on the experience of group annuitants and was widely used in computing rates and reserves for group annuities.

When interest rates increased to levels substantially higher than the level used in determining minimum reserves, new annuity business created a surplus strain for life insurance companies (see chapter 29). In 1971, two new mortality tables, the *1971 Group Annuity Table* and the *1971 Individual Annuity Table,* were developed to be used with the higher interest rates in setting reserves. Two new projection scales for males and one for females were also designed for use with the *1971 Group Annuity Table.*

In 1983, two further annuity mortality tables were adopted by the NAIC and are in use throughout the United States. The *1983 Individual Annuity Mortality Table for Males (1983 Table-a)* is for reserve and nonforfeiture purposes on individual annuity business—(Table 27-3)—and the other applies to group business (the *1983 GAM Table*). Figure 27-3 illustrates the mortality levels and slopes of the *1980 CSO Table* (male) and the *1983 Table-a* (for annuity mortality—males).

There has been growing concern over the adequacy of the *1983 Individual Mortality Table* as a valuation standard.[10] There is considerable interest and need for a comprehensive study of annuitant mortality. In the interim, *The Annuity 2000 Basic Mortality Table* (projected from the 1983 table) has been endorsed by the Society of Actuaries as a suitable basis for the statutory valuation of individual annuity business written in the United States.

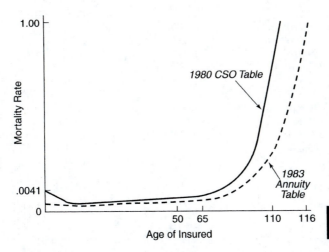

FIGURE 27-3 Graphs of Two Mortality Tables

---

[10]Robert J. Johansen, "Review of the Adequacy of 1983 Individual Annuity Mortality Table," *Transactions of the Society of Actuaries,* Vol. XLVII (1995), pp. 211–249.

TABLE 27-3 1983 Individual Annuity Mortality Table (Male Lives)

Age (x) at Beginning of Year	Number Living at Beginning of Year (l_x)	Number Dying during Year (d_x)	Yearly Probability of Dying (q_x)	Yearly Probability of Surviving (p_x)
5	10,000,000	3,770	0.000377	0.999623
6	9,996,230	3,499	0.000350	0.999650
7	9,992,731	3,328	0.000333	0.999667
8	9,989,403	3,516	0.000352	0.999648
9	9,985,887	3,675	0.000368	0.999632
10	9,982,212	3,813	0.000382	0.999618
11	9,978,399	3,931	0.000394	0.999606
12	9,974,468	4,040	0.000405	0.999595
13	9,970,428	4,138	0.000415	0.999585
14	9,966,290	4,236	0.000425	0.999575
15	9,962,054	4,333	0.000435	0.999565
16	9,957,721	4,441	0.000446	0.999554
17	9,953,280	4,559	0.000458	0.999542
18	9,948,721	4,696	0.000472	0.999528
19	9,944,025	4,853	0.000488	0.999512
20	9,939,172	5,019	0.000505	0.999495
21	9,934,153	5,215	0.000525	0.999475
22	9,928,938	5,421	0.000546	0.999454
23	9,923,517	5,656	0.000570	0.999430
24	9,917,861	5,911	0.000596	0.999404
25	9,911,950	6,165	0.000622	0.999378
26	9,905,785	6,439	0.000650	0.999350
27	9,899,346	6,702	0.000677	0.999323
28	9,892,644	6,964	0.000704	0.999296
29	9,885,680	7,226	0.000731	0.999269
30	9,878,454	7,498	0.000759	0.999241
31	9,870,956	7,759	0.000786	0.999214
32	9,863,197	8,029	0.000814	0.999186
33	9,855,168	8,308	0.000843	0.999157
34	9,846,860	8,626	0.000876	0.999124
35	9,838,234	9,022	0.000917	0.999083
36	9,829,212	9,515	0.000968	0.999032
37	9,819,697	10,134	0.001032	0.998968
38	9,809,563	10,928	0.001114	0.998886
39	9,798,635	11,915	0.001216	0.998784
40	9,786,720	13,124	0.001341	0.998659
41	9,773,596	14,582	0.001492	0.998508
42	9,759,014	16,327	0.001673	0.998327
43	9,742,687	18,375	0.001886	0.998114
44	9,724,312	20,703	0.002129	0.997871
45	9,703,609	23,279	0.002399	0.997601
46	9,680,330	26,069	0.002693	0.997307
47	9,654,261	29,050	0.003009	0.996991
48	9,625,211	32,177	0.003343	0.996657
49	9,593,034	35,437	0.003694	0.996306
50	9,557,597	38,775	0.004057	0.995943
51	9,518,822	42,178	0.004431	0.995569
52	9,476,644	45,602	0.004812	0.995188
53	9,431,042	49,023	0.005198	0.994802
54	9,382,019	52,455	0.005591	0.994409
55	9,329,564	55,921	0.005994	0.994006
56	9,273,643	59,435	0.006409	0.993591
57	9,214,208	63,016	0.006839	0.993161
58	9,151,192	66,712	0.007290	0.992710
59	9,084,480	70,695	0.007782	0.992218
60	9,013,785	75,157	0.008338	0.991662

TABLE 27-3 *(cont.)*

Age (x) at Beginning of Year	Number Living at Beginning of Year (l_x)	Number Dying during Year (d_x)	Yearly Probability of Dying (q_x)	Yearly Probability of Surviving (p_x)
61	8,938,628	80,296	0.008983	0.991017
62	8,858,332	86,280	0.009740	0.990260
63	8,772,052	93,247	0.010630	0.989370
64	8,678,805	101,230	0.011664	0.988336
65	8,577,575	110,230	0.012851	0.987149
66	8,467,345	120,228	0.014199	0.985801
67	8,347,117	131,192	0.015717	0.984283
68	8,215,925	143,072	0.017414	0.982586
69	8,072,853	155,774	0.019296	0.980704
70	7,917,079	169,196	0.021371	0.978629
71	7,747,883	183,214	0.023647	0.976353
72	7,564,669	197,672	0.026131	0.973869
73	7,366,997	212,427	0.028835	0.971165
74	7,154,570	227,472	0.031794	0.968206
75	6,927,098	242,767	0.035046	0.964954
76	6,684,331	258,222	0.038631	0.961369
77	6,426,109	273,669	0.042587	0.957413
78	6,152,440	288,863	0.046951	0.953049
79	5,863,577	303,469	0.051755	0.948245
80	5,560,108	317,071	0.057026	0.942974
81	5,243,037	329,216	0.062791	0.937209
82	4,913,821	339,452	0.069081	0.930919
83	4,574,369	347,231	0.075908	0.924092
84	4,227,138	351,825	0.083230	0.916770
85	3,875,313	352,603	0.090987	0.909013
86	3,522,710	349,178	0.099122	0.900878
87	3,173,532	341,399	0.107577	0.892423
88	2,832,133	329,422	0.116316	0.883684
89	2,502,711	313,825	0.125394	0.874606
90	2,188,886	295,252	0.134887	0.865113
91	1,893,634	274,336	0.144873	0.855127
92	1,619,298	251,686	0.155429	0.844571
93	1,367,612	227,884	0.166629	0.833371
94	1,139,728	203,484	0.178537	0.821463
95	936,244	179,023	0.191214	0.808786
96	757,221	155,019	0.204721	0.795279
97	602,202	131,955	0.219121	0.780879
98	470,247	110,383	0.234734	0.765266
99	359,864	90,646	0.251890	0.748110
100	269,218	72,933	0.270907	0.729093
101	196,285	57,337	0.292111	0.707889
102	138,948	43,883	0.315823	0.684177
103	95,065	32,548	0.342376	0.657624
104	62,517	23,262	0.372091	0.627909
105	39,255	15,909	0.405273	0.594727
106	23,346	10,325	0.442260	0.557740
107	13,021	6,294	0.483373	0.516627
108	6,727	3,559	0.529062	0.470938
109	3,168	1,835	0.579230	0.420770
110	1,333	846	0.634659	0.365341
111	487	339	0.696099	0.303901
112	148	113	0.763514	0.236486
113	35	29	0.828571	0.171429
114	6	5	0.833333	0.166667
115	1	1	1.000000	0.000000

Application of the Laws of Probabilities to Mortality

Earlier in this chapter the statement was made that risk in life insurance is measured by the application of the laws of probability to the mortality table. Now that these laws are understood and the mortality table has been explained, a few simple illustrations may be used to show this application.

Suppose that it is desired to estimate the probability of a man's death within one, two, and five years from age 35. This probability, according to the laws explained earlier, is determined according to a chosen mortality table and is a fraction, the denominator of which equals the number living at age 35 and the numerator of which is the number that have died during the one, two, and five years, respectively, following that age. According to the *1980 CSO Table*, 9,491,711 men are living at age 35 and 20,028 die before the end of the year. Hence, the probability of death within one year is:

$$q_{35} = \frac{d_{35}}{l_{35}} = \frac{20,028}{9,491,711} = 0.00211$$

During the two years following the stated age, there are 20,028 + 21,217 deaths for a total of 41,245. Therefore, the probability of dying within two years (represented by $_2q_{35}$) is:

$$_2q_{35} = \frac{d_{35} + d_{36}}{l_{35}} = \frac{41,245}{9,491,711} = 0.00435$$

Similarly, the total number of deaths within five years is 114,486 (20,028 + 21,217 + 22,681 + 24,324 + 26,236). Thus, the probability that a man entering age 35 will die within five years ($_5q_{35}$) is:

$$_5q_{35} = \frac{d_{35} + d_{36} + d_{37} + d_{38} + d_{39}}{l_{35}} = \frac{114,486}{9,491,711} = 0.01206$$

Note that this last expression could be simplified as follows:

$$_5q_{35} = \frac{l_{35} - l_{40}}{l_{35}}$$

where the difference between the number living at age 35 (l_{35}) and at age 40 (l_{40}) equals the number who died during this five-year interval.

Probabilities of survival can also be expressed by the table. The chance of living at least one year following age 35 (p_{35}) will be a fraction, the denominator of which is the number living at age 35 and the numerator of which is the number that have lived one year following the specified age (i.e., to age 36). Thus,

$$p_{35} = \frac{l_{36}}{l_{35}} = \frac{9,471,683}{9,491,711} = 0.99789$$

The discussion in the following chapters utilizes the *1980 CSO Table* in illustrating the principles involved in rate making. As emphasized in chapter 2, the *1980 CSO Table* is not, however, used by life insurance companies as the primary basis for establishing premium rates. They use tables reflecting up-to-date experience (often based upon the insurer's own most recent experience) in establishing premium rates. The *1980 CSO Table* is used for reserve valuation and nonforfeiture-value purposes.

UNDERLYING PRINCIPLES

Interest

As pointed out in chapter 2, prefunding for life insurance protection via either a fixed, level premium or a flexible premium can lead to the accumulation of large sums of money, which are often held by insurers for many years before being used to pay benefits. The funds, in large part, are invested in income-producing assets, whose earnings permit life insurance companies to charge lower premiums than otherwise would be the case. Because interest plays such a vital role in the actuarial calculations and the actual operations of a life insurance company, it is essential to consider some of the more important concepts relating to it.

Terminology

Interest may be defined as the price paid for the use of money. The original investment, referred to as the *principal amount* or simply *principal,* accumulates by the end of a specified term to a sum referred to as the *accumulated amount.* The interest earned for this particular period is the simple difference between the accumulated amount and the principal.

Abbreviations are commonly used in dealing with interest. Some of the most common ones are:

$$I \ = \text{interest amount}$$
$$S \ = \text{accumulated amount}$$
$$A = \text{principal amount, or present value}$$
$$i \ = \text{interest rate}$$
$$n \ = \text{number of compounding periods, often expressed in years}$$

Using these abbreviations, the statement that an accumulated amount is equal to the principal amount plus interest may be expressed as $S = A + I$. The statement that interest is equal to the principal times the rate per annum may be expressed as $I = Ai$. By rewriting the statement for accumulated amount, one obtains $S = A + Ai$, or $S = A(1 + i)$. The equation $S = A(1 + i)$ states that the amount to which the principal will accumulate in one year at a given interest rate is equal to the principal multiplied by the sum of 1 plus the interest rate.

Interest that is credited or paid only on the original principal is described as *simple interest.* In many cases, as is the case for life insurance calculations, interest earnings will be left with the original principal also to earn interest. When interest is not distributed but used to earn additional funds, it is described as **compound interest.**

Compound Interest Functions

Four basic compound interest functions are used in insurance mathematics. An understanding of these functions is important for anyone interested in insurance or any other area of finance.

Accumulated Value of 1 The amount to which a principal will accumulate in one year at a given rate per annum has been expressed as $S_1 = A(1 + i)$. If this amount were invested for an additional year, the interest for the second year would be i times S_1. The amount at the end of the second year could then be expressed as:

$$S_2 = S_1 + iS_1$$
$$= S_1(1 + i)$$
$$= A(1 + i)^2 \ [\text{using } S_1 = A(1 + i)]$$

By continuing to use simple algebra, the accumulated value of A at the end of n years may be expressed as $S = A(1 + i)^n$. Because interest tables show the value for a principal of 1, the values $(1 + i)^n$ may be found in the appropriate interest table and multiplied by the principal amount to determine the future value. Appendix 1 in this chapter provides such compound interest factors at various interest rates. More efficient than the use of such tables is the rapid result provided by a basic handheld calculator.

Present Value of 1   In all financial areas, it is often necessary to provide a set amount of money at the end of some specified period of time. To achieve this goal, a sum of money is invested today. The principal that must be invested now to accomplish some objective in the future is referred to as the **present value.**

Because $S = A(1 + i)^n$, it is only necessary to divide both sides of this equation by $(1 + i)^n$ to determine the expression $A = S/(1 + i)^n$. To determine the present value of the amount—that is, the principal—it is only necessary to divide the amount S by $(1 + i)^n$.

Of course,

$$\frac{S}{(1 + i)^n} = S \left[\frac{1}{1 + i} \right]^n$$

The symbol v is commonly used for $\left[\dfrac{1}{1 + i} \right]$. Thus,

$$v^n = \left[\frac{1}{1 + i} \right]^n$$

Tables for the value v^n at various interest rates are available. Appendix 2 is such a table. The figures given in these tables are commonly referred to as the present value of 1 rather than $1/(1 + i)^n$ or v^n. Present value tables were developed in the precalculator era so that multiplication rather than division could be performed to obtain present value results.

Accumulated Value of 1 per Year   Suppose that an investment of $1 is made at the beginning of each year for three years. To determine the accumulated amount at the end of three years, it is only necessary to add the amounts to which each of the payments will grow. The first $1 will grow to an amount of $(1 + i)^3$. The second $1 will grow to an amount of $(1 + i)^2$, and the third $1 will grow to an amount of $(1 + i)$. The total amount at the end of three years may be expressed as:

$$\ddot{s}_{\overline{3}|} = (1 + i) + (1 + i)^2 + (1 + i)^3$$

where $\ddot{s}_{\overline{n}|}$ is the symbol for the accumulated value at the end of n years of 1 invested at the *beginning* of each year for n years. (See Box 27-1.)

| BOX 27-1

The notation $\ddot{s}_{\overline{n}|}$ is commonly read as "s double-dot angle n." The two dots above the s mean that payments are made at the beginning of each period. An s without the two dots means that the payments are made at the end of each period.

In general

$$\ddot{s}_{\overline{n}|} = \sum_{t=1}^{n} (1 + i)^t = (1 + i) + (1 + i)^2 + \cdots + (1 + i)^{n-1} + (1 + i)^n$$

Appendix 3 gives tables of $\ddot{s}_{\overline{n}|}$ at various interest rates.

Present Value of 1 per Year   Another common compound interest problem is to determine what principal (i.e., present value) should be invested now to provide equal annual payments at the *end* of each year for the next n years. The total present value of the payments is computed by summing the present value of each payment. For example, suppose that we wish to find the present value of $1 payable at the end of each year for three years. The present values of the first, second, and third payments are v^1, v^2, and v^3, respectively. The total present value may be expressed as:

$$a_{\overline{3}|} = v^1 + v^2 + v^3$$

where $a_{\overline{n}|}$ is the symbol for the present value of 1 paid at the end of each year for the next n years. (See Box 27-2.)

In general, then

$$a_{\overline{n}|} = \sum_{t=1}^{n} v^t = v + v^2 + \cdots + v^{n-1} + v^n$$

Appendix 4 gives tables of $a_{\overline{n}|}$ at various interest rates.

Annuities

An **annuity** is simply a series of payments or receipts (a series of payments by a payor is a series of receipts to the recipient or payee). Usually, the payment is a constant amount and the intervals are regular, such as, $100 payable at the end of each month for 10 years, or $5,000 payable at the end of each year for 20 years. The annuity payment may be certain or may be contingent on a particular person being alive. The former are called **annuities certain.** The latter are called **life annuities.** A life annuity for a set term of years (but terminating if and when the individual dies during the set term) is called a **temporary life annuity.** An annuity that pays for as long as either or both of two persons are alive is a **joint and survivor annuity.**

When the annuity payments are assumed to be made at the *beginning* of each period, the annuity is referred to as an **annuity due.** Using actuarial notation for an annuity due:

$a_{\overline{n}|}$ for an n-year annuity certain

$\ddot{a}_x$ for a life annuity

$\ddot{a}_{x:\overline{n}|}$ for an n-year temporary life annuity

Annuity theory plays an important role in actuarial calculations because premium payments to a life insurance company by a policyowner constitute an annuity due to the insurer.

BOX 27-2

The $a_{\overline{n}|}$ notation is commonly read as "*a* angle *n*." The absence of the two dots above the *a* indicates that payments are made at the end of each period. See Box 27-1.

Assumptions Underlying Rate Computations

When the problem of life insurance rate computation is approached, several questions arise at once, and the answers to these questions directly influence the results obtained. For instance, how often will the premium be paid? Annually, semiannually, or otherwise? For how long will premiums be paid? For 5, 10, or 20 years, or for life? There are additional questions: What disposition will be made of funds between the time they are received and the time they are paid out? How will mortality rates be determined for periods of less than one year's duration in case, for instance, monthly premiums are decided upon because standard mortality tables give only yearly rates of mortality? Clearly, these and many other questions must be answered before the computation of rates can be accurately made.

The premium may be paid in a single cash sum, called a single premium, which pays for the entire risk incurred during the term of the policy, or premiums may be paid over a period equal to or less than the life of the contract. Many policies are purchased by annual premiums. In this connection, two simplifying assumptions are made: (1) premiums are paid at the beginning of each policy year, and (2) claims are paid at the end of the policy year in which the policy matures.[11] Accordingly, if a policy is purchased by a single premium, this sum is to be paid at the inception of the risk. In the case of level annual premiums, the first payment is to be made on the date of issue of the policy, and equal amounts are then paid annually thereafter on the anniversary of this date.

It is evident in the case of single premiums, and it is true only to a lesser degree with annual premiums, that the insurer will have possession of the funds for some time before being called upon to pay claims. Amounts in excess of that needed to meet current expenses and other policy obligations are invested and earn interest while in the insurer's possession. These interest earnings are an important source of the funds available to pay claims. As the insurer does not know the rates of interest to be earned in the future, it is necessary to assume a rate that is reasonably certain of being earned each year throughout the potentially long life of a policy.[12]

In determining the interest rate to be assumed in computing guaranteed maximum premiums (or choosing a guaranteed minimum interest rate under current assumption policies), it is necessary to select a rate that the insurer believes it is sure of earning each year over a long period of years. The assumption of too liberal an interest rate (e.g., 9 or 10 percent) will be a problem if the actual portfolio rate is less than that assumed. In establishing gross premiums, if the actual portfolio rate earned is less than the guaranteed rate, the result can be disastrous. If the insurer failed to earn the assumed 9 or 10 percent rate, it would need to make up the difference from surplus accumulated in previous years, or, in the absence of the latter, it might become insolvent.

Insurers issuing participating or current assumption nonparticipating insurance policies generally select a conservative interest rate, with the intention and expectation of returning to the policyowner, through dividends or otherwise, earnings in excess of the rate selected. A typical rate used by U.S. companies for original rate computations might be 3 to 5 percent. In other markets, rates are used to reflect conservative pricing

---

[11] Of course, insurers do not actually wait to pay death claims until the end of the policy year. They are paid promptly. The assumption that they are paid at the end of the year simplifies the analysis while not doing harm to the concepts. Most insurers both price and reserve on a continuous basis. In fact, if reserves are set upon a curtate basis, the Actuarial Standards Board requires actuaries to set up an Immediate Payment of Claims Reserve.

[12] Amounts actually earned in excess of those assumed can be credited to the policyowner via dividends under participating policies, via lower premiums on indeterminate premium policies, and via higher cashvalue interest credits on universal life and other current assumption policies.

(e.g., the rate in Japan might be 2 percent because of prevailing low interest rates). The rate chosen may make little difference (other things being the same) as long as it is neither too high (which could endanger solvency) nor too low (which could produce an uncompetitively high premium) because much of the excess earnings under most cash-value policies sold today eventually will be paid or credited to policyowners.

The second simplifying assumption sometimes made is that claims are paid at the end of each policy year. If there is a fairly even distribution of deaths throughout the policy year (roughly equivalent to all deaths at the middle of year), the payment of claims would occur on the average six months after death.[13] From a pricing standpoint, the assumption of paying death claims at the end of the year is too generous, to the extent of six months' interest in discounting claims. If premium rates are computed at 5 percent, this would mean a loss to the insurer of $250 on a $10,000 policy. Even so, many insurers calculate net premiums on the assumption that claims are paid at the end of the year. The error introduced typically is corrected by a small adjustment in the expense-loading formula or in the timing of interest credits.[14]

The assumption of when in the policy year deaths occur is financially significant to insurance companies, primarily in the case of policies with premiums that are payable at more frequent intervals than once a year. In the case of monthly premiums, if only one-twelfth of the annual premium has been collected in the first month, but one-sixth of the year's total mortality costs occur during the first month, the insurer will have to use its surplus funds to pay losses. With some mortality tables, this situation occurs during the first 10 years of life, when the mortality rate is decreasing and proportionately more deaths occur at the beginning of the year than toward the end of the year. At other ages, the mortality rate generally increases, and the discrepancy between the assumption of uniform deaths and the actual situation is favorable to the insurer.

In addition to these assumptions, the following must be known to compute premium rates in life insurance:

1. age of the insured
2. sex of the insured (where this is permitted as a factor)
3. benefits to be provided
4. mortality table to be used (possibly involving separate tables for smokers and nonsmokers)
5. rate of interest
6. amount to cover the insurer's expenses of operation, profits, and a margin for contingencies

Also, an estimate is needed as to the proportion of policyowners whose contracts terminate each year for reasons other than death or policy maturity. Together, all of these assumptions are used to test the tentative gross premiums through asset-share or other studies (discussed in chapter 30).

---

[13]In the early experience of life insurance companies, this was not far from the truth, for it took about three months to establish proof of death, and old policies allowed the insurer three months after proof before the claim was payable. At the present, however, claims are paid promptly. One prominent insurer, for instance, advertises that over 95 percent of its claims are paid within one working day of receipt of proof of death.

[14]A company may adjust the death benefits in the calculation of 5 percent net premiums by a factor of 1.024796719 to reflect "immediate payment of death benefits." The effect of that factor is to add half a year's interest on the death benefits. The factor is a mathematical continuous function derived by dividing the interest rate by the natural log of 1 plus the interest rate.

Interaction of Probability, Mortality, and Interest Concepts

As pointed out earlier, the process of obtaining the present value of a dollar payable at a specified time in the future is referred to as **discounting.** Assuming that the payment of the dollar in the future is not a certainty but is contingent on some insured individual being alive, it is necessary to reduce the present value of the future dollar still further, reflecting the probability that the individual will be alive to pay it. The process of discounting for probability is referred to as taking an *expected value.*

For example, assume that it is desired to know the value today of a promise to pay $1,000 in 20 years if a male now aged 30 is alive at that time. Assume money is valued at 6 percent and that *1980 CSO Table* mortality rates apply. From referring to Appendix 2, we know that the value today of $1,000 to be paid in 20 years (ignoring the survival probability) is found by multiplying the present value factor (at 6 percent and 20 years) by $1,000. Thus, $1,000 \times 0.312 = $312.

The probability that a male aged 30 will live for at least 20 years, $_{20}p_{30}$, is the ratio of the number living at age 50 (l_{50}) to the number living at age 30 (l_{30}), that is, l_{50}/l_{30} or, referring to Table 27-1, $8,966,618 \div 9,579,998$, which equals 0.936. Thus, the present *expected* value of the $1,000 to be paid at age 50 is found by taking the product of the present value and the expected value—that is, $312 \times 0.936 = $292. This represents the value (or worth) today of the future promise, based on the stated assumptions.

If expenses are ignored and the net premium rate for a life insurance policy is calculated, at date of issue the present value of all future expected premiums must be equal to the present value of all future expected benefits, where values are discounted for both interest and mortality. In word form, therefore, we observe that at issue date for any life insurance policy:

$$\text{Present Expected Value of Future Premiums } (PVFP) = \text{Present Expected Value of Future Benefits } (PVFB)$$

This relationship is illustrated in Table 27-4 for a hypothetical $1,000 ordinary life policy issued to an 80-year-old. Column 1 shows the net level annual premium that hypothetically would be paid at the beginning of each year if the insured were then alive. Column 2 shows present value interest factors, in which the factor for the first year is 1 because the premium is paid now. Column 3 shows probabilities of survival to the attained age shown. Column 4 lists the present expected values for each premium payment. The $698.96 total at the bottom of column 4 is the total present expected value of all future premiums.

Column 5 shows yearly death benefits payable. The figures in column 6, the discounts for interest, are smaller than the corresponding figures in column 2 because death benefits are assumed to be paid at the end of the year, whereas premiums are paid at the beginning of the year. Hence, death benefits are discounted for one year more than premiums. Whereas column 3 shows the probability of survival to pay the premium at each age, column 7 shows the probability of dying and, therefore, likelihood of payment of the death benefits at each age. Column 8 shows yearly present expected values of each future benefit. The total of $698.96 at the bottom of column 8 is the total present expected value of all future death benefits and is the same as the present expected value of all future premiums. Thus, at date of issue, we see that $PVFP = PVFB$.

Table 27-4 reflects the interaction of probability, mortality, and money concepts. Each of these elements has been included in its proper place and has been combined with the other elements according to a precise mathematical blend. The result is that based on the given assumptions as to mortality and interest, an insurance contract represents an equal exchange of *expected* value between the policyowner and the insurer. The policyowner pays the premiums, the insurer agrees to pay the stated death benefits,

TABLE 27-4 $1,000 Ordinary Life Policy for Male, Age 80 (1980 CSO Table, 6% Interest)

| | Premiums | | | | Benefits | | | |
	(1)	(2)	(3)	(4)	(5)	(6)	(7)	(8)
ATTAINED AGE (x)	LEVEL ANNUAL PREMIUM	INTEREST DISCOUNT FACTOR (v^{t-1})	PROBABILITY OF SURVIVAL ($_t p_{80}$)	PRESENT EXPECTED VALUE OF PREMIUMS [(1)×(2)×(3)]	DEATH BENEFIT	INTEREST DISCOUNT FACTOR (v^t)	PROBABILITY OF DEATH (d_x/l_{80})	PRESENT EXPECTED VALUE OF BENEFITS [(5)×(6)×(7)]
80	$131.42	1.0000	1.0000	$131.42	$1,000.00	0.9434	0.0988	$ 93.25
81	131.42	0.9434	0.9012	111.72	1,000.00	0.8900	0.0969	86.20
82	131.42	0.8900	0.8043	94.07	1,000.00	0.8396	0.0943	79.18
83	131.42	0.8396	0.7100	78.34	1,000.00	0.7921	0.0911	72.13
84	131.42	0.7921	0.6189	64.43	1,000.00	0.7473	0.0868	64.87
85	131.42	0.7473	0.5321	52.26	1,000.00	0.7050	0.0814	57.38
86	131.42	0.7050	0.4507	41.76	1,000.00	0.6651	0.0749	49.79
87	131.42	0.6651	0.3759	32.85	1,000.00	0.6274	0.0675	42.34
88	131.42	0.6274	0.3084	25.43	1,000.00	0.5919	0.0596	35.28
89	131.42	0.5919	0.2488	19.35	1,000.00	0.5584	0.0516	28.80
90	131.42	0.5584	0.1972	14.47	1,000.00	0.5268	0.0437	23.04
91	131.42	0.5268	0.1535	10.63	1,000.00	0.4970	0.0364	18.08
92	131.42	0.4970	0.1171	7.65	1,000.00	0.4688	0.0297	13.92
93	131.42	0.4688	0.0874	5.39	1,000.00	0.4423	0.0238	10.52
94	131.42	0.4423	0.0636	3.70	1,000.00	0.4173	0.0188	7.86
95	131.42	0.4173	0.0448	2.46	1,000.00	0.3936	0.0148	5.82
96	131.42	0.3936	0.0300	1.55	1,000.00	0.3714	0.0115	4.29
97	131.42	0.3714	0.0185	0.90	1,000.00	0.3503	0.0089	3.11
98	131.42	0.3503	0.0096	0.44	1,000.00	0.3305	0.0063	2.09
99	131.42	0.3305	0.0033	0.14	1,000.00	0.3118	0.0033	1.02
				$698.96				$698.96

and the present expected values are equal. The following chapters consider premium calculations in detail. It is important not to lose sight of this basic goal in all insurance contracts: the exchange of equal expected values at date of issue.[15]

Questions

1. The laws of probability are fundamental to insurance. Explain the application of these laws in the construction of mortality tables. What are some of the limitations associated with using the laws of probability to price life insurance products?
2. How are different types of mortality tables (valuation, basic, select, ultimate, and aggregate) put to use?
3. Why is it necessary to consider interest rates in the pricing of insurance products?
4. Why is it necessary to use different mortality tables for life insurance and annuity rate making?

---

[15]This statement, of course, ignores insurer loadings.

Appendix 27.1

Accumulated Value of 1 at Various Interest Rates: $(1 + i)^n$									
Years n	**3.0%**	**4.0%**	**5.0%**	**5.5%**	**6.0%**	**7.0%**	**8.0%**	**9.0%**	**10.0%**
1	1.030	1.040	1.050	1.055	1.060	1.070	1.080	1.090	1.100
2	1.061	1.082	1.103	1.113	1.124	1.145	1.166	1.188	1.210
3	1.093	1.125	1.158	1.174	1.191	1.225	1.260	1.295	1.331
4	1.126	1.170	1.216	1.239	1.262	1.311	1.360	1.412	1.464
5	1.159	1.217	1.276	1.307	1.338	1.403	1.469	1.539	1.611
6	1.194	1.265	1.340	1.379	1.419	1.501	1.587	1.677	1.772
7	1.230	1.316	1.407	1.455	1.504	1.606	1.714	1.828	1.949
8	1.267	1.369	1.477	1.535	1.594	1.718	1.851	1.993	2.144
9	1.305	1.423	1.551	1.619	1.689	1.838	1.999	2.172	2.358
10	1.344	1.480	1.629	1.708	1.791	1.967	2.159	2.367	2.594
11	1.384	1.539	1.710	1.802	1.898	2.105	2.332	2.580	2.853
12	1.426	1.601	1.796	1.901	2.012	2.252	2.518	2.813	3.138
13	1.469	1.665	1.886	2.006	2.133	2.410	2.720	3.066	3.452
14	1.513	1.732	1.980	2.116	2.261	2.579	2.937	3.342	3.797
15	1.558	1.801	2.079	2.232	2.397	2.759	3.172	3.642	4.177
16	1.605	1.873	2.183	2.355	2.540	2.952	3.426	3.970	4.595
17	1.653	1.948	2.292	2.485	2.693	3.159	3.700	4.328	5.054
18	1.702	2.026	2.407	2.621	2.854	3.380	3.996	4.717	5.560
19	1.754	2.107	2.527	2.766	3.026	3.617	4.316	5.142	6.116
20	1.806	2.191	2.653	2.918	3.207	3.870	4.661	5.604	6.727
21	1.860	2.279	2.786	3.078	3.400	4.141	5.034	6.109	7.400
22	1.916	2.370	2.925	3.248	3.604	4.430	5.437	6.659	8.140
23	1.974	2.465	3.072	3.426	3.820	4.741	5.871	7.258	8.954
24	2.033	2.563	3.225	3.615	4.049	5.072	6.341	7.911	9.850
25	2.094	2.666	3.386	3.813	4.292	5.427	6.848	8.623	10.835
26	2.157	2.772	3.556	4.023	4.549	5.807	7.396	9.399	11.918
27	2.221	2.883	3.733	4.244	4.822	6.214	7.988	10.245	13.110
28	2.288	2.999	3.920	4.478	5.112	6.649	8.627	11.167	14.421
29	2.357	3.119	4.116	4.724	5.418	7.114	9.317	12.172	15.863
30	2.427	3.243	4.322	4.984	5.743	7.612	10.063	13.268	17.449
31	2.500	3.373	4.538	5.258	6.088	8.145	10.868	14.462	19.194
32	2.575	3.508	4.765	5.547	6.453	8.715	11.737	15.763	21.114
33	2.652	3.648	5.003	5.852	6.841	9.325	12.676	17.182	23.225
34	2.732	3.794	5.253	6.174	7.251	9.978	13.690	18.728	25.548
35	2.814	3.946	5.516	6.514	7.686	10.677	14.785	20.414	28.102
36	2.898	4.104	5.792	6.872	8.147	11.424	15.968	22.251	30.913
37	2.985	4.268	6.081	7.250	8.636	12.224	17.246	24.254	34.004
38	3.075	4.439	6.385	7.649	9.154	13.079	18.265	26.437	37.404
39	3.167	4.616	6.705	8.069	9.704	13.995	20.115	28.816	41.145
40	3.262	4.801	7.040	8.513	10.286	14.974	21.725	31.409	45.259
41	3.360	4.993	7.392	8.985	10.903	16.023	23.462	34.236	49.785
42	3.461	5.193	7.762	9.476	11.557	17.144	25.339	37.318	54.764
43	3.565	5.400	8.150	9.997	12.250	18.344	27.367	40.676	60.240
44	3.671	5.617	8.557	10.546	12.985	19.628	29.556	44.337	66.264
45	3.782	5.841	8.985	11.127	13.765	21.002	31.920	48.327	72.890
46	3.895	6.075	9.434	11.739	14.590	22.473	34.474	52.677	80.180
47	4.012	6.318	9.906	12.384	15.466	24.046	37.232	57.418	88.197
48	4.132	6.571	10.401	13.065	16.394	25.729	40.211	62.585	97.017
49	4.256	6.833	10.921	13.784	17.378	27.530	43.427	68.218	106.719
50	4.384	7.107	11.467	14.542	18.420	29.457	46.902	74.358	117.391

Appendix 27.2

Present Value of 1 at Various Interest Rates: $(v)^n$

Years n	3.0%	4.0%	5.0%	5.5%	6.0%	7.0%	8.0%	9.0%	10.0%
1	0.971	0.962	0.952	0.948	0.943	0.935	0.926	0.917	0.909
2	0.943	0.925	0.907	0.898	0.890	0.873	0.857	0.842	0.826
3	0.915	0.889	0.864	0.852	0.840	0.816	0.794	0.772	0.751
4	0.888	0.855	0.823	0.807	0.792	0.763	0.735	0.708	0.683
5	0.863	0.822	0.784	0.765	0.747	0.713	0.681	0.650	0.621
6	0.837	0.790	0.746	0.725	0.705	0.666	0.630	0.596	0.564
7	0.813	0.760	0.711	0.687	0.665	0.623	0.583	0.547	0.513
8	0.789	0.731	0.677	0.652	0.627	0.582	0.540	0.502	0.467
9	0.766	0.703	0.645	0.618	0.592	0.544	0.500	0.460	0.424
10	0.744	0.676	0.614	0.585	0.558	0.508	0.463	0.422	0.386
11	0.722	0.650	0.585	0.555	0.527	0.475	0.429	0.388	0.350
12	0.701	0.625	0.557	0.526	0.497	0.444	0.397	0.356	0.319
13	0.681	0.601	0.530	0.499	0.469	0.415	0.368	0.326	0.290
14	0.661	0.577	0.505	0.473	0.442	0.388	0.340	0.299	0.263
15	0.642	0.555	0.481	0.448	0.417	0.362	0.315	0.275	0.239
16	0.623	0.534	0.458	0.425	0.394	0.339	0.292	0.252	0.218
17	0.605	0.513	0.436	0.402	0.371	0.317	0.270	0.231	0.198
18	0.587	0.494	0.416	0.381	0.350	0.296	0.250	0.212	0.180
19	0.570	0.475	0.396	0.362	0.331	0.277	0.232	0.194	0.164
20	0.554	0.456	0.377	0.343	0.312	0.258	0.215	0.178	0.149
21	0.538	0.439	0.359	0.325	0.294	0.242	0.199	0.164	0.135
22	0.522	0.422	0.342	0.308	0.278	0.226	0.184	0.150	0.123
23	0.507	0.406	0.326	0.292	0.262	0.211	0.170	0.138	0.112
24	0.492	0.390	0.310	0.277	0.247	0.197	0.158	0.126	0.102
25	0.478	0.375	0.295	0.262	0.233	0.184	0.146	0.116	0.092
26	0.464	0.361	0.281	0.249	0.220	0.172	0.135	0.106	0.084
27	0.450	0.347	0.268	0.236	0.207	0.161	0.125	0.098	0.076
28	0.437	0.333	0.255	0.223	0.196	0.150	0.116	0.090	0.069
29	0.424	0.321	0.243	0.212	0.185	0.141	0.107	0.082	0.063
30	0.412	0.308	0.231	0.201	0.174	0.131	0.099	0.075	0.057
31	0.400	0.296	0.220	0.190	0.164	0.123	0.092	0.069	0.052
32	0.388	0.285	0.210	0.180	0.155	0.115	0.085	0.063	0.047
33	0.377	0.274	0.200	0.171	0.146	0.107	0.079	0.058	0.043
34	0.366	0.264	0.190	0.162	0.138	0.100	0.073	0.053	0.039
35	0.355	0.253	0.181	0.154	0.130	0.094	0.068	0.049	0.036
36	0.345	0.244	0.173	0.146	0.123	0.088	0.063	0.045	0.032
37	0.335	0.234	0.164	0.138	0.116	0.082	0.058	0.041	0.029
38	0.325	0.225	0.157	0.131	0.109	0.076	0.054	0.038	0.027
39	0.316	0.217	0.149	0.124	0.103	0.071	0.050	0.035	0.024
40	0.307	0.208	0.142	0.117	0.097	0.067	0.046	0.032	0.022
41	0.298	0.200	0.135	0.111	0.092	0.062	0.043	0.029	0.020
42	0.289	0.193	0.129	0.106	0.087	0.058	0.039	0.027	0.018
43	0.281	0.185	0.123	0.100	0.082	0.055	0.037	0.025	0.017
44	0.272	0.178	0.117	0.095	0.077	0.051	0.034	0.023	0.015
45	0.264	0.171	0.111	0.090	0.073	0.048	0.031	0.021	0.014
46	0.257	0.165	0.106	0.085	0.069	0.044	0.029	0.019	0.012
47	0.249	0.158	0.101	0.081	0.065	0.042	0.027	0.017	0.011
48	0.242	0.152	0.096	0.077	0.061	0.039	0.025	0.016	0.010
49	0.235	0.146	0.092	0.073	0.058	0.036	0.023	0.015	0.009
50	0.228	0.141	0.087	0.069	0.054	0.034	0.021	0.013	0.009

Appendix 27.3

Years n	3.0%	4.0%	5.0%	5.5%	6.0%	7.0%	8.0%	9.0%	10.0%
1	1.030	1.040	1.050	1.055	1.060	1.070	1.080	1.090	1.100
2	2.091	2.122	2.153	2.168	2.184	2.215	2.246	2.278	2.310
3	3.184	3.246	3.310	3.342	3.375	3.440	3.506	3.573	3.641
4	4.309	4.416	4.526	4.581	4.637	4.751	4.867	4.985	5.105
5	5.468	5.633	5.802	5.888	5.975	6.153	6.336	6.523	6.716
6	6.662	6.898	7.142	7.267	7.394	7.654	7.923	8.200	8.487
7	7.892	8.214	8.549	8.722	8.897	9.260	9.637	10.028	10.436
8	9.159	9.583	10.027	10.256	10.491	10.978	11.488	12.021	12.579
9	10.464	11.006	11.578	11.875	12.181	12.816	13.487	14.193	14.937
10	11.808	12.486	13.207	13.583	13.972	14.784	15.645	16.560	17.531
11	13.192	14.026	14.917	15.386	15.870	16.888	17.977	19.141	20.384
12	14.618	15.627	16.713	17.287	17.882	19.141	20.495	21.953	23.523
13	16.086	17.292	18.599	19.293	20.015	21.550	23.215	25.019	26.975
14	17.599	19.024	20.579	21.409	22.276	24.129	26.152	28.361	30.772
15	19.157	20.825	22.657	23.641	24.673	26.888	29.324	32.003	34.950
16	20.762	22.698	24.840	25.996	27.213	29.840	32.750	35.974	39.545
17	22.414	24.645	27.132	28.481	29.906	32.999	36.450	40.301	44.599
18	24.117	26.671	29.539	31.103	32.760	36.379	40.446	45.018	50.159
19	25.870	28.778	32.066	33.868	35.786	39.995	44.762	50.160	56.275
20	27.676	30.969	34.719	36.786	38.993	43.865	49.423	55.765	63.002
21	29.537	33.248	37.505	39.864	42.392	48.006	54.457	61.873	70.403
22	31.453	35.618	40.430	43.112	45.996	52.436	59.893	68.532	78.543
23	33.426	38.083	43.502	46.538	49.816	57.177	65.765	75.790	87.497
24	35.459	40.646	46.727	50.153	53.865	62.249	72.106	83.701	97.347
25	37.553	43.312	50.113	53.966	58.156	67.676	78.954	92.324	108.182
26	39.710	46.084	53.669	57.989	62.706	73.484	86.351	101.723	120.100
27	41.931	48.968	57.403	62.234	67.528	79.698	94.339	111.968	133.210
28	44.219	51.966	61.323	66.711	72.640	86.347	102.966	123.135	147.631
29	46.575	55.085	65.439	71.435	78.058	93.461	112.283	135.308	163.494
30	49.003	58.328	69.761	76.419	83.802	101.073	122.346	148.575	180.943
31	51.503	61.701	74.299	81.677	89.890	109.218	133.214	163.037	200.138
32	54.078	65.210	79.064	87.225	96.343	117.933	144.951	178.800	221.252
33	56.730	68.858	84.067	93.077	103.184	127.259	157.627	195.982	244.477
34	59.462	72.652	89.320	99.251	110.435	137.237	171.317	214.711	270.024
35	62.276	76.598	94.836	105.765	118.121	147.913	186.102	235.125	298.127
36	65.174	80.702	100.628	112.637	126.268	159.337	202.070	257.376	329.039
37	68.159	84.970	106.710	119.887	134.904	171.561	219.316	281.066	363.043
38	71.234	89.409	113.095	127.536	144.058	184.640	237.941	308.066	400.448
39	74.401	94.026	119.800	135.606	153.762	198.635	258.057	336.882	441.593
40	77.663	98.827	126.840	144.119	164.048	213.610	279.781	368.292	486.852
41	81.023	103.820	134.232	153.100	174.951	229.632	303.244	402.528	536.637
42	84.484	109.012	141.993	162.576	186.508	246.776	328.583	439.846	591.401
43	88.048	114.413	150.143	172.573	198.758	265.121	355.950	480.522	651.641
44	91.720	120.029	158.700	183.119	211.744	284.749	385.506	524.859	717.905
45	95.501	125.871	167.685	194.246	225.508	305.752	417.426	573.186	790.795
46	99.397	131.945	177.119	205.984	240.099	328.224	451.900	625.863	870.975
47	103.408	138.263	187.025	218.368	255.565	352.270	489.132	683.280	959.172
48	107.541	144.834	197.427	231.434	271.958	377.999	529.343	745.866	1056.190
49	111.797	151.667	208.348	245.217	289.336	405.529	572.770	814.084	1162.909
50	116.181	158.774	219.815	259.759	307.756	434.986	619.672	888.441	1280.299

Appendix 27.4

Years n	3.0%	4.0%	5.0%	5.5%	6.0%	7.0%	8.0%	9.0%	10.0%
Present Value of 1 per Year at Various Interest Rates: $a_{\overline{n}|}$									
1	0.971	0.962	0.952	0.948	0.943	0.935	0.926	0.917	0.909
2	1.913	1.886	1.859	1.846	1.833	1.808	1.783	1.759	1.736
3	2.829	2.775	2.723	2.698	2.673	2.624	2.577	2.531	2.487
4	3.717	3.630	3.546	3.505	3.465	3.387	3.312	3.240	3.170
5	4.580	4.452	4.329	4.270	4.212	4.100	3.993	3.890	3.791
6	5.417	5.242	5.076	4.996	4.917	4.767	4.623	4.486	4.355
7	6.230	6.002	5.786	5.683	5.582	5.389	5.206	5.033	4.868
8	7.020	6.733	6.463	6.335	6.210	5.971	5.747	5.535	5.335
9	7.786	7.435	7.108	6.952	6.802	6.515	6.247	5.995	5.759
10	8.530	8.111	7.722	7.538	7.360	7.024	6.710	6.418	6.145
11	9.253	8.760	8.306	8.093	7.887	7.499	7.139	6.805	6.495
12	9.954	9.385	8.863	8.619	8.384	7.943	7.536	7.161	6.814
13	10.635	9.986	9.394	9.117	8.853	8.358	7.904	7.487	7.103
14	11.296	10.563	9.899	9.590	9.295	8.745	8.244	7.786	7.367
15	11.938	11.118	10.380	10.038	9.712	9.108	8.559	8.061	7.606
16	12.561	11.652	10.838	10.462	10.106	9.447	8.851	8.313	7.824
17	13.166	12.166	11.274	10.865	10.477	9.763	9.122	8.544	8.022
18	13.754	12.659	11.690	11.246	10.828	10.059	9.372	8.756	8.201
19	14.324	13.134	12.085	11.608	11.158	10.336	9.604	8.950	8.365
20	14.877	13.590	12.462	11.950	11.470	10.594	9.818	9.129	8.514
21	15.415	14.029	12.821	12.275	11.764	10.836	10.017	9.292	8.649
22	15.937	14.451	13.163	12.583	12.042	11.061	10.201	9.442	8.772
23	16.444	14.857	13.489	12.875	12.303	11.272	10.371	9.580	8.883
24	16.936	15.247	13.799	13.152	12.550	11.469	10.529	9.707	8.985
25	17.413	15.622	14.094	13.414	12.783	11.654	10.675	9.823	9.077
26	17.877	15.983	14.375	13.662	13.003	11.826	10.810	9.929	9.161
27	18.327	16.330	14.643	13.898	13.211	11.987	10.935	10.027	9.237
28	18.764	16.663	14.898	14.121	13.406	12.137	11.051	10.116	9.307
29	19.188	16.984	15.141	14.333	13.591	12.278	11.158	10.198	9.370
30	19.600	17.292	15.372	14.534	13.765	12.409	11.258	10.274	9.427
31	20.000	17.588	15.593	14.724	13.929	12.532	11.350	10.343	9.479
32	20.389	17.874	15.803	14.904	14.084	12.647	11.435	10.406	9.526
33	20.766	18.148	16.003	15.075	14.230	12.754	11.514	10.464	9.569
34	21.132	18.411	16.193	15.237	14.368	12.854	11.587	10.518	9.609
35	21.487	18.665	16.374	15.391	14.498	12.948	11.655	10.567	9.644
36	21.832	18.908	16.547	15.536	14.621	13.035	11.717	10.612	9.677
37	22.167	19.143	16.711	15.674	14.737	13.117	11.775	10.653	9.706
38	22.492	19.368	16.868	15.805	14.846	13.193	11.829	10.691	9.733
39	22.808	19.584	17.017	15.929	14.949	13.265	11.879	10.726	9.757
40	23.115	19.793	17.159	16.046	15.046	13.332	11.925	10.757	9.779
41	23.412	19.993	17.294	16.157	15.138	13.394	11.967	10.787	9.799
42	23.701	20.186	17.423	16.263	15.225	13.452	12.007	10.813	9.817
43	23.982	20.371	17.546	16.363	15.306	13.507	12.043	10.838	9.834
44	24.254	20.549	17.663	16.458	15.383	13.558	12.077	10.861	9.849
45	24.519	20.720	17.774	16.548	15.456	13.606	12.108	10.881	9.863
46	24.775	20.885	17.880	16.633	15.524	13.650	12.137	10.900	9.875
47	25.025	21.043	17.981	16.714	15.589	13.692	12.164	10.918	9.887
48	25.267	21.195	18.077	16.790	15.650	13.730	12.189	10.934	9.897
49	25.502	21.341	18.169	16.863	15.708	13.767	12.212	10.948	9.906
50	25.730	21.482	18.256	16.932	15.762	13.801	12.233	10.962	9.915

CHAPTER

28

NET PREMIUMS

Objectives

■ Describe the methods used to calculate net single premiums for term and whole life insurance.

■ Describe the methods used to calculate net level premiums for term and ordinary life insurance.

■ Describe the methods used to calculate endowment and life annuity premiums.

■ Explain how the selection and use of mortality tables for the calculation of term, whole life, endowment, and annuity premium calculations may differ.

INTRODUCTION

With the preceding life insurance mathematical principles as a base, it is now possible to illustrate one process by which life insurance and annuity premiums are calculated.[1] The process shown includes the calculation of net premiums for term, whole life, endowment, and annuity policies, to which amounts to cover expenses, profits, and contingencies are added to develop a gross-premium rate structure. Net premiums take into account interest and mortality factors only. This study begins by first determining the net single premium, from which the net annual premium can be found. Next, various methods of loading to ascertain a gross-premium rate schedule will be studied.[2]

NET SINGLE PREMIUMS

The Calculation Process

The computation of net premium rates for life insurance generally requires information as to (1) the age and sex of the insured, (2) the benefits to be provided, (3) the mortality rates to be used, and (4) the rate of interest assumed. In the computations that follow, mortality will be assumed to be that of the *1980 CSO Table;* the rate of interest

---

[1] Another process was illustrated in chapter 2.

[2] This procedure is not always followed but illustrates the relevant pricing principals. In any case, the gross premium is ordinarily tested by asset-share studies under realistic assumptions. See chapter 30.

assumed will be 5 percent; the face amount of the policy, $1,000; and the insured a male. The age of the insured will be stated in each instance.[3]

Term Insurance

Term insurance is the simplest type of life insurance. Term policies usually cover a set period and promise to pay the sum insured if the insured dies within this period. (Nothing is paid if death does not occur during the designated term.) Yearly renewable term (YRT) policies, which are discussed in chapter 4, are the simplest forms of term life insurance and offer an excellent opportunity to explain the elements of rate making.

Suppose that the net single premium is to be ascertained on a one-year term life insurance policy of $1,000 on a male aged 45. Immediate use will now be found for two assumptions mentioned in chapter 27—that premiums are paid at the beginning of each policy year and that matured claims are paid at the close of the policy year. The question is: What amount of money must be paid at the beginning of the year by policyowners to enable the insurer to pay $1,000 at year-end for each insured who dies during the period? The insurer is interested in the probability of having to pay the death claim—in other words, the chance of a 45-year-old male dying during the year. This will be determined by means of the mortality table shown in Table 27-1.

Suppose that an insurance company issued 9,210,289 (number living at age 45) one-year term policies to males age 45. If the actual mortality experienced among this group coincided with the experience expected under the mortality table, there would be 41,907 deaths during the year. Because each of these deaths represents a liability of $1,000 to the insurer, and because the claims are assumed to be payable at the close of the year, the insurer must have on hand at that time $41,907,000 to pay claims. This entire amount, however, need not have been collected from the policyowners because they were required to pay their premiums at the beginning of the year and the insurer was able to invest the money at interest for one year at, say, 5 percent. One dollar discounted for one year at 5 percent interest equals $0.952. Therefore, the insurer needs to have on hand at the beginning of the year only $39,895,464 (0.952 × $41,907,000) in order to have at the end of the year sufficient funds to pay $1,000 for each of the 41,907 deaths. To obtain the premium each individual should pay, it is only necessary to divide the total fund by the group of 9,210,289 to be insured:

$$\$39,895,464 \div 9,210,289 = \$4.33$$

The net single premium for a one-year term insurance policy at age 45, or the amount of money that must be paid at the beginning of the year to supply each individual's contribution to the death losses of the group for the year, is, therefore, $4.33. This method of determining individual net single premiums has been termed the *aggregate approach* because it emphasizes the total fund necessary to meet death claims as they occur.

The same problem may be approached using the mathematically identical *expected value approach*. An estimated 41,907 males aged 45 will die out of the group of 9,210,289, based on the mortality table used here. This is equivalent to saying that the probability of death during the forty-sixth (q_{45}) year is 41,907/9,210,289 or 0.00455. The expected value of a death claim for an insured is, therefore, $1,000 × 0.00455, or $4.55. This is the value needed at the end of the year, and money is valued at 5 percent. The amount to be

---

[3]The reader is reminded that the *1980 CSO Table* is not generally used for rate making; it is used for valuing insurance companies' policy liabilities. Insurers use up-to-date mortality experience in deriving premiums to be charged.

paid at the beginning of the year will be $4.55 discounted for one year at 5 percent, or $4.55 × 0.952, which equals $4.33. This may be summarized as follows:

$$(\$1,000)\left(\frac{41,907}{9,210,289}\right)(0.952) = \$4.33$$

which, in actuarial notation, can be written:

$$(1,000)(q_x)(v) = (1,000)\left(\frac{d_{45}}{l_{45}}\right)(v)$$

It should not be assumed from this that an insurance company can insure a single person only. Instead, it should deal with a group sufficiently large to ensure that the law of large numbers can operate reasonably. It does not, however, need to insure this entire group with the same kind of policy or at the same age. Results will be satisfactory if the entire group of insureds, including all ages and all kinds of policies, is sufficiently large.

The method used here in determining the premium rate embodies the following process: Multiply the probability of the occurrence of the event insured against by the amount of the policy, and then multiply by the value of 1 discounted for one year at the assumed rate of interest. This is a **present expected value.** It is an *expected value* because it is based on probabilities and it is a *present value* because it is discounted for interest (the time value of money).

To continue, suppose that it is desired to compute the net single premium for a five-year term life insurance policy issued at male age 45—that is, the amount of money that, paid in a single sum at age 45, will purchase insurance against death at any time within the next five years. Two facts are apparent: (1) The premium is paid only once, in a single sum at policy inception, and (2) death claims will be paid at the end of the year in which death occurs, not at the end of the five-year period. This latter fact has an important bearing on the interest earned and, therefore, on the method of computing the cost.

Manifestly, the cost cannot be correctly determined by multiplying the total probability of dying during the five years by the face amount of the policy and discounting this amount in one operation because some of the money collected will draw interest for only one year, another part will earn interest for two years, and so on. It is necessary to compute each year's mortality costs separately. The probabilities insured against in this case are the chances that a male aged 45 will die during the first year, during the second year, the third year, and so on. In actuarial notation, these probabilities would be found as follows:

$$\frac{d_{45}}{l_{45}} = \frac{41,907}{9,210,289} = 0.00455$$

$$\frac{d_{46}}{l_{45}} = \frac{45,108}{9,210,289} = 0.00490$$

$$\frac{d_{47}}{l_{45}} = \frac{48,536}{9,210,289} = 0.00527$$

$$\frac{d_{48}}{l_{45}} = \frac{52,089}{9,210,289} = 0.00566$$

$$\frac{d_{49}}{l_{45}} = \frac{56,031}{9,210,289} = 0.00608$$

Each of these figures must be multiplied by the insurance amount and by the present value of 1, discounted in each instance by the length of time the money is held. The money available for the first year's claims will be held for one year; for the second year's claims, two years; and so on, the funds for the last year's claims being held five years. The relevant discount factors for one, two, three, four, and five years at 5 percent interest are, respectively, 0.952, 0.907, 0.864, 0.823, and 0.784. The cost of the five years of insurance, therefore, can be calculated as shown in Table 28-1.

This computation shows that, ignoring expenses, taxes, and so on, $22.75 paid to the insurer by each policyowner and placed at 5 percent interest will furnish enough money to pay all the expected death claims on this five-year term policy. By simply continuing the process of calculating the cost of insurance on a per year basis, the net single premium for a term insurance contract of any longer duration may be determined.

Whole Life Insurance

A whole life policy provides coverage for the whole of life as defined by the mortality table used to calculate premiums, promising to pay the face amount whenever death occurs. This policy is like the term contracts just considered with the exception that, instead of being limited to a set number of years, it continues to the end of the mortality table. Because the *1980 CSO Table* assumes that everyone dies by attained age 100, the maximum possible age for which the cost of insurance against death needs to be calculated is 99. The net single premium on a whole life policy issued at male age 45 must, therefore, provide against the possibility that the insured will die during his forty-sixth year, his forty-seventh year, his forty-eighth year, and so on, during every year up to and including his one-hundredth year. The separate probabilities insured against number 55—that is, for ages 45 to 99 inclusive.

The chance of dying in each separate year $\left(\dfrac{d_{x+t-1}}{l_x}\right)$ is multiplied by the face amount of the policy ($1,000), and this amount is discounted for the number of years between the issue of the policy (i.e., the payment of the single premium) and the payment of death claims. Table 28-2 illustrates the calculations.

TABLE 28-1 Illustrative Net Single-Premium Calculation for Five-Year Term Insurance (Male, Aged 45, *1980 CSO* Mortality, 5% Interest)

Policy Year (t)	Age (x)	Calculation	Year's Cost of Insurance
1	45	$($1,000$)\left[\dfrac{d_{45}}{l_{45}}\right](v) = ($1,000$)(0.00455)(0.952) =$	$ 4.33
2	46	$($1,000$)\left[\dfrac{d_{46}}{l_{45}}\right](v^2) = ($1,000$)(0.00490)(0.907) =$	4.44
3	47	$($1,000$)\left[\dfrac{d_{47}}{l_{45}}\right](v^3) = ($1,000$)(0.00527)(0.864) =$	4.55
4	48	$($1,000$)\left[\dfrac{d_{48}}{l_{45}}\right](v^4) = ($1,000$)(0.00566)(0.823) =$	4.66
5	49	$($1,000$)\left[\dfrac{d_{49}}{l_{45}}\right](v^5) = ($1,000$)(0.00608)(0.784) =$	4.77
		Total (net single premium)	$22.75

TABLE 28-2	Illustrative Net Single-Premium Calculation for Whole Life Insurance (Male, Aged 45, *1980 CSO* Mortality, 5% Interest)

Policy Year (t)	Age (x)	Calculation	Year's Cost of Insurance
1	45	$(\$1,000)\left[\dfrac{d_{45}}{l_{45}}\right](v) = (\$1,000)(0.00455)(0.952)$	$= \$ \ \ 4.33$
2	46	$(\$1,000)\left[\dfrac{d_{46}}{l_{45}}\right](v^2) = (\$1,000)(0.00490)(0.907)$	$= \ \ \ \ 4.44$
3	47	$(\$1,000)\left[\dfrac{d_{47}}{l_{45}}\right](v^3) = (\$1,000)(0.00527)(0.864)$	$= \ \ \ \ 4.55$
$\vdots$	$\vdots$	$\vdots$ $\qquad\qquad\qquad\qquad$ $\vdots$	$\vdots$
53	97	$(\$1,000)\left[\dfrac{d_{97}}{l_{45}}\right](v^{53}) = (\$1,000)\left[\dfrac{29,054}{9,210,289}\right](0.075) =$	0.24
54	98	$(\$1,000)\left[\dfrac{d_{98}}{l_{45}}\right](v^{54}) = (\$1,000)\left[\dfrac{20,693}{9,210,289}\right](0.072) =$	0.16
55	99	$(\$1,000)\left[\dfrac{d_{99}}{l_{45}}\right](v^{55}) = (\$1,000)\left[\dfrac{10,757}{9,210,289}\right](0.068) =$	$\underline{0.08}$

Total $\ \ \ \ \$270.84$

(net single premium)

This $270.84 is the present value of this policy's share of all the expected death claims payable from age 45. It is, therefore, the net single premium that will purchase a whole life policy issued at age 45, based on the stated assumptions. It is true that a few men outlive their one-hundredth year, but because the computations assume that the insured will not have survived this age, and because sufficient money will have been accumulated to pay the claim at the close of the one-hundredth year of life, the policy may then be terminated for its full face amount at that time.[4]

Note that the probabilities of death used in the net single-premium calculation are not the same as the yearly death probabilities shown in Table 27-1. An understanding of this difference is crucial. The death probabilities shown in column 2 of Table 27-1 give the probabilities of death *for a person who has attained the stipulated age,* whereas the death probabilities used in the preceding calculation give the probabilities of *dying in various future years for a person now aged 45.*

An examination of the two death probabilities at age 99 illustrates this important difference. The probability of a 99-year-old male dying within his next year of life is shown as 1 (a certainty) in Table 27-1. In other words, a person who has attained age 99 is, according to this mortality table, certain to die during the next year. On the other hand, the probability of a 45-year-old dying during his one-hundredth year is d_{99}/l_{45} or $10,757 \div 9,210,189$ or 0.00117—a small likelihood. This suggests that our 45-year-old male is highly *unlikely* to die during his one-hundredth year. Why? It is highly unlikely that he will live to attain such an advanced age in the first instance. (The only way that he could die then is if he survives to the end of his ninety-ninth year!)

---

[4]The policyowner might be able to leave the face amount with the company to grow with interest. By delaying payment, the policyowner might be able to delay any taxable gain on surrender until the funds are actually received or avoid all income taxes if the funds are paid to a beneficiary after the insured's death.

The net single-premium calculation for a whole life policy, in essence, apportions the probability of dying (a certainty) over the various years remaining in one's life. Thus, if the death probabilities in the preceding whole life net single-premium computation are summed, they would equal 1. By contrast, a summation of the yearly death probabilities in Table 27-1 would have no meaning.[5]

Endowments

Although endowment insurance is not very popular in the United States, it is very popular in other markets, and several important life insurance principles are illustrated in endowments. For this reason, an understanding of the way they function mathematically is important.

Pure Endowments

A **pure endowment** promises to pay the face amount if, and only if, the insured survives a specific period. Thus, a five-year pure endowment would pay the policy face amount if the insured is living five years from the date of issue. Table 27-1 shows, for example, that of the 9,210,289 males living at age 45, 8,966,618 are still living at age 50. Thus, the probability of a male age 45 surviving for five years, symbolized by $_5p_{45}$, is:

$$_5p_{45} = \frac{l_{50}}{l_{45}} = \frac{8,966,618}{9,210,289} = 0.97354$$

Stated differently, the probability of the occurrence of the event insured against is 0.97354. Because the money paid as a single premium for a five-year endowment would be held for five years before the policy matures, the formula for determining the net single premium for a $1,000 pure endowment policy (at 5 percent interest) is:

$$NSP = (\$1,000)(_5p_{45})(v^5) = (\$1,000)(0.97354)(0.784) = \$763.26$$

A clear distinction must be made between a pure endowment and a savings account that is left to accumulate at an agreed rate of interest. The insured cannot obtain possession of the money invested in a pure endowment before the expiration of the endowment period. Nothing is returned if the insured should die during this period. The money remains in the fund needed to pay the survivors. A bank savings account, on the other hand, is not lost through death of the saver. This fact makes it possible to divide the $1,000 that will be paid *in case of survival through the endowment period* into two funds, one of which might be called an *investment fund* and the other a *benefit of survivorship fund*. The investment fund element of our five-year pure endowment will equal $762.77 plus interest compounded for five years at 5 percent. Using the formula for the accumulated value of 1 per year produces these results:

$$S = (A)(1.05)^5 = (\$762.77)(1.276) = \$973.29$$

This $973.29 is the amount that would be obtained by investing the net single premium of this pure endowment policy at 5 percent interest for five years. The remainder of the $1,000, or $26.71, comprises the survivor's share of the amounts left by those insureds who died before their policies matured—the benefit of survivorship contribution. The possibility of losing the entire amount of one's investment by death before the endowment period has expired makes the pure endowment a policy that finds little

---

[5]Indeed, they would sum to greater than 1! This is also the reason why a comparison of YRT rates to age 100 and the level premium for an ordinary life policy is not meaningful mathematically without adjustment of the YRT premiums for the probabilities of survival. See Robert E. Cooper, "The Level Premium Concept: A Closer Look," *Journal of the American Society of Chartered Life Underwriters,* Vol XXX (July 1976).

favor with the insuring public in the United States.[6] For this reason, it is combined with, or constitutes a feature of, some other kind of policy. It is interesting to note that a life annuity is merely a series of pure endowments (discussed later).

Endowment Insurance

An **endowment** promises to pay a certain sum in case the insured dies within the term of the policy or (usually) a similar sum at the end of the term in case of survival. This contract includes the pure endowment feature just discussed and, in addition, insurance against death during the term of the endowment. Thus, a five-year endowment insurance policy issued at male age 45 will pay the face amount if the insured dies during the first, second, third, fourth, or fifth years, or it will pay the same sum at the end of the endowment period. The net single premium for these two promises can be found by adding the net single premium for five years of term life insurance coverage and the net single premium for a five-year pure endowment. Based on our assumptions, the net single premium for the five-year pure endowment is $762.77 and for the five-year term is $22.75 for a total of $785.52.

There are other types of endowment contracts: partial endowments, semiendowments, educational endowments, and double endowments. They differ from the preceding policy in that the amount due on survival (i.e., the pure endowment element) differs from the amount paid on death.

Policies Involving More Than One Life

The policies illustrated here involve only one life. Life insurance companies also issue policies that cover risks on two or more lives; joint life and second-to-die policies are examples.[7] The computation of premium rates for these policies follows the same principles as for single-life policies. The critical difference in computation relates to the probability of the occurrence of the insured event. Thus, with a joint-life policy that pays the face amount on the death of *either* of two insureds, the probability of the insurer paying a claim can be derived by summing the compound probabilities of an insured event occurring.

Thus, the insurer will have to pay the claim under a joint-life policy if any one of three combinations of events occurs:

1. Insured A lives (p_x^x) and insured B dies (q_x^y).
2. Insured A dies (q_x^x) and insured B lives (p_x^y).
3. Insured A dies (q_x^x) and insured B dies (q_x^y).

The probability of the occurrence of the first combination of events is given by the compound probability:

$$(p_x^x)(q_x^y)$$

The probability of the second and third events occurring is given, respectively, by:

$$(q_x^x)(p_x^y)$$

$$(q_x^x)(q_x^y)$$

The sum of the three compound probabilities gives the probability of the occurrence of an insured event—the figure that would be used in each year's probability of death (i.e., claim payment).

---

[6]In some jurisdictions, pure endowment contracts are prohibited by law. They are sold in other countries.

[7]See chapter 7.

Second-to-die policies pay the face amount only on the death of the second of two insureds. Conditional probability calculations, which are beyond the scope of this introductory treatment, are necessary to derive such premiums.

Life Annuities

The remaining class of contracts to be analyzed is life annuities. Life annuities promise to pay the possessor a stated income periodically (often at intervals of one year) during the annuitant's lifetime. They furnish a type of investment whereby the recipient can be assured of an income for life.

Annuities covering a single life are ordinarily of two kinds—immediate and deferred. An **immediate life annuity** begins payments one period hence. A **deferred life annuity** begins payments more than one period hence. Annuities may be temporary (i.e., limited to a term of years during the lifetime of the annuitant); they may continue for the whole of life; or they may promise a minimum number of payments irrespective of whether the annuitant is living. Each of these contracts will be considered in turn.

Immediate Life Annuities

An immediate temporary life annuity of $100, purchased, say, at age 70 and continuing for a period of 10 years will promise to pay the annuitant $100 one year from the date of purchase, if he or she is then living, and $100 at each anniversary of that date, if he or she is still living, until 10 payments have been made. The cost of this contract will be the net single premium (present expected value) at age 70 for the payments of the sums promised to the annuitant. Because a payment is made to the annuitant at the end of each year, the cost for each year must be determined separately and these amounts summed to obtain the net single premium. This annuity is equivalent to a series of 10 pure endowments, the first maturing in one year from date of purchase, the second in two years, the third in three years, and so on, until the 10 payments have been made.

Although the formulas are equivalent to those for insurance, the mortality table is different because annuity mortality experience produces lower mortality rates than does insurance mortality experience. The *1983 Individual Annuity Mortality Table for Males (1983 Table a)*, without projection, is a table widely used for U.S. annuity valuation.[8] According to this table, the probability that the first annuity payment will be made equals the probability that a man aged 70 will survive one year (p_{70}), or it can be expressed in the form of a fraction, l_{71}/l_{70}, which equals 7,747,883/7,917,079. The $100 paid in case of survival is paid one year from the date of purchase of the annuity, and, therefore, the net cost of the first payment will be the value of this sum discounted for one year at 5 percent and multiplied by the probability of survival. The process is continued through the second, third, and following years as shown in Table 28-3.

If the contract issued at male age 70 promises to pay an annuity for the whole of life, the computations must continue throughout the annuity mortality table, which in the case of the *1983 Table a* is through age 115. The computation of the cost of this whole life annuity is shown in Table 28-4 (the first 10 years being the same as for the term annuity just computed).

If this same annuity guaranteed that the first five payments were to be certain—that is, not affected by the death of the annuitant before their completion—this fact would have to be taken into consideration in computing the net cost. The distinction would

---

[8]The authors have computed this table complete with l_x, d_x, and p_x values, using a radix of 10 million lives at age 5 (see Table 27-3).

TABLE 28-3 Illustrative Net Single-Premium Calculation for a 10-Year Immediate Life Annuity (Male, Aged 70, *1983 CSO Table a* Mortality, 5% Interest)

Policy Year (t)	Age (x)	Calculation		Cost of Year's Annuity Payment
1	70	$(\$100)\left[\dfrac{l_{71}}{l_{70}}\right](v)$	$= (\$100)\left[\dfrac{7,747,883}{7,917,079}\right](0.952) =$	$ 93.17
2	71	$(\$100)\left[\dfrac{l_{72}}{l_{70}}\right](v^2)$	$= (\$100)\left[\dfrac{7,564,669}{7,917,079}\right](0.907) =$	86.66
3	72	$(\$100)\left[\dfrac{l_{73}}{l_{70}}\right](v^3)$	$= (\$100)\left[\dfrac{7,366,977}{7,917,079}\right](0.864) =$	80.40
⋮	⋮	⋮	⋮	⋮
8	77	$(\$100)\left[\dfrac{l_{78}}{l_{70}}\right](v^8)$	$= (\$100)\left[\dfrac{6,152,440}{7,917,079}\right](0.677) =$	52.61
9	78	$(\$100)\left[\dfrac{l_{79}}{l_{70}}\right](v^9)$	$= (\$100)\left[\dfrac{6,152,440}{7,917,079}\right](0.645) =$	47.77
10	79	$(\$100)\left[\dfrac{l_{80}}{l_{70}}\right](v^{10})$	$= (\$100)\left[\dfrac{5,560,108}{7,917,079}\right](0.614) =$	43.12

Total $667.29
(net single premium)

lie in the fact that these five payments would not be affected by death. In other words, the probability of payment is a certainty. Therefore, the first five payments would be discounted for interest only. The sixth and all subsequent payments would depend on the probability of survival, and their net cost would, therefore, be computed in the same manner as previously for the pure life annuity.

TABLE 28-4 Illustrative Net Single-Premium Calculation for an Immediate Whole Life Annuity (Male, Aged 70, *1983 CSO Table a* Mortality, 5% Interest)

Policy Year (t)	Age (x)	Calculation		Cost of Year's Annuity Payment
1	70	$(\$100)\left[\dfrac{l_{71}}{l_{70}}\right](v)$	$= (\$100)\left[\dfrac{7,747,883}{7,917,079}\right](0.952) =$	$ 93.20
2	71	$(\$100)\left[\dfrac{l_{72}}{l_{70}}\right](v^2)$	$= (\$100)\left[\dfrac{7,564,669}{7,917,079}\right](0.907) =$	83.67
3	72	$(\$100)\left[\dfrac{l_{73}}{l_{70}}\right](v^3)$	$= (\$100)\left[\dfrac{7,366,997}{7,917,079}\right](0.864) =$	80.38
⋮	⋮	⋮	⋮	⋮
43	112	$(\$100)\left[\dfrac{l_{113}}{l_{70}}\right](v^{43})$	$= (\$100)\left[\dfrac{35}{7,917,079}\right](0.123) =$	0.00[a]
44	113	$(\$100)\left[\dfrac{l_{114}}{l_{70}}\right](v^{44})$	$= (\$100)\left[\dfrac{6}{7,917,079}\right](0.117) =$	0.00[a]
45	114	$(\$100)\left[\dfrac{l_{115}}{l_{70}}\right](v^{45})$	$= (\$100)\left[\dfrac{1}{7,917,079}\right](0.111) =$	0.00[a]

Total $936.18
(net single premium)

[a]Less than 0.0005.

Deferred Life Annuities

Immediate life annuities are usually purchased by persons of advanced age, and they contemplate the payment of benefits at periodic intervals following the date of issue. Some persons are interested in a deferred life annuity, which is an annuity contract that can be purchased by annual sums paid during their wage-earning years. It bears a close resemblance to private pension plans, under which money is accumulated year by year in small amounts from the wages of the employees and contributions by the employer, and this money is paid periodically during the lifetime of the employee after he or she has attained retirement age.

In the United States, a traditional deferred life annuity was usually purchased by an annual premium. Of course, flexible-premium deferred annuities may be purchased with any desired, reasonable premium pattern. It is also possible to pay for such a contract by a single premium paid at the date of purchase of the contract.

Assume that it is desired to find the net single premium payable for a male, aged 40, that will purchase the right to receive a whole life annuity of $100 beginning at age 70. There are two steps in approaching the problem. It may be asked: What is the amount of money that must have been accumulated by the insurer by the time the annuity begins? This is equivalent to asking how much money must be available at age 70 to furnish $100 annually during life, the first payment to be made when the annuitant reaches age 70. The problem at this point is, therefore, identical to that of the immediate whole life annuity just discussed, with the single exception that here the first $100 payment is made at age 70, whereas in the former case, the first payment was made at age 71. Therefore, the insurance company must have on hand at the time the annuitant becomes 70 years of age the amount of money necessary to purchase an immediate life annuity, the first payment being at age 70. Taking the figures from the previous computations, we find a new net single premium of $936.18 + S100.00, or $1,036.18. This amount may be considered as the net cost *at age 70* of a whole life annuity *due,* the first payment of which is made to the annuitant at that age.

The amount payable by a man at age 40 that will furnish this sum ($1,036.18) at age 70 is the present value of this sum discounted for 30 years at the assumed interest rate:

$$A = (S) \times (v^{30}) = (\$1,036.18) \times (0.231) = \$239.36$$

A deferred annuity is almost always purchased on a basis whereby payments (single or periodic) made during the accumulation period are not forfeited in the event of death. The foregoing calculation is based on this premise. If the cost of this contract taken out at age 40 had been computed on the assumption that the single premium paid at age 40 or the level annual premiums paid from ages 40 to 70 were forfeitable (i.e., the purchaser relinquished any right to his or her contributions in case he or she failed to survive to age 70), the calculation would further discount the $239.36 figure for the probability of survival from age 40 to 70.

NET LEVEL PREMIUMS

The Level-Premium System

Insurance policies may be purchased by a single cash sum or by periodic payments made monthly, quarterly, semiannually, or annually, and, with flexible-premium contracts, as often or infrequently as desired. With traditional forms of life insurance, the determination of level premiums is made after the single premium has been ascertained.

If policyowners are given the choice of payment for insurance by single or annual premiums, the amounts of the latter must be determined on such a basis that the insurer will receive equivalent value under each method of payment. Because the manner of computing the net single premium is known, the problem can be solved by finding a series of net annual level premiums that is mathematically equivalent to the net single premium. Such premiums will be paid during the life of the insured or for a limited number of years, but always *cease upon his or her death.* Note that this is the definition of a life annuity.

It is helpful to view annual premiums as annuities. They differ, however, in four important respects from the annuities thus far considered.

First, they are paid *by* the policyowner *to* the insurer, whereas regular annuities are paid *by* the insurer *to* the annuitant.

Second, annuities are ordinarily purchased by single or annual premiums. If annual premiums are analogous to annuities, what does the insurer offer the policyowner as consideration for the series of annuity (premium) payments? It promises a cash payment (the policy face amount) upon the happening of the insured event.

Third, annuitant mortality is considerably lower than insurance mortality. This consideration, however, does not apply to the annuities represented by the annual level premiums, and regular insurance mortality tables are used in the calculations regarding life insurance annual level premiums. Obviously, life insurance purchasers will have the mortality experience of insureds, not that of annuitants.

Fourth, the time when annual level premiums and annuity payments begin is different. The immediate life annuity pays the first annual income installment one year from the date of contract issue. In practice, the first annual premium is payable when a life insurance policy is issued, and not one year later, as is the case with annuities. This series of premium payments is known as a *life annuity due.*

The net level premium cannot be obtained simply by dividing the net single premium by the number of agreed-upon installments. The net single premium is a discounted expected value, and the net annual level premium must reflect (1) the possibility that the insured may die and not pay future premiums and (2) the smaller sum that will be invested at compound interest, with the resultant loss of interest earnings to the insurer.

The problem stated previously may now be restated in the following terms: The series of net annual level premiums will be a life annuity due that is equivalent at issue to the net single premium.

Computation of the Net Annual Level Premium

Term Insurance

In computing net annual level premiums, one can begin by ascertaining the net single premium. The second step would be to define the *premium payment period* over which annual premiums are to be paid and for which the *life annuity due* is to be ascertained.

An example will help clarify the issues. Assume that we seek the net annual level premium for purchasing a five-year term insurance policy of $1,000 at male age 45 using the *1980 CSO Table* and 5 percent interest. It was found earlier that the net single premium on this policy was $22.75. Beginning, at date of issue, the annual level premium will be paid over a five-year period, or until prior death and is, therefore, a *five-year temporary life annuity due.* An annuity due of 1 on the policy in question equals a temporary immediate annuity for four years plus 1 paid initially (making it an annuity due). Note that the *1980 CSO Table,* not the *1983 Table a,* is used because the calculation is required for a life insurance policy.

The calculation for the present value of the five-year life annuity due is shown in Table 28-5. The 4.504 total is the present expected value equivalent of 1 per year for five

TABLE 28-5	Illustrative Five-Year Life Annuity Due Calculation (Male, Aged 45, *1980 CSO* Mortality, 5% Interest)		
Policy Year (t)	*Age (x)*	*Calculation*	*Year's Present Expected Value*
1	45	1 due immediately	= 1.000
2	46	$\left[\dfrac{l_{46}}{l_{45}}\right](v) = \left[\dfrac{9,168,382}{9,210,289}\right](0.952)$	= 0.948
3	47	$\left[\dfrac{l_{47}}{l_{45}}\right](v^2) = \left[\dfrac{9,123,274}{9,210,289}\right](0.907)$	= 0.899
4	48	$\left[\dfrac{l_{48}}{l_{45}}\right](v^3) = \left[\dfrac{9,074,738}{9,210,289}\right](0.864)$	= 0.851
5	49	$\left[\dfrac{l_{49}}{l_{45}}\right](v^4) = \left[\dfrac{9,022,649}{9,210,289}\right](0.823)$	= 0.806
		Total	4.504

years. The net single premium on the policy in question was found to be $22.75. If the present value of the preceding annuity due is divided into the net single premium on this policy, we obtain an annual level premium, the present value of which will equal the net single premium. From this analysis, it is possible to state a general rule for ascertaining the net annual level premium on any policy: *Divide the net single premium by the present value of a temporary life annuity due of 1 for the premium-paying period.* Thus,

$$NLP = \frac{NSP}{PVLAD \text{ of } 1 \text{ for } PPP}$$

The net annual level premium on a five-year term insurance policy of $1,000 issued at age 45 is, thus, $5.05, computed as follows:

$$NLP = \frac{NSP}{PVLAD \text{ of } 1 \text{ for } PPP} = \frac{\$22.75}{4.504} = \$5.05$$

Ordinary Life Insurance

The net single premium for a whole life policy of $1,000 issued at age 45 is $270.84, according to the earlier figures. To find the net annual level premium for an ordinary life policy, this sum must be divided by the present value of a life annuity due of 1 for the whole of life because premiums are paid annually through the life of this policy. The method of ascertaining the present value of the life annuity due of 1 is shown in Table 28-6.

Thus, the net annual level premium for an ordinary life policy of $1,000 issued at male age 45 with *1980 CSO Table* mortality and on a 5 percent basis is $17.69. This result is obtained as follows:

$$\frac{\$270.84}{15.312} = \$17.69$$

Limited-Payment Whole Life Insurance

If it is desired to pay for the preceding whole life policy over a period that is less than the whole of life, it is necessary to compute the annual level premium that, continued for the desired premium-payment period or ceasing upon prior death, will purchase this policy. In accordance with the formula, the annual level premium for a 20-year payment

TABLE 28-6 Illustrative Whole Life Annuity Due Calculation
(Male, Aged 45, *1980 CSO* Mortality, 5% Interest)

Policy Year (t)	Age (x)	Calculation	Year's Present Expected Value
1	45	1 due immediately	= 1.000
2	46	$\left[\dfrac{l_{46}}{l_{45}}\right](v) = \left[\dfrac{9{,}168{,}382}{9{,}210{,}289}\right](0.952)$	= 0.948
3	47	$\left[\dfrac{l_{47}}{l_{45}}\right](v^2) = \left[\dfrac{9{,}123{,}274}{9{,}210{,}289}\right](0.907)$	= 0.899
⋮	⋮	⋮ ⋮	⋮
53	97	$\left[\dfrac{l_{97}}{l_{45}}\right](v^{52}) = \left[\dfrac{60{,}504}{9{,}210{,}289}\right](0.079)$	= 0.001
54	98	$\left[\dfrac{l_{98}}{l_{45}}\right](v^{53}) = \left[\dfrac{31{,}504}{9{,}210{,}289}\right](0.075)$	= 0.000[a]
55	99	$\left[\dfrac{l_{99}}{l_{45}}\right](v^{54}) = \left[\dfrac{10{,}757}{9{,}210{,}289}\right](0.072)$	= 0.000[a]
		Total	15.312

[a]Less than 0.0005.

period would be found by dividing into the net single premium the present value of a *temporary* life annuity due for a term of 20 years following age 45. The calculation of the present value of this life annuity due at male age 45 for 20 years is shown in Table 28-7.

The net annual level premium, therefore, for a 20-payment whole life policy issued at male age 45 is $270.84 ÷ 12.333, or $21.96.

Note that in all cases, the net single premium for the whole life policy (the numerator in the formula) is the same regardless of the premium-paying period selected. In the case of a 30-payment whole life or a life-paid-up-at-65 policy, the same principle would

TABLE 28-7 Illustrative 20-Year Life Annuity Due Calculation
(Male, Aged 45, *1980 CSO* Mortality, 5% Interest)

Policy Year (t)	Age (x)	Calculation	Year's Present Expected Value
1	45	1 due immediately	= 1.000
2	46	$\left[\dfrac{l_{46}}{l_{45}}\right](v) = \left[\dfrac{9{,}168{,}382}{9{,}210{,}289}\right](0.952)$	= 0.948
3	47	$\left[\dfrac{l_{47}}{l_{45}}\right](v^2) = \left[\dfrac{9{,}123{,}274}{9{,}210{,}289}\right](0.907)$	= 0.899
⋮	⋮	⋮ ⋮	⋮
18	62	$\left[\dfrac{l_{62}}{l_{45}}\right](v^{17}) = \left[\dfrac{7{,}814{,}753}{9{,}210{,}289}\right](0.436)$	= 0.370
19	63	$\left[\dfrac{l_{63}}{l_{45}}\right](v^{18}) = \left[\dfrac{7{,}644{,}788}{9{,}210{,}289}\right](0.416)$	= 0.346
20	64	$\left[\dfrac{l_{64}}{l_{45}}\right](v^{19}) = \left[\dfrac{7{,}503{,}368}{9{,}210{,}289}\right](0.396)$	= 0.323
		Total	12.333

be followed—that is, dividing the net single premium ($270.84 at male age 45) by the present value of a life annuity due for the appropriate premium-paying period. This is because the net single premium is a measure of the present value of future expected policy benefits and is blind to the actual policy premium payment method.

Deferred Annuity

Deferred annuities often are paid for by flexible, periodic premiums or, less commonly, by fixed, periodic premiums. Even when premiums are flexible, the contractholder often will choose to pay a level amount into the annuity with the idea of building to a future target sum. In theory, premiums may continue through the entire period of deferment, or, as in the case of the whole life policy earlier, they may be limited to a stated number of years. As with life insurance premiums, the annual level premium on these contracts is paid only while the insured is alive. If, therefore, the deferred annuity issued at age 40 begins the payment of an annual income of $100 at age 70 and if the net single premium for it is $239.36 (discussed earlier), the annual premium on this policy may be paid until one year prior to the beginning of the annuity (until the holder of the contract is 69). In this case, the series of annual premiums becomes a temporary annuity due for a term of 30 years—ages 40 to 69 inclusive. The amount of this net annual premium would be found, therefore, by dividing the net single premium by the present value of an annuity due of 1 computed for the 30-year term stated.

The present value of the 30-year life annuity due is 16.141 (15.141 + 1), the present expected value of an annual level premium of 1 paid over the same term as the premiums on the deferred annuity. This figure divided into the net single premium for the deferred annuity gives a net annual level premium:

$$\frac{\$239.36}{16.141} = \$14.83$$

Note that, unlike the life insurance premium calculation, the divisor is not a *life* annuity due because almost no deferred annuities involve life contingencies during the accumulation period.

Questions

1. Explain why the probabilities of death used in the net single-premium calculation are not the same as the yearly death probabilities in Table 27-1.
2. Why is the net level premium for a 10-year policy not the net single premium divided by 10?
3. Using the *1980 CSO Table,* assuming a 5 percent interest rate and a face amount of $1,000, compute the net single premium (*NSP*) for a four-year term life insurance policy issued at male age 35.
4. Compute the net single premium at age 60 for a deferred whole life annuity of $100 to begin at age 70 for a male, using the *1983 Individual Annuity Mortality Table for Males* and assuming 5 percent interest.

CHAPTER

29

LIFE INSURANCE RESERVES AND CASH VALUES

Objectives

- Explain the purpose and definition of the policy reserve.

- Describe a number of methods in use for calculating the policy reserve.

- Explain the significance of actuarial assumptions in the valuation of liabilities.

- Describe the approaches to calculating surrender values, as they are implied in the concepts of equity in this chapter and as dictated in the Standard Nonforfeiture Law.

- Describe the statutory requirements governing minimum policy reserves.

One of the most difficult subjects for the layperson to appreciate in connection with the administration of a life insurance company is the need for the existence of the enormous assets possessed by the companies. The great majority of these assets is needed to back the insurer's liabilities to its policyowners. Without these assets, the security of life insurance protection as we know it would not be possible.

RESERVES

Most reserves reflect an insurer's obligation to its customers, although some reserves relate to the insurer's investments and others relate to taxes. Box 29-1 shows the various liabilities appearing on U.S. life insurers' balance sheets. The policy reserve liability constitutes more than 80 percent of a company's total assets and more than 90 percent of a company's total liabilities.

Policy reserves are liabilities that represent, for in-force business, the amount that, with future premiums and interest earned, is expected to be needed to pay future benefits under those policies. Thus, more than 80 percent of the total assets held by U.S. life insurance companies represents funds held to support their policy reserve liabilities.

The composition of life insurer policy reserves has been changing over the years, reflecting a shift in the basic types of business done by life insurance companies. As the U.S. population has grown older, annuity reserves have become a larger and larger proportion of total reserves held by life insurers (see Figure 29-1).

BOX 29-1

1997 RESERVES AND OTHER OBLIGATIONS OF U.S. LIFE INSURANCE COMPANIES (MILLIONS OF $)

Policy Reserves	$2,164,559	83.8%
Dividend Accumulations	20,456	0.8
Policy Dividends	16,197	0.6
Other Obligations	174,359	6.8
Asset Valuation Reserve	36,159	1.4
Interest Maintenance Reserve	11,398	0.4
Surplus Funds	157,373	6.1
Book Value of Capital Stock	2,713	0.1
Total	$2,583,214	100%

Source: 1998 ACLI Fact Book, p. 117.

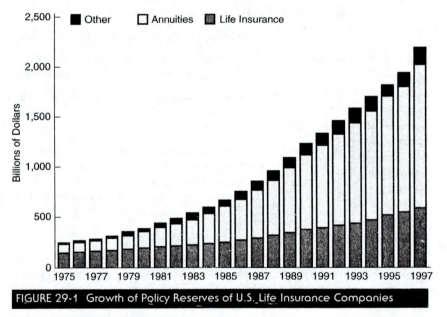

FIGURE 29-1 Growth of Policy Reserves of U.S. Life Insurance Companies

Source: 1998 ACLI Fact Book, p. 115.

As discussed briefly in chapter 2, cash surrender values are related to policy reserves in that they represent policyowners' demand claims against the insurer's assets. This chapter discusses both reserves and surrender values in more detail.

Origin and Definition of the Policy Reserve

Previously, it was stated that life insurance policies may be purchased by a single payment, by fixed annual premiums paid over a period of years, or by flexible premiums. It was also pointed out that mortality rates generally increase with increasing age. Thus, in the early policy years, fixed level premiums and (often) flexible premiums paid exceed the annual cost of insurance. In later years, the reverse may be true. The excess funds not used immediately to pay policy claims and expenses must be recognized by the insurer and preserved for the benefit of all the policyowners until needed at some future date. In a similar manner, when a policy is purchased by a single premium, this premium becomes the policyowner's only contribution toward claims to be paid and expenses incurred under contracts of the class, and a large share of this single premium must be held by the insurer to meet future obligations.

The **formula statutory policy reserve** is the amount that, together with future net premiums and interest, will be sufficient, according to the valuation assumptions, to pay future claims. This is the prospective definition of the reserve. Statutory reserve calculations ignore insurer expenses and lapse rates, being based instead solely on state-sanctioned mortality and interest assumptions and on the nature of policy benefits and method of calculation.[1] Another way of viewing the policy reserve is the retrospective view under which the reserve is considered as the difference between the accumulation at interest with benefit of survivorship of the net premiums received in the past and the accumulation at interest with benefit of survivorship of the claims paid, according to the valuation assumptions.

Reserve calculations (valuations) of policy liabilities require use of a mortality table and an interest rate. It is then necessary to calculate the net premium on the basis of the table and rate selected and in the manner that has been described in chapter 28.[2] With the selection of the policy duration for which the reserve is needed, the calculation may proceed, using either the prospective or retrospective method. The retrospective and prospective approaches are merely different ways of viewing the same issue and, therefore, with the same underlying assumptions, they will always yield identical results.

The statutory reserve has no relationship with the insurer's actual past experience. It is always calculated on the assumption that experience has been in accordance with the mortality table selected and interest rate assumed. The term *reserve* has come to have a technical meaning in life insurance because states' minimum reserve standards establish definite methods of valuing policy liabilities.[3]

The word *reserve* is somewhat misleading because it is not used here as it is used in the usual commercial dealings in which *reserve* is often synonymous with *surplus*. As pointed out earlier, the policy reserve of a life insurance company is a liability. It is a measure of the value of obligations to policyowners. As brought out in the following discussion, if the insurer underestimates its policy reserves, or fails to maintain sufficient assets to back its reserves, it eventually may be unable to pay claims. Of a life insurance company's liabilities, the policy reserve often is the most important one.

Methods of Calculation

Retrospective Method

The retrospective method looks back at a policy's *past* premiums and benefits to determine policy reserves. Thus, under this approach, the policy reserve is defined as follows:

$$\frac{\text{Policy}}{\text{Reserve}} = \frac{\text{Accumulated Value}}{\text{of Net Premiums}} - \frac{\text{Accumulated Cost}}{\text{of Insurance}}$$

The retrospective method may be explained in terms of either a group or individual approach.

---

[1]See Mark A. Tullis and Phillip K. Polkingham, *Valuation of Life Insurance Liabilities,* 2nd ed. (Winsted, Ct: ACTEX Publications, 1992).

[2]It is also necessary to select a specific valuation method. See later in this chapter.

[3]See "Regulation of Reserves and Cash Values" later in this chapter.

Group Approach   The reserve arises from the payment of a level net (valuation) premium in excess of that needed to meet current mortality costs. Under this approach, premiums in the early policy years usually are more than sufficient to pay the death claims that are assumed; they create a fund that can be used in later policy years, when death rates rise sharply and premiums alone may be insufficient to meet the then current claims. The retrospective reserve can be thought of as an unearned net premium reserve. It represents the provision in early premiums for prefunding of the benefits of surviving insureds and is shown on the insurer's financial statement as a liability item.[4]

Individual Approach   The retrospective reserve valuation method also may be illustrated with reference to an individual policy. The retrospective terminal reserve for any particular policy year can be obtained by adding the *net premium* for the year in question to the *terminal reserve* of the preceding year, increasing the combined sum (called the *initial reserve*) by one year's interest at the assumed rate, and deducting the *cost of insurance* for the net amount at risk for the current year utilizing the assumed mortality table.

Consideration of the process by which this reserve is built involves an understanding of the cost of insurance concept. Reference was made in previous chapters to the *net amount at risk,* which is the death benefit less the terminal reserve at the end of the policy year.[5] When an insured dies, the reserve held for the policy is, of course, no longer required. Under this approach, the value of assets corresponding to that reserve is considered to be freed to help pay the claim. The balance of the claim (the net amount at risk) is paid through charges against all policies in the group, including those that mature as a death claim.

The contribution each insured must make as his or her pro rata share of death claims in any particular year—the **cost of insurance**—is determined by multiplying the net amount at risk at the end of such year by the tabular probability of death during that year. This procedure, of course, is identical in concept to that in which the mortality charge of a universal life (UL) policy is determined, except that the cash value rather than the reserve is used to derive the net amount of risk.

Prospective Reserve

Although the retrospective method of computation provides a clear exposition of the origin and purpose of the reserve, it typically is not used. The prospective method is more commonly used.

As mentioned earlier, the reserve is the balancing factor in the basic insurance equation—that is, in prospective terms, the reserve is the difference between the present value of expected future benefits and the present value of expected future net premiums. (Of course, the assumptions underlying the calculation may or may not be reasonable.)

At the inception of a contract, the present value of future benefits (*PVFB*) is identical to the present value of future net premiums (*PVFP*): thus,

$$PVFB = PVFP \text{ (at date of issue)}$$

As soon as the contract goes in force and the first premium is paid, the present value of future benefits almost always exceeds the present value of future net premiums.[6] This should be apparent because fewer premiums remain to be paid and the present value of future benefits is greater because the policy is nearer to maturity. The difference between these two quantities is a measure of the obligation (reserve) of the insurer. Thus,

---

[4]A simplified example was given in chapter 2.

[5]See chapter 2.

[6]This statement is true in general of ordinary life policies but can be inaccurate for level-premium, decreasing term insurance.

$$\frac{\text{Terminal Reserve}}{\text{(age of valuation)}} = \frac{PVFB}{\text{(age of valuation)}} - \frac{PVFP}{\text{(age of valuation)}}$$

It has already been shown that the net single premium (*NSP*) for a given policy is the present value of future expected benefits, so the preceding equation may be written as

$$\frac{\text{Terminal Reserve}}{\text{(age of valuation)}} = \frac{NSP}{\text{(age of valuation)}} - \frac{PVFP}{\text{(age of valuation)}}$$

The present value of future net premiums necessarily must equal the net level annual premium (*NLP*) for the contract under consideration, multiplied by the present value of a life annuity due (*PVLAD*) of 1 for the remaining premium-paying period. Finally, then, the equation may be written in word form as follows:

$$\frac{\text{Terminal Reserve}}{\text{(age of valuation)}} = \frac{NSP}{\substack{\text{(age of} \\ \text{valuation)}}} - \frac{NLP}{\substack{\text{(age of} \\ \text{issue)}}} \times \frac{PVLAD \text{ of 1 for}}{\substack{\text{Remaining Premium-} \\ \text{Paying Period}}}$$

This same approach may be illustrated more analytically and concisely as follows:

$$_tV_x = A_{x+t} - (P_x)\ddot{a}_{\overline{x+t}|}$$

where $_tV_x$ is the net level terminal reserve for an ordinary life policy issued at age x at the end of any number of years t, P is the net level premium, and the other variables have the same meaning as discussed in chapter 28.

The manner in which the present value of future benefits and the present value of future net premiums diverge to create the necessity for a reserve is illustrated in Figure 29-2 (not drawn to scale). The computation of the present value of future net premiums involves the determination of the original net level annual premium applicable to the contract, which is multiplied by the present value of a temporary life annuity due of 1 for the remaining premium-paying period.

By way of further illustration, the computation of the twentieth-year terminal reserve on a 15-payment whole life policy issued at age 35 is:

$$\text{Terminal Reserve}_{55} = NSP_{55} - (NLP_{35})(PVLAD_{55})$$
$$_{20}V_{35} = NSP_{55} - (NLP_{35})(0)$$
$$= NSP_{55}$$

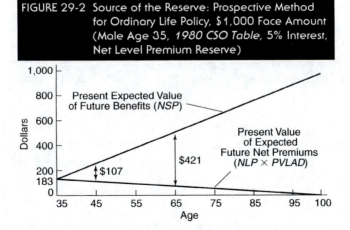

FIGURE 29-2 Source of the Reserve: Prospective Method for Ordinary Life Policy, $1,000 Face Amount (Male Age 35, *1980 CSO Table*, 5% Interest, Net Level Premium Reserve)

The result illustrates the principle that, because no further premiums are due on a paid-up policy, the reserve must equal the present value of future benefits, which can be measured by the net single premium of the policy at the attained age of valuation. The principle is even more graphically illustrated by the single-premium policy, which is paid up after the payment of the first premium. Thus, a single-premium whole life policy issued at male age 35 would produce a twentieth-year reserve identical to that of the twentieth-year reserve on the preceding 15-payment whole life policy, both of which would equal the net single premium for a whole life policy at male age 55. The reserves at a given attained age on all paid-up policies of the same type and amount and calculated under the same assumptions must be equal to each other, at the age of valuation, and they all must equal the net single premium for that generic type of policy.

For a policy not yet paid up, consider the tenth-year reserve on a 20-payment whole life policy issued at age 25. It would be formatted as follows:

$$\text{Terminal Reserve}_{35} = NSP_{35} - NLP_{25} \times PVLAD \text{ of 1 for 10 Years}_{35}$$

Table 29-1 shows the actual computation of reserves for this policy and for two other policies issued at age 25, utilizing the principles developed here and in the previous chapter.

TABLE 29-1 Computation of Prospective Net Level Reserves
(*1980 CSO Table*, 5% Interest)

	Net Single Premium per $1,000			*Payment Value of Life Annuity Due of 1*		
Age	*Whole Life*	*20-Year Endowment*	*10-Year Endowment*	*Life*	*20 Years*	*10 Years*
25	$124.316	$386.254	$616.655	18.389	12.889	8.050
35	183.559	393.167	617.928	17.145	12.743	8.023
45	270.840	412.730	622.701	15.312	12.333	7.923
55	387.005	457.051	634.199	12.873	11.402	7.682

Net Level Terminal Reserve (age of valuation)	=	NSP (age of valuation)	−	NLP (age of issue)	×	PVLAD of 1 for Remaining Premium-Paying Period

Computation

1. Twentieth-Year Net Level Terminal Reserve, Ordinary Life Issued at Age 25:

$$\text{Net Level Reserve}_{45} = NSP_{45} - (NLP_{25} \times PVLAD \text{ of 1 for Life}_{45})$$

$$= \$270.840 - \frac{\$124.316}{18.389} \times 15.312$$

$$= \$167.33$$

2. Tenth-Year Net Level Terminal Reserve, 20-Payment Whole Life Issued at Age 25:

$$\text{Net Level Reserve}_{35} = NSP_{35} - (NLP_{25} \times PVLAD \text{ of 1 for 10 Years}_{35})$$

$$= \$183.559 - \frac{\$124.316}{12.889} \times 8.023$$

$$= \$106.18$$

Tenth-Year Net Level Terminal Reserve, 20-Year Endowment Issued at Age 25:

$$\text{Net Level Reserve}_{35} = NSP_{35} - (NLP_{25} \times PVLAD \text{ of 1 for 10 Years}_{35})$$

$$= \$617.928 - \frac{\$386.254}{12.889} \times 8.023$$

$$= \$377.50$$

Terminal, Initial, and Mean Reserves

Reserves may be classified as terminal, initial, or mean depending on the point of time within the policy year when valuation occurs. The calculations illustrated earlier concerned primarily the **terminal reserve**—that is, the reserve at the end of any given policy year. The **initial reserve,** the reserve at the beginning of the policy year, equals the terminal reserve for the preceding year, increased by the net level annual premium (if any) for the current year. The **mean reserve** is the arithmetic average of the initial reserve and the terminal reserve for any year of valuation. As discussed in chapter 30, the initial reserve is used principally in connection with the determination of dividends under participating policies. The initial reserve generally is selected as the basis for allocation of interest earnings in excess of those assumed in the reserve.

The terminal reserve also is used in connection with dividend distributions because mortality savings are allocated on the basis of the net amount at risk, and the terminal reserve is used to determine the net amount at risk. The terminal reserve concept also is used to determine nonforfeiture values, although a so-called adjusted premium is used rather than the net level premium in such determinations.[7] The terminal reserve also is used in connection with the form of reinsurance based on yearly renewable term insurance for the net amount at risk.[8]

The mean reserve is used in connection with the annual statements of life insurance companies. Because policies are written at different points throughout the year and insurer annual statements are prepared as of December 31, it has traditionally been complicated and expensive to attempt a precise calculation for each individual policy. Changing technologies, however, make such calculations feasible. Consequently, for purposes of the annual statement, it is generally assumed that policy anniversaries are uniformly distributed throughout the calendar year of issue, and the mean reserve is used for such valuation purposes.

Significance of Actuarial Assumptions

In measuring or valuing its liabilities under outstanding contracts, a life insurance company must make assumptions as to the rate of mortality among its insureds and the rate of earnings on the assets standing behind the reserves. These assumptions are reflected in the mortality table and rate of interest assumed in making the valuation and the purpose for which the valuation is made, all of which may themselves be constrained by various tax and other laws. The preceding discussion assumed the *1980 CSO Table* and 5 percent interest—reasonable assumptions for the United States. Other assumptions, however, can be and are used in reserve valuations, especially in other countries. It is important, therefore, to consider the impact on reserves of the choice of the mortality table and interest table used.

Mortality

In practice, it frequently is impossible to determine which of two mortality tables will result in larger reserves at a given age and duration simply by reviewing the mortality rates. A change in mortality not only affects the number of deaths at a given age, but it also affects the number surviving at subsequent ages. Under the net level premium method, the effect of a change in mortality is somewhat spread over the premium-paying period. Because the impact of a change in mortality is not uniform from age to age and duration to duration, it may result in either an increase or a decrease in reserve at

---

[7]See later in this chapter.
[8]See chapter 25.

TABLE 29-2	Net Level Terminal Reserves per $1,000, Different Mortality Tables (*1941, 1958, and 1980 CSO Mortality Tables,* 5% Interest, Issued at Male Age 35)						
	Ordinary Life				*Endowment at Age 65*		
Duration (Years)	*1941 CSO*	*1958 CSO*	*1980 CSO*	*Duration (Years)*	*1941 CSO*	*1958 CSO*	*1980 CSO*
1	$ 11.01	$ 11.06	$ 9.15	1	$ 16.71	$ 16.51	$ 16.24
10	125.57	117.60	106.90	10	199.86	200.48	197.63
20	283.07	269.83	249.19	20	497.23	502.04	500.21
30	459.52	443.84	420.57	30	1,000.00	1,000.00	1,000.00
50	769.48	750.08	749.22				
60	872.51	869.15	868.26				

any given age and duration. The simplest way to analyze the effect of a change in mortality is to calculate the reserves on both mortality bases for representative plans and issue ages. Without actually calculating the reserves, the determination of the effect on reserves of a change in mortality assumptions is a complex mathematical problem and is beyond the scope of this volume.[9] Table 29-2 shows a comparison of reserves under the *1941 CSO Table,* the *1958 CSO Table,* and the *1980 CSO Table,* assuming an interest rate of 5 percent in each case.

Interest

The impact on reserves of a change in the interest assumption can be easily visualized. If the rate of interest assumed is decreased, the result will be an increase in reserves. This may be explained simply by the fact that the smaller anticipated earnings must be offset by a larger reserve at any point in time. The impact of a change in interest assumptions on the reserves of an individual contract utilizing the *1980 CSO Table* is presented in Table 29-3.

An explanation of the impact of the change in interest assumption in terms of the conventional prospective and retrospective methods of calculation is not as easily grasped. Such an explanation is complicated by the fact that both the assumed earnings on the assets backing the reserve and the net premiums are affected by the change, and the net effect on these modifications leads to the final reserve level. Even so, in general, we observe that the prospective approach utilizes a present value calculation. The higher

TABLE 29-3	Net Level Terminal Reserves per $1,000, Varying Rates of Interest (Ordinary Life, 1980 CSO Table, Male, Age 35)		
	Rate of Interest		
Duration (Years)	*3%*	*5%*	*6%*
1	$ 13.32	$ 9.15	$ 7.63
10	145.56	106.90	91.93
20	315.30	249.19	221.77
30	496.89	420.57	386.81
50	799.91	749.22	724.36
60	898.55	868.26	852.77

---

[9]See Newton L Bowers, Jr., Hans U. Gerber, James C. Hickman, Donald A. Jones, and Cecil J. Nesbitt, *Actuarial Mathematics,* 2nd ed. (Chicago, IL: Society of Actuaries, 1997).

the interest rate used in any present value calculation, the lower the present value, all else being equal. Thus, with reserve (and cash-value) derivation, the higher the interest rate used, the lower the values, other things being held constant.

Lapse or Withdrawal Rates

Life insurance statutory policy reserves are calculated based on the assumption that no policies will withdraw from coverage (lapse). This requirement makes the present value of future benefits for statutory reserves considerably greater than the insurer's actual present value of future benefits. Withdrawal rates are considered in pricing and in calculating reserves based on generally accepted accounting principles (GAAP).[10]

Plan of Insurance

The relative net level reserves for various plans of whole life insurance based on the indicated assumptions are illustrated in Figure 29-3. The figure illustrates that all limited-payment policies, assuming the same age of issue, amount, and underlying assumptions, have the same reserves after they are paid up. In terms of the formula discussed earlier, the temporary life annuity due becomes zero after all premiums have been paid, and the reserve becomes the net single premium in question at the insured's attained age.

Modified Reserves

Ideally, each class of policies should pay its own cost. From the standpoint of the insurer, however, the problem of meeting the expense when it occurs is of greater immediate importance. The primary difficulty is that the expenses of the first policy year greatly exceed those of any subsequent year and frequently exceed the entire premium. That first-year expenses are high can be seen by considering that selling expenses, such as agents' first-year commissions and expenses of physical examinations, of approving applications, and

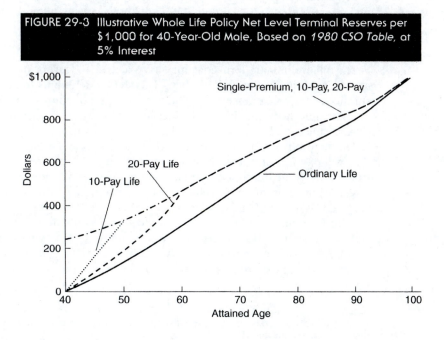

FIGURE 29-3 Illustrative Whole Life Policy Net Level Terminal Reserves per $1,000 for 40-Year-Old Male, Based on *1980 CSO Table*, at 5% Interest

---

[10]See later in this chapter and chapter 34.

of preparing policies for issue, as well as the expenses of setting up records for new policies, are all incurred in the first policy year.

Thus, the major problem of the incidence of expense is that policies typically cannot pay their first-year expenses from the amount available from the first premium. These expenses must be met when incurred, yet the insurer faces the necessity of maintaining a reasonable premium level, of paying death claims during the year, and of holding in reserve the remainder of the net premium.

Consider, for example, an ordinary life policy whose gross premium per $1,000 is $13.39 at age 35. Its valuation net premium of $10.71 (using the *1980 CSO Table* and 5 percent interest) would be increased at 5 percent interest to $11.25 at the close of the policy year. Of this amount, $2.01 is necessary to pay the estimated cost of insurance for the year. Thus, $9.15 ($11.25 – $2.01) constitutes a measure of the assets that should be earmarked (reserved) in anticipation of future claims against the policy. Under this statutory approach, the loading of $2.68 ($13.39 – $10.71) is the only portion of the first premium available to pay the first year's expenses, and this would be insufficient. This incidence of expense problem is referred to as **surplus strain** and is particularly severe when a small company increases its new business rapidly.

These first-year costs must be provided from some outside source, or some modification of the system of level reserve valuation must be made. For a well-established insurer with a large surplus, the solution to the problem is comparatively simple, for it can pay expenses of new business from surplus and depend on replacing the amount from margins in the loadings of the later premiums. This, however, is not possible for new and small companies, for they have less surplus from which to borrow to supply the demands of a rapidly increasing business.[11]

Another possible way of dealing with this problem is through some modification of the system of valuing reserves, whereby the policy reserve of the first year or of the first few years can be reduced. The two important methods of modifying full net level terminal reserves used in the United States are known as the **full preliminary term method** and the **commissioners' reserve valuation method**.[12]

Full Preliminary Term Method

The full preliminary term concept was conceived in Europe but is now used in many markets, including in the United States The technique entails treating the first year of insurance as term insurance, irrespective of the type of contract actually involved, and to assume that the original contract goes into effect at the beginning of the second policy year. Hence, *preliminary term* is a logical name for it.

This method of valuation provides that the first year's premium under any form of policy will pay for term insurance for one year and that the regular policy for reserve purposes will come into operation one year later than the age of issue and will be for a one-year-shorter premium-payment period and coverage period. By this means, the insurer need not earmark against the policy liability (terminal reserve) any portion of the first-year premium; the entire premium becomes available for payment of first-year claims and expenses. Because the amount required for first-year claims is the net premium for one-year term insurance (typically a relatively small amount), the amount available to cover expenses is the excess of the gross premium over the one-year term net rate.

---

[11]Smaller insurers often rely on reinsurance to provide some relief from the strain on surplus caused by new business. See chapter 24.

[12]GAAP does not allow insurers to use modified reserve methods. See "GAAP versus Statutory Reserves" section in this chapter.

For example, the net level premium on an ordinary life policy at male age 35 (using the *1980 CSO Table* and interest at 5 percent) is $10.71. The net premium for one-year term insurance at age 35 is $2.01 ($1,000 × 0.00211 ÷ 1.05). Thus, the excess amount released to help defray first-year expenses would be $8.70 ($10.71 − $2.01). On the 20-payment whole life plan at the same age, the corresponding excess is $12.39, whereas on an endowment-at-age 65 plan, it is $15.43. The net premium for the later years of the policy is then increased and the loading is correspondingly reduced because the gross premium paid by the policyowner does not change. The net premium becomes that for insurance issued at an age that is one year higher, at a date one year later, and for a term that is one year shorter.

The reserves held on the policy for the second and later years are the reserves based on this new net premium. Thus, an ordinary life policy's reserve at the end of the first year would be zero. The reserve at the end of the *second* year would be equal to that of the *first-year* terminal reserve for an ordinary life policy issued at age 36. The renewal (age 36) net premium equals the net level premium for age 36, and it is sufficient to provide benefits for an ordinary life policy issued at age 36 with level net premiums. The remainder of the gross premium is available each renewal year for expenses.

The net effect of the full preliminary term method compared to the net level method is to defer funding the first-year reserve and amortize this amount over the remaining premium-paying period of the contract. This method of valuation makes no distinction between various types of cash-value contracts.

For most low-premium policies written by a typical life insurance company, the additional first-year loading made available by treating the first year of insurance as term insurance is inadequate to cover fully substantial first-year expenses. The remainder of the amount needed must be drawn from assets backing the insurer's surplus. Thus, it is possible for a rapidly growing company to have a capacity problem, despite the fact that it is using the preliminary term plan.

On higher-premium plans, on the other hand, the first-year reserve borrowed is correspondingly greater, as the cost of one-year term insurance remains the same. The logic of this position has led regulatory authorities to prescribe the use of some modification of the full preliminary term method of valuation, the most important of which is the commissioners' reserve valuation method.

Commissioners' Reserve Valuation Method

The commissioners' reserve valuation method (CRVM) in effect makes the 20-payment whole life policy the maximum basis on which deferred reserve funding is permitted, and, in doing so, it divides policies into two groups:

1. The full preliminary term method is used if the net premium for the second and subsequent years of the plan does not exceed the corresponding modified net premium for a 20-payment whole life plan.
2. For plans with higher premiums, the additional amount for expenses is limited to the same amount as is permitted under the preliminary term method for a 20-payment whole life policy. It is not exactly the same as the 20-payment life amount in the case of policies that require more or less than 20 years' premiums because the amount "borrowed" is "repaid" by a level premium payable for each year of the premium-paying period, including the first.

For example, for ordinary life at male age 35, the CRVM calls for the full preliminary term method because the net premium at male age 36 is less than the corresponding 20-payment life preliminary term basis premium for the second and subsequent years of $15.46 (i.e., the 19-payment life rate at male age 36).

In the case of the endowment at age 65 issued at male age 35, however, the modified method applies because the rate at male age 36 for an endowment at age 65 of $18.52 exceeds the 19-payment life rate at male age 36 of $15.46. The additional amount available for expenses is found to be $12.29 (following the method described in paragraph 2); this amount is equal to that given earlier for the 20-payment life plan under the preliminary term plan. Where the premium-paying period differs from 20 years, however, the result will be slightly different. Table 29-4 presents terminal reserve values under the several methods of valuation discussed previously, using 5 percent interest.

Other Types of Reserves

In addition to reserves related to products, insurers maintain a number of other types of reserves to provide a more complete picture of their financial obligations. This section discusses several of these types of reserves.

Premium Deficiency Reserves

In the past in the United States, if gross premiums charged by a life insurance company for a particular class of policies were less than the valuation net premiums, the insurer was required to maintain a supplemental reserve, called a **deficiency reserve.** Valuation net premiums historically have been considerably less than gross premium. In recent years, however, continued improvement in mortality and increasing price competition brought gross-premium levels down to or even below valuation net premiums. The establishment of deficiency reserves was particularly difficult for smaller insurers with limited surplus.

Deficiency-reserve requirements (or their equivalent) are founded on the theory that the use, in the prospective reserve formula, of a valuation net level premium larger

TABLE 29-4 Terminal Reserves per $1,000, Various Methods of Valuation (*1980 CSO Table*, 5% Interest, Male, Age 35)				
Plan	*Policy Year*	*Full Preliminary Term Method*	*Commissioners' Reserve Valuation Method*	*Net Level Premium Method*
Ordinary life	1	$ 0.00	$ 0.00	$ 9.15
	5	40.42	40.42	49.20
	10	98.66	98.66	106.90
	15	165.90	165.90	173.54
	20	242.25	242.25	249.19
20-Payment life	1	0.00	0.00	13.04
	5	59.62	59.62	70.83
	10	148.35	148.35	156.71
	15	255.93	255.93	260.67
	20	387.01	387.01	387.01
Age 65 endowment	1	0.00	3.01	16.24
	5	73.55	76.33	88.59
	10	184.38	186.83	197.63
	15	321.21	323.26	332.24
	20	491.96	493.49	500.21

than the actual gross premium overstates the present expected value of expected future premiums and, consequently, understates the amount of the reserve. The deficiency is represented by the present value of the expected excess of the valuation net premium over the gross annual premium.

U.S. law no longer requires the establishment of deficiency reserves, as such. Rather, the law defines a new minimum required reserve as the present value of expected future benefits less the present value of expected future valuation net premiums calculated by the method (commissioners' or net level) actually used in computing the reserve for the policy, but using the minimum valuation standards of mortality and rate of interest. The gross premium on the policy is substituted in this reserve calculation at each contract year in which it is less than the valuation net premium. If the reserve calculated in this way is larger than the reserve otherwise required, it becomes the minimum reserve for the policy. In practice, however, the term *deficiency reserve* is still used to denote these special situations.

Reserves for Individual Deferred Annuities

There are three basic forms of annuity policies: the flexible- or fixed-premium deferred annuity, the single-premium deferred annuity, and the single-premium immediate annuity. The policy reserve, for the large majority of annuities, is equal to the present value of future benefits because most annuities sold today are either flexible-premium deferred annuities (FPDAs) or single-premium immediate annuities. In the case of FPDAs, the insurer cannot know for certain what future premium payments the policyowner may make. Therefore, the policy reserve is calculated on the assumption that the policyowner will pay no future premiums. Thus, the policy reserve is equal to the present value of future benefits for both single-premium and flexible-premium policies.

When any annuity becomes income paying, it is reserved on the basis of a legally recognized mortality table and interest rate, using the annuitant's attained age and the monthly income, and taking into account any minimum benefit guarantees. The mortality standard generally used is more conservative than that used for life valuation. (*Conservative* for life insurance means higher mortality rates, whereas *conservative* for annuities means lower mortality rates.)

Fixed-premium deferred annuities are policies in which the owner pays annual premiums during an accumulation period until such time as the annuitant begins to receive income. At income commencement, an annuitant receives the monthly income based on the cash value of the policy at that time and an annuity factor for the annuitant's attained age.

In 1976, a **commissioners' annuity reserve valuation method** (CARVM) was defined. It requires the comparison of the present value of future guaranteed benefits at each duration to the present value of future required premiums at that duration. The present value of the greatest excess revealed by these comparisons at the valuation date is the minimum reserve for the contract. Supplementary contracts involving life contingencies generally are valued according to the mortality and interest basis upon which the payments were calculated.

Reserves for Paid-Up Contracts

Under contracts in which no further premiums will be received, reserves are merely valuation net single premiums (i.e., the present value of future benefits). This would include (1) single-premium life and endowment contracts, (2) immediate life annuities, (3) paid-up life and endowment policies, and (4) supplementary contracts issued to beneficiaries in lieu of a lump-sum payment.

Reserves for Second-to-Die Policies

The procedure for deriving these reserves is identical conceptually to that for single-life policies. An adjustment, however, is necessary in the calculation to recognize the conditional probabilities involved with two insureds. Reserves under second-to-die policies are low while both insureds are alive. When one insured dies, however, the traditional second-to-die policies required reserves increase substantially as the policy, at that point, becomes in effect a regular single-life policy.[13]

Reserves for Substandard Policies

In the case of substandard policies, an additional reserve liability is recognized to anticipate the additional mortality risk over that expected for a standard policy. This reserve is calculated by any one of numerous methods, and the approach followed varies from insurer to insurer.

Similarly, the adverse selection reflected in the mortality experience under group and term conversions may be recognized by establishing an additional reserve for the extra mortality experienced. Reserving for these items is not uniform.

Reserves for Dividend Liabilities

Insurers are required to create dividend liabilities to account for policy dividends and experience-rating refunds that are owed but not yet paid. Dividends and experience-rating refunds are based on the policy year, which rarely coincides with the accounting year. An insurer's financial statement must reflect a liability for dividends and refunds that will be paid in the next accounting period. For GAAP statement purposes,[14] the reserves are equal to only that portion of the projected dividend that applies to the accounting year represented by the financial statement.

Reserves for Premiums Paid in Advance

A liability reserve must be reported for premiums paid in advance in one accounting period for coverage that is not effective until the next period. This type of reserve differs from an unearned premium reserve in that premiums are paid in advance for coverage that does not begin until the next accounting period whereas unearned premium revenues are for coverage that begins in an earlier accounting period and extends to a later period.

Reserves for Special Benefits

State laws require that a minimum reserve liability be maintained for accidental death and waiver-of-premium benefits, and an appropriate liability for supplementary contracts without life contingencies, dividend accumulations, and similar benefits.

Accidental death benefit minimum reserves are determined in a similar manner to ordinary policy reserves, using a mortality table (e.g., in the United States the *1959 Accidental Death Benefits Table*) based on accidental deaths.

Reserves for waiver of premium are, of course, based upon appropriate morbidity and mortality tables. These form the basis for predicting the probability of dying or becoming disabled, and, assuming that the waiver of premium annuity has been entered upon, the probability of death or recovery.

---

[13]It is possible to design a second-to-die policy in which there is no increase on the first death. These policies, called "Frasier-type" policies, are based on "Frasierized" mortality. Premiums, cash values, and dividends also do not change.

[14]Statement based on generally accepted accounting principles—see chapter 34.

Supplementary contracts without life contingencies, dividend accumulations, premiums paid in advance, and similar benefits are easily valued because they involve only compound interest calculations.[15]

Voluntary Reserve

In addition to the specific policy/benefit reserves (legal and voluntary) held to meet specific policy obligations, life insurance companies set aside various voluntary reserves that really represent earmarking of surplus for particular purposes and may not be liabilities.

GAAP versus Statutory Reserves

As discussed earlier, in the United States statutory minimum reserves are calculated on the basis of the **Standard Valuation Law.**[16] The law specifies the mortality table and other factors that must be used by companies in calculating minimum policy reserves for their statutory financial statements.

Reserve requirements for flexible-premium or interest-sensitive life products are spelled out in the NAIC's **Universal Life Insurance Model Regulation.** Not all states have adopted the NAIC's Universal Life Model Regulation; individual company approaches may vary in this regard.

Because minimum statutory reserves are conservative, they are generally larger than net GAAP reserves. Net GAAP reserves are equal to GAAP policy reserves minus deferred acquisition costs (DAC) (discussed later). Calculating U.S. GAAP policy reserves differs in several ways from calculating statutory policy reserves. For interest-sensitive products covered by FAS 97, such as universal life products, GAAP policy reserves are equal to the account value. For traditional life products, GAAP policy reserves are less conservative than statutory policy reserves.

The following factors account for the less conservative nature of GAAP reserves for traditional products:

- *Mortality Rate.* Under GAAP, insurers may use mortality rates they feel approximate their own mortality expectations. They generally assume mortality rates based on basic tables, but they often use a higher percentage of the rate shown in the basic table than they use for pricing, adding a margin for adverse results.
- *Interest Rate.* Under GAAP, insurers may use interest rates that reflect their best expectations but also with a margin for adverse results.
- *Lapses and Withdrawals.* Insurers recognize that not all life insurance policies will remain in force until maturity. Under GAAP, they may use withdrawal rates that approximate their expectations. Lapses and withdrawal rates may *not* be used in calculating statutory reserves.

The assumptions used for GAAP reserves generally must be used for the life of the policy even if the insurer's expectations at issue turn out to be wrong. In contrast, under certain conditions, insurers may be permitted to strengthen or destrengthen their

---

[15]Most insurers permit policyowners to prepay premiums by discounting them at a given rate of interest. The discounted premiums so paid are applied at the appropriate premium-due dates. If the insured dies, all unapplied premiums (less unearned discount) are paid to the beneficiary.

[16]This section is adapted from Susan Conant, Nicholas L. Desoutter, Dani L. Long, and Robert MacGrogan, *Managing Solvency and Profitability in Life and Health Insurance Companies,* (Atlanta, GA: LOMA, 1996), pp. 334–338.

statutory reserves. After business has been in force for some time, assumptions may be changed but remain subject to the *minimum standards* in the Standard Valuation Law.

Another important difference between GAAP and statutory reserves involves the definition of the present value of future benefits (*PVFB*). For statutory reserves, the *PVFB* includes only the present value of future death benefits. Under GAAP, the *PVFB* for traditional products includes four elements:

- the present value of future death benefits
- the present value of future surrender benefits
- the present value of all expected policy dividends
- the present value of the insurer's expected maintenance expenses for the business

Of course, the present value of future surrender benefits is a factor only for products that offer a surrender benefit, and the present value of future policy dividends is only involved with participating policies. The present value of future level maintenance expenses generally influences the size of policy reserves only for single premium and other limited-payment whole life plans. As suggested earlier, GAAP reserves contain a provision for adverse deviation, a safety margin to allow for unfavorable variations from actuarial assumptions. Despite this provision, GAAP reserves are generally considerably smaller than statutory reserves (see Table 29-5).

In calculating GAAP reserves, statutory modified reserving systems described earlier may not be used. Instead, GAAP limits surplus strain by permitting insurers to amortize excess first-year expenses over several years. Although the insurer must still pay all first-year expenses, only a portion of the first-year expenses are charged to income in each year of the period over which the first-year expenses are amortized (usually over the premium-paying period).

In order to keep their books balanced, insurers create an asset account called deferred acquisition costs (DAC). The DAC account includes those first-year expenses not charged to the current period. Each year a portion of the expenses being amortized is charged to current income and the DAC account is reduced accordingly. The effect of this process is that an insurer's first-year acquisition expenses reduce surplus over a period of years minimizing the impact (strain) on surplus. Thus, in examining GAAP reserves, it is necessary to deduct the DAC account from the GAAP policy reserves, resulting in **net GAAP reserves.** Net GAAP reserves are similar to modified statutory reserves, both reflecting the need to ease the strain on surplus of excess first-year expenses.

Voluntary Strengthening and Destrengthening of Reserves

Periodically, an insurer may conclude that its resources are inadequate for a particular type of policy, block of policies, or product line.[17] As a result, the insurer may engage in reserve strengthening. This *increase* in reserves may be, for example, accomplished by recalculating them with a lower interest rate. Similarly, if an insurer decides that its reserves are too conservative, it may destrengthen them by an increase in the interest assumption, thus *decreasing* the amount of its reserves.

As discussed earlier, the minimum size of an insurer's statutory reserves is determined by law at the time a product is issued. Insurers may set up more conservative

---

[17]This discussion draws on Elizabeth A. Mulligan and Gene Stone, "Accounting and Financial Reporting," in *Life and Health Insurance Companies,* (Atlanta, GA: LOMA, 1997), pp. 274–275.

TABLE 29-5 GAAP versus Statutory Reserves

For Age	Statutory Assumptions			GAAP Assumptions			Policy Year	Cash Value per 1,000	Statutory Reserves per 1,000	GAAP Reserves per 1,000
	Mortality per 1,000	Lapse (%)	Interest (%)	Mortality per 1,000	Lapse (%)	Interest (%)				
Annual Premium									11.87879	6.23597
35	2.173	0.00	4.50	0.998	28.80	8.50	1	0.00	10.27	6.69
36	2.320	0.00	4.50	1.088	16.80	8.50	2	0.00	20.87	14.72
37	2.491	0.00	4.50	1.185	11.40	8.50	3	5.00	31.81	23.34
38	2.685	0.00	4.50	1.305	9.00	8.50	4	15.00	43.09	32.24
39	2.904	0.00	4.50	1.440	7.80	8.50	5	25.00	54.70	41.45
40	3.154	0.00	4.50	1.590	5.40	8.38	6	36.00	66.63	50.75
41	3.429	0.00	4.50	1.770	4.80	8.25	7	47.00	78.89	60.41
42	3.713	0.00	4.50	1.958	4.80	8.13	8	58.00	91.48	70.57
43	4.029	0.00	4.50	2.175	4.20	8.00	9	69.00	104.40	81.17
44	4.371	0.00	4.50	2.393	3.60	7.88	10	81.00	117.66	92.23
45	4.730	0.00	4.50	2.640	3.60	7.75	11	94.00	131.26	103.79
46	5.123	0.00	4.50	2.888	3.60	7.63	12	106.00	145.20	115.89
47	5.528	0.00	4.50	3.165	3.60	7.50	13	120.00	159.40	128.52
48	5.975	0.00	4.50	3.458	3.60	7.38	14	133.00	174.16	141.69
49	6.459	0.00	4.50	3.780	3.60	7.25	15	147.00	189.17	155.42
50	7.001	0.00	4.50	4.140	3.60	7.13	16	162.00	204.53	169.67
51	7.632	0.00	4.50	4.568	3.60	7.00	17	176.00	220.20	184.42
52	8.332	0.00	4.50	5.048	3.60	6.88	18	192.00	236.15	199.63
53	9.135	0.00	4.50	5.603	3.60	6.75	19	207.00	252.37	215.25
54	10.009	0.00	4.50	6.203	3.60	6.63	20	223.00	268.82	231.28
55	10.964	0.00	4.50	6.870	3.60	6.50				

Product is $1,000 nonparticipating ordinary whole life insurance issued to a male, age 35.
Statutory and GAAP reserves are calculated on the net level premium basis.

(higher) reserves than the legal minimum, but in no case can the reserves be less than the legal minimum.

Assuming reserves are larger than the law requires, then the insurer may be able to destrengthen its statutory reserves by changing assumptions. In the United States, the insurer must have the permission of the state insurance commissioner. The accounting treatment for reserve strengthening or destrengthening involves a direct change in the insurer's balance sheet (reserves increased and surplus decreased); it does not go through the statement of operations.

Under U.S. GAAP, as opposed to statutory requirements, insurers normally *cannot* alter their actuarial assumptions to change the strength of their reserves. In contrast, in Canada, actuaries review actuarial assumptions annually and an insurer may change the amount of reserves as necessary, without obtaining regulatory permission. Many other countries allow a more flexible reserving practice than the United States.

CASH VALUES

Whether the reserve derives from a level-premium or a flexible-premium policy, the result is the same—prefunded mortality charges. What is an appropriate, fair disposition of these prefunded charges if the policyowner surrenders his or her policy? Clearly, under such circumstances, the insurer no longer requires the assets backing the reserve liability because its future liability under the policy ceases. Experience has shown that it is not necessary, for the protection of the insurer or other policyowners, to insist that the terminating policyowner forfeit an amount equal to the policy's entire reserve. The practice in perhaps all countries is to permit the policyowner who surrenders his or her policy to receive a cash surrender value.

Although the practice of allowing a cash surrender value in some form is old, for many years the matter was entirely optional on the part of U.S. insurers and remains technically optional in many markets. At one time, some insurers voluntarily granted cash surrender values whereas others did not. All U.S. states today, however, have nonforfeiture laws that define the minimum amount that must be returned upon policy surrender. Many insurers provide cash surrender values that exceed the legal minimums.

Insurer practice in determining the proper value to be granted discontinuing policyowners is based on certain principles. These principles are considered briefly.

Concepts of Equity

The actual treatment of withdrawing policyowners generally can be based on any one of four possible concepts of equity. One view is that the policyowner should receive nothing, on the grounds that the sole function of a life insurance contract is to provide certain designated benefits in the event of the insured's death or survival to the maturity date of an endowment policy. Under this approach, the policyowner bears the primary risk of loss associated with policy termination. Premiums could be discounted for anticipated surrenders (or dividends could be increased on participating policies) and the forfeiture thereby reflected in a reduction in the cost of insurance. In the early days of insurance, this view generally was accepted and applied, in many cases without an adjustment in the contract premium. Such practices led to the introduction of nonforfeiture legislation in the United States, and this approach probably would be difficult to sell today in the absence of complete, effective buyer disclosure. Discussions have taken place at the U.S. regulatory level about the possibility, for example, of allowing no cash values within whole life policies but, to date, they have not resulted in any relaxation of past nonforfeiture standards. Cash values remain purely optional in many other national markets, although the accepted practice is to provide them.

At the other extreme, it might be considered that the withdrawing policyowner is entitled to the return of all premiums paid (less dividends), plus interest at the contractual rate, less a pro rata share of assumed death claims—that is, to the full reserve under the contract, irrespective of the policy year in which the surrender occurs. This view, of course, ignores the incidence of expense and assumes that unamortized acquisition expenses under policies surrendered during the early years after issue should be borne by persisting policyowners or charged to the insurer's general surplus or the agent's commission.

Proponents of this view note that a substantial proportion of purchasers of cash-value policies terminate their policies within the first few policy years, even though it is accepted wisdom that these policies should be purchased only for long-term needs. A high rate of early policy termination results in substantial consumer loss—loss that arguably is traceable, to a large degree, to the policy not having been suitable for the customer in the first instance. This unsuitability could have stemmed from improper or incomplete counseling during the sales process, from the policy offering poor value, or from a host of other reasons. Of course, unforeseen changes in the consumer's circumstances also undoubtedly increase the rate of early policy termination.

This view of equity insists, in effect, that terminating policyowners should receive the full policy reserve and that the insurer and, perhaps, the agent should be held primarily accountable for early policy terminations. This accountability would take the form of having the insurer (via a charge to surplus) and also the agent (through a charge against his or her commission) bear the costs of early surrender.

This view received support through a report issued by the Committee on Consumer Policy of the Organization for Economic Cooperation and Development (OECD). After noting that a frequent cause of consumer concern in several countries arises from the low amount of surrender value granted in early policy cancellations, the report goes on to conclude:

> Further consideration should therefore be given to either greater disclosure
> of surrender values in the early years or to a reasonable burden-sharing which
> better balances the interest of the [insurance] company, the agent and the
> policy-holder and which gives the agent more of an incentive to counsel the
> consumer about the long-term nature of the contract.[18]

According to this concept, insurers and agents, by having a greater financial stake in whether a policy terminates early, will do a better job of matching policy to customer needs and a better job of disclosure. With this view, the insurer (and possibly, the agent) bears the primary risk of loss associated with policy termination. A modified form of this approach would have the acquisition expenses due to early terminations borne partially by the insurer, agent, and persisting policyowners and partially by the terminating policyowners themselves. This would result in a surrender value of something less than the full reserve but more than the asset share (discussed later), until the acquisition expenses had been fully amortized, after which it would equal the full reserve.[19]

---

[18]*Consumers and Life Insurance* (Paris: OECD, 1989), p. 38.

[19]Key to any discussion about who ultimately bears the cost burden associated with early policy terminations is an understanding of the elasticities of demand and supply of each of the stakeholders (a discussion beyond the scope of this text). It is worth noting, however, that because of elasticity differences, the cost may not be borne ultimately by the apparent person or entity. For example, were the intent to have insurer surplus absorb the costs of early termination, it would be unclear whether those costs were ultimately borne by the insurer's stockholders in the form of lower dividends, by the policyowners in the form of higher premiums, or by the insurer's employees or agents in the form of lower wages and commissions.

The third concept of equity, and the one generally applied, is that withdrawing policyowners should receive a surrender value that is as nearly as possible equivalent to their contribution to the funds of the insurer less (1) the cost of protection received, (2) any expenses incurred by the insurer in establishing and handling the policy, and (3) perhaps a contribution to insurer surplus. This view has as its objective that the withdrawal of a policyowner should neither benefit nor harm continuing policyowners in a substantial way. Under this concept, the amount received by the withdrawing policyowner would be based on the pro rata share of the assets accumulated by the insurer on behalf of the classification of policies to which his or her policy belongs—that is, the asset share—although further deductions from the asset share can be justified as discussed later.

The fourth concept of equity is that parity be maintained between terminating and persisting policyowners. This can be done by giving the terminating policyowner the present value of future benefits less the present value of future premiums based on market interest and other conditions at the time of termination. In this way, neutrality is maintained—terminators receive the "market value" of their policy.

Reasons Justifying Paying Less Than the Asset Share

The asset-share value equals the pro rata share of the assets accumulated by the insurer on behalf of the block of policies to which a particular policy belongs. This value reflects the incidence of expense and its relationship to policy duration. It has been argued that the actual cash surrender benefit may be somewhat less, for several reasons, including (1) adverse financial selection, (2) adverse mortality selection, (3) contribution to a contingency reserve or profits, and (4) cost of surrendering the policy.

Adverse Financial Selection

A reason advanced for not allowing the policyowner to obtain the full asset share on the policy at any time is the possibility that during periods of rising interest rates, financial stringency, or business depression, policyowners may avail themselves of the privilege of surrendering their policies to such an extent that the insurer's financial standing may be weakened to the detriment of remaining policyowners.

In normal times, life insurance companies have an excess of income over expenditures that is more than sufficient to meet demands for loans and cash surrender values. During difficult economic times, however, demands by policyowners may be so great that it becomes necessary to liquidate assets at depressed prices. The option of the policyowner to demand the policy's cash surrender value at any time also necessitates a more liquid investment policy than would otherwise be required.[20] Many insurers believe that the policyowners who surrender their policies should be charged with the loss of investment earnings (including capital losses) arising from their actions, and they take this into account in establishing the termination value.

Adverse Mortality Selection

An additional argument for granting a surrender value that is less than the full asset share (although some writers question its importance) relates to the adverse mortality selection that is assumed to be brought about by the allowance of liberal surrender values. The position taken by the supporters of this view is that a life insurance policy is a unilateral contract to which the insurer always must adhere but which the policyowner

---

[20]See chapter 30 for a discussion of the financial nature of insurers' obligations. U.S. insurers have the legal right to postpone payment of the cash surrender value for a period of six months. From a practical standpoint, however, this right should be invoked only under the most severe financial circumstances.

has the option of terminating at any time. Whenever, therefore, the payment of premiums seems a hardship, healthy insureds not feeling the immediate need for insurance may discontinue coverage. Insureds in poor health will, on the contrary, appreciate fully the value of their insurance and will exert themselves to the utmost to pay the premium. Hence, according to this view, policies on the good risks are likely to lapse on a larger scale if surrender values are liberal, whereas impaired risks will stay with the insurer. The result is a reduction in the average vitality of remaining insureds. It is, therefore, argued that terminating policyowners should receive less than the pro rata share of their policies in order to provide a fund to meet the higher death rate among the poorer risks who remain. Although the argument is logical, this tendency has been difficult to substantiate statistically.

Other Reasons

Some insurers believe that each contract should make a permanent contribution to the insurer's surplus, both to absorb adverse fluctuations and to enhance the insurer's overall financial security and profitability. To the extent that such a permanent contribution is required, the surrender allowance should be reduced.

In a stock insurer, an adjustment may be made in the surrender allowance to account for that policy's contribution to profits, which is in recognition of the risk borne by stockholders' investments. Finally, a certain amount of expense is incurred in processing the surrender of a policy. Some insurers adjust the surrender value to reflect this factor rather than taking it into account in their premium-loading formula.

REGULATION OF POLICY RESERVES AND CASH VALUES

All states in the United States have laws that explicitly stipulate the requirements that insurers must meet in calculating reserves and cash surrender values. In other countries, such as Canada and the United Kingdom, the actuary has more latitude in determining reserves and cash values. These U.S. laws have the effect of establishing minimum values below which insurers may not venture in establishing reserves and surrender values. The **Standard Valuation Law** defines the minimum reserves for life insurance and annuity contracts. The **Standard Nonforfeiture Law** defines minimum cash surrender values. Insurers are free to maintain reserves at a level higher than those required by the valuation laws and may have surrender values higher than those required by the nonforfeiture laws, but values cannot be lower. Most states' laws are patterned closely after the 1980 NAIC model laws, which are discussed later.

The basis for both reserve and surrender value computation is stated in terms of the mortality table to be used, the maximum rate of interest to be assumed, and the method to be applied. The requirements differ as between life insurance and annuities and as among ordinary, group, and industrial life insurance. Supplementary agreements relating to proceeds left with the insurance company are subject to special rules.

Background

Early nonforfeiture laws were enacted to prevent the forfeiture of equities built up in level-premium policies, and early valuation laws were designed to ensure company solvency. Traditionally, the surrender values required to be returned have been called **nonforfeiture values,** and the form in which these values may be taken are referred to as **nonforfeiture options.**[21]

---

[21]See chapter 9.

Prior to 1948, the legal minimum standard in most U.S. states for computing reserves and surrender values for ordinary insurance was the *American Experience Table* and 3½ percent interest. The minimum basis (mortality table) for valuing reserves and surrender values for newly issued ordinary policies was changed in 1948 to the *1941 CSO Table*. Previously, nonforfeiture benefits were linked directly to reserves. They were determined by subtracting a surrender charge from the reserve. This led to the situation that, when an insurer moved to strengthen its policy reserves (e.g., because of falling interest rates), it simultaneously increased the surrender values, thus increasing the demand claims on the very policies that the insurer felt needed more conservative reserves. Under the 1948 law, this close tie-in was obviated with the result that greater equity could be maintained between insureds at different ages and also with respect to different plans of insurance. The elimination of the former linkage recognized that reserves are an aggregate measure of future liabilities, whereas nonforfeiture values are meant to recognize to some degree the policyowner's interest in a particular contract. The 1948 law also established a new method for calculating nonforfeiture values. Variations of this method have been used in the United States since that time.

The use of the *1958 CSO Table* and 3½ percent interest was made mandatory for reserves on ordinary policies issued on or after January 1, 1966. The interest rate was changed to 4 percent and later to 4½ percent.

Minimum surrender values could be based on 5½ percent interest for annual premium policies and on either 5½ percent or 6½ percent for single-premium policies. Changes in 1972 updated the valuation mortality tables for both group and individual annuities. Under the 1976 amendments, the maximum nonforfeiture interest rate that could be used was 1 percent higher than the statutory interest rate specified for determining minimum reserves.

In spite of the seemingly continual updating of the earlier valuation and nonforfeiture laws, the need for further changes appeared to be constant. Each time a change in mortality tables or interest rates was needed, an amendment was necessary in every state's valuation and nonforfeiture laws. This was both a time-consuming and expensive process. It was widely recognized that the *1958 CSO Table* was out-of-date and that with interest rate volatility, further changes would be needed in the interest rate assumptions.

The 1980 U.S. Valuation and Nonforfeiture Laws

In response to these converging problems, a revised NAIC **Model Standard Valuation Law** and a revised NAIC **Model Standard Nonforfeiture Law** were adopted by the NAIC in 1980, the effects of which were intended to introduce greater flexibility into the laws and to render them more suitable for contemporary conditions. All jurisdictions in the United States adopted the new NAIC models or close variations thereof.

The revised laws had no effect on existing life insurance policies and individual annuity contracts. They do not affect the reserves that had already been set up on existing group annuity-type contracts, but the future growth of these reserves could be affected.

Changes from Earlier Laws

Three important aspects of the 1980 model laws deserve comment: (1) dynamic maximum interest rates, (2) new mortality bases, and (3) certain technical changes.

Dynamic Interest Rates The 1980 model laws define the maximum interest rates that can be used to calculate reserves and nonforfeiture benefits on a dynamic basis. The maximum permitted interest rate is automatically adjusted if a recalculation produces a significant change. The laws make use of the *Moody's Corporate Bond Yield Average-Monthly Average Corporates,* as published by Moody's Investors Service, Inc., as the applicable index. The maximum interest rates themselves, however, depend on the type of insurance contract, and they may be much smaller than this composite yield rate. These maximum interest rates are recalculated at 12-month intervals. The maximum interest rate for a particular life insurance policy or individual annuity contract is fixed at its date of issue. A change in the maximum interest rate applies only to newly issued life insurance policies or individual annuity contracts—not to those already in force.

The dynamic interest basis is an improvement over previous methods in that it automatically can adjust maximum interest rates to current conditions without the need for legislative action. Of course, the laws permit an insurance company to use lower interest rates than the permitted maximums if the insurer wishes to do this.

Mortality Tables   The model laws make use of revised mortality tables for individual life insurance, which were developed by a committee of the Society of Actuaries. These tables are constructed separately for males and females, for smokers and nonsmokers, and they are styled as the *Commissioners 1980 Standard Ordinary Mortality Tables,* the *Commissioners 1980 Standard Ordinary Mortality Table with Ten-Year Select Mortality Factors,* and the *Commissioners 1980 Extended Term Insurance Tables.*[22]

The model laws also contain a procedure whereby new mortality tables developed in the future can become effective in a state without being specifically named in the text of the laws. First, the NAIC must adopt any such new tables. These new tables must then be approved through a regulation promulgated by the commissioner of insurance for the state. The new mortality tables can be tables for individual life insurance or tables for other classes of contracts described in the laws.[23]

Certain Technical Changes   The model laws contain many technical changes, although the fundamental calculation processes remained unchanged. This summary identifies only a few of the changes.

The laws changed the formula for the expense allowance used in the Standard Nonforfeiture Law for life insurance, so as to reflect current patterns of expenses more accurately. The laws allow the state's commissioner of insurance to promulgate regulations describing appropriate minimum reserves and minimum nonforfeiture benefits for certain new or complex plans of life insurance that might not have been contemplated when the laws were originally written. The laws also cause the minimum reserves and minimum nonforfeiture benefits for some life insurance policies in the early policy years to be increased over what they would be otherwise, in certain cases in which the plan provides relatively high guaranteed benefits or cash values in one or more of the later policy years.

Requirements

As mentioned earlier, valuation and nonforfeiture laws stipulate (1) the mortality table to be used, (2) the maximum interest rate to be assumed, and (3) the method to be applied. The maximum interest rates permitted vary between annuities and life insurance and, within each of these categories, variations are based on duration and plan types. The permissible maximums change periodically in accordance with changes in Moody's bond yield figures, as discussed previously. The longer the policy duration, the lower the maximum permissible interest rate, all else being equal. Maximum rates to be used for valuation (reserve) calculation purposes are lower than permissible maximums to be used for nonforfeiture (cash-value) calculation purposes.

---

[22]Other specialized *1980 CSO Tables* exist. See chapter 27.

[23]New mortality tables were being devised as this book was going to press.

The nonforfeiture law stipulates that the nonforfeiture interest rate cannot exceed 125 percent of the reserve interest rate. Of course, insurance companies are free to use rates lower than the maximum permitted by law and many do so in the interest of being conservative. Presently, due to the definition of life insurance in Internal Revenue Code Section 7702, most cash values now have an implicit ceiling based on the *1980 CSO Table* and 4 percent interest.

The valuation laws stipulate that the method used for calculating minimum reserves can be the CRVM (discussed earlier). The net level premium method, in other words, is not required but may be used because it develops higher reserves than the CRVM.

The minimum nonforfeiture value at any policy duration is the present value of the future benefits under the policy less the present value of future *adjusted* premiums. This definition is essentially the prospective reserve formula utilizing an adjusted premium in lieu of the valuation net level premium. The **adjusted premium** is the level premium necessary to pay the benefits guaranteed by the policy (the net level premium) *plus* the level equivalent of a defined special *first-year expense allowance*.

Under pre-1980 laws, the maximum allowance for special first-year expenses was defined as a constant of $20 per $1,000 of insurance, plus a percentage (40 percent) of the adjusted premium for the policy, and a percentage (25 percent) of either the adjusted premium for the policy or the adjusted premium for a whole life policy issued at the same age for the insurance amount, whichever was less. Each of these percentages is limited to $16 and $10, respectively. According to the previous legislation, the first-year expense allowance could not exceed $46 per $1,000 of insurance. With this earlier formula, the percentage allowance was a function of the adjusted premium—the item being sought.

This circularity was removed by the 1980 changes to make the formula a function of the net premium rather than the adjusted premium. Thus, under the law, the maximum allowance is defined as 125 percent of the lesser of (1) the nonforfeiture net level premium or (2) $40 per $1,000; plus a constant of $10 per $1,000 of insurance. This approach simplified the calculation. The maximum first-year expense allowance per $1,000 face amount is, therefore, $60 ($1.25 \times $40 + 10).

Illustration of Adjusted-Premium Method

The first step in deriving surrender values under the Standard Nonforfeiture Law is to determine the special first-year expense allowance. This may be based on the insurer's expense situation, competitive pressures, or other considerations but is limited by the maximum amount permitted under the law.

The second step in the process is to calculate the adjusted premium. This may be approached from two standpoints. It may be regarded as the net annual level premium required to amortize a principal sum equal to the present value of the benefits under the policy and the special first-year expense allowance. Thus, the present value of future benefits (*PVFB*) for a $1,000 ordinary life policy issued at male age 35 (based on the *1980 CSO Table* and interest at 5½ percent) equals the net single premium for such a policy, $159.59. The net level premium is $9.90. The maximum special first-year expense allowance for such a policy is, therefore, $22.38.[24] The total of $159.59 and $22.38 yields a principal sum of $181.97. The net annual level premium that will amortize this sum may be obtained by dividing $181.97 by 16.121, the present value at 5½ percent of a life annuity due of 1 as of age 35. The result, $11.29, is the adjusted premium.

The second way of considering the adjusted premium is that it is the sum obtained by adding to the regular net annual level premium the annual amount needed to amor-

---

[24]$(1.25)($9.90) + $10.00 = $22.38.$

tize the special acquisition expenses over the premium-paying period. Thus, by dividing $22.38 (the maximum special first-year expense allowance) by the present value of a life annuity due of 1 for the premium-paying period, 16.121, the annual amount of $1.39 is obtained, which, when added to the net level premium for an ordinary life policy issued at male age 35, $9.90, gives $11.29, the same adjusted premium determined previously.

The final step in determining the minimum surrender value is to substitute the adjusted premium for the regular net level premium in the formula employed in the computation of prospective reserves. The following summary of the calculation of the tenth-year minimum nonforfeiture value for an ordinary life policy issued at male age 35 (*1980 CSO Table* and 5½ percent) will illustrate the application of the principles developed here:

$$
\begin{matrix}
NFV \\
(\text{age of} \quad = \\
\text{valuation})
\end{matrix}
\quad
\begin{matrix}
\text{Present Value} \\
\text{of Future} \quad - \\
\text{Benefits}
\end{matrix}
\quad
\begin{matrix}
\text{Present Value of} \\
\text{Future Adjusted} \\
\text{Premiums}
\end{matrix}
$$

$$
\begin{matrix}
NFV \\
(\text{age of} \quad = \\
\text{valuation})
\end{matrix}
\quad
\begin{matrix}
NSP \\
(\text{age of} \\
\text{valuation})
\end{matrix}
\quad -
\left[\left(\dfrac{\begin{matrix}NSP & \text{Special} \\ (\text{original}) + & \text{Expense} \\ \text{age}) & \text{Allowance}\end{matrix}}{\begin{matrix}PLVAD \\ \text{of } 1 \, PPP\end{matrix}} \right)
\left(\begin{matrix}PLVAD \text{ of 1 for} \\ \text{Remaining} \\ \text{Premium-} \\ \text{Paying} \\ \text{Period}\end{matrix} \right) \right]
$$

$$
NFV_{45} = NSP_{45} \quad -
\left[\left(\dfrac{\begin{matrix}& \text{Special} \\ NSP_{35} + & \text{Expense} \\ & \text{Allowance}\end{matrix}}{\begin{matrix}PLVAD \\ \text{of } 1 \, PPP\end{matrix}} \right)
\left(\begin{matrix}PLVAD \text{ of} \\ 1 \text{ for Life} \\ \text{at Age 45}\end{matrix} \right) \right]
$$

$$
= \$242.87 - \left(\frac{\$159.59 + \$22.38}{16.121} \right)(14.523)
$$

$$
= \$78.94
$$

Note that the only difference between this formula and the minimum reserve formula utilized earlier is the addition of the expense factor to the original net single premium, resulting in a net level adjusted premium. Thus, in prospective terms, the nonforfeiture value is the present value of future benefits less the present value of future adjusted premiums.

Modifications of the Adjusted-Premium Method

The preceding illustration demonstrates the calculation of minimum surrender values under a 5½ percent interest assumption. As mentioned earlier, many companies provide surrender values in excess of the minimums of the law. This may be accomplished by (1) assuming lower first-year expenses than the maximum permitted, (2) assuming the maximum expenses and amortizing them over a shorter period or at an uneven rate over the premium-paying period, (3) assuming a lower rate of interest than that permitted by law, or (4) a combination of the three methods.

If lower first-year expenses are assumed, the adjusted premium will be smaller, making the present value of future adjusted premiums smaller and resulting in larger surrender values. Similarly, in the case of amortizing the maximum permitted excess first-year expense allowance over a shorter period or at an uneven rate, the adjusted premium is itself adjusted, resulting in appropriately modified surrender values. In those cases in which the premium is adjusted to produce surrender values, the modified adjusted premium is known as a **nonforfeiture factor.** Similarly, the term **adjusted-premium method** refers to the derivation of minimum values only. Where larger values are derived through the use of nonforfeiture factor(s), the term **standard nonforfeiture-value method** is applied. The law requires only that values provided be no less than those derived by the adjusted-premium method.

Table 29-6 illustrates the variation in cash surrender values with changes in the interest assumption only, holding mortality and expense allowances constant. The interest assumption is of great importance in determining the level of surrender values, especially at early policy durations. Table 29-7 shows how results differ under various mortality tables with each using the adjusted-premium method and interest at 5 percent.

TABLE 29-6 Effect of Interest Rate Assumption on Surrender Values (Ordinary Life, Male, Age 35, $1,000 Basis, Based on 1980 NAIC Model Law)

End of Policy Year	Interest Rate			
	3%	5%	7½%	9%
1	$ 0.00	$ 0.00	$ 0.00	$ 0.00
2	0.00	0.00	0.00	0.00
3	13.22	5.78	0.00	0.00
4	27.82	16.20	6.74	2.87
5	42.69	26.97	14.08	8.79
10	120.95	86.02	56.05	43.39
15	205.55	154.21	108.05	87.80
20	295.59	231.63	171.11	143.79
25	388.46	316.33	245.03	211.18
30	482.40	407.03	329.06	290.57

TABLE 29-7 Effect of Mortality Assumption on Surrender Values (Ordinary Life, Male, Age 35, $1,000 Basis, Interest at 5%, Based on 1980 NAIC Model Law)

End of Policy Year	1941 CSO	1958 CSO	1980 CSO
1	$ 0.00	$ 0.00	$ 0.00
2	0.00	0.00	0.00
3	6.51	7.22	5.78
4	18.90	18.73	16.20
5	31.64	30.62	26.97
10	100.64	95.60	86.02
15	178.05	169.71	154.21
20	262.63	251.62	231.63
25	352.29	339.45	316.33
30	444.11	429.98	407.03

Requirements for Nontraditional Products

The valuation and nonforfeiture laws in the United States permit state insurance commissioners to promulgate special reserve and surrender requirements for policies whose cost and benefit structures do not fit easily into the classical mold.[25] Some commissioners have taken advantage of this legislative opportunity by stipulating special requirements for universal life (UL) and current assumption whole life (CAWL) insurance plans. These special requirements usually are patterned after the NAIC **Universal Life Model Insurance Regulation,** so discussion will center on this model.

In viewing reserve and surrender value requirements for UL policies, it should be recognized that the UL account-value mechanism is the cost structure of the policy. The guarantees of interest, mortality, and expense charges take the place of the premium rate in more traditional forms of insurance.

The flexible-premium aspect of universal life policies means that future premiums and policy benefits are not determinable at issue or at date of valuation, so the traditional methodology of "present value of future benefits minus present value of future adjusted premiums" is impractical. This quandary was solved in different ways for valuation and nonforfeiture by the regulation.

For valuation, the regulation defines a future premium to use for calculating policy reserves based on the level premiums needed at issue to endow the contract at its maturity date. The reserve calculations require that a projection of future benefits be made, using the fund value at the valuation date and assumed future premiums. This policy-by-policy projection requires extensive computer use. Some products' parameters permit simplified calculations. In many cases, it can be demonstrated that the cash surrender value is as large as the reserve, so separate reserve calculations need not be performed.

For UL nonforfeiture values, the regulation breaks with the methodology required in the Standard Nonforfeiture Law and bases minimum values on a retrospective accumulation. Minimum required cash surrender values equal the accumulation, at interest, of premiums less acquisition and administrative expense charges, mortality and other benefit charges, service charges, and deductions for partial withdrawals. Acquisition expense charges are limited to the allowance provided in the Standard Nonforfeiture Law for a fixed-premium, fixed-benefit plan that would endow for the specified amount at the policy maturity date. Surrender charges are permitted and may not exceed any unused, unamortized acquisition expense allowance plus any excess interest credited in the previous 12 months. There are no limits on administrative, benefit or service charges. There is no minimum interest rate.

The section specifying surrender values for current assumption whole life plans differs from that for UL policies and basically is a restatement of the nonforfeiture law with an explanation of future guaranteed benefits, as indicated by the following quote from the regulation:

> Future guaranteed benefits are determined by (1) projecting the policy value, taking into account future premiums, if any, and using all guarantees of interests, mortality, expense deductions, etc., contained in the policy or declared by the insurer; and (2) taking into account any benefits guaranteed in the policy or by declaration which do not depend on the policy value.

The last term, referring to benefits guaranteed that do not depend on the policy value, may seem odd. Policies may have guarantees in addition to those of the account

---

[25]This section draws from Douglas C. Doll, "Universal Life: A Product Overview," *SOA Study Note 340–41–91* (Schaumburg, IL: Society of Actuaries, 1991), pp. 10–11.

value. Many policies utilize such guarantees. They usually are found in policies in which the account value will not support whole life benefits on a guaranteed basis. The policy form will contain an additional guarantee that the policy will turn out to be at least whole life, regardless of the performance of the account value. Obviously, if the guaranteed plan of insurance is whole life, then the minimum cash surrender values must be those of whole life. With these secondary guarantee forms, the minimum surrender value can be greater than the full account value.

A number of states have not adopted the NAIC's Universal Life Model Regulation. The State of New York passed legislation with nonforfeiture provisions that are substantially different from the model regulation. More states have not adopted the regulation for two reasons. First, these states accept policies that meet the regulation requirements, even though they have not adopted the regulation; thus, there is little incentive to promulgate the regulation in these states. Second, several state insurance departments are dissatisfied with the model regulation's valuation and nonforfeiture provisions.

The method for calculating minimum reserves is the same for both CAWL and UL plans and is prospective in nature. The calculation procedure is complex, and there is concern that the regulation method is too complicated, difficult, and costly to apply and verify. There also is concern that, more so than for traditional whole life products, the reserves ought to be affected by cash surrender values after the valuation date—for example, any short-term cash-value guarantees that are more liberal than those within the valuation law should be recognized in the reserve liability. This is an attempt to apply annuity-type valuation procedures to a life product, and it may be prompted by the perception of universal life as a combination of term life insurance plus side fund rather than an integrated life product. Several proposals have been made to revise the valuation provisions of the regulation, but none has received much support.

Regulators have been more concerned with nonforfeiture values. The lack of limits on charges and interest credits is perceived by many to produce no meaningful minimum cash surrender values. This possibility is acknowledged in the regulation: "If benefit charges are substantially level by duration and develop low or no cash values, then the Commissioner shall have the right to require higher cash values." Some regulators prefer to have explicit maximum benefit charges and minimum interest rates, or a minimum interest rate of 3 percent, or both. Proposals to place these limits in the regulation have met significant resistance from life insurance companies that perceive them as a form of rate regulation.

The 1990 Standard Valuation Law Amendments

In 1990 the NAIC adopted an amended version of its 1980 Standard Valuation Law. Implementing model regulations were adopted in 1991. This new model, effectively a restatement of the 1980 model law, differs in one important respect. It requires the filing of an **actuarial opinion** about selected aspects of the insurer's operations. Every insurer must establish the position of **appointed actuary.** The appointed actuary is responsible for annually rendering opinions as to whether the reserves and related actuarial items are computed appropriately, are based on assumptions which satisfy contractual provisions, are consistent with prior reported amounts and comply with applicable laws of this state.

Larger insurers and insurers that do not meet certain financial tests must also file their appointed actuary's opinion as to whether reserves and related actuarial items, in light of the insurer's assets, make adequate provision for the anticipated cash flows required by the insurer's contractual obligations and related expenses. Extensive asset adequacy analysis, often by cash flow testing, is required to render this opinion.

The model law establishes minimum standards for the appointed actuary and seeks to provide him or her with greater independence. The actuary may, however, be a company employee.

While specifying specific minimum reserve standards, the law further requires insurers to maintain aggregate reserves sufficient for the appointed actuary to be able to render the required opinion. This requirement means that insurers should maintain greater reserves than those resulting from the minimum reserve standards if, in the actuary's opinion, they are necessary.

This model law provides regulators with another tool for evaluating insurer solidity. As noted in chapter 35, the United Kingdom, Canada and other countries have a history of reliance on the accounting and actuarial professions for insurer financial monitoring.

Current Developments

The NAIC Life and Health Actuarial Task Force (LHATF) has requested that the American Academy of Actuaries initiate a thorough study of current valuation methodologies for life and health insurance and annuities and recommend changes.[26] The study was to start with a clean slate and not be bound by history.

Existing Valuation Requirements

Early on, the academy assigned a working group to identify the advantages and disadvantages of the existing valuation requirements. These are discussed briefly next.

Advantages   Standardization is the major advantage of the existing formula-based reserves. For most liabilities, these reserves provide predictably consistent results from year to year and from company to company. This predictability results in reserves that are sufficiently immune from a company's ability to manipulate results to protect the consumer from inadequate reserves as well as provide a well-defined basis for tax reserves.

Insurance regulators and auditors find the present system easy to audit and monitor for compliance as well as to use for related purposes such as providing a foundation for risk-based capital requirements. With relatively minor differences between states, the core methodology for life and annuity products is consistent across state boundaries. The industry and regulators have been able to work together to develop reasonable approaches to new products.

The simplicity of the existing formula-based reserves facilitates automated reserve calculations that can be readily validated regardless of the size of the company. The inherent conservatism of current reserves has produced adequate reserves for many years and worked reasonably well, particularly for products offering one type of benefit. When combined with asset-adequacy testing, formula reserves provide an appropriate adequacy measure. Policy reserves, in conjunction with the asset valuation reserve (AVR) and risk-based capital (RBC), provide an adequate solvency cushion against most risks. With the interest maintenance reserve (IMR), formula reserves on a book-value basis maintain consistency with the book value of assets.[27]

Disadvantages   Many product designs (e.g., multiple-benefit contracts, guaranteed investment contracts, universal life, and equity-indexed products) have been developed to respond to a dramatically changing environment. The failure of the current system to

---

[26]This section draws on Robert E. Wilcox and Norman E. Hell, "Life and Health Company Valuation: Cleaning the Slate," *Contingencies* (November/December 1997), pp. 31–33.

[27]See chapter 34.

address these products has created problems. This has led to delays in introducing new products while the industry and regulators sort out how to force the new products into existing requirements, discouraging innovation and making companies less responsive to customer needs.

In general, under the present system, all companies must use the same assumptions for all products without the ability to reflect variations in emerging company or industry experience. Interest assumptions are not based on actual earned rates or the investment risks of underlying assets. Expense allowances that are permitted bear little relationship to actual acquisition expenses. The current formula inadequately addresses certain risks such as investment risk differentials, diversification of risk through pooling arrangements, policyowner expectations regarding nonguaranteed elements, and future flexible premiums.

Formula reserves are based on book value, which assumes assets are held to maturity. This assumption fails to recognize market-value risks associated with liabilities and supporting assets.

The use of implicit margins is a major shortcoming of the current system. The amount of margin is very difficult, if not impossible, to measure. The actuarial focus is on meeting minimum requirements and not on the true adequacy of reserves, shifting reserve accountability from the actuary to the regulator. Although asset-adequacy tests can address many of these concerns, not all companies are required to perform testing. Formula reserves are required even if tests indicate a lower reserve would be adequate. If extra reserves are indicated, they are not tax deductible.

Current valuation methodologies are not consistent in concept or technique. The inability to respond readily to new products and a changing environment have resulted in a proliferation of additional valuation requirements. The real purpose of the valuation process is to assure the adequacy of reserves, but valuation actuaries are increasingly required to issue written opinions demonstrating compliance with each part of this complex set of standards. Attempting to demonstrate compliance with each part of this complex set of standards results in a lack of focus on the real purpose of the valuation process.

The task force has determined that a valuation system should meet three objectives:

- Evaluate the ability of a life insurance company to execute various business alternatives.
- Evaluate the adequacy of resources relative to obligations.
- Measure changes in resources relative to obligations.

In carrying out its assignment, the Academy of Actuaries is analyzing the valuation systems used in other countries, including the role of the actuary. The study compares the current valuation systems in the United States against those of 14 other countries including Canada[28] and the United Kingdom. The interim report gave the U.S. system an "above average" rating.

Non-U.S. Valuation Requirements

The reserve requirements in the countries studied can be categorized in three groups:[29]

1. Brazil, Chile, Germany, Italy, Japan, Mexico, and Spain require statutory formula reserves only.

---

[28]See Joseph H. Lau, "A Comparison of Canadian and U.S. Statutory Reserve Methodology," *Contingencies* (November/December 1997), pp. 46–48.

[29]This section draws from Shirley Hwei-Chung Shad, "The Global Game of Insurance Company Valuation," *Contingencies* (July/August 1998), pp. 38–41.

2. Hong Kong, the Netherlands, the United Kingdom, Singapore, and South Africa all use a broader net premium reserve system in which all guaranteed benefits must be included. Most allow the actuaries some flexibility in choosing the assumptions underlying the reserve calculation. None, however, requires explicit asset-adequacy testing except some justification for the valuation interest rates or some demonstration of a prudent and satisfactory relationship between assets and liabilities.

3. Australia and Canada use gross-premium reserves and rely on the actuarial profession to define best-estimate assumptions. A provision for adverse deviation is required in Canada but not in Australia.

Although half the countries have formula reserves, there is a trend toward allowing the actuary more flexibility and discretion in valuing the inherent risks. Brazil, Chile, Germany, Italy, and Spain require compliance with the formula reserve provisions of their regulations. Some countries, however, require that technical notes addressing company experience be filed at the time products are priced.

Japan, Mexico, the Netherlands, and South Africa require actuaries to provide a reserve adequacy opinion/certification. Mexico requires that an external actuary provide such an opinion. Japan requires certification that policy reserves are suitable, including at least five years of projections.

Hong Kong, Singapore, and the United Kingdom also require that appointed actuaries provide a reserve adequacy report. A report on minimum solvency margins is also required for these countries. The appointed actuary in Singapore is further responsible for performing capital adequacy analysis.

Australia and Canada require annual valuation reports to demonstrate reserve adequacy, solvency, and capital adequacy. None of the countries in the study require asset-adequacy analysis for reserves only.

In most of these countries, the appointed actuary is also required to provide reports to the regulators. Even in countries where the appointed actuary system is not in place (Italy, for example) the actuary is required to report any ongoing problematic situations to the appropriate authorities.

Questions

1. Define the term *reserve* and explain its function in the life insurance context.
2. Show how reserve levels might be affected by:
   a. changing the mortality table assumed
   b. increasing the assumed rate of interest
3. Compare the merits of GAAP and the statutory reserving methodologies for assessing a life insurer's policy liabilities.
4. Describe the statutory regulations that govern the minimum reserves required to be set up as liabilities by life insurers.
5. Compare and contrast the full preliminary term an the commissioners' reserve valuation methods of modifying full net level terminal reserves.
6. Using the *1980 CSO Table* and assuming a 5 percent interest rate, calculate the fifteenth-year terminal reserve on a 11-payment whole life policy issued at age 30.

CHAPTER

30

GROSS-PREMIUM RATE STRUCTURES AND NONGUARANTEED POLICY ELEMENTS

Objectives

- Describe the process by which life insurers derive gross-premium rate structures.

- Explain how an insurer's assumptions and stated objectives may affect its gross-premium rates.

- Explain how asset-share calculations are used to test a tentative gross-premium rate structure's ability to meet company objectives.

- Identify sources from which additions to surplus arise.

- Describe procedures used to allocate divisible surplus among policyowners.

The concept of the net premium was analyzed in the preceding chapters. An insurer must, however, collect premiums that, supplemented by interest, will enable it to meet all costs under the contract, including the policy's share of the insurer's operating expenses and perhaps a planned contribution to surplus. The tentative premium charge is intended to meet these multiple objectives and is referred to as the gross-premium rate structure. The premiums actually paid by policyowners are determined from this rate structure.

One should not examine gross-premium rate structures without also recognizing that most policies sold worldwide provide for some mechanism of lowering the effective cost of policies below that inherent in the guaranteed assumptions. Historically, the payment of dividends (bonuses) under participating policies has served this function. Today there are other techniques such as excess interest credits and indeterminate-premium rate structures available under both participating and nonparticipating policies.

GENERAL CONSIDERATIONS IN DERIVING GROSS PREMIUMS

A gross premium may be regarded as either (1) the valuation net premium increased by an amount called loading or (2) a sum derived independently of the valuation net premium and based on all factors that enter into a gross-premium computation (i.e., mortality, interest, expenses, taxes, lapse rates, contingency allowance, and an allowance for a contribution to surplus or profit). The gross premiums of mutual insurers historically were derived by using the first method, whereas the premiums of stock insurers typically were derived by the second method. In recent years there has been a trend toward use of the second approach by both stocks and mutuals, and the second approach typically is followed in establishing the structure of charges and credits under universal life (UL) policies.[1] Loading, in the UL context, is represented by the explicit expense charges, the margins that exist between the benefit charges assessed and the actual benefit costs, and the margin between the interest actually credited to the account value and the interest actually earned on assets supporting the policy's liabilities. This pricing trend, driven by competitive considerations, may result in the selection of a gross-premium level first and then working back to determine what expense charges or benefit levels can be supported and yield the desired profit.

The combination of mortality, expense and surrender charges, and interest credits is a UL policy's rate structure. The only difference conceptually between UL and traditional forms is that the structure is unbundled under UL and similar policies, and it is bundled under the more traditional forms. For purposes of discussion, it should be understood that for UL and similar unbundled policies, the account value mechanism, comprised of benefit and expense charges and interest credits, serves the same function as and, in effect, is the same as the gross-premium rate structure under more traditional forms of life insurance.

Basic Criteria and Parameters

In developing a gross-premium rate structure for a block of policies, considerations such as adequacy, equity, legal limitations, competition, target market, and specific insurer objectives all enter into the process. Adequacy clearly is the most important requirement of a gross-premium rate structure because insurer solvency can be jeopardized by inadequate charges. Equity in a premium structure primarily is for the benefit of policyowners, although there is a practical limit to the degree of equity that can be attained. At some point the marginal cost of efforts to improve equity becomes greater than the value of the improvement due to expense considerations. Charges must not be in conflict with any law. Deficiency reserve statutes or their equivalent may indirectly influence premium charges for practical reasons.[2] Competition will, obviously, affect an insurer's premium rates. In setting growth and profit goals, other objectives, such as markets selected, products emphasized, or compensation philosophy, can all affect the gross-premium rate structure finally adopted.[3]

Nature of Insurance Company Expenses

Insurer expenses may be classified as direct expenses and indirect expenses. Direct expenses are those expenses that can be directly attributed to a specific product (e.g., agent's commission). Identifying direct expenses and allocating them to a particular product line or product type is relatively straightforward. All product pricing systems include direct expenses in a product's pricing structure.

---

[1] Risk theory can be the basis for premium development. See N. L. Bowers, Jr., H. U. Gerber, J. C. Hickman, D. A. Jones, and C. J. Nesbitt, *Actuarial Mathematics*, 2nd ed. (Chicago, IL: Society of Actuaries, 1997).

[2] See chapters 4 and 29.

[3] See chapter 23 for a discussion of product development in the context of an insurer's marketing plan.

In contrast, indirect expenses include those expenses that cannot be attributed to only one specific product. Expenses such as senior management compensation, accounting expenses, utilities, and information systems exist and continue whether or not the insurer offers a particular product. Identifying and allocating indirect expenses to a product during the pricing process is complex and often arbitrary. In fact, the arbitrary nature of the allocation process has led some pricing systems to avoid allocating indirect expenses to a product when determining the product's price.

In discussing insurer expenses, the first step is to divide them into investment expenses and insurance expenses. **Investment expenses** include the costs of making, processing, and protecting investments. Because they are related directly to the production of investment income, they are deducted from the gross investment income. They are, therefore, taken into account in determining the net rates of interest to be used in calculating premiums or excess interest credits and are not considered explicitly in connection with the loading.

Insurance expenses are those of a noninvestment nature and may be classified in various ways, depending on the purpose they serve. The costs of procuring, underwriting, and issuing new business—including commissions attributable to the first year's premiums—are regarded as **first-year expenses.** The various costs of maintaining and servicing outstanding policies, as well as renewal commissions, are regarded as **renewal expenses. Claims expenses** include claim litigation costs and appropriate amounts for salaries, rent, utilities, and so on, which are attributable to the claim department. Finally, there are **administrative expenses,** such as salaries, rent, and utilities, which are attributable to the nonclaim, nonmarketing executive and administrative functions.

For purposes of determining a proper amount of loading, these various insurance expenses may be assigned to three major groups:

1. expenses that vary with the amount of premiums—for example, agent's commissions and premium taxes
2. expenses that vary with the amount of insurance—for example, underwriting costs that tend to vary with policy size
3. expenses that vary with the number of policies—for example, the cost of preparing policies for issue, establishing the necessary accounting records, and sending premium notices

There are two major problems associated with reflecting expenses in the rate structure: (1) achieving the equitable distribution of expenses among different classes of policies and among policyowners of different ages—that is, the problem of making each policy pay its own cost, and (2) recognizing when the expense is incurred. The solution to these problems is complicated by the objectives of complying with statutory requirements, maintaining a consistent policy regarding surrender values and dividends, accommodating those expenses that do not fall neatly into one of the groups, and meeting the competition.

Because the objectives of adequacy and equity are sometimes in conflict with the objective of maintaining or improving the competitive position of the insurer, the final gross-premium rate structure normally represents a compromise. Nevertheless, in the aggregate, adequacy must be maintained.

Nature of Loading

An equitable system of loading should result in every policyowner paying the expenses properly attributable to his or her policy. The foregoing analysis of insurance company expenses suggests that loading should consist partly of a percentage of premium charge, partly of a charge for each $1,000 of insurance, and partly of a charge for each policy. In fact, the expense charges of many UL and other unbundled products are structured in this tripartite manner. Many unbundled products, however, omit one or more of the three elements in their expense charges, with some having no identifiable expense charges. In the latter situation, of course, the insurer's expenses must be met from margins built into the mortality charges and interest credits.

The expense-loading formulas of more traditional forms of life insurance often convert the "per-policy" expense element to a "per $1,000" charge by relating it to the average-size policy issued. To meet competition and to provide greater equity between classes of policies in which the average-size policy issued varies considerably, most insurers assume a separate average-size policy for each policy band (discussed later) or for the principal plans of insurance and age groups in their premium calculations.

The loading formula includes, in addition to an allowance for expenses, a provision for contingencies, a margin for contribution to surplus and/or profits, and perhaps an explicit element for dividends. With the per-policy expenses converted to an "amount per $1,000 basis," the hypothetical loading formula for traditional products may be reduced to two factors: (1) a percentage of the premium and (2) a constant per $1,000.

In the case of traditional bundled products (e.g., ordinary life), the insurer does not specify to the policyowner the portion of the gross-premium to meet expenses, the portion to cover the cost of benefits, or how much interest the insurer is crediting. In contrast, under unbundled products (e.g., universal life), the insurer discloses to the policyowner that part of the product's total price that reflects the insurer's expenses, that part of it intended to cover the cost of benefits, and how much interest is being credited to the policyowner.

The preceding discussion assumes that both direct and indirect expenses are allocated to each product in the pricing process. Identifying indirect expenses and allocating them to a product is complex, difficult, and often arbitrary. In view of the arbitrary nature of the allocation process, some companies allocate only direct expenses to a specific product. This approach is known as **marginal costing** in contrast to the traditional **full costing** in which both direct and indirect expenses are allocated to each product. In the case of marginal costing, indirect expenses are allocated to each *product line* rather than to a particular product. Both approaches, of course, must lead to a gross premium that reflects the company's aggregate expenses.

DEVELOPING THE TENTATIVE GROSS-PREMIUM RATE STRUCTURE

Although the gross-premium rate may be viewed as a net premium augmented by an amount called loading, it is more frequently regarded as an amount derived independently of the valuation net premium and based on all the factors that enter into the gross premium. The five elements basic to the calculation are: (1) the expected amount and incidence of claims, (2) an appropriate rate of investment return, (3) withdrawal rates and amounts withdrawn, (4) amounts and incidence of expenses and taxes, and (5) margin(s) for contributions to surplus or profit. Under traditional policy forms, assumptions as to each of these elements can be selected, a formula embodying all of them derived, and a premium rate calculated. Under unbundled product forms, assumptions are still required but the ability to explicitly tailor the margins on each element to meet specific competitive or profitability objectives complicates the analysis. For example, decreased expense charge margins may be offset with increased mortality margins. In any event, with both bundled and unbundled product forms, the tentative gross-premium rate structure is tested and refined by conducting profit studies to be certain it is consistent with insurer objectives.

The determination of unit expense rates involves both the amount of expense incurred, as shown by cost evaluations, and the time of its occurrence. Although the derivation of the individual unit expense rates is beyond the scope of this volume, a few additional comments are appropriate. Claim expenses and the costs of paying surrender values, dispensing policy loans, processing beneficiary changes and other service activities may be accounted for separately and treated as additional benefits. If this is done, the cost of writing the policy and establishing records would be assessed on a per-policy basis; any fees paid the government would be on a per-$1,000 basis and underwriting expenses would be split two ways, with one part on a per-$1,000 basis and one part on a per-policy basis. Salaries would be allocated on the basis of the nature of the work done, using time studies or other appropriate measures. Utilities, rent, and the like usually follow the salary distributions.

Once all unit expenses are developed, they are then combined to give a pattern of (1) per-policy, (2) per-$1,000, and (3) percentage expenses separately for the first year and renewal years. As pointed out previously, the expense-loading formulas for traditional forms of life insurance often convert the per-policy expense element to a per-$1,000 charge by relating it to the average-size policy issued. The unit expense rates developed on the basis of careful cost evaluations can be tested for accuracy by applying them to new sales and in-force policy exhibits and comparing the results to the actual costs of appropriate insurer functions. If this application results in total calculated expenses approximating those actually incurred, it may be presumed that they do in fact represent the insurer's operating costs. Judgment modifications can be made, depending on management's optimism or pessimism regarding the future. Table 30-1 presents a set of hypothetical expense factors reflecting the principles discussed.

For traditional policy forms, a tentative gross premium could be calculated by determining the premium payments necessary to equal the present value of all durational expenses, taxes, and benefits, and adding a percentage of premium and per-unit margins for profit, desired permanent surplus contributions, contingencies, and (in the case of participating insurance) dividends. For unbundled products, the initial rate structure can be determined by a source of profit analysis as discussed later in this chapter.

TABLE 30-1   Hypothetical Expenses

EXPENSE ITEM	First Year			Renewal				
	PER POLICY	PER $1,000	PERCENTAGE PREMIUM	PER POLICY	PER $1,000	Percentage Premium by Duration (Years)		
						2–9	10–15	16–20
Premium taxes			2.0			2.0	2.0	2.0
Commissions			60.0			7.3	5.0	3.0
Expense allowance			20.0			2.7	1.8	1.1
Medical and inspection	$22.15	$0.90						
Acquisition	20.93	0.21	14.0					
Maintenance	22.12	0.05	___	$22.12	$0.05	___	___	___
	$65.20	$1.16	96.0	$22.12	$0.05	12.0	8.8	6.1

Claim expense: $32.25 per policy plus $0.20 per $1,000

For participating insurance, it is customary to insert an additional allowance in the loading for the specific purpose of creating additional surplus from which dividends can be paid. In addition, in most cases, provision is made for a minimum dividend to be augmented by favorable deviations from the conservative assumptions underlying the premium rate. Such decisions involve broad managerial policy and vary from company to company. A moderate provision might be 5 percent of the gross premium, or alternatively, the equivalent amount expressed per premium dollar and per $1,000. The loading formula for participating business usually is expressed in terms of the tabular (the reserve basis) net premium.

TESTING THE TENTATIVE GROSS-PREMIUM RATE STRUCTURE

A gross-premium rate structure derived by applying a loading formula to a set of net premiums commonly is only tentative and is tested. The purpose is to determine whether, under realistic assumptions as to mortality, investment earnings, expenses, and terminations, the rate structure would develop sufficiently high asset accumulations to provide the surrender values and death and other benefits under the contract, to ascertain whether the structure is expected to yield the desired financial results to the company, to determine if it meets legal requirements, and to assure that the resulting net costs are competitive, reasonable, and consistent.[4]

Asset-Share Models

When insurers price insurance and annuity products, they must forecast the long-term impact of their pricing decisions in advance of policies being sold. Asset-share models are used to test the tentative gross premium and for profit testing the design of life, annuity, and health insurance products.

Asset-share models test the growth of a product's assets based on assumptions about the product and the economic environment. When developing asset-share models for insurance products (life, annuity, health, and disability), insurers make a number of assumptions including:

- type of product and product features included
- tentative gross premium
- investment income rate
- mortality and/or morbidity and disability tables
- expense assumption
- commission and other compensation schedule
- lapse rate assumption
- rate of taxation
- method of calculating dividends and cash values
- set of profit objectives

Asset-share models use asset shares to calculate the cash inflows and the cash outflows created by an insurance product. The tentative gross premium is examined to determine whether a proposed pricing structure will generate enough revenue to cover the product's costs and attain the company's profit objectives. The model allows the insurer

---

[4]This section draws on Susan Conant, Nicholas L. Desoutter, Dani L. Long, and Robert MacGrogan, *Managing for Solvency and Profitability in Life and Health Insurance Companies* (Atlanta, GA: LOMA, 1996), Chapter 6.

to change the underlying actuarial assumptions and see the effect of those changes on the profitability of the proposed product.

Asset-share models do not automatically take into account the demand for a product in their analysis of a pricing structure. In general, asset-share models allow insurers to set the assumptions concerning sales revenue and the number of policies lapsed. The asset-share model evaluates the effects of various proposed premium structures on the product's ability to cover its costs. Insurers use other forecasting methods to evaluate the effects of the various pricing structures on the product's likely sales performance and persistency.

The basic purpose of an asset-share calculation is to determine, for any block of policies (with the same plan and ratebook), the expected fund per $1,000 of insurance held by the insurer at the end of each policy year after payment of all policy benefits and expenses, taking into consideration all premiums paid and expected (realistic) investment earnings. Modifications of this model can be used to determine annual profit results and amounts that can be distributed to the owners of the insurance entity. Each year's accumulated fund divided by the number of surviving and persisting insureds produces the **asset share.** Asset-share studies are simulations of expected experience for blocks of policies using the best estimates of anticipated operating experience.[5] The purpose of such an asset-share calculation is to determine if the individual elements of the policy are well balanced and will produce acceptable results for both the insurance company and policyowners. The gross-premium rate structure is only one of the many factors being evaluated.

In a product's first year, insurers typically incur considerable costs. These first-year costs include the cost of underwriting and issuing a policy, setting up records, establishing reserves for the policy, and compensating the salesperson. Product sales usually cause an initial net cash outflow because first-year costs are high relative to the gross premium. The sale of a product requires an insurer to invest capital in its product line. This **initial investment** is the amount of capital that an insurer must invest to launch a new product. It should be noted that a product can produce earnings in a given period even though the total initial investment required has not been recovered.

Profitability Measures

Methods of measuring profitability are based on either the *net cash flows* or the *earnings* that a product is expected to generate. In contrast to net cash flows, earnings take into account noncash items, such as a product's contributions to reserve liabilities. Asset-share models generate a number of different profitability measures based on a given set of assumptions affecting the product's cash flows, earnings, and initial investment. These include:

1. payback period
2. validation period
3. net present value (NPV)
4. internal rate of return (IRR)
5. profit margin (ratio of the present value of profits to the present value of premiums)

---

[5]Asset-share studies also are made using historical data. This asset-share research is an integral part of monitoring developing experience and, for insurers writing participating insurance, evaluating the adequacy and appropriateness of dividend scales.

The five profit measures are basic capital budgeting tools that apply to any investment of long-term funds.

Profit measures are used by companies in deciding to accept or reject a proposed investment of any kind. Whether a proposed investment is accepted or rejected based on a given profit measure depends on the decision criteria the company employs. Decision criteria are rules or guidelines that help determine which of two or more possible decision alternatives to select. In examining a proposed product, an insurer might, for example, employ two decision criteria and accept the product if (1) the validation period is not longer than nine years and (2) the profit margin is at least 10 percent.

In examining the cash flows generated by the product, important characteristics of the cash flows under the preceding profitability measures must be taken into consideration. Some of these characteristics include:

- *amounts* of the cash flows
- *expected life* of the series of cash flows
- *timing* of the cash flows
- *predictability* of the cash flows

The more precisely and completely a given profitability measure takes into account these characteristics, the more useful the information the measure provides.

The **payback period** is defined as the number of years that pass before the earnings produced equal the insurer's initial investment. The payback period is the time required for an investment to produce a net contribution to a company's capital and surplus. The point in time when this occurs is known as *break-even point*. The drawback of this profitability measure is that it automatically takes into account only the *amounts* of cash flows.

The key comparison in an asset-share model is the comparison of reserves and cash values to asset shares. By comparing the asset share at each duration with the comparable cash surrender value and reserve and expected profit position, the insurer can evaluate the adequacy and equity of the tentative gross-premium rate structure. From an accounting standpoint, the amount taken from surplus to cover excess first-year expenses for a given block of policies is not fully recovered until the asset share equals the reserve. Up to that point, funds are "borrowed" from surplus. The extent of the strain on surplus may be mitigated through a modified reserve system.[6] Determination of the duration at which the full policy reserve is to be accumulated (when the asset share equals the reserve) is a management decision influenced by the competitive situation. The length of time over which this takes place (while the insurer has a "book" loss on the block of policies) is known as the **validation period.** The shorter the period, the larger must be the gross premium or the lower must be policy benefits or margins for contingencies and profit.

It is not unusual for a well-established insurer to take 5 to 10 years to amortize the acquisition expenses of a particular class of policies. Insurers with a large volume of new business relative to their total volume in force or insurers that expect termination rates to be high may amortize their acquisition expense within a period of 5 to 15 years.

The validation period, like the payback period, does not automatically take into account the *expected life* of the cash flows and the *risk* that the cash flows will not actually materialize.

---

[6]See "Modified Reserve Systems" in chapter 29.

The **net present value (NPV)** measure is calculated by subtracting the project's initial investment from the present value of the product's projected earnings. The discount rate used reflects the *risk* associated with the product. The higher the risk, the larger the discount used. The NPV measure provides for all four elements of a product's cash flows. It takes into account the timing of cash flows by discounting them to the initial date. In addition, this process automatically accounts for the *amount* and *expected life* of the series of cash flows. Finally, it also reflects the *predictability* of the cash flows through selection of the rate of discount used.

The internal rate of return (IRR) is commonly used as a measure of product profitability among insurers. For an insurance product, the **internal rate of return** (IRR) is defined as the percentage rate at which the product's earnings must be discounted in order to repay exactly the insurer's initial investment. The IRR method takes the *amount* and *timing* of cash flows into account by using present value calculations to reflect cash flows that occur at different points in time on an equal footing. An insurer can take cash flow *predictability* or risk into account by comparing a product's estimated IRR to the insurer's required return or hurdle rate.

Most insurers expect policies to make some permanent contribution to surplus, the extent being a management decision limited by considerations of safety, regulatory requirements, equity, and competition, in terms of both policyowner cost and company financial strength ratings assigned by various rating organizations.[7] The actual contribution as opposed to the book contribution of a block of policies (negative or positive) depends on the relationship between the asset share and the surrender value of the policy. When a policy is terminated by surrender, the reserves are released because, of course, the company is not required to maintain a reserve liability on its balance sheet for policies that are no longer in force. If the asset share exceeds the surrender payment, the company has a real gain. This typically occurs after the first few (e.g., 3 to 10) policy years. The asset share commonly is less than the surrender value in the early policy years, so the insurer has a real loss from surrenders during this period.[8] Determining the point at which the asset share for a block of policies should equal or exceed the surrender value is an important management decision. Once a surrender has occurred, the impact of that policy on the insurer's gain or loss is fixed.

If the asset shares produced by the tentative gross-premium rate structure are deficient in the light of insurer objectives, the premiums may be increased or some specific item of expense or outgo (e.g., dividends, cash values, or expenses) decreased. If the fund accumulation appears excessive, premiums can be reduced or benefits increased.

Selection of Most Probable Assumptions

If the asset-share calculations are to be a reasonable test of premium adequacy and equity among blocks of policies, the values or range of values entering into the calculation must be chosen with great care. The assumptions underlying any mathematical model are critical to its effectiveness as a predictive device.

Mortality

Selection of the most probable assumption as to future mortality is complicated by the secular trend toward mortality improvement. It might be argued that the asset-share study should reflect anticipated improvement in future mortality. The majority of in-

---

[7]The state of New York regulates the contribution that participating policies can make to surplus in the aggregate as do many countries (e.g., France, United Kingdom, and Singapore).

[8]This statement is not true for so-called lapse-supported policies. See later in this chapter.

surers do not reflect this anticipated improvement in their computations, but they do test under varying mortality scenarios. Regardless of this feature, all insurers utilize the latest available experience.

The best source of information on current trends, incidence, and levels of U.S. mortality among ordinary insureds has been the reports of the Committee on Mortality under Ordinary Insurance and Annuities, published periodically by the Society of Actuaries. These data are compiled by the committee from statistics supplied by a number of the largest life insurance companies. The experience is published on a select and ultimate basis. The death rates generally are shown for all ages on juvenile lives, but only at quinquennial age groups with respect to adult lives. Periodically, the committee publishes a graduated mortality table based on these data. Most larger insurers use mortality from their own experience, and many insurers rely on their reinsurers for guidance on mortality rates.

Interest

Determining the rate of interest to be used in asset-share calculations involves estimates of investment returns over the next 20 or more years. These estimates must be made with knowledge that the long-range impact of interest on life insurance is great. From the standpoint of the shareholder in a stock company, the leverage based on the margin between actual and assumed interest rates is enormous.

The rate selected normally will fall within a range of possible rates, the upper limit of which (during a period when interest rates are increasing) is the rate being earned on new investments, and the lower limit the valuation rate of interest for policies currently being issued. For both mutual and stock insurers, allowance is made in selecting these rates for the impact of taxes.[9] Furthermore, recognition can be given to the possibility of changes in earned interest rates in future years. For example, a higher interest rate might be assumed for policy years 1 to 10, with a lower rate assumed thereafter.

Operating Expenses

Mutual and stock insurers compute their expense rates in a similar manner. The average size of new policies is computed by plan and age at issue, and applied to the constant expense per policy to permit the expression of expense rates in terms of a percentage of the premium plus a number of dollars per $1,000 of insurance. Since the expense factors are based on the average collection frequency of the insurer's business, the expenses within the asset-share study must be adjusted to reflect the estimated proportions of the types of premium payment frequency. If the tentative gross-premium rate schedule was based on a detailed analysis of current expenses, these same expense rates could be used as a basis for estimating future expenses. Otherwise, a detailed cost study must precede the asset-share calculation.

Termination Rates

Predicting future lapse (termination) rates usually is a difficult task. The difficulty is caused by the extreme fluctuations over the years, largely as a result of economic conditions. Although for many insurers lapse rates may not be as important to the adequacy test as are the other three factors, for other insurers, the financial implications can be significant.

---

[9]A potentially significant problem arises for life insurers when products are priced assuming a particular tax burden and the government increases insurers' taxes. Depending on the types of products, insurers may not be able easily to adjust experience participation to accommodate the increase.

As in the case of the other assumptions, it is customary to use termination rates based on the insurer's individual experience.[10] Termination rates are influenced by many factors, including the quality of the agency force, age of issue, amount of premium, frequency and method of premium payment, as well as income levels and other economic conditions of the likely customers for the policy. In practice, termination rates usually are differentiated by plan of insurance, age of issue, and frequency and method of premium payment. Under most plans, they are highest during the first two years and lower thereafter. Lapse rates for UL policies have tended to be somewhat more uniform from year to year.

Ordinarily, the higher the lapse rates, the lower the insurer's profit (or surplus contribution) and, therefore, the lower will be dividends or other nonguaranteed policy benefits. This is the result whenever the asset share is less than the cash surrender value. Recently, however, some insurers have designed and sold policies wherein the higher the lapse rates, the *higher* the profit. Some survivorship life policies and policies with interest rate bonuses are designed in this fashion. The insurer designs products such that the surrender values are less than the corresponding asset share in the early policy years. The hope is that lapse rates will be sufficiently high so that gains from surrenders can be used to augment later-year policy values. The problem with such **lapse-supported policies** is that lower than expected lapse rates can result in lower future asset shares and, therefore, potentially lower product value.

Termination rates are necessary in premium calculations because of the disparity between cash surrender values and asset shares. If surrender values exactly equaled each year's asset share, lapse rates could be ignored for purposes of calculating asset shares but would remain important to overall insurer profitability and asset growth.

Special Unbundled Product Pricing Considerations

Bundled versus Unbundled Products

Traditionally, insurers offered only bundled products.[11] Today both bundled and unbundled products are available. A *bundled product* is one for which the policyowner is charged a single gross-premium amount reflecting three pricing elements—benefit costs, expenses, and investment returns. In contrast, an **unbundled product** is one for which the insurer expresses (discloses) the pricing elements separately. Traditional individual insurance products (term, whole life, etc.) are bundled products with a single gross premium disclosed to the policyholder. Unbundled pricing is used most often in connection with investment-sensitive products such as universal life, variable life, and fixed and variable annuities.[12] In the individual insurance product area, universal life was the first policy under which the internal operation of the elements affecting the product's price was disclosed.

The pricing of universal life (UL) is complex. The flexible nature of UL brings with it the need for additional assumptions. The premium payment pattern can vary. The ben-

---

[10]See M. A. Linton, *The Record of the American Institute of Actuaries,* Vol. 13 (1924), pp. 283–316; see also C. F. B. Richardson and John M. Hartwell, *Transactions of the Society of Actuaries,* Vol. 3 (1951), pp. 338–372; and Ernest J. Morehead, "The Construction of Persistency Tables," *Transactions of the Society of Actuaries,* Vol. 12 (1960), pp. 545–563. In recent years, industry persistency studies have been conducted and published by LIMRA International.

[11]This section draws from Douglas C. Doll, "Universal Life: A Product Overview," *SOA Study Note 340-41-91* (Schaumburg, IL: Society of Actuaries, 1991), pp. 16–17 and Susan Conant, Nicholas L. Desoutter, Dani L. Long, and Robert MacGrogan, *Managing for Solvency and Profitability in Life and Health Insurance Companies* (Atlanta, GA: LOMA, 1996), Chapter 7.

[12]Such products would also include mutual funds and separate account funds.

efit pattern also can vary according to changing specified amounts and type of coverage. Withdrawals or policy loan activity may result from client investment antiselection (disintermediation). Changing margins of interest earned over interest credited imply that adjustments will have to be made periodically. Inflation and other economic factors are likely to remain in a state of flux. Prudence requires that various scenarios be tested for each of these assumptions.

Of course, from this vast set of possible alternatives, only the most likely scenarios would be intensively examined. In doing so, it is important to determine the sensitivity of asset-share and other profit studies to deviations from the assumptions and equally important to monitor actual experience and to compare it with expected results.

The original UL concept was that product loads would match product expenses and that the result would be a significantly lower expense persistency risk to the insurance company. This was true for the first few products introduced, but most products since then have had first-year expense assumptions that were larger than expense loads, with excess expenses covered eventually by mortality margins, interest margins, and surrender charges.

Although not all costs will be covered by corresponding direct charges, it is important to balance the sources of margin so that most scenarios of premiums and persistency will result in acceptable profit results. Otherwise, policyowner antiselection might cause profits to be less than anticipated. This requires that the pricing actuary be aware of and measure each of these sources of profits:

1. interest earned more than interest credited
2. cost of insurance charges less than death benefits paid
3. expense charges less than expenses and commissions
4. surrender charges

The source of profit analysis is easier to interpret when calculated using the policy's gross cash (fund) value as the reserve basis. If actual reserves are different from the cash value, net profits should include a reserve adjustment factor.

Asset–Liability Analysis

Universal life carries a risk of interest rate antiselection. If external interest rates are higher than the rate credited to the cash value, the policyowner may withdraw the cash value (via lapse or partial withdrawal) and invest it elsewhere. If the assets held by the insurer have a reduced market value (which is likely if interest rates have risen), the insurer suffers a capital loss if these assets have to be sold. The reverse is true also. If interest rates have fallen, there will be an inflow of funds, which will have to be invested at these lower rates.

This risk is not unique to UL. It is argued, however, that, because of the attention paid to the credited interest rate, UL policies are more subject to this risk than are other life insurance policies. Prudence dictates that the actuary perform an analysis of the UL product combined with the possible investment and interest crediting strategies under different interest scenarios to determine the appropriate strategies and the appropriate charge to make for the interest rate risk.

Sample Asset-Share Calculation

The process by which a gross-premium rate schedule is tested was illustrated with an example in chapter 2, shown in Table 2-6. That table is reproduced here as Table 30-2. It may be recalled that the tentative gross premium for the ordinary life policy being tested

TABLE 30-2   Asset-Share Calculation, $1,000 Ordinary Life Issued at Male, Age 35 ($15 Rate per $1,000)

(1) Policy Year	(2) Number Paying Premiums at Beginning of Year	(3) Number Dying[a]	(4) Number Withdrawing[b]	(5) Number Alive at End of Year after Withdrawals [(2) − (3) − (4)]	(6) Expense Rate per $1,000	(7) Cash Value per $1,000 on Withdrawal[c]	(8) Dividend per $1,000
1	100,000	88	10,000	89,912	$22.00	$ 0.00	$ 0.00
2	89,912	92	5,394	84,426	2.25	0.00	0.50
3	84,426	101	4,221	80,104	2.25	4.31	1.00
4	80,104	111	3,524	76,469	2.25	13.91	1.50
5	76,469	118	3,058	73,293	2.25	23.86	2.00
6	73,293	132	2,638	70,523	2.25	34.16	2.50
7	70,523	142	2,256	68,125	2.25	44.81	3.10
8	68,125	152	1,975	65,998	2.25	55.82	3.70
9	65,998	164	1,781	64,053	2.25	67.19	4.30
10	64,053	175	1,601	62,277	2.25	78.94	5.90
11	62,277	198	1,494	60,585	2.25	91.05	6.60
12	60,585	212	1,393	58,980	2.25	103.56	7.30
13	58,980	226	1,297	57,457	2.25	116.46	7.90
14	57,457	240	1,206	56,011	2.25	129.78	8.50
15	56,011	256	1,120	54,635	2.25	143.51	9.20
16	54,635	273	1,092	53,270	2.25	157.66	9.90
17	53,270	293	1,065	51,912	2.25	172.19	10.60
18	51,912	315	1,038	50,559	2.25	187.10	11.40
19	50,559	340	1,011	49,208	2.25	202.35	12.20
20	49,208	368	984	47,856	2.25	217.92	13.00

(1) Policy Year	(9) Fund at Beginning of Year [(16) Prior Year]	(10) Premium Income [($15.00) × (2)]	(11) Expense Disbursements [(2) × (6)]	(12) Death Claims Paid [$1,000 × (3)]	(13) Amounts Paid on Surrender [(4) × (7)]	(14) Total Dividends Paid [(5) × (8)]
1	$ 0	$1,500,000	$2,200,000	$ 88,000	$ 0	$ 0
2	−847,520	1,348,680	202,302	92,000	0	42,213
3	184,874	1,266,390	189,959	101,000	18,193	80,104
4	1,158,873	1,201,560	180,234	111,000	49,019	114,704
5	2,075,453	1,147,035	172,055	118,000	72,964	146,586
6	2,952,197	1,099,395	164,909	132,000	90,114	176,308
7	3,793,916	1,057,845	158,677	142,000	101,091	211,188
8	4,608,572	1,021,875	153,281	152,000	110,245	244,193
9	5,402,822	989,970	148,496	164,000	119,665	275,428
10	6,178,178	960,795	144,119	175,000	126,383	367,434
11	6,878,634	934,155	140,123	198,000	136,029	399,861
12	7,544,670	908,775	136,316	212,000	144,259	430,554
13	8,187,206	884,700	132,705	226,000	151,049	453,910
14	8,814,338	861,855	129,278	240,000	156,515	476,094
15	9,428,459	840,165	126,025	256,000	160,731	502,642
16	10,024,395	819,525	122,929	273,000	172,165	527,373
17	10,595,212	799,050	119,858	293,000	183,382	550,267
18	11,137,988	778,680	116,802	315,000	194,210	576,373
19	11,645,673	758,385	113,758	340,000	204,576	600,338
20	12,115,010	738,120	110,718	368,000	214,433	622,128

	(15) Interest Earned during Year $[0.08[(9) + (10) - (11) - \frac{1}{2}(12)]]$	(16) Fund at End of Year $[(9) + (10) - (11) - (12) - (13) - (14) + (15)]$	(17) Asset Share at End of Year $[(16) \div (5)]$	(18) Reserve[d] at End of Year	(19) Surplus per $1,000 at End of Year $[(17) - (18)]$	(20) Surrender Gain per $1,000 at End of Year $[(17) - (7)]$
Policy Year						
1	$ -59,520	$ -847,520	$ -9.43	$ 9.15	$-18.58	$-9.43
2	20,229	184,874	2.19	18.65	-16.46	2.19
3	96,864	1,158,873	14.47	28.49	-14.02	10.16
4	169,976	2,075,453	27.14	38.68	-11.54	13.23
5	239,315	2,952,197	40.28	49.20	-8.92	16.42
6	305,655	3,793,916	53.80	60.07	-6.27	19.64
7	369,767	4,608,572	67.65	71.25	-3.60	22.84
8	432,093	5,402,822	81.86	82.79	-0.93	26.04
9	492,984	6,178,187	96.45	94.67	1.78	29.26
10	552,589	6,878,634	110.45	106.90	3.55	31.51
11	605,893	7,544,670	124.53	119.48	5.05	33.48
12	656,890	8,187,206	138.81	132.43	6.38	35.25
13	706,096	8,814,338	153.41	145.75	7.66	36.95
14	754,153	9,428,459	168.33	159.45	8.88	38.55
15	801,168	10,024,395	183.48	173.54	9.94	39.97
16	846,759	10,595,212	198.90	188.01	10.89	41.24
17	890,232	11,137,988	214.56	202.83	11.73	42.37
18	931,389	11,645,673	230.34	217.99	12.35	43.24
19	969,624	12,115,010	246.20	233.45	12.75	43.85
20	1,004,673	12,542,524	262.09	249.19	12.90	44.17

[a]Deaths are based on select and ultimate experience mortality table. Deaths are assumed to occur in middle of policy year on the average.

[b]Withdrawals are based on Linton A lapse rates and assumed to occur on anniversary at end of policy year.

[c]Cash values using *1980 CSO Table* at 5½% interest.

[d]Net-level-premium reserves using *1980 CSO Table* at 5% interest.

was $15.00 per $1,000 and that cash values (column 7) were calculated on the basis of the *1980 CSO Mortality Table* and 5½ percent interest and that net level terminal reserves (column 18) were used (at 5 percent and *1980 CSO*).

Other needed assumptions included expected death (column 3) and withdrawal rates (column 4), expected expenses (column 6), and illustrated dividends (column 8). A net investment earnings rate of 8 percent was assumed to be reasonable over the next 20 years. Column 17 gives the yearly asset shares for the hypothetical policy being tested, with column 19 providing the anticipated net surplus position of the insurer for this policy.[13]

The assumptions used in an asset-share calculation are supposed to represent the best estimates of what the actual experience will be. Invariably, however, actual results deviate from those assumed. Insurers expect this. As a result, they conduct asset-share

[13]No further discussion of the example based on the stated assumptions is presented here. See chapter 2 for such a discussion.

calculations using a range of underlying assumptions. This enables the actuary and management to judge the sensitivity of the results under varying possible future conditions.

Tables 30-3 through 30-9 indicate a type of gross sensitivity analysis as we alter only one factor in the Table 30-2 calculations. Thus, we show the impact on the calculation of the following changes in assumptions and benefits:

1. interest rate decreased from 8 percent to 7 percent
2. mortality increased by 20 percent
3. expenses increased by 5 percent
4. gross premium increased from $15.00 to $15.50
5. dividends reduced by 10 percent each year
6. cash values increased
7. lapse rates increased

In examining these tables, it is instructive to note the impact on the validation period in each case (see column 19). Similarly, note the point at which the block of policies would begin realizing a gain from surrenders (i.e., the time at which the asset share exceeds the surrender value).

Practically, of course, several factors will be adjusted simultaneously to examine the effects of the combined changes. When a combination of adjustments is made, the strength and direction of change in asset-share values cannot always be determined intuitively. Computers permit a wide range of experimentation in finding a combination of factors that is compatible with the insurer's objectives.

TABLE 30-3	Asset-Share Calculation with 7% Instead of 8% Interest Rate			
(1)	*(17)*	*(18)*	*(19)* *Surplus per $1,000* *at End of Year* *[(17) – (18)]*	*(20)* *Surrender Gain per* *$1,000 at End of Year* *[(17) – (7)]*
Policy *Year*	*Asset Share at* *End of Year*	*Reserve at* *End of Year*		
1	$ –9.34	$ 9.15	$–18.49	$–9.34
2	2.25	18.65	–16.40	2.25
3	14.39	28.49	–14.10	10.08
4	26.78	38.68	–11.90	12.87
5	39.46	49.20	–9.74	15.60
6	52.35	60.07	–7.72	18.19
7	65.36	71.25	–5.89	20.55
8	78.52	82.79	–4.27	22.70
9	91.81	94.67	–2.86	24.62
10	104.23	106.90	–2.67	25.29
11	116.44	119.48	–3.04	25.39
12	128.52	132.43	–3.91	24.96
13	140.57	145.75	–5.18	24.11
14	152.56	159.45	–6.89	22.78
15	164.34	173.54	–9.20	20.83
16	175.91	188.01	–12.10	18.25
17	187.17	202.83	–15.66	14.98
18	197.95	217.99	–20.04	10.85
19	208.13	233.45	–25.32	5.78
20	217.57	249.19	–31.61	–0.34

TABLE 30-4 Asset-Share Calculation With 20% Increase in Mortality

(1) Policy Year	(17) Asset Share at End of Year	(18) Reserve at End of Year	(19) Surplus per $1,000 at End of Year [(17) – (18)]	(20) Surrender Gain per $1,000 at End of Year [(17) – (7)]
1	$ –9.64	$ 9.15	$–18.79	$–9.64
2	1.73	18.65	–16.92	1.73
3	13.68	28.49	–14.81	9.37
4	25.96	38.68	–12.72	12.05
5	38.62	49.20	–10.58	14.76
6	51.57	60.07	–8.50	17.41
7	64.76	71.25	–6.49	19.95
8	78.20	82.79	–4.59	22.38
9	91.89	94.67	–2.78	24.70
10	104.85	106.90	–2.05	25.91
11	117.69	119.48	–1.79	26.64
12	130.57	132.43	–1.86	27.01
13	143.56	145.75	–2.19	27.10
14	156.64	159.45	–2.81	26.86
15	169.70	173.54	–3.84	26.19
16	182.72	188.01	–5.29	25.06
17	195.63	202.83	–7.20	23.44
18	208.27	217.99	–9.72	21.17
19	220.51	233.45	–12.94	18.16
20	232.23	249.19	–16.96	14.31

TABLE 30-5 Asset-Share Calculation with 5% Expense Increase

(1) Policy Year	(17) Asset Share at End of Year	(18) Reserve at End of Year	(19) Surplus per $1,000 at End of Year [(17) – (18)]	(20) Surrender Gain per $1,000 at End of Year [(17) – (7)]
1	$–10.75	$ 9.15	$–19.90	$–10.75
2	0.54	18.65	–18.11	0.54
3	12.46	28.49	–16.03	8.15
4	24.75	38.68	–13.93	10.84
5	37.45	49.20	–11.75	13.59
6	50.50	60.07	–9.57	16.34
7	63.84	71.25	–7.41	19.03
8	77.49	82.79	–5.30	21.67
9	91.46	94.67	–3.21	24.27
10	104.78	106.90	–2.12	25.84
11	118.11	119.48	–1.37	27.06
12	131.56	132.43	–0.87	28.00
13	145.24	145.75	–0.51	28.78
14	159.16	159.45	–0.29	29.38
15	173.20	173.54	–0.34	29.69
16	187.39	188.01	–0.62	29.73
17	201.68	202.83	–1.15	29.49
18	215.93	217.99	–2.06	28.83
19	230.09	233.45	–3.36	27.74
20	244.07	249.19	–5.12	26.15

TABLE 30-6 Asset-Share Calculation with Gross Premium Increased from $15.00 to $15.50

(1) Policy Year	(17) Asset Share at End of Year	(18) Reserve at End of Year	(19) Surplus per $1,000 at End of Year [(17) − (18)]	(20) Surrender Gain per $1,000 at End of Year [(17) − (7)]
1	$ −8.83	$ 9.15	$−17.98	$−8.83
2	3.46	18.65	−15.19	3.46
3	16.48	28.49	−12.01	12.17
4	29.98	38.68	−8.70	16.07
5	44.04	49.20	−5.16	20.18
6	58.58	60.07	−1.49	24.42
7	73.56	71.25	2.31	28.75
8	89.01	82.79	6.22	33.19
9	104.96	94.67	10.29	37.77
10	120.46	106.90	13.56	41.52
11	136.19	119.48	16.71	45.14
12	152.31	132.43	19.88	48.75
13	168.92	145.75	23.17	52.46
14	186.07	159.45	26.62	56.29
15	203.67	173.54	30.13	60.16
16	221.82	188.01	33.81	64.16
17	240.51	202.83	37.68	68.32
18	259.68	217.99	41.69	72.58
19	279.31	233.45	45.86	76.96
20	299.42	249.19	50.23	81.50

TABLE 30-7 Asset-Share Calculation with 10% Reduction in Dividends

(1) Policy Year	(17) Asset Share at End of Year	(18) Reserve at End of Year	(19) Surplus per $1,000 at End of Year [(17) − (18)]	(20) Surrender Gain per $1,000 at End of Year [(17) − (7)]
1	$ −9.43	$ 9.15	$−18.58	$−9.43
2	2.24	18.65	−16.41	2.24
3	14.62	28.49	−13.87	10.31
4	27.47	38.68	−11.21	13.56
5	40.85	49.20	−8.35	16.99
6	54.69	60.07	−5.38	20.53
7	68.95	71.25	−2.30	24.14
8	83.69	82.79	0.90	27.87
9	98.91	94.67	4.24	31.72
10	113.77	106.90	6.87	34.83
11	128.88	119.48	9.40	37.83
12	144.37	132.43	11.94	40.81
13	160.35	145.75	14.60	43.89
14	176.88	159.45	17.43	47.10
15	193.86	173.54	20.32	50.35
16	210.40	188.01	22.39	52.74
17	228.36	202.83	25.53	56.17
18	246.79	217.99	28.80	59.69
19	265.67	233.45	32.22	63.32
20	285.01	249.19	35.82	67.09

TABLE 30-8 Asset-Share Calculation with Increased Cash Values

(1) Policy Year	(7) Increased Cash Value per $1,000 on Withdrawal	(17) Asset Share at End of Year	(18) Reserve at End of Year	(19) Surplus per $1,000 at End of Year [(17) − (18)]	(20) Surrender Gain per $1,000 at End of Year [(17) − (7)]
1	$ 0.00	$ −9.43	$ 9.15	$−18.58	$−9.43
2	0.00	2.19	18.65	−16.46	2.19
3	5.78	14.39	28.49	−14.10	8.61
4	16.20	26.95	38.68	−11.73	10.75
5	26.97	39.93	49.20	−9.27	12.96
6	38.09	53.26	60.07	−6.81	15.17
7	49.54	66.89	71.25	−4.36	17.35
8	61.34	80.85	82.79	−1.94	19.51
9	73.51	95.16	94.67	0.49	21.65
10	86.02	108.83	106.90	1.93	22.81
11	98.89	122.53	119.48	3.05	23.64
12	112.15	136.40	132.43	3.97	24.25
13	125.78	150.52	145.75	4.77	24.74
14	139.80	164.91	159.45	5.46	25.11
15	154.22	179.47	173.54	5.93	25.25
16	169.02	194.23	188.01	6.22	25.21
17	184.19	209.13	202.83	6.30	24.94
18	199.70	224.07	217.99	6.08	24.37
19	215.52	238.97	233.45	5.52	23.45
20	231.63	253.78	249.19	4.59	22.15

TABLE 30-9 Asset-Share Calculation with 150% Increase in Withdrawal Rates

(1) Policy Year	(17) Asset Share at End of Year	(18) Reserve at End of Year	(19) Surplus per $1,000 at End of Year [(17) − (18)]	(20) Surrender Gain per $1,000 at End of Year [(17) − (7)]
1	$ −9.98	$ 9.15	$−19.13	$−9.98
2	1.56	18.65	−17.09	1.56
3	13.99	28.49	−14.50	9.68
4	26.87	38.68	−11.81	12.96
5	40.28	49.20	−8.92	16.42
6	54.08	60.07	−5.99	19.92
7	68.23	71.25	−3.02	23.42
8	82.73	82.79	−0.06	26.91
9	97.58	94.67	2.91	30.39
10	111.79	106.90	4.89	32.85
11	125.93	119.48	6.45	34.88
12	140.13	132.43	7.70	36.57
13	154.44	145.75	8.69	37.98
14	168.80	159.45	9.35	39.02
15	183.02	173.54	9.48	39.51
16	197.11	188.01	9.10	39.45
17	210.90	202.83	8.07	38.71
18	224.07	217.99	6.08	36.97
19	236.33	233.45	2.88	33.98
20	250.13	249.19	0.94	32.21

OTHER ASPECTS

Fractional Premiums

The calculations earlier in this text illustrate the determination of an annual premium. It would be possible to follow the same principles for any unit of time, but the existing mortality tables are not graded for periods of less than a year. When the policyowner pays premiums other than annually, a carrying charge is added to the fractional (also called modal) premiums, based on the company's experience.

The purpose of the carrying charge is to reimburse the insurance company for the additional expense associated with more frequent premium collection, to offset the loss of interest stemming from the deferment of part of the year's premium, to compensate for the higher lapse rates that may arise when premiums are paid other than annually, and to compensate for fractional premiums not paid in the year of death. The carrying charge is sometimes viewed as including an element of life insurance protection because companies disregard any remaining fractional premiums due in the year of death.

A fractional premium often is calculated by multiplying the annual premium by a specified factor and sometimes adding to the result a flat amount. Common factors for semiannual premiums are 0.5100, 0.5150, and 0.5200; for quarterly premiums, 0.2600, 0.2625, and 0.2650; and for monthly premiums, 0.0875, 0.0883, and 0.0900. (See Box 30-1.)

Premium Rates Graded by Policy Size

Two quantity discount systems have developed in which size classifications are used. Under the **band system,** a number of "size bands," often three to five, are established, with different premium rates applying within each band. The following might be typical under this system:

Size Band[a]	Premium per $1,000 for a Particular Plan and Age
$ 25,000 to $90,000	$14.00
$ 100,000 to 240,000	13.00
$ 250,000 to 490,000	12.50
$ 500,000 to 990,000	12.25
$1,000,000 and over	12.00

[a]Companies may use "blackout periods" (e.g., $90,001 to $99,999) to avoid putting policyowners into the position of paying more or less.

Under the **policy fee system,** the premium for a policy is expressed as the product of the policy amount and a basic rate per $1,000, plus a flat amount (known as the policy fee). For a particular plan and age, the premium might be $12.00 per $1,000 plus a flat $25. Thus, the premium is $265 for a $20,000 policy, $625 for a $50,000 policy and $1,225 for a $100,000 policy. Often the two systems are combined.

With both systems, the loading formula is modified so that the expense amount deemed to be independent of size is treated accordingly in determining the premium. The total amount necessary to cover expenses is not changed by such gradations, and the lower-amount policies must of necessity pay a higher rate to offset the discount granted to the larger-amount policies. Insurers most often use a policy fee with a banded system.

BOX 30-1

RETURN OF PREMIUM POLICIES

Policies sometimes include a provision whereby, on the death of the insured, an additional death benefit equal to the sum of the premiums paid will be paid to the beneficiary if death occurs within a stipulated time period. In actuality, of course, the insurer does not return the paid premiums. It simply calculates its premiums on the basis that the amount of life insurance protection each year equals the policy face amount plus an additional death benefit equal to the then sum of the premiums paid to date. This additional death benefit is simply an increasing amount of term insurance set equal to the amount of premiums paid.

SURPLUS AND ITS DISTRIBUTION

The earlier chapters made it clear that life insurance policies often contain elements that are not wholly guaranteed. Participating life insurance policies always have been characterized for their nonguaranteed aspect—that is, by dividends (bonuses). With the advent of indeterminate-policy charges and of excess interest credits (all on nonparticipating policies), the entire area of nonguaranteed policy elements has become blurred.

The actuarial aspects of the ways insurers determine excess interest credits and mortality and expense charges are not covered as thoroughly in the literature as that covering surplus distribution. In many ways, however, they are similar. Each shifts portions of the risk of deviations in the interest, mortality, and expense experience from the insurer to the policyowner. This shift permits insurers to offer potentially better valued products because they need not guarantee a fixed, rigid benefit package and attendant prices for decades into the future.

As discussed in earlier chapters, current assumption products differ from participating products primarily in the mechanism by which experience deviations are addressed.[14] For the indeterminate aspects of current assumption policies, the insurer typically examines its *current and likely future* operating experience in light of the competitive environment to decide upon the current year's *explicit* mortality and expense charges and excess interest credits.[15]

For participating products, the insurer typically examines its *past and current* operating experience in light of the competitive environment, to decide upon the current year's *implicit* mortality and expense charges and excess interest credits.[16] Because participating products involve greater reliance on past rather than probable future experience, their nonguaranteed element (dividends) tends to be more stable than the nonguaranteed elements (excess interest credits, mortality charge deviations, and possibly expense variations) of current assumption nonparticipating products.

The following discussion deals primarily with surplus distribution under participating policies. Many aspects, however, are also applicable to current assumption products.

---

[14]See chapters 2, 6, and 9.

[15]Of course, not all policy elements necessarily would be indeterminate. Often only the interest and mortality elements are subject to annual redetermination (see chapter 6).

[16]With participating products, the insurer normally considers all three of these aspects of product pricing in determining the distribution of surplus.

Nature of Surplus

Guaranteed life insurance premiums are calculated conservatively. This is essential if an insurer is to avoid jeopardizing its long-term viability. Consequently, insurers are expected over time to show a gain from operations. The immediate result of a gain is to increase the insurer's surplus position. The size and disposition of this gain depends, among other factors, on whether the business written is on a participating basis; a guaranteed cost, nonparticipating basis; or a current assumption basis.

In the aggregate, statutory surplus will develop only if an insurer accumulates funds in excess of those needed to establish policy reserves and other liabilities.[17] Surplus arises from favorable deviations from the assumed experience as to mortality, interest, and loading contained in the gross premium. These constitute the primary sources of additions to surplus and usually are designated as mortality savings, excess interest, and loading savings. The word *savings* is used here to connote both the residue arising from operations that were more efficient, economical, or profitable than anticipated and margins intentionally provided in fixing the gross-premium rate schedule. Even though insurers usually make participating premiums conservative, capable management can make a significant difference by adding yearly amounts to surplus.

An insurer's statutory surplus arising from a given block of policies consists of the sum of the excess interest, mortality savings, and savings from loading, plus gains from minor sources. For some policies, ages at issue, and durations, some or all of the three gains could be negative. In particular, the saving from loading is almost always negative in the first policy year, when the insurer's expenses are high.

Gains from Investment Earnings

Because life insurance policies often are written for a long term of years, it is essential that insurers assume a conservative rate of interest for their net premium and reserve computations to assure its being earned throughout the life of the contract. If an insurer bases its reserves on the assumption that it will earn 4 percent but actually earns 7 percent, that 3 percent difference represents the excess of investment earnings over the return necessary to maintain reserve liabilities, and it may be returned to policyowners who were responsible for its existence, if this is considered advisable.

Gains from Mortality

Gains from mortality arise because life insurance companies ordinarily do not experience mortality that is as heavy as that indicated by the mortality table employed in reserve calculations. Because the reserve mortality table is deliberately made to be conservative, it is natural that a surplus gain normally results from operations. Too much reliance should not be placed on a single year's mortality experience, however, because it tends to fluctuate from year to year. In the interest of stability and safety, therefore, most insurers average mortality experience over a period of years. Any surplus gain does not necessarily mean that the block of policies is profitable. The surplus gain or loss relates actual experience to the reserve liability value, which usually is conservative.

Gains from Loading

Sound insurance company management dictates that the gross premium should be more than sufficient to meet normal requirements, so that the insurer and its policyowners may be protected against exceptional conditions. In fact, as pointed out earlier,

---

[17]Insurers' decisions regarding surplus distribution to policyowners are heavily influenced by the accounting procedures required by insurance regulators. As a result, these decisions focus on *statutory surplus* as opposed to surplus as measured by a realistic assessment of the insurer's cash flows. The difference in approaches should not affect the ultimate amount of surplus generated by a block of policies—only the time of its recognition.

the loading on participating policies frequently includes an amount for policyowner dividends together with gains from other sources. Competitive conditions—especially in the matter of agents' commissions—as well as inflationary pressures on expenses have at times caused expenses to exceed loadings in the aggregate. This has been a particular challenge for insurers selling universal life policies. In recent years, life insurance companies have made a marked effort toward economical management.

Gains from Surrenders

Cash surrender values, as previously explained, normally are less than policy reserves. The difference between (1) reserves released as a result of surrender and (2) surrender values allowed constitutes another source of surplus gain. Such a gain frequently represents, in whole or in part, amounts returned to surplus that originally were taken from it to establish the reserves. In general, a surplus gain from surrenders will be a "paper" gain—a repayment of previously borrowed surplus—when the asset share is less than the policy surrender value. The gain will be "real" when the asset share is greater than the surrender value. Real gains derived from this source are generally used to offset expenses when calculations are made to apportion the divisible surplus to policyowners.[18]

Distribution of Surplus

Divisible Surplus

Following each year's operations, an insurer typically determines how much of the total surplus (previously existing surplus plus additions for the year) should be retained as a contingency fund or other special surplus appropriation and how much should be distributed to policyowners. No fixed relationship may exist between the surplus gain in a particular calendar year and the dividends distributed to policyowners on the next policy anniversaries. The directors or trustees of the insurer, as a matter of business judgment, make the decision. The amount earmarked for distribution is designated as **divisible surplus,** and once it is set aside by action of the directors or trustees, it loses its identity as surplus and becomes a liability of the insurer.

In deciding the portion of the total surplus that should be retained as contingency funds, a balance must be maintained between the need for a general contingency fund and the competitive advantages of a liberal dividend scale. When the surplus earned for any given year is insufficient to permit the insurer to maintain its current dividend scale, management may decide to use a portion of the general contingency fund for this purpose.[19] On the other hand, if, during a temporary period, additions to surplus are more than adequate to support the existing dividend scale, the excess often is added to the general contingency fund to avoid the expense and complications involved in changing the scale. If the excess is substantial and is expected to continue over a reasonable period, competitive considerations will usually lead to a change in the scale.

In the interest of security of the benefits and good management, life insurance companies maintain surplus and general contingency funds that bear a reasonable relationship to liabilities. As policy reserves increase through new business and the natural accretion under older policies, surplus and general contingency funds should also increase. With many insurers, each policy is expected to make a permanent contribution

---

[18]In the apportionment of surplus, as explained in a later section, it is more practical to treat all surpluses as coming from the three main sources previously mentioned: loading, interest earnings, and mortality. Surplus from other sources, such as forfeitures and appreciation in the value of assets, is, therefore, not treated separately but instead is considered in connection with expenses and interest earnings, respectively. An exception to this general statement occurs with lapse-supported policies when the gain from surrender is explicitly counted upon to support future policy values.

[19]An insurer may earmark a special fund for dividend fluctuations, but the principle is the same.

to the insurer's surplus. These contributions enable insurers to fulfill their contractual obligations even in the face of a catastrophe of the type that may occur only once in several decades. Thus, over the lifetime of a class of policies, aggregate dividend distributions made often will be somewhat less than the contributions of the class to surplus. On the other hand, some insurers' dividend practices result in substantially complete liquidation of each generation's contributions to surplus by the time that generation of policies is eliminated from the books.

Although insurers may, in the absence of legislation, use their discretion in determining the amount of surplus to be distributed, some governments regulate this matter by statute. New York limits the amount of surplus an insurer can retain on its participating business to an amount not exceeding $850,000, or 10 percent of its policy reserves and other policy liabilities, whichever is the greater amount. The United Kingdom, France, Germany, Singapore, and many other countries have similar limitations. Their purpose is to prevent insurers from retaining more surplus than is judged necessary to offset factors such as fluctuations in the mortality rate and interest earnings that may interfere with the payment of stable dividends. Many commentators today question whether such limitations serve the public interest and are warranted, especially given the great concern over insurer solvency and need for growth.

Frequency of Distribution

Unlike the situation in many other countries, in the United States surplus is distributed annually on practically all participating policies. This is required by statute in many states. There are still a few policies on which deferred dividends are paid.

Deferred dividends are dividends payable only at the close of a stipulated number of years, such as 5, 10, 15, or 20. Policies providing for payment of dividends in this manner are commonly called deferred-dividend, accumulation, distribution, or semitontine policies.[20] According to the underlying principle of the plan, policyowners who fail to continue premium payments to the end of the designated period (because of death, surrender, or lapse) lose the dividends they would have received under the annual-dividend plan. The lost dividends revert to those policyowners who continue their premium payments throughout the deferred-dividend period.

The traditional deferred-dividend plan lost favor with the U.S. public, having been almost wholly superseded by the annual-distribution system. The latter plan, it is argued, is well adapted to the policyowner who wishes to keep his or her net annual outlay to the lowest possible amount, and it also serves to encourage managerial economy because extravagance could be revealed by a reduction in the annual-dividend distribution.

The deferred system in a modified form is still used to some extent in Canada and elsewhere. Under Canadian law, for example, dividend distributions may be made every five years, but the amount of surplus set aside for deferred dividends during a five-year period must be carried as a liability until it is paid. Most Canadian insurers pay an interim dividend in the event of death during the period, but not in the event of lapse or surrender. (See Box 30-2.)

The Contribution Principle

The allocation of divisible surplus among policyowners is a complex matter. Equity is the basic objective, but consideration must be given to competition, flexibility, and simplicity. That the allocation should be competitive is obvious. Flexibility can be viewed

---

[20]Interest rate bonuses under current assumption policies are similar in effect to deferred dividends under participating policies. **Retroactive bonuses** provide that, after a predefined time period (e.g., 10 years), a bonus interest rate will be retroactively applied to all previous periods. **Prospective bonuses** provide that, after a predefined time period, future interest credits will be augmented by a bonus rate.

BOX 30-2

DIVISIBLE SURPLUS (BONUSES)

In the United Kingdom and in many other countries, divisible surplus (bonuses) under participating (with-profits) policies are declared at the insurer's discretion or as required by law at fixed intervals often greater than a single year. A reversionary bonus is commonly used, whereby the divisible surplus is used to increase the policy's face amount (the sum assured) and its surrender value.

The amount is often calculated as a percentage of the face amount without regard to the insured's age or the time that the policy has been in force. Sometimes an additional or terminal (or capital) bonus is paid on policy maturity, the intent of which is to allow the policyowner to share more equitably in the favorable operations of the insurer (office).

as a facet of equity because adaptability to changing circumstances is essential if equity is to be attained. Simplicity is desirable both from an expense viewpoint and from the viewpoint of understanding by agents and policyowners. The earlier discussion of the sources of surplus would suggest that one way of obtaining reasonable equity would be *to return to each class of policyowners a share of the divisible surplus proportionate to the contribution of the class to the surplus.* This concept is known as the **contribution principle.** The principle does not require the return of all or even most surplus. It merely requires that whatever the amount of divisible surplus, it be allotted to policyowners in the approximate proportion in which they contributed to it. This principle underlies the equity implicit in participating insurance.

The Three-Factor Contribution Method

The contribution principle provides the underlying philosophical base for surplus distribution in the United States and many other countries. The most widely used approach for applying the principle is referred to as the **contribution method.**[21]

This method is based on an analysis of the sources of insurer surplus and develops dividends that vary with the plan of insurance, age of issue, and duration of the policy. In the interest of simplicity, consideration usually is limited to the three major sources of surplus: excess interest, mortality savings, and loading savings. When special benefits are involved, such as disability and accidental death, an additional factor sometimes is included for these features.

The Formula Generally the three-factor contribution method may be expressed as:[22]

$$D_t = I_t + M_t + E_t$$

where

$$D_t = \text{dividend per \$1,000 payable at the end of policy year } t$$
$$I_t = \text{excess interest factor for policy year } t$$
$$M_t = \text{mortality savings factor for policy year } t$$
$$E_t = \text{expense savings factor for policy year } t$$

---

[21]Other methods exist. The so-called experience-premium method is used by many insurers. Its purpose is to avoid decreases in dividends on any plan, even with a low excess interest factor.

[22]See Joseph M. Belth, "Distribution of Surplus to Individual Life Insurance Policy Owners," *The Journal of Risk and Insurance,* Vol. 45 (March 1978), pp. 10–11. The symbols used here have a different meaning in traditional actuarial notation.

Each of the three factors, in turn, can be determined by the following formulas:

$$I_t = (i_t' - i_t)(_{t-1}V_x + {}_tP_x)$$
$$M_t = (q_{x+t-1} - q_{x+t-1}')(1{,}000 - {}_tV_x)$$
$$E_t = (_tG_x - {}_tP_x - {}_te_x)(1 + i_t')$$

where

x = age of issue

i_t' = dividend interest rate in policy year t

i_t = reserve interest rate in policy year t

$_tV_x$ = tth policy year's terminal reserve per \$1,000 for a policy issued at age x

$_tP_x$ = tth policy year's valuation annual premium per \$1,000 for a policy issued at age x

q_x = reserve mortality rate at age x

q_x' = dividend mortality rate at age x

$_tG_x$ = tth policy year's gross annual premium per \$1,000 for a policy issued at age x

$_te_x$ = tth policy year's expense charge per \$1,000 for a policy issued at age x

The following sections consider briefly the operation of the preceding formula. The discussion of each factor includes a sample calculation for that factor. The sample is based on a hypothetical \$10,000 ordinary life policy issued 15 years ago to a male *then* aged 25. The gross annual premium is \$170.00 (\$17.00 per \$1,000). Net-level terminal reserves are assumed to be calculated on the *1958 CSO Table,* with interest of 3 percent. The valuation net annual premium calculated on these assumptions is \$11.28 per \$1,000. Policy reserves per \$1,000 face amount at the end of the fourteenth and fifteenth policy years are \$162.97 and \$176.80, respectively.

Interest Factor   The interest factor (I_t) is the simplest element of the dividend, consisting of the excess interest on, usually, the initial reserve for the policy period at the end of which the dividend is payable.[23] Recall that the initial reserve is the previous year's terminal reserve ($_{t-1}V_x$) plus the valuation net-level premium ($_tP_x$).

Assume that the dividend interest rate is 8 percent for this policy.[24] Under these circumstances, the rate of excess interest ($i_t' - i_t$) would be 5 percent. Thus, on the \$10,000 ordinary life policy issued at male age 25 that had been in force 15 years, the interest factor of the dividend would be calculated as follows:

$$I_t = (i_t' - i_t)(_{t-1}V_x + {}_tP_x)$$
$$I_{15} = (i_{15}' - i_{15})(_{14}V_{25} + {}_{15}P_{25})$$
$$I_{15} = (0.08 - 0.03)(\$162.97 + \$11.28)$$
$$I_{15} = (0.05)(\$174.25)$$
$$I_{15} = \$8.71$$

The interest factor has a strong influence on the dividend, particularly at later durations when the initial reserve is large.

---

[23]Many insurers utilize the mean reserve on premium-paying policies and the initial reserve on policies for which premiums have been fully paid.

[24]Actual dividend interest rates can vary significantly from insurer to insurer.

Under the three-factor contribution approach, the correct base against which to apply the dividend interest rate is the initial reserve less one-half a year's cost of insurance. The difference between this theoretically correct base and the mean reserve is small. Although the mean reserve would be a more accurate measure of the policy funds available for investment, the difference in results is so insignificant that most insurers continue to use the initial reserve without the adjustment for one-half year's cost of insurance.

Although the interest factor is simple in concept, several complications arise in application. Several bases can be and are used to compute the rate of investment yield.[25] For purposes of asset-share studies underlying the dividend formula, it is common to use a base consisting of the interest-bearing liabilities and surplus. Interest-bearing liabilities include policy reserves, funds held under settlement agreements, dividend accumulations, and advance premiums. If certain items, such as dividend accumulations, have a minimum guarantee, some insurers credit such items with the guaranteed rate only and increase the net effective rate for regular policy dividend purposes. The final rate utilized in the dividend formula may be less than the rate used in the asset-share studies. This results in a contribution to the assets backing the general contingency reserves, part of which ultimately may be distributed as a termination dividend (discussed later).

With many insurers, the excess interest factor reflects the general trend of the insurer's investment earnings and would be set at a level that, according to the insurer's best judgment, should be appropriate for several years. For short periods of time, the factor could be based on a higher rate than that actually being earned.

Some insurers vary the dividend interest rate by the length of time the policy has been in force. Such insurers artificially segregate policies into different "generations" and use a dividend interest rate for each generation, which is based on the investment return on the assets accumulated on behalf of that generation. Thus, different generations easily could be credited with different interest rates. This **investment generation method** of investment income allocation tends to produce a dividend pattern that can change rapidly as earnings change, especially for generations of only a few years' duration.

Other insurers base their dividend interest rate on the average investment return of their entire asset portfolio. This **portfolio average method** does not segregate policies into generations; instead it uses the same dividend interest rate for all participating policies. This method produces a more stable dividend pattern than one based on the investment generation method. Both of these methods of investment income allocation, as discussed in earlier chapters, have been the subject of discussion and debate, and they render cost comparisons between such policies more difficult.[26] Questions have been raised about possible incomplete disclosure and the possibility of an insurer switching from one method to the other, depending on market rate changes.[27]

Many insurers tie their dividend interest rate directly or indirectly to the policy loan rate or activity. Thus, under the **direct recognition provision** discussed earlier, the excess interest rate is influenced directly by any policy loan activity and rate.[28] If a policyowner borrows heavily under his or her policy at a favorable interest rate relative to the market rate, this could cause lower dividends.

---

[25]For example, the base logically could be ledger assets, admitted assets, or invested funds.

[26]See chapters 6, 9, and 10.

[27]The NAIC Model Life Insurance Disclosure Regulation requires U.S. insurers to disclose their practices in this regard.

[28]See chapters 6 and 9.

The treatment of capital gains and losses on assets also can vary between insurers. Some insurers take these into account in fixing the dividend interest rate when they reflect actual market transactions as opposed to unrealized gains or losses arising out of adjustments in book value. The more common practice, however, is to transfer these gains and losses to an investment fluctuation fund or to a general contingency reserve in which over a period of time the gains and losses offset each other to some degree. This stabilizes net interest earnings.

Insurers also differ in the treatment of investment expenses. They particularly differ in their treatment of general overhead expenses and income taxes. This can make a significant difference and, although this should not affect the aggregate amount of surplus distributed, it does affect the pattern of distribution between blocks of policies.

With a constant dividend interest rate, the excess interest contribution increases with duration if reserves increase. At all ages of issue and durations, it is larger for higher-premium than for lower-premium policies. Thus, assuming the same duration and age of issue, excess interest makes a greater contribution to the dividend of a 20-payment whole life policy than to the dividend of an ordinary life policy, particularly at longer durations. The interest factor has a strong influence on the dividend.

Mortality Factor   The mortality factor in the three-factor formula can be derived by multiplying (1) the difference between the mortality rate used for reserve computation (q_x) and the (usually) lower rate to be used for dividend purposes by (2) the year's net amount at risk $(1,000 - {}_tV_x)$. In a continuation of the earlier example, the mortality savings for the 15-year-old ordinary life policy, with reserves based on the *1958 CSO Table* and 3 percent interest, would be calculated as follows:

$$M_t = (q_{x+t-1} - q'_{x+t-1})(1,000 - {}_tV_x)$$
$$M_{15} = (q_{39} - q'_{39})(1,000 - {}_{15}V_{25})$$
$$M_{15} = (0.00325 - 0.00225)(\$1,000 - \$176.80)$$
$$M_{15} = \$0.82$$

Many insurers express the mortality savings factor as a percentage of the assumed cost of insurance.[29] The percentage for any block of policies generally depends only on the attained age of the insured and the insurer's experience among all insureds at that age and duration. The mortality factor of the formula normally takes the form of a scale of percentages of the assumed cost of insurance, decreasing with attained age, and reflecting the insurer's actual mortality table assumed in calculating reserves. The scale of percentages may range from a high of 40 to 50 percent at the younger ages to a low of 5 to 10 percent at the older ages. Because mortality experience under term policies often is considerably different age by age than under cash-value plans, a separate scale of mortality savings often would be applied to these classes of policies.

The percentage utilized in the final dividend calculation normally is based on the ultimate mortality experience under the insurer's basic mortality table, although select experience is utilized in the asset share underlying the development of the dividend distributions. Otherwise, a decreasing dividend scale by duration could result because of large mortality savings at early durations. The savings from the effect of selection are assumed to be applied toward the payment of excess first-year expenses and, hence, are distributed indirectly in accordance with the method used to assess expenses to the various blocks of policies.

With an increasing incidence of deaths because of acquired immunodeficiency syndrome (AIDS), insurers have made appropriate adjustments within their dividend for-

---

[29]See chapter 29.

mulas. Most AIDS deaths and, therefore, attendant insurer death claims are of males from the 20 to 40 age range. The mortality factors for policies on males in this age range are, therefore, adjusted downward by many insurers to account for the increased mortality.

The mortality contribution normally is smallest on the higher-premium plans and higher ages of issue because the net amounts at risk are smaller. With advancing duration, a declining percentage factor is applied to a steadily smaller net amount at risk and, hence, in the usual case, a smaller cost of insurance. The higher the premium (because of plan or age at issue), the more pronounced is the decline in mortality savings. This is not invariably so, however. The cost of insurance actually increases at the higher ages under certain types of policies. In these cases, the increase in the rate of mortality more than offsets the decrease in the net amount at risk, resulting in an increase in mortality cost for the year. In general, however, the mortality factor results in a decreasing contribution with greater durations.

In contrast to the interest factor, the mortality contribution is highly significant for term insurance policies. The percentage factor is applied to a larger net amount at risk and, hence, cost of insurance, resulting in a relatively greater proportionate contribution to the dividends distributable to term policies.

Loading Factor   The loading factor (E_t) of the dividend consists of the difference between (1) the gross premium and (2) the valuation net premium and an expense charge, with the difference taken as a year-end figure by increasing the amount for a year's interest at the dividend interest rate. In the example, the gross premium per $1,000 is $17.00 and the valuation net annual premium is $11.28. Assume that the fifteenth year's expense charge is $5.00. The expense savings factor for the example would, therefore, be calculated:

$$E_t = (_tG_x - {_tP_x} - {_te_x})(1 + i_t')$$
$$E_{15} = (_{15}G_{25} - {_{15}P_{25}} - {_{15}e_{25}})(1 + i_{15}')$$
$$E_{15} = (\$17.00 - \$11.28 - \$5.00)(1 + 0.08)$$
$$E_{15} = (\$0.72)(1.08)$$
$$E_{15} = \$0.78$$

Thus, the expense factor for policy year 15 is $0.78.

The assessment of expenses probably presents one of the greatest difficulties connected with the distribution of surplus, as discussed earlier in this chapter. In general, the expense charge frequently is in the form of a percentage of the premium and a constant of so much per unit of face amount. The constant may vary to allow for differences in the average amount of policy by plan of insurance. The percentage element of the expense charge usually is on a decreasing basis, at least for the first few years, to reflect the lower expenses after the first two years. There are wide differences among insurers, both in gross premiums charged and in the manner of computing the expense charge. Consequently, the importance of the loading factor varies considerably, the amount being much higher in an insurer with "high" gross premiums than with an insurer utilizing "low" gross premiums. The pattern in most cases, however, is for the loading contribution to increase for the first few years and thereafter to increase slightly or remain roughly constant.

Combining each of the three factors, the fifteenth year's dividend per $1,000 face amount for the hypothetical policy is, therefore:

$$D_t = I_t + M_t + E_t$$
$$D_{15} = I_{15} + M_{15} + E_{15}$$
$$D_{15} = \$8.71 + \$0.82 + \$0.78$$
$$D_{15} = \$10.31$$

Dividend Pattern   For most plans of whole life insurance, the annual dividend under the contribution plan usually increases with duration. This is entirely aside from an increase in the scale itself. The normal increase of dividends with duration occurs because the interest factor normally increases with duration. In the usual case, this more than offsets the tendency for the mortality and loading factors to decrease with duration, but this is not always so. An unfavorable investment market may well cause just the opposite to occur, as happened in the 1940s, when the average rate of return dropped to below 3 percent. Also, the fact that many insurers have switched to the investment generation method of interest allocation renders dividend patterns less stable.

Special Forms of Surplus Distribution

Insurers often pay extra dividends or terminal dividends in addition to the regular annual dividends. An **extra dividend** may consist either of a single payment made after a policy has been in force a specified number of years or of a payment made periodically at stated intervals. The single-payment extra dividend is usually used when no first-year dividend is paid, the extra dividend serving as a substitute. This practice has the practical advantage of reducing the surplus strain of initial expenses, and it also may have a tendency to reduce the first-year lapse rate. It has the effect of assessing a larger share of first-year expense against those policies that terminate prior to the time when the extra dividend is paid.

Extra dividends paid periodically (say, at every fifth year) have little justification in theory unless regular dividends have been calculated on a conservative basis and equity insists that extra dividends be paid periodically to the policyowners as the experience develops. A practical advantage, however, is that illustrative net costs over a period of years are reduced by these extra amounts; only those policies remaining in force get the additional payments. This is particularly true of an extra dividend payable only at the end of the twentieth year.

Some insurers pay a **terminal dividend** in the event that a policy terminates by maturity, death, or surrender. In most cases, these dividends are payable only if the policy has been in force for a minimum length of time (e.g., 15 years). Terminal dividends, in theory, have the purpose of returning to terminating policyowners part of the general surplus to which they have contributed, or adjusting for a guaranteed cash value that is something less than the asset share. Some insurers, however, in effect use terminal dividends as a means of making their policies appear more attractive from a cost standpoint than they really are. This occurs when an insurer uses particularly high terminal dividends only at the duration required for cost index calculation purposes.[30]

The distinction between a postmortem or mortuary dividend and a terminal dividend payable at death is important. A **postmortem dividend** is payable at death, but either it is paid in proportion to the part of the policy year of death for which premiums have been paid or represents a one-time distribution of surplus, mainly on term insurance, in lieu of dividends on each policy anniversary while the insured was living.

Practical Considerations

In establishing a scale of dividends, several practical considerations impinge on the decisions made. For example, the dividend scale should be satisfactory to existing policyowners. They probably would have been conditioned by the existing scale to a pattern of dividends, and significant changes, as a practical matter, normally would be accomplished by a series of adjustments. Also, the net cost position of the insurer under a proposed scale must be checked against those of competitors to avoid dissatisfaction among

---

[30]See chapter 10.

sales personnel and to assure a competitive product from the buyer's viewpoint. Similarly, the administrative cost of developing and implementing a new scale must be considered. At some point, the increased cost of greater equity outweighs the benefit involved. These and other practical considerations are an integral part of the process of establishing a scale of dividends for participating contracts.

The various options under which dividends may be taken were discussed in chapter 9. Chapters 6 and 9 discussed some of the problems connected with "frozen" dividend scales and the comparability of dividend scales.

Questions

1. Describe the assumptions behind the asset-share model for determining the adequacy and equity of gross-premium rate structures.
2. How can various assumptions determine the degree to which asset-share calculations are a reasonable test of premium adequacy and equity between blocks of policies?
3. Describe briefly the so-called three-factor system of surplus distribution.
4. From time to time, special forms of surplus distribution are made as extra dividends and terminal dividends. Explain the basis of these distributions.

CHAPTER

31

THE PRICING OF HEALTH INSURANCE

Objectives

■ Describe the variability that can be expected in factors that affect health insurance premium rates.

■ Describe some approaches taken to estimate net annual claim costs for various medical expense benefits.

■ Describe risk classification factors used to underwrite health insurance coverage.

■ Explain differences between the rating practices of managed care organizations and of health insurers providing traditional indemnity products.

■ Describe different types of reserves set up by health insurers.

Premiums for individual and group health insurance policies are affected by many factors, such as the rates of morbidity, provider payment arrangements, interest, expense, and lapse rates. Other factors, however, such as the method of selling, the underwriting philosophy, and the claims administration policy, as well as the overall philosophy and objectives of the insuring company, may result in different claims experience by insurers issuing similar types of coverage. Similarly, changes and variations in hospital administration and medical practice, both geographically and from time to time in the same locality, and the impact of varying regulatory, economic, and business conditions make it difficult to predict reliably the future net annual claim costs. Nevertheless, pricing health care products necessitates estimating future net annual claim costs because pricing must reflect the risks involved.[1]

PRINCIPLES OF HEALTH INSURANCE RATE MAKING

The Rating Process

Rate making involves the analysis of available data and the development of premium rates that are *adequate, reasonable,* and *equitable* for the various classifications of insureds. Thus, in pricing benefits, insurers typically classify insureds according to charac-

---

[1]See Susan Conant, Nicholas L. Desoutter, Dani L. Long, and Robert MacGrogan, *Managing for Solvency and Profitability in Life and Health Insurance Companies* (Atlanta, GA: LOMA, 1996), Chapter 8.

teristics that are expected to drive claims experience such as age, sex, geographic area, and occupation depending upon the type of benefit involved as well as legal and competitive constraints. These classifications are considered necessary if reasonable equity between policyowners is to be realized.

If all insureds were charged an average premium rate regardless of the loss exposure presented by a particular individual, adverse selection by those with a higher than average probability of loss would result, and individuals with a lower loss exposure would tend not to purchase the insurance. There are, however, practical limitations on the process of refining classifications in the interest of equity. As in life insurance, the number of rating classes is limited by the increasing administrative expense of dealing with multiple classes and the need to have a sufficient volume of business within a class to provide reliable experience and stability in the rate structure.

Competition usually is relied upon to keep premium rates reasonable in relation to the benefits provided, but this is not always the case. Some jurisdictions require filing of health insurance rates, and most require approval of premium rates on individual policies.

Adequacy is arguably the most important criterion against which a premium rate should be measured. When a new type of coverage with unreliable experience is introduced, the margin of safety built into the premium is larger than in an established type of coverage that has its own body of experience. In addition to developing premium rates for new policies, there is the problem of revising rates on existing groups and individual policies when they are issued on an adjustable-premium, guaranteed-renewable basis. As discussed later, insurers normally test the level of their premiums with asset-share studies, utilizing various assumptions as to expense rates, lapses, morbidity, mortality, and interest.

Measures of Morbidity Experience

In establishing premium rates for any type of health insurance coverage, it is necessary to begin by providing a measure of the expected net annual claim cost per policy in an established line of business. The actuary has several sources of information to assist in predicting future claim costs. For established lines of business, the primary and best source is the insurer's own morbidity experience. Such experience reflects the effects of contract language the company has used in its underwriting practices and its customer base. In new lines of business, if an insurer has not written enough business to have credible statistics, other sources such as industry experience studies routinely conducted by the Society of Actuaries and other industry organizations must be used.

For instance, the Society of Actuaries regularly publishes studies analyzing claim costs for various types of benefits. Published morbidity and mortality data are also available from various actuarial consulting firms.

A relatively few insurers write a substantial amount of disability insurance and are able to price their products using their own proprietary morbidity data. For insurers needing published morbidity data, in the United States, the NAIC publishes public disability morbidity tables. The current individual disability morbidity tables are the *1985 Commissioners Individual Disability (1985 CID)* tables. The current group disability morbidity table is the *1987 Commissioners Group Disability (1987 CGD)* table. Although both the individual and group tables were developed primarily for valuation purposes, both show the basic morbidity rates underlying the valuation rates. Also, the Society of Actuaries periodically publishes reports of recent disability morbidity experience. In the final analysis, the actuary must use informed judgment in interpreting the data available to him or her.

Unit Benefit Costs

The net annual claim cost of any benefit is the product of the frequency of claims and the amount of the average claim (severity). The unit benefit cost method entails the calculation of the cost of providing a unit benefit, so that the net annual claim cost of benefits actually provided can be determined by multiplying the unit benefit cost by the appropriate benefit amount (see Figure 31-1).

The unit of exposure may be $1 (or other national currency unit) of daily hospital benefit, $1 of monthly income disability benefit, a standard maximum surgical schedule, or other suitable units selected. Unit costs can be subdivided to reflect the combination of age, sex, occupation, geographic location, and other factors.

It is possible to obtain the net annual claim cost without separately determining the frequency and average amount of claim for the benefit under consideration.[2] For example, all hospital miscellaneous benefits paid during the year under policies providing the same maximum benefit can be divided by the appropriate exposure to determine the average annual claim cost per life. In a similar manner, the net annual claim cost per unit of monthly income under disability income insurance with a particular elimination period and maximum benefit limit may be determined by dividing the value of total incurred claims at each age of disablement by the total monthly indemnity exposed. The result is the same as the rate of disability (frequency) multiplied by the value of the disabled life annuity (the average amount of claims).

Continuance Tables

The determination of (1) the expected claim frequency among insured lives and (2) the average claim value are two important problems that confront the actuary. The mathematical measurement of the effect on claims cost of various elimination periods usually involves development of a **continuance table,** which shows the probabilities of claim continuance for various durations or amounts.

Hospital confinement, for example, may be expressed as the number of patients remaining in the hospital at the end of *t* days out of an assumed initial number of patients confined to a hospital, such as 10,000. Figure 31-2 reflects a study of the probability of continuance of hospital confinement among 10,000 lives confined (adult males).

In disability income insurance, the elimination period has a dramatic effect on the rate level required. Figure 31-3 reflects a study of the probability of continuance of disability among 10,000 lives disabled at age 40.

FIGURE 31-1   Determination of Annual Claim Cost

Frequency × Severity = Claim Cost

Frequency of Hospitalization	Average Claim per $1 Daily Benefit	Annual Claim Cost per $1 Daily Benefit
0.12	6	0.12 × 6 × $1 = $0.72

Unit Cost		Coverage		Annual Claim
$0.72	×	60	=	$43.20

---

[2]It can be done the other way, however, using one body of data for frequency and another for claim size.

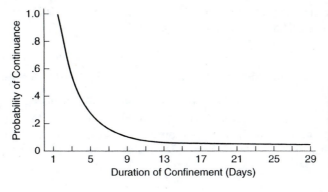

FIGURE 31-2 Probability of Continuation of Hospital Confinement among 10,000 Lives Confined

Source: 1997 Milliman & Robertson Inc. Health Cost Guidelines™.

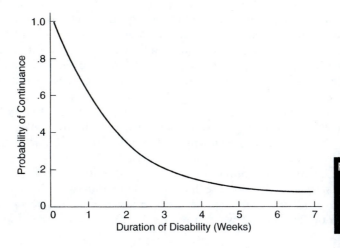

FIGURE 31-3 Probability of Continuation of Disability among 10,000 Lives Disabled or Age 40 (Adult Males)

In a similar manner, a major medical continuance table could express the probability that the claim experience will equal or exceed various dollar levels, from which the effect of varying deductibles and varying maximum amounts could be determined. Continuance tables are helpful in computing the average-sized claim. These average claim values, in combination with the expected claim frequency (rate of claims), produce the expected net annual claim cost for the pattern of benefits under consideration. The method is easy to apply in practice when a single benefit, such as a monthly disability income benefit, is being considered. When benefits are combined in various ways with different elimination periods and different maximum benefit limitations, the problem of measuring the expected net annual claim cost becomes exceedingly complex.

Net Level Premiums

The net level (valuation) premium for a disability income contract or long-term care insurance, as in the case of life insurance, is the level annual payment needed to pay benefits (1) if future claims exactly follow the average claim amounts assumed, as well as the frequency rates shown in the morbidity tabled adopted; (2) if decrements due to lapse and mortality among persons insured occur at the rates given by the assumed lapse and mortality tables; and (3) if the rate of interest earned is that assumed in the rate basis. Thus, the net level premium (*NLP*) at date of issue is found as follows:

$$NLP = \frac{\text{Present Value of Future Net Annual Claim Costs}}{\text{Present Value of a Life Annuity Due of 1 for the Premium-Paying Period}}$$

The present value of future net annual claim costs is the value at date of issue of all benefits that are expected to be paid until the termination date of the contract, appropriately discounted with interest. Table 31-1 illustrates the calculation of a net level premium for a five-year term, guaranteed-renewable hospital expense policy issued to males aged 60.

Loss Ratios

This method of establishing the level of morbidity costs is based on the ratio of benefits (claims) incurred to premiums earned. It is an acceptable method for developing premium rates on business issued on a one-year term basis but not for business issued on a level-premium basis. The loss ratio approach is used in developing the total amount of premium required for any particular experience-rated group. Several methods are used including the permissible loss ratio and the incurred loss ratio. The **permissible loss ratio** represents the proportion of each premium dollar, which is assumed to be used to pay claims. The remainder of each premium dollar is assumed to be used to pay expenses and taxes, and provide for an insurer's profit objective. Thus, the permissible loss ratio is the expected loss ratio in a given premium structure. Applying the permissible loss ratio to earned premiums develops the dollar amount of premium required for claims.

The **incurred loss ratio** represents the proportion of each premium dollar actually used to pay claims. Comparing the incurred loss ratio with the permissible or expected loss ratio produces the percentage rate increase or decrease needed to bring the pricing in line with the evolving experience.

TABLE 31-1 Illustrative Calculation of Net Level Premium Five-Year Guaranteed-Renewable Hospital Expense Policy (Male, Age 60)

(1) Attained Age	(2) Annual Claim Cost during Year Following Attained Age	(3) Average Period from Date of Issue of Contract to Commencement of Claims (Years)	(4) Proportion of Those Insured Who Will Survive Average Period	(5) Amount of 1 Discounted at 4½% per Annum for Average Period	(6) Present Expected Value of Claim Cost [(2) × (4) × (5)]
60	$210	0.5	0.9933	0.9782	$ 204.052
61	224	1.5	0.9860	0.9361	206.745
62	238	2.5	0.9779	0.8958	208.490
63	240	3.5	0.9690	0.8572	199.362
64	241	4.5	0.9592	0.8203	189.631

Total of column 6, present value of future annual claims costs $1,008.280

Present value of a five-year temporary life annuity due of 1 at age 60 (*1980 CSO Table,* 4½%) 4.436

$$\text{Net Level Premium} = \frac{\$1,008.280}{4.436} = \$227.29$$

Source: 1997 Milliman & Robertson Inc. Health Cost Guidelines™.

Regardless of the method used, all take into account expected future claims, a margin for higher than anticipated claims, expected future expenses, taxes, and the insurer's profit objective. Expenses, taxes, and contribution to profit are often combined in the premium rate formula and referred to as retention. **Retention** indicates the amounts to be retained by the insurer for items other than claims charged to the group.

The loss-ratio method should be used with great caution when comparing morbidity costs among different insurers. These comparisons can be misleading because of differences in (1) premium levels for the same types of benefits, (2) types of policies with varying benefits, (3) reserve requirements, (4) persistency rates, (5) claims and underwriting practices, and (6) rates of insurer growth.

Gross Premiums

The gross premium must provide for benefits, expenses, taxes, profit, and contingency margins in the event that claims and expenses are higher than anticipated.[3] Gross premiums usually are calculated on the assumption that they will be paid annually, but they may be paid semiannually, quarterly, or monthly. On some individual health insurance policies, gross premiums are paid on a level basis, which means that the same premium is payable each year, from the date of issue to the end of the term period of the policy, such as to age 65. Gross premiums also may be developed on a one-year term basis or a step-rate basis. Many insurers issue comprehensive major medical benefits with premiums increasing each year to keep pace with annual increases in medical costs and changes in morbidity.

Factors Affecting the Premium

The premium rates for a particular benefit depend on (1) morbidity, (2) provider payment arrangements, (3) expenses, (4) taxes, (5) persistency, (6) interest, and (7) profit and contingency margins.

Morbidity   In dealing with mortality rates, the only element considered is the number of deaths during a year compared with the total number of persons exposed in the class. In contrast, in the measurement of morbidity, the annual claim cost for a given age-sex-occupational class is the product of (a) the annual frequency of a particular event and (b) the average claim when such an event occurs. For example, the annual frequency of hospitalization for a given age and sex might be 10 percent, the average duration of hospital stay might be four to five days, and, therefore, the annual claim cost for a $500 daily hospital benefit would be $250 ($0.1 \times 5 \times \$500$).

In health insurance, although mortality is a consideration, the primary consideration is the morbidity cost. Annual claim costs may vary, depending upon the kind and amount of benefits, according to such factors as age, sex, occupational class, and geographical area. Inasmuch as most policies contain more than one benefit, it is necessary to obtain separate annual claim costs for each type of benefit.

Most morbidity tables used to calculate net annual claim costs of disability income benefits exclude the experience during the calendar year that a policy is issued. Attempts to identify the influence of underwriting on experience by policy year (select experience)

---

[3]This section draws from *Individual Health Insurance, Part B* (Washington, DC: Health Insurance Association of America, 1994), pp. 85–105 and William F. Bluhm, ed., *Group Insurance,* 3rd ed. (Winsted, CT: ACTEX Publications, 1999.)

have not been very successful in contrast to the success of the practice for life insurance. The pattern of select experience under disability insurance is quite different from that for mortality under individual life policies.

It is even more important to note that there is apparently substantial adverse selection by those applying for disability income policies whose elimination periods are short and maximum durations are long. Studies show that at ages 50 to 65 there is a substantial increase in morbidity by policy duration that continues until the coverage terminates. Applicants who become insured in their twenties and thirties develop a higher level of morbidity after age 50 than those applicants who become insured after age 50. Furthermore, the experience varies considerably, depending on the type of benefit under consideration. The experience is further complicated in the case of medical expense insurance by the continuing inflation in the cost of medical services, and in the case of disability insurance, by levels of employment and personal income. Obviously, consideration should be given to the relationship of select to ultimate experience in establishing gross premiums, so that the premiums for insurance issued at advanced ages properly reflect the savings from selection.

Provider Payment Arrangements   Premium rates for HMOs and other medical care organizations are affected by the degree to which providers participate in the cost. Having providers participate in benefit plan costs is intended both to reduce the costs of plan benefits through rate concessions and to provide incentives for the providers to control utilization, particularly in the areas of referrals to expensive specialists and in hospital admissions.

Under traditional indemnity insurance products, providers are paid on a fee-for-service (FFS) basis. Managed care plans have typically negotiated fee arrangements with hospitals, physicians, pharmacies, and other providers. Provider cost sharing can take on many forms, each of which have their own subtle impacts on underlying costs and behavioral incentives. These include:

- discounts from billed charges
- fee schedules and maximums
- per diem reimbursements
- hospital DRG (diagnosis related groups) reimbursement, ambulatory diagnostic groups, or global payments
- bonus pools based on utilization
- capitation
- integrated delivery system

Some of such arrangements act only to reduce the underlying benefit cost but provide no incentive for controlling utilization. A **capitation** model is one in which the insurer subcontracts with a provider to perform a defined range of services in return for a set amount per month per enrollee. This arrangement represents the very end of the spectrum in risk sharing in that virtually all risk is passed along to the provider. The only risk remaining with the insurer is the solvency of the providers and their ability to deliver services.

The fundamental purpose of these arrangements is to increase the providers' awareness of costs and utilization. Such mechanisms must be constructed to be beneficial for both the providers and the insurer. Otherwise, the contractual arrangement will eventually dismantle the entire program.

Expenses   To obtain suitable expense rates for determination of premium rates, it is necessary to make detailed cost studies in which the various expense items may be expressed as (a) a percentage of the premium (e.g., premium taxes and agents' commissions); (b) an amount per policy (e.g., cost of underwriting and issuing a policy); and (c) an amount per claim paid (e.g., cost of investigating and verifying a claim). Because of the nonlevel commission rates, the per-premium types of expenses usually are larger in the first policy year, decrease during the next few policy years, and then are level for the remaining policy duration. The per-policy types of expenses are much larger in the first policy year, reflecting the cost of underwriting and issuing the policy. The per-policy type of expense after the first policy year is relatively constant, except for the impact resulting from inflation.

Persistency The **persistency rate** for a group of policies is defined as the ratio of the number of policies that continue coverage on a premium-due date to the number of policies that were in force as of the preceding due date. Thus, if out of 100 policies, 75 policies are in force on the first policy anniversary, the first-year annual persistency rate is 75 percent. The persistency rate usually improves with policy duration, and for some types of coverage the annual persistency rate will be 95 percent or higher after the fifth policy year. Naturally, other factors affect persistency rates. In general, persistency rates usually are higher at the older issue ages and better for the less hazardous occupations. Persistency usually is better in connection with major medical expense and disability income coverages than on basic hospital expense coverages.

Persistency is important in health insurance rating for two reasons. First, expenses are higher during the first year than in subsequent years because of the expenses of issuing the policy or certificate and because of the typically higher first-year commission rate. Also, claim rates under health insurance tend to increase as the age of the insured increases. In view of these factors, which vary by age at issue and policy duration, the premium-rate level will depend on the rate of lapse.

Interest When a level premium is used, the insurer will have, after the first few policy years, an accumulation of funds arising from the excess of premium income over the amounts paid for claims and expenses. As in level-premium life insurance, the funds accumulated during the early policy years will be needed in the later policy years, when the premium income is not sufficient to pay claims and expenses. In computing premium rates, therefore, it is necessary to assume a suitable interest rate to reflect the investment earnings on these accumulations.

Interest rates are of less significance in the calculation of medical expense premiums than in calculating life insurance premiums. The ratio of claims to premiums under health insurance during the early policy years is substantially greater than under level-premium life insurance. Accordingly, more of the premium is used for claim payments soon after it is received by the insurance company, and it is, therefore, not available for investment, as is the case of level-premium life insurance. It is important to consider interest in measuring the average claim cost under long-term disability income and long-term care coverage. The value of the disability annuity can be significantly reduced because of the interest discount.

Profits and Contingency Margins As with life insurance premium rates, it is necessary to introduce a margin for contingencies and profit into the premium-rate calculation. One method of doing so is to calculate a premium on the basis of most probable assumptions and then increase the premium by a percentage to provide some margin for contingencies and profit. Another method is to introduce conservative morbidity, expense, persistency, and interest assumptions and determine a premium on that basis. Still another would be to develop a gross premium that is consistent with a specific minimum required internal rate of return.

Derivation of the Gross Premium

Having determined for a particular type and amount of benefit all the assumptions for a given issue age, sex, occupational class, area, and so on, as to morbidity, expenses, persistency, and interest rate, the actuary estimates what the gross premium will be. This tentative gross premium is tested against realistic expense, claim, persistency, and interest assumptions over an arbitrary period, commonly 20 years.[4] If the tentative gross premium produces a fund accumulation that is too high or too low at the end of the projected period, based on the insurer's objectives, an adjustment is made in the tentative premium to establish the appropriate gross-premium level needed to support the particular policy under consideration.[5] In the case of participating policies, if it is subsequently determined that the accumulated fund at any time, together with future premiums, exceeds the amount needed to pay future claims and expenses, dividends may be paid. Similarly, if the policies are nonparticipating, the insurer will realize a profit that it is entitled to for insuring the risk. In general, the margins in the premium rates are smaller on nonparticipating policies than for participating policies. Margins should be larger on noncancellable policies because premiums cannot be increased.

Gross premiums usually are not derived for every age by the method described previously but possibly for every decennial age, such as ages 20, 30, 40, 50, and 60. Premiums for intervening ages can then be derived by fitting a curve through the premiums for these ages. Another approach utilized by some insurers is to determine for each plan the net level premiums (based only on morbidity, persistency, and an interest rate) for each age and to find a loading formula, usually in the form of a constant plus a percentage of the net level premium, that will approximately reproduce the gross premiums that are obtained for decennial ages.

Significance of Judgment

The morbidity statistics used by an actuary assigned to compute health insurance rates for an insurer about to enter the business may come from several sources and may involve several modifications of the basic data based on experience and judgment. In view of the lack of reliable data and the multiplicity of factors producing variable cost levels, informed judgment plays an important part in health insurance rate making. This fact is especially relevant for new health insurance products being sold in many developing countries. A comparison of the gross premiums charged by other insurers for similar benefits, if available, can help an insurer determine whether the premiums it contemplates charging are competitive.

ANNUAL CLAIM COSTS

The net annual claim cost can be viewed as the product of the claim frequency and the average claim value. As many types of benefits with varying claim values are issued in the field of health insurance, it is necessary to consider each type of benefit separately in developing the necessary formulas and in applying the appropriate morbidity data for rate-making purposes.

---

[4]The tentative gross premium is tested against less likely assumptions—a range of scenarios—to examine the sensitivity of each assumption.

[5]With the appropriate assumptions and parameters, it also is possible to solve the asset-share formula with the gross premium as the unknown and, thus, to derive the appropriate gross premium directly. For a detailed description of how asset shares are used to determine premium rates, see Health Insurance Association of America, *Individual Health Insurance, Part B* (New York: HIAA, 1994), Chapter 3.

Accidental Death and Dismemberment

If r_x represents the accidental-death rate at age *x,* if the principal-sum death and dismemberment benefit provided is $1,000, and if *k* equals the percentage of total accidental death and dismemberment claims that are dismemberment claims, then an equation that expresses the pure annual premium P_x for accidental death and dismemberment is:

$$(1 - k)P_x = \$1,000r_x$$
$$P_x = \frac{\$1,000r_x}{1 - k}$$

Dismemberment claims usually represent about 10 percent of total accidental death and dismemberment claims. In such a case, *k* = 10 percent and

$$P_x = \frac{\$1,000r_x}{0.90}$$

Because accidental death rates vary only slightly with age at most ages at which this benefit is issued, the same premium is usually charged at all issue ages. Another method is to charge the same premium rate for all issue ages less than age 45.

Medical Expense Benefits

Hospital Room and Board Benefits

The average net annual claim cost varies considerably with the type of hospital benefit, the level of benefit provided, the maximum duration of hospitalization benefits, geographical area, the age and sex of the insured, and, in the case of managed care, payment arrangements with providers. Separate net annual claim costs may be developed from available statistics for males, females, and children, on the basis of $1 of hospital benefits payable for varying maximum durations. Occupational hazards and variations in claim costs by geographic area are recognized by adjusting the net annual claim cost. This method might be used on individual health insurance. With group insurance, adjustment factors might be applied to the gross premiums.[6]

Hospital Miscellaneous Expense Benefits

The hospital miscellaneous expense benefit is intended to provide coverage for hospital services not covered by the room and board benefit. Net annual claim costs may be developed from available statistics. These claim costs vary by age and sex for adults but not for children.

Hospital room and board and miscellaneous expense benefits, until recently, were determined without regard to geographic location within a given country. Because with regular hospital and surgical coverage, consumers buy a fixed amount of daily benefit, they tend to buy what is needed for their area, and geography was not considered to be very important. The trend today is toward using net annual claim costs for miscellaneous hospital coverages that vary by geographic location. This trend has developed since the introduction of major medical coverage, in which experience studies have confirmed the

---

[6]Policies available in the United States range from a minimum of $100 a day to maximums that exceed $500 a day for this benefit. Many insurers are moving away from the concept of a stated maximum by reimbursing for whatever the hospital usually charges for a semiprivate room.

necessity for such refinement to establish equity between various policyowners, both for individual and group coverages.

Maternity Benefits

Maternity benefits normally are dealt with separately because they have a separate cost pattern. Under individual policies, if the maternity benefit is included as an optional benefit that may be removed by the policyowner at any time, a gross annual premium of as much as $25 or more per $100 of maternity benefit may be considered appropriate.

Surgical Benefits

Surgical expense benefits may be provided on a scheduled or nonscheduled basis. In the United States, most are on a nonscheduled basis. The surgical benefit schedules in common use are fairly standard, and the costs of providing these standard benefits are fairly well established. In addition, the relative frequencies of certain procedures have been recorded on a basis unrelated to the benefit schedule (relative value schedule). It is possible, therefore, to develop rates for varying surgical benefits quite reliably. The process includes examining enough claims to determine the expected average claim cost under the new schedule as compared with the standard schedule, and adjusting the rate used for the standard schedule by multiplying it by the ratio of the average net annual claim cost under the new schedule to the average net annual claim under the original schedule. Such cost variations for nonmaternity surgical benefits usually are determined separately for adult males, adult females, and children. The additional cost for maternity claims is determined separately.

Under a nonscheduled plan, instead of a specific allowance, reimbursement of the surgeon's fees is based on the usual and customary charge, often as a percentage of the usual and customary charge, for the procedure performed. There is no published schedule of allowances. A usual and customary charge is defined by each insurer based on the charges normally made by surgeons for similar services and the amount most frequently charged by most surgeons for comparable services in the locality where the service is received.

Major Medical Benefits

The most difficult part of determining realistic rates for major medical coverage, whether on an individual or a group basis, has been the problem of adjusting available morbidity statistics to the types of benefits provided under major medical coverage. Factors other than the age and sex of covered persons that influence the cost of benefits include:

1. The effect of inflation, increased utilization, and better technology on medical care costs.
2. The effect on benefit costs of increased earnings and occupation of the insured.
3. The effect of geographic area on benefit costs for both employee and dependent coverages.
4. The effect on benefit costs of various recognized deductibles, maximums, and percentage participation (coinsurance) factors.
5. The difference in the level of cost between "per-illness" plans and "all-cause" plans.
6. The effect on benefit costs of inside limits, such as (a) a maximum hospital daily room and board benefit or (b) a maximum surgical fee schedule. These limits tend to affect the utilization of private-room facilities in the hospital as well as

the amount payable for standard surgical procedures. The charges for these items may vary greatly depending on the geographical location and the nature of the individual hospital confinement or surgical procedure required.

Cost Variations by Benefit Type

The cost variations according to the type of benefit are illustrated in the following tables, which show annual claim costs for hospital and surgical, maternity, major medical, and disability income benefits. Table 31-2 shows that the annual claim costs for hospital medical/surgical, hospital psychiatric, and hospital outpatient benefits generally increase by age. The annual claim costs for females are normally higher than for males and benefit types. Usually, no distinction is made by sex or age in deriving the annual claim costs for children.

Table 31-3 shows annual claim costs for a $1,000 maternity benefit. The cost of maternity benefits decreases by age. The cost of the benefits during the first policy year will be low because of the effect of the maternity waiting period (usually 10 months). The maternity claim rates at the younger ages are much greater than at the older ages, and, therefore, the cost of the maternity benefits is higher at the younger ages. If the maternity benefit is included on an optional basis, however, there is likely to be adverse selection by the insured; therefore, the claim cost probably would not vary by the age of the insured.

Table 31-4 shows the monthly claim costs for a plan of major medical benefits. The costs of the benefits increase with age, but the increase by age is much greater for major medical benefits than for the basic hospital and surgical benefits shown in Table 31-2. As indicated in the heading for Table 31-4, the costs shown reflect the plan provisions. They will be different for other plans, depending upon their specifications.

It must be kept in mind that studies of morbidity experience are based on experience that is already out of date, and because morbidity costs that are applicable to the future are needed, it is necessary, particularly when it comes to major medical coverages, for the actuary to use projection or trend factors.

TABLE 31-2	Annual Claim Cost for Certain Hospital and Surgical Benefits per Insured					
	$1,000 Inpatient Hospital Medical/Surgical Benefit		**$500 Inpatient Hospital Psychiatric Benefit**		**$500 Outpatient Hospital Surgical Benefit**	
Attained Age	**Male**	**Female**	**Male**	**Female**	**Male**	**Female**
25–29	$ 20.40	$ 39.90	$2.15	$2.80	$ 23.50	$40.00
30–34	21.70	43.80	2.55	2.80	25.50	51.50
35–39	29.70	50.60	2.60	3.10	28.50	61.50
40–44	40.30	62.40	2.05	3.15	34.50	65.50
45–49	54.50	67.10	1.75	3.15	43.50	69.00
50–55	73.30	74.20	1.95	3.35	56.00	77.50
55–59	113.80	98.40	1.85	3.40	79.00	78.50
60–64	131.70	126.40	1.75	3.40	102.00	91.00
	Child		***Child***		***Child***	
All ages	$44.70		$1.35		$19.50	

Source: 1997 Milliman & Robertson Inc. Health Cost Guidelines™.

TABLE 31-3	Annual Claim Cost for $1,000 Maternity Benefit per Adult Member
Attained Age	**Annual Claims Cost**
To 25	$54
25–29	64
30–34	43
35–39	21
40–44	7
45–49	2

Source: 1997 Milliman & Robertson Inc. Health Cost Guidelines™.

TABLE 31-4	Monthly Claim Cost Comprehensive Major Medical Expense Benefits $100 Deductible Amount, 80% Coinsurance, $2,500 Out-of-Pocket Maximum		
	Per Member Monthly Claim Costs		
Attained Age	**Male**	**Female**	**Child (All Ages)**
25–29	$ 68.51	$176.32	$63.80
30–34	76.83	176.50	
35–39	92.55	181.74	
40–44	112.30	191.94	
45–49	144.80	208.72	
50–55	194.10	237.15	
55–59	280.34	292.94	
60–64	391.02	357.26	

Source: 1997 Milliman & Robertson Inc. Health Cost Guidelines™.

There is a variation in the cost of medical care by geographical area. Under hospital and surgical expense coverages, benefits usually are subject to a daily hospital benefit limit and to a surgical schedule; therefore, there usually is no need to vary premium rates by area. In the case of major medical expense coverages, however, the cost of the benefits will be higher in high-cost areas. To a certain extent, this can be controlled by using so-called inside limits for room and board benefits, and by using a surgical schedule. If inside limits are not used, premium rates often are varied by geographical area. For a major medical policy providing comprehensive medical expense benefits with no inside limits, the cost of the benefits in the highest-cost areas of the United States is about three times higher than in the lowest-cost areas. Competitive concerns generally soften this effect.

Through the use of a deductible, major medical policies often provide for the elimination of initial hospital or medical expenses incurred. The amount of the deductible depends on the type of plan being offered. In U.S. group insurance, comprehensive major medical coverage often provides for payment of all covered physician's hospital charges (usually at semiprivate room rates) at a rate of 80 percent, but with a maximum "out-of-pocket cap" of $500 to $1,000 or more on the insured's payment. After the insured has incurred the out-of-pocket expenses, the insurer pays 100 percent of all further covered expenses. Benefits would be subject to a deductible of $100 to $500 or more. It is customary to provide a fixed maximum benefit of $1 million or more, except for certain inside limits. Most insurers issue comprehensive major medical benefits on individual policies with benefits similar to those described previously for group insurance, although, in general, benefits provided under individual policies tend to be less liberal than those provided under group plans.

Table 31-5 illustrates claim costs for a comprehensive major medical plan comparing Montana's costs with national experience. In addition to demonstrating geographical differences in claim cost, the table also reflects cost differentials due to age and sex.

Dependent Classifications

For individual insurance, it is customary to charge a rate for each child rather than a rate for all children, as is done in group insurance.[7] The premium for children varies by type of plan but generally not by age or sex. The hospital stay usually is short for most surgical procedures performed on children; therefore, the level of miscellaneous benefits provided by the plan affects the claim cost most dramatically and may vary the relationship between the cost of coverage for adults and for children.

The premium rate for dependent coverage under group insurance depends on the age of the employee and may or may not be independent of industry, depending upon the insurer. For group coverages, as opposed to individual coverage, normally there is no additional charge for children after the first child, whether the plan is basic hospital and surgical or comprehensive major medical. Some HMOs charge for the employee and two dependents and others for the employee and family. Although charging for each

---

[7]In major medical, it is feasible to use an all-children rate on individual insurance because of the cost-reduction effect of a large deductible. This effect is lacking on basic individual coverages, and, hence, a per-child rate usually is considered necessary.

TABLE 31-5 Monthly Claim Cost of Comprehensive Major Medical Expense Benefits: Montana versus National Experience

Attained Age	Average Monthly Market Premium Rates	Loss Ratio	Montana Monthly Claim Cost	Area Factor Montana versus National	National Monthly Claim Cost	Sex Factors		National Annual Claim Cost	
						Male	Female	Male	Female
0–17	$ 64.07	70%	$ 44.85	0.859	$ 52.21	1.10	0.89	$ 690	$ 560
18–24	97.15	70%	68.01	0.859	79.17	0.72	1.29	680	1,230
25–29	102.45	70%	71.72	0.859	83.49	0.67	1.33	670	1,330
30–34	111.23	70%	77.86	0.859	90.64	0.76	1.24	830	1,350
35–39	125.03	70%	87.52	0.859	101.89	0.91	1.09	1,110	1,330
40–44	141.77	70%	99.24	0.859	115.53	1.02	0.98	1,410	1,360
45–49	161.23	70%	112.86	0.859	131.38	1.05	0.95	1,660	1,500
50–54	188.13	70%	131.69	0.859	153.31	1.09	0.92	2,010	1,690
55–59	224.61	70%	157.22	0.859	183.03	1.12	0.89	2,460	1,950
60–64	255.29	70%	178.71	0.859	208.04	1.13	0.89	2,820	2,220

Source: The Montana Comprehensive Health Association and Statistical Abstract of the United States, 1996.

additional child would produce greater equity, it complicates administrative procedures. Because a portion of the premium normally is paid by the employer, the insured employees still receive equitable treatment under a properly designed group plan covering their dependents.

Disability Income Benefits

The annual claim costs for a disability income benefit vary significantly by occupational class. Table 31-6 shows the annual claim costs for one particular disability income plan. The costs vary according to age, sex, occupational class, elimination period, and maximum duration of benefits. If the elimination period and maximum duration of benefits are different for sickness benefits than for accident benefits, it is necessary to develop separate costs for accident and for sickness. Occupation Group I shown in the table covers white-collar types of occupational classes, and Occupation Group II covers blue-collar types of occupational classes.

Long-Term Care Benefits

The annual claim costs for a long-term care policy vary significantly depending on many factors in addition to age, sex, and amount of coverage. These include:

1. type of coverage (e.g., nursing home only, home care only, comprehensive, assisted-living facility, and hospice)
2. elimination period (varies significantly, ranging from 0 to 365 days)
3. benefit maximum
4. benefit triggers
5. state of issue
6. cause of claim
7. marital status

Table 31-7 presents annual claim costs for nursing home coverage, and Table 31-8 presents annual claim costs for home health coverage. It is clear that the difference in

TABLE 31-6 Annual Claim Cost Per $100 of Monthly Disability Income Benefit (First Year of Benefit Period—All Durations; Seven-Day Elimination Period) 1986–1991 Experience

Attained Age	Male Occupational Group I	Male Occupational Group II	Female Occupational Group I
Under 30	—	17.44	—
30–34	3.58	17.26	4.44
35–39	10.73	16.35	27.98
40–44	12.63	21.62	14.52
45–49	19.25	21.43	20.07
50–54	28.25	79.63	29.31
55–59	32.45	38.28	27.70
60–64	35.90	53.03	70.30
65–69	43.05	103.28	27.84

Source: Preliminary Report of the Committee on Individual Disability Income Experience, Society of Actuaries, 1998.

TABLE 31-7 Nursing Home Annual Claim Costs ($100 Benefit, per Day, per Person)

Attained Age	Male			Female			Total		
	M	*NM*	*T*	*M*	*NM*	*T*	*M*	*NM*	*T*
20	0.00	1.10	4.50	0.00	4.20	2.70	0.00	2.60	3.60
30	0.06	38.90	11.60	1.40	41.80	11.90	1.10	40.40	11.80
40	1.40	112.20	21.00	5.00	115.00	28.80	3.20	114.50	25.50
50	11.90	258.10	51.60	7.10	210.70	53.10	9.60	230.00	52.20
60	23.00	514.90	99.60	38.50	345.50	126.50	30.40	395.80	113.00
70	162.50	1,258.20	361.00	190.40	914.30	551.30	183.00	987.90	460.10
80	623.80	2,656.00	1,209.80	1,416.30	3,612.00	3,137.50	892.10	3,440.80	2,404.90
90	4,183.20	5,529.60	4,625.80	6,140.80	8,749.30	8,481.30	4,749.20	8,034.50	7,198.30

Legend: M = Married
NM = Not Married
T = Total (weighted average of Married and Not Married)

Source: 1985 National Nursing Home Survey.

TABLE 31-8 Home Health Claim Costs ($100 Benefit, per Person, per Year)

Attained Age	Male			Female			Total		
	M	*NM*	*T*	*M*	*NM*	*T*	*M*	*NM*	*T*
20	0.00	5.50	5.30	0.00	4.10	2.80	0.00	4.80	4.10
30	1.30	18.50	5.80	0.70	11.20	4.50	1.00	11.30	5.20
40	0.80	25.70	6.70	1.50	18.70	6.30	1.10	21.30	6.50
50	1.90	35.80	8.80	3.10	60.00	17.00	2.50	50.10	13.00
60	39.20	80.50	46.50	15.80	148.10	57.30	28.40	123.60	51.80
70	126.60	215.70	145.60	165.90	279.50	205.40	141.70	261.40	179.40
80	498.10	586.60	511.70	490.70	695.00	649.00	497.80	675.80	592.30
90	816.10	1,550.90	1,049.50	469.30	1,577.10	1,310.30	650.80	1,568.00	1,239.10

Legend: M = Married
NM = Not Married
T = Total (weighted average of Married and Not Married)

Source: 1992 Home Health and Hospice Care Survey.

claim costs between males and females can be explained by marital status. The majority of costs are incurred between ages 70 and 90.

As with any new product, the lack of reliable experience data provides new challenges to actuaries in pricing long-term care products. As more insured experience becomes available, forecasting costs and properly pricing long-term care products will improve.

PREMIUM-RATE VARIABLES

Because of the instability of health care costs, monitoring and adjusting prices are extremely important for medical expense insurance. In the case of noncancellable disability income policies, the insurer is obligated to offer a guaranteed premium for the life of the policy. In the case of guaranteed renewable and conditionally renewable disability income policies, the insurer is permitted to raise the premium in certain circumstances. Thus, if the product experiences higher claim costs than expected during pricing, the insurer can raise the premium on an entire block of policies, though not separately for individual policies.

The inability to work because of accident or sickness is subjective in nature and involves an attitude as well as a physical or mental impairment. Because disability is at least partially a state of mind, experience is subject to many factors, including the level of unemployment, the attitude of insurers, individuals' work ethics and their attitudes toward retirement, and the attitudes of physicians who certify disability. In an attempt to cope with these problems, insurers underwrite health insurance coverage carefully and use several risk classification factors, as discussed next.

Age and Sex Classifications

Age is of major importance in almost all forms of health coverage, as previously discussed. The premium rates for females for hospital, surgical, and medical expense benefits and disability income benefits are higher than for males at the younger ages. With increased age, however, the costs become lower for females. For group insurance—but not for individual insurance—the relationship also varies between employed females and dependent females. Female group rates may be calculated as a percentage increase over the male rate, or they may be based on an analysis of actual experience of female lives.

Disability income benefits usually are issued to regularly employed persons only. The rates for females generally range from 1½ to 2 times the male rate.

Occupational Classifications

Most hospital and surgical plans do not pay benefits from work-related illness or injury that would be payable under workers' compensation. Because this exclusion eliminates much of the adverse effect of hazardous occupations, some insurers charge the same premium for hospital and surgical benefits regardless of occupation. Industry loadings are often used for group insurance.

Accidental death and dismemberment benefits and disability income benefits may be issued on an occupational basis. In these cases, it is customary to subdivide the various occupations into at least three classes, with appropriate extra premiums depending on the degree of extra morbidity and mortality expected. Some occupations may be eliminated entirely because of an extreme occupational hazard.

Geographical Area Classifications

Within the United States, traditionally, the location of the insured individual has rarely been a factor for determining premium rates for disability income or accidental-death insurance. The indications are, however, that there are cost variations by area on disability income insurance.[8] This may be related to the level of employment by state. Therefore, the actuary often will determine whether the variations are significant enough to introduce them into the premium structure. Geography is very significant in health insurance costs mainly because of wide variations in hospital rates and other

---

[8]Nearly all companies have higher rates in California, and several other states carry higher rates in many companies.

medical care expenditures. Variations in claim frequency also occur in some areas, due largely to variations in medical management practices. Certainly, variations between countries are great, especially as between developing and developed countries.

Elimination Periods

The elimination of income benefits for varying periods (such as 7, 14, 30, 60, 90, 120, 180, or 365 days) is a method used to provide benefits that suit the various income-replacement needs of insureds in the event of disability. Many persons have underlying employer-provided or other disability plans that cover the first several weeks of disability. The cost of benefits decreases as the elimination period increases.

If a continuance table is used for disability income benefits, it is easy (superficially) to make the necessary adjustments in rates for various elimination periods. However, there should be a continuance table for each elimination period, or else modification values by elimination period, because the experience for policies with different elimination periods differs. Those who take longer elimination periods are healthier than those who select short elimination periods and have more incentive to return to work, improving claims experience.

Other Premium Classifications

Smokers exhibit higher morbidity and mortality experience than nonsmokers. As a result, many U.S. insurers have adopted premium differentials for individual policies for smokers and nonsmokers. The differential can range as high as 25 to 50 percent.

Increasingly, insurers issue individual noncancellable disability income or guaranteed-renewable medical expense policies to impaired risks, subject to the payment of an extra premium. Numerical morbidity ratings have been established for each insurable impairment, and these vary from approximately 125 percent to 300 percent. Two ratings are required for each impairment—one for accident-only policies and another for accident and sickness, including hospital and surgical and major medical. Some impairments are standard for accident only but are rated for accident and sickness coverage.

Some relatively undesirable hospital and surgical risks can be accepted for disability income coverage if there is, say, at least a 30-day elimination period. On the other hand, there are some poor disability income risks that are acceptable hospital risks. Some companies also use exclusion riders in which specific conditions are excluded from coverage.

MANAGED CARE PRICING

The financial management of managed care organizations in the United States is parallel in many ways to that of a health insurer.[9] A key difference, however, is the focus of financial management. Health insurance providing indemnity coverage projects health care expenditures as an independent third party. The emphasis is more on accuracy of projections as measured by loss and expense ratios and less on influencing the health care expenditure results themselves. Under managed care, however, the financing and delivery of health care are integrated. Projections and management (control) of health

---

[9]This section draws on "Financing, Budgeting, and Rating," in *Managed Care: Integrating the Delivery and Financing of Health Care, Part B* (Washington, DC: HIAA, 1996), Chapter 6.

BOX 31-1

CATEGORIES OF MEDICAL SERVICES

Hospital Services		Physician Services
Inpatient	*Outpatient*	Physician Encounter
Medical	Medical	Inpatient Visits
Surgical	Surgical	Surgery
Maternity	Emergency	Emergency Room Visits
Mental Health	Radiology/Pathology	Lab/X-Ray
Substance Abuse		Maternity
Skilled Nursing Facility		Referrals
		Drugs

Source: Lee E. Launer, *Group Insurance*, 3rd ed., p. 408.

care expenditures on the delivery side and projections used for pricing and budgeting are both considered together.

Claim costs and premium rates for HMOs and other managed care programs are generally calculated using a different methodology than that for traditional indemnity products. As discussed earlier, for indemnity plans, costs are estimated by aggregating projected claims per unit of population for hospital, surgical, and major medical services. In contrast, HMO costs are usually based on separate detailed utilization and cost rates for each category of medical service offered. Box 31-1 presents a sample of such categories of services.

The pricing of HMOs and other managed care plans must also account for the possible reimbursement and incentive programs made available to the providers of health care, whereas traditional indemnity plans have been based on open-ended, fee-for-service payments.

HMO Rating

Originally, and for many years, Blue Cross and Blue Shield plans used **community rating** (i.e., charging the same premium rates to all plan members). Most HMOs also used some form of community rating. In the United States, the laws of each state govern the rating flexibility of managed care plans operating in that state. In addition, HMOs serving Medicare and Medicaid beneficiaries have special licensing requirements. Furthermore, federally qualified HMOs must meet special pricing requirements. An HMO may be qualified by a state only or be both state and federally qualified.

Federally qualified HMOs must set their rates according to one or more of the following community rating approaches:[10]

- In **community rating** all groups are priced using the same per-member, per-month (PMPM) rates.
- **Community rating by class** is a modification that allows for variations in the community rate for a given group based on the age, gender, and other acceptable risk factors of the group.

[10]HIAA, *Managed Care: Integrating the Delivery and Financing of Health Care, Part B*, p. 118.

- **Adjusted community rating** allows greater flexibility in setting the prospective rates of a group (including consideration of experience of the group) provided that:
  1. The rating method is documented and released to the customer on request.
  2. The rating method is filed and approved by state regulators.
  3. Rates for groups with 100 or fewer eligible employees cannot be more than 110 percent of the community rate.
  4. The Health Care Financing Administration is notified that the plan is using this method.

Federally qualified HMOs are not allowed to experience rate retrospectively.

The vast majority of HMOs use a premium rate development method called a *benefit cost* or *actuarial method* that builds a claim cost on a service basis. That is, the calculation develops a rate needed for each service (the utilization of that service multiplied by the cost of that service) and then adds this value for all services to get a total premium. The resulting composite claim cost is then increased by appropriate administrative expenses, profit, and margins to develop the premium rate. Table 31-9 shows the determination of a gross-premium rate.

Most staff-model HMO plans use what is defined as a *budgeting* approach to determine annual revenue requirements. Revenue requirements are developed by projecting member demand for health care services and then determining how much professional time will be required to service the plan. The professional time can then be equated to the total dollars or budget needed for the staff model to operate. Enrollment figures are then used to develop premium rates that will be adequate to cover these services.

TABLE 31-9   Determination of Gross HMO Rate

	Cost per Member per Month
Plan Services	
Hospital services	$ 38.48
Prescription drugs	14.11
All other benefits	57.54
Subtotal, Net Benefit Costs	110.13
Adjustments and Loadings	
Administration, marketing, and overhead	10.07
Premium tax	2.01
Profit/contribution to reserves	2.01
Reinsurance premiums	3.53
Reinsurance recoveries	−1.77
COB recoveries	−1.70
Out of area/out of plan costs	2.25
State reserve	3.02
Subtotal, Adjustments and Loadings	19.43
Gross HMO Rate, PMPM	129.56

Source: Milliman & Robertson, Inc. 1997 Intercompany HMO Rate Survey.

PPO and POS Rating

In the United States, PPO and POS plans usually are regulated as insurance products and are subject to the same rating restrictions as indemnity medical insurance. Some states require that rates and/or rating methodologies be filed with (and, in some cases, approved by) state regulators. In general, however, there is much flexibility in setting rates for a specific group based on reasonable factors.

In general, PPO and POS rates are developed in much the same manner as HMO rates. A key difference is that some of the PPO and POS services may not be delivered through the organization's own network of providers. Also, when PPO and POS plans replace another insurer's health plan for a group, the experience of the prior insurer often is considered in setting the rates.

HEALTH INSURANCE RESERVES AND OTHER LIABILITIES

In health insurance, as in life insurance, it is important that proper provision be made in the insurer liabilities for all the obligations assumed by the insurer under its contracts, irrespective of whether it is required by law.[11] Liability accounts are established for present or future claims against the insurer's assets that must come from the premiums already received. **Reserve** is the term used to refer to the amount of the insurer's liability to fulfill future contingencies and unpaid obligations already incurred.

Health insurance reserves and other liabilities may be classified broadly as follows:

1. **Policy reserves** refer to the amounts necessary for the fulfillment of contract obligations as to future claims, which include pro rata unearned premium reserves and additional (active life) reserves for level-premium policies.
2. **Claim reserves and liabilities** include those amounts necessary to cover payments on claims already incurred but not yet paid.
3. *Expense liabilities* include those amounts necessary to pay loss adjustment expenses and taxes under obligations incurred by the insurer from operations prior to the annual statement date.

Table 31-10 shows a hypothetical insurer statement illustrating the various health insurance reserves and liabilities discussed later.[12]

Policy Reserves

Unearned Premium Reserves

In the United States, the amount of the unearned premium reserve to be included in the annual statement for individual coverage is the pro rata portion of the full gross - premium from the statement date to the end of the period for which premiums have been paid on the policy, regardless of the renewal provision of the policy. The amounts or reserves usually are smaller due to the way premiums are paid. In establishing the appropriate amount, approximation methods often are used. It is often assumed that premium-due dates are distributed uniformly over the year so that, on the average, one-half of the total premiums in force, regardless of the mode of premium payment, are unearned as of the end of the year. This normally is the largest item among the policy reserves, unless

---

[11] This discussion draws on Conant et al., *Managing for Solvency and Profitability in Life and Health Insurance Companies*, pp. 542–544.

[12] In the Life Insurance Company Annual Statement Form, provision is made for a breakdown of health insurance reserves in Exhibit 9, and liability for policy and contract claims in Exhibit 11. See chapter 34.

TABLE 31-10	XYZ Insurance Company Annual Statement of Financial Condition, December 31, 19XX	
Assets:		
Cash		$ 170,000
Bonds		675,000
Stocks		
Preferred		75,000
Common		25,000
Mortgage loans on real estate		316,000
Real estate owned		40,000
Premiums due and unpaid		43,000
Total assets		$1,344,000
Liabilities, capital, and surplus:		
Unearned premium reserve		$ 320,000
Net level premium reserves (additional reserve for noncancellable policies)		35,000
Premiums paid in advance		40,000
Liability for claims in course of settlement		140,000
Liability for claims incurred but unreported		50,000
Reserve for future amounts due on claims		110,000
Reserve for future contingent benefits (deferred maternity and similar benefits)		20,000
Liability for dividends declared		20,000
Liability for expenses and taxes due and accrued		85,000
Asset valuation reserve		36,000
Capital		250,000
Unassigned surplus		238,000
Total liabilities, capital, and surplus		$1,344,000

the insurer has large amounts of noncancellable or guaranteed-renewable business. In other countries, this reserve may be estimated to be 40 percent of the total annual gross premiums.

The unearned gross-premium reserve automatically provides a reserve allowance for the payment of expenses that will be incurred after the statement date, as well as for the benefit payments that will be incurred and must be paid from premiums already received. Premiums paid on or before the statement date but due after the statement date are classified separately as premiums paid in advance.[13]

Policy Reserves for Long-Term Health Insurance Policies

For long-term health products that are priced on a level annual premium basis and may or may not offer premium guarantees for a number of years such as individual disability policies, long-term care policies, and hospital benefit policies, insurers must establish policy reserves similar to those established for individual life products.

Noncancellable and guaranteed-renewable health insurance policies usually provide coverage to a specified age, such as 60 or 65, and often are issued on the basis of

---

[13]Advance premiums are not a part of the unearned premium reserve but appear as a separate liability because the premiums paid are not yet due. The insured may change his or her mind and request the return of the premium, and, therefore, sound accounting practice indicates separate treatment.

level premiums payable each year after the date of issue. Because of increasing morbidity costs as age increases and the use of a level premium, excess funds are accumulated in the early years (measured by the reserve liability or active life reserve). These funds eventually are consumed through increased claim costs by the expiration date of the benefits, in much the same manner as reserves on term-to-age-65 life insurance policies build in the early years and decrease to zero at age 65. As in life insurance, the so-called active life reserve calculated prospectively is equal to the difference between the present value of future benefits and the present value of future valuation net premiums.

Health insurance reserving practices are governed by the **NAIC Model Minimum Reserve Standards for Individual and Group Health Insurance.** For noncancellable and guaranteed-renewable disability income and other long-term health products, insurers are allowed to use a two-year full preliminary term reserve (although one-year full preliminary term is recommended), which allows the insurer to maintain a $0 reserve for the policy's first two years. **Statutory policy reserves** are calculated using the prospective method with designated morbidity tables, persistency assumption based on recommended tables, and a maximum interest rate. As with life products, long-term health policy reserves must be valued according to the minimum reserve requirements in effect at the time the policy is issued. **GAAP reserves** for long-term health products may be calculated using the insurer's realistic expectations for morbidity, mortality, persistency, and investment return on a net-level premium basis.

In the United States, the *1987 Commissioners Group Disability Tables (CGDT),* adopted by the National Association of Insurance Commissioners in December 1987, is the minimum standard for the valuation of disability income benefits due to accident and sickness. In contrast to previous tables, the *CGDT* is based on group experience, and its claim and termination rates vary by gender and elimination period. For accidental-death benefits, the minimum standard is the *1959 Accidental Death Benefit Table.*

As in the case of life insurance, to establish a minimum standard for reserves, regulatory authorities specify particular morbidity and mortality tables and a maximum rate of interest. For health insurance benefits, insurers are permitted to use as an interest assumption the maximum rate currently permitted by law for the valuation of new life contracts, and for mortality, any table permitted by law in the valuation of currently issued life insurance. Insurers may use a net-level, or a one- or two-year preliminary term method of valuation for active-life reserves. Although the additional reserve is required only on noncancellable or guaranteed-renewable policies or on policies in which the right of nonrenewal is limited, the need for this reserve exists on any level-premium type of coverage in which the incidence of cost increases with advancing age.

Claim Reserves and Liabilities

Claim reserves are liabilities reflecting amounts that an insurer expects to pay in the future on claims that have been incurred prior to the date of the financial statement but that have not yet been paid in full. In view of the frequency and sometimes long-term nature of health claims, claim reserves are particularly significant in health insurance.

There are many acceptable methods of estimating the insurer's liability for outstanding claims that have not been paid in full on the annual statement preparation date. Any method selected to determine the amount of outstanding claim liability should be one that assures adequacy and fairly reflects the actual liability, which will later be developed after sufficient time has passed to permit the insurer to tabulate the actual results that occur subsequent to the statement date. In discussing claim reserves, it is important to recognize the distinction between claim reserves and claim liabilities. Claim reserves refer to future payments that are not certain. This, like all other reserves, is subject to actuarial estimation. Claim liabilities refer to items due, unpaid claims, and claims in course of settlement.

Reserve for Amounts Not Yet Due on Claims

The reserve for amounts not yet due consists of two parts. The first part deals with reported claims. This reserve is for future "unaccrued" payments only; such payments can be identified as those that the insurer would not be required to pay if the claimant were to recover from disability at the close of the year. The second part of this reserve is the same as the first part except that it refers to unreported claims.

Because of the problem of determining the reserve liability for disabled lives, disability income benefits provide the best example of the complicated nature of health claim liability items. As the rate of recovery decreases with increasing duration of disability, the value of the claim annuity for a long-duration benefit period normally increases, until the value of the claim annuity reaches a peak, and then it gradually decreases to the end of the period for which benefits are payable. In estimating this liability item as of the valuation date, it is, therefore, desirable to show for each claim the age at date of disability, the number of months or years the claimant has been disabled, and the number of years of benefit remaining, in order to be able to apply the appropriate claim annuity factor to the monthly benefit amount being provided. If the monthly income is not payable for more than one year, the claim annuity valuation factors may be based on an average age and on average durations that vary with the type of benefit being considered.

Hospital, surgical, and medical expense benefits are usually settled in a single sum, and it is not practical, in most cases, to obtain the claim liability for each claim. Instead, by making a reconciliation of previous years' claims, one can develop a factor such that by applying the factor to the cash claims payable during the calendar year, a reasonable estimate can be made of the claim liability at the end of the year.

Liability for Claims Due and Unpaid

This item normally is a relatively small portion of total health insurance claims and represents claims approved but not yet paid. This is often a timing lag. Most insurers pay amounts due on a claim as soon as the amount can be determined and the claim approved.

Liability for Claims in the Course of Settlement

The liability shown for this item is based on claims on which notice of claim has been received, but on which all the proofs of loss or other documentation have not been received, so that the claim cannot be approved on the statement date. Some insurers examine each claim individually and prepare a list showing each item involved. Others use approximate methods. One method is to add the total amount of outstanding claims and apply to it a factor obtained from the experience on previous valuation dates. Another method is to analyze a sample of claims and determine a percentage factor that is applied to the total liability for claims, including both accrued and unaccrued amounts.

Liability for Claims Incurred But Not Reported

Experience will show that many claims that were actually incurred prior to the statement date are paid after that date each year because the insurer had no knowledge of the claim until after the statement date. It is usual to tabulate these claims each year and relate the amount to some base, such as volume of business in force or earned premiums on the type of coverage involved. The total liability for incurred but unreported claims is sometimes divided into two parts: accrued and contingent. The accrued liability is reported as "incurred but unreported," as part of the policy claim liability. The contingent liability accruing after the valuation date is included under "Reserve for Amounts Not Yet Due on Claims" discussed previously.

Liability for Expenses

It is necessary to provide in insurer liabilities a reasonable estimate of the claim expenses that will be paid on unpaid losses incurred prior to the statement date. This liability may be computed as a cost per claim, as a percentage of the liabilities for claims incurred, or as a combination of both. In major medical coverage, in which the cost of settling claims may be much higher per claim than under base-plan coverage, it usually is necessary to develop separate factors for each type of coverage based on actual cost studies.

Other than claim expenses, the reserve for expenses may be accounted for in the unearned gross-premium reserve, or, if this reserve is not adequate, an additional amount may be established in the expense liability. This situation might occur during the first year if unpaid commissions or other expenses end up being greater than the loading provided in that year's premium calculation.

Group Reserves and Liabilities

An insurer's liabilities under group health contracts create the need for the same types of policy and claim reserves as for individual health insurance contracts. The amounts of the reserves, however, usually are smaller. In general, premiums are paid monthly under group health contracts, and the insurer reserves the right to adjust premium rates on any policy anniversary. Nevertheless, it is an important objective to keep the level of premiums and, therefore, the insured's costs on a stable basis.

Other Reserves and Liabilities

On the statement date, participating health insurance policies will have dividends declared that will not be payable until after the statement date. This **liability for dividends payable** should be set up as a liability on the statement date.

Contingency reserves, which are not liabilities, are sometimes established on a voluntary basis to allow for the possibility of an upward trend in claim costs or an unusual occurrence. In state disability plans, these reserves may be established to offset decreasing premiums without a corresponding decrease in liability. This treatment may be necessary because premiums are paid on current wages whereas benefits depend on wages during a base period. Some states require the accumulation of a contingency reserve for group health business.

SURPLUS DISTRIBUTION

Individual health insurance policies are issued on both a nonparticipating and participating basis. Overall U.S. experience has not been favorable, and, therefore, dividends have either not been payable or the amount payable has been small. Large group health insurance policies (i.e., 100 or more employees) are virtually always participating through a variety of experience-rating devices. The concepts underlying both divi-

---

[14]In view of the generally unfavorable experience in recent years, there are virtually no individual participating policies available.

dends and experience rating are similar but may differ somewhat in basic philosophy. In any case, the process should take into consideration the surplus position of the policy-owner or class, the extent to which losses are pooled (averaged) among cases, the expenses incurred as between policyowners or classes, and the total surplus available for distribution.

Individual Policies

In the case of individual policies, funds are accumulated separately for each class of policy (sometimes referred to as policy form). In this way, the amount of surplus accumulated for any dividend class, in which the policies are participating, is ascertainable. The dividend formula usually is simple, taking into account only broad equities. For example, for policies that have been in force for, say, three years, a specified percentage of the premiums (varied in some insurers by duration) may be returned as a dividend. In connection with dividends, the asset-share calculation is used principally as a test of the adequacy of the accumulation for any dividend class. As pointed out earlier, the adequacy of the insurer's contingency reserve for this type of business will affect the proportion of current earnings that is added to the contingency reserve for a particular class of policies. Table 31-11 presents an example of a fund account for a class of policies issued at age 50 providing coverage to age 65. The actual experience will undoubtedly be different, and this will be reflected in both pricing and dividend distribution.[14]

Group Policies

An approach similar to that used for individual classes is used in dealing with small group cases. Groups are classified, and surplus distribution is determined through the use of fund accounts for each class of groups. Again, only a limited number of variables are considered. In small cases, morbidity experience must be averaged because of the low credibility of the individual case's experience. Expenses are relatively high, but because of the smaller-size discounts granted these cases, they may develop reasonable dividend distributions over a period of time. For very small groups, the possibility of adverse selection by the employer against the insurer is high and can lead to some medical underwriting. Individual states frequently have regulatory restrictions on pricing of small groups.

For the larger group health cases, it is practicable to develop the appropriate dividend or premium refund through the use of fund accounts. As in the case of life insurance, this involves the accumulation from date of issue of the premiums paid, increased in some cases by interest earnings. From this amount, losses incurred, accumulated expenses incurred directly or allocated to the case, taxes, and allowances for contingencies and profit are deducted. From this net accumulation, total dividends paid previously and charges for deficit recovery are deducted, and the result is the surplus amount available for distribution.

The chief problems in large group cases involve the development of unit expense charges for indirect expense items, the determination of the period of amortization of acquisition expenses, and the individual-case contribution to contingencies or profits. In all but the largest cases, it is necessary to establish a limit on the maximum level of losses considered in the experience-rating formula. This usually is achieved by imposing a limit on an aggregate basis or, in some cases, an aggregate limit and a maximum for a single claim during a given experience period.

In all cases, the experience-rating formula considers (1) premiums paid, (2) incurred losses (modified by loss limits and credibility), (3) direct and allocated expenses, and (4) allowances for contingencies and profits.

TABLE 31-11 Fund Account for Policies Issued at Age 50—Term to Age 65—Annual Premium $199.69

	Basic Data				Income during Year			Disbursements during Year			Fund Account	
									Expenses			
POLICY YEAR	LIVES ENTERING YEAR	DEATHS	TERMINATIONS	NET ANNUAL CLAIM COST	PREMIUM INCOME	INTEREST EARNINGS ON FUND	CLAIMS	PER PREMIUM EXPENSES	PER POLICY EXPENSES	CLAIM ADMINISTRATIVE EXPENSES	INCREASE DURING YEAR	ACCUMULATED FUND
n	1	2	3	4	5	6	7	8	9	10	11	12
1	1,000	4	199	$ 68.14	$199,690	$ –486.00	$68,004	$149,768	$27,000	$5,440	$51,008.00	$–51,008.00
2	797	4	119	82.36	159,153	675.00	65,476	47,746	2,391	5,238	38,977.00	–12,031.00
3	674	5	67	98.04	134,591	1,621.00	65,834	26,918	2,022	5,267	36,171.00	24,140.00
4	602	5	30	115.28	120,213	2,493.00	39,110	24,043	1,806	5,529	22,218.00	46,358.00
5	567	6	22	122.00	113,224	2,938.00	38,808	22,645	1,701	5,505	17,503.00	63,861.00
6	539	7	16	129.09	107,633	3,331.00	69,128	21,527	1,617	5,530	13,162.00	77,023.00
7	516	7	10	136.55	103,040	3,592.00	69,982	20,608	1,548	5,599	8,895.00	85,918.00
8	499	8	5	144.38	99,645	3,760.00	71,468	19,929	1,497	5,717	4,794.00	90,712.00
9	486	8		152.58	97,049	3,800.00	73,544	19,410	1,458	5,884	553.00	91,265.00
10	478	9		161.50	95,452	3,741.00	76,305	19,090	1,434	6,104	–3,740.00	87,525.00
11	469	10		170.09	93,655	3,541.00	78,922	18,731	1,407	6,314	–8,178.00	79,347.00
12	459	10		179.40	91,658	3,205.00	81,448	18,332	1,377	6,516	–12,810.00	66,537.00
13	449	11		189.08	89,661	2,729.00	83,857	17,932	1,347	6,709	–17,455.00	49,082.00
14	438	12		199.13	87,464	2,077.00	86,024	17,493	1,314	6,882	–22,172.00	26,910.00
15	426	12		209.55	85,068	1,366.00	88,011	17,014	1,278	7,041	–26,910.00	0.00

Source: Individual Health Insurance, Part B (Washington, DC: Health Insurance Association of America, 1994), p. 100.

Questions

1. What factors affect the cost of health insurance?
2. Health insurance premium rates should ideally be adequate, reasonable, and equitable. Describe the difficulties that market and/or regulatory conditions may pose for a health insurer that is trying to meet these premium objectives.
3. Describe the nature and purpose of three classes of reserves that are generally found in health insurance.
4. Why are interest earnings not as important in the calculation of disability benefits as they are in the calculation of life insurance benefits?
5. Describe three measures of morbidity experience.

LIFE INSURER FINANCIAL MANAGEMENT: I

Objectives

- Explain the benefits that financial intermediaries bring to an economy.

- Explain the incentives thought to be behind firms' efforts to manage risk.

- Describe the risk–return trade-off associated with investments.

- Describe and reconcile the actuarial and financial views of the risks faced by insurance companies.

- Describe some of the methods used by life insurers to manage actuarial, systematic, credit, and liquidity risks.

The financial management of life insurers today is vastly more challenging than that which existed just a few years ago. Not only has competition between life insurers intensified enormously, but more importantly, competition from other financial intermediaries such as banks, securities firms, and mutual funds has forced insurers to recognize that they must respond with far greater efficiency and effectiveness in all operational areas. This increased competition has by no means been limited to the United States. Resultant competition has led to increasingly complex products with lower margins and often with greater risk. Today, it is more likely that good financial management rather than good mortality or morbidity management will separate successful from other life insurers.

At the same time that competition has intensified, we also have seen great volatility in asset prices and numerous insolvencies of financial firms including many large life insurers. As a consequence, stronger financial reporting and regulatory oversight have ensued, forcing increased attention to the risks inherent in asset and liability portfolios. Together, these factors have further enhanced the importance of financial management.

This and the following chapter explore the theory and practice of financial management by life insurers. This chapter lays much of the conceptual foundation for understanding life insurance as a cash flow business. Chapter 33 explores the more applied elements of the subject.

LIFE INSURERS AS FINANCIAL INTERMEDIARIES

A life insurance company is a financial intermediary. A **financial intermediary** is a firm or other entity that brings together providers and users of funds. In addition to insurers, financial intermediaries include depository institutions such as commercial banks and thrifts (savings and loan associations, savings banks, and credit unions). Investment banks, finance companies, and mutual funds (unit trusts) also are common financial intermediaries.

Financial intermediation of all types decouples the savings and investment functions. All issue their own claims **(secondary securities),** whether in the form of insurance policies, certificates of deposit, mutual fund shares, and so on, to individuals and businesses and receive funds for doing so. These funds are then invested in financial markets in **primary securities** such as bonds, mortgages, and stocks. By doing so, investment is not confined to the sector in which the saving takes place. Funds can flow to the most productive sectors in an economy, which in turn implies the possibility of larger productivity gains.

Why Financial Intermediaries Exist

In economic models of perfect competition and complete markets, financial intermediaries would not exist. Firms and households, each with perfect information and incurring no transactions costs, would deal directly with each other, avoiding the expense of and having no need for the services of intermediaries. The real world, of course, affords less than perfect information and transactions are not costless.

In fact, investors do not have the time, resources, or ability to gather complete and adequate information about each possible financial transaction (i.e., lemon problems exist; see chapter 1). Financial intermediaries help solve these problems. Moreover, owner-investors cannot be certain that managers of the firms in which they invest will always work in their best interests (i.e., agency problems exist; see chapter 1). Owner-investors cannot constantly monitor managers. Financial intermediaries can help monitor the management of firms in which they invest and can conduct the research needed by investors.

Moreover, complete markets do not exist in which individuals can, in a frictionless environment, trade all possible financial claims among themselves to achieve their preferred mix of risk and liquidity. Financial intermediaries and financial markets enable individuals and businesses to change their existing risk and liquidity profiles. Hence, a household's risk profile can be changed by purchasing a life insurance policy on the principal wage earner's life, thus, in effect, providing an option, exercisable at death, for earnings lost because of premature death. Also, the household need not try to build a contingency reserve against the adverse financial consequences of premature death, thus allowing it to maintain less liquidity and, thereby, achieve a higher expected return on its resources.

In this transformation process, financial intermediaries price risk, a necessity for competitive market success. Life insurers do this at two levels. First, they price insurance (actuarial) risk, making for a more efficient allocation of society's limited insurance resources. In the process, of course, they must deal with their own information asymmetry problems (i.e., adverse selection and moral hazard). Second, they price risk through their investment activities, just as other financial intermediaries do. This pricing ensures a more efficient allocation of society's scarce financing resources.

Finally, financial intermediaries can lower transaction costs. Such costs would be quite high if each, typically small, investor dealt directly with firms.

Thus, the traditional rationale for financial intermediaries is that they help rectify the information asymmetry that exists between buyers and sellers, facilitate risk and liquidity transformation, and, through economies of scale, offer lower transactions costs than would exist otherwise.

Why an Understanding of Financial Intermediaries Is Important

Students of the life insurance business should understand, at a conceptual as well as a practical level, why financial intermediaries exist. Such an understanding permits a critical examination of the strategic role and functioning of life insurers. With the pace of technological, financial, and other change worldwide, we might find that the traditional rationales for and functioning of all financial intermediaries are evolving in ways that, if ignored, could doom a life insurer to failure. For example, transaction costs and costs associated with asymmetric information have fallen, yet intermediation has risen. Intermediation has become the major source of new financial resources flowing into the capital markets during the last several decades. Reconciling these changes with traditional theory is difficult. Some have suggested that a theory of intermediation based on risk trading and participation costs provides a more satisfactory contemporary explanation for the growing role of intermediaries in financial markets as well as their emphasis on the management of risk.[1]

With increased communication among buyers via the Internet and other media, we could find that technology allows more direct forms of risk and liquidity transformation. If insurer management fails to understand this evolution, business opportunities could be lost to other financial intermediaries or markets. Similarly, insurer owners and managers must consider thoughtfully the effects that declining asymmetric information and transactions costs could have on marketing, underwriting, pricing, and other insurer operations. Decisions grounded in a deep understanding of the theory of financial intermediation are likely to prove more enduring than those not so grounded.

FINANCIAL MANAGEMENT FUNDAMENTALS

Before exploring the financial management of life insurers, it will prove helpful to remind the reader of some underlying fundamentals. In this section, we examine briefly the concept of risk and return and the role of diversification in financial management.

The Goal of the Firm

The objective of any firm, including a life insurer, is to maximize the value of its owners' interest in the firm. With stock insurers, this means maximizing shareholder wealth; with mutual insurers, it means maximizing policyowner wealth. How, in principle, should managers of firms accomplish this goal? They should undertake projects whose net present value is positive. Stated differently, managers should maximize the firm's net cash flow.

Of course, the separation of ownership and management is a practical necessity for large firms today. We know that owners want to maximize their wealth, but each also has unique risk and liquidity preferences for lifetime consumption. If management is to act in the best interest of the firm's owners, how can it balance these conflicting owner objectives? The good news is that managers, at least in theory, need concern themselves only with maximizing owners' wealth and need not concern themselves with other owner objectives and preferences.

By assembling their own portfolio of financial assets, owners can determine their own consumption and risk profiles. They do not need management's help to do this. In fact, owners would not ordinarily want management to take their lifetime liquidity and

---

[1]See Franklin Allen and Anthony M. Santomero, "The Theory of Financial Risk Intermediation," *Journal of Banking & Finance,* 21 (1998), pp. 1461–1485.

risk preference goals into consideration. They want managers simply to maximize net present values, acting as risk-neutral agents for the owners and undertaking every project whose net present value is positive, irrespective of its risk.

Agency Problems

Regrettably, what is in the best interests of owners is not always in the best interest of management and vice versa.[2] This classic agency problem has been the focus of much study. Thus, managers may attempt to benefit themselves in terms of salary and perquisites at the expense of the owners. They may not work as diligently as they should and might not make financial decisions exclusively on net present value analysis; that is, they may consider riskiness.

Of course, the board of directors could fire insincere management. In theory, owners select the members of the board to look after their interests and to engage managers who will do likewise. In practice, it is not unusual for management to suggest nominees sympathetic to *their* interests and for such directors to have a stronger allegiance to management than to owners. The solution to this agency problem is to establish a system to monitor management and to try to seek a better alignment of management and owner interests. Managers can be monitored through audits, appropriate financial reporting, rating agencies, regulators, and other means. A better alignment of management–owner interests can be attained through offering management stock options, bonuses, and perquisites that are directly related to how closely management's actions benefit owners. The threat of an actual takeover by outside interests of the firm also encourages management to work for the interests of existing owners, for a takeover could mean a loss of their jobs.

Why Firms Manage Risk

If firms, including insurers, had strong monitoring systems and could address the incentive problem of aligning owner/manager interests better, there would be less motivation for the firm to reduce the volatility of its financial results. In practice, we know that financial intermediaries, in particular, devote considerable effort to manage their risks; in other words, they do not behave as risk-neutral decision makers. Four general reasons have been offered for this result:[3]

- managerial self-interest
- the nonlinearity of taxes
- the cost of financial distress
- the existence of capital market imperfections

As for managerial self-interest, besides the agency problems mentioned earlier, the concentration of managers' wealth (stock holdings and capitalized career earnings) in the firm they manage affords them little ability to diversify their personal wealth. This fact gives them an interest in avoiding volatility because, other things equal, stability improves their own situation. This logic applies especially to family-owned and other closely held insurance firms.

Also, under a nonproportional tax structure, stability of income can reduce the long-term average tax rate. Therefore, activities that reduce the volatility of reported earnings may actually enhance shareholder value.

---

[2]Agency problems, of course, exist in other relationships as well. The interests of debtholders and owners do not align perfectly, nor do the interests of insurance agents and management.

[3]This section draws on Anthony M. Santomero and David F. Babbel, "Financial Risk Management by Insurers: An Analysis of the Process," *The Journal of Risk and Insurance,* Vol. 64, No. 2 (1997), pp. 233–234.

The third reason offered for financial risk management by firms is the avoidance of the costs of financial distress. Financial distress is the threat of bankruptcy. This reason is believed by some to be the most compelling of the four and to be particularly relevant to regulated industries such as insurance. Financial distress leads to costs being imposed by regulators and the courts, which require various audits and accountings and place great demands on management time. Additionally, bankruptcy itself can be costly. Direct costs include payments for legal, accounting, actuarial, and other external advice as well as management's time. Numerous indirect costs are incurred, such as loss or suspension of licenses, loss of a market-dominant position, customers canceling their business, a falloff in new business, and, in general, the loss of intangible firm value, such as its reputation. For these reasons, firms may choose lower-risk strategies than if the costs of financial distress were minimal. In the process, they are actually maximizing owner value.

Finally, capital market imperfections are hypothesized to induce management to seek to reduce profit variability. With such conditions, finance external to the firm is more expensive than internal finance. These imperfections may be in the form of transaction costs associated with external finance, imperfect information about firm riskiness, or the high cost of financial distress. As long as the firm can finance positive net present value projects from internal funds, it need not rely on the more expensive external finance. However, because of volatility, external funds will be necessary at times if the firm is to take advantage of all appropriate projects. At such times, the higher cost of capital means that some projects exhibiting positive net present values at the internal cost of capital discount rate will reveal negative values at the higher external cost of capital. This results in underinvestment. Thus, the cost of volatility is the forgone investment in each period that the firm is forced to seek external funds. Because of this, the firm logically seeks to reduce volatility, thereby enhancing owner value.

Clearly, therefore, managers *are* concerned not only about expected profitability but also with the risk or variability of reported earnings and market values. To the extent that government, financial intermediaries, and markets can minimize the effects of any or all of the foregoing imperfections, expected returns to owners would be enhanced. Again, the challenge for insurer owners and executives is to develop a deep understanding of the means to ameliorate the factors that lead to motivations for *not* maximizing expected returns.

The Risk–Return Trade-Off

All financial intermediaries seek an adequate return on equity. To do this, management focuses on two features of performance—return and risk. The greater the risk of an investment (project), the higher will be the expected return.[4] The financial success of the firm is dependent on how well management balances these conflicting goals; management seeks an adequate return on equity while limiting the insurer's exposure to risks that might destroy it.

Behind this well-understood maxim resides a host of financial concepts. We explore some of them here. Note that the focus is on *expected* returns, for no one can know what *actual* returns will be. Figure 32-1 illustrates the concept.

Expected Return Defined and Measured

To achieve acceptable returns, management must be concerned with both the asset and liability sides of the balance sheet. For life insurers, liabilities arise principally in the form of policy reserves, which, in turn, flow from selling insurance policies. If prices are

---

[4]This section draws on A. J. Keown, J. W. Petty, D. F. Scott, Jr., and J. D. Martin, *Foundations of Finance* (Upper Saddle River, NJ: Prentice-Hall, 1998), Chapter 8.

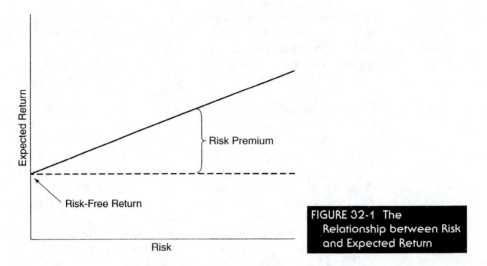

FIGURE 32-1 The Relationship between Risk and Expected Return

set too low, the insurer, in effect, is paying too much for its financing, thus depressing returns. On the asset side, loans and other primary securities similarly must be priced to achieve an adequate return, taking into consideration the possibilities of defaults. The key to acceptable financial performance is, therefore, the spread between what the insurer earns on its assets and what it must pay for its funds (liabilities).

Expected benefits or returns come in the form of cash flows. Cash flows, not accounting profits, is the relevant variable that the financial manager uses to measure returns. This principle holds true regardless of the type of security, project, or line of business.

Accurately measuring expected future cash flows is not easy in a world of uncertainty. To illustrate, assume ABC Life Insurer is considering offering a new annuity product, which will cost $10 million to launch, with future cash flows depending on the state of the economy, as estimated in Table 32-1.

In any given year, the investment could produce any one of three possible cash flows depending on the state of the economy. The expected value of the cash flow is simply the weighted average of the possible cash flow outcomes (CF_t), in which the weights are the probabilities of the occurrence of the various states of the economy [$P(CF_t)$]. Thus, the expected cash flow, *ECF,* may be calculated as follows:

$$ECF = \sum_{t=1}^{3} P(CF_t)(CF_t)$$

For this simple example, therefore, the expected cash flow is:

$$ECF = (0.2)(\$1,000,000) + (0.3)(\$1,200,000) + (0.5)(\$1,400,000) = \$1,260,000$$

In addition to computing an expected return from an investment, we can also calculate an expected rate of return earned on the $10 million investment. Similar to the expected cash flow, the expected rate of return is a weighted average of all the possible returns, weighted by the probability that each return will occur. The last column in Table 32-1 shows the rate of return for each state of the economy. The reader might verify that the weighted average is 12.6 percent.

If we were investigating the expected return of a portfolio of investments, we would simply weight each investment's expected return by its share of total investment. Thus, assume that an insurer held one-third of its portfolio in the foregoing investment whose

TABLE 32-1 Measuring ABC Life's Expected Return

State of the Economy	Probability of the State	Cash Flows from Project (000s)	Percentage Returns (Cash Flow/Investment)
Recession	20%	$1,000	10% ($1,000/$10,000)
Moderate growth	30%	$1,200	12% ($1,200/$10,000)
Strong growth	50%	$1,400	14% ($1,400/$10,000)

expected return was 12.6 percent, one-sixth in a bond whose return was 6.0 percent, and the balance in a security whose expected return was 10 percent. The portfolio's expected return, therefore, is 10.2 percent—the weighted average of the individual returns—calculated as follows:

$$[(1/3 \times 0.126) + (1/6 \times 0.06) + (1/2 \times 0.10)] = 10.2 \text{ percent}$$

The general formula for *n* securities is

$$r_i = \sum_{i=1}^{n} (x_i)(r_i)$$

where

$$x_i = \text{proportion invested in security } i$$
$$r_i = \text{expected return on security } i$$

Risk Defined and Measured

The second challenge facing insurer management is the control of risk. As we will see later, risks can be classified and managed in several ways. Additionally, risk carries multiple meanings. For purposes of financial management, however, we limit our attention to the financial meaning of **risk,** which is variability of future cash flows. The wider the range of possible events that can occur, the greater the risk. A common quantitative measure of risk is the standard deviation. The **standard deviation** (σ) is the square root of the variance. **Variance** is the weighted average squared deviations of each possible return from the expected return. Thus, we calculate the standard deviation as follows:

$$\sigma = \sqrt{\sum_{i=1}^{n} (r_i - \bar{r})^2 P(r_i)}$$

where

$$n = \text{number of possible outcomes or different}$$
$$\text{rates of return on an investment}$$
$$r_i = \text{the value of the } i\text{th possible rate of return}$$
$$\bar{r} = \text{the expected value of the rates of return}$$
$$P(r_i) = \text{the probability that the } i\text{th outcome or}$$
$$\text{return will occur}$$

The standard deviation is a useful measure of risk, especially for distributions of returns that are normally distributed ("bell shaped"). With normal distributions, we know that two-thirds of the time an event will fall within one standard deviation of the expected value. We know that it will fall within two standard deviations 95 percent of the time and within three standard deviations 99 percent of the time. Thus, as between two investments or projects having the same expected returns, we would prefer the one with the lower standard deviation (risk). Similarly, as between two projects with the same standard deviations, we would select that with the higher return.

Risk and Diversification

How Diversification Reduces Risk   The standard deviation is a useful measure of risk for an individual security.[5] Measures of variability also can be calculated for portfolios of securities. Returns on portfolios of securities are generally less volatile than returns for individual securities because diversification reduces risk. Diversification works because prices of different securities do not move exactly together. Stated differently, security prices are less than perfectly correlated.[6]

Figure 32-2 illustrates how portfolio variability decreases as we add securities to a portfolio of common stocks. The decrease occurs because some of the volatility of expected returns of each stock is unique to that stock; this is labeled **unique risk.**[7] The unique risk of each stock is countered to some extent by the unique risk of other stocks, thus reducing overall risk. Unique risk derives from the uniqueness of each firm, perhaps including its (and its competitors') unique environment. However, in practice, it is almost impossible to eliminate portfolio risk completely, as stock prices tend to move together. There is some risk—called **market or systematic risk**[8]—that cannot be avoided, regardless of diversification. Market risk stems from the fact that all businesses are subject to broad societal influences and factors that have a tendency to move together. Investors, therefore, will be exposed to some risk irrespective of the number of securities held.

Figure 32-2 shows that, for a portfolio holding only one or a few securities, unique risk is quite important. At about 20 or so securities, however, diversification has eliminated the great portion of unique risk. For reasonably well-diversified portfolios, therefore, only market risk matters.

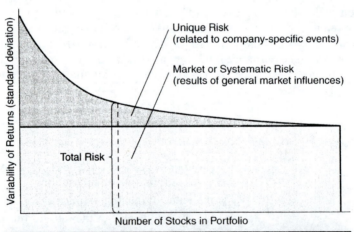

FIGURE 32-2   Variability of Returns Compared with Size of Portfolio

---

[5]We use the term *security* to refer to any asset or project.

[6]This and the following section draws on Richard A. Brealey and Stewart C. Myers, *Principles of Corporate Finance*, 5th ed. (New York: McGraw-Hill, Inc., 1996), pp. 153–165.

[7]Unique risk is also called unsystematic risk, diversifiable risk, specific risk, and residual risk.

[8]Market risk is also called undiversifiable risk.

TABLE 32-2	Calculating the Risk in a Two-Stock Portfolio	
	Company A's Stock	**Company B's Stock**
Company A's stock	$x_A^2 \sigma_A^2$	$x_A x_B \sigma_{AB} = x_A x_B \rho_{AB} \sigma_A \sigma_B$
Company B's stock	$x_A x_B \sigma_{AB} = x_A x_B \rho_{AB} \sigma_A \sigma_B$	$x_B^2 \sigma_B^2$

Measuring Market Risk We now explore more explicitly how the risk of a portfolio depends on the risk of the individual securities. Suppose that 60 percent of an insurer's investment portfolio is invested in the shares of Company A with the remainder in Company B. Expected returns for the coming year are 15 percent and 21 percent, respectively. The portfolio's expected return, therefore, is 17.4 percent $[(0.60 \times 0.15) + (0.40 \times 0.21)]$—the weighted average of the individual returns.

Assume that we know from past experience that the standard deviation of returns has been 18.6 percent and 28.0 percent for Companies A and B, respectively. We believe that these figures are a fair measure of the spread of possible future returns. To calculate the portfolio's overall risk, we cannot simply take the weighted average of the standard deviations of the individual securities; that is, 22.4 percent $[(0.60 \times 0.186) + (0.40 \times 0.28)]$. This would be correct *only* if the two securities' returns were perfectly correlated. In any other case, diversification will reduce the risk below this figure.

The procedure for calculating the risk of a two-stock portfolio is shown in Table 32-2. To complete the top left box, we weight the variance of the returns of Company A (σ_A) by the *square* of the proportion invested in it (x_A). Similarly, to complete the bottom right box, we weight the variance of the returns for Company B by the *square* of the proportion invested in it.

The entries in the diagonal boxes depend on the variances of the securities issued by Companies A and B; the entries in the other boxes depend on their **covariance,** which is a measure of the degree to which two values vary in tandem. The covariance can be expressed as the product of the correlation coefficient $\rho_{A,B}$ and the two standard deviations σ_A and σ_B.

Stock returns tend to move together. In this example, therefore, we assume a positive correlation coefficient and, therefore, the covariance is positive. If the prospects of the two stocks were wholly unrelated, both the correlation coefficient and the covariance would be zero; if the stocks tended to move in opposite directions, the correlation coefficient and covariance would be negative. Just as the variances were weighted by the square of the proportion invested, so we weight the covariance by the product of the two proportionate holdings in x_A and x_B.

Once the values of each box are computed, we simply add the entries to obtain the portfolio variance. Taking the square root yields the portfolio's standard deviation, our preferred measure of risk.

Thus, using past experience as a guide, we find that the correlation between the two stocks is 0.2. Portfolio variance is calculated as follows:

$$\text{Portfolio Variance} = [(0.60)^2 \times (18.6)^2] + [(0.40)^2 \times (28.0)^2]$$
$$+ 2(0.60 \times 0.40 \times 0.2 \times 18.6 \times 28.0)$$
$$= 300$$

The square root of 300 is 17.3. Thus, at a 17.3 percent standard deviation, the risk is now less than 40 percent between 18.6 and 28.0—in fact, it is less than the risk of either security separately.

The method of calculating portfolio risk can easily be extended to portfolios of any number (N) of securities. The matrix simply enlarges to $N \times N$ cells, with the individual security variances on the diagonal weighted by the square of the proportion invested in each, and the other boxes containing the covariance between each pair of securities, weighted by the product of the proportions invested.

With just two securities, the number of variance cells equals the number of covariance cells. With a portfolio of many securities, the number of covariances is much larger than the number of variances. Thus, the variability of a well-diversified portfolio reflects the covariances much more than individual security variances. An investor's portfolio is tied together by a web of positive covariances that set the limit to the benefits of diversification; that is, they collectively constitute market risk. The risk of a well-diversified portfolio, therefore, depends on the market risk of the securities included in the portfolio.

Measuring a Portfolio's Beta   Often we want to know the contribution of an individual security to the risk of a well-diversified portfolio. Such a contribution depends on how the security is liable to be affected by general market movements. It is of little benefit to think about how risky it is in isolation because investors care only about systemic risk and will not be compensated for risk that they can eliminate.

The sensitivity of a security's return to the market return is measured by **beta** (β). Beta measures market (systematic) risk, that is, the risk that remains after a portfolio is diversified. It is the amount that investors expect the stock price to change for each additional 1.0 percent change in the market. This is the only risk that matters for investors with diversified portfolios.

In statistical terms, a stock's beta is calculated by taking the ratio of (1) the covariance between the stock's and the market's returns to (2) the variance of the market return. The formula is as follows:

$$\beta_i = \sigma_{im} \div \sigma_m^2$$

Of course, the market is the portfolio of all stocks, so the average beta for all stocks is 1.0. Securities with betas of zero have no systematic risk. One-year Treasury notes have zero betas; their values are unaffected (if held to maturity) by changing market conditions. Securities with betas greater than 1.0 exhibit market risk greater than the typical stock. Stocks with betas below 1.0 tend to move in the same direction as the market but not as far. The betas for most stocks fall between 0.6 and 1.6.

Investors are interested in whether their portfolios as a whole are more or less sensitive to market changes, that is, whether their portfolio betas are greater or lesser than 1.0. To calculate the beta for a given portfolio, we simply take the weighted average of the individual stock betas. The weights equal the proportion of the portfolio invested in each security. Thus, if 50 percent of our portfolio is held in stocks with betas of 1.3 and the other half is held in stocks with betas of 1.1, our portfolio beta would be 1.2. We expect our portfolio, on average, to realize a 1.2 percent change in value for each 1.0 percent change in the market.

It is worth emphasizing that diversification is good for the individual investor because it lowers risk, and individual investors are risk averse. Were it not for the reasons discussed earlier as to why firm's manage risk, this same logic would not apply to firms whose shares are widely held. Corporate diversification would be redundant.

Constructing Efficient Portfolios   Most of the preceding ideas date back to Harry Markowitz's seminal 1952 article wherein he set out the basics of portfolio construction.[9] Using mean-variance analysis, Markowitz showed that it was possible to devise a set of portfolios that dominated all others, that is, portfolios that yielded the highest returns for a given risk.

---

[9]H. W. Markowitz, "Portfolio Selection," *Journal of Finance,* 7 (March 1952), pp. 77–91.

We can illustrate this concept using the earlier example of Companies A and B. Recall that the expected returns were 15 and 21 percent and that standard deviations were 18.6 and 28.0 percent, respectively. Company B offers a higher expected return but at considerably additional risk.

There is no reason, however, to limit our portfolio to a single stock only. We noted earlier that a portfolio composed of 60 percent Company B securities and 40 percent Company A securities would have an expected return of 17.4 percent with a standard deviation of 17.3 percent. Figure 32-3 shows expected return and risk values for different combinations of the two stocks. The investor can select from an array of possible risk–return combinations. If maximum expected return is the objective, irrespective of risk, a portfolio composed solely of Company B securities is called for. A minimum-risk portfolio, irrespective of return, would be composed 26.2 percent of B's securities and 73.8 percent of A's securities. Any portfolio composed of more than 73.8 percent of A's securities is dominated by some other portfolio in the sense that a higher return can be expected for the same risk.

Figure 32-4 shows this same principle applied to the entire market of securities. Each cross represents combinations of risk and return for individual stocks. By mixing

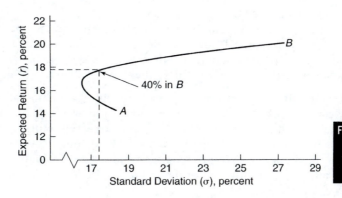

FIGURE 32-3 Expected Return and Risk Values for Different Combinations of Two Stocks

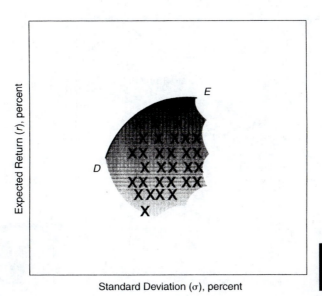

Standard Deviation (σ), percent

FIGURE 32-4 Expected Return and Risk Values for Entire Market of Securities

securities in different proportions, an even wider range of combinations can be obtained, perhaps something like the tinted area. The curved line DE is called the **efficient frontier** because it represents the set of efficient portfolios that dominate all other portfolios below and to the right of the line. From this set, the investor would select the portfolio that best matches his, her, or its risk–return preferences.

In 1958, James Tobin extended the Markowitz model to include the possibility of investor borrowing and lending at the same rate. The result was surprising: All investors would hold the same portfolio of securities. We explore this result briefly.

Assume that our investor puts some money in risk-free Treasury bills (i.e., lends money) and the remainder in common stock portfolio S, shown in Figure 32-5. Any combination of expected return and risk is possible along the straight line joining r_f and S. Because borrowing is simply negative lending, we can extend the range of possibilities to the right of S by borrowing funds at an interest rate of r_f and investing them along with other funds in portfolio S. (The model's validity is unaffected when borrowing and lending rates differ; only the slope of the line changes.)

Thus, the investor can lend money and end up somewhere between r_f and S or borrow and extend the range of risk–return choices beyond S. Regardless of the level of risk chosen, the highest expected return is achieved by a mixture of portfolio S and borrowing or lending. There would be no reason ever to hold portfolio T or any other portfolio along the efficient frontier, except S.

The investor, therefore, faces two decisions. First, find the optimum portfolio of securities, S in our example. Under certain rigorous conditions, it can be proven that this portfolio will be the market portfolio that, as we know, has a beta of 1.0. Second, decide how much to borrow or lend to achieve the desired balance between risk and return.

The Required Rate of Return   We complete our examination of financial fundamentals by connecting market risk to the investor's required rate of return. Risk is important, after all, only to the extent that it affects expected return. Security prices can be expected to reflect their risk, so we are also investigating the valuation of securities.

The minimum rate of return required by investors to acquire or hold a security depends on the opportunity cost of funds, that is, the return available from alternative,

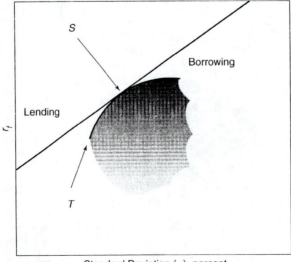

Standard Deviation (σ), percent

FIGURE 32-5 The Effect of Lending and Borrowing Treasury Bills on Expected Return and Risk Values

equivalent assets. We can think of this return (r) as being decomposed into two basic components: the risk-free rate (r_f) of return plus a risk premium (r_p); thus,

$$r = r_f + r_p$$

The risk-free return typically is measured by the U.S. Treasury bill rate. The risk-premium rate is the additional return expected for assuming the security's risk. The higher the risk, the greater the expected incremental return. But what is an appropriate risk premium?

Financial managers often use the **capital asset pricing model (CAPM),** which equates the expected return of a security to the risk-free rate plus a risk premium for the security's systematic risk.[10] The CAPM provides an intuitive way of thinking about the return that an investor should require from an investment, given the asset's systematic risk.

We can rearrange the preceding equation to solve for the risk premium as follows:

$$r_p = r - r_f$$

which simply indicates that the risk premium for a security equals the required return less the market's risk-free return. For example, if the required return of a security is 15 percent and the risk-free rate is 5 percent, the risk premium is 10 percent. Also, if the required return for the *market* portfolio (r_m) is 12 percent, the risk premium for the market would be 7 percent. This 7 percent risk premium would apply to any security having systematic (i.e., nondiversifiable) risk equivalent to the general market, or a beta of 1.0.

In this same market, a security with a beta of 2.0 should provide a risk premium of 14 percent, or twice the 7 percent risk premium existing for the market as a whole. Hence, in general, the appropriate required rate of return for the jth security, r_j, should be determined by the following formula:

$$r_j = r_f + \beta_j(r_m - r_f)$$

This formula is the CAPM. The equation designates the risk–return trade-off existing in the market in which the risk is defined in terms of beta. Figure 32-6 is a graph of the CAPM, assuming a risk-free return of 5 percent and an expected market return of 12 percent. This graph shows the appropriate required rate of return given a security's systematic risk and is called the **security market line.** For this figure, securities with betas equal to 0, 1.0, and 2.0 should have required rates of return as follows:

$$\text{If } \beta_j = 0: \quad r_j = 5\% + 0(12\% - 5\%) = 5\%$$
$$\text{If } \beta_j = 1.0: \quad r_j = 5\% + 1(12\% - 5\%) = 12\%$$
$$\text{If } \beta_j = 2.0: \quad r_j = 5\% + 2(12\% - 5\%) = 19\%$$

CAPM suggests that investors need not worry about the market portfolio; they need only decide how much systematic risk they wish to accept. Market forces will ensure that any stock can be expected to yield the appropriate return for its beta. Thus, if a stock is overvalued for its risk, fewer investors will hold it, thus depressing its price and increasing its expected return. Conversely, if a stock is undervalued, increased demand will drive up its price, thus lowering its expected return.

Assumptions underpinning all of modern portfolio theory are that transaction costs and taxes are negligible, that market participants have full information, that the information has been impounded in the security's price, and that no individual investor can influence market prices. These assumptions obviously do not comport with reality. However, the usefulness of a theory lies in its prediction accuracy, not the validity of its

---

[10]This presentation follows Keown et al., *Foundations of Finance*, p. 242.

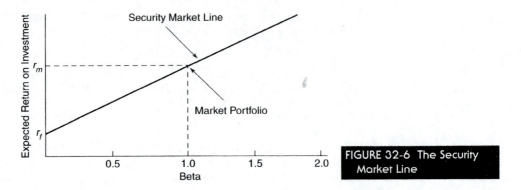

FIGURE 32-6 The Security Market Line

underlying assumptions, and many studies of CAPM suggest that it works reasonably well.

The CAPM, however, is not without its critics. Its theoretical foundations and accuracy have been questioned. An alternative theory posited by Stephen Ross has gained much acceptance in the financial community. Under the **arbitrage pricing theory (APT),** a security's price is explained by multiple economic factors rather than the single systematic risk factor. In effect, systematic risk is divided into smaller, undefined component risks. In some forms, the APT seems to price securities more accurately than the CAPM. However, the APT remains quite complex and difficult to grasp and use. For these reasons, it appears that the CAPM will remain the model of choice for financial management for the near term.

RISKS IN PROVIDING INSURANCE SERVICES

Insurers are in the risk business. They assume various types of actuarial and other risks in providing their services to the public. Insurers in the past, and to a great extent today, identify and manage these risks according to a classification of risks developed by the U.S. actuarial profession. Other financial intermediaries utilize a more general and more developed risk classification scheme. With increasing financial services convergence, we can anticipate a parallel convergence of the actuarial and financial views of risks. We explore both next.[11]

The Actuarial View of Risk

Traditionally, insurance companies have utilized a risk classification framework proposed years ago by a Society of Actuaries' committee. Under the actuarial view, the sources of risk to companies are grouped into four broad categories: (1) asset risk, (2) pricing risk, (3) interest rate risk, and (4) miscellaneous risks. Designated as contingency risks by the committee, these risks are labeled as C-1, C-2, C-3, and C-4 risks, respectively.

Asset Risk
Asset Depreciation (C-1) Risk is the risk that assets will lose value because of the possibility that (1) borrowers of insurer funds may default on their obligations to the company or (2) the market value of an insurer's investment assets may decline, except if

---

[11]This and the following sections draw from Santomero and Babbel, "Financial Risk Management by Insurers," pp. 233–270.

caused by interest rate movements. Clearly, a decrease in asset value reduces capital funds dollar for dollar, assuming no change in liability values. Because of leverage, however, the effect on capital is multiplied. Thus, if an insurer's capital equals 20 percent of its assets, a 10 percent decline in asset values will result in a 50 percent decline in capital.

In the case of bonds, the major bond rating agencies estimate the probability of default on bonds categorized by a given set of characteristics (see chapter 33). Their published ratings on bonds are based on historical default experience over a large number of bonds. Asset quality, of course, is not limited to bond investments. Ultimately, it is the risk that the insurer, because of poor asset quality, will be unable to pay its policyowners' claims in full or on time (claims-paying ability). Careful financial management through credit and investment analysis is the best risk management tool against asset risk. Readily available asset market values have facilitated management of this exposure. Historically, only the insurer's investment staff concerned itself with this risk.

Pricing Risk
Pricing Inadequacy (C-2) Risk is the risk that liabilities will increase in value because future operating results are worse than those implicit in product pricing. Negative deviations can occur because of higher than anticipated mortality, morbidity, lapse, or expense experience. Similarly, the possibility of lower than expected investment income or sales gives rise to pricing risk.

Pricing risk historically has been the primary province of product development and pricing actuaries. Capital decreases dollar for dollar with increases in liabilities, and, as with asset risk, the effect of this decrease relates directly to insurer leverage. Management of this risk is challenging because little market valuation information is available on insurers' liabilities, unlike the situation with asset risk. If an insurer's premium and investment income is based on assumptions that prove inadequate, it may be unable to meet its obligations to policyowners. As illustrated in Figure 32-7, inadequate pricing can eventually produce liabilities that exceed assets (i.e., insolvency).

Interest Rate Risk
Interest Rate (C-3) Risk is the risk that asset and/or liability values will be negatively affected by interest rate movements. Note that changes in asset and liability values occasioned by interest rate movements fall within the C-3 risk category, not in the C-1 or C-2 categories. The effect on an insurer's balance sheet of fluctuating rates is complex and, if different for assets than for liabilities, the insurer could be exposed to insolvency. Fortunately, the effects are subject to reasonable measurement and management,

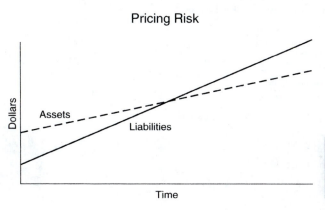

Pricing Risk

Dollars

Assets

Liabilities

Time

FIGURE 32-7 The Impact on Company Net Worth of Inadequate Insurance Product Pricing over Time

using the financial concepts of duration and convexity, as discussed later in this chapter. The precise linkage between interest rate movements and asset and liability values will depend on whether interest rates are rising or falling.

In a rising interest rate environment, both asset and liability values ordinarily will decrease. The financial manager's worry is that the asset decrease exceeds the liability decrease, thus reducing capital. Also, with rising interest rates, more policyowners than projected may exercise their policy surrender and loan options, necessitating the forced sale of assets at depressed prices, leading to a liquidity crisis.

In a falling interest rate environment, both asset and liability values ordinarily will increase. The risk here is that liabilities increase at a more rapid pace than assets, thus reducing capital. Also, more policyowners than projected may exercise their option to add funds to their contracts, necessitating the purchase of additional assets at high prices.

As a result of asset–liability mismatching, an insurer may incur a liquidity shortage. This lack of liquidity can arise even though the total book value of investments is more than sufficient to satisfy the total book value of obligations. Figure 32-8 illustrates conceptually that, although assets may exceed liabilities, current or cash assets may be insufficient to meet current or cash liabilities.

Miscellaneous Risks

The fourth actuarial classification of risk, **miscellaneous (C-4) risks,** includes risks associated with social, legal, political, technological, and all other changes not included in the three preceding classifications. This category includes risks associated with product obsolescence, tax and regulatory changes, loss of confidence in the insurer by policyowners, and liability arising from market misconduct of company employees or agents. C-4 risks lend themselves neither to prediction nor to quantitative analysis. The extent to which these risks are appropriately controlled depends to a great degree on the quality of insurer management, which is itself a type of C-4 risk. It is for these reasons that rating agencies place great weight on management quality in their company reviews and ratings.

Box 32-1 provides a summary of the actuarial view of risks. The box includes short definitions of each risk class and descriptions of the types of risk included in each category.

The Financial View of Risks

In contrast to the actuarial decomposition of risk, financial risk definitions are used by noninsurer financial intermediaries and are coming under increasing consideration by insurers. The classification scheme suggested by Santomero and Babbel (S&B) serves

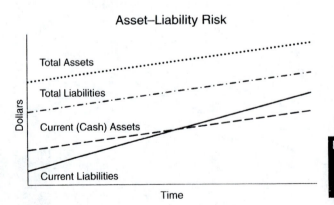

FIGURE 32-8 The Impact on Liquidity of Asset–Liability Mismatch Despite Long-Term Solvency

BOX 32-1

THE ACTUARIAL RISK CLASSIFICATION

ASSET RISK (C-1)

- Loss in assets' market value, except if caused by interest rate movements
- Borrower's default in payment of interest
- Borrower's default in payment of principal

PRICING RISK (C-2)

- Adverse change in mortality or morbidity experience
- Increase in cost of providing health care
- Increase in company's operating expenses

INTEREST RATE RISK (C-3)

- Assets' loss of value because of interest rate increases; loss on forced sales of assets when interest rates rise

- Withdrawals by customers when interest rates rise
- Loss on bond calls and mortgage prepayments when interest rates fall
- Losses due to asset–liability mismatches

MISCELLANEOUS RISKS (C-4)

- Market risk from expansion into new lines of business
- Market risk from geographic expansion
- Changes in tax law
- Fraud
- Mismanagement
- Lawsuits
- Guaranty fund assessments
- Runs on assets caused by fear of insolvency

Source: Adapted from S. Conant, N. L. Desoutter, D. L. Long, and R. MacGrogan, *Managing for Solvency and Profitability in Life and Health Insurance Companies*, LOMA, 1996, p. 391.

our purposes well and is followed here.[12] Of course, this list is not exhaustive—many other types of risks exist, such as reputational risk, environmental risk, and off-balance-sheet risk. Moreover, some overlap between categories exists. S&B decompose risk into these six categories:

- actuarial risk
- systematic risk
- credit risk
- liquidity risk
- operational risk
- legal risk

This section briefly reviews each of these risks.

Actuarial Risk

Actuarial risk is the risk that arises from an insurer developing funds via the issuance of insurance policies and other liabilities. In financial terms, it is the risk that the insurer has charged too little for the options that it has sold insureds in the form of the provisions and promises embedded in their insurance policies. In such cases, the insurer cannot expect to achieve satisfactory cash flow in the long run.

The finance profession's definition of actuarial risk probably encompasses all of the actuarial profession's C-2 (pricing) risk. As conceptualized, however, actuarial risk

---

[12]Ibid.

would be valued and analyzed more from an options pricing point of view than from the traditional actuarial pricing point of view.

The most obvious actuarial risk, of course, is the risk that mortality or morbidity experience deviates negatively from that implicit in the insurer's pricing. This could happen because either projections themselves were based on an inadequate knowledge of the loss distribution or losses exceed projections in the normal course of business. The degree to which they deviate from the projected basis (the mean) will depend on the precise nature of the risks insured. In many instances, however, this risk is actually less important than that which arises from other policy options, particularly the policy surrender and loan options.

Because of the relative stability historically of voluntary termination rates in the United States, policy loans and surrenders were viewed as contract design features that provided convenience to customers, increased the marketability of life insurance products, and satisfied the requirements of state law. These contractual features had been viewed as ancillary matters when they were actually embedded financial options with real economic value.

The policy loans and surrender option features of U.S. cash-value life insurance contracts represent book value withdrawal rights to policyowners. Indeed, all life insurance policy provisions providing policyowner flexibility are embedded options. Because of the unilateral nature of life insurance contracts, the policy can be viewed as a package of options. These options provide an opportunity to select against the insurer, and policyowners should be expected to exercise the options in their own best interest. Thus, the policyowner has the right to receive cash values on demand in the same way a checking account owner has the right to receive the account balance on demand.

Liquidity problems can arise for insurers when cash values are guaranteed at book value, while the market value of investments backing the cash-value guarantee fluctuates with market interest rates. Policyowner demand for withdrawals, whether by loan or surrender, is highest at precisely the wrong time for the insurer, that is, when interest rates are rising and market values are declining. These options are particularly valuable when policyowners have investment opportunities that yield higher returns than their insurance policies.

Actuarial risk also arises when the external investment opportunities for policyowners are less attractive than the embedded investment options in their insurance policies. As interest rates fall, cash-value earnings may become more attractive than other market opportunities. This is particularly true of insurers that employ the portfolio average method of interest crediting. Additionally, fixed-interest policy loans may be repaid and flexible premiums increased.

During the late 1970s and early 1980s, many U.S. life insurance companies were heavily invested in long-term bonds when inflation and interest rates were rising rapidly. Table 32-3 summarizes expected client behavior and company impact under different interest rate scenarios. The expected results ensued.

Systematic Risk
Systematic risk, also called **market risk,** is the risk of asset and liability value changes associated with broad economic factors. We know that this risk cannot be eliminated by diversification. It can be hedged against, however, as we discuss in the following chapter. Systematic risks come in numerous forms, such as foreign exchange risk, inflation risk, basis risk, interest rate risk, and a host of others. Most large insurers track and manage each of the major systematic risks individually. The most important of these systematic risks for most financial intermediaries, especially life insurers, is interest rate risk, which we focus on here.

TABLE 32-3 The Expected Impact of Different Interest Rate Environments on Policyowner and Investment Client Behavior

	Rising Interest Rates	*Declining Interest Rates*
Expected investment client behavior	Mortgages and bonds held as long as possible—the number of refinancings declines	Call bonds Repay mortgages at a higher rate
Expected policyowner behavior	Make policy loans Surrender policies Suspend flexible premiums	Increase flexible premiums Repay loans Persist
Insurer impact	Cash shortage	Cash glut
Insurer options	Sell investments at a loss Borrow at high new-money rates	Reinvest at low new-money rates

Of course, interest rate risk follows from the fact that life insurers facilitate the transformation of insureds' liquidity and risk positions. They sell their own secondary securities (insurance contracts) to customers, investing the proceeds in primary securities (bonds, stocks, mortgages, etc.). These primary securities often have maturity and liquidity characteristics that differ from the insurer's secondary securities. This mismatch is the source of interest rate risk (as well as most other systematic risks). This financial risk classification conforms most closely to the interest rate (C-3) risk within the actuarial risk classification but also subsumes a portion of the asset (C-1) risk that relates to decreases in the market value of assets, other than those caused by interest rate changes.

A deeper exploration of this important risk is justified because of its importance to life insurers.[13] We do this through an example. Assume that an insurer sells one-year endowment policies guaranteeing a yield of 9 percent and invests the proceeds in two-year bonds yielding 10 percent per annum. The following illustrates the time lines for the securities:

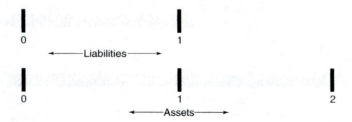

Refinancing Risk At the end of the first year, the insurer realizes a positive spread of 1 percent from having "borrowed" short term (one year) and lent long term (two years). Profits in the second year, however, depend on the rate of interest that it is required to credit to endowments in a possibly changed interest rate environment. If the insurer is able to maintain the same crediting rate during the second year, it can again benefit from

[13]This summary follows that of Anthony Saunders, *Financial Institutions Management*, 2nd ed. (Chicago: Irwin, 1997), pp. 73–75.

a 1 percent spread. If market interest rates have fallen and it can credit a lower interest rate, say, 8 percent, it will enjoy a 2 percent spread. The insurer, however, runs a risk that market interest rates will rise to 11 percent during the next year, in which case the insurer must credit that rate to be able to sell its one-year endowments to meet its financing needs. It must obtain new funds to avoid having to sell the two-year securities to meet cash needs. In this latter case, the insurer's profit spread in the second year would be –1 percent, offsetting its first-year profit.

Whenever an insurer holds longer-term assets relative to its liabilities, it exposes itself to refinancing risk. **Refinancing risk** is the risk that the cost of rolling over or refinancing funds could be more than the return earned on assets. The financial difficulties incurred by thrift institutions in the United States during the late 1980s are classic examples of this mismatch.

Refinancing risk also exists because of the tendency of borrowers whose instruments carry relatively low interest rates to delay repayments to the maximum extent possible. This practice effectively lengthens asset maturity, aggravating the mismatch.

Reinvestment Risk   Assume now that the insurer sold single-premium, two-year endowment policies crediting 9 percent per annum, investing the funds in one-year bonds to yield 10 percent. This situation is shown as follows:

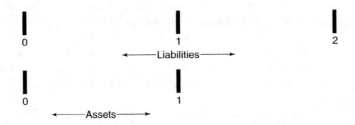

As before, the insurer locks in a 1 percent profit spread in the first year. At the end of the first year, the asset matures and the maturity proceeds must be reinvested. If market interest rates have fallen to 8 percent, the insurer would suffer a negative 1 percent spread during the second year. This is an example of reinvestment risk, which exists by holding shorter-term assets relative to liabilities. **Reinvestment risk** is the risk that the return earned on newly acquired assets is less than the cost of financing. The recent financial difficulties incurred by several Asian countries illustrate the risks associated with this type of interest rate risk. (It also illustrates exchange rate risk.)

Reinvestment risk also exists because of the tendency of borrowers to call bonds and to prepay mortgages. These practices aggravate the gap by further shortening asset maturity.

Market-Value Risk   In addition to potential refinancing and reinvestment risk that occurs when interest rates change, insurers also face **market-value risk,** which is the change in asset and liability values caused by a change in interest rates. Recall that the market value of an asset or liability equals the present value of its cash flows. Rising interest rates increase the discount rate, thus lowering the market value of assets and liabilities. Conversely, falling interest rates increase market values of assets and liabilities. Moreover, if asset maturities are longer term than liabilities, a rise in interest rates will cause a greater decline in asset than liability values, exposing the insurer to losses and potential insolvency.

Maturity Matching If holding assets and liabilities with mismatched maturities exposes insurers to reinvestment, refinancing, and market-value risk, they can be approximately hedged against interest rate changes by matching the maturity of their assets and liabilities. This has resulted in the general philosophy that matching maturities is somehow the best policy for insurers averse to risk. Note that matching maturities works against an active asset-transformation function for insurers. That is, they cannot be asset transformers and direct balance sheet hedgers at the same time. While reducing exposure to interest rate risk, matching maturities may also reduce the profitability of being an insurer because any returns from acting as a specialized financial intermediary are eliminated.

Finally, matching maturities hedges only interest rate risk in a very approximate fashion. The reasons for this are technical, relating to the difference between the average life (duration) and maturity of an asset or liability and how the insurer funds its assets. We take up this more technical treatment later in this chapter.

Credit Risk

Credit risk is the risk that promised cash flows on primary securities held by the insurer may not be paid in full. The actuarial C-1 (asset) risk includes credit risk (and more—see Figure 32-9). Nonperformance can be a result of either an inability or unwillingness on the part of the borrower to meet his, her, or its contractual obligations. Such nonperformance (default) affects not only the investor holding the bond or loan contract but other investors and lenders to the creditor as well. As a result, the financial condition of the borrower and the current value of any underlying collateral are of considerable interest to investors.

Firm-specific credit risk is diversifiable in accordance with the law of large numbers. Some portion of credit risk, however, stems from broad economic factors—so-called systematic credit risk—and is undiversifiable. Credit risk also includes **country (sovereign) risk,** which arises when governments interfere with their nationals paying foreign creditors.

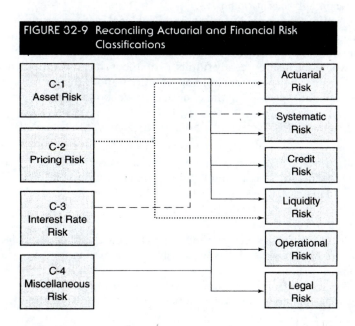

FIGURE 32-9 Reconciling Actuarial and Financial Risk Classifications

Liquidity Risk

Liquidity risk is, in essence, the risk of a funding crisis. The actuarial risk classification subsumes liquidity risk in the C-3 (interest rate) risk and, perhaps, also in part of the C-1 (asset) risk.

Ordinarily, insurer cash outflows are predictable; in fact, cash inflows usually are larger than cash outflows, thus minimizing the need for insurers to hold excessive amounts of cash. A cash crisis can arise, however, from unexpected events, such as a very large claim, a writedown of assets, a loss of confidence, or a legal crisis. Insurers operate in markets in which they can face massive requests for policy loans and surrenders due to changing interest rates.

Investments in private placements and real estate have relatively limited liquidity. It is important that an insurer maintains sufficient liquidity to respond easily to any demands for cash. Unless in such a position, an otherwise solvent insurer may have to sell illiquid assets at sacrifice prices, which can lead to significant losses. This in turn could lead to further demands for cash and even insolvency.

Operational Risk

Operational risk is the risk that system failures or human errors will substantially disrupt operations. Operational risks include technological problems or failure, fraud, negligence, accident, acts of God, failure of supply or marketing channels, and any other disruptive factor. These risks often reflect inadequate internal controls and procedures. Record keeping, processing system failures, and compliance with various regulations are other sources of operational risk.

Although well-run organizations normally face a low probability of a significant loss in this area, in unusual circumstances, the exposure can be quite expensive. Operational risk would fall within the actuarial C-4 (miscellaneous) risk classification.

Legal Risks

Legal risk is the risk that new government laws, regulations, or court opinions may decrease the value of the firm. Legal risk also falls within the C-4 actuarial risk category. This risk permeates financial contracting, separate from the legal problems involved with credit and operational risks.

Insurers are exposed to another type of legal risk as a result of the activities of their management, employees, and agents. Violations of laws or regulations, fraud, and other actions can lead to massive fines or court awards. Current examples demonstrate that, even where the insurer legally fulfills all of its contract obligations, massive litigation can result if some policyowners hold expectations about the performance of their policies other than that specified in the contracts (see chapter 9).

Reconciling the Actuarial and Financial Views of Risk

Depending on an insurer's business mix, its exposure to each of these risks will be different. In establishing corporate targets, each insurer must weigh both the return and the risk embedded in its asset and liability portfolios. Good risk management requires that expected net cash flows be measured and the various risks discussed previously evaluated in developing strategic plans that will achieve the goal of maximizing shareholder and policyowner value.

Box 32-2 lists the foregoing six financial risk classifications, along with a short definition of each. Figure 32-9 offers a schematic relating the actuarial risk and financial risk classifications.

The actuarial and the financial views of risk differ. This difference is considered by many to be an important barrier impeding progress toward effective financial risk man-

BOX 32-2

FINANCIAL RISK CLASSIFICATION

ACTUARIAL RISK

- Firm is paying too much for the funds it receives
- Firm has received too little for the risks it has agreed to absorb (e.g., pricing and underwriting losses)

SYSTEMATIC RISK

- Asset and liability value changes associated with broad economic factors (e.g., variations in the general level of interest rates, market-value variation, and inflation)

CREDIT RISK

- Borrower does not perform in accordance with a precommitted contract

LIQUIDITY RISK

- A funding crisis associated with an unexpected event (e.g., a large claim or a writedown in assets, a loss of confidence, or a legal crisis)

OPERATIONAL RISK

- Inaccurately processing claims, and inaccurately processing, settling, and taking or making delivery of trades in cash
- Record keeping
- Processing system failures
- Lack of compliance with various regulations

LEGAL RISK

- New statutes
- Court opinions
- Regulations

Source: Anthony M. Santomero and David F. Babbel, "Financial Risk Management by Insurers: An Analysis of the Process," *The Journal of Risk and Insurance,* Vol. 64, No. 2 (1997), pp. 238–239.

agement in the insurance business.[14] Both views encompass most of the same risks, but the contexts in which they are measured and weighted are different, resulting in different treatments of risk. The actuarial view, with its focus on risks in isolation and their impact on statutory accounting statements, is said to foster risk measures that do not aggregate well at the firm level and leads to a piecemeal rather than a holistic approach to risk management. The advantage of the financial view is that it examines risk in terms of its impact on firm economic value. Risk aggregation and covariance are the focus. Until a unified view of risk is accepted, there will continue to be too wide a range of ways by which financial risk is managed by insurers. The insurance industry is currently in a transitional period as it moves from using the actuarial view of risk toward using the financial view of risk.

Risk as Central to a Life Insurer's Franchise

What Risks Are Being Managed?

Insurers assume various kinds of actuarial and financial risks in providing their services. In some cases, they will transfer the risk to third parties through a combination of reinsurance, pricing, and product design. In other cases, insurers will eliminate or mitigate the actuarial and financial risks through proper business practices. Sound risk

[14]Santomero and Babbel, "Financial Risk Management by Insurers," p. 241.

management principles dictate that life insurers should absorb and manage only those risks at the firm level that are uniquely part of the services insurers offer. Two classes of activities should and must be actively managed at the firm level. The first of these includes exposures in which the nature of the embedded risk may be complex and difficult to transfer to third parties. It also includes complex proprietary assets (e.g., private placements) in which there are only limited or no secondary markets. Transferring such risks will be difficult and expensive. As a result, it may be more appropriate to hedge the underlying risk.

The second class of risks are those that are central to an insurer's business purpose—actuarial and financial risks inherent in key insurance lines—and must be absorbed and managed efficiently by the insurance company. Risk management is essential to life insurer financial management.

How Are These Risks Managed?

In general, an insurer relies on a variety of risk management techniques in managing risks. These include (1) standards and reports, (2) underwriting authority and limits, (3) investment guidelines or strategies, and (4) incentive contracts and compensation design. These tools are used to help control risk exposures and encourage managers to manage risk in a manner consistent with the insurer's goals and objectives.

Standards and Reports   Management must understand the risks on both sides of the balance sheet and in cash flows. Consistency in evaluating and rating asset and liability risk exposures is essential in determining the extent to which risks should be mitigated or absorbed. Underwriting standards and standards of review are basic tools of risk control. An important element in this connection is the standardization of financial reporting. In addition to statutory and GAAP statements, management needs standardized information on actuarial risk, asset quality, and overall risk posture with a frequent reporting schedule (daily, weekly, and monthly, as is appropriate).

Underwriting Authority and Limits   As discussed in chapters 25, 26, and 33, internal control of management activity is effected through the use of limits and minimum underwriting and asset quality standards. Risk taking is restricted to those customers or assets that pass some prespecified quality standard. In addition, limits are imposed to cover exposures to counterparties, credits, and overall position concentration relative to various types of risks. Management monitors the evolving experience through accurate and timely reports. In large organizations, accurate and timely reporting of evolving experience can be difficult. Timely reporting, however, is even more essential in such organizations.

Investment Guidelines or Strategies   As discussed in chapter 33, investment strategies are communicated by establishing policy guidelines in terms of concentration and commitments to particular areas of investment, the extent of desired asset–liability mismatching, and the need to hedge against certain systematic risks (discussed later). As a result of these limits and guidelines, passive risk avoidance takes place and/or diversification is obtained because managers generally operate within the established guidelines. In addition, securitization and derivative activity are available to the individual manager to keep risk exposure in line with policy guidelines.

Incentive Compensation Schemes   As discussed earlier in this chapter and in chapter 23, the objective of well-designed compensation systems is to align the goals of managers with the firm's owners. To the extent that an insurer can enter into properly designed contracts with senior management and other employees (including sales agents), relating compensation to the risks borne by those individuals, the cost and extent of risk management controls can be lessened.

LIFE INSURER RISK MANAGEMENT

Traditional approaches to life insurer financial management worked well in a stable economic and improving mortality environment. The probability of loss due to asset default, inadequate pricing, or asset–liability mismatch could be effectively managed through asset diversification, conservative pricing, and simple bond dedication. Virtually all life insurer products were profitable, net cash flow was almost always positive, and loss of market share was considered to be the principal exposure to adverse financial performance.

Because of the new volatility exhibited by life insurer cash flows and an increasingly integrated and competitive financial intermediation market, it has become critically important to measure and manage risk more effectively. As noted at the beginning of this chapter, the concept of variability as a measure of risk was developed and applied to investment portfolio management in the middle of the twentieth century. New financial tools have followed, ultimately to build a reasonably complete modern portfolio theory. Its application to the management of life insurer asset and liability cash flows involves (1) the identification of key control variables and (2) the establishment of constraints that define the maximum level of variability acceptable to management (risk posture), given its philosophy regarding profitability and the risk of insolvency.

For most life insurers, the key control variables are solvency (on both a statutory and cash flow or liquidity basis) and profitability. At a minimum, life insurers should establish risk management constraints designed to avoid:

- regulatory intervention due to statutory insolvency
- the forced sale of assets or need to assume debt obligations to meet cash flow solvency requirements

To define, measure, and control insurer financial risk, effective financial management requires application of modern statistical and financial techniques. In this section, we structure an examination of life insurer risk management practices around the financial risks discussed previously.

Actuarial Risk

As discussed earlier, when interest rates are volatile, policy options gain in value and their utilization rates can fluctuate widely. Today, standard valuation methods are available to permit these embedded options to be explicitly valued. Available software uses modern stochastic valuation techniques to estimate the values of insurance policies in a manner consistent with that used to value assets. Although this represents an important step forward in risk valuation, the stochastic valuation methodology most commonly used still relies on only one stochastic factor. A more serious problem is that most insurers have inadequate data collected and assembled with which to reliably model the interest sensitivity of policy option utilization.

Perhaps the greatest concern in the area of actuarial risk management is the agency problem of alignment of incentives between owners of the company and its sales and marketing staff. The payment of commissions on heavily front-loaded contracts creates strong incentives to replace existing policies. Sales managers and marketing personnel are often compensated based on volume of sales. Experience has shown that too rapid growth is one of the factors commonly associated with insolvency. Employees and agents, whose compensation is tied to sales growth, tend to be strong proponents of more "competitively priced" policies. Pricing actuaries are often under tremendous pressure to alter their assumptions so that the company's products can be priced more competitively.

Sales agents often represent a number of insurers and can shift new business to maximize their own earnings. Furthermore, they can shift existing business before an insurer can recover heavy acquisition costs.

Systematic Risk

In recent years, managing interest rate risk has become a major focus of attention of life insurers. Most insurers now recognize the importance of understanding, measuring, and managing interest rate risk.

To understand the management of systematic risk, it is necessary to understand the statistical measures of risk used in life insurer risk management systems. The two most important measures are duration and convexity.[15]

Understanding Duration

We discussed earlier that financial intermediaries are exposed to interest rate risk through refinancing, reinvestment, and market-value risks. Life insurers can somewhat hedge these risks through a policy of matching the maturities of assets and liabilities, but such a policy is of limited effectiveness because it fails to take fully into consideration the timing of cash flows or, stated differently, the average life of assets and liabilities. Duration is a more complex but more complete measure of asset and liability sensitivity to interest rate movements than is maturity. It takes account of the timing of all cash flows, not just maturity cash flows.

Intuitively, **duration** can be thought of as the average life of an asset or liability. A way of visualizing duration is to imagine future cash flows as discreet weights on a plank, with the maturity value usually being the heaviest. The fulcrum that just balances the plank is analogous to the duration. Technically, duration is the weighted-average time to maturity using the relative present values of the cash flows as weights.

The Duration Formula The calculation of duration begins with cash flow estimation for each asset and liability. The cash flows are then discounted by the current market interest rate. These discounted cash flows are used as weights that are applied to each cash flow to derive the weighted-average maturity. The weighted-average maturity is the duration.

The formula for the calculation of duration is:

$$\text{Duration} = \frac{\displaystyle\sum_{t=1}^{n} \frac{CF_t}{(1+r)^t} * t}{\displaystyle\sum_{t=1}^{n} \frac{CF_t}{(1+r)^t}}$$

where

CF_t = cash flow at end of period t

n = the last period in which cash flow is received

r = the market yield to maturity

Note that the denominator is the present value of the asset or liability cash flows, in other words, its economic value.

Table 32-4 shows the calculation of duration for a six-year bond with a face value of $1,000, an annual coupon of 8 percent, and a market interest rate of 8 percent.

---

[15]This discussion draws from and follows partially that presented by Saunders, *Financial Institutions Management*, chapter 7.

TABLE 32-4 Calculation of Duration for a Six-Year Bond, Face Value $1,000, Annual Coupon of 8 Percent and a Market Interest Rate of 8 Percent

t	CF_t	$\dfrac{1}{(1+r)^t}$	$(CF_t)\left(\dfrac{1}{(1+r)^t}\right)$	$(CF_t)\left(\dfrac{1}{(1+r)^t}\right)(t)$
1	$ 80	0.9259	$ 74.0741	$ 74.0741
2	80	0.8574	68.5871	137.1742
3	80	0.7938	63.5066	190.5197
4	80	0.7350	58.8024	235.2096
5	80	0.6806	54.4467	272.2333
6	$1,080	0.6302	680.5832	4,083.4990
			$1,000.0000	$4,992.7100

$$\text{Duration} = \frac{4,992.71}{1,000.00} = 4.993 \text{ years}$$

Characteristics of Duration   Several important characteristics of duration are worthy of note. First, it should be obvious that *duration increases with increases in the maturity of fixed-income assets or liabilities.* Because duration relies on a present value calculation, however, duration does not increase as rapidly as does maturity.

Second, *duration decreases with increases in the yield to maturity.* This makes sense as later cash flows are discounted more heavily at higher yields (r) and their relative importance declines.

Third, *the lower the coupon or interest payment, the lower the duration.* This also makes sense because the larger the early payments, the sooner cash flows are received and the higher (lower) the present value weights of those flows.

The Economic Meaning of Duration   Duration directly measures the sensitivity or elasticity of an asset or liability to small interest rate changes. As such, it can be used to predict a change in the price (P) of an asset due to a small change in interest rates. The larger the value of an asset's or liability's duration, the more sensitive it is to interest rate changes. Thus,

$$\text{Duration} = \frac{\dfrac{\Delta P}{P}}{\dfrac{\Delta P}{1+r}}$$

or

$$\frac{\Delta P}{P} = -D\left(\frac{\Delta r}{1+r}\right)$$

and

$$\Delta P = -D\left(\frac{\Delta r}{1+r}\right)P$$

Thus, duration measures the price elasticity of an asset or liability with respect to changes in interest rates.

Consider the six-year bond shown in Table 32-4. If interest rates decline by 1 basis point (0.0001), the percentage change in price is predicted to be

$$\frac{\Delta P}{P} = -(4.993)\left(\frac{-0.0001}{1.08}\right) = 0.0462\%$$

and the predicted change in price is

$$\Delta P = -(4.993)\left(\frac{-0.0001}{1.08}\right)(\$1,000) = \$4.62$$

and

$$P' = P + \Delta P = \$1,004.62$$

Were market yields to fall by 25 basis points, the expected price change in the bond would be

$$\Delta P = -(4.993)\left(\frac{-0.0025}{1.08}\right)(\$1,000) = \$11.56$$

so, $P' = \$1,011.56$.

To restate, the economic interpretation is that duration is the **interest elasticity** of a security's price to *small* changes in interest rates.

Duration and Immunization

Duration is relevant as a measure of a life insurer's interest rate risk exposure. It allows the financial manager to so select assets and liabilities as to immunize all or a portion of the balance sheet against interest rate risk. We explore how this is accomplished in this section.

Immunizing Future Payments   Life insurers know that they face future cash payments to policyowners and beneficiaries. They want to match their asset cash flows to these payments. Assume XYZ Life's actuaries have concluded that its life insurance claims exactly five years hence will be $1,469,000. The company's chief financial officer (CFO) wishes to invest assets now so that XYZ will have exactly $1,469,000 five years hence to honor its obligations to the beneficiaries. The CFO calculates that, at 8 percent, the present value of those claims is $1 million. Current-issue, five-year bonds pay an 8 percent annual coupon, and the current market yield for the bond is 8 percent. Thus, if $1 million is invested in these bonds today, they should produce $1,469,000 in five years.

The total return on a bond is comprised of (1) coupon payments, (2) interest earned on the coupon payments (reinvestment income), and (3) proceeds from the redemption or sale of the bond. Thus, the three components of XYZ's income are calculated as follows:

1. Coupon payments equal $400 (five annual coupons of $80 each).
2. Reinvestment income equals $69 (as the annual coupons are received, they can be reinvested at 8 percent, generating an additional $69 after five years).[16]
3. Proceeds at redemption equal $1,000, the bond maturity value.

---

[16]The coupons represent an immediate annuity certain (the payments are made at the end of each period).

The formula for the accumulated value of an immediate annuity is $S_n, n, r = \left[\frac{(1+r)^n - 1}{r}\right]$ or, in this case,

$S_n, 5, 8 = \left[\frac{(1+0.08)^3 - 1}{0.08}\right] = 5.687$. Reinvestment income is, therefore, $5.687 \times \$80 - \$400 = \$69$. We subtract the $400 because we have already counted the coupons.

The total return for $1 million in bonds should be $1,469,000, and XYZ will have precisely funded its fifth-year expected claims.

Suppose, however, that interest rates decline to 7 percent immediately after the bonds are acquired. What would be the total return? The $400 in coupons and the $1,000 maturity value would be unaffected, but reinvestment income would fall to $60 from $69.[17]

If market interest rates fall, XYZ would find itself vulnerable. Because of the reduced reinvestment income, total return would be about $9,000 ($9 × 1,000 bonds) less than expected. This result would directly reduce XYZ's expected surplus by that amount.

We saw in Table 32-4 that the duration of a six-year, 8 percent, annual coupon bond at 8 percent current yield to maturity is 4.993 years. The total return of this bond to approximately five years (one year *before* maturity) can be accurately predicted whether there is an upward or downward shift in interest rates. (See, however, qualifications relating to convexity later.)

Suppose XYZ's CFO applies the duration concept to the problem at hand: investing a sum of money whose total return over five years will be adequate to pay XYZ's fifth-year claims while rendering the company invulnerable or immunized to a change in interest rates. If the CFO invested XYZ's $1 million in *six*-year bonds to fund the *fifth*-year claims, the CFO would find that the bonds could be sold after five years with some confidence that the total return would be $1,469,000 whether there is an upward or downward shift in interest rates.

Consider the results per $1,000 when interest rates remain stable, fall immediately to 7 percent, and rise immediately to 9 percent.

INTEREST RATES ARE STABLE

Coupon payments	$ 400
Reinvestment income	69
Proceeds from sale	1,000

INTEREST RATES FALL TO 7 PERCENT

Coupon payments	400
Reinvestment income	60
Proceeds from sale	1,009[18]

INTEREST RATES RISE TO 9 PERCENT

Coupon payments	400
Reinvestment income	78[19]
Proceeds from sale	991[20]

---

[17] $S_n, 5, 7 = \left[\dfrac{(1 + 0.07)^5 - 1}{0.07} \right] = 5.751.$ Reinvestment income is, therefore, $5.751 \times \$80 - \$400 = \$60$.

[18] At the end of five years, the bond will pay the last coupon of $80 and the redemption value of $1,000 one year later. In other words, a cash flow of $1,080 is due in one year. With a market interest rate of 7 percent, the market value of the bond at year 5 is $1,080/1.07 = $1,009.

[19] $S_n, 5, 9 = \left[\dfrac{(1 + 0.09)^5 - 1}{0.09} \right] = 5.985.$ Reinvestment income is, therefore, $5.985 \times \$80 - \$400 = \$78$.

[20] $1,080/1.09 = $991.

Consider the total returns produced by the six-year bonds under different scenarios:

	Interest Rate Scenario		
Cash Flows	**7%**	**8%**	**9%**
1. Coupons	$ 400	$ 400	$ 400
2. Reinvestment income	60	69	78
3. Bond sale proceeds	1,009	1,000	991
Total return after five years	$1,469	$1,469	$1,469

In every interest rate environment—up, down, or stable—the total five-year return should be $1,469, and XYZ is immune from an upward or downward shift in market interest rates. Immunization of surplus from interest rate risk is what duration is all about.

Immunizing the Balance Sheet   The process that allows one asset or a group of identical assets to be immunized from the effects of interest rate changes can be used, in theory, to immunize the entire balance sheet and, consequently, a company's surplus. The duration of a portfolio is the market-value weighted average of the duration of the individual assets and liabilities.

If X_{At} is the value of asset t divided by the total value of assets, then D_A represents the duration of a portfolio of assets. Thus,

$$D_A = X_{A1} * D_{A1} + X_{A2} * D_{A2} + X_{A3} * D_{A3} + \cdots + X_{An} * D_{An}$$

$$= \sum_{t=1}^{n} X_t * D_{Lt}$$

Similarly, if X_L is the value of liability t divided by the total value of liabilities, then D_L represents the duration of a portfolio of liabilities. Thus,

$$D_L = X_{L1} * D_{L1} + X_{L2} * D_{L2} + X_{L3} * D_{L3} + \cdots + X_{Ln} * D_{Ln}$$

$$= \sum_{t=1}^{n} X_t * D_{Lt}$$

Assume XYZ Life has $1 billion of corporate bonds, $500 million of government bonds, and $200 million of policy loans with durations of 2.0, 4.73, and 7.2 years, respectively. It has issued immediate annuities in the amount of $200 million with average duration of 9.2 years, and guaranteed investment contracts (GICs) in the amount of $1.4 billion with an average duration of 1.86 years. These portfolio averages would have been determined using the same market-value weighting process for a portfolio that we use here for the balance sheet. The duration of the asset portfolio is calculated as follows:

Asset	Market Value (000s)	Market Value/ Portfolio Value	Asset Duration	Portfolio Duration
Corporate bonds	$1,000	0.4762	2.00	0.9524
Government bonds	900	0.4296	4.73	2.0320
Policy loans	200	0.0952	7.20	0.6854
	$2,100	1.0000		3.67 years

The duration of the liability portfolio is calculated as follows:

Liability	Market Value (000s)	Market Value/ Portfolio Value	Liability Duration	Portfolio Duration
Annuities	$ 200	0.125	6.3	0.7875
GICs	1,400	0.875	1.86	1.6275
	$1,600	1.000		2.42 years

We can use the durations of the portfolios of assets and liabilities to estimate the effects of a change in interest rates on their values using the following formulas:

$$\Delta A = -D_A\left(\frac{\Delta r}{1 + r}\right)A$$

and

$$\Delta L = -D_L\left(\frac{\Delta r}{1 + r}\right)L$$

Recall that capital equals assets less liabilities, so that estimates for changes in the values of assets and liabilities can be used to estimate the impact of a change in interest rates on the value of a company's capital. The foregoing two formulas can be combined to evaluate the impact on surplus. Thus,

$$\Delta S = -(D_A - D_L k)\left(\frac{\Delta r}{1 + r}\right)A$$

where k is an adjustment term equal to total liabilities divided by total assets reflecting the leveraging of capital and surplus.

Effect of interest shocks on capital. For the foregoing formula, it can be seen that the effect of interest rate changes on the market value of an insurer's capital decomposes into three effects:

1. *The Leverage Adjusted Duration Gap* $= [D_A - D_L k]$. This gap is measured in years and reflects the degree of duration mismatch in an insurer's balance sheet. The larger the gap in absolute terms, the more exposed the insurer to interest rate shocks.
2. *The Size of the Interest Rate Shock* $= \Delta r/(1 + r)$. The larger the shock, the greater the insurer's exposure.
3. *The Size of the Insurer.* The term A measures the size of the insurer's assets. The larger the scale of the insurer, the larger the dollar size of the potential net worth exposure from any given interest rate shock.

Thus, we can express the exposure of an insurer's net worth to interest rate movements as follows:

$$S = -[\text{Adjusted Duration Gap}] \times [\text{Interest Rate Shock}] \times [\text{Asset Size}]$$

Where the duration of assets and the adjusted duration of liabilities is the same, the adjusted duration gap is zero and a change in market interest rates will leave insurer capital unaffected. A portfolio is said to be **duration matched** when the changes in asset values will be exactly offset by changes in adjusted liability values.

Applying duration gap to XYZ life. Recall the balance sheet for XYZ Life:

Assets (000s)		Liabilities (000s)	
Corporate bonds	$1,000	Annuities	$ 200
Government bonds	900	GICs	1,400
Policy loans	200		
Total assets	$2,100	Total liabilities	$1,600
		Capital	500
		Total liabilities and capital	$2,100

Assume interest rates are at 9 percent and increase at all levels by 1 percent. In this situation, the assumed increase in interest rates will cause the value of surplus to fall by $426.06, calculated as follows:

$$\Delta S = -(D_A - D_L k)\left(\frac{\Delta r}{1 + r}\right)A$$

$$\Delta S = -\left(3.67 - \left(2.42 * \frac{\$1,600}{\$2,100}\right)\right)\left(\frac{0.01}{1.09}\right)(\$2,100)$$

$$\Delta S = -\$35.18$$

Thus, the insurer would suffer a greater than 7 percent decline in its capital from such a change. XYZ is clearly not immunized against changes in market interest rates. XYZ can move toward an immunized position by undertaking one of the following strategies.

- Decrease the duration of its assets to equal the adjusted duration of liabilities (1.844). This could be accomplished by acquiring shorter-term assets or variable-rate assets.
- Increase the adjusted duration of its liabilities to equal the duration of assets (3.67). This could be accomplished by issuing longer-term GICs or entering the structured settlement annuity market in which there are no surrenders.
- XYZ could change its capital structure to affect k.

Despite the obvious intuitive appeal of this analytical structure for eliminating interest rate risk, two important constraints limit its practical utility. First, uncertain assumptions, both explicit and implicit, underlie the preceding analysis. These are discussed in the next subsection. Second, competitive pressures often make an immunized portfolio an unachievable objective.

When the duration of assets exceeds the duration of liabilities, a company's surplus is vulnerable to a rise in interest rates. Conversely, when a company's adjusted liability duration exceeds its asset duration, falling interest rates could cause a loss of surplus. When a company's target market expects interest rates to rise, a company will be able to sell more attractive products if its asset duration exceeds its liability duration, and the more severe the mismatch, the more attractive the products can be. Competitive pressures will normally require companies intentionally to mismatch the duration of their assets and liabilities, and to assume some asset–liability matching risk in order to market products that will sell.

Challenges in Applying the Duration Model in Practice

The simple duration model presented here describes the basic procedure for using duration to immunize an insurer's net worth. In practice, however, a number of complications require adjustments, some of which are more elegant than others.

Immunization as a Dynamic Process   First, the model predicts the change in values of the asset and liability portfolios *for a one-time change in interest rates.* Once the interest rate has changed, so has the duration of the portfolios. Similarly, each instrument in the portfolios comes closer to maturity as time transpires, and the duration of the portfolio changes. Consequently, portfolios need to be continuously rebalanced.

Large Interest Rate Changes and Convexity   Second, the accuracy of the price sensitivity predicted using duration degrades with the magnitude of the interest rate change. This difference between the actual asset or liability value and its value as predicted by duration is known as **convexity.** Conceptually, duration is the slope of the price-yield curve and convexity is the change (derivative) of the slope. The actual price-yield curve ordinarily is curved, not linear.

To understand the importance of convexity, consider the six-year bond with an 8 percent coupon and yield, discussed earlier.[21] Recall that its duration was 4.99 years and that its price was $1,000 at an 8 percent market rate. If market rates increase to 10 percent, the duration model predicts a change in price as follows:

$$\Delta P/P = (-4.99)(0.02/1.08) = -9.2457\%$$

which translates into a price change from $1,000 to $907.54. These prices are shown as points *A* and *B*, respectively, in Figure 32-10.

We know that the price of a security is the discounted value of its cash flows. The actual price of this bond at a 10 percent market rate, therefore, is:

$$P = \$80/(1.1) + \$80/(1.1)^2 + \$80/(1.1)^3 + \$80/(1.1)^4 + \$80/(1.1)^5$$
$$+ (\$80 + \$1,000)/(1.1)^6$$
$$= \$912.89$$

This is point *C* in Figure 32-10. It differs from the price as predicted by duration by $5.35 or just over 0.5 percent.

---

[21]This example follows Saunders, *Financial Institutions Management*, p. 121.

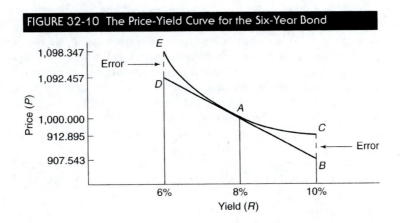

FIGURE 32-10 The Price-Yield Curve for the Six-Year Bond

The reader can verify that a fall in market rates to 6 percent results in a predicted price of $1,092.46, shown as point *D*. By comparison, the actual price is $1,098.35, as calculated based on the discounted value of the bond's cash flows. It is shown as point *E*. Again the duration model has underpredicted the bond price increase, in this instance by $5.89 or 0.5 percent.

Results of this type will occur for any fixed-income security. Several techniques, the mathematics of which are beyond the scope of this text, have been developed to adjust the model for convexity.

In normal interest rate environments, the convexity error is a good one in the sense that the duration model overpredicts a decrease in values when interest rates rise, and underpredicts an increase in values when interest rates fall. This phenomenon is referred to as **positive convexity.** Thus, positive convexity tends to err conservatively.

When the interest rate environment is characterized by an inverted yield curve (i.e., short-term rates are higher than long-term rates), the reverse is true, and the convexity error will cause a decline in surplus to be underpredicted. This is called **negative convexity.** Negative convexity is also found with fixed-income securities that have call or prepayment options, that is, when the issuer can redeem the security if interest rates fall.

Dependence of Asset and Liability Cash Flows   Finally, the model assumes that both asset and liability cash flows are independent of interest changes. In fact, a high degree of correlation exists between interest rate changes and cash flows. This is a result of the financial options embedded in both assets and liabilities. For example, policyowners may surrender their policies when interest rates rise, and bonds may be called and mortgages repaid when interest rates fall.

As pointed out earlier, the life insurance contract is a bundle of options, and one of the more important options is the right to surrender a policy for its cash value. Assume now that the CFO of XYZ forecasts the need in five years to fund $1,469,000 for anticipated cash surrenders and policy loans rather than death claim liabilities. If interest rates were to rise from 8 percent to 9 percent, the demand for policy loans and surrenders likely will increase. If we assume a 10 percent increase in demand, then XYZ's investment strategy to develop a fund of $1,469,000 in five years will be insufficient to fund its cash flow need of $1,615,900,[22] and its surplus will not be immunized or protected.

Predicting the results of the behavior of option holders requires a solution to at least two very difficult problems. First, the future pattern of interest rates must be predicted. Second, the reaction of option holders to interest rate changes must be predicted. Further complicating the issue is the fact that no market for life insurance liabilities, other than limited reinsurance contracts, exists.

When assets, liabilities, or both contain embedded options, ideally both duration and convexity should be adjusted to take account of these options. This is done by application of the concepts of **option-adjusted duration** and **option-adjusted convexity** (also called **effective duration** and **effective convexity**), which are measures of duration and convexity that have been adjusted for the risk of options embedded in asset or liability contracts. Although beyond the scope of this text, the process involves the adaptation of options pricing theory to immunization theory to recognize and account for the fact that assets and liability cash flows are themselves influenced by interest rates and will not remain static as they change over time. Commercial software is available to measure option-adjusted duration and convexity.

The use of option-adjusted duration and convexity measures represents a significant step forward in managing systematic risk. However, the lack of reliable data on

---

[22]$1,469,000 × 1.1.

lapses and surrenders leads to inaccurate measures of duration and even greater errors in measures of convexity.

Although not as crucial as it is for liabilities, interest rate risk is still of major concern to life insurers in measuring asset values. Fluctuation in the value of fixed-income assets is to a considerable extent the result of interest rate volatility even though values are affected by other risks including basis risk, credit risk, liquidity risk, call and prepayment risk, real estate, and equity risk. Insurers estimate the duration and convexities of their investments using their own or commercially available software. Some outsource the impact of interest rate risk to outside software and pricing services.

Asset–Liability Management

Most insurers develop estimates of liability duration and convexities for each line of insurance and for each class of assets. Weighting them appropriately with the fair value of liabilities and market value of assets (discounted value of cash flows) produces overall asset and liability duration and convexity measures. Taking into account any leveraging involved, the insurer can obtain measures of net worth duration and convexity. These measures provide an assessment of the impact of interest rate movements on the value of the company.

Asset–liability management (ALM) models and related ALM statistics have grown in sophistication. As pointed out earlier, duration and convexity measures have been refined to account for options embedded in assets and liabilities (effective duration and convexity). Models have also been adjusted to provide simulations that reflect potential yield curve movements. Until recently, conventional measures of durations and convexities assumed flat yield curves and parallel shifts in these curves.

ALM is a multidisciplinary undertaking. It involves both insurance product contract design and asset management. Although the primary purpose of contract design is to make products that have the features consumers want (price, service, performance, and flexibility), from an asset–liability perspective, a significant aspect of contract design is to discourage or prevent book value cash withdrawals under conditions likely to cause liquidity problems.

Because of the importance of the relationship between contract design and asset management, the actuarial and investment departments of life insurance companies are developing a much closer working relationship than has been the case in the past. In some companies, the position of CFO has been created to manage at a senior level the activities of both the actuarial and investment departments.

The asset–liability cash flow relationship, must, of course, be integrated with the primary objectives of contract design and asset management, namely, to develop marketable, actuarially sound products and to produce a maximum return on invested assets that is consistent with the company's tolerance for risk.

The impact of other systematic risk factors is considered much more informally. The essence of asset–liability management is to place limits on the insurer's selected portfolio structure reflecting the variety of risks to which it is exposed. Limits are set on individual asset holdings in a risk-based capital context. A limit also is imposed on the amount of duration mismatch allowed. This limit can be applied either by product line or across all assets and liabilities. The segmentation approach widely used currently imposes discipline on the pricing process so that long-term yields are not used in pricing short-term liabilities. However, some believe that an aggregate overall basis can permit needed pricing discipline and control with better asset portfolio management. Another control used by management is to establish a restriction on the number of scenarios that reveal losses due to asset–liability mismatches.

Credit Risk

Insurers, rating agencies, and regulators all focus critically on credit risk. Credit risk includes the risk of default on significant investments as well as the basis risk in the systematic risk factors discussed earlier.

Insurers rely on outside rating agency services (e.g., Moody's, Standard and Poor's, Duff and Phelps, and Dunn and Bradstreet) to assess the credit risk implicit in potential and actual investments. As discussed in chapters 33 and 34, the Securities Valuation Office (SVO) of the NAIC also assigns credit ratings to virtually all investments that are used for statutory reporting purposes. Regardless of these outside sources, many insurers carry out their own due diligence before accepting an investment that has credit risk. Management monitors the credit risk of assets through weekly and monthly experience reports. They maintain "watch lists" of companies that are deemed to be in financial difficulty, likely to be downgraded by rating agencies, or in danger of becoming insolvent. Investment policy sets limits on portfolio exposure by industry, geographic region, type of business, and individual company. Guidelines are also established relating to choice of outside counterparties, implemented primarily through approved lists of eligible firms. Development of investment policy and operational guidelines are discussed further in chapter 33.

The duration models examined previously ignore credit risk; that is, there is an underlying assumption of no defaults or delays in asset cash flows. We can incorporate credit risk into the duration model by recognizing that a default or delay in loan or other asset repayment is synonymous with lengthening cash flows. Thus, the financial manager unsure of future cash flows because of credit risk can discount (multiply) the promised cash flows by the estimated probability of repayment, substituting this expected value into the duration and related calculations.

Liquidity Risk

In the 1980s, liquidity was a major concern for life insurers. Policy surrenders reached 12.3 percent and, in some companies, surrenders approached 60 percent. Policy loans reached an all-time high. Insurers responded by developing liability and asset control techniques to reduce the probability and magnitude of adverse cash flows. As a result, today liquidity generally is not a major concern to life insurers because most of their policies (liabilities) are less liquid than their assets.

Liability Controls

The purpose of liability controls is to discourage or prevent book value cash withdrawals under conditions that are likely to cause liquidity problems. Liability control is accomplished during the contract design process through the inclusion of contractual provisions that create either additional cash flows to the policyowner who persists or additional cash flows to the insurer when withdrawal options are exercised.

The development of the entire new generation of current assumption products in the United States can be viewed as withdrawal liability control on a grand scale. When interest rates began to rise in the 1970s, many insurers (particularly stock companies writing guaranteed cost, nonparticipating products) had no mechanism for passing higher investment returns to policyowners. Mutual company dividend practices and regulations created delays in passing favorable results to participating policyowners. On a comparative basis, these policies were expensive, and as the practice of illustration selling gathered momentum, they became highly vulnerable to replacement (see chapter 24).

It became clear that some method of responding rapidly to changing interest rates was essential to the development of competitive new products. New interest-sensitive contracts, such as universal life, current assumption whole life, and market-value annuities, are examples of the industry response. This new generation of products has mechanisms for adjusting values as market interest rates change. When interest rates rise, interest can be credited to policyowners at rates that are competitive with other financial instruments, and, thus, the incentives to withdraw are reduced or neutralized.

These experience-participation features also protect a company when interest rates decline. An insurer can thereby reduce its credited interest and, to a great degree, not be burdened with long-term interest guarantees that current investments would not fund adequately.

In addition to provisions that permit crediting of additional interest to policyowners who persist, other contract features represent disincentives to withdrawal by creating additional cash flow to the insurer when withdrawal options are exercised. Surrender charges are the most obvious example of liability controls that generate additional cash flow to an insurer when policyowners withdraw. To the extent permitted by nonforfeiture laws, charges against the policyowner's cash value are available to offset any costs associated with surrender.

Direct recognition features also reduce the amount of interest credited or dividends paid to policyowners to the extent that funds have been withdrawn under policy loan options. Thus, interest withheld under the direct recognition provision is available to offset any financial consequences of cash flow antiselection.

Again, variable policy loan rates permit the adjustment of policy loan rates to reflect the interest rate environment existing throughout the life of the policy. The company will receive a current rate of interest for its loan and is not compelled to invest its assets at low rates agreed to years before.

Insurers, of course, can also offer fixed loan rates and deal with the risk of interest rates increasing by engaging in appropriate interest rate swaps that provide additional cash when rates increase. Some customers may prefer a known, fixed loan rate.

Thus, liability controls implemented by life insurers have been successful, to an extent, in reducing interest rate risk. Research indicates a significant reduction in the sensitivity of policy loan demand to changes in market interest rates.[23] Although such liability controls are essential, surrender charges have a cost in that some potential customers may be attracted to other financial products that provide lower withdrawal charges. This is another example of the need for a multidisciplinary approach to contract design.

Asset Controls

The purpose of asset control techniques is to maintain a portfolio with sufficient liquidity to pay current obligations under a variety of economic conditions, while achieving a maximum rate of return for a given level of profitability and solvency risk. The need to balance asset and liability cash flows is a special risk associated with the management of a financial intermediary that both borrows money (premiums) from its customers and reinvests the borrowed funds.

This asset–liability matching risk results from the manner in which this risk interacts with the operation of an intermediary institution. The investment portfolio construction process is discussed in chapter 33, but it will be seen there that the asset control techniques are investment constraints that govern the portfolio construction process. In other words, investments must be selected that are consistent with any asset control strategy undertaken. Just as policy contract design is an important element of liability

---

[23]James M. Carson and Robert E. Hoyt, "An Econometric Analysis of the Demand for Life Insurance Policy Loans," *The Journal of Risk and Insurance,* Vol. 59 (June 1992), pp. 239–251.

control activity, investment contract design is an important element of asset control activity. Although more than one-half of the average life insurer's assets are purchased in the open market and obtained on the same terms as those purchased by the general investing public, a significant portion of life insurers' assets is invested in privately placed and individually negotiated corporate bonds and mortgages. These private investments provide an opportunity to negotiate terms so as to support an insurer's asset–liability risk management strategy.

Another liquidity problem was inherent in the practice of reporting virtually all bonds at amortized values. Under these circumstances, the market-value risk was essentially ignored and, over time, some companies found themselves with balance sheet values well in excess of current market values and a questionable surplus position. Today, a significant portion of fixed-income investments are identified as "available for sale or trading" and are marked to market (see chapters 33 and 34). In effect, this is a form of risk control.

A number of other risk management techniques are used in liquidity management. They include bond portfolio dedication, hedging, and securitization. These are covered in the next chapter.

The responsibility for evaluating and managing liquidity risk typically rests with an asset–liability management committee. Liquidity risk decisions are part of the analysis and cash flow testing used by an insurer. Scenario testing usually includes running scenarios under a wide range of yield curve changes. For each path created by a scenario, the objective is to ensure that net cash flows are positive and that the solvency of the company is assured.

Cash flows are projected for up to 30 years for each product line. Such testing provides a sense of the company's liquidity status even though they are just estimates. This information is used appropriately in establishing and adjusting investment polices.

The volatility of interest rates has had a profound impact on the life insurance industry. Life companies have come to understand their business as a cash flow business, and this new understanding is now apparent in virtually every aspect of their operations. Matching asset–liability cash flows has become a necessity in managing the risks associated with operating a life insurance business.

As pointed out earlier, the importance of controlling for the impact of changing interest rates on asset–liability cash flows is perhaps best exemplified by the entire new generation of life insurance products. Virtually every feature that distinguishes these products from their traditional predecessors (direct recognition, surrender charges, separate accounts, variable loan rates, indeterminate- and flexible-premium structures, etc.) is designed to control company cash flow responses to changing market interest rates. These efforts to manage cash flows, of course, must be balanced against the need for products that are attractive to customers.

Asset–liability management influences insurer management policy in organization, investment management, product design, and marketing. The regulatory environment is also rapidly changing. The asset valuation reserve, the interest maintenance reserve, the valuation actuary, and risk-based capital concepts will be seen in chapter 34 as efforts to promote policyowner security within the context of the recognition that life insurance is a cash flow business.

Other Risks

In addition to the four financial risks just discussed, insurers face other risks no less important. Areas such as technological, regulatory, reputational, legal, and environmental risk are of concern to senior management and require substantial commitments of time and resources. However, they typically are not addressed from a risk management standpoint in any formal, structured way because they are, today, less amenable to a priori financial management.

Questions

1. Explain the role that life insurers play as financial intermediaries in an economy.
2. How do insurers help policyowners diversify various risks?
3. Compare and contrast the actuarial and financial views of risk as they relate to insurers.
4. Describe some of the systematic, credit, and liquidity risks that life insurers face and some of the approaches taken to manage them.
5. What macroeconomic or microeconomic events could increase a number of the financial risks faced by insurers?

33

LIFE INSURER FINANCIAL MANAGEMENT: II

Objectives

■ Distinguish between market and regulatory demands placed upon an insurer's capital.

■ Identify potential discrepancies between the market and book values of a life insurer's capital.

■ Describe analytical techniques used by life insurers to assess the sensitivity of their cash flows to changes in interest rates.

■ Explain how investment management can affect life insurer profitability and product competitiveness.

■ Describe the asset classes that comprise the investment portfolio of a typical life insurer.

■ Describe the regulatory treatment of various asset classes in a life insurer's investment portfolio.

This chapter continues our examination of the financial management of life insurance companies. Here we note the importance and purposes of capital management. We then examine how life insurers manage their cash flows and how they identify and manage their investments, including the nature and methods of investment portfolio construction.

CAPITAL MANAGEMENT

Insurance executives and managers face two critically important, yet somewhat conflicting objectives. On the one hand, they must satisfy the owners of the firm. Owners are interested in maximizing the return on their equity (ROE) in the firm, which means that their interests generally lie in *minimizing* their equity investment (i.e., the firm's capital). On the other hand, executives and managers must satisfy their customers (policyowners) and regulators. Policyowners and regulators are interested in the financial solidity of the firm, which means that their interests generally lie in *maximizing* the firm's capital. Capital management is concerned with balancing these interests. We will use the terms *capital, capital and surplus, net worth,* and *equity* synonymously, all to refer to the difference between assets and liabilities.

Capital within a life insurer (and any other financial intermediary) serves four functions.[1] Thus, it is necessary to

1. protect policyowners and beneficiaries in the event of insurer insolvency
2. minimize or eliminate the direct costs to other insurers and, ultimately, to taxpayers from insolvency assessments
3. absorb unanticipated losses with enough margin to inspire confidence and enable the insurer to continue as a going concern
4. provide the basis for future growth

Capital and the Risk of Insolvency

In examining how capital protects against insolvency, we should first define *capital* more precisely. The problem is that economists and accountants often define capital differently, each of which can differ from the regulator's definition of capital. To the economist, an insurer's capital is the difference between the *market value* of its assets and its liabilities. At the other extreme, regulators usually view an insurer's capital as the difference between some measure of the *book* (or *historical*) *value* of its assets and liabilities. Accountants often define capital in ways that blend the economic and regulatory approaches.

Our conceptual examination of capital and the insolvency risk begins by exploring the role of capital in insulating the firm against two of the major risks that life insurers face: credit risk and interest rate risk. We focus first on the economic concept of capital and then compare this with the book-value concept of capital. As we will see, the book-value concept can mislead managers, owners, policyowners, and regulators.

The Market Value of Capital

We begin with a simple balance sheet for our insurer, wherein all assets and liabilities are stated in market value terms; that is, all assets and liabilities are marked to their market values. (We ignore for now the problems in doing this.) As Table 33-1 shows, the insurer's capital is 10. It is economically solvent, which means that its liquidation today would impose no costs on policyowners or on other insurers or taxpayers through the state guarantee associations (see chapter 35).

Market Value of Capital and Credit Risk   We now consider how credit risk can affect the market value of capital. The insurer has $20 in long-term (e.g., mortgage) loans. Suppose that, because of recession, many borrowers are unable to make timely loan repayments. As a result, the market value (i.e., the present value of cash flows) of loans falls to $12. The insurer's revised balance sheet is shown in Table 33-2.

TABLE 33-1   A Life Insurer's Balance Sheet (millions)

Assets		*Liabilities and Net Worth*	
Long-term securities	$ 80	Policy reserves	$ 90
Long-term loans	20	Net worth	10
Total	$100	Total	$100

---

[1]This and the following discussions draw from Anthony Saunders, *Financial Institutions Management,* 2nd ed. (Chicago: Irwin, 1997), pp. 391–401.

TABLE 33-2	A Life Insurer's Market-Value Balance Sheet after a Decline in the Value of Loans		
Assets		**Liabilities and Net Worth**	
Long-term securities	$80	Policy reserves	$90
Long-term loans	12	Net worth	2
Total	$92	Total	$92

The loss of $8 in the market value of loans is absorbed fully by the firm's owners. The policyowners (liability holders) are fully protected because their claims are superior to those of equity holders. Note, however, that because of leverage, an 8 percent decline in assets equates to an 80 percent decline in net worth.

What if the decline in the market value of the loans were $12 rather than $8? The owner's equity would be wiped out completely and the policyowners would take a $2 hit. In the absence of a guarantee fund arrangement, policyowners would receive an average of 88/90 or 97.77 cents on the dollar. Of course, had the insurer's net worth been $15 rather than $10, policyowners would have been fully protected. The larger the insurer's net worth relative to the size of its assets, the more insolvency protection there is for policyowners and liability guarantors. It is for this reason that regulators focus on minimum capital requirements such as risk-based capital standards (see chapter 35).

Market Value of Capital and Interest Rate Risk   Consider the same market-value balance sheet in Table 32-1 after a rise in interest rates. As we discussed in the preceding chapter, rising interest rates reduce the market value of long-term, fixed-income securities and loans. Assume that the market value of the long-term securities falls from $80 to $75 and that the market value of the long-term loans declines from $20 to $17. The total decline is $8.

Rising interest rates also can reduce the market value of liabilities whose values are contractually fixed, although adjustable-rate contracts, such as many interest-sensitive annuities and life policies, provide for changes in their crediting rates so as to keep pace with market interest rates. We assume here that most policy reserves back interest-sensitive contracts whose crediting rates are adjusted instantaneously to market rates. Hence, we would see only modest change in the market values of liabilities—a decline of $2.

After the interest rate shock, the market-value balance sheet might look as in Table 33-3. The asset loss of $8 and the liability decline of $2 are reflected on the balance sheet, resulting in a decline in net worth of $6. Owner's equity is sufficient to absorb the decline. Only if the net of asset and liability declines exceeds $10 would policyowners be affected.

These examples show that market valuation of the balance sheet produces an economically accurate portrayal of the change in an insurer's net worth occasioned by credit and interest rate risk and, thus, its solvency position. As long as the owner's equity is adequate, policyowners (and implicitly, guaranty funds) are protected from insolvency risk.

The Book Value of Capital
As we discuss in the next chapter, insurance regulators require insurers to prepare their financial statements in accordance with statutory accounting principles (SAP). The accounting profession requires the preparation of insurer financial statements in accordance with generally accepted accounting principles (GAAP). Although SAP and GAAP differ in important respects, both rely on variations of book-value accounting.

TABLE 33-3	A Life Insurer's Market-Value Balance Sheet after a Rise in Interest Rates		
Assets		**Liabilities and Net Worth**	
Long-term securities	$75	Policy reserves	$88
Long-term loans	17	Net worth	4
Total	$92	Total	$92

To appreciate better the effects of book-value accounting on insolvency risk, let us now assume that the asset and liability values shown in the Table 33-1 balance sheet are calculated in accordance with SAP (or GAAP) rather than based on market values. Thus, the $80 in long-term securities (e.g., bonds) and the $20 in loans reflect the values when the bonds were purchased and the loans were made (see chapter 34 for details of SAP and GAAP valuation of these items). Similarly, the $90 in policy reserves is calculated in accordance with SAP, which means that they are not adjusted for changes in market interest rates.

The book value of capital is the difference between the book values of assets and liabilities. It usually comprises the following four components:

1. *par value of shares, for stock insurers*
2. *contributed surplus* (i.e., the difference between the original offering price of the stock and its par value or the amount of surplus contributed to form a mutual insurer)
3. *retained earnings*
4. *special reserves* (see chapter 34 for a discussion of the interest maintenance and asset valuation reserves)

We assume that the book value of capital shown in Table 32-1 is $10, the same as the market value of capital. However, book-value equity rarely equals market-value equity. We can understand why this is true by examining the effects on book-value capital of the same credit and interest rate shocks discussed earlier in connection with market-value equity.

Book Value of Capital and Credit Risk   We again assume that a portion of the $20 in loans exhibits repayment problems. We noted earlier that market-value adjustments lead instantaneously to a loss of $8 in this portfolio. Under GAAP and, to a lesser degree, under SAP also, insurers have greater discretion in reflecting such adjustments on the balance sheet. Indeed, insurers (and other financial institutions) may well resist writing down the values of bad assets as long as possible to try to present a more optimistic financial picture to policyowners and regulators. Such action can be expected particularly if executives and managers believe that revealing the true (market value) picture of the insurer's financial condition might result in their being fired (i.e., we have an agency problem).

Suppose that, in our example, the insurer is forced to recognize a loss of $3 rather than a loss of $8 on its loan portfolio. The $3 decline in statutory assets results in a $3 charge against capital—resulting in a net worth of $7. The insurer's actual capital is $5 less.

Book Value of Capital and Interest Rate Risk   Although book-value accounting systems do recognize credit risk problems, albeit only partially and usually with a long and discretionary time lag, their failure to recognize the impact of interest rate risk is more extreme. In our foregoing market-value example, a rise in interest rates lowered the market value of assets by $8 and liabilities by $2. This led to a reduction in net worth to

$6. With book-value accounting, a rise in interest rates would result in no change in value of either the assets or liabilities of our insurer and, therefore, no change in net worth.

The Discrepancy between the Market and Book Values of Capital

The degree to which an insurer's book value capital deviates from it true economic value depends on several factors, two of which are especially important:

1. *Interest rate volatility.* The higher the interest rate volatility, the greater the discrepancy.
2. *Examination and enforcement.* The more frequent the on-site and other examinations and the more rigorous the examinations and the regulatory standards, the smaller the discrepancy.

In practice, the discrepancy can be approximated for large publicly traded insurers, even if they do not mark their balance sheets to market. In an efficient capital market, we know that a firm's shares are valued based on the firm's current and expected future cash flows, as we discuss in chapter 32. The stock price, therefore, reflects the market capitalization (total value of the shares outstanding). Thus, the market value (*MV*) of equity per share is:

$$MV = \text{(Market Capitalization)} \div \text{(Number of Shares Outstanding)}$$

By contrast, the book value (*BV*) of equity per share is:

$$BV = \text{(Par Value + Contributed Surplus + Retained Earnings} \\ \text{+ Special Reserves)} \div \text{(Number of Shares Outstanding)}$$

The *MV/BV* ratio is often called the **market-to-book ratio** and shows the degree of discrepancy between an insurer's market value as perceived by the capital market and its book value as measured by SAP or GAAP. The lower this ratio, the more the book value of capital *overstates* the true equity of an insurer as perceived by investors, and vice versa. Given such discrepancies, we might question why regulators and insurers generally oppose implementation of market-value accounting rules. We take up this important topic in the next chapter.

Life Insurer Capital and the Short Straddle Position

Among financial intermediaries, life insurance companies have particularly complex interest rate risk exposures because of the options embedded in both their assets and liabilities.[2] We noted in chapter 32 that products sold by life insurers grant policyowners numerous options, and that we should expect policyowners to exercise these options in their favor. These options reinforce the positive convexity in insurer liabilities.

Simultaneously, life insurers seek high-yielding investments, such as collateral mortgage obligations (discussed later) and callable corporate bonds. These debt issuers retain the option to prepay or call away the mortgages and bonds at some book value (with mortgages) or at a specified premium over book value (with callable bonds). This results in these assets exhibiting negative convexity.

With options on both the liability and asset sides of the balance sheet, the company has created a capital position known as a **short straddle.** For companies in a short straddle position, movement of interest rates in either direction can cause depletion of economic capital. If interest rates remain stable, however, the company can reap large profits. Figure 33-1 illustrates this position. The solution to a short straddle position is to restructure the assets and/or liabilities so that the convexities are better balanced.

---

[2]This discussion draws from Anthony M. Santomero and David F. Babbel, *Financial Markets, Instruments, and Institutions* (Chicago: Irwin, 1997), pp. 646–647.

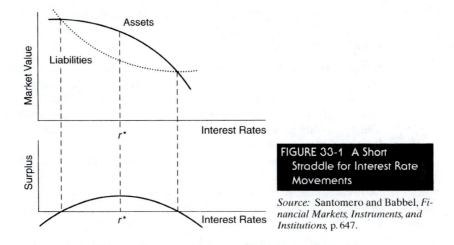

FIGURE 33-1 A Short Straddle for Interest Rate Movements

Source: Santomero and Babbel, *Financial Markets, Instruments, and Institutions,* p. 647.

Evaluating Capital Needs

As we see, insurers face a solvency–profitability trade-off, a balancing act directly related to the risk–return trade-off.[3] Insurers must hold enough capital to remain solvent, yet not so much that return on equity drops too low. To evaluate its needs for capital, an insurer must first have evaluated its risk exposures. This section provides an overview of capital management as practiced in the U.S. life insurance industry.

As we noted previously, capital provides both a cushion for adverse operational deviations and the basis for future growth. In establishing the amount of needed capital, insurers typically distinguish between capital needed for existing commitments and that needed for future commitments. Capital needed to support existing business is sometimes referred to as **required capital.** Capital needed to support future business is termed **growth capital.**

Required Capital

Objectives for determining the amount of required capital are established with consideration for regulatory requirements, rating agency guidelines, and the risk posture of management.

Regulatory Capital In the United States, minimum capital standards are set by the NAIC's risk-based capital formula (see chapter 35). Risk characteristics are a function of insurer size, asset quality, lines of business written, and other factors. To determine an insurer's risk-based capital ratio, an insurer's total adjusted capital (statutory capital plus the asset valuation reserve and any voluntary reserves) is compared with the risk-based capital amount obtained from the risk-based capital formula. Book-value accounting standards generally apply.

In determining the capital needed to support the various risks inherent in an insurer's business, a risk-weighted formula is applied using risk-based capital ratios that compare an amount of capital to a measure of risk. For example, an insurer would multiply the amount of its various investment classes by different risk-adjustment factors to provide for the risk of loss of value in each class. It would also multiply its various product lines by appropriate risk-adjustment factors. The accumulated amounts of capital

---

[3]This section draws on Susan Conant, Nicholas L. Desoutter, Dani L. Long, and Robert MacGrogan, *Managing for Solvency and Profitability in Life and Health Insurance Companies* (Atlanta, GA: LOMA, 1996), pp. 375–384.

needed for the several risk types constitute the minimum regulatory capital requirement. State laws also have usually lower fixed-dollar minimum capital requirements, established without regard to the risk profile.

Rating Agency Guidelines Rating agencies, acting independently of regulators and insurers themselves, evaluate insurers' financial positions and assign a **quality rating** to insurers according to their standards of claims paying ability, creditworthiness, and financial strength (see chapter 11). Rating agencies employ proprietary rating systems. They generally set higher standards and employ market-value accounting to a greater degree than do regulators.

For most life and health insurers, a favorable quality rating is essential because it can affect insurer efforts to attract capital, secure a favorable cost of capital, and improve marketing, both in terms of agent loyalty and customer confidence. Maintaining a high-quality rating reflecting the insurer's perception of its capital needs can be crucial to the company's business persistency and future sales.

Management Capital Targets Each insurer uses its own standards to establish the minimum amount of capital needed to support its portfolio of risks. These internal standards, often incorporating market-value accounting approaches, reflect the need to provide enough capital to cover expected obligations, including a cushion against short-term adverse developments. In general, the effects of adverse deviations smooth out over the long term. Management's decision as to the capital needed reflects its current objectives to assure solvency, maintain a selected quality rating, and achieve growth and profitability.

Maximum Limits on Capital In view of the risk–return trade-off, insurers must guard against holding too much capital. An insurer that holds excessive capital will find it difficult to earn a satisfactory ROE for the company owners and other stakeholders and can lead to additional expenses being incurred. This could lead rating agencies to downgrade the insurer's quality rating below the rating that management desires to maintain. Rating agencies tend to interpret excess capital as an indication that the company is not aggressive enough in seeking a reasonable rate of return.

Some state laws impose limits on mutual insurers' net worth. These limits require mutual companies to distribute, in the form of policy dividends, any surplus in excess of the statutory limit. The limit does not apply to stock insurers.

Growth Capital

The amount of capital that management decides is needed to support its new business plans in light of its unique risk profile is frequently labeled *growth* (or *uncommitted*) *capital*. Growth capital is needed to deal with both the cash outflow and surplus strain usually associated with new business development. An initial negative cash flow can result from expenses being greater than initial premiums and some expenses being incurred before any premiums are received. Surplus strain is a consequence of being unable to rely on economic (market-value) accounting. In addition, growth capital provides funds for such needs as providing returns to shareholders, paying dividends on participating policies, paying debts, and funding corporate stock repurchase programs.

Capital Planning Process

Management normally uses a capital planning process to establish its capital needs. Capital planning begins with development of a proposed strategic plan at the corporate level and then moves down the organizational hierarchy to the various lines of business. Once the separate capital management reports are developed for each line of business (existing products and proposed new products), they are submitted to and consolidated by the corporate planning staff. The capital management reports and projections include, for each product line, a target capital need and a target return on capital. To estimate these amounts, the line-of-business staff uses asset-share studies to evaluate forecasts of the following:

- return on capital
- cost of capital (hurdle rate)
- sales growth
- expenses
- profit margins
- surplus strain
- operating leverage

In consolidating and analyzing the separate capital management reports and forecasts, the corporate planning staff seeks to identify and understand the following:

- the combined effect of the proposed capital plans on future financial results
- interaction of risk exposures among different lines of business
- opportunities to invest capital in highly profitable lines of business
- opportunities to withdraw from unprofitable or otherwise undesirable lines of business
- opportunities for new capital investment (e.g., new information systems or a new line of business)
- the company's ability to raise capital from external sources and its cost

Once the line-of-business reports have been consolidated and analyzed, the process of developing a corporate-level financial plan can begin. **Target capital** is the total amount of capital that management believes is necessary for its required and growth capital needs. To establish a corporate target capital, corporate planners first sum the target capital objective amounts for all the insurer's lines of business. Then all of the various components of target capital are considered to ensure that all required and growth capital will be supplied at all times during the planning period selected. Following this, adjustments to reflect interactions (covariances) between risk exposures for the various lines of business are made. The concern here is with both positive and negative covariances; that is, there could be risk augmentation or risk offset, and adjustments must be made for the interaction of risk exposures.

Unfortunately, accounting for this interaction remains highly subjective. Insurers generally have inadequate data from which to model such covariances. Thus, they generally are forced to rely on financial simulations of cash flows. The year-by-year patterns of net cash flows and capital positions can reveal potential cash flow shortfalls or capital shortfalls that might arise under a variety of sets of adverse circumstances. The value of this information comes from providing management with insight into the relatively long-term impact of key variables on net cash flow and capital.

As discussed earlier, neither SAP nor GAAP financial reporting provides as complete or as accurate information as management needs. Most life insurers employ special financial reporting systems for management purposes. These unique systems—placing greater reliance on economic accounting concepts—attempt to correct perceived inadequacies in SAP and GAAP relating to the timing of recognition of income, expenses, gains, and losses. The objective is to produce more accurate market-value measures of an insurer's financial status. These internal reporting systems enable the insurer to evaluate its current capital position, establish a capital plan, and monitor the performance of its various operations.

Although the basic capital planning process has many intermediate phases, it essentially involves a three-step procedure:

1. *Set a target capital objective* (i.e., estimate the insurer's capital needs).
2. *Determine whether the company is facing a projected shortfall or excess of capital.* This is done by comparing the target capital with the amount of capital that the company anticipates.
3. *Develop appropriate capital management strategies that will enable the insurer to meet its target capital objective.*

In the case of excess capital, a company must find profitable ways to invest or reinvest the available capital. With a shortfall, ways must be found to secure additional capital.

MANAGING LIFE INSURANCE CASH FLOW

Preceding discussions have made clear that effective financial management requires an understanding of the *dynamic* nature of assets and liabilities that reflects the potential deviation in expected cash flows that may arise when interest rates change.[4] Insurers have developed analytical techniques based on interest-sensitive cash flow analysis. Implementation of an interest-sensitive cash flow model typically involves a four-step process requiring (1) segmentation of the insurer's business by product line, (2) forecasting the insurer's expected liability cash flows, (3) forecasting the insurer's expected asset cash flows, and (4) testing the cash flow results under a wide range of possible interest rate scenarios.

Traditional assumptions used in life insurance financial modeling such as commissions, expenses, mortality rates, and death benefits are supplemented by assumptions regarding the impact of interest rate and other risks on various cash flows. The credibility of all financial projections, however, ultimately depends on the assumptions used in developing the financial model. Some of the problems inherent in life insurance cash flow modeling include unanticipated (1) economic conditions, (2) policyowner behavior, or (3) the market responses to investments.

Segmentation by Product Line

Different insurance company products obviously have different cash flow patterns. For example, policyowners are more likely to exercise policy loan options if they hold an older policy with a low-interest loan rate than if they hold a new policy with a variable loan rate. To evaluate cash flow patterns effectively, then, it is necessary to consider distinct product lines independently. It is also necessary to manage different products independently.

Segmentation by product line is the process of independent management of different products. In the cash flow modeling process, the expected asset cash flows and liability cash flows are forecast for each product. In the management of products, a notational investment account is established for each line of business within the insurer's general account.

The segmented general account should not be confused with the separate account (discussed later). Even though a portion of general account investments may be assigned

---

[4]This section draws from Stephen W. Forbes, *Managing a Life Insurance Company in a High-Risk Environment* (Atlanta, GA: LOMA, 1997).

to a particular segmented product line, from a solvency perspective, the assignment is a conceptual management tool only. The collective assets in the general account are available to back all liabilities supported by the general account.

In other respects, segmentation has a practical effect on the company's policyowners. For example, interest crediting and dividend policy may be based on the investment experience of the segmented account. The implications for the company's management, therefore, include the need to ensure that investments available to the insurer are allocated fairly among different segments, that the transfer of investments from one segmented account to another is established on fair terms to policyowners of both product lines, and that intersegment loans are similarly equitable. Although different product lines behave differently, correlation across lines of business can exist that lessens the problem. In other words, a so-called natural hedge may exist.

There is a need for an overall, holistic risk profile for the general account. It is important that the costs of assuming the risks of different lines of business be allocated to those lines in a way that reflects the riskiness of the product line. Ultimately, the insurer's investment managers should address the specific requirements of each product, and the investment objectives established for each product line should be compatible with the insurer's overall investment objectives.

Liability Cash Flows

Understanding the impact of interest rate changes on liability cash flows is essential to effective cash flow analysis. Historically, insurers have had limited experience with lapses and surrenders within a volatile interest rate environment and, to date, have only limited data available on cash flows in volatile interest rate markets. Voluntary terminations, therefore, may be the most difficult liability cash flows to predict. A clear relationship exists between voluntary terminations and rising interest rates.

Other factors can be expected to influence lapse and surrender experience as well. Lapse-control contract features such as surrender charges may be effective disincentives to lapse, as may be a partial surrender option. Interest crediting/dividend strategy should also help determine whether the lapse option will be attractive to policyowners.

Policy loan activity should be influenced by variable policy loan rates and direct recognition features. Potential loan activity must also be considered together with factors that influence the attractiveness of the lapse alternative. The public perception of a company's financial and operating performance, as reflected in agency rating downgrades or negative publicity, may also influence policy surrenders. Although the volatility of interest rates has abated since the 1980s, the significant bond market decline of 1994 and increase of 1998 are compelling reminders of the need to anticipate unexpected market interest rate fluctuations. The proximate cause of the widely reported 1991 insolvencies of several major life insurers was investment oriented (overconcentration in junk bonds and real estate). The insolvencies demonstrated the "run-on-the-bank" phenomenon that can develop even in otherwise healthy insurers in which policyowners withdraw their money in a precautionary move.

Asset Cash Flows

The third step in interest-sensitive cash flow modeling is the forecasting of asset cash flows. Asset types and maturities must be established and the sensitivity of interest, dividends, rents, and asset sale proceeds to changes in the interest rate environment must be considered. As discussed before, the market value of investments may decline when interest rates rise, and extreme economic conditions could result in the default of some investments.

Consideration should also be given to the asset mix. Just as interest rate changes may affect the expected cash flows from individual investments, investment strategy and the types of investments acquired will also be likely to change as interest rates change. The implications of interest rate changes would be particularly important in times of declining interest rates and cash inflow antiselection.

With flexible-premium products, premium payment patterns should change as interest rates change. Increased premium cash flow may be expected in times of declining interest rates, particularly with insurers employing a portfolio average interest crediting strategy. When interest rates rise, premium cash flows may decrease, particularly when withdrawal control features such as variable loan rates and the surrender charges typical of newer products are present.

Evaluation of the impact of changing interest rates is essential to develop strategies for dealing with negative cash flows. Unexpected negative cash flows conceivably could require the liquidation of assets or the borrowing of funds from outside sources. The expected negative cash flows associated with new product introductions would normally be planned for and financed internally. Reinvestment strategies for positive cash flows must be considered as well.

Finally, consideration must be given to the interaction or correlation of events under different interest rate scenarios. For example, mortality antiselection should be expected during periods of high lapse rates, and extreme economic conditions such as high interest rates and unemployment could generate both asset defaults and increased disability income claims simultaneously.

Interest Rate Sensitivity Analysis

Once a determination has been reached as to the impact of changing interest rates and other risks on asset and liability cash flows, and an appropriate financial model constructed, the aggregate cash flow results are forecast under a wide range of potential interest rate scenarios. Most life insurers use stochastic modeling techniques and run thousands of simulations to examine resulting surplus distributions. At a minimum, an effective model tests results under the following general conditions:

- both rapidly and gradually rising interest rates
- both rapidly and gradually falling interest rates
- stable interest rates
- combinations of these conditions over time

It is also necessary to consider the impact of the shape of the market yield curve reflecting the relationship of short-term interest rates to long-term interest rates.

It is perhaps frustrating that interest-sensitive cash flow analysis will not produce a "correct answer." A predictable pattern of future interest rates cannot be known, as certainty is, of course, impossible. This is the nature of forecasting under conditions of uncertainty.

The usefulness of interest-sensitive cash flow analysis results from the analyst's ability to view probable results over a range of possible interest rate environments, and to identify the interest rate environments that might produce unacceptable solvency or profitability results. The analyst can then make judgments as to the probability of troublesome environments actually developing. When there appears to be a reasonable probability of interest rate environments developing that could adversely impact cash flow, management action is necessary. When the likelihood of adverse interest rate environments is remote, an insurer can plan for profitable results under reasonable economic conditions.

Interest-sensitive cash flow analysis does not eliminate interest rate risk, but it is a helpful tool in describing risk. The insurer is able to make a reasonably informed judgment as to the level of interest rate risk it can tolerate, and to understand better the potential consequences of the risk it decides to assume.

Figure 33-2 presents the results of a hypothetical interest-sensitive cash flow analysis for a particular product. Twelve interest rate scenarios are tested for their contribution to insurer surplus. (In practice, hundreds or thousands of scenarios would evolve from the process.) As the results indicate, scenarios 2, 4, and 5 represent the potential for significant adverse impact on solvency and profitability. Given these results, the company will evaluate the probability of these troublesome environments actually developing, and compare these results against the significant profits that may be achieved under other scenarios. In addition to the ending surplus analysis, companies also analyze cash flow periodically to ensure continuous solvency.

Applications of Cash Flow Analysis

The most compelling reason for the development of interest-sensitive cash flow analysis has been the need to manage the asset–liability matching risk effectively. Both *product design* and *pricing* and the construction, management, and performance measurement of *investment portfolios* are derivatives of cash flow analysis.

Chapter 34 covers both statutory accounting principles and generally accepted accounting principles. We know from the discussion at the beginning of this chapter that each accounting convention is a static method of financial analysis and that the sensitivity of aggregate corporate cash flows to changing interest rates must be considered to evaluate effectively the ability of an insurer to meet its future obligations and to produce profits. Performance measurement based on *economic value analysis* is derived from the cash flow model, and *value-based planning,* discussed in chapter 23, is driven by the economic value revealed in cash flow analysis.

Additional financial management efforts requiring cash flow analysis include *surplus management,* discussed later, and *scenario testing,* which are requirements of the valuation actuary regulatory initiatives discussed in chapter 34. As pointed out earlier, most insurers run thousands of economic simulations in addition to the required regulatory scenario tests. Simulations are asset-share studies using randomly generated variables.

Interest-sensitive financial modeling has become critical to identifying, describing, and managing life insurer cash flows. Figure 33-3 presents interest-sensitive cash flow analysis as the central engine for the major elements of life insurer financial management.

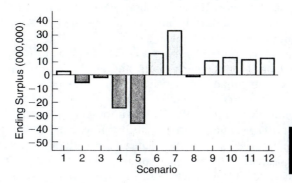

FIGURE 33-2 Forecasted Product Cash Flows—12 Possible Scenarios

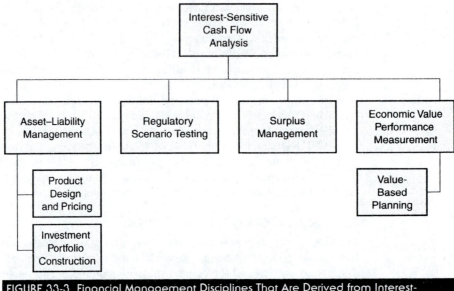

FIGURE 33-3 Financial Management Disciplines That Are Derived from Interest-Sensitive Cash Flow Analysis

FINANCING LIFE INSURANCE COMPANIES

As with any business enterprise, life insurers require financing. The typical sources of financing for businesses are equity and debt. As we discuss here, insurers also rely on these traditional sources. However, the major source of insurer finance is its customers. As we highlighted previously and in chapter 32, we can think of policyowners, *from an economic point of view,* as being debtholders, even though *from a legal and practical viewpoint,* policyowners are not the same as debtholders. Nonetheless, it is true that annuity, life, and health reserves—representing amounts owed ultimately to insurer customers—are the sources of greater than 80 percent of insurer financing.

The second most important source of insurer finance is equity. Equity financing is created by issuing common or preferred stock and by retaining earnings. A company's capital is directly increased by the amount of the issue or retention and, thus, an issuer's solvency position is improved. A company's shareholders are its owners, and they hold residual claim on all surplus and dividends after the company's obligations are satisfied. Conversely, all of a company's obligees must be satisfied before a distribution of surplus can be made to shareholders. Because policyowners hold the ownership interest in a mutual company, it cannot issue equity instruments, and this situation can create significant problems for mutual company financing.

Debt financing is created by issuing bonds (or debentures). Debt obligations are owed to the holders of the issuer's bonds and must be satisfied to maintain the company's solvency. Debt financing is available to both stock and mutual companies, although its use by insurers historically has been limited. Debt financing is a source of liquidity only; it is not a source of capital. Although the proceeds of a debt offering increase the assets of the issuing company, its liabilities are increased by the same amount and surplus remains unchanged. The financial strength of the insurer is not improved.

Two other sources of financing are unique to the insurance industry: surplus notes and reinsurance. Surplus notes are a form of hybrid debt, akin to preferred stock, but, because of special characteristics, they are carried on insurance company sap balance sheets as net worth, not as debt. Surplus notes can be issued by insurance companies only with the approval of regulatory authorities. Their special characteristics are:

1. All liabilities take priority over the payments of principal and interest on the notes.
2. Payments of interest and principal can be made only with approval of regulatory authorities.
3. Failure to make payments does not represent default.
4. Proceeds of a surplus note issue are treated as surplus only for statutory accounting purposes (see chapter 34).

Finally, insurance companies use reinsurance, not only for risk management purposes but also as a source of financing. Both indemnity reinsurance, used for risk management purposes, and financial reinsurance, designed specifically for financing purposes, are sources of financing for life insurers. Reinsurance agreements with recapture provisions are similar to debt agreements in that the insurer may at some point in the future end its relationship with the reinsurer and recover all future cash flows for itself. Reinsurance arrangements without recapture provisions are similar to equity financing in that the primary insurer has forever given up a share of cash flow on the covered business. It should be noted that use of both surplus notes and reinsurance financing depends entirely on favorable treatment by regulators, and that both are subject to substantial regulatory review.

INVESTMENT MANAGEMENT

The investment function is a critically important subset of the overall financial management of a life insurance company. Drawing on the discussions in chapter 32, the remainder of this chapter provides an overview of the formulation of investment strategy and the investment management process.

Life Insurer Investment Activity

Investment management is a significant element in the successful operation of an insurer and in its relationships with clients. The aggregate investment activities of any country's life and health insurance industry are also a major source of capital for national economic growth. Successful asset management is a primary objective for all life and health insurers.

Life insurers invest in the debt and equity issues of all types of corporations and make direct investments in and mortgage loans for office buildings, shopping malls, apartment buildings, and other real estate. They are major purchasers of government securities. Among U.S. financial intermediaries, life insurance companies rank behind commercial banks, mutual funds, and pension plans in total assets under management. Figure 33-4 illustrates recent trends in capital contributions of life insurers, commercial banks, mutual funds, and private pension plans for 1987 and 1997.

The total investment portfolio of a life insurance company can be separated into two categories: (1) assets supporting the insurer's general account and (2) assets supporting separate accounts. The accounts are classified primarily according to the nature of the liabilities for which the assets are being held and invested. Assets used to support contractual obligations providing for guaranteed, fixed benefit payments normally are held in the company's **general account.** Other invested assets, used to support the liabilities associated with investment risk pass-through products or lines of business (e.g.,

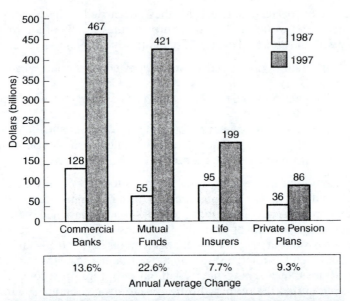

FIGURE 33-4 Life Insurers, Commercial Banks, Mutual Funds, and Pension Plans as Sources of Funds in U.S. Money and Capital Markets ($ billions)

Source: 1998 Life Insurance Fact Book, American Council of Life Insurance, p. 92.

variable annuities, variable life insurance, and pension products) are held in special accounts labeled as **separate accounts.** Separate accounts were first used by U.S. life insurance companies in connection with their pension business in the early 1960s. A separate account is a fund established by a life insurance company and held separately from all other assets.

State laws provide that assets in appropriate separate accounts may be invested without regard to the restrictions that are usually placed on the general account investments of life insurers. Thus, a separate account portfolio might be comprised of only common stocks, only bonds, only mortgages, or any combination of these or other investments. Almost 25 percent of all assets of U.S. life insurers are held in separate accounts. Figure 33-5 presents the growth in general account, separate account, and total assets of U.S. life insurers. The greater growth of separate compared to general accounts is due to higher demand for variable products.

Importance of Investment Performance

Life insurer investment activities cut across all product lines and have wide significance for a company's relationship with its customers. The investment performance of the general account of a life company affects profits, dividends, and interest credits on term, traditional whole life and universal life and other current assumption products, as well as traditional annuity products and guaranteed investment contracts. Separate account performance affects variable life and annuity products and pension funds when benefits by contract depend upon investment results that are passed directly to contract-holders. A growing number of insurers also offer pure investment vehicles such as money market funds, mutual funds, and other asset management services.

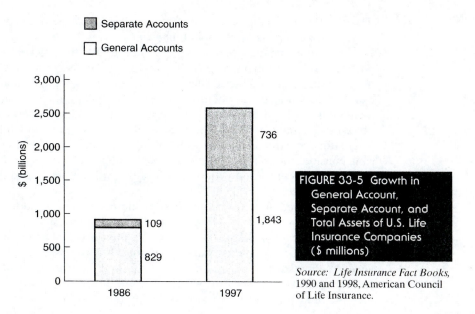

FIGURE 33-5 Growth in General Account, Separate Account, and Total Assets of U.S. Life Insurance Companies ($ millions)

Source: Life Insurance Fact Books, 1990 and 1998, American Council of Life Insurance.

The price of insurance products is highly dependent on the investment returns an insurer earns. Insurers that earn above-average returns can price products more favorably than others, and insurers that earn below-average returns may not be able to retain customers in a competitive market.

The importance of the investment management process has increased significantly in recent years. The traditional methods of life insurer financial management that were prevalent until the 1970s proved to be inadequate as economic and investment conditions began to change rapidly. Inflation was a key motivator of change. Increased competition in financial services generally and the life insurance industry in particular squeezed margins on policies that were traditionally a source of profit, and linked sales growth and profitability more closely to investment performance.

The development of interest-sensitive, variable, and flexible-premium products has created significant interdependence between investment performance and product performance. Investment management has become considerably more complex because asset–liability management concerns demand the integration of investment management and product design and management into a coherent process.

Investment markets themselves have become increasingly complex because of the volatility of interest rates. The universe of available investment alternatives has expanded rapidly as capital markets continue to develop synthetic and derivative investment vehicles designed to address the portfolio manager's need to manage the impact of market volatility on the investment portfolio. As with all aspects of life insurer management, the investment management process has become more sensitive to the wide range of simultaneous influences that changing market interest rates can bring to investment values, product performance, and customer behavior.

Establishing Investment Policies

The board of directors or trustees of an insurer has ultimate responsibility for establishing an insurer's investment policies. This responsibility is usually delegated to a finance or investment committee that is charged with developing investment policies designed to achieve the company's strategic objectives; the stated policy then guides the day-to-day activities of investment managers.

In establishing the investment policy constraints that define the parameters of the portfolio construction process, the finance or investment committee considers a number of environmental influences. These typically include general economic conditions and expected inflation, government monetary and fiscal policy, the state of various investment markets, the insurer's market posture and that of its competitors, tax liabilities, and other factors that may have an impact on investment values and policyowner behavior. Regulatory constraints and the views of rating agencies, brokers, and agents are significant considerations in setting investment policy. Insurers operating internationally would also be concerned with currency rates, trade balances, and the geographic location of liabilities.

As discussed in the previous chapter, life insurers must address the asset–liability risk inherent in all financial intermediary activities. Investment policy for life insurers establishes a level of risk tolerance not only for individual assets and collective portfolios, but also for the risk associated with mismatched assets and liabilities. **Risk tolerance** is defined as the largest amount of risk that an insurer is willing to accept for an appropriate expected return. At a minimum, insurer investment objectives include meeting obligations to policyowners, maintaining the insurer's ability to compete for market share, and contributing to the growth of earnings and surplus. The primary objective is to create an investment portfolio with cash flow properties that are consistent with an insurer's expected liability cash flows and asset–liability risk management strategy, and with its solvency and profitability constraints.

Investment Risk

Special Characteristics of Life Insurer Investment Risk

One of the central concepts of investment risk is the commonly acknowledged relationship of investment risk and expected return. Greater degrees of risk associated with an investment typically imply greater expected returns. The objective of investment portfolio management is to maximize investment return for a given level of risk (or to minimize risk for a desired level of return). **Investment risk** is generally defined as the potential variability of returns.

The traditional concept of the risk–return relationship applies to life insurers as it does to other investors. However, two aspects of the operating nature of the life insurance business require special portfolio management considerations that do not typically affect all investors.

The insurance pricing (actuarial) risk encompasses the first investment aspect special to insurers and other financial intermediaries. The rate of return assumed in calculating premiums is used to discount the price of insurance to policyowners. This is an implied long-term interest rate guarantee (interest rate guarantees on interest-sensitive products are explicit). The discounting practice has two important implications: (1) To meet solvency and profitability objectives, investment returns at a minimum must equal the returns assumed in its pricing practices, and (2) absolute yields are less important than the spread between pricing assumptions and actual earnings.

The asset–liability matching (systematic) risk incorporates the second investment consideration that is special to financial intermediaries. Changing market interest rates can simultaneously affect the value of a company's assets and liabilities and the behavior of its customers. The investment management discipline, along with contract design, is, therefore, a subset of the asset–liability management process.

Despite these special characteristics, life insurers, like other investors, prefer higher returns to minimize the cost of insurance products and to maximize profitability. When insurers seek to maximize return for a given level of risk, however, the concept of return must incorporate the idea of investment margins or spreads. The **investment margin** or **spread** is the difference between the amount of investment income the insurer earns and the investment income the insurer credits to a product or assumes when pricing that product.

Because of the special financial intermediary characteristics of life insurer operations and the special risk profile that results, fixed-income investments make up the significant majority of a life insurer's assets. As discussed later, bond portfolio dedication techniques are used to (1) ensure returns that exceed pricing assumptions and (2) maintain an appropriate relationship between a life insurer's asset and liability cash flows.

The Forward Commitment Aspect of Interest Rate Risk

Some life insurer investment opportunities, known as **forward contracts** (or **commitments**), are structured such that the commitment to make the investment is followed by a period of deferral before the investment is actually funded. Forward commitments are particularly common with private placements and commercial mortgages, as discussed later. These commitments are problematic for insurance companies because the commitment is not always mutual. The insurance company is bound to make the investment at the agreed time of funding, but the borrower is not bound to accept the loan. The risk in this unilateral agreement is termed **forward commitment risk.**

Life companies traditionally were able to plan ahead and make forward commitments because their cash flows were predictable, their liquidity needs were stable, and interest rates varied little. As interest rates have become more volatile, forward commitments evolved into valuable call options for borrowers. If interest rates had risen when the time for funding arrived, borrowers followed through on their relatively low interest rate loans; if interest rates had fallen, they declined to accept the insurance company loan and borrowed at lower rates elsewhere. To minimize the adverse impact of borrower behavior when interest rates change, life insurers now underwrite loans made on a forward commitment basis more carefully, often charging fees for commitments and shortening the commitment period. In fact, quite a few companies no longer make forward commitments. The margin between private placement and public bonds has sharply narrowed since the mid-1980s.

U.S. Life Insurance Industry Mix of Assets

U.S. life insurance companies hold and manage assets of more than $2.6 trillion. The largest investment category consists of corporate bonds, representing just over 40 percent of total industry assets. Real estate mortgage loans account for 8 percent of total assets, whereas directly owned real estate abort 2 percent. Life insurer holdings of U.S. Treasury and federal agency securities represent another 15 percent of assets. Corporate equity holdings are 23 percent of total assets, which is a significant increase over past years due primarily to growth in separate account business.

Investments in securities of other countries' governments and international agencies have always been small, amounting to 1.5 percent of total assets. Investments in both long- and short-term non-U.S. corporate debt obligations represent less than 5 percent of industry assets, of which a major share is in Canadian securities.

Policy loans make up another 4 percent of industry assets. These loans are taken at the option of the policyowner. Although policy loans are considered invested assets, they are not the responsibility of the investment department. Figure 33-6 shows the distribution of assets of U.S. life insurers at the end of 1997.

Investment Asset Classes

This section provides an overview of the major asset types that comprise the investment portfolio of a typical U.S. life insurer, particular U.S. regulatory constraints that affect their acquisition by life insurers, and their major cash flow properties. In today's highly diverse capital markets, a virtually limitless variety of cash flow patterns can be associated with most investments; the cash flow properties discussed here are those that are most broadly offered and acquired.

As will be discussed in chapter 34, **admitted assets** are those that qualify for listing in the insurer's *statutory* balance sheet. Investment regulation rules apply to these admitted assets; an insurer may hold an unrestricted amount of nonadmitted assets (e.g., furniture, certain equipment, and agents' balances), but no value for minimum capital, surplus, or reserves is granted under statutory accounting rules.

Corporate Debt Obligations

Fixed-income obligations of corporations have been the leading investment asset for most U.S. life insurers since the mid-twentieth century. As discussed earlier, fixed-income investments are well suited to the objectives of attaining pricing assumption yields and managing the asset–liability relationship.

Corporate Bonds   Since World War II, the U.S. life insurance industry has funded a significant portion of the long-term capital requirements of industrial corporations, and since the 1960s, it has also provided significant capital for oil and gas pipelines, aircraft, and other transportation equipment. The cash flow properties of publicly traded corporate bonds are determined primarily by periodic payment of interest at the coupon rate and the lump-sum payment of principal at maturity. Deviations from expected cash flow can be caused by credit deterioration, default by the issuer, and prepayment of principal under call provisions. Changing market interest rates can affect the market value realized if a bond is sold before maturity, as well as the probability that a bond may be called by the issuer.

Public issues of corporate bonds are rated for credit quality by rating agencies such as Standard & Poor's and Moody's. Table 33-4 shows the rating definitions used by these agencies.

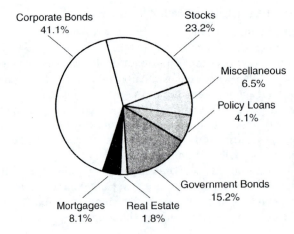

FIGURE 33-6 Distribution of Assets of U.S. Life Insurers (1997)

Source: 1998 Life Insurance Fact Book, American Council of Life Insurance, p. 94.

TABLE 33-4		Bond Ratings
Moody's	*S&P*	*Definition*
Aaa	AAA	*High-grade investment bonds.* The highest rating assigned, denoting extremely strong capacity to pay principal and interest. Often called "gilt edge" securities.
Aa	AA	*High-grade investment bonds.* High quality by all standards but rated lower primarily because the margins of protection are not quite as strong.
A	A	*Medium-grade investment bonds.* Many favorable investment attributes, but elements may be present that suggest susceptibility to adverse economic changes.
Baa	BBB	*Medium-grade investment bonds.* Adequate capacity to pay principal and interest but possibly lacking certain protective elements against adverse economic conditions.
Ba	BB	*Speculative issues.* Only moderate protection of principal and interest in varied economic times.
B	B	*Speculative issues.* Generally lacking desirable characteristics of investment bonds. Assurance of principal and interest may be small.
Caa	CCC	*Default.* Poor-quality issues that may be in default or in danger of default.
Ca	CC	*Default.* Highly speculative issues, often in default or possessing other market shortcomings.
C		*Default.* These issues may be regarded as extremely poor in investment quality.
	C	*Default.* Income bonds on which no interest is paid.
	D	*Default.* Issues actually in default, with principal or interest in arrears.

Source: *Moody's Bond Record* and *Standard & Poor's Bond Guide.*

Life insurers developed and have long used a lending technique known as private placements. **Private placements,** in contrast to securities traded on public exchanges, involve loans in which the terms of an offering are negotiated between the borrower and the insurer. Private placements can be advantageous to both issuers and life insurer investors because (1) legal, accounting, and brokerage commissions associated with public offerings are avoided; (2) the issuer is certain that the entire offering will be acquired; and (3) the terms of the offering are negotiated directly, providing an opportunity for the parties to better define or customize their agreement. Private placements are less liquid and marketable than public offerings; however, insurers acquiring private placements normally expect increased yields to compensate for illiquidity.[5] At year-end 1996, 16.3 percent of general account assets were invested in privately traded bonds.

Life insurers also benefit from negotiating investment terms in a way that helps control asset–liability matching risk. The cash flow properties of private placements can be tailored to meet the needs of both the issuer and the life insurer.

Large insurers typically employ a special staff devoted to analyzing and acquiring private placements; the analysis of private investments differs significantly from the analysis of public offerings, in large part because of the directly negotiated terms. Private

---

[5]An increasingly active secondary market for private placements has been developing among sophisticated institutional investors in recent years. The SEC has adopted Rule 144A for this purpose (leeway for large operators; protection for small investors).

placements are sometimes made to a small group or syndication of insurance companies. Participation in a syndication can be an attractive option for small insurers that do not have extensive research staffs and, therefore, rely on the investment judgment of larger companies in the group.

Through the 1960s and 1970s, life insurers acquired 75 percent or more of their corporate bond investments through private placements. In the 1980s, however, the share of private placements fell sharply, as the need for marketability of assets shifted acquisitions toward public issues. Nevertheless, the ability to negotiate the cash flow properties of private placements directly has led to a significant share of corporate bond holdings of life insurers being private placement issues, although there has been a distinct shift to publicly traded bonds in recent years.

Unlike private placements, public issues are readily marketable. This became an important consideration for portfolio managers after 1980, when liquidity needs took on higher priority. Liquidity needs increased because policyowners demanded policy loans or surrendered their policies to place the proceeds in other investments with significantly higher yields. The introduction of interest-sensitive insurance products after 1980 led to greater uncertainty about cash flows and moved insurers toward more liquid portfolios with shorter maturities. In practice, this brought about a new interest in resalable public issues, along with a shortening of original maturities from around 20 years to about one-half that duration.

Collateralized Mortgage Obligations   Prior to the late 1960s, life insurers had been a major source of financing for single-family mortgages. The relative attractiveness of corporate yields, however, led to a decline in single-family residential financing, and only a few companies remain active in such direct lending.

In the late 1970s, financial instruments known as mortgage-backed securities or collateralized mortgage obligations (CMOs) were developed in the capital markets. A **collateralized mortgage obligation** is a type of bond that is secured by a pool of mortgages. CMOs have been originated by banks, thrifts, life insurers, and other financial intermediaries and by quasi-governmental agencies such as the Government National Mortgage Association (GNMA) and the Federal National Mortgage Association (FNMA). Principal and interest payments of mortgages are passed through to the owners of CMOs. Because CMOs derive their value from other securities, they are classified as derivatives (see later in this chapter).

The cash flow properties of CMOs differ from those of typical bonds because periodic payments of interest and principal are passed through to the bondholder, matching the self-amortizing home mortgage loan. The amount of interest and principal payments depends on the lending rate.

The CMO market is growing, with insurers being important purchasers of them, especially to back GIC obligations. They appeal to insurers because of their attractive yields and high quality. However, they can be volatile investments because of their cash flow properties. Changing interest rates as well as prepayments and payment extensions can result in significant changes in their price, total returns, and cash flows. As we noted earlier, they exhibit negative convexity, which can lead to a straddle position. Because of this, derivatives are often used along with them, as we discuss later.

Regulation of Corporate Debt Obligations   Because of the safety of corporate debt relative to equity investments, and because these investments are well suited to the financial management needs of life insurers, there are generally no state restrictions on the aggregate amount of corporate debt obligations that may be held as admitted assets in insurer portfolios. There are, however, restrictions with respect to the credit quality of corporate debt and to the concentration of investment in the securities of a particular issuer.

In 1992, the NAIC adopted a model regulation, **Investments in Medium Grade and Lower Grade Obligations Model Regulation,** to protect the interest of the insurance-buying public by establishing limitations on the concentration of medium-grade and lower-grade obligations. The Securities Valuation Office (SVO) of the NAIC rates bonds into six quality categories from 1, the highest, to 5, the lowest for bonds in good standing, and category 6 for bonds in or near default. *Medium-grade obligations* refers to bonds rated 3 by the SVO. *Lower-grade obligations* refers to bonds rated 4, 5, or 6 by the SVO. The regulation provides that the aggregate amount of all medium- and lower-grade obligations may not exceed 20 percent of admitted assets. No more than 10 percent of admitted assets may consist of obligations rated 4, 5, or 6 by the SVO, no more than 3 percent may consist of obligations rated 5 or 6, and no more than 1 percent may consist of obligations rated 6 by the SVO.

In addition to these general limits, insurers may not invest more than an aggregate amount of 1 percent of their admitted assets in medium-grade obligations issued, guaranteed, or insured by any one institution, nor more than 0.5 percent in lower-grade obligations of any one institution. In no event may an insurer invest more than 1 percent of its admitted assets in any medium- or lower-grade obligations of any one institution.

This model law has been adopted in a number of states, with legislation pending in still others. New York has had such regulation in place for some time.

At year-end 1997, 94 percent of general account bonds were investment grade.

From an investment standpoint, the most important state laws are those of New York. The extraterritorial dimension of New York law requires all New York licensed insurers to comply in substance with New York investment law, even for insurers domiciled outside New York. A significant majority of all life insurance sold in the United States is sold by New York–licensed companies and, hence, is subject to New York investment laws.

The quantitative New York rules regarding concentration of investment in the securities of a particular issuer limit this investment to no more than 5 percent of the insurer's admitted assets. This requirement promotes asset quality by implicitly requiring diversification of bond investments among issuers. Figure 33-7 shows the distribution of U.S. life industry general account assets, including corporate bonds in 1986 and 1997.

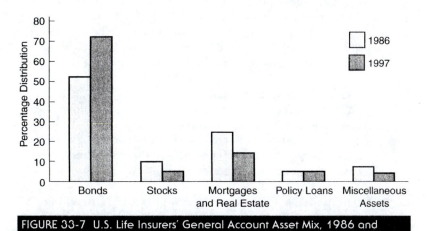

FIGURE 33-7 U.S. Life Insurers' General Account Asset Mix, 1986 and 1997

Source: 1998 Life Insurance Fact Book, American Council of Life Insurance, p. 101.

Commercial Real Estate Mortgages

As with corporate debt obligations, commercial real estate mortgages are generally fixed-income obligations. Historically, long-term commercial mortgage loans were considered an ideal way to match the long-term obligations assumed by life insurers under their whole life policies. Terms as long as 30 years were common. Commercial mortgages are generally illiquid investments; due to increasing liquidity requirements, the bulk of commercial mortgage lending is now closer to 10-year maturities.

Commercial mortgage loan commitments are generally made in advance of construction, and the proceeds are used to repay short-term bank construction financing. As discussed earlier, the forward commitment risk is increasingly being addressed by insurers through shorter commitment periods and more stringent underwriting and loan terms.

Commercial mortgages, like privately placed bonds, are directly negotiated between the insurer and borrower. The cash flow properties of mortgage loans vary widely. The negotiations represent an opportunity for insurers to match investment cash flows with expected liability cash flows, and to incorporate provisions that adjust investment cash flows to changing market interest rates.

The cash flow properties of mortgages are determined by the interest rate, principal repayment, and maturity provisions agreed upon in the loan document. The interest rate may be fixed or variable; principal may be repaid periodically or in a "bullet" or "balloon" lump sum. Additional returns supplementing earned interest are sometimes negotiated in the form of a limited equity interest or additional interest payment based upon the rental performance of the property.

Deviations from expected cash flows can be caused by default, prepayment of principal, and, in the case of variable-rate mortgages, changing market interest rates. There is no significant secondary market for commercial mortgages, and most loans are held to maturity by the insurer.

State investment laws affecting admitted mortgage loans are both qualitative and quantitative in nature. The qualitative restrictions generally focus on limiting the principal amount of the loan to a stated percentage of appraised value. The limit in New York is 75 percent. Regulatory loan to value ratio requirements are applicable only at the time of the making of the loan. When real estate values are depressed, mortgages may exceed the applicable limit.

Quantitative restrictions apply to both aggregate mortgage investment as a percentage of assets (or capital and surplus), and to the percentage of assets (or capital and surplus) that may be devoted to a single property. In New York, the limits are 50 percent of assets in the aggregate and 2 percent of assets to any one property.

U.S. Government Securities

U.S. government fixed-income obligations, including Treasury bills (1-year maturity or less), notes (1- to 5-year maturities), and bonds (5- to 30-year maturities) are generally considered free from credit risk. Certain obligations of government agencies are similarly backed by the full faith and credit of the U.S. government. The yields on U.S. government issues are, therefore, less attractive than relatively more risky corporate obligations.

In the 1980s, life insurer interest in U.S. government issues grew significantly. The increased interest was in part due to the need to balance the unexpected high risk associated with many bonds and corporate mortgages acquired during the 1980s. Additionally, the highly liquid nature of government issues is ideal when the potential cash flow fluctuations resulting from interest-sensitive products may require the sale of assets.

The cash flow properties of U.S. government issues, like corporate obligations, are determined primarily by the coupon rate and maturity date. Because there is no credit risk, deviations from expected cash flow are possible only when an investment is sold or called before maturity. Because there is no credit risk, life insurer investment in U.S. government issues is generally unlimited.

Corporate Equities

The cash flow characteristics associated with common stocks are far more variable and, therefore, riskier than those associated with fixed-income obligations. As a result, U.S. life insurer interest in these investments is significant only in connection with separate account business.

The cash flow properties of common stock are determined by the nonguaranteed, periodic payment of dividends, and by the market value of the shares. There is no maturity value for common stock.

Although over relatively long time horizons common stock returns generally exhibit favorable risk-adjusted results, the irregular nature of the cash flow is considered not well suited to U.S. life insurer investment. U.S. life insurers need to seek relatively certain returns over specified time horizons that are consistent with their pricing assumptions and asset–liability management strategies, and the more predictable cash flow results associated with fixed-income investments are generally desirable. Worth noting is that some countries (e.g., the United Kingdom) allow life insurers to issue (nonvariable) cash-value policies with no interest guarantees. In such instances, the logic that favors bonds and shuns equities is less compelling.

State investment laws at one time prohibited the acquisition of common stock. Restrictions on general account investment have been liberalized, reflecting the inflation protection, diversification, and long-term performance benefits that stocks have exhibited. New York limits admitted common stock investment to no more than 2 percent of any issuer's stock, 0.2 percent of insurer assets in the stock of any one issuer, and 20 percent of insurer assets in the aggregate.

As discussed earlier, insurers sought, and regulators accommodated, the approval of separate accounts. Institutional clients of U.S. life insurers in the 1950s and 1960s perceived the constraints on insurer stock holdings negatively, fearing the prohibition of significant equity investments would impair the real return on long-term pension investments during times of inflation. Because separate accounts pass investment experience and risk directly to the insurer's clients, common stock holdings in separate accounts are generally not restricted. The separate account option became available to individual policyowners with the introduction of variable life insurance and annuities. Common stocks frequently comprise more than 50 percent of separate account assets. Insurance companies now sponsor mutual funds apart from any insurance content and/or own mutual fund complexes.

Preferred stocks exhibit characteristics of both debt and equity investments. These shares pay a stated dividend when declared, and the preferred dividend liability must be satisfied before common stock dividends can be paid. Preferred stocks comprise less than 1 percent of life insurer assets.

Investment Real Estate

Direct investment or ownership in real estate is an equity investment like common stock. Real estate equity can be attractive to an insurer by producing higher current returns than equity in stocks, while providing the same opportunity for appreciation in the capital value of the investment. Real estate ownership is viewed as an attractive asset during times of inflation because rents can be raised periodically as long as market conditions are favorable, thereby increasing property values.

The cash flow characteristics of investment real estate are determined by occupancy rates, rental fees, and operating expenses. Deviations from expected cash flow can result from tenant defaults and from variable occupancy rates.

The unpredictable cash flow properties of investment real estate are not well suited to U.S. life insurer investment needs. In recent years, real estate holdings have amounted to no more than 3 percent of total assets. About one-eighth of the total represents the value of insurer head offices and branches used for their own operations.

Investment laws limit real estate ownership, as with other invested assets. Under New York law, an insurer cannot own more than 2 percent of assets in any particular admitted property or more than 20 percent of assets in admitted real estate held for investment purposes. Up to 10 percent of admitted assets, however, can be devoted to properties used by the company, as long as total admitted real estate holdings do not exceed 25 percent.

Quantitative limits generally do not apply to real estate assets acquired through foreclosure. Regulators often require, however, that such properties be disposed of within a stipulated period of time.

Policy Loans

Policy loans are unique among life insurer investments for two reasons. First, policy loans are not made as the result of an investment management decision—they are options exercised at the discretion of the policyowner. Second, because loans should never exceed policy cash values, and unpaid principal amounts may be deducted from cash surrender proceeds or policy proceeds at the death of the insured, the safety of principal associated with most loans is absolute. (In the case of variable products, declining cash surrender values can reduce the value of the insurer's cash surrender collateral below the value of the loan.)

As discussed in chapter 32, the historical experience with policy loans was troubling for life insurers, despite their safety of principal. Together with cash surrenders, they produced book-value liquidity requirements that were unpredictable. With the advent of variable loan interest rates and direct recognition dividend provisions, policy loans associated with newer policies have become well suited to maintaining investment spreads and asset–liability risk management strategy.

The cash flow properties associated with principal payments and withdrawals are determined by policyowner preference; interest income is determined by the applicable loan rate in the case of variable loan rate policies, and, in the case of direct recognition policies, the effective interest is the sum of interest paid and the amount of policyowner benefit forgone in the form of reduced dividends.

Risk Management Assets

Key Terms Defined   To minimize their asset–liability risk exposure, life insurers often enter into various types of hedging arrangements. **Hedging** is a strategy of acquiring securities whose gains and losses offset gains and losses in other securities or portfolios of securities. Hedging often is achieved through the purchase of **derivatives,** which are securities whose values are *derived* from the value of other securities such as stocks, currencies, or indexes of stocks, interest rates, and so on. Derivatives transfer some business risk, such as a rise in interest rates or declines in currencies or stock markets, from one party to another. No principal is at risk with derivatives. Only the cash flows derived from notional values are at risk. Common derivatives include forward and futures contracts, options, and swaps, all of which typically expire in less than one year after issuance.

As discussed earlier, a *forward contract* obligates one party to deliver on a specified financial (or other) arrangement at a specified future time at a price and on terms agreed to now. Forward contracts ordinarily are not sold on organized exchanges; they are individually tailored transactions and, therefore, are somewhat illiquid. They can, however, be bundled to create swaps (discussed later).

A **futures contract** obligates one party to buy and another to sell a financial instrument (or anything else) at a specified future time at a price and on terms agreed to now. Futures contracts are standardized, sold on organized exchanges, and have ready markets. Futures contracts require buyers and sellers to post margins as collateral as the market value of the contracts changes, which substantially reduces their credit risk.

Options grant their holders the right to buy (a **call option**) or sell (a **put option**) assets within a limited time period at a stipulated price. The option holder pays a premium for the right to buy or sell, and, if the option is not exercised within the stated time period, it expires with the option seller retaining the premium. Options are traded on organized exchanges and, therefore, are readily marketable. Because the premium is small compared to the value of the underlying asset, option trading offers substantial leverage, which can translate into great profits or enormous losses, as several recent notorious examples (e.g., Barings) well illustrate.

Swaps are agreements between two parties to exchange securities (i.e., cash flows). Four types of swaps exist: interest rate swaps, currency swaps, commodity swaps, and equity swaps. All swaps have as their objective the restructuring of asset or liability cash flows to suit the transacting parties. Interest rate swaps are by far the most common swaps.

Interest rate swaps permit an insurer to trade the fixed-rate interest payments it has a right to receive for the variable-rate interest payments another market participant will receive. The insurer's assets and liabilities are thus better matched, while the insurer has shared its natural advantage in acquiring fixed-income investments with another participant who shares its natural advantage in variable-rate credit markets.

Illustrative Use of Derivatives   To demonstrate use of derivatives as risk management tools, we consider an interest rate swap.[6] Insurer A has a four-year, $100 million investment with a return set at LIBOR. (**LIBOR** is the London Interbank Offered Rate—the most widely used floating-rate index in the interest swaps market.) The CFO wishes to convert the yield to a fixed rate, so the company enters into an interest rate swap with a dealer for a notional amount of $100 million. The company receives a fixed rate of 6 percent and agrees to pay the six-month LIBOR. The company's net yield, therefore, is 6 percent, as shown in Figure 33-8.

We now assume that the CFO is concerned about a rise in interest rates in connection with the insurer's interest-sensitive policy liabilities. The company can purchase a 7 percent interest rate cap with a notional amount of $100 million. Assume that it must pay 0.25 percent per year for this hedge. The company's net cost, therefore, is LIBOR plus 0.25 percent with a lifetime maximum of 7.25 percent, even if the LIBOR rate rises to 8.0 percent or higher. The cap allows the company to put a ceiling on its floating-rate liabilities. Figure 33-9 illustrates this transaction.

The Derivatives Market   The derivatives market is composed of end users and dealers. Besides insurers, other financial intermediaries as well as general business firms use

---

[6]This illustration is taken from Lehman Brothers.

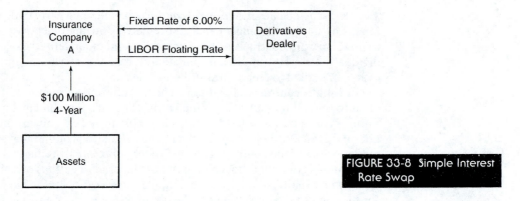

FIGURE 33-8 Simple Interest Rate Swap

derivatives. Dealers are primarily banks and securities firms, and a small number of highly rated insurers. Far more insurers are users than are dealers.

The Use of Derivatives by Life Insurers   Life insurers are major users of derivatives. They use them to achieve a better duration match of assets and liabilities and to help manage interest rate fluctuations, credit risk, and currency risk. Life insurers purchase futures to achieve a more acceptable duration for their portfolios. They purchase options to correct an unacceptable portfolio convexity.

Derivatives can serve multiple purposes, including the following:

- Exchange expected interest income patterns for other patterns better suited to the insurer's asset–liability matching requirements.
- Hedge floating rate debt.
- Lock in a rate for future debt.
- Protect the balance sheet against erosion in asset duration in a declining interest rate environment.
- Lock in current investment yields for premium income that will be received and invested in the future.

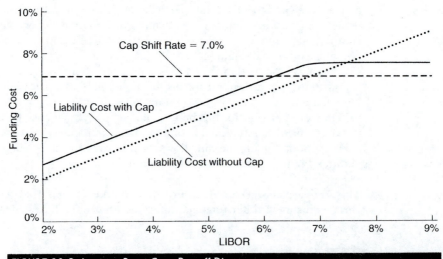

FIGURE 33-9 Interest Rate Cap: Payoff Diagram

Two studies by Cummins, Phillips, and Smith (CPS) found that large life insurers were much more intensive users of derivatives than smaller insurers.[7] They also found that insurers that made relatively greater use of derivatives were those with:

- relatively high proportions of their assets in real estate, CMOs, privately placed commercial bonds, and non-U.S./non-Canadian bonds
- relatively high proportions of group annuity and GIC reserves
- large maturity gaps.

These findings are consistent with the expectation that insurers use derivatives to hedge interest rate risk, volatility risk, liquidity risk, and exchange rate risk. CPS also investigated empirically whether the motivations for use of derivatives as a risk management tool seemed consistent with the standard explanations for why widely held firms would manage risk (as discussed at the beginning of chapter 32).

Their results supported the hypothesis that insurers hedge to maximize firm value and to reduce the expected costs of financial distress. They found some evidence that tax considerations influence insurer participation in the derivatives market. Finally, their results supported the hypothesis that significant economies of scale attach to derivatives operations. Thus, only large firms and/or those with higher than average risk exposure would find it efficient to incur the fixed cost of establishing a derivatives operation.

CPS reported that the largest single category of derivative usage by life insurers is interest rate swaps, followed by interest rate caps and floors. Life insurers also show significant activity in foreign currency derivatives.

Future Derivative Use by Life Insurers   The adoption of FAS 115 is expected to spur insurer usage of derivatives. As noted earlier, FAS 115 requires insurers to mark-to-market, under their GAAP financial statements, those fixed-income securities held for trading or available for sale. This standard moves GAAP financial statements closer to market (economic) accounting and, therefore, as discussed at the beginning of this chapter, exposes insurers to greater balance sheet volatility. Derivatives can reduce this volatility.

Derivatives have been the cause of substantial financial difficulties, and even failures, of some well-publicized financial and other organizations. These organizations represent a distinct minority of firms using derivatives, and their difficulties stemmed from their taking large positions in hopes of achieving profits rather than using derivatives as hedges. To date, only one insurer has suffered a similar fate. The great majority of derivative purchases by life insurers is intended to offset risks generated by insurance operations and not as a speculation.[8]

Changes in accounting rules, risk-based capital requirements, greater completion, interest-sensitive products, and risky investments have all worked to increase the use of derivatives by insurers. More insurers likely will find it necessary to use derivatives to ensure better asset–liability management and to reduce risk.

International Investments

Investing in a foreign security involves all the risks associated with investment in a domestic security but involves additional considerations and risks as well. The cash flows from international investments will be realized in a foreign currency. If the insurer expects claims in that currency, the investment will reduce the currency risk associated with

---

[7] J. David Cummins, Richard D. Phillips, and Stephen D. Smith, "Corporate Hedging in the Insurance Industry: The Use of Financial Derivatives by U.S. Insurers," *North American Actuarial Journal,* 1996, and J. David Cummins, Richard D. Phillips, and Stephen D. Smith, "Derivatives and Corporate Risk Management: Participation and Volume Decisions in the Insurance Industry," (unpublished), 1998.

[8] Ibid.

policies whose claims are denominated in the foreign currency. If no such claims are expected, there is the possibility that exchange losses (or gains) could arise when investment cash flows are converted into the domestic currency. **Currency risk** refers to uncertainty about the rate at which future foreign cash flows can be converted into the domestic currency. Currency risk can usually, but not always, be hedged in the futures and options markets, although some believe that the transaction and maintenance costs associated with hedging may outweigh the reduction in risk. Another risk is **political risk,** which refers to uncertainty regarding the ability to repatriate foreign cash flows when expected, including the possibility of imposition of exchange controls by foreign authorities or even expropriation.

Investments in securities or equities issued by non-U.S. governments or companies have been severely limited by state investment laws for many years. More recently, life insurer interest in international investments has increased. The leeway provisions of existing laws have been used by companies to take advantage of investment opportunities available internationally. The imposition of more stringent U.S. capital requirements has also led to a search for new sources of capital. As financial markets become more integrated and international, the logic for seeking better yielding international investment opportunities becomes more compelling.

U.S. Life Insurance Industry Mix of Separate Account Assets

As pointed out earlier, separate account assets are used to support liabilities associated with investment risk pass-through products or lines of business such as variable annuities, variable life insurance, and pension products. In contrast to general account assets, separate account assets may be invested without regard to state laws regulating the investment of general account assets. In these products, the investment risk has been transferred to the customer and investment managers are free to allocate assets among any investments available in the market. Pension customers may, and frequently do, participate in the allocation decisions.

The emphasis on corporate stocks, compared to general account assets (see Figure 33-5), reflects the flexibility available to investment managers in investing separate account assets. Figure 33-10 shows the distribution of separate account assets as of year-end 1997. The recent rapid growth of pass-through products is reflected in the volume

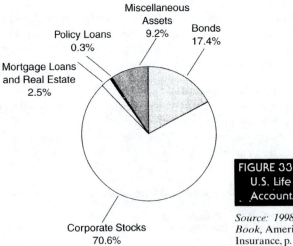

FIGURE 33-10 Distribution of U.S. Life Insurers' Separate Account Assets (1997)

Source: *1998 Life Insurance Fact Book,* American Council of Life Insurance, p. 101.

of assets supporting such products. Separate account assets have grown from 13 percent to almost 30 percent of total assets.

Investment Portfolio Construction

Before examining the process of constructing an investment portfolio, it will be useful to review measures of investment performance. In a competitive environment, sales growth and profitability are closely related to investment performance, and investment markets have become more complex and volatile. Measuring the effectiveness of investment performance is increasingly critical to effective life insurer financial management.

Investment Performance Measurement

Traditional investment performance measurement has focused on achieving high yields while minimizing risk assumed for a given level of return. Refocusing performance measurement on the creation of value for shareholders and policyowners is more consistent with every insurer's primary objective, and it better promotes the construction of an investment portfolio that is consistent with the cash flow nature of the life insurance business.

Traditional measurement of investment performance generally involves three steps: (1) An investment yield is calculated for the asset portfolio under examination; (2) a benchmark, typically an investment index, is chosen; and (3) the portfolio yield is compared to the benchmark yield. To the extent investment yield exceeds the benchmark, performance is considered to be superior.

Because of the risk–return relationship discussed earlier, comparing an investment manager's performance to an index tends to create an incentive for the manager to select the riskiest investments available from the universe that is consistent with the insurer's investment policies. Traditional investment performance measurement also fails to take account of the fact that investment spreads may produce satisfactory solvency and profitability results without the necessity of assuming the risk necessary to exceed the performance of a market index.

Although traditional measures of investment performance will continue to be used in the financial management process, the following discussion identifies significant weaknesses in the traditional approach and describes the need for a comprehensive approach to performance measurement. This broader approach is needed for a better response to the dynamic nature of life insurer financial management, and it underlies a portfolio construction process that is consistent with an understanding of life insurance as a cash flow business.

Four general calculations have been widely used in the process of life insurer investment performance management. **New investment yield** measures the income yield on investments purchased during the measurement period and can be helpful in determining the marginal impact of purchase decisions. This calculation produces relatively volatile results from period to period, reflecting changing market interest rates.

Portfolio book yield measures the income yield on all investments and, therefore, it produces relatively stable results from period to period. The current impact of prior purchase decisions is reflected. **Portfolio book income** measures aggregate cash inflows and outflows of principal and interest during the measurement period. It does not fully reflect the expected returns associated with prior purchase decisions, and its use is limited to comparisons with business plan projections. Finally, **portfolio total return** measures both income and market-value changes during the measurement period.

Both the new investment and portfolio book yield measures fail to reflect fully the investment risk associated with the portfolio. Both credit risk and interest rate risk are either ignored or inadequately reflected. New investment yield does not reflect credit or interest rate risk because market values are not taken into account. Portfolio book yield reflects the results of realized defaults and realized income associated with variable-rate investments, but credit deterioration and interest rate risk are again ignored because market values are not taken into account.

Portfolio total return, because it reflects the market value of investments, is sensitive to interest rate and credit risk reflected in the market at the time of measurement, as well as income generated during the measurement period. Future interest rates and credit deterioration are not taken into account, however. As pointed out in chapter 32, there is growing interest in using total return measures.

Traditional measures of investment performance, at best, retrospectively reflect the exposure to risk during the measurement period, but they do not reflect changes in the prospective risk position assumed by the insurer for its future results. The economic value of a company is measured by the present value of expected future cash flow, discounted at an interest rate reflecting both the cost of capital and risk inherent in the company's products and ventures. If other factors remain unchanged, an increase in risk assumed by an insurer reduces the value of a company, whereas a reduction in risk increases its value. Because traditional measures of investment performance take no account of a change in risk profile assumed by the company, increased current yields achieved by the acquisition of risky investments may produce superior performance results measured by traditional methods, while at the same time reducing the value of the company.

The important issue in investment performance measurement is less whether a particular portfolio has outperformed a particular index during the measurement period but whether the portfolio has contributed to the value of the firm. Investment portfolio construction, monitoring, and measurement must reflect potential risk, or variability of future cash flows, and they are best undertaken as integrated objectives within the context of interest-sensitive cash flow analysis discussed in chapter 32.

Portfolio Selection

Modern portfolio theory can be viewed as a risk management concept insofar as it attempts to reduce systematically the scatter or standard deviation of portfolio returns. Complex optimization algorithms have been developed to determine the optimum weighting ratios for many possible markets. Theoretical models regard the absolute risk of a financial asset as irrelevant. Prevalence is ascribed to the asset's risk relative to the portfolio containing it. The key to diversifying a portfolio lies not simply in the number of stocks it contains but in the correlation of their returns, as we discussed in chapter 32.

Diversification can eliminate company-specific, nonsystematic risk. As we have seen, however, broad economic factors (e.g., interest rate risk) that affect all firms provide systematic risk that cannot be eliminated (but can be hedged).

The capital asset pricing model (CAPM, see chapter 32) is widely used by analysts to value securities. CAPM focuses on the relationship between systematic risk (beta) and returns. Insurers need not worry about the market portfolio; they need only to decide how much systematic risk they wish to accept. Market forces then ensure that any stock can be expected to yield the appropriate return for its beta.

In selecting securities, then, the important point is the amount of risk that each contributes to the total risk of the portfolio. This depends upon the systematic or market risk of each security, that is, the extent to which its returns are correlated with the market's returns (its beta).

The choice of securities for a portfolio also will be influenced by the desired duration and convexity of the balance sheet. As pointed out in chapter 32, increasingly sophisticated software is available to facilitate the measurement of the effective duration and convexities, including the impact of varying yield curves. Weighting them appropriately with the fair value of liabilities and market value of assets (discounted value of cash flows) produces overall asset and liability duration and convexity measures. Taking into account any leveraging involved, the insurer can obtain measures of surplus duration and convexity. These measures assess the impact of interest rate movements on the value of the company.

The Construction Process

The portfolio construction process is designed to produce an investment program with cash flow properties that are consistent with an insurer's anticipated liability cash flows, pricing assumptions, and asset–liability risk management strategy. Although the formal process may vary from insurer to insurer, five general steps are fundamental to building a portfolio effectively. The process described here is essentially a restatement of the interest-sensitive cash flow modeling process described in chapter 32 from the perspective of the investment manager.

1. ***Establish Proper Control Parameters.*** Selecting an appropriate benchmark reflecting the insurer's solvency and profitability constraints for the planning of the portfolio and the measurement of its success is the first step in portfolio construction. In most situations, the objective will be to create growth in the value of the firm,[9] and a target or desired rate of growth will be established as a control parameter.

2. ***Establish Portfolio Constraints.*** Certain aspects of the investment portfolio or of insurer operations are necessarily limited for various reasons. Regulatory constraints are obvious. Less obvious may be the need of insurers operating internationally to invest in different currencies, or limitations arising from the expected tax or financial reporting consequences of particular investment decisions.

    An insurer's level of risk tolerance is established by the degree of variability in investment returns that is acceptable to management. The acceptable potential deviation of actual from expected results is always a significant constraint. The objectives of dedicated bond portfolio management techniques are discussed later and represent additional constraints for the typical life insurer.

3. ***Establish Alternative Strategies.*** Cash flow analysis should be conducted under a variety of possible economic scenarios. Alternative investment strategies are established to respond to the development of different market conditions. These strategies are developed in conjunction with dividend and interest crediting strategies, as well as other responses available to the insurer.

4. ***Conduct Cash Flow Analysis.*** Cash flow analysis produces a range of possible outcomes that includes the expected or targeted results. The cash flow analysis includes both liability (product) cash flows and asset cash flows. The range of outcomes is examined, and strategies that produce unacceptable results are rejected. Strategies producing results that are consistent with solvency and profitability criteria and with portfolio constraints are adopted for implementation.

5. ***Monitor and Adjust Portfolio.*** Monitoring the portfolio is accomplished by the periodic determination of two issues:

    1. Was actual performance during the measurement period within the distribution of acceptable outcomes?
    2. Does the distribution of possible future outcomes remain acceptable?

    A negative response to either determinant signals the need for readjustment of the portfolio.

---

[9]Occasionally, short-term goals such as reported earnings, liquidity, or even solvency may override this objective.

The cash flow–based portfolio construction and management process should (1) avoid the unnecessary risk associated with high-yield incentives that may be embedded in an insurer's performance measurement techniques; (2) reflect the potential variability of future cash flows; and (3) reward value-creating activity rather than index-beating activity.

Bond Portfolio Management Techniques

As discussed earlier, investment risk for life insurers incorporates not only the potential variability of investment return but also the possibilities of inadequate pricing (actuarial risk) and mismatched assets and liabilities. Bond dedication techniques can be used to ensure that investment yields consistent with pricing assumptions and solvency and profitability constraints are achieved, and that the relationship of asset and liability cash flows remains relatively constant through changing interest rate environments.

Bond dedication involves dedicating a portfolio to servicing a prescribed set of future liabilities so that the possibility of interest rate changes impairing the sufficiency of the portfolio to satisfy the designated liabilities will be limited or eliminated. Stated differently, bond dedication is an asset–liability risk-reduction technique that is designed to control the anticipated cash flow properties of a portfolio servicing prescribed liability cash flows. In essence, future funds are locked in and fluctuating interest rates should not affect the expected cash flows. Although there are many variations, the most prominent dedication techniques include cash matching and duration matching.

Cash matching involves the construction of a portfolio whose interest and principal payments exactly match a set of nominal liabilities. Cash matching normally requires fixed and certain liabilities. Because life insurer liabilities have become far less fixed and certain than has been historically the case, the cash matching technique has become less useful as liabilities have become more volatile.

Option-adjusted duration and convexity are used by many insurers. The adaptation of options pricing theory to immunization theory attempts to recognize and account for the fact that asset and liability cash flows are functions of interest rates and will not remain static as interest rates develop over time. Table 33-5 shows the option-adjusted duration and convexity values that would be expected to emerge for a particular life insurance product (e.g., a GIC) given various interest rate shifts. Table 33-6 shows a hypothetical duration analysis conducted for a life insurer's balance sheet.

TABLE 33-5   Option-Adjusted Duration and Convexity for a GIC

Interest Rate Shift	Assets			Liabilities			Surplus		
	Option-Adjusted Value	Effective Duration	Convexity	Option-Adjusted Value	Effective Duration	Convexity	Option-Adjusted Value	Effective Duration	Convexity
−200	1,600	2.9	N.A.	1,545	4.1	N.A.	55	−30.8	N.A.
−150	1,500	3.0	−66	1,405	2.9	60	95	4.5	−3,000
−100	1,400	3.1	−85	1,330	2.1	450	70	22.1	−25
−50	1,300	3.3	−176	1,243	1.8	700	57	36.0	−125
0	1,200	3.5	−190	1,151	1.5	680	49	50.5	−10,000
50	1,100	3.8	−121	1,061	1.4	390	39	69.1	−8,555
100	1,000	4.2	−50	975	1.2	85	25	121.2	−6,000
150	900	5.0	0	901	1.1	20	−1	−3,508.9	100
200	800	5.9	N.A.	845	1.0	N.A.	−45	−86.1	N.A.

Source: Santomero and Babbel, *Financial Risk Management by Insurers,* p. 249.

TABLE 33-6   XYZ Insurance Company Surplus Duration Analysis

Asset Class	Market Value	Effective Duration	Liabilities	Fair Value	Effective Duration
Bonds	10,000,000	6.5	SPDA 1	8,500,000	3.2
Mortgage-Backed	5,000,000	4.2	SPDA 2	4,000,000	2.0
Preferred Stock	200,000	8.1	Universal Life	400,000	7.9
Common Stock	3,000,000	2.1	Term Life	300,000	1.3
Mortgage Loans	6,000,000	5.7	Whole Life	12,000,000	6.8
Equity Real Estate	2,000,000	1.0	Endowment	500,000	8.5
Short-Term and Cash	1,500,000	0.8			
			Total Liabilities	25,700,000	4.85
			Surplus	2,000,000	3.36
Total	27,700,000	4.74	Total	27,700,000	

Source: Santomero and Babbel, *Financial Risk Management by Insurers,* p. 249.

Financial Simulation

The financial management process as practiced by many insurers involves simulations of investment results (e.g., interest rate spreads), operating results (GAAP and SAP earnings), and other important financial outcomes such as the internal rate of return and risk-based capital position. These simulations take into account different interest rate scenarios and investment strategies, including the use of derivative securities. The results provide management with insight into the impact of the company's risk exposures on the company's financial objectives, facilitating the setting of appropriate policies in light of the wide variety of economic conditions likely to be encountered.

Worth noting is that simulation analysis is no substitute for duration and convexity studies. Rather, they should complement each other.

ASSET QUALITY AND U.S. REGULATORY INITIATIVES

An inherent tension in the management of life insurer investment results from (1) policyowner preference for low-cost insurance and (2) the need for safety and the security of policyowner claims. Safety and security of policyowner claims has been the primary stated objective of insurer regulation. The concept of statutory solvency discussed in chapter 32 is intended to protect policyowners, and investment regulations are intended to promote insurer solvency. At the same time, because consumers are attracted to low-cost, high-yielding insurance products, successful, aggressive investment practices can increase an insurer's market share and profitability.

As reflected in the preceding discussion of regulatory restrictions on the admissibility of particular asset classes and assets, traditional investment regulation has focused on qualitative and quantitative standards. Investment laws and regulations in some states set forth a number of prohibited investments. Other states use legal lists of permitted investments. Diversification of nonbond asset types and of particular assets is required by limiting the percentage of total assets that can be held in certain types of assets—for example, mortgage loans, common stocks, or bonds of a single issuer, and so on. These percentage restrictions are widely used in the investment laws of most states. Quantitative limits may also apply to a percentage of an issuer's securities that may be held by one insurer.

Qualitative limits relate to the quality of eligible investments. For example, the earnings of a corporate bond issuer must be in a certain ratio to the interest charges on outstanding debt or the mortgage or real estate cannot exceed a specified percentage of appraised value. In the case of common stocks, requirements may include that the stock be traded on a national exchange and have a record of paying dividends for three years. In 1983, New York substituted a prudent-person rule for many of the inside prescriptions within each category of permitted assets, although the general quantitative limits by asset categories remained in effect.

Many new investment media and industries have emerged during the last few decades, and many of such investments did not qualify as admitted assets under existing rules. As pointed out earlier, to provide some relief from these and other quantitative constraints, several states, including New York, provided **basket** or **leeway clauses** in their laws, permitting a certain percentage of assets to be invested in any type of asset. This percentage has gradually been increased (currently, it is 10 percent in New York). The use of leeway or basket clauses allows insurers to enter new investment areas, such as equipment leasing and oil and gas pipeline finance, and facilitates the use of risk management assets such as futures and options. As mentioned earlier, the provisions also facilitate non-U.S. investing activities.

Before 1987, insolvencies in the life insurance industry numbered 10 or less and involved smaller insurers with assets below $50 million. By 1989, however, more than 30 insolvencies were occurring each year, many of which involved assets in the hundreds of millions of dollars. Major life insurer insolvencies in 1991 led to wide-scale public attention and calls for reform in regulatory standards. These insolvencies were directly related to investment problems arising from (1) overinvestment in noninvestment-grade "junk" bonds that had fallen sharply in price and (2) defaults on commercial real estate mortgage loans, leading to sizable book losses. Regulators seized the insolvent companies to halt mounting withdrawals of policyowner funds that developed after asset quality problems became widely publicized, also known as the run-on-the-bank phenomenon.

The decline in asset quality was due in part to aggressive investment policies developed during a highly competitive period, and in part to a general decline in the market values and performance of high-yield bonds and a weak real estate market. Although the greatest investments in junk bonds were concentrated in a relatively small number of insurers, a drastic general reduction in the market value of junk bonds—and the publicity associated with the insolvencies in 1991 of insurers that had invested heavily in them—contributed to a movement toward investment regulation reform.

The deterioration of asset quality was generally the result of investment policies that were developed in compliance with existing regulatory restrictions. The qualitative standards associated with the regulation of corporate debt obligations did not exclude the possibility of heavy investment in noninvestment-grade bonds, and leeway clauses were used, among other reasons, to admit commercial mortgage values that would not otherwise qualify under the mortgage-specific rules.

In 1996, the NAIC adopted a new version of its 1992 model investment law, **Investments of Insurers Model Act (Defined Limits Version),** similar in structure to the current regulatory scheme. It includes refinements intended to address the asset quality concerns that have developed in the industry. The most significant new provision permits the subjective determination by a commissioner that specific investment activities endanger an insurer's solvency and provides authorization to limit or proscribe those activities. Such a provision considerably expanded regulatory powers over investment activity.

In 1998, the NAIC adopted the **Investments of Insurers Model Act (Defined Standards Version).** This model investment law (called the "prudent-person model") is intended to serve as an alternative to the Investments of Insurers Model Act (Defined Limits Version).

Unlike the Defined Limits Model Act, this act is structurally designed so that an insurer is subject to the following type of investment regulation:

1. An insurer is obligated to fulfill the *minimum asset requirement* as that term is defined under the act. The minimum asset requirement is made up of an insurer's liabilities and what is called the "minimum financial security benchmark." This benchmark equals either the company's minimum capital as required by statute or the authorized control level risk-based capital, which applies to the insurer as set forth in the risk-based capital law of the state, whichever is greater; and

2. An insurer is obligated to invest its assets after fulfilling the minimum asset requirement in accordance with a prudency standard. In this respect, the act sets forth factors that must be evaluated and considered by the insurer in determining whether its investment portfolio or policy is prudent.

As structured, therefore, it differs markedly from the Defined Limits Version, which requires that investments be made only in assets that are specifically identified as within quantitative limits for assets invested in each category.

Each state was urged to determine which methods are best suited to its needs and whether its existing regulatory structure may be improved by using provisions from either or both of the model laws recommended by the NAIC. Individual state decisions will determine which version will have greater impact on investment regulation.

It should be noted that the decline in asset quality among U.S. life insurers has been reversed and there is considerable evidence that the financial condition of the industry, on average, is sound. Regulatory reform can be expected to better suit the requirements of a changing and evolving industry, but the conservative nature of traditional solvency, accounting, and investment regulations, together with management practice, has been generally responsible and successful. Investment risk, for an ever-increasing percentage of assets, has been switched to the client (see Figure 33-5). This change is favorable in terms of an insurer's survival in a poor investment climate.

Questions

1. Compare and contrast the market and book valuation of a life insurer's capital. What limitations are associated with using book values as a means to assess the solvency of a life insurer?
2. How can the various procedures outlined in this chapter for managing cash flow help a life insurer maintain a targeted level of capital?
3. Liquidity is not as important an investment objective for life insurers as for many other investors. Explain.
4. How does the practice of asset–liability management help a life insurer meet the concerns of its various stakeholders?
5. How can investment management affect life insurer profitability and product competitiveness?

CHAPTER

34

LIFE INSURER FINANCIAL REPORTING

Objectives

- Describe the various uses of different types of financial reports.

- Explain the objectives and limitations of both SAP and GAAP accounting principles.

- Describe SAP and GAAP treatment of accounting items.

- Outline the contents of the NAIC Annual Statement.

- Describe the way that managerial accounting and economic value analysis are used to analyze and improve the performance of life insurers.

- Describe some of the regulatory developments in life insurer financial reporting.

INTRODUCTION

The purpose of this chapter is to introduce the different financial reporting techniques that are commonly used in the U.S. life insurance industry. All of the principles and most of the practices enunciated here are relevant to other countries. The requirements of different users of life insurer financial reports have led to the evolution of different reporting methods, some required by law or regulation and some developed for internal company purposes. In all instances, however, the purpose of financial reporting is to allow an assessment of the financial condition and current operating results of a company.

Perhaps most companies undertake primarily short-term transactions. In the sale of goods, for example, delivery and payment typically take place within a short period of time. Single-year results produce a highly accurate financial report in which the great majority of transactions are completed during the year.

By contrast, life insurance contracts are, on average, long term. The current-year profitability of a block of contracts ultimately may depend on results over a period of decades. Persistency, mortality, morbidity, interest, and expense experience determine whether a block of contracts will produce a profit over time.

As a result, to report the financial condition and current operating results for a life insurance company requires the construction of a valuation. A **valuation** is a measure and comparison of an insurer's assets and liabilities based on estimates of future persistency, mortality, morbidity, interest, and expense experience. The construction of a valuation is problematical because minor changes in the assumptions regarding future experience can produce a dramatic impact on current financial statements.

State regulators require what traditionally were thought to be conservative assumptions to test the solvency of an insurer and to protect its policyowners. In the past, this conservatism reduced the earnings and shareholder's equity in stock companies to economically unrealistic levels. As a result, separate requirements for reporting to regulatory authorities and shareholders have evolved.

The development and presentation of a fair life insurer valuation are further complicated by the interest-sensitive nature of insurer cash flows as discussed in chapter 32. The assumptions required by regulators were historically conservative within the context of a relatively stable interest rate environment. As discussed later, the more volatile nature of contemporary interest rates raises questions about the probative value of regulatory accounting rules in solvency determination.

FINANCIAL REPORTS

Alternative methods of calculating and presenting financial information are available, depending on the needs of the user. We can classify users as being either external or internal to the insurer.

External Users

Regulators are most interested in the solvency of an insurer and require the use of *statutory accounting principles* (SAP) in order to test a company's ability to meet its obligations to policyowners. *Investors,* in addition to preservation of capital, are interested in the return on invested capital a company can generate. The use of *generally accepted accounting principles* (GAAP) accounting is required by the Securities and Exchange Commission (SEC) for publicly traded insurers and is a condition for listing on major stock exchanges. SEC regulations also require GAAP for insurers selling variable insurance, annuity, and pension products and for general-purpose financial statements of mutual life insurance companies.

Current policyowners and *potential customers* are interested in the solidity of the company and its ability to satisfy its future obligations, as well as its ability to maintain competitive dividends, interest crediting rates, and other nonguaranteed policy benefits. Both SAP and GAAP statements are relevant to them.

Rating agencies report opinions of insurer financial strength. These agencies usually rely on a variety of information sources, including management interviews. See chapter 11.

Creditors are interested in the insurer's cash flow and its ability to repay debt. GAAP is helpful in predicting long-term cash flow, but SAP analysis is equally important because assets are useful from the creditor's perspective only if they can be used to repay the debt. They are not useful if regulation requires that they be devoted to reserves or minimum capital and surplus requirements.

Potential buyers of an insurer are also interested readers of financial reports. The acquisition of a company must take into account its expected solvency and solidity positions and the appearance of its expected SAP and GAAP financial statements. In addition, the buyer is interested in statements prepared on the basis of **economic value analysis,** which reflects the value of the insurer's distribution system, goodwill, and other features that represent opportunities for expansion and growth—that is, the vitality of the insurer.

The *Internal Revenue Service* requires that insurers prepare reports of taxable income in accordance with the Internal Revenue Code and its regulations. Following the code and its regulations, in effect, constitutes still another accounting basis—*tax-based accounting.*

A variety of other parties may also be interested in the financial condition of a life insurance company. They include employees and suppliers of the insurer, as well as the general business communities in which the insurer has significant operations.

Internal Users

In addition to external users of insurer accounting information, corporate managers require two additional, internal classes of measurement tools: managerial accounting and economic value analysis. *Managerial accounting* includes budgeting, cost accounting, and the audit and control functions. *Economic value analysis* is used to evaluate the long-term financial results of current management actions. We explore each of these later in this chapter.

Also, management must respond to the needs of each group of external users of its financial reports. Therefore, management decisions must be made with an understanding of the impact decisions can have on the company's SAP, GAAP, and tax-basis statements. Operating decisions such as product pricing and interest crediting/dividend strategy, as well as strategic decisions such as possible acquisitions, entry into new lines of business or change in distribution system, must be analyzed from the standpoint of their effect on financial reports.

Management must also accord careful attention to financial reports derived from its statements but issued by others. The informal regulatory role of independent rating agencies can be a significant factor in the way an insurer is viewed by its customers and investors. Figure 34-1 summarizes the different accounting objectives and approaches required by principal users of life insurer financial reports.

FIGURE 34-1 Accounting Objectives and Approaches Required by Principal Users of Life Insurer Financial Reports

Accounting Objectives	User	Accounting Approach
Solvency	→ State insurance regulators →	Statutory accounting
Solidity and profitability	→ SEC (shareholders) →	GAAP accounting
Taxable income	→ Internal Revenue Service →	Tax-basis accounting
Operational information	→ Insurer management →	Managerial accounting

LIFE INSURANCE SAP AND GAAP ACCOUNTING

SAP and GAAP accounting underlies the most important external reporting requirements. In this section, we explore the principles underpinning each with particular reference to fundamental differences in objectives and accounting treatment.[1]

Statutory Accounting Principles

Objectives

SAP financial statements are intended to present an insurer's financial condition from the viewpoint of the regulator. The main purpose is to provide proof of an insurer's ability to meet its contractual obligations to policyowners.

The concept of solvency for a life insurance company has two dimensions. Economic solvency is the same as it is for any company: the ability to pay obligations when they come due. Life insurers must also be concerned with statutory solvency.

The insurer must, on an annual basis, present financial statements that meet the statutory definition of solvency in terms of investments, reserves, and minimum capital and surplus that is defined by law. Economic solvency does not necessarily imply statutory solvency, and perhaps more importantly, statutory solvency does not necessarily imply economic solvency.

Because life insurers hold large amounts of money for the benefit of their policyowners, SAP treatment required by state law is similar to the accounting required of a trustee or fiduciary. The insurer must also demonstrate that its assets, together with future premiums and conservatively estimated interest income, will be sufficient to meet all promises to policyowners. Other sources of income, such as profits on existing or new lines of business, are not taken into account. In effect, the entire insurer is viewed as a trust account for the benefit of policyowners, and the insurer's ability to generate additional profits as an operating business, or going concern, is secondary.

Limitations

Statutory accounting principles limit the usefulness of statutory reports in two respects. First, the stated objective of solvency determination is not well served by its static, balance sheet orientation, nor by valuation conventions that artificially stabilize reported values. Second, the solvency determination objective itself limits the usefulness of SAP to parties interested in other aspects of the financial condition.

One of the principal limitations of SAP solvency determination results from the "snapshot approach" it utilizes. Results are reported at a specific point in time under a set of static assumptions that ignores the possibility (indeed certainty) of changing economic conditions in the future. A NAIC model law, however, requires an insurer to certify reserve adequacy under a variety of economic scenarios, and the role of the valuation actuary in this process is discussed later in this chapter.

Bond values are recorded on the statutory statement at amortized value (discussed later) rather than market value. This valuation convention is based on the premise that most insurer bonds are held to maturity and that fluctuating market values would not significantly impact solvency. As discussed in chapter 32, the simultaneous impact of

---

[1] This section draws on *Life Insurance. Statutory Accounting Principles for the Life Insurance Industry* (KPMG Peat Marwick Executive Education, 1987), Chapter 7.

changing market interest rates on asset and liability values casts considerable doubt on this assumption.[2]

During periods of relatively high interest rates, the artificial stabilization of asset values by the amortized value convention may cause an insurer's statutory statement to exhibit a state of solvency, when in reality it would be unable to satisfy its cash obligations as they come due. Figure 34-2 illustrates the relationship of amortized values to market values in different interest rate environments. The asset valuation reserves discussed later could, under extreme conditions, contribute similar distortion in statutory reporting.

Statutory accounting also proves to be inadequate for the needs of investors and creditors because of its balance sheet orientation. With the exception of asset valuation conventions discussed previously, SAP treatment generally examines an insurer as if it were not an operating entity but rather a company in runoff or liquidation. This results from the conservative approach that requires accounting for all policyowner funds at all times and ignores the long-term benefits to be expected from investing in the future of the company. Additionally, the conservative assumptions required in the valuation of an insurer's liabilities normally do not reflect the potential profit that can be generated by in-force policies.

The solvency approach that is central to SAP tends to penalize current results without recognizing the long-term potential of a company's operations. As discussed in chapter 30 and reflected in the sample asset-share calculation, an increase in new business typically creates cash shortages in the early years of any new block of policies. Under SAP treatment, the high expenses associated with the writing off of acquisition costs of new business, together with reserving requirements, reduce current earnings. Under SAP, lapses of even profitable business increase current earnings because of the gains from surrenders created when reserves released exceed cash values paid (see chapter 30).

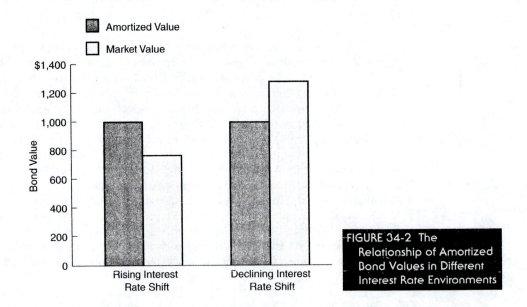

FIGURE 34-2 The Relationship of Amortized Bond Values in Different Interest Rate Environments

---

[2]Life insurers more actively manage their portfolios than ever before, with the result that a declining proportion of bonds is held to maturity. When reported under GAAP, FAS 115 causes a new valuation basis to be applied to bonds for which the insurer has neither the positive intent nor ability to hold to maturity.

As a result, earnings under SAP rules are penalized as an insurer grows, with faster growth producing a greater punitive impact on earnings. Conversely, earnings can be exaggerated when an insurer is losing market share to competitors. SAP treatment also tends to penalize current earnings when an insurer invests in its distribution system or makes other capital expenditures because such expenses generally are not capitalized but directly expensed.

The balance sheet liquidity focus of SAP is designed to prove an insurer's ability to pay future benefits that arise under its current policies. As such, it is an inadequate tool for measuring a company's ability to generate long-term profits or for comparing results with other insurers or its own past experience.

Generally Accepted Accounting Principles

Objectives

Although solvency is the primary focus of statutory accounting, the principal purpose of GAAP accounting is to report financial results for a company in a manner that is comparable to those of other companies and of other reporting periods. This comparability is essential to investors who need to be able to evaluate the relative merits of alternative investments both in the insurance industry and other industries. Comparability is necessary when financial reports are used in any analysis designed to predict future financial results. Generally accepted accounting principles are established through the issuance of Financial Accounting Standards (FAS) by the Financial Accounting Standards Board (FASB).

Quarterly and annual reports incorporating GAAP are required of all publicly traded companies. The most important of the required reports is Form 10K, which annually sets forth a statement of the insurer's business properties and business proceedings, its financial statements and supporting schedules, and exhibits and information regarding the insurer's officers and directors. Form 10-Q provides similar but less comprehensive information on a quarterly basis. Both reports include management's discussion and analysis of the company's experience during the covered period, a valuable source of information.

Limitations

GAAP accounting requires presentation of assets, liabilities, and cash flows. Although GAAP accounting is designed to *report* consistently on revenues, benefits, expenses, and current operating profit, it is often found to be inadequate as a *financial management* tool. GAAP does not recognize potential future profits on existing and future policies and, therefore, it is not well suited for evaluating the long-term financial impact of current management action.

Three aspects of GAAP accounting limit its usefulness as a financial management tool. These shortcomings are in large part the result of reporting the arbitrary, one-year profits of organizations that are engaged in an essentially long-term enterprise.

First, GAAP generally includes an accounting convention known as the **lock-in principle,** which prevents a restatement of assumptions regarding interest, expense, and mortality for traditional policies in force. The principle was designed primarily to deal with guaranteed-cost, nonparticipating policies. Today's product environment is dominated by policies that reflect actual operating experience and offer guarantees that are likely to be important only in the event of extreme interest rate or mortality developments. The accuracy of expected results for a block of policies can be considerably improved by periodic reevaluations, and FAS 97 and FAS 120 now effectively exempt interest-sensitive products and participating business from the lock-in principle. Lock-in continues to apply to other traditional life products.

Second, as with their treatment under statutory accounting, unrealized capital gains are not recognized in the GAAP income statement.[3] As discussed in chapter 33, capital gains and losses are an integral element of the total return generated by an actively managed investment portfolio.

Finally, GAAP accounting in many respects does not reflect the future impact of current events. As in statutory accounting, GAAP treatment of surrenders may produce increased current-period earnings without reflecting the loss of future profits on lapsed policies, and investment in distribution systems and other capital expenditures may produce decreased current earnings without a concurrent recognition of the insurer's increased capacity to generate future profits.[4]

SAP and GAAP Treatment of Accounting Items

Both SAP and GAAP financial statements are derived from the same source: the Blanks Committee of the NAIC, which develops the general form and content of life insurance company annual statements. The SAP statement in each state follows closely the form prescribed by the NAIC. GAAP statements are usually developed by adjustments to an insurer's SAP statement. This is increasingly untrue as insurers move to systems that develop SAP and GAAP statements independently.

The differences in SAP and GAAP statements are produced by the differing treatment of items that are entered into each statement. We can group the differences into four broad categories:

1. valuation of assets
2. valuation of liabilities
3. recognition of income
4. recognition of expense

Valuation of Assets

The primary differences in SAP and GAAP accounting regarding the valuation of assets involve the classification of assets that may be listed as approved assets, and the reporting of realized and unrealized capital gains and losses. Assets approved by state regulatory authorities as sound and accepted as such in the NAIC Annual Statement are known as **admitted assets.** Asset values that do not conform to legally prescribed methods to determine permitted asset values are known as **nonadmitted assets** (e.g., furniture and equipment and agents' balances). Only the value of admitted assets may be shown on the statutory balance sheet. By contrast, all insurer assets, including nonadmitted assets that do not meet regulatory approval, may be reported on the GAAP balance sheet.

The term *fair value* is used in GAAP statements reflecting the fact that some assets have no readily available market and are valued on the basis of the judgment of insurer management. Although, technically, independent auditors do not value assets, they do assess the fairness of value determined by management.

Valuation of Liabilities

The principal differences in SAP and GAAP treatment of the valuation of insurer liabilities involve life insurance policy reserves and the payment of dividends. SAP requires the posting of reserves that are based on statutorily defined, conservative as-

---

[3]Although unrealized gains and losses on most fixed-maturity investments are not reflected in the income statement, their effect is disclosed and can be used for analytical purposes. FAS 115 does provide for inclusion in the GAAP income statement of unrealized gains and losses on any "trading portfolio" securities that an insurer may have.

[4]Under GAAP accounting, investment in distribution systems and other capital expenditures must be capitalized and depreciated over time when there is a demonstrated future benefit.

sumptions regarding mortality and interest. GAAP is primarily concerned with insurer profitability, and more realistic assumptions are used with respect to mortality and interest. For interest-sensitive life products covered by FAS 97 (e.g., universal life), GAAP policy reserves are equal to the policy's account value. For traditional life products, GAAP policy reserves are less conservative than statutory reserves.

In addition, a major assumption used for GAAP but not used for SAP is the lapse rate assumption or, inversely, persistency. This assumption can have a large effect on GAAP liabilities. An insurer uses GAAP assumptions that follow its own experience or industrywide experience.

Policyowner dividends reported under SAP are limited to the anticipated liability for the insurer's following year. Because of the underlying assumption of continued company existence as a going concern, GAAP financial statements reflect, as a liability, policyowner dividends over the premium-paying periods of the contracts. As dividends are paid, the balance sheet liability is reduced accordingly.

Recognition of Income

One of the principles of generally accepted accounting dictates that income is recognized when it is earned and not when it is received. This means that earnings should be recognized when the service (insurance protection) is provided. GAAP premiums are recognized as earned over the coverage period of policies in force, whereas SAP premiums are recognized as earned over the premium-paying period.

Recognition of Expense

SAP rules are generally based on an implicit assumption that solvency should be demonstrable if the insurer were to be placed in runoff or liquidated during the current reporting period. GAAP assumes the continued existence of the insurer as a going concern. These approaches require a significantly different treatment of the high first-year acquisition expenses associated with new policies.

Although some statutory accounting relief can be provided through the use of modified reserving techniques, first-year acquisition expenses generally are charged in full to the current year's statutory income. Despite the fact that these first-year expenses are associated with policies that will generate future income, the conservative requirements of SAP do not allow for their amortization over the anticipated premium-paying period.

GAAP, by contrast, assumes the continuing existence of the insurer and seeks to match the timing of expenses associated with the production of income to the period when the income is produced. GAAP thus recognizes that future income will be associated with first-year expenses, and requires the deferral of those expenses in a way that reports the expenses ratably over a period of time. Costs related to future income are charged to future periods.

Under GAAP, acquisition costs are capitalized as a deferred asset. In traditional policies, deferred acquisition costs (DAC) are amortized in proportion to anticipated premiums and charged in future periods. With interest-sensitive policies, in which premiums exceeding mortality and expense charges are considered deposits, these costs are amortized over the policies' life as gross profits emerge.[5] As the expenses are charged, the value of the DAC is reduced accordingly.

Figure 34-3 summarizes the important differences in SAP and GAAP treatment of different accounting items.

---

[5]Gross profits arise principally from investment, mortality, and expense margins. Deferred policy acquisition costs are reviewed regularly to determine that the unamortized portion of such costs does not exceed recoverable amounts from future margins.

	SAP	GAAP
Valuation of Assets Accepted values:	Admitted assets only	All assets
Valuation of Liabilities Reserves: Policyowner dividends:	Defined by law Following year	Company and industry experience Present value of all future dividends
Recognition of Income Premiums earned over: Fees earned on deposits:	Premium period	Coverage period Coverage period
Recognition of Expenses First-year acquisition expense:	Full charge	Deferred and amortized

FIGURE 34-3 Comparison of SAP and GAAP Treatment of Specific Accounting Items

THE NAIC ANNUAL STATEMENT

An annual statement prepared according to statutory accounting principles is required in all states where an insurer is licensed to write business. The statement is prepared on a calendar-year basis on forms generally developed by the National Association of Insurance Commissioners (NAIC), and its accuracy is sworn to by the officers of the insurer. All states and many countries require insurer financial statements to be audited by an independent accounting firm. Additional information is sometimes required because some states adopt NAIC forms and regulations with changes. New York, for example, requires that the cash flows associated with certain product lines be tested under a range of differing economic scenarios. All states require estimated statements on a quarterly basis, and many prohibit insurers from publishing any financial statement that shows admitted assets or surplus in amounts differing from the statutory annual statement

As discussed in chapter 35, the power of the NAIC is generally indirect in the sense that it typically develops model laws that have the force of law only when adopted by the various states. In financial reporting, the NAIC influence is more direct. It controls the standards for financial reporting through the prescribed form of annual statement, as well as the valuation of securities through the Securities Valuation Office. These responsibilities have been delegated to the NAIC by the states.

SAP and GAAP financial statements follow the same general pattern. The following discussion of life insurer annual statements follows the form of the statutory statement. Significant differences in GAAP accounting treatment and conventions are noted.

The primary elements of the annual statement required by state insurance regulators are the balance sheet and the summary of operations. These statements are reconciled from year to year in the capital and surplus account. A cash flow statement is required. Supplementary exhibits and schedules provide a more detailed supporting analysis of items that appear in the primary financial statements.

The Balance Sheet

The purpose of the balance sheet is to demonstrate an insurer's solvency by comparing its assets and liabilities. Under statutory accounting, if assets exceed liabilities, the insurer is solvent and the excess assets represent, in general corporate terms, the capital of the company. The life insurance industry designates its capital as capital stock and paid-in surplus, which represents funds paid into the company by shareholders, and as surplus, which is the remaining excess of assets over liabilities. The final accounting equation for a company's balance sheet is:

$$\text{Assets} = \text{Liabilities} + (\text{Capital Stock} + \text{Surplus})$$

Figure 34-4 illustrates the general relationship of assets and liabilities and surplus.

Additional information is sometimes required. Most states, for example, require that the cash flows associated with various product lines be tested under a range of differing economic scenarios. All states require estimated statements on a quarterly basis, and many prohibit insurers from publishing any financial statement that shows admitted assets or surplus in amounts differing from the statutory annual statement.

Assets

Insurer assets can be divided into three major categories: invested assets, other admitted assets, and nonadmitted assets. Because of the regulatory concern for safety, legally prescribed methods determine permitted asset values. Asset values that exceed or do not conform to these legal methods are nonadmitted assets; asset values that conform to the legal requirements are admitted assets.

Invested assets produce interest, dividend, and rent and capital gain income (see chapter 32). Invested assets are reported in the following classes and statutory values:

- *Cash* consists of actual cash held in the insurers' offices on the date of the statement, and amounts on deposit in solvent banks.
- *Bonds* determined by the NAIC to be in good standing are listed at their amortized values.[6] The market value of a bond typically differs from its par or face value because of changing market interest rates. Amortized value refers to

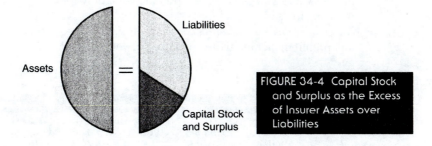

FIGURE 34-4 Capital Stock and Surplus as the Excess of Insurer Assets over Liabilities

---

[6]The NAIC Committee on Valuation of Securities specifies the bases for determining the eligibility of various classes of bonds for amortization. The committee submits an annual report that sets forth these requirements in great detail, and the Securities Valuation Office develops a Valuation of Securities manual each year as the source for uniform treatment of securities values. It includes values for all securities, including privately placed bonds.

adjustments of the original cost (original book value) by which the value is reduced or increased by successive stages until it equals the par value on the maturity date of the bond. Table 34-1 illustrates the amortization process for a $1,000
bond that is two years from maturity and upon which the interest rate is 6 percent (semiannual coupon rate of 3 percent). It is assumed that the bond was purchased for $1,018.81 to yield 5 percent. Bonds not in good standing are listed at
current market value. Due and accrued interest on these bonds is a nonadmitted
asset because the interest is reflected by the bond's market value.

- *Common and preferred stocks* (not subject to a mandatory sinking fund) are
  listed at market value as of the date of the annual statement.
- *Preferred stocks* in good standing are valued at cost. Preferred stocks not in good
  standing are valued at the lower of cost or association value.
- *Mortgage loans on real estate* are listed at unpaid principal balances net of unamortized premiums or discounts. Mortgage interest overdue for more than one
  year is a nonadmitted asset as well.
- *Real estate* is listed at book or market value, whichever is lower. Book value is
  original cost less accumulated depreciation, mortgages, liens, and other encumbrances under SAP rules. Some states allow depreciated cost less an impairment
  allowance. GAAP treatment does not record net values. Under GAAP, separate
  asset and liability entries are made for each property.
- *Policy loans and premium notes* are valued at the unpaid principal balance of the
  loan at the date of the statement. To the extent that the outstanding principal
  balance of the loan or note exceeds the *cash surrender value* of the policy, the excess balance is treated as a nonadmitted asset.
- *Collateral loans* are valued at the unpaid principal balance of the loan at the date
  of the statement unless the value of the loan exceeds the legal relationship to the
  market value of the collateral. To the extent that the unpaid principal balance of
  the collateral loan exceeds the legal limit, the excess cost is treated as a nonadmitted asset.

Certain assets included on the balance sheet are not "investments." These include
the following:

- *Risk management assets* such as futures and options are valued at either cost or
  market value generally based upon the valuation approach of the asset or liability being hedged.
- *Investment income due and accrued* is an asset category that includes investment
  and premium income that is due but not yet received.

TABLE 34-1 Amortized Bond Values

Period (Half-Years)	Book Value at Beginning of Half-Year	Coupon Payable at End of Half-Year	Six Months' Interest at 5% on Book Value at Beginning of Half-Year	Excess of Coupon over Interest Required (Amortization)	Book Value at End of Half-Year (Amortized Value)
1	$1,018.81	$30	$25.47	$4.53	$1,014.28
2	1,014.28	30	25.36	4.64	1,009.64
3	1,009.64	30	25.24	4.76	1,004.88
4	1,004.88	30	25.12	4.88	1,000.00

- *Premiums due and uncollected* is an asset category for policy premiums that will become due after the date of the annual statement and before the next policy anniversary date. The deferred premium asset for net premiums deferred and uncollected is established to offset the overstatement of the policy-reserve liability brought about by the difference between the assumptions as to premium payments in reserve calculations (made once a year assuming an annual premium received at midyear) and the actual modes of paying premiums. In essence, there is an overstatement of both assets and liabilities, resulting in an appropriate net liability. This item also accounts for premiums that are overdue because the reserve is overstated in this case also.
- *Accrued interest* (in the absence of a default) is a sound asset. During normal times, overdue interest is likely to be small. In periods of economic recession, overdue interest on mortgages may become sizable. In such periods, its size may be helpful in giving some indication of the quality of the mortgage portfolio. Its usefulness as such an indicator, however, is impaired by the fact that insurer practices, relative to charging off overdue interest as a nonadmitted asset, vary considerably. No item of overdue interest is an asset on bonds in default because the market value of these bonds reflects any interest in default.
- *Noninvestment assets,* such as computer equipment and amounts owed to the insurer by authorized reinsurance companies, are permitted by most state laws because they are closely related to the operations of the business. Computer equipment is generally valued at cost less accumulated depreciation under rules that may vary from state to state.

Most life companies have also established **separate accounts,** which are funds held separately from all other assets of the insurer. The primary purpose of separate accounts is to make investments exempt from the usual investment restrictions imposed by state law. Separate accounts are authorized by states to permit insurers to offer customers investment strategies that would not otherwise conform to insurance regulations. Separate accounts are maintained primarily for pension funds and variable life and annuity products. Generally, the customer, rather than the insurer, is responsible for all investment gains and losses. A separate account usually holds the funds of many policyowners or annuitants in a combined investment arrangement—a so-called **pooled investment account.** An individual separate account may be provided for a large corporate client, holding only its contributions.

The treatment of invested assets under GAAP accounting is different from FAS 115 that requires, except in rare circumstances, securities be carried at fair (market) value. Under GAAP, FAS 115 requires investments to be classified in three categories and accounted for as follows:

1. *Held-to-maturity securities*—reported at amortized values (e.g., private placements, public bonds, and mortgage-backed securities).
2. *Trading securities*—reported at fair value, with unrealized capital gains and losses included in earnings (e.g., Treasury bonds).
3. *Available-for-sale securities*—reported at fair value, with unrealized capital gains and losses excluded from earnings (e.g., public bonds and mortgage-backed securities).

This requirement applies only to GAAP financial statements and makes an insurer's equity more volatile. FAS 115 does not apply to unsecuritized loans. If mortgage loans are converted to mortgage-backed securities, however, they are subject to the provision.

Liabilities

The greatest part of a life company's liabilities is represented by policy reserves supported by assets held to fund future benefits under the company's insurance contracts. Other liabilities are also incurred in the course of operations.

- *Policy reserves* represent amounts needed to provide future benefits under the company's policies. Reserves are calculated on the basis of current assumptions as to future mortality, morbidity, and interest assumptions. These assumptions and the method of calculation are prescribed by state law in the case of statutory accounting. GAAP assumptions are derived from the insurer's best estimates based on its own experience and industry averages, and include assumptions regarding lapse rates.

- *Amounts held on deposit* are funds owed to policyowners and beneficiaries including (a) amounts held under settlement options without life contingencies; (b) dividends left to accumulate by policyowners; and (c) premiums paid in advance. Interest is credited to customers while the funds are deposited with the insurer in much the same way a bank credits interest to its depositors.

- *Policyowner dividends allocated but not yet payable* to policyowners are measured under statutory accounting by the insurer's estimate of all dividend payments for the following calendar year. Policyowner dividend liabilities under GAAP are measured by the estimated present value of future policyowner dividends in excess of the dividends, which represent a level percentage of premiums. Shareholder dividends are booked at the time they are declared by the board of directors.

- *Claims incurred but not yet paid* include (a) claims due but unpaid at statement date; (b) contested claims; (c) claims in the process of being settled with beneficiaries; and (d) the estimated amount of claims incurred but unreported to the company at the date of the statement (valued on the basis of the company's past experience).

- *Amounts held for the account of others* are liability items for funds in the possession of the insurer as an agent or trustee for another. Examples include taxes and property insurance premiums of mortgagors and payroll taxes.

- *Other amounts unpaid* include liabilities for incurred but unpaid items such as expenses and surrender values.

- *The asset valuation reserve (AVR)* and the *interest maintenance reserve (IMR)* are statutory accounting mechanisms designed to prevent volatile fluctuations in reported surplus due to the changing market values of securities. The AVR absorbs both realized *and* unrealized related capital gains and losses attributed to other than interest rates. The IMR applies to realized capital gains and losses attributable to changing market interest rates. The AVR applies to real estate, mortgage loans, and short-term investments as well as bonds and corporate stocks. Because the AVR does not reflect interest-related changes, its importance is limited to the asset quality of included investments. As pointed out earlier, the AVR and IMR are not recognized for GAAP purposes.

Within limits, capital gains and losses are reflected in the appropriate reserve and do not affect reported surplus from year to year. Under AVR more significant gains and losses exceeding prescribed limits directly affect surplus. Absent these valuation reserves to offset realized and unrealized capital gains and losses, the amount of reported surplus each year would fluctuate directly with changes in the values of securities owned by the company that are marked to market. The purpose of the AVR in addition to stabilization is to absorb losses (credit losses or fixed-maturity securities and mortgages and declining market value of real estate and equities) at unexpected levels. It is important to remember that all assets are not marked to market under SAP; therefore, the AVR and surplus are not and would not be impacted by changes in market value of all assets.

The IMR absorbs *realized* capital gains and losses caused by changes in market interest rates. The IMR reflects only those interest-related gains and losses realized by bonds, preferred stock, and mortgages which are the asset types most directly influenced by changes in interest rates.

- *Special reserves* are sometimes established by insurers for general contingencies such as epidemics or other unexpected claims or liabilities, when no reserve is required by statute. Some insurers choose to establish special reserves, whereas others will instead designate *special surplus* for the same purposes. For example, some insurers have established special reserves in anticipation of the higher mortality arising from AIDS-related claims.
- *Policyowner account balances* required under GAAP are policyowner account liabilities representing deposits arising from flexible-premium policies such as deferred annuities and universal life–type policies. For fixed-premium products, GAAP policy reserves are less conservative than statutory reserves.
- *Postretirement benefits.* Under GAAP accounting, employers are required by FAS 106 to recognize a liability for the cost of providing postretirement benefits (other than retirement income benefits) to retirees. The most substantial postretirement benefit is retiree health care. A statutory equivalent of FAS 106, based on vested benefits rather than benefits earned, is required by the NAIC.
- *Federal income taxes* under statutory accounting represent only the current-year tax payable under tax-basis accounting rules. Because of inconsistent tax-basis rules, determinable amounts of tax liability may be deferred beyond the current SAP or GAAP reporting period. GAAP requires recognition of the future tax liability pertaining to current operations on the insurer's balance sheet.

Capital Stock and Surplus

The excess of a company's assets over its liabilities represents its **capital stock and surplus.** In other commercial companies, this excess may be known as *capital* or *net worth.*

- *Capital stock* represents the par value of all common and preferred shares issued and not owned by the insurer.
- *Contributed surplus* represents the excess, if any, paid to the corporation for shares that exceed par value.
- *Special surplus funds* are voluntarily earmarked surplus designated to meet general contingencies; they serve the same purpose as special reserves.
- *Unassigned surplus* consists of all other surplus amounts and represents the corporation's "free" capital. It is not legally earmarked for any particular purpose and may be used for distributions to policyowners or shareholders in the form of dividends or for the expansion or diversification of the insurer's operations.

Table 34-2 presents the balance sheet, in SAP format, of a hypothetical life insurance company.

TABLE 34-2	Annual Statement for the Year 1998 of the XYZ Life Insurance Company

ASSETS

	Current Year				Prior Year
	1	*2*	*3*	*4* *Net Admitted* *Assets*	*5*
	Ledger *Assets*	*Non-* *Ledger* *Assets*	*Assets* *Not* *Admitted*	*(Columns* *1+2–3)*	*Net Admitted* *Assets*
1. Bonds (less $0 liability for asset transfers with put options, Schedule D, Part 1)	2,360,096,992		203,095	2,359,893,897	2,416,922,767
2. Stocks:					
2.1 Preferred stocks (Schedule D, Part 2, Section 1)					2,000,000
2.2 Common stocks (Schedule D, Part 2, Section 2)	113,094,988	(7,112,132)		105,982,856	82,824,432
3. Mortgage loans on real estate (Schedule B, Part 1, Section 1):					
3.1 First liens	706,520,056			706,520,056	652,499,040
3.2 Other than first liens					
4. Real estate (Schedule A):					
4.1 Properties occupied by the company (less $0 encumbrances)	22,024,936			22,024,936	22,871,167
4.2 Properties acquired in satisfaction of debt (less $0 encumbrances)	20,539,797			20,539,797	26,640,599
4.3 Investment real estate (less $0 encumbrances)	1,193,120			1,193,120	1,193,120
5. Policy loans	155,184,696		1,072,452	154,112,244	155,310,200
6. Premium notes, including $0 for first year premiums					
7. Cash ($(3,290,080), Schedule E, Part 1) and short-term investments ($57,270,057, Schedule DA, Part 1)	53,979,979			53,979,979	3,058,591
8. Other invested assets (Schedule BA, Part 1)	45,202,634	109,216		45,311,850	53,415,669
9. Receivable for securities	3,131,561			3,131,561	4,562,500
10. Aggregate write-ins for invested assets	4,984,344			4,984,344	1,876,737
11. Subtotals, cash and invested assets (Lines 1 to 10)	3,485,953,103	(7,002,916)	1,275,547	3,477,674,640	3,423,174,822
12. Reinsurance ceded:					
12.1 Amounts recoverable from reinsurers (Schedule S, Part 1)		1,753,928		1,753,928	921,516
12.2 Commissions and expense allowances due		246,116		246,116	251,171
12.3 Experience rating and other refunds due		31,224		31,224	
12.4 Other amounts receivable under reinsurance contracts					
13. Electronic data processing equipment	4,862,451			4,862,451	4,186,392
14. Federal income tax recoverable and interest thereon		6,379,072		6,379,072	3,698,405
14A. Guaranty funds receivable or on deposit	2,157,004			2,157,004	2,807,074

TABLE 34-2 *(cont.)*

	ASSETS				
	Current Year				**Prior Year**
	1	*2*	*3*	*4* *Net Admitted* *Assets* *(Columns* *1+2–3)*	*5*
	Ledger *Assets*	*Non-* *Ledger* *Assets*	*Assets* *Not* *Admitted*		*Net Admitted* *Assets*
15. Life insurance premiums and annuity considerations due and uncollected on in force business (less premiums on reinsurance ceded and less $1,004,526 loading)		11,479,569		11,479,569	12,355,232
16. Accident and health premiums due and unpaid		629,769		629,769	954,928
17. Investment income due and accrued (Exhibit 2)		41,221,248		41,221,248	42,922,860
18. Net adjustment in assets and liabilities due to foreign exchange rates					
19. Receivable from parent, subsidiaries and affiliates	1,023,819			1,023,819	344,468
20. Amounts receivable relating to uninsured accident and health plans					
21. Other assets nonadmitted (Exhibit 13)	4,211,523		4,211,523		
22. Aggregate write-ins for other than invested assets	21,955,666		12,434,519	9,521,147	3,598,968
23. TOTAL assets excluding Separate Accounts business (Lines 11 to 22)	3,520,163,566	54,738,010	17,921,589	3,556,979,987	3,495,215,836
24. From Separate Accounts Statement	1,530,754,537			1,530,754,537	1,288,348,863
25. TOTAL (Lines 23 and 24)	5,050,918,103	54,738,010	17,921,589	5,087,734,524	4,783,564,699

Details of Write-Ins

1001. Derivative instruments	4,984,344			4,984,344	1,876,737
1002.					
1003.					
1098. Summary of remaining write-ins for Line 10 from overflow page					
1099. TOTALS (Lines 1001 through 1003 plus 1098) (Line 10 above)	4,984,344			4,984,344	1,876,737
2201. Application software	5,548,095		5,548,095		
2202. Unearned annualized commissions	5,215,158		5,215,158		
2203. COLI cash surrender value	5,004,899			5,004,899	
2298. Summary of remaining write-ins for Line 22 from overflow page	6,187,514		1,671,266	4,516,248	3,598,968
2299. TOTALS (Lines 2201 through 2203 plus 2298) (Line 22 above)	21,955,666		12,434,519	9,521,147	3,598,968

(Continued)

TABLE 34-2 *(cont.)*

LIABILITIES, SURPLUS AND OTHER FUNDS

	1 *Current Year*	2 *Prior Year*
1. Aggregate reserve for life policies and contracts $1,469,771,293 (Exhibit 8, Line 9999999) less $0 included in Line 7.3 (including $0 Modco Reserve)	1,469,771,293	1,406,513,865
2. Aggregate reserve for accident and health policies (Exhibit 9, Line 17, Column 1) (including $0 Modco Reserve)	174,485,254	165,543,977
3. Supplementary contracts without life contingencies (Exhibit 10, Line 11, Column 1) (including $0 Modco Reserve)	58,982,695	57,699,473
4. Policy and contract claims:		
4.1 Life (Exhibit 11, Part 1, Line 4d, Column 1 less sum of Columns 9, 10, and 11)	23,759,138	18,307,643
4.2 Accident and health (Exhibit 11, Part 1, Line 4d, sum of Columns 9, 10, and 11)	2,141,451	2,158,972
5. Policyholders' dividend and coupon accumulations (Exhibit 10, Line 16, Column 1)	5,809,423	6,047,446
6. Policyholders' dividends $30,791 and coupons $0 due and unpaid (Exhibit 7, Line 10)	30,791	77,236
7. Provision for policyholders' dividends and coupons payable in following calendar year—estimated amounts:		
7.1 Dividends apportioned for payment to 12/31/1999	16,528,106	16,848,056
7.2 Dividends not yet apportioned		
7.3 Coupons and similar benefits		
8. Amount provisionally held for deferred dividend policies not included in Line 7		
9. Premiums and annuity considerations received in advance less $0 discount; including $464,340 accident and health premiums (Exhibit 1, Part 1, Column 1, sum of Lines 4 and 14)	926,942	780,003
10. Liability for premium and other deposit funds:		
10.1 Policyholder premiums, including $0 deferred annuity liability	502,575	613,480
10.2 Guaranteed interest contracts, including $0 deferred annuity liability		
10.3 Other contract deposit funds, including $1,382,014,368 deferred annuity liability	1,382,014,368	1,396,495,010
11. Policy and contract liabilities not included elsewhere:		
11.1 Surrender values on canceled policies		
11.2 Provision for experience rating refunds, including $0 A & H experience rating refunds		
11.3 Other amounts payable on reinsurance; including $0 assumed and $0 ceded		
11.4 Interest Maintenance Reserve (Page 40, Line 6)	23,365,781	15,448,090
12. Commissions to agents due or accrued-life and annuity $567,816 accident and health $183,166 and deposit-type funds $0	750,982	603,385
12A. Commissions and expense allowances payable on reinsurance assumed	67,822	110,964
13. General expenses due or accrued (Exhibit 5, Line 12, Column 5)	24,092,892	24,712,075
13A. Transfers to Separate Accounts due or accrued (net) (Including $(26,659,596) accrued for expense allowances recognized in reserves)	(52,296,064)	(19,491,197)
14. Taxes, licenses and fees due or accrued, excluding federal income taxes (Exhibit 6, Line 9, Col. 5)	3,815,347	3,321,439
14A. Federal income taxes due or accrued, including $0 on capital gains (excluding deferred taxes)		
15. "Cost of collection" on premiums and annuity considerations deferred and uncollected in excess of total loading thereon		
16. Unearned investment income (Exhibit 2, Line 9, Column 2)	49,290	197,518
17. Amounts withheld or retained by company as agent or trustee	1,346,868	1,471,016
18. Amounts held for agents' account, including $1,142,941 agents' credit balances	1,142,941	2,577,363
19. Remittances and items not allocated	35,013,476	7,672,297
20. Net adjustment in assets and liabilities due to foreign exchange rates		
21. Liability for benefits for employees and agents if not included above	5,649,338	4,176,346
22. Borrowed money $0 and interest thereon $0		

TABLE 34-2 *(cont.)*

LIABILITIES, SURPLUS AND OTHER FUNDS

	1 Current Year	2 Prior Year
23. Dividends to stockholders declared and unpaid		
24. Miscellaneous liabilities:		
24.1 Asset Valuation Reserve (Page 41, Line 13, Column 7)	36,644,070	56,861,696
24.2 Reinsurance in unauthorized companies		
24.3 Funds held under reinsurance treaties with unauthorized reinsurers		
24.4 Payable to parent, subsidiaries and affiliates		
24.5 Drafts outstanding		
24.6 Liability for amounts held under uninsured accident and health plans		
24.7 Funds held under coinsurance		
24.8 Payable for securities	549,299	341,413
24.9 Capital notes $0 and interest thereon $0		
25. Aggregate write-ins for liabilities	3,884,166	8,176,088
26. TOTAL Liabilities excluding Separate Accounts business (Lines 1 to 25)	3,219,028,244	3,177,263,654
27. From Separate Accounts Statement	1,524,810,149	1,288,348,863
28. TOTAL LIABILITIES (Lines 26 and 27)	4,743,838,393	4,465,612,517
29. Common capital stock		
30. Preferred capital stock		
31. Aggregate write-ins for other than special surplus funds	(242,150)	(250,850)
32. Surplus Notes	50,000,000	50,000,000
33. Gross paid in and contributed surplus (Page 3, Line 33, Column 2 plus Page 4, Line 44a, Column 1)		
34. Aggregate write-ins for special surplus funds	17,110,000	17,300,000
35. Unassigned funds (surplus)	277,028,281	250,903,032
36. Less treasury stock, at cost:		
(1) 0 shares common (value included in Line 29 $0)		
(2) 0 shares preferred (value included in Line 30 $0)		
37. Surplus (Total Lines 31 + 32 + 33 + 34 + 35 – 36) (Including $5,944,388 in Separate Accounts Statement)	343,896,131	317,952,182
38. TOTALS of Lines 29, 30 and 37 (Page 4, Line 48)	343,896,131	317,952,182
39. TOTALS of Lines 28 and 38 (Page 2, Line 25, Column 4)	5,087,734,524	4,783,564,699
Details of Write-Ins		
2501. Due to reinsuring company (reserve amount)	2,386,782	2,204,759
2502. Accrued interest on policy or contract claims	405,646	308,719
2503. Amounts held for benefit of group life policyholders	394,458	490,700
2598. Summary of remaining write-ins for Line 25 from overflow page	697,280	5,171,910
2599. TOTALS (Lines 2501 through 2503 plus 2598) (Line 25 above)	3,884,166	8,176,088
3101. Surplus note discount	(242,150)	(250,850)
3102.		
3103.		
3198. Summary of remaining write-ins for Line 31 from overflow page		
3199. TOTALS (Lines 3101 through 3103 plus 3198) (Line 31 above)	(242,150)	(250,850)
3401. Reserve for group life insurance	15,960,000	16,150,000
3402. Reserve for Separate Accounts	750,000	750,000
3403. Reserve for state guaranty funds	400,000	400,000
3498. Summary of remaining write-ins for Line 34 from overflow page		
3499. TOTALS (Lines 3401 through 3403 plus 3498) (Line 34 above)	17,110,000	17,300,000

Summary of Operations

The summary of operations represents an income statement for the reported year, providing a summary of the insurer's income, disposition of income, and a reconciliation of beginning and ending surplus. The summary of operations is an aggregated total of operations reported for each of the insurer's insurance products in the analysis of operations by line of business.

Income

Under SAP, the income of a life insurer includes premiums, investment income, deposits, and miscellaneous income. When policy benefits are left with the company under dividend or settlement options, the amount is treated simultaneously as a disbursement to the policyowner or beneficiary and as income to the company.

- *Premium* income consists of life and health insurance premiums and annuity considerations, together with dividends used to purchase additional insurance and policy proceeds left with the company under settlement options having life contingencies. Under GAAP, FAS 97 requires that cash received on interest-sensitive products, such as deferred annuity and universal life–type policies, not be recorded as premium income but be considered a deposit and reflected directly as a liability. Under SAP, all cash received is recorded as premium income.
- *Considerations for supplementary contracts and deposits* are funds left with the company under settlement or policy dividend options without life contingencies.
- *Investment income* is comprised primarily of interest, dividends, and rents derived from the insurer's investments. Under GAAP, realized capital gains and losses are recognized in the income statement as part of operating income. Under SAP, investment income also includes an accounting entry for rent paid by the company to itself for the use of owned and occupied real estate in order to reflect an appropriate yield on investment in corporate real estate. On a statutory basis, real estate is reported net of encumbrances; therefore, the interest expense on such debt reduces statutory investment income. Similarly, the effect of consolidating certain investments for GAAP reporting versus the equity method of presentation for SAP will create additional differences between GAAP and statutory investment income.
- *Miscellaneous income,* typically not significant in relation to total income, includes revenue arising from administrative service contracts and other consulting fees as well as other noninsurance operations.

Disposition of Income

A life company's income is devoted to the cost of doing an insurance business, including benefits and the maintenance of reserves.

- *Benefits* include regular death, endowment, health, and annuity benefit payments, as well as waiver-of-premium and disability income payments. Benefits also include payment of cash surrender values, dividends, and amounts due under supplementary contracts without life contingencies.
- *Operating expenses and taxes* include all expenditures paid in the course of doing business, such as rents, salaries, and agent commissions. Both federal income taxes and state premium taxes may be substantial. As noted previously, there is a significant difference in SAP and GAAP treatment of first-year policy acquisition expenses.

- *Increases in required policy reserves* are usually a significant item in the disposition of income. Increased reserves are established whenever the current-year valuation requires reserves that exceed those of the previous year. If a company's insurance in force is declining, required policy reserves may decrease. In the past, policy reserves were generally not actually entered on corporate accounting books but were determined annually at the time of the actuarial valuation. Today, most accounting systems do reflect liability balances in the general ledger. The net increase or decrease is determined by reference to and reconciliation with the previous year's valuation.
- *Net income* represents the excess of income over the foregoing disposition items. If an insurer is growing rapidly, substantial reserve increases and acquisition expenses may cause surplus strain when the total disposition of income exceeds sources of income. The surplus strain phenomenon is far less evident or nonexistent under GAAP rules because (1) the majority of first-year acquisition expenses are capitalized and deferred, and (2) reserve calculations are typically based on more realistic assumptions.

Changes in Surplus Account

The difference in income and disposition of income is determined in the summary of operations. This net gain or loss from operations is a primary source of surplus change. There are also direct sources of surplus change:

- *Capital gains and losses* in the operating statement before net income directly affect surplus if they are (a) realized during the reporting year through sale or other disposition (other than those captured by IMR in statutory net income) or (b) realized through a change in the admitted value of assets.
- *Changes in the AVR* flow directly to the surplus account without being reflected in the summary of operations.
- The *IMR* does not affect surplus. The amounts of gains and losses realized that are interest related are credited to the IMR and charged to the realized gain or loss account in the statement of operations without direct impact on surplus.
- *Dividends paid to shareholders,* unlike policyowner dividends, are a distribution of surplus, which is reflected in the summary of operations.

Table 34-3 presents the Summary of Operations and Reconciliation of Capital and Surplus Account for a hypothetical life insurance company in SAP format.

Cash Flow Statement

The NAIC requires a cash flow statement to be included in the annual statement. As discussed earlier in this chapter and in chapter 32, the balance sheet focus of statutory accounting does not adequately account for short-term cash flow activity. The cash flow statement reports an insurer's cash activities and may reveal potential liquidity problems in responding to potential disintermediation or other cash flow problems.

The cash flow statement reports the sources and uses of all insurer cash for a given reporting period both for insurance operations and investment activity, and it reconciles the cash and short-term investment holdings from period to period.[7] Table 34-4 presents the cash flow statement for a hypothetical life insurance company in SAP format.

---

[7]The format and classification of cash flows as operating, financing, and investing activities follows FAS 95 when a cash flow statement is presented for GAAP.

TABLE 34-3   Annual Statement for the Year 1998 of the XYZ Life Insurance Company

SUMMARY OF OPERATIONS
(Excluding Unrealized Capital Gains and Losses)

	1 Current Year	2 Prior Year
1. Premiums and annuity considerations (Exhibit 1, Part 1, Line 20d, Column 1, less Column 11)	271,912,004	251,808,030
1A. Deposit-type funds	530,509,495	424,326,106
2. Considerations for supplementary contracts with life contingencies (Exhibit 12, Line 3, Column 1)	274,262	43,479
3. Considerations for supplementary contracts without life contingencies and dividend accumulations (Exhibit 12, Lines 4 and 5, Column 1)	65,788,363	57,716,809
3A. Coupons left to accumulate at interest (Exhibit 12, Line 5A, Column 1)		
4. Net investment income (includes $0 equity in undistributed income or loss of subsidiaries) (Exhibit 2, Line 15)	280,351,487	273,053,665
4A. Amortization of Interest Maintenance Reserve (IMR) (Page 40, Line 5)	2,375,249	805,177
4B. Separate Accounts net gain from operations excluding unrealized gains or losses	(140,566)	
5. Commissions and expense allowances on reinsurance ceded (Exhibit 1, Part 2, Line 26a, Column 1)	2,658,164	2,388,497
5A. Reserve adjustments on reinsurance ceded (Exhibit 12, Line 9A, Column 1)	(65,000)	(168,618)
6. Miscellaneous income		
6.1 Income from fees associated with investment management, administration and contract guarantees from Separate Accounts	16,165,049	
6.2 Aggregate write-ins for miscellaneous income	5,952,791	3,742,383
7. Totals (Lines 1 to 6.2)	1,175,781,298	1,013,715,528
8. Death benefits	79,231,333	67,432,936
9. Matured endowments (excluding guaranteed annual pure endowments)	878,530	834,545
10. Annuity benefits (Exhibit 11, Part 2, Line 6d, Columns 4 + 8)	114,465,399	85,267,999
11. Disability benefits and benefits under accident and health policies	26,492,339	25,383,431
11A. Coupons, guaranteed annual pure endowments and similar benefits (Exhibit 7, Line 15, Columns 3 + 4)		
12. Surrender benefits and other fund withdrawals	446,429,057	418,034,192
13. Group conversions		
14. Interest on policy or contract funds	1,609,183	1,230,429
15. Payments on supplementary contracts with life contingencies (Exhibit 12, Line 20.1, Column 1)	2,238,706	2,401,742
16. Payments on supplementary contracts without life contingencies and of dividend accumulations (Exhibit 12, Lines 20.2 + 21, Column 1)	67,103,051	61,694,968
16A. Accumulated coupon payments (Exhibit 12, Line 21A, Column 1)		
17. Increase in aggregate reserves for life and accident and health policies and contracts	72,198,705	39,037,777
17A. Increase in liability for premium and other deposit funds	(16,014,891)	(22,115,027)
18. Increase in reserve for supplementary contracts without life contingencies and for dividend and coupon accumulations	1,045,200	(1,321,122)
19. Totals (Lines 8 to 18)	795,676,612	677,881,870
20. Commissions on premiums, annuity considerations, and deposit type funds (direct business only) (Exhibit 1, Part 2, Line 30, Column 1)	33,696,349	29,712,361
21. Commissions and expense allowances on reinsurance assumed (Exhibit 1, Part 2, Line 26b, Column 1, less Column 11)	1,012,884	1,273,169
22. General insurance expenses (Exhibit 5, Line 10, Columns 1 + 2 + 3)	95,881,782	85,303,316
23. Insurance taxes, licenses and fees, excluding federal income taxes (Exhibit 6, Line 7. Columns 1 + 2 + 3)	10,283,192	10,028,371

TABLE 34-3 *(cont.)*

SUMMARY OF OPERATIONS
(Excluding Unrealized Capital Gains and Losses)

	1 Current Year	2 Prior Year
24. Increase in loading on and cost of collection in excess of loading on deferred and uncollected premiums	(1,001,721)	(471,258)
24A. Net transfers to or (from) Separate Accounts	158,317,744	115,702,663
25. Aggregate write-ins for deductions	1,489,539	863,583
26. TOTALS (Lines 19 to 25)	1,095,356,381	920,294,075
27. Net gain from operations before dividends to policyholders and federal income taxes (Line 7 minus Line 26)	80,424,917	93,421,453
28. Dividends to policyholders (Exhibit 7, Line 15, Columns 1 and 2)	16,469,889	16,915,332
29. Net gain from operations after dividends to policyholders and before federal income taxes (Line 27 minus Line 28)	63,955,028	76,506,121
30. Federal income taxes incurred (excluding tax on capital gains)	20,248,242	26,921,891
31. Net gain from operations after dividends to policyholders and federal income taxes and before realized capital gains or (losses) (Line 29 minus Line 30)	43,706,786	49,584,230
32. Net realized capital gains (or losses) less capital gains tax and transferred to the IMR (Exhibit 3, Footnote (a), Line 3C)	(13,144,935)	1,667,018
33. Net income (Line 31 plus Line 32)	30,561,851	51,251,248
Capital and Surplus Account		
34. Capital and surplus, December 31, prior year (Page 3, Line 38, Column 2)	317,952,182	277,201,210
35. Net income (Line 33)	30,561,851	51,251,248
36. Change in net unrealized capital gains or (losses)	(19,757,039)	(5,603,731)
37. Change in nonadmitted assets and related items (Exhibit 13, Line 6, Column 3)	(1,678,673)	211,260
38. Change in liability for reinsurance in unauthorized companies		
39. Change in reserve on account of change in valuation basis (increase) or decrease (Exhibit 8A, Line D, Column 4)		
40. Change in asset valuation reserve (Page 41, Lines 2 through 4 plus Lines 8, 11, and 12, Column 7)	20,217,627	(4,911,898)
41. Change in treasury stock (Page 3, Lines 36 (1) & (2) Column 2 minus Column 1)		
41A. Surplus (contributed to) withdrawn from Separate Accounts during period	(6,000,000)	
42. Other changes in surplus in Separate Accounts Statement	6,084,953	
42A. Change in surplus notes	8,700	8,700
43. Capital changes: A. Paid in B. Transferred from surplus (Stock Dividend) C. Transferred to surplus (Exhibit 12, Line 24, Column 1, capital portion)		
44. Surplus adjustment: A. Paid in B. Transferred to capital (Stock Dividend) (Exhibit 12, Line 25, inside amount for stock $) C. Transferred from capital (Exhibit 12, Line 24, Column 1, surplus portion) D. Change in surplus as a result of reinsurance		
45. Dividends to stockholders		
46. Aggregate write-ins for gains and losses in surplus	(3,493,470)	(204,607)
47. Net change in capital and surplus for the year (Lines 35 through 46)	25,943,949	40,750,972
48. Capital and surplus, December 31, current year (Lines 34 + 47) (Page 3, Line 38)	343,896,131	317,952,182

(Continued)

TABLE 34-3 · *(cont.)*

SUMMARY OF OPERATIONS
(Excluding Unrealized Capital Gains and Losses)

	1 Current Year	2 Prior Year
Details of Write-Ins		
06.201 Miscellaneous income and reinsurance experience refund	5,952,791	3,742,383
06.202		
06.203		
06.298 Summary of remaining write-ins for Line 6.2 from overflow page		
06.299 Totals (Lines 06.201 through 06.203 plus 06.298) (Line 6.2 above)	5,952,791	3,742,383
2501. Miscellaneous deductions and interest paid	1,489,539	863,583
2502.		
2503.		
2598. Summary of remaining write-ins for Line 25 from overflow page		
2599. Totals (Lines 2501 through 2503 plus 2598) (Line 25 above)	1,489,539	863,583
4601. Net gain/loss on sale of furniture and equipment	(498,586)	(204,607)
4602. Adjustment of prior years annuity reserves	(2,994,884)	
4603.		
4698. Summary of remaining write-ins for Line 46 from overflow page		
4699. Totals (Lines 4601 through 4603 plus 4698) (Line 46 above)	(3,493,470)	(204,607)

Supplementary Schedules and Exhibits

In general, the subsidiary exhibits and schedules required by statutory reporting requirements provide further details in regard to some of the items that appear only in total in the primary financial statements. Among the exhibits, the more important are those that furnish details or classified information about (1) premium income; (2) investment income; (3) capital gains and losses; (4) expenses; (5) taxes; (6) policy reserves; (7) policy and contract claims; (8) life insurance issued, terminated, and in force (the "policy exhibit"); and (9) annuities issued, terminated, and in force (the "annuity exhibit"). General interrogatories and footnotes follow the exhibits.

The most important schedules found in the NAIC statement are those relating to real estate, mortgage loans, and securities (bonds and stocks). The schedules for real estate and securities show, in considerable detail, the amounts owned at the end of the year and the purchases and sales during the year. Somewhat similar information is given for mortgage loans but with less detail. Other important schedules show detailed information regarding (1) individual bank balances, month by month; (2) resisted claims; (3) premiums by state; (4) transactions with affiliates; (5) derivatives; and (6) reinsurance.

A statement of the company's business in the state in which the report is being filed is included. The statement shows the numbers and amounts of policies issued, terminated, and in force, together with a statement of premiums collected and policy dividends and benefits paid in the state. Naturally, the necessity of furnishing this information by state requires that the insurance company maintain its records in such a way as to be able to report its business by state.

TABLE 34-4 Annual Statement for the Year 1998 of the XYZ Life Insurance Company

CASH FLOW

Cash from Operations	1 Current Year	2 Prior Year
1. Premiums and annuity considerations	274,230,262	251,761,792
2. Deposit-type funds	530,509,496	424,326,106
3. Considerations for supplementary contracts with life contingencies	274,262	43,479
4. Considerations for supplementary contracts without life contingencies and dividend accumulations	65,788,362	57,716,809
5. Coupons left to accumulate at interest		
6. Net investment income	284,568,820	265,486,758
7. Commissions and expense allowances on reinsurance ceded	2,598,219	2,224,659
7A. Fees associated with investment management, administration, and contract guarantee from Separate Accounts	16,165,049	
8. Aggregate write-ins for miscellaneous income	6,134,814	3,748,952
9. TOTAL (Lines 1 to 8)	1,180,269,284	1,005,308,555
10. Death benefits	81,299,165	70,348,418
11. Matured endowments	866,724	909,472
12. Annuity benefits	110,463,239	85,335,887
13. Disability benefits and benefits under accident and health policies	23,836,911	21,385,567
14. Coupons, guaranteed annual pure endowments and similar benefits		
15. Surrender benefits and other fund withdrawals	446,429,057	418,034,192
16. Group conversions		
17. Interest on policy or contract funds	1,512,821	1,174,077
18. Payments on supplementary contracts with life contingencies	2,238,706	2,401,742
19. Payments on supplementary contract without life contingencies and dividend accumulations	67,103,051	61,694,968
20. Accumulated coupon payments		
21. TOTAL (Lines 10 to 20)	733,749,674	661,284,323
22. Commissions on premiums, annuity considerations, and deposit type funds	33,548,753	29,636,289
23. Commissions and expense allowances on reinsurance assumed	1,056,026	1,245,443
24. General insurance expenses	96,047,057	84,938,497
25. Insurance taxes, licenses and fees, excluding federal income taxes	9,681,211	10,272,324
26. Net transfers to or (from) Separate Accounts	192,583,247	125,563,459
27. Aggregate write-ins for deductions	1,489,539	863,583
28. TOTAL (Lines 21 to 27)	1,068,155,507	913,803,918
29. Dividends paid to policyholders	16,836,284	15,779,777
30. Federal income taxes (excluding tax on capital gains)	22,154,912	34,800,105
31. TOTAL (Lines 28 to 30)	1,107,146,703	964,383,800
32. Net cash from operations (Line 9 minus Line 31)	73,122,581	40,924,755
Cash from Investments		
33. Proceeds from investments sold, matured or repaid:		
33.1 Bonds	2,047,566,088	2,878,743,863
33.2 Stocks	13,954,633	47,755,668
33.3 Mortgage loans	136,039,446	81,433,955
33.4 Real estate	5,570,452	16,099,993
33.5 Other invested assets	26,937,856	7,543,982
33.6 Net gains or (losses) on cash and short-term investments	(82)	(327)
33.7 Miscellaneous proceeds	(3,107,607)	(1,665,912)
33.8 TOTAL investment proceeds (Lines 33.1 to 33.7)	2,226,960,786	3,029,911,222

(Continued)

TABLE 34-4   *(cont.)*

CASH FLOW

Cash from Operations	1 Current Year	2 Prior Year
34. Net tax on capital gains (losses)		
35. TOTAL (Line 33.8 minus Line 34)	2,226,960,786	3,029,911,222
36. Cost of investments acquired (long-term only):		
36.1 Bonds	1,989,570,638	2,848,858,528
36.2 Stocks	50,486,433	53,084,802
36.3 Mortgage loans	186,928,995	151,212,848
36.4 Real estate	2,261,085	7,313,184
36.5 Other invested assets	34,968,591	12,363,260
36.6 Miscellaneous applications		
36.7 TOTAL investments acquired (Lines 36.1 to 36.6)	2,264,215,742	3,072,832,622
37. Net increase or (decrease) in policy loans and premium notes	(1,136,625)	(2,766,223)
38. Net cash from investments (Line 35 minus Line 36.7 minus (plus) Line 37)	(36,118,331)	(40,155,177)
Cash from Financing and Miscellaneous Sources		
39. Cash provided:		
39.1 Surplus notes, capital and surplus paid in		8,700
39.2 Borrowed money $626,983,000 less amounts repaid $626,983,000		
39.3 Capital notes $0 less amounts repaid $0		
39.4 Other cash provided	13,917,138	2,117,983
39.5 TOTAL (Lines 39.1 to 39.4)	13,917,138	2,126,683
40. Cash applied:		
40.1 Dividends to stockholders paid		
40.2 Interest on indebtedness		
40.3 Other applications (net)		
40.4 TOTAL (Lines 40.1 and 40.3)		
41. Net cash from financing and miscellaneous sources (Line 39.5 minus Line 40.4)	13,917,138	2,126,683
Reconciliation of Cash and Short-Term Investments		
42. Net change in cash and short-term investments (Line 32, plus Line 38, plus Line 41)	50,921,388	2,896,261
43. Cash and short-term investments:		
43.1 Beginning of year	3,058,591	162,330
43.2 End of year (Line 42 plus Line 43.1)	53,979,979	3,058,591
Details of Write-Ins		
0801. Miscellaneous income and reinsurance reserve adjustments	6,134,814	3,748,952
0802.		
0803.		
0898. Summary of remaining write-ins for Line 8 from overflow page		
0899. TOTALS (Lines 0801 through 0803 plus 0898) (Line 8 above)	6,134,814	3,748,952
2701. Miscellaneous deductions and interest paid	1,489,539	863,583
2702.		
2703.		
2798. Summary of remaining write-ins for Line 27 from overflow page		
2799. TOTALS (Lines 2701 through 2703 plus 2798) (Line 27 above)	1,489,539	863,583

ANNUAL REPORTS

The NAIC statement is not an especially convenient or direct source of information for policyowners, shareholders, and the general public. As a result, condensed and simplified financial statements are included in the published annual reports issued by companies to their policyowners and shareholders. These statements and the excerpts from the annual reports are also used by many companies in their advertising and other publicity activities.

Any statutory figures in these reports are prepared, in part, from information in the NAIC statement. Any financial statements in the annual report are condensed versions of those in the NAIC statement or those that might be prepared based on GAAP principles.

The scope of annual reports and the kind and detail of the information included in them vary greatly from company to company. Most of these reports contain supplementary information on the company's operations, plans, and other matters usually also found in the trade press. Among other things, there frequently is a narrative presentation of a promotional nature. If GAAP financial statements are included, there is also likely to be a reconciliation of the principal GAAP statement items with the corresponding statutory statement items. In both SAP and GAAP, "Management's Discussion and Analysis" is an important source of information reflected in the annual report.

MANAGERIAL ACCOUNTING

In addition to using them for financial reporting systems, insurer management requires accounting tools for managerial purposes. Budget accounting is used for business planning purposes; cost accounting is used to identify the cost of creating, marketing, and operating discrete aspects of a company's business; and audit and control procedures are applied to minimize the possibility of accounting mistakes and irregularities.

Budget Accounting

Financial reporting systems account for the historical financial performance of a company. Management also requires projections of future financial results for planning purposes. *Budget accounting* becomes central to the planning process by detailing expected income and expense over a specified period of time for a company or department. Planning can be characterized as operational or strategic, as summarized in Box 34-1.

BOX 34-1

OPERATIONAL AND STRATEGIC PLANNING

Operational planning is short term in nature—typically two to five years—and focuses on the day-to-day financial activities of a company. Operating budgets are primarily concerned with income and expense statements for specified periods, and they can be presented by department or on an aggregate, companywide basis.

By contrast, *strategic planning* is more long term in nature, and it often involves fixed assets, capital expenditures, and long-term sources of capital. Strategic planning has been called capital budgeting on a grand scale, and it is essential for determining whether a company's capital will be invested efficiently.

Differing approaches to budget preparation include top-down budgeting, bottom-up budgeting, and zero-base budgeting. *Top-down budgeting* is prepared by senior management based on past experience and current objectives, with little input from middle management and employees. This approach ensures that budgets reflect management wishes and can be prepared relatively easily, but it may not enjoy the full support of non-participating managers and employees.

Bottom-up budgeting is prepared with significant contributions from employees and middle managers and most likely maximizes their support. This approach typically generates high-quality management information but is relatively time consuming. *Zero-base budgeting* begins with the assumption that past expenditures are not a good measure of future expenditures and that each department's expected outlays must be justified in full.

Cost Accounting

The primary purpose of **cost accounting** is to identify the cost of creating, marketing, and operating discrete aspects of an insurer's business. The ability to distinguish costs among different products, services, and operations is necessary for effectively supporting the pricing of products and the analysis of budgets and capital investments.

With reliable cost information, management is better able to make informed operations decisions, such as:

- Identifying less productive areas of insurer operations for the purposes of cost control.
- Budgeting insurer resources to hold, expand, or contract market share where appropriate.
- Determining premium and dividend scales.
- Evaluating and controlling operations by checking procedures and personnel.

Cost accounting is conducted on both a marginal and functional cost basis. *Marginal cost accounting* measures the additional expense of producing one additional product or service unit, and it is helpful because marginal cost and initial cost usually differ. Marginal costs will be less than initial costs because of the nonrecurring nature of many start-up expenditures. Understanding the marginal cost of a particular action reveals the true monetary effect that can be expected and is helpful in determining the prudence of proceeding or not proceeding with an action.

Functional cost accounting involves the identification of the cost associated with a series of operations that often crosses departmental lines. As pointed out earlier, the actuarial department plays an important functional role in a number of areas within the insurer. For example, new-product development may be basically an actuarial responsibility, but a new product necessarily involves marketing, investments, underwriting, systems, and other areas within the insurer. Functional cost accounting further refines the cost analysis procedure, and it is necessary to prepare the allocations by line of business, as is required for the statutory annual statement.

Audit and Control

Internal control and audit procedures are concerned with limiting the risk of loss associated with mistakes, fraud, and other irregularities in the processing of transactions and the handling of assets. To ensure that records are kept appropriately, audit and control personnel should work independently of regular accounting personnel and have access to both senior management and the board's audit committee.

Accounting control is intended to promote the following objectives:

- Transactions should be executed in accordance with the general or specific authorization of management.
- Transactions should be recorded in a way that permits preparation of financial statements that conform to GAAP, SAP, and other necessary criteria.
- Transactions should be recorded in a way that permits the proper monitoring of company assets.
- Access to assets should be permitted only under authorized circumstances.
- The company's record of its assets should be compared with existing assets at regular intervals in order to identify discrepancies.

Accounting audits provide confirmation to interested parties that financial results as reported are accurate. External audits are performed by accounting firms for the benefit of interested third parties such as shareholders and regulators. These audits are conducted in accordance with generally accepted auditing standards. The primary objective of the audits is to certify, with reasonable assurance, that a company's financial statements are free of material misstatements and that the statements are in accord with GAAP or SAP, depending on the purpose of the audit. The audit is conducted on a risk-based sample that reflects the state of the company's internal controls and the identified critical and significant areas that represent the most important areas of exposure. Internal audits may be performed by company personnel for the benefit of management and directors. Where appropriate control procedures are utilized, the audit should substantially confirm the company's regular financial reports.

ECONOMIC VALUE ANALYSIS

As discussed earlier, both SAP and GAAP accounting exhibit significant limitations in describing certain aspects of life insurer financial condition. In order to measure adequately the long-term financial impact of current-year management decisions, it is necessary to avoid these limitations to the extent possible. Specifically, these are the goals of management-oriented measurement:

- It should not distort the long-term results of surrenders (lost future profits) and new sales (additional profits).
- It should recognize anticipated profits on future business.
- It should recognize the long-term value resulting from current investment in distribution systems.
- It should recognize the unrealized capital gains and losses associated with active investment management programs.

As discussed in chapter 32, the primary management objective for virtually every life insurer is to create value for shareholders, and in mutual companies, for policyowners. Performance measurement systems based on the creation of value are increasingly being adopted by life insurers as a standard for judging the effectiveness of management activity.

The two most important of these are the value-added and return on equity methods. Students of investment analysis will recognize these methods as derivations of net present value analysis and internal rate of return analysis, respectively.

Value-Added Analysis

Value added for a given planning or analysis period is measured as follows:

	Ending Net Worth
Less:	Beginning Net Worth
Plus:	Stock and Policyowner Dividends Paid
Less:	Capital Infusions
Equals:	Value Added for the Period

Net worth is defined as statutory surplus plus the present value of future statutory earnings on existing business, plus the present value of future statutory earnings on future business. Statutory earnings, rather than GAAP earnings or cash flow, are probably best used as profit measures because statutory earnings represent the only source of capital for the payment of dividends or increases to surplus. Present values are calculated by discounting cash flows at the insurer's hurdle rate or cost of capital.

Adjustments to the discount rate may be made to reflect the different risk properties of different products and ventures. For example, a higher discount rate would most likely be appropriate for discounting profits on future business relative to future profits on existing business.

The value-added method, by incorporating future statutory earnings, recognizes the long-term value that can be expected to develop from current-year management actions. Value-added analysis can be applied to individual product lines, as well as to insurer net worth in the aggregate. Whenever the present value of future cash flows exceeds the investment under analysis, management is creating value for shareholders or policyowners.

Return on Equity Analysis

Return on equity methods are used to calculate profitability as a return on an insurer's investment in a product line or other venture. **Return on equity** is the implicit internal rate of return associated with the cash flows or statutory profits of a product line or other venture.

When return on equity exceeds the insurer's cost of capital, value is created for shareholders or policyowners. As with the value-added method, the incorporation of future earnings recognizes the long-term value of current-year management actions.

A more sophisticated form of return on equity analysis is used by some companies. The level return on equity method attempts to account better for the special risk-taking nature of life insurance by incorporating the idea that equity includes not only cash invested in reserves and expenses for a product line but also reflects some part of an insurer's surplus that supports the product line.

The idea of benchmark surplus, discussed in chapter 32, is central to recognizing the risk-taking nature of insurance in the measurement of financial performance. Management practice dictates that statutory reserves are not sufficient in and of themselves to support a particular product line. Some level of surplus is required to protect against unforeseen contingencies and to satisfy the requirements of regulators, rating agencies, policyowners, shareholders, and other outside evaluators of life insurers.

Although the mathematical and conceptual complexity of level return on equity makes a full discussion beyond the scope of this text, the method is intended to recognize that the equity devoted to a particular product line is not limited to cash outlays for expenses and reserves but also includes the benchmark surplus that effectively supports the product line. It is consistent with this recognition that after-tax earnings on benchmark surplus are combined with product earnings to calculate the implicit internal rate of return associated with the product, and the incidence of profit recognition is in part determined by periodically redetermined benchmark surplus requirements.

REGULATORY DEVELOPMENTS IN FINANCIAL REPORTING

The Valuation Actuary

Regulators historically examined the statutory statement to evaluate an insurer's current and future solvency. The statutory statement is a static, nondynamic view of an insurer's financial position. It also suffers from rules that value assets and liabilities independently. Bonds not in default are valued at amortized cost without regard to current market values, yields, or scheduled maturities. Liabilities are valued on the premise of interest and mortality assumptions permitted or required at the time of issue without regard to current experience or asset values. The statutory statement remains an inadequate tool for fully evaluating company solvency. This inadequacy reflects the inherent cash flow nature of the life insurance business, the vulnerability of its pricing and reserving assumptions to changing market interest rates (both discussed in chapter 32), and the use of artificially stabilizing asset valuation conventions (discussed earlier in this chapter).

In 1985, a joint committee of the American Academy of Actuaries and the Society of Actuaries recommended that each life company appoint a valuation actuary who would issue a "statement of actuarial opinion" on an annual basis, certifying a company's expected solvency under a variety of possible economic scenarios that recognize the interdependence of asset and liability cash flows.

In 1991, the NAIC adopted the Actuarial Opinion and Memorandum Model Regulation, which requires companies to appoint a valuation actuary to perform cash flow testing. The intent of the law is to encourage responsible asset–liability management. **Cash flow testing** can be defined as a process of projecting and comparing, as of a given valuation date, the timing and amount of asset and liability cash flows after the valuation date. The required actuarial opinion by an appointed actuary is a public document that must be filed along with the annual statement.

The law changed the role for actuaries in valuation. The appointed actuary is responsible *by law* for the liability reserves. The responsibility includes asset consideration and an asset adequacy opinion. The Actuarial Standards Board (ASB) provides the *professional base* for the appointed actuary's work.

Maintaining a balance between adequate regulation in the public interest and the insurer's need for management flexibility in investment to compete effectively is an ongoing process. What has become clear, however, is the need for increased awareness at both the regulatory and insurer level of the interplay between investment and marketing in the valuation process.

Risk-Based Capital Requirements

Historically, regulators have not given detailed attention to the nature of particular risks assumed by insurers. Reserving requirements for broad classes of business were established, which, together with minimum admission and valuation requirements for assets, were intended to promote insurer solvency. Minimum capital requirements represented nominal amounts for most insurers.

The NAIC developed a risk-based capital formula establishing target surplus amounts that are required above reserve requirements, which are intended to reflect the risk inherent in an insurer's contractual obligations and asset portfolio. The required amounts of capital are classified into five major categories: asset default risk—affiliates (C-0), asset risk—other (C-1), insurance risk (C-2), interest rate risk (C-3), and miscellaneous business risk (C-4).

The asset default risk components (C-0 and C-1) are intended to support all risks associated with losses related to assets. Insurance pricing requirements (C-2) apply to both mortality and morbidity risks. Requirements attributable to mortality are based on the relative weight of group and individual business, as well as the level of insurance in force. Morbidity requirements likewise reflect the mix of group and individual business, as well as the nature of coverages provided.

Interest rate risk (C-3) capital requirements depend on classification by the nature of the risk characteristics of individual product lines, as well as their withdrawal provisions. Miscellaneous risk (C-4) capital requirements include amounts derived from an insurer's risk exposure with respect to guaranty fund assessability. The general requirements also provide for a reduction in capital requirements for which risks may be offsetting.

Risk-based capital requirements have led to significant increases in companies' capital needs. As insurers manage their operations to develop a favorable risk-based capital profile, policyowners may expect generally increasing asset quality, whereas industry investors may expect generally declining return on equity results.

Codification of Statutory Accounting Principles

For several years, a NAIC working group attempted to define and document a means by which the statutory-basis accounting principles can be codified. It was felt that consistency in statutory accounting would be helpful to the industry at a time when insurers must compete with other financial institutions that do not have to keep track of accounting standards in the United States or maintain two separate bases of accounting—SAP and GAAP. Those favoring codification believed that consistency also is the foundation for sound financial analysis and solvency regulation and would be beneficial to consumers.

The NAIC working group reviewed and adopted, with modification in some cases, substantial portions of the GAAP literature applicable to insurers. They have produced, in effect, a technical foundation for codification. There were, of course, those who disagreed with some decisions made by the working group regarding the various accounting issues it addresses. Given the diversity that characterizes the industry, it would have been unrealistic to expect that all of the decisions would be popular with all parties.

The codification project was adopted by the NAIC plenary session on an almost unanimous basis at the 1998 spring national meeting. Shortly after, the chairperson of the AICPA's Insurance Committee (ICC) announced that SOP95-5 (*Auditor's Report on Statutory Financial Statements of Insurance Enterprises*) was based on a faulty premise and that, contrary to the SOP, a company may receive an unqualified audit opinion on limited distribution statutory statements when it follows accounting guidance based on its domiciliary state's prescribed or permitted practices rather than on codification. It is anticipated that most states will adopt codification as the baseline for statutory accounting.[8]

---

[8]American Council of Life Insurance, *General Bulletin*, no. 5475, March 19, 1998.

Questions

1. Explain the objectives and limitations of both SAP and GAAP accounting principles. To what extent are differences in their assessments of an insurer's financial position justified by different concerns their users may have?
2. How are concerns within SAP accounting reflected in the contents of the NAIC Annual Statement?
3. Explain how the following managerial accounting and economic value-added analysis methods are used to analyze and improve the performance of life insurers:
   a. budget accounting
   b. cost accounting
   c. accounting control
   d. value-added analysis
4. Discuss the origin and purpose of the following regulatory developments in financial reporting:
   a. the valuation actuary
   b. risk-based capital requirements
   c. the codification of statutory accounting principles

CHAPTER

35

REGULATION AND TAXATION OF LIFE AND HEALTH INSURANCE

Objectives

- Explain the public policy rationale for government intervention in insurance markets.

- Describe theories of regulation.

- Describe the scope of and mechanisms used in the state regulation of insurance markets.

- Discuss the regulatory concerns arising from the integration of financial services.

- Discuss the nature of life and health insurer taxation at the state and federal levels.

G overnments worldwide intervene into their insurance markets. This intervention takes many forms, some direct, some indirect. The nature and the degree of government intervention vary with each country's sociocultural and economic circumstances and its government's prevailing political philosophy. Perhaps all governments, even those strongly committed to a capitalist, market-driven philosophy, acknowledge the need for some level of government-provided social insurance protection, as we discuss in chapter 22. The hand of government is also evident in insurance markets through regulation and taxation.

Whatever the nature and degree of intervention, the avowed purposes are usually noble—typically to protect consumers, to raise revenue to support worthwhile social objectives, or to ensure orderly, well-functioning markets. This chapter examines the purposes, rationales, nature, and mechanism for insurance regulation and taxation. Our focus is on U.S. policies and practices.

THE PURPOSE OF GOVERNMENT INTERVENTION INTO MARKETS

The Efficiency Objective

All government intervention into markets should seek to maximize society's welfare. One widely accepted economic construct for conducting such an analysis builds on the goal of having society's scarce resources allocated in the most efficient way possible. Such an allocation ensures that resources are employed for maximum benefit for society.

935

Efficiency versus Fairness

A competitive market can lead to an efficient allocation of society's resources under certain conditions. Thus, in theory, a market-based economy automatically allocates resources efficiently without the need for government intervention. However, two problems arise with this idyllic world. First, society may not necessarily prefer an efficient allocation of its resources. Resource efficiency has never been any society's only goal. Certain social objectives are common goals also. Concepts of fairness and of taking care of the less fortunate are universally pursued. A society may support universal health insurance, public assistance, and other such programs because of fairness and compassion concerns.

With insurance, governments have routinely felt justified in a greater intensity of regulation than that found with most other businesses. Because the business of insurance is considered vital to citizens' well-being, it has been labeled as "affected with a public interest." Insurance bears directly on individuals' and businesses' economic security. Because of this fact and because insurers are important financial intermediaries, governments routinely intervene into their insurance markets before they might with most other services and goods.

The Existence of Market Imperfections

A second problem with the efficiency model arises when the rigorous conditions under which we hypothesize it to operate are not met. Efficiency assumes, for example, that *complete* and *efficient* markets exist for *all* products and services both now and in the future. Of course, markets do not exist for all products and services; for example, markets do not exist for all possible causes of loss to individuals and businesses. Moreover, markets are incomplete and inefficient. In practice, therefore, many products and services will be unavailable, with others available only through imperfect markets. Resources, therefore, will be allocated inefficiently to various degrees.

Recall that *perfect* competition requires that certain conditions must be met (see Box 1-1 in chapter 1). Obviously, no market fully meets the idealized conditions. Markets exhibit imperfect competition. Fortunately, the conditions need only be approximately met for the benefits of competition to be realized—so-called *workable competition*. Of course, the more distant a market's characteristics are from the ideal conditions, the more imperfect the resulting competition and, therefore, the poorer will be resource allocation and attendant consumer value and choice. As we noted in chapter 1, we term market-based situations causing an inefficient allocation of resources as *market imperfections*. In the economic model, the existence of market imperfections leads to a reduction in overall social welfare and, therefore, is undesirable.

Government Intervention and Market Imperfections

Throughout this book, we have emphasized the importance of market imperfections in driving insurer operational and management practices and in influencing government actions. Recall from chapter 1 that we classify market imperfections into four broad categories:

- market power
- externalities
- free rider problems
- information problems

The insurance business exhibits market imperfections in all four categories. Examples abound.

- Insurers seek market power (the ability to influence price) through market segmentation and product differentiation strategies.

- The failure of several large life insurers could harm a nation's entire financial structure—a negative externality.
- Public policy makers seem increasingly to consider health insurance as a public good.
- Insurers' product design, underwriting, and claim settlement operations are shaped by information asymmetry concerns—the buyer knowing more than the seller, thus leading to adverse selection and moral hazard problems.
- Conversely, the typical insurance buyer suffers from information asymmetry by virtue of being poorly informed about potentially important technicalities associated with insurance contracts, policy performance, and insurer financial solidity.

These and hundreds of other examples provide the basis upon which policy makers justify government intervention into insurance markets through regulation. In each instance, the avowed purpose of the regulation is to help rectify imperfections in the market, that is, to move the market toward greater efficiency and, thereby, greater social welfare.

Thus, within a competitive insurance market, we deem government intervention desirable only if these three conditions exist:

- Actual or potential market imperfections exist.
- The market imperfections do or could lead to meaningful economic inefficiency or inequity.
- Government action can ameliorate the inefficiency or inequity.

Conversely, if at least one of the three conditions is not met, no government intervention should be warranted. Thus, no intervention is justified for those aspects of insurance markets that exhibit no market imperfections or in which imperfections exist but do not lead to important inefficiencies or inequities. Additionally, even if market imperfections exist and they are judged to be meaningful, no intervention is justified if government's actions could not ameliorate the imperfection. Indeed, government regulation can make matters worse. Just as there is no perfect competition, there is no perfect regulation.

THEORIES OF REGULATION

Several normative and positive theories (see chapter 1) attempt to explain why regulation exists. Under the normative *public interest theory of regulation,* regulation exists to serve the public interest by protecting consumers from abuse. This regulatory theory flows directly from the goal of government seeking to rectify market imperfections. The objective is to maximize economic efficiency, including preventing or making right significant consumer harm that results from market imperfections. The premise that government can and will correct market imperfections presumes that government will function for the overall public good, and that it will be indifferent to conflicts of interest and special interest groups. The theory has its detractors who posit less noble purposes for regulation.

Under *private interest theories of regulation*—all positive theories—regulation exists to promote the interests of private parties. Thus, Peltzman suggests that self-interested regulators engage in regulatory activities consistent with maximizing their political support.[1] Under this theory, regulators might exhibit pro-industry biases to gain industry financial and other backing. Conversely, regulators might engage in activities that appeal to consumers (voters), such as price suppression to gain their support, even if the long-term effects were detrimental.

---

[1]Sam Peltzman, "Toward a More General Theory of Regulation," *Journal of Law and Economics,* Vol. 19, No. 2 (1976), pp. 211–240, and George Becker, "A Theory of Competition among Pressure Groups for Political Influence," *Quarterly Journal of Economics,* Vol. 98, No. 3 (1983), pp. 371–400.

The best-known private interest theory is the *capture theory of regulation* in which regulation is "captured" by and operated for the benefit of the regulated industry. Stigler and others contend that special interest groups, being well organized and well financed, influence legislation and regulation for their own benefit.[2] Special interest groups in insurance could include insurers, reinsurers, agents, banks, securities firms, brokers, and the firms that provide services to these industry participants. Thus, for example, U.S. banks complain about being denied full insurance marketing powers because agents have been able to unduly influence legislators and regulators.

Consumers, being widely dispersed, ill organized, poorly financed, and, on a given issue, not as well informed as special interest groups, may be ineffective by comparison. Regulation unduly influenced by special interests could be expected to result in

- restrictions on entry of new domestic and especially foreign insurers
- suppression of price and product competition
- control of interindustry competition from those selling similar or complementary products

Each of these phenomena is found in all life insurance markets to varying degrees. Under appropriate conditions, however, each can be and is justified under the public interest theory. Government's difficult task is to recognize when an interest group's public interest arguments mask self-interested, private motivations.

Finally, in what might be termed a *political theory of regulation,* Meier asserts that regulation will be shaped by a type of bargaining that occurs between different private interest groups within the existing political and administrative structure.[3] Interest groups include consumers, the regulator, political elites (courts and the legislative body), and the regulated industry. Political resources, saliency, and the complexity of regulatory issues determine interest group influence. These groups are not homogeneous, so bargaining outcomes vary from issue to issue.

There is little research to confirm or refute whether life insurance regulation has been meaningfully shaped in accordance with the foregoing theories. According to the conclusions of one researcher, "the overall impression . . . is that the insurance industry does not dominate the regulatory process."[4] Another researcher found evidence of the capture theory in one element of Canadian insurance regulation that could apply equally to U.S. regulation.[5]

OVERVIEW OF INSURANCE REGULATION IN SELECTED MARKETS

Insurance regulation is universal but different approaches are followed worldwide. This section surveys insurance regulation within selected large markets worldwide.[6] Some 95 percent of life insurance worldwide is accounted for by the United States, Canada, the

---

[2]George J. Stigler, "The Theory of Economic Regulation," *Bell Journal of Economics* (Spring 1971).

[3]Kenneth J. Meier, *The Political Economy of Regulation: The Case of Insurance* (Albany, NY: State University of New York Press, 1988).

[4]Ibid., p. 166. In his study of the property/liability (P/L) insurance industry, D'Arcy concluded that none of the popular theories of regulation adequately explained P/L regulation. Stephen P. D'Arcy, "Application of Economic Theories of Regulation to the Property-Liability Insurance Industry," *Journal of Insurance Regulation* (September 1988), pp. 19–51.

[5]G. F. Mathewson and R. A. Winter, "The Economics of Life Insurance Regulation: Valuation Constraints," in *The Economics of Insurance Regulation: A Cross-National Study,* Jörg Finsinger and Mark V. Pauly, eds. (London: The Macmillan Press, 1986), pp. 257–290.

[6]This section is adapted from Harold D. Skipper, Jr., "The Nature of Government Intervention into Insurance Markets," in *International Risk and Insurance* (Boston: Irwin McGraw-Hill, 1998), pp. 266–267; R. M. Hammond, "Life Insurance Regulation in Canada," *Canadian Journal of Life Insurance,* Vol. 9, No. 54

European Union, and Japan. For this reason, we focus our attention on these markets. Other life insurance markets are large (e.g., Korea and Taiwan), and numerous Latin American, Eastern European, and Asian markets are growing rapidly.

Regulatory philosophies and practices have a profound effect on the performance, structure, and operation of a nation's life insurance industry. At one end of the international regulatory spectrum, some governments only lightly regulate insurance with their primary emphasis being on insurer solvency. Competition is encouraged and relied upon as the primary consumer-protection force. Hong Kong, the United Kingdom, Ireland, and the Netherlands are examples of this approach.

At the other extreme, government regulatory involvement can be extensive, covering not only solvency but also policy content and pricing. Germany, Japan, and Korea are traditional examples. Such heavy regulation is rationalized as being conducive to a more orderly, stable market. Many markets, including those of the United States and Canada, fall between the two extremes.

Regulation in Canada

Supervision of insurance in Canada is shared by the federal and provincial governments. A life insurer may choose to incorporate and be regulated at the federal or the provincial level. The federal government is responsible for the solvency supervision of all non-Canadian companies operating in Canada on a branch basis and all federally incorporated insurers. These companies account for about 90 percent of the life insurance business in Canada. The Office of the Superintendent of Financial Institutions (OSFI) is the federal supervisory agency for insurance companies, banks, and other deposit-taking institutions. Provincial governments are responsible for the solvency supervision of all provincially incorporated insurers. In addition, provincial governments have exclusive jurisdiction over insurers' marketing practices such as contract wording and its interpretation, licensing of agents, and premium rates.

The Canadian life insurance market has become exceptionally competitive. The 10 largest life insurers, mostly mutuals, account for 70 percent of the business in Canada by premium volume. In 1990, their share was 61 percent. At the same time, the market is consolidating, with the number of insurers now at 130, from a figure of 160 three years earlier. Several Canadian life insurers have significant operations in the United States, United Kingdom, and other countries.

Canadian life insurance companies aggressively compete with deposit-taking institutions for savings through the issuance of deferred annuities. The main deposit-taking institutions in Canada are banks and trust and loan companies. These companies can and do own life insurers, although they are prohibited from distributing insurance directly through their retail branches. The Canadian banks make formidable competitors. Six Canadian banks—soon likely to be four because of mergers—dominate the scene with an extensive system of branch offices across the country. As measured by assets, all Canadian life insurers combined are only slightly larger than the largest bank.

Control of Entry

The approach to supervising federally incorporated insurers and the Canadian branch operations of foreign companies is basically the same. The main difference is that Canadian branch operations of foreign companies must maintain sufficient assets to cover their Canadian liabilities, plus any required capital margins, under the control of Canadian supervisory authorities.

(1991), pp. 23–27; Mike Lombardi, "A New Era for Financial Services," *Emphasis*, No. 1 (1992), pp. 20–22; and *Industry and Trade Summary: Insurance* (Washington, DC: U.S. International Trade Commission, 1991).

Incorporation of a new federal insurance company requires at least C$10 million of capital, an acceptable business plan, and reputable owners and managers. Foreign insurers can choose to operate in Canada either by establishing a branch operation or by incorporating a new federal insurer. Companies wishing to establish a branch operation in Canada must have at least C$200 million in assets, adequate capital, and a track record of successful operations.

Financial Regulation

All federally incorporated insurance companies must submit an annual financial statement in a prescribed format, accompanied by an opinion from an auditor. All Canadian branch operations must also submit an annual financial statement in a prescribed format, but an auditor's opinion is not required. The possibility of requiring an auditor's opinion is being considered. On-site financial examinations by OSFI examiners are carried out every two years, and more frequently if needed.

Subject to certain concentration limits and limits on real estate and share investments, previous quantitative tests for investment have been replaced by the prudent portfolio approach. Under this approach, the onus is on companies to develop prudent investment policies and implement appropriate control procedures.

To promote equity between generations of participating policyowners, regulations require some portion of unrealized gains and losses to be reflected in income. Another motivation of these regulations is to encourage the making of investment decisions for investment rather than income-reporting reasons.

Canada requires use of an appointed actuary, similar in concept to that used in the United Kingdom. Appointment is made and terminated by the insurer's board of directors, and the appointed actuary has access to the board. The actuary is responsible for determining the appropriateness of the actuarial reserves and for reporting to the board at least yearly on the insurer's financial prospects. If the appointed actuary becomes aware of circumstances that may have a material impact on the insurer's ability to meet its obligations, he or she must bring the matter to the attention of management and the board. If, in the opinion of the appointed actuary, satisfactory action is not taken within a reasonable time period, he or she has a statutory obligation to make the superintendent aware of the situation.

Regulation in the European Union

The European Union (EU) regulatory situation is unique. As discussed in chapter 3, one of the principal means of establishing minimum regulatory harmonization among the EU member countries is through directives. A *directive* is an order issued by the EU's Council of Ministers that requires member countries to enact new national laws or alter existing laws to come into compliance with the directive's provisions. Directives are meant to establish minimum harmonization of essential regulation throughout the EU. They are the principal means by which the EU is creating its single insurance market.

Each member state is free to regulate as it wishes subject to full implementation of EU directives. Historically, regulatory philosophy has varied enormously among EU states. The United Kingdom, the Netherlands, and Ireland have always regulated lightly, focusing chiefly on insurer solvency. The other EU member states have varying degrees of more intense regulation. Austria and Germany, for example, have exercised the strictest regulation, focusing not only on financial regulation but also exercising detailed oversight on policy terms, conditions, and prices. Recent EU directives call for less detailed oversight.

The EU market is said to be ahead of the legislators in rather comprehensively restructuring how insurance is bought and which companies might dominate certain markets. Indeed, banking and insurance company linkups have become so common that the French now speak of *bancassurance* and the Germans refer to *allfinanz.*

When the insurance directives are enacted fully, an EU-domiciled insurer holding a license in one EU nation will be able to underwrite and sell insurance in all member states without authorization from the host country. Insurers will be regulated primarily by their home country.

The insurer wishing to write insurance on a services (cross-border) basis is required to notify the host country of its intentions to do so. The insurer's home country regulator is to complete a certificate indicating the lines of insurance that the insurer is authorized to write and stating that it does not object to the insurer providing services on a cross-border basis. With certain exceptions, member states may no longer strictly regulate premiums (e.g., neither mandated premiums nor collective rate-setting activities are permitted) or policy forms. The host state may require disclosure of the actuarial aspects of premium and reserve calculations but not as a condition of market entry.

Distribution concerns are driving the insurance market within the EU and in Europe generally. Banks already have excellent distribution networks. Several European countries permit universal banking, which includes the sale and sometimes the underwriting of insurance. Merger and acquisition activity between insurers and between banks and insurance companies is brisk. One of the primary motivations behind this trend is the desire to quickly obtain an insurance distribution network that will compete effectively when all of the single-market directives take effect.

Regulation in Japan

The Japanese life insurance market is the world's second largest. The industry is characterized by a small number of very large companies. The Japanese Ministry of Finance (MOF) regulates both insurance and banking. The insurance sector reports to the banking division within the MOF. The system favors insurer financial stability over other factors.

Japanese insurance regulation has been characterized as being based on a "convoy" philosophy. The convoy members (insurance companies) move no faster than the slowest ship (weakest or least innovative insurer). Historically, price competition has been severely circumscribed, with insurers generally charging the same rates. This practice—which is changing—ensured that the financially weakest insurer would survive.

The MOF has placed priority on insolvency prevention, although a mutual life insurer failed in 1997, the first such failure in recent Japanese history. Market stability is of overriding concern, although this is changing. Volatility is to be minimized, which means strict regulation of policy forms and prices. As in Germany, Japan historically has viewed unfettered competition as unstable and ruinous.

The Japanese government has undertaken to deregulate and liberalize the nation's financial community, breaking down the walls that traditionally separated banking, securities, and insurance. Each of these sectors increasingly offers overlapping products, and this trend is expected to continue. Competition among sectors is rising.

BACKGROUND OF U.S. INSURANCE REGULATION

In democracies, people create governmental bodies to serve them and vest powers in these bodies. In the United States, the people granted broad general powers to their state governments. In creating a federal government, the people delegated to it certain specific limited authority to act on matters affecting the welfare of the entire nation. As no provision of the U.S. Constitution specifically limits the authority of the states to legislate on matters over which the federal government was given specific authority, both governments may exercise power in these areas. Any conflict, however, must be resolved by considering the fact that the delegation of a specific power to the federal government limits a general state power. The power of the federal government to act on matters over which it has specific authority is supreme.

The framers of the U.S. Constitution, recognizing that the economic welfare and the safety of the nation would be jeopardized by trade barriers restricting the free flow of trade among the states, gave Congress the exclusive power to regulate commerce with other nations and among the states. The right to regulate *intrastate* commerce was reserved to the states. As the specifically delegated powers of Congress are supreme to the states' general powers, no state may restrict or impede interstate commerce where Congress has taken action. No state laws are valid that contradict or contravene federal law regarding interstate commerce or matters affecting interstate commerce. Yet, traditionally, insurance has been regulated exclusively by the states. Some background on this issue will be helpful.

Paul v. Virginia

In 1869, in *Paul v. Virginia,* the U.S. Supreme Court refused to declare an insurance contract an instrumentality of commerce, and, as the following quote shows, it asserted the doctrine that a state clearly had the power to prohibit foreign insurance companies from doing business within its limits:

> Issuing a policy of insurance is not a transaction of commerce. . . . These contracts are not articles of commerce in any proper meaning of the word. They are not subject to the trade and barter. . . . They are like other personal contracts between parties which are completed by their signature and the transfer of the consideration. Such contracts are not interstate transactions, though the parties may be domiciled in different states. . . . They are, then, local transactions, and governed by the local law. They do not constitute a part of the commerce between the states.[7]

South-Eastern Underwriters Case

For three-quarters of a century following *Paul v. Virginia,* accepted practice was to regard the general supervision of all forms of insurance as falling solely within state government jurisdiction. In 1944, however, the Supreme Court, in *United States v. South-Eastern Underwriters Association, et al.,* abandoned this view.[8] It held that insurance was commerce and, therefore, the proper subject of federal regulation under the terms of the commerce clause of the U.S. Constitution.

In holding that insurance was commerce, and interstate commerce for the most part, the Court swept away the foundation on which the structure of state regulation of insurance had been built. It appeared that insurance was subject to any regulations Congress desired to impose, as well as several existing federal laws that could be construed as applying to the insurance business.

The McCarran-Ferguson Act

On the theory that it had the power to redefine the distribution of authority over interstate commerce, and consistent with the granting to other industries of complete or partial protection from antitrust laws, Congress passed the McCarran-Ferguson Act in 1945. The purpose of this act may be found in its title:

---

[7](1869) Wall. (U.S.) 168. See also *New York Life Insurance Co. v. Deer Lodge County* (1913), 231 U.S. 495.
[8]322 U.S. 533 (1944).

An Act to Express the Intent of the Congress with Reference to the Regulation of the Business of Insurance.

In this act, Congress redefined the authority of states and established a plan for cooperative regulation. In retrospect, it seems clear that Congress desired that there be some amount of collaboration between federal and state governments in a complete system of regulation.

According to the terms of the McCarran-Ferguson Act, the federal government retains exclusive or primary control over certain matters that it deems national in character—that is, matters in which regulation should be uniform throughout the states. Employer–employee relations (National Labor Relations Act and the Civil Rights Act) and fair labor standards (Fair Labor Standards Act), as well as agreements on or acts of boycott, coercion, and intimidation (Sherman Act), are deemed by the McCarran-Ferguson Act to be matters of national character and, thus, subject to the exclusive control of Congress.

Furthermore, Congress may expand its area of insurance control by relating an act specifically to insurance. Such a federal law would be applicable to the business of insurance and would supersede all state statutes in conflict with it. Prior to 1964, the principal federal acts relating specifically to insurance were limited in application to the District of Columbia. In 1964, the Securities and Exchange Act of 1934 was amended to relate specifically to the business of insurance. Since then, other measures have been enacted that assert federal jurisdiction over and even federal operation of selected aspects of the insurance business, such as flood insurance, crop insurance, and Medicare. Employee retirement plans were declared a matter for federal jurisdiction by the 1974 Employee Retirement Income Security Act.

Although the McCarran-Ferguson Act declares that the continued regulation of insurance by the states is in the public interest, the law states that certain existing federal statutes (the Sherman Act, the Clayton Act, and the Federal Trade Commission Act), which are general in nature and do not deal with insurance specifically, are made specific to the business of insurance to the extent that "such business is not regulated by state laws." Hence, a basic purpose of the McCarran-Ferguson Act was to encourage improved, more uniform state regulation of insurance in the public interest.

The Efficacy of State Regulation

In the years following enactment of the McCarran-Ferguson Act, the National Association of Insurance Commissioners (NAIC, discussed later), together with representatives of the insurance industry, drafted model legislation intended to place the regulation of insurance among the several states on a more uniform and adequate basis. Of course, the intent was to meet the challenge of the proviso clause of the act.

Today the states retain primary responsibility for the regulation of the insurance industry. Congress, however, retains oversight responsibility of state insurance regulation. In recent years, the adequacy of state insurance regulation has come under increasing scrutiny. Particular attention has been given to the continued validity of the antitrust exemption now afforded to the insurance business, the effectiveness of the states' solvency regulation, and inconsistencies in regulation among the states.

The issue of whether the public interest is best served by state regulation is an old one. The controversy could result in (1) the states continuing to be the primary regulators of insurance, (2) the federal government becoming the primary regulator of insurance, or (3) some system of dual regulation. The states could continue their primacy role, yet alter aspects of the system in an effort to be more efficient and effective. For example, the states could adopt a mutual regulatory recognition policy akin to that of the EU.

Such a policy would continue state regulation but place much greater reliance on home state control.

Under another proposal, the states would enter into a regulatory interstate compact. An interstate commission would be established with authority to promulgate statutes, regulations, and rules that would bind competing states. There is concern about state sovereignty, but many proponents see this as a vehicle for promoting greater regulatory uniformity while retaining the best aspects of state regulation. The state regulators have undertaken activities to strengthen the regulatory oversight role of the NAIC itself and to enhance programs in education and training, financial services, research, and other areas.

Under still another proposal, a two-tier insurance regulatory system would allow insurers to choose state or federal regulation. Insurers that elected federal regulation would be exempt from most state regulation. Insurers could elect to remain under state supervision, but state regulation itself would be subject to minimum federal solvency standards. Large insurers could be expected to be drawn to federal oversight, whereas smaller insurers could be expected to choose the state option.

A full discussion of this issue is beyond this chapter's scope. Box 35-1 shows the traditional competing arguments advanced by both sides in the debate.

BOX 35-1

ARGUMENTS FOR AND AGAINST U.S. STATE REGULATION OF INSURANCE

Some of the arguments for continuing state regulation include:

- State regulation already exists. It would be expensive to change and great uncertainty exists as to whether any other approach would be superior.
- Decentralization of government is a virtue in itself and consistent with U.S. citizens' views as to the appropriate locus of responsibility.
- States can be more responsive to local needs.
- There is no reason to believe that other regulation arrangements would be more effective or efficient than state regulation, especially given the unsatisfactory federal banking regulatory experience.
- Whatever uniformity is desirable can be achieved through the NAIC.
- The effects of ill-advised insurance legislation are localized.
- States serve as laboratories for insurance regulation.

Arguments advanced in favor of some form of national, including federal, regulation include:

- The expense of having to file financial reports in and deal with each jurisdiction's insurance department is high and leads to insurer inflexibility, ultimately hindering U.S. domestic insurers in their competition with international insurers.
- Ill-advised legislation can be passed easily in states where legislators cannot devote resources to studying legislation, as can the U.S. Congress.
- The political nature of the appointment or election of state insurance commissioners may produce poorly qualified regulators.
- Insurance commissioners and state legislatures are sometimes overly responsive to domestic insurance companies' pressures, to the point of placing extra burdens on nondomestic companies (e.g., discriminatory premium taxes).
- Conflicts arise between standard federal regulations and state rulings that adversely affect insurer operations.
- States find it increasingly difficult to solve regulatory problems involving non-U.S. insurers.
- Whereas U.S. insurers wishing to do business in other nations typically need deal with only one national regulator, non-U.S. insurers wishing to do business in the United States must deal with dozens of regulators.

AREAS OF FEDERAL INSURANCE REGULATION

Although insurance regulation in the United States remains the primary province of the states, the federal government plays a significant regulatory role in selected areas. Before exploring state insurance regulation in detail, a brief overview of federal involvement in insurance regulation is presented.

Committees of both the U.S. House of Representatives and the Senate periodically conduct investigations and hearings on important contemporary insurance issues. An express or implied threat of corrective federal legislation often follows. State regulators are thereby spurred into developing a state-based solution to the perceived problem to preclude a possible federal solution. This process has been repeated time and again over the years. It is through this nonstatutory mechanism that the federal government exercises its greatest influence over insurance regulation. In addition to this indirect approach, federal involvement also has more tangible avenues.

The *Internal Revenue Service* (IRS), especially through its enforcement authority, exercises substantial influence over life insurance policy design and value (see chapters 6 and 13). Additionally, through its influence in shaping tax legislation and in promulgating interpretative regulations, the IRS influences the demand for insurance and the taxation of insurers themselves.

The impact on insurance product design and operation of the *Employee Retirement Income Security Act* (ERISA) has been made clear earlier (see chapter 21). The 1974 enactment of ERISA probably has had a greater influence on insurers' marketing, design, and management of employee benefit plans than any other contemporary federal activity.

The *Securities and Exchange Commission* (SEC) is involved in regulatory oversight of the design, operation, and sale of variable life and annuity products (see chapter 6), and of publicly owned insurers themselves. Publicly owned insurers must file certain forms with the SEC disclosing detailed financial, personnel, and other information. The SEC is charged with protecting investors via mandated disclosures and enforcing laws prohibiting fraud and manipulative security practices.

The *Federal Trade Commission* (FTC) has, from time to time, exerted various degrees of regulation over insurance activities, and it remains involved in the oversight of direct-mail insurance solicitations. Its 1979 report on life insurance disclosure caused substantial controversy within the business (see chapter 12).

Other agencies of the federal government are involved in insurance activities by virtue of their role in international trade and commerce. Thus, the Department of Commerce, the Department of State, and the U.S. Trade Representative's office all have been involved in trade negotiations and other actions, the effects of which have been felt directly by U.S. insurers. Other countries' insurance markets may be more or less open to U.S. insurers depending on negotiations undertaken by these agencies. Their activities can also influence domestic regulation. For example, the North American Free Trade Agreement (NAFTA) among Canada, Mexico, and the United States permits insurers of each country relatively free access to the others' markets and prohibits discrimination between national and nonnational insurers.

Finally, the federal government, primarily through the Bank Holding Company Act, controls the extent to which banks may become involved in insurance. Banks have long sought full access to the U.S. insurance market, but concerns persist about undue concentration of economic power and competition. Changes in federal law permitting such involvement could have a major impact on U.S. insurance distribution and operations. We cover some of the important issues associated with bank-insurance arrangements later in this chapter.

THE MECHANISM OF STATE REGULATION

Regulation of insurance is shaped and influenced by the legislative, judicial, and executive branches of governments. This observation applies in virtually every market worldwide, including the United States. In the United States, the NAIC also performs a vital role in the development of model regulations and laws and in the coordination of legislative activities and of state regulators.

The Legislative Branch

The legislative branch of government enacts laws—called *insurance codes*—establishing the broad legal framework for insurance regulation and taxation. These codes also specify the scope and standards that govern the administration of the law. The law of each jurisdiction usually relates to the requirements, procedures, and standards for

- the organization and operation of the insurance supervisory department
- the formation and licensing of the various types of insurers for the various classes of insurance and reinsurance
- the licensing of agents and brokers
- the filing and sometimes approval of insurance rates
- the filing and approval of policy forms
- unauthorized insurers and unfair trade practices
- insurer financial reporting, examination, and other financial requirements
- complaint handling
- the rehabilitation and liquidation of insurers
- guaranty funds
- insurance product and company taxation

Most jurisdictions also incorporate into their insurance law certain standards for the insurance contract with specific standards for individual life and health insurance, group life and health insurance, industrial insurance, and fire insurance, among others. In addition, the code usually prescribes penalties for insurance law violations.

The Judiciary

The judiciary has a threefold role in insurance regulation. Most obvious to the average insured is its function of deciding cases of conflict between insurers and policyowners. The courts further protect insurers and insureds by enforcing criminal penalties against those who violate insurance law. Finally, insurance companies and their agents occasionally resort to the courts to overturn arbitrary or unconstitutional statutes or administrative regulations or orders promulgated by the insurance department.

The Executive Branch

The role of the court in the regulatory process, although important to individual and corporate rights, is relatively less so when compared with that of the legislative and executive branches. Generally, courts are not equipped to give protection in matters on which only experts are informed; and legislatures, in addition to their lack of experience, find it impractical to pass laws involving every phase of a highly technical and rapidly changing industry. Thus, insurance codes authorize the creation of specialized departments or agencies that are given broad administrative, quasi-legislative, and quasi-judicial powers over the insurance business.

Within the United States, of course, regulation resides primarily at the state level, so the insurance regulatory departments are found there. These state insurance departments usually are under the direction of a chief official who may have the title of commissioner, superintendent, or director. In a few states, the responsibility of direction is placed in a commission or board, which, in turn, selects an individual commissioner to carry out established policy. In 12 states, commissioners are elected;[9] in the remainder of the states, they are appointed, usually by the governor. In many states, the state official who has this responsibility also has other duties, such as state auditor, comptroller, or treasurer; or the department of insurance is associated with some other department, such as the department of banking or securities.

In other countries, enforcement responsibility may rest within the ministry of finance (common), the economics ministry (e.g., Thailand), the ministry of industry and commerce (or a similar name), or the ministry of justice (e.g., Switzerland). In Canada, regulatory oversight responsibilities are split between the federal and provincial governments, with the latter being charged with policyholder protection matters.

A formal advisory body assists regulatory authorities in most countries (but not typically in the United States). This body is composed of representatives of insurance companies, consumer groups, insurance experts, and others with an interest in insurance. The number of members varies from 5 to 60, depending on the country. The body advises the supervisory authority on important decisions. In some countries, the regulator must consult the advisory body before taking certain actions.

As the right to conduct the insurance business, to represent an insurer in doing insurance business, or to represent the public in placing insurance is considered to be a privilege, it is limited to those who qualify by obtaining a license. Thus, insurance is brought under the control and supervision of the insurance regulator through the licensing function.

The National Association of Insurance Commissioners (NAIC)

Structure and Operation

The NAIC is a voluntary association of the chief insurance regulatory officials of the 50 U.S. states, the District of Columbia, American Samoa, Guam, Puerto Rico, and the Virgin Islands. The NAIC (formerly the National Insurance Convention) was formed in 1871 to address issues concerning the supervision of interstate insurers within a state regulatory framework. The objectives of the association are as follows:

- the maintenance and improvement of state regulation of insurance in a responsive and efficient manner
- ensuring reliability of the insurance institution as to financial solidity and guaranty against loss
- fair, just, and equitable treatment of policyowners and claimants

The association operates through a committee structure wherein tasks are assigned by line of business (e.g., life, health, property/liability) and activity. Committees are composed of selected states that are represented by officials of the states' insurance departments. To assist the committees, *advisory groups,* composed mostly or exclusively of insurance industry representatives, prepare background papers, conduct research, and draft tentative model bills and regulations. The NAIC has been criticized by consumer groups for relying heavily on advisory groups whose membership is dominated by industry interests. In response, the NAIC began inviting greater consumer representation on such groups.

---

[9]The 12 states are California, Delaware, Florida, Georgia, Kansas, Louisiana, Mississippi, Montana, North Carolina, North Dakota, Oklahoma, and Washington.

Model bills and regulations are those agreed upon by the NAIC as being worthy of state adoption for purposes of addressing some regulatory issue. The models themselves have no authority. They have force only when enacted by a state.

The NAIC has been successful in several respects and has served as a unifying and harmonizing force. Some of its more significant accomplishments include the following:

- adoption by all states of a uniform blank for insurers' annual financial reports
- acceptance by most states of a certificate of solvency by an insurer's home state, thus eliminating much duplication and expense
- acceptance by most states of the principle that a deposit of securities should be required only in a company's home state
- adoption of uniform rules for valuation of securities
- development of a zone system of insurer examination
- preparation of new standard mortality tables
- preparation of standard valuation and nonforfeiture laws
- creation of a state certification program to help strengthen and harmonize state solvency regulation
- drafting of many other model laws and regulations in the fields of life and health insurance
- coordination of liaison activity with the federal government on insurance matters and with other state government associations

There can be no question of the important role that the NAIC has played in state regulation of insurance. The NAIC has adopted more than 215 model laws, regulations, and guidelines applicable to virtually all aspects of insurance regulation. In addition, the NAIC has undertaken a number of major research projects and expanded its services to members.

The State Accreditation Program

No state is bound to follow the recommendations of the NAIC. Although the NAIC has no enforcement power, its *state accreditation program* suggests that the NAIC's role is evolving from a purely deliberative or consultative body to one attempting to instigate change. The accreditation program has as its premise that any system of effective regulation has certain basic components. It requires that regulators have adequate statutory and administrative authority to regulate an insurer's corporate and financial affairs. It also requires that regulators be provided with the necessary resources to carry out that authority. Finally, it requires that insurance departments have in place organizational and personnel practices designed for effective regulation.

To guide state legislatures and state insurance departments in the development of effective regulation, particularly as it relates to solvency, the NAIC adopted a set of Financial Regulation Standards. These standards establish what the NAIC believes to be minimum requirements for an effective regulatory regime. To provide guidance to the states regarding these minimum standards and as an incentive to put them into place, the accreditation program was adopted in 1990. Under this plan, each state insurance department seeking accreditation is reviewed by an independent team whose job is to assess that department's compliance with the NAIC's Financial Regulation Standards. Departments meeting the NAIC standards are *accredited*. Departments not in compliance are given guidance by the NAIC as to how to bring the department into compliance. Accredited states are not to accept examination reports prepared by nonaccredited states on those states' domestic insurers. Companies domiciled in nonaccredited states are required to obtain a second examination from an accredited state. This sanction increases pressure on nonaccredited states to become accredited.

Almost all states have attained accreditation, but accreditation is subject to five-year reviews. The NAIC has yet to set out its longer-term view of the program. Many observers believe that the program could be made more effective if accredited states refused to license insurers domiciled in nonaccredited states, although this approach would face legal and political problems. It has also been suggested that state licensing could be streamlined if insurers licensed in an accredited state were accorded a presumption of financial solidity for purposes of obtaining licenses in other states. Reciprocal licensing recognition could follow, thus resulting in an EU type of mutual recognition and home state control.

Although the program has been praised, it also has its critics who contend it will prove ineffective. The U.S. General Accounting Office, for example, found that the program suffers three problems: (1) The standards are too general and have been interpreted permissively; (2) the program focuses too little on actual state implementation of the standards; and (3) documentation of accreditation decisions has not always supported decisions to accredit states.[10] The NAIC counters that the program continues to evolve and criticisms are either premature or unfounded.

AREAS OF STATE REGULATION

Because of the peculiar nature of the insurance business and the position of public trust that it holds, the authority of the state over the activities of insurance companies is exerted from their birth to their death. The insurance enterprise must meet certain requirements to be organized and to obtain a license in the various jurisdictions in which it wishes to do business. Its agents and brokers usually must be licensed, its contract forms approved, and, in some instances, rates may be scrutinized. Advertising and sales practices are considered and standards of fair competition established. Insurer expenses may be regulated. Deposits may be required in various jurisdictions as a guaranty of the willingness of the insurer to comply with state statutes and to discharge obligations under its contracts.

Insurer solvency is a matter of particular interest. Limitations may exist on the size of risk that may be accepted. Specific requirements are established for reserve liabilities, minimum capital and surplus, and investments and their proper valuation. Finally, the state presides over the conservation or liquidation of companies whose solvency is in danger.

In the following, we set out the broad areas of insurance regulation that are applicable to virtually all insurance markets worldwide. We, however, focus particular attention on the U.S. scene.

Organization and Licensing of Insurers

Although the organization of insurance companies is governed to some extent by the law applicable to the organization of general corporations, states have supplanted most of their general corporation law with special acts pertaining only to insurance companies. State insurance laws describe specifically the requirements for the organization of a life company. Health insurance may be written by a life, a casualty, or a monoline specialty company. When health insurance is written by a life company, the requirements for organization and licensing of a life company usually apply. Generally, a monoline health company may organize under either the life or casualty sections of the law.

---

[10]*Insurance Regulation: The Financial Regulation Standards and Accreditation Program of the National Association of Insurance Commissioners,* GAO/T-GGD-92–27 (1992).

State insurance codes require the drafting of a charter that specifically describes the insurer's name and location, the lines of insurance it plans to write, the powers of the organization, and its officers. Frequently, the method of internal organization must be specified. Minimum amounts of paid-in capital and surplus for stock companies are stated, varying from a few hundred thousand to $2 million and more of capital, plus an initial surplus varying from 50 to 200 percent of the minimum paid-in capital for each line of insurance (life and health) to be written. Minimum surplus and participation requirements for mutual insurers also are specified with minimum surplus requirements that are similar to the minimum capital and surplus requirements for stock insurers. Risk-based capital requirements (duscussed later) augment these fixed minimum standards.

Before issuing the certificate of incorporation, a responsible state official investigates the character of the incorporators, the company's proposed plan of operation, and its marketing and financial projections. After meeting these and other requirements, the company is prepared to seek a license to conduct the insurance business.

For purposes of establishing an insurer's domicile, the United States recognizes three types of insurers. A **domestic insurer** is one domiciled in the concerned state. A **foreign insurer** is an insurer domiciled in another U.S. jurisdiction. An **alien insurer** is domiciled in another country. In other countries, foreign insurers are what the United States calls alien insurers.

The requirements for licensing foreign and alien insurers may be similar to those for licensing domestic companies (i.e., they are accorded national treatment), but sometimes they are more stringent. All insurers (domestic, foreign, and alien) are required to maintain a substantial deposit of securities of a specified quality in trust with the state. To meet this requirement, foreign insurers may substitute a certificate from the insurance commissioner of another state in which they are licensed, to the effect that a deposit is being maintained in trust in that state for the purpose of protecting policyowners and creditors.

The deposit in trust for alien insurers operating through branch offices is usually substantial, equaling its U.S. liabilities plus surplus equal at least to the minimum capital and surplus required of a domestic insurer licensed to transact the same kinds of business. In addition, several states require a security deposit with the state's treasurer for the purpose of protecting the state's policyowners. Also, a foreign or alien insurer generally must appoint a resident of the state in which it wants to do business as its attorney for purposes of serving a legal process.

Unauthorized Insurance

One of the more vexatious problems confronting state insurance regulation involves the question of control over the activities of unauthorized insurance companies. By refusing to apply for a license, the unauthorized insurer may attempt to escape regulation in all states except its state or country of domicile, on the basis that it has no representatives within the state and, consequently, it is not legally "doing business" there. Unauthorized insurers generally make no reports to the state insurance department. As their business may be conducted through the mail or the Internet, the state commissioner may be handicapped in rendering any service to the policyowner in a dispute with the insurer.

At present, seven principal types of regulation are utilized by the states in an effort to control the operations of unauthorized insurers:

1. Under the NAIC Unauthorized Insurers Model Statute, as adopted by most states, no person may (a) represent an unauthorized insurer in the solicitation,

negotiation, or effectuation of insurance, or in any other manner in the transaction of insurance with respect to the subjects of insurance in the state involved; or (b) represent any person in the procuring of insurance from such an unauthorized insurer.

2. Although states' unauthorized insurers' acts generally exclude from their scope group life and health policies delivered in other states, the NAIC has recommended that mass-marketed life and health insurance offered by direct-response solicitation be subject to state advertising and claims settlement practices laws and be required to meet minimum-loss-ratio guidelines that states may have in effect.

3. Several states make such contracts legally voidable by the insured, unless, during the life of the contract, the insurer becomes licensed to transact the class of insurance involved (e.g., life or health insurance).

4. Advertising originating outside the state and designed to solicit insurance from persons located within the state may be prohibited. Usually, this prohibition is aimed at the publisher, radio station, and so on, as well as the insurer.

5. Under the NAIC Uniform Unauthorized Insurers Service of Process Act, as adopted by many jurisdictions, the insured may bring a legal action involving a claim against an unauthorized out-of-state insurer by serving process on the insurance commissioner of his or her home state.

6. The NAIC Nonadmitted Insurers Information Office—a central clearinghouse for the collection of information about nonadmitted foreign and alien insurers—may be used by individual states.

7. A significant number of states have enacted provisions of an NAIC model assuming jurisdiction of plans providing health care benefits. The purpose of this legislation is to assert jurisdiction over uninsured or partially insured multiple employer trusts or other trusts.

Despite the existence of laws of this type, numerous regulatory problems persist. They arise because the state of domicile does not adequately control the market practices and financial solvency of these insurers.

Insurance Policy Regulation

Once an insurance company is organized and licensed to transact business in the state, almost every phase of its operation is subject to supervision. This section covers the policy form and rate oversight role of the regulator.

Policy Forms

In most lines of insurance, including life and health insurance, policy forms are subjected to some regulation in an effort to protect insureds, policyowners, and beneficiaries against unfair and deceptive provisions and practices—in other words, to help rectify their information asymmetry problem. Contract regulation involves (1) the requirement that a policy form may not be used until it is filed with and (usually) approved by the state insurance department, and (2) the various requirements or standards for policy form approval.

The insurance commissioner utilizes both general and specific legal standards as a guide to determine the appropriateness of forms in the public interest. Much of this statutory and administrative law is based on NAIC recommendations. As the application of general standards creates problems for both the commissioners and the industry, the NAIC has developed specific standards designed to implement the general standard.

Every jurisdiction requires (or will accept) life insurance contract forms that contain, in substance, certain provisions as prescribed in the laws of most of the states. These statutory provisions, as recommended by the NAIC, include clauses related to the grace period, premium payment, incontestability, entire contract, misstatement of age, annual apportionment of dividends, surrender values and options, policy loans, settlement options, and reinstatement. We discussed these provisions in chapters 9 and 10. The required provisions for group life insurance contracts and certificates are treated separately.

In 1946, following the *South-Eastern Underwriters Association (SEUA)* decision and the passage of the McCarran-Ferguson Act, the NAIC and the All-Industry Committee recommended to the states the enactment of an Accident and Health Regulatory Law. In addition to establishing the requirement that contract forms, classifications, rates, and endorsements must be filed and that forms and endorsements must be approved, this law established the general standard that contracts must not be unjust, ambiguous, unfair, misleading, or encourage misrepresentation. Furthermore, the model law states (although this provision was omitted by some jurisdictions) that forms may be disapproved if "benefits are unreasonable in relation to the premium charged" (discussed later).

All jurisdictions have adopted the NAIC Uniform Individual Accident and Sickness Policy Provisions Law or a similar statute. This law includes specific language for both required and optional provisions and policy readability tests (see chapters 9 and 10).

The insurance commissioner of each jurisdiction has developed specific guidelines by administrative regulation. Requirements are established for the clear labeling of limited policies. Certain types of provisions are prohibited or restricted, and certain practices with respect to the policy contract are controlled.

Increasingly, regulation of health insurance policies is built upon minimum benefit and disclosure requirements. The NAIC, for example, adopted an Individual Accident and Sickness Insurance Minimum Standards Act as well as a regulation to implement the act. These regulatory measures separate accident and sickness coverages into nine categories, each of which is subject to particular minimum benefit standards and disclosure rules. This classification of policies and the public demands for coverages that may be compared in the marketplace have led to increased pressure for policy standardization.

Insurers wishing to sell Medicare supplemental policies must model their policies after one or more of 10 standardized policies promulgated by the NAIC. These 10 policies were developed by the NAIC in response to stipulations in the 1990 Omnibus Budget Reconciliation Act authorizing the NAIC to do so. Failure to act by the NAIC would have resulted in the federal government doing so. This requirement was in response to what was perceived as a bewildering variety of policies formerly available and a lack of standards.

Rates

In many lines of insurance, the supervision of the product involves the regulation of rates—the product price. Life (occasionally) and health insurance rates must be filed with the contract forms to which they apply. Generally, life rates are not subject to approval. They are filed principally to make them a matter of public record for the benefit of persons who come under the misstatement-of-age provision and other provisions involving an age proration of premium.

Life Insurance Life insurance rates in the United States for individual insurance are regulated only in a most indirect sense. Competition is believed to be an adequate regulator over any tendencies to rate excessiveness. As a practical matter, rate adequacy may be a problem, and it is believed that minimum reserve requirements (discussed later) and expense limitations are an adequate safeguard. The states of New York and Wisconsin have complex laws limiting the amount of expenses that can be incurred in the production of new business and the maintenance of old business in force.

The laws of most jurisdictions assume that, for stock insurers issuing nonparticipating contracts, competition is an adequate guarantor of rate equity among the different classes and generations of insureds. Where premiums prove to be redundant, equity demands that the excess be returned in the form of a dividend to each class or generation of insureds in proportion to their contributions to the surplus. Most states require that dividends be apportioned and paid annually. A few states limit the amount of aggregate surplus that may be accumulated by a mutual insurer. Although announced specific standards do not exist, some commissioners review dividend apportionment formulas from time to time—generally at the time of company examination.

In a few states, limits (e.g., 10 percent) apply to the maximum proportion of earnings attributable to a stock insurer's participating business that may be paid as dividends to stockholders. The limitation is intended to ensure fair treatment of par policyowners. These types of limitations are common in Canada, the United Kingdom, France, and many other countries.

Health Insurance   Health insurance rates are often subject to regulation, probably because health insurance has characteristics of a public good (see chapters 1, 19, and 25). An important standard for the approval of health insurance contract forms is that premiums charged under the contract must be reasonable considering benefits provided under the contract. This standard often is implemented by requiring a minimum loss ratio (ratio of claims incurred to premiums earned) under the policy form.

Although the distinction is somewhat tenuous, the law appears more nearly to establish standards for the approval of policy forms than for rates. Technically, it is the policy form that is subject to disapproval—not the rates—if there is a question about the reasonableness of benefits.

Loss-ratio guidelines have been the focus of renewed interest within the regulatory community as a means for monitoring and controlling pricing activities of health insurers. The NAIC adopted guidelines for the filing of rates for individual health insurance forms. The guidelines establish loss-ratio requirements for medical expense, loss of income, and long-term care coverages, depending on terms of renewal. It is anticipated that heightened regulatory interest in health insurance pricing will continue in the coming years.

Marketing Practices

Broadly interpreted, state regulation of marketing practices includes control over the licensing of agents and brokers and over unfair trade practices.

Licensing of Agents and Brokers

The statutes of all U.S. jurisdictions contain provisions for the licensing of resident and nonresident agents and brokers. A few jurisdictions license counselors—fee-paid advisors. No person may act as agent, broker, or counselor within the jurisdiction without first obtaining a license. No insurer may issue a contract through or remunerate any person (other than on renewal business or other deferred compensation for which the agent has ceased to participate in new business development), unless the person holds a valid license.

The procedure that must be followed in obtaining a license is similar for all lines. The applicant must first file an application for a license in which he or she gives information regarding his or her character, experience, and general competence. Each insurer for which the applicant is to be licensed must submit a notice of appointment (or intention of appointment), together with a certificate of trustworthiness and competence signed by an officer of the insurer. After these formalities, the applicant must then pass an examination covering the lines of insurance for which a license is sought.

In many states, the new applicant (usually defined as a person who has not held a license in the recent past, e.g., two years) may receive a temporary license with a permanent license being issued following the successful completion of the examination. Several states require new licensees to undertake a certain minimum number of hours (e.g., 40) of formal training in insurance before they can sit for the state examination. In addition to establishing a minimum standard of competency, these examinations are said to reduce turnover and to contribute to the general upgrading of insurance representatives.

The agent's license may be perpetual until it is revoked, or it may be subject to renewal at stipulated intervals. Licenses must be renewed through the payment of license or appointment fees. The license may be refused, revoked, or suspended by the commissioner, after notice and hearing, on the any of the following grounds:

- willful violation of the law in his or her capacity as an agent
- fraudulent or dishonest practices
- untrustworthiness or incompetence
- material misrepresentation in the application for his or her license

In addition, the license is terminated by death or termination of the agent's appointment by the insurance company. In states making provision for brokers, the requirements and procedures for obtaining a broker's license are similar to those already discussed.

Several states also require agents and brokers annually to undertake specific continuing education in their fields. The individual must either demonstrate that he or she has met the minimum number of hours' requirement or face nonrenewal of his or her license.

Many other countries do not require insurance agents to be licensed. Some require only registration and others do not even require this. Such countries note that the insurer is legally responsible for its agents' actions, so it has a strong incentive to select and manage agents appropriately.

Unfair Trade Practices

Although states have long exercised control over certain unfair practices—especially misrepresentation, twisting, rebating, and unfair discrimination—the impact of the *SEUA* decision and the McCarran-Ferguson Act led all jurisdictions to adopt the NAIC Model Unfair Trade Practices Act. The act was designed to be sufficiently comprehensive to oust the Federal Trade Commission from jurisdiction over these matters. Usually, these acts give the commissioner the power to investigate and examine and, after notice and hearing, to issue cease-and-desist orders with penalties for violations. The acts are designed to prevent numerous activities deemed to be unfair, some of which are discussed next.

Rebating is an inducement to buy insurance that is not specified in the contract. The practice of an agent returning a portion of the premium (e.g., the agent's commission) to an insurance applicant is the most common rebate. Rebating historically has been illegal. Antirebating statutes evolved decades ago in response to perceived marketplace abuses. Traditional arguments against rebating have focused on concerns about insurer solvency, about unfair discrimination, and about the unique nature of insurance. Critics of antirebating statutes claim that the prohibition unfairly prevents buyers from negotiating fully with sellers—a result that is offensive in a competitive system. The states of Florida and California allow rebating, although guidelines for rebating generally require no unfair discrimination in the granting of rebates.

Twisting refers to the practice by an agent of inducing a policyowner through misrepresentation to discontinue an existing life insurance policy in order to purchase a new one. In contrast to simple **replacement**—discontinuing one policy to purchase another—twisting is illegal. The purchase of a life insurance policy can be a complicated transaction. The consumer easily could be misled, either intentionally or unintentionally, by an agent. In recognition of this fact, several states have promulgated versions of the NAIC Model Replacement Regulations, which require the disclosure of certain information considered pertinent to the proposed replacement decision, as discussed in chapter 12.

Agents often handle large amounts of their policyowners' money. **Misappropriation** or misuse of these funds even on a temporary basis is illegal. Related to misappropriation is the practice of **commingling** of funds. Agents are not to combine monies belonging to policyowners with their own funds.

The NAIC has developed model regulations to deal with life insurance replacements, sex discrimination, discrimination on the basis of blindness, and discrimination on the basis of physical or mental handicaps. The NAIC also is focusing on the broader subject of classification of risks and on sex-based rate differentials in health insurance, as discussed in chapter 26.

Unfair Advertising Practices

The Federal Trade Commission's Trade Practices Rules Relating to the Advertising of Mail Order Insurance, promulgated in 1950, represented the first attempt of the commission to regulate the practice of insurance companies (other than actions regarding boycott, coercion, and intimidation) under the proviso clause of the McCarran-Ferguson Act. To strengthen its contention that advertising was adequately regulated by the states, the NAIC developed for state adoption the Rules Governing Advertisements of Accident and Sickness Insurance with Interpretive Guidelines in 1955 and revised them in 1974. These rules are composed of standards designed to guide commissioners in the implementation of the general advertising standards contained in the model Uniform Trade Practices Act.

The NAIC's Model Life Insurance Advertising Regulation has been adopted in many states with others devising similar rules to regulate life advertising. Some states' regulations (e.g., in Virginia) have considerably expanded the scope of the NAIC model. The rules recommended by the NAIC regulate the form and content of advertisements, set forth minimum disclosure requirements, and provide for enforcement procedures.

Solvency Surveillance

State insurance regulators are charged with the protection of the public interest by ensuring a financially healthy insurance industry. As with any other industry in which a fiduciary interest is involved, this entails a careful balancing of the goal of insolvency prevention with the goal of available, affordable insurance products. It is possible to design a regulatory system for insurance so restrictive that insolvency would be virtually impossible, but coverage would be expensive or simply unavailable for many consumers. The objective must be to establish the proper incentives for efficient as well as safe operation and to institute safeguards that keep insurer failures to an acceptable minimum. This entails early detection of financially troubled companies, taking corrective action to restore them to financial health when possible, and minimizing the negative effects of the financial difficulties that do occur. Financial failures are a natural economic consequence of a competitive market and are to be expected.

State insurance solvency regulation has been continually challenged to meet the demands of a dynamic industry. About 0.5 to 1 percent of U.S. life insurers become insolvent each year. Most insolvencies are of relatively small companies, but some have entailed large insurers, especially during the early 1990s.

This section sets out the policies and procedures that states have adopted to regulate life insurer solvency. Solvency surveillance is accomplished primarily through four mechanisms: (1) financial statement filing requirements, (2) the Insurance Regulatory Information System, (3) examinations, and (4) enforcement and market surveillance.

Financial Statement Filings

Each state requires that all licensed insurers file financial statements detailing their financial condition and operation. Statements must be filed at least annually and more frequently if financial problems are suspected. These filings are to include supplements to the annual statement entitled "Management's Discussion and Analysis." This supplement must include material events known to management that would cause the insurer's reported financial information not to be indicative of future operating results or of its future financial position.

Insurance supervisory authorities require that insurance companies maintain at all times assets that are at least equal to their currently due and prospectively estimated liabilities plus the required minimum capital and surplus levels. A large body of law has been enacted that specifically relates to these items.

Asset Limitations and Valuation   Although state insurance codes exhibit a decided lack of uniformity pertaining to insurer assets, all jurisdictions are concerned with the types of investments that are permitted and the techniques of asset valuation, as discussed in chapter 33. Nearly all jurisdictions distinguish between (1) capital and surplus and (2) reserve investments. New York follows the traditional pattern. It requires that funds equivalent to the minimum capital and surplus required by law for the line or lines of insurance being transacted be invested in certain secure types of assets (cash, government bonds, and mortgages). Life insurance companies may invest all remaining funds in so-called reserve investments, which are capital investments plus other permitted investments of second quality.

The laws in most jurisdictions require that no insurance company make any investment or loan unless it is authorized or approved by the company's board of directors, or by a committee authorized by the board and charged with the supervision or making of such investments. The laws further require that the minutes of any such committee shall be recorded, and that regular reports of the committee shall be submitted to the board of directors.

The valuation of the assets held by an insurer for annual-statement purposes is a complicated and detailed procedure. Most insurance codes state that the commissioner may specify the rules for determining the value of securities, subject (in some cases) to the limitation that these rules not be inconsistent with those established by the NAIC. Through its Securities Valuation Office (SVO), the NAIC values on a uniform basis the securities held in the portfolios of virtually every U.S. insurance company.

Most states impose quantitative (and qualitative, see chapter 33) investment restrictions on life insurers. Some refer to such quantitative approaches as "pigeonhole" investment guidelines. A few states regulate under the prudent-person standard, affording insurers greater investment latitude. Still other states rely on a blend of the two approaches. As noted in chapter 33, NAIC model laws exist for both approaches.

Investments in obligations or equities issued by non-U.S. governments and businesses have been severely limited by state investment laws for many years. Regulatory concerns about these investments relate to exchange rate fluctuations, expropriations, wars, and the difficulties of monitoring such investments. The state of New York permits an insurer to hold up to 10 percent of its assets in Canadian investments, whereas no more than 3 percent may be invested in securities from other countries.

Liability Valuation   The principal liabilities on insurers' balance sheets are policy reserves. Policy reserves are balance sheet accounts established to reflect actual and potential liabilities under outstanding contracts. Life insurers are required by law to establish minimum reserves as a liability. In this regard, the NAIC's Standard Valuation Law has been enacted or otherwise made effective in all jurisdictions. Its provisions are applicable, in general, to all policies issued since its enactment or amendment. (The valuation of life insurance reserves is discussed in chapters 2 and 29 and annual-statement health insurance reserves in chapter 31.)

Although the continued financial soundness of an insurer depends on proper investments, together with the correct valuation of all assets, the establishment and proper valuation of reserves is just as important and, in the health insurance line, a much more difficult task. In most jurisdictions, the standards utilized in measuring the adequacy of the various health insurance reserves are left to individual insurer determination, with many companies making this determination in consultation with the actuaries of the respective state insurance departments.

Two final reserve classes deserve comment. The asset valuation reserve (AVR) and the interest maintenance reserve (IMR), both discussed in chapter 34, cause larger reserves to be established. The AVR applies to all major investment classes. The IMR requires that interest-related realized capital gains and losses be deferred in the IMR and amortized to income over the remaining maturity of bonds sold.

As discussed in chapter 29, jurisdictions require the filing of a report by the insurer's appointed actuary wherein results of certain mandated cash flow testing are provided. This requirement, coupled with the NAIC annual-statement instruction that insurers annually must file an audit by a certified public accountant (CPA), means that regulators will receive a more complete view of insurers' operations.

Minimum Capital and Surplus   Requirements for minimum capital and surplus for insurer establishment were discussed earlier in the chapter. For ongoing insurers, regulators often establish internal minimums, which are greater than the statutorily prescribed minimums, against which they assess insurer solvency. These minimums may take into consideration some or all of the following factors:

- size
- lines of insurance written and their riskiness
- nature and extent of the reinsurance program
- quality, diversification, and liquidity of investments
- reserve adequacy
- surplus trends and the surplus levels of comparable insurers

An important new component of life insurer solvency regulation was added by the NAIC through its 1992 adoption of the Risk-Based Capital for Life and/or Health Insurers Model Act and of a risk-based capital formula and reporting requirements. These actions have altered the means by which minimally acceptable capital and surplus levels are defined and applied in the United States.

Risk-Based Capital Requirements   The risk-based capital (RBC) concept and requirements were discussed in chapters 32 and 33. Briefly, according to the concept, minimum required capital and surplus should reflect the differences in insurer risk characteristics. Risk characteristics are a function of insurer size, asset quality, lines of business written, and other factors. To determine an insurer's risk-based capital ratio, an insurer's total adjusted capital is compared with the risk-based capital obtained from the risk-based capital formula. **Total adjusted capital (TAC)** equals statutory capital and surplus plus the AVR, any voluntary reserves, and one-half of any policyowner dividend liability. If TAC is below the formula amount, one of three levels of regulatory authority is triggered, depending on the extent of the deficiency.

Figure 35-1 provides a stylized illustration of how risk-based capital requirements affect insurers. Insurers with capital and surplus below the threshold level are subject to various levels of regulatory attention. With this change, life insurers on average can be expected to maintain greater levels of surplus.

The model act defines four levels of concern between threshold RBC levels and the TAC. Affected insurers and regulators would be required to take specific actions as the insurer's TAC passes these levels.

Insurers are required to report their TAC and their authorized control-level RBC. The *authorized control level* (ACL) is derived by a formula that reflects the insurer's particular asset risks (C1), insurance risks (C2), interest rate risks (C3), and business risks (C4). The riskier the element, the larger is the weighting for the factor and, hence, the larger the insurer's ACL, all else being equal. The four RBC trigger points and accompanying required regulatory responses are shown in Table 35-1.

Thus, if an insurer's ACL were $100 million and its TAC were $200 million or more, the insurer would be above the company action level, and, therefore, no special regulatory or company action ordinarily would be required. If the insurer's TAC were between $200 and $150 million, the company must file an RBC Plan with the commissioner of its domiciliary state. An **RBC Plan** describes the cause of the threat to the insurer's solvency, offers proposals to correct the situation, estimates five years of financial projections, and includes other relevant information. This is referred to as the *company action level* because the company is required to take action.

If the insurer's TAC were between $150 and $100 million, an RBC Plan would be required to be submitted and the regulator must perform appropriate analysis and ex-

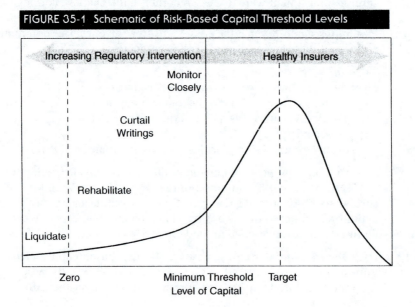

FIGURE 35-1 Schematic of Risk-Based Capital Threshold Levels

TABLE 35-1	U.S. Risk-Based Capital Trigger Points and Required Regulatory Responses	
RBC Level	**Trigger Point (as % of ACL)**	**Required Regulatory Action**
Company Action Level	200 to 150	RBC Plan required
Regulatory Action Level	150 to 100	RBC Plan and examination required plus corrective action order
Authorized Control Level	100 to 70	Insurer may be placed under regulatory control
Mandatory Control Level	Below 70	Insurer must be placed under regulatory control

aminations and may issue corrective orders—hence, the name *regulatory action level.* TAC between $100 and $70 million—the *authorized control level*—would subject the insurer to regulatory seizure. TAC below $70 million—the *mandatory control level*—requires regulatory seizure.

The RBC requirements were developed to aid regulators in identifying financially troubled insurers while time remained for corrective action. The formula is not intended to be used by competitors or others to rate or rank companies. In an apparent effort to ensure that RBC calculations are not used in this way, the model act prohibits agents and insurers from disseminating such figures. The act also exempts certain other RBC information from public disclosure.

The adoption by the NAIC and ultimately by the states of risk-based capital standards represents a potentially important evolution in solvency surveillance, although its accuracy in terms of assessing overall corporate risk has been questioned. The approach, because of its necessarily broad nature, renders only gross approximations for insurers' true risk-based capital.

Early Warning Systems   States utilize systems intended to alert if an insurer is trending toward financial difficulty. Most states rely on the NAIC's Insurance Regulatory Information System (IRIS), which includes the Financial Analysis Solvency Tools (FAST), to prioritize insurance companies for further regulatory review. States also secure information from other sources such as insurers' SEC filings, rating agencies, market conduct examinations, and any other source deemed reliable.

As discussed in chapter 11, IRIS consists of two phases. The first is a statistical phase that employs 12 financial ratios to flag companies that show unusual results. This is followed by an analytical phase, in which a team of financial examiners, on loan from state insurance departments, analyzes the annual statements and ratio results of the flagged companies. Upon more detailed analysis, insurers may be prioritized for further regulatory review by the domiciliary state.

The NAIC expanded IRIS in 1990 to focus special attention on insurers considered to be nationally significant, which means that they write business in 17 or more states and have gross premium writings in excess of $50 million. Such insurers are subject to additional statistical analysis.

The NAIC's Financial Services Division conducts further analysis under IRIS through the FAST, which involves an analytical routing using some 20 financial ratios, with separate analysis for life and health insurers. Unlike the original part of IRIS, FAST results are confidential. FAST develops a score for each insurer that is used to prioritize insurers for closer review. Each insurer's score is derived by assigning points based on the financial ratios. FAST also allows state insurance departments to develop financial reports on insurers, using the 20 FAST ratios or other screening criteria.

Examinations

On-site financial examinations of insurers are particularly useful regulatory tools. State laws typically require that the insurance regulator examine domestic insurers at least once every three to five years, depending on the state. These examinations involve a detailed review of all important aspects of operations. Investments are confirmed and their correct valuation checked. Liabilities are verified, as are income and expense items. Recent criticisms led to an NAIC study of the examination process and to the revamping of certain procedures.

Targeted exams can be and are conducted more frequently, if circumstances dictate them. A targeted exam typically focuses on certain aspects only of an insurer's financial operations, such as reserves, investments, capital changes, and so on. The call for a targeted examination could be based on a CPA audit report, analysts' work papers, annual or quarterly statement filings, or IRIS results.

Enforcement and Surveillance

State insurance regulators address potentially fraudulent activities and problem individuals and insurers operating in their state through the use of administrative sanctions and civil actions, usually in the form of agency or company license revocations, cease and desist orders, or injunctions. The federal Racketeer-Influenced and Corrupt Organizations (RICO) Act is one of the most useful tools available to aid insurance regulators' enforcement activity. Civil rights actions routinely filed by insurance regulators and receivers—especially those containing RICO charges—have proven to have a deterrent impact on the future activities of problem individuals in the industry.

The NAIC provides a formal method of information exchange. It publishes a bimonthly newsletter, available to insurance regulators only, which provides information on potentially fraudulent schemes that affect the industry, tracks the activities of problem individuals, and alerts regulators to problem alien and offshore insurers that operate in the United States.

Additionally, the NAIC has implemented a **Special Activities Database** (SAD) to expand the information available to insurance regulators and to provide a formalized vehicle for states to exchange information and inquire into the activities of companies and individuals of insurance regulatory concern, including persons who may be involved in fraudulent activities. This new database complements the **Regulatory Information Retrieval System** (RIRS), which is a computerized database containing information on regulatory actions taken against insurers and individuals.

Mergers and Acquisitions

Merger and acquisition activity continues at high levels worldwide as financial service firms seek a competitive advantage. Within the United States and most other countries, regulatory approval is required for any change of insurer structure or ownership. In the United States, almost all state laws regarding mergers and acquisitions are patterned after the NAIC Model Insurance Holding Company System Regulatory Act or its predecessors.

If control of an insurer is sought, the prospective acquirer must file a detailed disclosure statement—called Form A—with the state insurance regulator. Form A filing includes disclosure of the following types of information:

- the identity and background of the acquiring individuals or entities
- the source, nature, and amount of the consideration involved in the transaction
- audited financial information concerning earnings and financial condition of each acquiring party

- the acquiring party's intentions as to material changes in the insurer's operations, assets, corporate structure, or management
- a full disclosure of the terms and conditions of the proposed acquisition
- current ownership and recent purchase of the insurer's securities by the acquirer
- a description of any recommendations to purchase the insurer's securities, a copy of all tender offers and solicitation materials, and terms of any broker–dealer agreements

The insurance commissioner is accorded broad discovery powers in connection with the transaction. After review of the filings, the commissioner holds a hearing on the issue, and then, after due consideration of the information, renders a decision as to whether the transaction is acceptable. Grounds for disapproval include such circumstances as the following:

- The domestic insurer, after the change, would be unable to qualify for a license.
- The merger or acquisition would substantially lessen competition or tend to create a monopoly within the state.
- The acquirer's financial condition might jeopardize the insurer's financial stability or prejudice policyowners' interests.
- Any plans of the acquirer to liquidate, sell assets, or make other material changes in the insurer are unfair and unreasonable to policyowners and not in the public interest.
- The competence, experience, and integrity of persons seeking control are such that the acquisition would not be in policyowners' and the public's interest.
- The acquisition is likely to be hazardous or prejudicial to the insurance-buying public.

Control is defined as the power to direct management and is presumed to exist if the transaction involves 10 percent or more of an insurer's voting shares.

Rehabilitation and Liquidation

A regulator's typical first responses to a troubled insurer are informal. The regulator may attempt to work with management to identify and deal with the sources of difficulty. A friendly merger or acquisition might be arranged.

States also take formal actions against financially troubled licensed insurers. Formal actions vary by state, but ordinarily they consist of written directives—often called *corrective orders*—requiring an insurer to (1) obtain state approval before undertaking certain transactions, (2) limit or cease its new business writings, (3) infuse capital, or (4) cease certain business practices. The regulator also may revoke an insurer's license. All these actions are subject to court review.

Sometimes, despite the best efforts of regulators, insurers get into perilously troubling financial difficulty. In such circumstances, the state insurance regulator in most jurisdictions has the responsibility of assuming control over the entire company, in the case of domestic insurers, or over its assets, in the cases of foreign or alien insurers (if the largest amounts of the U.S. assets of the alien insurer are located within the state). The commissioner may petition the proper court for an order appointing him or her (in his or her official capacity) receiver for the purpose of rehabilitation, conservation, or liquidation.

If the commissioner determines that reorganization, consolidation, conversion, reinsurance, merger, or other transformation is appropriate, a specific plan of rehabilitation may be prepared. Under an order of **rehabilitation,** the commissioner is granted title to the domestic insurance company's assets and is given the authority to carry on its business until the insurer either is returned to private management after the grounds for issuing the order have been removed or the insurer is liquidated. Among the statutory grounds under which the commissioner may apply for a rehabilitation order are (1) a finding that further transaction of business would be financially hazardous to policyowners, creditors, or the public; (2) a determination that the insurer's officers or directors are guilty of certain acts or omissions; and (3) where a substantial transfer of assets, merger, or consolidation is attempted without the prior written consent of the commissioner. Many state regulators place financially troubled insurers in rehabilitation to avoid adverse publicity and possibly massive policyowner withdrawals and then move the insurer to liquidation.

Liquidation of a domestic insurer is the ultimate power of the commissioner. When it is found not advisable to attempt rehabilitation or if rehabilitation becomes impracticable, the commissioner must petition the proper court for a liquidation order. Grounds for liquidation include those listed for rehabilitation and the additional condition that the insurer is insolvent. Under **liquidation** proceedings, the commissioner is given title to all assets of the insurer and is directed to take possession of them as soon as possible. Notice is required to be given to other insurance commissioners, guaranty funds, insurance agents, and all persons known or reasonably expected to have claims against the insurer. Priorities for distribution of assets are established, with the cost of administration, employee salaries, and policyowner claims receiving highest priorities. Irrespective of whether ancillary receiverships have been establisned, the distribution of assets in nondomiciliary states will be controlled by the statutes of the domiciliary state.

In a technical sense, the statutes of several jurisdictions use the term **conservation order** to refer to the court order directing the commissioner to act as receiver for the conservation of assets of a foreign or alien insurance company within the jurisdiction. Grounds for the insurance commissioner's request are similar to those for liquidation and rehabilitation.

The procedure of naming the insurance commissioner (rather than another person) as receiver was developed to reduce the delay and expense associated with the ordinary receivership procedure, the hope being that it would speed the return of a larger payment to the insurer's creditors and policyowners. In some cases, it makes possible the rehabilitation or merger of a company, with little or no loss to those involved. In some jurisdictions, the commissioner still must petition the proper court for the appointment of a receiver (other than the commissioner), who then liquidates the insurer under the direction of the court.

Life and Health Insurance Guaranty Associations

Some insurer insolvencies are inevitable in a competitive market. Policy makers must decide what protections they should afford insureds of insolvent insurers. Perhaps the marketplace itself could evolve solutions to the problem assessing insurer solidity, but few policy makers seem willing to permit this potentially painful evolution. Consequently, many countries have some mechanism to guarantee insurance benefits. Several have insolvency guaranty associations or funds. Funds may involve modest (as in the European Union) or generous (as in the United States) indemnity limits. The insured may be fully indemnified to a maximum amount (United States) or some loss sharing by the insured may be included (United Kingdom). The fund may be government run (some EU countries) or operated and financed by the insurance industry (United States and Canada).

Every U.S. state has some type of insolvency guaranty law. Generally, the laws provide for the indemnification of losses suffered by policyowners of insolvent insurers through an association that derives funds for this purpose from assessments against solvent insurers doing business in the state.[11] Indemnification may be by payment of claims or cash values or by continuation of the insolvent insurer's policies.

History

The life and health guaranty association mechanism can be traced to 1941, when the first life and health guaranty law was enacted in New York. Several bills were introduced in 1969 into the U.S. Senate to create a federal guaranty mechanism. In response to the possibility of federal intervention, the NAIC adopted two guaranty association model laws—one for property and liability insurance and another for life and health insurance. These model acts formed the basis for most state insolvency laws.

The 1985 NAIC Model Act

The most recent NAIC guaranty association model act was adopted by the NAIC in 1985 and amended several times thereafter. Individual state laws often differ in important respects from the model. The model act creates a nonprofit legal entity called the (state) Life and Health Insurance Guaranty Association. All insurers, as a condition of their being licensed to transact any type of insurance covered by the act in the state, must be members of the guaranty association. An assessment mechanism is specified for general administrative costs and for costs associated with settling the claims resulting from insolvent or impaired insurers.

The guaranty association is generally under the immediate supervision of the insurance commissioner. The act primarily covers policyowners who are residents of the state where the member insurer is determined to be insolvent or impaired. Beneficiaries are covered regardless of their residence.

Several coverage limits apply. A maximum of $300,000 will be paid in life insurance death benefits, but not more than $100,000 in net cash surrender values. Coverage is limited to $100,000 for annuity cash values and payments, including tax-qualified annuities and structured settlement annuities. Health insurance maximum payments are $500,000 for medical expense insurance coverage, $300,000 for disability income coverage, and $100,000 for all other health coverages. These limits apply on an individual insured and not on a per-policy basis.

Advertising the guaranty association and its statutory obligations is prohibited. However, the model act does provide for a disclosure to the purchasers of policies that coverage may be available from the guaranty association. Not all states have enacted this disclosure provision.

The Assessment Process

Two kinds of assessments are possible under the Guaranty Association Model Act. Class A, the first type of assessment, is made for the administrative, legal, and examination costs associated with reviewing the financial condition of member insurers and other expenses. Class B, the second kind of assessment, is made to cover the costs associated with insolvent or impaired insurers. The latter assessment is undertaken after an insolvency or impairment.

Class B assessments are made of member insurers in the proportion that their state premium writings bear to the total writings for the relevant line of insurance. In total, for each calendar year, all assessments cannot exceed 2 percent of the member insurer's average premiums received in the state on covered business during the three years pre-

---

[11]This section draws on Lew H. Nathan, *Life and Health Guaranty Associations and Insurer Solvency* (Atlanta, GA: LOMA , 1990). Adapted with permission.

ceding the year of impairment or insolvency. The assessment of any member can be abated or deferred if payment would be harmful to the member insurer in fulfilling its contractual obligations.

Many states permit a tax offset for any assessments paid by a member insurer. This offset can be applied against the insurer's premium tax, franchise tax, or income tax liability to the state. The credit equals 20 percent per year of any assessment paid, for a maximum of five years. The effect of tax offsets is to shift most of the financial burden for insolvencies from insurers and their policyowners and stockholders to the state's taxpayers. Additionally, payments to the guaranty association are deductible for federal income tax purposes.

An Evaluation of Guaranty Associations

Guaranty associations and funds are rationalized in insurance because of consumer information problems. However, they diminish market discipline to some degree. If buyers know that they will be made whole if they purchase insurance from an solvent insurer, they have less incentive to investigate and monitor solvency. This assertion is more relevant for informed buyers than for less informed individuals. Also, if no distinction for insurer financial solidity is made in the guaranty fund assessment mechanism, the opportunity for moral hazard by firms is enhanced, thus further weakening market discipline.

The guaranty association structure has weaknesses. Coverage is not uniform among states. Each state's association also can act independently from the other associations, although the National Organization of Life and Health Insurance Guaranty Associations (NOLHGA) helps to achieve uniformity of the guaranty association process across the country. Another problem is the potential for a very large insolvency or series of insolvencies that might overwhelm the assessment ability of each state's guaranty association to provide immediate indemnification.

REGULATION IN AN INTEGRATED FINANCIAL SERVICES WORLD

Markets increasingly view insurance in the context of a larger, more integrated financial services world. Already, *bancassurance* and *allfinanz* are realities in Europe with some financial services conglomerates aiming to be *universal banks*—financial groups that manufacture and offer virtually all financial services. The United States and Japan remain the only major economies that legislatively require substantial separation among the major components of financial services—commercial banking, investment banking, and insurance. Markets are, however, moving faster than policy makers, with the merger of Citicorp and Travelers, among others, seemingly forcing the issue. This section reviews the U.S. laws requiring separation, examines recent court cases that have weakened these laws, and sets out the policy concerns related to financial services integration.[12]

The Glass-Steagall Act

During the 1930s, the U.S. Congress became convinced that banks' errant recommendations for and investments in stocks helped precipitate the Great Depression. (Today many historians disagree, noting that falling real estate and other values undermined

---

[12]This section draws partially from Robert H. Myers, Jr., "Are We Witnessing the Beginning of a New Era in Financial Services?" *Insurance/Healthcare Review* (Morris, Manning & Martin), Summer 1997, pp. 1, 5–6, and Andrew F. Giffin and Brian Clontz, "Integration and Globalization of Financial Services," in Harold D. Skipper, Jr., ed., *International Risk and Insurance,* pp. 160–189.

bank loans.) To rectify this perceived abuse, Congress passed the Glass-Steagall Act in 1933, effectively erecting a wall between commercial and investment banking.

Over the decades, banks argued futilely for the act's repeal, contending that such limitations harmed bank competitiveness and profitability and limited consumer choice. The intensity of their reform fervor grew in the 1970s and 1980s.

By the 1990s, banking regulators had done through regulatory interpretation much of what the banks had been unable to convince the Congress to do. Regulators had interpreted the law to allow banks to trade and underwrite securities through subsidiaries, provided their activities accounted for no more than 10 percent of the group's revenues. This limit was raised to 25 percent in 1996, thus effectively allowing the largest banks to acquire the largest brokerage firms, whereas the Glass-Steagall Act continued to bar brokerage firms from acquiring banks.

The National Bank Act and the Bank Holding Company Act

U.S. banks may have state or national charters. Banks are subject to three sometimes overlapping federal regulatory agencies. State-chartered banks are regulated by their state's banking regulatory authorities and by the Federal Deposit Insurance Corporation (FDIC). National banks are regulated under the National Bank Act by the Office of the Comptroller of the Currency (OCC), an independent agency of the U.S. Treasury. Bank holding companies are corporations that own banks and "nonbank" subsidiaries. They are regulated under the Bank Holding Company Act by the Federal Reserve System, the nation's independent central bank.

These regulatory regimes limit banks' ability to market insurance. The Bank Holding Company Act generally prohibits bank holding companies and their subsidiaries from marketing insurance. The National Bank Act restricts banks to the marketing of insurance from a "place of 5,000 or less" and other "bank-related" activities. Under the OCC interpretation, subsidiaries or branches of national banks, located in small towns, do not have to limit their insurance marketing activities to those small towns.

State-chartered banks historically have been similarly limited by their state laws. However, almost all states now grant their banks some insurance sales powers, with more than one-half of the states granting their state banks broad powers to sell virtually any type of insurance.

The *VALIC* and *Barnett* Decisions

For decades, the insurance industry, led by insurance agents, has been successful in limiting banks' insurance marketing. According to one observer, this result " . . . was accomplished through a combination of political clout and savvy, relatively favorable legislation, and the bureaucratic proclivity to protect the status quo."[13] Two U.S. Supreme Court cases have had a profound effect in the debate.

Thus, in *NationsBank v. Variable Annuity Life Insurance Company* (1995),[14] the Court held that the sale of annuities, which had been authorized by the OCC as the sale of investment products, was allowable under the National Bank Act. The Court held that annuities were investments and not "insurance." As such, banks would be permitted to both manufacture and sell annuities. Under state insurance law, however, banks can manufacture annuities only if they obtain a Certificate of Authority from the insurance regulator—which seems unlikely as banks are not "life insurance companies." To date,

---

[13]Myers, "Are We Witnessing the Beginning of a New Era in Financial Services?" p. 5.
[14]115 S.Ct. 810 (1995).

therefore, banks have been unsuccessful in manufacturing annuities but quite successful in marketing annuities underwritten by life insurers.

In the second case, *Barnett Bank v. Nelson, Florida Insurance Commissioner* (1996),[15] the Supreme Court held that a national bank with a branch and insurance agency in a "place of 5,000" may sell insurance as an agent despite state law prohibiting bank and insurance agency affiliations. Furthermore, the Court held that preemption of state law applies to any law that "prevents or significantly interferes" with the authority of national banks as provided by the National Bank Act.

The *Barnett* decision has potentially wide applicability. The Court effectively held that the small-town exemption under the National Bank Act is an insurance statute for purposes of the McCarran-Ferguson Act. As such, the OCC presumably is the controlling regulatory agency as relates to bank insurance sales. However, the OCC has insisted that banks comply fully with state insurance licensing and other requirements in their marketing of insurance. This OCC position could change if it perceives state insurance regulators are intruding in areas of bank examination that traditionally have been the OCC's purview or if insurance regulators show some bias against banks.

Regulatory Concerns about Integration

Together, these two cases have led to a substantial readjustment of U.S. regulatory authority and likely presage further regulatory reform, especially given mergers such as Citicorp and Travelers. Concerns about the integration trend persist, as we discuss next.

Contagion

The risk of *contagion* or financial infection refers to the exposure (or damage) that a tainted activity or component might inflict upon the financial services conglomerate. A bank, for example, may have a property and casualty subsidiary that has experienced enormous losses. If the bank transfers significant amounts of capital to the insurer, it might jeopardize the entire group's financial security. This transaction may be completely transparent or accomplished surreptitiously depending upon management's objectives (e.g., off-market or intragroup transactions).

Although no one questions the possibility of financial contagion within a financial services conglomerate, financial conglomeration could lead to greater diversification. If true, this fact theoretically should lower overall firm risk, not increase it.

Information disclosure and analysis by customers, intermediaries, rating agencies, and governments have been suggested as means of controlling the contagion exposure. Many observers believe, however, that a completely different approach is necessary whereby deposit insurance is privatized and regulation focuses on a narrow range of financial services activities.

Transparency

Transparency is concerned with the assurance that accurate information needed by customers, intermediaries, rating agencies, and governments will be readily available. The more complex the organizational structure, the less transparent it is ordinarily. To assume that customers have the time or the resources to perform due diligence on a financial conglomerate is unrealistic.

Traditionally, so long as there was enough unrestricted capital to meet contingencies, organizations were deemed safe. Although this approach may have worked reasonably well when institutions stayed within sectoral boundaries and like institutions

---

[15]116 S.Ct. 1103 (1996).

were roughly comparable, the new world of mixed services requires a broader consideration of factors (e.g., competitive position).

Management Responsibility

Management responsibility is concerned with the possibility that managers compromise their entity's sound operation in favor of the conglomerate's fiscal health (e.g., through unwise loans to connected parties). Where a financial services group is regulated functionally, how can each sector's regulator be assured that managers will fulfill their responsibility to meet regulatory requirements given other interests within the group?

Financial services regulators have struggled with this problem for many years as regulated units have become part of broadly based financial and commercial groups. Although there are serious analysis and enforcement limitations on regulatory agencies, some believe the solution is to include a broad obligation to disclose major intragroup transactions. Disclosure would entail transactions that affect the regulated entity or the basic integrity of the regulated unit's assets and operating capacity. At a minimum, these data should constitute a prerequisite for continuing authority to operate.

Double-Gearing

Double-gearing, a European term, exists when a company includes the capital of subsidiaries to meet its own solvency requirements. This double counting acts to artificially inflate the conglomerate's capital adequacy. Supervision becomes more complex if certain operations within the conglomerate are unregulated.

Clear, uniform accounting standards and requirements are necessary to identify double-gearing. Issues related to appropriate disclosure and the appropriate locus of regulatory responsibility must be resolved.

Market Power

Consistent with the chapter 1 definition, *market power* relates to the ability of one or a few sectorally dominant firms (e.g., through oligopoly or monopoly) to influence market prices. A highly concentrated market or the existence of vertical agreements could lead to market power that hinders market efficiency. Many countries have granted regulators supervisory powers over merger and acquisitions to curtail such risk.

In the past, traditional indicators have proven effective for sectoral analysis. The introduction of integrated financial services, however, renders this supervisory function more arduous. Moreover, with the exponential growth of cross-border trade and foreign penetration into domestic markets, many believe globalization will thwart any domestic concentration of power.

We have seen significant concentration of market shares, particularly among traditional banks and insurance companies, in many major markets. Simultaneously, we have seen considerable new entry. When a subsidiary, such as Predica, can enter the life market in France and become a leading company in a few years, the risk of oligopoly or monopoly power seems limited.

Overall, the trends toward cross-sector and cross-border entry (and new technologies) would seem to reduce the potential for concentration of market power. Most countries will retain antimonopoly authorities to protect against the rare cases of potentially sustainable market control combinations. Openness and rapid change in financial services markets are likely to preserve strong competitive forces.

Conflicts of Interest

The potential for **conflict of interest** exists when a financial institution offers multiple financial services and promotes proprietary products through coercion or other power for the organization's benefit over the best interest of the customer. In the United

States particularly, some have argued that banks should not be permitted to sell insurance because they may condition the availability of other products on the customer's agreement to purchase insurance. The Glass-Steagall Act was born from this concern.

Most financial services regulatory systems, including those of the United States, prohibit tying the purchase of one product to another, although discounts are permitted for joint purchase. As with prior points, some believe information disclosure and competitor exploitation of potential abuses may minimize such conflicts.

Regulatory Arbitrage

Regulatory arbitrage is the tendency of financial services conglomerates to shift activities or positions within the group to avoid or minimize certain regulation. For example, a conglomerate might shift the production and sale of a particular savings product to its insurance company if insurance regulation were judged less intrusive than banking regulation. In the absence of comprehensive cross-sector and international regulatory harmonization, opportunities for such arbitrage will always exist. To control this practice, some believe sectoral regulators should engage in extensive cross-sector information sharing. This is beginning to take place between state insurance regulators and federal bank regulators under the auspices of the NAIC. Internationally, regulators of multinational financial services firms could also engage in informational reciprocity with trading partners to help identify possible distress situations. The possibility of regulatory arbitrage encourages cross-sectoral and international regulatory harmonization.

TAXATION OF U.S. LIFE AND HEALTH INSURERS

U.S. life and health insurers are taxed by the federal and state governments. Federal taxation is based on insurers' net income, whereas states continue to tax insurers primarily on premium income. Before covering the essential elements of federal and state taxation, an overview of desirable goals of a tax system is presented.

Desirable Goals of a Tax System

Ideally, tax systems should be:

- simple
- equitable
- neutral

A tax system is *simple* if it is not complex administratively, it is not easily evaded, its costs of collection are low, and taxpayers can comply with the law with minimal expenditure of time and money. The system should be compatible with the country's level of economic development and sophistication of administrative apparatus. This goal often conflicts with the other two goals.

The concept of *equity* means that each taxpayer should contribute his, her, or its fair share in taxes. This goal poses theoretical and practical difficulties for tax-system designers. For businesses and individuals in the United States, net income has generally been adopted as an appropriate measure of the taxpayer's ability to pay and, therefore, the basis for calculation of the fair share. Equity in taxation in some situations also has meant taxing those who benefit from a government-provided product or service in some direct proportion to the extent of that benefit. Fuel taxes are examples.

A tax system, ideally, should be economically *neutral*, meaning that government should tax economically equivalent entities, products, and services equivalently. A tax system should minimize interference with the economic and social behavior of individuals, businesses, and other taxpaying entities in the absence of an overriding economic or social goal to be served by the tax system.

The concept of economic neutrality suggests also that the tax system (1) should not benefit one industry at the expense of another, (2) within a single industry, should not benefit one set of competitors relative to others, and (3) should not influence a firm's choices of production factors or product outputs. The concept of economic neutrality connotes that market forces, not the tax system, should drive business decisions. The principle underpinning this goal is that social welfare is enhanced if resources flow naturally to their highest-value uses.

State Taxation

States subject insurance companies to one or more of several types of taxes. The common types are discussed next.

Premium Taxation

Many countries and all states in the United States impose a premium tax of some sort. Ordinarily, the premium tax takes the place of net income or related taxation. A complete premium tax system is defined by the premium tax base, the premium tax rates, and any special deductions, credits, or exemptions provided for in the law.

Nature of Premium Taxation   Under the typical state premium tax structure, the tax base is the simple total of the insurer's premium revenue from the state with certain alterations. Premiums received from assumed reinsurance are usually excluded from the tax base because the original insurer that wrote the business would have already been subjected to premium tax for the direct premiums. Most states permit a deduction from the tax base for dividends paid to policyowners. The premium tax base may include premiums received for accident and health insurance, or such premiums may be taxed separately. Insurers' investment income is not included in the tax base.

Most states do not levy any premium tax on either domestic or out-of-state annuity considerations paid to insurers. Even the states that tax annuity considerations typically exempt federally qualified annuity plans (e.g., individual retirement annuities, tax-deferred annuities, and so on) from premium taxation. States that tax annuities place life insurers at a competitive disadvantage with banks and other savings media.

The tax rates on out-of-state insurers range from about 1 to 4 percent. Tax rates on domestic insurers vary from 0 percent to 4 percent. Several states violate the neutrality goal by providing preferential tax treatment for their domestic insurers, although most states have changed their laws to eliminate some or all such discriminatory elements. Some states tax health insurance premiums at a higher rate than that for life insurance premiums, whereas others do the opposite.

Selected forms of insuring organizations enjoy preferential treatment in many states in violation of the neutrality goal. Both domestic and out-of-state fraternal life insurers are typically exempt from premium taxation. Blue Cross/Blue Shield organizations and other nonprofit health care service plans, until recently, were exempt from premium taxation in most states. The trend is toward taxing them as any other health insurer. Self-insurance arrangements by commercial enterprises for health and other employee benefit coverages are generally exempted from premium taxation—a fact that encourages self-insurance compared to group insurance.

Evaluation of Premium Taxation   The premium tax system has both desirable and undesirable attributes. A system of taxation based on an insurance company's premium income is a simple approach to taxation. It is easy to administer by both insurers and tax authorities. Compliance verification is not particularly difficult. This taxation produces a steady and usually increasing revenue flow to the state. Another possibly positive attribute of the premium tax system is that it already exists. Insurers and state (and some local) governments are accustomed to it.

The premium tax has been criticized on the grounds that (1) it constitutes a direct tax on savings that is applicable only to insurers, (2) it is regressive in that it hits lower-income persons who purchase life insurance relatively harder than higher-income persons, (3) it discriminates unfairly against higher-premium (and cash-value) forms of life insurance because it is levied on the premium, (4) it discriminates unfairly against those who must pay higher premium rates, such as the elderly and those who are rated substandard, and (5) it must be paid irrespective of insurer profitability.

A premium tax that is higher for out-of-state insurers than for domestic insurers is an interstate trade barrier that, were it not for the McCarran-Ferguson Act, would almost certainly be unconstitutional. Such discriminatory taxation has the same negative effects on trade as tariffs, and it has been condemned by the NAIC for distorting competition and ignoring the national character of the U.S. market.

Although the rate appears low, it is applied to a large tax base and few tax concessions are provided. The net result, therefore, is a low tax rate but a high effective tax burden. Studies have found that the effective tax burden on insurers arising from premium taxation is consistently higher than that on other financial and nonfinancial institutions. With increasing competitiveness within the financial services community, economically neutral tax systems become more critical.

Income Taxation

Nine states subject out-of-state insurers to state income taxation. Three of these states provide that the income tax can be offset against the premium tax, and five provide that the premium tax can be offset against the income tax.

Fourteen states subject their domestic insurers to state income taxation. Six of these states exempt domestic insurers from premium taxation and, in essence, tax insurers as they do any other domestic corporation, with recognition for their special characteristics. Five permit offsetting premium taxes paid by domestic insurers against the state income tax obligation. Two states permit offsetting the income tax against the premium tax due, and New York provides that domestic insurers must pay both premium taxes and income taxes up to a stated maximum.

Retaliatory Taxation

Retaliatory tax laws are intended to promote the interstate business of domestic insurers by discouraging other states from imposing excess or discriminatory taxes. These laws have been held to be constitutionally valid. All states, except Hawaii, have retaliatory tax laws. Retaliatory laws usually provide that, when the laws of another state or country create a greater burden on a state's domestic insurers than the state's domestic laws impose on similar foreign insurers, the insurance commissioner of the state of domicile may impose similar obligations on foreign insurers seeking to do business in his or her state.

Other Taxation

States levy various other forms of taxes, fees, and assessments on insurers. These might include ad valorem taxes on real estate, personal property taxes, license fees, and franchise taxes. Also, a few states permit their cities and counties to levy premium taxes on insurers. This taxation can place a disproportionate administrative burden on insurers. Alternative revenue-sharing means of accomplishing the same purpose are far more efficient.

Federal Taxation

Life insurers operating in the United States are subject to taxation at the federal level in addition to their state tax obligations. Federal taxation, based on net income, has undergone considerable evolution over the years.[16] Taxation of life insurers on their net income is complicated by these considerations:

- the long-term nature of life insurance products and the complexity in ascribing operating gain to any particular year
- the desire for economic neutrality between mutual and stock companies
- the need to recognize that interest credited to policy reserves is economically allocable mostly to policyowners

Taxable Income

U.S. life insurers are taxed under the Deficit Reduction Act of 1984. Under the act, a life insurer is taxed on its **life insurance company taxable income (LICTI),** defined as gross income less applicable deductions. This general approach is the same as that of other corporations, but many of the details necessarily differ, as discussed next.

Gross Income   Gross income of a life insurance company can be divided into five categories:

> premiums
> investment income
> capital gains
> decreases in reserve
> all other items of gross income

The Internal Revenue Code (IRC) includes as income all *premiums and other considerations* received on insurance and annuity contracts. These receipt items include fees, deposits, assessments, advance or prepaid premiums, reinsurance premiums, and the amount of any policyowner dividends reimbursable to the insurer by a reinsurer. Also included are premiums or deposits on supplementary contracts and policy proceeds left with the company. These amounts may be reduced by any returned premiums (e.g., premiums returned because of policy cancellations or errors in determining the premium) and premiums paid for reinsurance. Approximately 60 to 80 percent of a typical life insurance company's gross income is included under this section.

The other principal source of income of a life insurance company is its *investment* activities. The investment earnings of an insurer consist primarily of interest, dividends, rents, and royalties. Approximately 20 to 40 percent of a typical life insurance company's gross income consists of investment earnings. Life insurance companies are taxed on capital gains the same as other corporate taxpayers.

Any net *decrease in certain insurance reserves* produces an income item. Life insurers are allowed tax deductions when net additions are made to reserves. Thus, when the reserves are released, their release produces an income item for the company.

Finally, the law contains a provision that encompasses all items of gross income not included under any of the other foregoing four categories. The sum of the five categories described earlier produces life insurance gross income.

---

[16]This section draws on William B. Harman, Jr., "The Structure of Life Insurance Company Taxation: The New Pattern under the 1984 Act," Parts I and II, *Journal of the American Society of CLU,* Vol. 39 (March 1985 and May 1985).

Deductions   Life insurers are allowed three categories of deductions:

- general corporate deductions
- deductions peculiar to the insurance business
- the small life insurance company deduction

First, life insurers are permitted all deductions allowable to other corporate taxpayers, with certain technical modifications. Second, life insurers are permitted certain deductions that are *peculiar to the insurance business.* Thus, a deduction is allowed for all claims, benefits, and losses incurred on insurance and annuity contracts. These payments are analogous to income tax deductions permitted manufacturing organizations for production costs.

A life insurance company also is granted a deduction for any net annual additions to specified insurance reserves that it must maintain for its insurance and annuity contracts. This reserve deduction includes two items: (1) an amount to represent the prefunding of mortality (i.e., the "savings" element included in premiums) or considerations received plus (2) interest credited each year to reserves to ensure that they are sufficient to meet its future obligations. The deductible net increase in reserves is computed by subtracting the opening balance of the reserves (January 1) from the closing balance of the reserves (December 31).

the six insurance reserves taken into account are:

- life insurance policy reserves
- unearned premiums and unpaid losses included in total reserves
- discounted liabilities for insurance and annuity contracts not currently involving life, accident, or health contingencies
- dividend accumulations and other amounts held at interest under insurance and annuity contracts
- advance premiums and premium deposit fund liabilities
- reasonable special contingency reserves under group contracts for retired lives and premium stabilization

Under earlier U.S. tax law, insurers were able to use statutory reserves. The 1984 act changed this practice, generally resulting in a decrease in tax reserves. Under current law, a reserve for any contract shall be the greater of (1) the net cash surrender value of the contract or (2) the reserve for the contract as computed under federally prescribed standards. In no event may this amount exceed the statutory annual-statement figure.

The reserve computed under federal standards uses the same methods and assumptions used for calculating statutory reserves but modified to take account of the following five federal standards:

- The Commissioners' Reserve Valuation Method must be used for life insurance contracts (see chapter 29).
- The minimum valuation interest rate to be used is the greater of (a) a federal interest rate determined using the average of the yields of midterm government bonds over the previous five years for the year in which the contract was issued or (b) the prevailing state interest rate, defined as the highest assumed interest rate that at least 26 states permit to be used in computing reserves for the particular insurance or annuity contract.
- The mortality tables to be used must be the most recent standard tables for mortality and morbidity prescribed by the NAIC that at least 26 states permit

to be used in computing reserves for the type of contract involved at the time of issue.

- Reserves for any amounts in respect of deferred and uncollected premiums must be eliminated, unless the gross amount of these premiums is included in gross income.
- Reserves for excess interest (i.e., interest exceeding the prevailing state assumed interest rate) and guaranteed beyond the end of the taxable year must be eliminated.

Another deduction peculiar to the life insurance business is policyowner dividends. This term is in the law as any dividend paid or payable to a policyowner in his or her capacity as such, and it includes any distribution to a policyowner that is economically equivalent to a dividend. Accordingly, it includes excess interest, premium adjustments, and experience-rated refunds, as well as any amount paid or credited to policyowners (including an increase in benefits) in which the amount is not fixed in the contract but depends on the insurer's experience or the discretion of management.

Stock life insurers are allowed unlimited deductions for policyowner dividends paid or accrued during the taxable year. Mutual life insurers, however, may be subject to a limitation on the deductibility of its policyowner dividends (discussed later).

The third major deduction allowed is the so-called *small life insurance company deduction.* This deduction, which was included primarily for political reasons and is consistent with the general congressional policy of encouraging small business, equals 60 percent of the tentative LICTI, up to a maximum of $3 million. Thus, the small company deduction can never exceed $1,800,000 (i.e., .60 × $3,000,000). If a life insurance company's tentative LICTI exceeds $3 million, the amount of the small company deduction is phased out by an amount equal to 15 percent of tentative LICTI in excess of $3 million. Thus, for an insurer with tentative LICTI of $15 million or more, no small company deduction is allowed.

Policyowner Dividend Treatment

According to current tax law, distributions to customers should be fully deductible by a corporation, whereas distributions to owners of the enterprise should not be deductible. In the case of mutual organizations, however, the customers are also effectively the owners.

Mutual insurers often charge comparatively high premiums and return the unneeded excess premiums as dividends to policyowners. This excess is properly deductible at the corporate level. Also included in policyowner dividends, however, may be distributions of investment and underwriting earnings of the mutual company (as the policyowner is effectively an owner of the company, as well as a purchaser of its services). Many believe that, in contrast with the return of excess premiums, these earnings should not be excluded from corporate income taxation, just as dividends payable to stockholders are not deductible by corporations.

Intertwined with the dividend deductibility issue at the time Congress was debating life insurer taxation was the issue of the amount of revenue to be raised from the life insurance industry and its apportionment between stock and mutual companies. With a 100 percent policyowner dividend deduction, a mutual insurer may have paid little or perhaps no tax. On the other hand, if no deductions were permitted, legitimate payments to policyowners as customers (rather than as owners), which should be deductible under general tax principles, would be denied to mutuals—an unfair result as it would have overtaxed those companies. Thus, it was (and is) crucial to impose appropriate relative tax burdens on each segment, so that the tax law does not favor one segment over the other. Accordingly, in an effort to treat the stock and mutual segments equitably and to raise appropriate revenues from the industry, it was judged necessary to limit the dividend deduction for mutual companies.

The assumption underlying the segment balance (55/45) was that an appropriate guide to the profitability of mutual life insurers is the profitability on equity of stock life insurers. The mechanics of the limitation on the deductibility of policyowner dividends by a mutual insurer involve the determination of a differential earnings rate on "equity" between stock and mutual companies. The imputed earnings rate on equity for stock insurers is assumed to be higher than that for mutual insurers, and this difference is assumed to represent a return to policyowners in mutual companies on their ownership interests in the companies. The procedure results, in effect, in a tax on mutual insurer surplus.

The 1990 DAC Tax

The Revenue Reconciliation Act of 1990 added a new provision to life insurer tax law that purports to defer (capitalize and amortize) acquisition costs of life insurance and annuity contracts. This provision is known as the DAC (deferred acquisition costs) tax.[17]

The theory for this tax is that certain insurance company expenses—commissions, underwriting expenses, agency expenses, and other costs of acquiring and retaining business—should be capitalized and amortized to produce a better matching of deductions with revenues. Such a capitalization is done under generally accepted accounting principles but not under statutory accounting principles. The DAC provision, however, came about because the Treasury Department and Congress believed the life insurance business should pay more in federal income taxes.

In form, the provision is a proxy for true deferral, which was seen as administratively complex. For each year, the amount of the insurer's general deductions to be capitalized is the sum of specified percentages of premiums by line of business:

- 1.75 percent of annuity contract premiums
- 2.05 percent of group life insurance premiums
- 7.70 percent of other life and noncancellable accident and health insurance premiums

In determining the amount to be capitalized, premiums on pension plan contracts are not included, nor are imputed premiums (e.g., where dividends are applied to reduce premiums). Generally, reinsurance ceded reduces premiums and reinsurance assumed increases them.

The capitalized amounts are to be amortized in a straight-line fashion over a 10-year period starting at the middle of the year of capitalization. It is of interest to smaller companies that the amortization period for the first $5 million capitalized in any year is five years. This $5 million amount is phased out as the capitalized amount moves from $10 million to $15 million, so large insurers obtain no benefit.

The DAC tax substantially raised the U.S. life insurance industry's federal income taxes. In turn, life insurers have had to make appropriate adjustments in existing and new-product pricing to account for this increase. Interest rate credits, dividends, and other nonguaranteed benefits are somewhat lower than they otherwise would have been.

---

[17]This section draws on Wayne E. Bergquist, Nicholas Bauer, and Douglas N. Hertz, "Principles of Taxation," SOA Course 200 Study Note (Schaumburg, IL: Society of Actuaries, 1995).

Questions

1. Why is it necessary for the life and health insurance business to be closely regulated? What are the general goals of the regulatory authorities?
2. Although rates are closely regulated in property and liability insurance, they are not regulated in life insurance. Why?
3. What reasons are advanced by the proponents of federal insurance regulation? What relevance do changes taking place in financial services regulation and in international insurance markets have for this discussion?
4. Why is there a need for the standardization of policy forms or the regulation of policy forms by state insurance authorities?
5. Describe the nature and purpose of state premium taxes.

Recommended Readings

Chapter 1
Economic Security and the Economics of Life and Health Insurance

Akerlof, G. A. "The Market for 'Lemons': Quality Uncertainty and the Market Mechanism." *Quarterly Journal of Economics* 84 (1970), pp. 488–500.

Bernheim, B. Douglas. "How Strong Are Bequest Motives? Evidence Based on Estimates of the Demand for Life Insurance and Annuities." *Journal of Political Economy* 99 (1991), pp. 899–927.

Briys, E. and H. Schlesinger. "Risk Aversion and the Propensities for Self-Insurance and Self-Protection." *Southern Economic Journal* 57 (1990), pp. 458–467.

Dionne G. and S. E. Harrington, eds. *Foundations of Insurance Economics.* Boston: Kluwer Academic Publishers, 1992.

Duesenberry, J. S. *Income, Saving, and the Theory of Consumer Behavior.* Cambridge, MA: Harvard University Press, 1949.

Ehrlich, J. and G. Becker. "Market Insurance, Self Insurance and Self-Protection." *Journal of Political Economy* 80 (1972), pp. 623–648.

Fischer, Stanley. "A Life Cycle Model of Life Insurance Purchases." *International Economic Review* 14 (1973), pp. 132–152.

Friedman, Milton. *A Theory of the Consumption Function.* Princeton: Princeton University Press, 1957.

Friedman, M. and L. J. Savage. "The Utility Analysis of Choices Involving Risk." *Journal of Political Economy* 56 (1947), pp. 279–304.

Goldsmith, A. "Household Life Cycle Protection: Human Capital versus Life Insurance." *Journal of Risk and Insurance* 50 (1983), pp. 33–44.

Hirshleifer, J. and J. G. Riley. "The Analytics of Uncertainty and Information." *Journal of Economic Literature* 17 (1979), pp. 1375–1421.

Holmstrom, B. "Moral Hazard and Observability." *Bell Journal of Economics* 10 (1979), pp. 74–91.

Keller, R. L. "Properties of Utility Theories and Related Empirical Phenomena." In *Utility Theories: Measurement and Applications.* Ward Edwards, ed. Boston: Kluwer Academic Publishers, 1992.

Modigliani, F. "Life Cycle, Individual Thrift, and the Wealth of Nations." *American Economic Review* 76 (June 1986), pp. 297–313.

Pfeffer, Irving and David R. Klock. *Perspectives on Insurance.* Englewood Cliffs: Prentice Hall, Inc., 1974.

Rothschild, M. and J. Stiglitz. "Equilibrium in Competitive Insurance Markets." *Quarterly Journal of Economics* 90 (1976), pp. 529–649.

Rubinstein, A. and M. E. Yaari. "Repeated Insurance Contracts and Moral Hazard." *Journal of Economic Theory* 30 (1983), pp. 74–97.

Slovic, Paul and Sarah Lichenstein. "Preference Reversals: A Broader Perspective." *American Economic Review* 73 (1983), pp. 596–605.

Tversky, A. and D. Kahneman. "The Framing of Decisions and the Psychology of Choice." *Science* 211 (1981), pp. 453–458.

Von Neumann, J. and O. Morgenstern. *Theory of Games and Economic Behavior.* Princeton, NJ: Princeton University Press, 1944.

Wu, Chunchi and Peter Colwell. "Moral Hazard and Moral Imperative." *Journal of Risk and Insurance* 55, 1 (1988), pp. 101–117.

Yaari, Menahem E. "Uncertain Lifetime, Life Insurance, and the Theory of the Consumer." *Review of Economic Studies* 32 (1965), pp. 137–150.

Chapter 2
Life and Health Insurance Pricing Fundamentals

Bailey, Richard, ed. *Underwriting in Life and Health Insurance Companies.* Atlanta, GA: LOMA, 1999.

Dearborn-R&R Newkirk. *An Introduction to Life Underwriting,* 10th ed. Chicago, IL: Dearborn-R&R Newkirk, 1991.

Huggins, Kenneth and D. L. Robert. *Operations of Life and Health Insurance Companies,* 2nd ed. Atlanta, GA: LOMA, 1992.

Rothschild, M. and J. E. Stiglitz. "Equilibrium in Competitive Insurance Markets: An Essay on the Economics of Imperfect Information." *Quarterly Journal of Economics* 90 (1976), pp. 629–650.

Smith, M. L. and S. A. Kane. "The Law of Large Numbers and the Strength of Insurance." In *Insurance, Risk Management, and Public Policy: Essays in Memory of Robert I. Mehr.* S. G. Gustavson and S. E. Harrington, eds. Boston: Kluwer Academic Publishers, 1994.

Chapter 3
The History and Importance of Life and Health Insurance

Atchley, R. C. *Social Forces and Aging: An Introduction to Social Gerontology,* 8th ed. Belmont, CA: Wadsworth, 1997.

Bedore, James M. *Industry and Trade Summary: Insurance.* Washington, DC: U.S. International Trade Commission, 1991.

Bernstein, Peter L. *Against the Gods, The Remarkable Story of Risk.* New York: John Wiley & Son, Inc., 1996.

Burnett, John J. and Bruce A. Palmer, "Examining Life Insurance Ownership Through Demographic and Psychographic Characteristics." *Journal of Risk and Insurance* 51 (1984), pp. 453–467.

Campbell, Ritchie A. "The Demand for Life Insurance: An Application of the Economics of Uncertainty." *Journal of Finance* 35 (December 1980), pp. 1155–1172.

Cutler, N. E., D. W. Gregg, and M. P. Lawton, eds. *Aging, Money, and Life Satisfaction: Aspects of Financial Gerontology.* New York: Springer Publishing Company, 1992.

Hirshorn, R. and R. Geehan. "Measuring the Real Output of the Life Insurance Industry." *Review of Economics and Statistics* 49 (1977), pp. 211–219.

Neugarten, B. L. "Age Groups in American Society and the Rise of the Young-Old." *Annals of the American Academy of Political and Social Science* 415 (1974), pp. 187–198.

Outreville, J. F. "The Economic Significance of Insurance Markets in Developing Countries." *Journal of Risk and Insurance* 57 (1990), pp. 487–498.

Schulz, J. H., A. Borowski, and W. Crown. *Economics of Population Aging: The Graying of Australia, Japan, and the United States.* New York: Auburn House, 1991.

Skipper, H. D., Jr. *International Risk and Insurance: An Environmental-Managerial Approach.* Burr Ridge, IL: Irwin/McGraw-Hill, 1998.

World Bank. *Averting the Old Age Crisis.* Washington, DC: World Bank, 1994.

Chapter 4
Introduction to Life and Health Insurance Products

Bloomstein, H. J. "Structural Changes in Financial Markets: Overview of Trends and Prospects." Chap. 1 in *OECD Documents: The New Financial Landscape—Forces Shaping the Revolution in Banking, Risk Management and Capital Markets.* Paris: OECD, 1995.

Graves, Edward E., ed. *McGill's Life Insurance.* Bryn Mawr, PA: The American College, 1998.

Huggins, Kenneth and Robert D. Land. *Operations of Life and Health Insurance Companies,* 2nd ed. Atlanta, GA: LOMA, 1992.

Kellner, S. and F. Mathewson. "Entry, Size Distribution, Scale and Scope Economies in the Life Insurance Industry." *Journal of Business* 56 (1983), pp. 25–44.

Koguchi, K. *Financial Conglomerates.* Paris: OECD, 1993.

Thomas, Mitchell G. "Timing Is Everything in Term Renewability." *National Underwriter (Life/Health/Financial Services)* 102, No. 37 (1998), p. 8.

Chapter 5
Whole Life Insurance Policies

Anderson, Buist M. *Anderson on Life Insurance.* Boston: Little, Brown and Company, 1991.

Babbel, David F. "The Price Elasticity of Demand for Whole Life Insurance." *Journal of Finance* 40 (March 1985), pp. 225–239.

Crosby, Lawrence A. *Consumer Attitudes Toward Whole Life Insurance.* Atlanta, GA: LOMA, Inc; Washington, DC: National Association of Life Underwriters, 1984.

Plona, Martha E., ed. *A Long-Term Look at Whole Life Lapsation in Canada: 1983–1986 Experience.* Hartford, CT: Life Insurance Marketing and Research Association, 1988.

Chapter 6
Universal Life Insurance Policies

Belth, Joseph M. *Life Insurance: A Consumer's Handbook,* 2nd ed. Bloomington, IN: Indiana University Press, 1985.

"Choosing a Universal Life Policy." *Consumer Reports* 58 (August 1993), pp. 525–539.

Ernst & Whinney. *Universal Life: A Summary of the Product. An Analysis of Accounting, Actuarial, and Tax Considerations.* Cleveland, OH: Ernst & Whinney, 1981.

Life Insurance Marketing Research Association (LIMRA). *Universal Life Persistency: Premium Payment Patterns and Cash Value Experience.* Hartford, CT: LIMRA, 1988.

Polk, Ken E. "Variable Premium Life Insurance." *Transactions of the Society of Actuaries,* Vol. XXVI (1974), pp. 449–465, 467–478.

Practicing Law Institute. *Insurance Products Under the Securities Laws: New Regulatory Initiatives.* New York: Practicing Law Institute, 1985.

R&R Newkirk. *Variable Universal Life.* Chicago: Longman/R&R Newkirk, 1988.

Tromblay, Dan. *Variable Contracts.* Chicago: Dearborn-R&R Newkirk, 1995.

Chapter 7
Health Insurance Policies

Bound, John. "The Health and Earnings of Rejected Disability Insurance Applicants." *American Economic Review* 79, 3 (June 1989), pp. 482–503.

Cox, Larry A., Sandra G. Gustavson, and Antonie Stam. "Disability and Life Insurance in the Individual Insurance Portfolio." *Journal of Risk and Insurance* 58, 1 (March 1991), pp. 128–137.

Coy, Jacquelyn S. and Paul J. Winn. "Long-Term Care—A Vital Product in an Evolving Environment." *Journal of American Society of CLU & ChFC* (September 1997), pp. 68–75.

Cutler, N. E. "Caring for Elderly Parents: Where Do You Look for Help?" *Journal of the American Society of CLU and ChFC* 48 (July 1994), pp. 38–41.

Cutler, N. E. and S. J. Devlin. "Framework for Understanding Financial Responsibilities among Generations." *Generations* 20 (May 1996), pp. 31–36.

Cutler, N. E. and D. W. Gregg. "The Human 'Wealth Span' and Financial Well-Being in Older Age." *Generations* 15 (Winter 1991), pp. 45–48.

Fundamentals of Health Insurance, Part A. Washington, DC: Health Insurance Association of America, 1997.

Health Insurance Association of America (HIAA). *Individual Health Insurance.* Washington, DC: HIAA, 1994.

Health Insurance Association of America (HIAA). *Long-Term Care: Knowing the Risk, Paying the Price.* Washington, DC: HIAA, 1997.

Life Underwriter Training Council. *Disability Income Course.* Bethesda, MD: The Life Underwriter Training Council, 1996.

O'Brien, Raymond, and Michael T. Flannery. *Long-Term Care: Federal, State, and Private Options for the Future.* New York: Haeworth Press, 1997.

Pauly, Mark V. and Peter Zweifel. *Financing Long-Term Care: What Should Be the Government's Role?* Washington, DC: AEI Press, 1996.

U.S. General Accounting Office (GAO). *Private Health Insurance.* Washington, DC: U.S. Government Printing Office, 1996.

Chapter 8
Annuities and Optional Benefits

Baldwin, Ben G. *The New Life Insurance Investment Advisor: Achieving Financial Security for You and Your Family Through Today's Insurance Products.* Chicago: Probus Publishing Co., 1994.

Chandler, Darlene K. *The Annuity Handbook: A Guide to Nonqualified Annuities.* Cincinnati, OH: National Underwriter, 1994.

Ernst & Whinney. *Accounting for Life Insurance and Annuity Products: Understanding and Implementing FASB Statement No. 97.* Ernst & Whinney, 1988.

Institute of Financial Education. *Annuities, Mutual Funds & Life Insurance as Investment Products.* Chicago: Institute of Financial Education, 1988.

Kennedy, Jena L. *Introduction to Annuities.* Atlanta, GA: LOMA, 1996.

Murray, Michael L. and Stuart Klugman. "Impaired Health Life Annuities." *Journal of the American Society of CLU and ChFC,* Vol. 44 (September 1990).

Poterba, James M. *The History of Annuities in the United States.* Cambridge, MA: National Bureau of Economic Research, 1997.

Wells, Bruce F. *All About Variable Annuities: From the Inside Out.* Chicago: Irwin, 1995.

Chapters 9 and 10
Life and Health Insurance Contracts: I & II

Clarke, Malcolm A. *The Law of Insurance Contracts.* London: Lloyd's of London Press, 1989.

Crawford, Muriel L. and William T. Beadles. *Law and the Life Insurance Contract,* 6th ed. Homewood, IL: Richard D. Irwin, 1989.

Dobbyn, John F. *Insurance Law in a Nutshell,* 2nd ed. St. Paul, MN: West Publishing Company, 1989.

Farnsworth, E. Allen. "Precontractual Liability and Preliminary Agreements: Fair Dealing and Failed Negotiations." *Columbia Law Review* 87 (1987), pp. 217–294.

Furrow, Barry R. *Health Law.* St. Paul, MN: West Publishing Company, 1995.

Keeton, Robert E. and Alan I. Widiss. *Insurance Law: A Guide to Fundamental Principles, Legal Doctrines, and Commercial Practices.* Student edition. St. Paul, MN: West Publishing Company, 1988.

Kennedy, Richard T. and Michael A. Knoerzer. "Freedom of Contract and Choice of Law in Insurance." *AIDA Quarterly Update* 1, No. 3 (Summer 1995), pp. 12–16.

Kessler, Friedrich and Edith Fine. "Culpa in Contrahendo, Bargaining in Good Faith, and Freedom of Contract: A Comparative Study." *Harvard Law Review* 77 (1964), pp. 401–449.

Lorimer, James J. et al. *The Legal Environment of Insurance,* 4th ed., vols. 1 and 2. Malvern, PA: American Institute for Property and Liability Underwriters, 1993.

Organization for Economic Development (OECD). *Consumers and Life Insurance.* Paris: OECD, 1987.

Ware, Stephen J. "A Critique of the Reasonable Expectations Doctrine." *University of Chicago Law Review* 56 (Fall 1989), pp. 1461, 1463–1475.

Wiening, Eric A. and Donald S. Malecki. *Insurance Contract Analysis.* Malvern, PA: American Institute for Chartered Property Casualty Underwriters, 1992.

Chapter 11
Insurance Advisor and Company Evaluation

Ainsworth, Jim H. *The CPA's Guide to a Successful Financial Planning Practice: Selling Financial Investments and Marketing Advisory Services.* New York: Wiley, 1995.

Belth, Joseph M. "The Quandary of the Life Insurance Agent in a Time of Uncertainty." *Journal of the American Society of CLU & ChFC* 46 (May 1992), p. 76.

Mathewson, G. "Information, Search and Price Variability in the Individual Life Insurance Contracts." *Journal of Industrial Economics* 32 (1983), pp. 131–148.

National Association of Insurance Commissioners (NAIC). *Insurance Company Rating Agencies: A Description of Their Methods and Procedures.* Kansas City: NAIC, 1992.

Puelz, Robert. "A Process for Selecting a Life Insurance Contract." *Journal of Risk and Insurance* 58, 1 (1991), pp. 138–146.

Schwartz, Richard A. and Catherine R. Turner. *Life Insurance Due Care: Carriers, Products, and Illustrations,* 2nd ed. Chicago: American Bar Association, Section of Real Property, Probate, and Trust Law, 1994.

Sloane, Leonard. *The New York Times Personal Finance Handbook.* New York: New York Times Books, 1995.

Smith, Michael L. "The Life Insurance Policy as an Option Package." *Journal of Risk and Insurance* 49, 4 (December 1982), pp. 583–601.

Chapter 12
Life Insurance Policy Evaluation

Belth, Joseph M. *Life Insurance: A Consumer's Handbook,* 2nd ed. Bloomington, IN: Indiana University Press, 1985.

Belth, Joseph. "The Rate of Return on the Savings Element in Cash-Value Life Insurance." *The Journal of Risk and Insurance* 35 (1968), pp. 569–581.

Kamens, Matthew H. "What to Look For in Analyzing a Proposed Life Insurance Policy." *Estate Planning* 16, 4 (1989), pp. 200–206.

Miller, Walter N. "The Problem with Sales Illustrations: Why It Exists and How It Should Be Addressed." *Journal of the American Society of CLU and ChFC* 47, 3 (May 1993), pp. 64–71.

Murray, Michael L. "Analyzing the Investment Value of Cash Value Life Insurance." *The Journal of Risk and Insurance* 43 (1976), pp. 121–128.

Rattiner, Jeffrey H. *Evaluating Life Insurance Decisions.* San Diego, CA: Harcourt Brace Professional Publishers, 1994.

Schwartz, Richard A. and Catherine R. Turner. *Life Insurance Due Care: Carriers, Products, and Illustrations,* 2nd ed. Chicago: American Bar Association, Section of Real Property, Probate, and Trust Law, 1994.

Chapter 13
Life and Health Insurance Taxation

American Bar Association. *Federal Income Taxation of Life Insurance.* Chicago: American Bar Association, Section of Real Property, Probate, and Trust Law, 1989.

Millard, Kevin D. *Federal Gift, Estate, and Generation-Skipping Transfer Taxation of Life Insurance.* Chicago: American Bar Association, Section of Real Property, Probate, and Trust Law, 1998.

Organization for Economic Cooperation and Development (OECD). *Policy Issues in Insurance: Investment, Taxation, Insolvency.* Paris: OECD, 1996.

U.S. General Accounting Office. *Tax Treatment of Life Insurance and Annuity Accrued Interest.* Washington, DC: U.S. Government Printing Office, 1990.

Chapter 14
Life and Health Insurance in Personal Financial Planning

Cambridge Reports, Inc. *Consumer Planning and Preparation for Retirement.* Cambridge, MA: Cambridge Reports, Inc., 1988.

Consumer Reports. "When It's Time to Buy Life Insurance, How Much Coverage Do You Need?" *Consumer Reports* 58 (July 1993), pp. 431–450.

Dolan, Ken and Daria Dolan. "Here's How to Figure Out How Much Life Insurance Coverage You Need." *Money* 24, 5 (1995), p. 47.

Dorfman, Mark S. and Saul W. Adelman. *Life Insurance: A Financial Planning Approach,* 2nd ed. Chicago: Dearborn Financial Publishing, 1992.

Goldsmith, Art. "Household in Life Cycles Protection: Human Capital versus Life Insurance." *Journal of Risk and Insurance* 50 (1983), pp. 33–44.

Gordon, Harley. *How to Protect Your Life Savings from Catastrophic Illness and Nursing Homes: A Handbook for Financial Survival.* Boston: Financial Strategies Press, 1996.

Hakansson, N. H. "Optimal Investment and Consumption Strategies under Risk, and Uncertain Lifetime and Insurance." *International Economic Review* 10 (1969), pp. 443–466.

Hallman, G. Victor and Jerry S. Rosenbloom. *Personal Financial Planning,* 3rd ed. New York: McGraw-Hill Book Company, 1983.

Kahnemman, D. and A. Tversky. "Prospect Theory: An Analysis of Decisions under Risk." *Econometrica* 47 (March 1979), pp. 263–291.

Karnie, Edi and Itzhak Zilcha. "Uncertain Lifetime, Risk Aversion and Life Insurance." *Scandinavian Actuarial Journal* (1985), pp. 109–123.

Lewis, Frank D. "Dependents and the Demand for Life Insurance." *American Economic Review* 79, 3 (1989), pp. 452–466.

Munch, James C. *Financial and Estate Planning—With Life Insurance Products.* Boston: Little, Brown, 1990.

Smalhout, James H. *The Uncertain Retirement: Securing Pension Promises in a World of Risk.* Chicago: Irwin Professional Publishers, 1996.

Walker, David M. *Retirement Security: Understanding and Planning Your Financial Future.* New York: Wiley, 1997.

Chapter 15
Estate Planning

American Law Institute-American Bar Association. *Uses of Life Insurance in Estate and Tax Planning, October 26–27, 1989, Boston, Massachusetts: ALI-ABA Course of Study Materials.* Philadelphia: American Law Institute-American Bar Association, Committee on Continuing Professional Education, 1989.

Casner, A. James. *Estate Planning.* Boston: Little, Brown, 1995.

Kaye, Barry. *Save a Fortune on Your Estate Taxes: Wealth Creation and Preservation.* Homewood, IL: Business One Irwin, 1993.

Leimberg, Stephan R. et al. *The Tools and Techniques of Estate Planning,* 10th ed. Cincinnati, OH: National Underwriter Company, 1995.

Millard, Kevin D. *Federal Gift, Estate, and Generation-Skipping Transfer Taxation of Life Insurance.* Chicago: American Bar Association, Section of Real Property, Probate, and Trust Law, 1998.

Mitchell, William D. *Estate and Retirement Planning Answer Book,* 2nd ed. New York: Aspen Publishers, 1997.

Plotnick, Charles. *How to Settle an Estate: A Manual for Executors and Trustees.* Yonkers, NY: Consumer Reports Books, 1991.

Soled, Alex J. *Estate Planning: Easy Answers to Your Most Important Questions.* Yonkers, NY: Consumer Reports Books, 1994.

Chapter 16
Retirement Planning

Delsen, L. and G. Reday-Mulvey. "Gradual Retirement in the OECD Countries: Macro and Micro Issues and Policies." *The Four Pillars Research Programme on Social Security, Insurance, Savings and Employment* 18 (November 1995), pp. 3–12.

Ferber, Robert and Lucy Chao Lee. "Acquisition of Life Insurance in Early Married Life." *Journal of Risk and Insurance* 47, 4 (1980), pp. 713–734.

George, Linda K. *Financial Security in Later Life: The Subjective Side.* Philadelphia: Boettner Institute of Financial Gerontology, University of Pennsylvania, 1993.

Lewis, Frank D. "Dependents and the Demand for Life Insurance." *American Economic Review* 79, 3 (June 1989), 452–467.

Pissarides, C. A. "The Wealth-Age Relation with Life Insurance." *Economica* 47 (November 1980), 451–457.

Walker, David M. *Retirement Security: Understanding and Planning Your Financial Future.* New York: Wiley, 1997.

Chapter 17
Business Planning

American Law Institute-American Bar Association (ALI-ABA). *ALI-ABA Course of Study: Life Insurance in Business and Tax Planning.* Philadelphia: ALI-ABA Committee on Continuing Professional Education, 1980.

American Society of Certified Life Underwriters. *Split Dollar Life Insurance.* Bryn Mawr, PA: American Society of CLU, 1982.

Floridis, Ronald G. *Comprehensive Split Dollar.* Cincinnati, OH: National Underwriter Co., 1983.

Gallop, Gerald D. and Edward M. Burgh. "Variable Life Insurance Can Fund a Supplemental Executive Retirement Plan." *Pension World* 23, 12 (1987), pp. 26–28.

Goldstein, Michael G., Michael A. Swirnoff, and William A. Drennan. *Taxation and Funding of Nonqualified Deferred Compensation: A Complete Guide to Design and Implementation.* Chicago: American Bar Association, Section of Real Property, Probate, and Trust Law, 1998.

Klein, William D. *S Corporations and Life Insurance.* Chicago: American Bar Association, Section of Real Property, Probate, and Trust Law, 1992.

Wynn, Stanford A. *Split-Dollar Life Insurance.* Chicago: American Bar Association, Section of Real Property, Probate and Trust Law, 1991.

Chapter 18
Group Insurance

Beam, Burton T. *Group Health Insurance,* 2nd ed. Bryn Mawr, PA: American College, 1997.

Beam, Burton T., Jr. and John J. McFadden. *Employee Benefits,* 4th ed. Chicago: Dearborn Financial Publishing, 1996.

Bluhm, William F., principal editor. *Group Insurance.* Winstead, CT: ACTEX Publications, 1992.

Health Risk Pooling for Small-Group Health Insurance. Executive Office of the President, 1993.

R&R Newkirk. *Introduction to Group Insurance,* 3rd ed. Chicago: Dearborn-R&R Newkirk, 1990.

Reynolds, Frank. "Introduction to Actuarial Aspects of Group Insurance." *Study Note,* Society of Actuaries, 1994.

Roberts, James E. *Group Life Insurance.* Washington, DC: Tax Management, Inc., Annual.

Rosenbloom, Jerry S. *Employee Benefits Planning.* Englewood Cliffs, NJ: Prentice Hall, 1991.

Chapters 19 and 20
Health Care Plans: I & II

Altman, Stuart H., Uwe E. Reinhardt, and Alexandra E. Shields. *The Future U.S. Healthcare System: Who Will Care for the Poor and Uninsured?* Chicago: Health Administration Press, 1998.

Andersen, Ronald M., Thomas H. Rice, and Gerald F. Kominski, eds. *Changing the U.S. Health Care System: Key Issues in Health Services, Policy, and Management.* San Francisco: Jossey-Bass Publishers, 1996.

Arrow, Kenneth J. "Uncertainty and the Welfare Economics of Medical Care." *American Economic Review* 53, 5 (December 1963), pp. 941–973.

Browne, Mark J. "Evidence of Adverse Selection in the Individual Health Insurance Market." *Journal of Risk and Insurance* 59, 1 (1992), pp. 13–33.

"Can HMO's Help Solve the Health Care Crisis?" *Consumer Reports* 61, 10 (October 1996), pp. 28–35.

Consumer's Guide to Health Plans. Washington, DC: Center for Study of Services, 1996.

Danzon, Patricia M. "The Hidden Costs of Budget-Constrained Health Insurance Systems." In *American Health Policy: Critical Issues for Reform.* Robert B. Helms, ed. Washington, DC: American Enterprise Institute Press, 1993.

Feldstein, Martin S. "The Welfare Loss of Excess Health Insurance." *Journal of Political Economy* 81 (March/April 1973), pp. 251–280.

Folland, Sherman. *The Economics of Health and Health Care,* 2nd ed. Upper Saddle River, NJ: Prentice Hall, 1997.

Grossman, Michael. "On the Concept of Health Capital and the Demand for Health." *Journal of Political Economy* (1972), pp. 223–253.

Ham, Chris, ed. *Health Care Reform: Learning from International Experience.* Philadelphia: Open University Press, 1997.

Health Insurance Association of America (HIAA). *1996 Source Book of Health Insurance Data.* HIAA, 1996.

Manning, Willard G. et al. "Health Insurance and the Demand for Medical Care: Evidence from a Randomized Experiment." *American Economic Review* 77 (June 1987), pp. 251–277.

Miller, Irwin. *American Health Care Blues: Blue Cross, HMO's, and Pragmatic Reform since 1960.* New Brunswick, NJ: Transaction Publishers, 1996.

Roemer, Milton I. *National Health Systems of the World,* Vol. 2. Oxford: Oxford University Press, 1991.

Sultz, Harry A. and Kristina M. Young. *Health Care USA: Understanding Its Organization and Delivery.* Gaithersburg, MD: Aspen Publishers, Inc., 1997.

Wilkerson, John D., Kelly J. Devers, and Ruth S. Given, eds. *Competitive Managed Care: The Emerging Health Care System.* San Francisco: Jossey-Bass Publishers, 1997.

Zeckhauser, Richard J. "Medical Insurance: A Case Study of the Trade-off Between Risk Spreading and Appropriate Incentives." *Journal of Economic Theory* 2, 1 (March 1970), pp. 10–26.

Chapter 21
Retirement Plans

Allen, Everett T., Jr., Joseph J. Melone, Jerry S. Rosenbloom, and Jack VanDerhei. *Pension Planning: Pension, Profit Sharing, and Other Deferred Compensation Plans,* 8th ed. Burr Ridge, IL: McGraw-Hill Companies, 1997.

Delsen, Lei and Genevieve Reday-Mulvey. "Gradual Retirement in the OECD Countries: Macro and Micro Issues and Policies (A Summary)." *The Four Pillars,* no. 18, Geneva: Geneva Association, 1995.

ERISA Industry Committee. *Getting the Job Done—A White Paper on Emerging Pension Issues.* Washington, DC: ERISA Industry Committee, 1996.

Kaster, Nicholas, et al. *1997 U.S. Master Pension Guide.* Chicago: CCH Incorporated, 1997.

McGill, Dan M., Kyle N. Brown, John J. Haley, and Sylvester J. Schreiber. *Fundamentals of Private Pensions,* 7th ed. Philadelphia: University of Pennsylvania Press, 1996.

Organization for Economic Development (OECD). *Private Pensions and Public Policy.* Paris: OECD, 1992.

Palmer, Bruce A. *RETIRE Project Report.* Atlanta, GA: Georgia State University/AON, 1997.

Samwick, Andrew A. *New Evidence on Pensions, Social Security, and the Time of Retirement.* Cambridge, MA: National Bureau of Economic Research, 1998.

Steinberg, Richard M., Ronald J. Murray, and Harold Dankner. *Pensions: A Financial Reporting and Compliance Guide,* 3rd ed. New York: Wiley, 1993.

Turner, John A. and Noriyasu Watanabe. *Private Pension Policies in Industrialized Countries: A Comparative Analysis.* Kalamazoo, MI: W. E. Upjohn Institute for Employment Research, 1995.

Chapter 22
Social Insurance

Chelius, A. "Liability for Industrial Accidents: A Comparison of Negligence and Strict Liability Systems." *Journal of Legal Studies* (June 1976), pp. 293–309.

Diamond, A. "A Framework for Social Security Analysis." *Journal of Public Economics* 8 (1977), pp. 275–298.

Holmlund, Bertil. "Unemployment Insurance in Theory and Practice." *Scandinavian Journal of Economics* 100, 1 (1998), pp. 113–141.

Kingson, Eric R. and James H. Schulz, eds. *Social Security in the 21st Century.* New York: Oxford University Press, 1997.

Medders, Lorilee. *The Value of Workers Compensation Insurance Incentives in Reducing Occupational Injuries and Illness in the Presence of Moral Hazard,* Chapter 3, Ph.D. Dissertation, Georgia State University, 1995.

Myers, Robert J. *Social Security.* Philadelphia: University of Pennsylvania Press, 1993.

Pestieau, P. A. "Social Protection and Private Insurance: Reassessing the Role of Public Sector versus Private Sector in Insurance (and Comments)." *The Geneva Papers on Risk and Insurance Theory* 19 (1994), pp. 81–100.

Quinn, Joseph F. "Social Security Reform: Marginal or Fundamental Change?" *Journal of the American Society of CLU & ChFC* LI, 4 (July 1997), pp. 44–53.

Reishauer, Robert D., et al., eds. *Medicare: Preparing for the Challenge of the 21st Century.* Washington, DC: National Academy of Social Insurance: Distributed worldwide by Brookings Institution, 1998.

Rejda, George E. *Social Insurance and Economic Security,* 5th ed. Englewood Cliffs, NJ: Prentice Hall, 1994.

Reno, Virginia P., Jerry L. Mashaw, and Bill Gradis, eds. *Disability: Challenges for Social Insurance, Health Care Financing, and Labor Market Policy.* Washington, DC: National Academy of Social Insurance, 1997.

Reno, Virginia P. and A. Price. "The Relationship between Retirement, Disability and Unemployment Insurance Programs." *Social Security Bulletin* (May 1985).

Report on the 1994–1996 Advisory Council on Social Security, Vols. I and II. Washington, DC: U.S. Government Printing Office, 1997.

Robertson, A. Haeworth. *Social Security: What Every Taxpayer Should Know.* Charlotte, NC: Retirement Policy Institute, 1992.

Ruser, A. "Worker's Compensation Insurance, Experience Rating and Occupational Injuries." *Rand Journal of Economics,* 1985.

U.S. Dept. of Health, Education, and Welfare, Social Security Administration, Division of Program Research. *Social Security Programs Throughout the World.* Social Security Administration. Government Printing Office, 1958 (updated periodically).

Wadhawan, Sadhev K. "Provident Funds Serve as Main Source of Old Age Benefits in Many Countries." *IBIS Review* (July 1995), pp. 18–20.

Chapter 23
Life Insurance Company Organization and Management

Adkins, Jason B. "The Policyholder Perspective on Mutual Holding Company Conversions." *Journal of Insurance Regulation* (Fall 1997), pp. 5–15.

Eakins, Stanley G., Kenneth Huggins, and Robert D. Land. *Operations of Life and Health Insurance Companies,* 2nd edition. Atlanta, GA: LOMA, 1992.

Fama, E. and M. Jensen. "Agency Problems and Residual Claims." *Journal of Law and Economics* (1983), pp. 327–349.

Fama, E. and M. Jensen. "Separation of Ownership and Control." *Journal of Law and Economics* (1983), pp. 301–325.

Fields, J. "Expense Preference Behavior in Mutual Life Insurers." *Journal of Financial Services Research* 1 (1988), pp. 113–129.

Forbes, Stephen W. "The Life Insurance Organization: Then and Now." *Resource* (June 1996), pp. 46–49.

Grace, Martin F. and S. Timme. "An Examination of Cost Economies in the United States Life Insurance Industry." *Journal of Risk and Insurance* 59 (1992), pp. 72–115.

Hemmings, Richard A. and Robert S. Seiler. "An Economically Viable Model for Insurers to Demutualize." *Best's Review, L/H* (November 1995), pp. 45–49.

Huggins, Kenneth and Robert D. Land. *Operations of Life and Health Insurance Companies*, 2nd ed. Atlanta, GA: LOMA, 1992.

Jensen, M. C. and W. H. Meckling. "Theory of the Firm: Managerial Behavior, Agency Costs and Ownership Structure." *Journal of Financial Economics* 3 (1976), pp. 305–360.

Lamm-Tennant, Joan and Laura Starks, "Stock vs. Mutual Ownership Structures: The Risk Implications." *Journal of Business* 66 (1993), pp. 29–46.

May, D. O. "Do Managerial Motives Influence Firm Risk Reduction Strategies?" *Journal of Finance* 50 (1995), pp. 1291–1308.

Mayers, D., Anil Shivdasani, and Clifford W. Smith, Jr. "Board Composition and Corporate Control: Evidence from the Insurance Industry." *Journal of Business* 70 (1997) pp. 33–62.

McNamara, Michael J. "An Examination of the Relative Efficiency of Mutual and Stock Life Insurance Companies." *Journal of Insurance Issues* 14, 1 (January 1991), pp. 13–30.

Pottier, Steven W. and David W. Sommer. "Agency Theory and Life Insurance Ownership Structure." *Journal of Risk and Insurance* 64, 3 (1997), pp. 529–543.

Ross, S. "The Economic Theory of Agency: The Principal's Problem." *American Economic Review* (1973), pp. 134–139.

Shapiro, Robert D. and Sidney A. LeBlanc. "The Merger of Mutual Life Insurance Companies: A Possible Answer to the Demands of the 1990's." *Journal of the American Society of CLU & ChFC* 46, 6 (November 1992), pp. 78–82.

Chapter 24
Marketing Life and Health Insurance

Barrese, J., H. Doerpinhaus, and J. Nelson. "Do Independent Agents Insurers Provide Superior Service? The Insurance Marketing Puzzle." *Journal of Risk and Insurance* 62 (1995), pp. 297–308.

Barrese, James and Jack M. Nelson. "Independent and Exclusive Agency Insurers: A Reexamination of the Cost Differential." *Journal of Risk and Insurance* 59, 3 (September 1992), pp. 375–397.

Bedore, James M. *Industry and Trade Summary: Insurance.* Washington, DC: U.S. International Trade Commission, 1991.

Bloomstein, H. J. "Structural Changes in Financial Markets: Overview of Trends and Prospects." Chap. 1 in *OECD Documents: The New Financial Landscape—Forces Shaping the Revolution in Banking, Risk Management and Capital Markets.* Paris: OECD, 1995.

Booth, Allen D. and Robert D. Shapiro. "The Product Development Program for Insurance Companies." *SOA Part 9L Study Note.* Shaumburg, IL: Society of Actuaries, 1982.

Browne, Mark J. and Kihong Kim. "An International Analysis of Life Insurance Demand." *Journal of Risk and Insurance* 60 (1993), pp. 616–634.

Cummins, David and Jack VanDerhei. "The Relative Efficiency of Property-Liability Insurance Distribution Systems." *Bell Journal* (Autumn 1979), pp. 709–719.

Cummins, David and J. Francois Outreville. "An International Analysis of Underwriting Cycles in Property-Liability Insurance." *Journal of Risk and Insurance* 54 (1987), pp. 246–262.

Damhoeri, Khairudin Bin. "A Cross-Country Analysis of the Determinants of Life and Nonlife Insurance Supply and Demand." Ph.D. dissertation, Georgia State University, 1992.

Gardner, L. M. and M. F. Grace, "X-Efficiency in the U.S. Life Insurance Industry." *Journal of Banking and Finance* 17 (1993), pp. 497–510.

Goodwin, Dennis W. *Life and Health Insurance Marketing.* Atlanta, GA: LOMA, 1989.

Kellner, S. and G. Mathewsen. "Entry Size Distribution, Scale and Scope Economies in the Life Insurance Industry." *Journal of Business* 56 (1983), pp. 23–44.

Koguchi, K. *Financial Conglomerates.* Paris: OECD, 1993.

Laporte, Paul W. "Compensation Breaks Loose—The Modernization of New York's Section 4228." *LIMRA's Marketfacts* (September/October 1997).

Saunders, A. and I. Walter. *Universal Banking in the United States: What Could We Gain? What Could We Lose?* New York: Oxford University Press, 1994.

Schroath, F. "Analysis of Foreign Market Entry Techniques for Multinational Insurers." Ph.D. dissertation, University of South Carolina, Columbia, 1987.

Truett, Dale B. and Lila J. Truett. "The Demand for Life Insurance in Mexico and the United States: A Comparative Study." *Journal of Risk and Insurance* 57 (1990), pp. 321–328.

United States Department of Commerce. "Insurance." In *US Industrial Outlook*, Annual.

Chapters 25 and 26
Life and Health Insurance Underwriting: I & II

American Academy of Actuaries. "Genetic Information and Voluntary Life Insurance." *Issue Brief,* American Academy of Actuaries (Spring 1998).

American Council of Life Insurance (ACLI). *The Need for Genetic Information in Risk Classification.* ACLI, 1994.

Anderson, R. M., ed. *Human Genetics: Uncertainties and the Financial Implications Ahead: A Discussion.* London: Royal Society, 1997.

Brackenridge, R. D. C. *Medical Selection of Life Risks: A Comprehensive Guide to Life Expectancy for Under-*

writers & Clinicians, 2nd ed. New York: Nature Press, 1985.

Case, D. "Arguments Against Risk Classification in Life Insurance." *Medical Section Report, Vol. XVIII* 1 (Spring 1994).

Lee, Kwangbong, Bruce A. Palmer, and Harold Skipper, Jr. "An Analysis of Life Insurer Retention Limits." *Journal of Risk and Insurance* 59 (June 1992).

Life Office Management Association. *Introduction to Reinsurance Guidebook.* Atlanta, GA: LOMA, 1998.

Life Office Management Association. *Underwriting in Life and Health Insurance Companies.* Richard Bailey, ed. Atlanta, GA: FLMI Insurance Education Program, LOMA, 1999.

Privacy Protection Study Commission. *Personal Privacy in an Information Society.* Privacy Protection Study Commission, Washington, DC: G. P. O. 1977.

R&R Newkirk. *An Introduction to Life Underwriting,* 10th ed. Chicago: Dearborn-R&R Newkirk, 1991.

Sankey, Keith. *Guide to Life Assurance Underwriting,* 3rd ed. London: Buckley Press, 1991.

Stanford, Miller. *Health Insurance Underwriting.* New York: Eastern Underwriting Company, 1962.

Chapter 27
Life and Health Insurance Actuarial Principles

Batten, Robert W. *Mortality Table Construction.* Englewood Cliffs, NJ: Prentice-Hall, Inc., 1978.

Batten, Robert W. *Life Contingencies: A Guide for the Actuarial Student.* Englewood Cliffs, NJ: Prentice Hall, 1990.

Department of the Treasury. *Actuarial Values, Alpha Volume: Remainder, Income, and Annuity Factors for One for Use in Income, Estate, and Gift Tax Purposes Including Valuation of Pooled Income Fund Remainder Interests.* Dept. of Treasury, IRS, U.S. G.P.O., 1989.

De Vylder, F. Etienne. *Life Insurance Theory: Actuarial Perspectives.* Boston: Kluwer Academic Publishers, 1997.

Habert, Steven and Trevor A. Sibbett, eds. *History of Actuarial Science.* London: William Pickering, 1995.

Life Insurance Marketing and Research Association (LIMRA). *Agent Service Tables Handbook: Actuarial Calculations for Marketing.* Hartford, CT: LIMRA, 1981.

Chapter 28
Net Premiums

Bowers, N. L. et al. *Actuarial Mathematics,* 2nd ed. Chicago: Society of Actuaries, 1997. (chapter 6, "Net Premiums")

Cooper, Robert E. "The Level Premium Concept: A Closer Look." *The Journal of the American Society of Chartered Life Underwriters* 30 (July 1976), pp. 24–32.

Shapiro, Robert D. "The Process of Premium Formulation." *SOA Part 7 Study Note,* Schaumburg, IL: Society of Actuaries, 1982.

Chapter 29
Life Insurance Reserves and Cash Values

A. M. Best, Inc. *Best's Illustrations of Net Costs, Cash Values, Premium Rates, Policy Conditions of Most Legal Reserve Life Insurance Companies Operating in the United States.* New York: A. M. Best, annual.

Bowers, N. L. et al. *Actuarial Mathematics,* 2nd ed. Chicago: Society of Actuaries, 1997.

Conant, Susan, Nicholas L. Desoutter, Dani L. Long, and Robert MacGrogan. *Managing for Solvency and Profitability in Life and Health Insurance Companies.* Atlanta, GA: LOMA, 1996.

Lau, Joseph H. "A Comparison of Canadian and U.S. Statutory Reserve Methodologies." *Contingencies* (November/December 1997).

Tullis, Mark A. and Phillip K. Polkingham. *Valuation of Life Insurance Liabilities,* 2nd ed. Winstead, CT: ACTEX Publications, 1992.

Wilcox, Robert E. and Norman E. Hell. "Life and Health Company Valuation: Cleaning the Slate." *Contingencies* (November/December 1997).

Chapter 30
Gross-Premium Rate Structures and Nonguaranteed Policy Elements

A. M. Best, Inc. *Best's Illustrations of Net Costs, Cash Values, Premium Rates, Policy Conditions of Most Legal Reserve Life Insurance Companies Operating in the United States.* New York: A. M. Best, Annual.

Belth, Joseph M. "Distribution of Surplus to Individual Life Insurance Policy Owners." *Journal of Risk and Insurance* 45 (March 1978), pp. 7–26.

Eakins, Stanley G., Kenneth Huggins, and Robert D. Land. *Operations of Life and Health Insurance Companies,* 2nd ed. Atlanta, GA: LOMA, 1992.

Chapter 31
The Pricing of Health Insurance

Bisbee, Gerald E. Jr., and Robert A. Vraciu, eds. *Managing the Finances of Health Care Organizations.* Ann Arbor, MI: Health Administration Press, 1980.

Dorn, Lowell M. "New York Life Morbidity Experience under Individual and Family Medical Policies." *Transactions of the Society of Actuaries, Vol. 15.* Chicago: University of Chicago Press, 1963.

Eakins, Stanley G., Kenneth Huggins, and Robert D. Land. *Operations of Life and Health Insurance Companies,* 2nd ed. LOMA, 1992.

Miller, Morton D. "Gross Premiums for Individual and Family Major Medical Expense Insurance." *Transactions of the Society of Actuaries, Vol. 7.* Chicago: University of Chicago Press, 1955.

Chapters 32 and 33
Life Insurer Financial Management: I and II

A. M. Best, Inc. *1997 Best's Aggregates and Averages,* Oldwick, NJ: A. M. Best.

Allen, Franklin and Anthony M. Santomero. "The Theory of Financial Risk Intermediation." *The Journal of Banking & Finance* 21 (1998), pp. 1461–1485.

Brealey, Richard A. and Stewart C. Myers. *Principles of Corporate Finance,* 5th ed. New York: McGraw-Hill, Inc., 1996.

Carson, James M. and Robert E. Hoyt. "An Econometric Analysis of the Demand for Life Insurance Policy Loans." *Journal of Risk and Insurance* 59 (June 1992), pp. 239–251.

Casualty Actuarial Society. *Fundamentals of Casualty Actuarial Science.* Casualty Actuarial Society, chapter 8, "Investment Issues in Property-Liability Insurance." pp. 485–509.

Collier, P., and C. Mayer. "Financial Liberalization, Financial Systems and Economic Growth." *Oxford Review of Economic Policy* 5, 4 (Winter 1989), pp. 1–12.

Cummins, J. D. and Elizabeth Grace. "Tax Management and Investment Strategies of Property-Liability Insurers." *Journal of Banking and Finance* 18 (1994), pp. 43–72.

Forbes, Stephen W. *Managing a Life Insurance Company in a High-Risk Environment.* Atlanta, GA: LOMA, 1997.

Harris, S. and J. Katz. "Organizational Performance and Information Technology Investment Intensity in the Insurance Industry." *Organization Science* 2 (1991), pp. 263–295.

Hull, John C. *Options, Futures, and Other Derivative Securities,* 3rd ed. Englewood Cliffs, NJ: Prentice Hall, 1996.

Kellner, S. and G. Mathewsen. "Entry Size Distribution, Scale and Scope Economies in the Life Insurance Industry." *Journal of Business* 56 (1983), pp. 23–44.

Keown, A. J., J. W. Petty, D. F. Scott, Jr. and J. D. Martin. *Foundations of Finance.* Upper Saddle River, NJ: Prentice-Hall, 1998.

Marshall, John F. and Vipul K. Bansal. *Financial Engineering: A Complete Guide to Financial Innovation.* New York: Allyn & Bacon, 1992.

Marshall, John F. and Kenneth R. Kapner. *Understanding Swap Finance.* Cincinnati, OH: South-Western Publishing, 1990.

Mishkin, Frederic S. *Financial Markets and Institutions.* New York: Addison Wesley, Inc., 1998.

Santomero, Anthony M. and David F. Babbel. *Financial Markets, Instruments, and Institutions.* Chicago: Irwin, Inc., 1997.

Santomero, Anthony M. and David F. Babbel. "Financial Risk Management by Insurers: An Analysis of the Process." *Journal of Risk and Insurance* 64, 2 (1997), pp. 233–234.

Saunders, Anthony. *Financial Institutions Management,* 2nd ed. Chicago: Irwin. 1997.

Stoll, Hans R. and Robert E. Whalley. *Futures and Options Theory and Applications.* Cincinnati, OH: South-Western Publishing, 1993.

Weiss, Mary. "Efficiency in the Property-Liability Insurance Industry." *Journal of Risk and Insurance* 58 (1991), pp. 452–479.

Yuengert, A. "The Measurement of Efficiency in Life Insurance: Estimates of a Mixed Normal-Gamma Error Model." *Journal of Banking and Finance* 17 (1993), pp. 483–496.

Chapter 34
Life Insurer Financial Reporting

American Institute of Certified Public Accountants. *Accounting by Stock Life Insurance Companies for Annuities, Universal Life Insurance, and Related Products and Accounting for Non-Guaranteed-Premium Contracts.* Prepared by the Insurance Companies Committee and Nonguaranteed-Premium Products Task Force. New York: American Institute of Certified Public Accountants, 1984.

American Institute of Certified Public Accountants. *Checklists and Illustrative Financial Statements for Stock Life Insurance Companies.* New York: American Institute of Certified Public Accountants, 1990.

Ernst & Whinney. *Accounting for Life Insurance and Annuity Products: Understanding and Implementing FASB Statement no. 97.* Ernst & Whinney, 1988.

Ernst & Whinney. *Financial Reporting Trends: Life Insurance.* Ernst & Whinney, Annual.

Gardner, Lisa M. "An Analysis of Cost Inefficiencies in Life Insurance Companies: Sources and Measurements." Ph.D. Dissertation, Georgia State University, 1992.

Insurance Accounting and Systems Association (IASA). *Life Insurance Accounting,* 3rd ed. IASA, 1994.

Klynveid Peat Marwick Goerdeler (KPMG). *Insurance Company Financial Reporting Worldwide,* 2nd ed. Summerhouse Communications, 1991.

Klynveid Peat Marwick Goerdeler (KPMG). *Life Insurance, Statutory Accounting Principles for the Life Insurance Industry.* KPMG, 1987.

Mulligan, Elizabeth A. and Gene Stone. *Accounting and Financial Reporting in Life and Health Insurance Companies.* Atlanta, GA: FLMI Insurance Education Program, Life Management Institute LOMA, 1997.

Saunders, Arthur R. *Life Insurance Company Financial Statements: Keys to Successful Reporting.* Chicago: Society of Actuaries, 1986.

Upton, Wayne S., Jr. *A Primer on Accounting Models for Long-Duration Life Insurance Contracts Under U.S. GAAP.* Norwalk, CT: Financial Accounting Standards Board of the Financial Accounting Foundation, 1996.

Chapter 35
Regulation and Taxation of Life and Health Insurance

Aaron, Henry J. *The Peculiar Problem of Taxing Life Insurance Companies: A Staff Paper.* Washington, DC: Brookings Institution, 1983.

Angerer, August. "Insurance Supervision in OECD Member Countries." In *Policy Issues in Insurance.* Paris: OECD, 1993.

BarNiv, Ran and Robert Hershbarger. "Classifying Financial Distress in the Life Insurance Industry." *Journal of Risk and Insurance* 57 (1990), pp. 110–136.

BarNiv, Ran and James B. McDonald. "Identifying Financial Distress in the Insurance Industry: A Synthesis of Methodological and Empirical Issues." *Journal of Risk and Insurance* 59 (1992), pp. 543–573.

Bergquist, Wayne E., Nicholas Bauer, and Douglas N. Hertz. "Principles of Taxation." *SOA-Course 200 Study Note,* Schaumburg, IL: Society of Actuaries, 1995.

Best's Insolvency Study Life/Health Insurers, 1976–1991, Executive Summary and Recommendations, *Best's Insurance Management Reports* (July 1992).

Brown, Mark, J. and Robert E. Hoyt. "Economic and Market Predictors of Insolvencies in the Property-Liability Insurance Industry." *Journal of Risk and Insurance* 62 (1995), pp. 309–327.

Carson, James M. and Robert E. Hoyt. "Life Insurer Financial Distress: Classification Models and Empirical Evidence." *Journal of Risk and Insurance* 62 (1995), pp. 764–775.

Dickinson, G. M. and E. Dinenis. "Investment Regulation of Insurance Companies across the OECD." In *Policy Issues in Insurance: Investment, Taxation, Insolvency.* Paris: OECD, 1996.

Finsinger, Jorg and Mark V. Pauly, eds. *The Economics of Insurance Regulation: A Cross-National Study.* London: The Macmillan Press, 1986.

Geehan, Randall. "Economies of Scale in Insurance: Implications for Regulation." In *The Insurance Industry in Economic Development.* Bernard Wasow and Raymond D. Hill, eds. New York: New York University Press, 1986.

Hamilton, Karen L. *The Changing Nature of Insurance Regulation,* 2nd ed. Malvern, PA: Insurance Institute of America, 1996.

Harman, William B. "The Structure of Life Insurance Company Taxation: The New Pattern under the 1984 Act." Parts I and II, *Journal of the American Society of CLU* 39 (March 1985) and (May 1985).

Harrington, Scott E. "Policyholders Runs, Life Insurance Company Failures, and Insurance Solvency Regulation." *Regulation: The Cato Review of Business and Government* 15, 2 (Spring 1992), pp. 27–37.

Jannott, Edgar. "Effects of the Deregulation of Supervision on the Selling of Insurance." *Geneva Papers on Risk and Insurance* 20 (January 1995), pp. 7–15.

Jump, G. V. "Tax Incentives to Promote Personal Savings: Recent Canadian Experience." In *Saving and Government Policy.* Conference Series no. 25, Federal Reserve Bank of Boston, 1982.

Klein, Robert W. "Insurance Regulation in Transition." *Journal of Risk and Insurance* 62, 3 (September 1995), pp. 363–404.

Kotlikoff, L. J. "National Savings and Economic Policy: The Efficacy of Investment and Savings Incentives." *American Economic Review* 73, 2 (1983), pp. 82–87.

Lin, Shun-Lan. "Financial Distress Classification in the Life Insurance Industry." *Journal of Insurance Regulation* 14 (1996), pp. 314–342.

Meier, Kenneth J. *The Political Economy of Regulation: The Case of Insurance.* Albany, NY: State University of New York Press, 1988.

Nathan, Lew H. *Life and Health Guaranty Associations and Insurer Solvency.* Atlanta, GA: LOMA, 1990.

Peltzman, Sam. "Toward a More General Theory of Regulation." *Journal of Law and Economics* 19, 2 (1976), pp. 211–240.

Skipper, Harold D., Jr. "Insurer Solvency Regulation in the United States." In *Policy Issues in Insurance.* Paris: OECD, 1993.

Skipper, Harold D., Jr. "International Trade in Insurance." In *International Financial Markets: Harmonization versus Competition.* Clause E. Barfield, ed. Washington, DC: AEI Press, 1996.

Skipper, Harold D., Jr. "Protectionism in the Provision of International Insurance Services." *Journal of Risk Management and Insurance* 54 (1987), pp. 55–85.

Skipper, Harold D., Jr. "State Taxation of Insurance Companies: Time for a Change." *Journal of Insurance Regulation* 6 (1987), pp. 121–142.

Skipper, Harold D., Jr. "The Taxation of Life Insurance Products in OECD Countries." In *Policy Issues in Insur-*

ance: Investment, Taxation and Insolvency. Paris: OECD, 1996.

Stigler, George J. "The Theory of Economic Regulation." *Bell Journal of Economics* (Spring 1971).

Tennyson, Sharon. "The Effect of Rate Regulation on Underwriting Cycles." *CPCU Journal* 44 (1991), pp. 33–35.

U.S. General Accounting Office. *Insurance Regulation: The Financial Regulation Standards and Accreditation Program of the National Association of Insurance Commissioners,* GAO/T-GGD-92-27 (1992).

U.S. General Accounting Office. *Insurance Regulation: The Insurance Regulatory Information System Needs Improvement.* GAO/GGD-91-20 (November 1990).

Weiss, Mary A. "A Multivariate Analysis of Loss Reserving Estimates in Property-Liability Insurers." *Journal of Risk and Insurance* 52 (1985), pp. 199–221.

Wheaton, William. "The Impact of State Taxation on Life Insurance Company Growth." *National Tax Journal* (March 1986), pp. 85–95.

Wright, Kenneth M. "The Life Insurance Industry in the United States: An Analysis of Economic and Regulatory Issues." *Working Papers,* The World Bank, 1992.

Glossary

10-payment whole life Whole life insurance with level premiums payable for 10 years.

15-payment whole life Whole life insurance with level premiums payable for 15 years.

20-payment whole life Whole life insurance with level premiums payable for 20 years.

401(k) plan A profit-sharing plan established by an employer in which up to three types of contributions are permitted: employer contributions, employee contributions from after-tax income, and employee salary reduction (elective) contributions. Neither employer nor elective contributions are included in the employee's taxable income.

403(b) annuity A tax-deferred annuity in which an employer sets aside a portion of the money that would otherwise be part of an employee's pay. These funds eventually will be subject to tax, but not until the money with accumulated interest is actually received, either as a cash withdrawal or as annuity payments.

5-by-5 power In estate planning, a situation in which the surviving spouse is given the right to take the greater of $5,000 or 5 percent of the trust corpus per year.

absolute assignment The complete transfer by the existing policyowner of all of his or her rights in the policy to another person.

absolute income hypothesis One of the theories of consumption stating that the larger a person's income, the smaller the proportion devoted to consumption (and the larger the proportion devoted to saving).

Accelerated Benefits Guideline for Life Insurance Regulation that prospective buyers of life coverage must be given numerical illustrations that reflect the effects of an accelerated payout on the policy's death benefit, cash values, premium, and policy loans.

accelerated death benefit Provisions or riders involving the payment of all or a portion of a life insurance policy's face amount prior to the insured's death because of some specified, adverse medical condition of the insured (also referred to as *living insurance*).

accident and health insurance See *health insurance.*

accident and sickness insurance See *health insurance.*

accidental bodily injury A clause stating that a bodily injury must meet one test to be a covered loss: The result (the injury itself) must be unforeseen or unexpected. (Contrast with *accidental means.*)

accidental death benefit Provides that double (or other multiple) of the face amount is payable if the insured dies as a result of an accident (also known as a *double indemnity*).

accidental means A clause stating that a bodily injury must meet two tests to be a covered loss: Both the cause of the injury and the result (the injury itself) must be unforeseen or unexpected. (Contrast with *accidental bodily injury.*)

accrued benefit See *benefit-allocation method.*

accrual rate or aggregate-cost ratio Derived by dividing the present value of future payroll into the excess of the present value of future estimated benefits over plan assets.

accumulation period The time during which annuity fund values accumulate, commonly prior to age 65.

accumulation period provision Defines the period of time during which incurred medical care expenses may be accumulated to satisfy the deductible.

active life fund Funds accumulated on behalf of pension plan participants who have not yet retired.

activities of daily living (ADL) Activities such as eating, bathing, dressing, toileting, continence, transferring, and taking medicine.

actual authority That granted to an agent by the principal in specific language or terms (also called express authority).

actuarial cost method A particular technique for establishing the amount and incidence of the annual contributions for funding pension plan benefits.

actuarial equity Charging proposed insureds rates that reflect their expected loss potentials with no planned subsidy between rate classes.

actuarial opinion Statement by an appointed actuary as to whether the reserves and related actuarial items are computed appropriately, are based on assumptions that satisfy contractual provisions, are consistent with prior reported amounts, and comply with applicable laws of the state.

actuarial risk The risk that arises from an insurer developing funds via the issuance of insurance policies.

actuarially fair price The expected value of benefit payments. The contribution of an insured to the pool that matches precisely the loss potential that he or she transfers to the pool.

actuaries Individuals who determine insurance premiums and reserves using their best estimates of future losses and expenses, with an eye toward competitiveness.

additional or guaranteed purchase option See *guaranteed insurability option (GIO)*.

add-to-cash-value option A dividend option under which the dividend can be applied to increase the policy cash value without increasing the insurance protection.

adhesion A contract whose terms and provisions are fixed by one party and, with minor exceptions, must be accepted or rejected *en totale* by the other party.

adjustable life insurance A level-premium, level-death benefit life insurance policy that can assume the form of any traditional term or whole life policy (within certain guidelines) and that offers the policyowner the ability, within limits, to change the policy plan, premium payment, and face amount.

adjusted community rating A method by which federally qualified HMOs can set their rates, which provides greater flexibility.

adjusted gross estate The gross estate less all allowable deductions except bequests to the surviving spouse and to charities.

adjusted premium The level premium necessary to pay the benefits guaranteed by the policy (the net level premium) *plus* the level equivalent of a defined special first-year expense allowance.

adjusted premium method A method of calculating cash values in which the premium is adjusted to produce minimum surrender values.

adjustment provision Permits the policyowner of an adjustable life insurance policy to change the plan by requesting the insurer to change the policy configuration.

administrative services only (ASO) Arrangement in which the employer purchases specific administrative services from an insurance company or from an independent third-party administrator.

administrator A person appointed to administer a decedent's estate.

admitted assets Assets that may be included in determining an insurer's statutory solvency.

adult day care Facilities where individuals receive assistance with activities of daily living and benefit from socialization.

adverse selection problem An asymmetric information problem in which the customer knows more than the seller about the customer's situation.

adverse selection spiral The tendency of insureds who are charged premiums sufficiently greater than the expected value of their losses to withdraw from the insurance pool, thereby precipitating premium increases for the remaining insureds, from among whom another round of withdrawals occurs, leading to still higher premiums, and further withdrawals. Can ultimately lead to the collapse of the insurance pool.

Age Discrimination in Employment Act U.S. federal law enacted in 1967 and amended in 1986 that prohibits age discrimination and limits mandatory retirement for most U.S. workers.

age of majority The minimum age at which a person can enter into contracts (age 18 in the United States).

agency building distribution Strategy under which insurers recruit, train, finance, house, and supervise their agents.

agency manager An employee of an insurer who heads a branch office.

agent A person who represents another.

aggregate level-cost recovery methods Analogous to individual level-cost methods, except for the calculation of costs and contributions on a collective rather than an individual basis. As with individual level-cost methods, supplemental liability for past service may or may not be determined separately.

aggregate mortality table Table including mortality data from both select and ultimate experience.

aleatory Involving the element of chance.

alien insurer In U.S. terminology, an insurer domiciled in another country.

all-cause deductible All expenses incurred are accumulated to satisfy the deductible regardless of the number of illnesses or accidents giving rise to the expenses.

alternate valuation date The value of an estate six months after death, if a lower estate value would result (e.g., because of investment losses).

alternative minimum tax A tax intended to ensure that no taxpayer with substantial economic income avoids tax liability.

ambulatory instrument An instrument such as a will that does not take effect until the death of the testator.

Americans with Disabilities Act Act passed in 1990 that prohibits a person with a disability, who does not pose increased risks, from being denied coverage or being subjected to different terms based on the disability alone.

analytical phase Review period required of insurers with four or more ratios outside of a prescribed "usual range" from the statistical phase of the NAIC's IRIS.

annual renewable term (ART) Term policies with level death benefits and premiums increasing annually.

annualized first-year commission A commission payment based on all or most of the year's premium.

annuitant The insured person to whom an annuity payment is made.

annuity A contract that promises to pay the insured a periodic (usually monthly) payment.

annuity certain A series of payments or receipts of a certain amount for a specified time period.

annuity due When the annuity payments are assumed to be made at the *beginning* of each period.

any gainful occupation A definition of disability stipulating that insureds are considered totally disabled only when they cannot perform the major duties of any gainful occupation for which they are reasonably suited because of education, training, or experience.

apparent authority That which a third person believes the agent possesses because of circumstances made possible by the principal and upon which the third party is justified in relying (also known as *perceived authority*).

applicant The person who applies for the insurance policy.

appointed actuary Individual responsible for filing an actuarial opinion about a company.

approval conditional premium receipt Provides that insurance will be effective only after the application has been approved by the company.

arbitrage pricing theory (APT) A theory under which a security's price is explained by multiple economic factors rather than a single systematic risk factor.

assessment basis Wherein members are assessed as needed to provide the promised benefit payments.

asset depreciation (C-1) risk The risk of losses in bonds, mortgages, stocks, real estate, and other investments through either default on payment of interest or principal or through loss of market value.

asset share Each year's accumulated fund, divided by the number of surviving and persisting insureds.

asset-share calculation A simulation of the anticipated operating experience for a block of policies using the best estimates for each future policy year.

assignment The transfer of ownership rights, of life insurance policies or other property, from one person to another.

assisted-living facilities Facilities that provide supervision, assistance, and limited health services to relatively healthy senior citizens.

assumed interest rate (AIR) The interest rate that, if earned uniformly throughout the period, would not lead to a reduction in benefit payments or cash values (also known as *target return*).

assumption reinsurance Life reinsurance undertaken to transfer all or a specific portion of a company's existing liabilities to a reinsuring company.

asymmetric information problems When one party to a transaction has relevant information that the other does not have.

attained-age method Method of conversion of term life insurance involving the issuance of a whole life or other cash-value policy at the insured's attained age.

automatic premium loan (APL) Provides that, if a premium is unpaid at the end of the grace period, and if the policy has a sufficient net cash value, the amount of the premium due will be advanced automatically as a loan against the policy.

automatic (treaty) reinsurance Where the direct-writing company *must* transfer an amount in excess of its retention of each applicable insurance policy to the reinsuring company immediately upon payment of premium and the issuance of the policy, and the reinsurer *must* accept the transfer that falls within the scope of the agreement.

average earning clause Provides that, if the total benefits under all valid disability income policies exceed the average monthly earnings of the insured over the previous two years or his or her current monthly earnings, whichever is greater, then the company will pay only such a portion of the amount of benefit due as the amount of such earnings bears to the total benefits under all such policies.

average indexed monthly earnings Method used in the U.S. Social Security system designed to ensure that monthly cash benefits reflect changes in wage levels over the worker's lifetime so that the benefits paid will have a relatively constant relationship to the worker's earnings before retirement, disability, or death.

average or portfolio rate The net rate of interest earned on the insurer's total investment portfolio.

aviation exclusion Excludes coverage if the insured dies in an aviation accident.

backdating The practice by which an insurer calculates premiums under the policy based on an age earlier than the proposed insured's current age.

bailout provisions Provide that if the credited interest rate falls below a certain level, the policyowner may surrender the policy and incur no surrender charge.

band system A quantity discount system in which a number of "size bands," often three to five, are established with different premium rates applying within each band.

bank trust A type of IRA whereby contributions usually are invested in one or more of a bank's interest-bearing instruments or, in some cases, self-directed accounts.

bankruptcy The application of bankruptcy laws to a debtor who may not be insolvent. One becomes bankrupt when one comes under the protection of the bankruptcy laws.

basic illustration Part of NAIC illustration regulation to ensure that illustrations do not mislead purchasers of life insurance that requires inclusion of a table of values based on the insurer's current pricing (experience) factors.

basic mortality table Table that reflects the actual mortality experience of the population from which it was drawn.

basket or leeway clauses Clauses that permit a certain percentage of assets to be invested in any type of asset.

beneficiary The person for whose benefit a trust property is held or to whom the proceeds of a life insurance policy are paid.

beneficiary clause Permits the policyowner to have policy death proceeds distributed to whomever and in whatever form he or she wishes.

benefit allocation cost Methods used with pensions that allocate benefits and then derive the actuarial present value of benefits.

benefit-allocation method Method that sets aside, in one sum, an amount needed to fund one unit of benefit.

benefit period The period following the satisfaction of the deductible during which benefits are paid.

beta Measurement of the sensitivity of a security's return to the market return.

binding premium receipt Provides insurance that is effective from the date the receipt is given.

block of policies All policies issued by the insurer under the same schedules of rates and values and on the same policy form.

Blue Cross Nonprofit hospital expense prepayment plans.

Blue Shield Nonprofit organizations offering prepayment coverage for surgical and medical services performed by a physician.

bond dedication An asset/liability risk-reduction technique that is designed to control the anticipated cash flow properties of a portfolio servicing prescribed liability cash flows.

bonuses The distributable surplus paid to policyowners (also known as *dividends*).

branch office system Office system in which an insurer establishes agencies in various locations, each headed by an agency manager.

broker The legal representative of the insurance purchaser. In the United States, brokers who sell to individuals are considered legally to be agents and, therefore, they represent the insurer.

brokerage general agent An independent representative who serves the same function as a brokerage supervisor.

brokerage supervisor The insurance company employee through whom brokerage insurers gain access to agents.

bullet GIC Guaranteed investment contract structured to accept a single-sum deposit (generally $100,000 or more) for a specified period of time (usually three to seven years).

Buyer's Guide Booklet containing an explanation of life insurance products and how to shop for them that regulators require a life insurance company to provide a prospective buyer.

buy-term-and-invest-the-difference (BTID) Where an individual with sufficient funds to purchase cash-value life insurance purchases a term policy carrying a lower premium than an equivalent amount of cash-value life insurance. The difference between the higher-premium cash-value policy and the lower-premium term policy is invested in a mutual fund, a savings account, an annuity, or other investment media.

bypass trust A trust that holds property not left to the surviving spouse (also known as *credit shelter trust, nonmarital trust,* and *residuary trust*).

cafeteria plan Allows participating employees to select among an array of benefits using a predetermined allowance of employer funds.

call option The right to buy assets within a limited time period at a stipulated price.

capital asset pricing model (CAPM) Model that equates the expected return of a security to the risk-free rate plus a risk premium for the security's systematic risk.

capital liquidation approach Assumes that both principal (capital) and interest are liquidated over the relevant time period to provide the desired income.

capital retention approach Assumes that the desired income is provided only from the investment earnings on the principal and that no part of the desired income is from capital.

capital stock and surplus The excess of a company's assets over its liabilities.

capitation A method by which providers are paid for services on a per-member, per-month basis; a common form of prepayment.

captive agent An agent who sells exclusively for one company (also known as *exclusive* or *tied agents*).

career agent Commissioned life insurance agent who primarily sells one company's products.

carry-over provision A clause that allows expenses incurred in the last three months of a calendar year (which are applied toward satisfaction of the deductible for that year) to be carried over to be used in satisfying the deductible for the next calendar year.

carve-out plans Health care programs managed separately from an employer's general health care plan for retired employees.

case management programs Involve professionals assessing a case, taking into account the patient's needs and treatment plan, managing the use of available resources, and evaluating the work environment situation.

cash accumulation method Cost comparison method that compares two plans that are set at equal levels in which annual premium differences are accumulated at some assumed interest rate, and one simply observes the cash-value/side-fund differences over time in an effort to draw meaningful cost-based conclusions.

cash balance plan A hybrid form of defined-benefit plan that combines some of the features of defined-benefit plans with some features of defined-contribution plans.

cash flow testing A process of projecting and comparing, as of a given valuation date, the timing and amount of asset and liability cash flows after the valuation date.

cash matching Involves the construction of a portfolio whose interest and principal payments exactly match a set of nominal liabilities.

cash refund annuity Pays a lump-sum amount to the beneficiary of the difference, if any, between the purchase price of the annuity and the simple sum of the installment payments made prior to the annuitant's death.

cash surrender value The amount of prefunded mortality charges that is available to a terminating policyowner.

cash-value accumulation test Test applying mainly to traditional cash-value policies requiring that the cash surrender value not at any time exceed the net single premium required to fund future contract benefits.

cash-value corridor requirement Under U.S. tax law applicable to life insurance policies, fulfilled if the policy's death benefit at all times is at least equal to certain percentage multiples of the cash value.

cash-value option Permits the dividend to accumulate as additional cash value but involves no additional pure insurance protection.

catastrophic illness coverage Provides for accelerated death benefit payments on approximately the same terms and conditions as terminal illness coverage, except that the insured must have been diagnosed as having one of several listed catastrophic illnesses.

catastrophic reinsurance Contract that covers multiple insured losses arising from a single accident or occurrence.

caveat emptor "Let the buyer beware."

certificate of annuity (COA) Provides for a fixed, guaranteed interest rate for a set period of time, typically 3 to 10 years.

change of insured provision Clause permitting a change of insureds under the policy.

change of plan provision Clause granting the policyowner the right to change the policy form.

charitable remainder annuity trust (CRAT) A trust that pays a fixed amount, which does not change during the life of the trust, to the income beneficiary at least annually.

charitable remainder trust (CRT) A living, irrevocable, tax-exempt trust in which the donor contributes property to the trust, reserving to himself or herself (or someone else) an income stream from the trust, with the residual trust corpus ultimately passing to a charity.

charitable remainder unitrust (CRUT) A trust that pays a fixed percentage of the fair market value of its assets to the income beneficiary at least annually. Trust assets are revalued each year, so the income will vary each year.

child's benefit The benefit under the U.S. Social Security system to which each unmarried child under 18 (or under 19 if the child is attending a primary or secondary educational institution on a full-time basis) or disabled before age 22 may be entitled: equal to 50 percent of the worker's PIA.

choses in action Ownership rights evidenced by something tangible but which itself does not have value, such as an insurance policy.

choses in possession Ownership of tangible objects (e.g., jewels).

churning The systematic and indiscriminate replacement of existing insurance for purposes of securing new, higher commissions.

claim fluctuation reserve See *premium stabilization reserve.*

claim reserves and liabilities Those amounts necessary to cover payments on claims already incurred but not yet paid.

claims expenses Claim litigation costs and appropriate amounts for salaries, rent, utilities, and so on that are attributable to the claim department.

claims personnel Persons who negotiate and settle claims.

classification The process of assigning a proposed insured to a group of insureds of approximately the same expected loss probabilities as the proposed.

close corporation See *closely held corporation.*

closed corporation See *closely held corporation.*

closely held businesses Businesses whose ownership interests have no ready market. Characterized by unity of ownership and management, small number of owners, and ownership interest not readily marketable.

closely held corporation A closely held business in a corporate form.

codicil An alteration to a will that changes the part of the will with which it is inconsistent.

cognitive impairment Clause that permits benefit payments with respect to those who cannot safely perform essential ADLs.

coinsurance The percentage of covered expenses paid by a medical expense plan: A plan with 80 percent coinsurance will pay 80 percent of covered expenses while a person who receives benefits under the plan must pay the remaining 20 percent.

coinsurance plan Plan under which the reinsurer assumes a proportionate share of the risk according to the terms that govern the original policy.

collateral assignment A temporary transfer of only some policy ownership rights to another person.

collateral assignment system A classical split-dollar insurance plan in which the insured employee applies for and owns the policy.

collateralized mortgage obligation A type of bond that is secured by a pool of mortgages.

combination See *home service distribution system.*

commingling Holding policyowners' money in an account with other funds of the insurer.

commissioners' reserve valuation method Method of modifying full net-level terminal reserves, which makes the 20-payment whole life policy the maximum basis on which deferred reserve funding is permitted.

community property A form of joint ownership stating that property acquired during marriage is the property of the marriage community.

community rating One method by which federally qualified HMOs must set their rates in which all groups are priced using the same per-member, per-month (PMPM) rates.

community rating by class One method by which federally qualified HMOs must set their rates that allows for variations in the community rating for a given group based on the age, gender, and other acceptable risk factors of the group.

commutative An exchange involving approximately equivalent value between the parties.

comparative interest rate The rate of return that must be earned on a hypothetical side fund in a buy-term-and-invest-the-difference plan, so that the value of the side fund will exactly equal the illustrated cash surrender value of the higher-premium policy at a designated point in time.

compound interest Interest that is not distributed but is reinvested to earn additional funds.

compound probability The chance that two independent events will occur. It is the product of the probabilities that the events, taken separately, will occur.

compound reversionary bonus Similar to the simple reversionary bonus except that the percentage addition is of the sum assured and previously declared bonuses.

comprehensive major medical expense insurance Covers virtually all types of medical care services and supplies.

comprehensive medical insurance Plans providing broad coverage and significant protection from large, unpredictable medical care expenses.

concealment The withholding of information.

concurrent review An ongoing monitoring of a patient's hospital stay to determine whether the patient is in need of continuing inpatient treatment.

conditional Characteristic of insurance contracts in which the insurer's obligation to pay a claim depends on the performance of certain acts, such as payment of premiums and furnishing proof of loss.

conditionally renewable A contract that gives the insured a limited right to renew the policy to age 65, or some later age, by timely payment of the premium.

conflict of interest When a financial institution offers multiple financial services and promotes proprietary products through coercion or other power for the organization's benefit over the best interest of the customer.

consanguinity A blood relationship.

conservation order A court order directing the insurance regulator to act as receiver for the conservation of assets of a foreign or alien insurance company within the regulator's jurisdiction.

consideration clause Summarizes the factors that led the insurer to issue the policy and represents the insured's part of the insurance agreement.

Consolidated Omnibus Budget Reconciliation Acts of 1985, 1986, and 1990 (COBRA) Require that group health plans allow employees and certain beneficiaries to elect to have their current health insurance coverage extended, at group rates, for up to 36 months following a qualifying event that results in the loss of coverage.

constant returns to scale When the firm is at a certain size and further growth neither adds to nor detracts from efficiency.

constructively received Income made available to the employee or if he or she could have taken it but chose not to.

consumer report Under the U.S. Fair Credit Reporting Act, a written, oral, or other communication of any information by a consumer reporting agency that has a bearing on the consumer's creditworthiness, credit standing, credit capacity, character, general reputation, personal characteristics, or mode of living, and which is used or expected to be used in whole or in part to establish eligibility for credit, personal insurance, employment, or certain other purposes.

consumer reporting agency Under the U.S. Fair Credit Reporting Act, an inspection company that collects and sells information about individuals' employment history, financial situation, creditworthiness, character, personal characteristics, mode of living, and other possibly relevant personally identifiable information.

contingency reserve The account that accumulates the excess when experience turns out to be better than was expected in prospective rating asusmptions.

contingent beneficiary A person named to receive death proceeds if the primary beneficiary is not alive at the insured's death (also called *secondary beneficiary*).

continuance table Shows the probabilities of claim continuance for various durations or amounts.

continuing care centers Facilities that provide a range of sensitive living arrangements and services that reflect each person's level of needed care and assistance (also known as *life-care centers*).

continuous-premium whole life Whole life insurance with premiums that are payable for the whole of life insurance (also known as *straight life* and *ordinary life insurance*).

contribution method Method of surplus distribution based on an analysis of the sources of insurer surplus and that develops dividends that vary with the plan of insurance, age of issue, and duration of the policy.

contribution principle Principle that holds that insurers selling participating policies should distribute surplus accumulated on behalf of a block of policies in the same proportions as the policies are considered to have contributed to the surplus.

contributory plan Employee contribution plan under which the employee provides part of the funds necessary to purchase his or her benefits, with the employer assuming the remaining cost.

convexity The difference between the actual asset or liability value and its value as predicted by duration.

coordination of benefits (COB) A situation in which two insurance companies must work together to ensure that an insured entitled to benefits under two insurance plans does not recover more than 100 percent of the expenses.

corporate-owned life insurance (COLI) Life insurance policies owned by and payable to a corporation.

corridor deductible Used in connection with supplemental major medical plans and applies after the basic plan benefits have been exhausted.

cost allocation cost method Method that computes the actuarial present value of total benefits to be paid and then assigns a portion of that value (or cost) to each plan year.

cost allocation method Method that allocates benefits and then derives the actuarial present value of benefits utilizing level amounts contributed over the remaining years of service.

cost basis With respect to life insurance under U.S. income tax law, the sum of the premiums paid less the sum of any dividends received in cash or credited against the premiums.

cost of insurance The contribution each insured must make as his or her pro rata share of death claims in any particular year.

cost recovery rule The general rule for taxation of lump-sum cash surrender value payments on life insurance policies under which the amount included in the policyowner's gross income upon policy surrender is the excess of the gross proceeds received over the cost basis.

cost-of-living-adjustment (COLA) Automatic increases in accordance with increases in inflation, as measured by a national cost-of-living index, such as the consumer price index (CPI) in the United States.

cost-plus funding A funding alternative for group insurance benefits under which loss payments are based on the employer's own experience plus an allowance for expenses, contingencies, and profit.

country (sovereign) risk The risk that a government will interfere with its nationals paying foreign creditors.

covariance A measure of the degree to which two values vary in tandem.

credit insurance Life and health insurance issued through lending institutions to cover debtors' obligations if they die or become disabled.

credit risk The risk that promised cash flows on primary securities held by the insurer may not be paid in full.

credit shelter trust Trust that holds property that is not left to the surviving spouse outright.

cross-purchase buy-and-sell agreement Where each owner binds his or her estate to sell his or her business interest to the surviving owners, and each surviving owner binds himself or herself via the agreement to buy the interest of the deceased owner.

Crummey trust A trust in which the annual $10,000 gift tax exclusion is available for gifts made to the trust if funds are withdrawn by a beneficiary within a limited time period.

currency risk Uncertainty about the rate at which future foreign cash flows can be converted into the domestic currency.

current assumption policies Allow policy values to deviate from adjustments illustrated at policy inception—both favorably and unfavorably—but adjustments are based on the insurer's anticipated future experience.

current assumption whole life (CAWL) insurance Provides (usually) nonpar whole life insurance under a nontraditional, transparent format that relies on an indeterminate-premium structure.

currently insured Social Security status attained by being credited with a minimum of six quarters of coverage during the 13-quarter period ending with the quarter in which the individual dies.

custodial account See *bank trust.*

custodial care The most basic level of nursing care, typically takes the form of assistance with the activities of daily living.

daily benefit A schedule of benefits offered in some types of health insurance policies.

death benefit The payment made on the death of an insured.

death benefit only (DBO) plans Plans in which the employer promises to pay an income benefit to the employee's survivor upon the employee's death.

death proceeds The policy face amount and any additional insurance amounts paid by reason of the insured's death, such as accidental death benefits and the face amount of any paid-up additional insurance or any term rider.

death-based IRR Derived by solving for the interest rate that causes the accumulated premiums (net of dividends, if appropriate) at selected durations to equal those durations' death benefits.

debit insurance Any type of insurance sold through the debit (home collection of premium) system of marketing.

decreasing returns to scale When the marginal cost of production increases with increasing production (i.e., further growth diminishes efficiency).

deductible A specified amount of initial medical costs that the participant must pay before any costs are paid by the plan.

deferred age theory Theory that retirement benefits should be thought of as employee agreement to defer current wages in favor of payments during retirement when income is presumably lower.

deferred dividends Dividends payable only at the close of a stipulated number of years, such as 5, 10, 15, or 20.

deferred life annuity An annuity purchased with either a single premium or periodic premiums. The first annuity benefit payment is made after the passage of more than one payment interval.

deficiency reserve A supplemental reserve required when gross premiums charged by a life insurance company for a particular class of policies were less than the valuation net premiums.

defined benefit plans Guarantee a monthly retirement benefit based on some combination of salary and length of service.

defined contribution plans Plans that include profit-sharing and 401(k) plans in which the employer contributes a certain amount annually to each participant's account.

delay clause Grants the company the right to defer cash-value payment or the making of a policy loan (except for purposes of paying premiums) for up to six months after its request.

deposit administration contract Contract in which the life insurance company takes all the risks and provides all services, but *only with respect to employees who have retired.*

deposit term A form of term insurance popular in the United States in the 1970s that provided for payment of a modest endowment whose amount was set equal to a multiple of the difference between the first-year and renewal premiums.

derivatives Securities whose values are *derived* from the value of other securities such as stocks, currencies, or indexes of stocks, interest rates, and so on.

diagnosis related group (DRG) Reimbursement system based on a set reimbursement to a hospital for a stay regarding a given diagnosis, regardless of the length of stay or the level of services provided.

direct contract model Model under which HMOs maintain contractual relationships with individual physicians in contrast to physician groups as in the IPA and network models.

direct recognition provision A provision permitting the insurer to recognize directly in its excess interest or dividend formula the extent of policy loan activity within the policies.

direct response Distribution channel in which the customer deals directly with the insurer without any intervening intermediary or firm.

direct-writing or ceding company The company that originally issued a life insurance policy.

disability The inability to engage in any substantial gainful activity by reason of any medically determinable physical or mental impairment.

disability income insurance Insurance under which payment is provoked because physical or mental incapacity prevents the insured from being able to work.

disability insurance See *health insurance.*

discharge planning Identifies the appropriate level of care a patient may need when a hospital setting is no longer necessary.

disciplined current scale The scale of dividends defined by the insurer's actual recent experience.

discounting The process of obtaining the present value of a dollar payable at a specified time in the future.

disintermediation When a person borrows at one rate and can invest the loan proceeds at a higher rate.

distribution channel The means by which products or services are provided to customers and encom-

passes the entirety of a company's marketing network.

distribution systems See *distribution channel.*

dividend The distributable surplus paid to policyowners (also known as *bonuses*).

dividend history The schedule of dividends actually paid under an insurance policy.

dividend illustration Shows the insurer dividends that would be paid under the policy if the mortality, expense, and interest experience implicit in the current scale of illustrated dividends were to be the actual basis for all future dividends.

dividends actually paid Amounts paid as dividends under an insurance policy.

divisible surplus The amount earmarked for distribution, and once set aside by action of the directors or trustees, loses its identity as surplus and becomes a liability of the insurer.

doctrine of substantial compliance When the policyowner has done all that he or she can to effect a beneficiary change but did not follow the procedure because of factors beyond his or her control, a beneficiary change will be deemed to have been accomplished.

domestic insurer An insurer domiciled in a given state.

donee A gift recipient.

donor A gift giver.

double indemnity See *accidental death benefit.*

downstream holding company Formed by a mutual insurance company and sits in the middle of the intercorporate structure.

dread disease Individual insurance that pays a variety of benefits up to substantial maximums solely for the treatment of a disease named in the policy, most typically cancer or heart disease.

due care The process through which an insurance advisor investigates the quality and value of the insurance program recommended to the client.

durable power of attorney A legal instrument in which an individual can protect himself or herself in the event of becoming incapacitated or incompetent by naming a person to complete and sign tax returns, pay bills, and generally make and execute other financial decisions on the incapacitated individual's behalf.

duration The average life of an asset or liability.

duration matched Offsetting exactly the changes in asset values by changes in adjusted liability values.

economic value analysis Process used to evaluate the long-term financial results of current management actions.

economies of scale When a firm's average cost of production falls with increasing production.

economies of scope When a single firm can produce multiple products or services at lower costs than can multiple firms.

education IRA A tax-favored trust or custodial account created to pay the cost of a beneficiary's education.

educational plan Provides a fixed income during 9 or 10 months of each college year, with a modest "graduation present" in cash after the final installment.

effective convexity See *option-adjusted convexity.*

effective date The date from which insurance protection commences.

effective duration See *option-adjusted duration.*

efficient frontier Represents the set of efficient portfolios that dominates all other portfolios.

eligibility period Period of time in which an employee is entitled to apply for insurance without submitting evidence of insurability.

elimination (waiting) period Time period before benefits become payable.

embedded-value analysis See *value-based planning.*

employee assistance programs (EAPs) Provide a broad range of services including counseling for marital and family problems, job-related problems, and emotional disturbances as well as alcohol and drug abuse problems.

employee benefit plans Employer-sponsored plans that provide benefits to employees as part of their total compensation.

Employee Retirement Income Security Act (ERISA) Enacted to protect the interests of participants in employee benefit plans as well as the interests of the beneficiaries.

employee stock ownership plan (ESOP) A qualified employee benefit plan that is designed to purchase the employer's stock.

employer-pay-all approach Premium payment arrangement in which the employer pays the full premium each year.

endorsement system A split-dollar plan in which insurance on the employee's life is applied for and owned by the employer. The employer is primarily responsible for premium payments.

endowment A promise to pay a certain sum in case the insured dies within the term of the policy or the same sum if the insured survives the period.

endowment insurance Pays benefits if the insured dies during the policy term and also pays benefits if the insured survives the policy term.

enrolled actuary An individual employed to apply IRC Section 412 to determine the minimum and maximum contributions that should be made to an insurer or trust under defined benefit plans.

entire contract clause A clause that provides that the policy itself and the application, if a copy is attached to it, constitute the entire contract between the parties.

entity buy-and-sell agreement Partnership arrangement in which the business itself is obligated to buy out the ownership interest of any deceased or disabled partner, with each partner having bound his or her estate to sell if he or she is the first to die.

entry-age normal method Funding method that permits a flexible policy with regard to funding the past-service liability.

equal outlay method A method to compare the costs of two or more policies, which assumes that equal amounts of money are expended under each of two or more proposed insurance arrangements.

equity split dollar Split-dollar plan in which the employee obtains ownership of the excess of the cash value over any premium payments.

equity-indexed annuity (EIA) A nonvariable annuity contract whose interest crediting mechanism is tied directly to some external index, such as the Standard & Poor's 500 Index in the United States (also called an *indexed annuity*).

equivalent level annual dividend (ELAD) That portion of the pricing of a participating policy that is not guaranteed.

escheat To transfer all of a decedent's property to the state when there is no will and no relatives exist.

excess SERPs Supplemental executive retirement plans that seek to replace the retirement benefits that highly compensated employees lose because of IRC or ERISA limitations.

excess-of-loss reinsurance Coverage under health insurance in which a reinsurer reimburses a portion of the claim payments of the ceding insurer, but only after the ceding insurer had made payments for a specified number of months of incapacity or after its retention is exceeded.

excess-of-time (extended elimination) reinsurance Coverage under which the extended wait period extends beyond the elimination period found in the policy itself. The extended wait period can be 1, 2, 5, or even 10 years before the reinsurer becomes responsible for payment.

exclusion ratio The ratio of the investment in the contract to the expected return under the contract.

exclusive agents An agent who sells exclusively for one company (also known as *captive* or *tied agents*).

exclusive provider organizations (EPOs) Groups of participating providers that contract with employers, insurance companies, union trust funds, or others to provide medical care services at a reduced, negotiated fee.

executive bonus plan An arrangement under which the employer pays for individually issued life insurance for selected executives.

executor A person appointed by a decedent's will to administer an estate settlement process.

expected return The total amount that the annuitant or other policyowner can expect to receive under the contract.

experience rating Approach to group insurance rate making in which the past claims experience of a group is considered in determining future premiums for the group and/or adjusting past premiums after a coverage period has ended.

experience rating refund With a stock company, the refund from a premium stabilization account.

expires The termination of an insurance policy with no maturity value at the end of the stated period of coverage.

express authority See *actual authority*.

extended family One or more nuclear families plus grandparents and possibly aunts, uncles, and some cousins.

extended term insurance (ETI) Gives the policyowner the right to use the net surrender value to purchase paid-up term insurance for the full face amount of the policy.

externality When a firm's production or an individual's consumption has direct and uncompensated effects on others.

extra dividend May consist either of a single payment made after a policy has been in force a specified number of years or of a payment made periodically at stated intervals.

facultative reinsurance Reinsurance basis under which each application is underwritten separately by the reinsurer.

family deductible provision Provision that waives the deductible for all family members after any two or three of them individually have satisfied their deductibles in the same year.

family income policies Designed to appeal to young men and women whose family responsibilities call for a monthly income to be paid to the surviving spouse (typically) until a certain age or for a set period of usually 10, 15, or 20 years from the date of policy issuance.

Family Medical and Leave Act of 1993 Requires employers of more than five persons to allow eligible employees up to 12 weeks of leave during any 12-month period for personal illness, birth, adoption, or illness of spouse, child, or parent.

family policy or family rider A policy or rider that insures all or selected members of the family in one contract.

father's benefit Under the U.S. Social Security system, if a widower has under his care a dependent and unmarried child under age 16 of a worker, or a child who has been disabled since before age 22, he can be entitled to a benefit equal to 75 percent of the PIA.

final or postmortem expenses Expenses and taxes created by death.

financial intermediary A firm or other entity that brings together providers and users of funds, such as commercial and investment banks and insurers.

first-to-die insurance Pays the face amount of the policy on the first death of one of two (or more) insureds covered by the contract (also known as *joint life insurance*).

first-year expenses The costs of procuring, underwriting, and issuing new business, including commissions attributable to the first year's premiums.

five-year renewable term Term insurance with level death benefits and premiums that increase in five-year increments.

fixed-amount option An annuity certain with the income amount fixed.

fixed-period option An annuity certain with the time period fixed.

flexible enhanced ordinary life Policy that permits the combination of whole life, term, and paid-up additions in such proportions as to allow the policyowner to establish a comfortable premium level, within limits, and to adjust the policy face amount, also within limits.

flexible spending account An interest-bearing account that allows an employee to fund certain benefits on a before-tax basis by electing to take a salary reduction, which can then be used to fund the cost of any qualified benefits included in the plan.

flexible-premium deferred annuity Permits the contract owner to pay premiums at whatever time and in whatever amount he or she wishes, subject to insurer minimums.

flexible-premium variable life A policy that combines the flexible characteristics of universal life with the investment flexibility of variable life (also known as *variable universal life [VUL]*).

foreign insurer Under U.S. terminology, an insurer domiciled in another U.S. jurisdiction. Under non-U.S. terminology, an insurer domiciled in another country.

formula statutory policy reserve The amount that, together with future net premiums and interest, will be sufficient, according to the valuation assumptions, to pay future claims.

forward commitment risk The risk of a unilateral agreement such as where the insurance company is bound to make the investment at the agreed time of funding, but the borrower is not bound to accept the loan.

forward contract Investment opportunities structured such that the commitment to make the investment is followed by a period of deferral before the investment is actually funded.

four-in-seven exception Exception to the rule that a business-related deduction does not hold when policy loans are used to finance life insurance under a systematic plan of borrowing, under which a deduction is allowed if no part of at least four of the first seven annual premiums due on a policy is paid through borrowing, either from the policy or elsewhere.

fraternal benefit society An organization operating under a lodge system, which provides social and insurance benefits to members and family dependents.

free rider problem When public goods and services are available to others at low or zero cost.

full costing Where both direct and indirect expenses are allocated to each product.

full preliminary term method Method of modifying full net level terminal reserves that entails treating the first year of insurance as term insurance, irrespective of the type of contract actually involved, and to assume that the original contract goes into effect at the beginning of the second policy year.

fully insured Social Security status attained by being credited with either (1) 40 quarters of coverage earned at any time after 1936 or (2) at least one quarter of coverage (whenever earned) for every calendar year elapsing after 1950 (or after the year in which the worker attains age 21, if later) up to the year in which he or she reaches age 62, or, if earlier, dies or becomes disabled.

fully insured pension plans Plans that rely exclusively on insurance contracts as the funding media.

funded An employee benefit plan under which the employer establishes and maintains assets in an escrow account or trust fund as security for its promise to make future payments.

funding media The legal instruments, such as pension contracts, issued by insurance companies under which the actuarial cost arrangements operate (also called *funding vehicles*).

funding vehicles See *funding media.*

future increase option Allows an insured to purchase additional life insurance or disability income insurance in future years without evidence of insurability (also known as a *guarantee of future insurability*).

future interest Any interest in property that does not pass into the donee's possession or enjoyment until some future date.

future service Defined benefit formulas based on service that is provided after the installation of the plan.

futures contract Contract that obligates one party to buy and another to sell a financial instrument (or anything else) at a specified future time at a price and on terms agreed to now.

GAAP reserves Calculated, for life insurance and long-term health products, using the insurer's realistic expectations for morbidity, mortality, persistency, and investment return on a net-level premium basis.

gainful occupation A clause stipulating that insureds are considered totally disabled when they cannot perform the major duties of any gainful occupation for which they are reasonably suited because of education, training, or experience.

general account Where assets used to support contractual obligations providing for guaranteed, fixed benefit payments normally are held.

general agency system The older of the two career agency systems and aims to accomplish through general agents what the branch office system accomplishes through agency managers.

general agent An individual who has powers coextensive with those of his or her principal within the limit of the particular business or territory in which the agent operates.

general business (C-4) risk Such risk factors as expansion into new geographic areas or lines of business, changes in the tax law, fraud, lawsuits, contingent liabilities, and other environmental sources of risk that do not fit into the C-1 through C-3 categories.

general insurance Insurance sold to protect property (also known as *non-life insurance* and *property/casualty insurance*).

general partnership A partnership in which each partner is actively involved in the management of the firm and is fully liable for partnership obligations.

general power of appointment When an individual has the right to dispose of property that he or she does not own, including giving it to himself or herself.

generation-skipping transfer (GST) tax Tax levied when a property interest is transferred to persons who are two or more generations younger than the transferor.

gift The transfer of property ownership for less than an adequate price.

gift tax marital deduction Permits tax-free transfers between spouses without limit.

grace period Provision requiring the insurer to accept premium payments for a certain period after their due date, during which period the policy remains in effect.

graded premium whole life (GPWL) insurance Provides that premiums begin at a level that is 50 percent or less than those for a comparable ordinary life policy and increase to a maximum over time.

graded-assessment system System of determining premium payment amounts under which assessments are graded upward by age at entry.

gradual retirement or phased retirement Where individuals move from full-time to a part-time employment plan and then to full retirement at a later date.

graduation An adjustment in which the rates are smoothed into a curve, which is made because the volume of experience is not uniform at all ages and is insufficient to provide completely creditable or reliable statistics.

grantor The person who establishes a trust.

gratuitous-indemnity benefit Government life insurance payable only in monthly installments for 10 years, and only to a restricted group of beneficiaries.

gross estate The value of all property or interests in property owned or controlled by the deceased person.

gross proceeds The amounts paid on surrender, including the cash value of any paid-up additions and the value of dividends accumulated at interest.

gross rate The amount charged policyowners—after loadings are added to the net rate.

group deferred annuity Contract under which employer contributions are used to purchase single-premium deferred annuities for employees based on the amount of annuity benefit accrued by the participant each year.

group dental insurance plan One of the fastest-growing employee benefit plans, which provides coverage for dental expenses.

group health insurance Health insurance purchased for a group of insureds, typically by employers for the benefit of their employees.

group insurance Life and health insurance purchased typically by employers for the benefit of their employees.

group model Model in which the HMO contracts with a multispecialty physician group practice to provide all physician services to its members.

group permanent Contract under which benefits, usually including a life insurance feature, are funded by a level-premium group annuity contract issued to the employer with certificates of coverage given to the employees.

growth capital Capital needed to support future business.

growth stage Stage of the product life cycle in which sales and profits increase dramatically.

guarantee of future insurability See *future increase option.*

guaranteed insurability option (GIO) Permits an insured to purchase additional insurance without providing evidence of insurability (also known as *additional or guaranteed purchase option*).

guaranteed investment contracts (GICs) Contracts under which the insurance company accepts a specific amount of money, usually $100,000 or more at a given interest rate, and agrees to return the money at a fixed date (1 to 15 years) in the future.

guaranteed minimum death benefit (GMDB) A variable annuity promise that often equals the greater of the cash value or the amount invested in the contract, if the annuity owner dies during the accumulation period.

guaranteed renewable Contractual right of the insured to renew the policy to some specified age. The insurer can alter premiums only on a class basis.

guaranteed-cost insurance policies Life and health insurance policies that fix policy elements (i.e., the premium, the face amount, and the cash values, if any) at policy inception.

guideline level premium Element of U.S. income tax law under which a premium is computed using interest at the greater rate of 4 percent or the rate guaranteed in the contract.

guideline premium requirement Requirement in U.S. income tax law that the cumulative premiums paid under a life insurance contract must not at any time exceed the greater of the guideline single premiums or the sum of the guideline level premiums at that time.

guideline single premium Utilized in one of two alternative tests to determine if a universal life and related policies qualify as a life insurance contract under IRC Section 7702.

health insurance   Any form of insurance whose payment is contingent on the insured incurring additional expenses or losing income because of incapacity or loss of good health (also known as *accident and health insurance, accident and sickness insurance,* or *disability insurance*).

Health Insurance Portability and Accountability Act (HIPAA)   Model law that helps to ensure that individuals will not lose their medical coverage or be subject to new preexisting condition periods when they change or lose their jobs.

health maintenance organization (HMO)   Organization that provides comprehensive health care services for members for a fixed periodic payment.

hedging   A strategy of acquiring securities whose gains and losses offset gains and losses in other securities or portfolios of securities.

holding companies   Financial corporations that own or control one or more subsidiary companies.

home health care benefits   Skilled nursing care, physical therapy, and related professional services as well as personal services such as assistance with activities of daily living.

home service distribution system   An agency-building life insurance distribution channel that relies on exclusive agents who are assigned to a geographic territory.

home service life insurance   Marketing system for industrial life insurance and monthly debt ordinary insurance.

hospice care   Special care and emotional support, provided in a facility or in the individual's home, for persons diagnosed with terminal illnesses.

hospice care expense benefits   Typically pay usual and customary charges made by a hospice.

hospital bill audit   Used to verify that a patient received the hospital services and items for which he or she was billed.

hospital confinement indemnity   Coverage paying a fixed sum for each day of hospital confinement.

human life value   A measure of the actual future earnings or values of services of an individual—the capitalized value of an individual's future net earnings after subtracting self-maintenance costs such as food, clothing, and shelter.

husband's benefit   Under the U.S. Social Security system, the benefit to which the husband of a retired worker may be entitled. The benefit equals 50 percent of the wife's PIA if she is at the NRA or older at the time of claim, or, regardless of age, if the husband has under his care a dependent and unmarried child of the wife under age 16, or, regardless of age, if the child has been disabled since before age 22.

illiquid assets   Assets not available to meet income or other monetary needs because they cannot be liquidated with reasonable price certainty.

illustration actuary   An appointed individual who must make certain annual certifications to the insurance regulator regarding the insurer's practices and compliance.

immediate life annuity   An annuity purchased with a single premium with the first annuity payment due immediately.

immediate participation guarantee contract (IPG)   Contract in which the employer's contributions are placed in an unallocated fund and the life insurance company guarantees that the annuities for retired employees will be paid in full.

implied authority   Authority of an agent associated with the basic job duties.

incentive compensation   Arrangements of compensating executives that are intended to align their and the business's interests.

income elasticity of insurance premiums   The relative change in insurance premiums written for a given change in national income.

incontestable clause   Provides that the validity of an insurance contract may not be contested after it has been in effect for a certain period of time.

incurred loss ratio   The proportion of each premium dollar actually used to pay claims.

indemnity   Contract in which insureds suffering a covered loss are entitled to recover an amount not greater than that which would be necessary to place the insured in the same preloss financial position.

indemnity disability income policies   Require insurers to pay the maximum amount specified in the policy regardless of the actual value of the lost income at the time of the claim.

independent agent   An insurance agent who represents several insurers.

independent property/casualty agents   Independent, commissioned agents whose primary business is the sale of property/casualty insurance for several insurers.

indexed annuity   See *equity-indexed annuity (EIA).*

indirect property loss exposures   Exist when an individual, family, or business can suffer a reduction in income (revenues less expenses) from the loss of use of property or when the value of property that is not damaged is lessened because of direct damage to other property.

individual equity   A social insurance plan in which participants receive benefits equal to their contributions plus interest.

individual health insurance An arrangement in which coverage is provided to a specific individual under a policy issued to an individual (and sometimes covering multiple family members).

individual level-cost method Method in which the total benefits to be paid to an employee are estimated and the sum required to provide the benefits is accumulated through level amounts contributed over the remaining years of service. This cost method may be calculated with or without supplemental liability (past-service liability) being determined separately.

individual level-cost recovery methods Methods under which benefits are funded on a level-amount basis or as a level percentage of pay over the employee participant's *entire* working lifetime. As with aggregate cost methods, the supplemental liability for past-service benefits is separately ascertained.

individual policy pension trust Trust in which benefits are funded by separate, individual policies issued on the lives of employees, the policies generally being issued to and held by a trustee.

individual practice association (IPA) Physicians' organizations comprised of community-based independent physicians, in either solo or group practices, who provide ambulatory services to HMO members.

individual retirement account A tax-deferred retirement plan for individuals with earned income.

individual retirement annuity Generally either fixed- or variable-annuity contracts that are issued by insurance companies.

industrial insurance Life and health insurance policies issued to individuals in small amounts, usually less than $2,000, with premiums collected on a weekly or monthly basis at the home of the policyowner.

inflation protection Ensures that the benefit amount increases with the cost of living.

informal funding Reserve funds established to meet future obligations of a retirement plan in which the fund is not formally linked to the obligation and remains a general asset of the business subject to attachment by its general creditors.

initial investment The amount of capital that an insurer must invest to launch a new product.

initial past-service liability The total cost of the credits granted for past service at the date of plan installation.

initial reserve The reserve at the beginning of the policy year, which equals the terminal reserve for the preceding year, increased by the net-level annual premium (if any) for the current year.

insolvency The inability to pay one's debts.

inspection company Company that collects and sells information about individuals' employment history, financial situation, creditworthiness, character, personal characteristics, mode of living, and other possibly relevant personally identifiable information.

installment refund annuity Promises that, if the annuitant dies before receiving income installments equal to the purchase price, the payments will be continued to a beneficiary until this amount has been paid.

insurability conditional premium receipt Provides that the insurer is considered to have made an offer conditional upon the proposed insured's insurability, and the applicant accepts the conditional offer by payment of the premium.

insurable interest When an individual can reasonably expect to receive pecuniary gain from that person's continued life, or, conversely, if he or she would suffer financial loss on the person's death.

insurance From an *economic* perspective, a financial intermediation function by which individuals exposed to a specified contingency each contribute to a pool from which covered losses suffered by participating individuals are paid. From a *legal* perspective, an agreement under which the policyowner pays a stipulated premium to the insurer in return for which the insurer agrees to pay a defined amount of money or provide a defined service if a covered loss occurs during the policy term.

insurance agent An individual who represents an insurance company, usually in sales.

insurance contract or policy A legal contract in which one party pays a stipulated consideration to the other party, an insurer, in return for which the insurer agrees to pay a defined amount of money or provide a defined service if a covered loss occurs during the policy term.

insurance density The average annual per capita premium within a country.

insurance penetration The ratio of yearly direct premiums written to GDP.

insurance programming The risk management process applied to personal insurance planning.

insured The person whose life, health, or property is the object of the insurance policy.

insurer An insurance company.

integrated deductible Deductible used in supplemental plans, determined by the greater of (1) a fairly high amount, such as $500, or (2) the basic plan benefits.

inter vivos A trust created during life (also known as a *living trust*).

interest The price paid for the use of money.

interest option Option in which the proceeds remain with the company and a guaranteed amount of interest earned thereon is paid to the beneficiary.

interest rate (C-3) risk The risk that asset and/or liability values will be negatively affected by interest rate movements.

interest-adjusted net cost Method developed to correct for the omission of the time value of money within the TNC method.

interest-sensitive whole life Term for current assumption whole life insurance derived from its use of new-money interest rates and current realistic mortality charges in cash-value determination.

intermediate nursing care Similar to skilled nursing care except that the patient neither receives nor needs 24-hour attention.

internal rate of return (IRR) Method for comparing insurance policies that solves for a rate of return but makes no allowance for the policy's internal mortality charges.

interplead Pay the proceeds to a court for it to decide the rightful recipient.

interpolated terminal reserve An amount equal to the policy reserve interpolated to the date of a gift.

intestate A person who dies without a valid will or without having made a complete disposition of his or her property.

intestate succession statutes Directions made by the state to whom and how an intestate decedent's property is to be distributed.

invested assets The income-producing assets of an insurer.

investigative consumer report A consumer report in which information on a consumer's character, general reputation, personal characteristics, finances, or mode of living is obtained from personal interviews with the consumer's neighbors, friends, or associates.

investment bank Financial intermediary engaged in bringing together investors and issuers of securities.

Investment Company Act of 1940 Regulates investment company management and operation including rules regarding security owners, maximum sales charges, investment management of contributions, and distribution of periodic financial reports.

investment expenses The costs of making, processing, and protecting investments.

investment generation method For purposes of determining interest rates to be credited to blocks of

policies, situation in which the insurer segregates policies into different generations based on the time of issuance.

investment in the contract Under U.S. income tax law, the premiums paid net of dividends received and not previously taxed.

investment margin The difference between the amount of investment income the insurer earns and the investment income the insurer credits to a product or assumes when pricing that product (also called *spread*).

investment risk The potential variability of returns.

investment year or new money Approach in which assets acquired during each calendar year are treated as a separate cell with the net investment income (including realized capital gains and losses) derived from these assets credited to the cell.

Investments in Medium-Grade and Lower-Grade Obligations Model Regulation A model regulation adopted by the NAIC in 1992 to protect the interest of the insurance-buying public by establishing limitations on the concentration of medium-grade and lower-grade obligations.

Investments of Insurers Model Act (Defined Limits Version) A model investment law updated by the NAIC in 1996 to address the asset quality concerns that had developed in the industry.

Investments of Insurers Model Act (Defined Standards Version) A model investment law (called the "prudent-person model") adopted by the NAIC in 1998 to serve as an alternative to the Investments of Insurers Model Act (Defined Limits Version).

irrevocable designation A beneficiary designation that can be changed only with the beneficiary's express consent.

irrevocable life insurance trust (ILIT) An insurance policy on the grantor's life owned by an irrevocable inter vivos trust, with the policy proceeds payable to the trust as beneficiary.

irrevocable trust A living trust in which the grantor permanently relinquishes ownership and control of the property.

joint and last-survivor annuity Provides income payments for as long as either of two or more persons lives.

joint and survivor annuity An annuity that pays for as long as either or both of two persons is alive.

joint and survivorship life income option Life income payments continue for as long as at least one of two or more beneficiaries (annuitants) is alive.

joint and two-thirds (or joint and one-half) annuity A modified form of a joint and last-survivor annuity that provides that the income will be reduced following the death of the first annuitant to two-thirds or one-half of the original income.

joint life annuity Provides a specified income for two or more named persons, with the income ceasing upon the first death among the covered lives.

joint life insurance Pays the face amount of the policy on the first death of one of two (or more) insureds covered by the contract (also known as *first-to-die insurance*).

joint tenancy with right of survivorship Property owned by two or more persons and, on the death of any owner, his or her ownership interest passes automatically to the survivors.

juvenile endowment policies Policies maturing at specified ages designed to cover expenses associated with a child's education, marriage, or independence.

Keogh or HR-10 plans Special tax-advantaged pension plans for self-employed individuals.

key employee disability insurance Provides for payment of a monthly indemnity to a business entity during the total disability of an essential employee who is the named insured under the policy.

key employee (key person and key man) insurance Purchased to indemnify a business for the decrease in earnings brought about by the death or disability of a key employee.

lapse rates Measure the proportion of policyowners who voluntarily terminate their insurance during a year.

lapse-supported policies Policies so constructed that their future values are in part dependent on the assumption of incurring gains from high early lapses and surrenders.

law of large numbers Theory that the greater the number of similar exposures (e.g., lives insured) to a peril (e.g., death), the less observed loss experience will deviate from expected loss experience.

legal risk The risk that new governmental laws, regulations, or court opinions may decrease the value of the firm.

level-premium contract with lifetime guarantees See *group permanent.*

level-premium group annuity See *group permanent.*

"lemons" problem An information asymmetry in which the insurance customer knows less than the seller about the seller and its products.

liability for dividend payable A liability posted on an insurer's balance sheet to reflect dividends declared but not payable until after the statement date.

liability loss exposures Arise from an individual's intentional actions or failure to exercise a sufficient degree of care such that another person or property is harmed.

LIBOR London Interbank Offered Rate—the most widely used floating rate index in the interest swaps market.

Life and Health Insurance Policy Language Simplification Model Act Act requiring that life and health insurance policy language meet an ease of readability test, and that policies be printed in at least a minimum type size, with an accompanying table of contents or index.

life annuity A contract that promises to pay the insured periodic payments that cease on the annuitant's death.

life annuity certain and continuous See *life annuity with installments certain.*

life annuity due A contract that makes the first annuity payment when the policy is issued.

life annuity with installments certain Calls for a guaranteed number of monthly (or annual) payments to be made whether the annuitant lives or dies, with payments to continue for the whole of the annuitant's life if he or she should live beyond the guarantee period (also called a *life annuity certain and continuous*).

life cycle hypothesis Ando-Modigliani's theory of consumption, which states that an individual's income will be low in the beginning and end stages of life and high during the middle period of life.

life-care centers See *continuing care centers.*

life income option with period certain The most widely used life income option; installments are payable for as long as the primary beneficiary lives, but should this beneficiary die before a predetermined number of years, installments continue to a second beneficiary until the end of the designated period.

life insurance company taxable income (LICTI) Gross income less applicable deductions.

Life Insurance Disclosure Model Regulation Regulation currently followed in about 40 U.S. jurisdictions requiring disclosures to prospective life insurance purchasers.

life insurance yield comparison index A yield index calculated by using a standard, prescribed set of term (mortality) rates that are applied to the policy's net amount at risk.

life-expectancy term Provides protection for a number of years equal to the life expectancy for a person of the proposed insured's age and sex, based on some specific mortality table.

life-paid-up-at-age-65 whole life policies Whole life policies with level premiums paid up to age 65.

limited partnership Partnership having at least one general partner and one or more limited partners who are not actively engaged in partnership management and who are liable for partnership obligations only to the extent of their investment in the partnership.

limited-payment whole life insurance Policy remains in full force for the whole of life, but premiums are payable for a limited number of years only, after which the policy becomes paid up for its full face amount.

Linton yield See *comparative interest rate.*

liquid assets Assets available to be liquidated with reasonable price certainty.

liquidation Situation in which the insurance regulator is given title to all assets of the insurer in order for him or her to wind down the insurer.

liquidation period The time during which annuity fund values are paid to annuitant(s).

liquidity risk The risk of a funding crisis.

living trust A trust created during life (also known as an *inter vivos trust*).

living will A legal instrument setting forth the individual's wishes as to the use of life-sustaining measures in case of terminal illness, prolonged coma, or serious incapacitation.

loadings Amounts to cover expenses, taxes, contingencies, and profits.

lock-in principle An accounting convention that prevents a restatement of assumptions regarding interest, expense, and mortality for traditional policies in force.

long-term care (LTC) insurance Insurance that covers physical or mental incapacity that prohibits the insured's activities of daily living.

Long-Term Care Insurance Model Act Act that specifies minimum standards that products must meet to be considered long-term care insurance.

loss of income insurance Provides periodic payments when an insured loses income because of injury or sickness (also known as *loss of time insurance*).

loss of time insurance See *loss of income insurance.*

maintenance of solvency Statute requiring that a fraternal benefit society provide in its bylaws that, if the reserves for any or all classes of insurance become impaired, the board of directors may require insured members to pay an equitable portion of the deficiency.

managed care An approach to health care financing that integrates the financing and delivery of appropriate health care services. It involves the active management of the services and providers.

managerial system See *branch office system.*

manual rating Approach to group insurance rate making in which the premium rate is determined independently of a particular group's claims experience.

marginal costing Where only direct expenses are allocated to a specific product.

marital deduction Deduction of the value of property left to a surviving spouse.

marital trust A trust established to receive property that qualifies for the marital deduction when the first spouse dies.

market conduct Practices associated with agents' and insurers' sales, counseling, and servicing activities.

market failures or imperfections Variations of actual market performance and structure from the ideal.

market power The ability of one or a few sellers or buyers to influence the price of a product or service.

market risk The risk of asset and liability value changes associated with broad economic factors that cannot be avoided, regardless of diversification (also called *systematic risk*).

marketing The provision of products well suited to consumers' needs through effective, appropriate distribution channels.

marketing channels See *distribution channel.*

marketing intermediaries Individuals who sell an insurer's products, typically on a face-to-face basis with customers and usually for a commission on each sale.

marketing program A tactical plan that deals primarily with the product, price, distribution, and promotion strategies that a company will follow to reach its target markets and to satisfy consumer needs.

market-to-book ratio Ratio that shows the degree of discrepancy between an insurer's market value as perceived by the capital markets and its book value as measured by SAP or GAAP.

market-value adjusted annuity A type of single-premium deferred annuity that permits contract owners to lock in a guaranteed interest rate over a specified maturity period, typically from 3 to 10 years (also called a *market-value annuity*).

market-value risk The change in asset and liability values caused by a change in interest rates.

mass marketing Seeking business from individuals through their affiliation with an organization or group.

material Information of such relevance that its misstatement could change some essential element of an underwriting decision.

mathematical reserves Liabilities for future claims (also known as *policy reserves*).

maturity funding contract Contract in which the life insurance company holds no funds prior to retirement and receives money to purchase the guaranteed annuities only as employees retire.

maximum benefit The largest benefit amount that a policy will pay; may be written on a lifetime or a per cause basis.

mean reserve The arithmetic average of the initial reserve and the terminal reserve for any year of valuation.

medical expense insurance Hospital, physician, or other health care expenses.

medical savings accounts Tax-exempt, custodial accounts established for the purpose of paying medical expenses in conjunction with a high-deductible major medical policy.

Medicare A two-part program of federal health insurance.

Medicare Part A A hospital insurance plan that covers essentially all persons aged 65 or over and all persons who have been receiving Social Security disability benefits for at least two years for extensive hospitalization benefits.

Medicare Part B Optional coverage that provides a supplementary program for surgical and physician's care, and certain other benefits, for persons aged 65 or over and all persons who have been receiving Social Security disability benefits for at least two years.

Medicare supplement A policy that meets specific minimum standards set out in insurance law or regulation.

Medicare Wraparound Provides benefits that cover the deductibles and coinsurance amounts that individuals must pay personally under Medicare.

Mental Health Parity Act Act passed in 1998 requiring some plans to have the same benefit maximums for mental health benefits as for all other benefits.

minimum efficient scale (MES) When a firm is at a certain size and further growth yields no additional efficiencies—long-run average costs are at a minimum.

minimum premium plan (MPP) The contract owner assumes liability for all but the largest claims or very unfavorable total experience of the plan.

misappropriation Misuse of policyowners' funds.

miscellaneous (C-4) risks Risks associated with social, legal, political, technological, and all other changes not included in the C-1, C-2, or C-3 classifications.

misrepresentation A false statement made to an insurer for the purpose of inducing it to accept a risk.

misstatement of age Provision stipulating that if the insured's age is found to have been misstated, the amount of insurance will be adjusted to be that which would have been purchased by the premium had the correct age been known.

Model Annuity and Deposit Fund Disclosure Regulation Regulation to help a prospect select an appropriate annuity and to understand its features. It applies to individual deferred annuities, selected group annuities, and deposit funds accepted in connection with life insurance and annuity contracts.

Model Group Life Insurance Definition and Group Life Insurance Standard Provisions Act Model act defining eligible groups and standard provisions for group life insurance coverage.

Model Policy Loan Interest Rate Bill Permits variable interest rates to rectify the imbalance presented with disintermediation.

Model Standard Nonforfeiture Law Model law prescribing minimum amount that must be returned to the policyowner upon surrender of a policy.

Model Standard Valuation Law Model law providing the legal basis for calculating minimum reserves for ordinary insurance.

Model Variable Annuity Regulation Provides guidelines for separate account investments and requires that variable-annuity contracts state clearly the essential elements of the procedure for determining the amount of the variable benefits.

modified coinsurance plan Reinsurance arrangement similar to a coinsurance plan with a provision that requires the reinsurer to pay the ceding company a reserve adjustment, the net effect of which is to make the arrangement yearly renewal term insurance.

modified endowment contract A life insurance policy entered into after June 20, 1988, that meets the IRC Section 7702 definition of life insurance, but that fails to meet the so-called seven-pay test.

modified endowment policies Popular in markets such as Thailand, these policies provide for the payment periodically of a set percentage of the insured amount over the policy term, as well as a maturity amount.

monthly debit ordinary Ordinary life policies typically written in the $5,000 to $25,000 range with premiums collected monthly at the policyowner's home.

monthly indemnity Fixed payable amount of a personal disability income policy.

moral hazard problem An information asymmetry problem in which individuals alter their behavior because they are insured.

morbidity tables Tables showing yearly probabilities of disability.

mortality tables Tables showing yearly probabilities of death.

mortgage protection term Provides for face amount decreases that match the projected decreases in the principal amount owed under a mortgage loan.

mother's benefit Under the U.S. Social Security system, if a widow has under her care a dependent and unmarried child under age 16 of a worker, or a child who has been disabled since before age 22, she can be entitled to a benefit equal to 75 percent of the PIA.

Mudarabad A form of partnership, necessary to be compatible with Islamic principles, in which one party provides the funds while another provides the expertise and management.

multiple-employer trust (MET) A subset of multiple-employer welfare arrangements.

multiple-employer welfare arrangements (MEWAs) Market group benefits to employers that have a small number of employees.

multiple-line exclusive agents (MLEAs) Commissioned exclusive agents who sell the life and health and property and liability insurance products of a single group of affiliated insurers.

mutual fund A pool of commingled funds contributed by investors and managed by professional managers.

mutual life insurance company A corporation authorized to sell life and (usually) health insurance, which is owned by and operated for the benefit of its policyowners.

mutualization A procedure involving the retirement of the outstanding capital stock of the insurer, coupled with the transfer of control of the insurer from the stockholders to the policyowners.

mutually exclusive The occurrence of one event precludes the possibility of the occurrence of another event.

NAIC Model Minimum Reserve Standards for Individual and Group Health Insurance Standards that govern health insurance reserving practices.

narrative summary Part of the Basic Illustration that provides a description of how the policy functions.

National Service Life Insurance Government insurance program established by the National Service Life Insurance Act of 1940, providing up to $10,000 (minimum of $1,000) coverage in multiples of $500 for individuals entering military service between 1921 and 1940.

natural monopoly When efficiency increases over an industry's entire relevant output range.

necessaries Legal term defining costs appropriate for a minor's circumstances.

negative convexity When the interest rate environment is characterized by an inverted yield curve, the convexity error will cause a decline in surplus to be underpredicted.

negative externality When a firm's production or an individual's consumption imposes costs to others.

net amount at risk The actual amount of pure life insurance protection, calculated as the difference between the policy reserve at that point and the face amount.

net GAAP reserves The result reached by deducting the DAC account from the GAAP policy reserves.

net gain from operations Approximate SAP equivalent of net income under GAAP.

net payment cost comparison index An estimate of the average annual net outlay (premium less illustrated annual dividend), adjusted by interest to reflect the time when premiums and dividends are paid during a 10- or 20-year period.

net present value (NPV) Project calculation calculated by subtracting the project's initial investment from the present value of the product's projected earnings.

network model Model in which an HMO contracts with more than one group practice to provide physician services.

new investment yield Measures the income yield on investments purchased during the measurement period and can be helpful in determining the marginal impact of purchase decisions.

nominal interest rates Prevailing interest rates.

nonadmitted assets Assets not recognized by regulatory authorities in assessing solvency and including items such as furniture, certain equipment, and agents' balances.

non-agency-building distribution Strategy under which insurers do not seek to build their own agency sales force.

noncancellable Basis meaning that the policy can neither be canceled nor the premium changed.

noncontributory plan The employer bears the total cost of a benefit program—the employee does not contribute.

nondisabling injury benefit Pays up to a specific sum, usually one-quarter of the monthly indemnity, to reimburse the insured for medical expenses incurred for treatment of an injury that did not result in total disability.

nonforfeiture factor The modified adjusted premium when the nonforfeiture premium is adjusted to produce surrender values.

nonforfeiture options Alternatives provided policy-owners who choose to terminate their insurance policies as to how to utilize the cash surrender value.

nonforfeiture provision Stipulates the options available under a cash-value policy if the policy-owner elects to terminate the policy and explains the basis or method used to determine these optional values.

nonforfeiture values Cash surrender values.

noninsured plan Pension financing vehicle that involves no element of insurance and requires the creation of a trust.

non-investment-grade bonds The sum of an insurer's investments in below-investment-grade ("junk") bonds and bonds in or near default.

non-life insurance Insurance sold to protect property (also known as *general insurance* and *property/casualty insurance*).

nonmarital trust See *bypass trust.*

nonmedical life insurance New ordinary insurance written without the benefit of a medical or paramedical examination.

nonproportional reinsurance Provides for the reinsurer to pay a claim only when the amount of loss exceeds a specified limit (excess-of-loss coverage).

nonqualified deferred compensation plan A contractual arrangement under which compensation for services rendered is postponed, usually until retirement, and does not qualify under IRS regulations as "qualified."

nonscheduled plan A health insurance plan in which reimbursement of the surgeon's and other fees is based on the usual and customary charge for the procedure performed.

normal cost The cost, under any actuarial cost method, that would be attributable to the current year of a plan's operation if from the earliest date of credited service, the plan had been in effect and costs had been accrued in accordance with a particular actuarial cost method.

normal retirement age (NRA) The youngest age for which an employee is entitled to retire with full benefits.

nuclear family Husband, wife, and dependent children living together.

numeric summary Part of the Basic Illustration that shows values based on (1) guarantees alone, (2) current assumptions, and (3) a midpoint set of assumptions, all at specified years.

old-age insurance benefit The insured worker's monthly retirement benefit under Social Security.

open contract Provision that requires a fraternal insurance certificate to state that the society's constitution and bylaws, and any future changes therein, are a part of the contract with the member/insured.

operation An organization's day-to-day activities.

operational risk The risk that system failures or human errors will substantially disrupt operations.

option-adjusted convexity Measures of convexity that have been adjusted for the risk of options embedded in asset or liability contracts.

option-adjusted duration Measures of duration that have been adjusted for the risk of options embedded in asset or liability contracts.

options Grant their holders the right to buy or sell assets within a limited time period at a stipulated price.

ordinary life insurance Includes individual life and health insurance policies with premiums payable for life or for a specified period.

original-age method Involves a retroactive conversion, with the whole life or other cash-value policy bearing the date and premium rate that would have been paid had the cash-value policy been taken out originally instead of the term policy.

other financial institutions Mutual fund organizations, banks, investment banks, pension funds, and insurers.

other hospital services Drugs and medicines, diagnostic X-rays and laboratory tests, and use of an operating room and ambulance service.

out-of-pocket cap A stop-loss provision that stipulates a maximum annual cap on expenses paid by the insured individual.

outpatient or ambulatory surgery A program under which a patient has surgery performed and is released on the same day to recuperate at home.

outsourcing Hiring an outside company to perform specific tasks.

overhead expense insurance Covers the monthly business expenses of business owners and professionals in private practice when they are disabled.

override or overriding commission A commission that the general agent receives on other agents' sales.

own occupation A clause that deems insureds to be totally disabled when they cannot perform the major duties of their regular occupations.

owner See *policyowner.*

paid-up policy A life insurance policy for which no further premium payments are due contractually but the policy remains in effect.

parent's benefit Under the U.S. Social Security system, dependent parents who are 62 and over are each entitled to a benefit equal to 75 percent of the PIA.

partial disability benefit Typically 50 percent of the monthly indemnity for total disability and payable for up to six months or, if less, for the remainder of the policy benefit period when the insured has returned to work on a limited basis after a period of compensable total disability.

participating insurance policies Life and health insurance policies that provide their owners the right to share in surplus funds accumulated by the insurer because of deviations of actual from assumed experience (also known as *with profits policies*).

partnership A voluntary association of two or more individuals for the purpose of conducting a business for profit as co-owners.

past service Credit for service prior to the installation of a pension plan.

payback period The number of years that pass before the earnings produced equal the insurer's initial investment.

payor benefit Provides a death (and typically a waiver of premium) benefit on the life of the premium payor (usually a parent).

Pension Benefit Guarantee Corporation (PBGC) A government corporation set up by ERISA in 1954 to provide termination insurance for participants in qualified defined benefit plans up to certain limits.

pension maximization Strategy wherein the participant in a qualified retirement plan who otherwise would receive income in the form of a joint and last survivor annuity (1) chooses instead to receive income under the single life annuity option and (2) purchases life insurance to replace the value of the survivor annuity to the spouse.

per-cause deductible All expenses incurred because the same or related causes are accumulated to satisfy the deductible.

perceived authority See *apparent authority*.

percentage participation See *coinsurance*.

peril A cause of loss, such as fire or windstorm, with respect to property, or disability or death with respect to persons.

permanent income hypothesis Friedman's theory for consumption, which assumes that individuals wish to smooth their level of lifetime consumption but do so through an assessment of their permanent level of income.

permissible loss ratio The proportion of each premium dollar that is assumed to be used to pay claims.

persistency bonuses Incentives such as interest rate bonuses or mortality refunds, which encourage policyowners to continue their policies.

persistency rate The ratio of the number of a group of policies that continue coverage on a premium-due date to the number of policies that were in force as of the preceding due date.

personal financial planning The process whereby an individual's or a family's overall financial objectives are used to develop and implement an integrated plan to accomplish the objectives.

personal insurance Life, accident, and other insurance covering a *person* in contrast to insurance covering property or liability.

personal loss exposures Arise from the possibilities of death, incapacity, illness or injury, retirement, and unemployment.

personal property Movable property, such as automobiles, furniture, stocks, and insurance policies.

personal-producing general agents (PPGAs) Independent, commissioned agents who typically work alone and focus on personal production.

phantom stock plan Incentive compensation plan under which an executive is granted a set number of hypothetical units in the business and receives the value of the units at the end of a specified period, including the appreciation in value over the period of those hypothetical units.

physician-hospital organizations (PHOs) Organizations that are jointly owned and operated by hospitals and their affiliated physicians, and typically are developed to provide a vehicle for hospitals and physicians to contract together with other managed care organizations to provide both physician and hospital services.

planned premium The rate at which insurance companies bill, according to the policyowner's preference, in order to overcome the concern that policyowners may inadvertently allow their policies to lapse (also known as a *target premium*).

point-of-service plan (POS) Hybrid health care plan that combines aspects of a traditional medical expense plan with an HMO or a PPO, under which a participant's access to a provider network is controlled by a primary care physician.

policy fee system System under which the premium for a policy is expressed as the product of the policy amount and a basic rate per $1,000, plus a flat amount known as the policy fee.

policy illustration Provides key policy information and values over time, usually 20 years.

policy loan provision Provision required by all U.S. jurisdictions under which insurers must make requested loans to policyowners, subject to certain limitations.

policy reserves Conservative measure of the amounts necessary for the fulfillment of contract obligations as to future claims.

Policy Summary Explanation containing pertinent data about the particular policy under consideration that the insurer is required to provide to the potential buyer.

policyholder See *policyowner.*

policyowner The entity or individual who pays a premium to an insurer in exchange for an insurance contract or policy.

political risk Uncertainty regarding the ability to repatriate foreign cash flows when expected, including the possibility of the imposition of exchange controls by foreign authorities or even expropriation.

pooled investment account A separate account holding the funds of many policyowners or annuitants in a combined investment arrangement.

pooled rates Method insurance companies use for small groups under which a uniform rate is applied to all such groups, although it is becoming more common to apply separate pooled rates for groups with significantly better or worse experience than that of the total class.

portable pensions Vested pension benefits that would follow the employee and be put into any new plan under which he or she is covered, or vested benefits that would be transferred to some central pension clearinghouse.

portfolio average method Average investment return of an entire asset portfolio on which some insurers base their dividend interest rate.

portfolio book income Measures aggregate cash inflows and outflows of principal and interest during the measurement period.

portfolio book yield The average yield on all investments, calculated on the investment's book values.

portfolio reinsurance Reinsuring specified blocks of business.

portfolio total return Measures both income and market value changes during the measurement period.

positive convexity In normal interest rate environments, the duration model overpredicts a decrease in values when interest rates rise and underpredicts an increase in values when interest rates fall.

positive externality When a firm's production or an individual's consumption causes others to benefit.

postclaim underwriting When the insurer purposefully issues insurance with minimal underwriting investigation so as to save money but then underwrites at the time of any claims, thereby allowing insureds to believe falsely that they had coverage when they, in fact, did not.

postmortem dividend Dividend payable at death, but either it is paid in proportion to the part of the policy year of death for which premiums have been paid or represents a one-time distribution of surplus, mainly on term insurance, in lieu of dividends on each policy anniversary while the insured was living.

preadmission certification Programs requiring prior review of a hospital admission for nonemergency conditions and often outpatient surgery as well.

preadmission testing Performing diagnostic tests and X-rays on an outpatient basis, avoiding unnecessary hospitalization.

preexisting condition Sickness that started or an injury that occurred prior to the issuance of an insurance policy.

preferred provider organizations (PPOs) Groups of health care providers that contract with employers, insurance companies, union trust funds, or others to provide medical care services at a reduced, negotiated fee.

Pregnancy Discrimination Act Act passed in 1978 requiring that pregnancy be treated the same as any illness.

premium A stipulated consideration that the policyowner pays to the insurer for the insurance policy.

premium deposit rider An additional policy feature that allows the policyowner to deposit amounts to pay future premiums.

premium stabilization reserve See *contingency reserve.*

premium waiver See *waiver of premium (WP).*

preneed funeral insurance Life insurance intended to fund a prearranged funeral.

present expected value An expected value discounted for the time value of money.

present interest Gift for which the donee must have possession or enjoyment of the property immediately rather than at some future date.

present value The principal amount that must be invested now to accomplish some objective in the future.

presumptive disability The presumption that an insured is considered totally disabled, even if he or she is at work, if sickness or injury results in the loss of the sight of both eyes, the hearing of both ears, the power of speech, or the use of any two limbs.

price discrimination When a firm offers effectively identical products at different prices to different groups of customers.

pricing inadequacy (C-2) risk The risk that premium rates will be unable to cover unfavorable changes in interest, mortality, morbidity, and so on.

primary beneficiary The person named as the first to receive policy death proceeds.

primary insurance amount The monthly amount paid to a retired worker under Social Security at normal retirement age (age 65 for workers born before 1938) or to a disabled worker.

primary securities Investments such as bonds, mortgages, and stocks.

principal The person whom the agent represents.

principal sum benefit A lump-sum amount payable if the insured dies accidentally.

principal–agent problem Information asymmetry problem arising when a principal delegates authority to an agent.

private placements Investments for which the terms are negotiated directly between the borrower and the insurer.

probate The judicial process by which a will of a deceased person is authenticated to a court.

probate property Property that passes by will or state intestacy laws.

probationary period A waiting period before new employees become eligible for group insurance.

producer groups Variation of the non-agency-building distribution strategy in which independent marketing organizations specialize in the high-end market.

product differentiation Where insurers attempt to design their products so that buyers have less reason to comparison shop.

product implementation The process of moving a product from its design stage to its actual introduction to the market.

product life cycle A theoretical construct that attempts to describe the key turning points and stages in the life of a product.

professional reinsurers Specialized insurers whose exclusive business is reinsurance.

profit-sharing plans A type of defined contribution plan in which employer contributions are typically based in some manner on the employer's profits.

prohibited transactions Transactions such as the sale, exchange, leasing, lending (except for certain loans to the participant), and furnishing of goods or services between the plan and a disqualified person that are not allowed by ERISA.

projected unit credit method Method in which the normal cost is the present value of the participant's projected benefit attributable to the current year's service, and the past-service liability is the present value of the participant's projected retirement benefit attributable to service earned prior to the calculation date.

property As used in law, refers not to the object itself, but to the ownership rights associated with the property (i.e., rights of possession, control, and disposition).

property/casualty insurance Insurance sold to protect property (also known as *non-life insurance* and *general insurance*).

proportional reinsurance Plans in which the reinsurer and the ceding company share both premiums and claims on a given risk in a specified proportion.

prospective bonuses Bonuses that provide, after a predefined time period, that future interest credits will be augmented by a bonus rate.

prudent-person standard Standard that requires the fiduciary to act with the care, skill, prudence, and diligence under the prevailing circumstances that a prudent person acting in a like capacity and familiar with such matters would use.

public goods Collectively consumed goods and services desired by the public.

public employee deferred compensation Deferred compensation plans established for persons who perform services for states, political subdivisions of states, agencies or instrumentalities of states or their political subdivisions, and certain rural electric cooperatives.

pure assessment system System for fraternal benefit society members in which premiums are required only when a member of the insured group dies.

pure endowment Promises to pay the maturity amount only if the insured is living at the end of a specified period, with nothing paid in case of prior death.

pure life annuity See *life annuity*.

pure life income option Policy option in which installments are payable only for as long as the primary beneficiary (the income recipient) lives.

put option The right to sell.

qualified terminable interest property Property passing from the decedent in which the surviving spouse is entitled to a lifetime income payable at least annually from the property, no one can appoint (e.g., by gift) any part of the property to anyone except the spouse during the spouse's lifetime, and the executor makes an irrevocable election to have the marital deduction apply.

qualifying events Events that entitle any employee, spouse, or dependent child to elect continued COBRA coverage without providing evidence of insurability.

quality rating A rating given to an insurer by a rating agency according to its standards of claims-paying ability, creditworthiness, and financial strength.

quarter of coverage Provided for each full $700 unit of annual earnings on which Social Security taxes are paid, up to a maximum of four quarters for the year.

quota-share reinsurance Proportional plan under which the insurer and the reinsurer share in a predetermined proportion of every risk underwritten in a specified category.

rabbi trust An irrevocable trust that accepts employer contributions and holds assets from which deferred compensation payments will eventually be made.

radix An arbitrary number of persons chosen for presentation of a given mortality table.

RBC Plan Describes the cause of the threat to the insurer's solvency, offers proposals to correct the situation, and includes five years of financial projections and other information.

real property Land and objects permanently attached to land, such as buildings.

real interest rate The difference between the nominal interest rate and the inflation rate.

reasonable expectations doctrine States that the objectively reasonable expectations of applicants and intended beneficiaries regarding the terms of insurance contracts will be honored even though a painstaking study of the policy provisions would have negated those expectations.

rebating An inducement to buy insurance not specified in the insurance policy.

recurrent periods of disability A provision that considers consecutive or recurrent periods of disability to be from the same cause as one continuous period of disability, unless each period is separated by a recovery of six months or more.

redetermination provision A policy provision stating generally that, after the initial guarantee period, the company can redetermine the premium using the same or new assumptions as to future interest and mortality.

reduced paid-up insurance Policy option permitting the policyowner to use the cash surrender value

as a net single premium to purchase a reduced amount of paid-up insurance of the same type as the original basic policy, exclusive of any term or other riders.

reentry A life insurance policy feature that allows the possibility of paying a lower premium than otherwise if the insured can demonstrate meeting certain continuing insurability criteria.

refinancing risk The risk that the cost of rolling over or refinancing funds could be more than the return earned on assets.

reformation An equitable remedy wherein a contract is reformed—redrafted—to conform to the original intention of the parties.

regular IRA An individual retirement account established by an individual to provide retirement income for himself or herself.

regulatory arbitrage The tendency of financial service conglomerates to shift activities or positions within the group to avoid or minimize certain regulation.

Regulatory Information Retrieval System (RIRS) A computerized database containing information on regulatory actions taken against insurers and individuals.

rehabilitation An order that grants the insurance commissioner title to a domestic insurance company's assets and the authority to carry on its business until the insurer either is returned to private management after the grounds for issuing the order have been removed or the company is liquidated.

rehabilitation benefit Allows a specific sum to cover costs not paid by other insurance or public funding when the insured enrolls in a formal retraining program that will help him or her return to work.

reimbursement disability income policies Business continuation plans in which insurers pay the lesser of the policy benefit amount or the actual value of the business at the time the buy-sell occurs.

reinstatement provision Gives the policyowner the right to reinstate a previously lapsed policy under certain conditions.

reinsurance The purchase of insurance by an insurance company.

reinsurer or assuming company An insurance company that assumes the risks of another insurance company.

reinvestment risk The risk that the return earned on newly acquired assets is less than that earned on maturing securities.

relative income hypothesis Duesenberry's theory of consumption that consumption depends on the household's income *relative* to the income of households with which it identifies rather than the *absolute* level of income.

relative value schedules Plans that show payment scheduled in units rather than dollars and provide a factor for various geographic areas. To determine the maximum amount the plan will pay for each procedure, the factor is multiplied by the number of units listed.

renewal expenses Various costs of maintaining and servicing outstanding policies, as well as renewal commissions.

replacement The exchange (termination) of one policy to purchase another.

replacement cost The single premium that an insurance company would charge for a comparable contract issued at the insured's/annuitant's attained age.

representation A statement made to an insurer for the purpose of giving information or inducing it to accept a risk.

required capital Capital needed to support existing business.

rescission An equitable remedy wherein a contract is canceled or voided.

reserve A conservative measure of the insurer's liability necessary to fulfill future contingencies and unpaid obligations already incurred.

residual disability benefit Provides reduced monthly indemnity in proportion to the insured's loss of income when he or she has returned to work at reduced earnings.

residuary trust The trust that holds property that is not left to the surviving spouse outright, in the marital trust, or not used to meet expenses, taxes, and other benefits (also known as a *bypass trust,* a *credit shelter trust,* and a *nonmarital trust*).

respite care Provides temporary relief for family members providing care in the individual's home.

results clause Clause in which the insurer is excused from paying the face amount only if the death is a *result* of war.

retention The excess of premiums over claims payments and dividends.

retired lives reserve (RLR) A group reserve accumulated prior to retirement to be used to pay premiums on term insurance after retirement.

retirement annuity contract An annuity contract that provides for a schedule of fixed periodic premiums.

retirement income policy The amount payable at death is the face amount or cash value, whichever is greater.

retroactive bonuses Bonuses that provide, after a predefined time period, a bonus interest rate that will be retroactively applied to all previous periods.

retrospective premium arrangement Fully insured plan variation in which premiums are set realistically to cover expected claims and expenses without the margin for contingencies usually included to cover higher than expected levels of either.

retrospective review A review of large claims enabling employers and health insurance providers to evaluate the utilization review process itself as well as the effectiveness of the professionals involved. Such reviews also include hospital bill audits.

return on equity The implicit internal rate of return associated with the cash flows or statutory profits of a product line or other venture.

return-of-premium feature Provides that, if the insured dies within a set number of years (e.g., 20 years) from the policy issue date, the death benefit will be augmented by an amount equal to the sum of all premiums paid to that point.

reverse annuity mortgage Where a (typically) elderly person enters into an agreement with a financial institution, such as a bank, under which the individual who owns a debt-free home receives a lifetime, fixed monthly income in return for gradually giving up ownership of his or her home.

reverse split-dollar (RSD) plan Plan in which the traditional roles of employer and employee are reversed, with the pure death protection payable to the corporation and death proceeds equal to the cash value payable to the employee's beneficiary.

revocable designation A beneficiary designation that may be changed by the policyowner without the beneficiary's consent.

revocable trust A living trust in which the grantor can terminate or alter the trust as he or she wishes and regain ownership of the property.

rider An attachment to a life or heath insurance policy that either adds benefits or excludes certain losses. Also, a passenger.

right to commute Policy option that permits policyowners to give the beneficiary the right to receive the present value of all remaining installments in a lump sum.

risk From a financial point of view, variability of future cash flows.

risk management The identification, measurement, and treatment of exposures to potential losses.

risk reduction Reducing the chance that a loss will occur or reducing the magnitude of a loss if it does occur.

risk retention Retaining or bearing the risk personally.

risk tolerance The largest amount of risk that an insurer, or an individual, is willing to accept for an appropriate expected return.

risk transfer Transferring the financial consequences of any loss to some other party.

rollout The transfer of a life insurance policy owned by a corporation to the insured, often by sale.

room and board charges Hospital expenses that typically include the cost of a room, meals, and nursing services routinely provided to all inpatients.

Roth IRA An individual retirement account in which withdrawals after age 59½ are completely free of income tax provided the account has been open for at least five years.

salary-reduction SEP A simplified employee pension plan in which an employee may agree with his or her employer to have a reduction in salary to fund the SEP.

savings incentive match plan for employers (SIMPLE) A simplified retirement plan for small business available to eligible employers as a tax-favored means of providing a retirement option for employees that does not have to satisfy many of the normal qualified plan requirements.

savings plan A defined-contribution plan offered by an employer under which employees have separate accounts.

scheduled plan Plan under which a specific payment maximum is allotted for each surgical procedure.

second opinion Required for surgery under some plans, the purpose is to eliminate unnecessary surgery and to encourage plan participants to make a more informed decision regarding surgery.

secondary beneficiary See *contingent beneficiary.*

secondary securities Investments such as insurance policies, certificates of deposit, and mutual fund shares.

second-to-die life insurance Insures two (or more) lives and pays the death proceeds only on the death of the second (or last) insured to die (also known as *survivorship life insurance*).

Section 303 redemption An income tax–free stock redemption allowed for qualifying estates in an amount to cover federal and state death taxes, funeral expenses, and estate administration expenses.

Section 457 deferred compensation Arrangement in which the employer agrees with each employee to reduce his or her pay by a specified amount and to invest the deferrals in one or more investment outlets that may include insurance products.

Section 2503(c) A trust for a minor that requires the trustee to have the discretion to distribute both principal and income; the beneficiaries are entitled to receive the principal of the trust when they reach age 21; and should any of the beneficiaries die before reaching maturity, his or her share of the assets would pass through his or her estate.

secular trust A type of trust in which assets are not subject to the claims of the employer's general creditors.

Securities Act of 1933 Sets registration, financial, and disclosure standards for securities.

Securities Exchange Act of 1934 Whereas the 1933 act deals principally with new securities issues, this act regulates secondary securities.

security market line The required rate of return given a security's systematic risk.

select mortality table Table reflecting the mortality experience of newly insured lives only.

selection The process whereby an insurer evaluates individual applications for insurance to determine the degree of risk represented by the proposed insured and to classify them equitably.

self-directed account A trust arrangement offered by investment bankers under which the owner is permitted to select and manage his or her own individual investments from a wide range of available stocks, bonds, mutual funds, and direct participation programs.

semi-endowment policy Pays upon survival one-half the sum payable on death during the endowment period.

separate account Account distinct from the insurer's general account to reflect the experience of a distinct pool of investments.

settlement options Policyowners' (and beneficiaries') options as to how death proceeds will be paid.

settlor See *grantor.*

seven-pay test Satisfied if the cumulative amount paid under the life insurance contract at any time during the first seven contract years exceeds the cumulative amount that would have been paid had the policy's annual premium equaled the net-level premium for a seven-pay life policy.

short straddle The capital position created with options on both the liability and asset sides of the balance sheet.

sickness Generally defined by insurers to mean sickness or disease that first manifests itself while the policy is in force.

simple probability The chance that an event will occur.

simple reversionary bonus Bonus declared periodically as a percentage addition to the sum assured (face amount).

simplified employee pension plan (SEP) An expanded version of an employer-sponsored IRA with features similar to a qualified plan.

single-premium deferred annuity A deferred annuity payable with a single premium.

single-premium endowment policy A long-term endowment policy commonly purchased as a mortgage-loan companion, the idea being that the endowment maturity value will pay off the outstanding loan balance at a preset time.

single-premium group annuity contract Contract in which the employer determines the benefit that will ultimately be payable to each of its employees and makes a single payment for each to an insurance company to guarantee that all these benefits will be paid as they become due.

single-premium immediate annuity (SPIA) An annuity that provides payments to the annuitant, which commence immediately after the insurer has received a single (typically large) premium payment.

single-premium method See *benefit allocation method.*

single-premium whole life (SPWL) insurance The extreme in limited-payment life insurance wherein the policy is fully paid up from inception with a single payment. Such a policy has immediate, substantial cash value.

skilled nursing care Twenty-four-hour care ordered by a physician and provided by a registered nurse, licensed practical nurse, or licensed therapist.

skilled nursing facility expense coverage Provides reimbursement for medical expenses incurred when an insured individual is confined in an extended care facility and requires ongoing active medical and skilled nursing care.

skip persons Heirs beyond those of the immediately following generation.

social adequacy Benefits paid that provide a certain minimum standard of living to all participants.

social insurance substitute See *social insurance supplement.*

social insurance supplement (SIS) Provides a benefit, under the conditions of the policy for total disability, when the insured is not receiving benefits from any social service plan.

sole proprietorship An unincorporated business owned by a single person who usually also manages it.

Special Activities Database (SAD) NAIC database that expands the information available to insurance regulators and provides a formalized vehicle for states to exchange information and inquire into the activities of companies and individuals of insurance regulatory concern.

special agent An agent with limited powers extending only to acts necessary to accomplish particular transactions for which he or she is engaged to perform.

special power of appointment The individual may appoint anyone other than himself or herself or his or her estate or creditors to receive property and not cause property to be included in the gross estate.

spendthrift trust clause Provides that the beneficiary has no power to assign, transfer, or otherwise encumber the installment payments to which he or she is entitled under the settlement option.

spinout Approach to unsplitting a policy in which the corporation merely transfers its interest in the policy as a bonus to the insured.

split option Allows a survivorship policy to be split into two individual policies, one on each insured.

split-dollar life insurance An arrangement for providing funding for individually issued, cash-value life insurance.

split-funded plans Pension programs in which two or more types of insurance contracts are combined or an employer makes use of an insurance contract in conjunction with a noninsured arrangement.

split-funding contracts Variations of split-funded plans.

sponsored arrangement Arrangement under which the insurer arranges with an association or similar group to offer products to its membership.

sponsored demutualization When a converted mutual insurer is acquired by another company.

spousal IRA Provision of the Tax Reform Act of 1986 that allows working employees who are eligible for regular IRAs to establish IRAs for their nonworking spouses.

spread See *investment margin.*

spread-loss reinsurance Plan under which excess claims in a year are covered by the reinsurer, which are then, in effect, reimbursed over a period of time, thus allowing the ceding company to spread its loss over several years.

staff model Model in which the physicians who serve the HMO members are employed by the HMO and typically are paid on a salary basis but may also receive bonus or incentive payments that are based on their performance and productivity.

standard deviation A common quantitative measure calculated by finding the square root of the variance.

Standard Nonforfeiture Laws U.S. laws stipulating that cash-value life insurance policies must state the mortality table and rate of interest used in calculating life insurance nonforfeiture values to be provided by the policy, as well as a description of the method used in calculating the values.

standard nonforfeiture-value method Where larger than minimum values are derived through the use of nonforfeiture factor(s).

Standard Valuation Law Basis used to calculate statutory minimum reserves.

static tables Tables that do not provide for changes in their rates depending on the calendar year to which they applied.

statistical phase Under the U.S. insurance regulatory information system, the calculation of 12 financial ratios based on data extracted from each life insurer's annual statement filed with the NAIC.

status clause Clause stating that the insurer need not pay the policy face amount if death results while the insured is in the military service, regardless of the cause of death.

statutory policy reserves Reserves calculated using the prospective method with designated mortality and morbidity tables and a maximum interest rate.

stock bonus plan A plan established and maintained by an employer to provide benefits similar to a profit-sharing plan except that the benefits are distributed in the form of stock of the employer.

stock life insurance company A corporation authorized to sell life and (usually) health insurance, which is owned by its stockholders and is organized and incorporated for the purpose of making a profit for its stockholders.

stock option plan Incentive compensation scheme that offers executives the option of purchasing the corporation's shares at fixed prices.

stock-redemption An entity buy-and-sell agreement.

stop-loss reinsurance Reinsurance that becomes payable if and when aggregate claims experienced by the ceding company in a year exceed some predetermined level.

straight life Whole life insurance with premiums that are payable for the whole of life (also known as *continuous-premium* and *ordinary life insurance*).

structured settlement annuity An SPIA contract issued by a life insurer whereby the plaintiff (the injured party) receives periodic payments from the defendant in a personal injury lawsuit.

subrogation The substitution of another party (in this case the employer or the insurer) in place of a party (the employee or a dependent) that has a legal claim against a third party.

substandard Group subject to a higher than average mortality or morbidity.

suicide clause A clause protecting the insurer against a policy being purchased when the individual is contemplating suicide.

supplemental executive retirement plan (SERP) A non-qualified retirement plan that provides retirement benefits to selected employees only.

supplemental liability A separately funded measure that separates past-service benefits from future-service benefits in pension plans.

supplemental major medical plan A plan superimposed on a basic plan provided by an insurer or another company such as Blue Cross and Blue Shield.

surplus strain Where the loading is the only portion of the first premium available to pay the first year's expenses.

surplus-share reinsurance Reinsurance under which the reinsurer assumes the liability above the ceding company's retention.

surrender charge A penalty for early policy termination.

surrender cost comparison index See *interest-adjusted net cost method.*

surrender-based IRR Policy comparison method that solves for a rate of return but makes no allowance for the value to the policyowner of the insurance protection.

survivorship clause Provides that the beneficiary must survive the insured by a fixed period after the insured's death to be entitled to the proceeds (also called a *time clause*).

survivorship life insurance Insures two (or more) lives and pays the death proceeds only on the death of the second (or last) insured to die (also known as *second-to-die life insurance*).

swaps Agreements between two parties to exchange securities.

systematic risk See *market risk.*

table with projection A table that shows the (lower) rates of mortality anticipated in the future rather than the rates that have been experienced in the past.

Taft-Hartley plan A collective-bargaining agreement in which benefits and the contributions are defined.

Takaful A type of solidarity or mutual fund, separate from the management operation, that relies on a pact among participants to guarantee each other. Necessary to be compatible with Islamic principles.

target capital The total amount of capital that management believes is necessary for its required and growth capital needs.

target premium See *planned premium.*

target return See *assumed interest rate.*

target SERPs A supplemental executive retirement plan that seeks to replace retirement benefits lost by ERISA-imposed limits *and* counteract the Social Security benefit bias in favor of low-income workers.

target-benefit plan Plan in which the employer chooses a target level of retirement benefit using a benefit-formula approach similar to that used in designing a defined benefit plan.

tax-deferred annuities (TDAs) Agreements in which an employer sets aside a portion of the money that would otherwise be part of an employee's pay. These funds eventually will be subject to tax, but not until the money, with accumulated interest, is actually received, either as a cash withdrawal or as annuity payments.

tax-sheltered annuities (TSAs) Agreements in which an employer sets aside a portion of the money that would otherwise be part of an employee's pay. These funds eventually will be subject to tax, but not until the money, with accumulated interest, is actually received, either as a cash withdrawal or as annuity payments.

temporary life annuity A life annuity payable for a fixed period or until the death of the annuitant, whichever is earlier.

tenancy by the entirety A joint ownership of property created between spouses only, which provides a right of survivorship.

tenancy in common A joint-ownership arrangement wherein each member owns his or her share outright.

term insurance Policies that promise to pay benefits only if the insured dies during the policy term.

terminal dividend Dividend paid, if the policy has been in force for a minimum length of time, in the event that a policy terminates by maturity, death, or surrender.

terminal illness coverage Provides that a specified maximum percentage (typically 25 to 50 percent) of the life policy's face amount can be paid if the insured is diagnosed as having a terminal illness.

terminal (or capital) bonus Bonus or dividend paid as an additional benefit on the insured's death.

terminal reserve The reserve at the end of any given policy year.

terminally ill When an individual has been certified by a physician as having an illness or physical condition that can reasonably be expected to result in death within 24 months or less.

term-to-age-65 (or 70) insurance Policy providing protection for a somewhat shorter period than a whole life policy and carrying a lower premium.

test of materiality With regard to misrepresentations, determines whether the insurer, had it known the actual facts, would have issued insurance, would have issued it with as favorable a premium, or would have issued it on terms as favorable as it did.

testamentary trust A trust created at death through a person's will.

testator Person making a will.

thrift plan A contributory profit-sharing plan designed to encourage employees to save from after-tax income.

tied agents An agent who sells exclusively for one company (also known as *exclusive* or *captive agents*).

top-heavy plan Plan under which the value of accrued benefits for key employees (certain officers and owners) and their beneficiaries exceeds 60 percent of the value of accrued benefits for all employees and their beneficiaries.

total adjusted capital (TAC) Equals statutory capital and surplus plus the AVR and one-half of any policyowner dividend liability.

total disability Covered when an insured cannot perform either any gainful occupation or the major duties of his or her regular occupation or one for which he or she is qualified by education or experience.

traditional net cost Cost comparison method calculated by adding the illustrated premiums over a selected time period and subtracting from this figure the sum of the policy's illustrated dividends, if any, taken to the end of the period. From this result is subtracted the policy's illustrated cash surrender value at the end of the chosen period.

transfer for value rule IRS provision applying to any transfer for a valuable consideration of a right to receive all or a part of the death proceeds of a life insurance policy.

transparency The assurance that accurate information needed by customers, intermediaries, rating agencies, and governments will be readily available.

trust A legal arrangement whereby one party transfers property to someone else who holds the legal title and manages the property for the benefit of others.

trusteed pension plans See *noninsured plan.*

twisting The practice by an agent of inducing a policyowner through misrepresentation to discontinue an existing life insurance policy in order to purchase a new one.

ultimate mortality table Table reflecting the mortality experience beyond the select years (i.e., of those who already have been insured for several years).

unbundled product A product for which the insurer expresses (discloses) the pricing elements separately.

underwriter An individual who determines whether and on what terms to issue a requested insurance policy.

underwriting The process by which insurers decide whether to issue insurance to a person and the terms and prices.

unemployment insurance Payment of periodic cash income to workers during periods of involuntary unemployment.

unfunded A retirement plan that provides that the employee must rely exclusively on the employer's unsecured promise to make payments.

unification of mortality An important feature of savings bank life insurance, under which the mortality experience of the banks in a state is pooled.

unified credit A tax credit that can be applied to offset estate and gift taxes.

Uniform Simultaneous Death Act States that "where the insured and beneficiary in a policy of life or accident insurance have died and there is not sufficient evidence that they have died otherwise than simultaneously, the proceeds of the policy shall be distributed as if the insured had survived the beneficiary."

Uniform Transfers to Minors Act and Uniform Gifts to Minors Act Under these acts, an adult is named custodian for the minor and manages the property through a custodian account. The property is distributed to the minor at age 18 or 21, depending on state law.

unilateral A contract in which only one party gives a legally enforceable promise—the insurer in the case of life insurance.

unique risk That risk associated with a particular stock or situation rather than the overall market risk.

unit credit method A funding method for trust fund plans and administration contracts where the normal cost is the present value of benefits expected to accrue in the current year, and the past-service liability is the present value of all benefits earned by the participant as of the calculation date.

United States Government Life Insurance The oldest of the U.S. government life insurance programs, established by Congress in 1919 and granted renewable term insurance, to a maximum of $10,000, to those in the military and naval services, for the benefit of selected beneficiaries only.

unit-linked life insurance A type of whole life insurance whose values may vary directly with the performance of a set of earmarked investments (also known as *variable life insurance*).

Universal Life Insurance Model Regulation Regulation establishing minimum valuation and nonforfeiture standards for UL and CAWL policies and mandating certain policy provisions.

upstream holding company A holding company formed by one or more stock companies.

usual and customary charge Charge based on the charges normally made for the service provided by physicians in a given geographic area.

utility A measure of consumer satisfaction derived from economic goods.

utilization review programs Cost containment programs concerned primarily with the appropriateness of care delivered in hospital settings.

utmost good faith A contract in which each party is entitled to rely in good faith upon the representations of the other, and each is under an obligation not to attempt to deceive or withhold material information from the other.

validate Amount of business agents are required to produce.

validation period The duration at which the full policy reserve is to be accumulated (when the asset share equals the reserve).

valuation A measure and comparison of an insurer's assets and liabilities, based on estimates of future persistency, mortality, morbidity, interest, and expense experience.

valuation mortality table Table that contain margins, rendering them conservative, used as the basis for calculating minimum reserves and cash surrender values.

value added The amount derived by taking the ending net worth, subtracting the beginning net worth, adding the stock and policyowner dividends paid, and subtracting the capital infusions.

value-based planning Focuses on the economic net worth of a company and its relative increase from planning period to planning period.

valued policies Policies in which one party, the insurer, agrees to pay a stated sum of money irrespective of the actual economic loss.

vanish pay A policy with a rapid buildup of cash values, structured with the expectation that, after the policy has remained in force for a specified period, no further premiums are expected to be necessary. Also misleadingly called a vanish premium.

variable annuity An annuity contract whose cash values and benefit payments vary directly with the experience of assets designated to back the contract.

variable life insurance (VLI) A type of whole life insurance whose values may vary directly with the performance of a set of earmarked investments (also known as *unit-linked life insurance*).

Variable Life Insurance Model Regulation Established certain mandatory policy design characteristics and policy provisions.

variable universal life (VUL) Product that combines some of the flexible characteristics of universal life with the investment flexibility of variable life insurance.

variance The weighted average squared deviations of each possible return from that expected.

vesting The employee's nonforfeitable rights in employer contributions.

vesting schedule A schedule that shows that portion or amount of an employer-provided retirement benefit to which the employee has a contractual right.

viatical settlement An arrangement under which a policyowner sells a life insurance policy to a viatical settlement firm.

viatical settlement firm A specialized company (or group of investors) that purchases life insurance policies usually from terminally ill individuals.

Viatical Settlements Model Act Regulation that requires certain disclosures to be made to the viator including the impact of the transaction on eligibility for government benefits, possible tax implications, rescission rights, and alternatives to viatical settlements, such as accelerated death benefits.

viator The person who sells his or her policy.

vision care expense plans Provide reimbursement for the cost of eye examinations to determine whether the individual needs glasses and, if so, for the cost of required frames and lenses.

void An agreement that has no legal force or effect.

voidable agreement One that can be made void at the option of the innocent party.

voluntary AD&D An elective benefit offering substantial amounts of coverage available and the employee's privilege of selecting the amount of coverage.

voluntary life insurance Plans in which each employee can choose an amount of additional insurance in increments up to a maximum that is based on the employee's earnings (e.g., three times salary).

waiver of premium (WP) Provides that premiums (or mortality and expense charges under universal life and current assumption policies) otherwise due will be waived if the insured becomes totally and permanently disabled before a certain age, typically 65 (also called a *premium waiver*).

war exclusion Excludes coverage if the insured's death occurs under certain military conditions.

warranty Requires that the warranted statement must be absolutely and literally true.

wealth replacement trusts Irrevocable life insurance trusts containing insurance whose death benefit roughly equals the value of the property transferred to the charitable remainder trust.

welfare benefit plan Defined by ERISA as any plan, fund, or program established or maintained by an employer (or by an employee organization) for the purpose of providing employee benefits through the purchase of insurance or otherwise.

whole life annuity A life annuity payable for the whole of the annuitant's life.

whole life insurance Life insurance that typically provides level death benefits coverage for the whole of the insured's life.

widow's/widower's benefit Under the U.S. Social Security system, a benefit due to the unremarried spouse of a deceased, fully insured worker.

wife's benefit Under the U.S. Social Security system, the benefit to which the wife of a retired worker is entitled.

will A legal declaration of an individual's wishes as to the disposition to be made of his or her property on death.

window GIC Designed to meet the need for periodic contributions inherent in some defined contribution plans, which credit an employee's account balance with the plan contribution (frequently monthly or semimonthly) as salaries are paid.

with profits policies Life and health insurance policies that provide their owners the right to share in surplus funds accumulated by the insurer because of deviations of actual from assumed experience (also known as *participating insurance policies*).

without profits policies Life and health insurance policies that fix policy elements (i.e., the premium, the face amount, and the cash values, if any) at policy inception, are guaranteed, and make no allowance for future values to differ from those set at inception (also known as *nonparticipating* and *guaranteed-cost policies*).

workers' compensation A law that requires employers to provide employee benefits for losses resulting from work-related accidents or diseases.

yearly price of protection method Cost comparison method that assumes a rate of return and derives a yearly price of protection figure.

yearly rate of return (YROR) method Cost comparison method that assumes a mortality cost (or price of protection) and derives a yearly rate of return figure.

yearly renewable term (YRT) plan Term policies with level death benefits and increasing premiums.

yearly renewable term (YRT) See *annual renewable term*.

Index

I